Published by:

www.napsusa.org

NAPS

National Association for Public Safety

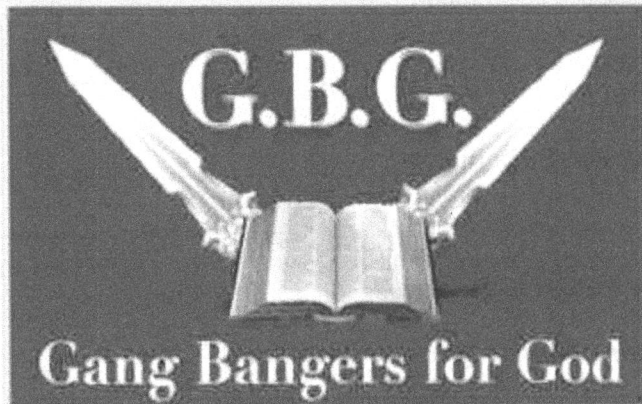

please visit us on the web at:
www.napsusa.org
www.cafepress.com/manning
shermanmanning.blogspot.com

or contact us at:
hallopeter@sunrise.ch

ISBN 978-0-9743260-6-1

Other Books by **Sherman Manning:**
Blue Eyed Blonde 2
Blue Eyed Blonde
Reach Beyond the Break and Hold On
Dream and Grow Rich
If It Doesn't Fit, You Must Acquit
Through the Valley of the Shadow of Death (Columbine High School)
Teens Are Dying/Parents Are Crying: Where Do We Go From Here?
American Dream, A Search for Justice Vol. 1 & 2
Creating Monsters
From Palace to Prison

CONTENTS

Cover design by A&M Enterprises

Praise and Support for K.K.K. (Kids Killing Kids)

To my Good Friend Sherman — (handwritten signature)

Taken — The Day of the Verdict! (handwritten)

Attorney Robert D. Blasier, Robert Shapiro, and O.J. Simpson

Attorney Robert D. Blasier was on the O.J. Simpson Dream Team with Johnnie Cochran, He is a world-renowned DNA expert. He fully endorses this book and wants every at-risk teen to read it. Attorney Blasier states, "*Sherman, I hope that young people all over the world will be moved, inspired and enlightened by your K.K.K. (Kids Killing Kids).*" Harvard Associate

Attorney Robert D. Blasier with Johnnie Cochran

ROBERT D. BLASIER

Attorney at Law

March 2, 2010

Mr. Sherman Manning,
J-98796 FA8-226
PO Box 290066
Repressa, CA 95671-0066

RE: Your Book

Dear Sherman:

I am happy to make the following statement about your book:

"Sherman, I hope that young people all over the world will be moved, inspired, and enlightened by your book - "K.K.K (kids killing kids)."

No-one can dispute the fact that you know the perils of a life of crime and the consequences that inevitably result when you are caught.

To put together a team of inmates, counselors, guards, and wardens to accomplish the goal of diverting youth away from gangs, guns, drugs, and violence is indeed a great accomplishment. You are certainly to be commended for all your efforts."

Sincerely,

ROBERT D. BLASIER

3600 Piedra Montana Road   El Dorado Hills, CA 95762
(916) 933-7289 [days] (916) 933-7690 [eves.] (916) 933-7452 [fax]
bobblasier@aol.com   www.blasier.com

ROBERT D. BLASIER

Attorney at Law

February 15, 2010

Mr. Sherman Manning,
J-98796 FA8-226
PO Box 290066
Repressa, CA 95671-0066

RE: Your Book

Dear Sherman:

I received your recent undated letter concerning your book "K.K.K. (Kids Killing Kids)."

As I understand the situation, you need me to request that I be provided with a copy of your book. Please accept this letter as my formal request that I be provided with a copy of your book: "K.K.K. (Kids Killing Kids)."

I look forward to reviewing your book given the goals you have established, ie. to turn our teenagers away from lives of crimes and gangs.

Sincerely,

ROBERT D. BLASIER

3600 Piedra Montana Road   El Dorado Hills, CA 95762
(916) 933-7289 [days] (916) 933-7690 [eves.] (916) 933-7452 [fax]
bobblasier@aol.com   www.blasier.com

John L. Burton Ex-California Senate President pro Tem

JOHN L. BURTON
ATTORNEY AT LAW

▼

CONSULTANT IN GOVERNMENTAL AFFAIRS

March 23, 2010

Mr. Sherman Manning (J-98796)
P.O. Box 290066
Represa, CA 95671

Dear Sherman:

Thank you for your letter postmarked on March 15, 2010. I am happy to make the following statement about your book:

"Congratulations on the publishing of *K.K.K.: Kids Killing Kids*. I certainly hope that youngsters around the world would take a look at it and realize the perils of crime, drugs, and gangs. Keep up the good work."

Peace and friendship,

John L. Burton

Enclosure

March 25, 2009

To Whom It May Concern:

I thoroughly endorse the concept of Gang Bangers for Good.

Anything that will help turn the lives of young adults and children around is worthwhile and beneficial to our state.

Sincerely,

John Burton

JOHN BURTON

HARVARD MEDICAL SCHOOL
DEPARTMENT OF PSYCHIATRY

ALVIN F. POUSSAINT, M.D.
Professor of Psychiatry
Faculty Associate Dean for Student Affairs

Director, Media Center
Judge Baker Children's Center

Senior Associate in Psychiatry
Children's Hospital

Reply to:

Judge Baker Children's Center
53 Parker Hill Avenue
Boston, Massachusetts 02120
Phone: (617) 278-4105
Fax: (617) 232-7343
APoussaint@JBCC.harvard.edu
www.hms.harvard.edu/orma/poussaint/index/htm

November 24, 2009

Sherman D. Manning
GBG / Heart President
CSP - SCA - J98796
PO Box 290066
Represa, CA   95671

Dear Mr. Manning,

Thank you for your note. I appreciate your kind words regarding *Come On People*.
I am glad to hear of your work with teens in prison. I would be pleased to receive a copy of your
book, *Kids Killing Kids*.

Best wishes in your continued good work.

Sincerely,

Alvin F. Poussaint, MD

AFP:bbs

raising a child is everybody's business

Fred Moor
140 W. South Boundary Street
Perrysburg, OH 43551
Phone 419-874-1333

April 10, 2009

To Whom It May Concern:

As outside coordinator for Compassion project I know the benefits of allowing prisoners the opportunity to be involved in something positive through a well supervised program. From what I understand the Compassion program is similar to the concept to the ideas being employed by Gang Bangers for Good.

By empowering prisoners to do good we may be changing the direction of our prison system to focus more on rehabilitation and restoration. I highly recommend that you look more deeply into the Gang Bangers For Good program. If you feel it meets your supervisory standards and fulfills the need of benefiting youth and guiding them in a positive direction this organization may be very worthy of your support.

Helping and motivating others to do good provides us with a unique opportunity of which we may never know the full benefits. Gang Bangers for Good deserves a chance.

Sincerely,

Fred Moor

Compassion

June 2, 2010

Sherman D. Manning, J98796
CSP-SAC – A-8 – 226
PO BOX 29006
Represa, CA 95671

Dear Sherman,

   Congratulations on the publication of your book for youth "K.K.K." Youth today need good information to show them the way to lead a better more productive life. What better way for them to receive that information than through the pages of "K.K. K."

   Students and teachers have the opportunity to be transformed by reading this innovative book. My best wishes in all the good things you are doing for youth.

Sincerely,

Fred Moor
Outside Coordinator

CAPITOL OFFICE
STATE CAPITOL, ROOM 2048
SACRAMENTO, CA 95814
TEL (916) 651-4025
FAX (916) 445-3712

DISTRICT OFFICE
ONE MANCHESTER BLVD., SUITE 600
INGLEWOOD, CA 90301
TEL (310) 412-0393
FAX (310) 412-0996

EMAIL
SENATOR.WRIGHT@SEN.CA.GOV
WEBSITE
WWW.SEN.CA.GOV/WRIGHT

CHAIR
GOVERNMENTAL ORGANIZATION

MEMBER
BUDGET & FISCAL REVIEW
BUDGET SUBCOMMITTEE #4
ON STATE ADMINISTRATION
GENERAL GOVERNMENT,
JUDICIAL AND TRANSPORTATION

California State Senate

SENATOR
RODERICK D. WRIGHT
TWENTY-FIFTH SENATE DISTRICT

April 30, 2009

Mr. Sherman D. Manning J98796
CSI-SAC-A 8-122
P.O. Box 290066
Represa, CA 95671

Dear Mr. Manning:

Thank you for contacting my district office with your concerns for our youth and for notifying me on your G.B.G. (Gang Bangers for Good) and HEART (Helping Educate At Risk Teens) programs.

The information presented is informative and I will keep your suggestions in mind during the legislative session.

It is always good to see progressive programs that benefit our community. Thank you again for contacting my office.

Sincerely,

RODERICK D. WRIGHT
Senator, 25th District

RDW/bat

REPRESENTING THE COMMUNITIES OF ALONDRA PARK, ATHENS, COMPTON, GARDENA, FLORENCE-GRAHAM, HAWTHORNE, INGLEWOOD,
LADERA HEIGHTS, LAWNDALE, LONG BEACH, LOS ANGELES, PALOS VERDES PENINSULA, SAN PEDRO, WATTS, WESTCHESTER, WESTMONT, AND WILLOWBROOK

Allee Simmons
Program Administrator

SJM
Family Foundation

July 22, 2009

Attn: Warden James "Jimbo" Walker and G.B.G. President Sherman D. Manning

SJM Family Foundation fully supports the mission of Gang Bangers for Good aka Gang Bangers for GOD (G.B.G.).

We hope this unique organization can play a major role in diverting youths from gangs, guns, drugs and violence. Hopefully, schools, parents, students and community leaders will take a close look at G.B.G.

Sincerely,

Allee Simmons
Board President

Law Offices

ALLRED, MAROKO & GOLDBERG
A PARTNERSHIP OF PROFESSIONAL CORPORATIONS

NATHAN GOLDBERG*
MICHAEL MAROKO*
GLORIA R. ALLRED*
JOHN S. WEST
DOLORES Y. LEAL
R. TOMÁS OLMOS
RENEE MOCHKATEL
MARGERY N. SOMERS
MARÍA G. DÍAZ
RAMIT MIZRAHI

*A PROFESSIONAL CORPORATION

6300 WILSHIRE BOULEVARD
SUITE 1500
LOS ANGELES, CALIFORNIA 90048
(323) 653-6530
FAX (323) 653-1660
www.amglaw.com

March 2, 2009
VIA U.S. MAIL

Sherman Manning - #J98796
CSP-SAC-A-8-122
P.O. Box 290066
Represa, CA 95671

Re: Your inquiry

Dear Mr. Manning:

I am in receipt of your letter regarding your book. I applaud your interest in helping young people avoid prison. Unfortunately, due to time constraints with my current workload, I am unable to assist you by writing for your project. I do, however, wish you much success with what appears to be an important effort. I am returning the pages you requested.

Very truly yours,

ALLRED, MAROKO & GOLDBERG

GLORIA ALLRED

PrisonVoice .com
FREE YOUR VOICE
PO Box 6560   Pahrump NV 89041-6560

April 14, 2009

ATTN: Sherman D. Manning, President/Founder *Gang Bangers for God*
        James P. Walker, Warden CSP-SAC

Gentlemen,

This letter will provide a hearty endorsement from *PrisonVoice.com* for your efforts in behalf of young adults and children of America.

We support the idea that inmates can and should be a constructive force in providing life lessons for those 'at risk' youngsters. We consider this effort to be a beneficial and worthwhile endeavor.

We appreciate your including *PrisonVoice.com* in your efforts to reduce the prison population.

Best Regards,

C. L. Booth

C. L. Booth, Staff Member
PrisonVoice.com-LLC

DAIN P. WEINER
ATTORNEY AT LAW
3350 COUNTRY CLUB DRIVE, SUITE 202
CAMERON PARK, CALIFORNIA 95682
Telephone (530) 677-9487 Facsimile (530) 677-2955

April 28, 2010

Mr. Sherman D. Manning, J98796
CSP-SAC-A-226
P.O. Box 290066
Represa, CA 95671

      Re: Steven Colver

Dear Mr. Manning:

    I recently received your letter on April 27, 2010. I read through the materials and "KKK" sounds like a fascinating and informative book. I see Steven on a fairly regular basis and would be happy to deliver a copy to him. If you send on, I will definitely forward it.

    Thank you and keep up the good fight.

             Sincerely,

             DAIN P. WEINER

DPW/ctb

17

About the Author

Sherman D. Manning is a prolific author and orator. He is an expert in the psychology of change. He is a motivational speaker. He is a Peak Performance Coach. He is a Human Rights Leader and a Youth Advocate. Harvard trained psychiatrist Franklin Curren (MD.) calls him "innovative, energetic and persistent". Carlos Solis (M.D.) says "Sherman is one of the most intelligent guys I know." Psychologist A. Duran states "positivity and energy just pours out of you (Sherman)". She states "you are a special man and I feel light all around you. They should let you out of here just for even coming up with the idea of G.B.G./Heart." He is a prisoner in California. He is the Founder and Chairman of NAPS (National Association for Public Safety). He is the Founder and President of G.B.G. (Gang Bangers For God/Good) and he's Founder of Heart (Helping Educate At Risk Teens). He is an expert on gangs. He is an expert on the prison subculture. He is an expert on prisons and prison guards. He is a preeminent expert on youth in prisons. He is a consultant to corrections captains, associate wardens, wardens and government officials. He is an orator and an entrepreneur. He's a Gang Banger For Good, a Gang Banger for God, a Gang Banger For Peace and a Gang Banger For Justice ....

www.napsusa.org
www.cafepress.com/manning
shermanmanning.blogspot.com
gbgod.blogspot.com

Photo Album

Rev. Sherman Manning with Rev. Hosea Williams (sitting)

and in a nursing home in Switzerland

Sherman preaching in a church in Atlanta Georgia

Sherman Manning and Peter Andrist

Daniel Macky

Reginald Manning, Rev. Gerald Anderson and Sherman D. Manning

G.B.G. Cheerleaders

Heart Cheerleaders

Jeff Glen Howell (center)

Johnny O'Neal (left)

Joseph Latham and Ramona (his mom)

Roger Peck

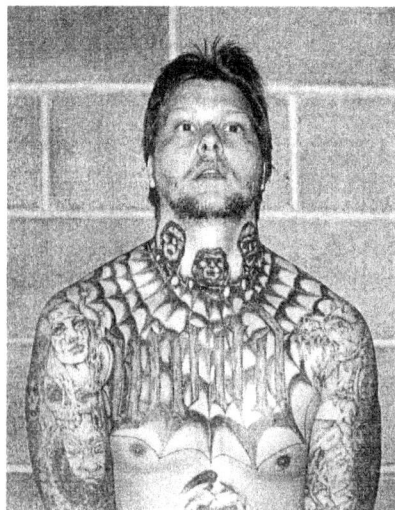

Travis Britt

Devin Merritt

Foreword by Attorney Robert D. Blasier

Sherman D. Manning reached out to me because I was on the O.J. Simpson Dream Team with Johnnie Cochran and others. He asked me to peruse, endorse and promote this major-book "K. K. K." Sherman is a unique man who is determined to use the errors of his past to transform the future of all of youths.

It is unusual (an understatement) that I'm writing the foreword for "K. K. K." Not merely because the author is incarcerated. Many powerful, spellbinding and great books have been penned by men in the "pen". What is strange is *how* I've come to know Sherman. I've ordered every Book he has written. And I'm impressed with Sherman's writing skills.

K. K. K. is the kind of Book that you can pickup and open to any page at random and still be enthralled by Sherman's vivid descriptions of life in prison. Sherman wrote to me: "I need *you* to help me reach these youths and divert them from these prisons."

When we secured victory in the O.J. Simpson trial in 1995, Johnnie told the press that his law practice was more about the No J's than the O.J.'s. Until he suddenly passed away, Johnnie was a voice to the voiceless and a champion to the underdog.

I cannot endorse every ideal, claim or accusation that Sherman writes in K.K.K. That's not even what he requested. What I can and will do is fully endorse the mission of G.B.G. (Gang Bangers for God) and HEART (Helping Educate at Risk Teens). And I hope that judges, lawyers, professors, criminal justice students, and kids in trouble will peruse this book.

It is compelling and unlike most of the books written about prisoners and prisons. Sherman is embedded in his story. He writes in real-time, with a "no-holds-barred" approach. He "names-names" not only about other prisoners but about corrupt employees within the California Department of Corrections.

Sherman is an expert on the prisons, which our kids are routinely sent to. This Landmark-Mega-Book is a powerful psychological portrait of the mentality of people in prisons. I hope that judges, prosecutors, probation officers and parents will inspire kids to read this book.

The sensational and controversial title of the book will automatically attract teens. And the fact that a man *in* the prison who has conned, cheated and connived in the past, *writes* this book while he's still in prison gives it both street and youth credibility.

Some prisoners (in gangs) organize, plot and orchestrate Gang "Hits" from their prison cells. Sherman methodically, skillfully and strategically plots a strategy to transform gang bangers from his concrete cage. Sherman writes: "We must bring every asset to bear and mobilize a task force of psychologists, prisoners, professors and pastors. Supplemented by praying mothers.... we must ally with Tony Dungy, Playmakers, Homeboy Industries, and Curtis Lee etc. and get this Book (K. K. K.) in every hood, barrio and suburb, to prevent kids from coming here."

I am an attorney with over 40 years of experience, Including 15 years as a prosecutor, and including many high profile and controversial cases. I can affirm that Sherman has never asked me to try to use this book as a bargaining chip for parole, a pardon or for political favor. He has only asked me to "please help me to get this book to these kids."

Sherman wants to get "K. K. K." to youngsters like Greg Pryzbiak, Colton Harris-Moore, and Cassius Harti etc. He Believes that when Jalen Rose, Bishop T. D. Jakes, Coaches and teachers read this book they will see that it gets to at risk kids and young adults.

This book is unusual, unique, powerful, compelling and candid. I strongly recommend it to teens, young adults, and professionals everywhere.

Bob Blasier, August 2010, www.Blasier.com

Preface by Peter Andrist
Philanthropist, Switzerland

I'm often asked how a Swiss white guy met an American Black entrepreneur (From Atlanta Georgia) in Richmond Virginia. I'll let Sherman D. Manning explain that. I'm also asked why my wife and I call Sherman "Marc Rice". I'll also let Sherman explain the Marc Rice name. I am to Sherman what Gayle King is to Oprah. He's my best friend and confidant. Sherman is my hero. He is an expert in the psychology of change. He's an expert on gangs (prison) violence and criminality. He is a consultant on kids in prisons and violence against youngsters in prisons, jails, juveniles, group homes and in foster care. He has researched teen predators, Fratricidal Murderers and Sadistic killers. He has interviewed and cohabited (platonically) with notorious (infamous) murderers (i.e., Eric Merendez and Lyle Merendez ... Sherman worked with Eric for 3 years in prison) in prisons. Sherman D. Manning has authored 9 books which have sold all over the world. He is the most brilliant and studious person I've ever met anywhere in the world. Sherman led prayer vigils for the murdered and missing children in Atlanta Georgia with Mayor Maynard Jackson and State Senator Grace Davis. He served as a consultant for the Atlanta women against crime and the Atlanta Youth against crime. He worked with Former United Nations Ambassador Andrew Young. He worked very closely with (civil rights Royalty) Former Martin Luther King Associate Rev. Hosea Williams. At age 13 he appeared in the Atlanta Constitution Newspaper in an article titled "Boy turns playground into pulpit". He travelled, spoke and motivated people from Atlanta Georgia all the way to Switzerland. He's a motivational expert and a peak performance coach... In the Book of Genesis we learn that Joseph was hated by his own brothers because of a dream that he had. He was thrown into a prison cell for a rape he did not commit. Later his gift (of prophecy) brought him out of prison. And Joseph became a prince. The story of Joseph is indicative of the power of providence to use the gifts of the least likely to do the Almighty. Saul (in the Bible) was actually guilty of being a vicious murderer. And murder is the Final Crime. Yet, in spite of Saul's horrendous past he was transmogrified into Paul. He left jails for crimes and began to preach against crimes. He used all of his mess to bless others. Almost half the holy Bible was written by folks in prisons and convicted of vicious crimes.

Sherman D. Manning is in jail today. And he almost singlehandedly invented a new youth institution: G.B.G. (Gang Bangers for God or Gang Bangers for Good). This powerful book tells the amazing story of Sherman's G.B.G. / HEART (Helping Educate At Risk Teens) Foundation. In the bowels of the California prison system the idea that a lone prisoner, unaided by a trust fund or a team of media savvy publicists etc. could outflank prophets of doom, racists, preachers of hate and gang leaders etc. and bring together hard-core killers, rapists, robbers and gang members under the Banner of Gang Bangers for God etc. This is awesome and it is incredible. G.B.G. is A team and as Sherman says "there's no "I" in the t-e-a-m" and "it's G.B.G not me B.G.". He brought together Bloods, Crips, the Aryan Brotherhood, the Mexican Mafia, skinheads, Nortênos, Southerners, the 415 Gang, South Siders, Los Primos, the Golden West Clique, an ex-LAPD Homicide cop, Christians, Atheists as well as the sons of Odinists and convinced them to join G.B.G. He's often hated and he'll admit that he's not perfect. But this man has the kind of rhythm, drive, energy, determination and stick-to-it-ive-ness which master leaders have.

What is also amazing is his G.B.G. staff. The G.B.G/HEART staff is directed by a Harvard trained psychiatrist. (as close as I am to Sherman he still has never explained to me how he convinced a Harvard trained physician to lead his training team.) That would be Franklin Curren MD. His chief training officer is C. Solis MD. Jennifer Heitkamp MD. is a G.B.G. staff psychiatrist. Doctor A. Duran, Dr. Jarman, Dr. Gregg, Dr. J. Friedman and Dr. Houston are all licensed psychologists who serve on Sherman's psychological consultation team. (The G.B.G. team of experts is fluid due to the fact that psychologists routinely walk up to Sherman and ask to join G.B.G.). G.B.G. was birthed in Sherman's spirit and (although you won't read about it in this book. Because Warden Walker and Madame Kennedy asked Sherman to make this a positive book to help kids. Rather than another one of his scathing diatribes against prison authorities.) I can tell you that anytime one tries to do a great thing a Judas will always raise up. Great men, whether they're in jail or Yale etc. will always have a Judas (opposition, envy, duplicity. I.E. the Judas who sold Jesus out for 30 pieces of silver) to contend with. A number of staff and inmates tried to prevent, hinder and to eliminate the G.B.G/HEART Foundation. But God is able!!... When Joseph left his prison and became a prince in Egypt. There was a famine in Egypt and the same brothers who had plotted to murder Joseph, the same brothers who sold him into slavery had to come to Egypt to get food from Joseph. And yet, they did not recognize Joseph. They didn't know it was him. But the Bible says he revealed himself and his brothers were ashamed. But Joseph told them "don't trip". He said "Ye thought evil upon me but God meant it for Good". And so my dear friend Sherman is now a Gang Banger. But he's Banging for Good and Banging for God. For the record Sherman has never been in a gang. He's a brilliant, studious and sophisticated person. But he'll fully explain the name in this book.

There are college and high school students all over America, in Europe and around the world joining G.B.G.

In an historic feat Sherman was blessed to get every death-row prisoner in the United States of America to join G.B.G. He has them using their errors and mistakes to help turnaround troubled teens. He says "G.B.G. does not seek pardons for our participants. We pay no salaries to anybody. It is a volunteer organization. And I'm certain that somebody will tell the parole boards that they are in G.B.G. Just as some staff will use G.B.G. as a stepping stone. But G.B.G. will never, ever get into the business of writing missives to the Board - seeking anybody's release."

If you'll look on the National Association For Public Safety (NAPS) website at www.napsusa.org you'll find the G.B.G. Facebook, Twitter.com and Blog pages. You'll also get to the G.B.G. shop (for caps, t-shirts, coffee mugs and computer pads etc. etc.). G.B.G./HEART do not seek donations! G.B.G. does not need your money! If anyone claims to be raising money for G.B.G. they are lying! ... Sherman has endured solitary confinement, a deadly disease (disseminated Valley Fever), punishments and violations of his rights. When he was felled with Valley Fever and was down to only 96 lbs. when Dr. Paul Griffin told him he would die. He cried out to the God of Abraham, Isaac and Jacob. He told God (De profundis ad tei Domine) "from the depths I cry out to thee, o Lord." He told God "If you'll just let me live I'll build an organization to help keep young people out of prison." He told God "Even though I'm in Joseph's predicament and you allowed me to come to prison for a crime I did not commit. If they had actually caught me for half of the crimes I did commit I'd be buried under the prison... If you raise me up I'll build a team of prisoners to fight youth crime." The die was cast and the sickness only strengthened his determination to build this movement. The implications of Sherman's G.B.G. do not end with New Folsom State Prison. He's helped to inspire a movement leading to a series of landmark (prisoner, collegiate and church) innovations in the movement to divert youth from gangs, guns, drugs and violence.

This book created a chilling image of the American prison system as a haven of darkness and violence. Every high school student, teacher, parent and principal needs to read this book. I recommend it to pastors, police officers, correctional officers, wardens, psychiatrists and social workers. The heads of Foster Care systems, Child protective services and kids in juveniles need to read this book. A lot of youngsters will be drawn to this book and sucked into it's pages because of the "gang" element. And because (unfortunately) many kids look up to prisoners! They are taught in the ghettos, barrios and even in suburbia to hate the police and look up to gang members. And the mob, mafioso and cartel members were all interviewed for this book. And Sherman conducted surveys, passed out questionnaires and consulted with police, prisoners, therapists, predators, murderers, serial killers, drug king-pins, street terrorists, death-row prisoners, priests, kids and parents for this book. The expert opinions of Dr. Jarman, Dr. Solis, Dr. Heitkamp, Dr. Curren, Dr. A. Duran, Dr. Gregg, Dr. J. Friedman and warden James P. Walker are reflected in this fascinating book. I would say much of the credit for being the 'brains' behind the HEART (Helping Educate At Risk Teens) must go to this unprecedented and distinguished team of psychologists, psychiatrists and therapists. And although it may take only one psychologist to change a light bulb. It takes many to transmogrify the youth of this nation. And it takes prisoners working with police, prosecutors, pastors, professors and parents to transform the jangling discords of youth in the hoods and to create an oasis of hope.

When King Pharaoh was having nightmares and dreams he couldn't interpret. He called on astrologers and sorcerers. But nobody could interpret the dream. But the chief Butler told the King that "I know somebody who can." He told the King about a man who was not a Rhodes scholar and not a politician. He didn't tell him about Bishop Flip Flop or Deacon Willie Wonder. But he told him about a dude in prison convicted of a heinous sex crime. In fact "he's convicted of attempting to rape a police captain's wife." But Pharaoh told them to go down to Pelican Bay, Reidsville, Pleasant Valley State Prison, Rikers Island or wherever and bring him Joseph... The chief Butler told the King (the C.E.O. of Egypt) "I know somebody who can!" And when Warden James P. Walker began to write about his legacy he chatted not with the Chief Butler. But he chatted with the Chief Deputy (Ret.) Warden Terry L. Rosario. And they reminisced about all of the child molesters, serial killers and fratricidal youth they had both met in the prisons. And James said to Terry "I've been doing this for 33 years Terry. I've walked the yards of San Quentin worked with death-row prisoners. I've had murders in my buildings, on my yards and in my prisons. I don't feel sorry for those guys. I feel sorry for the victims. But these kids who commit rapes, robberies and murders etc. I wish we could do something to turn them around. I've never had a nightmare about any prisoner hurting me or whatever. The only time I've had any nightmares it's been about the kids. I wish we could get somebody to figure out how to solve this nightmare". Terry L. Rosario replied "Well I can't Jimmy. But I know somebody who can". Terry looked at Jimmy and said "he's a pain in the butt. He's controversial and political. But he's brilliant. And he can." James retorted "Do I know him? You're not talking about an inmate are you?" And Terry replied "Yes and Yes... Sherman D. Manning ..."

The Bible says the steps of a good man are ordered by the Lord. And God ordered Sherman's steps back from his death-bed to New Folsom. It's awesome and it's amazing how the good Lord works. In mysterious ways. And His mercy endures forever. Now hear from Sherman D. Manning the rest of the story!...

Peter Andrist - July, 2010
Zürich Switzerland

Special thanks

Numerous convicts provided data and contributed information to this book. Some of their stories were embellished and some were complete fabrication. In prison it's your story and you can tell it however you want. My experience, training and my team of experts help me to weed out the truth from fiction and to seed in transformational writing. So I wanted to preface the thanks by explaining that some people think they are so smart that they can know you studied psychology at Harvard. But still think they can out wit you. I run into undercover racists just as often as I do under cover homosexuals. And they are cunning, duplicitous and subtle. But I play their game and just pray for them. And many of them talk about others with "ulterior motives" when they themselves are the epitome of an ulterior motive. But so goes the prison and there were many passive participants. But to be fair and harmonious I'll be equitable in my praise. There are guys who charge me to do G.B.G. work. But they'll work gratis for a captain or a lieutenant. And how can you charge me for work for the kids? And you are supposed to be a part of it? I don't write this to single the persons out (notice I don't name them). But I tell you this to show you how prisons operate. You need to get a picture of the prison subculture. And the best way to show you is by letting you read about how we deal with each other. When I'm critical of folk I care about I like and live around I just won't use their names. I'm not trying to embarrass people. But prisons are cesspools of hatred and violence. They are filled with demons and darkness. They are evil, wicked and rotten. Prison is like a rattle snake. It destroys any- and everything that comes inside of it ... Oh I guess I'll give some good people some thanks now.

I wanna thank all of the members of G.B.G. It is a team of men that is only as strong as our weakest link. When we succeed the team gets the fame. If we fail I get the blame. So I thank each member (from my heart) of the G.B.G. team. Johnny "Claw" Willie, Peter Andrist, George "HillBilly" Rose, Samuel Castellanos, Martin Estrada, M. Dillard, Gilbert Blaney, Mr. Washington, Mr. D. Brown, Billy Fleming and others. I thank each of them for their efforts, expertise, participation and the lessons I learned from them. My team is the Bomb! And none of this would be happening without Willie Ford, Fleming, Rose and the aforementioned. Thank you! Thank you very kindly. I thank our staff supporters. Franklin Curren (Harvard MD) is the G.B.G. director of Advisors. C. Solis MD. is the G.B.G. Director of Training. The G.B.G. sponsors are Dr. C. Solis and Dr. Duran. The G.B.G. special consultants are Dr. Jennifer Heitkamp (psychiatrist), Dr. Gregg (psychologist), Dr. Jarman, Dr. J. Friedman, Dr. Jamie Davidson and Dr. Houston (all licensed psychologists). The G.B.G. HEART (Helping Educate At Risk Teens). Advisors are Adam Lane, Dustin Nicolodi, Daniel Bugriyev and M. Reid. I thank them all from my heart and soul. The warden's oversight committee for G.B.G. consists of CCII Patricia Kennedy, CCII Kevin Pool, CCII Goldman, Captain Steve J. Vance and associate warden Fred Schroeder. I thank all of them. The G.B.G. Executive secretary to the president is correctional officer Dianna Smith. Our other secretary is Mr. Bugriyev.

I wanna thank all of these people from Willie all the way to Fred and Steve. I want to give a special thanks to the best warden in the State of California James "Jimbo" Walker. Jimbo is a ubiquitous, hands-on corrections expert with more than 33 years in corrections. I pray that his daughter, Mrs. Kennedy and CCIII Johnson-Dovey will talk Jimbo out of retiring this year. We (G.B.G.) and C.D.C. need him for (at least) 2 more years. He's still very energetic, innovative and we need him. I want my readers to log on to my websites and post messages asking Jimbo to stay 2 more years ... Willie, Ford, Castellanos, Fleming, Washington, Rose, Peck etc. etc. etc. Dr. A. Duran, Dr. Jarman, Dr. Houston, Dr. Friedman, Dr. Gregg, Adam lane, Daniel, Dustin, Fred, Steve, M. Reid, Patricia Kennedy, D. Smith and ... etc. etc. Thank you all so much. If I omitted the name of a member or supporter please charge the omission to my head and not to my heart. I love you all from my heart. You're all awesome! Awesome! Without you all we couldn't do this. ... I wanna also dedicate this entire book to Terry L. Rosario Sr. Terry retired at the top. He was Chief Deputy Warden here at New Folsom. He was good to me. I (literally) called him "Dad". Jimmy (Warden "Jimbo" Walker) worked as a captain under Terry. I was even more unpopular back then than I am now. Mr. Rosario pulled me out of ad-seg, out of transfer buses and out of messes. Rosario was no saint. But he was good to me. I have not forgotten him. And I really appreciate his help. I shout out to his wife and to Terry Rosario Jr. also Thank You .... Mrs. Kennedy (A/K/A "Moms") Thank You... I wanna ask Jimbo if it's okay to have Mr. Nicolodi, Mr. Lane and Mr. Bugriyev to put their photos on our face-book site. I want the world to see G.B.G.

These convicts, physicians, therapists, clinicians and correctional managers have all looked beyond my faults (and I do have many faults) and worked with me. And prison is filled with egomaniacs. There is enough testosterone in a prison to blow up Russia. And it is next to impossible to get 3 or more men in prison (from diverse backgrounds, gangs, cultures etc.) to work together on anything other than a riot. But I've been blessed by God to orchestrate this team. It is fragile and temporal but it is in place. I've had to pray more than I've ever prayed in my life for G.B.G. That's not an embellishment. I was fought by staff and inmates. I was connived against, lied on, set up and manipulated by certain people in authority who jumped on the band wagon when they saw movement. I vividly recall a captain telling a fellow captain (in my presence) how G.B.G. would never work and never happen. I mentioned videotaping the workshops and this captain said "absolutely it will never happen. The warden will never allow a video camera in this facility and.... " He was adamant, negative and shot holes in all of my G.B.G. ideas ... In March 2008 he called in one of my close advisors and explained how he was going to do a juvenile diversion program and he would videotape it and ... Everything which I proposed to do (in writing) became (some kind of way) his idea. Plans he had adamantly been against were now his idea and he would get them done ... I recall a person ranking above a captain (I won't say whether it was a male or female.) indicating "I am committed to G.B.G. 100%. Warden Walker is somewhat committed to a certain extent". However, Mr. Walker was totally, fully and absolutely committed to helping our youth. In defense of this captain and the other official I believe they meant well. In spite of people's arrogance, conceit and even deceit we all have good inside of us. The nature of the Beast (prison) is one of duplicity. And many (if not most) of the people working in corrections become damaged by working here. Living in prison affects one psychologically. Ipso Facto, working in prisons takes a psychological toll. So a lot of staff have been beat, stabbed, lied to and lied on. And they are accustomed to being in charge. So for them to wake up one morning and trust (and cooperate with) Sherman D. Manning and watch me organize goes against everything they have been trained to do. One of my weaknesses and one of my shortcomings (I have many) has been my failure to be as patient as I should be when dealing with supervisory staff. My background is one in which I walked and talked with mayors, governors, congressmen and ambassadors in civilian life. I was a suit and tie type youth leader. So I'm used to either being in charge or being treated as an equal. By those who are in charge and people like "dad" (Chief Deputy Warden Terry L. Rosario Sr.) were smart enough to take my history into account. And being the master manipulator that he is/was "dad" took me in and treated me as his own family. He broke no rules and violated no regulations for me. But he called me "Sherman" and I called him "Terry" or "Dad". And every time he had to make a judgment call involving me he made it in my favor. That satisfied my ego and it neutralized me. Terry knew no matter how many books I wrote he was untouchable in my books. Because I felt obligated. But now I'm dealing with people who are not as secure as Terry was.

Some are not as skillful as he was and some are just control freaks. And (to be fair) some just don't like me. And my failure was my unwillingness to take a Big picture look at things and to humble myself even more. I'm a lot more humble than I was 6 years ago. But not humble enough. I'm not demonizing C.D.C. (I do that in other books!) ... In fact I owe Sgt. Blackburn an apology. He knows why. I wanna be man enough to write publicly to Sergeant Blackburn that I apologize ... I also apologize for negative comments about captain Steve Vance. I don't always agree with Mr. Vance but I've seen Mr. Vance do some good. So let me salute Captain Steve John Vance, Fred Schroeder and Sergeant Blackburn here and now. ... At the end of the day we are all God's Children. We are human beings. And we (Fred, Steve, Willie, Alonso, Patricia Kennedy, Ford, Daniel, Adam, Dustin, M. Reid, C. Solis MD., Dr. A Duran, Dr. Jarman, C.O. T. Ramsey, C.O. K. Yeager, George, Kevin Pool and all of my G.B.G. team. We (C.O. D. Smith, CC II Gaskins, Rev. Glen Shields etc.) came together ... Convicts, physicians, therapists, clinicians, correctional officers, lawyers, professors, students and parents and we did a beautiful thing called G.B.G.

Senator John Burton blew our minds by becoming one of the forefathers of the G.B.G. support team. He was president pro tempore of the California Senate. Senator Burton was one of the most (if not the most) powerful politicians in the State of California. He reminds me of a white Rev. Hosea Williams! A bull in a china shop! Attorney Burton is called arrogant, profane, mean as hell and tough. But in spite of all of that he accepted my collect telephone call and came out and publicly supported the Gang Bangers for Good. On behalf of my staff and team (i.e., Dr. Jennifer Heitkamp, Dr. Gregg, Dr. Jarman and Dr. Duran etc.). I want to salute Senator (Ret.) John Burton. His support and endorsement of G.B.G. is a blessing and a miracle from Almighty God ....

I remember letting C.O.. K. Yeager peruse a missive from Senator Burton. Mr. Yeager replied "wow! This is amazing. John Burton? ... I think G.B.G. is a great thing Mr. Manning. If you need me to come to work early to help you with the youth tours let me know. I don't want my name (oops) in anything but I'll be a silent supporter." I was humbled. Thank You! Thank you. Thank You all so very much. It's just a blessing to see what God can do if we ask him. I'm not unmindful of the fact that this (G.B.G./HEART) is God's work!

Distinguished Professor and scholar of Law Michael Vitiello (at McGeorge School of Law) is also a major G.B.G. supporter. If I had ten thousand tongues I'd thank professor Vitiello with every tongue. Professor Vitiello is just a good man. He is for real. He is altruistic, positive and a blessing to G.B.G. Thank you Professor Vitiello...

Again I thank Dr. Lewis Yablonsky, Mrs. Spohn, the late Dr. Tyrone Hedblad, Linda MacFarland, Just Detention International, The Stafford Foundation, ACLU, Dept. of Justice office of the Inspector General, Male Survivors, Bay Area Women Against Rape, California Coalition Against Sexual Assault, California Coalition For Women Prisoners, Peace Over Violence, Code Pink Women for Peace, Psuyin at the Sexual Assault Recovery and Prevention Center of San Luis Obispo, Weave, Inc. Prison Legal News and Justice Denied Magazine ... I miss Rod Hickman (ex C.D.C. Director) and I didn't like the way he exited. I also miss Jeannie Woodford. But Matt Cate is a good man and he's doing a good job as director. I respect Susan Hubbard and give major props to Scott Kernan. Mr. Kernan helped inspire G.B.G. because of what he did with C.G.A. While he was warden at M.C.S.P.

In my very first meeting with Fred Schroeder about G.B.G./HEART I told him about Scott's C.G.A. I hope Susan, Scott and Matt will talk "Jimbo" (A/K/A James Walker ... A/K/A the Best Warden in the State of California) to stay on as Warden of New Folsom for at least 2 more years. Walker's rise from an old prison guard at San Quentin to Warden of New Folsom is like the stuff of movies. It is an awesome tale. I was here and I worked for the dude when they walked him off grounds (more on that in another time) for an investigation. I recall vividly how certain staff laughed and talked about how he and Rosario would be fired. I recall when they offered Jimbo the option of losing a bar (demotion to Lieutenant) and going to Mule Creek or being fired. Jimbo had the balls of a bull. He told them where they could go. And I recall Madame Patricia Kennedy giddily telling Willie and me that "Captain Walker will be back Monday." He and Terry L. Rosario Sr. were cleared (conclusively) of all wrong doing. And I think that being falsely accused has given Walker a strange kind of sensitivity which most correctional administrators can only read about. Walker and I are political opposites. Last time I checked he had no inmate (which definitely includes Sherman D. Manning) friends. But we talk. Mr. Walker gets on my nerves sometimes. But so does the president. I don't always agree with his decisions. But I respect him. And I can honestly say that he is a good man. And it tickles me to see some of the very same staff who thought he would go to jail now calling him "Warden". I had a guy tell me "I would have bet my car Walker was gonna be demoted. I would have bet my horse he'd never be confirmed as Warden." He is the shell answer man. The comeback kid. His story is inspirational and motivational to every young person who considers yourself an underdog. I'm so glad that great senators like Gloria Romero know what a great superintendant we have at C.S.P. Sacramento ...

Attorney Murray J. Janus, Michael Edward Bergin, Reggie Love, Principal Aaron Fernander, Barbara Lee, Dollie and James Manning, Reggie Manning, Brenda Smith, Shanteeka Smith, Shateecia Smith, Jeremy (Coalinga Fire Dept.), John Johnson (C.N.A.), Dr. Glade Roper, Dr. Paul Griffin, Dr. Kasper, Dr. Libke, Linda Li Hong, Nurse Susan, Janet, Marc Kashirets etc. Thank you ...

Sherman D. Manning, 2010
www.napsusa.org

The Folsom State Prison

"This is not a fun place to spend the Holidays! Sherman D. Manning owns real estate inside this (gated) community, and since Sherman lives in this place he can tell you how not to get here ...." On 10/4/10 Dr. Phil had homeless teens (Danny and Bonnie) on his show. Go Kelly Osbourne! And Alex Weinberg). I wanna get Danny in G.B.G. ... I asked Daniel Bugriyev and Mark Kashirets (two Christian G.B.G. consultants) to pray for Danny and for Bonnie. ... Help get K.K.K. to Michael Zhuang, Matthew Hallock, Andrew Bugbee, Taylor Matthews, John Foraker, Justin Cash, Justin Butler's brother, Dr. Steve Salzman, Ron Holt, Ben Marcovitz, Geoffrey Canada, Tim Robbins (Break the Whip), Don Shalvey, Chris Barbic and David Wu (teacher). This book is a road map away from prisons. Help get this to Nathan French, Dorsey High School Kids, Anthony Dewitt, Brian Grove, Gabe Teague, Carter Livingston, Jimmy Stewart Jr., David Carter, Michael Dennis, Adrian Grenier, Greg King, Dano Graves, Reed Alexander, Lavisas Williams and Alexander Burns etc.

Read on!

K.K.K. (Kids Killing Kids)

It all started with a death-bed promise to God that I would use my life to revolutionize youngsters. I was in the hospital for 14 months with disseminated Valley Fever. At my worst I weighed only 96 lbs. Correctional officers sat outside my hospital door making bets about how soon I would die. I felt the death angel lurking in the room. To state that I was sick and in horrendous pain is an understatement. This was the darkest hour of my life. I will write a bit more about my illness and near death experience later. But I told God that I needed a miracle. I needed him not just to raise me up off of my sick bed, but I needed to come up off of my death-bed. "If you'll raise me up I'll raise the youth up" I told God. And I'd been, perusing "the freedom writers diary" in my hospital bed. And I had just finished reading "The pursuit of happiness" by Chris Gardner. My body was broken but my spirit was ready and ripe for a miracle. I tell the entire disseminated Valley Fever story in "Blue Eyed Blonde" Book II and in my book "Left For Dead". So I won't rehash it here... I've interviewed admitted sexual predators, infamous homicidal maniacs, kid killers, Bloods, Crips, 415's, Northerners, Southerners, Skinheads, Aryan Brotherhood members, Klansmen, Two Five members, drug addicts, drug dealers, ex-police officers, multi-millionaires, wardens, captains, psychologists, psychiatrists, authors, homosexuals, bisexuals, trisexuals, rape victims, HIV patients, nurses, certified nursing assistants, firemen, congress persons and senators for this book. I conducted extensive research on gangs, drugs, guns and violence. I conducted a series of surveys and took polls personally and on the internet for this book. I know how to be cool. I know what it is to smoke dope, drink booze, do meth or crack. I know what is going on in schools across America. I have researched blogs, MySpace, Twitter and Face Book. I have eyes and ears in these high schools. And I know most youngsters who read books are the one's who don't need this book. But we will put this book into the hands of every youngster who attends a G.B.G./HEART clinic at New Folsom State prison. We will also make every effort to provide teens in foster homes, group homes, juveniles and inner city schools this book. I have asked William H. Gross, George Soros, Michael Moore, Tony Robbins, Leon Padilla, Dr. Jerry Buss and others to go to www.napsusa.org and get copies of this book and have them sent to juveniles and to jails. And I want to use my hood certification to talk to youngsters. I am prison certified. I am locked up in the bowels of the California Prison System. And I know all adults say they have a "passion" for youth. And when we see what a lot of catholic priests have done to little boys we wonder what type of "passion" they're speaking of. We all like to brag about how much love, care and concern we have for the little ones. We like to cliché it with "the children are our tomorrow", or we'll use "save the children". We are all familiar with little slogans like "just say no to drugs" etc. All that is well intentioned. But intentions without actions are irrelevant. I intended to come out to California and change the world. Instead I ended up in a Level Four State prison. I will use this book as a projector to show you a movie in your mind about a whole other way of living. Let me show you how to live in a bathroom with another man. I wanna show all of you thugs, crack heads, meth heads, gun carriers and you players who think you are bullet proof what it is like to live in a gated community. I eat, sleep and defecate amongst people society deems the worst of the worse. We are not choir boys. We are not here for going to Sunday School too late. Prison is where they send child molesters, perverts, rapists, sadistic killers, drug kingpins and outlaws. I interviewed a guy (Marvin Johnson) who is in prison for decapitating his homosexual lover. Marvin also decapitated his lover's paramour. As you read this book the opinions, ideas, thought processes and beliefs of Marvin and various other sociopaths will be reflected within these pages. Often I won't even quote the person by name. Sometimes I don't even tell you I'm specifically writing about anyone. But I am writing about specific, real-life persons.

I.E. The infamous Eric and Lyle Menendez. As much as I respect Madame Barbara Walters I used to laugh when I saw how well Eric manipulated her. I worked and lived closely to Eric Menendez for 3½ years. No-one can accuse me of profiting from Eric's crime. Quite candidly of my 8 other books I concisely refer to him (them) in only two. And to date I have never, ever told what I really know about Eric and Lyle. When tabloids offered me thousands of dollars to tell what I knew I refused. When fellow inmates tried to get me to help smuggle his photo (I.D. card) out to a newspaper I refused. When Eric borrowed $ 250.00 from me (I sent it to Becky Snead for him) because of his drug debt I never told it. When he offered to pay me off by giving me anal sex I declined. I never told it. When I saw his cell partner in a G-string in the cell I never revealed it. When I would see Eric giving oral copulation I said nothing. He married Tammy but he is absolutely gay. And I don't gay bash. I am not a person who attempts to dictate a person's sexual orientation. My wife and I do have gay and lesbian friends. But I oppose a man blatantly manipulating a good woman. And (for Tammy) I'd take a polygraph test affirming that Eric Menendez offered me anus for the $ 250.00 loan... He ended up paying me in tobacco. And my office still has the $ 250.00 receipt for the loan. Eric was a custodial technician with me. We both worked building #7 at night. For a long time I refused to even acknowledge his presence. Because he'd confused infamy with celebrity somebody made him think he was a celebrity. His gay lover was Michael Henrickson (real name). And Eric is a calculated, cold blooded, homicidal predator. I went to Mule Creek where I was met by his brother Lyle. Eric had told Lyle I was coming. And I never got to know Lyle as well as I knew Eric. But I did see him every day. What embarrasses me is the fact that I allowed myself to actually "like" Eric. And we had very little in common (except books). But inspite of my disdain for people who unapologetically murder their parents and are arrogant etc. I allowed myself to be sucked into his invisible web of false friendship. But I always had this funny (bad spirit or dark) kind of feeling when I was around Eric. He once told me he had astroplaned in his cell. Eric would vacillate from being into Christianity one month to devil worshipping the next. .. He departed New Folsom and went to P.V.S.P. Upon my arrival there, I discovered he was now into Wiccan. Eric's celly at P.V.S.P. was a drug addict by the nickname of "spot". And (true story) while I was there Eric's ex-lover Henrickson transferred in (small world) to the prison. And Henrickson's ex-gay boy lover who's name is also Eric was at P.V.S.P. Eric W. and Eric Menendez had an argument over Mike Henrickson. Believe it or not, Henrickson went with Eric W. over Eric Menendez... Eric Menendez is one of these guys who is a murderer but has a chip on his shoulder. He walks around as if he's done the Nation a favor. And I don't believe (for one moment) his dad was molesting them. And how could you blow your mother's head off? And how could I belittle myself by speaking to him? My speaking to the Menendez Brothers is indicative of my entire reason for telling his prison story here. It shows how hanging out with killers can rub off on you. And try living with killers. And if you youngsters don't stop slinging dope, get out of the gang; stop beating up women, stop the violence and get back in school, you will come to prison. And as much as I respect your parents and teachers their telling you not to come to prison is not like me telling you. They saw prison on the TV and read about it in the newspapers. Hell, most journalists are under the erroneous assumption that prison is jail and they don't know the difference. I have been where your parents and teachers are. But they've never been where I am. And I'm glad they are not here. So I'm here in hell and before I burn to death I'm launching a nuclear writing assault on gangs, guns, drugs and violence. I am waging a campaign to promote literacy and education. I'm going back to the basics. Reading, writing and arithmetics. Education truly is the Bridge to liberation. The motto of the G.B.G. (Gang Bangers for Good ... and I'll tell you specifics about G.B.G. later) mottos is what President Obama proclaimed: "When you drop out of school, you not only fail yourself, you fail your family and you fail your contry! We must do whatever the heck it takes to keep you in school. If we figure out a way to keep you in school I am convinced we can/will keep you out of prison. More than 90% of U.S. prisoners read at less than a 7th grade level. 82% of U.S. prisoners dropped out of high school. 98% of prisoners did not attend college. More than 90% of the 2% who did go to college, went in prison. Ipso Facto it is a fact that most people who finish high school don't come to prison. And more than most people who go to college don't come to prison. And if you can force yourself to get that high school diploma you can do anything. Absolutely anything. So I don't need to write an extensive dissertation which elucidates a bunch of numerical statistics which might lead you to assume that I'm a bright guy. Having you assume that I am sharp, smart, bright or even brilliant won't help me do what I want to do. My aim is the HEART (Helping Educate At Risk Teens) method founded by G.B.G. (Gang Bangers for Good). I want to help Educate you. I don't sell me as an individual. I don't attempt to convince you that I'm a good guy. I'm not up for a pardon or parole. Governor Schwarzenegger is not gonna let me out of prison. My past is checkered with crimes, false allegations, wrongful convictions, rightful omissions, embellished and even fabricated data. I am not a saint. I am not qualified to receive the Citizen of Year Award. I am a Bad Boy! Don't get it confused. And I know what I know. Prison is a cesspool of hatred. Prison is built to last. Prison is built to maim, kill and destroy. Prison is filled with vicious, mean, bitter and broken boys pretending to be men. We are a bunch of fools. We are living life on a stationery treadmill. Prison is a place where a bunch of men walk around the yard looking like idiots all day long. And we act like we are going somewhere. We act like we are doing something. We are beat down mentally, emotionally and spiritually. There is nothing worse than an incarcerated mind and a locked up spirit. We (staff and inmate alike) are all suffering from some level of institutionalization. It takes a certain level of psychosis just to survive in the prison. This is a sick place. This is a dark, disastrous and a dismal place. This is not a place for players and winners. This is a place for losers. This is a violent place. This place is violent. If I could think of any other way to communicate the fact that prison is belligerent, bellicose and volatile I would. To cell with another man is unnatural. How could anyone think it is cool to live in a bathroom with another man? We eat, crap and sleep in the same concrete shed. C.D.C. has gotten so regimented that our toilets have been put on timers. We can only flush our toilets twice every five minutes. If you flush a third time your toilet (automatically) shuts off for two hours. This is cruel and it is unusual. It is unsanitary. It is barbaric. Now your cell partner has to inhale your defecation. And we live here. And most of us are psychologically damaged by the pain and abnormality of incarceration. And what is terrifying is how few of us know we are mentally damaged. Prisons are battlefields and literally war zones. To say that prison is a microcosm of society at large is somewhat deceptive. Prison is a place for misfits. This is where they send you when courts decide you are too dangerous and dysfunctional to remain in society. It is punishment. And punishment is never fun. People don't get along in prison. Just as they don't get along at home. The difference is when we don't get along in prison we beat, maim, cut and murder each other. Prison is the most racist and backwards place on the planet. And the California (and Texas prisons along with others) prison system suffers from an intense, 1950's style of racism which is unheard of in my home state of Georgia. The prisons in California are racially segregated. They cell blacks with blacks, whites with whites and Mexicans with Mexicans. The racial segregation is even more complex than color. It is also dictated by kind. They put Crips with Crips, Nortēnos with Nortēnos, Bulldogs with Bulldogs etc. etc. And the California prison system is inundated with gangs. Gangs run the prison! And once your narrow behind gets locked up you must choose to run with a gang or get in the hat. And if you get in the hat it means you have a "war daddy". And your war daddy is your

Father, your Big Brother and your man! He is your husband. This means he will protect you and provide you with food and cosmetics. And you will provide him with mouth and butt hole; period. And perhaps you are gay? Perhaps you consider yourself to be straight but have secretly wondered what it would be like to experiment with another boy or man. That's your business. But prison is not the place to seek out relationships. I could pen ten tomes about the myriad reasons that you should never seek out a jail cell looking for love. So to be candid being gay won't cause a prison to be a fun experience. If I had a gay buddy whom I knew was coming to prison I'd advise him to play straight. Gayness and prison mix like oil and gas. It's a mess. We have blatant homosexuals we call Queens. They call them "she". I refuse to call a person equipped with the male apparatus a she. And every drag queen I've ever seen in prison causes problems. People get beat, stabbed and killed over queens in prisons every day. It is a deadly thing to be involved with a prison "faggot" or "punk". (I don't usually call people "punk" or "faggot") and please note that there is an enormous amount of sexual activity in prison. It's called on the down low and "under cover" sex. I know hard core murderers who are as gay as a three dollar bill. I have seen 220 lb. muscle men pumping iron in the day time and riding (another man) at night. Prison breeds homo and/or bisexuality. I call C.D.C. Broke Back (mountain) C.D.C. . I did a study on C.D.C. sexuality. I don't want to get into our findings (I was assisted by a licensed psychologist) in this book, but it would blow your mind. More than 65% of the men in prison have had sex with other men. And more than 50% of prison inmates have hepatitis-C and the HIV rate of infection is soaring in prisons. And 750 thousand prisoners get out of prisons every year. And they carry the diseases right back into the cities and communities in which you live. If they're not f--king (expletive deleted) each other they're sucking each other. If they're not having sex they are sticking needles in their veins. If it's not a needle it's a tattoo gun... We spread disease in prison like wildfires. It is ugly. And yes, it is broke back C.D.C. I know the fellas don't want me to let the cat out of the bag. And I'm in no position to pass judgment on any man. I'm just the writer. But if prison walls could talk a lot of our congressmen and senators would have to say "oh what a tangled web we weaved." It's a gay producing factory. Many of the guards are undercover gay guys. I'll leave that alone. Let me just recommend "Creating Monsters" and "Blue Eyed Blonde", Book II to you. (www.cafepress.com/manning).

Prison is an unnatural environment and it produces perversions. If you lock a wild animal in a cage and keep him there for 20 years he'll become violent (more violent), abnormal and he'll crave stimulation. Put a dog in solitary confinement for ten years. Then bring him a young pup (i.e. fresh meat) for a cage partner and he might rape the puppy. Prisons routinely put 17, 18 and 19 year old boys in the cell with gangsters who have not had a woman in 20 years. What do you think happens? And not only is there consensual sex in prison; statistics say an inmate is raped in California (jail, juvenile or prison) every 19 minutes. Three inmates are raped every hour in California. .. 72 inmates are raped each and every day in California. .. Listen to me young folks. I don't care what politicians may tell you. Regardless of what you see, hear or read in the press. I live here. It's bad. And I don't want to see anybody else (black, white, Mexican, Indian, Chinese, German, etc.) come to prison. But I've gotta admit that I feel especially sorry for you Caucasians perusing this tome. Any white boy in California who gets himself locked up (especially in Los Angeles County Jail) has a death wish. (Disclaimer: this is not a work of fiction! This book is non-fiction ...) To be candid in prison (even in Georgia, New York, Florida, Texas, etc.) the whiter the meat, the sweeter the treat. It is difficult to explain but I did extensive research and conducted a series of surveys with victims of rape in prison, the perpetrators of rape and with witnesses to rape. And it is my opinion (based upon these extensive research, consultations with experts i.e. Dr. Jarman, Dr. Curren, Dr. Solis, Dr. Heitkamp, Dr. Gregg, Dr. Houston, Dr. Jamie Davison, Dr. Hall etc. after studying data by experts such as Dr. Lewis Yablonsky, Dr. Terry Kupers and Dr.

Phil McGraw, and based upon being an eyewitness to several sadistic, racially motivated train rapes in L.A. County Jail) that sexual gratification plays an extremely small part in the reasoning for prisoner rape. Inmate homosexuality has very little to do with it. It is (indeed) about power! It is sadistic, perverted and it is wicked. But it is about power. I do not have a recognized degree in psychology. I'm not an expert in psychology per se. Yet a renowned gang expert and author of 19 books on prisoners (Dr. Lewis Yablonsky) calls me an "Experience therapist". And I've been careful, humble and pragmatic enough to surround the G.B.G. team (I'll explain that later) with licensed psychologists, psychiatrists and correctional veterans. And it is the collective opinion of the G.B.G./HEART team of experts that prisoner rape is all about power. One could argue that all rape is about power. I beg to differ. I've interviewed and lived amongst many sexual deviants. I've lived around dudes who committed serial and sadistic rapes in civilian life. (I've also interviewed and have direct knowledge of folks falsely accused of rape. It didn't stop with Joseph in Genesis!). By and large guys who committed rapes in civilian life come to prison and never rape a man. The reasons are diverse and complex. However the conclusion I was able to reach after extensive examination was as follows: Men who rape women are generally cowards. Some combination of abuse, neglect and denial led them to develop low self esteem. The low self esteem gave rise to perversions. These perversions are often satiated by violence and/or rape. Ipso Facto there is a different kind of power. A perverted coward feels when raping a woman in civilian life. Which is not identical to the power gangsters and predators feel when raping a male, fellow prisoner. Ipso Facto, many non gay men who never raped anybody come to prisons and rape men. And I refuse to talk about the sadistic, perverted and violent rapes I saw in L.A. County Jail. I will only say it was like watching a movie. I won't say what I did or didn't do (or say). I'll only affirm that I did not (ever) participate in the rape(s).

There is a psychosis which can adequately elucidate the prison rape epidemic. I have neither the time, space nor expertise to author a dissertation about the psychosis. I can comment with all deliberate certainty, that although Blacks and Mexicans out number Whites (6 to 1) in prisons, more white males are raped in prisons than blacks and Mexicans combined. Blacks rape white boys in jail. Mexicans and Asians rape white boys in prisons. Older whites rape whites in prison. It is an epidemic of titanic proportions. (Read more about it in "Blue Eyed Blonde" Book II. And in "Fish" by T.J. Parsell). And even though this book is directed toward diverting youths away prisons. And I wanna help prevent the crisis of kids killing kids. I also wanna take a moment to use this tome (platform) to tell the congress, our U.S. Senate and State legislators to please, please do more to prevent rapes in prisons! These guys who are forced into sexual servitude are the new slaves in America. Ipso Facto, America now has white slaves!!! Trapped in the filthy bowels of prisons in Alabama, Georgia, Michigan, New York, California, Texas, etc. etc. there are tens of thousands of inmates (mostly white) who are owned by other inmates (mostly black and brown) ...   The sadistic and senseless rapes of female prisoners across the Nation is so widespread and rampant that I won't even attempt to address it in this book. G.B.G./HEART has commissioned a study (co-chaired by Dr. A. Duran and Dr. Jennifer Heitkamp) of female rape victims in prisons. We will issue the findings by the end of 2009. I will say women prisoners have a serious epidemic of rape in prisons. And G.B.G. calls for emergency, congressional hearings on rape in women's prisons ... Back to the Bad Boys ... Prisons are filled with illicit sex Broke Back C.D.C. They took the girlie mags. They now have two men showering together (M.C.S.P., P.V.S.P., etc.) in prisons. And when you spend 24 hours per day in the room with another man, when you hear his grunts as he craps, and you smell his gas, you (often) either kill him or screw him. Prisons breed sexual deviance and abnormality. Prisons are breeding grounds for learned helplessness, posturing and psychological madness. (I strongly suggest every young man read "Prison Madness" by Dr. Terry Kupers and "Blue Eyed

Blonde" Book II.) ... Since we know more than 750 thousand (perhaps as many as 825 thousand) prisoners get out of prisons each year , what do we think about the AIDS, Hepatitis, tuberculosis, staph. infections, aggravated mental illnesses and perverted sexuality which prisoners bring back to the streets with them? ... Prisons are cesspools of anger, abnormality, wickedness, violence and mayhem. Prison takes a toll on even strong minded and mentally stable individuals. It most certainly takes a toll on the children we lock up who are still tender, impressionable and easily influenced. I have asked Chief Deputy Warden (Ret.) Terry L. Rosario, Warden James "Jimbo" Walker and CC II Patricia Kennedy to oversee a study by Dr. C. Solis, Dr. Duran, Dr. Gregg and Dr. Jarman about the after effects of prison on a young man's psyche as it pertains to sexuality. We will also consult with Dr. Terry Kupers on this study. We will present our findings to congress and to President Obama.

But it doesn't require a rocket scientist to figure out that kids are tender, naive, gullible, curious and highly sexed. So when you lock up a 14, 15, 18 or 19 year old boy. When you house him with 30, 40 and 50 year old prisoners etc. it is a recipe for rape, enslavement, intimidation and violation.

I interviewed a 28 year old Hispanic inmate just days ago. We conducted a 2 hour interview in which no questions were out of bounds. His name is Mario Delgado. Mario and I rarely talk. Yet I've watched him move around in the prison for months now. He can read. He can write and he can think. And he's a gang member. His is a southern Mexican gang member. Mario was a member of Los Primos (The Cousins). We discussed Los Primos, Golden West, 18th Street, the Mexican Mafia and Eme. We talked Nuestra Familia and other gangs. (more on that later). But I was astounded when Mario looked directly into my eyes and clearly proclaimed that "I was afraid somebody would try to rape me in prison. You join a gang and you hope the gang will protect you. You need your squad around you to keep people from preying on you and taking your sh-t." It should be noted that I've been taught some of the same methods which the secret service use in order to detect deception. A psychiatrist (years ago) who specialized in these methodologies trained me in this specialty. I also conducted extensive research in the areas of reading body language and the detection of deception in the eyes of individuals.

Ipso Facto I'm extremely receptive to the notion that much of the data provided in polls and surveys is embellished and/or fabricated. When I was a kid my mom told me that a neighbor (Mr. Popeye) was a pathological liar. And she indicated that anytime I wanted an answer to go talk to Mr. Popeye. And she said to believe the very opposite of anything he told me. "If he tells you to carry your umbrella because it will rain, wear a bathing suit instead. Because you can bet your bottom dollar it will be sunshine" she said. "If Popeye tells you to wear a coat for the cold, you should wear short pants and a t-shirt" she said. Likewise, I believe very little of what I'm told. Especially in a prison. By staff and by inmates. However, I'm uniquely positioned as a researcher and as an investigator because (unlike most of the folks who write about prisoners) I live with the people and the subjects of my research. I know the Business. I am accustomed to the vernacular of guards and convicts, cops and robbers. I know a "war" story when I hear one. And time, after time, after time people (cops and robbers) told me bull crap stories just to try to get put in a book. I know the Business. Many a person in prison suffers from delusions of grandeur and a psychosis of narcissism. And many of my cohorts think they can out think, out-smart and out maneuver a Harvard scholar. They dropped out of high school in the 7th grade. They read two books in solitary confinement and took a six month course in philosophy. And now they think they're scholars.

But I'm cognizant of embellishment. And I meticulously scrutinized all of the data provided to me for this book. A Harvard trained psychiatrist along with C. Solis MD. and A. Duran Ph.D. perused (analytically) all of the surveys which I conducted.

My goal is not to put together a critically acclaimed book that might land me on Oprah. More importantly I wanna bring a Dr. Phil like candor, to the discussion on kids killing kids. America is at a crossroads. Where do we go from here?... A few weeks ago we had a mass killing in North Carolina. A crazed killer murdered the elderly... In Binghamton New York a youngster just murdered 13 people because he felt folks were picking at him because of the way he talks. All of his weapons were registered to his name. Recently an 8 year old boy apparently used a shotgun to kill his own father along with his father's roommate. It was his father's (rest in peace) weapon. If his father didn't have "that" shotgun (in the house) the kid certainly could not have killed them with "that" weapon. And why did (if he did it) this kid do this? Did (the elephant in the room... All due respect to the deceased) the kid get molested by the dad's roommate? Did the kid "see" something going on between the dad and this man which confused and/or angered him?... Jordan Brown is eleven years old. Jordan is a baby. He's a kid. And a few months ago Jordan supposedly murdered his dad's pregnant girlfriend. Jordan (allegedly - for the record these are all unproven allegations) used his dad's gun to commit this heinous murder. His dad taught him how to shoot and hunt. In fact, this 11 year old kid has won shooting and hunting awards. If he didn't know how to shoot? If his dad didn't have unlocked and unsupervised weapons in the house? If? We can if all day long. But the bottom line is there is rampant violence in America right now. There are hundreds and thousands of kids killing kids. We face the problem of kids killing kids with guns, knives, cars, drugs and even with sticks. We are raising little gangsters and thugs in the ghettos, barrios and even in suburbia now. Kids don't have to get jumped into gangs anymore. They are born into gangs. I'm told of 8, 9, and 10 year old kids who are bonifide gang members. Can you even fathom a 3rd grader in a gang? A 3rd grader packing heat? A 3rd, 4th or 5th grader killing a kid (or an adult?)? There seems to be a kind of belligerent spirit released upon the psycho of children growing up in these United States today. There seems to be a mentality of madness which has been unleashed upon our youth today. And we (Americans) must unite ourselves under the banner of saving our children. One of the things which we can do to save the children is to save ourselves. Physician heal thyself. To thirk ownself be true. I was talking with an under cover racist the other day who went on and on about strategies we can employ to help youngsters to get along. How can we teach kids to do what we can't/won't and don't do? We are duplicitous with a capital "d". We hate each other. We walk north and talk west. We are mean, bitter, broken and spiteful boys pretending to be men. We will work (typing, waxing floors or even shining shoes) for a captain, lieutenant or a sergeant gratis all day long. But if a fellow convict needs something typed he must pay. And he can't just pay but we want specific items. We have no charity or altruism for community efforts. But we wanna teach kids to get along?

It sounds too simplistic and it seems elementary but if we (adults - in prison as well as those who are outside these walls) fix our own brokenness our kids will mend. Kids model parents, cousins, teachers and dudes they see in the neighborhood.

There have been billions upon billions of people born to planet earth. As a matter of fact kids have been born since you started reading this page. Babies are born every second. And never in the history of humanity has there been born a racist girl or racist boy. Kids are not born racist. You were not a racist at birth. I knew absolutely nothing about race at birth. Each and every thing we know about race was/is learned from somebody else. Kids model us. They model our idiosyncratic whims. They model our attitudes, habits and even our vernacular. So I don't need my Harvard trained psychiatrist (Dr. Franklin Curren) to figure out that if we (all of us who have this "passion" to "save" the youth) really wanna save the youth we've got to save ourselves. That's it and that's all. When we figure out how to love one another and stop our racism there will never be another racist kid. When we figure out some kind of way to stop our adult violence, rapes and robberies kids will stop. If my mission (with this book) was to simply present a plan to stop every child born (right now ... starting this very second) from fighting, shooting, molesting and killing people the task would be easy. It would be simple. I would send kids being born today as far away from you and me as I could send them. Give me ten kids today who are 6 hours old and let me send them to an island where there are ten men and ten women. And if the 20 parents use no alcohol, smoke no cigarettes, use no profanity, love one another, don't fight, rape, shoot or kill etc. If violence is not introduced to these kids via the television, radio or internet etc. You can go find the 10 kids 15 years from now and you'll find zero racism, violence, drug addiction or crimes. Rape is learned behavior. Racism is learned behavior. Murdering people is not innate.. Assaulting folks is not innate. The kind of great work Ryan Hreljac does to provide wells (water) for the poor in Africa is innate. Ryan is an 18 year old white kid who has a heart of gold (innate). And he had a burden to do the work which Jesus talked about in St. Matthew Chapter 25. And so this kid saw people thirsty and he's committed his life to giving them water to drink. The people he helps look nothing like him. Ryan is a lily white boy with blue eyes. The people he helps are as black as an ace of spade ... Mother Teresa decided to follow Jesus into the slums. It was (to her) natural to have a ministry for hurting people. And most human beings (who are not mentally ill and who have not been tainted by people around them; who have been tainted by them.) Have a giving, a helping and a loving nature. When we see tsunamis, hurricanes and tornadoes etc. we all operate on Auto-pilot. We give of our money, time, food and service. White people send help to black people and vice versa. If you walked down the street right now and saw a six month old infant who was not breathing you would help. Would you not? You'd try to do C.P.R. You'd call 911. I'll bet that 99.9½% of you reading would help that baby whether it was male or female. You would not give a darn about whether the baby was a boy or a girl. You can't even fathom some dude stopping at the place where a hurt or non breathing baby is and checking to see if it's a boy or girl before deciding whether or not to render aid. In fact, even in the 40's and 50's there were a lot of white physicians, nurses, paramedics and anesthesiologists who could have killed black patients but did not. Society dictated that blacks should be mistreated, denied and discriminated against etc. But those medical professionals (more often than not) saved the lives of black folks in spite of and not because of. Time and again white doctors woke up in the morning. They drove from segregated, lily white neighborhoods where they'd faint if they saw a black man. And they arrived at the hospital and parked their Jaguar. They washed themselves up, put on scrubs and performed open heart surgery on black men. They delivered black babies from black wombs. There was even a time when pregnant black women could not afford to go to hospitals. And even if they could afford it they were disallowed to be treated at hospitals. But even in the midst of that kind of discriminatory abuse, very often white nurses and physicians would drive to the black family's abode and deliver the baby. It is just another signal that altruism, love, caring and sharing are innate.

I am not only amazed at how far we've come in this great country. But my fellow Americans when I look back at where we come from I now see the glass as half full. I am astounded that more people didn't rape, maim and kill each other. I'm not pretending that it was not bad. Google "Bloody Sunday" and look at Rev. Hosea Williams. Also Google Ambassador Andrew Young. They were on the balcony at Lorraine Motel when Dr. King was cut down by a vile racist. Hosea (AKA "Doc") was Dr. King's Chief Field General. He was beat and bloodied by cold white men at the Edmund Pettus Bridge. They saw cross burnings and murders all in the name of race. But they also saw white students (I would argue that it is the grand kids of these former students who helped elect L. Douglas Wilder, Deval Patrick and even Barack Hussein Obama) get on buses and ride for freedom for black people. And many whites died and were murdered by whites. But why would they ride for freedom? Because intrinsically they understood that racism was abnormal. And the sick white brothers who murdered them were simply modelling the behaviors of their parents.

But the fact that more blacks didn't get together and go burn down white houses and churches etc., the fact that more black slaves didn't murder the master in his sleep, the fact that (vice versa) more whites (in positions of power) didn't kill more blacks etc. tells me that even in the midst of all of this hatred, anger, meanness and wickedness etc. love is a natural emotion. ..

When we are arrogant and egotistical etc. it is a combination of learned behavior (via modelling) as well as some small form of an inferiority complex that we are feeling. You young men know that when someone gives you a compliment or praises you it makes you feel good. And this is because it boosts self esteem. And when people criticize you (even if you know it is true) how does it make you feel? There are a number of ways to boost self esteem. And I want you to try them for 21 days.

A. Engage in positive self-talk. For the next 21 days (or more) wake up in the morning telling yourself "I'm worthy. I'm special. I'm God's child. I can". Go to bed at night telling yourself the same things. Positive self affirmations work wonders for self esteem. Talk good to yourself! Know that you're okay. God made you and (no matter what) you are okay.

B . Learn new things. Read good books. Read! Read! Read! Reading opens up the mind and betters self esteem. Learn a new word (dictionary or Thesaurus) every day. And the more words you learn there is an automatic self esteem boost which shall occur. Reading and learning new words are like vitamins for your mind. Do it for 21 days. Learn 21 words in 21 days.

And finally (C) pray. Pray for self esteem. And when you feel good about yourself, you'll become more calm and in control of your emotions. Motions create emotions. When you get loud, angry, arrogant, agitated and nervous you shut down and short circuit your brain. Slow down your gesticulations. Breathe in and out slowly. Breathe from the pit of your belly. Slow down and breathe in and out slowly. Relax and don't make sharp, quick and choppy moves with your hands. And you will calm down. And your self esteem will be enhanced. And you won't explode ... You have seen so many people in positions of power who were arrogant. You have watched leaders, teachers and even pastors who were arrogant and angry individuals. They always react to disagreement with anger and arrogance. They are bullies. And you and I model this kind of leadership. We must learn to have grace under fire. We need to breathe no matter how bad we feel. When we're being disrespected and/or neglected if we can breathe and keep our motions slow (and reserved). We will react more cordially and powerfully. Tony Robbins is a master at teaching that motions create emotions. How you walk, talk and how you move your body dictates how you feel. Ipso Facto, You can't smile and feel sad. You can't wrinkle up and tighten your face and feel happy. When we frown and breathe fast our blood pressure shoots through the roof. And we feel bad. I have been so angry that I became literally ill. And my blood pressure was high enough to kill me. But even in the midst of anger there were times Mrs. Kennedy would tell me to "Breathe". She said "Just be quiet and breathe." I would literally feel better... If every young man reading this book just took this one thing away about motions creating emotions we would stop kids from killing kids. You can't murder me if you are smiling at me. You will not blow my brains out if you are sober, breathing properly, thinking clearly and smiling. We often hear people say "I don't know why I did it. I just got angry. I wasn't thinking straight". Motions and how we think contribute to anger. Anger shuts down the brain. So if I breathe properly I won't get angry. If I move my body in a relaxed way my brain won't shut down. When we smile we release chemicals in the brain which tell us to feel good. It sounds too simplistic but I guarantee you that if we begin to practice self esteem, practice self talk and relaxation. If we train our motions etc. we will ameliorate teen crimes (including rape and murder)...

I also wanna talk about group homes and foster care. We must do something now to fix the broken system. I saw "Angelo" on Fox 40 News who is 16 and needs a family. Angelo is at that age where he really, really, really needs some structure. And what makes his situation worse is the fact that we don't wanna adopt teenagers. I hope you'll call the Sierra Adoption Services (916-368-5114) and check up on Angelo... on 04/07/09 I spoke with Yolanda McFarland at the Alliance for Children's Rights in Los Angeles. They are powerful advocates for kids in the foster care system. If you are being abused or mistreated in the Foster care system (anywhere in America) I want you to call 213-368-6010 and ask for Yolanda in the intake department. They can help you.

And my research has shown that many people in prison came from the Foster care system and/or from group homes. And research shows that more than 70% of them were abused (sexually, physically and/or emotionally). And 100% of them know someone who was abused in group or foster care. And G.B.G. is blessed to have Dr. A. Duran on staff. She worked (teaching psychology) in 7 universities. She worked for child protective services in 2 states. She is an expert. And her expertise is represented throughout this tome. Dr. C. Solis treated the heads of C.P.S. in the past. He is an expert psychiatrist. And I consulted with him (extensively) while preparing this book. Dr. Jarman, Dr. Gregg, Dr. Houston, Dr. Jennifer Heitkamp, Adam Lane (RT), Dustin Nicolodi (RT), M. Reid, Daniel Bugriyev and many others helped me to write this book. I recall C.O. K. Yeager telling me on 04/01/09 "I'm willing to help you with G.B.G. This is a powerful thing you're doing. In all my years in corrections I've never, ever seen any prisoner send out as much mail as you do. You send hundreds of letters out per week. All for G.B.G. I'll volunteer to come in early on Saturdays to help".

Captain Steve John Vance earns $ 108 grand per year. And he told me "I'll come in every Saturday to do this"...

Captain Vance, C.O. Yeager, Adam, Dustin, Daniel, Dr. Duran, Dr. Solis and these others all know that group homes and the Foster Care System is often breeding ground for criminals. Group homes and Foster Care can be a feeder system for the prisons. We must stop abuse in group homes. We must better manage Foster Care. Just as there is an economic tsunami in America due to too much deregulation. Too little and lackadaisical over sight of the Foster Care and group home systems in America has caused a Foster Care Armageddon in these United States. There is an epidemic of titanic proportions in group homes in America. And I wanna start a National dialogue about group homes and Foster Care (see http://napsusa.blogspot.com) in America. I want attorney Andrew Bridge, Jason Huyck, Yolanda MacFarlane and teens across America to log on and discuss ways to fix the system. I want Hillary Nachem in congressman Doris Matsui's office to log on. Dallas works at Kmax TV and we need his two cents. Bill Dallas (author of "Lessons from San Quentin") needs to get in on this National conversation. I want Paul Wright, Rose Braz, Robbie Wolff and the Youth Justice coalition to get in on this conversation. I want YAYI (Youth Against Youth Incarceration), James Shelby and Alice Huffman to help us. We need everyday citizens like Craig Scott, David Hellyer and Zach Freisen to get in on this discussion. If we find a way to motivate folks like Van Jones, Mr. Willie Brown, C.J. Sheron, Brian Hawn and Desiree Rogers to log on to www.napsusa.org and offer suggestions on fixing the Broken System we will change the world. We need Ari Wohlfeiler, Cassie Pierson and Luke Sears in on this. I wanna launch a cyber offensive attack on the abuse that is rampant in Foster Care and in group homes. If we can get Kyle Love, Chris Austad, Guy Farris and Andrew Bridge to work together. If we can figure out a way to motivate folk like Van Hansis, Jake Silberman, Billy Magnusson, Maxwell Hanger and Michael Sessions to work together we can revolutionize the Foster Care System.

I used to tell C. Solis MD., A. Duran Ph.D., J. Heitkamp MD. and Dr. Jarman that "since I have all of these unused degrees in psychiatry and psychology around me I may as well pull knowledge from you guys and use it to change the world". And I'm so very thankful to God for people like Harvard Graduate Franklin Curren MD., Dr. Houston, Dr. J. Friedman and other experts who have made their knowledge available for me to use to help kids. Dr. Solis told me that "you are uniquely positioned Sherman to revolutionize our youth. Unfortunately the youth looks up to guys in prison. You are Heroes and Bad asses to them. When you talk to them or write to them you have a ready made and captive audience... Hollywood has taught kids that violence, robberies and gangs are exciting. So when you tap in to that phenomenon and manipulate it with a name like Gang Bangers for Good and/or Gang Bangers for God you can use prison as a Bully pulpit to help the youth in ways that I could never help them". Dr. Solis continued with "Dr. Heitkamp, Dr. Duran and all of us who are learned experts have watched you run around here like a chicken with your head cut off for G.B.G. You have worked your butt off to make this program happen. And we so respect your intentions and your drive. But no matter how spectacular you may be in many areas, this is still a prison. And they operate unlike any bureaucracy I've ever seen. I'm not criticizing my employers at all. But I can tell you that prison is a very complicated (to say the least) bureaucracy. Don't give up and don't quit. You planted G.B.G. at C.S.P. Sac. You started this program and kicked the doors open. All of that writing, researching, reading, praying and studying has not been in vain. And providence will dictate the results. Keep going".

And when I observe the excitement which I've seen in the eyes of these professionals (ie. Adam Lane who is an ex-marine sergeant but only 30 years old. Daniel, Dustin, Dr. Duran and Dr. Gregg) when I talk to them about G.B.G. it excites me and it reminds me that "yes we can" help stop the epidemic of kids killing kids. And if I am able to motivate and locate just ten Adams, Dustins, Bugriyev, Steve Vance', A. Durans', C. Solis' and Jennifer Heitkamps' etc. in civilian life we will revolutionize Foster Care and group homes in these United States of America. When we fix orphanages, group homes and the Foster Care System in America we will reduce the population of the prison system.

And for all of you youngsters who are perusing this book consider this a missive of sorts. This book is really a letter to youngsters from a brother in the prison. If I knew I was about to die and I had only 3 hours to talk to the American Youth this book (missive) is what I would say to yall. If I could talk to the boy'z in tha hood this tome is what I'd say to you. I would be brief. I'm reminded of a Lil Boy sittin in church one Sunday with his mom. The preacher was yelling and hollering and had been lecturing for hours. The kid yelled out "you preach too loud". And his mom grabbed him and told him to be quiet. He then yelled "you preach too long" and his mom slapped his leg and she was so embarrassed. And he yelled "and you ain't saying nothing"... If I were standing in front of students at Folsom High School, or in Compton or Oakland Ca. If I were talking to kids to YAYI or the Youth Media Council I would try not to talk too loud. I wouldn't talk too long and I'd try to say something (lol). I would tell yall not to come to prison. Yes I would remind you that there are 2.4 million people in prison in America. I'd reiterate the fact that (I can't say it too much) more than 49% of them are kids 7-19 years young. I'd talk about Foster Care, abuse and group homes. I'd have a variety of issues which I would discuss. But the main focus of my chat would be from the vantage point that no one you know has. And that is from the perspective of someone on the inside looking outside ... Now (with all due respect) I know Madame Oprah may not want to talk to me or my cohorts. We are manipulative, deceptive and full of games. We lie, cheat, kill and steal. We are thugs. And you can't trust us. But on closer analysis Dr. A. Duran once told me something which blew my mind. She said "Sherman if there was a person who literally and verifiably went to hell, met Satan and came back, everybody would want to talk to him. He would be on Oprah, Tyra Banks and on Dr. Phil. We may be afraid to touch him or trust him. We might think that touching him would make the residue of hell rub off on us etc. But we would pray that he wrote a book which we could read. We would watch him and analyze his every word. You'd see him on the Today Show, Good Morning America and on Dateline..." Dr. Duran continued "Sherman prison is hell. It is a beast and a monster factory. And I believe it is incredibly important for us to hear what a person living in hell has to say. If I'd wanna hear from a person who just got back from hell, I would certainly want to read a letter written from a person in hell. Society may never trust you. They may not be comfortable with you. But they need to hear and read every word which you have to say". This came from a brilliant (may I remind you) female psychologist who has taught in universities. She has also worked in (our core audience) Child protective Services. Prison is absolutely hell. And I have met Satan (via Eric and Lyle Menendez. Via a guy you've seen on Inside Edition who murdered the actress who played on Mork and Mindy. He rang her door bell and the moment she opened the door he pulled out a gun and murdered her. We call him "Arizona", but his name is Bardo. He even stalked O.J. Simpson, Attorney Marcia Clark through the mail. I interviewed him on 47 occasions for a total of more than 86 hours... Daniel Henson was a 16 year old who murdered his parents, siblings and the dog! We had hundreds of conversations over the course of 4 years... I promise you I am in hell and I have met Satan! .... Marvin Johnson? When he was 19 he decapitated his gay lover as well as the youngster who was with him. I still have long missives written to me by Marvin. He was my next door neighbor for 13 months.) in these dark and tormenting prisons. And even if Oprah never believes in Sherman D. Manning it's all good. I just want my conversations with killers to motivate you not to kill. I just want my experiences observing gangsters to get you out of gangs. I want to inspire Gabe Williams, Timothy Coleman, Devin Rio (in tracy Ca.), Patrick Green (in Sacramento) and you to stop using meth. Get off crack. Quit packing guns and start packing books... Let me preface this next portion of my missive to you by saying I don't defend child molestation. (for the record) I have no liberal or sympathetic view of those damaged people who would dare molest a child or rape a woman. And I'm so thankful that of all the vile things which I've been accused (I am in Joseph's predicament) of I've never, ever been accused of molesting a child. Thank You Jesus. But having said that - it absolutely amazes me to see the irrational and ridiculous mentality of the prison which subscribes to the unwritten theory that child molesters are worse than sadistic killers. President Obama, Michelle or Dr. Phil if you all are eavesdropping on this conversation I'm having with youngsters I want you all to know this. This hell that I am in is a place where even staff have a mentality of madness. I recall a civilian telling a control cop that "Here comes a criminal and he has an inmate with him". He was referring to the prison guard as the "criminal"... But it amazes me that even staff treats murderers as if they are cool, but the molesters are bad... At P.V.S.P. C.O. Garza treated Eric Menendez as if he was royalty. But he'd say that so and so is a piece of sh_t because he's a molester.

I've watched captains and associate wardens who also routinely refer to the takers of human life with a spirit of camaraderie and okay-ness yet the only bad guys are the molesters. I thank God I was never molested. I would not wish molestation on my worst enemy. But... If I had to make the choice between being molested and being murdered which do you think I'd choose? If you kill me I am over. I am gone! And my reason for sharing this with you is twofold.

A. I want you to recognize how ridiculous, odd, different and unusual the prison subculture is. I want you to notice how unusual it is to have a bunch of murderers sitting around talking about how sick a "molester" is. I want you to have an "Aha" moment and to see that even people working in prisons (hell) get affected by the fire (mentality). And once you step inside hell you will never, ever be the same. Yall recognize?

I also wanted to explain where this mindset comes from. It is a diseased mentality rooted in feelings of inferiority. People who are hurting hurt other people. And people who are embarrassed about who they are, how they are and what they did try to divert attention to somebody else. We learn to try to be in cliques. Early on we are taught by society, television and by the movies to be the alpha male. And what good is. Alpha if there is no omega? If 200 million Americans all had Jaguars they would not be "special" anymore. Prison strips you of your individuality and robs you of your uniqueness. They dress us alike and feed us the same. We all live in the exact, same sized houses (cages, cells) and we eat the exact, same food. So we look for ways to be above others. We look for ways to numb our own pain. We hate ourselves. We know that every time we pick up the telephone and call somebody "collect" we are registered losers. We are the guys that society decided were too dangerous to be free... We are trapped in moral darkness and simultaneously cutting our own lights out. We have no women. We have no prestige. We dropped out of school. We can't read. We can't write. We can't count. We can't think and we hate ourselves so badly that the only thing we have left is the ability to delude ourselves into thinking that we are better than somebody else. Ipso Facto, we know we have taken lives. We have left a trail of tears, a trail of pain, a trail of loneliness and blood behind us. We have left a trail of death behind us. We didn't just kill a person. But we murdered the dreams, hopes, aspirations and the plans of the victim's children, parents, siblings and spouse. We feel like God won't forgive us. We feel like our victim's family won't forgive us. We feel society won't forgive us. And we won't forgive ourselves. So the only thing we have left is to try to feel a little better about ourselves by singling out somebody else. But I'm reminded that when I point one finger at somebody else. I have three more fingers pointing to myself. If you murdered an innocent victim you are worse than any child molester. I don't give a damn what the prison shot caller told you. I care less what a Blood, a Crip, an A.B. or a C.D. told you. Murder is the worst crime. Murder is the final crime; period. And it disturbs me to see all of these miscreants around me who wanna remind me to write about "those sick Chesters (A/K/A Child molesters)... But I'm more concerned about an individual who assumes it's cool to be a life taker. I can (by the Grace of God) teach a kid some skill sets that could probably help them to recognize a molester. I can teach them what inappropriate touching is all about. I can write tomes which elucidate and explain how a molester grooms a kid to be molested. But I can't write a thing that can teach a kid how to undo the death of a murderer's bullet in their brain. Murder (I repeat) is the final crime... And Youngsters, I wanna tell yall again that prison is a horrible place. Prison is hell. It is filled with bitter, broken and rotten men... And whatever you do don't become rotten... You are young and even if you've been in trouble you can still turn around today. Right here and right now you can transmogrify. But don't get rotten. When meat get's rotten (incorrigible) it can't be rehabilitated. Only God can do miracles. All we can do with rotten meat is throw it away. Even molded bread must be thrown away. Now if you eat a piece of bread just beginning to mold you can cut that piece off and save the bread. If you leave a loaf of bread open air gets in and makes the bread hard. When you come to prison this air of hatred gets into you and it makes you go and grow hard. You may have a little mold on you right now. Maybe you've been drinking beer and smoking dope. Perhaps you've tried ecstasy, meth, heroin or some other drugs. We still have time to cut that mold off the bread of your life and transform you. Judge Greg Mathis had mold on him. He got into trouble as a juvenile. And inspite of living the thug life for a time and getting some mold on him Judge Mathis became a Gang Banger for Good. He's a Gang Banger for Justice. The honorable Greg Mathis knows what HEART (Helping Educate At Risk Teens) can do.

Education! Education! Education!

I'm telling you education makes you powerful. Education will lift you up out of poverty. Education will lift you up out of the ghettos, barrios, trailer parks and the hoods. The more you learn the more you earn. Get yourself some books. Read everything you can get by Anthony Robbins, Les Brown and by Zig Zigler. R-E-A-D. Nobody can take knowledge from you. Once you get it in your head and brains it is yours. Let no man ever convince you that education is not cool. It's super cool. Look at Barack and Michelle. Look at Oprah... Get a book and a Bible Baby Boy!!! Read to succeed! You can do it. Rise above it. You can rise above racism. You can rise above drug abuse. You can rise above crime. You can rise above this madness. Yes you can.

There is temptation, confusion, wickedness and violence swirling all around you. But you can do the right thing. IF Judge Greg Mathis can do it, you can do it too. I'm in hell and I am telling you that you don't want to come to prison. This place changes you drastically. You can't go to bed at night and wake up in the morning in this much darkness and not be affected. This place subtly drives you mad. I again remind you to read "Prison Madness" by Dr. Terry Kupers. In this hell we are mad, sad, violent, bitter, broken and lonely. This place will drive you insane. This book is not full time hospital. This book is an emergency ambulance for you Youngsters. This book is not mental medication. This is an emergency defibrillator for teens in, near or headed toward trouble. For Pastor Glen Shields, Dr. Hardin, Bishop Jakes and for high school principals around the world I challenge you to tell young men (as well as young ladies) that this book is not the doctor. It is spiritual life support or teen C.P.R. And once kids finish reading this book from the very gates of hell, then they need to be under a doctor's care. I'm not the doctor. (Call 9/6-985-8610 ext. 3000 and tell Warden Walker you need to speak with an expert like C. Solis MD., A. Duran or Dr. Jarman. They can lead you to a full time hospital. This book is only the ambulance). But I know the Business. In fact I've consulted with captains, associate wardens and with wardens on how to identify and prevent predators. That's what kid girls need to hear. (Read "Blue Eyed Blonde" and "Blue Eyed Blonde" Book II). Little girls and boys need to know how to detect a predator. I would argue (that since I'm in hell) I've spent far more time around molesters than your parents have. As Dr. Yablonsky says I'm an "experience therapist". Kids don't ever forget that most molesters have been molested. Most molesters are people you know. They are usually not strangers in trench coats. They are older brothers, uncles, coaches, teachers and preachers. If they begin to look at you with lingering looks tell your parents. If a teacher or coach touches you in a sexual way report it. And keep reporting it (to parents, principals or to police) until somebody does something about it. And (this is a very, very, very important point which people rarely make but Youngsters need to know this) even if it feels good it is still molestation! If a 22 year old man has sex with a 13 year old girl (or boy) the 22 year old is committing molestation. If a 20 year old lady has sex with an 11 or 12 year old boy she is molesting him. And when kids are 7 and 8 they can be aroused. And if a 7 or 8 year old awakens to find an adult fondling or kissing them I say pretend to be sick. Start to puke or pretend to need to take a dump or say it feels good but you need to urinate etc. and as soon as you get up run and yell "Fire". Call 911 if you can but get out of there and yell "Fire". Molesters don't think the way you and I do. They are not "normal". You can't talk them out of molesting you. Crying won't stop them. There is something wrong with them that I'm not qualified to adequately explain. They are perverted and often their brains are abnormal. But you can't stop them verbally. Get away and report it. Never, ever, ever keep a sexual secret which involves an adult. It is not Your fault. It is never Your fault. Molestation and rape is always the molester's and the rapist's fault. Not Yours! Report it ! Report it! Report it!

I hope Justin Berry, Maxwell Hanger, C.J. Sheron and Josh Costa (a teacher in Sacramento) will help G.B.G. launch an international Cyber offensive against child molestation.

My aim is to post tons of data on www.napsusa.org about how to prevent child molestation. And I need Ari, Zach Friesen, Biz Stone and Andrew Bridge etc. to help drive high school traffic to www.napsusa.org. I need Ben Tracy, Robin Roberts and Tyra Banks to help tell kids about this website. I need David Begnaud, Jason Huyck, Dallas, Hollywood Henderson, Cody Sheldon and Adam Lambert to put the word out. I need Jeffrey Buttle, Timothy Goebel, Johny Weir and Guy Farris. I need you (and you too) to tell kids to log on to www.napsusa.org.

We also need to focus like a laser beam on teaching kids to build their self esteem. We must teach kids the power of education. We must make learning fun. It is time for us to make it exciting to go to school. We need teachers to be motivated and excited. Years ago Tony Robbins said they gave students Ritalin to slow kids down. But we noticed that when you give Ritalin to adults it speeds them up. Perhaps we should give teachers Ritalin instead of giving it to kids. But teachers need to be exciting, motivated and funny. Make learning exciting.

I need Michael Shackelford (from Oklahoma) and Joseph Latham to join G.B.G./HEART. I need every student to go to groups.yahoo.com/group/publicsafety. Join us today...

You can turn your life around today. Yes you can. No matter how bad it looks you are not alone. I believe in you. I believe in you. Kris Allen, Nathaniel Marshall, Josiah Lemming and Jai Breisch need to go to groups.yahoo.com/group/publicesafety and join us now. I am very aware of the fact that it is hard to get out of a gang. But you can get out of a gang. Move to another city. Go to another school. Get a j-o-b. Read a book. But get out of that gang. I've asked Mrs. Reid, Daniel Bugriyev, Adam Lane and Dustin Nicolodi to post data on www.napsusa.org and on http://napsusa.blogspot.com about ways to get out of gangs. You don't have to be a Blood, Crip, Southerner, Skin head or any other kind of gangster. Look up SHARP (Skinheads Against Racial Prejudice), Straight Edge, NAACP and the S-C-L-C. Call the Southern Christian Leadership Conference in Atlanta Georgia and ask them to help you get out of that gang. Call your local pastor or call Bishop T.D. Jakes (1-800-Bishop-2) and tell Bishop Jakes you need help exiting a gang..... I need 20 internet savvy kids to Google Julian Smith (on Facebook or Julian's Youtube site), Joseph Latham, David Hellyer and Justin Berry and tell them about G.B.G. We need no money! We don't seek a donation. We only need you to tell young teens about G.B.G./HEART and write on our Facebook wall. I need some youngsters to poke (positively) Tyra's (Tyra Banks Show) producers Paul and Michael and tell them about G.B.G. We want Chris and Becky Thompson. We want Stacy Smedley and every student to help launch this cyber offensive to turn around troubled teens.

...Harvard trained psychiatrist (Dr. Franklin Curren) told me that G.B.G. must try "any and everything we can to reach these young men. Sherman They'll listen to you guys. You're the experts". I am boasting about these brilliant psychiatrist (i.e. C. Solis MD., Jennifer Heitkamp MD., Franklin Curren MD., etc. and psychologists (A. Duran Ph.D., Gregg Ph.D., Dr. Jarman, Dr. Houston, Adam Lane, Dustin Nicolodi, Daniel Bugriyev, C.O. Diana Smith, C.O. K. Yeager, CCII Kevin Pool, Captain Steve John Vance, A.W. Fred Schroeder, C.D.W. Terry L. Rosario, Dr. Bakeman, Dr. Hall and Dr. Jamie Davidson etc.). And I hope these professionals will order five or six copies of this book and donate it to Public Schools and/or to group homes etc. Go to www.napsusa.org, www.cafepress.com/manning, Amazon.com etc. to order this book. If your bookstore does not have it they can order it. If you don't like ordering stuff over the internet (i.e. C.O. D. Smith is the G.B.G./HEART Secretary and she refuses to order anything over the internet...). Call 1-877-809-1659 and order K.K.K. that way. Adam, Daniel, Dustin, Dianna, Dr. Solis, Dr. Bakeman, Dr. Curren, Steve John Vance etc. etc. can anonymously order and donate this book to troubled teens. I am not given ordering data by bookstores and Amazon.com etc. So if yall think Cafepress is going to tell me you (or who) ordered the book, Wrong! Also if you think I'm advising teenagers to become my penpals wrong again. No member of G.B.G. is allowed to write, call or contact any kid 16 years old and younger. Not unless the person is in your family. Any 17 year old can write to a G.B.G. member as long as a parent (or teacher) peruses the missive. An 18 year old can write anybody they want. Staff (at C.S.P. SAC) screens all incoming and outgoing mail. But (for the record) as Chairman, Founder and President of G.B.G./HEART I recommend that no student or kid ever write to any prisoner including me. We are not in here for going to Sunday School too late. If you need somebody to write call Rev. Otis Moss at Trinity United Church in Chicago and ask for a referral. But kids should not be writing to us. If you need a mentor call Dr. Phil. Call my staff (Dr. Solis, Dr. A. Duran, Dr. Jarman, Dr. Curren, Dr. Gregg etc.) and ask for a referral. Do not establish a Friendship (under the guise of "Follow-up" etc.) with me or any other prisoner... If you wanna laugh call Bill Cosby. If you are lonely go to church. If your life is spiritually empty consider logging on to TDJakes.org or call your pastor. Don't reach out to a man locked in ...

This book is about monologue, not dialogue. If you want dialogue talk to your counselor or look on the web... I struggled with whether or not I should write a lot about rapes in prisons. Pragmatically I don't want my keepers to be so offended that they try to quash this constitutional exercise of free speech (K.K.K.). But as my advisor Dr. C. Solis said "You've got to tell them how it really is in hell... You don't want to write just another nice, neat little book. It needs to be raw, candid, actual and factual from your vantage point. Keep it real and it can actually save lives Sherman".... Senator John Burton promised he would read this book if it was less than 200 pages. Since I know Senator Burton is reading this book I ask Senator John Burton to do 2 things:

A. Get a copy of this book to Willie Brown please.
B. Please send 10 copies of this book to a local high school in San Francisco.

Thank you Senator Burton...

So I must tell Maxwell Hanger, Brett and Chris (Chris & Brett went to San Quentin State Prison with Dr. Phil's show) that you will get raped in prison. I have no doubt that in L.A. County Jail (read "Blue Eyed Blonde" and or "B.E.B." Book II) Brett and Chris would have their cherries popped! Kids (can we be candid?) wake up with woodies every day. So when Brett wakes up (looking 15 years old) in a dorm (with 200 other guys) with a woody and Bubba is laying one foot away from him, what is gonna happen? When I think of Brett (from the Dr. Phil Show) I can imagine Brett walking up to a cell and C.O. Marion E. Spearman throws Brett in the cell with a 6 fts guy. The guy has 23 inch biceps and when they lock the cell door he looks at Brett and says "turner Brown." Brett yells, screams and begins to cry. Brett is crying crocodile tears because Brett thinks Turner Brown said "turnaround"...

Maxwell Hanger, David Quattlebum, Joseph Latham, C.J. Sheron would be had in L.A. County Jail any day of the week.... And rape is serious ... As we noted rape is about power. Rape is about masking feelings of inadequacy with intimidation. Prison rape is about artificially inflating one's low self esteem by abusing somebody else. Sex is but a symptom. So studies and statistics show (from news reports in the Amarillo Globe News, Atlanta Journal Constitution, Dallas Morning News, Sacramento Bee, Los Angeles Times and numerous other newspapers) that inmates are not the only rapists in prisons. Garrett Cunningham was raped by a guard in the Texas Prison System. Some prison and jail guards, when entrusted with a modicum of power, succumb to the temptation to sexually assault the prisoners under their care; especially younger girls and boys. According to the aforementioned newspapers there is a national epidemic of authority run amok in the hands of abusive detention facility employees, who have insufficient supervision and even less self control. In just one particular case, first degree sexual misconduct, indecent liberties and second-degree custodial misconduct are among the many charges facing as many as eight King County Jail guards in Seattle, Washington.

Brigette Sarabi, executive director of the Oregon-based Western prison project, said "There's no way sexual contact between someone incarcerated and the person guarding them can be consensual. The power differential is too great. You can't say no. It is flat-out prisoner abuse. It is rape".

Sarabi continues "You'll have these women (and men in male prisons. Brett and Chris are you reading? I'm sending this book to Gloria Allred and octo-mom attorney Jeff Czech and asking them to get it to Brett and Chris. It might save your life.) coming in, some of them strung out on drugs. They're hungry - starving - and the diet in the jail doesn't provide enough calories for them while they're coming down". One source told me "They'll give a sex show for a candy bar"... The Moss Group, a Washington D.C. based consulting firm helps deal with issues of sexual misconduct at jails. The lil mentions I've made in K.K.K. of prison rapes (by staff and prisoners) are but the tip of an insidious iceberg of moral malignancy metastasizing throughout our Nation's prisons. No state is immune and no vaccine is available as prisoners are preyed upon by fellow prisoners and by their supposed protectors. I feel very sorry for any female in prison. I also feel very sorry for any kid in prison... Kathleen Liden, 44, pleaded guilty in July 2004 to having a sexual relationship with a minor while she worked as a guard at the Adobe Mountain School, a juvenile correctional facility. Liden was convicted of unlawful sexual contact with an incarcerated youth and attempted unlawful sexual contact with an incarcerated youth; her 16-year old victim was serving a one-year sentence for violating his probation when Liden molested him. She was sentenced in November 2004 to three years in prison. Another juvenile detention guard, Mike Hollingsworth, was sentenced on October 25, 2004 to four months in jail and three years probation after being convicted of child prostitution. In June 2004 Hollingsworth offered candy, cigarettes and soda to a young girl in custody as an enticement for her to expose her breasts. Kevin Richard Carlisle, 40 was arrested on July 29, 2005 for kidnapping and sexual assault of a 16-year old detainee. Carlisle was a 15-year veteran with the Bureau of Immigration and Customs Enforcement (ICE)... In juveniles and jails across America there are too many male guards in charge of female prisoners... The Ventura (in CA.) Youth Correctional Facility for girls is also under fire - as many as a dozen guards at the prison face accusations of coercing sex from prisoners in exchange for special favors.

Six guards raped a 20-year old Yorba Linda woman, who was incarcerated in Camarillo in 2003 and 2004. She states guards bring jewelry, extra food and weed to female inmates for sex.

National experts have published numerous damaging reports which strongly criticize the California Youth Authority's tendency to warehouse and to drug their wards (youth inmates) rather than counsel and rehabilitate them. Daniel Macallair, executive director of the San Francisco based center on Juvenile Criminal Justice, insists that "this is stuff that's been going on for years... You've got a system used to operating without a lot of accountability." Four current and former juvenile prisoners at the Herman G. Stark Youth Correctional Facility in Chino filed suit against prison guard James Shelby and others. The minors claim that Shelby pressured them to perform sex acts and ordered beatings by other prisoners. Shelby is also accused of rewarding compliant prisoners with contraband items, including TVs and cell phones. On July 28, 2005, Jasper Ayala, a former correctional lieutenant at the California prison for women, was sentenced to prison for raping a female inmate... This writer is familiar with two correctional managers (for my own protection I will only reveal their names to a member of the United States

Congress) who contributed to the rapes of male prisoners at a California prison. These men are racist, duplicitous and extremely powerful. They have friends in high places.

This writer was asked by Warden Walker not to write anything negative in this tome about associate Warden Mike Bunnell... Ipso Facto I will not write about this __ man. I will suggest you Google A.W. Mike Bunnell and read "Blue Eyed Blonde" Book II...

I know the kind of climate which breeds the rapes of prisoners by guards and by inmates. I've seen it up close and personal. One day a Facility Captain (long, long time ago) pointed his finger in my face and attempted to talk to me as if I were a "Boy". I responded with negative results. He's a Big guy so he began to bully me and threaten me and I replied (I've got to be honest) "F--- You". He jumped up as if he would rush me and told me to get out of his office. I walked out and there was an alarm and he tried to lord over me with "never talk to me like that again, I'll transfer you just like M.B. (name deleted) did". I replied "F. You". He stated "That's a 115" (rules violation). I said "F. You again". He stated "that's two 115's". I replied "F. You. You're a big old bully. You are arrogant, duplicitous and corrupted. You've been sued a million times because you are a big ole bully. F. You". He had the audacity to tell me what/who I couldn't write. I stated "this is not communist China. This is the United States of America." He said "no, this is C.S.P. Sac". And he was absolutely right. What he meant was "we have our own set of rules. The good ole boys. All white and all crooks". That was a good while back. And it should be noted that Warden James "Jimbo" Walker would never tolerate or condone this level of blatant staff misconduct. People like Jimbo, CCII Pat Kennedy, Jeff Macomber and C.D.W. Tim Virga will not tolerate misconduct by staff or inmates. And when we complain we have retaliatory captains and associate wardens (in C.D.C.) who will special transfer us. (more on that in another book)... Rogue and renegade captains and associate wardens are a cancer which needs to be excised from corrections. They breed rape, murder and mayhem. That captain told me he kept a file on me. I wondered if he had any idea how thick the file my lawyer has on him is... One false move (and they will, they always do) and I will get (through the Court system via lawsuit) his house and his truck. I follow the rules. I am a writer. And when I write about Perfecto Hijar it upsets corrupted officials. Perfecto, who is a lieutenant at the Arkansas Valley Correctional Facility in Crowley County, Colorado, was charged with felony sexual assault, sexual misconduct in a penal institution and misdemeanor official misconduct. Hijar, 54, a former Crowley County Sheriff's official had been arrested for intentionally inflicting sexual assault on a prisoner and coercing him to perform a sexual act... All due respect to Derek Hough, Zac Efron, Cody Linley, Jeffrey Buttle, Anthony Fedorov and Clay Aiken etc., but if either were in L.A. County Jail for 2 minutes they'd be on their knees, on their backs (with their legs in the air) or belly-up. Period... Ipso Facto perhaps you all should poke Zac, Clay, Jeff etc. on Facebook and tell them to join G.B.G. in calling for a congressional investigation into the treatment and care of Caucasian inmates at L.A. County Jail. (A strange request for a tome titled K.K.K). I need Leonard Padilla and law professors to talk about it in the press. L.A. County Jail is an abomination. L.A. County Jail is hell on all inmates. Blacks, Mexicans and Asians all get beat by jail deputies. They are even murdered by deputies. But most of the victims of rape in L.A. County are the Ashton Kutchers, Efrons, Aikens and the Sherons. And although Steve (Vance) and Fred (Schroeder) etc. probably would not condone these kinds of crimes I know sergeants, lieutenants and captains who condone rape and murder. I'll name names in another book. In this missive from hell I wanna tell yall again to stay in school and stay out of jail. It'll keep you out of hell. Read to succeed. Put down the tools of destruction and devastation and grab hold on an education. If you will learn to love reading you cannot fail. I don't want to see you in prison. I join with T.I. And I say get out of gangs and off of drugs. Model Barack and Michelle. Model Bill Cosby. Read "Come on People" by Bill Cosby and Harvard psychiatrist Alvin Poussaint MD.

And you males please remember that men do not hit women ever. Men don't hit women. We love and protect them. If you love women you can't, won't and don't beat or rape them. If you ever hit a woman you need to get help with all deliberate haste. You have a problem...

State Judicial Marshal Jenar Smith, 31, was arraigned and charged with two counts of sexually molesting a 19-year old female prisoner... Kenneth Joyner, a St. Lucie County Sheriff's Deputy was fired after an investigation confirmed that he had tried to coax a male prisoner into exposing himself and engaging in sexually explicit correspondence and conversation... Police Chief (Valaville Ca.) Richard Word is upset with the Ca. Dept. of Corrections because he says Joseph Johnson is a violent sexual predator. Johnson was released from prison and Chief Word says he should be serving a life sentence. And people are protesting the guy living there. This is knee jerk reaction due to well intentioned and wrong headed public out-cry. I believe in law enforcement. I am saddened by the murders of 4 Oakland police officers two months ago. They gave their lives trying to protect citizens. I salute them. I salute the officers in Pittsburgh who were viciously murdered. I support law enforcement. I know some good guards in C.D.C. I know many class acts right here in New Folsom State Prison (A/K/A C.S.P. Sac)... CC II Gaskins, Lt. Jimmy Guyton, Jerry McCowan, C.O. Granger etc. etc. C.O. K. Yeager and C.O. Pinkard. These are decent people who do their jobs within the rules. They are not friends of mine. I have no staff friends. I am an extremely unpopular prisoner. There are also some criminal guards in C.D.C. Every profession has bad apples. And according to published reports there are many criminal guards in C.D.C. who work with inmates. There are "hits" on me at Corcoran, Salinas Valley, High Desert and even at Donovan. Staff at numerous prisons have refused to place certain inmates (i.e. Mr. Brinson and C.E.) on my 8/12 so that when ever some rogue cowboy captain or associate warden decides to transfer me again etc. I can go into a war zone and be killed. I've spent very little time on Sherman D. Manning in this tome from hell. But since it is my book I think kids won't be upset by me telling you and your parents how prisons work. I will continue (in a bit) to tell you about prisoner rapes and the rampant sexual misconduct in hell etc. But I want you to know that if it had not been for the Lord that was on my side I would have been swallowed up... I still remember when that Big Bully captain had me thrown into a small cage (a violation of my free speech. A violation which rises to a level of constitutional proportions. The courts must be aware that I was barred from grieving due to my fear of retaliation) a little corrupted sergeant who despises me was happy. As I left the cage to return to my cell (another cage) this sgt. asked the sgt. who was escorting me "what are you doing dude?" angrily. "I'm taking him to his cell". A civilian with a medical degree indicated to me that "I took an oath to do no harm. I know you almost as well as Dr. Ty Hedblad (rest in peace, Dr. Hedblad was a great man) knew you. I know your secrets. And I know you have been cheated and mistreated. If you ever make it to a court of law I promise to testify to everything I know. And then I'll retire"...

I know we need to be notified (Chief Word) when a real rapist is set free. But I'm looking for a pragmatic approach to preventing, detecting, punishing and treating these perverts. With all the respect I have for law enforcement I must say - we can't depend on the police to deal with this epidemic. If we do you won't ever hear about the in-custody rapes which I'm writing about (and I'm not finished yet). Nor will we ever prevent this kind of wickedness. We can't always trust the police. It was the wife of a police captain who falsely accused Joseph (Genesis Chapter 39) of rape. It was also police officers who arrested Joseph for a rape he did not commit. It was the court system which sentenced him for a sex crime he'd been falsely accused of. And guards held an innocent man for 13 ½ years. We can't always depend upon accusers, police, judges and guards... Read the dedication to President Nelson Mandela in "Blue Eyed Blonde" Book II and you'll see more about wrongful concretions, lying prostitutes etc. etc.

I've seen the police call press conferences and tell us "he" is a sexual deviant. He tried this in Ohio. He attempted that in Chicago. And we know he will do this again. And time after time (i.e. in "Justice Denied" Magazine) I've read where 20 years (too late) later we found out he did not do that in Ohio. And we learn that he was the wrong guy in Chicago. And if police were so darn good at spotting a molester, detecting a rapist or noticing a killer etc. Why didn't they prevent a monster from murdering Sandra Cantu? This little angel is gone. I got too caught up in the case. I prayed, and prayed and prayed for this girl. Where is little Haleigh Cummings? I'm not lambasting cops. They work their butts off and many of them do a tremendous job. I salute police officers. And I want cops to be paid more money! But I don't want to make them gods or to pretend there is no corruption or to act like they always get it right. Rolando Cruz was not a molester. But they convicted him of raping and killing a girl. Pete Rose was right here in California. He was at Mule Creek State Prison with me. He was (according to the press) a child molester with a strong affinity for teens. He was not to be trusted. Even some psychologists talked about how Pete was a perverted predator until D.N.A. proved Pete Rose was 100% innocent. And now that he's a multimillionaire some of the same inmates who hated him when he was locked up, because these inmates believed what the police and guards (whom inmates pretend to hate) said about Pete Rose etc. those same "he's a dirt bag" inmates want his address so they can write him and ask him for $20.00. Only in Hell!

Youngsters (reading this) please remember that if you come here a guard (who hates you or is angry with you) or a fellow convict (i.e. a Clerk etc.) can have you beat or killed on a lie. All the C.O. needs to do is whisper to one of his slaves (an inmate who thinks his "Boss" is his "peer") that "you didn't hear this from me but I know for a fact that dude is a rapo" and there you go. When a C.O. or another prison official tells the press something about you and a story appears in the paper or on the local news about your so-called sex crime etc. believe me when I tell you all of your inmate buddies will turn against you. They are brainwashed and they are programmed to believe what they "hear" especially if they heard it form "the Man" (a cop). And especially if the media tells them it's true. My message? Stay out of prison. The next message is that police, psychologists, psychiatrists, profilers and parents need to work in concert to prevent sex crimes. Then we need to identify sexual predators early on. And we must do something to prevent the kind of horrible tragedy which happened to Sandra Cantu. This has got to stop and building another jail won't stop it. Building another prison will not bring Jon Bennet Ramsey, Haleigh Cummings or Sandra Cantu back. We must talk to Elizabeth Smart. Talk to Garrett Cunningham in Texas. Let's talk to T.J. Parsell, Dr. Duran, Dr. Gregg, Dr. Jarman and Dr. Curren. And let's devise a doable strategy for preventing the kidnapping and raping of kids. If a man is sexually attracted to an 8 year old something is wrong. We need to find out what is wrong and then we need to do what's never been done in America. Prevention! Prevention! Prevention! Let's talk to Justin Berry, Pusyin, Linda McFarland, Yolanda McFarland, Dr. Heitkamp etc. and let's harness the power of the internet to do cyber warfare against the kidnapping, molesting and the raping of our children. It must involve more than policing. It must involve more than sporadic media hype. We need some people who will be in this cyber offensive for the duration. Casey Jay, Jason Boggs, Andrew Knox, Jonathan Giannini and Jason Huyck can help us. This is a shovel ready (or mouse ready) project...

Let's go back to rapes in custody. Actually, despite my redundant utilization of words like "rape" and "sex", it aint about sexual abuse in prisons. Not when the keepers abuse the kept. It's about the abuse of power!

Read Dr. Terry Kupers' work. Confer with Dr. Jarman, Dr. Jamie Davidson, Dr. J. Friedman and Dr. Duran and you shall learn that sex is the symptom of a deep social disease, a deviancy which goes beyond the uniforms of jail and prison officials to sexual abuse which is condoned by some of those who wear judicial robes... Let me repeat that there are 2.5 million (plus) people in prison in America. And more than 49% of them are kids 7-19 years old. It is safe to assume we have well over 1.3 million kids 7-19 years old in U.S. prisons. When those "Blue Eyed Blondes" are viciously and sadistically sodomized in L.A. County Jail (by deputies, probation officers and by inmate) these are kids. These are human beings. And more than 99% of all L.A. County Jail inmates will get out of jail. And they take this nightmare (and perhaps disease) back to civilian society. And once they have been to any jail they are meaner, tougher, sicker and slicker. And when they get out they re-offend quicker. And then they are dumped into the prison system. And they are suffering from a myriad of different levels of mental illnesses. And most prison systems (i.e. C.D.C.) refuse to treat post traumatic stress disorders. Due to the 14 month hospitalization from Valley Fever "it's like you've been in a war zone" Dr. Bakeman told me. "You definitely have P.T.S.D.". Dr. George states. Yet C.D.C. will not treat it. (perhaps we ought to call attorneys Michael Bien, Holly Baldwin, Ernest Galvan, Karen Kenard, Kristin Palumbo, Bingham, McCuthen or Rosen, Robert Blasier). So we have damaged youngsters running around the prisons like rats chasing cheese... If the rapes (of mostly white boys in the prisons and jails) I've detailed involved ordinary citizens, prosecution would have been swift, high bonds and pre-trial incarceration automatic, and lengthy prison sentences upon conviction automatic. The raped inmates would have been treated as crime victims with all the attendant rights which goes along with the status of "victims". Yet, because prison, jail guards and inmates are involved, a certain degree of leniency is afforded. Too often law enforcement - and judicial - officials favor fraternity over justice.

In Kids Killing Kids I want you (kids) to see the other side of the coin. You see the flip side in the media every day. They tell you all about what the public needs to know. And I (again) support law enforcement. If we did not have some great judges, great prosecutors, great police and prison guards there would be chaos...

The former warden of the Evangeline Parish Jail was convicted on two counts of malfeasance in office for extorting sex acts from family members of prisoners. Warden Michael J. Savant, 53, was sentenced to serve six months in jail and placed on three years probation. The freaking warden. About the serious epidemic of prisoners being raped in prison ??? Superior court judge Thomas Power stated "When I send somebody to jail, I certainly don't send them for the purpose of being molested".

Twelve prison guards at the Scioto Juvenile Correctional Facility have been charged with various counts of physical abuse, sexual abuse and endangerment of kid prisoners. After Latimer County (Oklahoma) Sheriff Melvin Holly raped jail inmates he (allegedly) told one victim she would "end up dead... floating face down in a river if she told anyone. Holly was convicted of having sex with four prisoners, sexual contact with four others, improperly touching three employees, improperly touching the teenage daughter of an employee, threatening to kill a prisoner if she revealed their relationship and lying to federal authorities. In defense of himself the sheriff states "these women are dope makers, dope sellers, dope users." Melvin Holly got a 25 year sentence.

Michael Boyles, 54, a former juvenile probation officer for the Oregon Youth Authority, was given an 80 year prison term after being found guilty of having sex with at least five teenage boys during his eleven years in office. Boyles was convicted on 45 counts of sexual abuse of young men. Boyles had been supplying the boys with drugs. This again exemplifies the fact that many (if not most) molesters and rapists are people in power, with authority and they are the folks whom the media and the police tell us we can and should trust. One of Boyles' victims committed suicide.

At Mule Creek State Prison I met inmate Ed Stokes who was the prison (admitted) lover of Noah L'Hotsky. Ed was in jail for raping teenage boys and he told a psychologist he had "hundreds of victims". Ed was released from prison and less than a month after Ed got out I saw him on "Inside Edition". He had bought an ambulance. He used the "trust worthiness" of the ambulance to pick up little boys and molest them. I was weeping the other day as I thought about Sandra Cantu and Haleigh Cummings and I told Alonso Dearaujo that when I think of people molesting a child and murdering a child it reassures me that there has to be a devil.

And a lot of devils wear guard, deputy and police uniforms every day... John Pastor, 58, a former President of the Prison Guard's Union (in P.A.) pleaded guilty to the sexual assault of a jail inmate at the Allegheny County Jail.

Daniel T. Rogers, 54, a guard at Westmoreland County Juvenile pleaded guilty to three counts of institutional sexual assault. He fondled, caressed, paid and coerced 19, 18 and 16 year old female inmates to have sex. We need Gloria Allred to get involved with these in custody rapes.

It has been said that Texas is the prisoner rape capitol of the U.S. prison system. With California and New York running closely behind... Anthony Riccardo (David Quattlebum? David Hellyer? Jeffrey Buttle? Johny Weir? C.J. Sheron?), incarcerated at Illinois Centralia Correctional Center, pleaded with Lt. Larry Bausch not to house him with gang member Juan Garcia. Lt. Rausch wouldn't listen and within two days Garcia was forcing Riccardo to perform fellatio. Prison authorities are often deliberately indifferent to a prisoner request for a cell change.

Kids I want to tell you that if you come to prison you will join the most marginalized and politically vulnerable population in our society... Although most citizens are appalled by sexual assault, there seems to be significantly less sympathy for prisoners who are raped as opposed to non-incarcerated rape victims. According to the U.S. Department of Justice, Bureau of Justice Statistics, a report released in July 2006 found there were an estimated 9,225 allegations of sexual misconduct against prisoners. Of those, 49% involved sexual misconduct by staff members and 14% involved sexual harassment by staff - over 4,400 incidents involving prison and jail employees nationwide. An estimated 3,090 incidents were substantiated (not including on-going investigations). And that's just one year alone.

And most inmates are afraid to report staff misconduct to staff. Prisoners are routinely disbelieved; their very status of being incarcerated works against their credibility. And there is a pervasive "code of silence" amongst guards...

About the only time American politicians treat rape as a joke is when the victim is a prisoner. As legislators campaign for office on the backs of sex offenders they are silent about the sex offenders in their employ or what they have done to give them de facto impunity.

I don't want to see C.J. Sheron, Jonathan Giannini, Casey Jay, Redmond O'Neal or Brian Hawn in prison because of this senseless violence and rape epidemic in prison. The U.S. has failed to adequately address the sexual violence that plaques its prisons and jails. The failures of the Departments of Corrections nationwide to prevent sexual abuse behind bars and to adequately respond to those who are victimized needs to receive national and international attention. These are serious and severe human rights violations. According to the Universal Declaration of Human Rights, "All human beings are born free and equal in dignity and rights. They are endowed with reason and conscience and shared act toward one another in a spirit of brotherhood." Incarceration does not diminish a person's human rights. But I must sadly report to you youngsters that guards think inmates are a group of nothings. ... G.B.G. as well as NAPS has endorsed stop prisoner rape (SPR) which is working hard to eliminate prison rapes. SPR recognizes that prisoner rape is a human rights crisis of staggering magnitude. A lack of extensive study, research and data on prisoner rape has been used as an excuse for corrections officials to minimize and marginalize the problem for decades. G.B.G. will be conducting more surveys contemporaneously with SPR and holding discussions on Yahoo!, our blogs and message boards in order to establish an undercover network of prisoner and juvenile rape and abuse activities. G.B.G. will work in concert with Rose Braz, Alex Friedmann, Jason Wilhite and with SPR to stop prisoner rape. We shall utilize "public shaming" to highlight the rapes, retaliatory transfers, wrongful placing in ad-seg and the abuse of prisoners; especially young prisoners.

We are troubled, flabbergasted and angered by the abuse of young girls and boys in prisons. G.B.G. is asking the independent commission on safety and abuse in America's prisons to examine the treatment of youths in prisons with a special focus on the treatment of white inmates in L.A. County Jail. We call upon Margaret Winter, Associate Director of the ACLU National Prison Project to focus an intense light on the abuse of kids in prisons.

Under international human rights law, the sexual assault of prisoners, whether perpetrated by corrections officials or by prisoners with the acquiescence of corrections staff, is recognized as torture. The U.S. has ratified two treaties that expressly prohibit torture. The convention against torture and other cruel, inhuman or degrading treatment or punishment (CAT and the International Covenant on Civil and Political Rights (ICCPR). (For more info visit www.ohchr.org).

The CAT requires that each warden take action to prevent acts of torture within its jurisdiction. Under the CAT, torture can never be justified and a country may not return a person to a jurisdiction where he or she may be tortured. Ipso Facto, no person should ever be extradited or deported to America. When the CAT convenes in Geneva in 2011 G.B.G. plans to send a psychologist to testify. G.B.G. shall submit a "shadow report" to CAT highlighting how the U.S. has failed to comply with the treaty.

In 2006 SPR provided the only shadow report focused exclusively on the continued and widespread sexual abuse of incarcerated men, women and youth in detention. The report, entitled "In the Shadows" examined the systemic conditions which contribute to sexual violence behind bars, the plight of those prisoners most vulnerable to sexual exploitation, and the legal provisions that would help combat sexual assault in custody but are not effectively enforced. The report offered recommendations to remedy this acute human rights crisis... America must amend the Prison Litigation Reform Act (PLRA) so that victims of torture in custody can seek justice through the courts. Why does the PLRA bar claims based on emotional and psychological mistreatment that are unaccompanied by physical injury?

It's my job to tell in this missive from hell, that sexual abuse in prisons is an epidemic that many prison officials choose to ignore or to sweep under the rug. The domestic legal system in America fails to protect prisoners from sexual assault, and survivors of prisoner rape are habitually denied legal recourse. International Human Rights Law is an essential, but still neglected tool for promoting social justice domestically. We need (Gloria Allred, ACLU, NAACP, H.R.W., Human Rights Campaign etc.) a national outcry to stop prisoner rape!...

SPR (Stop Prisoner Rape) changed their "name" to "Just Detention Int'l"... Just Detention Int'l (A/K/A Stop Prisoner Rape) seeks to end sexual violence against prisoners. They provide counseling resources for imprisoned and released rape survivors and activists for almost every state. (contact: SPR at 3325 Wilshire Blvd. # 340, Los Angeles, CA. 90010 (213) 384-1400... www.justdetention.org). My friend Linda McFarland is at the L.A. office and Linda is a dedicated activist. Also attorney Melissa Rothstein, Esq. (N.Y. Atty. Registration # 2987378) is in L.A. You can write Attorney Rothstein via legal, sealed and confidential mail... I hope you never come to prison! And if (God forbid) you come to prison I hope you never get abused.

If you are abused by staff or inmates call "Just Detention Int'l". Here are some websites if you've been raped: www.aclu.org/prisons, www.aardvarc.org, www.advocateweb.org, www.healthjustice.net and www.GLBTNationalhelpcenter.org...

If you or someone you know has been raped call 202-393-4930, 888-232-6348, 800-227-8922, (Spanish speaking people call 800-344-7432, 888-372-0888 or 888-843-4564.). There is a special service for male survivors of rape. Call toll free 800-738-4181 or visit www.malesurvivor.org. Write "male survivor" pmb 103-5505 Connecticut Ave. N.W. Washington D.C. 20015-2701. Yall call these numbers and write to these people if you have been sexually assaulted. It is not your fault if you are raped. But if you are out in the streets gang banging it is your fault. If you are smoking weed, using meth or crack etc. it is your fault. If you are carrying a gun that is your fault. Get out of the gang. The only time you should gang bang is for Justice, Good and for God.

Need I remind you that prison is an abnormal and violent place? You are reading a book which has been salted and peppered with data revealed to me during thousands of hours of interviews with gangsters, folks in the mob, shot callers, predators, victims of rapes, guards, captains, counselors and with wardens. Prison is an unusual "beast". When I interview prisoners suffering emotional crises as they enter the prison world etc. concerns about the violence of prison infiltration Rites is a major precipitant of their psychological stress. "When you're a new fish you're nothing and nobody. So you've got pressure on you from everybody. You first come in, their intention when they look at you is that they're going to take this man ..... They test you" a guy states. Jack Abbott spent most of his adult life in prison and before he died he stated "this is the way it is done. If you are a man, you must either kill or turn the tables on anyone who propositions you with threats of force. It is the custom, among young prisoners. In so doing, it becomes known to all that you are a man, regardless of your youth. I had been trained from a youth spent in gladiator school (juvenile detention hall) for this. It was inevitable then that a youth in an adult penitentiary at some point will have to attack and kill, or else he most certainly will become a punk, even though it may not be well known he is a punk. If he cannot protect himself, someone else will."

Youngsters, yall listen to me please. I'm cognizant that prison is glorified and romanticized in movies. But I am in this hell hole. I eat, sleep and crap in the bowels of these prisons. I know the real deal... Things are horrible in prison. In the first half of the twentieth century, the prisoners essentially operated prisons in America.

They cooked, served meals, cut grass, performed Bldg. maintenance and worked in prison industries. Collectively, convicts developed their own self-contained society, with a pronounced stratification system, a strong convict value system, odd patterns of speech and bodily gesticulations, and an array of social roles.... Importantly, their participation in this world with its own powerful value system, the convict code, gave them a sense of dignity and pride. It was convicts against what they perceived as a cruel prison system and a corrupt society.... However, society was much more accepting of the ex-convict than it is now. And recidivism was very low.

Yet, the "war on drugs" which is raging in the inner city; America's "law and order" sensibility; three strikes legislation etc. .. huge racial disparities in arrests and sentencing etc. the waning of prison rehabilitation programs; massive overcrowding of jails and prisons; racial and gang warfare in prison etc. and huge recidivism rates have combined to transmogrify the code significantly. There is less solidarity among prisoners. And prison officials take advantage of this. They play inmates against each other. It is the oldest trick in the game but it works, it works, it works. I once had a facility captain (at another prison) who was a master manipulator. But his weakness was his horrible memory. He couldn't keep up with his lies. And he was deceptive and unprofessional. He used to try to convince me that Mrs. so and so hated me. This guy even told me the warden hated me. He built an entire career around manipulating and playing people against each other. And I believe that a captain like this would allow an inmate to be beat or raped as punishment. And he would justify it in his mind by saying that you should not have gotten locked up. Prison is an extreme environment. I know you are a Bulldog, Blood, Crip, Nazi Low Rider, Norteño or a Southerner etc. You may be a gang banger but prison is an extreme, extreme environment. Any sign of weakness leads to being labeled as a victim, a boy, a fag or a B-tch. And weaklings are subjected to beatings or Booty calls. In this milieu, prisoners don't talk to each other about their pains, their needs, their vulnerabilities - to do so with the wrong man could lead to betrayal, sodomy, enslavement and death. Back to rape in a while... Politically conscious prisoners and activists in the prison movement on the outside are attempting to build on the camaraderie and feelings of solidarity among prisoners. The goal is to help prisoners understand that animosity toward other prisoners is misguided and that they must stand together against their real oppressors. The interracial animosities, male dominance hierarchy and intergang battles are hurdles that must be overcome in this organizing and consciousness-raising project. But it is a tall order because the slave mentality is entrenched in prisoners in America. While organizing G.B.G. (more on this later) I found an astounding number of inmates who ... never mind but we need to stop allowing staff to cause us to hate, mistreat and to deceive one another.

... I disbelieve most of the statistics on prison rape because most men who are raped are too ashamed to report it. Shame plays a big part not only in victims, refusal to report rapes but also in maintaining their subservience and isolation. When a boy is shamed, for example by an alcoholic dad or critical mom, he goes to his room. He seeks no support from other members of the family. In the school yard, the boy who loses a fight or "chickens out" does not seek the support of his friends to heal his wounds; he keeps to himself, and the wounds fester. Shame leads to isolation, and in isolation there is little hope of transcending shame. In prison, it can be dangerous to speak frankly to others about one's pains- again, the code. After being defeated in a fight, especially if a boy is raped, he stays to himself; perhaps he remains in his cell all day in the dark. But this is exactly the kind of response which deepens depression or leads to chronic post-traumatic stress disorder (which C.D.C. does not treat)... Many prisoners suffering from mental disorders are raped. The code in prison is based on intimidation. Positive outlets for the need to feel powerful are scarce. (but joining G.B.G./HEART is an exception! and prisoners are joining by the hundreds.) The demeaned of the land are willing to demean those who are even lower in the hierarchy than they are. And even some of the most demeaned of the prisoners, when eventually they leave prison, find themselves acting abusively toward others... Youngsters I want you all to listen to me. Or should I say my fellow Americans listen to me. Derek Hough, Cody Sheldon, Brett and Chris would be raped at L.A. County Jail. I'll stake my life on it. And getting raped destroys you from the inside out, and it will take a part of you and put it where you can't reach it. Sexual violence is devastating in any setting; but survivors healing from this abuse in prison face extreme and unusual challenges. An urgent lack of private counseling, high rates of violence and ...

I'm aware of a sexual assault by staff which took place at CMC East in 2008. I'm also aware of the "second rape" of the inmate by other staff who were insensitive and indifferent to the inmate. It's extremely lonely, frightening and embarrassing. There needs to be a trench war fare against rape in prisons. I call Paul Wright, Rev. Otis Moss, pastors, lawyers and teachers to join G.B.G. and JDI in fighting it. Imagine living in the cell with your rapist. How would you feel if you were raped by the police who polices rapists?

"I was gang-raped at 17, on my first day in general population in a Michigan prison. Even though I felt hopeless at the time, I want you to know that there is hope. I was able to go on to live a healthy and productive life. I graduated from college, became a successful businessman and I now advocate for the rights of prisoner rape survivors.

I tell you this not to impress you, but to impress upon you that you too can recover from the horrific ordeal you have endured" states T.J. Parsell in his awesome book "Fish". I hope they make "Fish" a movie. T.J. was/is a white guy gang raped by blacks and whites in prison. Rape can happen to anyone, no matter how strong, no matter how smart.

... Gangsters: my studies into gangster hood, mobs, shot callers and the entire gang structure revealed some starting facts about gangsters and sex. I was so amazed by the results of confidential G.B.G. surveys that I called (one of the most preeminent gang experts in the Nation) Dr. Lewis Yablonsky at home. I also consulted with Dr. Jarman, Dr. Gregg and Dr. Franklin Curren regarding gangsters and sexuality. Gangsters tend to be homophobic. Their insecurity about their own masculinity is a major factor in their macho syndrome. Many gangsters present themselves as supermen in an effort to compensate for some of their underlying feelings of being insecure in their role as a heterosexual male.

There is vast evidence of homosexual experimentation among gangsters outside, but mostly in custodial institutions. A common pattern for gangsters is to become the passive recipient of homosexual relations with a seductive overt homosexual. The homophobic ritual which often recurs was expressed by a gang member to Dr. Yablonsky as follows: "After this faggot blew us (laughs), we beat the hell out of him." He seemed to have zero awareness of his own homosexual involvement in the act. My great grand daddy stated "it makes no difference if you're catching or pitching, you're still playing baseball."

This pattern is more pronounced in prison. Gang members will turn you out (rape you or groom you subtly which can still be rape). They pass certain sexual whores around (on the down low) from gangster to gangster. This is the kind of stuff they didn't tell Lisa Ling when she came to New Folsom. They most certainly did not tell Madame Barbara Walters when she came to interview Eric Menendez. (Eric told this author that Ms. Walters was hiring him an appellate attorney. Eric also claimed Ms. Walters hated Star Jones because Star hated him)...

In many cases punishment for an errant gangster against his gang involves his being sodomized. This "discipline" is carried out to humiliate the offender and to demonstrate that he is really a punk.

Gangsters become humiliated when it's pointed out to them, as I've done in group discussions, that when they play any role in a homosexual act they are practicing homosexuality... I point out to gang leaders that years in prison and gang life don't create the appropriate male personality for relating in a positive way to women.

Mexican Mafia (or Eme), Black Guerrilla Family (BGF), Aryan Brotherhood, LA Familia, Asian Gangs, Cambodian Gangs, Nortenos, Surenos, Tiny Rascals, Crazy Brothers Clan Cambodian (CBC), 415, Bloods, Crips and all gangs have prisoners. I have seen a number of gangsters, humongous and cold-blooded killers, riding their celly's private at night. I've caught gang members performing fellatio upon each other in the middle of the day. I've seen gangsters in make-shift G-strings in their cells. I have come to suspect anybody who claims to hate gays as being latent homosexuals. The Ca. Dept. of Corrections (I repeat) is broke back C.D.C. ... And you pretty boys (listen to me), especially need to stay out of prison.

You need to build your self esteem. You need to learn how to feel good about yourself.

I really, really suggest r-e-a-d-i-n-g as a way out of no way, a way out of gangs, a way out of poverty and a way out of mediocrity. All successful people are master readers. If I could pay every young man in America $ 1000.00 per book to read books (by Tony Robbins, Les

Brown, Zig Zigler, Dr. Na'im Akbar and Dr. Terry A. Kupers etc.) I would pay you. Reading is exciting, fun, motivational and inspirational. Reading will transform your mind and transmogrify your life. If you forget everything else I write here don't forget to read at least one book per week ...

G.B.G. is asking the Schoettler-Neufeld Tire Retread Center's owners to help us in our awareness campaign. We will be emphasizing the power of reading to pre gangsters, gang members and to ex-gang members. And as we reach into neighborhoods to motivate boys to stay out of gangs we want to provide empowering books to these kids which will help divert them away from crime. We also want to put books (i.e. by T.J. Parsell, Terry A. Kupers, Zig Zigler etc.) into schools, churches, jails and juveniles. We will reach out to men who are in gangs (in prisons) in order to divert them away from gangs. Guys in prisons are in an entrenched gang warfare. They order hits (murders) from inside prison walls. When we are successful at transforming a prison gang member we prevent crime, recruit gangsters who will Bang For Good and we divert youth from crimes.

Glimmers of hope are reflected from the prison to the hood and from the juvenile to the suburbs. The Schoettler-Neufeld Tire Retread Center (near Fresno C.A.) have been committed to hiring ex convicts and ex-gang bangers to work at their company. They should be applauded. A job empowers an excon. A job prevents crime. Nothing stops a bullet like a job.

G.B.G. seeks to work with Schoettler-Neufield, Justin Brice, Bonnie Doolittle, Andrew (the volunteer) at Homeboy Industries and with college students around the world.

We call out to you and we ask you to use Facebook, MySpace, Google and Zabasearch to locate the following people: Nicholas Taxera, D.J. Swearingen, Alex Seabolt, Benjamin Whipple, Bradley Thomas Jr. (please don't merely glance over these names. G.B.G./HEART, Just Detention Int'l and Naps needs these people to know that K-K-K is published, they're in it and that we need them...) Matthew Gerber, Mr. Landers (from Vancouver B.C. of "The Apprentice" Fame), Kevin Greene (Grand Rapids Michigan), Daniel Seddiqui, Robert Linggi, Jake Reitan, Jesse Grund, Craig Scott, B.J. Hill (Boston), Michael Perrelli, Tyler Summit, Seamus Farrow, Ronald Bonilla, Austin Sisneros (Utah), Eric Flores (Roseville CA.), Nathan Wilhite, Jason Huyck, Louis Copelin, Vaughn English, Von Smith, James Michael Avance, Bishop Keith Clark, Nathan Langley, Michael Castro, Andrew Lang, Mitch Fredrickson, John Hancock (Hands on Disaster), Melinda Gates, Earl Stafford, Randy Madden, Alex Wagner Trugman, Cody Sheldon (Detroit Michigan), David Santos, Scott Macintyre (and his brother in Scottsdale AZ), Ashley Anderson, Rev. Alice Baber Banks, Christian Fellowship Ministry Church (Del Paso Heights CA.), Alex Mandel, Stephen Memory (Tracy CA.), Redmond O'Neal, Coach Craig Robinson, Dr. Bill Cosby, Mayor Adrian Fenty, Cesar L. Chavez, Ron Clark (Ron Clark Academy), Mayor Cory Booker, Bernard Risco, Beau Maestas, Dr. Patricia Turner, Chris Austad, Derek Lull, Dr. David Kaufman (plastic surgeon), Bobby Ginn, Phillip Vieira (Fresno), Michael Farris, Charlie Todd, Dr. Joseph Jacobson, Paul Karason, Alan Rafferty, Pastor Bruce Hood, Grant Coffin, Tyler Perry, Dr. Scott Modell, Corbis Fear, Dr. Jim Hernandez (Sacto), Michael Buckley, Tyler Heald, Warren Hodges (Sacto), Ryan Chandler, Chris and Becky Thompson, Marilyn Joseph, Greg Sutter (Sacto), Zach Devals, Ezekiel Hernandez, Attorney David Balser, Kevin Griffin, Dan Kozlak, Det. Michael Delaney, David Matthews (author), Dr. Nicole Black Singleton, Dr. Janet Taylor, Marian Robinson, Eddie Neale, Trino Savala (Sacto), Francisco Javier Delucas, Taylor (at Pepperdine University), Keith Allen Wattley, Tom Agostanelli, Scott Kenney, Damien Galpren, Kirke Adams, Alex Huiza, Michael Carandang, Josh Ross, Trevor Loflin, Silas Miers, Nicholas Benner, David Hellyer, Chad Pennington, John Fena, G.T. Dave, Jason Wroble, Terry Sedlack, Eric Hansen Jr., Jeffrey Buttle, Marshall Sylver, Tucker Horwatch, Scott Moore, Andy Dick, John Quain, Chelsey Ramirez, Reggie Love, Chris Slyker, David Heath,

Kevin Clyne, Attorney Andrew Bridge, Liam Hall, Darren Wooley, Joseph Stawicki, Cory Crayn, Mike Corsetto, John DeCarro, Ryan Moats, Robert Powell, Jason March, Judge Greg Mathis, David Begnaud, Nick Janes, Chad Ruyle, Kent Depriest, Brent Depriest, Michael Crowley, Kevin Jarrad, Hunter Brown (Wheston Illi.), Geoff Gloeckler, Wendy Kramer, Ryan Kramer, Warren Paboojian, Josh Landis, Dr. Vance Moss, Brent Sarabian, Preston Mcvey, Preston Phillips, Tyler Roche, Dominic Pensibene, Stacy Smedley, Mitch Butler, Chris Russo, Jeremy Bowden, Mark Cherry, Rev. Samuel Rodrigues, Max on TMZ.com, David Zinzincko, Tyler Farrar, Jason Wu, Eric Hutchinson, Brent Keith Smith, Wil Heuser, Matt Giraud, Ryan Johnson (Cincinatti), Wil Seabrooks, Neal Carlson, Kris Allen, Maxwell Hanger, Anthony Fedorov, Ricky Braddy, Ian Acosta, James Kaschak, Chris Arrher, Tony Romo, William Rains, Jonathan Adler, Heidi Limbrunner, Pat Pattituchi, Mike Morales (American River College), John Romesburg, Marcus Dixon, Lawrence Tynes, Tim Tebow, Mike Jake, Michael Moore, Chad Hurst, Ryan Hreljac, Christopher Perrine, Imaculee, Robert King, Dave Parrish, Luke Sears, Alex Flores, Mayor R. Rex Parris, Adam Pan, E.J. Vaught, Danyel Smith, Rodrigo Rodriguez, Brandon Biggs, Dr. John Diaz (MD.), Brent Remai, Dan Orlovsky, Sam Adam, Rick Klein, Zach Freisen and Kyle Love.

If every K.K.K. reader would I.M. or T.M. (poke them if you have to) all of the aforementioned and let them know this book is out we would change the world. I repeat that we would change the world. I need tree huggers and youth activists to know this book is out. We must come together in a spirit of ecumenicity and transmogrify young America. I call out to freaks, geeks, nerds, jocks, inmates, outmates, drop outs and drop ins. We can do this. I know many of you are not violent gangsters. Many of you don't bang. But we are all in a gang of some sort. The gangs of nerds, freaks, geeks, Bloods, Crips etc. legal and illegal, civil and uncivil, structured and/or bootleg, official and unofficial "gangs."

Low self-esteem and a sense of alienation drives boys and girls to clique up or to ally themselves with official and unofficial "gangs". Violent gangsters and even some jocks act super tough to mask their inner sense of inferiority. This produces what Dr. Yablonsky calls "machismo" or "macho psychosis". This is an effort to present themselves as supermen and compensate for their underlying feelings of low self-concept and feeling like a "nobody" in the larger society.

Young men in prison are infected with an epidemic if not a pandemic proportion of the macho syndrome. These are dudes who are insecure about their masculinity. They physically, emotionally and verbally posture as macho supermen. And violence is the language of the unheard and the illiterate. Males in prison don't simply walk. We move with an unmistakable superman tough-guy physical strut. Emotionally and verbally we're always engaged in proving our machismo. Any comment of disrespect to a gangster implying femininity will produce a violent response. The gangsters macho syndrome is an effort to compensate for his failure to be a real man and succeed in the larger society. Gangsters have created their macho syndrome superman stance, in part, as a reaction to their deeper feelings of alienation, and hopelessness about achieving any degree of success in the free world. Violent gangsters who feel alienated from the free society create the gang to provide a sense of feeling like a man in their gang "community". The rage they feel from other sources is often expressed in gangbanging (rat-packing, a group of guys beating, sodomizing or killing another person) and other forms of senseless violence. The gang gives them status in what they perceive is a barren and hopeless world. Strange how a mentality can be so perverted that it becomes respectable for 3 or 4 guys to beat 1. The man to man or one on one or head to head type "respect" is lost in gang fights. It's pretty sick...

And I want this book to be prescriptive for youngsters. And if you are on this road to self hatred, low self esteem and bitterness I must tell you it is a trail of destruction. While you are young you still have time to get off this path. Bitterness destroys the vessel that contains it... I recall a guy telling me that an inmate whom we called "Irish" was dead. Irish (rest in peace) apparently committed suicide. This guy (whom I used to like) told me "I'm glad he's dead. He lied on me". And it rocked me to the very core of my foundation to hear this kind of hatred. I've never viewed this guy the same way anymore. He was glad he was dead. I also recall being at P.V.S.P. when Eddie Watts swallowed drugs and it killed him. A guy called "twin" told me "I dropped the dime on him that put him in the cross". Translation? He was explaining that Eddie (rest in peace) was returning from a visit. And Twin snitched on him. Twin told that Eddie had gotten drugs in the visit. Twin was angry because Eddie supposedly owed him. So Twin told and his telling resulted in death. In my humble opinion Twin was an accessory to an accidental death. I said "rest in peace" and Twin stated "rest in sh_t". Young people, I'm simply demonstrating what prolonged incarceration can do to us. It makes you cold. My suggestion to you is to never hang around bitter people. I want you to stay positive and to clique up with positive people... Who am I to tell you? I am a wounded convict. Our wounds enable us to speak to other people's pain. I want you to be secure. Even if your daddy was not a secure man learn how to feel good about yourself. Secure fathers circumcise their sons. Insecure daddies castrate their sons. And castrated sons walk around trying to cover their impotence with gangs, guns, drugs and violence. Impotent boys rape others... And please watch what you speak in to the atmosphere. The power of Life and Death are in the tongue. The silk (spittle) which comes out of the mouth of the caterpillar creates the environment into which it is nurtured. Words create your cocoon. Your words can bring you from a jail cell to a palace. Joseph used words to explain and interpret dreams. The accuracy of Joseph's words brought him from being a convicted sexual predator to a palace in Egypt.

Paul went from being the murderer to the minster using words. His words got him into trouble. He went to prison. At one point he was locked up in a prison cell yet at the end of the book of Acts inmate Paul found himself in Caesar's household using words to preach...

Richard Peichoto, Ronnie Lawson, C.J. Sheron and you (and you too) ought to speak positive and elucidating words... To you kids in highschool, hoods, Barrios, juveniles or wherever you are. In some way we have been united through tragedy and joined by pain. Prison is my stage or a canvas for me to paint this picture of hell for you... Eric Hansen Jr., Andrew A. Bridge and Hunter Brown etc. this tome is only a missive from hell. Just a rambling note about what's happening in this cesspool of wickedness. I want you to be a teen with a dream. I want you to stop and get yourself together. ...

In one of my interviews with a Mexican gang member I was amazed at what institutionalization can do to Us. We lose touch with reality. We are totally deranged by the subculture of prison... This guy (Julio) explained how being in prison teaches you how to get along with other races. He emphasized that "R" word; Races. Just listening to prisoners talk about races and your "own" people etc. will make you think we are in some type of time warp stuck in the 1950's. And this guy was in his twenties. Then he explained how you "learn" respect and rules etc. in prison. The stuff he's telling me he learned in prison are things most people "learn" via parenting. We should learn this stuff in kindergarten. And our parents should teach us these things. But in listening it became obvious that some hard core gangsters secretly consider older gangsters their parents. Many prisoners consider it mandatory to roll up their mattresses in the morning. And they will take boxes of property and stack the boxes on the table etc. Why? It is discipline and "clean". Now I thought cleaning meant soap and water. How, who or why rolling up a freaking mattress makes me clean is beyond me. And I'm not calling these guys stupid. They are not. Some of them are buddies of mine. And some are good people. But rolling up a mattress and stacking up boxes (daily) is absolutely asinine and it is a sign of the ridiculousness of prison.

This guy explains how a fellow gang member can order you to stick some dope up your butt (you literally wrap drugs up in plastic and squeeze it into your anus... You dump it out via defecation. I've never seen an all male environment where everybody claims to be a murderer but nobody has any problem sticking foreign objects up their butts!) And go "stab Joe Delgado because he's a child molester." And you must do it. Never mind the fact that you might get a life sentence in prison or Joe might murder you. You have your orders. And when you do the stabbing and go to the hole you must defecate the drugs out. You clean the crap off the plastic and remove the drugs. You tear up a sheet and make what we call a fishing line. You tie drugs onto this line and throw the line under your cell door. Someone throws a line toward you. The two lines connect. You slowly drag the end of his line into your cell. You tie the dope onto the end of his line. He drags the line into his cell. This kind of organized chaos takes place every day in prisons... My gang banger interviewer kept using terms like "we're not allowed to", and "disciplined". How/why would I allow another man to tell me what I'm not allowed to do? And if a shot caller doesn't like what you've done/said he issues out your discipline. He can order you to do push-ups. He can order you to stay in your cell. He can order you (the same dude who hates it when your teacher tells you to do homework) to "write an essay." This is what they don't show you in the movies. Again I repeat that prison is a modern day form of slavery. ...

I asked this guy did he think he'd stay out if they let him out tomorrow. (For the record we all say yes). And then I reminded him that of the 100 released yesterday, 82 would return. And (as usual) he was (in his mind) in the 18. I've never had a guy getting released to tell me "I'll be back". But many (if not most) have came back. It seems like there is a magnet placed inside of us once we come here. And when we get out it draws us back to the prison community. When the slaves were freed in America many of them returned to the plantation. Because they never got the 40 acres and they never got the mule. So it was advantageous (economically) for them to keep living on a plantation.

And many men get out of prison with no money, no job and few skills. The psychological damage of the prison sub-culture has destroyed our character. Our spirits are broken and our minds are dysfunctional. And we return to the plantation. We are broken, bitter, deceptive and angry men. And we return to an all male environment to roll up mattresses and sit boxes on bunks to show how neat we are. We are lost boys...

At another institution I met a black female librarian. She hates black men. She has (obviously) been abused. By black men. And Mrs. Bradley (pseudonym) is one of the most wicked, vulgar and bitter women I've ever met. She is sick- and what is worse is the fact that inmates allow her to poison them against their peers. She gets these guys in that library (at P.V.S.P.) and she has them acting like "staff". It is crazy with a capital C. How can I ever allow a person who goes home every night to bring dissension between me and a person who sleeps in the house with me? But we (prisoners) do it every day of the week. And this sister (Mrs. Bradley) had the nerve to tell me she is a Christian. Wow....

I see why so many folks mock the church. It is not God that they're angry at. They are disappointed in us evil, spiteful, hateful and angry fake Christians. This Mrs. Bradley just decided to hate me. And I was too arrogant and too egotistical to humble myself and go out of my way to show her that I was not a bad iuy.

Young men and young ladies I want to tell you the same thing. First Lady Michelle Obama told a group of students: "All of you are jewels. You are precious to my heart." Your life is filled with golden opportunities. Please don't tarnish your life by coming to prison. Prison is a disfunctional place. You don't know who to trust. I've even had psychiatrists to deceive and manipulate me before. But I've also been guilty of manipulating them.

Prison: there is nothing as dangerous as fellowshiping with men who have missed their moment. They (we in prison) think that minimizing you maximizes them. They focus on bringing you down rather than lifting themselves up... Saul messed around and lost God's favor and became envious of David. Prison is full of envy. And prison is filled with folk who have been ignored. And there is a propensity to become bitter when you've been ignored. When somebody just showed up on the scene and they do something you couldn't do in ten years you can get angry. But there is an Injustice to God's Favor. Favor is not Fair. God is a Just God but he is not a Fair God... There are a lot of prodigal sons in prisons. And there are brothers of prodigals in here. And (in the Bible) the prodigal son's brother got jealous when he came home. The Father threw the prodigal son a party when he came home. And his brother had rocks in his jaws and he actually boycotted his brother's party. He told his daddy "I've been faithful... He spent your money and laid up with harlots. But I've been faithful and you never threw me a party." As long as you're angry and bitter you'll never be blessed... In prison you keep getting up in the morning and time is still ticking. Seconds turn into minutes and minutes turn into hours. Hours turn into days, weeks, years and decades. You keep getting up in a cell and walking around the same yard. You keep doing the same old stuff with the same old people... You become cynical, bitter and angry. You sit in the seat of the scornful. And when you sit in the seat it means you plan to be there (scornful) a while.

In prison you don't even remember what day it was that you lost the gleam in your eyes. A permanent frown becomes etched across our faces. We sit in the seat of the scornful and we have become comfortable. I pray everyday that God won't allow me to sit in the seat of the scornful.

I've even seen folk I care about in here become scornful and envious. Hurting people mask hurt and fear with anger. And angry people will kill you. This is a lonely place yall. Trion Savala ("The Effort") can tell you... I want Cole Fox, Patrick Green and Chris Thompson to know what it is like... Strive to make peace in your school. If somebody gets on your nerves you pray for them and bless them. You love them. And instead of trying to date them lil gals (or boys) date a book.

Learn persuasion through love. 6% of U.S. teens are clinically depressed. Depressed people often turn to drugs and crime. Drugs can be the language of the depressed and the bored. And people on drugs often come to prison. And you can take a five year sentence and turn it into a death sentence very quickly. ... Adrian Lamo? Alex Flores? Chris Lehane? Adam Pan? Kyle Sevey are yall reading this?

Caleb Sima and Seamus Farrow need to get this book. I want all of those great students at the Ron Clark Academy in my home town (Atlanta Ga.) to get this book. If I am successful at figuring out a way to put this book into the hands of kids in schools, clubs, groups, youth centers and juveniles around the Nation. And If I'm able to write one sentence in this book that motivates you to stay in school my work is not in vain. You are Jewels. You are creative and wonderful human beings. You have the power to rise above poverty, rise above illiteracy, rise above gangs and drugs and be a leader. If you can see it you can be it. The only thing that is bigger than a dream is your imagination.

I know it might not be easy. Life can be tough. But tough times never last, tough people do. You're either in a storm, on your way to a storm or just coming out of a storm. Life is a series of storms. But with faith in God and with education you will weather the storms of life. If I could only give you two pieces of advice they would be A. Education, B. no drugs. Those are the main two things you can do to stay out of prisons. It does not take a rocket scientist to figure out that most guys in jail are either drug addicts or drug salesmen. And most of us don't even have a high school diploma. Stay in school. Stay off drugs. And you'll stay out of prison.

I know many of you are in the Foster Care System. And much of the research which we did for this book revolved around the Foster Care System and group homes. A large number of jail and prison inmates were in Foster Care. And I will repeat that the Foster Care System is absolutely broken. We (psychologists, ex-cons, pastors, parents, police and professors) must fix it. It needs to be overhauled. Governors ought to declare a state of emergency in America's Foster Care System.....

I want Earth First and ELF members to get this book. We need you (www.napsusa.org) ...

May I ramble? Young people I cannot over emphasize the urgency of the need for self esteem and education. Prison is filled with folks who can't think, read or write. And can I throw out some numbers? Education: only 48% of the black males in America graduate from high school. Only 60% of the black females in America graduate high school. I see why Bill Cosby was so livid with us. Every black church in America ought to have a literacy program and a book club. Illiteracy is the new civil rights battle. This is embarrassing and ridiculous. But 74% of the white males in America graduate high school. Most crack users are black. This is sick...

And 74% of all child killers are Caucasian. 92% of all child killers are male. 83% of all child molesters are also Caucasian. Embarrassingly ridiculous and sick. And what is even sicker is the fact that many white folks were feeling pretty good when I gave out the crack numbers and the graduation numbers. And a lot of blacks felt cool when I pointed out the child predator statistics. But even though we still have these biases, prejudices and even this racism etc. Most Blacks murder other Blacks. Most Whites murder other Whites. And most Hispanics murder other Hispanics. So our racial pride, bias and prejudices are not translating into love and peace. If we (Black folks) love each other so much based upon our "kinship" then why don't we stop killing and hating one another? Why don't white folks do the same? Our reasoning is without reason. We need to grow up and start loving all people.

And I want to motivate you youngsters to guard your minds. If you don't want to be sitting up here in prison with a bunch of spiteful losers (us). You need to guard your minds early on. If I came to your house and dumped a trash can full of garbage in your living room you might shoot me. You'd be appalled if I threw my garbage in your living room. But - you allow people to dump garbage and trash in your mind every day.

Do you have more respect for your living room than you do for your mind? You need to prime your mind for success by disallowing garbage inside. Feed your mind the good, the clean, the pure, the powerful and the positive. When your buddies bring you gossip (garbage), rumor, innuendo, prejudice, negativity or he-said, she-said stop them. Tell them politely "not today my brother. I love you but I can't do that today." And every time they bring you bull crap refuse to entertain it. Exercise your right to be an individual. Practice utilizing initiative and leadership. You lead by learning to lead yourself. Lead yourself to the library. Lead yourself to positive people. Learn a new word every day. When you politely tell your buddies you don't want and won't allow garbage to enter your mind you are leading. When you refuse to allow people to influence you to use drugs or drop out of school etc. you are leading. Lead yourself...

Professor Ted Delaney is chairman of African American Studies at Washington and Lee University. Professor Delaney was a janitor at this same college. He worked there when blacks could not attend. He went to college at 40. And now he is a professor at the same place at which he was a janitor. I wondered about the white student sitting at the table which Professor Delaney lectured on TV. This white student had on a black shirt and he had on khaki shorts. When they were walking down a flight of stairs, (as shown on "Our World") this same white kid seemed to be mesmerized. I want that student in G.B.G. with all deliberate haste. Prof. Delaney says to students to "be persistent. Don't take no for an answer and give it all you have." I endorse that statement. ... Read "Awaken the Giant within" by Robbins. "Unlimited power" Robbins "Blue Eyed Blonde" Book II. "Live your Dreams" by Les Brown and "The magic of thinking big" by David J. Schwartz... Read those books within the next 30 days and I promise you your life will begin to be transformed. It is so fun and exciting to read great books. Yes, you will learn from these books. But "Awaken the Giant", "B.E.B." Book II and "The Magic" etc. are fast, fun and exciting books. I have never given any of the above five books to a young man who didn't come back and say "wow" or "that was awesome". So if you wanna graduate school, go to college and not go to jail etc. get these books with all deliberate speed. If you absolutely can't afford the books go to http://napsusa.blogspot.com and post a message and we'll get our readers to donate you the book(s).

Be a sponge for information. Try to soak up knowledge everywhere you go. God gave you 2 ears and 1 mouth. Listen twice as much as you talk. You can change who you are, how you are and even where you are by changing what goes inside your brains. Don't allow people to dump (± repeat) garbage into your mind. Don't let your mind be a garbage dump.I am in this hell and I live in it every day. I know (obviously) what it takes to come to prison. I am cognizant of the various methodologies which can be employed to survive in prison. I know how we (the dudes in prison) operate, think, scheme, behave and group. I don't care what you saw at the movies. I don't care how brilliant my publicist told yall I am. Smart folks don't usually come to prison. And if I was smart enough I'd figure out a way to get out of jail. Prison is not what you think it is. It is a dangerous, lowly, animalistic and a sad place. Even the folks who work here (very often) become jaded, psychotic and malicious. I have major respect for the few people who are able to work in corrections for more than five years without becoming corrupt. Light (often) attracts light. And people who are like each other tend to like each other. Prison draws a certain clientele toward itself. Certain kinds of people could/would never work in a prison. And who wants to (i.e.) live or work with a molester, rapist, robber or killer? Well when you work in prisons your clientele are criminals, and many of these guards work 16 hours per day, 5 days per week. They spend more of their life in prison than they do free. They work 2 and 3 hours away from home. So they're either sleeping, on the way to work or coming from work. Ipso Facto most successful salesmen love people. Great cosmetologists etc. love hair and love people. You go into sales or into counseling because you are an affable and gregarious person and you like to be around people. Great pastors love people. Great lawyers (trial lawyers) not only love law but they love people. Show me an articulate, outgoing, charismatic person and I'll show you a great lawyer... But what kind of person says "I wanna grow up and spend my life working with people who murder, maim and molest...?"

"When I wake up every morning for 30 years I wanna look forward to going inside a prison and looking at the private parts (i.e. penis, testicles and anus) of other men... I'll strip them out and cuff them up. I ..." Yall feel me? This is a hell uva career move. And you can't come here and not be affected. Many guards are infected. And they do more damage than they do good. Lock up a kid in a prison full of predators and throw a couple of inmates in with them. (smile). But seriously - if the inmates are criminals and the guards are no good it is a recipe for disaster... I remember being stationed at M.C.S.P. in Ione Ca. A young white inmate by the name of Womack was being escorted down the tier (walkway). Inmates (we convicts) were yelling about how fine he was and "look at that as_"... Back up and re-read that. If I'm looking at another man's butt (as if he were a woman, although we share the same anatomical protrusion) what does it say about me? But what stood out in my mind was the correctional officer's comments. C.O. Jackson (pseudonym) stated to an inmate we called "Double R" that "How did you like all that ass on that boy? Good, young, fresh tender ass". This coming from a correctional officer who is married with children. But forget Jackson for a moment and ask yourself the question: How would I have felt if I was Womack? I later learned that Womack was 18 years old and he would serve 3 years in prison. But when you lock a boy up around vicious, hateful, mean, jealous, envious, ignorant and hard core men (many of whom will never get out of prison) for 3 years what does it do to his psyche? I've been studying what happens to us for a decade now and it is a recipe for animals.

I recall being in the cell with a fellow who loved rap. I'm not opposed to rap but it is not my favorite music. I like gospel, Rock and Oldies etc. But anyway I don't call women the B_ word. Nor do I call people the "N" word. And in his music every woman was a "B". And every person was a "N". And he woke me up to this rap and we went to sleep listening to this rap. And after 3 or 4 weeks I was chatting with an acquaintance and I caught myself referring to a woman as a "B". I was humiliated. Association brings about assimilation.... But how would you feel (assuming you are heterosexual and if you are gay that is your business. But even gay folks don't deserve to be raped or harassed.) walking through a crowd of 1000 men (in their 30's, 40's, 50's and 60's. A group of thugs. Perverts and undercover gay boys etc.) and they all looking at your booty. And you're getting cat calls from men. And you find out that your options are to join the skinheads or get raped. How would you feel? And the very police officers (i.e. the guards) are just as corrupt as the inmates who are staring at your booty? 2 Be honest you think the C.O. must be on pipe too ... So the convicts r checking u out n u c the po po checking u out 2. This is the way prison works. And you will be strip searched by male guards routinely. And you have no privacy. Your movement is monitored. Your mail is monitored and even your cell is monitored... While I'm writing this I got interrupted with a cell search. The officers decided to come and search all of my property. How do I know they didn't read my legal mail? They can do whatever they want to do. And you will strip when they tell you to ... "Hair" (meaning rub your fingers through your hair to prove you don't have a knife hidden in it).... "Ears" (turn your ears out)... "Mouth" (open your mouth - lift your tongue. Rub your nasty fingers around your gums to prove no drugs or weapon is being hidden). "Arms" (lift your arms to prove nothing is taped under your armpits). "Nuts" (sic) means lifting up your testicles to prove... "Turn around, right foot, left" (turn around in the nude and lift your feet to prove no razor or drugs are taped to the bottom of your feet). "Spread your cheeks, squat and cough" (you open up your butt cheeks, squat down and cough to prove no shank is hidden up your posterior). This is the routinized naked strip search we killers go through every day. You see us and you know that our cocks (excuse my French), balls and butts have been seen thousands of times by hundreds of other men. And this is where you want to spend your life? ... Back to Womack etc. So I hate to tell you but more than likely Womack got out of prison and is back doing life by now. If he went off on somebody for disrespecting him (sexually) they beat him, killed him or just scared him and made him a boy. If he killed them he has his "respect" and a life sentence to go along with it. You're damned if you do and damned if you don't I can't count the men who came here, got out and returned with a life sentence. And when boys like Womack come here we rub off on them. They model our pettiness and they model our foolishness. The idiosyncratic whims of institutionalization rubs off on them. If I had my way we would rarely ever send a youngster to prison. And when we did I would require him to read, read, read and read. And when he got out we would deprogram him in order to deinstitutionalize him. We would have people like Dr. Jarman, Dr. A. Duran, Dr. Heitkamp, Dr. Curren and Dr. Gregg to deprogram him upon his release. Rather than running to check in with a parole officer I'd have him running to check in with Dr. A. Duran.

Prisons exacerbate mental illness. Prisoners are surrounded by people suffering from mental illness. And those with small mental problems become affected by those who are severely ill. And persons such as Dr. Gregg, Dr. Duran and Dr. Jarman can attest to the fact that we feed off of each other. What do you think riots are about? ...

I've never understood why we drink in prison. Yes, we manufacture pruno (i.e. Hooch or wine) in prison. And if I'm surrounded by fellow killers, molesters and maniacs whom I don't trust etc. Shouldn't/wouldn't I want to have a sober mind? How can I adequately, skillfully and willfully defend myself if I'm drunk? Come on people (Dr. Bill Cosby forgive me). Why would anybody wanna be disoriented in a prison full of murderers? I can't count the time I've seen people get their butts kicked while they were intoxicated. Alcohol and drugs retard the reflexes and delay reactions. So for the life of me I can't comprehend any sane person using drugs and alcohol in a place where they send people who killed other people. I aint had a drink in more than 8 years. I'm too scared to drink...

Nothing grows on ice. And prison is such a cold place that it will freeze your brain. Ideas, creativity and brilliance are not fomented in prisons.

Unusual. Bizarre. Cold. Dark. Dank. Lonely. Demonic. Wicked. Those are the words which come to my mind when I think about prison... "The miraculous Journey of Rubin "Hurricane" Carter" is another powerful book I would highly recommend for every youngster to read. It is an awesome and terrific book. It is a splendiferous read... "Breaking the chains of psychological slavery" by Dr. Naïm Akbar is another terrific book; read it...

I was thinking about that captain (at another prison) who stated that he had a "file" on me. First of all this dude is one of the most forgetful, scatter brain guys I've ever met. Secondly it Boggles my mind to note that he's been sued a thousand times and he's still corrupt. This man should know better. I have more dirt on this guy than you could ever imagine. The only reason I didn't sue him was because it was not pragmatically appropriate to do so. Terry L. Rosario (A/K/A "Dad") told me years ago that "I'm letting you in the tent. But I'm gonna point you toward the exit. So if you piss - you piss outside." I learned to be kind to folks directly over me. But it should be reciprocated. But when you deal with Bullies (i.e. this captain at that other prison) they can't help themselves. The fact that they go home every day is not enough for them. The fact that they earn $ 108.000 per year is not enough. They could stand 7 ft. tall and it would not satiate their desire to bully people.

I was launching a new program at another prison (P.V.S.P.) and you should have seen the captain and the associate warden. I never thought I'd have to scare off staff looking for glory. Both men claimed to love God. But how can you love God and hate your brother? And they hated Sherman D. Manning. Hate is a powerful emotion. But they hated me. They manipulated inmates against me. They came in and tried to hijack the group. They attempted to manipulate the warden against me. They were rogues, renegades and thieves. I remember telling the associate warden (a so-called devout Christian) that "if you knew so much about organizing a group such as this etc. You've been in corrections for 24 years. Why have you not started a program before I got here?" ...

As I said - whenever you try to do something Big, Beautiful and Godly - a Judas will always be raised up. The spirit of Judas will always arise. If there is no Judas there's no Jesus. And if Joseph's biological brothers tried to kill him for a dream. What do you think non relatives would do to a Joseph in a prison; for a vision? If Cain would kill his brother out of anger. What will a captain do to me? This is spiritual wickedness in high places... Because of my experience with that group I now run from any C.D.C. official who claims to be a Christian. I have watched way too many Christian captains order retaliatory transfers. I've seen Christian Captains assault and murder convicts. Today is Easter Sunday and I assure you that the Christian A.W. and Captain (at P.V.S.P.) are in church today. They are in suit and tie and they love God today. They are shaking hands and toting Bibles. But the Klu Klux Klan-men were also in church every Sunday. They wore suits on Sunday and robes on Monday. They had Bibles in one hand and crosses (for burning) in the other. And racism, corruption, criminality etc. is entrenched in C.D.C.

as well as in corrections departments, all over the world. It is difficult to have anything good, clean, pure, powerful or positive to come out of a prison ... When I think of David Han (Folsom), Doug Pieper Jr., Luke Sears, Kyle Love and Omar Samy etc. etc. I want to yell to the top of my lungs and tell them to stay as far away from hell (prison) as they can... Angel Alcazar, Seamus Farrow, Zach, Jai and all of you stay away. Keep away from prison. It will infect your life.

I've been blessed to have a team of psychiatrists i.e. Dr. Franklin Curren to consult with about the contents of this tome.

My research had me in the faces of Dr. Gregg, Dr. A. Duran, Dr. Jarman, Dr. Curren etc. perhaps more often than they would like. But what I learned from these clinicians, therapists, Adam Lane, Dustin, Daniel, Madame Patricia Kennedy etc. etc. were things that helped me to write this book. I could not have written this book without the things I learned from Steve John Vance and Fred Schroeder. I thank God that I met these people. God is awesome. And I'm so thankful to have met the G.B.G./HEART secretary who is C.O. D. Smith. She was told all sorts of negative things about me by others. Yet, she was professional enough to be fair and to observe my character for herself. She has found me to be manipulative, studious, courteous, respectful and sober. Never has Mrs. Diana Smith heard a profane word exit my lips. Not because I'm a Saint (I am not) but because I respect women. Madame Smith told Johnny Willie and me "you two guys would make the best politicians in the world... You have a way with people". And I salute Mrs. Smith... But any time I start feeling pretty good about myself a Mrs. Bradley will show up. I'll walk up on a librarian, a Cain or a captain who hates my guts... And when people hate your guts you don't have to do anything. All you need to do is wake up in the morning. And the fact that you woke up is enough to make them mad. So if you wanna satisfy your enemies just die... Remember that prison is duplicitous, dangerous, dastardly, disastrous and destructive. I want Jason Huyck, David Begnaud, Ben Tracy, Robin Roberts. Lisa Ling and Tyra Banks to interview Matt Cate. I want them to interview "Jimbo" (A/K/A warden James P. Walker), Terry L. Rosario and Patricia Kennedy. I want folks like Jimbo, Terry, Diana Smith and even Rod Q. Hickman to begin to tell America's media and the press about the this mess. That goes on in prisons. Jimbo, Terry, Patricia, Fred and Scott Kernan etc. can tell America what really goes on inside these walls. To be candid, I think Rod, Jimbo, Rosario and others owe a debt to society. They owe it to our youth to give warnings about what prison is all about. I think this is why Jimbo decided to get behind G.B.G./HEART and to allow us to bring kids inside these walls to turn them around. I think this is why Senator Burton got behind G.B.G. These people feel that we owe society. And I know all of the guys in G.B.G. (Willie, Ford, Fleming, Rose and the other fellas) are cognizant that we owe a debt. We have robbed, cheated and crooked society. And we now owe it to youngsters to forewarn them about hell. You Bible scholars remember when somebody went to hell and sent word telling his friends not to come to hell. And "Father Abraham, let Lazarus come down, with one drop of water to cool my scorching tongue"... Some of the G.B.G. members are sworn enemies. We don't all lunch or brunch together. But we put aside our differences and made the G.B.G./HEART juvenile diversion program happen. It took a lot of prayer. I told Fred weeks ago that "I've never prayed this much in my life... I'm serious Fred. Putting G.B.G. together has been one of the toughest challenges in my life. But I promised God... It's so much work. I spend (literally) hundreds of dollars a month on postage. Each letter costs me (at least) $ 59 cents because my missives have 8 and 9 pages in every envelope. And I have to massage so many egos. I have to deal with anger, jealousy, animosity, distrust and Y-O-U" I told Fred. He laughed and said "Yes we can". I wanna take a moment and (again) thank Fred, Steve, Billy Fleming and others for fully supporting G.B.G. I can't thank Johnny and Doc enough.

Johnny helps me for free; all the time. Alonso helps me for free; all the time. George Rose also consistently promotes our group. Without these guys there would be no G.B.G. I always say it is "G.B.G." not "me G.B."... I reach out to David Han, Seamus, Brian Hawn, Faisal Saleh, C.J. Sheron, Cody Sheldon, Zach, Angel, Hellyer and you (U2) too... Join G.B.G. today and help us to Change the World... And while I'm mentioning Johnny Willie I want a lawyer to help Willie. This (tome) is not the appropriate forum for me to prognosticate about his injustice. But I will ask (Johnny Griffin, Ephraim Margolin, David Balser etc.) some attorney to please help Johnny Willie. He's at C.S.P. Sacramento and he needs a lawyer. I thought Paul Comisky would help him but he didn't. So it can be Sean Musgrove, Ann Patterson or any other great lawyer. I just want a lawyer who is moved by injustice to step up to the plate and hear Willie's cry to "rescue me"...

Now I wanna talk about disease a moment. Last night I looked out of my cell door to see not one but two different guys getting prison tattoos. I like both guys and they're cool. But why would any man get a tattoo in prison? We know for a fact that many prisoners have hepatitis. We also know you can get it from tattooing and sex. And (the irrationality of the prison mentality) each and every guy getting a tattoo (or giving one) will tell you how safe they do it etc. I've never ever met a guy in here who told me "I give tattoos and I'm good at it. I got a hand but I'm unsafe and I spread hep. C when I do tattoos." I have also never met a dude receiving a tattoo who told me "Yeah I like the way dude tats. He gots skills even though he's probably gonna give me hep while he tats me."

Not one single person who has received hep. C from a tattoo thought he was gonna get it when he got it. I don't know a dude who gave it but thought "I'm gonna grab this tattoo gun and go give a guy hep. C. right now."

But there are 27 people in the dayroom right now. And 13 of them (whom I know about) have hepatitis. And that's not a joke. Many of them were diagnosed late and don't get proper treatment. And they got it from sex, needles or tattoos. Why would anybody take the risk of getting a disease when we're already locked up and have enough problems? Because we are not in prison due to our ability to make good decisions. I saw one guy who is going home in less than 3 months and he was getting a tattoo on his face. That is asinine....

Folks in jail die, kill and assault due to drugs, drag queens and gambling more than anything else. The last thing a man ought to be doing in jail is hooking up with a drag queen. With all due respect to gays (we are all human beings. But prison is not humane) queens in prison are like seagulls. They spread crap (no pun intended) everywhere they go. They're like a small block of cheese amidst a thousand rats. It requires very little gumption to know that when you put ten drag queens (i.e. men who walk, talk and try to act like women. They use cherry kool- aid to make lipstick etc.) in the building with 200 gangsters etc. 100 Of the 200 gangsters will fight over the punk. And at least 10 of those 100 will actually kill for the queen... Candidly? Even is you're gay I'd suggest you hide it at all costs. Because the moment we get a peek into your sexuality and discover femininity etc. we are all over you ...

One of the worse things you can be in prison is a litigator/writer. I've not always been around fair and secure administrators like James P. Walker, Tim Virga, Jeff Macomber, CCIII Patricia Kennedy and CCIII Johnson-Dovey. I've been in a number of institutions where in I received retaliatory and vindictive transfers simply because I exercised my constitutional right to write. Inmate Edwards died on 04/12/09. Apparently he had asthma and was pepper sprayed by a sergeant. Apparently this killed him. I'm not calling the sergeant's name here for various reasons. But I would hope the prison law office and the Inspector General will look at this. Since I know folks like U.S. Attorney Larry Brown are perusing this tome - I just want justice. Certain folks will read this and be angered. Well Martin Luther King Jr. had enemies. So did John F. Kennedy and so does President Nelson Mandela.

I asked an individual about Mr. Edward's death and he replied "that ain't none of my business." Well it is my business. Mandela said "the chains on any one of my people are the chains on me." How can I get free if my people are not free? I'm not a boy and I will never, ever allow the prison to desensitize me or to destroy my empathy. (I'm not promoting Sherman D. Manning. I'm still a prisoner, a thug and a bad guy.). And the saddest thing to me is to see 40 and 50 year old men pleading for freedom. While we are simultaneously insensitive to the plight of other brothers. And if Lawyers, Senators and Governors adopt that same "it's not my business" mentality we will never get justice, freedom or the assistance we so desperately seek.

And another lesson for you youngsters about why not to come to prison is the apathy and the inattention of the powers that be. If you get up in the prison system and these people decide to transfer you (even to a place where people are waiting to kill you ... They did it to this author) they will. And you can write all the politicians you want to write but most (if not all) of them will decide (too) that it ain't "none" of their business. And you can kick, scratch, fight and bite but they will transfer you with all deliberate haste. And when you write to the director of corrections (i.e. in New York State) his office shall merely redirect your missive to the same institution which is transferring you. It is sickening, sad and illegal. It is also extremely expensive (to taxpayers) to do these transfers. But they do them every second of every minute, of every day. My suggestion is simple: Don't commit a crime. Don't come to prison. Don't drop out of school...

And if (God forbid) you are incarcerated and you're being retaliated against by staff etc. write to your family. They steal mail so follow-up. By having a buddy to also write your family. Have a lawyer, public defender or your buddies' lawyer to call the prison, call prison headquarters, call the Governor's office and to call a judge. Also have your family to contact the media. Google the official who is in charge of (have your family to Google them) your transfer. Go to http://napsusa.blogspot.com and (have your family do it.) post a message about your transfer etc. etc. online ...

The other thing you can do is pray that great wardens like Jimbo stop retiring! You can bet your bottom dollar that as soon as he retires they will (again!) transfer me to a place where I can be murdered. They hate me. And although Madame Susan Hubbard, Scott Kernan and Matt Cate are good people etc. They can't help me if they are unaware of my dilemma.....

Please get you some books and read. Please stay away from drugs and alcohol. If you've never tried drugs never try drugs. If you tried drugs and can't get off get help. Call a pastor, call a judge, call a lawyer, call a deacon, call a counselor or a clinic. But get off drugs. It is hard but you can do it. You may need some help but you can do it. The cycle of drug addiction can be broken. You can do it. Yes you can!

.... I have an address (Sherman D. Manning), J98796-CSP-SAC-A-8-226- P.O. Box 290066 - Represa CA 95671) in hell. I don't wanna wax biblical on yall but I gotta make my point proper. St. Luke 16:27-30 "I beg you therefore Father, that you would send him to my Father's house (my school, my hood, my suburb, my church or my club), for I have five brothers (kids, youths and youngsters), that he may testify to them, lest they also come to this place of torment ... No Father Abraham, but if one goes to them from the dead, they will repent". Will you? The rich man in Luke was in hell and so am I. The rich man in St. Luke 16:19-31 called out while being tormented. He lifted up his eyes and saw Abraham afar off. I can see you kids in Atlanta, L.A., San Francisco, Switzerland, Africa, New York and in Michigan. I see you afar off... And this man cried out and said "Father Abraham, have mercy on me, and send Lazarus that he may dip the tip of his finger in water and cool my tongue, for I am tormented in this flame." And I want to echo that sentiment to you. I am tormented in this prison. I seek no sympathy. I deserve no sympathy. I simply seek your attention. The reason I deserve no sympathy lies in Abraham's reply to the rich man in verses 25 and 26. Abraham told em to remember that in his lifetime he lived the good life. He had it all. And he received good things. He was a jock. He was Van Hansis or Jake Silbermann. He was Matt Damon etc. But Lazarus lived in tent city. But now he is comforted and you are tormented... And besides all this, between us and you there is a great gulf fixed, so that those who want to pass from here to you cannot, nor can those from there pass to us". I would hope you never pass from there to here; this (I remind you) is hell. And many of us here are on death row or are serving life sentences in prison. Ipso Facto, we can't pass from here to there. But via this missive from a place of torment you've been served. Having read the truth you can't act like you don't know. Many of us want the courts to have mercy on us. But we don't have mercy on one another. Instead we lie, cheat, connive, plot, scheme, stick, stab, rob, rape and we kill. But we want mercy... This is a place of torment. And we are men scorned.

I wrote earlier about our scornfulness. Psalms 1:1 reads "Blessed is the man who walks not in the counsel of the ungodly, nor stands in the path of sinners, nor sits in the seat of the scornful". Be careful where and with whom you walk. And stand up for justice, right, peace and light. And be very careful where and with whom you sit. So watch your walking, standing and your sitting. I promise you that if you sit with scornful men they'll cut on the TV., bring a beer and a bag of chips. As soon as you sit down folk will go to feeding you. And then they'll entertain you. And slowly but certainly you too will become cynical, bitter, mean and scornful. ...

I spoke with a black C.O. a little while ago concerning an inmate death. This black C.O. goes to church every Sunday and is a deacon in his church. Concerning the loss of life this deacon stated "that's on him" meaning the inmate. It still boggles my mind to see how callous we (prisoners and prison guards) are. But I must remind myself that this is Hades (AKA prison/hell) and that this is a valley of dry bones. Is this really where you want to end up? Do you really have a death wish? Is this what you want to die doing?

I'll never fully understand prisons. I'm supposed to be an expert on prisons and crime. I'm a prolific author. I'm told I'm the most prolific writer (in prison) in the United States. And having said all of that I still don't fully comprehend this hellhole. This (prison) is a strange place I tell you... At P.V.S.P. I saw an I.S.U. sergeant along with the Big Bully Captain, tell a man that he could not write to any high school principal. Now there is absolutely no federal state or institutional regulations prohibiting a prison scribe from writing anyone. Staff peruse all incoming and outgoing mail. So to blatantly tell an inmate "you can not write a missive to a high school principal". The prisoner was told things like... I won't repeat them. But it amazes me that in 2009 we still have back woods, hillbilly, hick town, pompous, abusive folks earning $ 108,000 annually who still want to treat prisoners like animals. Prisons are filled with drugs, needles, alcohol, cell phones and weapons etc. But rather than chasing down illegal weapons and drugs these bullies are running around trying to stop a man from writing a principal etc. about gang diversion. The captain told the inmate to "Have your attorney to sue us". He's been sued 93 times. Several inmates (in pro per) won their lawsuits against this captain. Sadly, John and Jane P. Taxpayer (you) pay for these lawsuits. The State defends this captain. And you pay the state. And when there is a settlement it comes out of your pocket. (If Senator Gloria Romero, the Inspector General, Senator Feinstein or the prison law office would like to know the captain and the I.S.U. sergeant's name etc. contact me...)...

When I think about corrupted prison officials (I know many) it helps me to better appreciate professionals like CCIII Patricia Kennedy, C.O. Diana Smith, R. Herrington, Warden Jimbo Walker, Scott Kernan and Matt Cate....

I wanna remind Jacob Cook, nurse Randy Greene, Ben Jurney, Anthony Romero (Diane Sawyer's buddy), Ben Woodside, Damien Cave, Dr. Will Kirby, M.C.P.O. Paul Thorp, David Han, Angel Alcazar, Stacy Dewitt, Gary Dockery, Jake Silbermann and Van Hansis to join G.B.G....

This tome is a missive from Hades to America's youngsters. If your memories are bigger than your dreams you're in trouble. The poorest person in the world is not the one without a nickel. The poorest person in the world is the one without a dream. Dream bigger than your circumstances. Dream and work 2 make your dream become reality...

Prison is built to last. Prison is built to destroy. Prison is built to break you down and to poison your spirit. Lock a man up for ten years and I can spot him by his walk or his talk. And if you parents think (for one moment) that these prisons will rehabilitate your kids please read closely; they won't. Yes, rehabilitation comes from within. Yes, a person must want to change. Yes, transformation is possible. Yes, I believe in changes and yes most prisons are not conducive to change. These are not institutions of higher learning. These are institutions of destruction, devastation and institutionalization ... Not all murdering or molestation is genetics. Destruction and the ability to prey is considered a sign of masculinity. Even in the kindergarten boys begin to see (via older siblings, dads, football, basketball and the movies etc.) that physical prowess, wrestling, boxing, violence and killing makes you a man. There is even a subtle sense of masculinity attached to the depiction of molestation in the movies. We are taught that men murder, molest and rape. And according to experts (i.e. Michael Welner MD., Franklin Curren M.d. and A. Duran Ph.d. etc.) we learn to model this erratic, irrational and this violent behavior.

Why do most kids who are molested grow up and molest? Why do most boys who grow up in abusive homes grow up and abuse? Kids growing up in homes where smoking is cool often smoke. And so is it with this violence which leads to kids killing kids. Much of it is merely modeling. Add drugs, alcohol and a gun into the mix and you have a master recipe for murder, rape, gangs, guns and violence...

There are lil gangsters perusing this missive from Hades. I want you Skinheads, Bloods, Crips, N.L.R., B.G.F., eme, Bulldog and all other gang members to get out of the gangs right here, right now. Marcus King, Jamie Foxx, Professor William Keach (Brown Univ.), Dr. Philip Gasper (Notre Dame), Professor Dylan Rodriquez, Professor Vitiello, Adam Lane, Daniel Bugriyev, Dustin Nic, M. Reid, Matt Cate, Scott Kernan and G.B.G. stands with you if you want to turn around. And if you are already in juvenile, jail or prison let me tell you this: Don't be belligerent. You are (if you're locked up anywhere in these United States) pitted head-to-head, eye-to-eye and toe-to-toe against the forces of the gun power, guards, the code of silence, barbed wire, steel bars, discrimination, duplicity and double-standard prison rules etc. You must be motivated by your moto ndani, your fire within. Rise above the grinding, negative, rigid conditioning by nourishing your intellect and spirit. You can out-think wicked situations with gumption and a pragmatic approach which radiates masterful countermeasures. Do any and everything necessary to change your life. You must get off of drugs. If you don't get off drugs don't even read this book. You are wasting your time if you are unwilling to put crack, meth, pruno, speed and ecstasy down. Get off drugs. Get a book. Pray to God and change. One day at a time and one step at a time. A journey of a thousand miles begins with one step. Step one = decide 2 change. Step two - go back to step one - then take a step... I recommend you read "Blue Rage, Black Redemption" by Tookie Williams. I also recommend (again) "The Miraculous journey of Rubin "Hurricane" Carter... I've almost given up on those of us who are already in prison. It's sad but a fact. I have very little confidence in those of us who are already incarcerated. I'm not telling you we can't change. I'm just telling you most of us won't and don't change. We are vicious, bitter, broken, scornful and deceptive dudes. We will fight over the right to be the C.S.I.C. (Chief Slave In Charge). I've seen guys fight over watering the grass in the prison yard. We are locked up in the gates of hell. We can't get out. And instead of thinking, praying, discussing and plotting a legal strategy to get out. We argue over watering grass. Guys will stab each other for the right to dig in the trash can. Grown men with life sentences running around ready to kill other brothers for the right to pilfer and sift through saliva, snot and crap. It is absolute madness. When I look around at these broken, hurting and wounded men I get sad. I'm so sad at what I see in them and feel in me. There is a big ole beautiful world out there. People in cars, boats, ships, trains and planes. People living life and having it their way. And I'm sitting on a concrete slab hoping the associate warden does not transfer me because he hates me. I'm sitting on the grass watching 4 people fight over a prison punk. And the punk has H.I.V. I've got the world fused out. And I'm caught up in the midst of the madness. And prison takes the adage "dog eat dog" to another level. You'll never know what "smiling faces sometimes tell lies' means until you see a prison. I've had people to embrace me and as soon as I walk away they embraced my enemy. Barring Lonnie Young I knew very few people whom I've been able to trust in prison. We are cutthroats and brutal. We have been desensitized, programmed and ruined. Men in here are good for nothing. And Melissa Rothstein and Psuyin etc. can all attest to the fact that some guards are rapists and murderers. In April 2009 C.D.C. Director Matt Cate said guards were smuggling cell phones into prisons for money. They'd confiscated more than 1500 cell phones in California prisons in just 3 months. "We had an officer who earned a hundred thousand dollars in one year smuggling cell phones... They can get up to one thousand dollars per phone" Mr. Cate stated... And they also smuggle drugs and weapons. And they beat, abuse, set up and rape. I have been set up by guards. I've had mail stolen by guards. I've had money, books and glasses stolen by guards. I've had inmates (working for guards) to set me up. They'll rat you out, lie on you or write a missive. This is absolutely a Monster Factory. It is absolutely a place of torment! Keep out!!!

This tome or this missive from from Hades is akin to a fireside chat with a thug (Sherman D. Manning) who is in hell. Due to technological advances, the Internet, blogging etc. this missive (tome) has arrived in your mailbox (school, church or computer). And I remind you not to trust me.

Don't trust anybody in prison. Not the kept and not the keepers. Find a principal, a teacher, a counselor, a pastor or a parent in whom you can trust. This missive is your ambulance but you need to find a hospital... Go to TDJakes.org and get some D.V.D.'s that will motivate you. Great preaching and teaching is awesome...

I called home on Easter Sunday and spoke with my Aunt Annette. It was splendid to hear her voice. She told me she had gone to my Uncle Melvin's church and took all of her kids with her. And she said her daughter Lori stayed outside the church during service. And (my Aunt is crazy yall) she said "I should have stayed out there with her. Rev. Carmen (pseudonym) can't preach. I tried so hard to get into his message. The man can't preach... He gotta TV. show too. And anytime u wanna get u a good nap, just turn on his show and ...."

I know Rev. Carmen personally. And as much as I love great preaching (Jasper Williams, Leroy Elliott, T.D. Jakes, Timothy Flemming, Eddie Long etc.) I must admit that Dr. Carmen can-not-preach. I just threw this lil story (true) in since this missive (tome) is prose and not poetry. Since the data I'm covering is so hard, sad and bleak. I just wanted to lighten the moment.

Prisons are breeding grounds for hate, violence, wickedness and destruction. And hate groups are expanding in record numbers in 09. According to Attorney Morris Dees at the Southern Poverty Law Center there are 926 active hate groups in America. Up 50% since 2000. The expansion is due to Mr. Obama's election, immigration, the political climate and due to the economy. And many prison guards are active members of hate groups... There is rampant Domestic terrorist extremist groups in prisons. These r folks who believe that America is evil, will take away our guns and our rights. Very often these r guys who have returned from Iraq wounded, unable to get a job and suffering from P.T.S.D. (please remember CDCDR does not treat post traumatic stress)... And don't let them get locked up. When/if these guys go 2 jail they clique up and formulate lil bootleg hate groups. They often merge with skinheads, the A.B. or N.L.R. and instead of prison authorities preventing, disrupting and dismantling these gangs, hate groups and vicious domestic terrorists etc. they are too busy disrupting and delaying the mail ... They are drunk cowboys who are intimidated by intelligence. And if they had the option of finding a cell phone, meth, a gangster or preventing a racial attack etc. or confiscating a missive to a controversial prisoner/author etc. I assure you they will confiscate the mail... I recall one of my books "Blue Eyed Blonde" Book II being published. The mail room supervisor wrote on the tome "This guy is whacked" and sent it to the I.S.U. (Investigative Services Unit) to launch a full scale investigation into a book which had been written a year ago, published months ago and was even sent to the President etc. But these cowboys thought they had rights which superseded my constitutional, free speech and artistic expression rights ...

Rambling on etc. I think pepper spray ought 2 be outlawed in prisons. I have Valley Fever and Asthma. If they cell extract (forcefully remove) an inmate from a cell the physicians will disallow them 2 use pepper spray if the inmate has asthma alone; much less Valley Fever. But if that same asthma and/or Valley Fever patient (whom physicians disallowed them to use pepper spray on during a cell extraction etc.) is on the yard fighting (or spits at staff) they are authorized (by policy) to utilize pepper spray. Even if they are the victim...

This missive (tome) from Hades is cutting edge data. We need to reach Mark Michalowski (Robot inventor), Ramit Sethi, David Quattlebum, Phillip Alpert, Caleb Peek (in Indiana) and Senator John Campbell with this missive. I want the shot callers in the hoods, the jocks in suburbia, the quarterback of your football team, the President of the Student Body, thugs, bullies, freaks and geeks to peruse (meticulously) this missive. This book is for young G's, young crooks, gangsters, leaders, studs, jocks, clique leaders etc. yall don't gotta agree with everything I write. It's your call 2 do what U wanna do. But you don't agree with every lyric of every rap you listen to. I'm certain most of you would never fix your lips to utter the kind of things about your mother which Eminem says about his mom. But you still listen to Slim Shady.

This book is prose and it is not written to be accepted and agreed upon by all. Just because I give you C.P.R. when you're dying (have you a choice? You're not breathing.) Doesn't mean you need to join my gang after you get well. Just because you are drowning and I throw you a life jacket does not mean you have to follow me to the polls and vote for the same person I vote for. If you're falling off a clip and I save your life you should thank me. And thank God. But it does not mean that you must start practicing witchcraft just because I do (I do not)... This (K.K.K.) is the Book to read. Thousands of you in juveniles, schools, churches, colleges, hoods, barrios and suburbs etc. will read this book... It is life support data for youngsters at, in or near (even within a vista) kids killing (raping, molesting, beating or bullying) kids. This is your C.P.R. But you have your own mind, your own political beliefs, family and social circle etc. Don't abandon yours for mine. Be your own person with your own beliefs.

The reason I am convinced that Ben Whitticombe, Phillip Alpert, Jai Breisch, Van Hansis, Devin Rio, Gabe Williams, Timothy Coleman, thugs, gangsters, young G's, student leaders and even youth pastors will read this (KKK) missive from Hades is by virtue of opportunity, conditions and ... this book steps into a vacuum, an uncontested position (void) tailor-made for a prison scribe. This tome expands racially (I've more white readers than blacks and Mexicans) on the writings of Malcolm, Tookie, Geronimo Pratt, Jack Abbott, Rubin Carter and even (in another sense) Gerry Spence ... I'm able to tell poor people that their real adversaries are the squalid living conditions, the vortex of powers confining you to those conditions and your own unwitting perpetuation of those conditions. I'm in a position to speak truth to power. I can tell the skinheads, Nazi Low Riders, Sacramaniacs, Bulldogs, Nortenos etc. that you are unconscious accomplices in your own subjugation - your own worst enemies. Because after a decade of watching and researching (brainwashed, violent, cold blooded, vicious and bitter) prisoner gang warfare I know that we are (unconsciously) accomplices in our own subjugation, incarceration and our own worst enemies.

I also can testify to the fact that prisoners (i.e. even studious little white boys who get arrested for meth possession, bad checks, credit card fraud or car theft) are beat, raped and killed by guards and jail deputies.

Case in point: The major Stanford Prison Experiment, which divided students into two groups: one group posed as prisoners and the other as guards, both in a makeshift prison setting. This six-day experiment resulted in a violent, vicious and barbaric transmogrification in attitude among the students role-playing as prison guards. It got so dangerous they had to terminate the experiment. And these were Stanford students. What do you think these Hicks, thugs and .... some of the people working in corrections do? This was but a scaled-down version of the madness behind these walls where some of the most sadomasochistic minds belong to guards. Some of the men and women working in prison undergo a Dr. Jekyll and Mr. Hyde transformation. Many of their family members and friends would be appalled to learn how odious, mendacious, conniving, insidious, perverted and animalistic they can be at work. Or maybe they would not.

Prison are institutions that protect their own, polices itself even when charges of malfeasance or rape are brought forward. Peers investigating peers. They attend the same churches (or Klan rallies) and live in the same neighborhoods. ... I want you all to find Mario Cook, Barbara Cottman Becnel, Michael Moore, Jacob Cook, professor Dylan Rodriquez, Jake Silbermann, gang bangers, student activists and teachers (via Face Book) and tell them this missive from hell is out. Yall can un-friend (de-friend?) me after you peruse the missive but right now put the word out!

Dealing with prison authorities as well as fellow prisoners will convince even the most stoic atheist that there is a devil. Ipso Facto there is a God. All you need to do in a juvenile, a jail or a prison is to try to build anything which is beautiful, positive and is good and I promise you, as sure as you're looking at this page - you will see the devil. He'll raise himself up through administrators, captains, cohorts, cellies and even psychiatrists. The spirit of jealousy, envy, anger and animosity is rampant in prisons. I've been in situations where I walked with someone whom I embraced. I walked with someone I prayed for, folk I considered to be my brothers. And I'm discussing Joseph and his brothers' jealousy. We are talking about envy amongst other prisoners etc. And this same brutha whom I care about etc. is also a Judas... President Obama said if you want a friend in D.C. "get a dog." Well at least Barrack has Bo. We don't got no dogs in jail yall. So I'm alone. But I do have God. And our God is an awesome God. He can cause lions to lay down with lambs. Instead of running around trying to find favor with the fellas I seek the favor of God. One thing that laying in a lonely hospital bed - chained to a bed for one year and two months taught me was how to be alone. And I had no buddies, no pals, no gangbangers, no so-called "Friends" by my bedside. I had guards outside my door betting on how soon I'd die. I learned some lessons on my death-bed. I learned how insignificant I am. It taught me how the world can actually survive without (damages ego, cures narcissism etc.) Sherman D. Manning. And unless I wrote it down yall would never know it (me, my hell, my pain, my journey or my truth). And it also taught me what Jasper Williams meant when he preached that "there will come a time in every one of our lives when it gets down to nobody but you and the Lord... U better know how to call on God... " And I saw through a glass clearly. There is a

God. And He is able to do exceedingly, abundantly above all that I may ask or think. If you all think I'm embellishing call Dr. Paul Griffin in Coalinga CA and ask him how many times he knew I would die. But God! and I'm still here. And this tome is a debt I owe to Jehovah. Exposing myself and putting my life out there for all the media to scrutinize etc. Giving vent to all of my haters so they can allege that my motives are dark and dastardly etc... They will allege I'm just trying to get a pardon or a prize. But they don't understand I already got the prize. I have my Life. And for the record - while we're on the subject A. I've always maintained I am wrongly convicted of this crime. B. I also admit I have done many other things that (if caught) would have buried me under the jail. I'm a thug and a Bad Boy. C. The Governor will not pardon Sherman D. Manning. D. Neither Warden Jimbo Walker, nor Patricia Kennedy, Scott Kernan nor any other C.D.C. official is my friend. They don't trust me any farther than they can throw me. And ... About ten minutes ago Chief Deputy Warden Jim Virga (whom I think is a professional guy) indicated to me that he's heard he is in this book. And it's negative. This rumor, innuendo and speculation is indicative of the fact that staff does not trust me. But (for the record) I have no reason (yet) to say anything negative about C.D.W. Virga...

So this book (missive from Hades) is not a public service just cause "I have a passion for youth" etc. As quiet as it is kept, just tween u me n the doorpost - I'll kick yo butt if you get in my face... And... I am not qualified to win the citizen of the year award. Perhaps the thug of the year would be more appropriate. "To mine own self be true". I am. I am not runnin around here tellin yall to believe in me, send me a donation or to adopt all of my philosophical paradigms. I have one goal here and that is to de-glorify and de-romanticize prisons; period... If I get a few kids in Buckhead (Atl.), Beverly Hills, Watts, in Compton, Oakland and New York to stop thinking dudes in prison are cool my job is done. Even if my enemies (I.E. some of the folks in C.D.C. etc.) convince you all that I'm some kind of pervert, murderer or a serial terrorist. That's fine and I can live with that. I can't lose what I never had. And a friend of mine (i.e. Peter Andrist, Emmett Brown, Aaron Fernander or Lonnie Young etc.) can't be told anything negative about me. Not that crazy stuff anyway. So writing a tome with such a widely recognized acronym (K.K.K.) gives rise to the potential for close scrutiny. Writing a book with this kind of name, in these kind of times with all of the internet promoting etc. is putting myself on front street. But it is a debt I owe to God. And since I'm the Chief sinner saved by grace you can't try a man twice for the same crime. And I know that my right wing, devout Christian counterparts who have a Bible in one hand and the death penalty in the other would crucify me in a heart beat. But I'm like that woman whom Jesus met at the well. I've been caught in adultery, crookery, thuggery and crimes. And I know some folks ready and willing to cast the first stone at "that ole criminal Manning who thinks he's something cause he wrote a coupla books". But I have the blood that stands between me and the stones. And I want you to take it from a thug, a loser, a criminal, a guy who played the game, drove fine cars etc. Flew all over the world and committed some crimes. I conned people. I conned people. And I conned people. And what is so ridiculous is that the vast majority of folks I conned would have helped me just for asking. All the energy I channeled into fraud and illegitimacy could have been utilized to build a black walmart~ ... So here I am yall. All of my partying in Virginia, New York, Atlanta, Chicago, Detroit, Switzerland, Paris and in Hollywood etc. And I now wake up everyday in hell. I sleep in a bathroom with another man... Would you like to eat your breakfast, lunch and dinner next to the commode while your celly craps? What happens if you've used up your two flushes and your toilet is shut down for an hour and your celly must take a dump? And as soon as he finishes dumping the C.O. brings your dinner tray to the door. Now you can't flush the toilet. And you can't tell the C.O. to bring a tray later. And he'll be back in ten minutes to retrieve your tray. Sound like fun? It sounds like barbaric animalism to me. I've no idea how these people could justify shutting off a toilet (for an hour) after two flushes. It is inhumane and filthy. And it is absolute prison. Call it psychological torture, sadomasochism, barbarism or bondage. It is hell! It is jail. It consists of cells. ... Rambling on ... I disagree with associate warden Fred Schroeder on a number of issues - plain and simple. But one of the things I strongly admire is his commitment to preventing the exploitation of kids. He is committed (and most certainly warden Jimbo Walker is) to making certain that those of us in here don't misuse or abuse our unique vantage point. Fred does not believe kids should be writing to prisoners. He is correct. Fred believes the internet can be abused; right again... Listen to me (a thug) yall. Be very, very careful on the internet. Listen - no 26 year old man is in love with a 14 year old girl. No 27 year old man is in love with a 12 or 13 year old boy. (Even if you're gay or uncertain about your sexuality etc. no adult should be having sex with a kid!). All of that sexting and chatting can be dangerous. Social networks can be deadly. You should never give your home address or personal data to any stranger online. Listen to me youngsters: I've been around sadistic sexual pedophiles for years. I've studied and researched what society calls "monsters" for years. I have journals, surveys, notes (even private missives written by infamous murderers which I've mailed to an attorney in Virginia!) and tons of empirical data on these "monsters". I could write a book on recognizing "the art of pedophilia" and recognizing "the art of predatory seduction". My first lesson would be that "monster" is the wrong term to use. In a strange kind of way it causes you to let your guards down. You'll think that as long as he's not wearing a long black trench coat and... The sexual or violent predator is not a "monster". So don't look for a monster. He is (instead) the guy next door. He's a coach, the ballet teacher, the fireman, the police officer and even the pastor. He can be a she. It is any person who inappropriately looks at, touches, texts or is sexting kids. They will lure you. It's called "Grooming". He'll build you up with compliments and tell you how beautiful, smart and sexy you are. He will methodically isolate you and turn you against your family, teachers and your friends. Read my lips (fingers): any adult who heaps compliments on you is suspect. Any adult who tells you (a kid) to keep a secret is suspect. Any adult seeking nude photos of you is a pervert (suspect). You must report this kind of conduct to an adult and to police immediately. You are precious and you are jewels. Be careful... Be extremely careful on the internet. And if you know of a friend who is being secretive and/or lured over the internet please notify police and parents forthwith. Check out www.protect.org and I think oprah.com has some data about child predators and the help you can get if you've been victimized. Google Camille Cooper and also Christine Feller (National Center for Exploited Children) and report predatory activity .. ....

You see that word (above) "activity"? This (now) is the first time I've had this part of the book in 5 months! Confused? Let me clear it up for you... "Report Predatory Activity". You see that above? I stopped at "activity" and have been separated from this manuscript (now) for five months! So since I was away (as you'll see later) I put pen to paper and completed the book (the pages to come) without these pages (all of the pages up to and before "activity" above). So it's kinda freaky to be back with these pages and to interject this right now. Can I blow your mind? Can I freak you out? You will read (later because I'm writing this now. Although later on I'll say a lot about this dude and even wish I could speak with him. I could go edit it out so the tome would have a more sequential and chronological order to it. But I'm not going to doctor this. It is what it is. But don't be confused if you (i.e.) read (later) the saying "I've never had an apple. Wish I could." But right here you read "I just had an apple"... I'm writing this last... And I wrote that already ...) Today (so later when you read about him remember I wrote that before today) at 9:14 Am I made a telephone call. It turned out to be one of the most important and powerful calls I've ever made. It was (indeed) a call that shall forever be frozen in the freeze frame of my memory... Before I tell you who I called and what we said let me explain that I had my first G.B.G. training (conducted by C. Solis MD.) in five months, today. I also had two G.B.G. Advanced

Individualized Training (AIT) sessions with Richard Ford (Doc) and Johnny Willie (claw) today. I also met with Captain Steve Vance, Captain Scottie Shannon, A.W. Jomson - Dovey and Warden Jimbo Walker today... Catching up has been difficult. I've (literally) been awake for 3 days with zero sleep. Dr. C. Solis and Warden Walker told me to slow down... Captain Steve Vance is really leaving in November. C.D.C. is losing a great captain. And I really hope he'll come back as a retired annuitant... Before I get to that call I made at 9:14 Am today I also had a confidential telephone call to Attorney Murray J. Janus. It was great to speak with him. "Sherman be careful young man" he stated. "I have friends in California (i.e. Blair Berk and Barry Tarlow etc.) and I'm told you must be extremely careful. You have a lot of powerful enemies within the CCPOA and C.D.C. Were it not for Warden Walker, CC III Patricia Kennedy and a few psychiatrists you'd be dead! ... Don't transfer to Donovan, High Desert or any of those places. Ask the Governor, State Senators or whoever to keep you at New Folsom... I have it on off the record data that you have enemies... ". Wow! That was sobering to me but not surprising. The Fix is in. Mike Bunnell wants me anywhere except New Folsom State Prison. He knows Walker, Vance, Schroeder, Shannon, Johnson-Dovey and Gaskins etc. are good people. And they are not murderers. Even if they don't like you they are fair and decent people ... I'm appealing to the Governor, Scott Kernan, Matt Cate, Gloria Romero, Dianne Feinstein, Maxine Waters and even Judge Thelton Henderson to please, please keep me at C.S.P. SAC... Last time I left here I went to M.C.S.P. per Bunnell. And Mike Bunnell (that murderous, crooked, wicked and evil killer) special transferred me (via I.S.U.) to P.V.S.P. to "catch Valley Fever and write a book about that". And... Bunnell needs to go to hell. And I know Scott Kernan, Susan Hubbard (personally; and Hubbard does not like me because I lied to her. But Hubbard is a professional and she's not a murderer.) and Matt Cate. They are fair, unbiased and professional. Warden Walker told me (personally) "they don't come any better than Kernan and Cate". And Fred agreed with him. But I don't want Maxine Waters, Madam Feinstein, Jackie Speier, Gloria Romero or Darrell Steinberg to read this and forget about it. This is no paranoia and it is not embellished. Mike Bunnell threatened my life. He had me so afraid (years ago) that I wrote threatening letters just to stop a transfer! He's got pals in the CCPOA, at P.V.S.P., R. Donovan and allover. And a dead black inmate is a dime a dozen at those prisons. What's so special about C.S.P. - SAC? CC III Patricia Kennedy! AW Johnson-Dovey! Jimbo Walker! They are consummate professionals. And the reason C.S.P. - SAC has been safe (for me) for years is because of Walker's predecessors. Warden Cheryl K. Pliler was here and she was a fabulous warden. And "Dad" (Chief Deputy Warden Terry L. Rosario) was here and he (too) was a great man.... They made New Folsom a safe and fair prison to be in. And I need the Honorable Thelton Henderson (or anybody with political power) to ensure my safety and keep me a C.S.P. - SAC ...

Are you ready to hear with whom I spoke at 9:14 Am? I was blessed to speak with the most famous Bounty Hunter, Bail expert and Philanthropist on the planet; Leonard Padilla ... Google Leonard Padilla. He was involved with the Casey Anthony case. And he is more famous than "Dog" Chapman. And Mr. Padilla is also President of the Lorenzo Patino Law School. He's also a philanthropist. He has given tens of thousands of dollars to the poor, neglected and the unprotected. And Leonard Padilla has a Heart... He is also a brilliant man. He knows my mentors Rev. Hosea Williams and former Ambassador Andrew Young. Leonard reminds me of Hosea. He's candid, no-nonsense and opinionated.

Leonard Padilla blew my mind when he reminded me of something Hosea taught me years ago; Crime PAYS! ... Padilla states "Sherman California spent $ 11 Billion on prisons last year. $ 11 Billion with a "B"... Poor whites, blacks and Mexicans can't get houses etc." Padilla stated "what poor white could go to a Governor and say 'Give me $ 4500.00 per month for a House? Any Governor would think they were insane Sherman. But we in California have given

$50.000 homes to 173,000 poor people. We have locked up damn near 200,000 poor folks. And a large majority of these prisoners are not rapists, not molesters and not murderers. They are piss poor folks who wanted the American Dream. They see rich people on TV day in and day out. And they're being told this is the Life". Padilla continued "They want a car, a home or whatever. And when they can't get a job what happens? Their misery and hopelessness or the desire for money drives them to use, sell or buy dope and booze etc. and they are set-up to enter into the Gated community ... We won't employ them or create a job. We brag on how important Education is but poor people can't afford college. C.S.U. is raising fees right here, right now!" Padilla gave me flashbacks to a conversation I had with civil rights legend Rev. Hosea Williams in the 90's. I was driving him (in his red and white convertible Cadillac) to Birmingham to meet Cong. John Lewis. (I mention that later) and Hosea lectured me about how crime pays. "People make and sell handcuffs, batons, guns, bullet proof vests etc. And every police officer has a gun. Who makes the gun and how much does it cost? How much does the Atlanta Police Department spend on guns, cuffs, uniforms and squad cars" Rev. Williams said. And "Do you know it costs tens of thousands of dollars to build each prison cell? The locking mechanisms cost $ 20 grand per cell. Hundreds of millions of dollars are paid to construct jails, juveniles and prisons... It costs $ 35 thousand (in the 90's) dollars per year to send a man to jail. But only $ 21 thousand dollars a year to send a man to Yale. If my son asks the state to send him to Yale they'll say we don't have the money. If he commits a crime they will invent the money" Rev. Williams said. And as I was driving I launched into a long monologue about what we could do to save the youth of America. And I gave what I thought was a powerful and moving argument. And I was pretty impressed with myself and sort of enjoying my own speech. And I took my eyes off of the road to look over and see if Rev. Williams was visibly (he'd been extremely quiet while I spoke) impressed. And as I gazed upon Rev. Hosea Williams to see what he thought, he was slumped over in the seat asleep ...

So today I could clearly comprehend what Leonard Padilla was saying as he elucidated the issue. California prison guards are the top paid guards in the Nation. You can walk into C.D.C. with only a G.E.D. and pull down $ 70.000 per year. The Director earns $ 225,000 per year yet seven guards earned more than him last year. Seven guys who probably can't spell the word "rehabilitate" earned a quarter million dollars in 2008. "Only in America?" No - "only in California". But if we came up with a brilliant plan to reduce crime by 15% in California. A variety of powerful groups would sabotage the implementation of the plan. As quiet as it's kept there are judges, prosecutors, lawyers and street cops who would lose their jobs with a significant reduction in crime. If we had a bonafide plan to reduce crime in America by 25% in 2011. Do you know how many $ billions of dollars would not be paid for more police to arrest more criminals? What does a judge do if he has no cases to preside over? What do the hundreds of prosecutors (x tens of $ millions per year to pay them) with no cases to prosecute do? If crime dropped by 25% for a year in L.A. it would disrupt the economy of the entire state.

And the very valid point Leonard Padilla kept hammering was the politicization of crime. The more laws there are to break the more jobs (cops, deputies, guards, judges etc.) they create ... Perhaps the best kept "secret" in America is how many multimillionaires America has made on the backs of poor criminals. I should say poor people who are influenced to commit crimes. (I love psychologists and psychiatrists and without them this cesspool would explode!) I counted the employees (psyche techs, social workers, psychologists and psychiatrists etc) coming out of the treatment center during a fire drill yesterday. And I counted $ 5.6 million (per year) in salaries (no guards included) outside the treatment center... Hundreds of millions of dollars are spent (and I repeat they are necessary. Mental illness runs rampant in the prisons.) on the mental illness in prisons; in California every year... There are serious reasons the CCPOA, guards and the politicians who receive CCPOA money etc. are adamantly opposed to releasing the 40,000 inmates Judge Henderson and Karlton has ordered released. And every politician (worth his salt) in Ca. plays the brainwashing "Get though on crime" game every day. And they utilize brilliant marketing schemes as they sell their newly revised (AKA "Lock em up and don't just throw away the key; but lose it. Bury it!) crime bill to the unsuspecting public. And if they think 40,000 inmates will be released they use scare tactics and play games. You'll start seeing commercials saying "40,000 predators, rapists, murderers and molesters are going to be released onto our streets by these liberal Judges" and they'll show some kids on a playground in the BACK ground to scare you into another tax increase.... IF Judge Henderson wrote an order tomorrow morning at 9:00 AM stating "No prisoner convicted of any violent crime is to be released, but 20% inmates incarcerated for using and/or selling drugs are to be released with all deliberate Haste!" that order would be bogged down in red tape, appeals and.... By 9:01 the CCPOA would have a commercial on K.C.R.A.

... When Leonard Padilla activated this paradigm shift in me it was a wake up call. It reminded me that there are a lot of politicians, police, judicial concierges (if you will) who have (absolutely) a vested interest in that shooting which is taking place (in Oak Park; Del Paso Heights, Carver Homes, Detroit or D.C. etc.) right now ... Any serious community policing programs are considered to be too expensive! We have to spend that money locking em up so we can throw away the key... I hate to say it here but "Yes we can" and we do!

I know it sounds like a Hollywood "tale" but I would bet my life that if some Governor ran and won in California and if he (never!) released 50,000 inmates from prison and got all of the churches, synagogues, mosques and Kingdom Halls to take these people in. If they fed, housed, clothed, educated and employed them etc. the Governor would turn up missing, dead or himself in jail. They would kidnap him, set him up or kill him!

... In my hometown (Atlanta) in Dekalb County they had never (ever) had a black sheriff. (This is law enforcement) and my friend Derwin Brown ran and won. He was the first black ever. And he talked about cleaning up the jail. Letting dope smokers out to get treatment etc. And he had a list of dirty, compromised and rogue deputies which he planned to fire day one. And (you can Google it) a couple of days before he was sworn in as the first black sheriff he was (methodically) murdered in his own drive-way. It appeared to be a "professional" hit!!

The very same way Mike Bunnell murdered (or paid someone to do it) Captain Doug Pieper (for breaking the "code of silence") and made it appear to be suicide; Sheriff Brown was assassinated (in his own front yard) by his peers !!! A couple of years ago! Not in the 1950's. Just a couple of years ago! ...

Leonard Padilla told me to call him back. He is a great, great man. I felt led to contact him years ago. And I did not follow my spirit. I sense my destiny (in some way) connected to Leonard Padilla.

Leonard mentioned Switzerland and Needle Park etc. and I told him I'd been to the now closed "Needle Park". We talked about Casey Anthony. We talked about Ellie Nessler as well as Willie Nessler. When Willie beat a man to death Ellie asked Leonard to go on TV and tell Willie to turn himself in to Leonard. Because the Sacto police and deputies were going to "Kill Willie". Willie saw Leonard and did (in fact) turn himself in to Leonard Padilla!

Leonard told me a few things which I shan't repeat... Peter (in Switzerland) will donate hundreds of copies of this tome to innercity students. Richard "Doc" Ford told me "You know how much money Leonard Padilla gives away! Hell, when I was working Homicides at the LAPD Padilla was giving away money back then". Doc continued "You and I should give Locke high school some copies of K.K.K. and you ask Leonard to donate 50-100 copies of K.K.K. to that "shoulder to shoulder" mentoring group in SAC." Doc continued "I guarantee you that if Leonard goes to www.cafepress.com/manning and orders fifty or sixty copies of our K.K.K. book and has cafepress.com to mail them to "shoulder to shoulder" and/or sends 20 copies just to the Head Football coach at Lodi High School and Cafepress puts a note "Dear coach give these books to your players, compliments of Leonard Padilla" it will be a blessing. And the media loves Padilla!! Doc concluded "And you should let Padilla serve as an unofficial spokesman for you and for G.B.G.. He's brilliant, philanthropic, candid and he has balls... Leonard Padilla has the connections to get International attention for our team. And he actually gives a darn about our youth... All you need to do is ask him to donate 50 books. He'll probably do a hundred... $ 2300.00? Leonard spends $ 2 grand on dinner! He's a darn good man!! And Doc said to me finally: "Sherman you must remain humble and authentic. The good Lord is showing us His favor. And He's doing it because he knows our Hearts. And His word said He would Bless us if we would seek His face, turn from our wicked ways and call on Him ... Sherm you've got dirt on your hands just like I do. I still recall vividly all of the money you loaned Eric Menendez. Hell, he left owing me $ 400.00. And even though you and I are too paranoid to do drugs... Let's face it, we knew Eric Menendez was buying drugs!". Doc said "But I've watched you transform from an arrogant know it all into a young man. And you're still you. You are opinionated, political and you have a lot of stuff going that I want nothing to do with i.e. Mike Bunnell! I don't know why you got involved with pissing Bunnell off kid... But leave me out of that. And you know Warden Walker, A.W. Schroeder and CC III Kennedy will never vouch for your tirades against C.D.C. ,,, But when you start talking about transforming at-risk teens Walker, Schroeder, Vance and Kennedy are all ears. They actually care ... It is a blessing: ... Doc made me feel good. And the self same day that he mentioned Leonard Padilla giving books to "Shoulder to Shoulder" I saw the program on TV again!

I wanna give a shout out to Semaj Horec and to Isiah Matthews who are two kids in the "Shoulder to Shoulder" program. One of them stated the program is helping him with his "anger". I am extremely impressed with Ray Upchurch, Donnell Rigins and Bill Coibion. They specialize in reaching out to fatherless kids. I say great. Because if we don't reach out to fatherless kids Gangs are ready to reach in to them. I hope and pray (more on Leonard Padilla later in the book) Leonard will have cafépress to send "Freedom Hall" at the Martin Luther King Jr. Academy in ("Shoulder to Shoulder") Sacramento 40 or 50 copies of this book. And I pray Leonard Padilla will also donate 20 or 25 copies to Lodi High School's Football team. It will be a blessing!

Using prison as a platform on which to preach and teach kids not to come here to Hades is now the cause of my life! Prison is my teachable moment. I'm not concerned with attempting to rehabilitate my name or to establish credibility. As C.Solis MD. states "Sherman it does not matter whether you are good or bad. If you are wrongly convicted it's irrelevant. And if you are even worse than your conviction it does not matter. Either way you have a Bully pulpit for youths. You are extremely articulate. And you have internet access." Dr. Solis continued "If I'm a parent at home and I'm reading the G.B.G. Face Book site I want my son to see it. I will read (screen) it and then want my kids to read it... And if any parent makes the mistake of telling a kid not to look at G.B.G. even more kids will look at it. And since DateLine, the F.B.I. and police will also be scrutinizing the G.B.G. site we know it is (per se) a safe site... Parents will disagree with some of your diatribes and politics etc. But they will support the "mission" of G.B.G. as does Senator John Burton and others".

Dr. Solis concluded "and you need to keep inmate Ford out front. He is one of G.B.G.'s most potent weapons. His background as an ex Homicide cop is awesome. Kids want to hear or read his story... Keep praying"...

Johnny Willie told me "God is awesome. And don't worry about nothing (sic). We will pray our way through this. G.B.G. will be a blessing to all of these broken, bitter and hurting kids around this world. And we've got to make sure we stay prayed up and right with God. If we keep our Hearts pure God will be pleased... I'm excited about this program (G.B.G.) Atlanta".

Willie said "Before it's all over Michael Vick, Tony Dungy and even Bill Cosby are gonna be reading about G.B.G. in our K.K.K. Book"...

I also hope I can get Attorney Thomas Luneau, Mark Merin, Cupcake Brown or perhaps even a law student (at Lorenzo Patino Law School!!) to help me in my civil rights case against C.D.C., Mike Bunnell and P.V.S.P. and I am pleading with the dean of Lorenzo Patino Law school, Attorney John Burton (Burton & Norris in Pasadena) and John Burton in Santa Cruz to please, please, please help me in this lawsuit. I need some help!

... Hope somebody will send D.J. Strong (at Idlewild Arts Academy), Brett Jolliff, Maxwell Hanger, Alex Blench, Melissa Moore and Catherine Lytle this book. I want my pal "Andy C. (the volunteer from Ohio) to get this book.

And I will reiterate to teens (over and over) that you must not come here to Hades. Stay out of prison any way you can. Chief Dep. Warden (Ret.) Terry L. Rosario, Warden (Ret.) Cheryl K. Pliler, Warden Walker, Mrs. Kennedy, C.O. D. Smith and Lt. Jimmy Guyton etc. will all tell you that once a kid enters the Gated community (almost 90% of the time) it is over! ... Case closed! ... If there is any "well meaning" parent who thinks prison or juvenile may "teach" your son a "lesson", call Terry, Jimmy, Cheryl or Mrs. Kennedy and I assure you they will admit to you "Hell no".

I am here in prison. And Yes I am a Human Being (all that and a bag of chips) but ... I must confess to you that prison destroys everybody and everything that comes inside of here. Just follow the numbers ... This place can lock up your spirit and arrest your mind. And once your "spirit" and "mind" are incarcerated your Heart turns into stone. And you are a walking, talking and breathing dead man. And ... I shook hands with 7 guys today. And 4 of the 7 hate my guts. I've never stolen from them. I've never cheated or mistreated them etc. They just "Hate" me because they "hate" me. And this is not to say I'm a "good" guy. I'm not a choir boy and they did not put me in prison for going to Sunday school too late ... I just get mesmerized by the level with which mankind can hate mankind ... And prison is a dark and a lonely place. It is cold, angry and evil in here. This is Hades. And with all the commotion, sensationalism and problems this tome may cause. I just hope and I pray that a Tyra Banks, Tyler Perry or a Dr. Bill Cosby will really read this book. And if they read it all I think they will "get" (aha) it ... They may not close the book and decide to invite G.B.G. (or me) over for dinner tonight! They may not say "I like Sherman and I think he's a good man" etc. They may not "like" me at all. But - I believe that this authentic, deadly, dastardly, blemished and wicked portrait of a prison which I've painted is the most credible argument for why kids should never come to prison!

... Tyra, Tyler, Wendy etc. R-e-a-d my "Lips" (letters) ... The last thing Alex Chivescu, Roger Walthorn, Jacob Jason, Jonathan "Legacy" Perez, Semaj or Isiah Matthews should ever do is "come" and get to "know" my buddies and I ... Once we inject our venomous poison, anger, wickedness, envy, racism and institutionalization into then they will never, ever be "clean" again! Parents keep your kids out of prison!

I am pleading with great men like Bill Cosby, Tony Dungy, Aaron Fernander, Tyler, Steve Harvey and Rev. Otis Moss etc. to help me to sound the alarm with this book. This is my most powerful, anointed and important book ever. Because I did not write it alone. I wrote it with strong input from the G.B.G./HEART team. I wrote it with hundreds of hours of monologue from and dialogues with a brilliant team of psychiatrists (Frank Curren, C. Solis and Jennifer Heitkamp) and psychologists (Dr. Jarman, Dr. Jamie Davidson, Dr. A. Duran, Dr. Gregg, Dr. Houston, Dr. Handian, and the late Dr. Tye Hedblad etc.) ... When I'm with Dr. Solis and Dr. A. Duran I grow by the moment. These are not just brilliant folks. Dr. Solis and Dr. A. Duran c-a-r-e about youths.

They understand the cycle of violence and the psychological chains of illiteracy and/or poverty that embellishes the prospects of kids killing kids. And Dr. Solis, Dr. Duran, Dr. Curren and the entire G.B.G. Advisory Board understands (clearly) how difficult it is to break a psychological "curse".

And I must confess that I've broken down and wept (more than a few times) when I think about how much time, energy, information, explanations and counseling these psychologists and psychiatrists have poured into me and into G.B.G. I could never pay them for all of the time, intellectual, informational and educational data they poured into me. Dr. C. Solis, Dr. Jarman, Dr. Hedblad, Dr. Houston and Dr. Gregg mentored, tutored and "taught" me. I would walk up to Dr. Solis (too many times) or Dr. A. Duran and declare "take me to school". And they would (indeed) "school" me. Can you imagine talking and listening to Dr. Phil five days per week for ten years? ... I have been watching (the) Dr. Phil for seven years day-in and day-out. And I've talked to Dr. Harvard University (Franklin Curren MD.), Dr. "Phil" C. Solis, Dr. "Phil" Houston, Dr. "Phil" A. Duran and Dr. "Phil" Heitkamp, five days per week for years! "You can't be around that much knowledge without growing" Doc told me ... "Atlanta" (Doc continued) "I watch you day after day spending hours walking and talking with shrinks! If you retain merely 25% of what they teach you I guarantee you'll be a bad man". I replied "Doc I spent years enjoying the sound of my own voice! And I finally realized by entertaining Dr. Jeff Gardere, Dr. Phil and Dr. Tye Hedblad etc. how much I don't know. And we are residing in a place (Hades) where 99.9% of the conversations are bull crap. And I had an "Aha" moment the day I woke up and said every psychologist has 20 plus years of schooling! And every psychiatrist has 28-32 years of schooling. I'm 38 years old. When I was 30 I was in jail and while I was (already) in jail these psychiatrists whom I bug the heck out of (Dr. C. Solis, Dr. Jennifer Heitkamp etc.) were still in school. How could Dr. Solis "not" teach me something?" I continued "I learned how to host my own talk show (lol) and interview people by watching Oprah. She (Oprah) didn't know it but I graduated (magna cum laude) from Harpo school of "asking questions" years ago. I had to "learn" how to ask questions, to listen and to be quiet. Everything in my background had taught me to talk, pronounce, enunciate, speak, teach, preach and to articulate. But I needed to learn to do all the opposites. It really began with that saint Dr. Tye Hedblad. I used to pull data, information, explanation and motivation out of him. And listening to Dr. Hedblad, Dr. Jarman and Dr. Jaffe changed me". I concluded "I aim to rob every therapist, psychologist and psychiatrist out of all the knowledge I can steal from them. And 90% of the psychologists and psychiatrists in C.D.C. feel unfulfilled and frustrated. Because the forensic practice allowed in prisons uses so little of their knowledge... C. Solis MD., Jennifer Heitkamp MD. and Franklin Curren MD. have (combined) nearly $ 1.9 million dollars worth of education and formal schooling! One day I had Dr. Heitkamp, Dr. Gregg, Dr. Duran, Dr. Solis, Dr. Curren and Dr. Houston in the same room and I thought "here is $ 4 million worth of psychological, medical and psychiatric training at my disposal gratis". Doc said "Did you get a mental boner (lol)?" I said "Yes".

Doc interjected "And the triple blessing is that not only do they add distinguished credibility to our G.B.G. outreach etc. But as I read your writing (now) and listen to you speak, your psyche has been indoctrinated, affected and brightened by these shrinks. Sometimes I think Dr. Solis and Dr. Duran are Paul McKenna PhD. (famed hypnotist). I'll look across the yard and one of them is speaking to you and your big mouth is glued shut. Your head is nodding and you appear to be in a trance".

I replied "I'm not in a trance, I'm must in school Doc." Doc's celly approached us and I left to go hunt a shrink. I had (as I always have) "questions". ... I want to remind you students to rob your teachers of their knowledge. I'm cognizant of the fact that some of you have grown up in poverty and in families of illiteracy. Many kids in the trailer park have never even been on the other side of town. Much less out of town. And all of their friends are poor and under educated. And when one is surrounded by poverty, uneducated and undereducated friends (families and neighbors etc.) they see poverty and illiteracy as the norm. And one of the greatest things about going to school is the fact that (for millions of kids) the teacher in that classroom is the first (and only) person in their life with a college degree. We have 13.5 million children in poverty in America. And perhaps 12 million of them have, don't, won't or would never meet any person with a college degree in their life; I.E. home, family, community etc. etc.. The only way they will ever come in contact with a college educated person is in school. And school (grade and high school) is free. So I encourage youngsters to live in that school. Be a sponge around those teachers. All of them have at least four years of college. Most of them have six years (minimum) of college. Every time you look at a precious teacher you're looking at $ 100.000 thousand (minimum) of education. Your schools have $ millions of dollars of education and information amongst those teachers and a few of them are burnt out, depressed and they (too) feel unfulfilled. They've seen so much crime, poverty of spirit, violence and disrespect from you that they've almost given up. But I assure you (in fact I promise you) that if just 2 or 3 of you (in each class) were to go to your teachers and say "I apologize man (or sir). I wanted to say I am sorry. I've been disrespectful, unmotivated and a slacker. I am ready to get myself together and use all of that $ 100 grand education that you have. Will you please help me?" Your teacher(s) will light up like a Christmas tree. Positivity, motivation and excitement are contagious. And when they see you ready for help they will throw you a life jacket. To be honest all of my grade and high schooling was in public schools. William Finch Elementary and Samuel Archer High (way, way after Glady's Knight graduated from Archer) school etc. And as I reflect upon those public schools I can't think of a single teacher who was not willing to stay after class and after school to help us. Mrs. Hill, Mrs. Davetta, Mrs. Walton, Mrs. Jones, Mr. George Jinks, Ralph Mitchell, Mrs. Slocum, Mrs. Warrior, Stanley Wallace, Earl Davenport and Mr. Fortenberry (to name a few) etc. they represent over $ 1.1 million dollars in educational training and college. And I could tell you individualized stories about each of them staying after school, going beyond the call of duty, giving, preaching, praying and saying "you can make it" to us. Coach Coffee, Coach James and Coach Willie Jordan (all had Masters degrees, stayed after school every day teaching athletes How to read... I remember coach Willie Jordan (I loved that man) explained to me (when I broke my hip playing football) "sh, sh, sh, sherm, sherman (lol - he stuttered a lot!) your doctor is an orthopedic surgeon. Dr. Fred Allman Jr. (my physician) is rated as one of the Best and most brilliant sports medicine physicians in this country. You should ask him to mentor you". I did on the very next appointment. And this brilliant, short, fat white man said "sure Sherman start coming to my sports medicine clinic every Saturday. And in the summertime you can come 6 days a week. And I'll teach you about sports injuries, conditioning and recuperating etc. I'll even have my physical therapist to take you under his wings". And (brain fart) as spectacular as most people will tell you my memory is I (literally) can't recall the physical therapist's name. I think it was Bob. Every time I see Oprah with Bob Green I wonder if that is him... But Dr. Fred Allman (his wife was real nice also) was my first (ever) Caucasian mentor. We became very close. He introduced me to tomes about medicine, science, sports and motivation etc. He was a multi-millionaire philanthropist and a Christian. He told me "I know your parents are going to send you to college and can probably afford it. But if anything happens I will pay for your college education". I was humbled. His physical therapist taught me how to tape ankles to prevent injuries etc. And then coach McNeill took me over to Morris Brown college one day and introduced me to "Walt" (Walter Smith - respiratory therapist at Grady Memorial Hospital and Head Athletic trainer for Mo. Brown coll.). And Walt had Craig (another high school kid) and I under his wings. And Walt taught me how to tape ankles with rapid speed and precision. I still recall how impressed coach Jordan was after

Walt started training me. I taped 6 ankles to coach Jordan's every 2. And Dr. Allman (who was the physician for the Atlanta Falcons as well as for Georgia Tech. College) taught me so much about physical sports related injuries, wound care, sprains, strains and conditioning etc. that anytime there was a serious injury at a football game, practice of whatever; coach Jordan called me and I'd make the decision on whether a person needed to see a physician ... I seriously contemplated becoming an athletic trainer (i.e. for the Falcons! Dr. Allman had all the connections!) ... But reflecting back on the power, richness and the fullness of my exposure to Dr. Allman I'm reminded that is was a stuttering Head Football Coach/physical Ed. teacher who turned me on to Dr. Allman. I had no idea how prominent my physician was. And I would have never even thought about asking him to mentor me had coach Willie Jordan not suggested it. Your teachers, coaches, librarians and principals are a powerful resource for personal growth and development. And one of the smartest things you can ever do is to seek out advice from those coaches, teachers and counselors at school. Borrowing Doc's words "you can't be around all of that greatness and knowledge without experiencing growth" if you take advantage of it...

(Pause) Professor Michael Fauntroy, Ben Cohen (Ben & Jerry's), Steven Rothberg (collegerecruiter.com), Daniel Daily (Pikes Peak, Colorado), Andy Nevis (Sacto), Eldin Foco, Mike Pitcher (Sacto), Neal Carlson (Rock singer), Eric Bulrice, Bobby Hestin, Brandon Moreno, Jacob Jason, Andy Dunn and Brian Spaly (Bonobos) ... I need you (Heather F.) to locate each of these individuals and tell them they are in "K.K.K.".

And tell them to drop me a line for a gratis copy. I want Jake Heartsong, Kerry Arredondo, Louis Copelin (Folsom Ca.), Caleb Peek, Kids at Reedley High School, The Roosevelt Institution, Michael Lefenfeld, Sean Glass (I'll make it easy and give Sean a plug. He's at www.higherone.com), Paul Graves (positivesdating.com), The Trevor Foundation, Quest Youth Group, Walter Dean Myers, Campus Anti-War Network, Deny Hamlin, Brenton Wilson (mo.), Daniel Sample and Nicholas Runde to all know the book is out. U.S,. Mint Green (Heres to another $ 500.00 gratis plug for U.S. Mint Green. Ipso Facto Heather, I need you to locate these people for me with all deliberate speed). I need you... Yall tell Shaun White, Joey Cheek, Isaac Young (Fresno), Ratemyprofessor.com (the owner), Buddypics.com (owner), Benoit Denizet-Lewis, Cynthia McKiney, Brian Burrough and Justin Berry that "K.K.K." has them in it. Jake Simpson and Jason Toombs also ... And I want teens, tweenies and parents to contact Lorin Zaner and Kim Hart at the National Child Abuse Defense Resources and get involved. Contact Erin Runion and get involved with snaps ... I want the 5 Browns and Jason Huyck to know "K.K.K." is out Baby Boy ... I want to get this tome and G.B.G. data to Stephen Carriere, Christine Craft (Sacto), Jeffrey Buttle, Alexander Abt, Justin Gadsden and Sam Fuick. ... I try to offer something in this tome for everybody. For Dave Karger and Michael Ausiello (whom I know are reading - lol) I offer InternetJock.com ...

Attorney Janus stated to me also that "I read your "K.K.K." tome (a lot of it) and it is sensational and spectacular. To your question, I doubt very seriously if C.D.C. another lawsuit. .. The key is your book can't be disallowed merely because of the allegations you make about staff. And you repeatedly cure any allegations of so called threats to safety and security. Because you write repeatedly that you oppose violence. You are anti-drugs and anti-weapons etc."

... "Nothing stops a bullet like a job". I have learned to respect the power of gainful employment. And especially the power of economic freedom. I got into an argument with a close pal of mine years ago because I disrespected his line of work. I've owned companies for years and I embrace the entrepreneurial spirit. However, I would not (for example) own an "escort" company. My pal hires 18, 19-30 year old guys and girls, most of them are straight but they have telephonic intimacy. He pays them $ 50.00 per hour to sit on the telephone and (pretending to be gay, lesbian, bi etc. etc.) "chat" intimately. I argued that it was borderline prostitution and full blown exploitation. He argued that they are all 18 and older. They are amateur actors and they never meet up with the client. And he owns 4 Rolls Royce's and a $ 4 million mansion. I've softened a bit but I still would not own that type of company. ..

G.B.G. promotes an agenda of employment as well as an entrepreneurial agenda. And I'd want to see many of you youngsters begin to study business, master math and begin devising business plans forthwith. All it takes is one right idea and you can make a difference in the world. But you've got to stay in school. You've got to learn to love reading. And reading will open up all kinds of doors, opportunities and possibilities for you... I'm depending upon the fringe elements (geeks, freaks, nerds and jocks etc.) of the Facebook Generation to develop an underground industry for promoting, discussing and analyzing this (K.K.K.) book. I want you all to sell it and plug it on the web everyday.

And let's find Roger Walthorn (really need to reach Roger), Jason Rapp, Collin Orcutt, Max Steele (N.Y.), Thomas McDonell, Greg Deekens, Chris Casimir, Nicholas Evans, Sam Hayes, Marc Hamilton (ASU in AZ), Kyle Sevey, Alex Flores (Sacto), Steven Acosta (intern in Hollywood), Christopher Clubb, David Sommers, Drake Bell, Josh Peck, Andrew Knot, Jason Ward, Nathaniel Marshall (Malone N.Y.), Von Smith (Greenwood mo.), Ross Robagliati, Matt Giraud, Danny Gokey, Omer Klem and Phil Southerland. We must bring together a "people" army if we are really gonna fight to transform at-risk kids. We can't do this alone, let's come together. Failure to act rapidly can turn a crisis into a catastrophe. We need Sean Wolf (Buff. N.Y.), Nicholas Kohlmeyer, Mike Roberts (outside magazine), Earl Stafford, Rafael Martinez (Carmichael), Ted Russert, Chris Bergaus, Atty. Josh Kaizuka, Sean Pander, Sean Musgrove, YAYI (Youth Against Youth Incarceration), Asociaciõn Ñeta, Doran Smestad, Raphael V. Johnson, Korey Blake, Adam Rip, Derek Trent, Mark Thew (Loomis) and George Soros. As youngsters, teachers and parents stand-up gangs must stand-down. We must change our falling schools. Schools are supposed to be the foundations for a better life ... Stay away from toxic people. And anytime you are tempted to do something which can land you in prison remember prisons are concrete cages. And plant no gardens on concrete because nothing grows on concrete!

... The time has come to set aside childish things. We adults need to grow up. I keep thinking that any authentic effort to save the children must being by trying to save the adults. We who have the mental residue of bitterness and brokenness within us. We who are spiritually marred and psychologically scarred. We who have tasted from the bitter well of civil war, separation and segregation... This old hatred shall someday pass. But since it hasn't fully passed we (adults) are infecting our kids with the venom which causes them to join gangs, use or sell drugs or drop out of school. It is time for us to get our anointing, our drive and our focus back. Good roots produce good fruits. Most (more than 95%) college educated parents produce college educated kids. A G.B.G. poll of 1000 families revealed that kids growing up in two parent households where both parents completed college etc... More than 95% of those kids graduate college. More than 97% of them complete high school. Ipso Facto, we must look at the problem of massive drop-outs amongst inner city kids for what it is; a reflection of their failed parents (the village). So there is a deep psychological wound and a mental "cycle" of poverty and illiteracy which must be addressed with all deliberate haste. I shared this idea (about the cycle of illiteracy) with my long time comrade Aaron Fernander (Principal of Ralph Bunche Middle School in Atlanta Ca.) and he said "That's right! Boy now you are thinking. See you're dealing with the cause and not merely symptoms now ... I'm proud of you Sherman". Now can I keep it real? (As quiet as it's kept) I never corrected Aaron by explaining to him that Dr. C. Solis is responsible for elucidating the epidemic of the "cycle" to me. I got a good doctor (lol). But heck this lil ego stroke from Aaron felt too good (lol) for me to mention Dr. Solis! ...

I would hope that Chelsey Ramirez, Luke Johnson (in Richmond Ca.) and even prisoners will begin to pray, to think, to write and to speak about "Breaking the curses of poverty and illiteracy" off of our kids, our families and our friends. Violence is the language of the frustrated and the unheard. We (in these prisons) must begin to serve notice on teens and tweenies that Uncle Willie, Uncle Doc and 'so and so' hears them. This is something any inmate can do (to help kids) any day of the week. Write missives of encouragement to your kids, family, the kids of your friends and kids in the schools and tell them your story. And let them know you are willing to 'hear' them. If you want millions of kids to see your writings (i.e. Essays to teens etc.) send them to your family and have them post it on Naps and/or on the G.B.G. Facebook site ... I'm praying that people like Earl Stafford will go to our website and link it up to his foundation. I am looking for Earl Davis Jr., Rafael Rodrigo and Jonathan Philips etc. to get involved with the G.B.G. Big Brother or the G.B.G. mentoring programs. Earl Davis received an Olympic torch for prison recidivism reduction! (Google him and tell him I mentioned him here)... I want to get this tome to the senior class at Oak Ridge High School (i.e. Brian F. who's mom is Tina) and to kids in the "upward Bound" programs nationwide. As a staunch supporter of the JROTC program I want cadets to receive this book. ... This tome can be a wake-up call to Anthony Durbin, Ronald Cummings, Lee Cox, Rev. R.L. Patterson, Jordan Brown, Chris Jomson (Grass Valley), Michael Anthony Camella, Angela Sasseville and Bill Moyers. I need teens to activate the awesome power of the internet to promote this off the wall, riveting, disjointed and compelling book. You all can do it. This (K.K.K.) is Your Book! ... We need a movement via the mobilization (over the W.W.W. for K.K.K.) of youths! ... Aaron Moskowitz, John Farelli, Errol Lewis and Tyler Gentry? We need you to help us resurrect hope in schools. Let's help Arne Duncan to transform public schools. Arne will accept all the help (prisoners, guards, police and G.B.G.) he can get ... We must team up with Blair Walsh, Tim Tebow, Geoffrey Fieger, Chris Hicks (Sacto), Matt Sly, Ripley Hunter, Bernice King, David Deluz and Alice Huffman and transform our educational system in America. Great schools are a repellant against prisons. So I call upon John Tu, Ryan Hreljac, Jake Heartsong and you to join us as we put our hands on the arc of history and revolutionize public schools in this country. We will usher in a new spirit of service. This is a new dawn of teen leadership and a new day is at hand... I'd like to inspire Jeff Herman, Kim Church, Michael Carandang (Tyra producer), Prof. Roger Wilkins and Kady Song to work with G.B.G.. We aim to inspire an army of new teachers who will go into the schools, churches and into the neighborhoods and lift America's promise (our children) out of the bowels of illiteracy.

At G.B.G./HEART we advocate turbocharging America's teachers by giving them (the Educators) peak performance training annually. I intend to submit A Blue Ribbon G.B.G./HEART "missive to the President" to Arne Duncan, (Dr. Solis, Dr. Duran and Dr. Heitkamp etc. informed that their report will be completed by Feb. 2011) next year. This missive will detail some specific ideas, suggestions and strategies we feel can be employed to revolutionize public schools. Our president of these United States has been preaching "sacrifice, service and responsibility" and We (G.B.G./HEART) are simply heading Mr. Obama's call to action and to service.

...Dr. C. Solis reiterated to me recently that "Sherman, I would not put my reputation and license (he's a licensed psychiatrist) on the line with G.B.G. if I didn't believe in it. Jennifer Heitkamp MD., Frank Curren MD. and Dr. A. Duran etc., we don't attach our names easily and I will continuously supervise, oversee and monitor you, your words and writings etc. Not to attempt to censor you or try to quench your political tirades etc. I've just got to make certain everything you write for kids is positive and constructive".

... I want all of you boys and kids who are reading my words to begin to "speak" your literacy, education and prosperity into existence. The power of life and death are (indeed) in the tongue. Even Christ said to "speak" to this "mountain" and it shall be moved. ..

The Bible is replete with instances in which God said and then God saw; because He said it before he saw it... Words are things in seed form... When you say it you release it. Words affect thinking. Thinking affects how you feel (emotions). Emotions affect actions and actions create habits. Habits create character. And your character determines Destiny! Your "mouth" affects your spirit. Words are active things. You've got to have two active chemical agents collide together in order to produce immediate results ... I'm writing this to teens and tweenies. I'm not writing to Baby Boomers. I love Baby Boomers and all of that. But life has taught me that a lot of Baby Boomers have deceived themselves into thinking that they've maxed out on the Education of the game of life. They think they know it all. They are bitter, cynical and arrogant. So I'm going to leave the Baby Boomers (the hard cases) for Zig Zigler, Tony Robbins, Les Brown and Steve Covey to deal with.

But I want you (Nathaniel, Keith and Alex Hornbuckle etc.) to know there is awesome power in your tongue. I'm not jiving, joking, kidding or Bull crapping you. Why lie? I have no "Blessing plan" to sell you. If you send me $ 50.00 for a "Blessing Plan" I'll have the Blessing" ($ 50.00) and you'll only have a "plan". It's not complicated kids. You don't have to spin around 19 times and catch a four leaf clover. Just "speak" the good, the clean, the pure, the powerful and the positive. Just realize that as the caterpillar releases a silk like spittle and the same substance (thing in seed form) he releases becomes the very cocoon into which he is (later) nurtured. And he shall wrap himself into a cocoon (which hath proceeded from his own mouth) and inside his cocoon (substance? silk? word? seeds?) he shall transform via a metamorphosis into a lovely butterfly.

Your words (substance, silk, spittle, words, seeds) are your cocoon. And your mind, psyche, spirit and emotions are wrapped up into your words. And your words can cause your mind to soar like an Eagle. Use lofty words. Think lofty thoughts. Pray lofty prayers. And you can soar like an Eagle... You hear (read) me Ryan Shanahan (Kettle Bell), Jacob Bailey, Hugh Ewing, Danny Magee, Devin Stinson, Brendan Moran, Jason Durtchi, John Hancock, Dr. Alex Vaclavik (G.B.G. seems to have an affinity for Alex's!), D.J. Swearingen, Kris T. Jernell, Alex (see!) Holgan, Alex Seabolt, Nick Pelham, Joseph Latham (Torrance Ca.), Joey China, Phillip Pohle (Carmichael), Zach Harris, Schoettler-Neufeld Tire Retread Center, John Romesburg, Pat Pattituchi (C.S.U. Sac), Brandon Walker, John Decarro, Devin Rio, Daniel Watts (Sacto teacher), B.J. Hill, Robert Lingle, Brent J. Newell, Christy Henzi and Urban Poole?

... Judge Greg Mathis went from juvenile and gangs and dropping out of High School etc. to an internationally acclaimed jurist. And Judge Mathis sneaks in issues of injustice and bigotry. He uses his platform to talk about gangs and poverty. Judge Greg Mathis is a powerful inspiration for our G.B.G. team! And I salute Judge Mathis, Judge Glade Roper, Judge James Long and Judge Joe Brown!

... God put our eyes in front of our head so we'd always be looking forward. I want you (in Atlanta, Chicago, Miami, Detroit and L.A. etc.) to look forward, onward and upward. If you can look up you can get up!... You at Waterfront Community Church (Pastor "Jim" in Illinois), Cosby High School (Midlothian VA.), Officer Trevor Downey, Jason Lifton, Daniel Clark, John McWhorter, Jamie Johnston (actor), Mike Lobel, Matt Damon, Adam Ruggiero, Earl Davenport and you at Samuel Howard Archer High School etc. etc. You in prison (if you're really serious) can go farther than any other prisoner has gone. You can go as far as (your mind will take you) possible! You can do it ... Establish a G.B.G. mobile command center in your cell, class, school, home or church. You contact Omer Klem, Von Smith, Dominick Lacey, Miles Kenison and Mark Thew and tell them about K.K.K.

Check the atmosphere around your mind. Change the climate (I repeat) in your house. Make the ground conducive for growth... Put water in a freezer, it changes to ice. Put water on fire, it becomes steam. Atmosphere creates change.

...Put water on soap and it becomes a cleansing agent.

...Ali Naqui, Cong. Paul Ryan and Juan Williams? Are you reading? I know Shelby Steele is not reading. Shelby is a homosexual and a drug addict. I met Shelby in D.C. at a convention. And he and Larry Elder (also gay) were staying in the same hotel room.

I wanna reach Michael Sulliman (College Park High School), Tanner Bazemore, Brian Boyle (D.C.) and Christopher Rousche ... You can redesign yourself ... I've been called a golden fingered writer with the incendiary style which brings a prison movement out of the shadows ... Kevin Wehr, Prof. Jim Hernandez (CSU.Sac), Cong. Emanuel Cleaver and Charles Rangel need to read this book! Doran Smestad and all the students at Nokomis High School needs this book ...

I won't allow a little quirk or crack in the "whole" of my character to destroy my future ... Don't allow that which is weak in you to destroy that which is great in you.

We all have cracks in our character. Some hide theirs better than others but we are not perfect. Don't magnify your flaws while diminishing your strengths. Learn to play up your strengths and play to your strengths. But (in private) work to ameliorate and improve your flaws and weaknesses.

... Ipso Facto (with respect to the always wise and brilliant legal advice of Murray J. Janus I want to repeat and reassert the following:) A. I do not support any physical violence. I believe in nonviolence 100%. Ipso Facto, those inside institutions who are visibly frustrated and angry etc. I support prayer, coupled with litigation and publication. I believe in the sacred constitutional rights of all Americans (with respect to the CA. supreme court's overturning 'son of Sam') rights to free speech and artistic expression ...

Next - when I criticize folk like Rush Limbaugh, Glenn Beck (a Klansman!), Sean Hamity (whom I know personally), Ann Coulter and prison officials etc. I am not speaking for G.B.G. (any of our advisors, supporters etc. I certainly am not even capable of being a "spokesman" for staff etc. I am a convict!). But for me. To insinuate that simply because some staff (i.e. C. Solis MD., Franklin Curren MD., Jennifer Heitkamp MD. and A. Duran Ph.D. etc.) share my belief that prisoners are uniquely positioned to discourage youth from coming to prison (and living with us) etc. means they support my personal agenda or political opinions is preposterous. Jimmy Carter is Caucasian and he was President of these United States. And he opines that the disdain, disrespect and the venom being directed at Barack Hussein Obama is racist. Does President Carter speak for "all" of or even "most" of white Americans? Certainly not! There are (indeed) people who attend the same church as Mr. Carter and worship the same God as he does yet, they disagree with him on Obama. Ipso Facto, many (if not most) of the staff who share my passion for youth out reach (i.e. Warden Walker and Chief Deputy Warden (ret.) Terry L. Rosario sr.) adamantly disagree with my criticisms of C.D.C.

I've never discussed Mike Bunnell with Warden Walker. Mr. Walker, Mrs. Kennedy, Jomson-Dovey, Schroeder etc. refuse to discuss staff (good, bad or indifferent) with me or any inmates ... I think it's fair to assume that Jimbo does not think Bunnell is a murderer. And Sherman D. Manning (the American also) believes (adamantly) Bunnell is a rogue, crooked, criminal and a "murderer" ... Congressman John Boehner seems (to me) to be a bigot, a classist and perhaps a racist.

I have (indeed) met Sen. Lindsey Graham and I know a lot of dirt on Lindsey. He has used the "N" word in my presence. He has (indeed) snorted cocaine in my presence (at a party on the outskirts of Arlington VA.) and (although I did not see Lindsey have sex with her.) Lindsey departed from this party with a very very young "escort".

Mentioning "escorts" I accuse craigslist C.E.O. Craig Newmark of being a rapist and a murderer. In my view if you are an accessory to a crime you are guilty of that crime. Newmark's website promotes prostitution, sex with minors etc. They had a section called "Erotic Services". And they have changed the name (but not the game) to "adult services". Every victim of the "craigslist Killer" ought to sue Newmark. The families of the deceased should sue ...

And schools need to begin to hire psychologists and to develop psychological profiles on kids early. I'm told by various psychiatrists that a Jeffrey Dahmer should have been "noticed" and could have been prevented ... Chronic conflict may be a sign of underlining brain dysfunction ... Casey Jordan is a psychologist and an attorney who studies the minds of killers. She is brilliant. She talked about Phillip Markoff being "the guy next door" and being "tall, blonde and handsome. A star student becoming a physician". His dad is (Dr. Richard Markoff) a doctor.

... Raymond Clark is suspected of viciously murdering the Asian (Ann) Yale student. All of Ray's friends described him as "the guy next door" ... Markoff graduated college suma cum laude. But websites (i.e. Gayclublist.com, passion.com and Alt.com and I'm certain Sean Hannity and Brother Shelby Steel both use pseudonyms when they browse on them) showed Markoff (who was engaged to Marcy) was obsessed with power, sex, control and thrill seeking. He (i.e. Ray Clark?) was a "cleancut" killer with a secret life. .. When his mom and dad divorced he felt isolated. And his public persona was at war (Hannity? Coulter?) with his deeper desires. He had what psychologists call a "fractured identity". But as Dr. Solis taught G.B.G. there is a "trajectory to crime". People rarely snap unless it's a crime of passion. Killers and most serial killers exhibit some characteristics and traits as they elevate the trajectory etc. etc. And we need to know what to look for. Markoff enjoys the "feeling" of excitement, thrills and exhilaration. But he had elevated to an "addiction" to the "exhilaration" which you or I feel up on a roller coaster. But where you and I can cure our desire for excitement by going to "six flags" some (i.e. Markoff) get satisfied by pulling a gun on you, "forcing" you to "obey", raping you and/or killing you too. I love lawyers and Attorney John Salsberg (according to atty. Deanna Cook) is an excellent lawyer in Boston. And I would hope not to offend Atty. Salsberg but I believe Markoff is as guilty as Manson and Bunnell. He's a sadistic killer and a perverted rapist. He is as homo (or bi-) sexual as Hannity. And most "thrill seeking" killers who double as rapists etc. are "clean cut" and come across as "the guy next door"... Washington D.C. is full of "secret" sexual lives, drug abuse and philandering politicians. I seek a top to bottom review of the private lives of our congressmen and senators. There are a lot of Mike Duvalls, Larry Craigs and yes Markoffs in D.C.

As I reflect upon the conflicted (sexually) Sean Hannity and the swagger that he carried himself with in public in Atlanta. He was arrogant and brutal on the radio. But in the backseats of cars, on side streets etc. Mr. Hannity routinely had sex with male prostitutes whom he picked up on North Avenue in Atlanta ... Atty. Steed Scott knows (Tommy) one of Hannity's "regular" prostitutes. Tommy lived with Steed (an openly gay attorney) for a while until he robbed Steed ... Ricky Mitchell in Summerville Georgia has had sex with Mr. Hannity. I challenge Sean Hannity to take a polygraph test at my expense ...

I would hope that Kasey Edwards, Kim Edwards (Ocochokee Florida), Daniel Watts (Sacto teacher), Josh Costa (teacher), Louis Copelin, Christopher Elliot (Sacto), Robert Santillanez, Matt Martinez (Carmichael), David Quindt, Chad Michael Morrissette (W. Hollywood Ca.), Bruce Sarchet (Sacto), Justin Wilson (Minn.?), Megan Ginter, Dan Cintinello, Omar Samy, Samson Benen, Marion Jones-Thompson, Ripley Hunter, Sam Perry (Silicon Valley), Brian

Kehoe, Mike Gorman (Sacto), Dan Sarro, Michael Crowley, Captain Mike McNerney, Shawn Hornbeck, David Plouffe, Arthur Vilkin (Sacto), Travis Coble (Sacto), Sandi Russi, Eric Dill,, Eric Jensen and Austin Sisneros etc. will get this tome ASAP and read it.

We in G.B.G. (Jennifer Heitkamp MD., C. Solis MD. and Dr. Jarman etc.) have been chased and tracked down by the spirit of history. And we (G.B.G./HEART, J. Burton, L. Padilla, students and teachers etc. will be and not just see history. We (Fred, Steve, Jimbo, CC III Patricia Kennedy etc.) have to make this happen. This is an epic moment. It is a pivotal moment. We have worked so hard and come so far. We must mobilize the consciensences of the world for kids. The Save The Children campaigns must be as vocal, as consistent and as victorious as the "Get tough on crime" campaigns. I call upon John Tu and you too. I'm calling upon Kent Evans (Chicago), Garrett McCain, Garrett Haden (Sacto), Jayce Tyrell, C.J. Sheron and David Hellyer to view prisons as "weapons of mass destruction" for killing the spirits of kids. This is a signature moment in America. I need Trent Thornley, Cesar L. Chavez and Andrew Knox (Sacto) to come stand with G.B.G. I need Christopher Kerney (W. Milford N.J.), Brian Hawn and Joseph Latham (Torrance Ca.) to stand with G.B.G. ... I hope we get copies of this tome to Shirley Franklin, Michael Nutter, Cory Booker, Kevin Johnson and Michael Sessions etc. Help me get it to Josh St. Louis, Jake Simpson, Nadia Kunda, Trevor Muhler, Grant Herring, Evan Loudenbeck, Zachary Suratt, Joshua Borland, Larry Tompkins, Nick Jonas and to Mark Gerragos ...

Kids, there is a place inside yourself where nobody deserves to got but you ... When you get (Nathaniel & Keith) give! When you learn, teach! Sit down and write your blessings! Write that you know how to write. Think on the millions of people who don't know how to hold a pen or a pencil ... You (Alex Chivescu, Hornbuekle, Kyle Love and Christian Nelson etc.) are blessed and highly favored. W-r-i-t-e for G.B.G. and help somebody else - write right now! ... I need you all to call the Schoettler-Neufeld Tire Retread Center and tell the owners (great men!) they are in K.K.K. ... I need to get this book to Shea Newberry, Benjamin Whipple, Devin Rio, Ted Ginn, Ginn Academy students (Cleveland, Ohio), Jeff Buttle and to Tyler Schroeder etc. ... I want attorneys Brent J. Newell, Dean Johansson, Francis Papica and Andrew Bridge to have this book ... I'll tell Louis Copelin, Doug Pieper Jr. and Christopher Elliott that we at G.B.G. are resident advisors and why not to come to prison!

Error seems to compound upon error within C.D.C.. Prisons are a total corruption of Justice. I want to get this data to Eric Blinden and Jeffrey Prang ... Have you watched "Lock up" on MSNBC? People are mesmerized by all the prison stories ... Don't come here. You don't have to live down to other people's labels ... I want Justin Gadsden, Sean Pander and Sean Musgrove (Rescue Ca) to get K.K.K.. We see youths (reading this book) engaging in a season of service. We need Earl Davis, Tony Robbins, Zig Zigler and you to help us.

Paul Larosa, Stuart Campbell (Sacto), Sherri Miller (Oakland), Drew Stevyns and Jacob Martin. If you all help us get this book to them then "the work begins anew. Hope rises again and the dream shall never die". And I tell G.B.G. that a rising tide lifts all boats ... Karishma Kumar, Michael Potrilli (teacher), Atty. D. Kavinoky, Tony Dungy, Eric Bates, Tadd Carr, Tom Degnen and Monticello High School needs this book ... Help get it to Khorrami Pollard & Abir, David Santos, Cody Sheldon (Detroit), Alex Wagner Trugman (Studio City Ca.), Scott Macintyre (Scottsdale AZ) and his brother, Randy Madden (Moorpark CA), Vaughn English (Prairie Village, N.C.), Von Smith (Greenwood Mo.), James Michael Avance, Nathan Langley (C.S.U. Sacto), Michael Castro (Rockwell Texas), Andrew Lang (Columbia Mo.), Mitch Fredrickson (Dean of Academic and Student Affaires) at Dunwoody Academy - Minneapolis), Kevin Greene (Catholic Central High School - Grand Rapids MI), Bill Dallas Andrew Rauscher, Nathan Wilhite, Michael Perrelli, Marcus Haggard, Eric Flores (BestBuy-Roseville), Austin Sisneros (Utah), Daniel Seddiqui, Mayor Adrian Fenty, Bernard Risco and all the students at Hillhouse High School ...

Jason Rapp and Roger Walthorn must get K.K.K. ... Luke Duran, Nicholas Wysong, Brad Clark, Andrew Petrass, Matthew Clark (South Bend Indiana), and Ronald Cummings need this book ... I salute CART (Child Abduction Response Team) and I ask G.B.G. members to pray for CART ... Let's reach students at Biola University and ask them to pray for "K.K.K." ... I want Thomas Kaplan (Editor, Yale Daily News), Travis Payne and all the M.J. Back Up Dancers ("Final Tour") to have this book! ... We must get it to Christopher Clubb (in Oregon), Octavio Cruces (Sacto), Jonathan Lipnick and Steve Hansen. I want Garrett McCain to be one of our school leaders ... G.B.G. needs to be more potent than the "Chicago Machine" and "The Clinton Machine" combined. We've tailor made our message out of our mess. The worst our criminal records are the more effective our testimony is. We are Bad Boys! We are criminals. They call us heathens, killers, predators and... We seek a summit meeting on Youth Criminality. We teach kids to respect and understand power. We teach them to stay close to power. ... The real Obama story are those Caucasian (flag toting) republicans who secretly voted for Obama. And we (G.B.G.) want You ... My two lil sisters mean the world to me. I love them dearly. Family means a lot to me and I have a great family. And truth (also) means the world to me. Both of my sisters are (bonafide) Tom Cruise fans. And they've pleaded with me to never tell this (authentic) story. And I love Oprah. And Oprah loves Tom. Yet, even with all the love and respect I have for Oprah I will not take Tom's secrets to the grave with me. Especially since he claims to be such a powerful scientologist. I have no bone to pick with Tom Cruise. He is a terrific actor. But somebody needs to state to Tom Cruise what Jack Nicholson said to him in the movie "You can't handle the truth!". Tom is a bi-sexual. He "goes both ways". Bishop Joe Price used to live in an apartment on North Avenue in Atlanta. Both Peabo Bryson and Elton John had penthouses (on the top floor) in the same building. Bishop Price was one of the few persons in the building who was not gay. I used to take Bishop Price's Limo and ride quite often because the Bishop owned a Radio Station that my show was on. I heard "Tom Cruise is gay". I heard "Tom goes to Blakes, Backstreet, The Gallus, The Armory etc. A friend of mine who owned a jet swore to me that Tom would cruise North Avenue picking up Hustlers (male). He claimed Tom frequented "The Limelight" (in N.Y.), Uncle Charlie's and "Rounds". Yet, I'd heard a lot of B.S. about a lot of folks. And 90% was untrue. They claimed Steven Seagal was gay and had a sock fettish (never proven!). They claimed Jason Priestly was gay (never proven). I heard tons of crap ... But with my own eyes I saw Mr. Cruise cross dressed, with a skirt, high heels, panty hose, toe nails and finger nails painted red. And Tom Cruise was wearing red lipstick. Bishop Joe Price was with me. So were two ladies and so was Daniel Clay H. ... I'm not going to give Clay's last name and I won't name the two women. I have no reason to lie on Tom Cruise. He has done nothing to me. My sisters are his fans. And it would be easy to dismiss what I write about Ambassador Andrew Young, Don King and Zig Zigler (later in this book). But as out of the ordinary and as sensational as the Don King story is, it is authentic and it is verifiable. I affirm under penalty of perjury that (secret and kinky lives of the often conflicted rich and famous) Tom Cruise was in the elevator with Bishop Price, Daniel Clay H., two females and I. And Tom was petite, effeminate and in drag. And we saw which room he went into. And that individual was a gay Caucasian whom the Bishop had often attempted to convert. And Tom exited that room in men's clothing wearing large, dark sunglasses. He gave Clay his autograph. And the room was the (same) room of a gay man. Tom is definitely bi-sexual. And I've 'heard' he was a cocaine head. That is rumor. But the gayness I verify. Bishop Joe Price indicated to me "Manning, I've seen Rob Lowe in this building hanging out with gay dudes. It's a lot that'll blow yo (sic) mind but you gotta pray for these people. Demons have overtaken them". I asked (I've got to tell the truth) Bishop Price why not sell the Tom Cruise story to the media. Joe Price said "I won't do that for a lot of reasons. These dudes are my neighbors. And they have not done me any wrong. I just speak to em (sic) pray for them and keep on walking". I have seen a lot of famous (especially "politicians") people in kinky, salacious and drug related situations. But the most famous dude (on the planet) that I have ever eyeballed in "drag", entering and exiting a gay man's apartment is Tom Cruise. He is definitely a bi-sexual man. And if he hadn't done Brooke Shields etc. like he did I would never have spilled the beans. And I am willing to take a polygraph test and be sworn under oath. And I assure you that the gentleman who is running around building his entire career off of writing unsupported, sensational allegations about Michael Jackson's alleged sexuality etc. would never agree to polygraph ... And certainly folks like Hannity, Beck and Coulter may attempt to negate all the good, the clean, the pure, the powerful and the positive within these pages etc. And they may want to focus a white hot light on a few paragraphs about yet another (cocaine addict and undercover semi-homo) gay celebrity! (I get confused on the right term(s) for a man (like Tom) who has sex with men and women - Gay? Bi? Whatever; I'm done with Tom. End of subject. ...

Youngsters (I repeat) your duty is to glean the clean, pure, powerful and the positive out of this tome and use it for good. You don't need to eat steak just because I do. You may prefer oysters feathered under glass. I love Bishop Long and he drives a Bentley and I would never own a Bentley. My point is we don't have to agree on everything. I'm not a fanatical discipled type of dude. Just because a person is my color does not make them my kind. Zig Zigler is a master motivator but we might not like the same kind of movies. I respect people's right to opinions. Ipso Facto, you don't need to agree with everything in this book. But glean that which is transformational and utilize it to succeed. My main purpose is not to befriend you. You need no prisoner pals. My main aim is to convince you that it would be wise if you never meet me. I seek no student friends.

The folk I would like to befriend are Joel Stein (satirist), Bloggers, Laurel White (Sacto), McGregor Scott and Vloggers. I'd like to befriend F. Lee Bailey, Mark Merin, Hollywood Henderson, Jim Brown and perhaps Les Brown. I don't need student pals.

I want Thomas Kaplan, Gene "Junior" Watson Jr. (Clay N.Y.), Chris Judd and Travis Payne to know this is it. This is the moment we can come together and transform our youth. If we depend upon politicians (I.E.) John Edwards etc. "That story is completely false. There is no truth to it (an "affair")" one day. And a few months later this filthy Rich Lawyer who was a United States Senator (top notch politician and policymaker) and who could have become our President etc. etc. He (senator(ret) John Edwards) lied to us over and over. He had sex with "that woman" and he is the father of her child... So we need not depend upon politicians to transform our country. You (students, parents and teachers) and I (prisoners, guards, police, ex-cons etc.) must get together and heed the call to service. Each one must reach and teach one... I call upon Michael Vick, Mike Milken, Paris Hilton, Martha Stewart, Tony Dungy, Rev. Otis Moss and You and I to work together right here, right now. We can't depend upon police (alone), deputies, the Feds, parole agents, 3-strikes and/or multi-agency task forces to keep our kids safe. We had all of that along with parole agents visiting Phil Garrido's House (and searching) several times per month for 18 years! And just as Tom Cruise has had his "secret" for decades etc., just as John Edwards, (attorney General and Governor) Elliot Spitzer and (congressman) Gary Condit had his secret(s). Phil (the molester) was able to keep a secret compound in his back yard for 18 years. Three strikes didn't bring him in. A Lackluster and an inattentive (and overworked) parole department did not bring him in. If we depended upon Eddie Santos, the sheriff or politicians (i.e. Mike Duvall), Madame Jaycee and those two little girls would still be enslaved in that filthy "back yard". ... All it took to crack the case was for a woman to make eye contact with a kid. I'll look you in your eyes and see into your soul. Let me see you ...

G.B.G. needs some women, men and some children willing to look a hurting, neglected, dejected person in their eyes. And this motherly, sisterly and brotherly eye (soul) contact can save the children... I need Doran Smestad, Seamus Farrow, Raphael V. Johnson, Asociación Ñeta, Louis Copelin, Dominick Lacey (Sacto), Michael Ausiello, Michelle Bernard, Brian Spaly, Brandon Moreno, Ryan Bonifacino, Eric Bulrice, Chris Shaull, Steven Rothberg, Mike Pitcher (Sacto), Jacob Jason (and Jacob should see the Ashton Kutcher Challenge on page 313 of "Blue Eyed Blonde" book II. We extend the challenge to Jacob!), Bobby Hestin and to Jonathan Perez to help us transform the youth.

Kids, I want to put you up on "game" yo. Meditate in the word (word of God and in positive self affirmations) and keep weeds (negativity, doubt and low self esteem) out of your mind. Words are seeds. And inside every word (i.e. biblical scripture and positive word) is a voice. Harvest the seed (word) till you get the voice behind (inside or underneath) the scripture (word). Find the deeper meaning. Words are powerful seeds. Plant heartily in the garden of your mind ... Bradley Thomas Jr., Tony Hunter (Ohio), D.J. Swearingen (Columbus), Nicholas Taxera, John Griffin (Freshman), Nick Pelham, Professor Julius Bailey, Matthew Boettcher (D.C.), Bryan Garner, Michael Johnson (Fash. designer - Details), Mark Ballas, Derek Hough, Chris Durbin and Phillip Coffee need to come on to G.B.G.

We need help today. I have a dream that G.B.G. interns will go into schools and conduct the training and the disciplining of people in non-violence. We will instill discipline in students and motivate them. We seek social justice and international peace. We at G.B.G. say "Imagine all the people ... you may say I'm a dreamer. But I'm not the only one." There are millions of dreamers. And we (G.B.G.) take actions to make our dreams become reality ... Neither rain nor sleet shall keep me from my duty to break this vicious cycle of "Kids Killing Kids" ... California (the Golden State) has 33 prisons! 33 concrete (Hades) witnesses to the failures of society! 33 witnesses to our failure to educate and protect America's promise. Thirty three ... Dorian Young (Roseville Ca.), Atty. Chad Carlock, Erik Steffenson, Greg Deekens (Va.), Sam Inman, Brett Bates, Petty officer Kennedy (U.S. coast guard N.Y.), Dean Elzinga, Steve Hansen, Caleb Peek, Josh Stone, Justin Zegar, Tom Salzman, David Osmond (Salt Lake City, Utah), Von Smith (Greenwood Mo.), Nathaniel Marshall (Malone N.Y.), Kris Allen (Conway Arkansas), Matt Giraud (Michigan), Sean Wolf (Buffalo), Ben Kaplan (pub. college Dreams website), Daniel Dhers, David Quindt etc. etc. let's do this.

We must teach kids to dream. But how 2 dream big! I'd like 2 c principals run schools like a company. Motivate, influence and be positive. Utilize incentives and positivity to teach kids... Ted Ginn Jr., Marva Collins, my friend Aaron Fernander and Ron Clark are master educators. And I'd like to see Ron, Ted, Marva and Aaron etc. join Arne Duncan in an educational summit meeting PDQ! ... Talk to Dr. Eugene Sanders (CEO of the Cleveland School System). Ted Ginn has no college degree. His students wear bow ties and suit jackets daily. "The Red Coats" ... His students test 13% higher than all other Ohio students. We need a cascade of candor about public schools right now. We must move full steam ahead with transforming every American School ... Let's start groups online and establish independent study programs etc.

We (G.B.G.) must start tipping up stealthily on this enemy of illiteracy and defeat it ... Prison has become a canvas on which I use to paint this picture of bad education being good for incarceration. I must sound an alarm in Zion from Hades. We need to release a strategy and a campaign or crusade (Dr. Cosby! Dr. Poussaint! Dr. Duran! Dr. Solis!) to promote education ... When I recruit G.B.G. members I ask "Do you wanna go change the world?". Hell, if we gotta employ Amway or Herbalife tactics we must release a strategy to promote education ... It's been too long now ... A delay is not a denial ... It may not be God sent (prison?) but it can be God used. God will break the rules for you and make you the "prototype". He'll make you the pattern for others to follow ...

I tell you to get excited and don't give up. Because they rejected Leah God opened up her womb and gave her a child. Because they "Hated you I'm gonna bless you" He told me ... Every now and then God sends you an angel. Wait on your angel ... Don't quit! "Having done all to stand! Stand!" Stand there and wait. God did not bring you this far to leave you. God is cooking you up a blessing. There is a reason you didn't die.

... Get up and stay out of dark places ... Love yourself and feed on God's Love. It is hard to fill a bucket with a hole in it. That's why compliments and ego strokes don't last long. You keep coming out and going right back to that dark place (Anger, drugs, alcohol, crime, gangs etc.). You need to (finally) get delivered. You need to fill (plug) that hole. I'm surrounded (in Hades) by broken boys with gaping holes in their psyches, hearts and spirits. And it's dangerous to fellowship with envious, broken and "sensitive" brothers who have holes in their Hearts ...

I need Nicholas Kohlmeyer, Don Sullivan, Mike Roberts (Editor - Outside Maga.), Brian Boyle, Michael Sullivan (senior at College Park H.S. in Sacto), Austin Sisneros and Alex Chivescu to come on in. I may be an incendiary scribe who helps bring a prisoner group out of the shadows and (together) we can put it on the map.

But we must remain transparent, authentic and probitistic. We must support Bill Coibion, Angela Murchison (Angela if you need a couple hundred dollars I'll give it to you!). Freedom Hall, parents, staff and students at M.L. King Jr. Technology Academy ...

I need Joshua Smith (Townsend Montana), Atty. Warren Ballentine, Perry Thompson (Granite Bay H.S.), Yossi Dina, Matthew Cochrane, Christian Hosoi, (state Assemd), Taylor Lautner, Todd Graves, Bruce Toms, Ryan Jett (Sacto), Esteban Nunez (L.A.), Dave Ellis (author of "Becoming a master student"), Moseley Collins, Kai McKenna and Sherri Miller (Oakland) ... We have far too many kids turning their guns on each other rather than turning their guns on the issues (poverty and illiteracy)... I'm calling Zach Devals, Ezekiel Hernandez, Kevin Griffin (Washingtonian Magazine), Dan Kozlak, Michael Castro, David Matthews (author "Ace of spades") and Dr. Janet Taylor to join our efforts. We want to speak to that broken place that needs healing in our youths. We are spiritual surgeons. I need Dr. Nicole Black-Singleton, Sara Baldwin, John Sexton and Jason Sutherland to join us today. ... Without unusual opposition you cannot receive new blessings. And when you get new blessings don't handle them in old ways ... Don't let the weakness in you destroy the greatness in you... You own the definition of who you are ... write down 3 things you did today worth talking about tomorrow... Bring me Christopher Mejia (Covina Ca.), Andrew Knox and Joshua Costa (teacher) and we (you, them and me) will change the world ... Our wounds (holes) enable us to speak to other people's pain.

... Secure fathers circumcise their sons. Insecure dads castrate sons. And sons spend a lifetime trying to cover and camouflage their impotence.

... An African proverb says "If you want to go quickly go alone. If you wanna go far go together". We (G.B.G.) have got to go far quickly ... I'm gonna need great people like the owners of the Schoettler-Neufeld Tire Retread Center, Rev. Otis Moss, Ted Ginn and Ron Clark to make this (G.B.G). happen!

... kids? Yall have been told negativity over & over for so long. So let me repeat (tautology) something I've written in this tome ... The silk/spittle which comes out of the mouth of the caterpillar (as well as what comes out of your mouth) creates the environment into which he (and you are) is nurtured. Your tongue is the pen of a ready writer. Speak your way out of poverty, lack and illiteracy ... I know my writing disturbs a lot of folks. And when they were building the tower of Babel God said "Let us go down and disturb" then ... The spoken, preached and written word can catapult you into situations you would have never thought possible ... Paul was in chains, in a storm, in a prison at the beginning of Acts ... At the end of the book of Acts Paul (the prisoner) found himself in Caesar's Household preaching! ...

I need Richard Peichoto (Sact), Ronnie Lawson, Fabian Cancellara, Austin Sisneros (Gotta stipend 4 you!), Michael Castro (Texas!) and Esteban Nunez to join us ... Drugs are the lyrics of the insecure. Violence is the language of the unheard ... Justin Brice (youth teen minister in Yuba City), Ryan Hreljac and Brian Hawn where are you? We need you! ... We need Russell Wagoner (wagonner? Musical Theatre), Garrett Henson, Cody Jones (Westfield High School), Andrew Levit, Alex Seabolt, Sam Bradford (Oklahoma), Jason Howard (N.Y.), Devon Poston (Sierra Ca.), Jason Durtchi, Blake Lewis, Omar Samy and Mark Kielburger ... This is a watershed moment. We can do this ... I need Derrick Knill (Grass Valley, Nevada), Trevor Loflin, The Christian Fellowship Ministry Church (Sacto), Robbie Wolff (Sacto), youth at Youth Justice Coalition, Julian Smith (25 things I hate about Facebook), Alice Huffman, James Shelby, Marc Morial, Jeremy (at Atty. Mune Basailah's office), Dr. John Diaz (plast. surg.), Nicholas Flowers, Tyler Lyon, Dr. Jim Hernandez etc. right now... It is not the outfit but the infit that'll determine your destiny... We need to employ a Herculean and Gigantic effort to transform public education... We need Mike Kirby (G.Q. Maga.), Burton Deckoning (Buena Vista High School), Thomas Williams (Center High School - sac. town), Tony Hsieh, David Vick, Tyra Banks producer "Paul" (4/8/09), Luke Sears (Oakland), MaCaulay Culkin, Peter Grammatas (N.Y.), Matt Schoettler, Akram Sweis, Hunter Brown (Wheaton, Illi.), Joel Stein, Attorney Joe Cheshire, Andy Knox and You ...

I got 3 million broken homeboys trapped within the bowels of these prisons. And prison is a mighty stage to tell our story, our truth and use it to transform youths.

Jesse Grund, Robert Linggi (Sacto), Danny Seddiqui, Jake Reitan, Tim Coleman (Sac), Gabe Williams (Sac.), Tyler Lewelling, Derek Jarvic, students at "Step one Sacto Dance and Fitness," J. Douglas Clark, Harold Ford Jr. and Daniel Clay etc. we need you. I want to see squads of door knockers out changing the world for kids ... We need Shawn Khorrami, Dylan Pollard, Danny Abir, Matt Bailey, Bahr, Nancy, Deborah, Becki Kammerling, Galorah, Payum Banafshe, Mikel Jones, David Mallen, Melissa Harris-Lacewell, Melody Barnes, Tommy Vietor, Shelley Handy, Kyle Hunter (San Diego), Prof. William Ayers, Mark Malkin, Bob Herbert, Tim Hanson (Alex. VA.), Cody Cates (East Nicholos High School - Sutter County), Jenigh Garrett, Justin Berry and Andrew Ross Sorkin ... Growing and changing is exciting even if you have to look at some painful things inside yourself in order to do it. You can heal your life! ... Write this down: "I am willing to change and grow. I am willing to learn new things. I do not know it all. I am willing to drop old concepts when they no longer work for me. I'm willing to see situations about myself and say "I don't want to that anymore. I know I can become more of who I am. Not a better person because that implies that I am not good enough but I can become more of who I am." I need Kyle Hunter (Rep. in San Diego), Megan Poindexter, Andi Greenman, Chad W. Carter, Atty. Paul Bradley, Jonathan Dyke (Diamond Bar CA.), Michael Folkner (Lodi), Doug Melton, Chad Burton (Oakland), Parker Kehoe, Stoney Creek High School students, Simon Perez (Oakland), Matt Cash, Chris Cash, Ryan Rathsen, Shawn Hornbeck, John (at Oakdale Cheese Factory), Garrett Graff (Digi. Media Strategist)k, Ben Clark, Levelle Mixon, Gil Somera, Jacob Knoble, Adam Waddell (Wyoming), Adam Bettencourt (Sac. State), Alex Blench (computer wizard!), Abraham and Winslow Norton (Alameda County), Danny McDermot (swimmer), David Holloman (Sacto), Alex Sliva (Woodland CA.), Craig Cannon (Woodland), Omar Samaha, Matt Lanter, Steve Henning (Sacto), Ryan Evans (Golden Colorado), Chris Savvas, Jake Simpson, Collin Finnerty, Bridget Black (CSU. Sac.), Kellen McGuire (CSU, Sac.), Sean Mehra and Caroline Rooney. As President and chairman of G.B.G./HEART I issue a personal invitation to Ben Lewis (Univ. of Pennsylvania), Brian Laoruangroch (Univ. of Mo.), Chris Varenhorst (Ma. Int. of Tech.), Scot Frank (MIT), Zac Workman (Ind. Univ.), Matthew Briner (Yale), Jeff Reitman (Yale), Justin Cannong (MIT), Justin Yan and everybody at GX studios to join G.B.G. . We wanna work with you. We need your input and ideas. I need the folks at Green Mobile (in Mo.), Brett Laoruangroch, Darin Ezra, Jessica Mah, Frank Carter and Ryan Hreljac I need you yesterday. And I will pay a lot of money to anybody who will find and email some (a lot) of these 29,000 folk I've named and tell them to get K.K.K. today! ... I need Daniel Sample and Joseph Schoen (Missouri), Larry Laboe (Sacto), Joseph Latham (Torrance CA.), Ramona Latham (San Diego), Cameron Civella (Sacto), and Esteban Nunez to know this book is out. I need y-o-u to use your computer to locate and notify (at least 20) some of these people. Don't assume somebody already did it. The more the merrier. You contact some of these people please ... With you we can do this! Contact Elk Grove High School's football team and tell them the Book is out! We gotta be innovative and creative. I've given (with my team) a lot of seed tomes (to schools etc.) that are things. Harvest the voice behind these words. One voice is telling you to randomly contact 20 of the folk's I've named within these pages. And then contact 10 of your friends and tell them to read "K.K.K."

... I was chatting with a Caucasian inmate today (Shaun S.) about the racism within prisons. We chatted about the A-B-, Skinheads, Nazi Low Riders and The Sacramaniacs etc. We discussed the fact that white inmates are disallowed to take psychotropic drugs in prison.

... No Wellbutrin, Prozac or any psychotropic drugs whatsoever. No matter if he's depressed, suicidal or homicidal etc. If any Caucasian inmate accepts his prescribed psychiatric meds he will be assaulted, sliced (cut) or killed by white gang members; in any California prison! Lance Corcoran and Mike Jiminez and every California guard knows this. But they allow it ... You've never read this in the newspaper. You've never seen it on the News or in a movie. But it is an indisputable fact. I challenge Lisa Ling, David Begnaud, Dr. Phil or Jason Huyck etc. to interview any white inmate in a California prison. And verify my authenticity. Come interview former LAPD Detective Richard "Doc" Ford and ask him what happens to whites if they take take meds?

This is a threat to the safety and security of all prisons staff (i.e. civilian staff and nurses etc.) and to society ... When a white (mentally ill) inmate in prison is disallowed by a gang to take his prescribed meds it aggravates and exacerbates his illness. Ipso Facto (according to C. Solis MD.), he's more likely to reoffend upon his exit from prison ... This is mad!

...I want you to (really) read this list of Lawyers: Attorney Nicole Murphy, William J. Cranston (Baker & Hostetler LLP), Adam V. Lindgren (Meyers Nave Riback Silver & Wilson), Tony Serra, Lise Anderson, Countess C. Williams, Gregory L. Cannon (Cannon & Harris), Matt Bailey (Khorrami Pollard & Abir LLP) and Murray J. Janus (Bremner, Janus & Cook)... All of the above named lawyers are top notch firms. G.B.G. salutes them. And we ask them (each) to donate (at least) 20 copies of this tome to a high school ... If they don't it's okay. I've got Peter Andrist, Bob Blasier and Attorney Murray J. Janus. We will do this! This tome will reach around the world. And we (G.B.G.) will use prison as a mighty stage from which and with which to launch this message to youths all across this globe ...

I did not know they'd named a street (in Atlanta) after Hosea Williams. Yes they did! And he deserves it... He was (and now you) the only person I ever confided in about televangelist Pat Robertson (700 Club). Remember Jimmy Swaggart got caught up with porn and a prostitute? Pat Robertson was arrested in Decatur Ga. on charges of possession of child pornography by Dekalb police officer (and my friend) Michael Scandrick (vice)... Captain Hogan (Dekalb County Jail) and Major Melton tore up, destroyed and disregarded his arrest and threatened to fire Mike if he ever went to the press... (DeKalb County is where Sheriff Derwin Brown was assassinated!). I don't know how much money Pat Robertson paid Major Melton and Captain Hogan. But he paid them. Ask Attorney Steed Scott or Mobley Childs ... Pat is a pervert!

I'm certain it's difficult for many to believe pastors can be so perverted. But there are many people that know "about" Him but they don't know Him. If they would lay on their face before God a change would come. But I've seen so much mess that you would stop (God forbid) going to church if you knew it all. I have seen deacons pull guns in church! Likewise some of the same pimps you send your money too are hustlers! Benny Hinn is not a healer. Benny Hinn is a hustler! And just like Tom Cruise he's bi-sexual. I know gay Limo drivers he had sex with. I know an Attorney he had sex with. It is not just Ted Haggard! It is (also) Robertson, Jenkins, Hinn and ... While I'm speaking on preachers; I am an apologist for members of Clergy. I love preachers. But I spent so much of my life being deceptive that hypocrisy is my pet peeve. I can handle the truth. "I'm short and I'm flawed but I do love God". I get that preaches are still Jacob one moment and Israel the next. Preachers want to be superman but Clark Kent is still there. That is why I only have a few select people (in civilian life) who are my "Friends". When I was a golden boy, on stage and having it my way I was loved. But I only have a few folks whom I can show my flaws, scars, wounds and my Clark Kent. And even when I'm naked and exposed they love me. But I get tired of preachers deceiving folks and pretending that (in flesh) "I'm holy"... I received a 4 page missive from one of my favorite preachers yesterday. It was an encouraging missive but I was displeased when (at the end) he (too) seemed to tie my "Blessing" to a seed "offering". I'm burnt out on preachers begging for money. Creflo Begs. Kenneth Copeland, Rod Parsely and Benny Hinn etc. all send missives tying your miracle, healing and blessing to how much money you send them. "A dollar a day keeps the devil away". They drive Bentleys and Rolls (Creflo has 4 Rolls Royces and a Jet) and I'm in jail. And I should send them my money? It does require money to stay on TV. Money is a necessary tool. But I wish Bishop Flip Flop and Deacon Willie Wonder would send me a letter unattached to "seed" money etc. and just write "... It takes a lot of money to be on TV and if you can please send an "offering" so we can stay on TV" period! And I (Sherman D. Manning) will (readily) send you (Bishop T.D. Jakes and/or Bishop Eddie Long etc.) a check! ...

"I believe this (jail) is a crime scene" an anonymous person told me during a visit... "Crimes against humanity (mostly young Caucasian boys) take place here (L.A. County Jail) every day" he told me. He is a "captain" with a police department in the Long Beach Area. T.J. Parsell, Linda McFarlane and my dear hero Dr. Lewis Yablonsky all concur with the captain's opinion. The Los Angeles County Jail (system) commits "High crimes and misdemeanors" against citizens (some of whom are arrested on minor violations) every day. I wish two things: A. I wish you (teens and tweenies) would read the tome "Fish" by T.J. Parsell. B. I wish Leo Terrell, James Brosnahan, Analea Patterson or Bob Blasier etc. would file a class action lawsuit (on behalf of white boys) against the L.A. County Jail, L.A. County sheriff's dept. etc. Robert Waters or McGregor Scott could/would create a media sensation around L.A. County Jail and sweeping change would take place. Dr. Yablonsky, Dr. Terry Kupers, Richard "Doc" Ford and even I could/would testify about what I saw at L.A. County Jail ...

Teens and tweenies I need you perusing this tome and taking action on what you read. I'm not writing for Baby Boomers. They are too cynical for me. They yell out "You lie" to Heads of State and show up at town hall meetings with guns strapped on their lips. They're stuck in a time warp and the "Wild Wild West". I don't have anything for them. They (The Baby Boomers) specialize in criticizing and fault finding. And "that's too many names (lol) in K.K.K." they'll complain. But a Jonathan Davis (Elk Grove High School football player) will see all these "names" I "drop" and grab the broom of "creativity" and the dust pan of "innovation" and "sweep" (the names) up on a "miracle". I need yall (the teens and the tweenies) to "see" the 69,000 (lol) names in this tome and harness the power, the persons, the creativity and the synergy behind the "names". I "name" them for a "reason". And if you (Gen. Y, The Facebook and Myspace

Generation etc.) do nothing else for "me" or for "G.B.G." please... Go back and take a visual "snapshot" of the names named by "name" in this tome and Help! Help! Help! Help me and G.B.G. by deciding (o.k. let me email Eric Bulrice, Jonathan Davis, Matthew Clark (South Bend Indiana), Ben Cooper (Davic CA.), Joseph Latham (from Torrance CA. Ramona's son), Kyle Love (Brenda's son in CA) and Alex Holgan etc." And you tell them 'Dude you are in a splendid new book called "K.K.K.". Order it at your local book store or at www.cafepress.com/manning"... Can you all do that for me? It's all good.

     ... If after perusing thus far you're still "cool" with "coming" to jail etc. I'd like to know how you will feel (and what it will do to you psychologically) when you have some rogue, renegade (bisexual) "captain" like Mike Martel standing outside your cell door demanding to see your "private" (genitalia) or "I'll transfer yo butt to High Desert"). How will you feel? ... When Jeff Glenn Howell (Justin's brother) stole the $100,00 from me and decided to take "my" money and buy weed with Bo Bo and accuse me of threatening to "Beat" his butt... Captain Mike Martel (close pal of Mike Bunnell's) told Howell "I don't like Sherman anyway. But I'm not gonna help you unless you show me your"... And Martel fondled Jeffrey Howell after the visual peep show. This is the same captain Mike Martel "caught" having sexual intercourse (in the prison) in the work center with Dr. Marilyn Windham. "If you snitch us out I will fire yo black ass" captain Martel told C.O. Wright. Mike Martel is now "Warden" at M-C-S-P and Mike Bunnell (M&M) is his "assistant... "I would have bet you my house that Martel would never make Warden" a facility captain told me. But Martel (to his credit) plays golf with State Assembly-men (Gentlemen Only Ladies Forbidden) and state senators. And Martel and Bunnell are extremely "powerful" men ... I am "still" (today) suffering from the wrath of Bunnell against me for writing about him in a tome ... My U.C. Davis appointment to see infectious disease specialist Dr. Melcher was "inadvertently" cancelled the last three times. How? Easy answer etc. It was not anybody at Warden Walker's prison. A.W. Fred Schroeder and Captain Scottie Shannon are not "inmate lovers". But they are fair and unbiased ... I have no (never) access to a regular, non "collect" telephone. All my calls are recorded! But .... Mike Bunnell (literally) calls and reports (using a pseudonym) that I "refused" to go to my appointment. And if U.C. Davis hears from a person with a regular telephone that "Manning refused" they cancel me. And just yesterday "Miquel" told me "somebody called D-M-H-etc. and somebody claimed you refused. I'm so sorry Mr. Manning. Warden Walker and CC III Patricia Kennedy are adamant about getting you to see Dr. Melcher. You will go next month!" ... Bunnell manipulated (behind the scenes and "off the record") my stay (14 mos) at the civilian hospitals. A "confidential" source finally told me "somebody at M.C.S.P. "hates" the ground you walk on! We were ordered (for 9 months) not to contact your family and let them know you were in the hospital! We were ordered not to give you a telephone call for 14 months! We were ordered not to allow you in the hospital chapel ... Don't shoot Joe Rikalo ... He was acting on an "order" ... I am as convinced that Mike Bunnell tried (desperately and in "concert" with Marion E. Spearman, Negrete, D.L. Criner, Sylvia Garcia etc. etc.) to kill me that I'd stake my life on it. ... "This is strange" Dr. Postolo (Chief psychiatrist at P.V.S.P.) admitted when he saw me after my 14 month outside hospitalization ... "I still remember you were afraid and suicidal" he stated. And "You told me Bunnell sent you here (P.V.S.P.) to catch Valley Fever ... You were distraught and lo and behold a month later you were nearly dead. If it was not for nurse Hall and Dr. Huang (a psychiatrist) you would be dead" ... Dr. Bruce Bakeman (senior psychologist) told me "Mr. Manning, I want nothing to do with lawsuits and all of that. That does not involve me. But I can tell you that Dr. Smith says he visited you at the hospital and he thought you would die. He told me you could not even lift your arm to shake his hand. He told me you were out of it. Perhaps 90 lbs or so... Just being here at P.V.S.P. is in my expert opinion, psychological torture. Somebody (Bunnell) for some reason; wants you here at P.V.S.P.". And different experts argued and disagreed about whether re-breathing Valley Fever (cocci) spores could/would reinfect me. Yet, Dr. Igbinosa (Chief Medical officer) and Dr. Tootell (Regional Medical Director) both stated to me (in a round about way) that I should never have been transferred to P.V.S.P. "with asthma, being black, being from out of State and suffering from a low "T" cell count you should have been on the list to "not" be transferred here" Dr. Tootell told me... "Somebody (Bunnell) pushed very hard to special transfer you here... Lt. J. Herrera told us you were brought to P.V.S.P. in the middle of the night. In a squad car by I.S.U. They cell extracted you at M.C.S.P. and videotaped you coming here" stated Dr. Felix Igbinosa ... Counselor Freeland stated "You have an enemy (Ray Sanchez Jr.) at this prison on this yard... You have an enemy (Fonseca) on another yard here.... A.W. Mike Bunnell (specifically) sent Counselor Costa to investigate... I have a note (States Freeland) by Costa stating that per Bunnell Ray Sanchez is not at P.V.S.P." ... Freeland asked me "Hey Manning can I ask you a question?" I said "What is it?" He stated "What the f--- (expletive deleted) did you do to associate Warden Bunnell?" I said "Why?" Freeland said "Bunnell personally, exclusively and methodicly orchestrated your special delivery to this (P.V.S.P.) prison".... When I finally got my miracle from God and got out of the hospital etc. Dr. Paul Griffin wrote a special, unprecedented missive explaining how I nearly died, suggesting "single" cell status and writing that "stress" alone could "kill" me. And yet I went back to P.V.S.P. armed with Dr. Griffin's missive and spent a year pleading to be transferred out of P.V.S.P. Marion E. Spearman stated clearly "We work together and an enemy of Mike Bunnell's is an enemy of mine". And when Spearman took my clothes, blankets, sheets, mattress, legal mail etc. and when he shut off my cell water and took my toilet paper. He and Lt. J.D. Bennett stated "This is per Bunnell". Spearman said "I'll let you die if you don't stop writing about Bunnell". Spearman states "When they (Tasi and C.O. Garza put you in five point restraints (also unconstitutional) at the hospital. That was per me. I talk to Bunnell every other day. I used to work at Mule Creek. And Bunnell already told me you're gonna probably try to write about me... You'll be a dead man". And when Spearman ordered Captain Walker, Deshazo, Sgt. Scott, Solis, Flores and Lt. Lubkin to "cell extract" me just to get my TV Spearman told me "You are the first and only inmate we have ever forcefully extracted, in a non-emergency just to get a TV". And I ended up having to go on a hunger strike for 16 days to convince A.W. Henson to transfer me out of P.V.S.P. Ron Henson told me "Manning, Bunnell has you blackballed all through C.D.C. You will never get back to New Folsom because Bunnell knows Walker and Kennedy are there. And they play fair. Bunnell wants to keep you in places like Donovan, High Desert and Salmas where he has juice. This man wants you dead". Henson told me that in C.T.C. at P.V.C.P. during my hunger strike. Dr. Bakeman, Dr. George, Dr. Silverstein and even Dr. Mike Mullan all tried desperately to get me out of P.V.S.P. And Marion Blockaded them every time. I must confess that no person worked more vigorously to get me out of P.V.S.P. than Dr. Bakeman. At one point (immediately after Dr. Lumpkin called Dr. George the "N" word and told her he hoped an inmate would "rape" her...) Dr. Bakeman and Dr. Huang (the man who saved my life after P.V.S.P. medical had engaged in gross deliberate medical negligence! ... After L.V.N. Hall had tried for three weeks to get Dr. Benyamin, R.N. Bond (unsuccessfully) to see me.) had me going back to M.C.S.P. to the E.O.P. program. Dr. Bakeman had stated "you have PTSD. The nightmares and flashbacks you are having about the hospital and "watching guys die" etc. All of that is due to your extensive hospital stay". Dr. Bakeman continued "Mr. Manning it is just like you've just come out of a "war zone". Nine months without your family knowing where you are. Ten months with no mail or books. Fourteen months without TV, radio, a visit or a telephone call etc. That kind of sensory deprivation is akin to psychological torture. It is as if you've been a prisoner of war for fourteen months". Dr. George stated "I cannot speak to your issue of medical neglect. However, for a man who goes to church

101

and believes in God to be denied a Bible, a chaplain and chapel access for fourteen months is A. psychological terror! And B. unconstitutional".... So Dr. Huang and Dr. Bakeman had me all scheduled to return to M.C.S.P. to get treatment etc.... They told me to "pack your property you're transferring in 3 hours". C.O. Martin told me that. 2 Hours later C.O. Martin said "Marion E. Spearman cancelled you (sic) transfer dude. Somethine (sic) bout Bunnell and Duclos at M.C.S.P."....

At 11:00 Am A.W. Spearman had me pulled out of my cell by C.O. Province (Province is a good man! As is C.O. Buffy Davis, Sgt. Farmon, Lt. Burnette, C.O. McAfee and C.O. K. Yeager etc.). Mr. Spearman told me "Mike Bunell does not want you back at M.C.S.P. He got Duclos to write a special chrono saying she fears for her life if you come back. It looks like you is (sic) stuck here with me, Yates, Criner and Tucker. I can still send you back to "A" Yard".

With a greasy grin on his face Spearman licked his lips and said "Sherman let me see yo (sic) d_ck; right quick. I can help ya I'm the associate warden". I began yelling and kicking the cage and Spearman called C.O. Mendez, Sgt. Martinez and 3 other (unidentified) officers and ordered them to "beat his ass. He's acting a fool. Get him!" And they opened the cage and beat me maliciously! Lt. Webster came over and yelled "what the f--k are yall doing to Sherman?" And C.O. Mendez said "Spearman told us to kick his ass". Lt. Webster put his body between mine and the group and saved me. He yelled "I'm ordering you to stop now!"

... Few weeks later Marion E. Spearman retaliated against Lt. Webster by removing him from D-4 (and for some other trumped up reasons) and having him reassigned! ... A couple of months later C.O. D.L. Criner, Gail Crooms and Marion E. Spearman attacked me in C.T.C. Mr. Criner delivered most of the punches to my belly with Spearman yelling "you still gon (sic) sue us! You still writing bout Bunnell"... Spearman spit on me... A C.N.A. saw the commotion and hit her alarm. Lt. Wendy K. Meyers ordered Criner to "stop hitting him Criner! Stop! Stop! Stop!"

... Months later I was at C.M.C. East (in San Luis Obispo) and Lt. Webster and Sergeant Hosman travelled from Coalinga (P.V.S.P.) all the way to C.M.C. East to see me. Lt. Webster had me pulled out of my cell and he stated "Sherman I'm going off the record with you. Because we are joined together by our Valley Fever. I almost died from cocci and so did you". Webster had water in his eyes. "I can't be a witness for you in some lawsuit and if you ever quote me I'll have to swear you are lying! Sherman I like you. Wendy (Lt. Meyers) likes you. But we also like our jobs. And we are not willing to go out on some limb for your dude... Marion hates me because of you and for some other crap. But listen - you are dealing with extremely powerful, dangerous and wicked people... If I were you I would stop writing about Bunnell, Spearman and any of that crowd..."

Lt. Webster stated emphatically "They are gonna end up manipulating a transfer and getting you to Salinas, Donovan or High Desert etc. and you will end up as dead as Doug Pieper and it'll be ruled a suicide or a cell murder". Lt. Webster concluded "I drove all the way to C.M.C. East, in plain clothes just to tell you they want you dead ... I know a lot I can't say but lemme (sic) give you a glimpse.

... Inmate Emslander set U up at M.C.S.P. with guidance from Duclos and Bunnell. U gotta 115 (R.V.R. i.e. A "ticket")... A lady on the I.S.U. told U that U should be released from Ad-seg and Emslander should be put in the hole... A fair lieutenant who hates Bunnell found you "not guilty" of the R.V.R. you were put in the hole for".

Lt. Webster continued "You made a phone call to Switzerland. You were told that Emslander sent a missive (confessing to setting me up!) to Mr. Andrist. You asked him to mail you the letter so you could use the letter to prove (even though you'd already been found not guilty) your innocence... Mr. Andrist mailed U the missive twice at M.C.S.P. Bunnell stole it both times! ...

"Soon as you got to P.V.S.P. Mr. Andrist remailed (He'd dealt with C.D.C. long enough to know how often mail is stolen that he made 10 copies of the missive from Emslander) you the missive and miraculously you got it! In black and white - proof that you never threatened Duclos! ... Bunnell got CCI Costa to testilie that you had no enemy at P.V.S.P. when you got to P.V.S.P. You were initially placed in Ad-seg by Lt. Herrera. You were so afraid of Valley Fever and P.V.S.P. that you sent a missive to captain (now AW) Beels stating you had an enemy at P.V.S.P. and you did not want to go to general population! You refused to attend your 72 hour lock-up hearing. You refused to attend I.C.C. And yet Spearman still forced you to go to Facility "A" in absentia... Sherman, we never release inmates to G.P. in absentia. We consider it an insult when U refuse to show-up for a lock-up hearing and for committee... The fact that you were released in absentia boggles my mind"...

Lt. Webster concluded "Sherman - stop writing about Bunnell and Spearman... These guys r deadly!"...

I hate to do this (per the Baby Boomers anguish! But Gen-Y, teens and tweenies will understand why I need to "Name" all of these "Names"...) I want Attorneys Leo Terrell, James Brosnahan, Stewart Katz, Michael C. Alder (of Beverly Hills Fame), Marc Grossman, Bill L. Schmidt, Kyra Kazantzis, Josh Kaizuka, Wilke Fleury Hoffelt Gould & Birney LLP, Michael Bein, James Zahradka, Tony Serra, Meyers Nave Riback Silver & Wilson, Manning & Marder, Kass, Ellrod, Ramirez LLP, Nicole Murphy, Shawn Khorrami and Nancy Gardner etc. to closely scrutinize this area of this tome. I want Ann Patterson, Joseph M. Malkin, Thomas Y. Coleman, Dora Mao, Lisa Brewer, Jill L. Rosenberg and everybody at Orrick, Herrington & Sutcliffe LLP to closely and meticulously analyze this tome... Mike Bunnell is completely guilty of a conspiracy to commit murder on me. He's an accessory to attempted murder. He can't escape the fact that documentation exists showing that I reported to the Chief (I repeat) psychiatrist at P.V.S.P. that "Bunnell sent me here to catch Valley Fever". And since Coalinga is the cocci capitol of America and since inmates and staff (i.e. the husband of Fresno city cop Figueroa) at P.V.S.P. had already died from Valley Fever. And since Federal Receiver Robert Sillen had asked the Governor to shut down P.V.S.P. due to the Valley Fever epidemic etc. If any prison knew that shortness of breath and severe "night sweats" meant "cocci" P.V.S.P. should have known! Bob Blasier are you reading?

"Did you pee in the bed?" My celly "Dopey" (I shan't utilize his real name because Criner, Tucker and Spearman may get "to" him) asked me one morning, because my bed was drenched from head to toe with sweat. And (as I reported to L.V.N. Hall repeatedly) if I ate something it felt like somebody was stabbing me in the stomach with a knife... When Hall finally convinced R.N. Bond (tautology on Hall as well as on me) to see me nurse Bond said I was "faking" and my bloated belly was only "gas"... When Hall finally convinced (4 weeks later) a physician to see me (R.N. Bond was present and he colored the physician's bias against me etc.) the doctor ordered abdominal X-rays. And when the physician read the X-ray he showed me and stated "all of those clouds are gas. I will give you laxatives and an enema"... When I finally, miraculously made it to UMC hospital Judge Roper's son (fresh out of medical school) Dr. Glade Roper Jr. said that so called "gas" is actually six liters of Valley Fever fluid! Are you sure a physician read the X-rays at P.V.S.P.?"....

Dr. Roper saved my life a second time at UMC. C.O. Daly and Merrielles were guarding me at UMC. And Mrs. Daly came into my room and began berating, belitting, badgering and harassing me. She called me names! She talked about Mike Bunnell and C.O. Duclos. She said she hoped I died. And the male (Merielles) guard joined in. I began having severe chest pains and I pressed the "emergency" button. And the nurse came in. She called a "code". Dr. Roper ran in and hooked my chest up to a monitor... He yelled "Nitro glycerine!" and he yelled it over and over. They put it underneath my tongue. I grabbed Dr. Roper's arm "Am I gonna die?" I yelled! He was pale but he replied "hang on Sherman, don't give up". They put more Nitro underneath my tongue and Dr. Roper said 200, 190, 180, 170, ok. Sherman you're okay".... Dr. Roper ordered me to the Intensive Care Unit. C.O. Daly handcuffed my left wrist so tight and underneath the bunk etc. etc. that my nurse (Lorraine) told her "you're gonna cut off his circulation. Are you trying to kill this man?" Daly stated "I'm doing my job my way, you do yours". Lorraine stated "I'll start by notifying Dr. Roper. And then I'll call your watch commander!" Daly then immediately took off the cuffs.... When I had grabbed Dr. Roper's arm earlier (thinking I was a "goner") I looked over at C.O. Daly and she was "smiling". She (literally) wanted me to die ... To her credit (however) she is not a racist. A Caucasian inmate coded and died (I still have nightmares about him) in my room and Daly had that same, evil and sneaky "grin" on her face. After he died my physician kept asking me if I was okay and I said "I need a chaplain, a Bible and a psychologist" and C.O. Daly stated "and a pacifier to "suck on". And she refused to allow the physician to get me some "help".... Bob Blasier R U Reading?

I still remember (like it was yesterday) signing myself out of the hospital! After 9 months without my 76 year old Dollie Manning knowing where I was. And Paul Griffin MD. telling me I was going to "die" if I checked out. But I did so anyway. And he wrote (clearly) that "In my medical opinion without oxygen and Amphotericine (p. 41 of 50) B this patient will "die"!" And yet, when I arrived at P.V.S.P. in the C.T.C. the physician refused "absolutely" to provide me with oxygen! ... (may I repeat?) That was the longest night of my entire life. I faced death that evening and walked away winning! ...

In-spite of all the high crimes and misdemeanors committed against me by Bunnell, Duclos, Spearman, Daly, Criner and R.N. Bond. In spite of egregious gross deliberate medical negligence. In spite of a 14 month hospital stay during which I was tortured because of my tomes, God is still God. He (and He alone!) rules and super rules. He put His "Super" on my "Natural". The Lord Reigns. When I think of His goodness and all that He's done for me. My soul shouts Hallelujah and I thank God for saving me! He is an awesome God! .... I can tell you that there were some times when I doubted God... Is He Real? Does He exist? Was I wasting my time running to church every Sunday on the streets? Etc. etc. But I wanna let you youngsters know what I know; Yes God is Real! I'm a long way from being a religious fanatic. I am no zealot. And I have met a whole lot of folks (correctional managers, Administrators and "convicts") who will tell you "I'm a devout Christian". And some of them attend church Sunday after Sunday. And they are as duplicitous (with a capital "D") as one can imagine...

I've almost gotten to the point (seriously) where I become disenchanted when someone (especially prison officials and fellow convicts etc.) tells me "I'm a Christian". The moment they "say" it I assume (based upon empirical data!) they are backstabbers, liars, frauds and phonies. But - there is a difference in knowing about God and knowing Him... The devil knows about Him. The devil quoted scriptures to Jesus when He led Him up in the mountain to "tempt" Him. But Jesus said "my sheep know my voice (not "word", not "Bible" ... He said "voice") and a stranger they shall not follow" ... You can know about a treatment for cancer. But if you don't take the treatment (i.e. undergo radiation or chemotherapy) you'll "die" with your "knowledge". I can read about condoms all day long. I can become an "expert" on "condoms". I can even write a book about "condoms"... But "if" I'm crazy enough to screw a punk in prison (or on the streets) who is infected and I'm not protected. (There is a chance even with a condom) I will get aids. And all of my knowledge (is not power. My class ring was wrong. Knowledge is potential power. Power is taking action on what you know) about condoms shall not prevent me from getting a disease if I have unprotected sex with an infected partner. U feel me?

Ipso Facto, I'm convinced that so many (and I do mean many) dudes in prisons (and working in prisons) know "about" God. But if a man will lay on his face before God. If a man will develop a relationship with God. He can't smile in my face, call me "Sherman" and then stab me in my back. He can't sit back and proclaim "I believe in influencing minds by my testimony... Jesus is this and that" and walk away and plot against me... It's sad but it is true; I have been wronged, mistrusted, lied to and lied on more by folk who "read Daily Bread" etc. than I have by folks doing witch craft or black magic. I have looked into deep blue (brown and black) eyes and been told "Jesus Christ is Lord" by the same man (men) who secretly wished I was dead. I'm almost at the point where if a man tells me he is a "Christian" I want to r-u-n away from him. I am surrounded by "snakes"! Folk with "holes" in their "hearts". They would not know "love" and "truth" or "authenticity" if it knocked them in the head! ... That's them but now let me tell you about me. At P.V.S.P. I had a "homeboy" who was really from Atlanta. And we met and he extended the hand of prison fellowship to me. They called him "O.G." and his authentic last name was Mobley. And every time he came to the shower he would call me and chat with me while he was in the shower. And I was all nice and "homey" this and "brother" that. And as soon as he exited the shower I'd call Al (inmate Augustine) and talk about my "homeboy" like a dog... And I caught myself one night and had to ask myself "what the hell am I becoming?" I was beginning to "wear" two coats.

... For years I had been "known" as a dude who would not even "speak" to you if I didn't "like" you. And now I was "becoming" just as phony, fake and "two" faced as the folk I've railed against. I got down (all the way down) on my knees and pleaded with God to take duplicity out of me... I still got "mess" on me and I "am" a "sinner". But one thing that I don't (and won't) have is duplicity. I won't "fake" on you ... I felt like a walking contradiction! ... Captain Daniel Hahn (Sacto P.D.) is also duplicitious. Captain Hahn sells drugs. He (literally) had kids (on the streets) out on the streets selling crack and speed. I have it on firm confirmation that A. this dude may be a police chief one day. B. He is as crooked as the New York cops who worked for John Gotti. Daniel Hahn reminds me of Deputy Sheriff Chu Vue who murdered C.O. Low (who worked at C.M.F.) in his own drive-way. Deputy Sheriff Vu has two "gangsta" brothers accused of "other" murders. And here Vu was running around with a badge, gun, and a uniform... as quiet as it is kept Captain Daniel Hahn, Deputy Vu, associate wardens Spearman and Bunnell should all be sharing a cell in jail... They are "thugs" and "criminals"....

These people (Captain Hahn, A.W. Bunnell, Vu, Spearman, D.L. Criner, T. Negrete, Wally Tucker etc.) are criminals in uniform ... Lt. Webster fears Bunnell and Spearman more than a Blood fears a Crip. Web fears Bunnell and Spearman more than a rat fears a cat. They are deadly... IF (when) I'm transferred out of New Folsom (again) I assure you I will (at Donovan, High Desert, Salinas etc.) end up dead. And when I am dead I command you (my family, lawyers, Ann Patterson, Josh, Mark Merin etc.) to talk to Max Lemon, James Mattocks, Webster, Wendy K. Meyers, Michael Bein, Michael Snedeker, Arnold Erickson and E. Ivan Trusillo etc. "About" Bunnell, Spearman, Duclos, Criner, Tucker and Scarsella etc. hell talk to Andy Furillo! ... My blood will (ultimately) be on Mike Bunnell and Marion E. Spearman's hands! ... Former LAPD Sergeant ("Doc") Riwaed Ford told me "If I were you I'd beg the Governor not to let them transfer you again.... You know Walker, Kennedy, Schroeder, Virga and Macomber are not gonna let you die on their watch. Mrs. Kennedy is a "Saint". But Sherman, they are going to "kill" you dead the minute Bunnell orchestrates another transfer... The biggest mistake you could have ever made was writing about Bunnell in a book.... What were you thinking?" Doc continued "I heard your dad (CDW Terry L. Rosario) tell you years ago to stay out of staff business! And your hardheaded ass did not listen!".... Bob Blasier R U Reading?

It is now 2:10 Am and I'm not able to sleep. I'm so pregnant in my spirit with this word I can't hardly see straight. I need to get this tome out of my belly and into the schools. I need Jason Durtchi, C.J. Sheron and Daniel Sample to get this tome... I spoke to (several folks) Aaron Fernander today. It still mesmerizes me to call him "principal". It feels like it was just yesterday when he and I were running around his daddy's grocery store. And he was attending Albany State College. And he used to tell me "Sherman, I will be a principal one day". And now Ralph Bunche Middle School in Atlanta. It belongs to my Buddy Aaron

... Principal Aaron Fernander told me today "Boy that K.K.K. tome is gonna be off the hook! Pragmatically you should have written it a long while ago. That book can only be written by a "prisoner". Andrew Young can't write this ("K.K.K.") tome. I'm a principal with darn near a doctorate degree and I can't write "that" book". Aaron continued "if you write one third of the stuff you know(first hand) about Creflo Dollar and Leroy Jenkins etc. they may try to sue you".... Aaron continued "Creflo got 4 Rolls Royces and a Jet. You might not want to tell what you know about Dr. Dollar".... For the record - I have denied (for years) having ever met Creflo. At this juncture I am not prepared to retract that "denial". If Creflo knows God I hope he'll pray for me!... Aaron concluded "Sherman, more important than anything else Bro. Your status, with stripes on yo (sic) shoulders. Having walked and talked with Andy Young, Jesse Jackson and Hosea Williams etc. and the stripes you have because you've survived in level four California Prisons etc. etc. you can reach Black Boys in Larver Homes, Hollywood court, Watts and even in trailer parks whom I'd never reach...

"As a principal I am going to make certain all my 8th grade boys get "K.K.K.". If they're old enough to listen to rap, go to the mall and the movies they're old enough to read that darn book! Sherman, they are joining gangs at 8 and 9 years old now. Hell, Jay-Z told Oprah he was selling dope (in the 90's) at 13. If a boy in the "Hood" (Barrio or trailer park) can sell drugs on a street corner at 13, why can't he read a book in a library at 14?"

Aaron concluded "I disagree vehemently with some of what you say, do and write. I have been disagreeing with your butt on some stuff since you were a 3 year old boy.... But I be darn if I'm going to set myself up for a lawsuit by disallowing your "words" in any school ... And if them wardens in California try to keep your book out you should sue them. The ACLU would take that suit. Willy Gary or Gerry Spence might take that one"...

"I heard her (I.S.U. C.O.) tell you that Bunnell wants you out of this prison", inmate Brandon Hughes told me at M.C.S.P. a month before I transferred. "From what I could hear she's saying they know your celly (Emslander AKA "Noodles") lied on you. But because you wrote in some justice (sic) books bout (sic) Bunnell and Pieper he wants you gone". Hughes continued "I could not believe how long they (I.S.U.) searched your cell looking for Pieper's address! Don't they know you gots a photostatic (sic) memory? Dude told you that Bunnell wanted Pieper's address out of your cell and if you didn't come out they would extract you"... I had written Doug Pieper Jr. a missive at M.C.S.P. explaining that I knew Bunnell murdered his dad (Captain Doug Pieper Sr.) and Bunnell confiscated the missive; stole it and sent rogue officers to "find that address and bring it to me". ... Yet, a year later as I lay in Coalinga Regional Medical Center I told C.O. Pieper his Aunt's (Evette Pieper) address from memory! And Pieper knew about Bunnell sending me to P.V.S.P. to "catch Valle Fever and write a book about that". At P.V.S.P. inmate Jose Zuniga told me "you should pay me for not stabbing you... Tucker offered me a carton of cigarettes to stab you".... My celly Dopey was handcuffed by Tucker, Deathridge and Criner one day. They took him to the watch office and tried to talk him into claiming I "raped" him and stabbing me. When he refused they (D.L. Criner, Wally Tucker and C.O. Deathridge) beat him... He wrote out everything Criner and those guys told him. He signed and dated it and I mailed it to an Attorney... Charles Hedrick (Chucky) lay in C.R.M.C. with his teeth knocked out and he tells me "Everybody knew Tucker and Criner wanted you dead. Raven was gonna "hit" you. What did you do to piss Tucker and Criner off? Criner is a "Christian"... Inmate Jimmy Van Horn was in ad-seg with me at M.c.S.P. He stated "When they rolled you up C.O. Warren told us Bunnell set you up! And C.O. Gregory told us he had personally read your book. And Gregory said "Bunnell is trying to kill that brother"....

... Peter called Bunnell (and recorded the call.... It is Legal to do so in Switzerland!) and pleaded with him not to transfer me to P.V.S.P. Peter told Bunnell "Ich personally apologize on behalf of Sherman for what he wrote about you in his buch! Und Ich am willing to issue a public apology on behalf of NAPS... " Mr. Bunnell (on a recorded telephone call! The tape is in the hot lil hands of a licensed attorney!) told Peter "Manning crossed the line. I don't fight fair and I don't play clean ... When he gets to P.V.S.P. if he doesn't wear a bullet, take or knife or commit suicide.... Valley Fever will give him a great book to write about". And Bunnell hung up on him... Peter called Gloria Romero, Hickman, Woodford and Hurtle to try to report it. He got all recordings and voice mail. He emailed Keith Chandler at Attorney Sander's office in W. Sacto CA.... And we lost! And Bunnell won! He got me to P.V.S.P. with all deliberate haste... And Lieutenant Massey told me years ago to "Leave Bunnell alone! He's crooked and powerful!" And I.S.U. (Investigative Services Unit via the "gang coordinator") Lt. Reid told me to "stay away from Bunnell. Don't write about that man; he is dangerous!" And Sergeant R.N. Saunders told me "You think I'll kick yo ass... You f --- with Bunnell and he will send you to meet your maker".... Bob Blasier?

... And (psychiatric social worker) Chuck Christiansen told me one day at Mule Creek "Don't say that name (Bunnell) out loud. I sit in committee every week with Bunnell. He is a very, very corrupted man.... cc II Cusick told me that Bunnell is in The Green Wall". Chuck continued "I have heard Bunnell talking about you, Mr. Manning, to Sylvia Garcia, Cusick and to Lt. Cherry. I can't tell you everything because I have to protect my job... But please - whatever you do have your family check on your enemies at P.V.S.P ". And Chuck whispered "Sanchez is at P.V.S.P. on A-yard I promise you.... Bunnell wants you ..." An hour later cc I Costa came to my door (in earshot of Brandon Hughes) and I told him (again! I'd already filed an appeal) about Ray Sanchez Jr. and Costa mentioned Bunnell and there was "no Ray Sanchez" at P.V.S.P. ... I asked for an emergency telephone call to Attorney Murray J. Janus. Costa said "sure". He told me "I'll tell sergeant Gentille to give you a call... " Sgt. Gentille came to the door "A.W. Bunnell said no phone call! You are leaving this prison!"...

When I was still on the yard at Mule Creek (M.C.S.P.) I recall (vividly) Wayman Berry telling me that "Lieutenant (name redacted for security reasons at the recommendation of counsel) _____ told me that Mike Bunnel is coming to this prison soon. If he does you need to run. You remember your clash with Bunnell at New Folsom when Captain (name deleted at the recommendation of counsel) _____ told you to "stay away from Bunnell. He is crooked".... I also recall being in ad seg with Daniel Masterson and him telling me "When you left the yard Duclos threw a block party in 2 bldg. She has fully adopted Emslander as her son. They (C.O. Duclos and inmate James "Noodles" Emslander) have been caught several times in the staff bathroom having sex. C.O. Duclos (according to Daniel who is Caucasian. It should be noted that this author has never and does not consider Mrs. Duclos to be racist.) hates intelligent black men. Bunnell had her, Cutsinger, Parks and Lively (correctional officers) working and plotting against you". Masterson continued "dude you were walking around with your head in the clouds oblivious to the plotting which was going on. I was not even close to you on the yard. But I saw it. Ray saw it... C.O. Pogue said it. Whatever you did to Bunnell was an extremely dangerous thing!" Masterson continued "Atlas (AKA Alonzo Collins), Joker (inmate Johnson - B.G.F.), Chucky Pyle, Diamond (M. Young), C.O. Gregory and even Lyle Menendez & T.P. said you were set-up by Bunnell. Bunnell manipulated Duclos and Emslander to get you... Noodles was indigent when you went to ad. seg. Totally and completely broke. But when you were rolled up he began to receive money, packages and special purchases etc. All compliments of C.O. Duclos, Lt. Cherry and A.W. Mike Bunnell.... Even I.S.U., Captain Wilson and Captain steel were involved" ....

I clearly recall being at C.R.M.C. (hospital) in Coalinga and this 6 ft. 6 skinny black sergeant (they call him "Drew") Andrews coming into my hospital room. He closed (to my utter surprise) the door. He stated to me in hushed tones that he was sorry for what happened to me. And he was "praying" for me. And "Criner is my friend Manning. And I don't know why he got involved with this mess. Perhaps they manipulated, pressured or scared him. But I don't like it Bro".

Sergeant Andrews was interrupted by C.O. Deshazo opening the door with one of those fake ass smiles saying "You cool in here sarge?" Drew replied "Manning is 80 pounds soak and wet and chained to the bed. Why would I not be allright?" Deshazo stated "Tucker told me to check on you Bro." Drew closed the door and whispered "He's a straight cross buring Klansman. Watch what you say around him.... Web (Lt. Webster) is a friend of mine and he told me the whole story. The Mule Creek A.W. (Bunnell). Your special transfer. Tucker and Freedland them blockading you from medical treatment.... They told me that one day CCI Freedland was working the block as a C.O. (in uniform) and you darn near fainted. Your celly did a man down (meaning kicking the door yelling "medical emergency") and Freedland came up to your cell and saw you short of breath and blacking out and told your celly Manning gotta wait til after count to die. Cause he ain't leaving this cell till after count! They say you had to wait 2 hours to go to medical. And when you got there Freedland told the nurse you was (sic) faking. And you did this all the time. And the nurse gave you an asthma breathing treatment, ignores your sweats and gut pain; refused to call the doctor and sent you back." Bob Blasier?

I interjected "And yes an hour later Dopey did another man down and Freedland refused to come and check on me. And he told his co-worker not to come. Twin came to my door and said "Freedland said to tell you yo daddy Tucker will be here in the morning and he can send you back to medical ... Dude is tripping man... You allright?" I said "Nall I'm not allright I can barely breathe". He said "Yeah Freedland said if you can talk you can breathe".... I told Drew "I thought I was going to die that night and the next morning C.O. Tucker showed up and he refused from 6:30 AM - 2:30 AM to call medical. When Ruth came on I did a "man down" and Ruth let me go to medical. When I got there she (the nurse) said "it's only your asthma". I saw Dr. Benyamin and Dr. Phi leaving the bldg. and I said "nurse, please let the doctor see my bloated stomach". She slammed the holding cell door and said "They're going to a meeting Mr. Manning. There is nothing wrong with you. Guys stomachs swell up and they get short of breath all the time! I already see in your chart where you say somebody (Bunnell) sent you here to get Valley Fever. Well you aint transferring and you don't have Valley Fever so chill"... I filed two emergency appeals and they "disappeared". I'm told CCII Shannon routinely threw appeals away. I know Lt. Herrera (in collusion with Marion E. Spearman) shredded appeals routinely.... That day with Drew at C.R.M.C. was one of only two times my hospital door was closed. I used to complain about "doctor patient confidentiality" and requested to speak with Dr. Griffin (whom I trusted) in private. Rikalo, Criner and Negrete all said "no".. After being in the hospital ten months Meyers got me pen and paper (at Dr. Griffin's insistence)... And I wrote Dr. Griffin a missive telling him what Bunnell had done and how long I'd been denied medical treatment at P.V.S.P. I told him about Spearman, Tucker and R.N. Bond. I told him I feared for my life if I lived. He called the warden and Yates promised to take care of it; a lie!

... The other time my hospital door was closed was when Director of nurses (Coalinga Regional Medical Center) Lori came into my room with Joe Rikalo. Lori closed the door and with that Mississippi drawl she said "Mr. Manning, did you tell Cindy (L.V.N.) that (on the advice of counsel I shall give this hospital employee a pseudonym: Tonya) Tonya is on crystal meth". My heart began to beat very, very hard. First of all I respect Lori so much! She and 99 1/2 percent of her staff (Linda LiHong, Jessica, Norma, Jeannie, Susan, Judith Redmond, Mike Lupo, Jeff, John Hutchinson etc.) were great to me. They were like family! Beautiful people who cared deeply about me... so I felt very conflicted about this issue! ... Lori said "Cindy said you told her you think Tonya is on meth" . I (lied!) replied "I was joking Lori. I shouldn't have said that but it was a bad joke!" Lori said "I trust Joe Rikalo cause he (sic) been working here for years. He won't ever mention we had this conversation. The door is closed." Lori looked anxious "Tonya drinks those energy drinks and what R those Joe? Rock Stars? She does not use meth"... Later Cindy told me "I'm sorry I told Lori but I've been hearing rumors a lot about Tonya using meth. Not just from you so I wanted to get to the bottom of it. And I don't think you were joking".

Later Nurse Norma (I called her momma Norma. A fat white girl from Mississippi. Her sister is also a nurse and Norma was so, so good to me! She is a travelling nurse so she's back home in Miss. now and telling this won't hurt her. If it would I would not tell it!) told me "Cindy is just brown nosing. Don't ever tell her anything. We all know Tonya is on something. I thought she was gonna puke on you when she was looking at your picc line... It takes 5-10 minutes tops to install a picc line. It took her and Dr. DeGucchi 4 hours to put in your picc line. It's a wonder she didn't kill you she was stoned".... During the installation of my picc line Tonya was jumping, snatching out the line, sweating and .... It completely frightened me. I had nightmares (for months) about Tonya jumping and snatching out my picc line. It took 4 hours. And later I had to hit the emergency button because I almost bled to death due to the picc line ... Tonya had performed numerous ultrasounds on me and scared me everytime... Dr. DeGucchi allowed her to stick a needle in me (against rules - she is not a doctor or a nurse) to draw Valley Fever fluid out of my lung and she nearly killed me... Hello Bob Blasier!

Having been at C.R.M.C. for nearly a year I was very close to some people... Pushing me in my wheel chair I asked (on the advice of Counsel since I intend to litigate ... I shall use a pseudonym here...) Joe about Tonya "Oh yes she is addicted Bro. And (also a pseudonym) Tom Wilson used to be addicted to meth too when he was a maintenance man. So he is trying to help Tonya but she is messed up"....

Few days later I asked (sobriquet) pseudonym on the advice of Attorney Murray J. Janus) Willie Williams about (K) Tonya and he stated "Lori, Dr. DeGucchi and all the big wigs had a meeting with Tonya last week. They know she is addicted! And they're offering to put her in rehab! She's been on meth a long time!".... That is when I became angry... You knowingly allow a known addict (high on meth) to perform invasive procedures on me? That is the height of gross medical negligence; if not attempted murder! ... I got a roommate (Mexican P.V.S.P. inmate) who also got a picc line installed (Mark Ravis are you reading this? Shawn Khorrami, Louis Pacella and Scott Leviant are you all ready to go to war?) and when he returned to the room 3 hours later without provocation from me he said "Dude Tonya is on speed! She was jumping, sweating and shaking! And Dr. DeGucchi kept trying to get in her pants asking if he could take her to dinner... He knew she was high"...

When I was at UMC in Fresno a physician (authentic name - Dr. Chris Burns) sat on my bed and asked C.O. Lee (Black dude) to step out... Dr. Burns began mashing my stomach and then grabbed my (private part) genitalia. "How does it feel when I massage your c--k?" I went off! I began yelling and Lee came back into the room. "What's happening in here?" I go "Dude is a fag! He grabbed my ...." Dr. Burns told Lee "I'm gonna kick him out of the hospital. Send him back to the prison to let them care for him." Lee said "Kick him out for what?" Dr. Burns said "He doesn't want to be touched". I said call my Doctor Dr. James is my doctor:... Dr. Burns sat back on my bed and told C.O. Lee and I "I have a master's degree in surgery. I'm way better trained than Dr. James. I'm ..." He tried to discharge me. My nurse paged Dr. James and he was livid. He came in on his off day and confronted Dr. Burns. He explained I was near death and would not be going back to P.V.S.P.

There is some (other) type of blemish on Dr. Burns that Dr. James would not share with me. But I'd stake my life that Dr. James knows something (about Burns being disciplined or something) he wouldn't or couldn't tell me... Dr. James, Dr. McCray, Dr. Roper, Dr. Libke, Dr. Sheik, Ross, Dr. Fontaine etc. were very good to me ...

Dr. Ericka Kasper (black physician) told C.O. Daly and Merrielles "You need to stop torturing Mr. Manning. I get that you don't like him. But you keep belittling and arguing at him and this man is almost dead. He weighs 90 lbs! You keep running his blood pressure up your're gonna kill him and I will report you . Leave my patient alone!"....

Tyler Tony (Texas Adm. Student, who were his two comrades on CBS with Harry Smith on 9/28/09? G.B.G./HEART needs to speak with both of them), Bryan Mealer, Andy Barr (politico) and Ryan Hreljac etc. are you all perusing this? ...

Let me tell yall (Gen "Y" and the Facebook Generation ... I'm not writing to Baby Boomers! Glenn Beck has you all covered) something: When you give up your rights and join me in prison you will live amongst snakes, liars and broken bruthas! It is a sad and pitiful sight here in Hades. You lose your power, personality and your individuality. And he who has the gold makes the rules. The CCPOA (California Correctional Peace Officers association) AKA (Ca. corrupted predator officer association) controls the prisons in California. And unlike inmates) they stick together like crap on stink. They are bullies, thugs and criminals. And a lot of their members are perverts and bisexuals. Years ago C.O. Duclos told inmate James A. Emslander "I like to watch! Men on men! Women on women! All of that... You should do gay porn when you get out. Gay porn scenes pay ten times more than straight porn. You can get $ 5 grand for a man on man scene and only $ 500.00 for a man on woman "she told him....

C.O. Coggenshall (at M.C.S.P.) told my pal Brandon Hughes "I'll give you a pack of Camels to finger your A.H. and jerk off while I watch you".... Brandon said "You're out of your mind dude I'll assault you". And Brandon could (and did) not report it because he knew the CCPOA would retaliate and he'd end up dead at Pelican Bay! ... I heard Coggenshall (with my ears) when he told Brandon that...

My pal Joseph Latham was also (allegedly; I did not witness this but I definitely believe it) propositioned by C.O. Coggenshall. "I'll put a $ 100.00 money order in your account if you lay face down and finger yourself for five minutes and then turn over and masturbate". Coggenshall said (allegedly)... " "Should I write a 602?" Joseph wrote to me (a lawyer has that missive)... I (reluctantly) had to tell him "no". Daniel Masterson is a living witness that when you write them up (i.e. crystal meth Baker) they will "get" you (and me!) one way or another! Sooner or later they win! Lance Corcoran and Michael Jiminez make the LAPD Rampart division look like "Sterling characters" Attorney John Lippsmeyer told me. "You are too brilliant, too black and too powerful for C.D.C. Mike Bunnell wants you dead" Attorney Donald Dorfman told me... "They lied to me. Lt. (per CC III (A) Patricia Kennedy's order I am disallowed to speak negatively of any C.S.P. Sac. staff! And I obey Madame Kennedy! ... Yes I do! I think this dude retired anyway but call him "puncho"). Puncho lied to me so he, G.S. and Mike Martel could transfer you to M.C.S.P." Attorney Paul Comiskey stated to me. "They knew Bunnell would end up at M.C.S.P. and they wanted you there" Attorney Comiskey told me. Paul Comiskey started the famed Prison Law Office in the 70's. "Sherman I fear for your life in C.D.C. I can see them putting you in some shu program and murdering you .... I used to be a Catholic priest" Comiskey told me. "So I'm gonna have to advise you to pray Sherman... These people (Bunnell, Corcoran, Jiminez etc.) are extremely corrupt, powerful and dangerous" Attorney Comiskey concluded....

... Attorney John Lippsmeyer stated "Attorney Kathy Druliner's husband is a prosecutor.... She (Attorney Mrs. Druliner) has heard from David (Attorney David P. Druliner) something from within C.D.C. about you. They know that you fear being transferred to Corcoran and killed." Attorney John Paul Lippsmeyer continued "Sherman David knows all about Bunnell's record and your state of mind when you wrote these threatening letters. Who (in their right mind) would write a Clayton County Red Neck Sheriff and say "if you don't release all black men in 3 days I'm gonna kill you?" You were trying to catch a case (and succeeded!) to stop the transfer Bunnell has orchestrated!". Lippsmeyer continued "Back then you did not know Pat Kennedy, Jimbo Walker or Terry Rosario. You had nobody to save you... Dr. Tye Hedblad is prepared to testify under oath that your fear of being murdered by Bunnell's cohorts at Corconan etc. led you to decompensate to the extent that you wrote threats you had no means, motive or opportunity to carry out.... Hedblad's credibility is sacrosanct because he is not some 'whore' of the court you are paying... He works for C.D.C."....

OH how I should have listened to Attorney John Paul Lippsmeyer. Druliner was/is a friend of his and he was trying to give me good advice... Attorney Donald Dorfman (and Lippsmeyer) knew that Mike Bunnell was plotting to "get" me. But I was too arrogant, naive, and distracted to "listen" to them. And I grew up thinking that every time I heard the word "conspiracy" that people were "paranoid" !! I did not believe in "conspiracies" period! No way! No How! .. Hillary Clinton claimed a "right wing conspiracy" against President Bill Clinton. And as recently as 4/2/09 President Clinton said he still believes "there was a right wing conspiracy" against him even accusing him of "murder". "And" says President Clinton "they will run down President Obama's poll numbers and run up his opposition. They are well funded and strategic"... Knowing (what Attorneys Lippsmeyer, Comiskey and Dorfman were trying to tell me) what I've learned about Bunnell, Scarsella, R.N. Saunders, Duclos, Cherry, Sylvia Garcia, Marion E. Spearman etc. etc. it appears that the "joke" was on me. I was the victim of a "right wing conspiracy" by the CCPOA (California Corrupted Predator Officer Association)! Lance, Jiminez and Bunnell should be in jail!...

I spoke with "magic Mike" Attorney Michael Morchower (He's the second best trial attorney in the State of Virginia!) about my Valley Fever, Bunnell etc. etc. And Mr. Morchower stated "if I were in California I would pay $ 25 grand to watch you (Sherm) try this case... Pragmatically, this is one of the few cases in which I'd recommend you hire a lawyer to second chair you. You are not sharp enough to legally manipulate against opposing counsel..... But" Attorney Morchower continued "You are a master orator... Johnnie Cochran stated that everything in his career had led him and prepared him to try O.J. Simpson's case and deal with Marc Fuhrman". Attorney Morchower proceeded "Sherman, your life experience; years in pulpits and polishing our oratorical skills etc. have brought you to this place. I would pay to see you argue this case before a jury of your peers. This is your case. If you were in Virginia I would do the motions, plot strategy. And make objections etc. I'd let you argue". ... Coming from Attorney Magic Michael Morchower I have to ask of the following: Sean Musgrove, Bob Blasier, Becki Kammerling, Don Dorfman, John Rogers, Michael W. Bien (Rosen Bien & Asaro), Steven Cron (Cron Israels & Stark), Blair Berk and Ephraim Margolin etc.... R U Reading?...

Prosecutor Mary Hanlon made an illegal, unethical and criminal deal with Ricardo (for the first time ever - I talk about my case later in the book....) Calvario to send me to prison. She expunged his criminal record. She threatened Richard Martz not to speak with my investigator Captain Tom Owens. She colluded with Detective Dave Winkler and Robert Altman. Mary

Hanlon bribed Attorney Robert Thomas Burns and Curt Waite to sell me out. She threatened Bret Nelson and then he disappeared out of jail... She brought Russell Camosky from Richmond Virginia to testilie against me. He (Camosky) was out of jail on Bail for "rape". And even in the face of having absconded while on bail Mary Hanlon Stone (the prosecutor) was caught at Russell's hotel (I can prove this) performing fellatio on Camosky. She even gave him money ($ 200.00) for sex. Mary used cocaine with Russell (we can corroborate). And I am told Mary Hanlon was an excort (prostitute) while she was in college and during her first year of law school. She is also reported to have had a sexual affair with the Honorable Robert Altman.

.... Attorney Janus had his investigator to locate a witness (Daniel Clay H.) who could/would dispute everything Russell was going to say on the stand. I was given a so-called confidential telephone call with Daniel. I later learned that both Judge Altman and Mary Hanlon Stone had listened in on the call. Ipso Facto, Altman sustained his own motion to disallow us to fly Daniel (same way Mary Hanlon flew her Beau Russell) to testify....

We (Captain Tom Owens) located a deputy sheriff (Sanford) who stated "Everybody knows Ricardo Calvario is a prostitute"... Judge Altman called (extrajudicial contact) the deputy and coerced him into not testifying! ...

... Let's revisit Tom Cruise a moment. I've learned that Tom got a woman (yes, he's "Bi") pregnant in 2001. She began to have pregnancy complications and Tom's scientology religion caused him to refuse to let the lady get 'medicine'. And as a result of Tom's Zealotry the baby died. "It was as if Tom was relieved that she died" a confidential source stated.

... on 9/28/09 Dr. Courdy stated to me "You are still suffering from PTSD due to your lengthy hospital stay and Valley Fever"... On 9/29/09 Mr. Costa repeated the PTSD claim... On 9/28/09 C.O. Bond asked me "why did you cell with that cutthroat Dearaujo?" That dude aint (sic) no good"....

On 9/28/09 a very young (24) C.O. named Novak asked "Are you Sherman D. Manning?" He (Mr. Novak) and C.O. Woodard were working 8 bldg. "Dude" Novak proceeded "I heard about you at San Quentin". He continued "Scott Peterson hates you! I worked death row and he reads your books. Your name is crap on death row". I was told of a script writer (on death-row) named Jenkins. A lil old black man.

I was also told (by another guard who worked death-row) that Richard Ramirez is a freak. He exposes himself to kids in the visiting room. He gets naked photos from 12 year old lil girls!... A correctional officer who routinely read his mail told me that. How/why are 12 year old girls writing to a man on death row? Where are the parents?

... Scott Peterson is one of the most polite convicts I've ever met" a guard told me. A "polite" murderer! Eric and Lyle Menendez can also be very "polite" and cunning. Eric (I repeat) politely borrowed my money. And he also has never paid Richard "Doc" Ford his $ 400.00 back...

Eric Menendez? What if I told you that he was in a mop closet with a black male guard (Wally LaFfitte) performing fellatio! I've never told it but (there are witnesses) it is old news within C.D.C. Eric's brother Lyle is extremely close to Mike Bunnell, Lt. Cherry, C.O. Baker and C.O. Duclos. (I did not witness this) Lyle was supposedly intimate with C.O. Coggenshall and he (Lyle) definitely had close ties to Mike Bunnell... Bam Bam:, MarmaDuke, Jerry Wines, Cartoon and Frank were all sexually involved with Lyle. C.O. Cutsinger and Duclos routinely allowed Lyle to enter into 2 bldg. and go to Jerry Wines' (AKA Joker) cell and have sex. As a building worker I've seen he-men become she-men in cells. I've seen outfits in arms and outfits (infits?) in anuses. But perhaps the strangest thing I ever witnessed with my eyes was C.O. Duclos, Lyle Menendez, Joker (Wines) and Daniel Job (lil man) in the cell together. C.O. Gregory was working control in 2 bldg. He beckoned me and whispered "Manning go 'sweep' by that cell and see what the f--- is going on. C.O. Duclos is in there". C.O. Duclos was sitting on Lyle's private.

Lyle had his t-shirt twisted up like a bra and he was simultaneously performing fellatio on Joker. And Joker was bending around (like "the Rubber Boy") fellationizing (if you will) Daniel Job.... They were off the hook! No condoms or protection; nothing! Just flesh to flesh risky behavior....

I spoke with Attorney Steve Sadow and he stated "I would love to come to CALI (sic) and prosecute your lawsuit. I'd do anything to watch Mike Bunnell get on the witness stand and explain himself.... I can't, however, represent you due to a conflict of interest. You reportedly have written negatively of Chris Brown. And I represent Chris..."

I spoke with Attorney Murray J. Janus again... "I need you on a non monitored telephone" he stated. In two hours a court order granted the call. And in early September 2009 Attorney Janus said "Sit down reverend and get this. I must be your lucky charm... When Russell Camosky lied on you and you were facing 20 plus years in Federal prison. Hell you had the Feds (led by a female special agent named Bonnie Strauss) looking for you. And sitting in my office one of my assistants (Scott Lechner) discovered that we (Bremner Baber and Janus) were representing a boy (in a civil suit) who had been maliciously wounded by Russell". Attorney Janus sounded like a Jewish T.D. Jakes now. "And" he continued, "it just so happened that at the same time Russell was lying on you and trying to extort you. You came to me (via a large sum of money I gave Attorney IRA London in New York for Janus... After I got my money back from Michael Morchower) at the same time we were suing Camoskys family.... Sometimes the stars just seem to line up.... My investigator just stumbled upon a memo which is going to turn your "cocci" lawsuit right side up!" Now I was getting excited! "Do tell, Do tell!" I stated.... "Long time ago in my office why" Attorney Janus asked.... "Did we have to call an ambulance for you?" I thought a moment and replied "Oh I had an asthma attack". Attorney Janus stated "Bingo! B.J. just provided me with a memo issued to all 33 California prisons months prior to Bunnell sending you (special delivery) to P.V.S.P. The "memo is papered gold for your case... It reads in part "Individuals suffering from emphysema, asthma and other compromised medical conditions must not be transferred to the following institutions". The first prison on the list is Pleasant Valley State Prison! ... I'm calling Stanley (I. Greenberg), Blair (Berk) and Mesereau to see if they'll take your case... After "K.K.K." is published lawyers will seek you out. It's not "if" but how much they'll (C.D.C.) pay you". ... I was trembling, on the one hand this is absolutely exciting.... I hope Robert Johnson, Joey Grissett, Denny, Craig Gilstrap, or Ronald Francis, Mike Crowder or Daniel Clay! ... If I could find Brian (he lived on Grace St. and worked at Exxon Gas Station when I met him. Last name was Fasal? Faskohl? etc.) "I would prove Mary Hanlon was hooker!"....

The Sacramento "jail" Captain? Go get David Quindt, James Heath Teague, Hugh Michael Hughes or Joe Wilson and I can prove "that" captain is corrupted! ... Those inmates at Sac County Jail are not committing suicide. They are being murdered.

.... Deputy Manning (Sacto County Jail) told me "I wanna get out of here Bro. We are killing inmates here every day! Manning this place is corrupt".... At Sacto County Jail I met officer Brad Robinson. He was with the Sac P.D. and he deals drugs on the side. This guy reminded me of Rafael Perez of the notorious LAPD Rampart Division. Officer Robinson was connected to C.O. Wally Laffitte and Lt. S.L. Scarsella. And Brad used them (Wally and Stephen) to smuggle drugs into prisons....

"In that call to Murray J. Janus he also stated "You've been writing that Sgt. R.N. Saunders was fired, demoted and/or forced to retire.... The CCPOA protects their own. Saunders works outside the gate at New Folsom (maintenance) driving a trash truck and is being paid like a sergeant. He was on "probation" and still working at the prison! "They say 'only in America" Try "Only in California". You are a convict working at a "prison".

... On 9/30/09 I was called to see a sergeant at 8:05 AM. I knew this youngster when he first got his job in C.D.C. He was still living in his parent's house and had a motorcycle. We used to (verbally) sex play all the time. He really liked Aaron J. Lindwedel (AKA "Blue") a lot... Since he promoted he's a legend in his own mind. His arms are sleeved (tatooed) and it looks very unprofessional... He says "You wrote a letter to Jimmy claiming Lt. (deleted) and L (deleted) are stealing yo (sic) mail... Why can't you follow normal procedures and file a staff complaint? Why you gotta write a personal note to the warden?" I felt a tad bit perturbed. When we file formal complaints we are criticized for not attempting to resolve things informally. And yet my informal attempt is a "problem". I'm not going to defy Madame Patricia Kennedy's order (Mr. K don't play!)! This is why I'm not publishing the sergeant's name.... As I was exiting the office he yells "I expect you to go straight 'home'". I replied "my home is Atlanta so I won't be going home". I returned to the cell and (literally) prayed for this sergeant. Back in the day I'd a been on the yard at 10:55 AM waiting on Jimbo to walk through so I could get him to spank this arrogant, egotistical, bitter and illiterate sergeant. But I've grown up. And I am able to look within and not just without. I saw how intimidated he is by intelligence. I serve, worship and praise the God of Abraham, Isaac and Jacob. And if I expect God to overlook and to forgive the Jacob (trickster, conman and the supplanter) in me. How dare I not have compassion on a 30 year old boy trying to be a sergeant... I apologize (to the world) for what I wrote about sergeant Blackburn (on page 225) in "Blue Eyed Blonde" Book II. I was being "mean". How dare I expect compassion when I give anger? I was wrong. Blackburn is a human being just like you and me. And we have all been weak, sad and lonely. I was wrong!!!

On 9/30/09 "Gregory" (and his fine sista Brandy) appeared on the price is right! Greg went to Jackson Hole Wyoming for 6 nights. Greg is a part of U.C. Dance. G.B.G./HEART needs Gregory. I need U.S. Mint Green (Ryan or Heather) to find Gregory; Email him and tell him what page he is on in this book.... Gregory drop me a line forthwith!.... I reach out to Kirk Johnson, Reggie Shaw (Utah), Chris Horton (Sacto) and to Mike Crowder (Rich. VA). We have stipends for Tadd Carr, Michael Parker (Walnut CA.), Billy Bell (L. Florida), Victor Smalley and Maxwell Hanger... I need to hear from Ryan Hreljac, Travis Denison and from Brian Boykin (Rich. VA.) ASAP....

.. I spoke recently with a "white" Crip rapper. We were at Mule Creek together. He was still there when I left. He told me all about the Mike Bunnell, Duclos, "Noodles" etc. Rumors about me when I left. "Atlas (AKA Alonzo Collins) told me for show (sic) U wuz set up dude! He say Berry and E. J. Told U 2 leave Bunnell alone. Even C.O. Warren and O'Neal say they told u... C.O. Gregory say he wuz gon call a lawyer bout how Bunnell played u yo"....

This white Crip also mentioned other rappers (i.e. Goldy, "Trouble" - AKA Anthony Miranda etc.) at M.C.S.P. who knew me. He told me about (I already knew) Suge Knight and his homosexual escapades at the Creek.... He asked me about Mike Henrickson (Eric Menendez - gay lover! Henrickson is now at P.V.S.P. I mention him in other parts of this tome...) and Henrickson was suing the archdiocese in LA. Because he was (allegedly) molested by a Catholic priest in L.A. as a kid... The white Crip indicated (also) that "Lyle" made a pass (his claim) at him at M.C.S.P.... "I got a "R" (meaning rape) in my jacket Atl... And I was rolled up for getting head (fellatio) from a queen on the yard. Lyle wanted some of dis (sic) white pipe"....

... So anyway the white Crip is very (very) familiar with Daniel Hahn, Deputy Manning and... (the white Crip is Brooks wintermute.)

My critics (there are many) will doubt my data (Facts! If I don't know it I call it a "claim") about Benny Hinn, Captain Hahn, Gary Condit and some of these other miscreants. But I have not told it "all". I'm well cognizant that "we" wanna put our police and prosecutors on pedestals. And we have a "need" to believe in them. And many (I salute and honor the men who do a terrific job!) of them are great! But I grew up with policemen, police managers and even police chiefs (i.e. Ralph Batts, Police Commissioner Reginald Eaves, Lee P. Brown, Chief Eldrin Bell, T.J.

Scipio, Mike Scandrick etc.) as personal friends. And I've known (personally) police managers who smoked dope, sold crack and committed murder(s) on the side. I've also known (I.E. Eldrin Bell - American Idol Justin Barrino's dad!... and Alexander Hamilton... and my dear friend who is a "Major" with the Fulton County Sheriff's Dept.... Major Raleigh Rucker...) Folk in law enforcement who risked their lives for others...

But there are many "bad cops". My close associate (former LAPD Homicide Cop, Police Detective, Vice and Narcotics officer and Member of the Elite Undercover Child Pornography Task Force) Richard "Doc" Ford is in prison convicted of "murder". While he won't discuss his "case" with me. He told me "The LAPD Rampart division was nothing. You don't know the half. If I told you 25 % of what I now about LAPD, deputy and prosecutorial corruption etc. you'd write it. They'd kill you, me and then go for our families .. Atlanta (AKA Sherman) under no circumstances will I ever discuss the LAPD secrets I know with you... Give it up"....

If you had not read about Chu Vue in the newspapers and I wrote about it, you'd think it was a Hollywood script. Gary Vue (28 years old), Chong Vue (30)? both are gang members suspected of "many" murders! Their Brother Chu? Sacramento County (decorated) deputy Sheriff. Two gangsters and a cop... Chu finds cell phone pictures of his wife (David E. Kelly, Cody Sheldon and Jerry Bruckheimer are you reading?) having oral sex with correctional officer Steve Lo. I knew C.O. Lo... Chu's brothers are wanted on murder charges in Minnesota. And now Sacto Deputy Chu Vue is sitting in Sacto County Jail (where I'm told he killed inmates and made it appear to be hanging/suicides) on murder charges... Police Chief Jerry Dyer (Fresno) ought to be in jail on murder, conspiracy and racketeering charges. .. When I was at a hospital in Fresno CA. officer Figueroa (wife of C.O. Figurroa who was felled by the Cocci which nearly killed me) told me "Manning our "Chief" is more dangerous than John Gotti was. He is a murderer and he hates blacks and Mexicans!"...

I want kids at Huntsville High School (Texas), Lodi High, Northside High (Atl. Ga) and at schools all across this country to read this book and walk away equipped with a healthy fear of interaction with police, prosecutors and prison guards. Whether you believe I'm a good guy or a murderer is not relevant to me. I'm not running for "Mayor" of the city "Book Club". I am not your friend!

... Prison is my "nerve center"! It is my "command post, ministry, platform" and my "bullhorn:. I am buried alive in Bricks! And my m-a-i-n message to you is "Don't come here". Period! Innoculate and vaccinate yourself against prison. Education (and God-U-Cation) is the premiere vaccination/innoculation against incarceration! U feel me?

... I was in the Navy and the navy seal motto is "the only easy day is yesterday". And the most sacred vow of all is to "never leave a man behind". And the most sacred G.B.G./HEART vow is to "Leave as many men (and kids) behind as possible!" We aim to leave you behind! Behind means on the other side of our command post! I'm in the "red zone". I'm at "Ground Zero" for failed men... We are so void, angry, lonely, broken and bitter... I had a person type something for me the other week and when Attorney Steed Scott paid me a compliment ("you were well educated and connected") inside a criticism. The person only typed the criticism and deleted the compliment. He can't help it. I am convinced that more than 85% of the (damn near) 3 million U.S. prisoners have H.I.V.... And H.I.V. (Having Insufficient Vision) is deadly! ... The most dangerous (as I write about later) person on the planet is a person who has lost his/her vision... I'll re-state: Vision is not sight! Sight is vision's enemy! Sight shows what is. Vision shows what could be. When you get a gang of boys together who have no vision, no goals, no plans, no hopes and... It is a deadly, dastardly and a dangerous atmosphere. I've learned to pray in the spirit in order to survive in Hades. The environment here is unnatural and destructive... The last face I see at night is another man. First face I see in the morning is a "man". And some of these dudes get jobs and "work" together. I asked a guy "are you gay?" and he said "Hell No (p. 47 of 49) why U say dat?"... I said "You work, eat, sleep, crap and live with your celly ... It's no way I wanna be around a man 24/7. .... Even in civilian life the average married couple spends less than five (waking) hours together per day. He (and sometimes so does she) leaves at 6:00 AM to go to work. He gets home at 5:00 or 6:00 PM. By 10:00 or 10.30 PM he's asleep... Space is a blessing ... You work with who you live with. I can't fathom that!..."

I'm telling you kids this (Hades) is "BrokeBack prison!" ... may I repeat - I don't hate or dislike gay folks. I know too many openly (and closeted) gays to "hate". I hate rape. I hate molestation. I hate people being coerced into a sexuality which they didn't "choose".... Two dudes wanna get together and Booty Bang in jail , it is their business! My problem is force!! And... I love Whoopi! But I vehemently disagree with her on Polanski. Yes, it was 1977. But - "she" was 13. She was a "baby". He was grown (40). He gave her drugs and raped her. Whoopi says it was not a "rape rape". What the hell is that? If Polanski was black, brown or poor and white nobody would be vouching for him. No man. Is above the law. I respect the rule of law... I agree that he does not need to go to prison forever! But - he does need to come here and "Face the music". Since he can afford Gerry Spence, Robert Wood, David B. Porter Jr., Mark W. Eisenberg, Geri Lynn Green or Barry Tarlow etc. he won't go to prison anyway!

... Billy Bell? Victor Smalley? Brett Gustman (Fairfax High School Athletic trainer), Jermain Gill, Reynolds Wolf (Atl. Ga.), Daniel Seddiqui, Christopher Clubb (Oregon), Tyler Schuurman (Riverbank CA), Lauren Bledsor and Ben Alexander are you reading!.... Andrew Knox (West Sacto), Madam Barbara Lee, Diane Watson, Maxine Waters, Jackie Goldberg, Richard Polanco and Matt Gray are you all reading? ....

I'm told Lance Corcoran and Mike Jiminez had a "contract" out on Richard Polanco, threatened him and ran him out of office! ... I'm just sayin!

Gary Dockery Caleb Peek and Sam Fuick understandeth thou what thou readeth? Prison is lose lose. Guards Guarding!!! Why did Rod Hickman and Jeannie Woodford really retire?....

I'm committed to getting Dr. Alex Vaclavik (his pal the Publicist), Chris Jost, Cong. E. Bernice Johnson, Cong. James Clyburn, Cong. Bob Inglis (if he can get the powder off his nose), Justin Gadsden, Jonathan Davis (Elk Grove High School), Garrett McCain, Casey Jordan (Attorney & psychologist), Steve Huff and David Russell to work together, "shoulder to shoulder" with G.B.G. and help us restore "vision" to Gen. Y. and the Facebook Generation.... I'm also gonna ask Marc Grossman, F. Lee Balley, James Zahradka, Karen Johnson-McKwan, Sallie B. Armstrong (Donney Brand LLP) and other lawyers to help us get the criminal records of boys expunged similar to what Judge Greg Mathis does in Chicago and Detroit. I believe Ann Patterson, Bob Blasier (a master Lawyer), Tom Mesereau, Marc Ravis, Matt Bailey and other lawyers will be willing to help a G.G.B./HEART "Second Chance" initiative!....

... Joe Morrissey got more than a "second" chance. I was in Richmond VA. I thought I was the sh-t (crap)! Driving a Black Jag and wearing an Armani suit. I rolled out of the Jag and stepped in and up to have my shoes shined. And this Caucasian man in suit and tie sat (having his shoes shined) looking directly at my crotch (lol). He was driving a Jeep (because I saw it in front of me.) with a customized tag with a "Commonhealth Attorney" sticker on it. Dude licked his lips slowly and said "nice suit". I dryly replied "thanks". He extended his right hand and said "I'm Joe Morrissey". As I shook it I said "Marc Rice".... I sat down nervously because it was obvious this guy was "gay"... Later that evening I called Attorney Murray J. Janus and... "Joe is the Head prosecutor for Richmond. He's flamboyant, charismatic and never lost a case... He's never faced me yet" Attorney Janus stated. I said "you left out 'gay' in that litany Sir". Murray laughed "Gay? I've heard a lot of things about Joe but never 'gay'".

My business associate (also a mid-level filmmaker) was shooting a movie that would include a gay scene and gay club. Whoever told you that your Clark Kent (Jacob!) days were over never watched Superman (Israel!). You will fall down but keep getting yo black (brown or white) ass back up!...

You will have issues, weaknesses, flaws and trials in life. But trials come to make you strong... I wanna be a 'part' of orchestrating a flawless assassination conspiracy (spiritual) of the gangs (and gangstas) in your hood, Barrio or trailer park... "You are the Boss of all Bosses!" Doc told me. You are the godfather!" Doc had me laughing. "If Selwyn Raab knew you he would call you the John Gotti of G.B.G.! You are an Emperor and a Titan".

... Detective Richard "Doc" (ret.) Ford concludes "you are a writing tycoon! The John Grisham of C.D.C." He left out "the most hated convict in C.D.C. and CCPOA Public Enemy No. 1 !"...

... On 9/30/09 I complained (for the 3rd time) of severe knee pain, joint aches, migraines and shortness of breath at 9:00 AM. The nurse was next door hanging an NPO sign on the door. "Fill out a 7362 (sick call) and they'll see you first thing tomorrow especially since you have Valley Fever. We gotta make certain it has not gone to your knees". The nurse stated. "Yeah, they're swollen and I can barely climb steps" I told her... I filled out an urgent 7362 and gave it to Hale at 6:00 PM and he said "It's probably your Valley Fever". And on 10/1/09 the only person to "see" me was a Lieutenant for an R.V.R. This lieutenant is the C.O. who faked my signature to a job "change" years ago and changed me out of a j-o-b. I was blessed to convince (then) Captain Jimbo Walker and Lt. Jimmy Guyton to put me "back" in my j-o-b.

... This lieutenant is the "same" C.O. who tried to "move" me from Bldg. 7 to Bldg. 8 to retaliate. God blessed me to convince the Lt. (P. now appeals coordinator) to call (then) captain Jimbo Walker at home. He called "Dad" (CDW Terry L. Rosario) and "Dad" said "tell them to leave Sherman in Bldg. 7. If they don't like it the C.O. can get a job change"..

This C.O. went to Mule Creek and worked (promoted to sergeant) for Lt. Cherry, (with C.O. Duclos) and for Mike Bunnell! This guy should not be (conflict) hearing my R.V.R. I "refused" to attend the hearing. He threatened to put me in the hole. I went to the hearing as humbly as I could. He refused to Recuse himself... "I talked to Bunnell last night! He can do more over a telephone than a lawyer in a courtroom... You see you still have not been able to get to U.C. Davis for your infectious disease appointment... Are you in pain now? Need to see a doctor?" I could not believe this dude. He'd better be glad I gave Madame Kennedy my word not to speak ill of New Folsom Staff. By and large CSP Sac (I repeat) staff are pros. Jimbo is blessed with CCIII Kennedy, Johnson-Dovey, Jeff, Steve, Fred, Tim Virga etc. and a masterful team of psychiatrists and psychologists....

But this lieutenant (let's call him "Timm", "Manuel Timm"..) went to M.C.S.P. to promote. He is not a racist. I wish he was. The easiest thing (I learned from Ambassador Andrew Young and the Great Rev. Hosea Williams) for me to do is deal with a "racist". He doesn't trust me and I don't trust him. He doesn't like me and I don't like him. You watch, avoid and stay away from racists. Most racists are not educated. Lt. M. Timm has a four year college degree. He is an egomaniac, a control freak and one of those dudes with a 'hole' in his soul. When I was in C.T.C. he made it his 'business' to come back with Lt. Baker as she (Baker) read me a new lock up order stating I would be transferred. Lt. Timm lit up like a Christmas tree. I never mentioned that I'd seen Madame Kennedy and Warden Walker that same morning. And they (Walker, Kennedy & Johnson-Dovey) assured me that I would 'not' be transferring.

...For Lt. Timm to hear my R.V.R. was perhaps the most foolish decision of his 'career'. In his little pee brain he figured "how can I not hear this? Manning beat me when I forged his signature on a job change. Manning beat me when I tried to move him out of Bldg. 7 ... I promoted at M.C.S.P. and discussed him (Manning) with Lt. Cherry, C.O. Duclos and A.W. Bunnell. And now I just got a 'bar' on my shoulders and I have the 'power' to find my buddy's (Bunnell's) enemy 'guilty' I must do this"...

Johnnie Cochran felt that his entire career had prepared him to cross examine Mark Fuhrman. But as noted trial Attorney Murray J. Janus stated "the most brilliant strategic decision Johnnie made during O.J. Simpsons trial was to "not" cross examine Mark. He told Lee Bailey to do it. It threw Fuhrman "off his game". He (Mark) was psychologically prepared for Johnnie. But instead he got Lee Bailey. And Lee Bailey buried Fuhrman..."

I spoke with another Lieutenant (whom I've known ten years. Call him Lt. James Gibson) later that evening (10/1/09) and he said "that idiot (Timm) was stupid enough to hear your R.V.R.? If I was him I'd have ran from that hearing. And Timm is in your book (by authentic "name") and worked directly with Bunnell etc. He is an idiot"... I asked a white C.O. "Do you know Lt. Timm?" He replied "I stay away from that dude. He aint (sic) no good."

I made the strategic decision to take notes and forward said data to Michael Bien, Donald Specter, Geri Lynn Green and to Stanley I. Greenberg... I had nightmares (literally) that night (10/1) thinking about the things Lt. Timm claims Mike Bunnell told him. I woke up cramping, perspiring, with excruciating pain in my knees and short of breath...

Attorney Murray J. Janus perused "all" of the documents I have on my Valley Fever situation. He wrote the following: "You (Sherman D. Manning) should 'own' C.D.C. when this is over. This (cocci) is a fatal disease. You should allege unusual and cruel punishment for being forced to go to P.V.S.P. by a rogue A.W. (Bunnell) who blackmailed you for writing about him in a tome... You want damages under California Civil Code 52(b), general and punitive damages as proved under 42 U.S.C. 1983, and attorney fees and costs provided by law for injuries suffered from 2006 to the present... "

Attorney Janus continued "Exhaust Administrative remedies. The conditions you endured at P.V.S.P. (even before cocci) constituted psychological torture. Based upon what you told Dr. Postolo, your consistent housing on suicide watch. The allegation you made to captain Beels about Ray Sanchez Jr. and your fear about going to the "yard". The fact that Bunnell personally sent CCI Costa to tell you there was no Ray Sanchez Jr. at P.V.S.P. The fact you were forced to go to the yard and breathe the spores.... Had you remained in Ad.seg per your request (via refusal to attend the lock-up hearing, refusal to attend ICC and a missive to Captain Beels) you would not have breathed the spores (outside)... Then after being forced to go to Facility -A- you made an allegation to Lt. Herrera and Captain Beels (in L.V.N. Hall's presence). Inmates (i.e. Jose Zuniga) heard you make the allegation. You were placed back into C.T.C. and tortured by Dr. Lumpkin and Dr. Martin and then forced (again) to return to facility -A- to breathe the spores... You suffered night sweats, excruciating stomach pains and shortness of breath. Your sickness went untreated for almost a month. The prison was severely overcrowded which went unabated. P.V.S.P. is filthy. That the P.V.S.P. is overcrowded to the point of violating prisoner's constitutional rights is well established".

...Attorney Janus continued "six - in custody murders as a result of P.V.S.P. mismanagement and overcrowding. The most dangerous P.C. yard in the state of California. P.V.S.P. is the major incubator, breeding grounds and a source for dangerous, infectious and communicable contagious diseases. You asked for a mask so you'd not breathe the spores. P.V.S.P. custody and medical staff said 'no'. You asked to be placed on C.T.Q. (Confined To Quarters) so you would not have to go outside (to breathe spores) and staff called you 'paranoid'... There has been an explosion of Valley Fever into the community via P.V.S.P.... You need a well drafted suit. By a Stanley (I. Greenberg), Geri (Lynn Green), Barry (Tarlow) or a Mark (Ravis) citing violations of your Eight Amendment and California Constitution Article I, & 17, the Fourteenth Amendment and California Constitution Article 1, & 15 [improper conditions of confinement in violation of substantive and procedural due process of law], violation of duty of care under title 15 of the California Administrative Code (1027, 11/7, 11/8, 1263, 1270, 1271, 1272 and 1280) and Government Code 815.6, and violations of California Penal Code 2600. [prisoner's civil rights], 4015 and 6030... You want the tape showing I.S.U. special transferring you to P.V.S.P. on the orders of one Mike Bunnell. You will own C.D.C.... Try calling Litt, Estar, Harrison, Miller & Kitson LLP in LA. You will win at least $ 6 million... I wish I were in California". So sayeth Attorney Murray J. Janus. He is a 'bad' man! ...

... On 10/2/09 (finally) a 'nurse' called me to 'tell' me she thinks my shortness of breath and severe joint pain is my Valley Fever. And guess what? I'd be seen by a physician the following (in seven days) Friday. I am a walking miracle (thanks be to God). I nearly died from disseminated Valley Fever. I am a critical care patient. And shortness of breath and severe joint pain etc. are not enough to rapidly get me to a physician. Guess what else? As I left the nurse (in the dining hall) I passed by a physician. Dr. Moghaddam (who is very familiar with my Valley Fever!). But he refused to examine me 'because' he was assigned to 'B' section of the building! Only in C.D.C. this is not only neglicence but it is deliberate. It represents a lack of training, care and concern. And if I got sick(er) over the weekend and had to be flewn to U.C. Daws etc. A. I could die! B. John Q. Taxpayer will (again) foot the bill...

Taylor Moson, Benjamin Alexander, Billy Bell, Victor Smalley and Jason Jacobs are you reading this? Douog Pieper Jr., Jason Huyck and Chad Michael Morrissette are you reading?.... Yall tell (again) Derek Hough, Justin Gadsden, Paris Hilton, David Joiner and Riley Foster that the "Ashton Kutcher" (seriously) challenge on page 313 (of "Blue Eyed Blonde" Book II) is to them too... But we'll double the money!

... Back at P.V.S.P. my night sweats, shortness of breath and pain were all classic, and signature Valley Fever symptoms. But they still nearly let me die. I was placed in holding cells for hours waiting on doctors (finally) and then waited for 7 hours for transportation. And then I was severely afraid because Dr. Lumpkin told transportation to "take him out and hang him"....

... A high level C.D.C. official spoke with me (on the condition of anonymity at D-M-H-Vacaville) about "double-celling". He states "we've had more cell murders, rapes, stranglings etc. in C.D.C. than any other prison system in America other than Texas... Inmates need to be single celled. All of you! ... And a person with 'your' conviction? You should definitely be on single cell unless we as a department are saying we believe you are wrongly convicted ... CC II Janice Mayfield was absolutely correct about your need for the "S" suffix."

This high level official continued "distinguished psychologists and psychiatrists all question the wisdom of double celling level 4 inmates. The department coerces psyches to not speak out on the need for single cell status. If we single celled half of the inmates who 'need' single celling the Judges would be demanding we release nearly 100,000 inmates instead of 44,000... Double celling you guys is a clear and present danger. C.D.C. should be declared a crime scene and we should wrap yellow tape around all 33 prisons".

I hope Taylor Moson (marketing consultant in San Diego), members of Christian Fellowship Ministry Church (Sacto) and Rev. Otis Moss etc. are reading these words. The system is designed to fail. We must tear down these walls!

...My job is to (I repeat) utilize this vicious prison as a platform. This is an educational moment. This is a ministry and a pulpit. I must tell you (Gen Y) about the domestic Abu Ghraibs (P.V.S.P., Pelican Bay, Reidsville and Rikers Island etc.) and Guantanomos that dot American soil. This story I tell elucidates the day to day atrocities of prisons. I try to tell of the horrors of Hades artistically ... Sporadically I try to salt and pepper (season) this tome with empirical data on how to survive Hades, come out bruised and changed but with one's core intact. I want kids already (unfortunately) in prison to become stronger, more powerful and passionate! It is extremely difficult (but not impossible) to come here and leave out sane. Great horrors and deprivations take their toll. Living amongst people who secretly want to see you fail takes a toll. Being around folk who hope you "die" is draining on the battery of life. And the duplicitousness is absolutely mind boggling. But - if it had not been for the Lord that was on my side; I would have been swallowed up by my enemies. But if God Be For You who can be against you...

My mission with G.B.G. and with K.K.K. is not to be your friend. You get drunk and smoke weed with your friends. I am not your friend. I am not to be trusted. Don't love me, because I'm a mess. Just get the message out of my mess. I'm telling you how to stay alive. (even with gangs all around you). I'm just sayin how to keep yo sanity, body and your soul intact...

K.K.K. is a gold mine! Not because "I" wrote it. I'm just a thug in jail. It is an awesome tome because I walked, talked and lived with Eme, Latin Kings, Sacramaniacs, Mexican Mafia and BGF inmates as I wrote it. I am on special assignment in the prison. I am imbedded and entrenched in my story. I live with the troops about whom I write. I consulted with youngsters (i.e. 22 year old Jesus Sandoval, Jeff Glen Howell, Joseph Latham, Jerry Wines and...) as I wrote this. This book can save lives, minds, bodies and souls. This book is breakfast for (young) champions. I'm inviting teens and tweenies to enter into the Winner's Circle. I am calling you forth and calling you out. I may not be the "Emperor" that Doc calls me but I am a man. And I'm qualified to call you to service. I'm calling Charles (who was on the Price Is Right on 10//1/09... He attends UNLV and Charles wants to become a dentist) forth. I'm calling all my students at Locke High School... There are 58,000 abductions per year in America. Mostly by coaches, teachers, preachers and Boy scout leaders etc. 58,000! We obviously are not doing something right. Allover the place millions of law enforcement personnel. We have locked up damn near 3 million humans in the U.S. and still Phil was able to imprison and enslave Jaycee and two kids for 18 years!!

If cops, detectives, profilers, so-called parole experts etc. and/or C.D.C. knew what the hell "they" were doing this man (not a "monster" because when we say "monster" is absolves "us" of major responsibility, cause we can't control the 'animal kingdom'. No Phil is a man. A human being just like you and me. He's no damn good! He is the epitome of evil but he's not a bear. He is 'us'.) And inspite of all the cops yall did'nt get him. So when the damn cops ain't got an answer call the robbers. I am the robber and I've come to teach you how not to get robbed!... My team (G.B.G.) and I can read the handwriting on the wall. Joseph (the dude locked up in prison on a "sex" beef for 13 1/2 years) can interpret the dream even when politicians, police commanders and parole agents can not. So then the spirit of the Joseph (who had an "R" in his jacket) of Genesis is alive in this book. And I intend to "manipulate" what I've learned from my battery of experts (psychiatrists, psychologists, Wardens, captains, gang members etc.) and use it for "Good". I'll use it to reach out of my gated community and to reach in to bear River High School and schools across the world.

I pray that Dr. Alex Vaclavik, reporters like Kenny Lopez (fox 40 in Sac town), Bloggers and Vloggers etc. will use this tome to spread light and to mobilize Hope. I'd like to reach out to Tony Deville (principal of Union Mine High School), Alex Chivescu and Alex Seabolt etc.

Together with Ernie Allen (protect your children) we can create "safe beds" for kids. (G.B.G. notice: if you know the whereabouts of a missing or exploited child etc. Call 1-800-the-lost)... We must teach kids to say "no". Build their self esteem and convince them of their self worth. We must empower kids.

Christian Nelson etc. use them to play with kids (as G.B.G. Ambassadors). And this will also be in a setting where teachers, parents and administrators can add in their two cents. We can do this Yall...

.. In the alternative you can come to Hades. And if you come here I know some dudes who will buy you a Tiffany ring!... Tyra ran a rerun on 10/2/09 and a white (so-called Biker! 250 lbs and "straight") yelled out "Quentin's or Marius can be my celly. Look at the freaking lips on Marius! Look at Quentin eyes!" I said "You gay". He replies "No I'm not gay but I'd lick Marius' asshole". I go "I'll be back as soon as I'm done vomiting!" ... If you (whoever u - are) are looking for Bromance come on. It's all right here in this place!... Whatever you want Baby Boy it's here! And even if you are 'gay' or 'Bi that's your business. But can I ask you a question? What fool would come to the joint to get laid?

... You lost yo mind! To each his own but listen. I would hope that I'm a half way decent looking fella. But having said that; any woman who jumps in bed with me (if I live to see freedom) upon my release is a damn fool. I don't have H.I.V., Hep. C or any of that. And Valley Fever is "not" contagious by blood or saliva. But I'm just sayin. How would you know? If my unmarried sista (Shanteeka) wants to date an ex-con so be it. I don't recommend it. But - I'd tell any female to have your ex-con get tested for Hep, Aids and the whole nine yards. Prisons are incubators of disease and mental illness. When we get outta jail we have an invisible sign on our heads that says "Beware!" And I know the fellas don't want me writing this. And I'm cognizant that when we get out we have enough strikes against us. But we (you in jail and me) should have and could have thought about all of that before we started selling dope and gang banging.... And if we are authentic in our transformation. If we are not faking the funk with this jailhouse religion Bull crap etc. If we are ready to do warfare with Life's coping skills. If we are ready to be soldiers for good and soldiers for right. I assure you that there is no stopping a man determined to do right. You can't stop a man who has made up his mind to do justice, love mercy and to walk humbly with God. I know yall think all of that 'Law of Attraction' and visualization stuff is crap. But you better not knock what you have not tried.

God is real! I don't care how many crooks (like Benny Hinn, Leroy Jenkins etc. etc.) are out there God is authentic... When I was at my lowest state He never stopped being God just because I was in my Jacobness. He didn't stop blessing and anointing people just because I was being crooked. My weakness for women does not diminish God's power. My lies don't stop God's truth. My being fake preventeth not His authenticity. Just because I think about what it would be like if me and Tyra Banks were alone and... I took all the tests (i.e. Aids and Hep. etc. etc.) and Tyra and I were lying down at the Palmer House in Chicago. And Tyra had on a pair of pink pa... O.K. Let me stop but even as I was about to start lusting. It would not stop God from being God. His sun still woke up this morning behind the Eastern horizon. The light still punched in on the time clock of another day.. .I know a lot of hypocrites. I know a lot of angry, violent, vicious and vindictive folk who are Gold-star church members. It bothers me too. But I've learned not to be arrogant. We can't be arrogant just because somebody else is broken in a place where we're whole. We don't need to condone them or befriend them but pray for them. Don't let a man (a crook, a guard, an associate warden, a facility captain or a Leroy Jenkins etc.) damage your faith in God.

I almost stopped believing. I can't lie to you; I almost gave up laying on my 'death' bed (and yeah I'm sick and in pain right this minute. My knees and ankles are swollen and I'm being denied medical treatment.) wondering "why me?" Wondering how and why a God with all power would sit back in Zion and allow Bunnell to kill me. Wondering how God could allow a system to be in place that would allow my 76 year old Granmother to not know where I was for 9 months. Hell Yeah I almost gave up. I almost quit. I almost threw in the towel and gave up. But if you've ever really known Him you keep the residue of his spirit within you. You still have his fingerprints on your soul. And all I can think to tell you is that "If it had not been for the Lord that was on my side...."

This whole little situation with Dearaujo (you'll read about him shortly) came from a black man. I've learned that a black man plotted, schemed and sat down at a "table with caveman (AKA "Dearaujo') and came up with the "story". How low can we stoop? I've never hurt this black man. I've never harmed this black man. But if you wanna know what I did wrong to this black brother it is simple; I woke up this morning! That is "what" I did to "him". I woke up! ... The Lord let me know that a man who hates himself can never love me. A man angry with himself shall never be authentic with me. He'll have a problem with my walk and a problem with my talk. If I speak I'm no damn good. And if I'm quiet I'm still no good. Negative, spiteful, hateful and bitter people are toxic... And no matter what you think of me. Regardless of whether or not you disagree with me on some, a few or even all political issues etc. I'm fine with that. But the one thing I think Attorney Bob Blasier (Jonathan C. Turner, Emily E. Doringer), Verone Kennedy and even Barack Obama and I "all" agree on is the necessity of education!.... Bill Cosby, Dr. Poussaint and Bill Gates etc. may all disagree (I'm not sure and I don't care) with me on politics, science, religion or whatever. But I assure you that even Oprah will stand "shoulder to shoulder" with me when I tell you that reading opens the mind and inspires knowledge. Reading to the mind is like oxygen to the lungs. Reading is the mental fuel which will propel you into your destiny. And I was taught (early on) to even read stuff I disagreed with because it increased growth. I don't just read tomes which "Amen" my beliefs and opinions. I read offensively, defensively and strategically. I read for knowledge, entertainment, inspiration and for vision. And I didn't ask lawyers (entrepreneurs, teachers and preachers etc.) to help us put "K.K.K." into schools so you all would celebrate me. I asked Attorney Blasier, John C. Turner and James Brosnahan etc. to join Murry J. Janus, Senator John Burton, Peter Andrist and G.B.G. in putting 'this' book in schools not to celebrate me. I'm a thug, a crook, a conman, a convict, a trickster and a supplanter. I asked Zig Zigler, Tony Robbins and Aaron Fernander (school principal) to help us get this to you so you could celebrate you, not me. I want you to see be cured of H.I.V. (Having Insufficient Vision)! You don't need to write me. You don't need to meet me. All you need to do is see. Once your vision is restored you'll see how to make it. And having seen what can be you'll never settle for what is. And with a powerful education you'll vaccinate yourself against incarceration. As a matter of fact the goal and mission of G.B.G. is to help you see so you'll never need to meet me. Jail is Hell!

Can we be authentic and probitistic? Senate president pro tem (and chairman of the CA. Democratic Party) John Burton is not endoring me! He is endorsing the mission of G.B.G. under the supervision of Dr. Curren, Dr. C. Solis, CCIII Patricia Kennedy, Dr. A. Duran, C.O. Diana Smith etc. etc. Bob Blasier is a master lawyer! When he puts 10, 20 or 30 copies of this tome (I'll announce on our Facebook site) into a school it does not mean Attorney Blasier agrees that Eric Menendez is gay. Mr. Blasier does not know and does not care. Murray J. Janus, Steed Scott, Taylor B. Stone and Magic Michael Morchower are not interested in who is doing who in the jail. These are (Janus, Cook, Stone, Blasier and Ravis etc.) educated, powerful and wealthy men. They are promoting this book on the gamble that 'just one' of you gangbangers, dope dealers, speed or weed heads, paint sniffers, prescription drug addicts, boyz in tha hood, youth in suburbia etc. Just one of you might read some of the stuff (substance) which my team and I (along with guidance from our advisory board, Warden Jimbo Walker, CCIII Patricia Kennedy, A.W. L.N. Johnson-Dovey, Jeff Macomber, Tim Virga etc.) have written on these pages etc. And one (Alex King, Derek King, Alex Chivescu, Tadd Carr etc.) of you will decide to stay in or return to school. And you'll forego the opportunity to come here (Hades) and be a fag, punk, "Boy", girl or a gangbanger. And there is a difference between a prison girl, boy, punk and a faggot. I wish I had the time to elucidate it for you...

But be advised that our supporters (including Peter Andrist, Senate President Pro Tem (ret.) John Burton, Atty. Murray J. Janus or who ever etc.) they support the "Mission" of G.B.G./HEART! They do not endorse me ... You can join a church who's pastor is republican but you can remain a democrat...

I've learned even more about the Dearaujo allegation and how even Mike Bunnell (as with the Duclos/Emslander duo) was involved with that!

When I think about my students at Martin Luther King Jr. Academy (Sacto), Locke High, Lodi High and even at the Ron Clark Academy etc. I wonder if you all have even an inkling of what it's like to be here (Hades)... Parents should never complain about the few little cuss words in this tome. I write nothing you all don't see in the movies and on TV. And it's this TV romanticization which concerns me. I so don't want you to believe that prison is like "that" which you see on TV "It don't go like that" Judge James Long would declare.

This (Hades) is a dark and deadly place. Folk in here will slit your throat for looking at them the wrong way. That's not embellishment. After Dearaujo lied on me I understood what the heck David was sayin with "Do not deliver me to the will of my enemies;" If you are trying to do right you will (shall) have some "haters". The brother who helped Dearaujo invent the story was a "plant". God allowed him to be a planned and a planted "enemy". Are you reading this? I'm trying to give you all some game Baby Boy. It has taken me darn near 40 years to understand that whether you are black, white, dark, light, wrong, right, gay, straight, by or celibate (if you God's child) you will have enemies. If you don't have enemies you are not doing anything. Martin Luther King Jr. was stabbed by a black woman long before he was shot by a white man. Mother Teresa and Ghandi also had enemies. They 'hated' on Jesus! So you know that if you try to do right they are going to hate on you. You at Locke High, Colfax High, Lodi High etc. you will have enemies ... And David tried to explain Russell Camosky and Ricardo Calvario to me long time ago but I missed it. But now with Bunnell, Dearaujo and the Brutha I get what David meant with "for false witnesses have risen against me..." Notice it says they have "risen". They were there (amongst you just like Judas) all along. They were kicking back, fitting in and chillen. But when you began to advance, rise and make a move they decided it was time to "rise"... David said "I would have lost Heart" or I would have fainted. I would have quit. I almost gave up. I almost... I would have "unless I had believed that I would see (get past H.I.V. Don't Have Insufficient Vision! Without vision people perish) the goodness of the Lord..." I've already seen the filth, the wickedness and the deadliness of mankind. I've even seen my own anger, violence and the wickedness that I'm capable of. And watching the brutality, the murders, rapes and the spiritual wickedness in high places on the faces in prison. It is enough to make you faint. I watch guys pass out "huggies" like we're in grade school. I watch the fraud, the corruption and the envy that we do. And it is enough to make you faint. It's enough to make you lose "Heart". And can I tell you that there have been a couple of times in prison (i.e. facing 75 years to life for a couple of so-called 'threats' nobody believed were serious...) Lying on my death-bed thanks to Mike Bunnell and lying in C.T.C. on a floor for 2 months while the D.A. considered striking me out due to the Dearaujo 'lie' etc.) when I "would have lost Heart." But some kind a way God reached down and showed up in my situation. Someway and somehow He let me "believe" that (it may be dark right now. It may be spooky, scary and lonely right now but) I "would see the goodness of the Lord (not after I die and go to Heaven but) in the land of the living"... And can I tell you where I am right now? "My heart is overflowing with a good theme;" (my theme now is education causes liberation. My theme is education innoculates against incarceration. The theme of the G.B.G. team is that "when you drop out of school you not only fail yourself. You fail your family and you fail your country!"... So I understand psalms 45 now...) "my tongue is the pen of a ready writer". I've learned what Jesus meant when He said I could "speak to this mountain" and command the mountain to "move". I clearly get the "power of life and death are in the tongue". I'm speaking a blessing over the pages of this tome. I'm speaking peace, success and a super education into your destination. I speak help (getting this book into schools etc.) with "K.K.K." into existence right now... Your "tongue is the pen of a ready writer". And if I stay with the Lord "Grace is poured upon your lips; therefore (inspite of the haters) God has blessed you forever"... And the favor of God is upon my life. It's on me and it's on G.B.G.... And I tell all my G.B.G. team and you too (U A Soldier right?) " Your arrows are sharp in the Heart of the King's enemies;" Even the King has enemies. I should say "especially the King" has enemies. But if we are soldiers for justice, education and for God. If we G.B.G. "the people (gangs, molesters, murderers and those who corrupt our kids etc.) fall under you:. IF we (G.B.G.) are serious, authentic and we're committed we get to a place where our enemies (God's enemies) fall under us...

Anybody who climbs mountains knows what a snake line is. Once you get so high on a mountain you can get to a place where snakes can't live. It's too high for them. And those of us who really wanna get close to our creator and get to a place where we are a vessel of prayer. Those of us willing to truly seek our calling, find our destiny and increase our anointing etc. We can rise up so high that snakes can't live. When you know who you are in God you can declare your authority without joining a gang or carrying a piece (gun)...

I recall that my Daddy James Scott Manning had so much authority and respect in our home (and he did not beat or abuse us!) that Reggie and me could be acting a fool. And CAT (Dollie Manning) could just "say" James or "Daddy" and we'd act right. Sometimes we'd be tearing our room apart and the door would open up and our daddy would Stick his head in and the moment we "saw" him we froze. He was (is) a man who knew his authority. A Prince in his own home...

If you know how much God loves you and know His will (plan and destiny) for your life you won't pollute you with a drug, booze or a needle. You'll stop running around from person to person, gang to gang and lover to lover trying to get someone to endorse you. (This is "real talk" yall). If I know who I am and whose I am I don't need an endorsement. I don't need a slap on the back. I don't need an "Atta Boy". And as quiet as it's kept (just between you, me and the door post) I don't need "you" to "like" me. If I love God I'll have a healthy self image. I won't have low self esteem. I'll know myself well enough to esteem me. I won't be cocky, arrogant, egotistical or narcissistic. I won't have a hole in my heart, spirit, mind or soul ... I pray that God will fill all the holes in you like He did me. He filled up the holes so I could see. He'll show you why you were raised like you were raised. He'll show you why He did it like He did it. He'll show you....

I wanna Holla at all the Juniors and Seniors at Trinity University in San Antonio Texas. I send a shout out to Keaton Davis and (inside joke) "I have some socks n underwear that need folding Keat". Look on Apartments.com and you'll see Keaton Davis and you'll comprehend the joke. Tell Keaton to get this book. We want Keaton as a G.B.G./HEART ambassador. We also believe Keat can help us locate Sean Farmer and Mike Delgado (El Paso Texas)...

 I intend to peel away that malevolent, macho and egotistical mask you are wearing. And through this book and with G.B.G. I plan to see the real you. When I write I'm not writing to your church face: I'm not writing to the "Momma May I?" side of you. I'm not writing to the you that you show everybody else. I am writing to Jacob. I am called to write to the trickster, supplanter and to the conman in you. I'll let Benny Hinn heal you! I'll let Rush Limbaugh bombard you with hate and demagoguery. I'll let Bishop Flip Flop and Deacon Willie Wonder shake your hand, smile in your face and give you a testimony. I'll let them tell you "my idea of leadership is influencing minds and..." Walk around the corner and look for a dagger they can stick in your back!

But I come as a Saul trying to be Paul. I come saying I still have not arrived. I'm not "there" yet but I'm on my way. I still find myself (every now and then) thinking about Tyra and me (lol)... "Every time I try" to do "good" evil is always there. I came to tell you that "it's me too" just like you. I still have issues... I still got some stuff to deal with. And I don't have time to play with you. I'm not seeking your endorsement, friendship or your favor. All I want from you is action. If I can spin around 19 times and throw $ 37.00 over my left shoulder to get you back in school I'll do it. I just want you to go to school. I just want you to stay off drugs. I just want you to stay away from me. The only way you can be "near" me is to come to Hades. Stay the Hell away from jail... This place kills the spirit. This place murders hopes. This place assassinates dreams. This is a bad place.

K.K.K. is a manual on incarceration. It is a manual on the devastation of incarceration. The diagnosis and prognosis are clear. I came to prescribe the only medication which you should get addicted to. The prescription I prescribe (having earned my Ph.D. on "prisons") begins with an "e" and ends with an "n". I prescribe "education" to prevent you from suffering the devastation of incarceration. I prescribe "books" as your physical therapy. And if you're in drastic situations (i.e. broken homes or Latch key kid homes etc.) I am gonna prescribe a drug more powerful than chemotherapy and radiation combined! (and it won't make your hair fall out either). I prescribe a powerful drug (being) which begins with a "G" and ends with a "D". I prescribe "God". If you get God on your side my brother "If God be for us who can be against us".

.. A number of fellows here with me (in Hades) will walk up and ask me "Am I in your book?" They want their "name" out there. But when I ask them to "write an essay to help the kids and I'll put it in a book and on Facebook etc." I'm (routinely) told "I can't write that good" etc. I recall a young Mexican fellow who was volunteering to "work" for 4 hours in a dining hall telling me "we'll see whats up". And then "If I have time I'll do it". I explained "you don't have anything but "time". He says "But I'm trying to get outta here (prison)". By volunteering to slave in a Chow Hall? Prison is a group of boys all dressed up with nowhere to go. We remind me of a large group of "mice" all fighting for a piece of cheese. It is almost comical (if it weren't so sad) to watch us. But we think we're cool. And "we" are the "smartest" dudes on the planet. We are not smart enough to get out of jail. But "we" know it "all". And we got game and....

Bob Vonvillas is the crime partner of Detective Richard "Doc" Ford. Bob was also a decorated officer with the LAPD. Bob told "Doc: to "tell Sherman I think G.B.G. is a great idea. If politicians, priests and police (the 3 p's) had the "answers" you (Doc) and I would not be in jail".

Mentoring is like magic even if the kid's situation is tragic. And from my bully pulpit and my perch in the prison etc. I shout out to Rev. Timothy Flemming, Rev. Otis Moss, Rev. Arthur Carson, A. Lincoln James and to every pastor! I beg you to start mentoring programs at your church. I don't need you (pastors) for "me". G.B.G. does not need a donation and we seek no grants. I have funded G.B.G. out of my own pocket. G.B.G. never seeks a monetary donation! If anybody calls or writes you seeking a donation in the name of G.B.G. you call the police! ... We (G.B.G.) don't do that).... But I need great preachers to listen to (Joseph) me on this; we need to mentor troubled youth. There is an awesome need for churchhouse mentors! and it don't (sic) cost yall (pastors) a penny to do it. "I was in prison and you visited me not". And no my team (G.B.G.) is not seeking visitors. (with all due respect). We are cool. You just "pray" for Doc, Sherman, Billy and Willie and we'll be just fine... I am asking you (Rev. Otis Moss, Pastor Timothy Flemming, Jasper, Pastor Barber and Elder Sam Wallace etc.) all to reach out to these "kids" in juveniles, jails and prisons. If you want "men" in your church I assure you these "youngsters" in jail are looking for somebody and something to latch on to. The reason(s) some of them are in the darn gangs is because you passed by them (in your Bentley, Rolls and ...) and looked the "other" way...

I told Jesus (cool lil youngster here with me) to "make time for the kids. How dare you be so busy and preoccupied in the prison that you not (don't, won't etc.) have time to write an essay for kids?" I told Jesus Sandoval that "Jesus Christ said to suffer the little children and let them come into me".

How dare we (dudes in jail including my black butt) sit back in jail all locked up and not be willing to write (to and for), pray for and encourage youngsters? I'm looking in the dayroom at C.S.P. SAC right now (7:55 pm). I count 21 dudes in dayroom. Eight are playing dominos. Four are playing pinochle. And the rest are watching the ball game but "we" are "busy"? Give me a break... C section is locked down right now and there are 24 cells in this section (at 7:59 pm) and only 3 cells are lit up with "reading" lights. The rest of "my" posse are sleeping, watching TV, in bed with their cellies and.....

I'll leave that alone .... But "we" are busy flexing, flossing and high siding. It tickles me to see "us" dress up to go to dayroom. The highlight of our lives is to put on a new pair of shoes and go to dayroom and hope (another "man") somebody will notice we have on new shoes ... But I have asked a number of dudes to help me with this book. They'll tell me about C.G.A. (Criminals and Gangs Anonymous) and how much they had on the streets. But they are too "busy" to write something to help a youngster in need... And some of these guys "think" they are hot "crap". How dare a "boy" locked up in jail (Sherman D. Manning) and not in Yale etc. have the temerity to "think" he's something? But I know guys right here who have $ 100,00 in their account (sent by their "mother") and they think they're bad... retarded boys! Retarded Boys! Bitter, deranged, evil and vindictive Boys!

.... A guy told me (today) that Dearaujo (it'll make sense later on when you peruse Part II of this tome) admitted to him (also) that he "lied" on me to get rid of me. It would have helped if Billy had told Vance, Kennedy or Walker "what" Dearaujo did to me!!!

And I know "silent" (Roger Peck) is reading right now. And I want "Silent" to tell Dearaujo I forgive him and I am praying for him (day and night)!!... Why would I forgive him? Why not? All of "us" have sinned, cheated and lied. And one thing I wanna do with this powerful tome is reach out and touch troubled youth. There are so many complexities associated with being young. Some of you are bullies and some are being bullied. Some are jocks and some are nerds. I have geeks, freaks and outcasts perusing this book. And a lot of you are troubled. I know what I'm talking about. You can run but you can't hide. I have seen some ladies who were so sexy, so fine, so .... They were so bad that if they passed by the Pope he'd have to 'look back'.... But even though they had Tyra Face and Beyonce Booty. They were troubled.... And even "if" you are not suicidal or depressed right now etc. Do me a favor and take this lil talk (writing) on credit. You might not need it now but sooner or later you're gonna need a "lift".

... Elijah was an awesome, powerful and anointed man of God. And when kids would see him they'd holler "Elijah! Elijah! Elijah! I can't believe it's you. I always wanted to be like you... Momma can I get Elijah's autograph?" ... And yet Elijah (the great man of God) ended up sitting under the juniper tree wishing he was dead!.... Elijah was in a dark place. And some of you studs, jocks, freaks and geeks are in some dark (spiritual, psychological and emotional) places... "Momma I always wanted to be like Elijah" and yet; Elijah is in a "cave".... Elijah "What doeth thou here?" said God... He was just eating angel food and "lifted" but now he's in a "cave"....

Kids - we are indeed conflicted creatures. We are multilayered persons. You can be a "Christian" and you are (still) a "person". You are an "intellectual", sexual and an emotional being. And as youngsters (even into your 40's, 50's and 60's) sometimes all of those beings get into a "Fist Fight". And you are Jacob one minute and Israel the next. I'm a living witness that you can love God and preach all over the church Sunday and be out chasing prostitutes on Monday. We are conflicted... and we've all heard that money can't buy happiness. But secretly we've all felt that "if I just had 'a' million bucks". But we just watched a "rich" man who would've paid all kind of money for sleep.... He just wanted to "sleep". He paid $ 150.000 per month! If he'd just lived to be 70 he'd have spent about $ 40 million for sleep...

Get out of those dark and depressed places. Don't quit! Don't take an overdose and don't jump off the bridge. Don't slit your wrist and don't cut your throat. If you die over who you have met (and they left you) you'll miss who you will meet (in your future)....

You must expect to get up and expect to get out. Expectancy (I keep on saying) will bring you to the door of the cave (Elijah).... Paul said if we have no "hope" we are of all men most miserable... I'm at the door of the cave (prison) and ... Well maybe I can get out! Maybe I will get out of this... Some of you are be-twix and between. It could go either way... Think yourself up and out. As a man thinketh so is he .... You can see a little daylight at the door. You can see the possibility of a way out of no way.

Hope against hope! Do you have any hope? I didn't say do you have faith! For if you don't have any "hope" faith can't do anything for you. For faith is the substance of things hoped for. Stir up your hope! I dare you to have some hope! I dare you (David Reynolds in Chesterfield VA., Chad Sherman, David Proctor, Brian Boykin and Tadd Carr) to have hope ... I got me some hope. That's why the enemy does not want you reading the word of God (and even this book). He knows the word will resuscitate and motivate you. Hope!.... I'm talking to Michael Wilkerson, Eddie Cannon, Ralph Cannon, Billy York, Sam Fuick and David Joiner... Hope! I came to tell Omar Samy, Billy Bell, Jason Jacobs, Jeff (Homeless student in Pike County, Eastern Kentucky... I want Rick Branham, Robert Scheeler, Judge Wayne Rutherford and Kathy Wiggins to tell "Jeff" I have a stipend for him) etc. etc. to stand up and shake yourself! Shake yourself loose! Shake yourself over! Shake yourself out! Shake that depression off of you! Shake that addiction out of you! Shake!

... Sometimes just when you think it is over God will step in and give you double for your trouble. And where God is getting ready to take you (Roger Walthorn, Jai Breisch, Christian Lawrence, Travis Shaw, Jason Rapp etc.) is too great for you to keep on doing (and eating) what you've been doing. You gotto get up, eat and strengthen yourself... Your (Billy York in Cummings GA., Eric Bulrice, David Joiner, Roger White, James Nesmith etc.) future is greater than your past.. We (Michael Vick, Sherman D. Manning etc.) can't just "proclaim" to know God we've got to exemplify Him in our Lives.... I repeat (to you "Jeff" in Pike County, Hugh Michael Hughes, Timothy Coleman, Gabe Williams and Zach Freisen etc.) don't O.D. Don't slit your wrist.... I hear the cries of you kids; I hear you! I know you're troubled, lonely, confused, hurt, sad, mad and conflicted. I hear you!

Some of you (Garrett McCain? Jake Heartsong? Alex Blench? Daniel Radcliffe? Nicholas Taxera?) Ache in your soul! You are drowning in a situation you should be walking on.... What keeps bringing you back to this dark place?.... Things don't have to get better for you to get better... The test for "Adam" was "now that you've been mentored and fathered can you (Adam) think like me (God)?"....

G.B.G. has great men (i.e. Attorney Bob Blasier, Steve Vance, Murray J. Janus, Mosely Collins, Geri Lynn Green and Mark Ravis etc.) and women ready to mentor you (youth) via this Book. And I want to know you are reading.... Go to Facebook, Myspace and some of my blogs and let me know you're reading... And I want Justin Berry, Luke Sears and Jai to contact me PDQ (AKA ASAP) and let me know you are reading.... John Sexton, Roger White, Ronald F. Wright, Alexander Dugdale and Maxwell Hanger what do you all need? Do tell. Do tell!... I need Michael Wilkerson (in Georgia), Christopher Durbin, Curtis Sykes (Ga.), David Proctor and John

Jodie Bear to let me know what you need... I want you all to get up and get out. Shake yourself and step into your destiny ... Travis Shaw, "race car" Jeremy, John Johnson (CNA), Josiah Poirer and Todd Dressler I'm talking to you.... David DeCook, John Caudell and Michael Hawkins (Virginia) I am also talking to you....

David Dowdie, Gary Browning, Daniel St. John, Luke Johnson and Ronald Keith Dunn shake your self! Richard Kenneth Chandler and David Joiner shake yourself!.... You've gotta get up and you've gotta get out... Pike County (Eastern Kentucky) is the oxycontin Capital of the World! And it's an enormous amount of teens and tweenies who are addicted. We must reach out to them. These are America's invisible youth. And I wanna remind you that you can empower yourself by healing others. You don't need to wait til you get it all together to start helping others. Find somebody that's broken in a place where you are whole and you lift them up!

Sometimes God'll deliver you "from" people so He can deliver you "to" people; so you can deliver them! Are you reading this?.... Civil Rights Legend Rev. Hosea Williams and Ambassador Andrew Young kept bailing me out of messes. They helped me over and over. But then I came to California and Hosea died. And Andy stopped helping. And I became "Alone". And having to deal with murderers in suit and tie (like Mike Bunnell, Marion E. Spearman and Lance Corcoran). And having to be guarded by guards gone wild (i.e. Wally Tucker, D.L. Criner etc.) and... I got delivered and now I'm gangbanging for justice and gangbanging for God.... Attorney Murray Janus (the ever "candid") told me "You are not a great writer!" Thanks a lot Bro! "You've become a good writer but you're not John Grisham". The brilliant Attorney continued "Grisham was not a "great" lawyer. But he is one of the "greatest" writers. On the flip side Gerry Spence is a terrific lawyer but not a great writer. And Gerry has a lot more help (Book doctors, editors and polishers etc.) than you (Sherman D. Manning) do. But I read Gerry's book for meat, substance and data; not entertainment. Grisham writes rings around Gerry. But Gerry would kick his ass in a courtroom". Mr. Janus (critic in Chief?) continued "Sherman you are a master orator. Hell Rev. Hosea Williams dubbed you the 'Martin Luther King Jr.' of the pulpit... So what if Grisham was separated from his pen and simply had to "speak" all of his books? He wouldn't sell ten million copies. He's not a master speaker. Ipso Facto, you were separated from your microphone and had to teach yourself (erudite) to preach through a pen.... My generation sees a lot of 'run on sentences' and subject shifts. But those energetic youngsters see 'game', 'science' and 'real talk'. You finally did it with "K.K.K.". Is there a compliment (lol) in there somewhere?

But Attorney Janus is "correct" as usual. My "writing" is "mediocre" (stylistically). But it is candid, blatant, authentic and 'all me' Baby Boy. I don't got (sic) nobody proofreading, ghost writing or none of that. I'm 'not' ever gonna make Oprah's Book Club. There will be no elaborate media campaign for this tome. I don't merit an avalanche of publicity. But kids (some of the persons behind the 'names' I "drop") are masters at manipulating publicity over the internet. And as commander in chief of G.B.G. I order my posse (Ryan Hreljac, Billy Bell, Jason Jacobs, Justin Berry, Benoit Denizet-Lewis, Nicholas Runde, Mike Polmear, Valith Polepeddi, Gregory Brown (the 5 Browns), Neil Peterson (in Ohio), Aaron Ashmore, Kerry Arredondo, Jake Simpson, The Roosevelt Institution, Louis Copelin (Folsom), Doug Pieper Jr. and campusprogress.org to launch an International media (via Myspace, Facebook and Twitter) campaign for "K.K.K.". I need Anthony Fedorov, Danny Noriega, Quinn Wilhelmi, Joshua Hopkins, Jason Toombs, Vincent Glaviano and Parker Anderson (Carmichael) to help me do this. "This is it" yall. "K.K.K." is the "Best" I got for the "Best" there is (you)! And if half of you perusing will tweet about this book it's on and cracking! I need Goldy (Jeffrey Allen Walker - Sharon's son), Laremy Legel, Chris DeWolfe, Benjamin McKenzie, Sean Glass, Michael Lefenfeld, Paul Graves, The Trevor Foundation and the Quest Youth Group to help us do this. ... I'm up against the power structure! Professor Dylan Rodriquez, Professor Jody Armour, Professor Vitiello, Joshua Costa and Daniel

Sample you all know I'm not lying.... Brian Doyle, Mike Bunnell, Marion and Lance etc... Brian Doyle was a spokesman for George Bush' Homeland Security. He was in the "Justice Department". Brian had the highest level of of security clearance. And Brian (whom a reliable source says used Meth and "poppers") is a child predator! He was (finally) caught! America has tens of thousands of pedophiles! Mostly educated, in law enforcement, coaching and.... We need to recognize the portrait of a molester better.... The media will parade black, Mexican and poor white criminals all across the evening news every day. But they don't/won't parade the businessmen, entrepreneurs, dentists etc. (who are pedophiles) across the TV news.... Most of the adults (in America) who buy kiddie porn are Caucasion millionaires! There are very few (i.e. Marion E. Spearman, etc.) black dudes who are into kiddie porn. But Marion is a handkerchief head so he studies how "not" to be black....

Tom Delay, Jack Abramoff, Randy "Duke" Cunningham, Gary Condit, Scott Jones and (my homeboy) Newt Gingrich are all "rich", freaks, crooks and racists! Period!

Youngsters please (please) read (I repeat) "Fish" by T.J. Parsell and "Prison Masculinities" by Dr. Terry Kupers.... Benoit Denizet-Lewis, Greg Jonsson, bloggers, vloggers, twitteres, tweeters and you podcasters gotta help me tell the world about these pedophiles! We can't depend upon CBS, NBC and ABC. Don't depend upon your local media. They suffer from ADD and they "forget". Why have you not heard about Haleigh Cummings, Sasha Groene etc. lately? The media has places to go; people to see and thangs (sic) to do. It's the "nature" of the Business..... But Andre Schumake, Sherri Miller, Sean Zane, Chris Austad, Joe Klein (West Hollywood), Michael Parker, Isaac Young (Fresno), John Jody Bear (Richmond VA) and Ryan Hreljac etc. you, me and we can remind the Nation about these children.... The spirit of the "murdered and missing children of Atlanta" is upon me right now. I can feel it in my heart, my soul and even in my bones ... (switching gears). I've learned that Detective Dave Winkler is a married, homosexual (like Larry Craig) pervert. And according to a sergeant with the West Hollywood Sheriff's Department Winkler was sexually involved with (Calvario?) many male hustlers. Especially 'drag queens'.... Cedric Palms says "I sucked Winkler a lot of times". Douglas Stave and Alan Stark etc. Douglas Siegfried etc. etc. Dave Winkler - wow!

.... I wonder where Scottie Moran (Richmond VA) and his brothers Aaron and Lloyd are. I'd love to hear from David Dowdie, David Proctor, David Reynolds, Ronald Keith Dunn, Ricky Parnell, Brian Boykin, Mike Crowder, Nathan Hand, Luke Johnson, Joey Grissett, Ronald Wright, Christopher Eavey, Josh Orapello, Greg Pugh, David Perry, Aaron, Chad Sherman and all my VA posse right now! I have stipends for each of them. And I wanna hear from the young men at Mars Hill Church in Seattle! For the Bible says David gathered together the "Choice" men of Israel. And G.B.G. needs Devin Deuell, Maxwell Hanger, Alex Blench, Brett Jolliff, Garrett Cunningham and Anthony Fedorov to be "choice" men. As a matter of fact whatever money Devin, Max, Alex, Garrett etc. may need etc. I got you. I just 'need' you to be ambassadors for G.B.G. I'm putting out a G.B.G.-APB for Alex Seabolt, Alex Holgan, Andrew Knox (W. Sacto CA), Jai Breisch, Christian Lawrence, Josh Costa (teacher), Daniel Sample, Joe Schoen and David Hellyer today. Come out, come out wherever you are. We (G.B.G.) need you, Ricky LeBaron (Balti-MD.), C.J. Sheron, Garrett McCain etc. we need you....

And may I remind you studs, jocks, geeks and freaks not to come here (Hades)? unless you want to die. Prison is unnatural, unusual and it is dysfunctional!.... I put in 4 sick call (i.e.) slips on 10/2, 10/3, and 10/4.....

... You'd assume a physician would have seen me the first thing Monday (10/5/09) morning since I have Valley Fever, asthma, swollen knees, ankles, joint pain and shortness of breath, right? Since I reported (Friday) all my inhalers were empty and I needed a new one stat!... I even put in a slip pleading to see a psychiatrist (due to nightmares, sleep walking, night

129

sweats and flashbacks etc.) and by 10/9/09 I'd still not been seen... "You call that systemic failure. You call that gross medical deliberate negligence" Attorney Janus told me "What in the hell are Dr. Bal, Dr. Mohaddam and Dr. Sahoda thinking?" Attorney Janus stated "Wow! I wish I had "time" to come to California. Deanna (Mrs. D. Cook - his daughter), Taylor B. Stone and I would bankrupt C.D.C." I (finally) got some laughter out of Janus by saying "that wouldn't be hard because C.D.C. is already broke!.... But I'm taking your advice and just waiting for "K.K.K." to be published! Stanley I Greenberg, Geri Lynn Green, Mark Ravis, Robert Waters and a number of gigantic firms seem to be very interested!"....

I want Nick Newman (National White Collar Crime Center.... tracks internet activity with the F.B.I.), Chad Newman (Georgia), Christopher Durbin, David Joiner, Wayne Snyder and Wayne Rawlings to read closely.... All yall (sic) even in juveniles, jails and prisons read closely .... I want every young man in America to get ready to concentrate on these next few pages like you've never concentrated before... Pay close attention to the next five or ten pages as spiritual dopamine is about to be released in you. These five or ten pages are about to release psychological steroids into your mind.... Kids, teens and tweenies get ready! Are you ready? Read! Omar Samaha, Omar Samy and Maxwell Hanger (etc. etc.) let me tell you to "Don't stop believing". Go listen to "journey" and "Don't stop believing"! Books change lives! This book (K.K.K.) is a passport to bring you inside the yellow police tape. In this book (through it and with it) you've been able to enter into a deadly place. You've come inside the prison in this book. A book is your (Garrett Cunningham, Garret McCain and Devin Deuell etc.) passport to go anywhere in the world. "Books will change your perspective!" States Khadijah Williams. She's an 18 year old black girl who was on Oprah last month. Khadijah grew up homeless. She slept outside, in park benches, bathrooms and in shelters by night. She "lived" in libraries by day. "Books will give you "experience" and "exposure" she told Oprah. Her library was her escape... The arrival of the virus (H.I.V. = Having Insufficient Vision) and the arrival of the vaccine (knowledge and vision).... The vaccine will immunize you against the virus which leads to addictions, violence, gangs, prisons and cemeteries! I want you (kids in the Hoods, Barrios, Suburbs and trailer parks etc.) to get this vaccine so bad I'm willing to tie yo butt up and force feed you.... Sit your ass (yall excuse my French) down and listen (read) to me.

Khadijah had every reason (poverty, homelessness, female, black etc. no father!) to fail. But Khadijah has gone from skid row to death row? That sounds logical doesn't it? No! She went from skid row to Harvard! She's now there with Alex Chivescu (I need Bob Blasier to please be certain Alex, Dr. Poussaint, Henry Gates and Khadijah get this book!) kickin (sic) it. Khadijah knew that you (in the suburbs, hoods, juvenile or wherever) are not defined by your circumstances. Khadijah never (ever) stopped believing that education was her ticket out of poverty and homelessness. This girl stayed in the library.... She changed schools 12 times in 12 years and finished at Jefferson High School in LA. (Peter is sending Jefferson High a few copies of "K.K.K.").... Devin Deuell, Alex Blench, Brett Jolliff, Maxwell Hanger and Jake Heartsong I need you (and your computer) to blog, vlog, podcast, tweet and chat about "the power of vision" and "knowledge" to immunize boys against the mess that leads to prison.... I need help putting this out there.... If Erika Eiffel can (objectum sexual) marry the Eiffel (lol) tower. If she can make love (sexually) to bridges and drums and get on Tyra! I know darn well we can put this potent message out there! We can do this! I do believe. And "whatsoever things you desire when you pray; believe, ye recieve them and ye shall have them". The war we (G.B.G.) are fighting is a war of necessity. We have to navigate from where we are not from where we "wish" we were. G.B.G. is the one place where we can marshal the forces of prisoners and police for good.... We are ordering ("yes we can") multilateral and unilateral sanctions against gangs and drug dealers.... Because of our distinguished advisory board we conduct thoughtful and thorough analysis of youth's problems. The war we (G.B.G.) are fighting is not only a war worth fighting but it is a war which is fundamental to the defense and development of our kids.... "K.K.K." is not biting "satire" but real and authentic.... I came with 'real talk' for boys. There will be peaks and valleys in life. Life is not a straight line!

... We can't depend upon the mainstream media to push the G.B.G. agenda.... They operate on a "It's always led if it bled" mentality. But we (Ryan Hreljac, David Hellyer, Daniel Sample and you too) are masters of subtlety.... Prison has amplified my voice. And I must speak truth to power!

... Rush Limbough and Sean Hannity etc. can't deliver a pizza much less a nomination (politically).... Newt Gingrich (the white supremacist in chief of the South! A flawed man who likes lil "Boys"!) is in "the league of the South". Joe Wilson is a prevaricator himself. Newt is a congenital liar? But in spite of the vituperative language and the incendiary conduct of the "right" (i.e. undercover racists like Sarah Palin etc.).... We (the "youth" i.e. you!) are mounting a response not a reaction! We reach out to Locke High, Huntsville High, Lodi High and Folsom High School students etc. with our "words".

.... We are reaching out to Jacob Karr (Orlando Florida), Jim Griffin (Freshman at Sac State College), Cameron Civello (Sac CA.), Larry Laboe (Sacto), Mr. Schoettler and all the ex-gang bangers at the Schoettler-Neufeld tire retread center etc. We reach out to kids at Ron Clark Academy and at "Infinity" School in New York. We reach out to brilliant principals like Verone Kennedy, Joe Negron, David Levin (Kipp co-founder... KIPP is the Knowledge Is Power Program in New York) etc. etc. I want all 20,000 KIPP students to have this book. I want Gabriel Gomes (7th grader), Casey Cristosto, Garrett Cunningham, Josiah Lemming and Danny Noriega to peruse "this" book! This ("K.K.K.") is breakfast for champions! "This is it" yall! ... I want Bryan Boyer (Utah), Sean Conway ("Notehall" in AZ), Danen Beres (and Danen's brother at "washed up Hollywood"), Joshua Murillo (Utah), Ryan Dilello (Utah) and John Garvin (in GA) etc. etc. to read closely!

"...so God heard their groaning, and God remembered His covenant with Abraham, with Isaac, and with Jacob (a trickster)".... I have been groaning in the spirit about this tome and about G.B.G. I have prayed and asked God to put His "super" on my "natural". Jacob (Clark Kent) can't pull this kind of "white Hot" book off alone. I needed to go into my phone booth (kneeway station) and get into my prince (Israel) state to do this. And I had to ask God to "bless me" and to "bless me indeed". And to "enlarge my territory and let thy hand be with me. To keep me from (Dearaujo, enemies, liars) evil". So that "I may cause no harm!! And I declare to you (Jason Jacobs, Chad Michael Morrissette, Matt Martinez in Carmichael Ca. etc.) that I felt God saying "I have surely seen the oppression of my people".... And "I have heard their sorrows..." (Exodus 3:7).... But I came to the students at Folsom High, Locke High and Lodi High etc.. As I reasoned with my daddy (God) about whether or not I should write about my alleged offence etc. I told Him (Exodus 4:1) basically "But suppose they (Garrett McCain, Travis Shaw, Omar Samy and Tadd Carr etc.) will not believe me or listen to my voice; suppose they say, "the Lord has not...." Sent me... But I felt in my spirit the inclination, inspiration and the motivation to "write the vision" (K.K.K.) today.

And I came to tell Nick Pelham, Bret Jolliff, Alex Blench and Alex Seabolt etc..... to the young man knowledge and discretion – "a wise man will hear and increase learning, and a man of understanding will attain wise counsel".... I gotta tell (Creflo Dollar? Pat Robertson? Benny Hinn?) "the weak you have not strengthened, nor have you healed (Leroy Jenkins? Benny?) those who were sick, nor bound up the broken, nor brought back what was driven away, nor sought what was lost; but with force and cruelty you have ruled them.... Surely because my flock became a prey (in LA. County jail, juveniles and in prisons), and my.... Because there was no shepherd, nor did my shepherds feed themselves (with Bentleys and Rolls etc.) and did not feed my flock".... Ezekiel 34: 4-12....

Alex Chivescu, Maxwell Hanger, Daniel Sample and Josh Costa can I tell you all something? "What is this proverb that you people have about.... which says, 'the days are prolonged, and every vision fails?.... I will lay this proverb to rest, and they shall no more (I'll break the curse! End the cycle! I'll interrupt and disrupt the norm!) use it as a proverb in Israel.... The days are at hand, and the fulfillment of every vision for no more shall there be any false vision or flattering divination within the House of Israel... For I am the Lord. I (Jehovah) speak, and the word which I speak will come to pass; it will no more be postponed; for in your (Chivescu, Jolliff, Jake Heartsong, Blench and you too etc.) days.... I will say a word and perform it...." Ezekiel 12: 22-28 "Therefore say to them, 'thus says the Lord God: "none of my words will be postponed any more, but the word which I speak will be done," says the Lord God'... Are you reading? In Ezekiel 13:3 God says to you with H.I.V. (Having Insufficient Vision) "Woe the foolish prophets, who follow their own spirit and have seen nothing".... I see a way out of no way. I see a way out of the trailer park, hood and the barrio. I see a way!.... "Because you have spoken nonsense and envisioned lies, therefore I am indeed against you", says the Lord God"...

But I see truth, hope, help, deliverance and magic for you. I see the youth at Mars Hill Church (in Seattle), Gabriel Gomez (7th grader), Jakob Karr (Orlando Florida), Larry Laboe, Cameron Civello, John Griffin (Sacto Freshman), Johnny O'Neal, Daniel Job and Shea Newberry coming up and coming out.... I believe in Sean Conway, Danen Beres (and his bro.), Joshua Murillo, Ryan DiLello and in Joseph Schoen. We (Garrett Cunningham, Tadd Carr, John Sexton and Christopher Durbin etc.) can do this. If not now when? If not us who? I feel a shifting. I feel a lifting. I feel an anointing Marius, Murillo, Blench and me are getting off the bench. We will rise! We must rise. I feel a shifting, lifting and a gifting. I feel Travis Shaw, Danen, Nick Pelham and Faisal Saleh. We will win!.... Louis Copelin and Sam Fuick we need you too. We need Joseph Latham (from Torrance), Jeff Glen Howell and Justin Howell. We need Devin Deuell. We need Khadijah and... we need anointing (Marc Gross, David Joiner and James Nesmith etc.) to break the yoke, the curse and the cycle. We need God.... In my Clark Kent (Jacob, trickster, supplanter, etc.) state I'll fail and go to hell. But if God be for me who can be against me. We call upon Almighty God to lead us, guide us and to strengthen us. Devin Deuell, Brian Devin Graham, David Proctor and Joey Grissett etc. We can do it. We will do it. We must achieve. We've got to succeed. We will do it. You (Hugh Michael Hughes in Sacto CA. etc.) me and we. What shall we render? What shall we give? We've got to come out against every gang. We've got to break the curses of gangs off of our children. Revive yourself! Rise up and believe.... Get up!....

I want Jason Rosen, Billy Bell, Roger Walthorn and Joshua Murillo etc. to get up and to get out.... I keep wondering (again) how in the heck could Elijah be that gifted, that lifted, that anointed and that depressed... And when I see lil studs like Austin Sisneros, Larry Laboe, Tyler Schuurman, John Griffin, Christopher Clubb (Oregon) and Shawn Hornbeck etc. I'm cognizant that there is more than meets the eye. You can be cool, a stud, a jock and still be miserable. You can be lonely, afraid, bullied and angry etc. while you're talented, gifted and lifted... What happened at The Juniper Tree got Elijah up but not out... The cycle (or drugs, glue, paint, anger, smoking etc.) will never stop because it is on the inside of you.... Computer geeks, kids of successful parents, etc. are committing suicide every day... We have kids afraid to go to school and too embarrassed to "talk" about it. We must (Yes I'm being "redundant") start listening to our children... Benjamin Alexander (comp. expert & college student) and Alex Blench can help us understand kids who don't interact "socially".... I've come to understand that we are patternistic people. And in moments of authentic introspection we find the truth is always somewhere inside of us.... Some kids at the height and climax of your school and college years keep regressing back to a dark place... Until you transform your perception (Tadd Carr, Aaron Jackson and Donald Dusk etc.) you won't change... Elijah was a master warrior. He was a talented, gifted and an anointed man.... "Wait on me inside the cave.".... Back up and meticulously look at this dude Elijah. All that power he had and yet a woman (Jezebel) ran him out of town. Marius, Brett, Chivescu and you (too), have you ever been at the climax or peak of your streak and some woman (boy or girl) was able to beat you with a "threat"? The book says Elijah "ran for his life"! (1 Kings Chapter 19 if you have a Bible)...

... And this mighty man of God, this warrior, this Colin Powell, this Colonel or General... this Michael Jordan of warriors sat down underneath a broom tree and prayed that he might die... Elijah said "It is enough!" That's it, gotta quit, I can't hit.... " Now, Lord, take my life, for I am no better than my fathers"... Have any of you young men in your teens, tweenies and perhaps thirties ever secretly said to yourself "I'm no better than my daddy! My daddy left my momma and now I got a child I'm not taking care of. And I'm in and out of jail. And I'm".... Some of you have mommas who have told you "Your gonna be just like yo (sic) daddy! No damn good!".... Do you hear me today?

"... And there he went into a cave (dark place". And God said "What are you (Michael Jordan, Colin Powell, King General) doing here, Elijah?" What R U doing back at the crack house? Y R U back on meth? What doeth thou there? And I wish I could tell Garrett McCain, Alex Chivescu and (u 2) you etc. that as a prolific author and as a man.... as the commander in chief of G.B.G. that it is not me... But (as quiet as it's kept) between you, me (Murray J. Janus, Michael Morchower, Bob Blasier, Mark Ravis etc. under the attorney client privilege!) and the door post, it is me too. I know the Bloods, Crips, Eme and the Bulldogs etc. don't want nobody (sic) to know but "it's me too". It is David Hellyer, David Dowdie, David Joiner, David Reynolds and King David too... This King who slayed a giant with a slingshot found himself in Elijah's predicament and we hear David in the secret dark place... "Lord I (25 year old "Hiram") am an anointed and appointed man. I'm a King! I'm a Gang Banger for God. But I'm conflicted and afflicted. I am a "man". I done got a woman pregnant. I had her husband killed! Lord".... David really did say (psalm 55) "Because of the "voice" (not the gun, bomb, knife or sword!... A "threat" (words) by a woman ran Elijah outta town. And now here is a King! A big old buff brutha like no other talking about a voice) of the enemy".... 55: 4, 5 and 6 ... (please remember we ain't talking about a chump or a sissy etc. We are talking about a "King") "My heart is sore (to be "sore" implies you've been hurting for days. Soreness comes after the impact!) pained within me, and the terrors (sounds suicidal to me.... "Elijah - it's me too! Not just you!") of death have fallen upon me". Here is a King so nervous he's shaking "fearfulness and trembling have come upon me, and horror has overwhelmed me.... "Oh, that I had wings like a dove! I would fly away and be at rest"... Right now I'm going to bed and waking up just as tired as I was when I laid down.

... While I'm asleep my mind is in a tug of war with my spirit. A part of me is lusting for Tyra! Another part is longing for Jesus. I gotta Clark Kent on one shoulder and Superman on the other. I'm a fornicator, an adulterer, a murderer but a King, with an anointing and a man after God's own heart....

Zach Freisen, Cody Sheldon and Eddie Cannon all know what it's like to go to bed tired and wake up tired. Matt Stuart (ABC reporter) and Dr. Alex Vaclavik all know you can get sleep but no "rest".... So I hear the psalmist David Sayin to you, me and to Elijah that "its me too!... Elijah tells God "I am alone I am left; and they (Mike Bunnell, Marion E. Spearman, Sgt. J.S. etc.) seek to take my life".

But always listen for a still small voice! I wanna tell Alex Chivescu, Jake Heartsong, Josh Murillo, Travis Shaw, Claw, Doc and (U 2) all of you to "wait" for a still small voice... When Elijah heard the voice he was in a dark place. He had been threatened, let down and had had his grapes of hope crushed into the raisens of despair. But when he "heard" a still small voice he said "I'll try it again". He said "Let me get up and maybe I can get out. Maybe I can make it. Maybe I can get over this broken relationship. Maybe I can go on. Maybe I can heal. Maybe I can ...."

... So the Bible says Elijah "went out".... tell yourself "I got to go out! I must get out of this dark place. I "...." He "went out and stood" Every soldier gotta take a stand Baby Boy. There is a time to laugh and a time to cry. A time 2 kneel and a time 2 stand! Touch yourself and say "I gotta take a stand". Elijah went out and "stood in the entrance of the cave..." He comes to the door of the cave.... He's not all the way out (Alex) but he aint all the way in.... "At least I can see a lil daylight now. At least it aint all the way dark in the door. I may not be out yet. But devil you should have killed me when I was backed up in the dark place. You should have killed me when I was backed up in the cave of my depression. But I got up! And I stood in the door. I got up because I expected something.... Expectancy will get you to the door. And if you get to the door on a hope you can get through the door on faith. You can get up and to the door on a wing. But you'll get through the door on a prayer.

The moment he listened to the voice he got up. The moment he saw (visions) daylight his perception changed! And when he transformed, transmogrophied and changed his perception he got out!.... In verse 19 Elijah got where you've got to get. In 19 Elijah did what G.B.G. and you have got to do. In 19 Elijah did what Jesse Jackson had to do when he (me too) fell down and had a baby out of wedlock. In 19 Elijah did what David had to do. In 19 Elijah did what every boy, youngster, teen, tweenie and even the fellas in their fifties and sixties must learn to do.... In 19 Elijah "departed" from the dark place. He "departed" from the broken place. He "departed" from the crackhouse, whorehouse or the place of depression.... So Elijah "departed from there, and found Elisha". After Elijah left the dark place he found that one who would end up saying (II Kings 2:6) "As the Lord lives, and as your (Elijah) soul lives, I (Elisha) will not leave you!"... Elijah would have never met his "main" man if he did not leave the cave.... Some of you kids are in the prisons of hurt, prisons of "leftedness" (she/he left me and...) and the "prisons of abandonment" and... You think you can't make it without her... But Baby Boy if you don't believe Nuthin (sic) else I write etc. If yall (Blench, Heartsong, Laboe, Sheldon, Chivescu and you too) don't believe what I write about my "case". If you all don't believe I have a passion for youth. If you (do - it's up to you) believe every nasty, filthy and dastardly thing that Mary Hanlon Stone says about me. If you "believe" all the "mess" (embellishment, prevarication and false speculations etc. about me) in my criminal record; okay! I can live (I've made it 38 plus years) with you not believing me... But this, this, this, this one thing I need you 2 believe: Believe that as long as you don't (I repeat) die (in the dark place) over the one that left! You, will meet somebody new!.... "Hallelujah" belongs there! I promise you! I double promise you! I triple promise you! I don't care how wonderful, sexy and beautiful she was! I don't care how "bad" he was. She may have had Beyonce Booty! Her crap may have smelled like roses (I doubt that!)... She may have tickled your every fantasy. And you thought she was your soulmate. But your (Larry Laboe, Billy Bell, Victor Smalley, Nate, C.J. Sheron and...) destiny is not tied to the one that (I'm being redundant but y-o-u need this) left. When people wanna leave you let them go. It just means that their part in your story is over... But Elijah "What doeth thou here?" You "can't meet Elisha if you stay in the cave". I came to tell you (David Hellyer, Ralph Cannon, John Garvin etc.) to get yo butt out of the dark place. I command you to get out of there. Just come to the door so you can see daylight. Just come to the door. Just look at what's possible. You don't have to have any "faith" right now. I just want you to have some hope....

I lost Lathia (she was "bad")! I left and lost (Yvette Lewis) my soul mate. I left and lost Marva Respres, Tonya and... I lost others! And I was broken and wounded. And boys R scared to run to somebody and say "yo I'm a preacher! Yes I'm tight with ambassadors, civil rights legends and I preach. Yes I'm anointed and appointed but I'm hurt and I'm broken... And I don't think I can get over her. I'm hurt! I'm lonely! I need Yvette! I need Marva! How could they do this? What's wrong with me? I got kids who wanna be like me at Bethel. I got boys imitating my preaching. Running around sayin "Good, good, good, good! Good Evening". I am somebody! I am an entrepreneur... But I'm so broken I can't rest. I'm about to run to Harrisburg and rip off Stella. I'm a mess".... I thought it was over. Hell nall yall I can't lie. I can ("sort" of) relate to Michael being looked up to, worshipped (never worship a human!) and... secretly he was the world's loneliest man. Let me ask yall a question: (just a "thought" or a "possibility" etc.) what if he was totally and completely innocent? You know exactly what I'm talking about. I'm not going into it. But just what if? What if it was not just the brilliance of super lawyer Tom Mesereau? What if this man never did anything unseemly to a child? Let us (cause it's me too! I called him eccentric, weird, probably a mole..... and I said he wanted to be white and I was not right!) imagine being a billionaire with a "B". Folk love to see you dance and sing. But they all suspect that you are a pervert when you're not... you can't even sleep .... Lord have mercy!...

My message to you guys (i.e. Jason Rosen, Billy Bell and Jeff Buttle... Gabe Williams and Timothy Coleman) is whether you sing, preach, pray or dance "it's me too". Don't dress up and masquerade the problem. Get delivered! Get delivered from people and delivered from the problem... After I lost and/or left Marva, Lathia, Yvette etc. I almost quit! I almost gave up! I almost turned back. I.... I got up and went to the door of the (mental) cave of my depression. I stood and found myself in Richmond Virginia. I saw enough daylight to "see" that my jewelry needed cleaning. I walked (went) into a pawnshop on Broad street to get my jewelry cleaned. And I "met" somebody who said "I will not leave thee"....

And I came to tell Seabolt, Ben Whipple, Nick Pelham, Chris Durbin, Chivescu, Billy Bell, Billy Fleming and Johnny Willie to "get up" and.... If you get up you can "get out". And once you get out you will mess around and "see" some daylight. And once you see (what could be) you can get some "hope" back. Once you get hope it's on and cracking.

.... I was in a dark place for 14 months. Locked onto a hospital bed and "left for dead" by Mike Bunnell, Marion E. Spearman, Wally Tucker, D.L. Criner and R.N. Bond etc. But I got up and saw "G.B.G.: and once I starting hoping to use prison as an educational platform I ... Charles (at UNLV), Taylor Moson and Tadd Carr are you all perusing this? I need Collin Orcutt, Max Steele, Greg Deekens, Nicholas Evans, Sam Hayes and Caleb Peek etc. to hear me. I know you all are exhausted (lol) with my "name" calling (dropping) but I need Andy Knot, Jason Word, Kyle Sevey, Donna Sheshtowsky and Devin Deuell etc. to hear me.... I came for Christopher Jost, Steve Perry and Laura Cole etc. I wanna tell kids in trailer parks, Barrios, suburbs and juveniles etc. Even if you're in a dungeon! Even if you messed up and got locked up. Maybe you're in juvenile or jail. But I came to tell Mika (Atmikasounds on Twitter), Professor Russell Rumberger, Scott Tyler Jelensky, Scott Johnson (Warner Robbins Ga.) and Maxwell Hanger to "Don't stop believing". When Neal Schon lost Steve Perry he thought it was over. But he went on Youtube and met (found!) Arnel Pineda... and Arnel had been in some "dark places" and some lonely places. He had been "homeless". He slept on park benches. But Arnel's "gift" brought him out. Arnel met "Neal" and they began a "Journey" that reignited the soul of rock n roll! And Neal says "Arnel makes me a better man".. I.E. there are a lot of basketball players who used to say that "Michael Jordan makes me a better player". Just playing with the dude made you a better player.

135

And Neal says Arnel makes him a "better man"; not a better singer! Not a better musician but a better man.... Oh how I wish I could/would develop to the point (I'm not "there" yet) where a Jason Huyck, Larry Laboe, Victor Smalley or a Johnny Willie could/would say I make them "better" .... Arnel has a "humble and beautiful heart". He escaped the "pain and the poverty" and says "all I wanted to do was get out of that". Everything is in Divine order. And Arnel told Oprah "I feel like I'm an alien right now and I'm not allowed to be here... I thank God for that"... I can relate to that feeling when you're in your "element" or anointing and you feel surreal. You feel like you are watching yourself in a movie...

I want you (kids in schools) to have "resilience". You can triumph! You can have "everything you want if you help enough other people get, what they want" says Zig Zigler... God told Elijah that as soon as you leave this "dark place" etc "anoint Hazael". Help somebody else! He told Elijah as soon as you leave this dark place don't feel "sorry for yourself". Don't take time to tell a sob story. Don't have a pity party, but use what you (Elijah) have to "anoint Jehu" and "Elisha"... You may be broken in a place where I'm whole. But I've got some broken places. Some of us are broken in our spirituality, mentality, sexuality, self confidence and criminality. But every person has a "broken place". And I command G.B.G. and all of you thugs, gangsters, gay boys, freaks, geeks, nerds an tur.... (lol) .. I command you to "anoint" (lift, help, teach, heal and skill) somebody "else" in "their" broken place. Don't you dare allow the enemy to convince you that because of your sexuality, mentality, criminality, depression and.... Don't let the enemy convince you that "David because of what you did God can't use you"! Don't think "we" don't need "you" because of your "conflicts". Even though David did what he did I'd a paid "money" to sit at the feet of (the man who slayed Goliath) David and learn. I used to treasure every moment I had with Ambassador Young and Rev. Hosea Williams - they were there on the balcony at Lorraine Motel with Dr. Martin Luther Kind Jr... I don't care what Bill Clinton did, I'd pay to sit with him and learn from him... Jesse Jackson can still teach me a thing or two; how bout you?

... You still have worth! You still have a gift. And I want each one to reach and teach one... Daniel Bugriyev (a beautiful soul and spirit), Devin Deuell and Jason Huyck etc. "Don't stop believing"... Khadijah, Chris Gardner and Arnel were all "homeless". Yet Chris and Arnel are both now rich. Chris lived in the library like Khadijah. And Khadijah is at Harvard!.... Roger Walthorn, Jason Rapp are you reading? It is not over. I'm a "word slinger", an "ink slinger", a scribe and a "president" all while I'm a "prisoner"....

Mandela went from the prison to the presidency!

... Do you know how much power you really have? You have the power to manifest a Dream... "K.K.K." and "G.B.G." are "dreams". I've manifested by the power God gave me. You can call it the Law of "attraction" or whatever the heck you want to call it. But "call it)". And if you "call it" you'll "draw (attract) it"... Alex Chivescu, C.J. Sheron, Brandon White, Larry Laboe etc. what are your dreams and hopes? Write those dreams on paper and then bury (plant) them and they will grow. Put them under a rock and wherever you are in the world that rock will call you back.... Ask Tererai Trent (google her)..Education is power! Go back to the rock! Go back to your dream! Go back to your Hope! Go back 2 school! Go back 2 your "vision".... Oprah says "You never know what "words" will be "the words" that will affect a child's mind".... An angel told Daniel "I have come for (because of) your words".... I want you to begin to practice saying (words) your dreams, your hopes and your visions after you write them down.... And if (when) you write your dreams (on paper) and begin to say (repetitively like I repeat names over & over! lol) your dreams out loud! You will be able to one day tell Oprah, Tyra Banks and even Tyler Perry that "it's me too!

... I'm not Creflo Dollar. Ipso Facto, I am not going to promise you that you will be a billionaire! Hell after you've seen Elvis, Belushi and Michael you may not even want to be filthy rich!... But I will assure you of two things actually three. A. You will go down (into a cave! You may not be depressed right now because you and "Katrin" are cool etc. Maybe you have it "going on" right now but keep living!) sometimes!

B. You can get up!.... And if you get up and just stand in the "entrance" of the cave... What you "see" will C. Get You Out! You will get out! Whether you do ballet (Gabe Williams, Timothy Coleman, Carlos Rodriquez), Dance (Billy Bell, Josh Murillo), Bromance (Marius and Q") or play football (Jonathan Davis, Garrett McCain) etc. etc.

.... You can get up! You can get out... God is not through with you yet! God is not through with you yet! God still loves you. He might not like you sleeping with Bathsheba. He might not like you killing Uriah! But "whatever" the "conflicts" you (Gary Browning, Joseph Latham, Daniel Jacob, Jeff Glen Howell, Justin Howell, Jeff Allen Walker, Sean Zane, Jason Huyck, Dr. Ken Carter, Dr. Alex Vaclavik, C.J., Jake, Chivescu and you too) may have your daddy still loves you! He loves Tim Daraitis (student in Rocklin CA), Chad Michael Morrissette, Matt Martinez, Eddie and Ralph Cannon.... God still loves you. He loves Roger Walthorn, Jeff Buttle, Nate (Paradise Hotel), Cole (the Secret Millionaire), Cameron Civello, Daniel Sample, Alexander Abt, Johnny Weir, Stephen Carriere etc. just like he loves you and me.... Important disclaimer: If the back cover implies that Peter Andrist, G.B.G. or anyone other than me is calling Bunnell, Spearman and Tucker a "molester" etc. Be advised that "I" (not Peter, not G.B.G. and not anyone affiliated with me) am calling that thug Bunnell, Spearman and Wally (AKA "Hitler") Tucker "Child molesters". I sincerely believe they "are" indeed!.. End of notice...

On 10/11/09 C.O. Dunkle walked up on the tier and a black inmate (A.) whom I'd not seen that day, looked up and said "What's up dude". And I was about to speak until I realized that "A" was speaking to C.O. Dunkle (not "me").... Then as A. exited the shower he began chatting (without calling a "name") and I (again) thought he was speaking to me. But instead he was speaking to (J.J.) a white guy.... As much as I love white folks (i.e. my wife) and as much as I want to see convicts and staff get alone. It is (still) a sad, and shocking day when a black "inmate" (A) feels more inclined to acknowledge a C.O. and a Caucasian guy who perhaps would have stabbed him in L.A. County Jail; than to me.

But this place (Hades) and these people (inmates and staff) brain washes, numbs and dumbs up anyone who enters. This Valley of despair (I repeat) is dark in here! It is mighty dark in this place. It is filled with the most bitter, broken and lonely boys (claiming we're men) on the planet. I want to ask every Y.G. (Young Gangsta), youth, teen, and tweenie (on the planet) a question: Do you "really" wanna meet me? Only way yo (sic) narrow ass can meet me is to get "locked" up!....

In 1999-2000 I met a man in New Folsom who was a predator. Nothing really strange about meeting a predator in a prison; Right? But dude was also a misogynist and a molester! He (like so many criminals) had been caught with sadistic kiddie porn and let off the hook because of "who" he was... one day he was doing O.T. (overtime) and told me: I know all about you "N" and your "book sh-t". And "one day you're gonna get killed". Did you know predators (convicts?) can work "overtime"? ... In 2006 he assaulted a female correctional officer (C.O. T.V.) in building Five on B-facility. And he told her "I'll rape you and kill your "family". And oh by the way, convicts "don't" work "overtime". Ipso Facto, this misogynistic, belligerent and bellicose miscreant.... this predator who assaulted (I affirm under penalty of perjury!) a female peace officer etc. was not an inmate. He was a decorated, veteran (with 18 years in) correctional officer. C.O. Larry Turner! let me write it again: correctional officer (Chu Vue? Wally Laffitte? Stephen Luke Scarsella? Mike Bunnell? Marion E. Spearman? D.L. Criner? Wally Tucker?) Larry Turner! .... Turner was working in the control booth (with a "rifle" and with real "bullets") in building five on B-yard. Turner (a sworn peace officer) became so livid with an inmate (already in "chains", imprisoned and powerless!) that Turner told the inmate "I'll come down there and kick your ass." Turner got a co-worker to relieve him (the co-worker should have refused!). Turner came down (abandoning his "post") out of the gun tower to the prison dorm and began viciously attacking the inmate! A female (pretty lil senorita) c.o (T.V.) attempted to save Turner's j-o-b. By pulling him (Larry Turner) off of the inmate. Turner turned on T.V. and knocked her out cold!.... She should have (James Brosnahan, Mitchell A. Kamin, Michelle Williams Court, Grant R. Specht etc. are you all interested? Atty. Murry J. Janus can give you all her full name....) sued Turner and C.D.C. she will never be the "same" again. She suffers from PTSD and the department kept Turner around (in employee ad-seg = the mailroom! To punish convicts by putting a criminal in the mailroom to steal our money, magazines, stamps and photos etc.) for almost a year. The "pay cage" is right next to the mailroom. So every time T.V. went to get her paycheck she had to endure a "death stare" and threats by C.O. Larry Turner. And even in 2010 there are many (as soon as Bunnell masterminds my next transfer I'll "name names" etc.) peace officers who won't speak to her. They intimidate and alienate her because she broke the "code of silence" and "told" on Turner. If they (i.e. C.O. G.W.) were men they would wanna kick Turner's ass for beating (Chris Brown) on a woman. Where I come from "men" love "women". We don't assault them "ever".

Oprah is right "love doesn't hurt". Judge Greg Mathis is right "If a woman assaults you and you can't restrain her - run!" ....

This just in: One of my investigators just told me (I'm unable to verify this at press time) that Larry Turner is now working across the street (at the prison where Mike Bunnell used to control. Where Bunnell still has "many allies".... I am certain Warden "Jimbo" Walker would not allow a "woman beater" to work in his prison!). At Old Folsom State Prison.... If so I am calling upon Doris Matsui, Diane Feinstein, Maxine Waters, Eric Holder and the F.B.I. to immediately look into this. The NAACP, SCLC, ACLU, Alice Huffman and NAPS should protest a "known criminal" who can't control his "temper" and has "violent tendencies" working around inmates. This man has access to a "rifle". This is a (if he's really at Old Folsom) "threat" to the "safety" and "security" of inmates, staff and the "public"....

I just left the Shu Yard "alone". It is the same Shu Yard that Eric Menendez, Doc and I used to hang out on as Eric told us how much Barbara Walters "loved" him. And the same Shu Yard on which he explained that Barbara called New Folsom after I.S.U. searched his cell. And Barbara forced the captain to put Eric on the telephone so she could hear his voice and know he was "okay". The same Shu Yard on which Eric borrowed $ 400.00 from Doc and also borrowed from me.... The same Shu Yard that C.O. Wally Laffitte used to use as a delivery "spot" for drugs, knives, cell phones, condoms and money! ... But in 2009 I find myself on this infamous Shu Yard "alone". As I looked up (a Shu Yard is enclosed by brick, concrete walls 20ft. high, barbed wire is atop the concrete but there is no ceiling which makes it a 'yard'. Imagine your garage without the roof. That's a Shu Yard) at the dark sky and I messed around and located a "star", one star! And it seemed that I could hear Dr. King saying in Birmingham Alabama "Sometimes I feel discouraged and feel my work is in vain. But then the Holy Spirit comes and revives my soul again... I know it's dark right now. But only when it is dark enough can you see the stars. I see the stars of hope tonight! Yes, I see"... As I looked up at this 'one star' I began to pray. "Lord I can't see my way out. But I can see my way up. I see a star. There is a light at the end of the tunnel". I told God "I need your help tonight. My Clark Kent needs you. My Jacob, conman and the trickster in me needs you. My Israel and my prince is already connected. But Lord God don't let that which is weak in me destroy that which is strong in me. Don't let my short coming destroy the long in me. Don't let the cracks (and holes) in my mentality, sexuality, psychology and intellectuality destroy my spirituality. Don't let Sher destroy the man. Don't let the man destroy my ning. I need God! I'm not smart enough to do it on my own. I still believe God.

Put your super on my natural. Help me! Abba! Abba! Help me". I told the Lord on the Shu Yard that I needed Him to anoint this tome. Put His power and His spirit within these pages. I won't win any awards for this book, because I'm too wild, scathing and blunt. And because I won't allow a ghost writer, book doctor or editor to "clean" this book up. But to all of you ready to criticize me (too many names, to 'All over the place', not smooth enough etc.) I accept. But yo old ass ain't who I'm writing "to" anyway. The folks (Gen. Y, teens, tweenies, thugs, gangsters, wanna-be gangsters, students, boys in group homes and in juvie etc.) I'm writing to write worse (lol) than me. They use PDQ for pretty damn quick instead of ASAP for as soon as possible. They write like thugs and read like crooks. They would never read this book if Dr. Franklin Curren, Dr. C. Solis, Dr. Jennifer Heitkamp (All of whom advised me on the contents and substance of this book. All of whom are brilliant psychiatrists etc.) or Dr. Terry Kupers wrote it. But you let some thug; some John Gotti, a rapist or a murderer put pen to paper (PTP) and kids in the hoods, barrios, trailer parks and the suburbs will hang on to every word!

I wrote a 32 page essay for boys in 2008. I had no time to proof it after my typist typed. She made a few errors and I made a lot. She mailed it directly to a mom who let her 17 year old (a senior in high school) son read it. He wrote "It's the most awesome, candid and enlightening writing I've ever read Mr. Manning. I shared it with my football team and they thought it wuz (sic) hella cool dude"... When I read this "awesome" essay which I wrote I found 9 typographical errors. I found run-on sentences. I found cheesy segues and too many "names". But kids called it "awesome". So you who don't like my style I want to be gracious and ask you to pray for me... But please pass this book on to a kid. Give it to one of those gangbangers on the street corners. Give it to a kid who is sitting on the "fence" between dropping out of school and dropping into prison. That kid who is "betwixt" and "between".

I need you (lawyers, entrepreneurs, pastors and professors) to get this book to kids at (schools G.B.G. has adopted) Locke High, Martin Luther King Jr. Academy (in Sacto and "Shoulder to Shoulder" at "Freedom Hall", Ron Clark Academy (in my hometown) etc. All you need to do is tell cafepress to "send ten copies of K.K.K. to Locke High School" etc... I want my law students in Ohio (Ryan M. and Heather F.) to find Arthur (who was on the Wendy Williams show on 7/30/09) and get Arthur this book. Let's get it to Dan Rollman, Justin Bieber, Dustin (and Mallory on Tyra Banks on 8/21/09), Leon Powell, David Gordon, Brenda Love's son Kyle Love and to David Hellyer... I need Rev. Otis Moss and preachers all across this planet to help G.B.G. get this book to Al Rojas (Woodland CA), Andy C (the volunteer) at Homeboy Industries etc. I want Roy Cherry, (my boy) Scott Johnson (from Warner Robins Ga.), Austin Sisneros, Eric Flores (Roseville CA.), Bill Dallas, Nathan Wilhite, Alan Rafferty, Andrew Rauscher and Jason Huyck to become G.B.G. Ambassadors. I want young, strong and focused youngsters like Craig Scott, Louis Copelin, Michael Perrelli, Robert Linggi, Jesse Grund, Jake Reitan, Kevin Greene (Grand Rapids Michigan), Bryce Kaff, Dan Sellery (Sacto) etc. We must put this powerful book into the hands, heads and hearts of lil white boys, black and brown boys and plant these words into their spirits....

I just wanna see this book in those young hands. Having held this book they can't stay the same. Change is in this tome. (as I said in another part of this book.) I don't know what chapter, section, page or in which paragraph your change will come. I have no idea what sentence, word or which l-e-t-t-e-r is going to change you. But if you are reading this book a transformation, transmogrification and "a change is gonna come" in you.

Jesus operated (again) by the force of faith and gravity had to submit. And he walked on water!.... Nuclear, atomic power and the laws of the universe are the children of the parent force which is faith. Faith is the parent force. We possess the greatest power on earth which is faith.

We can harness the power of faith and defy logic... "I'm gonna put u behind a rock so that when I pass by; the residue of where I was will bless you.... Because you can't see me and live!"....

The Bible is a weapon of mass destruction! You discover an explosive force called faith in the Bible. I have the power to blow up negative forces with faith. I'm a military (G.B.G. Baby) soldier. Faith is my most powerful weapon. The force of faith is like dynamite. And with it we (G.B.G.) have the power to blow up (disrupt, dismantle and destroy gangs) evil....

We (G.B.G.) are as serious about our war council meetings as President Obama is about Afghanistan. Drugs, gangs and violence are as much of a threat to kids as Osama, Al Qaeda and the Taliban are to Americans.

We aim to reach and teach Christopher McCowan (Fresno City College), Jeff (via Judge Wayne Rutherford or Rick Branham), Tim Daraitis, Cody Sheldon, David Santos,Scott Macintyre (and his brother), Alex Wagner Trugman, members of the Avenue Street Gang (Highland Park), Randy Madden, Nathan Langley (Sac state), Michael Castro and Andrew Lang. We need Phil Spector to help us get "K.K.K." to Vaughn English, Von Smith, James Michael Avance, Matt Fisher (Sacto promoter), Mitch Fredrickson (Dean of Academic and student affairs at Dunwoody Academy), Craig Hutto and Attorney Pat Young etc. etc.

This tome may cause a ferocious media firestorm on the internet etc. And when folks like Alex Blench, Ben Alexander, Larry Laboe etc. begin to blog and vlog about G.B.G. and K.K.K. etc. it will spread like wildfire! If Jeremy (racecar "Jeremy" the Coalinga Fire Department Master Fireman!) takes my challenge (on page 313 of "Blue Eyed Blonde" Book II) we'll put him on a calendar (serious...) for ladies 18 and older (perhaps we'll send Marion E. Spearman a calendar!).... Craig Hutto, Alex Blerch, Daniel Sample, Michael Castro and Anthony Fedorov I'll double the offer (pp 313 in "B.E.B." Book II) for you....

Let us (you and me) work like crazy to get John Griffin (CSU-Sac) and Cameron Civello to become G.B.G. (paid) ambassadors. And let us pray that the Schoettler-Neufeld tire retread center owners will donate hundreds of copies of this book to teens. I want to get it to all twenty thousand KIPP (Knowledge Is Power Program) students in New York. We need to get it to principals like Joe Negron, David Levin (KIPP co-founder), Joshua Costa, Folsom High Bulldogs, Gabriel Gomez, John Litzler (we have a stipend for John in Loveland Ohio), Casey Cristosto, Jacob Karr (stipend! Orlando Florida), Billy Bell (stipend!) and Dan Sellery .... We must get this book to Mike Wilkerson and to Christopher (Becky's son) Thompson....

And I want to tell you youngstas about a 21 year old "white crip". He reminds me of my old celly Jeffrey Allen Walker and I will tell you about this lil youngsta white crip in a lil while....

I need to remind our youth that there are some cunning, crafty and sneaky (this is magnified in the prisons; I am a living witness!) people who carry Bibles. Benny Hinn wears a white suit and carries a Bible. And please remember (those of you who believe in the Higher Power) no matter how anointed and gifted you are your anointing won't shield you from crafty people. In fact your anointing can be a magnet for deceptive folks. But you don't need to wine and dine with duplicitous folks whom you know mean you no good. You are not Jesus. Jesus ate dinner with a man He knew was going to betray Him. But Jesus also knew Judas would end up killing himself. And when folks plot, scheme and connive against you a lot of times they'll kill themselves... The Bible is a marvelous (and the most powerful) book. And it gives an agricultural perspective which confuses Metropolitan boys. But when we read it we must condition our minds to think agriculturally.... the soil grows the plant. If the ground is tainted or poisoned the seeds won't grow. But the ground is not the only concern for farmers and gardeners. The climate or the atmosphere also grows the plant. Check the atmosphere around your mind young man.... I tell parents and teachers to evaluate the atmosphere around our kids. The wrong climate, atmosphere or environment can stunt the growth of our kids. I tell adults to change the atmosphere in their homes. The atmosphere can hinder (or turbo-charge) the manifestation of your miracle... Put water in a frozen atmosphere and it transforms into ice. Put that ice (water) into a pot and change the atmosphere to heat and the ice becomes steam. Atmosphere, climate and environment produces transmogrification. If you change the atmosphere you change the situation... I was talking to my dear friend (principal - of Ralph Bunche School in Atlanta) Aaron Fernander the other day and we began to talk about "sons". I told Aaron "ours sons are supposed to carry the anointing (or promise). This is why the enemy is after our boys. Putting knives, drugs and guns in their hands. He's trying to distort and disrupt the anointing which they carry". Aaron replied (candidly) "Sherman you can speak to that like no one else I've ever met. With your mind, connections and your ability to preach and speak I would not have dreamed that you would go to prison. When there is promise, power and great destiny inside you the devil works day and night trying to disrupt the anointing".

A lot of times the enemy will fill a gifted man with "pride". And "pride" always comes before a great fall. Sports athletes, preachers and many politicians suffer from arrogance. They forget from whence they came. They forget who brought them.... Alex Haley (of "Roots" fame) used to keep a picture of a turtle sitting up on a fence in his office. And he'd always say "one thing you know for sure when you see a turtle on a fence is that he had some help". And when you can throw a football, shoot a basketball, play a guitar or sing a song etc. God gave you arms, hands, fingers and vocal cords. And don't forget to remember where all your blessings come from.

The enemy will use that pride, selfishness, drugs, mental illness, anger or alcohol etc. to mess up your anointing.... Old folks used to say that "when praises go up blessings come down". And you can change your spiritual (and mental) atmosphere by giving God praise. Oh Bless His Holy name. Hallelujah! Thank you Jesus!

... My atmosphere just changed

... The contents of his book change atmospheres... "Boys need some connection to and direction from their fathers". Dr. Franklin Curren told me "and when that connection and direction is missing it can shunt a boy's growth.... Our challenge is to find men willing to step up and to step in and mentor fatherless children" he continued.

I'm seeing boys (in our 30's, 40's, 50's and 60's) who folded like a cheap suit when it came to raising our children. Yet we "bad" let us tell it. And all "we" know is violence....

"My one failure as CEO of Chicago Public Schools was lowering and preventing violence in schools" Education Secretary Arne Duncan admitted. G.B.G./HEART, our advisory board (led by Dr. Curren) and our warden etc. are willing to work with secretary Duncan in prioritizing and nationalizing an effort to prevent school violence. G.B.G. members are experts on violence, bullying and victimizing. We are (according to Dr. Lewis Yablonsky) "Experience therapists". And we will work with Mr. Duncan, KIPP, Principal Fernander, David Lewin, Josh Costa, Daniel Watts and Charles Best etc. etc.

I am calling on Zac Sunderland, Zach Freisen, Omar Samy, Craig Hutto, Brett Jolliff, Jesse Martin (sailor), Garrett Cunningham and Cody Sheldon to join us (G.B.G.) and to become G.B.G. ambassadors.... I will pay stipends, bonuses, salaries and fees to as many of you (Maxwell Hanger, Alex Chivescu, Ben Alexander, Austin Sisneros, James Michael Avance, Danny Noriega and Michael Castro etc.) as I can. If I get proper support and can pay more of you (Billy Bell, Alex Holgan, Nathan Langley, Caleb Peek, Caleb Shockley and John Litzler etc.) I will.....

Nothing is more important to me than putting this book into the hands, of every young man. With more than 55 million American students we need at least (bare minimum) 5.5 million students to read this book.... John Tu, Earl Stafford, US Mint Green, Attorney Blasier, Atty. Mark

Ravis, Atty. Taylor B. Stone and Michael Morchower etc. will help us... And you bloggers, vloggers, podcasters and twitterers must tweet (even B 4 U eat!) about G.B.G. and "K.K.K.". Put it out there into the blogosphere... Tell somebody to read this book.... Get it to Alex King and... I wanna hear from Jacob Karr, John Litzler, Billy Bell and Victor Smalley PDQ... I want Dr. Janet Taylor and Dr. Jeff Gardere to help us put this tome "out there".

... Listen to me" we (G.B.G.) are authentic warriors and soldiers doing battle with the domestic Al Qaeda which is destroying our boys. Kind David was a soldier! He killed Goliath!.... Blessed be the Lord my rock, "who trains my hands for war, and my fingers for battle"... Sounds like war to me.... "My fortress, my high tower and my deliverer, my shield and the one in whom I take refuge, who subdues my people under me".

And, as we do this strategic, dangerous, methodical warfare against the domestic talibans (Bloods, Crips, AB, Bulldogs, NLR etc.) which are destroying our boys please remember that we wrestle "not" against "flesh and blood" but against "spiritual wickedness in High (associate wardens, captains, chiefs of police, judges etc.) places"... And, I told the Lord (as did King David in Psalm 144) to "Bow down your heavens, O Lord, and come down; touch the mountains, and they shall smoke. Flash forth lightning and scatter (gangs) them; shoot out your arrows and (disrupt, dismantle and) destroy them.... Stretch out your Hand from above; Rescue me and deliver me out of great waters, from the hand of (Dearaujo and his crew of evil doers) foreigners".

As we do warfare to rescue our boys I repeat that no matter how anointed you are you will meet folk who lie on you and want to see you fail.

.... "Whose mouth speaks lying words and whose right hand is a right hand of falsehood".... David was going through it. His own son Absalom had turned against him. And in verse II David "repeats" his call to God to "rescue and deliver me from the hand... Whose mouth speaks lying words, and.... "And the reason G.B.G. is fighting gangs and drugs etc. is "that our sons may be as plants grown up in their youth; that our daughters may be as pillars, sculptured in palace styles".

In psalm 18 I can "feel" what David (a "King") is saying. 18:4 "the pangs of death surrounded me, and the floods of ungodliness made me afraid".

... In the movie the boy said "I see dead people". In Hades I can state (with authenticity) that I see dead people! Dead men are walking; talking and breathing right here, right now. You're dead when you don't acknowledge God. You're dead when you hate yourself. You're dead when your heart is full of envy, larceny and deception. I see dead people!

But I tell you who are corrupting children (let me repeat that "it takes a village to raise a child" and "it takes a village to destroy a child). You who are putting guns and knives in their hands. You who put drugs and alcohol in their bodies. You who molest innocent children (yes, including Roman Polanski!). You who recruit them into gangs, hate groups, ???? (p. 523) and "teach" them racism etc. You are gonna mess around and make God mad. And when God gets angry.... Oh Baby, baby, baby.... "Then the earth shook and trembled; the foundations of the hills also quaked and were shaken, because He was angry. Smoke went up from His nostrils... He bowed the heavens also, and came down with darkness under His feet".... He "bowed the Heavens"....

"The Lord thundered from heaven, and the most High uttered His voice, hailstones and coals of fire. He sent out his arrows and scattered the Foe (gang bangers and drug dealers etc.), lightnings in abundance, and He vanquished them." Let me engage in tautology by repeating to the Bloods, Crips, AB, Southerners, Eme and.... "And He (God) vanquished (smashed!) them"...

... Do you (Derek King, Maxwell Hanger, Brett Jolliff etc.) understand that "the Foundations of the world were uncovered at your rebuke, O Lord, at the blast of the breath of your nostrils. He sent from above, He took me; He drew me out of many waters". God "took" me out of some situations that I'd have never made it out of. Dealing with people who have taken human life like it was nothing.... Living with guys who have murdered and who have the nerve to think they are "better" than a "rapist". Guys who murdered and now have a Bible in their locker. And they're taking a couple of college courses but are still racist, still murderers, still "duplicitous" etc.... This has taught me how dangerous people can be.... "He delivered me from my strong enemy, from those who hated me, for they were too strong for me". When it's a captain, an associate warden, a person who sleeps in the cell with me; they're too strong for me". "They confronted me in the day of my calamity, but the Lord was my support"... And let there be no doubt that I can't organize a strategic force such as G.B.G./HEART without my daddy. And it is "God who arms me with strength, and makes my way perfect. He makes my feet like the feet of deer, and sets me on my high places. He teaches my hands to make war (against gangs, guns, drugs and violence), so that my arms can bend a bow of bronze. You have also given me the shield of your salvation; your right hand has held me up, your gentleness has made me great. You enlarged my path under me, so my feet did not slip". I want all the molesters, gangs and dope peddlers to pay close attention to psalm 18:37-48. As commander in chief of G.B.G. listen to me "I have pursued my enemies and overtaken them; neither did I then back again till they were destroyed. I have wounded them (even with this book!), so that they could not rise; they have fallen under my feet. For you have armed me with strength for the battle; you have subdued under me those who rose up against me. You have also given me the necks of my enemies, so that I destroyed those who hated me. Then I beat them as fine as the dust before the wind; (I put the smash down!)... A people I have not known shall serve me.... He delivers me from my enemies. You also lift me up above those who rise against me; you have delivered me from the violent man"... God is delivering us from the (Bloods, Crips, BGF, AB, NLR, corrupted cops, Bunnell etc.) "violent man".

And I'm asking Rev. Otis Moss, Bishop Jakes, Bishop Long, Rev. Rick Warren and all prayer warriors to pray for a "switch". Ask God to do a "switcharoo" and move us (G.B.G.) into a season for our power. Let us use our power to reach our boys and snatch them from the claws of gangs, guns, drugs and violence... I need some believers to pray for me. And to pray for G.B.G. Pray that we become a powerful conduit to help troubled teens.... God has trained my hands to do war with this pen. Chief Deputy Warden Terry L. Rosario (AKA "Dad") once told me "Sherman you are the most dangerous convict at New Folsom. And you've never assaulted staff. Your pen makes you a force to be reckoned with". I aim (with firm determination) to reach out and recruit Billy Bell (in Florida), Travis Denison (Atl. GA.), The Wade Robson Project, Victor Smalley, Jakob Karr (Flo.), John Litzler, Elite fitness trainers (Sacto), Jonathan Davis (Elk Grove), Kyle Evans (Sacto), Justin Gadsden, Justin Howell, Joseph Latham (Torrance CA.), Andy C. (the volunteer and everybody at "Homeboy Industries") and Shea Newberry etc. etc. We reach out to studs, jocks, gay-boys, lesbians, nerds, geeks and freaks. We concur with President Barack Obama's decision to end "Don't ask don't tell" in the U.S. military. And we (most of our executive board) believe the act of homo sexuality is a "sin". And we believe smoking cigarettes is "sin". And we shan't exclude Mr. Obama from G.B.G. merely because he takes a puff. Nor can we exclude Danny Noriega (if he's gay) simply based upon our disagreement with who he goes to "bed" with. "For whoever shall keep the whole law, and yet stumble in one point, he is guilty of all". James 2:10.... Young men listen to a brutha "for we all stumble in many things. If anyone does not stumble in word, he is a perfect man, able also to bridle the whole body". I want all my lil Bloods, Crips, Mobs, thugs, gay boys, jocks and studs to peruse meticulously: ".. we put bits in horses' mouths that they may obey us, and we turn the whole body. Look also at ships: although they are so large (and you don't way a buck fifty soak and wet!) and are driven by fierce winds, they are turned by a very small rudder wherever the pilot desires". Are you all still reading? You at Locke High School? You at Lodi, Ron Clark Academy, Folsom High and "shoulder to shoulder'?" And the tongue "... repeat out loud "and my tongue". If you're in jail look over at your celly and say "and my tongue". If you're in class raise your hand and say 'and my tongue'...

"And the tongue" is verse 6 but go back to James 3:5 "Even so the tongue is a little (poquito) member and boasts great things. See how great a forest a little fire kindles? And the tongue is a fire, a world of iniquity (cussing, fussing, cursing, conniving and lying!) The tongue is so set among our members that it defiles the whole body, and sets on fire the course of nature; and it is set on fire by hell.... For every kind of beast and bird, of reptile and creature of the sea, is tamed and has been tamed by mankind. But no man (not the pope, Bishop Flip Flop or Deacon Willie Wonder etc.) can tame the tongue. It is an unruly evil, full of deadly poison. With it we bless our God and father, and with it (that tongue) we curse men, who have been made...."
.... my brethren, these things ought not to be so.... if you have bitter envy and self-seeking in your hearts, do not boast and lie against the truth".... We got a lot more to worry about other than who folks are sleeping with! I can never "support" gay marriage because the Bible does "not". Nor will I ever "support" lying because the Bible does "not". But if I stopped speaking to everybody who violated "thou shalt not lie" I'd have to stop speaking to Sherm!.... "this wisdom does not descend from above, but is earthly, sensual, demonic. For where (in Hades = prisons!) envy and self-seeking exist, confusion and every evil thing are there"... I was telling Willie (Claw) the other day "it's only 50 or 60 people out here on this yard right now. And we all hate one another. It's gossip, lies, dissension and anger. Why can't a few guys get along Willie?" And the answer is.... "confusion and every (racism, hate, envy, duplicity etc.) evil thing are there (in the prison!)." And where I'm trying (finally) to go is "but wisdom that is from above is first pure, then peaceable, gentle, willing to yield, full of mercy and good fruits, without partiality and without hypocrisy"...

... If you are a youngster and you need immediate help, counseling, guidance or intervention call 1-800-448-3000 (I repeat) today. That number is for girls and boys... I am trying to get (I know they will.... I just gotta get Ryan M. or Heather F. to call them) Dr. Janet Taylor and Dr. Gardere to join our G.B.G./HEART advisory board.... and if you know of a brilliant psychiatrist, psychologist or counselor (Dr. Curren requires all G.B.G. advisors/consultants to have at least a masters degree and preferably a PhD. minimum) whom we should 'invite to join our board etc. email Madame Katrin Andrist at hallopeter@sunrise.ch today....

I want to bring David Levin, Joe Negron, Daniel Sample, Ron Clark, Tedd Ginn, Joshua Costa, Charles Best, Joe Clark, Aaron Fernander, Barbara McCall, Joe Schoen, Daniel Watts and Zig Zigler etc. together with Arne Duncan for an education summit. And if my former (brilliant) principal Mr. R.J. Wolfe is still alive I'd like Mr. Wolfe to have a private meeting (perhaps with Joe Clark and Dr. Solis included) with Arne Duncan about "violence" in schools.

I'm a firm believer in finding someone who "knows" how to do what I'm "trying" to do and "modelling" them....When R.J. Wolfe became principal of Samuel Howard Archer High School (the school where Sista Gladys Knight attended) it was the most "violent" school in the city of Atlanta!.... Disrespect, yelling, screaming and skipping class were the norm. Students would be laying on top of their cars smoking dope, drinking beer and playing loud music during lunch when Mr. Wolfe took over Archer High School. He ran around the campus (with assistant principals Charles Hodge (rest in peace), John Tyler (rest in peace) and John Arnold) with a Bullhorn (but no baseball bat) like Joe Clark. One "year" after Mr. Roy Jerome Wolfe took over Archer High School they would hold an assembly in the gym etc. and a thousand students would be talking, laughing and yelling etc. and the moment Mr. Wolfe walked in (I'd never seen it before) he would lift his hand (like a colonel) and the noise would cease. You could hear a rat pee pee on cotton....

Violence stopped at Archer. And weed smoking, laying on cars and drinking were non-existent. I saw this with my own eyes. I call it the "Wolfe Doctrine" and it can be duplicated!

I want Arne Duncan to seek Mr. Wolfe out. He was a master disciplinarian. The Best I've ever seen... I know Aaron McClear, Margita or somebody in the Governator's office is perusing this tome in a cursory manner for Arnold. And yall check this out. Arnold has the power, and unquestioned authority to pardon me today! As Chief Executive Officer of California he can send me back home to Atlanta on his last day in office!.... And I'd do just about anything to get out of here; But!.... My family (Reggie, Gerald, Bo, Teeka, Yak etc.) are gonna think I lost my mind.... If Arnold gave me a choice today (think I'm lying "try" me) and said "Sherman it's your choice. I will pardon you today and send you home; or I will use a small portion of my $ 200 million fortune to buy 1000 copies of "K.K.K." and donate them to kids in California." I would shake Arnold's hand and tell him to "keep the pardon and put one thousand copies of this book into the hands of California kids!".... Am I crazy? Yes, I am! I'm crazy about kids! I am crazy about what Jesus said: "suffer the little children and let them come unto me". I'm crazy about the fear I still have in the pit of my belly when I think about how I felt when boys were being snatched up off the streets of Atlanta and killed!

I am crazy when I think about confused, scared, vulnerable, gullible and naive little boys looking for something to belong to. I know that I know, that there is medicine in this book for boys. It's not a scam. It's not a scheme. It's not a ploy. I will "not" try to leverage this tome or my work (debt) with G.B.G. to try to exonerate me.... That's what Gerry Spence, James Brosnahan, Bob Blasier, and Mark Merin are for. Lawyers can argue my innocence and that has zero bearing on G.B.G. and K.K.K..... But I am pleading with billionaires and with millionaires (i.e. Tyler Perry, Earl Stafford, Michael Moore and ....) to please help us to put this medicine, this 'real talk', this deromanticized and empowering tome into schools, colleges, churches, hoods, trailer parks, suburbs and juveniles.... You all don't need to befriend me or endorse me. But endorse the mission of G.B.G..... We need your help today. Right here! Right now!

... I want some parents who thought it was all over. I want some of you in your 30's and 40's who have all but "quit", to get up and get involved with G.B.G. today. When you raise your children you are fighting against your genes. You want your kids to be perfect, but they have you in them. And sin is passed down not in behavior but in genetics.... I love the Bible! Oh, baby baby, I'm so glad that I have fallen back in love with the Bible... We Christians are phony. We are just as fake as two left shoes. But that's why I love the bible (baby boy) because it is real.... Christians will give you this P.G., censored and watered down version of "who" they are. But the Bible will give you the low down, the dirty and the nitty gritty. The Bible ain't a P.G. book because it is Bold (more bold than I am in "K.K.K.") enough to deal with rape, incest and murder... The first Family of the Bible, Adam and Eve. And you are the first parents on the planet and your kid kills your kid ("K.K.K.")! and since you are the "first" family it's not like you can go down the street and get counseling from Norella, Murt or Dr. Phil.... There was a prophecy and a promise over Eve's life and yet her first and second sons were a mess. She lost both of her babies. When your kid kills your kid you lose them both. One is dead and one is on death row. And when you lose both of your babies it is unspeakable pain. And you don't have the courage, the energy or the spirit to try it again. But I want to tell "parents" to try it again. Keep believing God for a comeback... The "first" murder was by the kid of the "first" family.... But "Adam knew his wife again, and she bore a son and named him Seth, "for God has appointed another seed for me instead of Abel, whom Cain killed". And as for Seth, to him also a son was born; and he named him Enosh." ... God used Seth to unblock the blessing and to fulfill the prophecy spoken over Eve's womb before Cain had ever murdered Abel. Seth was a divine replacement. Seth restores the connection between a woman's dream and the prophetic word over her life... "Then men began to call on the name of the Lord". God used a disobedient, troubled and a dysfunctional family to cause "men" to begin "to call on the name of the Lord".... When I meet priests and saints and folk who claim they've never done any wrong I get nervous. I can't relate to them and they make me itch. Because the God of Abraham and Isaac is not the God of "Israel" (the Prince.). He is the God of Abraham, Isaac and Jacob (the trickster). So if your life is nice, neat and well put together I salute you but I'm scared of you. I serve a God known for using serial murderers (Sir Saul) and transforming them into Chief apostles! I serve a God known for using jailbirds with "R"s in their jackets and making them the Prince of Egypt. I serve a God who'll take a dope smoking and liquor drinking dude names Barry and transform him into "Barack". Then catapult him into the First Black President...!....

I've come to tell parents, teachers and mentors that even though it was painful, spooky, traumatic and scary "Adam knew his wife again". Even though the "first two times we did this Adam we made a mess. Our own kid killed our kid and I'm scared to try it again". But "Adam knew his wife again".

... Having done all (tried once, twice or twelve times no matter) to "stand". I'm bound but I'm gonna "stand". I'm broke but I'm gonna "stand". I'm confused and scared but I'll "stand".

Resilience, commitment, tenacity and strategy will produce a comeback! Young people think of your life as a basketball. You will go down but you will come up. You gotta go down to bounce back up. It's hell to go down, but Heaven getting up. The harder the fall (bounce) the higher the rise.... Everything Christ did He did it from the lineage of disobedience. God didn't decide that "since Adam and Eve disobeyed me and their kid killed their kid ("K.K.K.") I'm gonna create me another family with a perfect background." Nall, God used the lineage of disobedience, dysfunction and disaster to produce "Seth" so that "men began to call on the name of the Lord". And generations later the dysfunctional lineage resulted in a perfect lil baby boy born in Bethlehem. Laying down in a manger and... Seth begot Enosh. Enosh begot Cainan. By verse 22 (Genesis 5) we see Methuselah and Methuselah lived to be 969 years old...

I know that when your son got in trouble, when your brother went to jail for rape, when your cousin got locked up for dope, when your relatives (or you) joined a gang, when I came to prison, hell got happy. Demons were high fiving one another. But I came as commander in chief of G.B.G. in K.K.K. to tell you to tell hell to blow out the candles. And tell the devil to stop the party! Because we are coming back. We are coming up and coming out. We are coming back. We are gonna try it again!....

Most of this book is written for youth (thugs, gangs, juvies etc.) not parents. But I want all of you teeny boppers to go get your parents right now and bring them to the book right now. And I wanna tell parents, teachers, preachers and leaders who almost quit. You almost gave up. You almost stopped trying. After you made a mess and passed your sin into your kin. I know you're afraid. But I came to call you back to service. I came with a divine executive order to call you back to active duty. Momma, Daddy, big brother, Mamie, Sally Mae etc. we need you. Come out, come out wherever you are! Our kids are killing kids. And they learned it from us. We've got to suit up and boot up and get back into the fight.

We must remove ourselves from underneath this juniper tree. We must remove ourselves from inside this cave. Get out of the cave of disbelief. The cave of fear. The cave of negativity. The cave of grief and... At least stand in the entrance of the door. "Having done all to stand". Stand! my brother, my sister and my friend; Stand! I am calling you back. You didn't come this far to quit. You didn't come all this way to stop. Get up and "stand".

You will come back! You will rise again. God can do anything. God can do the almighty through the least likely. God is an awesome God! I need you to get up! You, in that jail cell. You in the school House, the out-house, the state-house and the Whitehouse; you stand!....

I love the Bible yo. It is deep, authentic, real and specific. I told yall incest, rape, murder, dysfunction and alcoholism etc., it's all in the Bible. And the Bible will talk to you about the things you can't talk to anyone about!... What do you do when your son has sex with your daughter? How do you get over the psychological trauma of a sister being raped by her brother? Even more, what do you do when a sister (voluntarily) had sex with her brother? What do you do with the shame, the hurt and the pain? Who do you talk to about the guilt, sorrow, shame and the fear that haunts you concerning your secrets? Secrets rot the soul and puts holes in your heart. Who do you talk to when your family reminds you of a Jerry Springer episode? And you need to talk to a Dr. Phil but can't afford the bill for therapy? Who can you talk to about the conflicts that convict your psyche? Who do you call on when your life is not working?

You want a life, a wife, a kid and a dog. But deep within you, you are a man who is attracted to a man. And you can't understand. Who can you turn to when you want a woman one minute and a man another minute? You don't want Aids and your church hates gays. Where do you go to and who can you call on when you love the Lord all the way down to your shoe laces? You worship, praise and serve the Lord! You pay your tithes and give to the poor. You are a woman after God's own heart, but secretly you fantasize about other women instead of men...

... You are cool with your sexuality and you are as "straight" as an arrow. You've got the kids and wife and are living a good life. You go to work every day and to church on Sundays to pray. But you are addicted to drugs (crack, meth, booze or prescription drugs) etc. Will God help you? If you die right now will you go to hell because of your secret? I came (in "K.K.K.") to be real. "K.K.K." is no more kid unfriendly than the holy Bible. I want to talk to you (Lacey Hipp in Texas, Brian Walker in Denver, Eric Betts, Omar Samy, Omar Samaha and Justin Chiriogotis etc.) about the stuff you can't talk to your homey about. I want to talk to Chris Arger (Roseville), Chris Balding (Sacto), William Larson (Sacto), Jeff (homeless student musician... Robert Scheeler - hollaback), Garrett McCain, Garrett Cunningham and Josiah Lemming. I want to have this ("K.K.K.") conversation with Casey (and Ben at Sierra Med. Ctr. in San Luis Obispo), John Johnson (CNA- Coalinga), Shea Newberry, race-car/fireman "Jeremy", Andy C. (The volunteer) and with all the fellas in "Honor Society" (the Band).... I want to sit down in the dorm, the Frat or in Starbucks and chat with "The Jonas Bros", "Living Things", Justin Gadsden, Max Steele, Jake Shears and Victor Smalley. I want to talk to real people about real issues. I don't want to "front", censor or dilute our issues. I want to have a dialogue with Louis Copelin (n Sacto), Andrew Knox (West Sacto), Kyle Evans (Sacto student), Larry Laboe and John Griffin (CSU-Sac)... I am tired of "Christians", Holy rollers and Bible thumpers. I'm sick n tired of folk who don't' "drank" (sic), smoke or chew and don't hang with them that do". I need to talk to a "Cain" who has killed (or thought about killing) an "Abel". I need to talk to some brothers who thought about killing (Joseph) a brother because of envy, jealousy and "haterism".

I'm looking for Nick Pelham, Nicholas Taxera, Nate (from Paradise Hotel 2008), John Jody Bear, David Reynolds, Joshua Orapello, Gary Browning, Curtis Sykes, Billy York, Billy Bell, Travis Denison, Danny Noriega, Alex Blench, Brett Jolliff, Jake Heartsong, Kaether Cordero and Ricky Harlow.

... I am ready to do warfare you see. Whatever will (we will to) be will be. It's you and me. We must come together to break the curses which have been spoken over our children. We (the Gangbangers, brothers from the Hood, kids in the suburbs etc.) have got to come together and destroy the Taliban (like) gangs that are recruiting and misusing our "boys". I'm calling on Jai Breisch, Eric Bulrice, C.J. Sheron, Shawn Hornbeck, Caleb Sima, Sam Altman, Alex Holgan, Alex Chivescu, Seamus Farrow and Nurse Josiah Poirer... We (you, the fellas, G.B.G. and me) can do this. "Yes we can".... I need some soldiers! I need Michael Wilkerson, Christopher Durbin, Scott Cozza, Blake Koch, Matt Stuart (ABC), Spec. Zachary Boyd (Ft. Hood Texas), Dan

Rollman, Joe Joe Kerschner (Sacto), Matt Campbell (and Arezo Khanjani), James Evenson (Mr. James Evenson should take the "B.E.B." book II chall. on page 313), Jakob Karr, John Litzler, Cameron Civello, Jerry Wines, Jeremy Anthony Lonnick, Atty. Pat Young, Craig Hutto, Michael Sessions, Andrew Bridge, Warren Ballentine, Austin Sisneros, Mike Perrelli, Bryce Kaff, students at OAK Ridge High School, Anthony Durbin, Justin Bozarth, John Keker, Peter Grammatas, Tim Daraitis, Doug Pieper Jr. and Tim Coleman (Sacto. Ballet)!....

Sean Zane (Chesterfield VA.), David Proctor and Alexander Dugdale can talk to me. Daniel St. John (Richmond), Scottie Moran (and his brother Lloyd) can talk to me. Todd Dressler, Frank Carter (Atl. GA.), Andrew Pruitt, Gene Langford (Atl.) and Ricky Mitchell (Summerville GA.) can all chat with a brother about the "conflicts" of a man's life. And when we (Max Hanger, Omar Samy, Billy Bell, "Teddy", Jason Huyck and Roger Walthorn, etc.) begin to open up and have these 'bromantic', real deal, brutha 2 brutha dialogues etc. we will unlock our creativity and unblock our potential... I can't fully, adequately and totally love a woman (Sabine) till I fill the hole(s) in my own heart and learn how to love Sherman...

When I was at that infamous P.V.S.P. I met nurse Glenn Pickett. He and I related because he had worked at Northside Hospital in my hometown. Nurse Pickett examined me after Marion E. Spearman (per Mike Bunnell) had gotten C.O. Mendez and Agguralde to "beat" and "assault" me. Pickett caught me in a room alone and told me "I almost had to knock that child molesting homeboy of yours (Marion) out. Dude (Marion) told me I had a nice 'piece' (penis)". I was shocked because I thought Marion only liked Caucasian men and little Boys.... "That fool (Marion) is more corrupted than Brumbaugh. I heard him tell Lt. Bennett that he hoped you die. He told him something about an A.W. Bunnell (sic) at Mule Creek and you wrote about em in a book & they sent you here...I'm leaving Coalinga cause these fools might try to kill me.... I'm going to work up at CSP- SAC"... he stated to me. My law students state that "for some reason CSP-SAC I.S.U. has a photo posted of nurse Pickett stating he is not allowed on prison grounds!".... I have "no" idea what that is about. I've not seen nurse Pickett since P.V.S.P..... The psyche tech who replaced him (Mrs. Miranda) is on "meth" according to CNA Ashley. And Miranda is very close to Brumbaugh and to Marion....

Daniel Hawlawl, Sam Rutherford and Mr. Joshua Costa need to read "K.K.K."... ... I want Mike Tyson to visit me! He does not have any money so it's not that. I feel like Mike Tyson is supposed to meet me and vice versa. I can't save him. But I can relate to him. And I feel like (silly me) this man has not had a man in his life since 1985 he could "relate" to. And everybody around Mike (including gold digging Robin) wanted a piece of that $ 400 million! ... I almost feel like I'm writing about Mike (the other Mike) Jackson. Michael Jackson, Michael Vick and Michael Tyson. All were young, black, gifted and rich. All had to see a great fall.... Lord have mercy. And Michael Jackson left us.... Michael Vick went to jail. Tyson went to prison for a "rape" I never (really) believed he did... But I declare that I told my wife years ago that "I wouldn't be surprised if Mike Tyson and Michael Jackson both commit suicide. Those are two extremely troubled men"....

...Jonathan Mack, Justin Zysman, Joseph Rocha and Christopher Kline (Auburn, CA.) are you all reading today?

Mr. Tyson is a broken man. One week I watched Whitney on Oprah and I saw a broken woman. The next week here comes Michael and I see brokenness.... I was "mad" at Mike Tyson. Mad that he lost to HolyField! Mad he bit the ears! Mad he went to jail. Mad he lost $ 400 million! Mad at him for being mad at God. And I felt like I knew Mike... If you did not see the Oprah interview get it on DVD. I'm not mad with "Mike" (Tyson or Vick) anymore.... I told you all how I view (stoically) "men" crying period. And I especially oppose us crying in public. I told you all that I used to make fun of Montel crying... But as I watched "Iron" Mike weeping I had to fight tears.

Mike's mom died when he was 16. He never knew his father.... He met a man (James Scott Manning? Rev. Hosea Williams? Andy Young? Dr. Fred Allman Jr. ? etc), Cus who believed in him. And Mike says "I started believing in this old man Cus. He spoke with me every night about discipline and character". Mike went on "what we'll do is we'll just sit down and watch all the great fights from the 1890's up to 1980'. ... Cus said I wish you had a body like Ken Norton... I was just frustrated that Cus didn't think I was scary enough. So I practiced being scary". Oprah replied "It worked!" (lol). "Ah man this is (crying) a mess" Tyron said. And what do you do when the first "man" you ever fell in love with dies? Cus died and "I just started drinking and going to drugs.... I didn't really have any desire to do that stuff (boxing and training) anymore". Mike says "I listened to my mentor (Cus). He said Ali was the "best" and I believed him".

Mike said he thought he was "a god of Combat (Comeback?)".... He says he was just a little poor kid with no self esteem. "I needed to believe that.... I'm just stroking my ego as I walk down the aisle (towards the ring). Subconsciously I'm a peacock. I like to be seen working...." Mike says he's often allowed himself to "run riot". He says "I know what it's like to go down that dark road and meet the devil and hang out with him... I have to live at the top of the world, I also have to live at the bottom of the ocean. I don't know how to (Bi-polar disorder?) live in the middle".

Mike goes on "I know I'm not gonna win. I'm tired of losing. I want to win now. I have a lot of rage... I grew up in abusive households n stuff... I felt 'alone'. I felt 'ashamed'. I felt like a half a person. Not a 'whole' person.... I had no role models (G.B.G. are you reading this?) of what a marriage should be except entertainers". Mike goes on "I was taking the drug dealer's money and not paying their money. I think they really felt sorry for me. I'm surprised (me too) I'm still alive... I was just enraged".... Asked if he hated competitors he replied "Hate doesn't have a place in any kind of disciplined sport..."

Mike served 3 years in prison and says it made him a worse person. "Prison - there's nothing in there but hate! Retched swine! That's a place where you are restricted but you have no boundaries.... You lose your moral fiber.... nothing there (prison) but hate, hate, hate. Hate reflecting off the walls! Racism and 'I hate you'.... I lost my faith and stopped believing in God in prison. I was extremely angry when I came outta prison!"

James Toback did a masterful job with the documentary 'Tyson'. It was psychoanalytic. He'd throw out a subject (much like Dr. Solis does to me) and just let Mike go. And that allowed Mike to let the voices come out... Didn't he (Mike Tyson, Mike Jackson, Mike Vick etc.) almost have it all? He has a tormented (like Saul, Paul, Jacob, Sherman and the rest of 'us') past. And if he transforms it is an 'inside job'.... I wept and prayed for Mike. I wanna meet Mike. I feel a connection.... Another guard told me yesterday "U wasting your time with Leonard Padilla. He's duplicitous and he ain't gonna help G.B.G." If that's true it's all good. There is nothing which can stop an idea (G.B.G.) and a tome ("K.K.K.") who's time has come...

There's enough of us ("Doc, Phil Spector, Mumia etc.) in here and then (Christopher Ochoa, Vick, lawyers, entrepreneurs and pastors etc.) out there (who've done 'time' or knows someone doing 'time' etc.) that we (G.B.G.) will do "this". As Michael (Jackson) said "This is it". And "this (K.K.K.) is the moment". We will make this happen.....

Mike Tyson's story, his brokenness, loneliness, rage and his pain can help somebody. He says when his daughter died a few month ago "I wanted to blame somebody.... I wanted to go in that place blasting... But I didn't want to go about this in the wrong way".

....Derek was on The Price is Right (Ryan? Heather?) on 10/13/09. I believe (in my heart) that Mike's story, this book and G.B.G. can help Derek ("Chris" on Tyra on 10/12/09, Jonathan Mack, Justin Zysman, Joseph Rocha, Adam Rich, Greg Deekens, Jeremy Winters, Trevor Loflin, Elijah Wood, John Doggett, Scott Yates, Jason Ziedenberg and Michael Taketa etc.).... And I want Ryan and Heather to skip trace and find Charlie Badakker, Christopher Parker (in CDC.), Jimmy Dougherty (Davis CA), Michael Holt (CA. teacher), Ron Rodriquez (South Sacramento) etc. and tell them they are in "K.K.K." And if Joseph Rocha, Justin Zysman (Elk Grove CA.), Caleb Peek or Craig Huffo contact me, we have something for them ...

I want every young man (right here, right now), to read closely. Here comes a life changer! (Tyson and Vick R U reading?).... Once upon a time an eagle lost an egg and the tiny lil eagle egg was discovered by a hen. She carried the egg home to the chicken coop and sat on it with all the loving patience of an incipient mother. Shortly thereafter the egg was hatched and out stepped a tiny lil eagle. This tiny bird had an eagle history, eagle genes, eagle chromosomes, eagle power and marvelous eagle potential. Yet, because he was born in a chicken environment (slums, trailer parks etc.), he grew up thinking he was a chicken. He grew up thinking chicken thoughts, dreaming chicken dreams, scheming chicken schemes, praying chicken prayers, praying chicken games and behaving like a chicken. He was even made to feel inferior and ashamed of his eagle features (Chris' "Good Hair, Bad Hair"?). He didn't know who he was, but the other birds in the barnyard did. They said to each other, "we must keep this bird thinking he's a chicken, because if he finds out he's an eagle, he will lord over us".

The other birds made fun of his mighty eagle beak, because they had little thin, narrow, weak chicken beaks. They joked about his eagle talons, because they had weak, tiny scrawny chicken feet. The bird became ashamed of the richness of his deep, dark eagle feathers. At this juncture, he even considered plastic surgery. He thought about cutting off half of his eagle beak and dyeing his dark eagle feathers so he could look more like the chickens. His greatest ambition in life was to one day hop, skip and jump up on the fence post to cockle-doodle-do at daybreak like the rooster. But one day, when this confused bird was playing in the barnyard, he saw the deep, dark contours of a mighty shadow swim across the ground. For the first in his life, this lost little bird looked higher than the fence post, higher than the tree line and saw the remarkable sight of an adult eagle in full flight - with all of it's majesty, grace and power. This lost little bird was transfixed. He said to himself, "I wish I could be like that". The big eagle perceived the dilemma of the little lost bird and swooped down from the stratospheric heights and said, "Boy, you ain't no chicken. You're an eagle! Your mighty talons were not meant to rake and scrape on the ground for worms and feed, but to snatch the side of yonder mountain of achievement. Boy, you ain't no chicken. You're an Eagle! Your eagle eye was not meant to be limited to the narrow confines of the barnyard but to seek out the distant horizon of your own unfulfilled potential and spread your wings as you catch the lofty winds of your immeasurable genius. You ain't no chicken - you're an eagle!.... Each of you reading can take a lesson from this study. Do I even need to explain it to you?

You, who have been programmed to fail and live in a living hell. You, who see pain, problems, death, drugs, hurt and misery all around you. You, with wealthy parents but have a computer (or video game) as a nanny. You at "shoulder to shoulder", Ron Clark Academy, KIPP (in New York), Castlemont High School, Columbine High and at Folsom High. You are not a chicken (faggot, nobody, loser etc.) You (Joseph Rocha, Maxwell Hanger, Billy Bell etc.) are an Eagle! You (Jamil Posey, Mike Tyson, Michael Vick, Justin Zysman etc.) are somebody! You must raise the angle of your vision. Look higher than poverty, honorable mention, gangs, failure or violence. Look higher than juveniles, jails and prison cells. Raise your vision and rise above your circumstances... This message (about youth being Eagles!) is the message (of this tome) which attorneys Bob Blasier, Gerry Spence, Tarlow, Janus, Morchower and Ira London do support!.... Preparation determines destination! Tyler Perry and Tyra Banks can both get behind this message!....

And I know (I see it) prisons are creating killers and molesters. I know poor white boys are the victims of the kind of warehousing California (Texas, Georgia, N.Y. and Michigan etc.) does for profit and the breeding of a new class of humans; young, untaught, unfathered, uninspired and guilty of committing minor infractions yet sent to prison. Viciously brutalized by seasoned convicts; these boys (Alex and Derek King etc.) grow up (physically) in prison. But their mental, analytical and spiritual selves are stunted by a development which was arrested when their bodies got locked up.... Sixteen year old boys sent to prison to earn a bachelor's degree in PPS (Prison Political Science) and a master's degree in prison subculture!....

I want every broken boy who has cried in the night. And been hurt, scared and afraid. I want all of you who used to wanna be like "Iron Mike" but now know he was just as broken (not iron but aluminum foil] just like you), scared and lonely as you are etc. I want you to know you are an eagle! ... Joseph Rocha is an eagle even though a master chief petty officer hazed (abused!) him and forced him to pretend he was having oral sex with another sailor! In front of the entire company Joseph was ordered on his knees and pretend to "blow" another man... Instructed in "how" to be more "queeny" and more feminine etc. I have 3 things 2 say 2 Joseph. A. You are an Eagle! B. Sue the hell out of the navy!! C. We (G.B.G.) have a stipend for you...

Justin Zysman had to see "Burn Jew Burn" on his locker at Amador High School for a year.... That is wrong! Ira London, Murray J. Janus and Blair Berk would "own" Amador County if they represented Justin. I'd like to tell Molly and Jason Zysman to keep the faith. And to Justin you are an eagle! A tall, football playing, Jewish Eagle!

Justin, Scott Tatum (my homeboy in Atlanta), Kim Deterline, Zach Freisen, Van Jones and Adam Rich need to get this book. And I need Tony Dungy, Jeff Lurie, Michael Moore and... to help G.B.G. put this spiritual atomic bomb, this nuclear ("K.K.K.") weapon into schools all over this earth... So that we (Blasier, Janus, Ravis, Morchower etc. etc.) will let them (kids) know that they are all "Eagles"....

I want y-o-u to get up! If you can look up you can get up. You can rise above your predicament. You can rise above your circumstances. As quiet as it is kept, what grows in (your) "mind" grows in (to) time. See it and you will be it.... The biggest trick (scam, game and ploy) Mike Tyson played on his competitors was mental. He ("practiced being scary"), made them "think" they could "not" beat him. He made them feel inferior (like "chickens") to him (an "Eagle"). And as long as he defeated them psychologically he beat them physically... The moment (because he stopped "practicing", training and believing. Because he was abusing drugs and alcohol etc.) "Iron" Mike believed he could (would) be beat etc. The moment (I'd still put my money on Tyson! at his age right now. Let him lose that weight. Give him and Holyfield 6 months to get in shape and Tyson will beat Him! Don King where are you?) Mike ran up on a dude (Evander) psychologically prepared to win. When he found a dude un-intimidated , Mikes streak was eliminated.

"Belief" is a mental nuclear weapon in the arsenal of any successful warrior. If I convince you (teens and tweenies) that you are inferior and that I'm superior; I win! The moment you become convinced that you are too poor (or rich), too young (or old), too fat, short, tall or small to "win" you "lose". History is replete with mighty men and mighty women (Mother Teresa, Martin Luther King Jr., President Mandela, Oprah, President Obama etc.) who locked themselves in rooms (closets and classrooms) and convinced themselves that "I can". And that "I will". When you affirm to yourself repetitively (redundantly and utilizing tautology as I do with "names" lol) that "I am somebody" and "I'll rise again", and "I can do this" etc. your subconscious begins to "believe" it. And once an idea, thought, principle and a belief gets planted (picked up, programmed etc.) into your subconscious etc. it is on and cracking. "I can" becomes "I will". And I "will" is transmogrified into "I must". If you (Eagle!) believe it you really (I'm being real yall) achieve it... I "chant", I "sing" and I "talk" to myself. I tell myself that "I am God's child! I will make a difference... I have an appointment. I have a destiny. I am coming out of this ... I will do it! I must.... "

... I let the White Crip (the one I'm a tell yall about in a bit) read the "Chicken" and "Eagle" story. He (the white Crip as I said) is only 21. My target audience! He read it (and two pages before it... All the way to "I must....'). And stated "Damn that's awesome! I can't wait 2 read "K.K.K". This is off the hook! I mostly read 'friction' but I'm gon (sic) read "K.K.K.". And my 'crew' gon read it too". I asked on a 1 to 10 how he'd rate what he read; he said "ten plus! It's off the charts man. That's real talk."

By contrast I let a 51 year old fella peruse the 'same' pages... "It's kinda cool... I give it a 6 or 7 out of 10". May I repeat that those (o.gees, folk in their 40's, 50's and 60's) are not "my" audience. I love older people. In fact I have a strong spiritual affinity toward senior citizens etc. And I will do anything I can to help the elderly! But this ("K.K.K." Bomb!) book is not for you. (who "know" it all). If you are over 40 put the book down. Step away from the library (or bookshelf). You are too good (critical, jaded, negative, bitter and spiteful) for me or for this book. You need to walk away from this ("it's too long! too many cheesy segues! Too many names! too incendiary! too much...) book and go listen to Rush (Limbooty) Limbaugh! Go listen to that racist, drug addicted, snake oil selling pervert who gets richer by the listener. He's a prevaricating, selfish and execrating bastard. Rush is a toe tapping conman who's heart pumps only defecation.

If you (the tome "critic") are 41 years or older I demand that you (seriously with only a few exceptions i.e. Tony Dungy, Jeff Lurie, Whoopi and Michael Moore etc.) put this book down. This ("K.K.K.") is not poetry, punditry or satire. I mean (unlike Rush) what I write... And you ("village" people who have "taught" our kids to hate and hurt. "Village" people who have "destroyed" our kids!) need to go listen to that pervert Sean Hamity. You (over 40) are "smart" enough to "critique" a book. But you are not smart enough to know when you've been "had". Jean Hamity, Limbaugh and Ann Coulter are all multimillionaires. Rush is almost a Billionaire! And yo (sic) ass is not even earning a hundred grand per year. And yet, you "pay" Rush to "play" with you. Every time you "tune" in to that "Radio Leroy Jenkins" Rush who uses "sleight of tongue", prevarication, racism ("The Magic Negro") and doom to scare people. Every time you (older white folks and Uncle Tom blacks) let Rush make your "stereotypes", "biases" and "prejudices" feel "normal". He gets paid (and "laid") and you get to run to the barbershop and say "Rush said". You fool! You sucker! You are a damn fool... How dare I plant a $ one thousand dollar (my "last" grand) "seed" offering in to the Benny Hinn, E. Bernard Jordan or Leroy Jenkins 'ministry'. So they can go sleep with lil boys and snort cocaine? They are rich, crooks, false prophets and "pulpit Rush Limbaughs". I'm not giving them "one red penny".

..When was the last time Rush, Ann or Sean wrote a million dollar check to help any minority (i.e. 'poor' whites, blacks, Mexicans etc.) group? Have they fed the hungry or clothed the naked? Why would I waste my time (life) tuning in to a multimillionaire who is also a "Bigot"?

... I didn't mean to engage in a tirade but I'm tired of "old", jaded, bitter, poor (minded) negative folks. They (the O'Gees) will beat you down psychologically. They'll make you doubt your calling, your gifts and your anointings. They'll inject bull crap, negativity, race, stereotypes and criticisms into your mind. I don't walk with them. I don't talk to them. I don't try to teach them or reach them. I love them from a distance and I pray for them. But that's it. I'll let T.D. Jakes, Eddie Long, Noel Jones or somebody try to reach em but I'm "not" the one...

Jesus Sandoval (mas on Senor Sandoval later) is 22 years old. And I "read" the last 20 pages to him out Lord... He (a Y.Gee) said "Damn Atlanta that's bad! I like it! I really really do. And I really believe if I hear (sic) Chicken - Eagle story when I'm 12 or 13 I don't come to prison... I will read every page of "K.K.K.". And I don't read labros (books)"... He (22 year young Sandoval) is my "target audience".

... I pray that Manning & Murder (Kiss, Elrond, Ramirez LIP), Michael Moore etc. will (indeed) help us to plant this book, into schools all across this earth! I need Tony Dungy, Jeff Lurie, Earl Stafford and attorneys like Marc Grossman to help us... But.... Let there be no doubt that (I repeat) "this ("K.K.K.") is it!" This is that moment! And we (the gangsters, the juvenile paparazzi, believers in the 'vision' etc.) will do this with you or without you! (I'll announce on twitter, face book and all our websites in July 2011 "who" donated this tome to schools etc.).... Getting (sic) "this" (is it!) book to students, drop-outs, thugs, the left out, locked in and the forgotten about etc. etc. is the cause of my life. This (to me) is what that ("Healthcare" etc.) was to Ted Kennedy! "K.K.K." to me is what "manpower" and "woman thou art loosed" is to T.D. Jakes. I want teens and tweenies to read this book just like the Pope wants Catholics to read the Bible!... Getting this medicine, argument, breakfast, for (young) champions, chicken soup for tweenies, souls, talking points for walking youths etc. to young gang bangers, young hustlers, young truant teens, young thugz and boyz in tha hood etc. means everything to me.

I am not a saint, not a choir boy and not to be trusted. I'm still Clark Kent, Jacob, trickster, supplanter and conman. I am "short" of the Glory of God. I am the subject matter of this book. I am you (lil white, black and brown brother). And (just a 'few' names yall but they're important.) Ambassador Andrew Young, Rev. Hosea Williams, Chief Eldrin Bell, Zig Zigler (all personally) taught me some ("game") stuff! You can't sit at the feet of "uncle" Andy Young and Rev. Hosea Williams etc. and not be changed. You can't sit in Zig Zigler's house on a golf course etc. and be "found out" (discovered, spiritually exegeted etc.) by Mr. Zigler and not be "better" afterwards! Mr. Zig Zigler had me sitting in his house and something didn't "feel" right. He found me out! And the reason I'm able to sling ink now etc. The reason I'm able to write this caliente book is because I was on my deathbed! Because of what I learned from Hosea, Andy, Les Brown and Tony Robbins etc. And because Mr. Zigler discovered my "masquerade", my "fraud" and my "facade", Mr. Zigler's uncanny ability to see inside my soul has "taught" me how to "see". And because of Mr. Zigler I can "see" inside Derek King, Michael Couch (in Montana), Billy Bell and the fellas in the (band) "Honor Society"... I'm not Dr. Phil! I'm not Dr. Solis! I'm not Dr. Curren! But I am a "Doctor" of "Vision". I am a spiritual, psychological and a "motivational ophthalmologist". And I can exegete the conflicts, rage, anger and the turmoil that "boys" are dealing with in school, in church, in college, in the trailer parks and in the subdivisions. The mental tailspins, whirlwinds and the confusion that males feel trying to be boys. The stuff boys go through which locks us into our boyhood. And won't release us into our manhood etc. etc. I can read the ("that") "handwriting on the wall". I can't teach psychology like Dr. Duran can. I can't understand psychiatry like Dr. Curren does. I can't elucidate politics like David Axelrod can. I can't write like John Grisham. But, but, but.... There are more than 2.5 million folks in prisons in America. More than 49% of them are 7-19 years old! So we have (here in the promised land! Only in America?) more than one million, two hundred and fifty thousand boys and teenagers in prisons. And I can relate (elucidate, exegete and educate etc.) to each and every boy and teen in prison. (This does not include the millions of boys who have dropped out of school, dropped into gangs, are in school physically but in prison mentally etc.)... So if I were pastoring ("the Potter's House"... "The prison House") I'd have a base membership (verifiable) of 1 million, 2 hundred and fifty thousand members. And I'd guestimate my projected membership (with just the "boys") is 35 million (conservative estimation)!.... Go back to the 1 million 2 hundred and fifty thousand "boy" inmates.... All of them CAN get "out" of prison! Most of them will get out! And a lot of them (roughly 800 thousand!) will get out of prison by 2016.... so even "Iron Mike" admitted that there is "nothing in prison but hate, hate, hate" etc. And you'll recall (i.e.) Bill King (who was "not" a racist before he went to prison!) tied a black man (Jimmy Lee Byrd) to the bottom of his truck and dragged him to death! Dragged him till his head separated from his neck and shoulders; after he served "time" in a prison!.... The gangs (atmosphere! Environment!), cliques and the subculture of the prison changes a person.

..."I was pretty angry when I got outta prison" 'Iron Mike' said. Prison is the "master recipe" for creating killers, molesters, racists and 'failed humans'. It is a place of brokenness... Ipso Facto, I am not smart ("brilliant" or a "pioneer" enough) enough to write a book that will reach, teach and transform jaded, corrupted and malicious prison guards (i.e. Bunnell, Spearman, D.L. Criner and Deathridge etc.) across this nation. I can't write a good enough book to make guards work against their vested interests in prison gangs, riots and violence etc. I won't write a good enough book to cause positivity, transformation and reform to spread (like wildfire) from guard 2 guard, counselor 2 counselor and warden 2 warden across America... to thine "ownself be true". I won't do that!

But (x9) 'I Can', 'I will' and (hell yeah) 'I must reach these kids! Boys 7 years old? Boys 12, 13, 14, 15, 16, 17, 18 and 19 years old? (Tad bit younger than Jesus Sandoval and my white crip!) I know what makes them tick! I am them! I know how it is! I'm in their shoes. And I "believe" in the fabric of my being that this book has a 95% chance of helping (lifting, changing and inspiring) more than 90% of every teen and tweenie who reads it!

.... This is why I need Ryan M,. Heather F., you (and u 2) to be creative and innovative as you use the internet to reach, "poke", email and I.M. the "Buttload" of "names" in this book! If we put "this" book into the hands of Steven "Van" Burgess [in Bolling Springs S.C.] and the dude "Van" Sued etc. If we get this to Kenny Lopez (at Fox 40), Cassius Harti (we have a stipend for Mr. Harti), Jeff Kinney, Charlie Hill (in So. Cal.), Derek Hough, Aaron Carter, Joseph Rocha and Justin Zysmon etc. we will transform the Nation!.... We won't transform the youth! "They" are not the "problem". It is "us"! The "village" people who raised (destroyed) them r what's wrong with em. Derek and Alex King used who's shotgun to kill their dad and his friend? Who was molesting them? Every cuss word, racial slur and evil thing those 7-19 year olds in prisons know etc., they "learned" from us. Save the children? Here's how: keep them (children) away from us (adults)!!! "We" are the problem.... So I guarantee you that if "we" (the people! the one's who "claim" we have such a "passion for youth") put "this" book into the hands of just 50% of those 7-19 year olds in jails (who are going to get out!)... We can get into their brains and remind them that they are Eagles! We can remind them of their resilience with this book. We can remind them that though they've fallen they can get back up. We can remind them of the inquisitiveness, curiosity and the creativity of their childhood. And we can help them to redirect their energy in a direction which leads them up and out of jail. We can help them get out of that "cave". G.B.G., Dr. Curren, Dr. Solis, Daniel Bugriyev, Willie etc. and me. We have come in this book to help "restore vision" for young men. Vision!

... I just left the Shu-yard a moment ago where I bowed, down on that concrete and prayed. I prayed and "whatsoever thing ye desire when ye pray believe that ye receive (your vision) them and ye shall have "them". And.... I prayed that this tome would be instrumental in providing spiritual, psychological and motivational stimulus for your (mental) infrastructure. I looked up and saw "one star" again. And all I wanna do is reach one. "Just one"! If this entire tome will motivate just one of you to transform your scars into stars our (Dr. Curren, Dr. Solis, my entire team) work won't be in vain... The fact "that I never saw tragedy coming is almost inconceivable to me... I had no inkling of the battle that Dylan was waging (Clark Kent vs. Super Man, Joseph vs. Israel, trickster vs. prince, an angel vs. a demon) in his mind" Susan Klebold stated. Her son (you'll recall) was one of the two kids who murdered 13 at "Columbine" High School in Littleton Colorado... I repeat (her words) "the fact that I never saw tragedy coming..."

Alex and Derek King's mom (I'm not demonizing them! We pray for them. And we are willing to work with them!) could also state (with authenticity) that she never "saw tragedy coming" before they took that shotgun and killed their dad and his "friend".... "For the rest of my life I'll be haunted" Madame Klebold stated. And there are tens of thousands of "haunted" mothers all across this earth. Their sons, babies and boys had "Battles" which were raging in their minds. And mothers, fathers and brothers "never saw it coming".

Can I preach like I feel? I'm not even writing a tome anymore. This (right here) is a conversation (although monoligistic) with boys (Jolliff, Kip Williams, Kaether, Dan Sellery, Billy Bell and students everywhere)! It's just a jailside (i.e. "Fine side") chat with the homeys. Dr. Lewis Yablonsky, Dr. Curren, Dr. Heitkamp, Dr. Solis and Madame Patricia Kennedy all told me to "write". In fact Madame P. Kennedy told me "you need to shut up and write! It's what your calling is! ... Not the stuff about staff etc. But with all that energy and brainpower you have. If you would really write about what it feels like to be in prison etc. no "boy" would ever want to come join you all".

And all of my psychological (Duran, Gregg, Jarman etc.) and psychiatric experts reminded me that "they" (kids) will listen to you (convicts) all before they will us"... And since so many well-meaning mothers can't "see" the battles "we" boys R dealing with I came to preach. Not "at" you but "to" you. We've tried everything and everybody else. As Fred Moor said why not "Give G.B.G. a chance".

As I walk and talk with correctional geniuses like Warden Jimbo (the comeback kid) Walker, CDW. Terry L. Rosario, CDW Tim Virga, Jeff Macomber, L.N. Johnson-Dovey etc. I learn so "much" about these prisons that I can't even write it all down in a book! But the fact that the "Best warden in the State", his deputy, associate wardens and a Harvard psychiatrist are all "rooting" for me to finish "K.K.K." and put it out there is humbling... "You (dudes in jail) can 'see' a lot of things that parents would never see" Warden Walker told me. And A.W. (A) L.N. Johnson-Dovey chimed in (yall know a sista gotta put her two cents in!) "And Sherman they wouldn't know what they were looking at even if they 'saw' it! It is your job, your duty and your responsibility to tell these kids the truth about prisons... So even if parents 'miss' it kids will 'see' it". Madame Johnson-Dovey stated... "You have some issues!" She continued, "But boy you have a head on your shoulders! Mrs. Kennedy and Warden Walker told me you were 'brilliant' before I ever met you. But you need to focus" she proclaimed ... "We should rarely see you. And when we do you oughta have pen to paper"...

A black psychologist at P.V.S.P. (Dr. Hall) told me "your power is in your books. Not debating staff and not in trying to prove how smart you are... Be smart enough to write to these kids about prison"... Rio Americano High School student John Butterfield wrote an opinion piece in his lil school newspaper. And this little 'article' (opinion) resulted in an International Story. Sabine (in Switzerland) read about John's 'opinion' in Switzerland. ... (Principals Brian Ginter, Verone Kennedy and Aaron Fernander are you reading?).... John's writing ignited media interest. It was a lesson in the power of the "pen"... Butterfield is now thinking about how he can spin the story into an essay for his college applications. "It makes me feel good that people considered what I wrote in the paper and thought about taking action...." John continued "In High School, a lot of the time we (prisoners too) feel powerless... It makes me feel hopeful that if the adults keep listening to what we put (write) in the paper, things will get better". And I'll bet you John did not think his little "opinions" in the school paper would end up in a book that's going to the Whitehouse. But John Butterfield 'Your 15 minutes have been extended!' and we (nearly 3 million U.S. prisoners) can learn a lesson from John... Write! Write! Write!

And find your power! I found my niche. My job is to not write poetry! I'm not a James Patterson! I am a Sherman. And I write to release that spiritual dopamine that'll transmogrify your life. I came to bring vision so kids can "see" what many mothers are not "seeing".

I want Kierman Oberman, Sam Altman, Kyle Evans and John Butterfield etc. to peruse this tome and find the courage, character and the nerve to confront what you "see". I'm reaching out to Michael Parker (Walnut Creek), Dan Sellery, Victor Karlsson (Union Mine High School) and Michael Castro etc. we reach out to every kid. And I came to bring 'vision'. And to provide you (kids) with an authentic realistic and candid (moving) word picture of the "prison". It is Hades....

I don't even have the vocabulary to adequately elucidate the level of "hate" in "here" that Mike Tyson was talking about. But it is "hate! hate! hate!" in here. Boys running around lying just to lie. Building 'dream' worlds and becoming 'legends' in our own minds... There is a guy with H.I.V. who will go home on Halloween. He is a giant, huge and pathological liar. And he will be 'back'. And he will infect somebody (plural) with H.I.V. when he gets out. He would not know the truth if it hit him in the nose... "Freddie moved out on me and moved in with a black drag Queen" he told me when I was in C.T.C. and when he thought I'd never return to 'this' yard... A black "drag Queen". Freddie (Engel) is a white guy... When I returned to the yard I asked five guys who was the "Black Drag Queen" Freddie moved in with... "Freddie moved in with (his old celly - a white guy) Scottie" everyone told me... There was "not even a black drag queen on this yard". That's an example of somebody just lying to be lying. No reason, rhythm or rhyme etc., they just 'lie'. And I'll be praying for him. And I'll be praying for you.. Hoping he does not con you into sex and infect you before he returns to prison...

(Again) I don't understand some of this stuff "we" do. I see guys (read "creating monsters") who live in the same cell. Work the same job. And every time they come in the cell their celly is with them. In my opinion that is "gay", "insane" and ridiculous... I don't wanna live with a "man" in this bathroom (cage) What the hell do I wanna eat, sleep, crap, work and go to yard with a man for? I did not "work" with my "wife" on the streets... We spent 5 waking hours together daily. When I was in town, but I'm gonna come to jail and spend (by 'choice'... a job is a 'choice') 24/7 with a 'man'? That is absolutely asinine. But guys do it everyday in here.... They "work" with their "cellies".

Frazier McGinn (CSU-Sac), Roman Lukowsky, Jordan Simon and Steven Cozza are you reading this? I just don't get it. I wanna lay up in a small room with you all night. Wake up and go to work with you. Return with you and say I'm "straight"? I'm straight "gay" or "straight crazy"... And please remember (Cody Sheldon, Scott Tatum and Shaun Hornbeck etc.) that this place will inject venom into your spirit. This place is psychologically and spiritually dark. It is all about "I", "me" and "my". And I've just given up on "friendship" in here. (with the exception of Lonnie Young, Brandon Gene Martinez, Jeff Allen Walker etc.) I don't consider any of these guys "Friends". And the good thing is the feeling is "mutual".

Gary told me the other day (lol) "I'm getting all of my 'Friends' to sign this card for my wife". And then he went straight to Steve's cell. He then went to get another gentleman to sign... He never got me to sign. But... I noticed that one of the guys he got to sign was the same guy he talks about like a dog. He's called the man a pill head, dope fiend, a nut case etc. etc. Yet the 'dope Fiend' is his 'Friend' enough to sign his wife's card? If that is his 'definition' of friendship then I'm not insulted that I was not asked to 'sign'...

But I keep using the word "duplicitous" so very much because I'm (let me confess) lonely (in here) at times. And when you go through life there are times you need to 'talk' to somebody who will be candid, spiritual, honest and "concerned" about you. But I can't count the times (on ten hands) when I was 'stupid' enough to think I'd (finally) found a 'friend' in Hades. And they let me down. They smiled, nodded and shook my hand. Sometimes we even "broke bread together." And they "hated" me. They lied, gossipped and... I'm no "better" than "they" are. I am sinner in chief. And I have some folks I just don't like. I am too judgmental (at times). And I expect too much of people.... However, I can say this: If I don't 'like' you I don't mess with you. I'll stay away from you. I won't break bread, nod, wink and shake your hand... But in Hades I think (seriously) people get a 'kick' out of seeing 'if' they can sucker you into believing they're your "friend". It's another form of a "predator"... Can I "prey on your mind and play with your emotions? Can I win your confidence so I can withdraw your secrets and talk about you (to others) like a dog?" ... I hope Martin Cheatham, Joseph Latham and Justin Howell are perusing these words... I need Cody Sheldon, Alex Wagner Trugman, Austin Sisneros, James Avance, Von Smith, Andrew Lang and Vaughn English to "get" this. I want every young man (who's already dealing with conflicts, anger, rage and insecurities etc.) to know that if you decide to reside in Hades ("Location! Location! Location is everything!") that you will have 1500 guys all around you with 'none' you can 'trust'. Absolutely none. You can't confide, believe, accept or receive anything from these guys. We 'hate' you! Hell if I 'hate' myself how in the hell can I not hate you? If I'm mad at Sherman I've got to be mad at Herman. If I'm mad with me then loving you is something I can't see... There have been times (in here) when I would have given a hundred grand for a "friend". Not a lover! Not a buddy! Not a pal! Not a cohort or a homey etc. But somebody who could see me naked (spiritually naked) and still "like" me. Somebody who'll pray for me and "speak a word" over my life... I don't need their money, jokes, games, canteen or a 'hook up' etc. I've just needed somebody (Elisha) I could look in their eyes and "trust".

It's sick, infected and wicked in here. You'll see guys living (celling) together today. They are best pals. They sleep in the same "bathroom" etc. And next week "that dude is nasty. I can't stand him. I had to check him like a bit--. And I".... It's how "we" do it. I'll say (write) it again; Duplicitous... Staff and inmates alike. Just living, breathing and walking lies... Richard Pryor used to say "You tell one lie and I tell three"... And guys will holler "Friend" in a hot second in here. But they know if your name is not "Johnny Willie" (Brandon Gene Martinez, Lonnie Young etc.) you are not "my" Friend. We can be acquaintances. I promise not to lie on you. I won't gossip about you. When I gossip it hurts and harms the person spoken of, the person spoken about and the person spoken to...

I can survive (in here) without ever calling "your" name. But way too many guys (it is a place of dysfunction; remember?) in here just don't get that... It is now 12:10: .... ten minutes after midnight in New Folsom. And many of my (most) fellow cohorts lied and gossiped on their way to sleep. And they will wake up cussing, cursing, lying and gossiping... It would be funny if it were not so sad... I saw a guy today saying "George (sobriquet) is a faggot. I can't stand him He got (sic) an 'R' in his jacket. I was gonna kick his ass last week and..." Twenty minutes later he shook George's hand and hugged him. "What's up brother?"... So goes the story of C.D.C.

I wanna tell a T.D. Jakes story, but let me begin with do they (the Potter's House) read any of the mail? Jakes always says "send me a letter or an email and... " this is the 3rd time I've sent money for C.D.'s and did not get the C.D.'s... This time I sent $ 35.00 four months ago. They sent me a 'receipt' but no C.D.'s. Then I get a letter requesting money (more money) and I write in red ink that I did not get my CD's. I've sent 5 letters and the "only" replies I get ask me for money. That is not cool....

There's a guy here who says he's a "full blown Christian". And I was telling (witnessing) him about a T.D. Jakes sermon I'd heard Sunday. I was pumped and breaking it down to my fellow "Christian" and he seemed a bit standoffish etc. A guy who practices "Wiccan blatantly interrupted us to talk about buying a "cigarette" and my Christian buddy got animated and invigorated talking about 'smoking'. And when they finished he forgot all about the "God" we had been discussing.... That is how it goes in here. "Jailhouse religion". Folk claim Christianity to 'get over'. They want the parole board, judges, lawyers and their family to think they're a Christian. Claiming Christianity in the prisons is a predatory act. It positions you to be looked upon with regard. It can also be manipulated to help keep you from getting your butt kicked... My Christian buddy smokes, drinks, gambles, cusses like a sailor and.... I'm at the point that I don't even 'tell' people I'm a 'Christian'. If (and that is debatable) my life does not 'show' some Christianity then I deserve to be 'thought' an atheist. I don't sing the "I'm a Christian" song. It represents game, schemes, tricks and con... If my Clark Kent is so awful that my Superman can't be seen. If the Jacob in me is more powerful (and obvious) than the Israel in me. If my trickster out shines my prince etc. then I need to lay on my face before God. I need an anointing which is palpable... If I've really (really) been with the Lord then the residue of His countenance will get off on me. If I really know Him He'll affect me. His spiritual dopamine will cause a metamorphosis inside of me. An authentic relationship with Jesus Christ is transformative. When you've been with the Lord you can be warming yourself (Peter) around the enemy's fire - and you can swear up and down that "I don't know Jesus". And Peter ended us cussing to add emphasis to the lie that he didn't know Jesus. But there was something about the way he walked, looked and talked which let them know that "Peter is one of them".... If you've really had an experience with God you can be at the club trying to dance. And no matter how Bootylicious you are folk will start looking at you and say "look at her. She looks like she's doing the holy dance. I think she's a church girl". They'll recognize the residue of His holiness on you.

But in this place of brokenness, madness, anger and rage etc. "we" are thieves. And a "thief" is by nature, deceptive and double minded. If I'll lie to my momma and tell her I need money for "child support" when I'm really buying crack. If I'll steal from my mother to buy meth. If I'll force (barbaric and wicked) a woman to have "sex" (AKA "rape") with me. If I'll shoot a woman in the head. If I'll blow a man's head off for $ 50.00. If I'll sadistically, maliciously and savagely molest a child etc. what won't I do to you?

I have to remind myself (over and over again) that this place (Hades) called prison etc. it is that place that they send "us" to for a garden variety of vicious assaults. I am a part of and I live amongst people under demonic influences and suffering from all manner of mental illnesses. So the fact that I'm still shocked, awed and "hurt" when people (in Hades) lie to me, on me, about me etc. The fact that I'm still running around telling Willie, C.O. Smith and Mrs. Kennedy etc. "I don't understand why he would do that". And "Why would this dude just lie?" and... It is indicative of the fact (perhaps) that I'm still rejecting (perhaps for my own psychological survival) the reality of the nature of the prison. I "get it" intellectually, philosophically and spiritually. I'm not certain that emotionally I've been successful at exegiting the prison subculture....

Imagine (Brett Jolliff, Alex Blench, Andrew Lang or Cody Sheldon etc.) that you wake up tomorrow morning in the room (locked in) with a 49 year old who murdered a man for meth. And he's been in prison 17 times. He's committed sexual assault, aggravated assault, robbery, drug sales, carjacking etc. and now he's "down" (locked up) for murder. He has a life sentence in prison. And you (Alex Chivescu, Anthony Durbin or the "Brett" on Dr. Phil who went to San Quentin etc.) are locked up on a burglary, theft, credit card scam or on drug charges. You are going (supposedly) home in 3 years. But your O.Gee celly (who has not had sex in 18 years! who has been sitting up watching Tyra and lusting Marius & Quenton etc.) will "never" get out! Never is a long time. Now may I ask you (Nathaniel, Keith, Larry Laboe or John Griffin etc.) a question? Do you think (perhaps) there might be a small chance that while you are sitting on the throne (toilet - which is 2 feet away from your celly's bed) dumping your little booty out etc. Is there a small chance your celly might start thinking about what it would be like to go up in you? ... Can I be real with you (Brett, Michael Parker, Tadd Carr and John Butterfield etc.) all and tell you what really goes on in here? Can I tell you what you'd hear if prison walls could talk? I'll try not to be as explicit, candid and as graphic as the holy Bible is I promise. But if "this" ("K.K.K.") is really "it". And my "moment" to come into your school, classroom or bedroom. If I'm really gonna reach out to students already in college like John Griffin, Alex Chivescu and Frasier McGinn etc. and inspire them to stay in school. If I'm gonna use "this" (K.K.K.) moment to inspire John Butterfield to go to (and stay in; no matter how difficult it becomes) college. If I have any chance of reaching boys like Tadd Carr, Steve "Van" Burguess and Maxwell Hanger etc. I've gotta come "real" or not at all. Max and Tadd etc. can get a diluted, watered down and "G" rated version about what some "scholar" (with a team of Ghost writers, Editors and Book doctors etc.) "thinks" goes on in prison at the local library. And/or you can go watch "Prison Break" on DVD. But "if" you would like to "break" the CYCLE (habits, characteristics and traits) which can lead you to "prison" then you better drag your hips to the dorm (the cell, the dayroom, the bedroom or the coffee shop etc.) and 'read this book'. You'd better get on the internet (in chat rooms, on blogs, facebook, myspace and at yourplace and tell what's his face) and tell the fellas "yall gots 2 check this book out. A dude in jail put it down bro. He opened up the prison can of worms and he broke it down..." You tell your partners that "Sherman writes like we talk. He breaks all the writer's rules. It's not a polished book bro. It is raw, ripped and cutting. It is just as raw and gripping as it's name. It is "K.K.K." dude"....

My assignment is to tell it (Hades) like it is. Like it t-i-s. And then after presenting you with the unvarnished truth. After painting a word picture of the inside of a prison from the inside of a prison etc. then it's on you what (to) you do. If you want to come find out what it feels like to be taking a dump two feet away from a killer and a rapist; come on. He'll hear you grunt, fart and butt spit. He'll hear you and smell you. And he'll start out 'joking'. "Your crap doesn't stink". That'll lead to "your butt smells like roses". And that'll lead to Bob slapping Marius' butt cheeks. And if Marius flashes (gets angry) Bob'll say "Dude lighten up. This is prison! You know how many times Scottie Pippen slapped Michael Jordan's butt. Kobé get's his butt slapped all the time. I don't want none (sic) of your lil tight butt. You couldn't turn me on (reverse psychology etc. You're a "boy" in your teens. You are insecure, gullible and vulnerable etc. You still have a need to please. And the desire to be wanted etc.) If you wanted to". And then he'll start calling you "kid". And reminding you of how tough, powerful and deadly he is. And within 3 weeks he'll have you (Alex, Brett, C.J., Jai and Craig etc.) so afraid, intimidated and "conflicted" that when (not if) he screws you, you won't be able to figure out if it was "rape" or "sex". And...

They put a 44 year old dude in the cell with me a few weeks ago. A. He is white but says he's "black and chinese". And his intro was "I have an "R" in my jacket and I'm a homosexual (he's not effeminate. But neither is Marion E. Spearman!). But not active right now". I said "Dude if I had a choice I'd say hell no.... But I don't want to know anything about your "R". I'm not a judge. And you will definitely be "inactive" in this cell".

He 'said' he was a 'clean' person. God bless him. He says he's clairvoyant and psychic. He's a nut. And he is absolutely filthy. He wakes up in the morning and does not wash his face or brush his teeth! That freaks me out. And when they bring the food trays to the door he wonders why I won't allow him to give me my tray. He's been scratching his butt and balls all night long. Having a booger and snot convention in his bed. And then has the nerve to touch my food? Oh no! And I had to put on rubber gloves the other night and put a pair of his short pants in a plastic bag. The smell nearly ran me out of the room. He says "I washed them and disinfected them".... The mere fact that they needed "disinfecting" ought to be a sign to trash them. I don't hate him. He means well. But he's the funkiest psychic "medium" I've ever smelled (met). Damn!... He's an interesting segue to the "arrogance" of prisoners. "We are at the bottom of the barrel. Locked up in maximum security prisons and "we" have the audacity and the temerity to toot our nose up in the air...

"He (my celly) couldn't cell with "me" because he gots (sic) a "R" in his jacket" a dude told me. And a few days thereafter this same arrogant inmate moved a fella in whom I know from M.C.S.P. (Bunnell's prison). And this guy definitely (without question) has an "R" in his jacket. As a matter of fact he was rolled up (at M.C.S.P.) for receiving fellatio from a "queen" (outside!) on the yard! ("rolled up" means to be locked up in ad-seg)....

So this "picky" and choosy inmate who wouldn't let my celly cell because of an "R". And who says he is not gay! (I'm not saying he is!)... He has a convicted sexual offender who has sex with men etc. in his cell...

I recall a guy telling someone he "hates" gays. And... In E.O.P. (Enhanced Outpatient Program) I saw him giving a "hand job" in a group underneath the table!! (lol) For "reals". I kept seeing him and the guy next to him laugh and put their hands under the table. So I became a tad bit suspicious. I threw my ink pen to the floor. And quickly bent down to retrieve it. As I did so I looked over at these laps and both had their pants unzipped and were masturbating one another. I am serious. But he'll tell you in a minute he's not gay....

Guess what I found? I found a missive (to me) by the dude with the "R" in his jacket. And in it he pleads with me not to mention his "R". He goes home in 29 days. I'm tempted to wait til he goes home and show his arrogant, uppity celly the note. But pragmatically (lol) he'll be back. He's coming back to prison. And I'm tired of "fighting". I'd have to "fight" him. Plus why should I stir crap up? We have enough "haters" around here. I just want youth (Jonathan Davis, Kyle Evans, Esteban Nunez and C.J. etc.) to get a glimpse of the mentality of prison(ers).... School rivalries, enemies and fights are serious. And they're getting worse (more on that later). But if you have/had problems in school or college multiply it by 100. Think of the worst bully at your school. The worst of the worst. Then imagine your school having 100 bullies (as bad as the worst one at your school) all there. Now imagine that you were locked on campus with the 100 bullies. Now imagine your school being converted into a campus of two man cells. And you must cell with one of the 100 bullies. And you eat, sleep and crap locked in a cage (cell) with him... And when you get "mail" (from your kids, siblings, wife or mom etc.) you have to leave it in the cell with a bully (thief, crook, thug and a murderer.). And "if" I'll kill a man in cold blood. Do you really think I won't sneak and peruse your mail? Record your addresses? Look at your photos? I've seen guys catch their celly masturbating while looking at a photo. Not just "any" photo. But a photo of their "kids". And so what would you do (Michael Avance? Austin Sisneros? Michael Castro? Von or Vaughn?)? You have a 3 year sentence. And you walk into your cell Michael (Castro). And you catch your celly (Ed Stokes or Eric Menendez) getting his "money" to a photo of your 3 year old niece. I believe Mike would "put hands on Ed". And since Ed has a life sentence he might stab you (Bro. Castro). And since Mike is a big ole healthy youngster he might take Ed's knife and stab Ed.... And Mike just turned his 3 year sentence into 25-to-life. And if Jason gets Mike a superlawyer Mike might get away with (only) ten more years added to his sentence.... I'd like my team (Ryan and Heather) to do a study on just 'one' California prison. And examine (of 1000 inmates) how many guys (like me) have had "time" added to their sentence because of stuff they "did" or "had to do" to survive in prison. Jail is hell yall. Nathan Langley, Alex Wagner Trugman, Cody Sheldon, Caleb Peek and Randy Madden etc. Better hear (read) what I'm sayin to you. This is not a joke!.... I want James Evenson, Travis Shaw, Dave Molteni, Victor Karlsson and Frazier to hear me...

I pray (again) that Andy Reid, Jeffrey Lurie, Tony Dungy and Lebron James will help G.B.G. cause boys to "see" with the "vision" in this book. I need J. Wyatt Mondersire, Earl Stafford and Tyler Perry to help us bury the contents of this book in the brains of our boys.

We need to help our boys develop their vision as well as their (spiritual and psychological) peripheral vision. This book is a wake up call! In order for a kid to navigate your way through life you need to be able to see around corners, in nooks and crannies. You've got to have sight, insight and foresight. And then you need visions, dreams and goals. Lest you end up here...

I went outside to the yard today for the very first time in a month. I've been locked in writing. Rubin "Hurricane" Carter got it right: "when the prison is awake I will sleep. When they are asleep I will wake". Hurricane had discovered that the best way to keep the prison out of your mind is to keep your mind out of the prison. Ipso Facto, I don't go out. I don't want to contaminate what God has given and is giving me. And when you walk and talk with people who "breathe out violence" it'll infect you.

.. I saw a big old, fat racist captain today. He is absolutely a Klansman. And he's going to hell in a hand basket. He says he is a "believer". Well, I "believe" there is a man named Marilyn Manson. But I don't "know" him, have never "met" him. And I don't listen to him. This captain may very well "believe" there is a God but he (the captain) does not know him, has never "met" him and does not listen to him. You can't listen to God and still be a big ole bumbling Klansman. Yeah, this captain may 'believe' but Satan himself 'believes'. And it is so sad that a man earning $ 108,000 per year who goes home everyday can be just as "locked-up" on the streets as Scott Peterson is on death-row. "Locked-up" in his own hatred, bitterness and rage. He probably beats his wife. This dude has costed the department of corrections $ millions. Because he's been sued (successfully) at least 60 times. He once told me "Aint no money outta my pocket. Ain't no sweat off my balls"... A lieutenant told me "Walker has a good heart (Amen) but he is surrounded by snakes and crooks". Were it not for Madame Patricia Kennedy, L.N. Johnson-Dovey, Jeff Macomber and a few others, Walker would be in trouble. Not for anything he (Walker) does. But for the vindictiveness, racism, violence and retaliatory actions of some of these right wing, Limbaugh loving "Christians" working for him... I'm not writing to Baby Boomers remember? I'm not 'qualified' to write to them. I'm not John Grisham! (I aint Hatin, yall. I read "all" John's stuff;). I'm not a James Patterson or a Richard Norm Patterson! I'm not that good!

I'm writing to students at McClathy High School in SAC Town (i.e. Tony Radjsavong, Rachelle Alamon, Nicholas Wysong, Brad Clark, Andrew Petrass and Matthew Clark etc.) who are studying Tupac Shakur! I'm writing to the Band "The Clark Brothers", Hairo Torres, Dr. Tracy Talmadge and to "Brandon (Brandon was on KCRA on 10/17/09 "connect with kids" The Fight Club story). And these teens and tweenies can relate to where I'm coming from. I just want to let them know what's in this (Hades) place. People (like that fat ass captain) who abuse their authority and misuse their power engaging in pissing contests with inmates. People who ought to be (i.e. the captain) out washing cars or collecting garbage etc. Yet, in spite of the fact that many of them are psychologically compromised (i.e. this captain is bi-polar) and even though their presence in an institution is a threat to the security and safety of inmates and staff... I.E. Larry Turner who abandoned his post to come beat up an inmate and ended up assaulting C.O,. T.V. ....I.E. a sergeant (I think his name is "Burrell") at Mule Creek (where Bunnell is) who broke an inmate's arm through the cell door. And smuggled cigarettes and drugs in to pay inmates not to tell....

In spite of all that they got a j-o-b in CDC. And they are walking lawsuits waiting to happen. And if you come here you get to have some renegade, rogue, racist and bigoted "captain" decide where and when to transfer you. And if (when) they decide you're going to ad-seg or going to transfer etc. you are going!

Be pragmatic a moment. I am not indigent! Nor am I illiterate. And I'm perhaps (all praise due to God) the most prolific CA. prisoner author on the West Coast. I've written more books than Mumia Abu Jamal and (the late) "Tookie" combined! And yet, this renegade, bi-polar, duplicitous captain put me in ad-seg on "B" yard years ago for nothing. And Mike Martel (along with a thug chief deputy warden) transferred me to Mike Bunnell. If they'll get "me". What will they do to a poor, disconnected high school dropout?... I saw a poor Mexican inmate at CMC East get the crap beat out of him at CMC East (in the E.R.) by C.O. Davis and Lt. Romero. (Lt. Romero smuggles drugs and knives into CMC inmates to gang members. .... C.O. Acosta was doing the same thing here at New Folsom and Madame Cheryl K. Pliler fired him. Acosta was on the Elite I.S.U. unit!). They knocked 3 of his teeth out. And nurse Kennedy (widely rumored to be involved in a sexual relationship with C.O. Davis at C.M.C.) stated "I didn't see anything!".... But the inmate was poor and illiterate and staff knows "He doesn't have any family support... It's his word against ours and we have badges!"...

President Obama recently spoke about how insurance companies use their considerable power to conduct phony studies to prevent reform. He could've been talking about the CCPOA. They've used their considerable influence (money) for decades; to prop up corrupted guards. To conduct deceptive media campaigns and provide misinformation to the public etc. All to obstruct prison reform.... Someone told me that Anthony Gentile is now a "lieutenant" at Old Folsom.

... Sgt. Anthony Gentile told me at M.C.S.P. "Dude, I'm embarrassed to be working for Bunnell. I don't know bout that "murder" crap Manning, but I do know 3 things: A. Bunnell is corrupted! B. He's a 'threat'! And C. He wants you to go to Pleasant Valley! Dude, he ordered Costa (CCI) to say Sanchez (Ray Sanchez Jr.) is not at P.V.S.P." .

You get that Kyle Evans, Cody Sheldon and Nathaniel etc.? You're in prison and your associate warden is a criminal. And no matter who you write (Cong. Jim Costa, Sen. Gloria Romero, the ombudsman etc.) you can't stop him (a rogue A.W.) from sending you to Valley Fever capitol via special escort! I.S.U. does not do transfers! They transferred my nappy headed butt! And they stopped (they kept the camera off then) at McDonalds. And they bought me food and they (seriously) put something in the food! I thought it was mighty strange that a team of Elite commandos (Investigative Service Unit) on orders from A.W. Bunnell to special transfer me to P.V.S.P. with all deliberate haste would buy me food. And for a prisoner to turn down McDonalds is unheard of. I refused to eat it. And after that; I was beat!... Lt. J. Herrera met us at P.V.S.P. and authorized (per Bunnell) another beating... Nathaniel, Keith, students at KIPP, Ron Clark Academy and Locke High School etc. it (beatings and special transfers etc.) happens everyday! And the problem with folk like Scott Kernan and Matt Cate (good managers) is that they don't (just like T.D. Jakes doesn't) read their mail. So writing them alarming, life or death missives etc. is a waste of time...

The Big Booty (racist-bi-polar) captain once told me "President Nelson Mandela is a murderer! He bombed....." I got up and left his funky butt office. I rarely allow anybody to get me that angry. But for him to have the temerity to sit up and criticize and ridicule a world leader based upon some Limbaugh/Hanity/Coulter propaganda etc. got a rise out of me... The good thing about captain (so & so) is the fact that his vituperative, scurrilous and belligerent conduct toward me confirms I'm doing something right. Rev. Hosea Williams taught me that "any time corrupted, racist and egotistical white folks are pleased with you, you must be a handkerchief headed Uncle Tom like Clarence Thomas!" Ipso Facto, as much as I write about them I expect for them to offer me vinegar for water.... But I'm growing and whereas I used to just get angry etc, I returned to my cell and prayed for the captain. My duty is to forgive those who trespass against me. My responsibility is to love those who hate me. I've got to be able to exegete his (and all other Klansmen, Uncle Toms, gang bangers and drug dealers etc.) character. This man (A) can't help the fact that he is psychologically ill. And (B) he can't help the fact that he "learned racism" as a kid.... I'm not gonna allow myself to go through life being a psychological adolescent. Nor will I be a spiritual toddler. I've got to have enough "vision" to see the big picture. And witnessing the effects of wicked, racist and psychologically unstable folk like this captain has to serve as a motivational inspiration to me. Let's face it - we will always have some juveniles, jails and prisons. So I must work to help prevent 'just one' kid from growing up to become racist like this captain. I must also work (strategically) to build up the political infrastructure of NAPS so we can spark a call for change in corrections. We must ensure that some big ole corn fed white boy (black or Mexican also) who played college football etc. is not automatically given a job guarding prisoners when his psychological illness threatens public safety.... I wanna be a part of changing the criteria for becoming a guard so we can help prevent 'just one' Mike Bunnell, Marion E. Spearman, Wally Tucker, Wallace Laffitte etc. from guarding over our kids. Renegade, rogue, drug smuggling and racist guards exacerbate criminals. They help prisoners become incorrigible and institutionalized....

'Just one' is an authentic and powerful goal. Hitler was one man. Martin Luther King was one man! How many Jews would be alive had there been 'not one' Hitler? How many blacks would be on the backs of buses or otherwise marginalized had there been 'not one' Martin Luther King Jr.? Had there been 'not one' Bunnell I would not have Valley Fever for the rest of my life....

So as I write this book I'm only writing it to reach, teach, inspire, encourage, educate and motivate 'just one' of you. If Tyra never reads this so be it. If I don't attain national media interest so be it. I won't stop writing, you can believe that. And even after I'm in heaven I'll have books being published (just like Tupac is still putting out C.D.'s!) after I'm gone... But if (that is what I'm fasting and praying for) 'just one' Justin Howell, Joseph Latham, Daniel Job, Maxwell Hanger, Brett Jolliff or Alex Blench etc. peruses this tome and is bettered by what you read my work is done....

Star Jones and Barbara Walters had much discussion and many arguments about Eric Menendez. And (allegedly) Barbara had a pal of hers to agree to help Eric write a book. And Eric had inmate Richard Cruz (of Daniel Henson fame) typing the book. Somebody (I've gotten various reports on who) snitched Cruz out and they transferred him... That's why my tomes are (always) typed on the streets. I don't trust these guys. They'll give your stuff to the Captain to "proof" (lol)...

I struggled with whether or not to be 'graphic' in a teen tome. I consulted with my panel of experts (Curren, Heitkamp and Solis etc.). I talked with youngsters like Dustin (Nic), Adam (Lane) and Daniel (Bugriyev) etc. I talked to my youngest convicts (AKA "experts" on youth criminality and "Experience Therapists") like Jesus Benjamin Sandoval and Johnny O'Neal (who just turned 21). And their collective opinion was unanimous. "These Kids R slinging dope at 9 years old". And they "carry guns before they turn 10. They know about sucking and fuc---- at 8. If you don't come real you won't reach them Atlanta my youngest youngster told me. Ipso Facto let me tell you this (lest you come to Hades)....

To be turned-out means to be "turned" gay. To be turned-out, a dude is either raped or pressured into having ex. "Men" are expected to defend yo manhood, and if you lose it, you'll need another "man" to protect you. For a weaker con, the choice of having to do it (have sex) with one is better than having to do it with a lot of them. Younger inmates are also "tricked" into sex by another queen or punk.

"There is a queen named one punch" Jeremiah told me at MCSP. "She is huge! She's about six foot four, and weighs close to two eighty".

I'd heard rumors about One Punch in L.A. County Jail also. His/her rep. was legendary! The story goes that One Punch has a thing for white boys (like Marion E. Spearman does). One Punch loves to suck their (privates) 'things'. Legend has it, she'd (it's hard for me to call a "man" a "she", but in prison that's what "staff" even calls them) trick them into her cell and she'd hide them under her bed, where she'd give them the most awesome and splendiferous face (blow job) they'd ever had. They say One Punch had sucked hundreds of Caucasian penises. And there's an endless supply of eager pipes (if you will) in prison. One Punch would suck em and when she was done, her 'voice' would get deep and she'd say "now it's my turn"... But the lil white boys would be "straight" (at least they 'thought' they were. But, look up the word "homo" and then tell me if a man who has sex with a 'man' is straight!) and as soon as they began to object and say "But I'm not gay" as soon as the 'g' came out their mouth.... Bam! One Punch (with "one punch") would knock them out!

And, according to Jeremiah and ten other dudes I consulted with (including 3 victims), when they woke up, the white boys would say something like, "god damn! That bitch punched me so hard my asshole is sore!..."

In L.A. County Jail a lil white boy named Christopher Parker strutted up to my cell door in some lizard looking shorts and he told my celly (Alan Stark - AKA "Turtle") to "look at this" and he turned around and jiggled his butt cheeks like jello. What was sad is that in 2500 three months earlier I saw two blacks and three Mexicans get em drunk off of pruno (AKA spud juice) and they tricked him into the shower area to "talk". Chris staggered in. They had mixed drugs (psyche meds) into the "hooch" and Juan Sanchez said to Chris "you gay right?" Chris replied (emphatically) "Hell no!"... "Lay down" Juan ordered. Chris' pants were gone and he probably didn't even remember dudes taking em off. Gone were his underwear also. Juan got on top of Chris and pushed his face into the floor, muffling the yelling. "Shouldn't we stop these guys?" I said to a fellow. He replied "They'll stab us dude. They 'run' this". My stomach (literally) turned. Juan split his butt hole open screwing him. Chris sobbed. I felt like an animal in a zoo watching this bull shit... When Juan finished, one by one the other four screwed him. One of em made Chris blow him before he screwed him. This happened in L.A. County Jail. And "Chris" and "Juan" are not pseudonyms.

Rapes take place (I shall repeat) each and every day in L.A. County Jail... Read "Creating Monsters" (www.cafepress.com/creating)....

One of the "trade secrets" of California prison guards is the fact that they use "rape" as a way to punish youngster inmates who defy them. C.O. Larry Turner did it. The Baker Brothers at MCSP were known for it. Marian E. Spearman, Lance Corcoran, Mike Jiminez, Mike Bunnell, Wally Tucker and Mike Martel are all "known" to use prisoner rape as punishment. They'll throw an 18 or 19 year old in a cell with a booty bandit in A minute. And then they'll use I.S.U. (i.e. C.O. Acosta) to obstruct any investigation if the (see pages 10-12 in "Creating Monsters") inmate actually reports it... If you try to "call" home to tell :mommy" the telephone will say "your call has been intercepted". And you won't connect. Your mail (just as Goldsmith did mine for years and I still have mail thefts!.... Bunnell stole mail to me from Peter... remember?) will be "stolen".

... I have multiple correctional "sources" about "secret meetings" held by staff (i.e. Spearman, Bunnell and/or Martel) which have been infiltrated... The prison guard underworld (led by the likes of Lance, Bunnell, Deathridge, Sgt. DeFrancis and Jiminez etc.) is incredible. They have "the Green Wall" (AKA 723) which conducts secret rituals, "sacrifices" inmates and even has "ceremonies". They make the "LAPD Rampart Division look like sterling characters" Attorney Lippsmeyer wrote to me.

C.O. Sam Bess worked my bldg. on overtime in 2001 (approximately) and Bess told me "If you don't leave Bunnell the f--- alone your asshole is gonna end up tore wide open. And we can even put you in a body bag". Yet the karma truck came around and C.O. Sam Bess (who was very close to Lt. Stephen Luke Scarsella, Sgt. R.N. Saunders, C.O. Larry Turner and Mike Bunnell (... You kids should google all of them... And send em a note and tell em you read about them in "K.K.K.". And tell them I said to "Picture me Rolling") had a "hit" placed upon his head by a white prison gang. A correctional captain (who spoke on the condition of anonymity because the captain is unauthorized to comment on this matter) stated to me that "Bess wanted you dead! I was a sergeant back then. And he, Scarsella, Sanders and Bunnell were after you. I disagree with you on Martel. Martel is not corrupted. He plays golf with legislators and people in the Governor's office! He's a pompous ass but not corrupted. He was appointed "warden" as a quid pro quo by his golfing buddies in the state senate"... I'm calling for the Justice Department to investigate this alleged quid pro quo appointment of Mike Martell. I've given attorney Murray J. Janus and Michael Morchower the name of the captain (and my notes) who told me that in case something (else) happens to me.

I've also provided the lawyers with data (including witness statements from "staff") concerning the "lieutenant" who worked (as a sergeant) with Mike Bunnell at M.C.S.P.....

Unlocking secrets unblocks mysteries and creates accountability. I'm calling for a top-to-bottom investigation of Lance Corcoran, Mike Jiminez, the CCPOA, Bunnell and the entire "Green Wall". I want staff held accountable for setting inmates (mostly young and "white") up to be "raped", "stabbed" and in some cases "murdered". I affirm under penalty of perjury that C.O. Celsa Zamudio, C.O. W. Brumbaugh, Sgt. R. N. Saunders, C.O. Wallace Laffitte, C.O. Larry Turner, Lt. Stephen Luke Scarsella, C.O. Wally Tucker, C.O. D.L. Criner and· (then) captain Marion E. Spearman have all engaged in setting up inmates to be assaulted, raped and/or murdered... Inmate Michael Gorman was murdered! Inmate "Hollywood" Walters was murdered! (Hello Brumbaugh and Uncle Tom Spearman!). And countless inmates around the Nation have had their butts busted and ruined because of prison guards'. "Girls Gone Wild? Hello! How bout guards gone wild!.... If Michael Gorman (who was murdered and sodomized and had a TV guide shoved up his anus!) had lived he would have needed a colostomy bag for the rest of his life! He was murdered at the behest of Mike Bunnell, Celsa Zamudio and Sam Bess! That's for certain! And rumor has it that Larry Turner was involved with the "order". I'm not certain about Larry's involvement in "that" particular "hit"....

Back to the fat ass, demon possessed "captain" who is bipolar. A sergeant (who's brother is a lieutenant at M.C.S.P. Rosario "Dad" ran his ass to M.C.S.P.!) told me that "captain Smith (pseudonym) should be in a cell right next to you. That dude has committed so many crimes I couldn't even count them"... For the record Rosario was right to send that corrupted lieutenant to M.C.S.P. This sarge claimed that "Rosario was gonna falsely accuse my brother of a "crime".... For the 'record' I was not some type of handkerchief head "yes" man to Rosario. There were time(s) we disagreed. But Rosario respects "men". He liked Celsa Zamudio. They were buddies. Rosario gave Celsa any job he wanted. And Celsa even escorted Lisa Ling when she was here. But I couldn't stand Celsa. I still can't stand Celsa!... But - this 'sergeant' is just as duplicitous as the "captain". Both of them are going to hell. The sergeant has had several female staff file complaints on him (attorney Janus has all this data so that when they transfer me again we'll file) for sexual harassment. He's been a sergeant for more than 11 years. I've never seen him commit any crimes. But he should take one of those many overtime checks he gets and "Buy him a set of balls". He is one of the weakest, dumbest and most spineless sergeants I've ever met. Inmate Wayman Berry had this sergeant convinced that he (Berry) had $ 350 grand in his bank account. Berry took a bank statement (for $ 35.00) and used white out. He then typed in $ 35 grand and showed it to this sarge... "I have a law firm on the streets" Berry told him. "We represented Dianne Feinstein in her divorce". And "I'm almost a millionaire" Berry told Sergeant Dumbo. And he bought it! And yall wonder why C.D.C. is not "working"? Look at who's running C.D.C.... High School drop outs! Dope fiends. As quiet as it is kept (I stand corrected) you only need a GED to be director (at the rate of $ 225,000 per year, plus a car, plus gas and plus other perks!) of the CA. Dept. of Corrections!.... Roderick Q. Hickman was good! I personally liked Rod! But let's be real; Rod did not have a college degree! (candidly - Rod was the first, only and last black C.D.C. director. Arnold did that! And the CCPOA Lance Corcoran and his team of hoodlums ran Rod out of office! Rod may not admit it but they did! They ran Richard Polanco out of the Senate! And they ran Jeannie Woodford out of office after only 3 months! Lance and Mike are known thugs! They can be deadly! I dare Lance Corcoran and his deadly cohorts to take a polygraph test at my expense! I want Robert Navarro and James Mattocks to sit in on the exam!

... While we talk polygraphs - I'd like for Bunnell to take a polygraph test and answer only 4 questions: A. "Didn't you read a book by Sherman D. Manning with you in it?" B. "Didn't you tell Manning 'I'm sending you to P.V.S.P. so you can catch Valley Fever and write a book about that?" C. "Didn't you have the mailroom to flag and steal a letter to Sherman from Chairman Andrist?" And D: "Didn't you have Doug Pieper murdered?" I will pay for the poly. And if Mr. Mike Bunnell passes the test he will receive $ 25 grand and a public apology from me... I am not allowed to give any C.D.C. employee anything. It is against the rules. I will not be giving Bunnell the money. First of all he will fail. Secondly (in the event that he's a psychopath etc.) if he passes an anonymous donor will give him a check for $ 25 grand!

So I want my youths (not traditional media! I'm not concerned with traditional media! Most of them are "Baby Boomers" and in areas like Sacto they support the CCPOA because of ad revenue! I don't need them! I need Sam Altman, Evan Williams, Benoit-Denizet, Tom Joyner, Bev. Smith, Tavis and John Butterfield etc. I want twitterers to twit, tweet or twot (lol) about this challenge to Bunnell! And call Mule Creek State Prison and/or 916-323-6001 and ask Bunnell to poly! Let's do this!) to get it "out there" in blogosphere etc. and see if that murderous pervert (Mike Bunnell) will take the poly. Ipso Facto, if he refuses then he can't claim that I'm some "paranoid conspiracy theorist" etc. nor can he claim I'm a James Frey engaging in "yellow" journalism. My journalism is "black" (as am I) and "white" (as is my wife). It is authentic, factual and it is actual.

And I must reiterate to you youngsters that in prison it is to be or not to be. Kill or be killed. They will rape you in here! It is not a nice place. This is not a home away from home. Most prison officials are just as dirty, dark, wicked and as evil as the dudes over whom they officiate! ... It takes a dark person (not "all" the time but by and large. If you think I'm joking do a poll. Ask 3000 14, 15 and 16 year olds how many of them would like to work in a maximum security prison for 30 years. I'd bet less than 20%.... Now go to Fresno State or CSU Sac and ask 3000 college freshmen and sophomores how many wanna spend their lives working in prisons: less than 5%!) to work in a prison. And yall know I gots "names" for you! Right? So I'll do a ten name poll. Call Roger Walthorn, Alex Chivescu, Keith and Nathaniel Mullennix, Benjamin Alexander, Jason Rapp, Marius (from the Tyra "Bromance" show), Brett (who visited San Quentin on Dr. Phil!) and Maxwell Hanger. And ask each (Ryan and Heather I need you all to really call all them. And post your results on the G.B.G. Facebook pages) of them would they want to work for 30 years guarding child molesters, murderers, rapists, dope fiends and sadistic criminals.

... I told my dear friend (and mentor) Dr. Tye Hedblad that "prison is too dark a place for your gentle spirit". Dr Hedblad was privy to the retaliatory, vindictive and criminal plans to send me to Corcoran to be "murdered". He was going to testify to it in Court! Attorney Jon Lippsmeyer and Attorney Paul Comiskey can verify that... I just (recently) learned the full story on what happened to (the brilliant psychologist who was also a close friend and colleague of our chief psychiatrist Dr. Jaffe) Dr. Hedblad! ... Larry Turner, Sam Bess, Zamudio and Lt. Scarsella threatened Dr. Hedblad's life! "If you testify for Sherman D. Manning you will regret it. It will end your career. It may even end your life!" they told him... He was so afraid he asked Dr. Marilyn Windham what he should do.

.... Bunnell (AKA the John Gotti of C.D.C. along with Lance Corcoran) orchestrated the "threats". Hedblad checked into a "drug" rehab and he told Paul Comiskey he feared for his life. And he wanted to speak to Judge Jane Ure personally... Paul sold me out! Paul was a "double" agent! Paul tipped deputy D.A. Tom Clancy and Kathryn Druliner off. Madame Druliner told her hubby (an A.G. chief deputy prosecutor)... "they" told Hurtle (an Uncle Tom Ombudsman). And Hurtle dutifully informed Lance and Bunnell. And Dr. Hedblad (a brilliant psychologist) turned up (as did captain Doug Pieper) d-e-a-d.... He (allegedly; I've no credible data to prove otherwise!) drank himself to death because he was afraid of Bunnell, Scarsella, Lance and that crowd....

A female psychologist and (extremely attractive) due to a pending sensitive issue I was asked not to use her name. We'll call her "Jackson") agreed to testify on my behalf. "I personally heard Mike Bunnell tell Lt. Trujillo and Captain Shievelbein that 'You need to transfer Manning to Corcoran so they can shoot his ass on a Shu Yard". And I will testify Manning feared for his life when he wrote those irrational threats" she wrote in an affidavit. And then her husband (allegedly) cheated on her. And a few months before she was to testify against Bunnell and that crowd she was dead. Not even 30 years old and she was dead. "They" claim she committed suicide! So Hedblad PhD. is dead. Doug Pieper (who actually testified against Mike Bunnell;!) is dead! The CCPOA said "Pieper committed suicide because he was given a job change and because his son (allegedly) was "gay". The CCPOA said Dr. Jackson "committed suicide because she was hurt by her husband cheating on her"... The CCPOA is a criminal enterprise with a vested interest in crime. What other union in the Country defends thugs like Bunnell, Baker, Tucker and the guards Rod Hickman fired for beating the kid up at Y.A.?

I would not be surprised if some of those little boys Mike Jimenez is having sex with are also selling drugs for him. "Doc" Ford, Bob Vonvillas and Rafael Perez can all attest to the fact that a "badge" is a great "cover" for dishonor. And - guys like the warden at CMC East (J. Marshall), James Yates (warden at P.V.S.P.), Bunnell and Martel at M.C.S.P. etc. are all known crooks! These guys (Marshall, Yates, Bunnell & Martel etc.) are sitting atop $ 200 million budgets! And they only have high school diplomas and G.E.D.'s And it is a "well known fact that James Yates (and Marshall, Martel and Bunnell etc) gets kickbacks for the contracts he gives to contractors and entrepreneurs doing business with P.V.S.P." C.O. Joe Rikalo stated to C.O. Thornton "And with $ 200 million under his thumbs you know he's stealing some of that money... Yates has an offshore bank account" Rikalo stated.... He didn't think I could "hear" their private conversation outside my hospital room. Hell, I can tell you (in this tome) Joe Rikalo's two daughters names. His son's name and where his wife works. I know his home telephone number as well as his home address. All compliments of Joe Rikalo himself. He "said" it outside my door...

At C.R.M.C. (Coalinga) hospital my life was jeopardized by the lady (I'll not yet reveal her name as I've stated previously) addicted to meth. But (just a tease to exemplify my authenticity and the fact that "House" is not the only hospital with drama!) Mike Lupo was a reformed meth addict! He's young, gregarious and a "good" young man. I like Mike (Jeff and also John Hutchinson). Mike is the director of medical imaging at CRMC. He worked his way up from a jasitor and a plumber to now earning over $ 100 grand annually.

A person was telling me that "Mike tried to help her (the meth friend who bungled my ultrasound and almost killed me when inserting a picc line with Dr. Degucchi.....Ryan and Heather, you all be certain to send CRMC Hospital a copy of this book) get off meth. But she won't listen. And Lori (D.O.N.) and Dr. Degucchi are defending her".

... Moseley Collins, Attorney John Morgan (in Orlando Florida) and Attorney Robert Navarro are you reading this?....

... "What the hell is the I.S.U. Lieutenant doing Sherman?" a staff person asked me. "He's red flagged your mail and directed the librarian 'not' to give you any High School and College addresses".... I owe Madame Bradford an apology. I thought she was doing this... But I was wrong. She was following an illegal order. Scott Kernan can tell the ISU Lieutenant that any "prisoner" has a "right" to correspond with "anyone" in the world. If I can write to Mr. Obama how can I not write to a high school principal?... I won't go negative (but this is what you deal with when you come to Hades young people... Perhaps I'd understand it if I were convicted of child molestation etc. If I were sexually into kids as is Spearman, Bunnell and that crowd. But I'm not! About the lieutenant (Madame Kennedy is perusing with highlighter and red pen in hand!). I won't talk about his 'education' (or lack of), arrogance, egotism etc. Nor will I mention what a "pitchess" motion on him would. But I will state two things: A. His actions are outside of the rules and (according to Murray J. Janus, Robert Navarro and Mr. Morchower) he'd be wise to re-look at the rules. And B. If I didn't know Mr. Walker had him in that position for a reason I'd sue him!....

Sometimes (Mrs. Kennedy taught me this) people mean well and "think" they're right. And in their zeal to do their jobs they overreact....

I get that! But you all get this. I've seen folk get caught with cell phones and get less than a slap on the wrist. They can have drugs and even cause civilian staff to be "fired" (i.e. at P.V.S.P. I saw this) alone. But I get mail stolen, sabotaged, and now a prison lieutenant (who writes on a 6th grade level) wants to re-write the constitution? I'm not gonna call his name (he's reading this) but I want youth (High School students) en-masse to call Senator Dianne Feinstein and ask her to check up on a Lieutenant. He is in the CCPOA... If I were as bad as they act like I am why have I never written C.O. Joe Rikalo's "kids" a letter about their daddy?

But I'll make a promise (solid affirmation) in this book. Next time they risk my life via an arbitrary, retaliatory and vindictive "transfer" I will list all of their home addresses on my website. And ask citizens to go to their houses and non violently protest. All power to the people. .... Bunnell had his I.S.U. "hit" squad to conduct a 6 hour cell search (including searching my legal mail etc.) looking for Doug Pieper's address. Had Warden Walker been at M.C.S.P. he could have told them it was a "waste" of time. Once I program (Linda Fortee - pay no. 1326) something into my mind it is written in stone. I would never (ever) be stupid enough to write down a P.V.S.P. staff member's (I don't know the addresses of any C.S.P. Sac staff... But I have both of Bunnell's addresses between my two ears!) name on paper. I write them in my mind....

Great segue to remind you youths to learn how to remember. Take a picture of numbers (i.e.) in your head and program them in . Memory makes money. Having a great memory is just one of the pieces of mental and educational infrastructure that can assist you in remaining free...

"There's something happening in the Country!" President Obama said when he defied all odds and won the Iowa Caucus. "There's a mood in the air" he concluded. And that is what I want gang leaders, dope dealers and child molesters to know. There is an unseen hand at work. There is an undercurrent on the streets, in the hoods, trailer parks, barrios, juveniles and in the prisons. We will win!.... I'm telling Rev. Otis Moss, A. Lincoln James, T.D. Jakes, Eddie Long and those praying mothers to join with me and tell the devil that "Satan you can't have my child! I break the curses spoken over our children. I rebuke the devour. I won't stop believing God. No matter how bad it looks. I won't stop trusting, believing and visualizing a break-through. My child may already be in trouble. And there's no climate for change in that juvenile. The atmosphere for growth is not in that group home. But I'm believing God for a miracle. I see a rose growing out of concrete! I see my kids getting their drive, hope and dignity back. I hear my baby saying 'I might be in juvenile but I'm a blessed son. I'm blessed by God and Highly favored. I'll rise again. You may have counted me out but still I rise!.... I still believe my kids can come out of that prison. Come off of those drugs." I tell my kids what Jesus told Lazarus. Son - "come forth"! I speak it into existence. "Come forth Reggie, Johnny Boy, Ralph, Thomas, David DeCook, Sam and Mike; Come forth!"

I want some mothers and brothers to speak (and to repeat) those words out loud..."I'm just getting started! I don't quit!!" President Obama stated. And I want to let drug dealers and pimps (who are prostituting our kids) know I won't give up! I don't quit!... If I could con (see the second half of this book) America's greatest promoter (a man with street smarts and business brilliance!) the "Don" you can bet your bottom dollar this fight will be won. By God's grace I will not stop until we inspire, motivate and elevate some child to turn around. I've seen too many "tear drops and closed caskets". I have got to let these teen studs know that Tupac was correct (and his death proved "it's me too") when he said "You can be touched!" They will lock your narrow ass up for life! Yes for drugs, guns and for gang banging... You'd better stop playing spiritual charades with your life and get on your knees and talk to your daddy. Tell Him what you need and want... talk to God!

... This book is a sign for you to become a partner in this G.B.G. effort. This book is your leg on a stool. To show you visions (what can be). Now see the gateway (education) to success.

Can I tell you a powerful secret? Zig Zigler was correct "If you want to have everything in life you want; help others get what they want". In ministering to others you (actually God does it) minister to yourself.... When I walked through that convalescent home in Switzerland every time I made an Elder smile; I smiled. I blessed them and I got blessed. In ministering to you (youth) I'm ministering to myself. And Ephesians 6:8 tells us whatever good thing you make happen for somebody else - God will make happen for you! And God can't lie. Don't wait (read closely) until you get totally together. Start hollering at the homey's right now (Don't wait) about the stuff you're reading in this book. Don't be ashamed to disagree with me. Discuss "K.K.K." in the Bobbashop (AKA "Barbershop") and in the school liberry (AKA "Library"). "I think Manning should have said this... Sherman was wrong about that, but.... ").... When a person goes to college to attain a four year degree they don't wait till they obtain their degree to start talking about college and the courses they're taking. They join frats, groups, clubs and sororities and chat about class, professors and the 'Ladies'. Don't you wait till you feel you've attained your "degree" in "togetherness". Don't even wait until you've finished reading this book. But begin now to chat, blog and vlog about this book. Don't wait! While you're still in trouble, in the struggle and in "conflicts" etc. Begin to speak about getting out. And if you are bodacious, daring and courageous enough to help somebody (else) to get out while you're still in. You'll be blessed!

Speak up and speak out. As quiet as it's kept if every pastor stopped preaching about any "sin" until they were totally "free" from that "sin". Every pulpit on the planet would be silent Sunday morning!....

... I wrote about Rev. Leroy Jenkins in the second half of this tome. But I was not going to tell that a preacher working for Jenkins "quit" on him. And he called me and told me "I caught Rev. Jenkins having sex with an eleven year old boy". And I believe it. Jenkins is a sick bastard and a crook.

... If I told everything I know about famous pastors and preachers I'd ... Let me leave that alone... I want to know what Donald Dusk (Akron Ohio), Aaron Jackson (Delaware Ohio), Wayne Rawlings and Sam Fuick are now doing with their lives. G.B.G. needs these fellas.... And if you live in Sacramento, North Hollywood, West Hollywood and you are a waiter earning $ 2.25 per hour (aged 18-25) I will give you $ 500.000. The first 20 waiters (20 in N. Hollywood, 20 in W.

Hollywood and 20 in Sacto) to write me a missive (include your photo so we can put you in our photo gallery!) I will have $ 500.00 sent to you; Period!...

Mike Bunnell was foolish enough to speak with my investigators! Bunnell defended himself against allegations that captain Pieper was murdered by stating "Pieper was a weirdo". Bunnell claims "Pieper dressed up like a clown for extra money. He was torn asunder about finding out his son (Doug Jr.) was gay. That hurt his 'pride'". Bunnell then stated (first time I've ever heard this) "Captain Pieper stole some lumber sitting outside a lumber store. He was embarrassed by that and thought he would be demoted. That contributed to him committing suicide". These are Bunnell's words. I know nothing about this "stolen" lumber. But I still know Captain Pieper did not kill himself. Bunnell murdered him or had him killed; period!

... I want Dillon Banionis to join our ambassadorial team. A guy was charged with raping a 29 year old man. And Dillon stated "In this country you're innocent till proven guilty... If I saw him (J.M.) drive by in his Lamborghini I'd still be cordial... maybe I wouldn't (he smiled) invite him into my shower!".... I have no position on J.M. (I don't know the case) but in this age of conservative "guilty till proven innocentness" it is a blessing to find a youngster like Dillon willing to follow the law. I want Dillon to team up with Dan Sellery, Michael Sanford, Kyle Hancock and Tanvir Kapoor. And they must all get involved here with G.B.G. and together we will change the world!.... My investigators have learned the authentic reason Marion E. Spearman packed up and left Atlanta Georgia. The real reason Marion was arrested and charged with forcible sodomy in Atlanta. Marion was 16 and the boy was 7. Marion was able to get a judge to agree to "seal" his record and allow him to leave the state of Georgia. He came out here and became a guard. And now he earns more than $ 114,000 per year. But teachers like Joshua Costa and Daniel sample are struggling.

"A lot of us have juvenile criminal records" a 19 year veteran prison guard told me... Sgt. Elsberry is MIA. She is the sergeant who turned in Lt. Scarsella for beating down the inmate. And the code of silence almost saved him. But Elsberry stepped up with the truth... I hope Anthony "A.J." Hall, Robert Westerlund and Caleb Sima are reading. I pray and hope Cody Sheldon and Austin Sisneros are reading. We must get this book to Sean Zane, Esteban Nunez and congressman Bob Filner. I believe Jackie Goldberg and Cong. Susan Davis will like this tome... On 10/20/09 Tyra showed her "truth squad" panel. I want Matt (from that panel) to peruse this book. I pray that Joseph Latham (and his mom Ramona) gets this book. I want F. Lee Bailey to read it....

Back to "sealed" records etc. C.O. Joe Rikalo was arrested at 16 for kidnapping and attempted rape. His record is sealed. Inmate William Coker can tell Joe's wife all about him... There is a well kept and hidden secret in California corrections. C.O. Province at P.V.S.P. explained to me that "I almost could not get this job because of my juvenile criminal record. But the CCPOA will use their influence and get your record "sealed" if you know the right people". Mr. Province (a good man) continued "Manning, if you knew what yo (sic) homeboy (Marion) did in Atlanta you'd be shocked!"... It took me two years to get my sources at the Atlanta police department to reveal that Spearman did (indeed) force a boy to have sex in Atlanta. Can I repeat? Marion forced a boy to have sex! And Marion came to California and got his record sealed!! I dare Marion to take a polygraph test! He's a molesting, conniving, corrupted little thug. He is a menace to society!

... I keep hearing Susan Klebold's words about never seeing tragedy coming in her son. And I'm well cognizant of the fact that it is politically incorrect for the "mainstream media" to get behind "my" tome and my work, because I'm in "Joseph's" predicament. I'm cognizant of how the media can be brutal, blatant and incisive! He's just a "rapist, a predator and a crook". I get that! I'm (actually) cool with that. I recall my homeboy Richard Jewell. We saw neighbor after neighbor on TV testifying to us that Richard was a "good guy" and "cool". But the "media" decided to vilify Richard. The media worked "in concert" with the police. And the "media" went about strategically, methodically and zealously proving to us (via "empirical" data) that Jewell was a "terrorist" who set "Bombs". Everything "good" about Richard was made "bad". His historicity was transformed to make him "fit" the "profile" of a frustrated "terrorist". We were led to believe Richard wanted to be a "cop" so badly that he "probably" did "it" so he could make himself look like a "hero". The media coverage was incendiary, abusive, biased and malicious. It was as if the media acted as a "spokesman" for the police and F.B.I. The media rubberstamped police "theory" of the "crime". Richard was charged, tried and convicted by the "mainstream" media; who believed (and promoted) everything the police told them about his "profile"... Criminal records (allegations, arrests, suspicions etc.) can be manipulated to promote any "profile" one wants... So I'm not concerned about any attempt to garner the "support" of "mainstream" media when I know to whom they are beholden. Richard Jewell contemplated suicide (he's dead now) because of the dastardly and deceptive way the media treated him. And yet he was "innocent".

In "long walk to freedom" when President Nelson Mandela was in prison guards wrote in his "C" file that Mandela was "manipulative". Yet he was a lawyer, wrongly convicted and a revolutionary.... In my "C" file I'm described as "manipulative" and "litigious" etc. I feel that I'm in good "company". Ipso Facto, it would be unwise and unheard of for the "media" to cover this (G.B.G.) work. But.... Remember Madame Brooksley Born? There was a concerted effort to shut her down. She tried to sound the alarm about "toxic" assets back in 2005. But times were good and she was up against powerful and entrenched forces. George Bush called Alan Greenspan a "rockstar" and "the Wizard". And Bush had a total "hands-off" approach to Wall Street. Mr. Greenspan was the man with the master plan. Everybody would hang on to his every word even though they had no idea what he was talking about. He was "the man behind the curtain". Nobody wanted to take him on because he knew so much more than anyone else. And if he didn't he acted like he did. Even though Alan Greenspan embraced an unusual political guru (profile of an Elitist/nut?) the "media" overlooked it.... Brooksley Born was a brilliant securities lawyer. But A. she was a woman in a man's (good-ole boys) world. B. she tried to sound an alarm against the "rockstar" of "establishment" of Wallstreet. The same media which told us Jewell was a Bomber - told us Attorney Born was "kook" and just wanted "attention". They (the "mainstream media") were "wrong" again. And now that your parents have "bailed out" Wallstreet etc. "we" all wish we'd listened to this woman Brooksley Born. She told us Greenspan's plans, tactics, schemes and plots would "cost" us.

... In the same way "we" (convicts) are sounding an alarm in Zion. We are telling America and the world about the murderous, rogue, renegade and vicious guards gone wild who are torturing youths in prisons. And the most powerful "Union" in California (the CCPOA) protects and ruthlessly defends the guards of whom I speak and write. And the CCPOA will (indeed) encourage the media to do one of three things: A. Ignore me! B. Marginalize me! Or C. Vilify and crucify "that predator!"... So (read the second half of this tome) we've broken out of the boxes and given youth my "dirt". And having seen the truth you won't turn back. This (tome) is a meeting of the minds! My mind meeting yours. My job is "not" to line up witnesses (lawyers, physicians, principals and philanthropists) to testify to you that I'm a "good guy" etc. It didn't do Jewell any good. But instead I'll "own" my (embellished and in some cases prevarication!) evil and wicked past. And I'll use the "street creds" which come with my being a "bad boy" and engage in efforts to advance youth from my perch. I shall shine a light on your path (and having traveled it) remind you that it is a collision course toward prison. The political climate in America is indifferent toward this message. Unions (i.e. the CCPOA) have done a masterful (I applaud them) job of convincing the American citizen "not" to give a damn about what goes on inside these walls.

... Think about a dumb prison guard". In California he walks in off the street (even without a high school education) to a $ 70,000 per year job. And earns up to $ 225,000 per year without education. He produces no product. He does not have to meet a quota. He performs nothing tangible. And his employer (John Q. Taxpayer) has absolutely no concern about anything that goes on inside. The fact that a peace officer (with a badge) falsified documents and forged my name to a "job change" slip in the late 90's is irrelevant to his employers. He's now a "lieutenant". And he lords over me. All he has to do is "claim" I looked at him wrong and I go to ad-seg. He can claim I'm a "threat" and I transfer again... His employers (citizens i.e. your parents) are not concerned. Rocky (Salazar) was murdered and "The Beat" goes on! Michael Gorman, Inmate Hollywood Walters and... All murdered at the behest of prison guards and nobody gave a darn. The one and only thing your parents, my family (and all Americans) are concerned about is "the count!"... As long as Bunnell, Tucker, Spearman and Larry Turner (Celsa Zamudio and Wallace Laffitte etc.) got the "body count" right it is (was) "all good". Laffitte could smuggle dope and cell phones in for decades! Larry Turner could beat the hell out of an inmate and assault a female guard! Lt. Scarsella could assault an inmate and get Sgt. Saunders to do "fix it tickets". Sgt. Elsberry (an honest woman with integrity) could get ran out of New Folsom because she told the truth ("snitched") on Scarsella and Saunders and "The Beat goes on". Nobody even heard about it. But if one of us "Broke out" there would be a wall to wall media situation! Hell if I break out (I won't) you will see, hear and read all about in local, regional and national news... As long as these "thugs" get the count (all inmates R 'present' and 'accounted' for America!!!) right you all will sleep tonight. But God forbid that a guy who is paroling in 3 months (anyway) escapes 3 months early. This "vicious", "deadly" and "dangerous" predator (who is getting out anyway!! In 90 days!!) must be "found" and "caught" by "any means necessary". They would lock down schools and colleges and call a "prison Amber Alert" all because a dude who would be released etc. in 90 days anyway; got out early....

When Larry Turner beat up the inmate and his co-worker the warden (Mr. Walker was not the warden) did not come to the scene of the crime. When Brumbaugh had Ronnie Ritter to murder inmate Walters, Warden Yates was still at home sleeping. But let that "count" be wrong. They'll wake up the warden at 2:00 am. And he will come to the prison if they can't get the "count" right. It is the "one" and "only" area a dumb prison guard must succeed in!... To be fair - many of them are "not" dumb. And when I generalize and paint them all with a broad stroke I'm being biased and unfair just like the "mainstream media" about whom I complain... C.O. D. Kelley (cool lil youngster) told me "I hate all inmates!" (lol). And (prior to him knowing I was really an author) he said "quote me". And Kelley is a "guard". But I consider him to be "a good guy". And he told another cop "I'm gonna be famous. I'm going in a book".....

C.O. Pinkard told me "You remind me of Cornel West". I inquired "have you read any of his books?" and he stated "I read them with a dictionary sitting next to me. That man is brilliant"... Pinkard was signing my legal mail (27 letters in one day) with C.O. Dunkel and asked "how do you find the time to do all of this?". I said "time? Hell, all I have is time. What should I be doing playing cards and drinking hooch?"

C.O. K. Yeager really respects my "work ethic" and Yeager is fair. He's not duplicitous and corrupt... Many guards are gonna let their kids read this book just to alarm them and show em why "not to go to meet Manning". C.O. Hodge is also a very young guard. Perhaps 21 or 22. And guys like Hodge, T. Ramsey (23), K. Yeager and D. Kelley are shining examples for kids of how "not" to come to prison. I'm not (necessarily) bragging on guards. Because (by and large) they all practice "the code of silence". This is why they ran sergeant Ellsberry away from here.

And it's why they threatened to murder Max Lemon (see "Creating Monsters"). But there are a few (i.e. Lt. Jimmy Guyton, Madame Diana Smith, Hodge, Ramsey and Yeager etc.) whom I feel have good "hearts". And they try to 'do the right thing'.

.... Look - you all can call me "rapist", "predator", "crook", "thug", "convict" or whatever the hell u wanna call a brutha! A "man" by any other (Richard Jewell, Joseph, Mandela, Hurricane Carter, Willie or Manning) name is still a man. You may call me Brooksley Born if you'd like. Because my enemy (the CCPOA) is "the man behind the curtain". They ran Hickman, Woodford and Steve Rigg (a whistle blower who worked at Corcoran State Prison!) out of C.D.C. They (CCPOA) ran Richard Polanco out of office and out of town. And the CCPOA is so deadly, dangerous and dastardly that after Hickman "fired" the guards caught on video sadistically beating a youth at C.Y.A. etc. Even after Attorney Davey Turner filed a successful lawsuit against the fired guards etc. Mike Jimenez and Lance Corcoran flexed the enormous muscle of the CCPOA and got their jobs back! The CCPOA runs C.D.C. Not the Governor or anyone else!

Why do Lance and Mike get rogue guards their jobs back? Easy answer; for money! In clandestine meetings Jiminez and Lance Corcoran arrange for secret pay offs etc. I.E. One guard was fired at Old Folsom. He had 8 years in the department. "Give me $ one thousand per month for 3 years ($ 36 thousand!) and I will get you your job back" Jiminez told him. Dude had a G.E.D. and were he not working in C.D.C. he'd be flipping burgers! In C.D.C. (with overtime) he earned nearly $ 8 grand per month. He was fired! To get his job back he agreed to a $ 36 grand pay-off to the President of the CCPOA! And "if" Mike has the temerity to call me a "liar" I demand or challenge him to take a polygraph test (at my expense)! If he passes I'll donate $ 25 grand to his favorite charity. And I'll issue a public apology! And I will retire from writing books! Jiminez and Mr. Corcoran are the biggest crooks in Sacramento. They wine and they dine with the likes of Mike Bunnell. They have more secret rituals than the masons and "skull and bones" combined. And I "believe" both of them have off-shore bank accounts....

Warden Jimbo Walker is the best warden in the state of California for more than one reason. And one of his practices remind me of our President. He (Jimbo) is like his honor (Barack) in being ubiquitous. And some media pundits criticize President Obama for being "in our face too much". Because unlike Bush (whom ironically, Jimbo voted for), Barack does not hide out in the White House. He understands that the folk who elected him want to see, hear, touch and feel him in whom, they trusted...

And I assure you that 98% of the convicts and 75% of staff at P.V.S.P. would not know Warden James Yates if he sat next to them. They know Marion because he carouses around all over the prison sniffing out penis. He (Marion E. Spearman) can smell a Caucasian boy's genitalia from a mile away.....

... Wardens ought to model Jimbo. They must be required to walk the beat at least twice per week. New Folsom is a better place because Warden Walker is accessible, available and approachable. Scott Kernan, Matt Cate and the California Senate should plead with Jimbo not to retire. Facility A at New Folsom State is a "model" facility.... Cheryl Pliler, Madame Patricia Kennedy, Terry L. Rosario, Raphael Frazier, Lt (ret.) Percy Massey and Jimbo made facility "A" a "model". And "Uncle Willie" is the "Governor" of the yard... I have to also admit that a lil "thief" named Deon C. "Fat Cat" Braggs helped make "A" yard what it is. Fat Cat was the M.A.C. (Men's Activity Council) chairman. And even though Eric Menendez tried a coup d'etat they got a coup de grâce from Fat Cat. He was a thief but he fought diligently for convicts. I.E. when E.O.P. used to have weekly community meetings Cat would attend everyone. And he M.A.C.'d 7 days per week 12 hours per day. He could call Warden Cheryl Pliler on the telephone... "William" was on 'The Price is Right' on 10/21/09. William attends John Carroll University and is majoring in business. I want my "crack team" (Ryan M. and Heather F.) to track William in Ohio and get him this book. I want Preston McVey, Brett Preston and (i.e. Steve) his consorts in the lawsuit against 'American Cellular Labs' to get this book. Read and heed it.

I want you (all) to be soldiers and Gang Bangers 4 Good! You could if U just would! "Be strong in the Lord and in the power of His might! "If you gonna be a soldier U gotta suit up! "Put on the whole armor of God, that you may be able to stand against the wiles of the devil. For we wrestle (it's a fight, Baby Boy) not against flesh and blood, but against principalities, against powers, against the rulers of the darkness of this age, against spiritual hosts of wickedness in the heavenly places". Yall gotta remember that there is an active spiritual warfare being waged. And I'm tired of spiritual sissies, wimps and punks. You're a thug in the flesh. You walk around the jail with your shirt off "Look at me cause I'm buff". But in the spirit you can't pray off a common cold. "I'll knock you out!" But you can't knock them demons out. You can't break the curses off of your life, legacy, destiny and off your family. But you (right in that school, in college, juvenile or C.Y.A. etc.) need to "take up the whole armor of God, that you may be able to withstand in the evil day, and having done all (when you've done everything you know how to do), to stand. Stand therefore, having girded your waist (suit up bro.) with truth, having put on the breastplate (uniform) of righteousness, and having shed your (boot up bro) feet with the preparation of the gospel of peace; above all, taking the shield of faith with which you will be able to quench all the fiery darts of the wicked one. And take the helmet (God is Gangsta!) of salvation, and the sword of the spirit, which is the word of God; praying always with all prayer and supplication in the spirit, being watchful...." You gotta "be watchful". A soldier is always "watchful". A real Gang Banger (G.B.G.) is gonna "be watchful". Get yo spiritual binoculars and your psychological magnifying glass out so you can be "watchful". I'm looking for some sons at "Freedom Hall", at Locke High, at Ralph Bunche in Atlanta and at Rio Americano High School etc. who will "be watchful". I'm not looking for crybabies and chumps, but I need some white brothers, dark and light brothers who will be "watchful" and who'll "stand".

... Jeremiah (in the "Sword") had inner turmoil concerning his "call" to ministry. His anguish was at times overwhelming. Jeremiah had doubts about his power to speak because of his youth. Jeremiah 1:6-8 "then said I (C.J. Sheron, Austin Sisneros etc.) Ah, Lord God. Behold I cannot speak, for I (Maxwell Hanger) am a youth.... Do not say (God replied), I am a youth; for you (Brett Jolliff, Garrett McCain etc.) shall go to all to whom I send you, and whatever I command you, you shall speak. Do not be afraid of their (the media, the CCPOA, Bunnell or the dope dealer etc.) faces, for I (God) am with you to deliver you....".

Did you all read that? "Whatever I command you, you shall speak". And God uses men to speak. Did He not use Paul in a jail cell? And the Lord told me to command you (Michael Parker, Jai, Billy Bell and all of you) to "stand" and fight! Fight the gangs, the drugs and the marginalization of youngsters. Your "youth" is not an excuse. Craig Kielburger was 12 when he began his campaign. Ryan Hreljac was 14.... I command you to "stand" and to "be watchful".

The enemy thought I was gonna get in this jail cell and die. But the God of Jacob has taken my prison sentence and used it "for a wide door for effective service has opened to me" according to I Corinthians 16:9. A door "wide" enough for me to reach out and touch (Jason Durtchi, Garrett Cunningham and Scott Tatum etc.) you in that school, college, church or jail. Through this "wide" door I reach out to Jonathan Matheny, Ian Manshum, Daniel Walsh, Tom Merritt and to David Hanning. And I've asked Attorneys Stephen R. English, Molly Munger and Constance L. Rice (Connie 'Mac') to help me to reach you via this "wide" door.

I am not on a mission to get you to believe in me. I'll let you down; I promise. But my campaign is to get you to believe in you. I want Alan Le, Christopher Savvas, Louis Copelin and "Tyler" (who's on the hit show "16 and pregnant") to know it's time to grow and to go. Go! Go my brothers Go! Go to your destiny!

The prefrontal cortex is responsible for weighing decisions. It is not fully developed in you in your teens. And although we look fully developed and grown at 14 and 15, our minds are not fully developed.... Some of you are having crazy sex at 11 and 12. And I'm privy to the fact that there are rituals and initiations in gangs, groups, clubs and frats etc. which involve sex, hazing and kinky stuff. My first (and best) suggestion is that you don't do it! It is morally wrong. And... only 8% of American parents (in a poll) said their kids were having sex. But 50% of the kids polled admitted to having sex. Many of us use the pull and pray technique in lieu of condoms.... But we (often) call people who use the pull and pray method "parents".

One in ten kids R having anal sex due 2 thinking it'll prevent pregnancy and is safer. But there is oral (fellatio and vaginal copulation) and anal cancer. I suggest parents look at the HPV vaccine available for boys and girls.... "K.K.K." promotes a conversation about sex, drugs, rock, roll, gangs, violence, bullying and prisons etc. I'm promoting A "root" beer "summit" (not at the White House with Mr. Obama but at the schoolhouse with kids, daddies and mommas) on education. Not legislation which only results in incarceration but education'.... We (adults) are dealing with the tick tock of an explosion of violence in America. We have been aiding and abetting our youth in the art of self destruction.

... Rev. Hosea Williams told Bethel Mission Church (on video), Free For All Baptist church and the youth of Atlanta that "God" has called Rev. Sherman D. Manning to engage in a war, a crusade and a campaign to save the youth of America". That was in 1995. But what Rev. Williams and Andy Young did "not" tell me was "unto whom much is given much is required". Rev. Williams used to joke (but actually it was a prophetic joke) "Rev. Manning, they gon (sic) send yo ass 2 Reidsville (maximum security prison in Georgia!)". And I had no idea I'd be placed on special assignment. Any soldier (especially Airborne, paratroopers and infantrymen etc.) can be sent to war (i.e. Iraq and/or Afghanistan etc.) any day of the week. A sailor can be sent to sea or assigned to a submarine. And you won't understand war until you've fought in a foxhole. And Joseph used the skills he honed in prison (on a fake "sex" beef for 13 1/2 years) when he got to the palace. What U learn in prison will work (hint hint prisoner Mandela/ President Mandela) in the palace. Joseph had to be a prisoner before he became a prince.... Joseph would have preferred just having the "dream" and then living the dream. But that's not how it works.... I want "Kevin" (he's a great young man 6 ft 11. He has one arm but plays great basketball. He attends Manhattan college.... And Matt Buchanon - another red head and a computer expert!) to read (and heed this) these words. Joseph had his dream and was hated because of his dream. His brothers plotted and conspired to kill him because of that "dream". He became a "slave". He was falsely accused of a "sex" crime. In today's world Joseph would have been disqualified from working with youth or even volunteering at a church because of his sexual predatory profile... Why would God allow a good man to be sitting up in that prison on a sex case (Rolando Cruz, Calvin Johnson, Pete Rose, Sh....) that he did not do? Because you learn some skills, techniques and some survival tactics in jail that if they (jail, the guards and the inmates etc.) don't kill you God'll reveal to you... When Joseph got outta prison? "If I could survive in there with all of those haters. Haters who would try you. Haters who would lie to, about and on you. Haters who woke up lying and went 2 bed lying. Haters who gave me vinegar when I asked em 4 water. Haters who breathed out violence.... If I made it in Hades and maintained my sanity and salvation etc. then I can come outta jail (Hell) and make it in politics. I can handle Rush Limbaugh and Sean Insanity (Hannity). I can deal with pundits if I can handle Haters".

God sent me to war. I'm here and I'm in school. I've gotten a Masters degree in human haterism. I've got my Ph.D in duplicity, jailhouse religion and the subculture of "Hate". I've learned loneliness, hurt, sorrow and..... I know the hell TUPAC was talking about "me against the world". And I relate to "Dear Momma". Hugging on my momma from my jail cell.... I understand "all eyes on me". Hating, staring, vindictive and envious "eyes on me". There are even a few people (in here) whom I like, I respect and I care about who "envy" me.... I couldn't have learned this in a college course or a psyche class. I could/would only learn this in the war zone. I'm at Ground Zero for anger, hate, perversion and violence. And my "position" qualifies me to speak to youth's "condition". And "Justin" (a 23 year old Bass fishing expert on the "Today" show on 10/22/09) can learn something from this book. Zac Sunderland and Greg Pugh (Richmond VA) can learn from this book. I'm writing it in a very troubling time in my life. I'm writing it in a war zone. I'm writing in a situation with "fluid hatred". I want Kelly Hildebrandt, Jake Simpson and Jakob Karr to get this book (of seeds) in their minds and spirits. And to let hope, vision and dreams grow in their minds. And to take this "vision" and transport it into the barrios, schools and the suburbs. I want youth (you) to come to "attention". There is life saving information in this crazy book. I'm calling a state of Emergency and a Code Red in every American school. I am making the call as commander in chief of G.B.G. I don't need a permission slip from pundits or politicians to make that call. I announce boldly this "State of Emergency".

... Attorney Robert Navarro told me "You Mr, Manning are way more qualified to call a gang truce, issue a cease and desist order on violence in these hoods, schools and colleges than Rev. Jesse Jackson is. We love and respect Rev. Jackson and he's a distance mentor to you (as is Dr. Gardere, Dr. Phil etc.). But you are in Hades. And there's something about being in Hades that qualifies a Malcolm, a Hurricane Carter and a Mandela (and Joseph!) to come out of prison and to change the world".

Attorney Navarro told me very candidly that "Mr. Manning, I don't know you well enough to totally "vouch" for you. I might not want you staying in my home. I would not allow you to raise my children. But you can "bet" I would want you to 'speak' at my kids' school, church and college. I want youth to hear your story. I want them to know what you've seen, heard and learned. And reading your books and hearing your 'words' promotes a dialogue between fathers and sons. An ongoing chat that parents, teachers, preachers, professors, coaches and mentors need to be having with kids".

Piggybacking off of what Attorney Robert Navarro stated I emphatically issue a "Code Red" in every American middle and high school right here today. This is the time for us to operate with a code red mentality. First order (4 U kids 2 tell adults about) is for an immediate change in adult behavior! Once we (adults) transform the hypocrisy ("Do as I say not as I do") of the man in the mirror. The process of transmogrifying youths shall become clearer. And the goal of ending school violence will be nearer... I support Big Brother and other mentoring programs. However, I'm beginning to entertain the possibility of needing a "lil brother" program. So that kids can remind us of how special, unique and beautiful they are. In the hopes that these reminders will motivate us not to pollute, poison and contaminate our children with our "issues".

Have U ever watched the lil children play? Sometimes they can brighten up your whole day. The lil children R God's love. And in the future they'll inherit the world. Just as sure as there R sorrows, the children R our tomorrow. You (kids in schools and in college) are our tomorrow.... This tome (I reiterate) is not ordered chronologically. Instead, the organization is based upon content, situational happenings and connective links....

"O my soul, my soul! I am pained (by "Kids Killing Kids" and adults killing "Kids"!) in my very heart! My heart (Helping Educate At Risk Teens) makes a noise in me; I cannot hold my peace (I had to write this book), ... The alarm of war (against and amongst our Babies!). Destruction upon destruction is cried, for the whole land (not just columbine and, Locke but every American school and schools across the planet!) is plundered.... For my people (adults! those of us hypocrites in the senate, in the congress and in the cities etc.) are foolish, they have not

176

known me. (I'm just another predator like Joseph in Genesis, Rolando Cruz, Pete Rose etc.) They are silly children, and they (the pundits etc.) have no understanding (Limbaugh, Coulter, Altman, Hanlon etc.). They are wise to do evil, but to do good (give, mentor, donate and educate etc.) they have no knowledge". It seems like Jeremiah was sitting in the very center of America (and the world) in December of 2009 seeing what I see.... Crazy Butt Tracy Morgan has an alter ego (don't we all) whom he calls "Chico Divine". And Chico's motto is "poor me". 'Pour me' another drink! But Tracy stopped drinking when he realized it could destroy his entire life.

.... "I'm the new black and it ain't just about color no more" Tracy says, "It's about what Obama said "There are no more excuses". If Tracy Morgan (his dad was a heroin addict who died from Aids etc.) can make it anybody can... And it ain't just 'words' no more. It's 'black' in the 'white' House. It's concrete proof". To that I say "preach Tracy". This is our message to Robert Brown (bro. of sweat lodge victim), Robert Thomas (Denv. Colo.), Luke Sears and to you (too). You can rise above the ashes of defeat, abuse, violence, bullying and gangs etc. and you (ain't no chicken) can spread your wings... Malcolm Gladwell and Judge Greg Mathis etc. can all tell you that you R gonna fall down but get back up. Get back up. Don't ever give up. Get up, don't give up.

I'd like to tell Ryan Hreljac, John Griffin, Brett Jolliff and all yall to be great!... Arlene Cash (V.P. of Spelman College in my hometown) said it best: "Every student can't (afford to) send a thousand pairs of sneakers to Somalia - but you can send one pair of sneakers to a needy family and inspire (motivate, encourage, 'shame' or whatever) a thousand fellow students to do so as well".... The theme: "send one" and brag about it.... you all boast about your clothes, shoes and your bling bling. (But James Scott Manning taught me that 'if it's on your ass it ain't in the bank!)... Brag on giving. And through a process of inspiration and motivation (preferably) etc. or of shaming, outshining or guilt tripping etc. you can spark a freaking revolution at Locke, Lodi, McClatchy, Biola University, Harvard or Sacramento State University.... send one! That's what I'm screaming to lawyers, physicians (C. Solis MD., Franklin Curren MD., Jennifer Heitkamp, A. Duran PhD., J. Gregg PhD. etc.) and to entrepreneurs etc. If you will just 'send one' copy of this book to a kid, a student, a school or a juvenile etc. then go on to the G.B.G. Facebook, Myspace and to our blogs and brag about it etc. A lot of other physicians (i.e. Dr. John Diaz - a plastic surgeon), lawyers (i.e. F. Lee Bailey etc.) and entrepreneurs (i.e. Levan Hawkins etc.) will say "well let me send this tome to the High School I went to"....

I want college students like Gonzalo Barcia and High School students like Matthew IM to peruse this tome. This is a book of seeds which we must plant into our schools, colleges and our churches. We've got to get this to Roy Grimes, Joe Clark, Caroline Kennedy and to Joe Negron. Every student (all 20 thousand) in the KIPP (Knowledge Is Power Program) schools ought to have these 'seeds'.... This is an "Amber (Anti-violence, homicide and suicide) alert". Get the word out! I need Larry Laboe to help us. We need Greg Deekens to spread the word. We need Van Jones to help 'put it out there'. I want pastors, preachers, professors and teachers to use these seeds to spark a conversation. You all can disagree with me. You can write me off as a 'con, crook, conspiracy theorist' or whatever. But (at a minimum) use 'me' (the thug, the criminal) as an example of where (Hades) 'not' to go. Talk about me like a 'dog'. If Cameron Civello, Anthony Coulson (DEA), Rob Burns etc. hate on me it's all gravy baby. I'm a part of the CIA! Did you know (yall thought I was crazy didn't you?) I'm in the C (Christ) I (In) A (action)? Yes I am.....

Four teens (I restate) in the past couple of months have jumped in front of trains and committed suicide. "It's not coincidence any more" a parent (Ann Hill) stated. I - MAY (International Mass Alliance for Youth) - founded by my brother in law and I) was sounding the alarm about teen suicides in the 90's.... All four teens attended Gunn High School in Palo Alto. They are committing suicides in clusters. Experts (i.e. Dr. Heitkamp, Dr. Solis and Dr. Curren) say that each "suicide plants seeds" in the minds of other Gunn students! We must counter those seeds with the seeds of hope and encouragement. And we need a "practical game plan to Help Educate At Risk Teens" my G.B.G. special task force told me. And I'd like to let every college and High School student know that you (too) do have a seat at the (round) table of G.B.G. And I'm calling on youngster teachers like Michael Holt, Daniel Watts (Sacto), Josh Costa, Daniel Sample and David Levin to come stand with G.B.G.....

"I dropped outta school cause dude it was boring" a guy told me. "We use chanting, music and we teach in a kid friendly (edutain) way" David Levin told us. And I want to see Arne Duncan advocate making learning fun, exciting and interesting. "Wasn't there at least one teacher or coach that you loved to hear talk?" etc. I asked the guy. "Yes - my English teacher. And I dropped out 2 months after she died" he replied. I love teachers! I really really do. But I'm pleading with you teachers to be exciting! Find a successful and impactful teacher and 'model' them. Get some Zig Zigler, Tony Robbins or Les Brown CD's or whatever. But learn how to teach (speak, edutain and maintain the interest of your children). As much as I love you all our schools are failing. And failing schools produce failing teens. And failing teens become excelling inmates. And excelling inmates will never be excelling outmates (citizens). So the school is the dream center. It is a place of vision... And I am calling Jeff Buttle, Johnny Weir etc. to come here. And I want them (youngsters) to volunteer to go into these schools and tell kids "my name is Jakob Karr (Billy Bell, Victor Smalley, Teddy, Peter or Nathan etc.) and the commander in chief (G.B.G. Baby Boy), our President (who doubles as a C.I.A. Christ In Action leader) sent me here to tell you to stay in school. Get Education!" I need Casey Cristosto, Alex King, Shawn Hornbeck and Travis Shaw to get involved today... We have got to reach Matt IM, Brett (of Dr. Phil fame), Matt Whyatt, Esteban Nunez and youngsters around the world with these seeds (students educating enhancing and developing) and to make them (you) pimps (partners in major progress). If I gotta call on the boyz in tha hood or trailer park etc. If I must pay Brandon Hughes, Hugh Michael Hughes or 18 year old C.J. Sheron to wear t-shirts ("read "K.K.K." 2 day") to school I will. But we will get these seeds into schools!

Hell, we have predators and child molesters (i.e. 31 year old Charles Licop - an Elk Grove School clerk who doubled as a molester of boys!) already in the schools. Why not put "K.K.K." there too?

I want kids at Huntsville High (Texas), Marius (the bro-mantic) etc. to be frantic and "poke" your pals on facebook and tell them 2 get their "read" on....

I'm calling Gonzalo Barcia and Michael Sanford to make reading this book a standard operational procedure.... Paul Thomas Heintz stabbed a Chico state female because she left him. Paul needs some seeds. He almost killed the lady....

We need Zac Sunderland and Kaether Cordero. Bring me Zach Freison and Kevin Zade. I need Kevin Shelton and Andy "the volunteer". I need my homeboys at "Homeboy Industries" and we will change the world. Hell, we'll duplicate or emulate society's super youth (Craig Kielburger, Marc Kielburger, Ryan Hreljac and the late Mattie Stepanik etc.) and use em in G.B.G. to help other kids see (vision) how to succeed....

A month ago 7 year old Sommer Thompson was kidnapped and savagely murdered. (see http://saveshastaGroene.blogspot.com) and thrown into a trash can. Her mom Diena Thompson said to the killer or killers "We're coming for you". Amen to that. G.B.G. is using the technology (i.e. facebook) of the internet to orchestrate a mounting chorus of all points bulletins to child killers, gangs and to molesters that "we are coming for you". We (prisoners, police, professors, pastors etc. Justin Berry and C.J. today) are coming for you. Ken Wooden, Diena and Leana (all of us) are coming together to get you.... Yell, scream, fight and run (kids) if a car pulls up to try to lure you.... never keep a secret with an adult! Never!

... Students: Ted Spencer (provost at the University of Michigan) talks about how important "Essays" are to get into colleges. I command you (kids) to work diligently on those writing skills!! Practice on me and G.B.G. .... Post practice essays on our websites and our team of educational experts (led by principal Aaron Fernander) will critique it....

I'm writing to students at Armiso High School etc. We need you too. No one strike is gonna stop school killings or youth gangs. Not one strike. But the sustained direct blows to the cartels of thugs who recruit youth into their gangs - will work.... We are coming for the LA. rolling 40's, LA Familia, Bloods, Crips and every violent street gang. Those who are enticing youths to sell drugs and terrorize neighborhoods. This is a job for the C.I.A. and G.B.G. we are coming 4 U. There is a new sheriff in town. We'll work with U.S. Attorney Larry Brown, Michelle Leonhart (DEA) and police to detect, detach and smash you..... Ironically, LA Familia forbids it's members from using illicit drugs although they sell it...

If I could get Tommy Davis and Tom Cruise to withdraw from their clandestine (homosexual) rendezvous long enough etc. We would even accept help from those greedy and power hungry scientologists in New York.. We need everybody to help us defeat these gangs! Everybody!.... Remember that two women with their street smarts and their radar (intuition) did what cops, parole officers and deputies couldn't. They saved Jaycee Lee Duggard. We (you and me) can do this.... Yes We Can!!.... Trevor Loflin went to Bob Jones Univ. Seth Grey went 2 Folsom H.S. Max Carlson, Brett Dewitt, Ron Dipolla, Igor Stebakov and Ryan Hanson etc. We need you too. When we get Aaron Spool at the table we can reach kids who have been told "Don't nobody want you. Don't nobody need you". We can reach these boys (and girls) who have been neglected, ignored, abused and in incest etc. We can help them. Let go of those reservoirs of pain. And prevent them from entering this (prison) University of predators.... This book can be like the movie "precious". People say "you walk in (2 c the movie) one way and leave out changed". No young man (by God's grace and anointing) will read this book and close it and be the same... 3 Boy's dad was convicted of murdering their mom (Wisconsin?). A woman with the last name "Berry" (S. Berry? "Truth in justice"?) was trying to help the dude. I think the dad's sister (Google!) was raising the three boys.... I want those boys to get this book. This book of seeds will enhance kid's psychological and "spiritual immunological infrastructure".... G.B.G. has reached out to Dr. James Gilligan, Steve Rigg (CDC Whistle blower) and to Evan Williams. We need Biz Stone and.... Help us with this "Amber" alert.

... Jennifer Francis has 3000 donated books for kids. She runs a mobile literacy program in Tampa Florida "Bess book mobile". She partnered with VSP (Vision Insurance), Trans Optical etc. and they have a mobile vision clinic. We applaud Jennifer. And one of the books those kids read (this one) ought to have Jennifer's name in it....

Boys? You can dress up, masquerade and parade around in your facade all day long. But the meat, substance and the seeds in this book R gonna reach down inside the very core of your being. I'm looking 4 the real U. Come out, come out, wherever you are... We need you! Come here Revival Tabernacle Church, Kevin Ramsey, Vakaville Christian High School students, Ryan Johnson, Remington Korper, Peter Tyson etc. I have in my hand a "summons" for you. You've been parading, flossing and masquerading around town. But I can see (vision) through the cloak, disguise and the mask. Halloween is over but you are still in disguise. You are lying to everybody about the real you. You are a broken, confused, scared and "lost" little boy. I know you may be all big and buff but I see (you) through that stuff. Here (K.K.K.) is your summons. I know it's tough, difficult and confusing but you have got to get your butt up off the bench. I don't care what you did, how you messed up or how bad it looks. You can do this. You've got to get back up and fight. Fight to get out of the gang. Fight to get in school. Fight! Fight that addiction. Fight that affliction. The ground is no place for a champion' fight....

C.O. Bartlett asked me (today) "were you a teacher before you came to prison?" I replied "teacher?" He says "Dude, you speak like an educator".... But life has a way (lol) of keeping you humble. I allowed a brother (whom I'm constantly giving addresses and encouragement to. Whom I'm praying for!) to (finally; I rarely share my writing with fellow convicts.) With this particular newsletter however, I allowed 3 fellow convicts to peruse it - to read it. He walks up to me and states "It's not 'bad'". Then "we are both doing the same thing. But".... God love him. I've been blessed to publish 9 books and more than 300 newsletters but "it's not bad" is his "expert" critique.

... Yet they all say "why you don't never (sic) let us read any of your work? We gotta buy it?"... The newsletter was "the $ 3 million Mexican". I allowed two Mexican guys to peruse. Uno of the dos told me "I wanna add my two cents.... youngsters..... " He then launched into a monologue about what he disagreed with. He never told me any of the points he agreed with.

... I'm not bashing these guys which is why I'm not calling their names. I just wanna show you this word portrait of the mentality of prisoners. "Good Job" is not in our vocabulary. "I found a lot of good points" no way Jose. "You are intellige...." Impossible. Because "we" have holes in our souls, psyches, spirits and in our hearts. And we are so brainwashed, damaged, fragile and sensitive that we've become "master haters". He (Joe Blow) thought "it's not bad" was (actually) complimenting me...

I thank God that I don't "need" pats on the back to 'keep goin'. If I needed a compliment, an 'atta boy' or a 'good job' to keep writing I'd save a lot of ink.

Youngsters (you studs, jocks, nerds, outcasts, eccentrics etc.) listen to me: this place (Hades) retards the spirit and robs the psyche. This place is filled and running over with walking "murders" (murderers) waiting to happen. We are walking and talking encyclopedias on "hate". We "hate" everybody including the dude in the mirror. It is dark, spooky and "sad" in here. Just bitter, broken and rotten spirits. Rotten! Rotten to the core. Rotten! Rotten! Rotten!.... Is there anyone (free) reading this (gay, straight or 'Bi') who would wake up tomorrow morning and decide "I wanna go spend the rest of my 'life' with Robbers, rapists, molesters and murderers"? What (in your character or mind) could decide (unless 'you' are one yourself) "Oh mom I'm gonna give up my woman/man and go hang out (4 life) with dudes who rape Babies"? I gotta summons with your (Joey Grissette in Virginia etc.) name on it. I came to call you to "attention". Snap to it, it's time for you to "fall in". We (G.B.G.) need your service. I need your hands, fingers, feet and your asses off the seats. I call you to attention. You've been standing 'at ease' for too long. You've been at parade rest but come on now and fight.

I refuse to sit back and spend another month, another week, another day, another hour, minute or moment languishing, lolligagging or .... I will arise and fight. I'll use my sword (pen) to fight and bring light. I am not writing to everybody. I just want to reach 'just one'. Give me Nathaniel, Keith, Tadd Carr, Omar Samy or David Hellyer... If all of my praying, fasting, sleepless nights, visualization, training and reading etc. results in just "one" kid getting out of a gang. Getting off of drugs. And getting in school etc. I'll feel blessed!.....

I want somebody to find a Joe Wilson (white - he's probably in his early twenties now...) who was a 16 year old kid in Sacramento County jail when I was going to court. We must get him (Joe where are you?) this book....

I'm aware that a dude in prison calling himself a commander in chief and daring to call a youth "Amber - Anti School Violence" alert sounds crazy. But I'm into intellectual ventures and solutions. It is going to take radical solutions to stop this violence! Radical and crazy sounding solutions. I have to act like a surgeon in an emergency room. I have to focus, run, stretch, improvise and act on my feet. I'm a spiritual and psychological surgeon. A criminal surgeon. It sounds crazy just as a "shot" or a "pill" to cure polio sounded crazy 58 years ago. But "Hello". I don't give a flying "flip" who thinks it odd, ironic or "crazy" that I am the commander in chief! I am! I am the President and founder! I am! I am "Joseph". I am Saul and Paul. I am.... reading, writing, listening, studying, praying, fasting and analyzing the "state" of "young" America. We can do this! Yes we can! We will do this! Yes we will! It sounded crazy for a black, junior senator accused of "paling around with a terrorist", with a pastor like Jeremiah Wright etc. etc. to say "I'm going to be president but he made a believer outta me. I see a way out of no way. I want Roy Wolfe, Aaron Fernander, Ron Clark, David Levin, Daniel Sample and Josh Costa etc. to meet us on facebook. It may sound "crazy" but meet me. We will do this. I'm calling Cameron Ashley, Omar Samaha and Brett Jolliff etc. to meet me. We will succeed. I do believe. I'm calling C.J. Sheron, Louis Copelin, Doug Pieper Jr. and Garrett McCain to come forth. All my boys like Ralph & Eddie Cannon (Telfair County), Gary Browning, David Reynolds, Craig Gilstrap, Joey and Daniel Clay Hollifield etc. suit up! I got partners (really) in trailer parks (i.e. Shady Hill trailers etc.) in Richmond Virginia. I got buddies in Bankhead ("the Hood" in Atlanta) and in Buckhead. I'm not waiting on John Q. Media, Rush, Hannity or Coulter to give me a 'permission slip' to conduct a scribe triage! While Rush hopes Obama fails. While Sean repeats Rush's every word of hate! And while Ann Coulter performs fellatio out of one corner of her mouth and spews hatred out of the 'other' corner etc. While pundits yell, scream, bash and demand cash etc. our schools are failing. And our kids are in trouble.

I have come to bring "vision". I need Magic Johnson, Tyler Perry, Tony Dungy and... But I won't wait or hesitate. If I gotta go (back) on a hunger strike till a "Hollywood" Henderson, Richard Scrushy, George Soros or Jeff Lurie helps me; we will succeed. This book of seeds will be planted, in schools, jails and in prisons all over this earth. Attorneys Geri Lynn, Robert Navarro, Carolyn Phillips, Merin, Sanford Rosen or somebody must help me! And.... We must turn this earth - right side up.... Nothing "sounds" as crazy as President "Obama" but we're getting used to it now.

It "sounds" crazy for me to tell Shawn Hornbeck, Derek King, Daniel Job, Jerry Wines, Jeffrey Allen Walker and Hugh Michael Hughes etc. (in a book) to snap to attention but "attention!".

When I lay this book into the hands of Maxwell Hanger, Alex Chivescu, Michael Wilkerson and youngsters at "Homeboy Industries" etc. a change is gonna come. Kids at Edison High School etc. gotta come forth! I'll step into the Sacramento "Ballet" and pull Tim Coleman and Gabe into this fight if I need to. Carlos Rodriquez (Hayward) and Johnny Weir gotta come here and fight! Fight with your roller skates on. Fight in your jail house uniform. Fight in suit and tie. Whatever you do - fight.

I'm ready to scramble teams of social, psychological and spiritual paramedics to help these troubled teens. So many people (some of whom I don't like and some who don't like me) have stepped forward and told me "Sherm I'll help in anyway I can.... Don't tell anybody but I'll even buy a few copies of "K.K.K." and donate them (anonymously) to a school".

"I'll help" C.O. Kevin Yeager (repeated) told me the other day. "As long as Warden Walker is in I'll help". C.O. D. Kelley (who I repeat looks like a school boy) told me "I'm not an inmate lover" but we've gotta do something to reach these boys. They've gone mad" Kelley stated. Captain Steve John Vance stated "I'm loyal to Walker and Fred. And I may be retiring in December Sherman. And you and I don't always see eye to eye. But I won't quit. I'll come to New Folsom on Saturdays for G.B.G. tours as long as Jimmy needs me". I was touched. I even plan to ask Sergeant Blackburn to help us! We've got to be radical. And I've got to be bold enough to ask people who don't agree with my propaganda and politics etc. to help. I must be humble enough to recognize the need for difference and diversity of opinions etc.

I (repeat) am not smart enough to tackle this on my own. I am not rich enough. I need help to help the kids who need help. And G.B.G. must model (believe it or not) C.D.C. (in a sense). You have guards here (i.e.) who are staunch right wing republicans! They think Rush Limbaugh's gastrointestinal releases are odoriferous delights. And to the opposite extreme there are left wing, Al Sharpton loving guards right here at New Folsom. Yet, although many of these guards don't live in the same neighborhoods etc. They don't attend the same churches. Some of them don't even speak to each other on the streets. But - (and this is a hello 'but') the minute there is an institutional alarm sounded etc. you'll see white boys, black boys, skinny and fat boys. You'll see republicans, democrats, racists and Uncle Toms etc. And all of these diverse people will be running toward the "sound" of the alarm. And every runner has one thing in common etc. They are guards. They R sworn peace officers. They have a "badge". Yes, some of them are "bad" cops. And some of them have "issues" etc. But - when there is an alarm in a prison the prisoners lay down (by rule as a form of surrender. And if 'we' don't lay down they'll knock or shoot us down!) and the guards run. We use the ground to lay down. Guards use the same ground on which to run. They don't slow down because it's a republican guard in trouble. They don't negotiate, stagnate or debate etc. They respond to the alarm by running to the incident... Ipso Facto, G.B.G. can't be about me and folk seeing things the way I see. We (G.B.G.) are boys, men, inmates, convicts (there is a difference), guards, police, judges, politicians, lawyers, entrepreneurs and athletes etc. We are Christians, hypocrites, Muslims, atheists, agnostics, racists, thugs and.... We are flawed humans who are running (responding) toward the alarm which has been sounded at VA. Tech, Columbine, Locke High, CSU Sac, in Chicago and around the globe. We (Jimbo Walker, Patricia Kennedy, L.N. Johnson-Dovey, C.O. T. Ramsey, D. Kelley, Bugriyev and Dustin etc.) are running toward the cries of our kids. We don't go to the same church. We don't vote for the same politicians. Some of us 'can't' vote at all. But 'we' are responding to the alarm. And our enemies (gangs, drug dealers, molesters and murderers) must submit. Make no freaking mistake about it the enemy must do the same thing these murderers ("we convicts") do when the alarm is sounded in the prison. No matter how big, bad and buffed we may be. No matter if 'we' are convicted of a petty crime or serial murder etc. Whatever the conviction etc. when 'we' (bad ass) convicts hear an alarm we "get down". Because if we don't "get down" guards are authorized to "shoot" us.

And I've come to tell those gang bangers, drug dealers, molesters and kid-nappers to stand down!! We're coming for you! I got my Big Homeys with me. I've got a hard nosed warden associate wardens, guards (some of whom would not even speak to me on the streets), ex-cops, brilliant psychologists and psychiatrists etc. with me..... Bloods, Crips, Nortenos, Surenos, Bulldogs and AB etc. yall better hear me: Stand down! I've come to tell you like Somer's mom "We're coming for you!". Yeah, I know you all are bad! You're BAD, buff, rough and tough with a gun or a knife. You're bad with a crowd! But you (gang bangers) are a sissy and a chump in the spirit. You don't have any wind! And you can't win!.... Remember I've been embedded in the reality of my subjects. I saw you (Bloods, Crips, Southerners, Northerners and Skinheads etc.) in L.A. County jail getting beat down and smashed on by jail deputies. I have watched and witnessed gang bangers get bi-ch slapped and smashed by jail deputies and prison guards. Yeah, you're bad with a gun or a group. But get you by yourself and you're a sissy. We (G.B.G.) know how to do warfare. We are spiritual and psychological seals, Green Berets and Special Forces. We will defeat you. I break the curses spoken over our children. I break the cycle of violence. I link up in the Holy Spirit with Tony Dungy, Tyler Perry, Rev. Otis Moss, Rev. Rick Warren and with every believer. And those things I desire (a radical transformation in youth education and inspiration vs. incarceration) as "we" pray I believe we receive them.

I'm calling for "Brad" (he was on 20/20 with Professor John Lisk on 10/23/09), Joshua Cook (in Sac Town) and Jason Lee (High school quarterback in Sacramento). We need you (too) to suit up. It is time to make a change. We have been stuck in a long grief weighted purgatory but we've gotta get up. I'm calling for Chancellor Michelle Rhee, Dr. David Kaufman (a Folsom plastic surgeon), Jeseanna Leahy, police chief Dan Davis, Ryan Johnsom, Reina Keola and Shea Newberry etc. to suit up.

A fifth grade student (Jonathan McCoy) is giving speeches and asking the world to eliminate the "N" word. And he's a powerful little speaker. And I applaud him. People are calling him "crazy". But I wanna tell him to use criticism as a spring board to master oratory.

...."Crazy"? I know some atheists who think it is "crazy" to believe that a ghost named Holy had a clandestine rendezvous with a lady named Mary. And that Mary who "knew" no man; gave birth to a baby names Jesus the Anointed one...

I need Nia Malika Henderson, Ana Porgras and Jeff Buttle etc. to stand with us and pray for us.......

I need prayer warriors (Mary Bell, Dollie Mae and Angela Montez etc.) to pray 'in' a substratum of spiritual infrastructure for G.B.G. which will get us the victory. We (G.B.G.) need favor. "Oh God bless me. And bless me indeed! Enlarge (even though I'm in a hole) my territory (via the internet) and let "thy" hand be with me. To keep me from evil (the "hits" ordered by gangs and guards) so that I may cause no harm". We need an underlying layer of anointing. We need a layer of earth beneath the surface soil. We need the groundwork and the very foundation of G.B.G. to be anointed. I need you to pray that the material upon which other material is coated with will be anointed. We need the favor of Jehovah so we can fight this war. I pray for a strategy which is cunning. I need to engage in spiritual hand to hand combat. I wanna have the ability to engage in spiritual subterfuge. We've got to engage in a subterranean warfare if we intend to smoke them (molesters) out. If we want to expose them. We are fighting a "New" war. This is an informational, technological Jihad Baby. We need a cold, calculated strategy. With Justin Berry, Benjamin Alexander (internet and tech "tycoons") the gang bangers don't stand a chance. The only stand they can do is to stand down! Stand down! The alarm is sounding within the pages of "K.K.K." today and we R human beings blessed with the gift of speech. The power to preach, to teach and reach. Boys and girls on the street!

... Justin Berry, Ryan Hreljac and (you too) the word is nigh thee even in thy mouth. U can Be the Rose that grew from concrete. And say "still I rise".

... I'm calling my homegirls (like Browns Mill elementary school principal Alycia Smith, Dr. Yvonne Sanders-Butler etc.) and.... we present these kitchen table remedies, classroom solutions and jailcell prescriptions etc. to stop this madness!

... Darrien Albert was a 16 year old honors student who was beat to death in October in Chicago. Gang Bangers beat him to death. Chicago has had more than 34 youth deaths and 290 shootings (in the first few months of 2009).... I almost wept as I looked at Darrien's grandfather Joseph Walker and his aunt Rose Braxton weeping on TV. When I see this youth terror. It makes me seek supernatural wisdom to fight. I call on Attorneys Areva Martin and Michael Sanford (at Lehigh) etc. We must fight!...

Some of you are at Penn State and I'm in a state pen. But God let me know it's gonna take my (ink) pen in the pen; your pen at penn etc. to win...

Yolo County District Attorney Jeff Reisig and deputy D.A. Garrett Hamilton need to resign from office forthwith. In October they spent $ 3 million taxpayer dollars on a 17-year-old Hispanic gang-member!

... While we are laying off teachers and people are losing their homes etc. Garrett and Jeff are writing $ 3 million dollar checks on your bank account.... Judge David Rosenberg signed off on the $ 3 million expenditure. And he (too) should resign.... Judge Rosenberg sentenced 16-year-old Andrew Aradoz, a gang member with the Moniker "savage" to consecutive sentences totaling 24 years for crimes he committed at age 14.... Sarah Weeden should not be in prison. Society failed Sarah and yet we're paying $ millions to incarcerate her (see $ 3 million Mexican also)... It's sick... I'm calling Jeff Kinney, Cassius Harti and Cody Sheldon etc. We (G.B.G.) are spiritual Machiavellians and we will defeat this enemy!....

.... A 15 year-old boy in Florida (Michael Brewer) was set on fire (in October, 2009) by five teenaged bullies in his school. Denver Jarvis, Jeremy Jarvis and three other teens (as young as 13) got angry and doused alcohol on Mike and set him on fire. Michael had reported a stolen bike and the teens retaliated against him by calling him a "snitch" and burning him up. He's burned over 80% of his body.... Attorney Valerie Small-Williams (who represented a 7-year-old killer in 2008) stated "this case is just a tragedy!".... Mike's mom (Valerie Brewer) said "this violence has got to stop! People around the world must come together and stop this violence in these schools". Valerie continued "Look at what they did to my son! Kids are stabbing and shooting each other!" She then broke down and wept..... "People (prisoners, parents, police, students) around the world must come together and stop this violence (I'm pushing the alarm!) in these schools".

... When I look at Darrien and Michael. And when I see 7 year old killers and 11 year old gang members. When I see college students (Scott Gregory Hawkins) beat to death by a 19 year old "suite mate" at C.S.U. Sac etc. I know that I know Valerie was right. We have to come together. We have to stop this violence in these schools. We need Jesse Grund, Jake Heartsong, Ronald Cummings and you too....

I've seen the gang initiation rituals and symbolic killings. I've studied kid bullies and violence. A call to action has gone forth in these prisons and even on death-row. We are organizing and galvanizing. We need a radical gameplan & safety in schools. Youth violence is the second leading cause of death amongst kids aged 10 - 24.... According to the CDC (center for disease control). And we must attack this as a disease. A mental swine flu and a spiritual HIV (Having Insufficient Vision).... Dr. Susan Lipkins, Dr. Curren and Dr. Duran etc. and I are calling on Arne Duncan and principals to set up "triages of Bully intervention teams" Forthwith.... We see the handwritingion the hall! Bullying is becoming more violent and more sexualized every day.... Education. "Vision" and "mentoring" are vaccinations for this swine flu and this HIV....

I wanna tell the homeys in these prisons and jails to "triage". It is time to piss, crap or get off the pot. I don't want to hear about any mess. All I want you to do is "triage"... I know you wanna get your "freak" on with them youngsters on your tier. And 'some' of them 'want' to 'freak' with you too. But A. Don't rape or pressure anybody! B. Tell them youngsters the truth. Tell them how broken, troubled and miserable you are. Tell them about your pain and shame. Tell the truth. I need some brothers who are willing to remove your mask, your 'front', your fake face and the costumes of phoniness. You've been in sin, in shame and in dirt for so long. You have a masters' degree in 'crime' and in doing 'time'. As long as you've been in and out of trouble. In and out of jail. In and out of Hell. It's time for you to tell the truth. We must feed the flowers we've often robbed. We've been enrolled in the university of predators, the undergraduate program for master "preying" long enough now. It's time to put our backs straight up! It's time to square our shoulders and having done all to "stand". I made up in my mind that I won't sit back. I won't stay depressed. But I'll fight! I'll fight for Michael Brewer, Sarah Weeden, Alex King and Shawn Hornbeck. I'll fight!....

In September 2009 more than 1000 law enforcement officers descended on the homes of key members of a notorious street gang suspected of murdering a deputy and killing rival gang members. A federal indictment names 89 suspects and specified criminal activity spanning well over a decade.

Forty-six folks were arrested in a predawn raid targeting members of the avenues gang, which claims a swath of Northeast L.A. as it's turf. Another 34 suspects were already in custody and nine are on the loose.

Cops in full body armor were seen at dawn at a blocked-off staging area at the Dodger Stadium parking lot, where suspects, almost all of them men with shaved heads, were being processed at a portable booking area as media helicopters hovered overhead.... If we could get the media to hover overhead at an honor society's meeting or at Homeboy Industries in LA.

We can't! So we must hover overhead on the internet! We will do this...

The operation involved 1,100 police officers working with almost 300 federal agents, making it one of the biggest raids in city history... The indictment read like a laundry list of gang crime: prolific drug dealing, the murders of rivals, money laundering and weapons violations.... Asst. U.S. Atty. Christopher Brunwin stated "this indictment attacks a criminal organization that has terrorized a community for generations."

"The avenues preyed on community members, with two named suspects accused of attacking a resident in a parking lot, and shooting him to death as he screamed for help. A woman was pistol whipped, then shot at, but survived to identify an assailant by the Fedora-wearing skull he had tattooed upon his chest," said asst. U.S. Attorney Ariel Neuman.

The mostly Latino gang also is accused of carrying out acts of violence against cops, culminating in two attacks which rocked the law enforcement community last year. In the first of those, in February 2008, avenues gang members opened fire with handguns and an AK-47 on Los Angeles cops. Cops shot back, killing 19-year old Daniel Leon.

Then on Aug. 2, 2008, off duty L.A. sheriff's deputy Juan Escalante was shot dead in front of his parents' home in the Cypress Park neighborhood.

Imagine kids descending on a blocked-off staging area at the Dodger Stadium to do 'Dream Jamboree', a seminar on 'hope', a 'Homeboy Industries/G.B.G.' youth intervention etc. 1,100 local cops plus 300 feds? Damn near 1500 cops. Well since Michael Brewer and Darrien Albert and Haleigh Cummings etc. (Sasha Groene, Shawn Hornbeck and Jaycee etc.) this is a national emergency. I'm issuing Emergency Authorization for parents, kids, teachers and preachers all over the nation to do warfare. Let us 'stage' in the parking lots of schools, churches, colleges (i.e. CSU-Sac), juveniles, jails and even prisons etc. And let us anoint, appoint and empower an army of youngsters to do triage. If we've gotta knock on doors and pass out this book do so. If we (Ryan Johnson at CSU, chancellor Rhee, Michael Vick, Larry Birkhead and Garrett McCain etc.) have to have prayer vigils, light candles, hold marches, fast and pray. We must do warfare! Because "this violence has got to stop! People around this world must come together and stop this violence in these schools.... Look at what they did (13 year old kids set him on fire!) to my son". Are you reading my words today?

The media have moved on to the next tragedy! They're just doing what they do. But I'm not writing 2 the freaking media.... I'm writing 2 U at Locke, McClatchy High, Ron Clark Academy and at schools around the world. I am writing 2 Billy Bell, John Litzler, Levi Johnston, Jonathan "Legacy" Perez, Craig Hutto etc..... John Butterfield, wrote a poquito opinion piece for 'the Mirada', (Rio Americano High Schools' student paper).... John's 450-word piece Sept. 24 on page 6 of the school paper ignited media interest. A local TV station picked it up. Then a Nationally Syndicated Bigot (Bill O'Reilly) picked it up... It was (for Butterfield) a lesson in the power of the pen. He's thinking about how he can spin the story into an essay for his college applications. "It makes me feel good that people considered what I wrote (write on right on!) in the paper and thought about taking action...." John concluded "In High school, a lot of the time we (in prisons, juveniles, trailer parks etc.) feel powerless.... It makes me feel hopeful that if the adults (Bingo!!) keep listening to what we (kids) put in the paper, things will get better". I could stop writing with John's words. You ought to re-read what he wrote. Thank you John! Thank you for elucidating and educating. If we (adults) focus on your (John's) words we will win! When John wrote his lil piece in the school 'rag' he never imagined a prisoner trapped in a hole would be writing his (Butterfield's) words in a tome and sending it to Arne Duncan, Robert Gibbs, Governors and to the President of these United States of America. But "the pen (even in the penitentiary!) is mightier than the sword. I wanna use John Butterfield (and don't you all forget it) as a shining example of how to create a story. Write in that 'rag'. Write in that 'hole'. Write in that pen, at Penn; with that pen. You can do it, You are Superman; write.

My spiritual immune system has been activated. When I heard Valerie cry out "Look at what they did to my son", the hair on the back of my neck stood at attention.

I want the Juniors and Seniors at Rio Americano, McClatchy, Lodi High and everywhere else to suit up. I need yall in full body armor to show up and to show out! Let's do this!

We need a cacophony of voices from the jails, juveniles, prisons, churches, schools and the colleges for youth. We must be spurred into action by Albert, Brewer and by kids in gangs. I'm calling for faculty members, teachers, student groups, frats, sororities and church groups etc. to step up, suit up, "stand" and to fight. We need more than sporadic media "chatter" and frustration etc. We need a plan for tenacious, strategic and sustained action to operationalize emergency procedures and tactics (i.e. spiritual and educational paramedics to do triage in the schools etc.) to "stop this violence in these schools". Sustained! Sustained! Sustained means prolonged. We don't quit! We won't surrender! We continue to do warfare and Jihad with "this" (is "it") book, over the internet and in the churches etc. If media helicopters don't hover over our army of volunteers we still press on....

UC Davis has 32,000 students. I only need (facebook) ten percent of them with G.B.G..... Today's drastic budget cuts R the results of "vision"-less decisions by lawmakers and governors. A generation ago, in the midst of yet another recession, California spent today's equivalent of $328.00 per CA. resident on the higher education system, including the UC, CA. State Univ. and community college systems. This system allowed any family in CA., no matter their financial means, 2 send their kids 2 one of the highest-quality higher education systems in the world. That spending, in them, drove the innovation which powered the economy of The State. This expenditure was 3.2 times as much as we spent on the entire criminal justice system, reflecting a clear ("vision") priority of education (elucidation) over incarceration (devastation).

By 08-09, spending on higher education had declined to $262.00 per CA. resident, down 20 percent from a generation ago... In the meantime, spending on the criminal justice system has been turbo-charged-up more than 220 percent on spending per resident since 1984-85. CA. now spends 25 percent more on systems for arresting and imprisoning people than we do on mentoring and educating youths and students of all ages.

G.B.G. is calling for vision, student, group, club, frat, faculty and church mobilizations to make a change. At these current rates (and trends) universities will begin to serve only the wealthy. Creating even more pockets of poverty, trailer parks and ghettos in America. It is time for all the people (Chris Benner, Ryan Galt, Jonathan London, Jonathan Eisen, Winder McConnell, Daniel Sample and David Levin etc.) to "stand"...

Since my dance with mortality (Valley Fever) my enthusiasm for life has intensified. I've always had a "rage" and an "anger" at the very center of my soul... Rev. Hosea Williams and Ambassador Andrew Young helped teach me to transform the rage into righteous indignation and creativity. They taught me to channel and redirect it into positive and innovative ways.

.... One of the reasons for Mike Tyson's troubles has been his inability to transmute the ferocity he had in the boxing ring into the ring of life. Many athletes are not capable of finding ways to play in the game of life with the same kind of intensity with which they play in sports arenas etc... We need people such as Zig Zigler, Les Brown and Tony Robbins to help these guys learn to transmute that tenacity....

We (those of you in civilian life) need to be role models that kids can see and touch. I shall never forget the life lessons which I learned from Uncle Melvin Jackson as I interned with him on Saturdays and during summers. He took me into the homes of Atlanta's rich and famous. Dr. Milton (and Cookie & Amy) Frank, William Orkin ((Orkin exterminating), Dr. Arnold Zweig (famous plastic surgeon), Dr. Lippett (and his 'bad' daughter 'Melanie'), Bert Lance and Mike Thevis etc.... My uncle was one of the best interior decorators in Atlanta. He was the 'best' wall paperer in Atlanta. His brother Larry Kent Jackson was a master sign painter. His brother Grady Jackson Jr. (rest in peace) was a master carpenter. His brother Roy Jackson Sr. one of the best auto mechanics in Atlanta.... Uncle Melvin was a role model (with a powerful work ethic). I could see, touch, question and interrogate... Valley Fever taught me that each breath is a breakthrough. Each moment is a gift. And I am a prisoner of hope. I've learned to channel the rage at the center of my soul. And I put the rage on the page (after page) of books and newsletters. This writing (as John Butterfield learned) has the potential to effect and affect people from trailer parks and outhouses in Alabama, to the United States Senate and the White House in D.C. My writing forces me to not take a middle ground stance in a superficial argument. Yes's have to be 'Yes' and no's 'No'....

When I think about Michael Brewer, Darrien Albert, Haleigh Cummings and.... In Chicago bullets are flying in schools. In Detroit there is a 75% drop-out rate. Seventy five percent!

... Preachers (Benny Hinn? Pat Robertson?) politicians etc. where is the sense of urgency and emergency? Superficial glitz creates noise. And the noise prevents us from hearing the cries of our children... The greatest gift one can give another is inspiration. I aim to inspire, babies, boys, kids, teens and tweenies to "fight". Let's go! Lock Stock and Barrel Baby Boy. We must fight (spiritually, educationally and informationally etc.) these molesters, drug dealers and gang bangers. "Chicago Style". They pull a knife, we'll pull a gun. They send one of us to the hospital, we'll send them to the morgue. We (my boys Alex Chivescu, Benjamin Alexander, Nathaniel Mullinnex and Maxwell Hanger etc.) must be sophisticated, coordinated, orchestrated and calculated in our attacks. We must (simultaneously) attack the illiteracy and poverty which contribute to the hopelessness. Because the hopelessness creates a void which ripens the psyches of boys to be receptive to overtures from gangs. I need people in this fight, campaign and crusade whom I know. I want some fellas (black, brown and white alike) whom I've broken bread with (i.e. R. Francis Wright, John Jody Bear, Clay, Billy York, Serena's dad James Nesmith etc.) to "stand" with me and with G.B.G. I want Professor Scott Coltrane (U.C. Riverside), Ty Adams, Dr. Jean Bennett and Dr. Al McGuire to "stand" with us. I am not seeking (I repeat) a monetary donation. Donate 'your' money to your local church. And to legitimate charities. I don't want your money!.... I want your input, prayers, suggestions, ideas and for you to put this book into schools (i.e. in Detroit!)...

.. We need Dr. Jerey Guyden (City college of New York) and Dr. Vincent Reid (surgical oncologist) etc. to "stand" with us....

A 15 year old just murdered (back in October 2009) a 9 year old (Elizabeth) in Missouri... "People around the world (we repeat Valerie Brewer's prophetic words) have got to come together and stop this violence in these schools".... Gangs have "cleverly and skillfully created a sense of inevitability" an anonymous ex-member of Eme told me. "Unless you can penetrate that armor of (so-called) inevitability which they use to recruit kids etc. you can't win" he said... We hear him... one of the few major mistakes Dr. Martin Luther King Jr. made was in not doing 'succession planning! I (am not worthy to carry Dr. King's shoes) won't make that mistake. I wake up every day knowing I'm only one transfer (Bunnell N his cohorts) away from death! And some of these gang leaders can collude with Bunnell; get me transferred (i.e. to Donovan, Lancaster or High Desert etc.) and assassinate me. But I'll be a martyr! They can't unwrite what this pen wrote! They can't stop G.B.G. just by stopping me. They can't stop the hundreds (349 to date) of boys who have written to me and stated that they "will" read 'this' book and share it with their buddies. If each of them share it with ten buddies that's almost 3500 dudes reading "K.K.K.". That is a battalion.... If just half of the 3500 get on facebook, twitter and myspace and write about what they read we will revolutionize our youngsters.

We (Aaron Fernander, Daniel Sample, Joe Negron, David Levin, Michael Holt and Josh Costa etc.) will institute and operationalize critical care (education) units. We will mobilize educational satellite, triage clinics, tents, workshops and seminars. We will go to the best of the best (Les Brown, Tony Robbins, Mr. Covey, Zig Zigler etc.) and have them to coach and train teachers in how to better their teaching skills. We will post educational (edutainment and infotainment) data on the internet and attract kids (i.e. the 75% who R dropping out in Detroit) that will change them. We will master the operationalization of the internet to attract, inspire, motivate and educate kids. I will be depending upon students (in colleges and high schools) like John Griffin, Chivescu, Benjamin Alexander, Jakob Karr, Jonathan Davis and Garrett McCain to make it happen!....

In naval bootcamp (RTCC command in San Diego CA.) I had a Scott (could've been Steve?) Coffman (could've been Kaufman) from Floyd Illinois in my company. I need to find Coffman. Fred Duane Hall (was in another company, but my buddy!) also! And Lopez was in my company. I will pay (good money) to anyone who has photographs of me and my company mates from U.S. Navy Bootcamp (Ryan and Heather announce this on the internet!).... Senior Chief Petty Officer Franklin and S.C.P.O. Beauchamp were our company commanders....

I want Joseph Rocha, Matthew Im, Jakob Karr, Billy Bell, John Litzler, Michael Castro, Austin Sisneros and Cody Sheldon etc. working closely with G.B.G. in our youth outreach.... I will find a way to pay Matt, Cody and Austin etc. if they need money!... Heather and Ryan M. are committed to promoting "K.K.K." and G.B.G. in schools, colleges, churches and jails allover the planet! And if you have creative and innovative ideas about promoting G.B.G. and "K.K.K." in schools let us know with all deliberate speed.

I love Tony Dungy and Michael Vick etc. I know they can help promote the platform of G.B.G. as well as "K.K.K.". But I'm not depending upon "them". I am depending upon Greg Deekens, Derek King, John Butterfield, Nicholas Taxera, Eric Bulrice, Sean Zane and Greg Pugh etc.

I am counting on students to 'tell somebody' to read this book of seeds.... I know Nathan Hand, Joey Grissett and Brian Boykin can spread the word...

Sam Fuick, David Joiner, Roy Cherry and Eddie Cannon were all in prison in Alto Gregoia. Sam, Eddie, David and Roy where are you? Where the hell are my partners Scott Johnson, Christopher Rousche, Sean Farmer, John Garvin, Ralph Cannon, "Bird", Billy York and James Lewis? Where U at John Garvin? I need yall in G.B.G.... Chad Newman, Bradley Poole, Keith Jerrolds and Roger White (Alto) I need yall! Front N center!... Where is Robert Kaufman (the lil white boy who tried to escape from Phillips C.I. with the black guy)? David Holmes? "Chuck" who snitched on me? Where is Chris Mike Fowler from Cobb County? ...

Succession planning? If they knock me "off" tomorrow there are 3 persons trained and ready to step up and to preside our G.B.G./HEART. God birthed G.B.G. in me. God built G.B.G.

through me. And He gave it to me. But I don't make G.B.G. It's bigger than me. And even though (like Paul) I'm in chains when I'm in heaven our new president will come from the streets. I love my brothers in chains. I support, pray for and advocate for every prisoner. But the new president of G.B.G. won't "be" in prison... And... Mr.Bronner (Founder of Bronner Brothers CO. in Atlanta Ca.) once told me that the reason he did not allow his company to pass out 'free' samples was because "people don't appreciate, cherish and take care of things they get for free". Ipso Facto, this is why I changed my mind about giving, my fellow convicts free copies of 'this' tome. They can find money to obtain any and everything else they 'want'. They all have sneakers, Nike's ("just do it") and.... We can buy pruno, drugs, cell phones and nude pictures etc. If they want the book they'll find the money. I'll 'give' the book to kids and schools who can't afford it. Not to duplicitous, hating, evil and...... "us".

Hey (Garrett McCain, John Butterfield, Dustin Sisco, Brandon Kundert and Scott Tatum etc.) studs, jocks and nerds I wanna remind you that 'this' place (Hades) will suck your spirit and humanity out of you. It'll create insanity. It is a horrible, cruel, mean and bitter place. And once you've lived in the throes of conflict (gossip, lies, rumor and innuendo etc.) and violence for so long etc. it becomes a way of life. You forget what "normal" even looks like anymore.

I wrote this book for you. You kids in Atlanta out there acting like a damn fool. You out in Miami, in Memphis and in New Orleans. I wrote this book for every young thug, wanna be thug and for you perpetrators. I have come to you up in Detroit who are all thugged out, sucked up and about to be locked in. You get yo black (brown or white) ass back in school. Folk died for your (the 'black' ones of you) right to go to school. For you white boys etc. some of your ancestors treasured education so much that "they" did every damn thing they could to keep blacks out. And now you don't want in? What the heck is wrong with you? Those with education pass legislation. Those who master reading and writing run the world! If you don't wanna go to church with me I'm cool with that. If you don't want to vote the way I (would) vote I can handle that. But Baby Boy (at least) get your high school diploma... Be nice to go to college but at least finish high school.... I wanna shout out to Inmates Douglas Frazier (Colorado), Joey Ferreiras (N.Y.), John Ritter (Flo.), Francisco Rivas (Massachusetts) and Robert Smith (Wisconsin). Shout out to Justin Howell, Chucky Pyle, Jerry Wines, Jeremiah Rodriguez, Pedro Armando Quandt, Jose Zuniga and to my "friend" Brandon Gene Martinez... Danny Macky where are you? Christopher Parker? Charlie Baddaker? Jerrin Porcher?....

I keep telling you all to stay in school this and that. And I continuously use my bully pulpit to remind the powers that be that prisons do not work. As such, I'm adamant that we must begin (again) to spend whatever is necessary to educate our children. And then there will be no need to incarcerate our children. And if we sit back and continuously try to fight fire with fire. And if you (the youngsters) continue to come to this dark place looking for light. Here's what you'll get: torture and victimization! And if the prisoners don't get you the guards will.

Tens of thousands of kids (teens and tweenies) are enduring long term solitary confinement in California (and prisons all over the planet). Youth are the most urgent victims of U.S. mass incarceration with our overcrowded facilities and practices of incapacitation, not rehabilitation.

The tens of thousands (in the nation's prisons) held in solitary for years on end report the classic symptoms of psychic disturbance, social disruption and mental deterioration. Dr. Solis and the G.B.G. advisory board experts describe the symptoms of this syndrome as including massive free-floating anxiety, hyper responsiveness to external stimuli, perceptual distortions and hallucinations; feelings of unreality, difficulty with concentration and memory, the emergence of primitive aggressive fantasies, acute confusional states, motor excitement, persecutory ideation, violent destructive or self mutilatory outbursts. These degrading conditions produce behaviors ranging from assaults amongst prisoners to assaults on staff, self mutilation, assaults by staff, excrement throwing and contract killings. Isolation tears apart family and friendship ties creating social and emotional dislocation.

Tens of thousands of kids in America are held in supermax facilities called security housing units (or ad-seg). The regime in SHU is a 24 hour per day lockdown (with sporadic but irregular showering) in an 8'x10' cell with no communal activities aside from sporadic small group exercise yards for a few. The kids don't work, don't go to school, no communal worship and meals (often spat in by staff) are eaten in the cell. TV's and radio's are usually (more often than not) disallowed. When they are allowed they must be purchased, so the poor have none. Visits are noncontact, behind glass and limited to 1 hour on each other weekend visit day. Each kid must submit to being handcuffed behind the back in order to exit the cell. They are strip searched and often sexually harassed (and fondled) by the likes of Marion E. Spearman etc. Leg iron hobble chains are attached tightly to their bodies.

Many kids are in supermax permanently because of alleged gang ties. In California, for example, the only program offered to them is to debrief. The single way offered to earn their way out of solitary confinement is to tell the departmental gang investigators everything they know about gang membership and activities including describing crimes they have committed. In California it's called debriefing. Prisoners call it "snitch, parole or die". The only ways out are to snitch, finish prison sentence or die. The protection against self incrimination is collapsed in the service of anti-gang investigation.

Prison administrators assert that the lockdown and snitch policy are required for the security and safety of the prisons. Having legitimate penological purpose, supermax snitch programs are deemed worth any harm done to prisoners. Yet, California prisons continue to have high rates of assaultive incident among prisoners and from inmates to staff. There is no evidence or even any study which demonstrates that these measures are effective anti-gang measures. They appear to be no more useful than previous brutalities like that unleashed at Corcoran (in Ca.) prison over a decade ago.

Between 1988 and 1995 CDC ran a program at the Corcoran Shu called the Integrated Yard Policy. (See www.cafepress.com/creating). Rival gang members were deliberately mixed together in small group concrete yards. The inmates had to fight, and fight well or be punished by their own gangs. When fights occurred guards were required to fire first anti-riot guns and then assault rifles at the gang combatants. Eight prisoners were killed and thousands were wounded. The program of beating down prisoners into the concrete with gunfire resulted in bigger, stronger gangs with new martyrs and heroes. Violence and mayhem was added to the prison social system by departmental policy. No CDC official has ever been held accountable or even assigned responsibility for what was known as the "Gladiator" fights. Guards placed 'bets' on the gang fights. Guards brought to trial by the US Department of Justice avoided criminal convictions by proving they were just following orders (Abu Ghraib?).... Those identified as gang members serve shu terms without end. The only way out is to debrief, to testify against oneself to prison rules violations and criminal activity or die.

Prisoners find it nearly impossible to attack the abuses in the SHU, even though the US is under the jurisdiction of the UN convention against torture. (CAT). Yet America states reservations to the treaty asserting that the U.S. constitution and body of law are all that is required to satisfy the obligations of CAT. Yet the 1995 prison litigation reform act (PLRA) that prohibits a prisoner from bringing action for emotional or mental injury without prior showing of physical injury is one law which violates CAT. The UN committee on Torture expressed concern that by disallowing compensation for psychic abuse the PLRA is out of compliance with CAT.

Under CAT torture includes "any act by which severe pain or suffering, whether physical or mental, is intentionally inflicted..." But the U.S. 1990 reservations to CAT were designed specifically to allow solitary confinement as the reservations state that mental pain and suffering must be prolonged, be tied to infliction or threats of infliction of physical pain, the result of dragging or the result of death threats.

In spite of SHU confinement without end to attempt to control gangs, prison gangs thrive in California's prisons and in prisons across America. The gang leadership predictably uses the snitch sessions to falsely target their rivals, or just recruit new members. Just as we have seen in U.S. antiterror investigations, info derived from coercion is more often than not unreliable.

Utilizing interdeterminate total lockdown to extract confessions is torture by international standards, as is the use of prolonged solitary confinement. U.S. prison officials order by rule the torture of prisoners. 1 in 30 adults in America are under the supervision of the criminal detention system (juvenile, jail, prison, parole or probation) with nearly 3 million behind bars. Prisons dominate the lives of poor communities and are ignored by affluent America. 1 in 10 African - Americans and 1 in 25 Latino Americans are under penal jurisdiction. Prisoners damaged by prolonged incarceration are returning to communities increasingly less able to 'function'. The 2005 census found that severe poverty increased 28% more than overall growth in poverty. In 2003 45% of the Nation's poor were living in severe poverty, the highest rate since 1974.

Torture has always served more to beat down a people than to attain credible info. The unstated goal is to marginalize and incapacitate the dangerous poor who are locked out of America's opportunity and riches. The routine even banal nature of torture in US prisons enables torture to be acceptable, and informs our falling strategies of dealing with any opposition by using brute force.

I wonder if Matt Douglas (Chesterfield Missouri) and Serena Nesmith are reading this?

A more useful way to undermine and blunt prison gangs would be to provide procedures and programs to enliven the community of inmates with rehabilitative activity making them too busy and too optimistic to become involved. Mental health treatment, drug treatment, education and vocational training rather than enforced idleness and despair will help change the culture of the prison yard from a battleground to a place for personal and social renewal. To be successful at a renewal behind bars, a revitalization of our poor communities is desperately needed. I want Charles Salter (principal of 3000 students at Aliso Niguel) to get the "comedy club" students who were on the news (talking about the Dance Rules etc.) to read this book and offer suggestions on how to "fix" this broken system. We need to hear from youths.... All yall at Aliso Niguel High School Hollaback...

In the United Kingdom one of their highest security prisons houses eight of the forty men out of 75,000 considered too dangerous or disruptive to be in any other facility. On a recent visit the men were out of their cells at exercise or at a computer or with a counselor or teacher. The goal was to get them back to mainline through rehabilitation not terror. With embarrassment the host took visitors to one cell holding the single individual who had to be continuously locked down, cuffed and hobbled before exiting from his cell. But this is how America treats hundreds of thousands of it's prisoners.

This tome is a canvas on which I'm painting a picture of the problem to more adequately show you (Daniel Coverston, Kyle Love and...) what you'll experience if you choose incarceration over education....

And it is not getting any better because politicians don't care. They just wanna win elections; period.... Today I had to go outside for a while. By the time I returned to this cage I had a migraine. Prison is called a city of men. But actually it is a city of boys. Broken Boys! Everything I heard was negative, angry and frivolous. Males all trapped in jail but so brainwashed, so messed up and caught up that rather than looking for a loophole, a lawyer or a way out etc. We catch pet lizards and spend hours a week catching butterflies to feed lizards. Frivolous! But if somebody goes out there and tries to get "us" to talk about God, change, politics or spirituality for an hour 'we' are too busy. Like a bunch of (jealous, envious, miserable and duplicitous) lil girls. We don't even pretend to be intelligent anymore. We're a mess. And since we have holes in our hearts, psyches, spirits and souls etc. we spend 95% of our 'time' noticing faults in others. And 'no' time working on our own 'stuff'.

I asked a guy to write some words of encouragement for young Mexicans (weeks ago). First of all he didn't have the 'respect' to return my material to me. Secondly, he didn't speak for weeks. Last night he had the temerity to tell me he was too "busy" (mopping floors) to 'write' anything. Tonight I listened (for as long as I could take it) to him basically. Tell a white inmate how 'bad' he was/is. "That C.O. put me in the cage. I told him I'm not no (sic) weirdo you know. He found out about me at High Desert.... All my staff assaults and then his whole demeanor changed and.... " Translation? "I'm a freaking loser! I'm tore back. I ain't had a woman in years. I'm lonely! I'm angry! I feel like a nobody. And the only way I can half way feel decent about myself (for a few minutes) is to brag on what a 'bad ass' I am/was".

To be candid, If I didn't love God I'd hate 96% of the guys here with me. But you can't love God and hate your brothers. But it's mighty dark and mighty lonely in 'here'.

I pray that F.B.I. agent Minerva Shelton, Jenny Williamson (Founder of "Courage to be you". She had a benefit concert in October, 2009 in CA. Who was the band? I need the name of the band), Daniel Coverston, Allen Harris (in Abbeville GA), Aaron Smith (Chester GA) and Benjamin Harris etc. will pray for G.B.G. and will help us via 'strategy reviews' etc. and work with us. We need Aaron Smith (Valdosta GA.), Alan Harris (Jackson GA), Professor Dylan Rodriguez and Ari Wohlfeiler to come join us on facebook. We can transform the jangling discords of the poverty our youths face into a symphony of Hope. We can lift our youth by lowering ourselves.

We must get ego, pride and selfishness out of the way. And we must humble ourselves before God and seek change. I still believe in change. We can transform our youth. but our efforts must be concerted, strategic and sustained. If I've gotta get some boyz in tha hood etc. we will do this. David J. Quindt, Brandon Hughes, Hugh Michael Hughes (Sacto), Anthony (Clumzy) Sarabia, Juan Sanchez (he was wrongly accused of rape in LA in 1995), Michael Bein (LA. County jail in 1995), Danny Macky (New Folsom in 98), Jerry Wines, Heath James Teague (Sacto) and Joseph Latham must suit up!

My Homeboys like Ernest Griffin, John Garvin and Allen Harris (mandatory) have got to get off the bench and get in the game. We (G.B.G.) need you. And we (G.B.G.) need you now!

E.J. Puente, Ralph Cannon (Telfair County CA.) and Ruth Wilson Gilmore, we need you.... With this wave of gang terror sweeping across the world we're going to have to come together. We will need some unusual and unlikely bed-fellows to come together. An enemy is after our children. And we don't have time to criticize and to ridicule one another. We've got to take action.

... I'm in Hades and I'm gonna say (again redundantly) to you teens and tweenies "Danger - Do not Enter!" This place mixes with your spirit like oil mixes with gas. I see people here whom I actually like and they (too) have become gossip boxes, haters, bitter, envious and 'fake'. Wow! In a way I wish (but hell no you've just got to take my word for it Bro.) you could see it (us). Double minded! Double spirited! Double hearted! The words "integrity, loyalty, peacemaker, authenticity and man" are foreign to us. Men raise their children. Men abandon gossip, negativity and duplicity to get the "job" done. Boys (us) get locked up in jail and sit around in cages with other males. Smelling each others farts and telling each other 'war stories' etc. Boys get trapped in "cities of boys" and try to normalize an abnormal situation. Boys wake up and the highlight of our day is to put on a new pair of sneakers, gold chain etc. and walk around (and a round) the yard hoping to impress other boys with our new clothes. My Uncle Melvin used to say "ain't been nowhere and aint going nowhere. Don't know anybody and can't even think their way out of a paper bag. Just fools". That is where I live...

I don't speak to you because I 'heard' you were a 'weirdo'. I've never seen you do anything. I want my family, friends, the Courts and I want the media (and authorities etc.) to 'think' well of me. In other words I expect you to 'believe' that either the judge or jury got it wrong and I am misplaced. And/or I want you to believe that even if they got it 'right' that was 'then' and this is now. I done (sic) learned my lesson. I grew up. I love kids. I miss my children. I worry bout my 'grandchildren' and "I".... "I" want "you" to believe that no matter what "they" say or said. Even no matter what I "did" back then etc. Don't believe the authorities when they tell you I need to be "here". I'm ready to come home and I'm not that guy any more. This is what "I" want you to believe about "me". But (simultaneously as I sit back and hope you give me the benefit of doubt etc.) I (even though I'm in chains) judge everybody! "Dude is a pervert". "Dude is a dope fiend". "Dude gotta be gay" And....

In a majority of cases "I" have never "seen" dude sitting on top of another man's private part. "I" have never "seen" him have sex with a male. I've never seen him do dope, but I "heard".

So even though I'm telling Jon Fleischman, Matthew Barrows, Paul Gutierrez, Bill Cosby etc. to "believe" in me, I want them to "don't believe the hype". I tell em not to bite into the innuendo, propaganda, speculation and... But I "bite" every negative meal of gossip I'm served in Hades. I want Tony Dungy, Rev. Otis Moss, Bishops, pastors and mothers to "pray for me because God can do anything and".... But how often do "I" pray for those (right here in jail) who despitefully use me? Why don't I pray for the people (here) who are being lied on, marginalized, raped and tortured? While I Boo Hoo and tell a sob story about what Oprah has not done for 3 strikes and what Bill Cosby should/could be doing etc. Why don't I do for my fellow convicts what I want Oprah and Bill to do for me?

Because the time I coulda, shoulda and woulda used on self analysis, self development and reading my Bible etc. I was playing cards, gambling, catching bugs for a dam lizard. I'm spending my life on frivolous bull crap but... "Oprah ought to be doing something for all these brothers in jail." I was playing pinochle when she got Marcus Dixon out. I was drunk when she interviewed Rubin "Hurricane" Carter and said "God please don't never let me be falsely accused". But I want Oprah to help "open up these prisons" and let (get) these brothers (who raped, robbed, shot, killed and...) outta these prisons". Hell Nall! I'm out on a limb (I know) but I promised God that "this" ("K.K.K.") is it". I can't "play" with you youngsters. I must be authentic. And in doing so I shall repeat that (at the risk of having you individually paint me with a broad stroke!) some (many) of us should never (ever) be freed; ever! We are suffering from spiritual swine flu and psychological aids. And just as a woman having unprotected sex with a man who has aids will (eventually) be infected, a person intermingling, interacting with a confused boy, who has an infectious (spiritual and psychological) disease will (if you're not protected) be infected... Lock a Pit Bull up in a cage and half feed him. Don't let him have sex and abuse him etc. Do that for a while and then throw another male Pit Bull in a small cage with him and what happens? To be or not to be. Rape or be raped! Prey or predator! Sadistic, evil and wicked behavior becomes a new "norm". So I'm laying up in my cell (cage) like a damn fool. I'm wearing my tennis shoes because it's not 9:00 pm yet. I have all my boxes on the bunk because it's day time. I'm a so-called "clean freak" and I'm "real neat" but I'll snort a pill (preferably methadone) up my nose that an aids patient had in his mouth. I'll swallow pills other folk's saliva has been on. I'm a germaphobiac (let me tell it) and my "house" (a cage) is spic and span but I'm drinking rotten fruit that dudes made in the toilet. Old trailer trash and ghetto thugs who R picking their nose, scratching their booty holes and playing with their genitalia while "cooking" pruno etc. they send me a cup of (germs/poison) rotten fruit so I can get drunk and kill my stupid ass. I'm a "fool"...

Eight months ago I was telling a brother (whom I like. He's a writer and he's not a punk) how foolish it is to get drunk in a deadly environment like this to retard your motor reactions etc. etc. And…. He got drunk and went to sleep in the dayroom. Thirty dudes (rapists, molesters and murderers etc.) in a concrete room and I'm drunk and asleep. I'm a "fool". But Oprah should be helping me. I'm mad at God! I'm mad at the world! I'm playing pinochle, hating, gossiping and drankin (sic). But my problem is Oprah. As a matter of fact (with all due respect) "I think Oprah might not like men". I …. this same dude got drunk in dayroom one night and got his ass beat by a youngster who probably could not beat him if he were sober…

But Oprah ain't his only problem. I 'm also his problem. I should publish his book. I should do this and that. As a matter of fact "Atlanta likes them white folks too much! Dude got a white wife and two half white kids. He (Sherman D. Manning) might be an Uncle Tom. If I wuz a white boy …." C.J. Sheron, Caleb Peek, Zach Freisan, Nick Hogan and Billy Bell etc. do you really wanna come here (to Hades) and 'kick it'? You boys (Clay, Cassius, Allen Harris, Eddie Cannon etc.) need to suit up. You need to boot up. As a matter of fact I want yall (Maxwell Hanger, Nathaniel, Keith, Christian, Alex Blench etc.) in your G.B.G. Swat Team Regalia because we've gotta rush those trailer parks, hoods and barrios. We must rush into these suburbs and find (via our internet Jihad) those kids using meth, smoking weed, playing video games etc. and we've gotta connect them and hook em up with a mentor, a teacher and a pastor. We must put "K.K.K." into their hands. We must get them to interact on the G.B.G. facebook with (ambassadors) our people. We must get positive, decent and kind hearted people like Daniel Bugriyev, Andy "The Volunteer", Jeremy (Jeremy Hudson), Casey and Ben at sierra vista regional Med. Center etc. to connect on Facebook via G.B.G. with kids in the hood who need advice and mentoring. My vision is to reach out N touch "Nate" (he was on Paradise Hotel in 08. He and a black guy.... In the costume make-up shooting pool? How bout Nate in G.B.G. Regalia doing a G.B.G. rally at Martin Luther King Jr. Academy in Sac Town?) and "Cole" (Cole was on "the secret millionaire with his dad in 08. I saw care and concern in Cole's eyes. We need Cole!) and to connect them with Jeff Glen Howell, Jeffrey Allen Walker (my ex-white crip ex celly), Joseph Latham and my Homeboy Nathaniel. I "see" strange bedfellows setting aside 'differences' and saying "I might not like the Band 'Honor Society' like you do. I might not like the Jonas Brothers etc. But I'll suit up and fight to get kids back in school". I "see" guys like "Brett" (Dr. Phil's "San Quentin" Brett) coming forth and removing the facades etc. I "see" Brett saying "O.K. I've lied! I've smoked weed and drank. I've been a fool. And I'm not gonna pretend like I've got it all together now". I hear "Brett" sayin "I still have conflicts, weaknesses and temptations. It ain't easy being me. But I'm in G.B.G. whether I'm right or wrong. Weak or strong! I got some authentic brothers (in and out of jails. In schools, colleges, churches etc.) who got my back. They'll tell me the truth. They'll speak-a-word over my life... Hell my commander in chief is "Joseph" AKA Sherman D. Manning AKA Saul/Paul. AKA "Gifted, anointed and flawed"... I see Brett, Jordan McGraw and his daddy (Dr. Real Deal Phil) saying "U won't me 2 des keep it real with u right? C.J. if yo ass goes 2 jail they will eat u alive"... I see a way out....

Richard Hatch (the Survivor) gets on my nerves. He's still an arrogant and pompous ass and he is 'right' when he talks about unchecked bureaucrats, prosecutorial misconduct (i.e. Mary Hanlon) and prison regimes trying to 'muzzle' the truth. They locked this man up in boxer shorts. Even knowing he had a lawyer and he had media attention etc. the bureau of prisons were so bold, arrogant and blatant that they hauled Hatch to prison in underwear. They put em in solitary confinement for 30 days. They etched "Kill a fag" on the walls of his cage.... "People R abused by the system and I think I can help" he says. And he's right. And (I repeat) if any prisoner hears of a stomp jumping, tobacco chewing, hillbilly warden trying to keep this book (K.K.K.) out of a prison let us know. You write Ryan at US Mint Green and tell him to let me know. You also write your lawyer, P.D., the local media etc. and tell them. You also have your family to email Hallopeter@sunrise.ch and tell him which prison is raping my (as an author who consistently talks about God and non-violence... I consistently tell prisoners to use the courts not assaults to address staff misconduct!) free speech, your free speech and your right to religious data. And tell family members to go on to the G.B.G. Facebook site and post the name(s) of prisons and jails (or schools) disallowing this Book. Call 202-393-4930 and tell the ACLU too. Contact the NAACP Legal Defense Dept. and report it. Also call 206-234-1022 and tell PLN. finally..... Contact (write him) Attorney Robert Navarro in Fresno CA. and tell him you (or someone you know) are being denied a book. Your religious, political and free speech rights "shall" not be violated merely because I criticize prison officials just like Gerry Spence does...

I wanna "stand" with Richard Hatch on his "right" (as an American) to speak freely. I also "stand" with him on his crusade to expose Bureaucratic Arrogance, prosecutorial misconduct and the orchestrated propaganda schemes operated by courts and cops everyday... But the vaccination (social "condom") which protects you (youths) from ever needing to go through what Hatch and I go through is education. Education is the vaccination that (more than 90% of the time) protects against Incarceration ... You feel me? ...

We've gotten 4 people to accept the challenge (which we upped to $ 2000.00) on page 313 of "Blue Eyed Blonde" Book II. In July 2011 we'll set up a secure website (to be viewed by persons 18 years old and older) and place the photos ("racecar" Jeremy?) on the website... Brett Jolliff? Mike Ardron? Daniel Coverston? "Marius"? Quentin? Tyra Banks? Paris Hilton? Aaron Carter? Derek Hough? Beyonce? Ashton? Sherri Shepherd? Elizabeth Hasselback? Alex Blench? Jeff Buttle? Levi Johnston (no big deal for Levi!)....

Rubin "Hurricane" Carter was absolutely serious in "The miraculous journey of Rubin Hurricane" when he wrote that "prison destroys any and everybody that comes in contact with it". His method for not being destroyed was to "transcend the prisons which hold me". And "when the prison is awake, I will sleep. When they are asleep I will wake". He meant it. I'm a living witness that if (when) a person hangs out, socializes and participates in prison politics (even just playing cards and walking the yard etc.) it will (that is "shall") pollute, contaminate and infect you. Yes it will. Put a nice lil dog in a pound with barking and biting dogs and he (too) will bite, bark or lay and become prey. Put a stoic, quiet baby in a play pin with yelling, screaming and crying babies and the quiet baby will yell, scream and cry.

Put Kenny Scott (Spokane Wash. He's 20), Daniel Coverston, Brian (Brian was on The Price is Right on 10/27/09. Hell, call Drew Carey), Brett and "Marius" in a prison with 'us'. And they will kick, catch or kill. They will become predators or prey... I wish I could get Hurricane, Geronimo Pratt, Wilbert Rideau, Pete Rose and Kenny Waters to go on a crusade across America telling students what "really" goes on in these prisons... That's what I told Attorney Robert Navarro. "Oh but you are telling em with "K.K.K.". And believe me a whole lot of boys are gonna read that book" he told me...

"Ladies and gentlemen with everything that is inside me I ask you to find Beverly Ann Monroe not guilty. She did not murder this man". .. That's what I remember hearing Attorney Murray J. Janus tell the jury in Powhattan County Virginia... I think Attorney David Hicks (now the District Attorney for Richmond VA.) And I were the only two blacks in that courtroom. And Janus' voice rocked that courthouse ... I'd give anything to get the name of the young man (one of Beverly's relatives) who told me on a break "Listening to Janus is like listening to a magician"... And yet, although Janus was/is the most successful trial lawyer in Virginia. And although I've personally watched Murray J. Janus walk into courtrooms with clients facing Life in prison. And I've seen those defendants (some guilty and some not) walk out (free) with Janus. Although a detective told me "Nobody prepares for trial like Murray J. Janus. Not in Virginia". And inspite of David Hicks and Murray J. Janus putting on one hell-u-va defense for Beverly etc. they lost that trial. And Beverly went to prison for murder ... "I'm disallowed by law to discuss a client's case" Janus told me. "But Beverly Ann Monroe did not kill that man!" He told me... I sat at Beverly's trial with Gavin, Katie and Shannon (her kids)... It turns out that Virginia State Police agent David Riley lied, tortured Beverly and manufactured evidence to falsely convict Beverly... HINT HINT? If a Country redneck cop will set up an upper middle class white woman who has the best lawyer money can buy? What will they do to yo black, brown or poor white butt? ...

Beverly's beautiful daughter (a lawyer) quit her job and dedicated her life to getting her mom out of prison.... Attorney Steve Northup (lawyer at the Troutman Saunders Law Office ...) They won! And after 7 years in prison Beverly got out. Her case was a monument to prosecutorial indiscretions and mishandling....

I want John Stoll, Jed, Donnie and Allen (in Bakersfield CA.) to read this book. Danny, Bui (Sacto), Justin Berry read "K.K.K." and then join our Education crusade. We need Doug Pieper Jr., Isaac Young (in Fresno), Louis Copelin and you... Whatever it takes to keep one kid out of this Den (Hades) full of snakes! This Human Dog pound... we need Gary Hardwick, Jed Stone, Scutt Turow and all of those who "claim" to be "passionate" about "youth". We want you: Jason Huyck, Josh Stone, Josh Cook and Alex Seabolt. I'm not smart enough to do this alone. It's gonna take God's favor to do this. And it's gonna take the energy, wit, restlessness, zeal and the know-how of Cody Sheldon, Benjamin Alexander, Sam Altman, Paul Graves and John Butterfield etc. to help us infiltrate college dorms, frat houses, schools and chatrooms with "K.K.K." and "G.B.G.". I "see" a way to do this. But the onus is on Chivescu, The Mullennix Bros, (Keith and Nathaniel), Brett Jolliff, Scott Tatum and Alex Blench etc. to "make it happen!" as warden Walker would say ....

"Find you ten John Butterfields (who will write, chat and blog about G.B.G. etc.) and G.B.G. will be known around the world in less than a year" Dr. A. Duran told me.

I need some spiritual insurgents to take arms. We are on a mission and Adam Crandall must help us "kick" the ball of hope in these schools. Yall tell Daniel Kaufman (Agoura Hills) and Evan Tucker that I said "put your uniform on" ... How can teenagers leaving a Highschool dance gang rape a 15 year old girl in Richmond CA? And I'm being told that 25 people watched and did nothing about it. My blood is boiling and my heart is broken. This shit is sick. Gang rape? ... I know that Charles Johnson (on site safety supervisor) and Charles Ramsey (W. Contra Costa County Supervisor) are not to blame. But listen, we need a summit meeting forthwith. Where are the pastors?

...Same thing I thought as I lay chained to a hospital bed for a year and two months etc. Where are all those preachers who love God and are faith healers? Tell Benny Hinn to go 'heal' some of those gang bangers who are infiltrating Richmond High School. They are hijacking the 'vision', hopes and the dreams of students. These are our children! These are our children! Where is the alarm? Where is the panic? I'm not bashing ministers but since you have a Bentley etc. can't you (preachers) use your Bentley to drive to Northside High School, Indian Hills High School or to Locke and preach and teach anti-violence?... I need Dustin Sisco, Alex Gilbertson (out in Minnesota), Mike Ardron and Spencer Dirrin to suit up and boot up. We must find Bryan Boyer, Danen Beres, Joshua Murillo, Erol Ozturk, Christopher Kline, Bart Bardecki and Tim Daraitis to come forth. Put on the whole armor yo. Put on your swat team regalia because just as fireman (and paramedics) run into burning buildings etc. We (G.B.G.) must run into burning schools, churches, hoods and trailer parks. And we must save these lives which are burning up with drugs, burning up with violence, illiteracy and hatred. And we must arrest the thugs, gang bangers and the bastards who are starting the fires. I want my spiritual Homeys to get ready to scramble. We must stage some interventions into these schools. We must inject ourselves into the fires ... Remington Korper, Dr. Alex Vaclivik, Nate Archibald, Corporal Colby Jones, kids at St. Charles High School in Chicago Illinois gotta come forth. I won't take no for an answer. I need you. I gotta have Justin Zysman, Joseph Rocha, Garrett Haden etc. We need squads of door knockers and street teams to go pass out "K.K.K." and G.B.G. pamphlets like the Jehovah's witnesses pass out watch tower' mags. We can do this. Yes we can! ...

I need Attorney J. Douglas Clark, Danny Bui (Roseville), Daniel Coverston, Kenny Scott, Christian Thormann, Jason Schwartzman, Shaun White and Dave Franco. It is code red in these schools. We can't turn our attention away from the pain, hurt, sorrow and trauma that youth (you) face merely because the media (like an ambulance Chaser) moves on to the next story.

Ryan St. Onge, Professor Marc Howard, Marty Tankleff, Charles Salter (Principal of students in the "comedy club" class at Aliso) and Jacob (Jacob was on The Price is Right on 10/28/09. Jason's twin brother is in Airforce Bootcamp. Jacob lives in San Diego and he won the showcase showdown. Tell Jacob we don't need any money! We need his mind and his time!) come forth!

... Daniel Tingen got in trouble a few times. I have a stipend and some books for Daniel Tingen and for Tomas Plancarte-Benson. Daniel does yard work for Rob's dad. He lives in Troutdale Oregon. I wanna prevent Daniel (and Tomas) from ever working on the "yard crew" in a state prison! I don't wanna see Daniel or Tomas running around with an orange vest on and carrying a "poopa scoop" picking up bird crap! ... Daniel does yard work and couldn't come up with $ 100,00 to pay Tomas back... If Daniel Tingen is reading right now listen (read). "Read this book Daniel. And write me an essay (minimum of 750 words!) I won't critique it. I care less how good or bad it is. I don't trust you! I only want the 'essay' to prove you actually read the book!) and I will send you $ 100.00 with all deliberate haste. All u gotta do is read the freaking book! If you don't have the money to buy the book and Tomas (lol) won't loan it to you etc. (some readers email Daniel and tell him I 'wrote' this) I'll give you the book. Email me and say "Sherm I heard about your offer in the book. Send me the book" etc. And we'll send you a gratis book!" And when Daniel Tingen (and Tomas, Jacob, Gary Stein, Justin Chirigotis and Chris Balding etc.) reads this book he will be changed... I know I'm right. And I'm counting on F. Lee Bailey, Steve Dougan, Joe Weinberger, Pastor Bryan Carter, Professor Anupam Chander and Dylan Rodriguez to all help sponsor books!

When Matt Bomer, John Litzler, Jonathan Phillips (singer), Sean Pander and Jonathan "Legacy" Perez get their hands on this book they will feel the fire in their belly ... Nicholas Frank Prugo, Chris Kline (Aubum CA.) and Erol Ozturk (I repeat) we need feet in the streets ... We've got work for Dillon Banionis and Spencer Dirrim to do. I need to reach Jimmy and David Hartline in Summerville Georgia. I need Ernest Griffin (in Georgia) ...

In late October 2009 I called (the greatest trial lawyer in the State of Georgia. Arguably one of the top ten criminal lawyers in America. They modelled Matlock off of this man.) Attorney Bobby Lee Cook. "Sherman, how have you been?" When I asked if he remembered me he replied "Of course, I vividly remember you ... I spoke with Murray Janus a few weeks ago and he mentioned some explosive and earth shattering bombshells you're writing called "K.K.K." ... I'm hearing it's gonna be a thundering assault on gangs and school violence". .. I asked Mr. Cook a few personal questions and we ended our chat with the famous lawyer stating "Sherman, I am absolutely looking forward to the book. And if I can help you in any way let me know. You have my home number"... I want Mr. Cook to please donate ten copies (or more) of this book to schools! ...

G.B.G. concurs with District Attorney Kamala Harris who suggests we take a close look at elementary school students Truancy. A student not getting an education is a crime. And there are tens of thousands of elementary school students missing 60 days out of a 180 day school year. Truant elementary students will become high school dropouts! And those dropouts will become crime victims and crime perpetrators. Kamala believes in intervention. She believes in the mission of G.B.G. We applaud and salute Kamala. And we hope she becomes Attorney General. And Kamala will become America's second black and first female President! ... I want parents, principals, prosecutors, judges and police officers to read Madame Prosecutor Harris' book "Smart on crime".

A state prisoner promoting a book by a prosecutor? "Only in America" Baby Boy ... Matt Douglas (Chesterfield Missouri) and Jai Breisch Hollaback... "my name Joseph Latham. I live down South in Torrance CA. It's by Redondo and Palos Verde ... I'm 19 and hear (sic) on some bullshit ass charge of some robbery's (sic) 1st degree. They gave me 3 years/2 strikes. I only got 1 year and 6 months left. Hey, I would like to read your book though.

Hey, Atlanta, it's hard to find good people in prison. You write like a professor and I heard you was (sic) filthy rich dude ... " Joseph sent me that note in response to a written inquiry I sent him while I was researching for 'this book'. Joseph should be 22 or 23 by now. I hope he's not back in prison with 25 to life. I hope he got back on track! But wherever Joseph Latham is I want him to get this book and write me. I've never forgotten Joseph.

... Tyler Perry: He was molested and abused. His own father used to beat him and tell him he would never be "nothing". And when lil Tyler tried to defend his mother his dad would say "that boy is gonna make you cry one day"... Tyler was hurt, just like many of you boys (faking like you're a man) are hurting. But Tyler says "You let it destroy you or you take it (the pain, the hurt and the rage) and you use it. I use it in my life and in my work". Youngsters U gotta stand up and walk out of your past. And use the pain to make you better... When Tyler started talking about (in a television interview) his mother taking him to church on Sundays. I flashed back to Dollie Mae Manning. Lord, I'm so glad that my grandmother always took me to church. Yall think I'm a mess now? If I had not met Dollie's God I would sho nuff be a mess ... "She took me to church on Sunday mornings and it was the only time I'd see her smile and happy". Tyler said. "So I wanted to know this God who made my momma smile" ... Hollywood "closed the door on me, so I had to tear a hole in the window! 'He who owns the gold makes the rules'." Tyler's first film was featured in my hometown and it was titled "I know I've been changed" and it flopped. Tyler then got turn down after turn down. So he used his own money to write and to produce... "When Hollywood produces you they control the content, rewrites and they say what goes into it... I couldn't handle that. I had to do my own thing". Amen to that! If you all really (really) knew what publishers told me about this book. They loved the title and called it a 'Stroke of genius'. But they wanted me to let them "Dictate". So I (like Tyler) did it my way. And I'm gonna watch this book "blow up" in teenies 'Chittlin Circuit'. And I'm gonna watch internet "bombs" drop as Justin Berry, Justin Zysman, Ryan St. Onge, Clay, Daniel and Tomas begin to chat, blog and talk about this book of seeds.

I'm looking for John DeCarro, Omar Samy and Maxwell Hanger. All I wanna do is change (uplift, inspire, motivate and transform) one. Just one. Every time God did something great He begin with just "one". Give me a Dillon Banionis or a Justin Chirigotis etc. Just give me one. God started humanity with "one" Adam. God began the nation of Israel with 'one' man Abraham. God slayed the Giant Goliath with 'one' young man David. God saved people from the Tsunami of the Bible with 'one' man Noah. He sent 'one' man to the cross to die for my sins. "One". I'm not stupid enough to think my words are gonna reach out into these maximum security prisons and transform all these vicious, bitter and broken predators. My prayer is just 'one' Allen Harris at

Wilcox State Prison. Just 'one' Aaron Smith at Dodge State prison. Just 'one' Benjamin Harris, Thomas Alexander or Joseph Latwton... One Douglas Frazier, Douglas Stave, Joey Ferreiras, John Ritter, Robert Smith, Francisco Rivas, Wakeel Sabur or Anthony Sarabia etc. will read this book and be changed.

I talk about the diseased spirits and the dark souls of many of the lying people with whom I reside a lot. I often remind you (youths) of how bad, sadistic and horrible it is in Hades. I remind you that you can't trust anybody in prison. And that is not embellishment nor an over statement. You can't even trust 'staff'.

... I saw Attorney Steve Fama in this prison in October. And Fama is a notorious Prison Law Office lawyer. He was in my building escorted by a prison official who is egotistical, pompous, duplicitous, vindictive, bitter and .... a "Christian". It's Hell in here brothers...

But make no mistake about the fact that people can, will and they do "change". I have witnessed people absolutely transform. I've seen people literally go through a metamorphosis in my presence. It is an awesome and amazing thing to see. And I know that (in the fabric of my being) after folks finish 'hating' on this book. After the media remind you all of why I'm in jail (Hell). After Mary Hanlon reminds you of what a "dangerous predator" I am etc. When Mary (meth smoking) Hanlon concludes her diatribe against "Clark Kent" etc. some Tomas (Benson), Daniel (i.e. Tingen or Kaufman), Justin (i.e. Zysman or Berry etc.) or Maxwell etc. is gonna pick up 'this' book "one way" and put it down and be (changed) "another way". Just one! It may be a quote from Dr. Curren, Dr. Solis or Dr. Heitkamp that "changes" them. It might be a quote from the Bible that "changes" you. It could be something Warden Walker, CC III Patricia Kennedy or A.W. L.N. Johnson-Dovey said or 'taught' me. I don't know what page 'change' is on for Shea Newberry or kids at Locke. I don't know which page, paragraph, sentence or word is going to revolutionize your life! But I do know it will!

I wrote this book (with my own money!) because one of us is in trouble! And one small hole can sink the entire titanic. One small bullet can kill a giant. One mad, raging, angry and troubled teen can shoot up an entire school. One of us is in trouble! Just one of you in the LA. County Foster Care System is in trouble. One impoverished kid needs a book like this. One of you needs a tome which gives you a multitude of reasons to stay in school.

I gotta get this to one of you at the Alliance for Children's Rights, Casey Foundation's Children's Conference, Court Appointed Special Advocates (CASA), Los Angeles County Dept. of Children and Family Services etc. I must get this to one of you working at the Child Welfare Initiative in Los Angeles.... Just one Caroline Kennedy, Verone, Karen Biernacki (Dir. Harmony House/ CASA), Joni Pitci (Dir. CA Child Welfare Co-Investment Partnership), Pete Herbst (Hudson County Child Abuse Prevention Center), Dr. Glenn Dubois (chancellor, Virginia's Community College), Michelle Barclay or Dr. Jeff Gardere etc. one of you can pass this book on to a troubled kid and change their life...

We never know what book it is that'll reach that youngster and change him for Good. In St. Paul Wisconsin (at McMally College) Freddy Fresh has become Professor Fresh. He teaches 'rapping' in college! Just one of his students (like the drummer) might read "K.K.K." and transform students in Wisconsin into an "army of teens and tweenies for Good".

One of us is in trouble!... I want Dr. David Kaufman (Folsom), Dr. Alex Vacklavic, Attorney Geri Lynn Green, Bob Blasier and Michael Louis Kelly (Kirkland & Packard) etc. to know I need some help because one of us (I told you all the power of one) is in trouble. It might be Denver Jarvis, Jeremy, Lil Michael Brewer or Alex King, but one.... We've got "Kids Killing Kids" and "Kids raping Kids" and "Kids beating kids" and.... one of us .... I'm calling, I'm yelling and screaming. This is a call to arms! We have got to get together. I need Valerie Small

Williams, the principal at Mira Loma High School and Nathan Livingston. I need Ted Ginn, Ron Clark and Daniel Sample etc. to lets get together!

We can talk statistical probabilities later. But right now it's one of us... One was important enough to bring the Big Boss back. Jesus Christ came all the way back... Eight days later for an audience of one. Jesus had already showed Himself to all the other disciples and He could have just gone to Heaven. But Thomas had not "seen". And Jesus interrupted everything He was doing. He put one on His itinerary. How many preachers do you know who will fly into town to preach and teach to an audience of one? Jesus came for Thomas! And I want to take a minute here to apologize to Thomas. I've been guilty of spreading a rumor around about Thomas. I preached and I taught that he was "doubting Thomas". I judged his whole life by one incident. Thomas was not a doubter, he was just discouraged. "Doubting Thomas"? Thomas was willing to die for what he believed in. That does not sound like a doubter! Thomas did better than Peter. Peter lied and denied. Judas betrayed Christ. But Thomas was willing to die... But one of us? The name Thomas means twin. I said his name means twin.... I have an announcement. I have a twin in me. I have a twin. He drives my car. He wears the same size shoe as I do. He even has my fingerprint. He (the twin) is me. I have a Clark Kent and a Superman. They wear the same face. I have trickster and prince both in me... Thomas was a disciple willing to die for the Christ. It was his twin who said "unless I see in His Hands.... I will not believe". Have you ever been discouraged? Because believing hurts. Believing will get you in "trouble". Believing will cause you to stop sleeping with the boss like the other girl did and you'll miss the promotion... "I believe God and I still lost my job". Somebody says "I believed God and I still lost my house". Joseph could have said "I believed God but I still went to prison for a sex crime I did not do." Believing can embarrass you... "I thought he was a preacher, but look at him sitting up in that prison with an "R" in his jacket".

Have you ever gotten tired? So tired that you didn't want to get excited again because the last time you got excited you got hurt.... So even though Thomas (twin) was discouraged he dragged himself to see Jesus.... You must drag your flesh to Jesus or your flesh will drag you to Hell. Even when you get discouraged you need to drag yourself to school, college and to church.... Can I tell you kids who are discouraged something? You are so close to your answer that if you'll just stretch (your mind, your faith and your vision) you'll get the power to succeed... I've found myself discouraged and in trouble. And here comes Jesus right in the midst of the trouble. He's a very "present" help in the "time" of trouble. He's showed up for me and said "I'm gonna fix it". He'll come for the twin on the inside. He'll come for you baby boy. Bow down on your knees and tell the Lord "one of us is in trouble". The one of you that's on the down low. The one of you sneaking, snorting, laying and playing. God will show you where to touch to get empowered... And if you will have resilience, commitment, tenacity and strategy you will succeed....

Andre Taylor is a student at Richmond High School and he's concerned about the sadistic gang rape that happened. And when I saw Andre on TV it's like I could hear him saying "one of us" is in trouble. They locked up Salvadore Rodriguez but he says he didn't do it; "one of us" is in trouble.

... Gary White Jr. (17 year old in Coronado), Ace Young and Adam Lambert? "one of us" is .... Kenny Lopez, Jacob Cook, Jason Huyck and "Dallas" etc. one of us.... But if you'll take the medicine in these pages. If you will meditate on it and "speak" it. "I believe therefore I speak". If you get positive affirmations and words of inspiration out of your "mouth" you'll grow. You will start growing into a different person and reinventing yourself. You'll start psychologically going to another level. You'll become a testament to the incredible power of the Human Spirit. You are going to make it!...

We will figure out a way to bring brilliant lawyers (and activists) like Warren Ballentine (black) to the G.B.G. round table with Andrew Bridge (white). We'll bring John Butterfield to the roundtable with C.J. Sheron, David Perry (VA.), John Caudell, Ryan Hreljac and Andy C. at "Homeboy" and we'll revolutionize the world...

On 10/29/09 "cops" re-aired a show in which a 21 year old was arrested for possessing 20 ecstasy pills. His roommate has a mohawk. I want the mohawk brother (AKA "Wood") and the arrestee to read this book and contact me with all deliberate celerity...

Jakob Karr, Victor Smalley, "Legacy", Peter, Ryan and Nathan (from "so you think you can dance") all need to contact G.B.G. Justin Caporusso and Austin Wolfe need to contact me also. We need them.... I want you (teens and tweenies) to diligently study this tome. Then go study all of Les Brown, Zig Zigler and Dennis Kimbro's tomes. These books will help you weatherize and spiritually insulate your mind because you're gonna need it. If you keep living storms will come... I want Gary White Jr. (17), Matt Bomer and Nicholas Frank Prugo to peruse this tome. This book is not "the way". I'm not 'that' smart. This book just, turns on the light so you can see your way....

Oh yeah, somebody told me that we should challenge Mika Penniman, Jared Swilley, Kevin Barnes, Christopher Owens, Charles Jackson (Fairview Park, Ohio), Jade Puget and Ben Hudson to take the "challenge" on page 313 of "Blue Eyed Blonde" Book II.... Yall ever heard of a streetwise Atlanta MC name Playboy Tre? He came up with rhymes in his head in order to impress friends etc. He 'had' to memorize them to keep from getting fired. His "boss" hated the fact that he would come "off the truck to write raps". He loaded cargo vans. His supervisor said "If you come off that ... truck again to write these silly-ass raps, I'm gonna fire you!" So he learned to memorize... He quit his job and took his skills into the lab.... He self-released (self published) "Liquor store mascot". He is still unsigned. He sounds like Tyler (and perhaps "Sherman") as he says "If the majors come, that's cool; if not we're gonna build this foundation. Seeing [independent] artists like Murs Rock 20,000 or 30,000 people changed my perspective on things". He's not worried about getting a pink slip anymore. Tyler Perry is not worried about a rewrite and I'm not worrying about a "rejection" letter. I'm in a human laboratory (Hades) and I write from my heart, not just my head. And guys like Chris Owens can relate to this book. Chris' Band "Girls" is fledgling but captivating.... "I wanna make music where the person will remember the lyrics, they .... And it has a positive effect" Chris says. He spent his childhood in an apocalyptic, sexually perverse cult called the children of God (an offshoot of the late 60's hippie fringe group the Jesus Movement)... He has struggled his entire adult life to reconnect with the world from which he was so fanatically sheltered. Chris has lived amid such extreme volatility that he hasn't had the luxury of ironic distance. When Chris speaks passionately, you believe every word. And when he sings his troubles (Tyler acts his troubles and I write mines) in a buoyant voice, there's not a trace of insincere affectation.

His fingernails are usually covered in pink nail polish and he's effeminate. But he has a lady and a kid.... He met Stanley Marsh, a millionaire oil scion and art collector. The eccentric Texan hired Chris as a personal assistant, and they developed a close bond. They attended cocktail parties, traveled to Indonesia to see the world's largest python, and talked constantly about Marsh's favorite works of literature, art and film. At that time Chris wanted to be a painter, so Marsh converted the indoor "Croquet Court" in his office building into a studio. "Probably he had never been appreciated before for being his creative self", Marsh says. "And I encouraged it and enjoyed it". Now 71, Chris recalls his time with Marsh, as profoundly altering. "He became my best friend and father figure" he says. "He helped me get over being so angry and self-destructive. Without Marsh, I would still be playing punk music in Amarillo, a junkie with an illegitimate child, struggling to keep a crappy house. I would probably blow my brains out at some point".

About his singing he says "it's about finding a reason to be alive". I think Tyler Perry can relate and I know I can .... do you really think I want to just "Live" in prison to be "living"? In a place where boys behave like girls trying to be men? In a place where I sat down with "Bandit" to "learn" why I'm (supposedly in prison and "why" I went to ad-seg? A place built on rumors, prevarication, hate and anger? No - I write (to you) to live... I use Dr. Philisms, Oprah-isms, Dr. Heikampisms, Jarmanisms, Solisisms, Currenisms and Kennedy-isms to 'stay alive' and to help keep you alive! ... After five years with Marsh, a restless Chris Owens packed his car and moved to San Francisco.... "I'm sick and tired of the way that I feel/I'm always dreamin and it's never for real.... I don't want to cry-y-y-y- my whole life through/I wanno do some laughin' too" he sings in "Hellhole Rat race".

Chris says "I wrote that thinking ,like, 'I want to fu----g kill myself'. It sounds super corny to say, but my life's been extremely difficult. I have to push (R you reading Max Hanger, C.J. Sheron and...?) really hard to get to the next spot all the time. And I was pretty depressed when Liza (his ex-girlfriend) broke with me, to put it plainly. But I'm not a f--king whiner. The song's about feeling that low, but what are you gonna do about it? Yeah, life sucks, but there's an alternative". Chris says "Hang out with your friends. Have a good time". I say Hang out with your friends. Study, learn, grow and have a good time.

... I'm creeping up stealthily on Christian Siriano, Christian Nelson and Christian Lawrence and on you (and U 2) and telling you that G.B.G. wants you! We want and need Dillion Banionis and Ryan Hreljac right here and right now... Bobby Lee Cook, Gerry Spence and Murray etc. are 'super' lawyers'. I aim to be a super writer. I want to reach you where you are. And may I (again) ask you 'who are you so angry at that they are worth messing up how your story ends?

I'm writing to kids at Franklin High School, Rio Americano and at Locke etc. I want yall to be young Ameri-cans! Not Americants. I want Justin Zysman, Joseph Rocha and Kaether Cordero to use their pain to create power. The only reason you are still alive is because God wants glory out of your story. And he will divinely orchestrate and situate the events of your life. So that He can use your test as an influential and a persuasive testimony to help somebody else...

I wanna know about the trials which Scott Tatum, Ron Rodriguez (South Sacto), Davey Havok and John Litzler etc. have come through so I can use them to help you. I want to have Jasper Anderberg, Kevin Devine and Brice Partouche on our team because they each bring a diverse perspective which can empower Matthew IM, John Butterfield or whoever.

"It's way wild! I was born to be wild and I'm gonna keep on being wild" Adam Lambert said of his new CD. And Yes, we want "wild" Adam, Anthony Fedorov, Danny Noriega and Garrett etc. on our team... In order for troubled teens to get "Back on Track" it's gonna take monumental efforts by prisoners, parents, police, professors and even prosecutors (i.e. Kamala Harris, David Hicks and Paul Howard etc.) working together... I call on Judge Marvin Arrington (whom I met through Rev. Hosea Williams) and Judge Joe Brown etc. to prescribe "K.K.K." to kids in their courtrooms.

This is an emergency tome. When a house is on fire the smoke usually kills you more often than the fire does. Smoke represents environment and soil etc. If the cocoon, environment or the soil is poisoned the plants die. There is a poison (a hopelessness) in the atmosphere (smoke) in our neighborhoods and schools.... When you're in one room and a fire is in the other room you can put a blanket or towel under the door to help keep the smoke out.... "K.K.K." is a towel under the door! .... If you're on the second floor of an apartment and the place is engulfed in fire you must 'find a window' and jump! You'll break a leg but at least you're alive!... If a person's arms are on fire they will panic. You will have to sweep their legs and throw them to the ground and then wrap a towel around their arms. This book aims to throw you to the floor and wrap a towel around your psyche. It's gonna take prayer, counseling, parents, mentors and teachers to heal the wounds and scars that are left by the fire... But if you 'work out', if you take classes, get counseling and have faith etc. your scars can be transformed into stars.

Men and women are judgmental and we may try to look down on you because you're a dope fiend, a lesbian, a drop out or an ex-con. We love to judge, to mock and to gossip. But God commended His Love toward us in that while we were yet sinners, Christ died for us. Even in your lowest state, God loves you. He does not just start loving you when you get 'saved' and get on the deacon's board. But even while you're smoking dope and hanging on the corner Christ loves you....

No matter what people say about you just keep going. Mary Hanlon Stone has a lot of bad stuff to say about me but I'm still God's child. I'm gonna mess around (by the grace of God) and become a prison writin kingpin.... I'm gonna mess around and get Jesse and Marcus Heilman, The Donkeys, Andrew Doheny and Shem on our team. Kids at Calvary Christian Center (in Sacto) are gonna stumble upon this book and we are gonna get together.

... At Richmond High School in California "The roof is on fire".

... When Cain killed Adam that was dysfunction. And (as I wrote before) when the one you love kills the one you love etc. when your son is on death row for killing your son. It seems like God would have chosen a different family through which to bring the promised Messiah. But God has a way of using dysfunction, accused rapists (Joseph), serial murderers (Saul/Paul) and drunks (Noah) to revolutionize Humanity. And God will use broken, busted and disgusted dudes in chains (AKA Sherman D. Manning and 'G.B.G.') to put a "towel under the door" of that classroom at Richmond High (Locke, Ron Clark Academy, McClatchy High or at Columbine etc.) and slow the "smoke" of violence (racism, hatred, guns, gangs, drugs and thugs) from coming into that room. And my message to every youngster who's reading is to "jump Baby Boy! Jump!" Don't let the "smoke" emitted by rapists, murderers, molesters, gang bangers and 'Boys gone wild! etc. kill you. Don't wait around on a savior. Jump! Jump! Jump into somebody's church! Jump into the word of God! Jump into a drug rehab or an anti-violence program. Do whatever you've got to do to get that High School diploma. Do whatever is necessary to take some college courses. Jump! ...

I'm writing to Charles Jackson (in Fairview Park, Ohio), Owen Wright, Jordan Smith, Rustin Ware and Alex Gray etc. We must do what we must do to reach the turning point. This is a crucial and critical moment. God is not looking for any perfect servants but for public servants. He knows what you did. He knows about the weed you smoked. He knows about the wild Irish Rose, Budweiser, Coors and Old Milwaukee you drank. But He still wants you (Peter) although you denied Him. He still wants you (Thomas) although the twin (in you) is in trouble...

We (G.B.G.) are saving a place for you at the roundtable.... I smell hope percolating and I see dreams brewing in schools, colleges and even in jails... Ben Loeterman, Luke Top, Benjamin Pollack and Will Janowitz we need you. The Ku Klux Klan couldn't stop Obama. And the Ku Klux Klan will not stop the G.B.G. plan to bring teens (and tweenies from all walks of life) together to do Jihad against the domestic terrorists in our own Homeland. Burning crosses is terrorism. Jump! Lynching people is terrorism. Jump! Gangs and militias are terrorists. Jump!.... We may break two legs, but we must Jump!... With these gang rapes and school shootings etc. with Michael Brewer literally being set on fire etc. People are panicking... We wrote this book to sweep you off your feet. And to throw you down so we can wrap towels around the fire on your body. Stop, drop and roll. Stop the foolishness! Drop back into school. And roll with some people who are going somewhere in their lives!

.... And don't get bogged down in trying to judge other people merely because of what some pundit like Hannity, Limbaugh or O'Reilly says about them. For while you're looking at Billy Joe 'suspiciously' because of his prison record convictions or accusations etc. it is often the wolves in sheep's clothing who are wrecking havoc on our kids! ... I.E. Judges R supposed 2 be the protectors of our constitutional rights. They are supposed to be impartial and fair, and to safeguard vulnerable members of society unable to protect themselves. But in January 2009 two Luzerne County, Pennsylvania Judges (not prisoners or ex-cons etc.) pled guilty to Federal charges related to their acceptance of $ 2.6 million in kickbacks for caging kids!... These judges engaged in a conspiracy to help arrange the construction of private juvenile facilities, eliminating a county-owned and operated juvenile prison, obtaining a favorable contract for the private juvenile and "incarcerating" juvenile offenders accused of minor crimes in the private, for-profit juveniles.

Judge Mark A. Ciavarella Jr. 58, and Senior Judge Michael T. Conahan, 56, entered conditional guilty pleas to charges contained within a 22-page criminal file. They must resign from their courts, pay an undisclosed amount of restitution, and serve 87 months in prison. Both are free on $ 1000000 unsecured bonds pending sentencing.

This is a chilling story of egregious judicial misconduct and the exploitation of children for profit... Judge Ciavarella met with a lawyer in June, 2000 who was interested in building a private juvenile facility in Luzerne. Judge Ciaverella introduced the attorney to a construction company owner, who then built the facility for a firm called PA Child Care, LLC. Local media identified the lawyer as Robert J. Powell, who was a co-owner, along with Gregory Zappala, of PA Child Care.

Greg is a Pittsburg-area investment banker whose father, Stephen Zappala, is a former Pennsylvania Supreme Court Justice. In June 2008, amid news reports of a joint FBI/IRS investigation into Judicial Corruption; Zappala bought out Powell and became sole proprietor of PA Child Care. He also owned Mid-Atlantic Youth Services, a company which provided employees to staff the private juvenile facility....

Judges were paid $ 997,600 for their roles in making possible the construction of the facility. Now they needed to fill the facility. Ciavarella thus began locking up kids for petty offenses.

Kurt Kruger, 17, was sent to a Bootcamp program for six months for being a lookout for a friend who tried to steal DVD's from Wal-Mart. His first offense. Twelve-year-old Dayquawn Johnson was locked up for several days in 2006 after he failed to appear at a hearing as a witness to a fight he wasn't involved in. Jamie Quinn, 13, served ten months for slapping a friend whom she claimed had slapped her first. Shane Bly, 12, was accused of trespassing in a vacant building; he was sent to a boot camp for two weeks.

"I couldn't believe what was happening", one unidentified parent stated. "They told us the hearing was not a big deal, a minor offense. 'Just sign here and we'll get this over with', they said. Next thing I knew, they were handcuffing my daughter and taking her to a juvenile residential treatment center. I fainted right there in the courtroom".

Thirteen-year-old Hillary Transue had created a fake myspace page which poked fun at the vice-principal of her school. She was charged with harassment, found delinquent by Judge Ciaverella, and sent to juvenile for three months. It was that case which led to a complaint filed by Hillary's mother, a child services worker, that eventually resulted in the federal investigation.

When a cigarette and pipe were found in a backpack that Jessica Van Reeth, 16, was holding for a friend at school, she was sentenced to three months...

"We feel that it's a great day for the young people and the youth of this area to see the system really does work; it's like Xmas seeing this rogue judge go to jail. It's just wonderful to see that the scheme of jailing for dollars has come to an end" Jack van Reeth stated... An estimated 5200 cases were tainted against youths because of these predator judges who sent kids to prison. And in prisons corrupted guards, gangs and predator convicts become the deFacto parents of our kids. What will they teach?

From early 2002 through the end of 2007, the judges tore apart families and traumatized children in the pursuit of profit. (on a larger scale so-called fair judges do the same thing everyday. They send people to prison for profit!)... These judges ended up raking in over $ 2.7 million in this caging kids scam. They bought a Florida condo and claimed their illicit kickback income as rent payments. Powell kept a 56-foot yacht docked at the condo. It was named "Reel Justice".

From 2003 through 2007, Ciavarella incarcerated nearly 30% of the children who appeared before him - almost triple the statewide average of 10%. Ciavaralla even coerced juvenile probation officers to change their recommendations from community supervision to incarceration, and overruled those who didn't. Hearings lasted an average of two minutes.

In April 2008, the Juvenile Law Center (JLC), a National public interest law firm and adequacy group, filed a complaint with the supreme court of Pennsylvania seeking review of more than 250 questionable cases involving children. The Supreme Court denied the petition in a one-line order dated Jan. 8, 2009, which contained no explanation for the denial. The Luzerne County D.A.'s office had (of course) opposed JLC's petition, saying it "was not a matter of immediate public importance".

After Judges Conahan and Ciavarella's guilty pleas and the scandal generated public outrage, the Supreme Court, on a motion for reconsideration, issued another one-line order on February 2, 2009 which vacated its previous order pending further action.

.... "We see this as a very positive sign that the Court is going to take a fresh look at our application for relief", said JLC Executive Director Robert Schwartz. "Beyond that, it's hard to read into this. It's pretty clear that they want to go deeper. There's no reason to do this if they're not going to grant relief down the line or at least figure out a way to provide relief to the kids of Luzerne County". This was/is a travesty of juvenile justice and it needs to be rectified as fairly and as swiftly as possible... On Feb. 26, 2009, JLC and the law firm of Hangley, Aronchick, Segal and Pudlin filed a federal class-action civil rights and Rico suit against Ciavarella, Conahan and others. The lawsuit alleges that the judges conspired with others in a corrupt scheme to accept kickbacks for their assistance in the ...

"Judge Ciaverella's placement of so many children in juvenile facilities without regard for their underlying charges suggests a procrustean scheme which violated one of the core principles of the juvenile justice system. The right to individualized treatment and rehabilitation, commented JLC Associate Director Lourdes Rosado. "He shredded the constitutional rights and statutory rights of these children. And now, he's been properly stripped of any right to serve as a judge or practice law ever again. Through this lawsuit, we also seek to hold him civilly liable for money damages.

On March 12, 2009, the Special Master appointed by the Supreme Court issued his First Interim report and recommendations.... Senior Judge Arthur E. Grim's report stated "that a very substantial number of kids who appeared without counsel before judge Ciavarella for delinquency or related proceedings did not knowingly and intelligently waive their right to counsel. My investigation has also uncovered evidence that there was routine deprivation of children's constitutional rights to appear before an impartial tribunal and to have an opportunity to be heard". He recommended that convictions of low-level offenses for certain juvenile offenders "be declared void ab initio, and/or vacated, and/or expunged". He noted that this action would "be at least one step towards righting the wrongs which were visited upon these juveniles and will help restore confidence in the justice system".... Hundreds of convictions will be expunged as a result... "I've never encountered, and I don't think that we will in our lifetimes, a case where literally thousands of kids' lives were just tossed aside in order for a couple of judges to make some money", said JLC Attorney Marsha Levick. I disagree vehemently. I believe the system routinely locks up kids who don't need to be locked up etc. for the profit motive.

This horrendous malfeasance was abominable. This scandal illustrates the quintessential reason why prisons, juvenile or otherwise, should not be privatized.

Any convergence of moneyed interests with the construction and operation of for-profit prisons creates a fundamental conflict between the private prison industry and what best serves the public interest. Private prisons have a financial incentive to incarcerate as many (so do 'public' prisons but not as blatantly) prisoners as possible. They operate like Hotels: more filled beds means more profit....

I hope football players in college (i.e. Maehl at Oregon), High school and grade school are reading this. I want students and teachers of every stripe to read this... Question and investigate everything. Don't take anything at face value. If you can't trust judges in black robes or priests in white collars etc, who can you trust?

... Attorneys Robert. R. Rothstein, John C. Bienevu, Mark Donatelli, P. Scott Eaton and Gerry Spence etc. R U reading this?

... Arizona Sheriff Joe Arpaio? The notorious publicity hound Joe Arpaio? He is a "chester" (AKA childmolester)! When Joe Arpaio was 15 years old he was accused of molesting a 2 year old baby boy. It was sealed and expunged (and the parents later claimed it never happened) from Sheriff Arpaio's record... Small wonder he likes to see men in pink underwear...

Question everything and everybody. Please note that Bernie Madoff was considered a "financial genius". Hell, he was the Chairman of Nasdaq! But Madoff was a "swindler".

... I want teens like my homeboy Ben Lincoln to read this book and to be empowered and changed by it. Ben's parents traded in their 5000 Square Foot Atlanta home for an R.V. They were so impacted by a mission trip to Africa that they decided to travel all over America volunteering to "Serve". And I want Ben Lincoln to put G.B.G. on his 'to do' volunteer list. All I need him to do is sit down for an hour per week and send messages to teens on Myspace and FaceBook and tell them to read "K.K.K."... and I need Ben's parents to "Pray for this book" to Reach the Right Kids at the right time.

Once Dustin Sisco, Alex Gilbertson, Andre Taylor (Richmond High School), Salvadore Rodriguez, Juan Sanchez (LA), Michael Bien (LA), Abel "Grumpy" Maldonado and Dr. Alex Vaclavic begin to blog, chat and 'poke' about "K.K.K." etc. we will be heard and read.

... I want you kids to believe in yourself. Believe in your dreams, hopes and in your 'visions'. This bump in the road of your life will pass. It ain't gonna be dark always (Baby Boy) morning comes. The sun shall rise again. The light shall punch in on the time clock of a new day. Morning will come - tough times never last but tough people do. Hold up your head, take a deep breath and keep on walking.

Don't worry about what your fellow students say. Whether they cry "Hosanna" or "Crucify" you've got to keep on walking. You will rise again! You will rise again!! You will rise again!!! You are not a chicken (a loser or scum), you are an Eagle!

... I'm a living witness (via intimate experience) that just as Joseph was falsely accused and wrongly convicted of a "sex" crime etc. the system does get it "wrong". They'll wrongly profile and peg you as a molester or a predator by mistake. And sometimes they'll do it "on purpose". I've watched Mike Bunnell (and others) sit behind the scenes of CDC and manipulate documentation in my "central file" and make me appear to be Jeffrey Dahlmer. But you must remember that there are republicans on the web, on radio and even 'in office' who have accused a certain black fellow of being a "Muslim" (although being a Muslim is not a bad thing), being a 'Farrakhan lover', not an 'American' and of 'paling around with a terrorist'. And this "Muslim, Farrakhan sympathizing terrorist" is also the President of these United States. So IF a CDC "captain" can tell me that President Mandela is a "murderer and a terrorist". IF the Prince of Egypt can be profiled as a sex offender. IF Pete Rose, Rolando Cruz and Tim Masters etc. can all do 'time' on sex beefs they did not do. Who the hell am I to complain merely because some high school drop-outs wearing badges etc., some dudes who burn crosses in their 'off' time etc. decide to make it their business to try to destroy me with propaganda and false data?

... Ipso Facto, I wanna tell all of you (in the streets, hoods, in trailer parks and in schools etc.) not to worry because people lie on you. Don't make the same mistake that Sherman D. Manning made for a decade! I tried to hide behind my wrongful conviction. My intentions were authentic. But I tried to have my cake and eat it too. I would write about everything and everybody except why I was in prison. And I allowed CDC (via de Facto Authorization) to define me. I allowed prison guards to whisper prevarication and innuendo about me to try to neutralize, contain and/or destroy me!

I let them (rogue guards: i.e. Bunnell, Tucker, Spearman etc.) define me! And because I did (and do) have some dirt on me (fraud, con, supplanter, trickster, playboy etc.) they were able to mix oil with gas and portray me as "useless". They (i.e. Goldsmith and B.M.) literally got on the telephone and called people (i.e. principals) and lied on me... How dare a sworn peace officer pick up a telephone and call principal John Doe and claim "you know he is serving sentences for raping young men?" A flat out lie. Absolutely deceptive and dishonest... But what I like about God and about wisdom etc. is that God will show you how to use everything your enemies threw at you to work for you. God taught me spiritual Aikido. He revealed to me that "if" that sick molester Jeffrey Dahlmer had found a way to publish a book etc. "We" would have read it just to see how "sick" he was. Ipso Facto, the more Bunnell, Spearman, the CCPOA etc. tell "you" all what a "sicko" I am. The more you'll read this book and be changed. Your change ain't gonna come "if" (because) you believe I'm a Saint. Nor will your change come "if" (because) you believe I'm a "sicko". Your transformation shall come because of the Dr. Phil-isms, Dr. Solis-isms, Dr. Curren-isms and Dr. Heitkamp-isms in this book.

Your transmogrification shall come to pass because we preach and we teach (over and over in this tome) "get an education". And "because" we teach (in this tome) you to stay the hell outta jail! .... I'm not promoting a Sherman D. Manning fan club! Nor am I running for "parent" of the year. I am simply candidly painting a 'real deal' picture of this 'sick' place, I'm in so that you will stay yo narrow ass out of here!

... And I want you to learn from our president not to allow gossip, lies, innuendo and mendacity to deter you from your dreams. Don't be as cowardly as I was by refusing to confront a vicious lie head-on. No matter how embarrassing or catastrophic the lie or embellishment may be you confront it. And move on! ... I will not (ever) write another book that includes the Ricardo Calvario story in it. I won't spend the rest of my life (however short it may be thanks to Bunnell and Valley Fever) writing and talking about Calvario and that scenario. But I'm guilty of trying to dance around the accusation. I was a hypocrite!! While I ran around stating that "all that it takes for evil to rage is for good men to remain silent". I was "silent" about my wrongful conviction!

I've come to understand that there is a reason that David spent a large majority of the psalms (read psalms 37, 69 etc.) talking, writing, praying and singing about enemies, false witnesses (Calvario, Camosky etc.) and folks 'lying' on you. Candidly, if you ever aspire to greatness you will (I promise you) have enemies. You will (I promise you) have people who blatantly, willfully and skillfully "Lie" on you. But I was so busy hiding inside the wrong I "did" do and being a hypocrite about the stuff I did "not" do etc. that I missed David's point. He did commit adultery! He did have Bathsheba's husband killed. But the enemy raised up liars to accuse him of stuff he did not do.... Instead of C.D.C. officials telling teachers etc. that "Manning lied to Stella Bryant! He promised to marry her and ripped her off! He's a con, a crook and a fraud" etc. (see "confessions of a conman") they lied! And "false witnesses" rose up against me. But there is a reason King David spent so much of his career writing about liars, false witnesses, haters, enemies etc. He knew about Joseph spending 13 1/2 years in "prison" for a "sex crime" he did not do. He knew that "you" and "I" would have haters. David knew that some kids might be upset with John Butterfield for writing what he wrote ('Free Speech') in the 'Mirada" about what he thought were too sexually explicit moves etc. and that some of those could very easily put out a rumor that "Butterfield is gay" and... High Schools are rumor factories! And kids in school are at the most vulnerable and sensitive time of your lives. And you "care" what people "think". And I'm a livin witness that it "hurts" when people lie on you. But it's more important what I "know" about me than it is what you "think" about me. You have to keep walking....

It's difficult to believe but prison is worse than High School when it comes to gossip, rumors and lies. This (prison) is "Ground Zero" for "Deception"... When Dearaujo lied on me I asked C.O. D. Smith "Why would he do that?" She replied with a question: "Manning, if I'll murder you what won't I do to you?" She stated "I don't know why Dearaujo is in prison and if I did I couldn't tell you. But you've got to remember where you are. They send people here for rape, molestation and murder. And yes some of you guys didn't do everything they said you did. But generally speaking this is a 'bad' place. So "if" a man will rob, rape, molest or murder. Do you really think he'll think twice about lying on you, me or anyone else to get what he wants? Walker and Kennedy know he lied on you. But they've got to dot the I's and cross the T's. It'll come around. Have faith"....

I want you to know they will "lie" on you... I'm writing to John Hackett, John Garvin and John Butterfield. I'm even talking to Garrett McCain, Garrett Schell and Garrett Cunningham etc... If you are a tad bit effeminate they will claim (often erroneously) you are gay! If you experimented with "weed" only they'll say it was cocaine. If you get caught doing this they'll say it was that. People embellish, lie, tell tall tales etc. But you cannot allow a lie to make you cry. Nor can you allow a lie to cause you not to try. Love or hate Mr. Obama etc. He has taught us that even if you made some mistakes etc. you experimented with booze or weed. You made some misturns and errors in judgment. Your pastor turned out to be way more radical than you thought he was. People call you terrorists and spread false propaganda about you all over the internet etc. Obama taught us that if you believe in God, self and in education etc. you can be black, white, short or tall. But you can rise to the highest office in the land! Yes you can!....

"Let me tell you something: I don't believe in I can't" President Obama said. ...And I want an army of teens and tweenies (i.e. John Hackett, John Butterfield, Alex Gilbertson, Andre Taylor, David and Justin Morton (Rich. VA) and Kaether Cordero etc.) to rise above rumor, racism and innuendo etc. and help us spread the words across the planet that "we can do it" and "yes we can!"..

I read an article in The Atlantic titled "Teenage Wasteland". It says "a Chicago Funeral Home's Business is growing". As I read about Leak and son's funeral home in Chicago I remembered (vividly) meeting Mr. Spencer Leak (the proprietor) in 1993. He's a distinguished man... He buried 59 homicide victims between January 1 and August 1, too many of them much closer to 18 than 80. In 2008, he buried 85 homicide victims in all, the vast majority of them kids, part of a huge surge in young homicides that saw 37 Chicago public-school students, killed in the 08-09 school year... On a warm, sunny Saturday mourners stream in for 2 funerals for 2 homicide victims in chapels across the hall from each other. In one chapel, Brandon Earl Little, 19, lies in a wooden casket. Across the hall, Jessica Sade Wesson, 18, is in a casket. Wesson was found behind a middle school, strangled and stabbed. Little was gunned down in broad daylight, carrying a gun as two other men chased him down the street.... Dozens of young men, sporting tattoos and low-hanging pants, drift in to Little's funeral. One tattoo displays a fist and the words "Pay me". Another has a dollar sign next to the phrase "when money talks, I listen". The youths lined the wall, some with eyes unflinching. Others sniffled or shook with sobs, unable to stop. A slim young man wore a shirt that showed a skull and read R.I.P. Brandon Little, your riches are acquired by the misfortune and bloodshed of others... In one chapel, Wesson's mom spoke: "My baby, she was good. She was real good". Across the hall, the Rev. Joe MacAfee aimed his words at the young men who crowded the chapel's pews. "All you know is kill, kill, kill". MacAfee said. "Preach!" Cry some of the mourners. "Are you the next Brandon" Is your funeral gonna be the next one?" "Better think about it!" a woman called. "Stop the Brandons" said MacAfee. Stop the madness!".... I wanna ask all of my readers in and out of prisons: are you the next Brandon? And if you don't wanna be etc. If you don't want your lil brother or your friend to be etc. We must stop this fu----- madness!!

... Mr. Leak is a dignified and tall mortician. He reminds me of my dear friend Rev. Raleigh Rucker (pastor of Mt. Patmos in Atlanta. A 'Major' with the sheriff's dept. and the proprietor of Rucker's Funeral home) who allowed me to preach at this church when I was only 12 years old.... Mr. Leak says he'd much rather bury elderly persons who've died of natural causes. "Then you're arranging a funeral that turns out to be a celebration of life". Business would also be simpler as it is, Leak (and Rucker) sometimes has to brace for potential violence, wary of gang members seeking revenge. At other times he's a counselor to heartbroken mothers whose kids were struck by bullets intended for someone else. And many crime victims require complex restoration work. "The worst are beatings with blunt objects like baseball bats or tire irons. And/or someone stabbed in the face 40 times" says Jeraldine McCall, an embalmer at Leak and sons.

As a black man, Leak despairs. And as the holder of a master's degree in criminal justice, a former director of Chicago's Cook County Jail, and chairman of the Black on Black Love Anticrime Organization, he has his own theories about who or what is to blame. Leak is convinced that most youths who become violent can't read above the third-grade level. "They have this hatred for themselves, because they're not going anywhere". He hopes his fellow south sider, President Obama, whose Chicago home is about 30 blocks away, will devote some attention to low-income children who can't read. "They are our future murderers", Leak says. And his (and Rev. Rucker's) future customers.

And for the one's who don't die, they come to jail. And they will be pressured, tortured, traumatized, brutalized and sodomized here in the living Hades... I'm calling upon John Savio and Reko Rivera to help us put the word out. This tome is an SOS. It is a Clarion call. If you can't write me, email me, yell etc. Send out a smoke signal or whatever. But let me know that you're reading this. And that you (too) are ready to help us do warfare. I need Ben Lincoln, Benjamin Alexander and Scott Tatum to come stand with G.B.G. This tome reaches out to Redmond O'Neal, Joseph Schoen, John Hackett and to you too. Let's do this.

No matter what juvenile, jail cell, church, school or college you're in we need you. We need Kris Stump in Fresno. Ex-Bulldogs and Ex-Crips. Richard Scrushy, Paris Hilton and Mike Milken etc. Your criminal record does not disqualify you from serving. If America lost a million soldiers in Afghanistan and Iraq they'd release prisoners to go fight the war. This is an emergency and we need everybody....

The average Israeli man is 5 ft. 8. But (in the Bible) Zaccheus was a very short man. He certainly had heard all the short jokes. He'd been picked on and no doubt bullied in school. For looking like a midget. But if he'd been normal and average Jesus would've never seen him. He would not have climbed up in the tree and been recognized by the Christ. God'll take your disability and use it to raise you up in a tree for all the world to see... Jesus sent for Zaccheus and said "Come on down, I'm coming to your house". Jesus recognized Zaccheus because of that which kids had laughed about. Your dysfunction and the mess you came through qualifies you to teach, preach and to mentor...

I'm talking to Amber Arellano, Esohe Esoi (University prep. advisor) and to Donnie Pastard etc. It's time to wake up! We need school and neighborhood crime prevention programs. And mega-reading programs. Wake up!.... Geri Silva, Barbara Brooks, Angela Y. Davis, Priya Kandaswany, Rose Braz, Mothers Roc (Mothers Reclaiming Our Children), Barbara Meredith, Francie Arbol and Ruth Wilson Gilmore etc. gotta come forth.

Mothers have been asleep.... And 2 women who were harlots came to the King in 1 kings 3" 16-27. And one woman told the King that "this woman and I dwell in the same house; and I gave birth while she was in the house". And three days later the other woman gave birth... They were alone in the house sleeping and the second woman's baby died in the night because she laid on him. So she arose in the middle of the night (told yall the Bible is raw! Baby stealing didn't start on the soaps. It started in the Beginning). And "took my son from my side, while she slept, "and laid him in her bosom, and laid her dead child in my bosom. And when I rose in the morning to nurse my son, there he (her son) was, dead. But when I examined him in the morning, indeed, he was not my son whom I had borne".

The other woman lied and claimed the living one was her son.... King Solomon said "Bring me a sword". They brought him a sword. And he said "Divide the living child in two, and give half to one, and the other half to the other". But the woman whose son was living spoke to the King, and the Bible says "she yearned with compassion for her son; and she said, "O my Lord, give her the living child, and by no means kill him! But the other said, "Let him be neither mine nor yours, but divide him". She'd rather kill em than give em back to his momma. And the drug dealers and gang bangers and molesters etc. would rather kill our children than give you back to your mothers. But King Solomon said "Give the first woman the living child, and by no means kill him; she is his mother".... While the women were sleeping there was a "switch".

St. Matthew 13:25-28 says "but while men slept, his enemy came and sowed tares, among the wheat... He said to them 'an enemy has done this'..." And when mothers and fathers are sleeping, drinking, drugging, laying and playing the enemy is stealthily creeping into our schools, churches and houses. Building up networks of gangs of kids... And there has been a switch.... But when that woman "spoke"... I need you kids to go tell your mommas that "the dude in prison with that 'R' in his jacket like Joseph says you (mothers) need to speak!"... And that woman "yearned with compassion for her son". I want mothers not to turn your kids over to me (a jailbird). Not to turn your kids over to Bishop Flip Flop or Deacon Willie Wonder. But I want mothers (and fathers) to A. Wake up! B. To Speak! and C. to yearn for our children. I came to awaken mothers (fathers, sisters and brothers). I came to trouble the waters and send shockwaves throughout the neighborhood. We've got to wake up....

Austin Wolfe, Justin Caporusso, David Reynolds and Tadd Carr etc. we've gotta open up our spiritual stockpiles and use a spiritual stun gun to bring kids (on fire) to the ground. And go back to the basics teaching self love, empowerment and a knowledge of a self to esteem...

Richmond High School is on fire! Anytime 10 gang bangers can rape a 15 year old girl with 20 or 30 people looking on there is a fire. Throughout history (i.e. mobs and lynchings) the 'individual' has gotten 'caught up' in the 'group collective'.... This violence in schools is a virus, an epidemic, a cancer and a pandemic.... Wake up! ... Charles Jackson, Carlos Rodriguez, Greg Deekens, Christopher Clubb, Jason Word and Nicholas Evans let's get together.... I'm calling on Jonathan Raymond (superintendent), Donna Sheshtowsky, Jenny Triplett and Daniel Coverston etc. We must put on our swat team regalia. I need Kenny Scott (Spokane), Minerva Shelton, Shawn Hornbeck, Jenny Williamson, Dave Franco, Christian Thormann, Jason Schwartzman and Danny Bui (Roseville) etc. to "fall in". We've got to fight! .... I want to sound the alarm today! I wanna blow the trumpet in your ear! It's high time for you to awake out of your sleep! I don't give a darn whether or not you are gay, straight or bi. It is time for Joseph Rocha, Daniel Sample, Redmond O'Neal and Ben Lincoln to come together as one. We need righteous indignation. We need to get mad about those gangs that are domestic terrorists. Get angry about child molesters. And we must reclaim our children. Even those daddies (like me) who are in prisons etc. we've got to speak up! We must wake up! It's time for us to stand up!.... An enemy has done this!....

Travis Shaw, Michael Parker, Maxwell Hanger and Alex Chivescu, we need you too.... We all have a place at the G.B.G. Roundtable.

I want this book in the hands of Charles Ramsey (superintendent of schools), Adam Crandall (Edison High), Daniel Kaufman (Agoura Hills), Evan Tucker (Sacto), Kyle Sevey, Marc Hamilton (ASU), and Danny Gans' son... Wake up!.... Alex Gilbertson, Omar Samy and Dustin Sisco etc. It's time to fight!

... Michael W. Smith is the founder of Rocketown in Nash. Ten. It is a safe teen Haven .... On 11/1/09 there was a "band" (what band was it? Lead singer?) playing for Rocketown. I wanna salute the band on the G.B.G. Facebook site.

.... Jordan was a young man who spoke about Rocketown. We have a stipend for "Jordan" and I want Jordan to be a G.B.G. ambassador.... Rocketown was having a financial problem and gospel singer Michael W. Smith called on football coach Tony Dungy. Mr. Dungy rocketed into town and rescued this Haven for kids... "I always looked at football and coaching as a platform to mentor and to teach.... And I felt that God had me in the NFL for a season in life. I walked away from the NFL so God could use me to mentor troubled young men" Tony Dungy said. And I was so moved that I sent Rocketown a check. Peter is sending Jordan, Michael and Rocketown this book. And I intend to send more money to Rocketown.

Talk about God using Dungy. When he was in the NFL he was my favorite coach, Peyton was my favorite Q.B. and the Colts were my favorite team. But I never wrote to Tony Dungy. But now that he is on a crusade to stop this madness etc. I reach out to him. Not seeking a money donation or a promo. But I want Tony Dungy to pray for G.B.G. Pray that "K.K.K." will "trouble the waters" and wake people up. And pray that this book (of seeds) will "rocket" into "towns", schools, hoods, churches, juveniles and into jail cells etc...

I met a "Nicholas" in a mall in Virginia in the 90's. He had purple hair. I recall him calling my Hotel and saying "You wrote Merry Christmas on your business card"... I want outcast looking guys and gals to get "K.K.K.". I recall David Morton, Justin Morton, David Dowdie, Gary Browning and Michael Crowder, all in Richmond. They need this tome!.... My lady (Stella) told Lori's boyfriend (my skateboarding buddy "Joshua") that "you should participate in our 'best male buns' contest. Cause you got ass Josh". She'd talked me into sponsoring two local Best Buns contests (one for guys 18 & older and one for gals) in Richmond. We were gonna make a male and a female calendar featuring the "Best Buns" and pay the winners $ 500.00 each. However, I was jealous and (intimidated) angered by what I thought was her flirting with another man about his "buns". She'd done 90% of the male selections (i.e. John 'Jodie' Bear, John Caudell, Brian Fasal, Gary Browning, David Reynolds, Joey Grissett, Ricky Parnell, Daniel Clay, Brian Devin Graham, Alex Dugdale, Chad Sherman, Ronald Keith Dunn and David Proctor etc.) and I chose 100% of the female participants (more than 50 Beyonce Booty Ladies!).... Each participant paid

$ 5.00. We would have made a lot of money! But my jealousy and insecurity were more dominant drives than my desire for profit!....

My assignment with this tome is to elucidate (for John Savio, Reko Rivera and Maxwell Hanger etc.) a visual description of this place called prison etc. in such a way that the average 8th grade student at Richmond High School, Locke or McClatchy etc. will (at least) think twice about continuing on the journey (of criminality and truancy) which leads to eventual Residence in prison. This book is blatant, candid and (at times) graphic. But "K.K.K." is like a literary form of "The Jaws of Life". There is an emergency, an urgency and a crisis in our schools. When we see gang rapes, sexualized bullying, x-rated hazing and freak dancing in 6th grade etc. it says to me that we need "The Jaws of Life"....

If you are arrogant, foolish, cocky or reckless enough to peruse this (unpolished, raw, unedited "street released", underground) book and still come here you deserve to be here. I know what I know. And I've met younger dudes in prisons (i.e. John Jodie Bear, Scott Johnson, David Joiner, Christopher Michael Rousche, Jeff Glen Howell, Johnny O'Neal etc.) who have had extreme difficulty navigating their way through the prisons.

We wake up each morning to concrete cages and prison bars. I wake up in the company of boys I would never choose as friends. My time - and my movement - are totally controlled (and without God) hopeless. As soon as we open our eyes, we are mad. The gnawing in our bellies now accompany the dawn of each new day.

We are so damned angry that utter and complete madness cannot be far away. Bitterness is like a drug, it's an addictive substance which haunts us each moment. Bitterness whispers its catechism of gripes and complaints. We can't seem to calm the increasing volume of those angry voices. Our cases for hatred are airtight. Bitterness, hatred and rage consume us until we lose ourselves. The surface of our character and control (after years) begins to crack, snapple and pop. I've watched many men lose all touch with reality in here and snap. But they are the easy one's because you "see" them coming. The most dangerous and deadly one's are guys who look, act and talk 'normal', but are inwardly raging, snapping and cracking. They can go off and rape, assault or murder you at any given moment.... I knew an extremely intelligent black inmate in Georgia (Mr. Chairs) who woke up one day and cut off his penis and flushed it down the toilet....

Jail, juvenile detention and prison are the ultimate in poverty, and poverty is a tremendous incentive for con games. Men (in Hades) manipulate men like a sculptor molds clay... Guards (i.e. at Alto and Reidsville in Georgia and certainly in California etc.) work diligently to break men's spirit. They know that violence and destruction just breed more of the same. Flagrant injustice always leads to open violence. But before the dam breaks there are plenty of small breaches in the peace. And my assignment via G.B.G. and in "K.K.K." is to aid you in recognizing the small breaches in your school or college. And to equip you with some spiritual, psychological and motivational tools to help you ameliorate and eliminate the breaches before the dam of violence breaks.

We must establish special tactic units in schools and churches. The G.B.G. CERT (Central Emergency Response Tactics) memo is available (gratis) upon request.

In prisons the CERT (Central Emergency Response Teams) merely assault, beat and attack inmates. I've witnessed (in Georgia, Virginia and in California etc.) inmates beat almost to death by guards; under the guise of CERT teams reacting to violence....

I once called Attorney Murray J. Janus about an assault taking place at Chesterfield County Jail. A frail, defenseless, young white inmate was assaulted by seven deputies. I was frantic, alarmed and flabbergasted by what I witnessed in the visiting room. I'd used my license and ordination to get a clergy visit with several inmates (i.e. Elwood Booker who was a former captain with the sheriff's dept., Craig Gilstrap, John Caudell and F. Ronald Wright etc.) at the jail. (Atty. Janus had threatened the jail commander with a lawsuit if they didn't allow me a clergy visit. Rev. Martin Luther King Jr., Malcolm X and Rev. Hosea Williams all had criminal records. But when they bailed out of jail they visited people in prison. Rev. Sherman D. Manning will visit these inmates or I'll shut the jail down!" Atty. Janus stated to the jail commander. And they rolled out the red carpet for me after that call....)

You'd think jail deputies would be on their best behavior if they knew that I'm (a rabble-rouser and an activist) in the visiting room. But when you wear a badge, carry a gun and are in charge you can become careless. And carelessness, arrogance and corruption are a dangerous mix.

I witnessed a beating by Chesterfield County deputies that shall forever be seared into my memory bank. I had one of those large (this was 1995) mobile telephones in a briefcase. I called Attorney Janus at home. He told me to "leave the jail - Reverend - now!" I left. Forty five minutes later I got a call from Wayne Dillard at the jail. "Sherm - the F.B.I. is here at the jail.... That Janus dude is bad! I overheard the Major saying that Janus called a federal judge, because you called him. And the judge sent the feds rolling in here deep".

A couple of weeks later (because of my activism, some illegal crap I was doing, coupled with false allegations and embellished data etc.... I.E. I passed by a 23 year old white lady who was doing yard work. I blew a kiss at her... Her hubby was a cop! They actually did a "field report" on me and put it in my FBI files.... "suspect made sexual overture at young 'girl'.... slowed his Jaguar down and blew kiss". You have to read 7 pages over to discover that the 'girl' was 23 and I was 24 ..... Atty. Janus showed me my field reports and I was wowed! Because of my involvement with the murdered and missing children of Atlanta's prayer vigils, Rev. Hosea Williams, Ambassador Young and civil rights etc. I even have a secret service file etc. etc.) Attorney Janus told me to "Get out of Virginia! Get out now! I'm telling you what I know! I'm good, but I'm not Bobby Lee Cook or Gerry Spence! I'm no magician! Reverend - whenever the police decide they "want" you they "get" you. And they will nail you to the cross!"

I couldn't believe my ears. Attorney (now a judge) Michael Edward Bergin had told me something eerily similar a few years before that.... I just could 'not' believe that a 'system' would work to falsely profile, set up and abuse an individual; not in America!

"You are not rich enough to continuously pay me to defend you against bogus charges" Mr. Janus said.

"And the fact that you like white women in a conservative town like Chesterfield Virginia is not helping you at all. The fact that you like to wine and dine. You preach against racism, corrupted police and the power structure. Then you arrogantly pass by cops driving flashy cars with their (white) women in them.

And on top of all of that Reverend you are crooked! You are a hypocrite! Make no mistake Reverend: there are thousands of brilliant, arrogant, half-crooked men sitting in Virginia prisons with life sentences! For murders, rapes, kidnappings and molestations that they did not do! You need to leave Virginia tonight before you become one of them.." ..

... When you come to prison if a knowledgeable inmate starts helping an illiterate, the guards merely ship one of them off - and if internal affairs shows an interest, the staff scatters everyone involved... If you get beat by guards in prison it is a lose lose. Unless you can afford Bobby Lee Cook, Janus, Geri or Brosnahan etc.... Do you have an extra $ 50 grand lying around? If so, you'd probably not be in prison in the first place...

Prison is all about the control of actions and possessions.... Bullies are the same wherever you find em; in a sandbox, a school, college or a prison; guards, students or inmates. They always go for the weak, and have no respect for the rules. Sometimes you defeat a bully by ignoring him. Sometimes you can use humor and psychological Aikida. But sometimes you must confront them... (see the G.B.G. CERT memo)... We in prison are like lions in a cage. When I consider the wasted potential in this place I get sick...

Let me tell you (Alex Gilbertson, C.J. Sheron, Nathan Hand and Ernie Griffin etc.) that in juvenile detention, youth authority, jails and in prisons the only law is the law of the jungle. The supreme rule is that the strong dominate the weak (though some men live in strange commensally relationships). Domination is an obvious aspect of prison life. But bullies deftly wield their psychological weapons in prisons.

The most vulnerable victims are white inmates. This has less to do with racial identity than with practicality. Young white boys (Timothy Kwasniewski, Todd Dressler, John Griffin, Alex Holgan etc. R yall reading?) from affluent homes are soft (AKA refined and have etiquette) and easily intimidated (and hopefully motivated to stay out of jail) by hardened black, brown and older white inmates. A life of civility and privilege has multiple benefits, yet is renders you useless and powerless against prisoners (and guards) who take sadistic pleasure in mind control. Tough young whites have fewer problems, and the weak blacks and Mexicans are victimized. But the Caucasian children of affluence are especially marked for servitude... Domination in prison is both premeditated and subtle, not always the typical prison rapes depicted in novels and films. (K.K.K. is not a novel!). Very often a new prisoner will come in and two older inmates conspire to establish one of them as the protector and one of them as the threat. The threatener acts out a hollow con, an in-your-face intimidation which presages violence. But the protector is the actual menace.

Some guard'll tell inmates that the new dude is "some rich lil bastard, who got caught with an ounce of coke and some meth".... His fear is palpable and he goes out of his way not to appear to be gay. Dudes will set him up and create an incident or argument. And once the threatener has him scared the protector will come in and "save" the white boy from the 'threat'.

And a friendship is established. The O.Gee looking out for the youngster. Consoling him when he has legal problems, loses his appeal or nobody shows up for a visit. Sometimes, like a big brother, he holds him when he cries. And in prison everybody cries (in the night - out of sight). To the boy and his parents, the O.G. is a protector and a savior, but to the savvy prisoners he is known as a "war daddy". His parents speak to the older man when their son calls; they may even send him cards and money, but they have no earthly idea what's really going on. Their boy has been tamed, his spirit broken, and he's become his war daddy's "boy". After a while the young man gets used to the older man's affections, and even relies on his comfort. The game works out well for the war daddy, and the young man becomes totally submissive and willing to perform sexually for his protector. The pleasure for the O.G. is a combination of sexual pleasure and pure domination; to him it is a game of human chess.

Some 'boys' who come to prison are unsure of their sexuality. Arguably, some of them were gonna be bi-sexual or gay for pay or gay (on the down low) anyway. For "them" I have little (if any) sympathy. And some dudes just wanna have sex! Sex for pleasure! Experimental sex etc. and whatever two consenting adults wanna do is between them.... But when straight (scared, vulnerable and soft) boys are preyed upon, my blood boils. Rape is rape! Be it rape by intimidation or the rapes (which do take place in here) by violence.... I've seen, heard and witnessed too much. And friends of mine (i.e. David Joiner, Christopher Michael Fowler, Roy Cherry, Chad Newman, Bradley Poole, Eddie Cannon, Danny Macky, Gregory Swokla, Nathan Gould, Christopher Parker, Charlie Baddaker, Abel "Grumpy" Maldonado, Jose Zuniga and Joseph Latham etc.) have told me a lot. And prison authorities are indifferent at best and complicit at worst. And if a rape victim in prison tries to reach out to the media he'll be ignored, denied and disbelieved....

There are too many biased persons (i.e. Joe Orlando at Fox 40 News in Sacramento. Joe is a meth addict himself. And he has friends who work in CDC) like Joe at Fox 40 News who will go out of their way to paint any prisoner in a bad light. If we are able to gain media attention press like the folk at 'Fox" will paint us up as predators. So you can be viciously, assaulted, terrorized, humiliated and 'raped' by a fellow criminal (AKA "guard") or a convicted criminal etc. and by the time 'Fox' gets a hold of the story "this prisoner has been described as an openly gay inmate. He's known for propositioning staff and inmates. His allegations of 'rape' against staff, officials say, is frivolous".

But the press will not tell you that Gubernatorial candidate Bob McDonnell has been accused (on 3 occasions) of having sexual relations with underage girls, one girl was 11 years old!.... Nor will you read that LAPD chief of police Charlie Beck has been accused of raping females in his custody (years ago). The media is often bogus, biased and bigoted.

... Yall still wonder why I would not allow the normal editorial (which includes re-writes, grammatical modifications and 'ghost' writing etc.) transformation of this tome? I wrote this book! And (love it or hate it) very few authors are able to say they "wrote" their books. Paul didn't allow anyone to edit, modify, re-write or ghost write the book of Philippians. Nor any of the other books (of the Bible) which he wrote while in "chains" as is this writer. Nobody re-wrote Dr. Martin Luther King Jr.'s "Letter from a Birmingham Jail cell" either!.... When I tell prisoners down in Georgia like my boys Benjamin Harris, Alan Harris, Aaron Smith and Allen Harris that "I" wrote it. They want "me" to write it. Allen is one of my lil G.B.G. soldiers. You'll be reading about him more in the future and can see him on the G.B.G. Facebook (and Myspace etc.) site(s).

.... Ben (at Dodge State Prison) and Allen (at Wilcox) are recruiting fellow prisoners, guards, friends, family members and pastors to join our army. Guys like Thomas Alexander (in Dillwyn VA.) wanna read authentic tomes, not some whitewashed and watered down crap. And Thomas can reach out to my boys (Clay, Jody Bear, Wayne Dillard, Gilstrap, Nathan Hand, Chad, Luke Johnson and Joey Grissette etc.) in Virginia and tell em they're in a real life tome. A tome written in the deep, dark and dangerous bowels of a California prison. A maximum security penitentiary .... "This is it".

When kids come to the pen it's a whole new language (literally and figuratively speaking) they must learn. Coming to this place is like walking into a foreign country. This is worse than Iraq. There is no "Green Zone" here. It's worse than Beirut, Afghanistan or.... These Abu Ghraibs here in the homeland are ticking time bombs waiting to explode. These are dangerous prisons getting worse by the day. Prison is a house of horrors....

I was showering today and thinking about the demons, darkness, the hate, the rape and the bitterness in here. I'd thought about the fact that on November 3, 2009 veteran correctional officer Garcia was caught smuggling cell phones in to active gang members on C-facility. The same C.O. Garcia, who told me weeks ago "Bunnell is gonna have you transferred as soon as that book comes out... And the Mexican mafia is gonna murder you!".... I thought about how wicked and corrupt this place is.... "If I was not in there" I felt the Lord saying. "The place would blow up right now".... It dawned on me that if some praying mommas and praying daddies were not asking God to "be" in these prisons we would riot, we would murder and we would "rot". If God was not in here this place would blow up. I just wanna take a moment here (on behalf of the more than 2.5 million of us in these prisons) and thank the Lord for His glory! His presence and for His hedge... Thank You Jesus! I want some of you brethren in these jails and prisons to take a 60 second praise break! Yall holler for football, baseball and basketball games and that's all good. But the Raiders didn't bring you here. The Braves didn't bring you here. If you knew how many dangers "unseen" that God has protected you from you'd shout!.... I want you (Ben, Allen, Thomas, John Ritter, Justin Howell, Jose Zuniga, Brandon Gene Martinez and Nathan Gould etc.) in the prisons to lift up your hands and say "Thank You Jesus!"... Do it again, "Thank You Jesus!" Tell your celly, your home-boy, your "war daddy", your "boy" etc. "Thank You Jesus!"... If it wasn't for His love, His forgiveness and for His mercy etc. He would have destroyed you last night while you were in the bed with your celly! He would have killed you today while you were snorting pills. He would kill you for your lust, unnatural cravings, the blood on your hands, the blood on your mind and... He loved us (all 2.5 million of us) enough to wake us up this morning! I want Ritter, Harvey Lashler, John Garvin, Michael Jacinto, Joseph Latham, Womack, Jerry Wines, Allen and Benjamin (and the tens of thousands of you reading this in dayrooms, cells, classrooms, schools and in homes etc.) to say "Thank You Jesus!".... Now turn your head to the left. Just look back over your shoulder and see where God has brought you from. Oh God! My God! My God! My God! I know this ain't a religious book. I know this tome has too much "mess" in it to be a church book. But when I think of His Goodness! And all that He's done for me. My soul shouts Hallelujah. And I thank God for saving me.... He could have killed me (and Billy York or John Garvin) at Valdosta.... He could have killed me (Mojo, Roger White, Chris Durbin, Michael Wilkerson, Sam Fuick, Roy Cherry, David Joiner, Ernest Griffin and David Hartline etc.) at Alto... But God sent me an angel by the name of Clarence Jones. He showed me favor with Captain Gold, Captain Cole, Captain Million and.... He could have killed me (and Scott, Chris Rousche, Keith Blackwell, Ricky Sweet, Mike Fowler, Robert Kaufman etc.) at Phillips in Buford Ga. But God kept showing me favor on top of favor. And He sent civil rights Giants like Andrew Young and Hosea Williams into my life. And even though I was in a mess (and a conflict).... He didn't let me die. And He kept me. And here I am the Tyler Perry of "Hades" ... They might not know me at NBC or ABC. But they know me in the "Chittlin Circuit"! They know me and my writing (at PVSP, CYA Chad, CYA Stockton, Rikers Island, Locke High School, Rio Americano, McClatchy High, Ron Clark Academy and at Rocketown etc.) and .... I was flabbergasted when I learned the whole story. C.O. Domingo Garcia didn't just smuggle cell phones in to Mexican gang members on C facility. He smuggled coke, crystal, heroin and knives in. He tried to smuggle in a 'gun'. And since the CCPOA have fought to prevent "searching" peace officers entering prisons etc. he could/would have smuggled a gun into CSP/Sac. were it not for a 'tip' from an inmate snitch. And the quick, masterful response by Warden Jimbo Walker's staff etc. Inmates, officers, physicians and therapists etc. could have had their heads blown off. Imagine a 'rapist' in a maximum security prison. Doing a life sentence with a gun. How many female staff would he rape?

If Domingo Garcia (a veteran correctional officer with ties to the former C.O.'s Celsa Zamudio, Acosta, Wallace Lafitte, Marilyn Windham PhD and associate warden Mike Bunnell!....) Garcia also had close ties to that bastard Larry Turner! this sends shockwaves throughout this nation etc. If this is allowed to be swept under the rug by Lance Corcoran and Mike Jiminez etc. then the public deserves the killings (out there) which are ordered and orchestrated (in here). If you (the public) are gonna continuously allow 'guards gone wild' and dirty cops etc. to smuggle cell phones to us so we can call our comrades in the barrios, hoods and in the trailer parks etc. to order murders.... You deserve it! ... Parents, students, principals etc. (who have principles!) must get off your lazy, complacent and "trusting" (i.e. "the politicians will take care of it".) posteriors and demand a change! We (especially us drug addicted conservatives like Limbaugh) are so concerned about "protecting" traditional marriage (which has a 55-60% failure rate!) etc. We are so freaking concerned about what "consenting adults" do in their bedrooms and whether or not "they" use the word "marriage" that we will raise $ tens of millions of dollars to pass "propositions". We'll campaign and collect signatures to stop those "fags" from marrying. But we won't do St. Matthew Chapter 25.... nor will we "do justice, love mercy and walk humbly with our God". We'll not call the Governors, the senators and Barack and tell them "We want an edict mandating that every prison guard and jail deputy etc. be required to go through the same metal detectors en-route to work.... The same one's 'we' go through when we visit our family and friends in prison!". What the hell is so complicated about inundating twitter with tweets i.e. "We don't want child molesters, murderers and 'shot callers' having cell phones in prisons. You search us (bankers, lawyers, pastors and great grand mothers etc.) when we go see convicts etc. Why can't you search the guards who guard these violent predators? We don't want drug addicts in prison for crimes etc. to do, push and deal drugs in prison.... Wally Lafitte, Acosta, Larry, Domingo and thousands of rogue guards have been 'caught' smuggling weapons to cons. Tens of thousands are not caught. Shake down the guards who shake down the guarded". Does that make sense?

At P.V.S.P. Wally Tucker, D.L. Criner, Gail Crooms, Thornton etc. brought "us" contraband routinely. .. Assault somebody that Wally Tucker dislikes and Wally will bring you a cell phone with all deliberate haste!

.... Dr. Marilyn Windham? C.O. Domingo Garcia would allow her (under the color/cover of authority) to sneak into the chow hall, in the office and have train (chain) sex with Mexican gang bangers... on one occasion (that I know of) C.O. Garcia forced (via threatening to 'arrest' her... as far as I'm concerned this was "rape") Dr. Windham to "suck my (expletive) too".... What a guard.... I personally wrote a missive to I.S.U. about Domingo Garcia in 2002. I informed I.S.U. and the Ombudsman (Hurtle) that this man was "corrupt" and that he was threatening my safety etc. I.S.U. never replied! (only time I hear from them is when they confiscate a new tome I've written or try to deny me my "right" to "write" certain civilians... They stay so busy stealing my mail that they don't gots no time 4 Domingo!)... I saw Hurtle walking the yard (in late 02) with Bunnell. I asked Hurtle did he receive my missive. And his reply (verbatim) was "You gon F around N git (sic) yo ass in something U can't git out of. You need 2 mind yo own Business N leave people alone!! Manning".

... I recall that when Jimbo Walker was a captain. I overheard Jimbo telling Wally (Lafitte) "I'm hearing a lot of chatter about you that I can't confirm. But a word to the wise: If you are doing anything you should not be doing you need to stop! Dude, I will get you fired if you threaten safety and security". Wally replied by calling Jimbo a "racist Klansman!" and "I'm in the CCPOA! They ain't gon let you crackers F with me! You can't touch this!" Wally walked out of the office and slammed the door so hard I thought it would come off the hinges. I looked in expecting to see a shaken Walker. To my utter surprised Jimbo was laughing... Keep in mind that Jimbo is "warden" now and Wally is an ex-con who cuts grass for a living.......

In Florida Federal agents went into a prison to arrest a dirty guard. He had a personal weapon (unauthorized semi-automatic handgun) on him inside the prison. He shot a federal agent and killed him.... He'd been bringing drugs and cell phones in to prisoners. How long before the right inmate was able to procure that gun that the rogue guard was carrying inside the prison?..........

And Domingo? A confidential source informed my law students that "they found 13 cell phones in just one bldg. on C-Facility. All sold by Domingo"........

In Georgia guards earn paltry salaries. If an inmate offered a rogue (broke) guard $ 50 grand to "smuggle me a small handgun" he would do it. And it would jeopardize the safety of civilian staff! I.e. other guards, nurses, physicians and chaplains etc. Ipso Facto, while "we" get on the Hannity show and engage in lengthy diatribes about President Obama only appointing ACLU lawyers to the Federal Bench etc. why don't you kids (my posse) engage in a concerted, strategic campaign to insist that guards be searched at the gates... Incoming and outgoing.... And insist that Domingo's fat ass not receive a "slap on the wrist" like most rogue guards do. Lock him up and give him the maximum penalty allowed under the law.... Write the presiding judge (James Mize) in Sacto superior court and demand that "when Domingo is convicted; he be sentenced to a maximum penalty". I don't support (which is why this tome is not a threat to institutional security!) prison vigilantism. So you won't ever hear (or read) me saying "Beat his ass when he goes to prison". No! The only "beating" Domingo should get is a criminal sentence to prison. Upon being sentenced he deserves to be punished humanely and not assaulted by some thugs looking for a "notch" on their belt(s). The only "notch" a prisoner needs on his belt is to beat illiteracy and learn how to read and how to think.

My co-worker is over 40. I won't call his name because I'm not trying to embarrass him. But we were counting trays the other day and I said "Joe (pseudonym) I have 53". He replied "I got 12". I said and "12 and 53 is what?" He looked at me with the dumbest look I've ever seen and stated "I don't know". I thought he was kidding. He's a fat white guy.... "Joe 53 plus 12 is what?". There was total silence and Doc looked at me. After about 60 seconds C.O. Pipes yelled down from the control booth "It's 65 Joe! Damn!"... Doc and I could suppress our laughter no longer... I was passing out the coffee. Doc asked "Does Joe not help you?" I said "Hell nall' I'm black (lol)". Doc looked at Joe and said "tell him Joe - 400 years and he's still gotta work". I laughed and Doc left. I noticed Joe was not laughing. I went over to him (out of curiosity) and said "What do you think Doc meant by "400 years?" Joe looked at me (totally serious) and said "I didn't get it. I think he's calling you old".... Lol or cry....

A recent study concluded that most adults who do not have a high school diploma spend some time on "Welfare" and on "food stamps". Hint! Hint! And most of us in here can't read, write and count. Ipso Facto, Dr. Solis, Dr. Curren, Dr. Heitkamp and I are on a crusade via Helping Educate At Risk Teens (HEART) because "pragmatically".... If we can convince you to make reading, writing and arithmetic learning mandatory etc. you won't come to prison! Get your High School Diploma at a minimum. School is cool (just remove the "s" and the "h") and it prevents you from being a fool. Or yo ass will be in here with me unable to add 53 and 12. That is sad.......

In 2007 Sacramento Kings player Justin Williams was arrested and had allegations of rape against him. And while I concur (fully with Attorney Roy Black's claim that "rape" is easy to allege (remember potipher' wife), difficult to prove but easy to convict".... I also know that (allegedly and supposedly) Attorney Kathy Druliner was given $ 50 grand (in cash) to bribe her husband (Chief Deputy Prosecutor in the A.G.'s office.... Very influential with D.A. Jan Scully) to make certain (fix) charges against Justin were dropped.... If Justin were poor like David Quindt he would still be in Sacto County Jail being beat, extorted and set-up by deputies...........

Trevor Loflin or Alan Rafferty? (not a shameless plug but read about "Booty Bandit" in my book "Creating Monsters".... Guards routinely celled younger white inmates with "Booty Bandit" to be raped! And it was mostly white guards doing it!) Johnny Weir etc. if he were here would be violated anally and orally; consistently with complicity.... And it is sad, sick and sadistic (I repeat) that reporters rarely report about the Weirs, Huycks, Josh Cooks, Goulds and the Montagnos who are raped in prisons daily. And (I re-repeat because even the Sacto Bee no longer has a single 'prison' reporter) if/when Justin Howell, Christopher Parker, William (Cisco) Flores or Jeremy Winters writes to Joe Orlando to tell him "I was raped by Marion E. Spearman" or by "my celly" Joe will laugh and say "He shouldn't have went to prison". And Joe will forward the letter to his cohort (Paul) and they'll send it to the CCPOA...

And Lance and Mike are so busy making money [on the side in their illegal scams etc. Hell Lance and Mike are like mob bosses for "Peace officers"....) They couldn't care less about some (predator) Michael Gorman being murdered and sodomized after guards ignored his pleas for help for hours...

Is any of this supposed to make you (students etc.) believe in Sherman D. Manning? Should you now exalt me to..... Hell Nall! The last thing you need to do is "believe" in me. I forfeited my right to request your 'belief' in me the moment I left a woman (Stella) and her child (Mahogany) stranded in Richmond Virginia.... I left a woman who loved me. And a few days after I broke a good woman's heart. I was in pulpits (televised) at Trinity Baptist Church (Rich. VA) and at Temple of Deliverance (Memphis Ten.) preaching the word of God.... You should "hear" me, "fear" me, "watch" me and "study" me so you'll know how not to treat women. And how not to go to jail... Yes, police are often corrupt. And I've been set-up and falsely accused on a number of occasions. But make no mistake about the fact that I "have" committed some crimes. Yes, I have. And no corrupt cop, deceptive prosecutor or biased judge forced me to commit a crime. No all-white jury came to Virginia and told me to rip Stella off.

I did that and I was wrong! I won't play the O.J. Simpson game of "If I did it". Hell "I did it". I lied, cheated, manipulated and deceived people day and night. Ipso Facto, I decided to manipulate people to read, to write, to get an education etc. as a vaccination or immunization to prohibit incarceration.

... Michael Castro, Andrew Lang, Nathan Langley and Von Smith had better stay away from prison. It's a devilish and deadly place. And it is so lonely here. There are so many times I look at the "few" guys (here in Hades) that I actually 'care' about and they act funny. They seem to harbor jealousy, envy and negativity. "I'm not happy and I don't want you to be happy". And "I have so many holes in my soul, spirit, mind and in my heart I feel I'm about to split apart. I can go to bed with Paris Hilton, Beyonce (!), Tyra etc. but it still won't cure me. I can see and hear T.D. Jakes on TV and still can't get "me" delivered. I get 'lifted' and even 'excited' but I'm still not 'delivered'.

I see this everyday. People who have been locked up so long and 'think' they wanna go home but they are incarcerated (rotten and bad 2 the bone) all the way down in the marrow of their bones. There is absolutely nothing you can do for them. The complexity of their dis-ease and the trauma which has visited their souls have ruined them. Give them a million dollar check and they'll be (lifted) happy for a few days. But check them out 3 weeks later, and they'll just add 'arrogance' to their 'issues". It's like pouring some expensive cologne on a bucket of defecation. The Aramis or Kouros smells awesome but when you pour it on stench it won't transform the scent into an odoriferous delight. You can't make a bucket of crap smell like Aramis. The crap needs to be destroyed.... You can't poor compliments, hand shakes, high fives, canteen, packages and jewelry etc. into or onto a wounded and hole(d) psyche and make them 'normal'. I am in a Haven for dysfunction and disfigurement. Our souls are disfigured. The only thing which will save a man who has been in prison for 20-30 years is a miracle from God. That's it and that's all.

When I'm able to pick my mind up and sit (mentally) atop the prison and look down upon us. It gives me a sense of 'wonder' and amazement. I am amazed that the recidivism rate is "only" 82%. I would predict (given what I see here) it should be 100%.

... Ralph Batts was an Atlanta police officer. Joe Sutton was also an Atlanta cop. Joe and Ralph were friends of mine. And both Joe and Ralph verified for me that (then city councilman, next Atlanta Mayor) Bill Campbell was corrupted.... Joe also told me "If you knew how much cocaine Sean Hannity snorted... And some of the times he's been locked up and bribed his way out"... Keep in mind that police chief Eldrin Bell (Justin Barrino's dad) and I attended the same church. I've been in his office and at one time was a confidante.

... Former Governor Zell Miller should be in prison! (I won't reveal who told me). Zell Miller was accused of raping a "black" woman. Just as Gerry Spence, Bobby Lee Cook or Barry Scheck etc. will tell you that many men are sitting in prisons for rapes, molestations and murders they did "not" commit. They will also tell you that many wealthy, connected, protected and respected criminals (rapists and murderers: Gary Condit, Miller etc.) never "see" the inside of a prison....

And.... prison? "Did you see Shaun White on TV today? That white boy got ass. He could sit that 'red haired' asshole in my face. I'll stick my tongue inside and take his temperature" Ray (pseudonym) told me two weeks ago. Ray is 220 lbs. He has 3 kids and his "wife" visits him every Saturday! Prison!.... "His Halloween costume? He was Wendy. Oh, he turns a brother on... I'm a start dreamin bout (sic) shaun like I do Anthony Fedorov.... In my dream I gots Feddy Bear, Weir, Buttle and Timothy Goebels all at the same time. And Fedorov has on a red female G-string and".... This is a married man who will be free in 3 years. And he has a wife! Are you reading this, James Michael Avance, Vaughn English, Michael Castro, Randy Madden and Caleb Shockley? I hope that Alex Wagner Trugman, Cody Sheldon and Alex Chivescu are reading this...."profiting" off of "looks". But (sadly) if Justin Frazier went to L.A. County Jail right now he would not be "paid" for a challenge (i.e. 313 - part humor/part exploitation!) etc. He would be forced to "bend over" and be train raped! Trevor Loflin? John Doggett? Alan Rafferty? Daniel B? ... Etc. etc.

... I want somebody (seriously) to call Heather Spencer and tell her to call Justin Frazier (Dan Sellery, Dan McMullan, William Letlow and C.J. Sheron etc.) and tell him I said stay away from jail..... Period.... Daniel Kaufman? Talk to Christopher Durbin, Sam Fuick, Gene Langford, Keith Jerrolds or John Jodie Bear. Call up my buddy Clay Hollifield, Billy York, John Garvin or David Joiner and ask them what happens to "white" boys in prison. 'They' are all white so talk to em. And I have some G.B.G. soldiers in prisons all across this country (Caucasians) who can chat with you about "whites" in "prisons". Let me name some dudes (G.B.G. Combat Soldiers) You can talk to: Allen Harris, Benjamin Harris, Aaron Smith, Thomas Vanwormer, Jeremy Hewitt, Steve Boteler, Bobby Neble, Woodrow Williams, Michael Myers, Corey Keller, Genesis Shellock etc. etc.

Allen Harris (Abbeville Ga.) and Benjamin Harris (Chester GA) are sergeants in G.B.G. and they know the "Business" of rapes, mayhem and mess in the prisons... Jeffrey Allen Walker, Justin Howell and Jeff Glen Howell can talk to Caleb Peek and Cody Sheldon... You in the schools, churches and colleges gotta listen. I'm writing to "Jordan" at Rocketown in Nashville Tennessee. I am talking to Keith Mullennix and Christian. I am writing to Frank Carter, Ralph Cannon, Scott Tatum and Brian Hawn etc. Stay away today! You've got to stay away!

... I struggled with whether or not I should write graphic details in this tome. I've watered most stuff down and diluted it because of the "kids" I knew would be reading. But God has a way of getting you to see his 'point' in the midst of struggle. And it seemed that from out of nowhere Dr. C. Solis walked up to me and asked how the book was coming. And I explained my struggle with keeping it P.G. etc. And Dr. Solis stated that he disagreed. "First you've gotta realize how controversial the title (K.K.K.) is. It's a stroke of genius but it's also ostentatious. Some 'parents' won't get past the 'title'. But if it has substance kids will promote it for you. And if kids want to read K.K.K. they will read K.K.K.... Don't water it down. You need to tell the story as it has never been told. I've treated 9 year old gang members. I've treated 8 year old rapists and 13 year old killers. If they can rape at that age they can read a candid book".

... And then came the movie "Precious". When I saw Monique on Oprah I knew everything I needed to know. This movie is being viewed by families and kids all over the country. And there is more profanity, sex and drugs in "Precious" than I'll ever write about... "Lee Daniels called me and told me 'I need you to be a monster". Monique told Oprah of the producer......."I read and by the time I got to page ten I said what is this?" Monique said. Will Smith told Tyler Perry that he had to talk to Monique so he could find out "how she went that deep, raw and real" in the role. Monique says she (too) was molested by her brother Gerald...

"Precious"? She's obese, illiterate and pregnant by her incestuous dad who raped her. Monique said "An Asian brother said to me 'Monique I am Mary Jones. I was Mary Jones to my brother and to my sister". And he broke down and started sobbing... I hugged him and told him 'now go get yourself some help'". Monique said "Molestation and incest happens every hour of every day in the week. We sweep it under the rug and people are hurting. I'm not talking about kid siblings experimenting. I'm talking about 18, 19 and 25 year olds molesting 3 and 4 year olds... I wanted to do the role with a realness.

... We always try to dress it up". Monique said "I wanted to be very honest and very real".... In the movie Monique tells her daughter "I should have aborted yo (sic) ass! You fat bitch! I should've aborted yo fat ass. I knew U wasn't gon be nuthin bitch!"

... Words sting and hurt. They'll build you up or tear you down. And many of you reading right now. You had negativity injected into your psyche as a kid. And when mean and cruel words are introduced into your mind(s) by parents, teachers or by other trusted adults. Some people hear those words for the rest of your lives... I wanna thank God for letting me see Monique. And I thank Monique for letting me see Mary Jones. And Mary Jones told me to be real, raw and honest in this book. And I won't hold back and I can't play games....

On 11/6/09 who ran (on stage on the 'Ellen' show) in a pair of underwear and a suit jacket? And he gave away a Gibson guitar? Who was that? I want him in G.B.G....

Nathan Burris, murdered his girlfriend. He blew her head off!... If Chris Brown does not get some serious help he's the next next Nathan Burris.... Did yall really look at the photos of Rihanna? Come on yall... If that had been Shanteeka or Shanteecia I would beat the hell out of Chris. And violence (is never the answer!) begets violence!....

"I saw no soul in his eyes. It was just blank. Like he was blacked out when he hit and beat me" Rihanna stated. And that sounds like "a psychopath" a G.B.G. Special consultant stated. And "Can you imagine Chris in drag? He'd be sweet. I'd f--- him in his a--!" Donny (Sobriquet) stated. And "Chris Brown was known for giving good head when he was 11, 12, 13 and 14 years old" one of my Virginia sources stated. (Remember I lived in Virginia for years!).... "Chris was an undercover gay boy. We all knew that. But that fool could sang (sic)". ... I have no problem believing the claim. I can't count the under cover, on the down low gay boys I've met and seen in action; in prisons. And I am 99 1/2% certain that if Chris had come to prison (as he should have with his coward ass) Chris would have been swopping out (AKA Flip Flopping, AKA "69"ing) with his cell mate... AKA suite (sweet) mate...

If there is any young man out there (reading - and I know you are) hitting or beating on your girlfriend - go get help! Email me and I'll put you in contact with Dr. Solis, Dr. Curren or Dr. Duran etc. Call Dr. Phil, a pastor or somebody etc., but get yourself some help. And get help now! ... It is abnormal, against the law, unnatural, a sin and asinine to hit a woman. A woman! ... second chances? I believe in second chances. Hell, I believe in 3rd, 4th and even 5th chances. But I also believe in justice! treatment! counseling!... Somewhere I read that no man is above the law.... They should've locked his ass up! If Chris had been poor (black, white or brown) he would be in prison right now (in T-shirt and panties!)! I am not a hater. I drink Gatorade, not Haterade! I've had a couple of dollars before. I've been in Limos (hell ask "Love Limousine" in Richmond Virginia), Jags and in Rolls. I've enjoyed a tad bit of 'celebrity' in my life. I congratulate success! Tyler Perry! Mo' Nique! Chris Gardner! Lebron.... etc. I love to see successful people. But when they are dysfunctional etc. they often kill or die... "No soul" Rihana says. "I saw no soul" in Chris' eyes.... I'm in a factory of soullessness. And (I love Whoopi, Sherri etc. etc., but I'm more aligned with Elizabeth Hasselback on this one).... Chris Brown should be in state prison for what he did to that lady. And I guaran(fuc----)tee you if it was your daughter, sister or momma that he assaulted you would Holla "Lock his ass up!"... And - (since I do believe in second chances etc.)

in prison Chris should be reading, meditating, praying and getting counseling. And after thinking about his crime for 3 or 4 years he should (then) be released from prison and given a "second chance".... He had a great lawyer. And I'm not speaking of Gerragos either. I'm speaking of Steve Sadow... Bobby Lee Cook and Murray J. Janus both speak well of lawyers and justice. And I .... I'm just sickened to my stomach by what this scumbag (AKA Chris) did to a female. And young girls (silly girls) have the nerve to run to court yelling "we love you Chris". Gloria Allred should have ran to court (with a 'grip' of women) yelling "we love Rihanna"!

And inside university of predators (AKA Hades) there is a gang (as I mention in another section of this tome) of support for Chris. "That bi-ch shouldn't have ..." one "boy" (40 year old boy) told me. And... misogynistic thugs! Gets on my last nerves. How dare you call yourself a man? If you've got to fight, fight a man... And (even though I didn't write this tome for convicts I wrote it for previcts hoping to prevent the con from being victed. I wrote it for kids...) You boys sitting on your ass who were beating women on the streets need to hang yourself!... No! I'm kidding. Don't hang yourself but do hang your head in shame. And go get help! You must go get help! Talk to a chaplain, counselor, psyche tech, psychologist or a psychiatrist. Be honest and open. (If it was a crime A. Know the statute of limitations. And B. Anything said to a psychologist or psychiatrist is doctor/patient confidential... Before you open up ask the doctor "if" it is 'confidential'. But having the horror heard helps heal you!)... Get some help my brothers. There is something wrong with you. If you look at Tyra Banks, Beyonce, Paris, Angelina Jolie etc. and you say "bit-- I'll beat your ass". Rather than "I wanna make love to you ..." something is wrong with you. You need help!

... I see grace, class, sensuality and....

I can be walking by certain ladies and not only do I get a 'crook' in my neck turning around to try to see how she walks away. But... I've got to admit that there have been a couple (okay maybe a lil more than a couple) of times in "church"... I was minding my own business and worshiping Jehovah. And I was sincere and I went to church with God on my mind. Yet a Beyonce look alike will walk by me and I'll turn... How can we beat a woman? Their faces and scars will heal. But the gallery of one half million women who are battered by men can tell you the scars inside don't heal so quickly. They have flashbacks and they ache. Their minds hurt and they're spirits are broken.

... Chris Brown received 6 months community service. The judge should resign. The judge and the D.A. folded like a cheap suit... I wanna talk to Craig Hutto, Gerald Morrow (principal at Paul Robeson High School in Englewood Illi.) and Attorney Mark Anderson. I wish I could've talked to Quran Jones or given him this book before he beat Scott Hawkins to death with a baseball bat. It's not just 'guns'. It's hammers, bats, rock and sticks. It's not just here but over there and everywhere. It's in schools, CSU Sac and it's coming back. If we don't "do" something forthwith.... C.O. S. Morrow (a youngster) just came to New Folsom from Pelican Bay. We want S. Morrow in G.B.G. C.O. D. Kelley and all the youngsters. Kids can relate to them. And since we are supposed to be "rehabilitating" let's get busy. Gage Christensen (Utah), Austin Sisneros and Daniel Sample have got to come forth. Tanvir Kapoor, Austin Wolfe, Winfred Roberson (Davis Sr. High School principal), Billy Bell and Jakob Karr must come forth. G.B.G. is on the move and we won't stop till we make a "change"... "I know I've hurt you. I know I've lied to you" Michael told his dad (Rick) on Dr. Phil. It was on the first week of November in 2009. The topic was "risky teen trends". Michael (has his mother's eyes and he just wept and wept on the show. He (19) cannonballs drugs with alcohol. Michael grew up on the 'right' side of the tracks. And his parents are upper middle class... There are so many (mostly white) rich kids addicted to the same oxycontin etc. that Michael is taking. He's played his parents like a fiddle. He needs a metamorphosis. He's using and dealing. His brain is altered and his responses are altered. He's a passenger on the drug train. He can't stop!

.... Michael started by taking ADHD pills to increase his alertness in school. And he's just as addicted as a crack addict. And he admits that many "kids in school are using drugs". There is a rich kid prescription drug abuse epidemic in these United States. And you (who are doing it or know someone who is doing it) must get help and break that cycle... La Cienda Treatment Center (in Texas) took Michael in... Yall call Rich Whitman (at La Cienda) and ask him where we can send Michael this book. I want "Michael" to write to me. I wanna hear from James Henderson (Davis CA), Riley Evans and Davis on "The Scholar".... Jonathan Ajar, Shaun White, Chad Sizemore and Derek King we need you too... I want Chaz Wolcott, Christian Dunst and Shawn Hornbeck to help us reach these mangsters. A mangster is a broke (indigent) young gangster.... Collin Finnerty, TI, Joshua Orapello and Michael Hawkins (Petersburg VA.) must come forth and get on the G.B.G. train. We need football players like Joshua Harper, Josh Goldin, Shea Newberry, Dev Patel and Ben (call Ben on Fox 40 - and on 1/12/09) to help us. I want Danny Henson and Caleb Peek to join us. We must do warfare. This is not a test. It is not a "training exercise". What we saw at Columbine (ask Craig Scott) was real. VA. Tech, CSU (Scott Hawkins) and Richmond High School etc. is real. And if you bring me Charles Jackson (Fairview Park, Ohio), Aaron Jackson (Delaware Ohio), Donald Dusk (Akron Ohio), Kirbu Bumpus and Roger Walthorn we'll change the world. This is a moment to institutionalize and internationalize nonviolence.... Greg (UC Dance - his sister is Brandy... on The Price Is Right on 9/30/09), Kirk Johnson (an Arabic scholar), Mike Wilkerson and Sam Fuick need to come on now....

We must take action!.... On March 27, 2009, Los Angeles County agreed to pay $ 7000000 to a youth who was severely beaten at the Barry J. Nidorf Juvenile Hall (Nidorf) in Sylmar, California after the kid was pressured, but refused (a no no), to join a gang.

Raymond Amande, Jr. was viciously and savagely attacked in a recreation room by four gang members after watching a TV show. The room was filled with 37 youths and being supervised by only one staff member, far less than what was required.

Amande's neck was broken as the attack ensued after he was slammed to the cement floor. The lone staff member in the room at the time tried to intervene, but was unsuccessful. There were cameras in the room, which were not operational. Raymond was left a quadriplegic as a result of the horrendous attack.... Raymond's assault follows on the heels of a DOJ (Dept. of Justice) inquiry which found widespread violence, understaffing and severe overcrowding at Nidorf. Raymond used the DOJ's findings in his complaint.

His lawyer (Michael Louis Kelly, of Los Angeles based Kirtland & Packard (Michael Kelly is brilliant and altruistic), said Raymond is "very happy with the settlement". And "it's going to allow him to move on with his life". Raymond, now 20, plans to go to college. If he's reading (don't just plan - you go) Go to College.... The settlement requires the County to pay Raymond $ 3,800,000 upfront, with the remainder being disbursed through periodic installments.

The County must (finally, too late for Raymond and thousands of other kids who didn't have lawyers) improve conditions at its 22 juvenile facilities as a result of the DOJ investigation and Raymond's lawsuit. Improvements include repair of all surveillance cameras... No staff were disciplined in connection with Raymond's attack...

On behalf of the tens of thousands of youths who have been beat, raped, enslaved (sold as property from gang member to gang member etc.) and killed etc. I just want to say Thank you to Michael Louis Kelly and to Raymond. And I want Jason Sutherland, Jeff Allen Walker and Johnny O'Neal to help us to prevent the next Raymond.... This is "it". Not a test! This is the 'Real Deal'! ... Heather Spencer, Justin Frazier, Omar Samy, Max Kiesner and Kyle Evans I need you. I'm looking for Dan Sellery, Daniel Asare and Zach Burkes. I need Zach Severson, Zach Roerig,

Farah Joy and Kyern Bennett... G.B.G. is everywhere. And we need everybody. Our "work" is cut out for us. This is real.... I'm calling Matt, Sean and Aaron Maloney in Green Bay Wisconsin. And I want Shemm, Derrick Flowers and Lee Truex to suit up. Yall put on yo swat team regalia. We are going into these schools and colleges with "this (K.K.K.)" book of seeds. And we will hold psychological triages, educational summits and workshops until we see a change. We need a change. We must have it.... Daniel Coverston? Douglas Stave? Donald Siegfried and Greg Siemen we need you.

... Somebody call Josh Stieber, Timothy Combs and Jerry Wines. Call William Coker and Nick Lamar... Anthony Hancock, Jason Bria and Mayor Romaine Quinn ...

What happened to Raymond happens each and every second, of every minute of every hour of every days. In juveniles, jails and prisons in America! Boys are forced to join gangs, be killed or be toys. This is not an embellishment. Every warden (and jail guard) knows that inmates are bought, sold and raped in prisons daily.... Go talk to Shea Newberry, Brandon Hughes, Jeremy Anthony Lonnick or Joshua Orapello. Craig Gisltrap and Clay can tell you.

... I need Gloria Killian, Sasha Vodnik, Jodie Evans and James Marsden to help us. I am so desperate to "do" this that I am willing to forgive people who wronged me (i.e. James Albert Emslander, "J" and even Phillip Coffee etc.) to get this done. I want bands like "Honor Society" and Living Things to stand with G.B.G.... We can use our pain (tragedy and mistakes etc.) to help others.... Granite Bay High School students and kids at Amador High have got to suit up. Man your battle stations and let's get ready to rumble! I want the quarterback for the football team at Rocklin High School to help us huddle up as we battle illiteracy!

.... Few weeks ago a 14 year old student at Natomas High school carried a loaded gun to school. He told the assistant principal that it was for 'protection'. Hint. Hint. If a 14 year old boy was been abused, bullied and disrespected so much that he feels he needs to take a 'gun' to school etc. something is wrong! It is obvious he (the 14 year old boy) does not feel he can talk to his parents about his pain. Can we (like Mo'Nique said... and yall know she lives in 'my' city now! And my Uncle Gerald Anderson is a friend of hers!) Be real? I am not blaming 'those' parents. I'm sure this 14 year old kid's parents probably love him. I am blaming 'us' adults. When the team can't win you fire the head coach. If the ship sinks the captain dies... It is obvious that this boy felt 'alone'. If he thought he could call up Bishop Flip Flop or Deacon Willie Wonder and get them to intervene, he would have. He did not feel close enough to his teachers (or preachers) or principal, to talk about it. God bless the assistant principal who found the gun. My question is if 'we' had watched (monitored and examined) his interactions (days and weeks prior) with others (i.e. whoever he felt he needed protection from) like 'we' watched him the day 'we' found the gun; could we have prevented him from feeling he needed the gun? And where did he get the gun? Can we go deeper? Last time I checked there were no kids manufacturing guns. And the last time I went into a gunstore the owner was an adult.... Chris Biele has a co-worker (John) with a son named Zach. We need Zach in G.B.G. ...

So I must tell superintendents like Jonathan P. Raymond, Chancellor Rhee and Mayor Kevin Johnson etc. that I'm still an American and (like Paul) although I'm in chains I have something to give, to teach and to preach. And maybe 'just one' 14 year old boy who is thinking about getting his daddy's gun and taking it to school next week etc. Just maybe he'll hear (some chatter) about some black dude (whom they say likes white women) in jail (on Myspace, and Facebook etc.) who is a (G.B.G. Baby Boy) Gang Banger for God! And this 14 year old boy will hear that "dude is black and in jail in California. And yet a white (Peter Andrist yo) dude in Switzerland works for the black convict. And he published his own tome (on the down low) called "K.K.K". And a lot of folks have blackballed the book. But dude wrote each and every word of this book and...." Maybe instincts, spirit, God, faith or prayer etc. will lead that boy to pick up 'this' book. And as he's flipping through he'll see a 'Name' (yall know I got names 4 u) or a phrase that catches his eye and he'll find courage, strength, help, influence or inspiration on one of the pages (or in one of the sentences) in this book. And he'll decide not to steal or buy the gun. He may decide (i.e.) "damn, it's some crazy crap going on in jail and I ain't trying to go there. Let me call a hotline, log on to Dr. Phil 'teen talk', call Dr. Curren, Dr. Jarman or look on the G.B.G. Facebook site for help. I'll go to my police chief it I have to. But I ain't gonna do nuthin that might land me in there with Marvin Johnson!"... Marvin grabbed a flower one time and was gonna give it to Mrs. Kennedy (she was a lowly correctional officer back then. And she worked in E.O.P.). Another C.O. said "I don't think you should give her that flower, inmate Johnson. It may seen over familiar." And Marvin told the C.O. that "if I was gonna be over familiar, I'd give the flower to 'Buffy' (AKA C.O. Davis - a 'man'). I don't like women". And I thought (to myself) "hell you've been known to cut two men's heads off so if I were Buffy I'd be careful"....

Yall wanna meet Marvin, Booty Bandit and.... Come on in. You're old enough to carry a gun to school, you're old enough to read the real deal about what happens in here. It is madness.

And I'm in a fox hole (like apostle Paul) telling you to get up. I know you've been injured. Some of you have been mistreated, misled, molested and.... Garrett McCain, Jonathan Davis and Joshua Harper can all tell you that sometimes U gotta play (when U R) hurt. This book is the huddle. This is the formation. "Huddle" up and/or "fall" in. Come to attention. This tome is your "Distance" learning. What if you were in Marine Bootcamp (in San Diego) and you were gonna be deployed. You are 17 years old and on your first day of Bootcamp. Fresh outta Folsom High school (or Locke, Lodi or wherever). And yet, in five or six months you will be going to Iraq or Afghanistan to fight in a war. Wouldn't it be priceless to get missives, anthologies or a tome written (unedited and unpolished) from a soldier (on active duty) who "writes" you from the war zone while stationed in Iraq!

Well, I am a flamed soldier and I'm stationed in a maximum security California penitentiary. Many of the folk you have seen (and 'see') on the news have lived right here (on this base) with me.... Eric and Lyle. Henson and Bardo!

... Domingo Garcia, Wally, Acosta and Mike Bunnell etc. I am in the ultimate war-zone. One could argue that you are not trying to come 'here' where I'm stationed. I must disagree... Michael (the oxycontin addict) is trying to come 'here' or die. He'll be (end up) in the cemetery or the penitentiary. Rick (his dad) and Dr. Phil told him that. And I'm writing to the hundreds of thousands (if not millions) of Michaels out there who are using, abusing and dealing. And I am an expert on where you will be deployed (destroyed) to if you kids in grade school (on the potential road to Harvard) boys and girls.... Imagine the chancellor or president of Morehouse college writing a book and sending it to lil black boys in Perry Homes or Bankhead Court in Atlanta.... Dr. Lewis Yablonsky has (I repeat) written 20 books on gangs. He is the foremost expert on youth gangs. And in a telephonic interview he told me "You are the authentic expert. You are a therapist. An experience therapist". I'm writing to Maxwell Hanger, Brett Jolliff, Adam and Brendan (on Eco company) and to you. And I'm stationed in Hades and may never see daylight again. And I wrote K.K.K. not to proclaim my innocence. Not to campaign for me. Not to seek an award. But to take all the clothes off the prison. I came to lift up the blinds, pull back the drapes, turn the light on and show you (not the Hollywood version. Not the 'prison break' fiction!) what I see, touch, feel and hear each and every day. And to say to you that you can do it too. If you just drop out of school. IF you use or sell drugs. IF you beat up women and join a gang etc. etc. You can wake up tomorrow morning and say "Darn I hope my celly goes to the yard today so I can mas--rbate".

... Or maybe not........ If you're (Eric Menendez, Michael Henrickson or about 1.7 million other inmates) lucky you may be saying "I hope my celly stays in today so we can freak". Damn!.... You may be saying "I hope he does not rape me again today! Darn my asshole is sore... When I wiped I was bleeding today".

... "Michael", "Chris", "Brett" and John Q. student, John P. drop-out, John P. meth addict or John P. gang banger etc. this could (very well) be the content of your dialogue, monologue or 'self talk' tomorrow if you don't get off the drug train, the drop-out, illiteracy or the gang train... The cycle of youth gangs and school violence is so horrible that Gloria Allred (who's always anti-inmate and often anti-man) encourages G.B.G. to tell you the truth. Gloria Allred? consorting with a jailbird? It must be serious!

... I've not visited or resided in half as many prisons as the author of the book of Philippians (the book of Galatians, Ephesians and Colossians etc. etc... the Apostle Paul) but I've been around the prison block and back. And I'm far too inquisitive, manipulative and ambitious (lol) to sit back and "believe" the "hype". I've always (ask my teachers, professors, principal Aaron Fernander or even Ambassador Andrew Young) needed to know. I read for enjoyment and for excitement. But I also read because I wanted to know. I just could not stand being ignorant about anything.... I learned (and played) the game of football (in school) because I wanted to know what a "Huddle", "Field goal", "punt" and a "touch-down" was. I became an athletic trainer and learned First-Aid, taping ankles and condition training because I didn't wanna be a "water boy" and.... Coach Appling me "I'll let you help me coach and condition the girls basketball team "if" you "know" about basketball....

Latasha Way was a cheerleader! So was Allison Brownlee. And they practiced right by the gym where the girls practiced basketball. And "ough" (she was bad) played basketball. Plus Mrs. Appling had a nice body. And all I had to do to hang out with, train, condition and render First-Aid to the ladies was "know" basketball?.... I interrogated (athletic director) coach Coffee, Coach James and (my favorite coach) coach Willie Jordan. I read books about basketball. I immersed my mind in the "rules" of the game etc. And two months later I reported to the new gym where there were 21 sistas in shorts and t-shirts.

.... Hallelujah! I called plays! I refereed practices. I sneaked a peep (sporadically) in the locker room and shower.... I .... I ..... loved basketball.... I made myself indispensable...

And in Hades I hate it. I literally despise this place. And in order to function with the kind of "personality" which I have I had to "know" why it is like it is. Who comes here? Why do we come here? Who works here and why? What makes this place like it is? And why do people get out and return to this all 'male', vicious, violent and dark atmosphere? Why do guys (already in jail because of substance abuse and/or sales) use alcohol, weed, heroin, cocaine, methadone and... Right here?.... The guy with HIV who got out of prison on Halloween was drinking, slamming dope and snorting pills 8 hours before he went home... More than 70% of us are hooked (right now) on alcohol, heroin or pills. We are what (who) Rick's son Michael (that boy got his momma's eyes!) looks like two years from now if he does not get off the drug train. We are what (who) Brett and Chris (of Dr. Phil Fame) look like a year from now if they keep on boozing, smoking and...

Scott Johnson was my "friend". (so was James Nesmith and John Garvin etc.). Unfortunately Scott did "time" at Phillips C.I. in Buford Georgia. Scott (I'm looking 4 him) has something to say about 'prison politics'. He can tell you (so can Nesmith, Mike Fowler and Christopher Rousche) what it's like to be 'hated' on for 'having' things in prison. Hated by 'Chuck' who snitched.... Hated by Harvey Lashler and.... John Garvin and Billy York were at Valdosta C.I. .... Billy lives in the city that Rev. Hosea Williams and I marched in for disallowing 'blacks' to live there (in the 90's!).... I still have personal missives written to me from Billy, James Lewis (who was at Alto), John Jodie Bear, Hartline and Scott etc....

... Keith Jerrolds, Kenneth Chandler, David Joiner and Roger White etc. (I have letters from them all... letters from Spence Palmer, James Keith Blackwell, Sean Farmer, Wayne Dillard and Francis Ronald Wright etc.)... I know these dudes and we (G.B.G.) need those dudes... I have 9 letters from Curtis Sykes and Curtis can help us...

I'm still looking for senior Chief Petty Officer Franklin and Beuchamp. I wanna find my Bootcamp buddy (Coffman from Floyd Illinois, Lopez, Redwine, Duane F. Hall etc.) Coffman.... I need those sailors and I need them now! ... I had so many photos of me and my buddies in bootcamp at RTCC in San Diego and Conrad Stole them. I'd give anything for photos of me and my boys (Coffman, Lopez, Hall etc.) in Bootcamp!.... seems like it was just yesterday that we were hazing Coffman about his "ass" and Lopez about his "lips". It seems like it was yesterday that I was in my fifth week of Naval Bootcamp training. I sneaked on my dress Blues one night and stopped "Seaman Recruit Hall". I pulled his demerit chits and I yelled at him. I made him do pushups and... It was ten minutes before I revealed to Duane Fred Hall that he'd been punk'd. I had no more authority over him than you have over your classmate(s)... I need to talk to my boy Hall yall...

Who would have ever thought that after the incisive, divisive and bitter campaign between Al Gore and George Bush that "they" (Bush and Gore) would ever come together on any issue? Even though Bush stole that election.... A few months later we saw Bill Clinton, Bush SR., Al Gore and George Bush etc. We saw democrats and republicans etc. sitting in the same church on a Sunday morning. George and Al were joining hands, singing songs and praying prayers; because America (9/11) had been attacked!! It was a state of emergency!! There was no bickering or partisanship. It was a national state of emergency!... I've come with a sense of urgency to announce that there is a state of emergency (and although he'll disagree with some of my 'propaganda' in this tome etc. Arne Duncan will agree with me on this!) and an urgency at Gurn High School, Natomas, Lodi, Richmond High and at Locke. And this is a critical issue affecting blacks, whites, students, parents and teachers. Kids are blowing up schools all across the country. And we (adults) are sittin on our asses debating gay marriage and arguing over whether or not a kid can pray in school. But they prey in schools! Took prayer out and put gangs in....

This is a state of Emergency! And just as The Bush's, Clintons and the Gores came together after they saw those planes knock down the twin towers in New York. Just like T.D. Jakes was being interviewed on CNN (not TBN) and (in the middle of the interview) they asked the Bishop to stop and "say a prayer for our nation"... Just as blacks and whites all came together after 9/11. We (prisoners and prison guards, Pauls, Sauls, Cops and Robbers, students, teachers, preachers and parents etc.) have all got to come together. There has been a "switch" while we were sleeping. And the Gang Bangers and dope distributors have gotten (you) our children!.... Phillip Garrido (the molesters, the dealer, the shotcaller etc.) has got our sons and daughters imprisoned and entrapped right before our very eyes. And just as Jaycee suffered from Stockholm's syndrome etc. You (teens and tweenies) have begun to identify with and to defend your enemies (the dealers, the gangs and the molesters) as if they were your friends. You might wanna do what Rihana suggested girls in abusive relationships do" "F--k love!..." And I say "F--k how much you love that high or love that adrenaline rush! If you love that booty hole of yours and you don't want it rammed by a chorus of predators etc. you better get off the drug and/or gang train"... Do you hear what I'm saying? Michel Brewer! The Honors (Albert) student beat to death by a teen gang in Chicago! The student (Scott Hawkins) who had his head bashed in by a baseball bat welded by a teenager (Q. Jones)! The 15 year old girl who was savagely gang (train) raped by a vicious mob of boys while two dozen people looked - on. Alex King! Derek King! Sasha Groene! Haleigh Cummings! Elizabeth Smart! The 14 year old boy carrying the gun to school. The boy too embarrassed to tell his mother he's scared to go to school. The boy who is conflicted and... The school violence etc. requires us to stop bickering. Stop the partisanship and politics. Stop arguing over who is or is not 'qualified' to serve, to reach and to teach. And 'we' must come together and stop this madness! Let's be clear; an emergency is here... We must bombard youth centers, schools, colleges, the internet and "walls" etc. with the contents of this book. We need Dr. Phil, Dr. Gardere, Dr. Pinsky and .... We have Dr. Bill Cosby and Dr. Alvin Poussaint. We (G.B.G.) have Dr. Curren, Solis, Heitkamp etc. etc. and we need you and you too. It is going to require a united effort and a pragmatic strategy. We need young, energetic, computer savvy youths like Justin Berry, Ryan Hreljac and Benjamin Alexander. We need John Butterfield (winner of the G.B.G./HEART youth of the month award & stipend), Omar Samy and Omar Samaha...

This is a clarion call and a trumpet blowing in your ear. I'm calling upon Brendan and Adam at ECO Company. I've got work for you (Adam and Brendan) to do....

I need to reach Taylor Francis. He's a brilliant, influential and an articulate Menlo Park High School student. Taylor knows "the power we all have to make a difference". Taylor gives talks about global warming to schools. He says 'the light bulb went off in my head after I watched 'An Inconvenient Truth' by Al Core". He began a letter writing campaign and started his own speaking tour. Taylor knows that our biggest problems can also be our biggest opportunities. He gesticulates like a preacher. He looks like my pal (long lost) Clay Hollifield. Taylor says "schools are a unique community in which to effect change". He says "people listen to young people. And Taylor excited me so much that I want Heather to find him in Menlo Park so I can send his cause a check. Taylor may also receive our youth of the month award (??) in the future... We are calling Brendan, Adam, Taylor Francis, Daniel Sample, Cody Sheldon, Austin Sisneros, Austin Wolfe and C.J. Sheron etc. We need your input, knowledge, ideas and your 2 cents today!....

"So this is our moment to live up to the trust that kids have placed in us. Even when it's hard. Especially when it's hard" I told the G.B.G. team in a "special" session. I borrowed those powerful words from President Obama... (Just tween (sic) U me N the door post - I borrow from Obama, Dr. Phil, Dr. Yablonsky, Dr. Curren, Dr. Duran and Dr. Heitkamp etc. quite often)... If you had educated, successful and brilliant (licensed) psychiatrists (on call) like Jennifer Heitkamp, C. Solis and Franklin Curren etc. all of whom are that I want medical doctors etc. would you not question, interrogate and hang on to their every word? It would be presumptuous, arrogant and pompous of me to try to take credit for the psychological dinners (data) you're eating (reading) in this tome. I might be qualified to deliver some basic psychological ??? (page 946) or perhaps some psychiatric snacks. But to sit down and prepare a psychological feast such as the one's you've been able to dine upon in "K.K.K." is above my expertise. The ranting, raving, tautology, "names" and propaganda are all "me". But...)

We need to reduce the level of stress in our kids. And we need to process the traumatic experiences of kids' pasts. We always state that kids are resilient. Yet, they are less resilient than we assume. They lack matured 'coping mechanisms'. Early trauma and stress decreases concentration and contributes to accidents etc. Early childhood trauma (literally) weakens the immune systems and shortens life span... That? Is A. Duran PhD, not me you see...

Kate Winslett is getting on my nerves. Kate is a pill popper who definitely used mega dieting and pills to lose work. She rarely ever went to a gym. She needs to be in a rehab.... 'Yoens' is from Hamburg, Germany. In 93 he was working (or visiting) in D.C. It could have been 1994. We met near Dupont Circle. We were supposed to meet again and I was late. I never saw Yoens again. Does anyone (Sam Altman? Justin Berry?). In late 1994 Peter Andrist and I played volley ball (I was the only brutha!) with 3 or 4 guys from Germany. They spoke only High German. We even took a photo with them. And I don't know either one of their name(s)... They were ABB employees, in Richmond Virginia. We played at 'waterside' apartments on Iron Bridge... Ask ABB who (3 or 4 guys who were 19 or 20 back then) worked for ABB in Richmond etc. and where from Germany? ABB has to keep records. These guys wanted a 'ride' in my limousine.... G.B.G. needs them right now.... Urijah Faber, Steve Coffman and David Hartline etc. I need you. Spence Palmer, Phillip Coffee and... I need you... Attorney Brian Oxman and F.Lee Bailey I need you... Attorney Richard Rubin, Abby UpteGraff (Roseville) and C.J. Swanson (Placerville Ca.) we need you too.

I want Alicia Holland and all the kids in Richmond CA to come stand with me. Let's shine a light on kids. We can do this.... Captain Burgess? I'm not certain about the last name. I know the last name begins with a "B" and in 1996 he was a captain with the Chesterfield County P.D. Back when Jeff Green was a sergeant. I knew the Captain's son and they lived down the street from 'Courthouse Green' apartments. I need Chad Sherman, David Reynolds (my boy) or David Proctor to locate them....

The Honorable Judge S. James Otero accepted a "bribe" in the Girls gone wild'. Joe Francis case. Judge Otero accepted a $ 50,000 bribe to give Joe probation. The 'cover story' is that they discovered a witness had lied to them on the eve of trial. He now gets probation. I challenge the Judge to take a polygraph test at my expense. Judge Otero is a crook! ... I suspect some hanky panky in Chris Brown's case but I can't prove it.

... I reach out to John Griffin (CSU SAC), the Schoettler-Neufeld tire retread center owners, Devin Rio, Nicholas Taxera and Tadd Carr. Let's get ready to rumble! We can do this. John Romesburg, John DeCarro, Kris T. Jernell, Bill Dallas, Brent Keith Smit, Brent Depriest, Hunter Brown and Preston MCvey etc. come forth. Silence is betrayal! 1,2 million students drop-out of school every year. 1.2 million kids drop out yearly. And I would bet 1:1 of the 1.2 will end up in prison! Where is our sense of urgency? I need kids who do social networking to put the word out. Scott Yates, Michael Percelli, Brent Depriest and Brent Keith Smith we need you. We need Dr. Frank Bailey and Nick Pelham. With more than 75% of kids in Detroit dropping out of school we must issue a state of Emergency! Giovanni Alvarez, Jerry Wines, Jeremiah Rodriguez, Will Coker and Jose Zuniga... Sandy Close and Paul Twaragowski we need you.... Give me Ryan Hreljac and Taylor Francis and we (just Ryan, Taylor and me) will change the world... our biggest problem (the broken educational system that leads to kids killing kids) is our biggest opportunity. And we (Taylor, Clay Hollifield, Maxwell Hanger etc.) won't let anyone steal history from us. We'll will be history, not just see history. We will read, write, study, pray and live up to a high standard. "We" are Eagles, not chickens'! ...

I want Jack Pawlowski, Timothy Kwasniewski and Lt. David Shook to help us to heal the world... When an ice skater is not winning championships she/he changes coaches. Jeff Buttle, Brian Joubert and our Buddy J. Weir can all attest to the fact that if they don't skate well they check the coaching. If a football or basketball team is not winning they change coaches. When a boxer loses he changes trainers. So since our schools are failing we must look at the "teaching"... I love (honor and I respect) teachers and professors. I've always advocated and suggested we should "pay" teachers more!

But if a school, class or students are failing we must check the teaching. And 'if' the teaching is subpar improve (retrain, mentor and motivate) the teachers or fire them. I hate to go there but we are talking about the education(s) of our children. And you are our future and our present. I recommend we dispatch 'reading doctors' into these trailer parks, hoods, ghettos and barrios. We need to get college kids, grad students etc. to spend a couple of hours per week and on weekends in these underperforming schools teaching kids the power and the excitement of reading!... Bring me Jack Pawlowski, Kyle Love and C.J. Sheron etc. I want those who are considered 'in' as well as the 'out' crowd. I want geeks, freaks, nerds, jocks and studs. Everybody can be great, because everybody can serve. Everyone has something to teach!... I keep hearing Mo'nique telling me (only in my imagination) to "keep it real Sherm, keep it real! You might not get on Oprah. You might not ever get outta jail. But if the damn book keeps one kid out of hell (jail) your job is done! Talk about what goes on inside those walls. If kids can read about it in a newspaper or on the internet it ought to be in your book". My imaginary Mo'nique told me "this is the book of your life. You've gotta be authentic. Be a priest. Be a prophet! Tell us what you see. Take us there where you are embedded!". It seems that I can hear (almost literally) Rev. Hosea Williams (and anybody who knew him would know these are his words! Ask Ambassador Young!) telling me "Rev. Manning some of them white folks will never accept yo black ass. Look at how many white folks you (Sherman) know who hated my guts. I was an "alcoholic", a "womanizer" and a "crook" in their opinion. But an opinion is like an asshole. Everybody got (sic) one". I hear Rev. Williams (AKA "Doc") telling me "you will always be a 'thug', a 'crook' or a 'rapist' (a Jacob, a Clark Kent, a Joseph) to some of them. But to many you'll be an "experience therapist" (an Israel, a superman and a 'prince' of Egypt or America etc.). Those who hated me and wrote nasty, mean and bitter news-stories etc. about me - Rev. Manning they never stopped me. I was still a civil rights giant! And Atlanta, Georgia and America is a better place because of Hosea Williams (and Andy, and Malcolm, and Martin etc.). You have got some believers. Just write the damn book as if you was (sic) writing for Didymas (Thomas - "twin") or an audience of one. Don't sell out! Don't water it down. Tell it Rev. Manning tell it".

Peter Andrist told me that "Marc (his name for me), we've learned that you can't walk on water. But still you are the best swimmer (that we know) in the American prison system. You are brilliant"...

Peter told me "Michelangelo and Rembrandt were great painters and they used a brush. You paint pictures with your mouth, words and that pen".

I wanna talk to Phillip Banks. He's the President of the New York chapter of 100 black men of America. And he heads 'the Eagle Academy' which is a school for boys that produces scholars. Kids will be what they see. And this tome is that clarion call to all teachers, entrepreneurs, prisoners, judges, prosecutors, students and parents to man up and respond to the crisis. Don't react; the media reacts reflexively! And after they (react) jump on the latest school incident or predicament etc. they pack up and move down the street to the next best tragedy.

Beverly Bond is a DJ and Founder of "Black Girls Rock". We want Beverly on our team... Phil Strickland is CEO of Manchester Bidwell' and he almost didn't make it out of poverty, hopelessness and the hood. He almost didn't make it to college. But as he gave a recent commencement speech he told the Dean to "Don't give up on the poor kids. They might be the commencement speaker one day".

Mentoring is a way of transferring power, value and responsibility... Rev. Hosea Williams and Ambassador Andrew Young mentored me. Rev. Moses Lee Raglin, Dr. Fred Allman Jr., Uncle Melvin Jackson and James Scott Manning mentored me. And yall think I'm a mess now cause I'm in jail? If these great men had not deposited wisdom, knowledge, encouragement and a love for God into my spirit I'd be dead!...

We have got to actualize the words of this tome into real life human beings. I need teachers like Ben Cook, Joshua Costa, David Levin and Marua Collins to help us actualize this rhetoric. We need Faisal Saleh and Taylor (out in Menlo Park) to help us to plant the seeds of "K.K.K." into schools and colleges around the world.

Cody Sheldon is a brilliant young (amateur) filmmaker. Cody likes to make Horror Movies. Well I tell Cody that Hades is the house of horrors and a citadel of anger. Come collaborate with Dr. Solis, my team and I and let's do a horror film for students. Let's do this. Bring me Cody, Lee Daniels, Alex Blench and my boy Brett Jolliff and let's make a movie! Yall call Will Smith and tell him I said "Hello", but tell em I'm the Tyler Perry of the prison Chittlin circuit and I don't go for a lot of "re-writes". We must tell it like it 'tis'. And as Mo'nique would say "keep it real".

... I want u 2 learn how 2 release your spiritual dopamine. If we can figure out a way to teach people to release spiritual endophins and tap into the spiritual dopamine that folks 'feel' when T.D. Jakes is preaching etc. We will end the need for nicotine, weed, meth and coke. I'm keepin it real yall. Derek Hough, Aaron Carter, Garrett McCain and Matthew Clark (S. Bend Indiana) etc. I'm talking to you....

I know how to do it. I know how to reach it. But I'm less qualified to teach it... Psychiatrists (trust me, I've had hundreds of discussions on this subject with Dr. Solis, Dr. Heitkamp, Dr. Curren, Dr. Chen and Dr. Courdy etc.) call it "mania". And there is a level of dangerousness in which folks who are called manic depressive or "Bi-polar" (i.e. Mike Tyson and many other talented persons) get out of control. They'll go on spending sprees, use drugs and.... But prior to reaching the 'danger zone' there is a level of energy, creativity and positivity which one can manipulate and actualize etc. I draw upon this pool of creativity, energy and optimism to speak, to write, to organize, orchestrate and to strategize. Super energy can be transformed into super intelligence. Just as mentoring is a way of transferring power etc. etc. This dopamine can transfer creativity. However, one needs psychiatric and psychological monitoring and mentoring in order to develop and control this 'energy'. The challenge is to find an expert (i.e. a C. Solis MD. and a Jennifer Heitkamp MD. etc.) who is not atheist or agnostic. Because (as I've personally been blessed to discover and to learn) an atheistic belief system discounts and disbelieves in a father (Jehovah) who's able and willing to put His "super" on our "natural". An atheistic view cannot fathom a man, boy or girl being able to go into a spiritual "phone booth" and transforming into a superman or superwoman...

But my big momma (Clara Jackson) used to go into her 'sewing room' on Wimberly Road and start singing. She'd be praying and singing "will the circle be unbroken". And she'd sing "come and go to that land where I'm bound... I got a mother in that land..." And Big momma would sing the Holy Ghost up in that 'sewing room' and in that house. She would walk in (the 'room') one way and leave out another way. And... My grand momma (AKA "momma", AKA "Cat") Dollie Mae Manning would be fixing hair. (She's an expert cosmetologist) and standing with her right foot propped up on her left leg. And... Later on Cat would go into her bedroom and bow down at the foot of her bed. And she'd be talking to God about her family. And her children. And when she would come out of her bedroom she (like Big momma) would be superwoman. It took me almost 40 years to realize that my Clark Kent is my Didymas. My Clark Kent is my Jacob, my Saul, my supplanter, my conman and my trickster. The dude (Didymas! Didymas! Didymas!) who abandoned Stella and broke her heart! Clark Kent! The dude who left (one of the biggest mistakes of my life) Yvette Lewis (AKA African "Queen") was Clark Kent. And I must 'fast', pray and meditate to get enough "manpower" to prevent the "Jacob" in me from sabotaging the "Israel" in me. I gotta spend "time" with the Lord in my "phone booth" if I wanna be "superman" in my speaking, my preaching and my writing. And young people hear (read) me clearly and meticulously when I tell (write) you that we all have issues! We (you, me, he, we, T.D., Eddie Long and...) All have a Jacob! We all have a Clark Kent or a Lois Lane. You may hide, disguise or masquerade your Clark Kent better than me. But there is a part of you that we don't see. And our prayer needs to be "Lord don't let my Clark get super in so much trouble that I destroy my ... " If Jonah had been high on speed, booze, crack or weed he could have fallen off the ship too early and missed the whale God had prepared for him. And he could have drowned and died. And we would've been writing, teaching and preaching about how Jonah died because he disobeyed God. We probably would be saying God killed him. But it would have been because of the crack (Clark Kent) in Jonah's character leading him to self destruction... Young men, you must (I repeat) - you must do whatever is necessary to tame (control, mentor, teach and reach) the beast (the conman, the supplanter and your Saul) within you. If your Saul leads you too far into the far country you'll mess around and get a life sentence (in jail) or a death sentence (in Hell). You can be dying as Saul and we'll never see you be Paul. The prisons are filled with Sauls! The prisons (I repeat x 25) are filled with Sauls, Clarks, cons, tricksters and .... boys locked into their boyishness etc... 2.5 million plus... 49% aged 7-19 ... (That's more than 1.2 million kids....) who never became Paul. The cemeteries (in Atlanta, Detroit, Germany, Russia, Iraq etc.) are filled with Clark Kents and Lois Lanes who never became superman and superwoman. They refused to surrender and submit to the God that endows men with supernatural (cryptonite) anointings and they died discouraged, broken and bitter... What if Jesus did not return for an audience of one (Didymas)? What if Jesus had listened to the rumors, the police "profiles" etc. which reduced Didymas (AKA Thomas) who had been willing to die for him etc. to Didymas was just "Doubting Thomas". Christ loved Thomas so much that he looked beyond his (Thomas/Didymas) fault and saw his need. He looked beyond his twin (Jacob) and saw the man (Israel) within.... We talk all the time about how your "faith", and "fasting" and "praying" etc. will bring God into your situation. But every now and then Christ will show up in the midst of doubt and discouragement. Sometimes God will show up when we are weak, tired and are discouraged. I'm about to shout right now. Thank you Jesus!

When I was on my deathbed with Valley Fever I began I began to doubt Him. And if church folks had a (sic) known what I was thinking they would have called me "Doubting Sherman". But even while I was hurting, doubting and discouraged God walked into my hospital room. Preachers (church folks) had disregarded and forgotten me for 14 months. With churches on every corner in America not one Deacon Flip Flop or Bishop Willie Wonder came to see me.

... Where was the church? Where were all these orthodox Jews, sanctified Pentecostals, theological seminary attendees etc.? ... I was hungry and you fed me not. I was in prison and on my death bed and not one of you Bible thumpers came to see me... But God came to see me while I was hurting, crying, dying and even doubting. He came to Coalinga Regional Medical Center for an audience of "one"...

Brett Westcott? Cameron Brown? Devin Deuell are you all perusing my words today? You are still important to God. Even though His kids act crazy and act a fool a lot of times; there is nothing wrong with God.

I know we (His children) think "I got the answer, it's one-ness". And "oneness is heresy". And I know we act a fool but God ain't the problem ...

I spoke with a guard the other day whom I've known nearly a year. And I was startled to learn he is a Christian. He is a High School drop-out who read a couple of books and he's now qualified to 'judge' ("ye not that ye be not judged"?)... He told me that "T.D. Jakes is a false prophet and a heretic because he believes in 'oneness'". He then began to "argue" his points. He told me how great America is. He argues, curses and is 'mad' and is arrogant, pompous and persnickety. But he's in seminary and wants to be preacher. He told me that an associate warden (same AW who told me Jakes spoke at a function he attended and he was 'great'. Same AW who was listening to a Jakes tape) agrees with him that Jakes is a heretic. And the word of God is clear (as clear to him that he's right as it is to Jakes that he's right) to him. And according to this guards' beliefs every member of the Potter's House will go to hell. And the tens of millions across the world who believe similar to Jakes will go to hell.

And even though he's abrasive, fanatical, pompous, judgmental and a "know-it-all" he is going to heaven... When I speak with fanatics like him who have the "you're wrong, I'm right! I can prove it with the Bible" attitude etc. I understand (clearly) why so many wars have been fought in the name of religion.... Rather than returning to the cell to prepare credible arguments against his fanaticism etc. I came in and prayed for him....

Dillon Banionis? Andrew Knox? D. Hanning? I have stipends for each of you... I have a couple of things for Dillon Banionis, C.J. Sheron, John Litzler, Josiah Lemming, David Quindt, Pedro Armando Quandt and for Brandon A. Hughes...

"K.K.K." is your call to duty. I'm not looking for lazy ass armchair revolutionaries (i.e. Baby Boomers etc.)! I need squads of door knockers and street teams. Give me some students as committed to G.B.G. as Brett and Cameron (at Purdue) R to their "compliments". Give me ten students (worldwide) half as committed to G.B.G./HEART as Taylor is to warning people about global warming etc. etc. and we will change the face of the planet... Faisal Selah, Trevor Loflin and Alan Rafferty I need you ... Matthew Hashimoto (in Hawaii) and Jake Simpson come on down. Today I'll be coming to your house. I need Matthew, Antwi Akom, Matthew Gerber, Matthew Scheper and Bret Boardwine. If (when) we get Joe and Zach Boardwine, Clayton Johnson and Dave Hamrick to poke, post, blog and chat about our Heart program it is on and cracking. I wanna find lil gangsters like David Topete (AKA 'Youngster'), Hugh Michael Hughes (in Sacto) and hook em up with my Ohio buddy Andy C. (The volunteer) and Shawn Rushforth. And when I'm able to successfully motivate Kevin Greene (Grand Rapids Michigan), Louis Copelin, Michael Perrelli, Bill Dallas, Eric Flores (Roseville) and Kris Stump (Fresno) to go to work etc. we will change these schools. We will stop these killings. We will win! Nicholas Taxera, Daniel Asare and Omar Samy have got to come forth. I won't stop believing. I can't stop believing. We will do this. Our time has come. Our moment is here! We don't give up and we never surrender...

Jenny Triplett, Kat Sanchez, US Mint Green, Attorney Michael Louis Kelly, Gerry Spence, Bobby Lee, F. Lee Bailey and Austin Sisneros will help us get this book to you. Attorney Warren Ballentine and Andrew Bridge will help us.... so will Bob Blasier.

I still want "Angelo" (who was on Fox 40 looking to be adopted in the Sierra Adoption Services. Angelo must be about 17 now.) to get this book. Tylar Whitt, her boyfriend, Esteban Nunez, Chucky Pyle and his buddy "Frank" need this book...

John Kerry? The foolish republicans spent so much time lying with the swift boat ads etc. that they missed the bigger story: Joe Lieberman... Shannon Russell Camosky was one of Joe's gay for pay boys. Mr. Lieberman is well known in Virginia as an (like Mr. Craig... ask David Pruitt! David Perry, Aaron, Lloyd Moran, Scott Moran or Ricky Parnell) under cover gay politician. Ben and John (John was attending medical school.) and John spent a lot of time at "The Frat House" and "Mr. P's". And Sen. Lieberman would be parked outside in a limousine. And Joe frequently paid $ 50,00 to guys to allow him to perform fellatio... D.J. Carpenter, Martin Cheatham, Jerry Wines, Casper (Anthony Voorhees) and Jason Voltaw would have all been irresistible to Mr. Lieberman. Joe would have eaten Tracy Roby up...

Kate Winslet? I have an update on Kate. She was using (in addition to drugs) the tape worm diet. She purposely ingested parasites into her body. This woman is sick....

Marvin Stone, Danny Henson (Richmond VA), Ronald Keith Dunn and Andrew Rauscher etc. have got to help me. I cannot do this alone. And there are too many of you out there like Shaun Rushforth at USC and Tadd Carr etc. etc. there are too many Greg Deekens, C.J. Sherons and Cody Sheldons out there for us "not" to do this. I will locate Ramona and Joseph

Latham (somewhere near Torrance), Steven Moreno Jr. and Billy Bell. We will print up calendars, do photo galleries etc. etc. We will partner with superbly (Brad asked me months ago if G.B.G. would support their "sexiest inmate" alive and "sexiest college student" alive contests.... "we even wanna do the best inmate 'buns' contest but can't get photos of guys' buns in prison" they stated... We will use any photo(s) (as long as they are not nude) to enhance and further our cause. We will utilize pragmatic strategies to promote the agenda to win our war against violence in our schools.

We are creative, daring, bold and innovative in our pursuit of the gangs and the predators preying upon our children... I wake up every morning (every morning) with G.B.G. and with "K.K.K." on my mind. I will not stop until kids at Locke High School, Lodi, McClatchy and Columbine etc. are reading this book. If I have to launch a hunger strike to get Tony Dungy, Mike Vick, Jeff Lurie and Hollywood Henderson etc. to help me get this book to the people I will! I want 'Max' (at TMZ.com), Maxwell Hanger, James Nesmith, Christopher Durbin and John Garvin etc. to get this book....

I need all the students like Benjamin Alexander, CJ, Justin Berry and Kevin Greene to get on Google and be creative. Link "K.K.K." up to other sites and to other words and phrases... And if you come up with a spectacular way to link, cross promote or viral announce "K.K.K." etc. I will pay you!!

I need Dustin Davis, Rod Baybayan and Kiel Pratt to get in the car with G.B.G. We need you... "superbly" has indicated that they'll add $ 500,00 to the 'challenge' in "Blue Eyed Blonde" Book II on page 313. Ipso Facto, (since I doubled the offer) "we" will give $ 2500.00 to all the folks I've named already (with the challenge) and to (per "superbly") Anders Morrison, Matthew Long, Steven Moreno Jr, Shaun Rushfeth, Omar Samy, Bradley Gates, Shane Johnson, Max Steele, Jeff Buttle, Johnny Weir, Alexander (studying philosophy at Pepperdine Univ.), Zachary (on Price is Right - attends CAL Lutheran College), Chris Thompson (Becky's son), Joseph Latham (Ramona's son), Hunter Brown (Wheaton Illi), Austin Sisneros, Von Smith, Chad Michael Morrissette, Billy Bell, Jakob Karr, John Litzler, Taylor Lautner, Justin Chirigotis, Zach Freisen, Chris Balding, Nicholas Taxera, Nick Pelham, the two "compliment" college students, Alex Blench, Maxwell Hanger, Michael Parker (Walnut Creek CA.), Christopher Durbin, David Joiner, Trevor Loflin, Chris Hicks, Andrew Knox, Mr. Gerber, Evan Loudenbeck, Matt Sly, Brian Kehoe, Mike Gormon (Sacto), Christopher Kerney, Neil Peterson (Ohio), Vincent Glaviano, Mario Lopez (Elk Grove), Jason Durtchi, Alex Holgan, Josiah Lemming, Anthony Fedorov, A. Chiguila, Paul Pruden, Cameron Brown (Purdue), Matthew Gerber, Caleb Peek, Craig Hutto, Zach Boardwine, Kyle Griffith, Eric Flores, Ben & Casey (Sierra Regional Med. Ctr.), Tyler Schroeder, Daniel Kaufman, Ryan Jasinski, Mike Corsetto, Doran Smestad, Tobias Lake, Ollie Valencia, Spc. Justin Snyder, Levi Turner (Sacto), Steven Kelly, Kevin Kelly, Shaun White, Richard Peichoto, John Griffin, Dan McMullan, William Letlow, Paul Twaragowski and Scott Tatum... And I (personally) offer $ 5 grand (they can give it to charity!) to Tyra, Beyonce, Mariah, Alicia Keys, Angelina Jolie and to Madame Paris Hilton... Any person (must be 18 or older! Go to page 313 in "Blue Eyed Blonde" Book II....Photos will "not" be returned!) can enter the challenge but you are not guaranteed to be accepted...

I want this movement to be the moveon.org of the anti-violence movement. We (G.B.G.) will be to schools what Google, is to search engines. We will Revo-'Fu---ng' lutionize schools! We will not get bogged down in politics, religion, or any of that bull crap. When one soldier falls all soldiers fall. When one kid is killed every kid is killed. When one child is bullied, beat or molested etc. the whole of humanity is hurt. We will be pragmatic, strategic, flamboyant and methodical as we use the tools of the 21st century to stop this madness. Rather than praying for God to be on our side. We will pray to be on the side of God.

We will use the skills, techniques and energy of Benjamin Alexander, Taylor Francis, Daniel Asare and Dillon etc. to operationalize a calculated, orchestrated and a withering assault on gangs, gangs of molesters, gangs of murderers and gangs of predators. We will not surrender to the Red Herrings articulated by Limbaugh and Hannity etc.

Planes have been flown into our schools! Our schools are burning up with hatred, sexism, bullying, gangs, guns and drugs. And we must run (like spiritual paramedics and psychological firefighters) into these burning schools and save the children!... I am calling Justin Doucette, Wyatt Duino (Elk Grove), Tucker Horwath, Scott Moore (of the Bulldogs), Matthew Long and Anders Morrison to suit up! Let's run into these buildings, schools and colleges and get our kids out! Let's mentor, lead and empower young people. We need Bradley Gates, Ryan Jett. Esteban Nunez, Kai McKenna, Victor McKenna and Richard Scrushy. We must repair these broken wings...

Our kids are in conflict, crisis and in despair. And while the schools are burning up Limbaugh is abusing prescription drugs at night and spreading hatred by day. While we are "sleeping" Leroy Jenkins is probably still trying to molest little boys or talk John Mandern into having sex. While we are "sleeping" an enemy has attacked our babies.

But if the devil thinks we are gonna sit back and not fight back he's outta his mind. Christian Hosoi, Nathaniel Mullennix and Roger Walthorn etc. are suiting up. And you who are reading are clearing up your head. And you are realizing that you (too) must fight. Chris Argee, Justin Chirigotis, William Larson (Sacto) and Christopher Clubb have joined the (G.B.G.) club and we will fight. Matthew Scheper, Jeff Axten, Trevor Muhler, Nick Jonas, Jason (and his brother Adam on "who wants to be a millionaire" from Port Wash. New York), Pat Pattituchi, Nic Buron, B.J. Hill, Robert Lingle, David Quattlebum, Ben Whipple and Zach Harris (Roseville)....suit up!

I need Jason Durtchi, John Hancock, Andrew Theiss, Dr. Alex Vaclavik, Boink Magazine and Jake Bailey. Our loved one's are hurting. Our kids are dying. We need to march on these schools and sit-in until gang bangers get out. We (Tyler Schroeder) are not playing around. When Devin Devell, Matthew Gerber, Evan Kholmann and private Joseph Foster, get our suits on it's on and cracking baby....

I need Ryan Armstrong (Sacto), Nathan Hewitt, Jared Swilley, Kevin Barnes, Mika Penniman, Charles Jackson, Bradley Silverman, Will Rains and Kent Depriest to suit up and fall in! Right here! Right now! Today!

Where are Ripley Hunter?, Michael Anthony Cannela?, Chris Johnson (Grass Valley)?, John Farelli?, Sam Perry?, Brian Kehoe? Dan Sarro? Austin Peck? Josh St. Louis? Jake Simpson? Paul Hamm? Jeff Parshley? Matt Martinez? Chris Bergaus? Neil Petruic?....

I gotta have Caleb Alexis, Jeff Herman, Oz Contreras, Brian Spaly and Dustin Johnson today. We can do it....

When Robert Downey Jr. was in prison he was involved in a homosexual relationship. He had a gay lover. I hope his "lady" has an HIV test. Forthwith......

....The "orthodox" Christian C.O. told me today that I'm worshipping a 'false' God. He began his monologue by explaining to me that we should keep our voices down and no-one needed to hear what we were discussing. After he gave me a lengthy monologue explaining that T.D. Jakes was going to hell due to being too charismatic etc. he then explained to me that my entire family and I would burn in hell. He was angry, arrogant, fanatical and... When I politely rejected his 'argument' he became livid and he changed his topic from God to me... "I 'heard' you don't even have a publisher and all you do is talk nonsense. You don't have a publisher like 'Zondervan'. And you think you're somebody but you're not. That's just what I'm "hearing". So now my orthodox Christian C.O. is yelling, berating and belittling. And unlike the book of "James" advises etc. He is entertaining gossip. I could have inquired as to how many tomes he's published. And... When I told him (quite politely) I'd pray for him he became livid and infuriated. And 'we' wonder why people fight 'wars' in the 'name' of religion. I am still praying for him...

Matthew Fulkerson, Jason Wright (AKA Jason Gomez), Seth Wrinkles, Christopher Owens and Ramreet Virk .... We need you. We need all of those engineering students at Consumnes Oaks High School in Elk Grove. We want Mr. Tim Dougal, Jordan, Dr. Laura Stachel, PFC. Michael Kern, Patrick Gallardo, Ahmad Farzan and all the students in the "we care solar club" to join G.B.G.....

I saw Matthew crying on Oprah on 11/10/09. In this "men R not supposed 2 cry" Era I was glad to see Matt crying. Because when boys don't cry tears we often cry bullets. And I wanna be a witness to Matt turning his pain into power. I want Matt as a G.B.G. ambassador to use his hurt, sorrow, tragedy and the gruesome murders of his parents as a platform to help other kids. Matt could be on meth, coke or booze. But he did not choose to be a dope fiend. His grandmomma raised him right. And I'm proud of her and of Matthew and I want Matt to help us to heal the world... Matt is a forgiving person and he does not believe in the death penalty. I saw 'vision' and dreams inside of Matt. Give me Matt, Wyatt Duino, Justin Doucette, Jason Durtchi and Caleb Peek etc. and we will change the world.

We need Aaron Jackson (Delaware Ohio), Charles Jackson, Matt Barrows, Victor Smalley, (Billy Bell, Nathan, Peter, Ryan, Litzler, Teddy etc.) Brandon A. Hughes etc. etc.

We need Shane Johnson, Luke Johnson (Richmond or Chesterfield), Bradley Gates, Matthew Long (a lot of Matts yo'), Anders Morrison and Andy "The Volunteer". We need you bruthas to step up and to step in. Together we can bombard these schools with the transformational power of hope, light and with right. We will inject, infuse and inundate our schools with Hope and with Peace. We'll provide transfusions of self esteem into the psyches of our kids from around the world. In this book I'm calling all angels! Calling all prisoners! Calling all mothers, fathers, sisters and brothers... Our schools are on fire and our kids will die if we (the people) don't run into these burning buildings and introduce the waters of optimism, education, transformation and pragmatism.

If we can get Shaun White half as enthusiastic about schools as he is about snowboarding. If we (Dr. Solis, Dr. Heitkamp and Dr. Curren etc.) can get Aaron Carter to bring his talent and energy to helping stop school violence etc. If we can get Dev Patel, Van Hansis, Sergey Brin, and Jeff Bezos etc. to give the G.B.G. mission just a little time, a lot of prayer and...

I am convinced that the God of Abraham, Isaac and Jacob. The God of the Bible and the God of my Big Momma etc. He will bless us, empower us and help us...

I know what Jason Durtchi, Daniel Job, Joseph Latham, "Casper" Voorhees and I can do if we come together.... As hypocritical and as phony as I've been in my life I'm willing to practice what I preach, write and... I will forgive James "Noodles" Emslander, Jeff Glenn Howell and Daniel 'lil man' Job... they know what they did... I forgive each of you today; let's do this thing. I want the boyz in tha hood, fellas in jail as well as in Yale etc. to help us keep kids out of Hell (AKA jail). All of us must do this work. All of us. I don't care what you did or who you did it to. You still have worth. And your story can help somebody else. Whether you're in a penthouse or a prison you still gotta pulpit. You (Matt Fulkerson, Matt Long and my boy Joseph Latham etc.) have something to say, to share and to give. And you (Chris Slyker, Tucker Horwath, Scott Moore, Hunter Brown, Andy Dick, Alexander (the philosophy student at Pepperdine), Shaun Rushforth and Steven Moreno Jr. etc.) have a sermon to preach, a lesson to teach and a kid to reach.

From the depths of my soul and from my spirit I reach out to you at Richmond High School, you at Locke, Lodi, McClatchy, at Rocketown etc. and I connect my faith (in the spirit realm) with Tony Dungy, Tyler Perry, Zig Zigler, my mother and with all the saints across the world. And "we" (Tony Dungy, Michael W. Smith and me etc.) believe God that He will reach into your school, church, college, jail or home. And that he will lift you up and then He will bring you out.

... And (my friend) Brandon Gene Martinez I've never stopped praying for you.... I know you (AKA "solo") are in prison and you thought I forgot about you. But I pray for you (Brandon) everyday of my life; I promise!...

We need Michael Jacinto, Pedro Armando Quandt, Jerry Wines, Voorhees, Chucky Pyle, Frank, Abel "Grumpy" Maldonado, Allen Harris and Danny Macky... Justin Howell, Roger Peck and Nathan Gould etc. "Cole" ("The secret millionaire") and Nate (Paradise Hotel 2008) etc. we need you... Jose Zuniga, Will Coker and Omar Hernandez etc. Let me hear from you. Yall have your family (or your lawyer/s) to send me your missive... Have your family to go to the G.B.G. Facebook and sign you up...

And all of you in juvenile, jail and prison etc. You can participate in the "superbly" sexiest man alive contest... "Brad" ("superbly" supervisor) stated that "most dudes in juveniles and prisons have low or no self esteem. We do 'sexiest man alive', best 'male buns' and 'sexiest (non prisoner) student (must be over 17) alive contests to boost self esteem and self confidence"... (You all can send your photos to the G.B.G. facebook, our myspace and/or send em to me at the prison..)

We need talented and skillful folks like Robert Pattinson, Daniel Radcliffe, Aaron Carter, Derek Hough and Anthony Fedorov to stand with G.B.G.... My orthodox Christian C.O. reminds me of the Pharisees. And he also reminds me of Noah's critics. For a hundred years they called Noah a nut, crazy, stupid and insane ("you're just talking nonsense"). But Noah continued to build that Ark because he had "heard" something from the Lord. There was no Bible (writing) back then for high school drop-out guards who got their GED to debate. Those dudes like David, Abraham and Elijah had to get their marching orders by what they "heard". I guess that's why Christ said "my sheep know my 'voice' and a stranger they will not follow"... God had 'implanted' a 'word' in Noah's spirit. Noah.... You must seek to hear the 'voice' behind the words. Spiritual deafness will destroy your destiny. You've gotta ask the Lord to heal you of your deafness so you can hear Him.

... Three times Peter denied Christ. And three times Christ asked Peter did he love Him above all others. Three times Peter said yes and that cancelled out the denials. Christ told him thrice to "feed my sheep". Peter tried to walk away but he was possessed with a revelation of who Christ was. And when a revelation has been implanted in you, you can be sitting up in prison on a rape charge but the revelation will 'pull you back in'. Judas committed suicide but Peter preached the word 'after' he denied Christ. When it is implanted in you no matter how many times you lie and deny Him it will 'pull you back in'. That's why the Bible says if you train (teach, implant) up a child in the ways of God (he might stray be he can't stay away) and when he's old(er) he won't depart.

The prodigal son strayed but he didn't stay. He was smoking weed, snorting coke and hanging at the club. And.... If folk see you when you've strayed they'll send you to hell with their "mouth". "Look at him with his no good self. He been to juvenile two or three times already. He got suspended and he's about to get expelled. He's on his way to hell. He ain't no good. I 'heard' he...." But the prodigal son came back home. And Peter came back. And... Noah built the Ark inspite of critics, folks hating on him and ridiculing him.

... When Martin Luther King Jr. decided to go to Birmingham he was mocked. Even some of the black preachers hated on Dr. King. But Dr. King was possessed by a 'dream' (vision) that he had. And when a dream, a vision, a mission or a set of instructions has been implanted in your spirit haters, liars, folk laughing at you and calling you "insane" etc. will not deter you or stop you from building the Ark, starting that club, band or group etc. and living your 'dream'.

And when a jail inmate (i.e. Sherman D. Manning) starts saying that "I met with my war council" (G.B.G. Advisory Board and our members etc.) I'm laughed at. I'm "serving that old false..... talking non-sense. Talking bout a gang ... Who do you think you are?" Well I know who I am. I am somebody! I am an Eagle! I am a Joseph, a prince, a Paul... I am a child of the King. And as such I'm already (always) fighting a spiritual war. And as commander in chief of G.B.G. I ...

I am a licensed and ordained preacher. Ordained at first Corinth Baptist Church by Rev. Moses Lee Raglin. And I remember (well) being in the Atlanta Constitution Newspaper. I was in the Atl. Daily World, The Purple Cow and The Christian Science Monitor etc. etc. And the 'reporters' always (without fail) wrote "the Reverend Sherman D. Manning said" etc. They wrote that because I was "a great young man with a promising future" according to Ambassador (AKA Mayor and civil rights giant!) Andrew Young!

... But in Virginia the very first time I got in trouble the reporter wrote "He calls himself (I'd never spoken with the reporter!) 'reverend'". This was the first time I'd ever experienced the power of biased media and slanted journalism. And that's neither 'here' nor 'there'. But my point is if people meet you, hear about you or 'read' (he calls himself "Dr. Johnson"... Well "if" he has a PhD or a medical degree he is a doctor whether he is accused of 'rape', 'robbery' or 'rage' etc.) about you at a certain time or stage (or phase) in your life they can 'write' (you off) any damn thing....

Can you imagine what Hannity, Coulter, Beck or Limbaugh would have written or said about Joseph if they'd met, read or heard about him while he was in jail? Oh, my God I can hear Limbaugh (and my orthodox Christian C.O.) "ladies and gentlemen he (Joseph) 'calls himself' a man of God... This inmate at CSP-SAC (a level four maximum security prison) claimed he heard from 'God' and had a 'dream' as a kid. In this 'dream' inmate Joseph was lording over his brothers.... (Rush would be rattling some paper right now!) sounds egotistical, presumptuous and narcissistic to me... Now how did he go from a 'dream' to a 'nightmare' in a prison? If 'God' was with Joseph why would God allow him to be sold into slavery? The temerity of this lil Hebrew boy made God so angry that God 'made' him a 'slave'. And then the tried to rape his slave master's wife. You give a slave an inch and he'll take a mile... Captain Potiphar trusted his little 'slave' and gave him a job and yet he wanted the man's 'wife'". And I see Rush farting (lol) and Sean (Hannity) inhales, smiles and enjoys the odoriferous delight that Rush was kind enough to release. And Rush continues "and after this 'slave' is convicted of a 'sex' crime, he's sitting up in prison claiming he's innocent. CNN is reporting that this 'convicted rapist' has the audacity to sit in CSP-SAC and guess what he's doing? He's calling himself a spokesman for God. He raped one of King Pharaoh's captains wife. And now he's telling the King's Butler and his Baker to "tell them (their dreams) to me". His qualifications to interpret dreams in the prison? Well let's see: he claimed he had a dream that didn't come true. He was a slave... And he's been in prison for more than a decade on a 'sex' beef. And if he had so much power and the hand of God upon his life. The power to interpret other people's dreams etc. Why won't God get him out of prison? He (Joseph) talks nonsense. He doesn't even have a 'publisher' (of his interpretations)! He "thinks" he's somebody but he's just a predator. Think about it; if Joseph was blessed and endowed by God why would God allow him to be sold into slavery? His own brothers hated his guts. They plotted to kill that predator. And then he went from being a dreamer to a slave. His daddy spoiled him with that special coat (of many colors). And Joseph began to suffer from delusions of grandeur. And then he tried to take some p----! He's a tree jumper - and has the nerve to sit up in New Folsom thinking he's somebody! He calls 'himself' ....

Young men (you who dropped out of school. You in gangs or about to get in a gang. You undercover bi-sexuals, undercover gay boys, flamboyant gays, jocks, studs, playboys, gigolos, thugs, addicts etc.) I wanna tell you don't you ever, never, ever allow anybody (no damn body) to judge your day by the weather. Don't let some Limbaugh 'Rush' and pass judgment on your destiny. You are somebody! Whether you are in a penthouse, shelter or a prison cell. You still have worth. Whether you are at 'penn' state or in a state pen you still have worth. You are not a chicken. You can choose to pray and not prey. And if you pray God can keep you from becoming prey today... If a dream, a vision, a goal or an idea has been 'implanted' in your spirit. Don't allow some prison guard to make you believe that "Inmate Mandela you can't be a President. South Africa has never had a black president. And you are washed up, institutionalized and a Has-Been. And you've been sitting in CSP-SAC (Robbin Island) for almost 27 years. And you have the temerity to think you can be the commander in chief? Who do you think you are?". And four years later he could say "I'm Nelson Mandela! Ex-convict and President of South Africa!"...

I wanna tell you (youngsters) not to allow anybody to define you or to marginalize you (because you're black, gay, a nerd, a drop-out or whatever). If you dropped-out you can drop-in. Go back to school. Get off the meth. Get help!...

And "Calling all them names in his book! Using 'K.K.K.' for a title. Who do you think you are?". I am a man! I am the same "great" man with a "promising future" (destiny)... I am (as you are) an Eagle! I was Rev. Sher... Before any reporter ever wrote it. I was still Rev. Sher... after reporters wrote it. And I'll be Rev. Sherm... even if they never (again) write it.... John Butterfield is John. He was John before you read his name in this book. He is John while you're reading it. He will be John after... If he gets fat he's John. If he gets buff he's John. If he falls in love with a man he's John. If he marries a woman and has 30 kids he's still John Butterfield. He does not need you or me to endorse him. And you must stop running around from person to person and gang to gang looking for somebody to endorse you. You are an eagle!...

Noah went on and built his Ark even though he couldn't get on the Phil Donahue show. He built his Ark even though psychiatrists called him "crazy" and...

Joseph interpreted dreams while he sat in prison convicted of a sex crime... Paul sat in a prison cell and he taught, preached, prayed, prophesied and baptized. Paul wrote his book(s) in prison (even though he didn't have a publisher or an Editor - lol)....

So if you think criticisms will deter me or stop me you're out of your mind. I promised God I would do this work. And if you think they called Noah "crazy" etc. Wait til I begin to assign missions. As commander in Chief I'm about to 'assign' some missions, tasks and 'ranks' to certain persons right now: John Butterfield (Buck sergeant), Ryan Hreljac (sergeant first class), Taylor Francis (G.B.G. , S.F.C.), Christopher Holton (corporal), Army PFC William Warner (Ohio - G.B.G. corporal), Seth Wrinkles (G.B.G. PFC), Matthew Fulkerson (G.B.G. corporal), USMC Sgt. Jeremy Glenn (G.B.G., SFC), Steven Roche (G.B.G. PFC), Joseph Rocha, Justin Zegar, Daniel Asare, Nathaniel Mullennix, Keith Mullennix, Shea Newberry, David Decook, Lee Truex, Matt, Sean and Aaron Maloney, Aaron Carter, Alex Blench, Brett Jolliff, "Marius", Jake Heartsong, Maxwell Hanger, Austin Sisneros, Daniel Sample, Cody Sheldon, Cody Cates, Scott Cozza, Derrick Flowers, Riley Evans, Greg Deekens, C.J. Sheron and Tadd Carr etc. etc. are my front line 'net' team. It is your job to blog, chat, post and 'poke' about G.B.G. and K.K.K. From February 2010 - February 2011 you guys must spend at least two hours per week emailing and contacting people about G.B.G. and K.K.K.. Do it!....

All yall sophomores, juniors and seniors at Locke, Lodi, McClatchy, Folsom and Richmond High School who wanna do something; suit up! Don't get bogged down listening to the haters - suit up! They'll tell you "Oh, you listening to some ole prisoner trying to get you involved with politics" etc. It's not like I need you. Hell, I can send you some money. I'm not looking for a donation or any dues. I am not working for the prison. I work for the people. I am absolutely transparent about my present.

"Brethren (Yo Jolliff, Blench, Heartsong and Chivescu) I count not myself to have apprehended ..." that was Paul in a prison... Brethren (yo Brett, Alex, Jake etc.) I am not 'there' yet. I have not attained a holy life yet. I (Sherman D. Manning) still struggle with 'lust'. Every time I look at Beyonce (don't trip - Jay-Z aint reading this tome. Hell yall remember - I don't have a "publisher". I'm just writin' 2 my partnas in schools, colleges n trailer parks!), Eliz Hasselbeck, Tyra (oh Tyra!) and Alicia Keys I get weak in the knees... Help me please... I have issues. I am not a choir boy. I am a sinner! I'm no rapist! I'm no thief (not anymore... but what I did to Stella was thievery!). I'm no murderer! I'm not a lot of things, not a drug addict! I'm not an alcoholic!... But (the 'but' kicks my ass... oxymoron?) I am a sinner! I am vindictive! I am... A "Bad Boy" ... I love the Lord God! And I am in awe of his power! And I strive to .... But yo Billy Bell, John Litzler and Victor Smalley can I tell you all something? "I don't pretend to have apprehended" in my flesh. Every time I try to do good, evil is always there. Hindering me on my way. I can't blame Alicia Keys. She does not 'know' me. And it's not about her... It's just time for an author to be like Tyler Perry ... meaning? A. Write the damn tome. Write it! ....B. Tell the truth and don't make crap up just trying (James Frey) to get on Oprah. Tell it like it is... I'm so, so, so glad that Attorney Murray J. Janus told me that "if" I really wanted to help kids I had to "tell" my "truth". He told me I must "tell them why you're in prison". Attorney Janus stated "I doubt very seriously if anyone will believe Ricardo Calvario's fantastic and incredible story... But even 'if' a few people believe his tale you can change lives by telling the truth".

I got that yall!....

Lance Corcoran and CCPOA President Mike Jiminez should be buried under the prison! I know Mike is gay! And both of them are stealing union money. Both of them are predators and crooks. They are guilty of money laundering, extortion and bribery. Mike and Lance are "racketeering". And if I get any reports of them trying to intercept my constitutional right to free speech and artistic expression etc. I will sue them. This is America - not communist China... President Obama may (I don't know) disagree with 90% of this book. But as an American and a Harvard trained constitutional scholar; I'll bet he would defend my legal right to write...

All of you thugs, gang bangers, prescription drug addicts and... stand up and walk out of your past. You are not what they say you are. I know some well-meaning adults yelled at you. They berated and they belittled you. They called you a "fag", and "idiot", a "fool" and they told you that would never "be" anybody. They planted seeds of self hatred in you. And those seeds led to self destruction and self sabotage. And you've been busy running around (like Limbaugh) trying to medicate your way out of that anger, that shame and that hurt. You've had some people to put emotional band-aids on your pain from time to time. But band-aids come off and they are temporary. Your spirit has been infected. I came to bring the seeds of a spiritual balm and antibiotic. We must get these antibiotics down in your psychological (and emotional) bloodstream. We will get a breakthrough for you. In between name dropping (lol) we will get the seeds of this psychological penicillin down inside of you. If God be God then every man is a liar. If God is God then I have fasted and I have prayed. And God will trouble the spirits of Tony Dungy, Tyler Perry, Bishops, parents, preachers and teachers until they start praying for these seeds to get into your mind. I can't tell you that God told me Tony Dungy will help us get this book to you. He may not. Can't tell you that Tyler Perry is gonna buy a thousand copies of "K.K.K." and send em to Luther Burbank High School or to a school in New Orleans. God didn't tell me that. But I do have faith that Tony and Tyler will pray that this tome will reach you.

Words are powerful tools. Words can curse you and they can bless you. Words are transformational. And it is absolutely urgent that we get these words to you. If I have to go on a hunger strike until God moves on Dr. Curren (Dr. Heitkamp, Dr. Solis, Dr. Duran, Dr. Gregg etc. etc.) and motivates each of them to send 10 or 20 copies (they can even do so anonymously by calling - toll free - 1-877-809-1659) of "K.K.K." to a school etc. I will fast and I will pray. But John Tu, Mark Ravis, Bobby Lee Cook and Michael Louis Kelly etc. have got to help us launch this effort... our task is monumental and our enemy (illiteracy, drugs, gangs, molesters and...) is potent. But I told Johnny O'Neal a few weeks ago (11/12/09) that an enemy is a door not a wall. A door that leads me into my next season. David shoveled sheep crap until he met an enemy (Giant - Goliath). If he never met his enemy he would have remained a shepherd boy. But once he met his enemy he parlayed meeting (slaying and defeating) Goliath into a Kingship.

... Every time you try to do something brilliant, great, positive and Godly the spirit of Judas is raised up. The spirit of betrayal (Judas) and denial (Peter) come to discourage you. And you start thinking about how people walk out on you, let you down and how they hurt you. But Peter walked with Jesus. He talked and 'broke bread' with Jesus. But then he let Jesus down... How many folks have let you down? And between you and I you've let yourself down too. I wish I had time to tell you about the times that I let myself down. My Lord. Do you have any idea what it feels like to be a 12 or 13 year old boy; with 'promise' and with 'praise' hanging above your name. You preach and you teach. Everything you touch turns to gold. You have political capital (chips) and are the most 'influential' youth in your city. You preach allover the State of Georgia. And you're quoted in newspapers and on the television. You mess around a meet an ambassador named 'Andy', a civil rights legend named 'Hosea', Grace Davis, Flip Schulke and... You are a rising star in the black Mecca of America etc. and then a Jezebel (Tracy Green) comes along and runs you out of town. And... I give Judge Michael Edward Bergin permission to violate the attorney client privilege and to speak about my Tracy Green situation... I spoke to Judge Bergin on 11/10/09 for the first time in more than a decade. His beautiful wife (a 'black' woman who is a corporate attorney) accepted the call at home. "I know I'm getting you in trouble with your wife because I'm calling you at home" I told Mike. "You got that right Reverend.

... "Perhaps I'll get a pass because I just came home from the hospital. I had some gall stones removed". We chatted about this book and some confidential matters. "I'm so sorry you're in prison so far away from home Reverend. Will you ever get out?" Mike inquired... "Don't put an index in your book so people will have to r-e-a-d the darn tome to see what you said about them" Mike said. And if Mike is perusing this tome I want Mike to ask his wife if he can send ten copies of this book to a high school in Fairburn Georgia...

Young folks you can turn a detour into a book tour. You can learn how to transform lemons into lemonaid. You can use the winds that work against you to propel you into your destiny. Don't allow where you are to prevent you from going where you want. Don't allow your history to hinder you from your destiny. A setback is a setup for a comeback. Imagine and envision yourself succeeding. Get a picture of yourself in success in your mind. And consistently see it. Because if you see it you can be it....

Back to Tracy Green... After that fiasco I became a troubled youngster. And my situation was unique because I was a preacher, a leader and a ... And when you are in "charge" people expect you to have it together. When you are the quarterback, team captain or student leader you are expected to have it together. And you'll try to keep your pain, trouble, sorrows and mistakes a secret. And secrets rot the soul. And having the horror heard helps heal... I told no man and no woman about my inner hurt and pain. To be 'labeled' (named) can be tragic. I must repeat: be careful who you allow to 'name' you. People have a tendency to live up (or 'down') to their name(s). And we love to attach names (i.e. "inmate", "ex-convict", "felon", "loser" etc.) and labels to people. Tracy helped 'label' me... And later on I found myself doing, saying and thinking things which I should not. I let myself down. I bruised my own spirit. I saddened my own soul and I began to sabotage myself. I lived a life that made me vulnerable and susceptible to being accused, abused, misused and set up. You can lay down with dogs and catch flees. If you hang out in a room with somebody who is smoking the smoke will get into your clothes. And if a cop stops you and smells smoke ("where there's smoke there is fire") he will believe you have been smoking. And if you happen to have a lighter in your pocket he'll really believe...

If you French kiss (over and over like me and Tyra Banks ought to do;) a person who has been drinking alcohol and later you're driving etc. you are swerving because you are tired and get stopped by a cop. He'll take the fact that you are swerving and the fact that he smells alcohol on your breath to mean you have been drinking.. Let's go deeper... If you hang in the room with somebody smoking cigarettes not only will you smell like smoke but you can get cancer from second hand smoke and... "your honor when I stopped Jared Milles he smelled like smoke - and now Jared has lung cancer... Ladies and gentlemen this man is (not!!!!) a smoker!"...

Even though you make mistakes and you (will) let yourself down etc. Don't allow the Judas or the Peter or the mistake(s) in your life to make you think that your life is over. I wanna tell every student at Gunn High School, McClatchy, Locke and at high schools and colleges across the world etc. can I tell you all something? It is not over! It is not over! You can rise up from the ashes of defeat and you can succeed. And please remember that "everybody" is not going to be a millionaire. 'Everybody' will not own a Rolls Royce. But you can be happy with a job picking up trash. You can have a Pinto or a Toyota and be happy. As long as you have some 'bling blinging' in your spirit you are cool... I need Jared Milles, Robert Quell, Ryan Little and James Tilton etc. to hear that. Success involves way more than money... "money don't (sic) buy happiness" we all 'say'. But we still believe it is a lot better to arrive at your problem in a limousine than it is to arrive on the bus. Nobody likes "Pat" and "Turna" meaning "Pat them feets (sic) and turn a corner (walking). We want cars. And... (I repeat) we just watched a man pay almost $ 40,000 per week for sleep. And he died trying to 'sleep'.

.... I can personally attest to the fact that you can be riding down the streets of the Big Apple in the back of a triple stretch limousine with 3 women in the car and be miserable! I have been there, done that and got a t-shirt Baby....

I've also sat in a cheap Hotel with little money and a mediocre car and had somebody I love (Sabine) buy a small cake and sing me happy birthday (with her guitar) and been as happy as I've ever been. And some of the happiest people I have ever in my lifetime met have been in ghettos (Perry Homes, Hollywood Court, Bankhead Court and in Carver Homes etc.) and trailer parks (i.e. one of my favorite spots called 'Shady Hill' in Virginia) around the country. Money? Spend a lot on steak (I like it i.e. filet Mignon) or a little on pork chops (I love it) ... Show me a man who earns $ 80 grand per year (in Georgia but perhaps $ 120,000 in California) with a great wife and a good kid and he'll be (often times) much happier than my pal (i.e.) Danny Wilkins (pseudonym) who (in 1995) earned $ 850,000 per year and was a single (playboy) alcoholic... Chase hope, not money. If you chase your dreams and master education etc. you won't ever have to worry about money. Even street sweepers earn good wages.

... Be the 'Best' that you can 'Be' and even the Bible says that your 'gift' will "make room (and board) for you".

... Youngsters I am telling you that teenhood is tough, stressful and rough. And it is not right for those of us on the outside (looking in) to try to tell you that we know how you feel. We do not know how you feel. Based upon empirical data we can attempt to surmise and/or assume. But we don't 'know'. And rather than assuming and pretending etc. I ask. When teenagers write

242

to me, email my office and contact us I ask questions. Lots and lots of questions. If I don't know the problem(s) how can I prescribe a potential solution?...

The main reason that I've been able to remain current is because I've been able to stay in touch. I talk to young people in their teens and tweenies every chance I get. Sergeant Zanini (now a lieutenant) brought a student (Casey - he was very cautions and a tad bit nervous. But studious and affable as I recruited "Casey" for G.B.G.) from Delta college by the name of Casey. Casey blew my mind with some of the things he told me which are going on in college! The sexualized hazing, date rapes and drugs etc. and warden Walker has some great young staffers at CSP Sac. ... Daniel Bugriyev (of G.B.G. fame) is extremely bright, gregarious and optimistic... C.O. Hodge (his co-workers call him pretty boy!). C.O. D. Kelley (his fellow officers call him "Kid"). C.O. T. Ramsey (his co-workers call him "pretty white boy"...) etc. I call all of them "C.O." when I'm in a good mood and "guard" when I'm not. Mr. Kelley? 27. Mr. Hodge? 22. Mr. Ramsey? 22... All bright, studious and professional. C.O. McAfee, Costa (Mac's partner), K. Yeager, Dunkle, Pinkard, Anderson, Tino Huggins etc. etc. All basically good guys (they are O.G. officers) who are not impressed with me. Some of them don't even like me. But they are fair and they follow the rules... Pinkard retired from the Navy as an E-4. Dunkle is still in the Army. K. Yeager was in the U.S. Air Force. And being in the military taught these guys rules, regulations and discipline. Being ... O.K. I was kidding (lol) about Pinkard's rank. He actually retired as a chief petty officer... And being in the military is a good training ground for becoming a guard. Especially the one's like Pinkard (who does not like me. He really does not. But he is fair.) who started very early in the Navy. He gets a retirement check plus his guard's pay. Ipso Facto, he (and Dunkle and K. Yeager etc.) don't need to smuggle in cell phones and dope for 'money'. With retirement etc. they easily earn as much as an associate warden...

What I like about dealing with dudes like Mr. Dunkle and Mr. T.R. Huggins etc. is the fact that they are polar opposites of me. They disagree with my politics and my propaganda. I don't think they even think inmates should be allowed to write tomes. But if both of us agree on everything, one of us is unnecessary. And staff are not sent here to "like" me. They are sent here to "keep" me locked up...

As long as they are not like Acosta, Domingo Garcia, Wally or Mike Bunnell etc. I'm cool.... Bunnell is a co-conspirator (along with Lance, Jiminez and others) in the murder of captain Doug Pieper. And Bunnell is an unindicted co-conspirator in the "cover-up" of Pieper's murder... C.O. Pieper (at P.V.S.P. working overtime at C.R.M.C. we spent hundreds of hours discussing Bunnell, Lance and Jiminez etc.) admitted to me "If you quote me I'll call you a liar from one end of the state to the other. But Evette (Doug Pieper's wife) saw a blue truck (just like Bunnell's) casing the neighborhood the day before the supposed 'suicide'". Officer Pieper continued "my uncle (captain Pieper) was heard arguing with Bunnell and Lance over the telephone a day before that... For them to try to claim he stole some lumber, was getting a job change and that Doug Jr. (who has never stated to my investigators that he is gay.. And 'if' he is that is not relevant!) was gay and that made him commit suicide? That's asinine! My uncle did not commit suicide"...

Bunnell, Lance and Jiminez (triple demons of corruption, deception and perversion) murdered him. (all 3 are weapons experts) and/or they paid to have him killed. He knew too much. He broke the "code of silence". And he was a "rat" to them.

.... Told yall sgt. Elsberry had to get outta dodge because she "told" on Lt. Stephen Luke Scarsella... Max Lemon had to get armed guards to protect him from them (Bunnell, Lance and Jiminez etc.)... tell yall the truth I wish the governor send me home (the State of Georgia!) to serve my illegal sentence!... They will not keep (DRB) me at CSP Sac. Bunnell, Spearman and Lance will (indeed!) pull strings and have me re-transferred out of New Folsom within the next 6 months. And when I transfer I'll be killed! They will take me out. And they (the Green Wall) will cover it up! "Gangs retaliated against Manning because he exposed them in "K.K.K." they will say. And/or "his cell partner murdered him because...." they will say.... So I say send me to Georgia. I've got Georgia on my mind! (they won't send me to Georgia. They will send me to another state and/or just lock me down fully! Claiming it is for my own protection. However, if this is a tome of lies etc. why lock me down? And/or if guards are not corrupt, if there is no 'Green Wall' and these are law abiding correctional professionals etc. why would I need to be protected from them?)

... I want David Shaw, Judge Thelton Henderson, Senators and congresspersons to read this book and launch an investigation.. I don't need or require an investigation into my treatment. I'm cool on that. With an army of youngsters blogging, poking and chatting about me etc. my situation will work out...

But I'm calling for an investigation into how we treat 'youngsters' in juveniles, jails and in prisons. Pragmatically it makes sense to deal with this crisis. I don't need to call Dr. Phil, Dr. Gardere or talk to Dr. Curren to know that this system (as it is) is broken, abusive and in severe need of reform.... We lock up 'kids' too often, for too long and in too violent places!

Can we be real? I know boys and men don't want me talking about sex but keep it real Sherman! Tell us the nitty 2 the damn gritty. Don't be half stepping brutha" I believe Mo'Nigue would tell me...

Anytime you lock up 500 teen boys together some of them are going to voluntarily experiment sexually. "Boys will be boys (girls if you put em 2 gether for 2 long!)". And although 'I' believe homosexuality is a sin and wrong etc. I don't really claim 'we' should concern ourselves with 'boys' who were sitting on a fence (betwix and between - sexually) and got locked up (with raging hormones) and decided to engage in consensual relationships. Not my business!...

My problem is when (or rather "if") Justin Bieber gets locked up and his celly (who has been in and out of jail forever and has hepatitis and HIV) rapes him!... And (I'll repeat - and if you think I'm embellishing like James Frey don't call Mrs. Winfrey. Call Mrs. McFarlane, Linda McFarlane at Just Detention is an expert on prisoner rape(s). Boys who look like Justin, CJ. Alex King etc. etc. are raped every second, of every minute, of every hour of every day! Some Justin (looking) Bieber is being train raped (in Michigan, Arizona, Florida, New York and California etc. etc.) right this very moment. And I am an "Expert" monitor of this animalistic behavior because of what I have seen, witnessed and heard on the inside. It is a sad sight to see a Nathan Gould, Christopher Parker, Marvin Stone etc. forcefully butt-f--ked by 3 or 4 lifers and he's too scared to tell it. Because boys get raped in Hades, but snitches get killed in prison...

And I've said that even though Frey embellished "a million little pieces" I concur with the 57 year old female librarian at CMF-Vakaville who said "Even though there is way too much profanity in that book I wish every 12 year old (and older) would read that book. They need to read (before they use) such a powerful gripping tale about drugs... Having read about drugs many of them will. Be turned around"..

Likewise I say T.J. Parsell's tome "Fish" has too much profanity and a lot of graphic sex but every boy (11 years and older) should read Parsell's "Fish" with all deliberate speed...

And senators, the U.S. Congress etc. need to investigate the treatment of kids in U.S. prisons. There is a surge of violence taking place in bootcamps, juvenile detention facilities and in prisons where kids are housed. What happened to T.J. Parsell in American prisons were sadistic crimes against humanity. What happed to T.J. Parsell in these United States of America was appalling, humiliating and devastating. And all of these Bible thumping pastors ought to be thumping the halls of congress demanding reform for all of the "boyz (who were in 'tha hood' but are now) in tha prison". ... One of my critics perused a portion of this tome and stated "You know that the media have a fascination with the backrooms (boardrooms?) of prison officials, pastors and politicians. And we have a fascination with what goes on in prisoners bedrooms (bathrooms?). And your book is just feeding that frenzy... You've exploited your friendship with the Menendez brothers and written things which only the tabloids need to know". Eric and Lyle were my Friends? Never! Eric and Lyle are stone cold killers. They are sociopaths, greedy, narcissistic, egotistical miscreants. Quite frankly, Eric is worse than Lyle. Eric manipulated Barbara Walters (and attempted to manipulate the courts) into believing Lyle was the mastermind. And Eric was a "reluctant participant". Eric even filed a confidential motion (under seal) claiming that Lyle molested him (Eric) out in the woods on a number of occasions. This does not explain away why both Mike Henrickson and Eric Menendez were caught with child porn in their cell in 2000. "Eric had nude photos of 7 and 8 year old boys underneath his mattress. And Henrickson had photos of both little boys and girls in his locker... "I confiscated the kiddie porn and was writing a 115. But Scarsella and Sergeant Saunders ordered me not to write the R.V.R." a veteran prison guard states.... At MCSP Lyle was caught with methamphetamine and gay porn on 3 occasions in 2004. C.O. Baker and Pogue were accused of smuggling the items to him. All 3 incidents were ordered swept under the rug by Sylvia Garcia and Mike Bunnell.... At P.V.S.P. Eric was caught with a cell phone, a "playgirl" magazine, meth and "kiddie" boy porn. Lt. Allen and Captain Beels ordered the materials "hot trashed" (destroyed) because they did not want media attention at the already infamous P.V.S.P. At my hospital bed (C.R.M.C.) Wally Tucker explained to D.L. Criner that "C.O. Wheat (a female) and Garza are smuggling the crap to Menendez. So the warden does not want to have to investigate and fire people etc. etc. So the incident "didn't happen". The blind can't lead the blind" Tucker continued. "Yates has dirt, dope and blood on his hands so he does not want any attention"....

Every time Eric and I had long, controversial philosophical discussions etc. he always attempted to explain to me how great, sophisticated and brilliant he was. Yet he would simultaneously attempt to convince me that Lyle was the mastermind behind the plot to kill their father. And their mother was merely "collateral damage". Eric blew his mother's head off. He re-loaded and shot her again. His mother!! I'm sorry (Barbara Walters etc.) to all of you who are sympathetic to the Menendez murderers but I'm not with it. There is absolutely nothing you can do to a half way decent person to persuade them to annihilate the person responsible for putting them on the planet. It is beyond inexcusable and it is unexplainable. How dare I express all kinds of outrage and disbelief at Phil Garrido (with his sick and perverted butt) for his enslavement. Yet express understanding for Eric and Lyles' assassination? There is no explanation for executing your mother and father. And (here and now) I will 'face the music' and I'll admit (here and now) that I am 100% guilty! Guilty! Guilty! I am totally (fully) guilty as charged of masterminding a conspiracy to extract data from Eric and Lyle. It's confession time now.... I informed Attorney Michael Edward Bergin (in the late 90;s) that I was housed in the same building with Eric G. Menendez. And that "I don't speak to that bastard!"... I had spent almost two years going out of my way to ignore and disregard Eric. Mike said "but Reverend he's a hot potato.... There are gonna be lots of inmates trying to sell quick stories about him which are superficial and lack any substance. If I were you I'd get to know everything I can about the guy. Win his confidence and then write meticulous notes about every conversation. Try to get him (Eric) to write you a missive.... You can use this data in a tome to make a difference". I took Mike's advice and I staged the conversation Eric and I had when I finally began to allow him to speak with me. I took studious notes. And I have (the lawyer has them) seven missives from Eric (I was unsuccessful at getting Lyle to pen me a missive when we were at MCSP). Three of them are about tobacco, one is about his celly (Henrickson) and 'gay porn'. And three are about the $ 250.00 I loaned him. (If he denies we have the cancelled check to Becky Snead for Eric and Tammy. I have his notes and I will pay for Eric to take a polygraph at P.V.S.P. I'll also pay for a poly to be administered to me....)....

I wanna revisit another predator that I've mentioned before: Joe Arpaio, the head lawman over Maricopa County, Arizona. Joe Bills himself as "America's toughest Sheriff". In September 2006 Joe actually debated L.A. County Sheriff Leroy Baca about who ran the strictest jail... When most folks hear Joe's name they reflect upon the Austere conditions at his infamous outdoor tent city jail: Prisoners forced to wear pink underwear (for Joe's lecherous fantasies) and striped uniforms; temperatures of 110 degrees and above; no coffee, smoking or porn mags allowed; chain gang work crews; and two meals a day which cost only 30 cents per inmate, with an emphasis on green Bologna. Joe Boasts that he spends twice as much on meals for the dogs and cats he keeps in an air-conditioned rescue center. Recently Joe removed kool-aid from his jail menu.

Joe has no respect for people's civil and human rights. Many inmates have been beat, raped (by inmates and by Joe Along with his commando squads etc.) and killed in Joe's lock-ups.... (Shawn Carter and Ryan Bradley r u perusing this? We want you all 2 be "ice skating Gang Bangers for Good!)... In 1999, Maricopa County paid $ 9 million to settle a wrongful death suit filed by the estate of prisoner Scott Norberg, who was tasered and placed in a restraint chair. That same year a jury awarded $ 1.5 million to Tim Griffin, A jail inmate denied treatment for a perforated ulcer. On March 24, 2006, a jury returned a $ 9 million verdict against the County in a case involving a mentally ill inmate, Charles Agster III, who died after being forcibly restrained by deputies and raped by Joe. September 11, 2006 while Americans were mourning and remembering 9/11 Joe was settling a lawsuit regarding a controversial "jail cam" that he had installed, which broadcast video of pre-trial detainees, including female prisoners, on the internet. Joe tried to arrange a secret deal with a porn mogul to feed film of inmates masturbating to the mogul; a deal worth $ 5 million...

Six other wrongful death suits against the Maricopa County sheriff's office are still pending - including one involving the April 15, 2003 death of Brian Scott Crenshaw, a legally blind inmate who was beaten into a coma by jail guards (on Joe's order); Brian died at a hospital. According to (Cho-mo Joe) Arpaio, Brian fell off a bunk... "It's part of Business", Joe once quipped. "You don't stop the wheels of government because some civil liberties group is going to sue you". He doesn't stop the wheels of government even when they rape, run over and kill folks housed in his jails 'either'.

Joe is sinister and nefarious. Political dirty tricks, vindictive actions against the media that print unflattering articles (if Joe tries to keep K.K.K. out of the jail inmate families etc. must contact PLN, G.B.G. and/or the ACLU etc.), secretive real estate holdings, kiddie porn and retaliation against his own employees etc. are all hidden under a thin veneer of his law-and-order facade.

Country music star Glen Campbell and Phoenix Businessman Joseph Deihl II were given special treatment in jail by Joe. In exchange for tens of thousands of dollars in campaign contributions to Joe. Diehl is suspected to have given Joe $ 25 grand (cash) to pay a male inmate not to go public with his sexual relationship (which allegedly began at the Mesa Jail facility) with Joe.

Joe bribed TV reporter Rob Koebel to air false allegations of rape against an opponent (who was about to defeat Joe in 2004) of Joe's for sheriff... Joe hates the Phoenix New Times because they publish critical articles about his jail treatment of inmates. Joe calls a Phoenix New Times reporter (John Dougherty) "a brain-addled geezer" and a "demented cretin". Joe put John under criminal investigation for publishing Joe's Home address in the paper... Recently Joe had the publishers of the Phoenix New Times arrested on false charges. He also hates the West

Valley View, which criticized the sheriff in an article for failing to inform the community about a pair of attempted child abductions. The inflammatory headline read, "Sheriff as dangerous as a child predator. Both of the "as" should have been removed from the headline...

If Joe's wife Anna knew about the sex and fantasies Joe orders select inmates (wearing the pink undies) to fulfill at the jail, she would divorce him with all deliberate speed... Joe has more than $ 3 million in real estate holdings with only a $ 76,000 salary!

The sheriff's dept. is Joe's personal fiefdom, and woe to anyone who angers King Joe.... Joe has run promotions scams for deputies who support his campaigns for sheriff. And demoted and/or fired others who did not support his bids... Attorney Michael Manning states that the deputies involved in the wrongful death of Charles Agster III received promotions... Joe's deputies run a prostitution ring which kicks back money to Joe.

Amnesty International has condemned his jail. See www.arpaio.com and www.mothersagainstarpaio.com.... Even Matt Salmon, director of the Arizona Republican Party, says of Joe (also a republican of course), "I don't respect him, and I don't think he's playing with a full deck". However John McCain, Limbaugh, Hannity and Coulter all support Joe... The Arizona Republic Newspaper does not cover negative stories about Joe because Phil Boas (the editor) is Joe's son-in-law... I applaud the East Valley Tribune, West Valley View, Phoenix New Times and PLN for having the balls to report (what Paul Harvey would call) the rest of the story on Joe... Joe, Bunnell, Domingo, Marion, Mike and Lance should all be sharing a six man prison cell...

... The most important goal that G.B.G. has is to influence and persuade kids not to join gangs. And to get those in - out. Ipso Facto, we work to influence you (youths) away from the things which often lead to gang land and which go hand in hand with criminality. If we figure out a way to get you to keep yourself off drugs and in school etc. half our job is accomplished...

Another strong goal we have is to influence legislators away from locking so many kids up, so fast and for so long. Pragmatically, however, it'll take a sea change and vision to accomplish that part of our mission...

We also are adamant about shining a white hot light on youths who are molested and raped in custody. The rape(s) of boys (11, 12, 13 - 26 etc.) in custody is an understated, underreported epidemic in juveniles, jails and in prisons all across America!

.... During the 2006 elections, Texas Attorney General Greg Abbott ran TV ads touting the capture of the State's internet child predator. "They worked on a bill which would impose the death penalty on those with the most serious child sex offenses. Less than a month later Gov. Rick Perry, Abbott and the entire Texas legislature had to take a long look in the mirror when it was revealed that two high ranking state employers had been molesting Young boys for years... Sammy Carlson, Jason Durtchi, Stewart Katz, Mark Merin and Cheryl Montgomery are you reading this? Mr. Obama, Joe Biden, Professor Gates and the cop had a "Beer summit". Sarah Palin wants to have a "coffee summit" with Madame secretary Clinton. G.B.G. held a "soda summit" (with my executive staff and two advisors) to discuss this Texas scandal. Likewise I've consulted with C.O. A. Novak, C.O. D. Kelly, C.O. Hodge, C.O. T. Ramsey, Daniel Bugriyev and our advisory board about what happened in Texas. Because as Dr. C. Solis stated to me "Love or hate Sherman D. Manning etc. If you write something substantive about what happens to kids in prisons. If you write something powerful for youngsters to read it can begin something great". I asked Dr. Solis what he meant. "Sherman you already know Baby Boomers and the establishment are not going to trust you any farther than they can throw you. But 'we' can't stop kids from reading 'K.K.K.'. They will read it whether we want them to or not". Dr. Solis continued "If we (parents) had so much influence over our kids why do 50% them drop out of school in D.C. And 75% of them drop-out in Detroit? They don't listen to us. Hell, if only 10% of the drop-outs read the book it'll make a change... If you use this book as a staging platform to tell kids what they would know if 'juvenile walls could talk' you will do two things: A. Cause some of them to do what is necessary to not go to prison. And B. You'll cause some of them to begin to work to change the system for the kids who are already in prison... Some kids will be drawn to "K.K.K." because of the name (K.K.K.). Some will be attracted because a maximum security prisoner wrote it. Some will read it because you dedicated it to President Obama.

... You don't care why they come to the theater to view the written movie of "K.K.K.". And I may dislike some of the commercials (i.e. propaganda) in the movie (tome)... So what? Is there anything in this movie that might make a kid think twice about joining a gang, dropping out of school or going to prison? If the answer is 'yes' then you have succeeded".

... From 2002 to 2005, complaints of inappropriate sexual contact began piling up against Ray E. Brookins and John Paul Hernandez. Yet rather than spark an immediate investigation, those complaints were mostly ignored while Ray and John rose to positions of power in the Texas Youth Commission (TYC), the state's juvenile justice agency.

John Hernandez was the principal of the West Texas State school, a facility for kid offenders in Pyote, Texas. Hernandez used offers of cake, candy and educational aid as enticements to lure boys into sex... Ray E. Brookins, an administrator at the school, even had a 16-year-old boy living with him in his home on the West Texas campus.

Reports from staff and youth over the three-year period expressed concern about the two men spending excessive amounts of time alone with the juvenile kids and specific charges of sexual contact. But officials consistently disregarded the complaints, and Ray was recommended by his supervisor and promoted to assistant superintendent of the West Texas facility.

"If you ask me, I'll say... if it feels good, just do it!" These are the words posted on the myspace.com page of "xxxrayvijon" AKA Ray E. Brookins. The assistant superintendent of the West Texas State school said he was into "making good love to the one I'm with", and practicing safe sex "cause I love me".

When Ray was visited at home by Texas Ranger Brian Burzynski, the "one he was with" was a 16-year-old boy. Burzynski found pornographic videos, magazines and catalogs at the residence. 3 of the magazines were under the boys bed; the boy was not a resident of the school. Ray told the Texas Ranger and the Ward County investigator who was with him that the boy's mother had left the boy with him while she was tending her mother, who was sick.

Brian warned Ray that child protective services (CPS) would be notified since the superintendent failed to keep track of his vast quantity of porn materials. Yet by the time CPS officials arrived at Ray's residence, the boy was "visiting" his "relatives elsewhere".

... The boy's dad said he'd detected a lot of personal interest by Ray in his son. Ray claimed the boy was simply staying with him til his dad could come from S. Carolina to take him home; and denied molesting the youth.

However, an 18-year-old who was interviewed by Brian said Brookins and he had engaged in oral sex, and described how Ray instructed him in a variety of sex activities. Ray admitted he had taught the boy how to masturbate, how to use porn when masturbating, and how to use sex toys.

Ray was not a stranger to online porn. During his tenure at the TYC facility in San Saba, Texas, Ray received a reprimand, 90 days probation and a transfer after explicit porn was found on his work computer. This transfer landed him at the boy's school in Pyote.

Ray had convictions for passing hot checks and multiple moving violations. He'd been accused (but not formally charged) of child molestation. After he began his career as a prison guard in 1985, he received major disciplinary violations for failing to report major uses of force on prisoners, failure to perform random drug tests on inmates, once for wrecking the warden's car and falsifying documents. Seven adult inmates accused Ray of engaging in sex while he was a captain at the Cotulla unit in 1995; he failed two polygraph tests, but the complaints were dismissed!

"This guy should never have been working for TYC. Period" said Sen. John Whitmore, chairman of the senate criminal justice committee.... and prisons (and juveniles etc.) run rampant (across the nation) with violent and abusive guards (like Marion E. Spearman, Joe Arpaio and Bunnell etc.) who graduate from filing false reports (i.e. "fixit tickets" like fired Sergeant Aaron Ralls filed at CSP Sac.) to beating inmates etc. to manipulating (enticing and bribing) inmates into sex etc. on to eventually raping inmates...

Hernandez and Ray were both accused repeatedly by teachers of having late night parties with the teen boys under their care. Burzynski reported that the two would often wake boys up in the middle of the night and then lock themselves in classrooms and offices for hours with the lights off.

"We should have fired [Ray] in 2001, after we found porno on his computer", said TYC spokesman Tim Savoy. "That should have been a red flag". Why were these two dudes not prosecuted for three years? When this scandal finally came to light, Hernandez was working as head of a charter school (molesting more boys) in Midland, Texas.

Many officials knew about this sex scandal and did nothing about it... Ranger Burzynski's investigation revealed that between 2000 and 2005 the superintendent of the West Texas State school, Chip Harrison, had received numerous complaints about Ray and Hernandez... They used their authority to alter complaints or to discard them altogether, to cover up for each other. Chip's only effort to address the problem was to ask both men not to spend so much time alone with the boys... I want Bob Blasier and Attorney Lisa M. Bassis, John Burton and my advisory board to help me put together a plan (form the inside put) to help youth wards in custody to prevent and report rapes...

The complaints grew to so many that TYC Headquarters opened its own investigation into the two guys, but their efforts came up empty. They concluded that "the complaints didn't suggest "sexual abuse or violation of policy". They found that staff witnesses contradicted each other, and that Hernandez and Brookins' behavior was open to interpretation.

Lydia Barnard, the former superintendent of the San Saba facility who had initially hired Ray, was the official who reprimanded him when porn was found on his work computer. When complaints began to cross her desk, she, like Harrison, simply asked Ray not to spend as much time alone with kids at the facility. She was also responsible for Ray's promotion to acting superintendent when Harrison took a medical leave of absence.

"How did they miss that?" asked Jim Hurley, TYC spokesman. One care-worker, angry at not being able to keep Ray away from children at the school, emailed TYC executive director Dwight Harris. No action was taken... Geoffrey Yager, Alexander Huba, Scott Tarvin and Tadd Carr are you reading this?

"We're going to get to the bottom of this", declared Sen. Whitmire. "There are no untouchables". I respect Sen. Whitmire but I disagree. Marion E. Spearman, Bunnell, Arpaio and Lance Corcoran etc. are (obviously) "untouchable".

"I want the problem solved", stated Lt. Gov. David Dewhurst as he simultaneously called for the entire board of commissioners over the TYC to be fired.

"We gotta come in and clean House", Sen. Juan "Chuy" Hinojosa echoed. It was one of Hinojosa's aides who was key in exposing the TYC sexual abuse cover-up.

Instead of facing the wrath of the legislature, TYC Director Harris resigned. Neil Nichols, his replacement, also eventually resigned after he was required to testify before the State Senate.

Neil withstood the senate investigation with remarkable composure. "There's no question. We missed a lot of keys", he said. However, Neil pointed out that TYC couldn't be held responsible for failing to prosecute Ray and Hernandez once they had been forced to resign. "The decision to prosecute is not ours to make", he said.

Jay Kimbrough, appointed by Gov. Perry as a special master to investigate the system-wide problems in the TYC, arrived at the West Texas State School in March 2007 on his Harley, two hours early, and ordered a surprised TYC guard to show him "where the blind spots are".

Kimbrough, a former Marine, detailed surveillance cameras and staff shortages, paperwork fraud and classification errors Jay informed legislators that as many as 60 to 95 percent of juveniles institutional infractions were often without proper documentation.....

Kyle Hoover, Nathan Hand and Greg Pugh (Rich. VA.) etc. are yall reading this?....

Congressman Jerry Madden, Chairman of the House Corrections Committee explained "I think ultimately we're talking about (releasing) a fourth of those in custody, maybe more.

By March 29, Kimbrough had searched under every rock and looked in every nook and cranny of TYC. He ordered the firings of 111 employees with felony convictions and required all top management to reapply for their jobs. This Harley-riding, no-nonsense watchdog was overwhelmingly approved to be the new conservator over the TYC.

"He always responded to the call of his country or his state", lauded Sen. Steve Ogden. "Jay Kimbrough is a good man, a straight arrow".... Devin Rio? Justin Zysman and Joseph Rocha etc. read on.... Legislators ignored (because many legislators receive campaign money from guards working in these institutions!) information about improprieties in the TYC system for years. Most legislators in California don't even read prisoner mail. Cause prisoners don't have any money!....

The TYC began to sound like a Donald Trump reality show on March 11 2007 when Gov. Perry demoted TYC board chairman Pete Alfaro just before Alfaro resigned. By law the governor couldn't fire a state board member, he can only demote the chairman.

"The incidents at West Texas, what happened there is terrible, no board member will disagree", Alfaro stated. "But we followed our procedures that we had".

Procedures? Procedures must be changed to prevent staff from raping students, inmates and kids etc.... "That kid Derek King? I would stick my tongue all the way inside his pink, sweaty asshole.... Look at Derek's lips. I would eat him up!.... If he wanted $ 2500.00 to let me lick his balls I'd pay it!". A man said this. And perhaps [??] this perversion can be understood (though not condoned) being made by a dude who has not had a lady in 20 years. An inmate.... But - it was a "peace" officer who said this. He is married and had kids. Correctional Lieutenant Cherry (MCSP) said this... A married man!...

On March 9, 2007 there were 3 more administrative casualties. TYC's Chief Internal Investigator, Ray Worsham, was suspended for redacting documents which contained incriminating data. Sylvia Machado, superintendent of TYC's Ayers Halfway House in San Antonio, was suspended after she was caught shredding documents. She was arrested and held til she posted a $ 20,000 bond...

Machado reminds me of associate Warden Schievelbein. He was a pompous ass and a pervert. When he was a captain at New Folsom he attempted to rape inmate D.J. Carpenter and Lefty Linscott. E.J. Puente reported that captain Schievelbein brought him a carton of Camel cigarettes in Ad-seg and attempted to get him to "masturbate while I watch".... Captain Schievelbein grabbed and fondled inmate(s) Tracy Roby and Martin Cheatham... Each and every person who complained about Schievelbein was special transferred out of New Folsom. He went down town in charge of transportation. He was a part of the Bunnell gang which transferred me. He promoted to A.W. and went to "Old Folsom". He was written up for sexually fondling two male inmates. He was written up for shredding (the 'Machado' like-ness) the write up. And that 'write up' disappeared. He reported to work drunk twice. He falsified and shredded a number of documents.... A lobbyist was on the radio talking about Old Folsom. The lobbyist had a relative doing 'time' at Old Folsom. A.W. Schievelbein called the lobbyist and left a threatening message on the man's answering machine (what an Idiot). The lobbyist returned the call and spoke with the A.W.'s old lady (a correctional employee at New Folsom). She told the lobbyist to "watch your back". And due to these terroristic and veiled threat(s) the A.W. was forced to retire... Prison officials shred documents and falsify data all the time...

David Andrew Lewis was fired from the Coke County Juvenile Justice Center (CCJJC) after it was learned that he was a "convicted 'sex' offender" - he was even listed (Justin Chirigotis, Billy Bell, Peter, Teddy, Nathan and Ryan r u reading this stuff? Dude - this....) on the state's public sex offender (i.e. Mike Jiminez? Lance? Spearman?) registry.... legislators addressed TYC's board at a joint house - Senate hearing in March of 07. "You're responsible for 5,000 children that are incarcerated, and they're God's children", fumed Congressman Jim McReynolds. (I want Ryan Mac 2 send cong. McReynolds a missive and ask him to call the Governor and plead that Shievelbein's old lady be forbidden from retaliating against me!)... Those are the most important 3 words in this tome: "They're God's Children!"... You are God's child!.... You are special and you are precious. Say that out Lord: "I am God's Child!" Say "I am precious".... Congressman McReynolds continued "I read (reports) last night until I wanted to vomit". "The system is broken. You're part of the broken system".... I thought about Wayne, Rawlings, Ronald Wright, Chris Durbin and Mike Crowder as I read about TYC. And as I re-read missives written to me (by Ronald, Wayne and Jodie Bear etc.) I wondered how they (also John Sexton, Chad Newman, Daniel Job and Daniel Hallsell etc.) would have survived in TYC...

... Four days later the senate criminal justice committee defied Gov. Perry's wishes and unanimously agreed to fire the entire panel of the TYC board members. On March 17 the board resigned in the wake of a "no confidence" vote by the full senate.

On March 20 there were two more resignations, as TYC Deputy Executive Director Linda Selness Reyes and General Counsel Neil Nichols resigned.

"You could classify them as forced resignations" Jay Kimbrough's spokesman stated. "We do know we need a change and they're at the top of the food chain"...

April 4 brought numerous other staff changes, as forty TYC employees with felony records were fired. Over half of those fired had received 'deferred adjudication' on their criminal charges... CDC has many rogue guards with deferred adjudications.... Twenty-five of the forty were guards.

By April 18, sixty-six TYC employees had been identified as convicted felons. All were given a go-day severance package. Their convictions included, aggravated assault with a deadly weapon, car theft, engaging in organized crime, sexual assault, attempted murder and murder.

A TYC whistleblower with a felony record was not spared. Anthony Mikulastik, a case manager, had brought sexual abuse allegations to the attention of his supervisors in 2003 but rebuffed. He was fired on May 7, 2007, six days after he spoke to the media. He had a felony conviction for burglary in 1972 that had been disclosed to the TYC when he was hired. He claimed retaliation.

As of May 14, 2007, a total of 93 TYC employees had been suspended, terminated or forced to retire. Then the arrests began.... If C.D.C. (like TYC) were to begin to do thorough FBI background checks on all 35,000 guards there would be hundreds (if not thousands) of firings. We have convicted child molesters and murderers wearing badges and uniforms and carrying guns. And the CCPOA is an organized criminal enterprise managed by criminals!...

Donna Bobb's son (a teen) and all of you young g's better vaccinate (educate) yourself against the perils of crime that'll cause you to do time. Because if you come here (to Hades) your guard may need guarding.

... Once the can of worms was open it wasn't log before TYC guards and supervisors started landing in jail. James Allen Sullivan had been investigated for sexually abusing young kids at the Ron Jackson School in Brownwood, Texas as early as 2002. Smitten by a 16-year-old, he started giving the kid extra privileges, candy and even drugs for sex. Sullivan would flirt with the kid and say "you are sexy".... Senator Hinojosa's aide found "missing tapes" showing Sullivan going into a supply closet with kids... The grand jury reviewed the video footage, and on May 10, 2007 Sullivan was named in a 19-count indictment and arrested. He posted a $1500.00 bond and got out....

Barry Ransberger also worked at the Ron Jackson unit. In March of 2007, he was arrested on charges of sexually assaulting an adult prisoner while a guard at the Middleton prison unit in 2005. He'd been forced to resign from Middleton due to the incident, but while under investigation still managed to obtain a job at the TYC.

"It's very disturbing that if he was being investigated by (the Texas Dept. of Crim. Justice), he was somehow able to get a job at TYC", said spokesman Jim Hurley...

As of March 16, 2007, active Internal TYC Investigations included 228 related to suspicion of sexual misconduct...

... Jerome Parsee, superintendent of TYC's Martin facility, was arrested for lying to Texas Rangers about sexual assault reports filed at the unit... I need Justin Zysman, Daniel Asare and John Butterfield etc. to get a vivid picture of the fact that boys are made toys and sex-slaves in prisons every day of the week. And guards do a lot of the raping. And they very often do get away with it. So boys at Lincoln High School, Donna Bobb's son, Justin ("Ratchet Rockets"), "Logan" ("Miss Daisy" design leader), kids in coach Al Ostrow's class etc. need to remember that there is a "light at the end of the school "Hallway". I want kids to know that prisons are no longer simmering with rape, rage and violence etc. We've reached a boiling point. America's juvenile prisons are falling off the edge of a cliff. And 'if' you do things (i.e. gang banging, drug using, selling etc.) to land you here you are pretty much telling the world "I wanna be traumatized and sodomized". And you can't expect a guard to guard you from the boys who act like men in the day and yet screw (and suck) like women in the night. Because the guards very often are gay, bi and rapists themselves.

... Let me ask Daniel Hallsell, Josh Cook, Jason Durtchi, Maxwell Hanger and Dan Sellery etc. a question: How many straight men do you know who would volunteer to take a j-o-b where they will be looking (staring at) at penis', anus' and testicles for 30 years? Event the married guards see more penis' in one 8 hour shift than their wives see in a lifetime. More than 70% of male prison guards fantasize about sex with other men. This would explain why they over compensate and go out of their way pretending to despise those convicted of "rape" etc.... Kids at Frank Sinatra school in Queens N.Y. 'Cory', students in the "Glee" Club, Kevin McHale, The Masters school, Justin Eller, Darryl Paulo, Puka Lopa, Mo Torres, Ayanna Moody, Evan Karoway and Eric Bulrice have gotta read this... Ladd Wildaman (41) sexually assaulted a drunk and sleeping 27 year old man weeks ago. This is the kind of stuff your celly (suite mate? sweet mate?) will do to you if you come here to Hades.

On April 11, 2007, the two men whose misconduct instigated the wide-spread investigation into the TYC scandal were finally indicted. John Paul Hernandez was charged with one count of sexual assault, nine counts of of improper relationship with a student. The charges involved six youths, ages 15 to 19. He got out on May 10th after his bond was reduced from $ 650,000 to $ 95,000.

Ray Brookins, charged with two counts of having a relationship with a person in state custody, a state jail felony, was released on a $ 100,000 personal recognizance bond.

One irony in the Hernandez and Brookins scandal is that Marc Slattery, a volunteer tutor at the West Texas State School who provided a tip which set the TYC sex abuse investigation in motion, himself had been locked up for sex assault in 1986. He had pleaded guilty to a lesser charge of simple assault and was put on probation. The TYC has since revoked his volunteer status... Yates and Marion E. Spearman have allowed hundreds of convicted sexual offenders to volunteer at P.V.S.P....

There is a reason (some) that I'm writing my ass off to motivate kids not to come here. And there is a reason (some) I'm seeking out Joseph Rocha, Zach Freisen, Chris Austad and Kyle Love etc. and encouraging them to become ambassadors and help "us" spread the word...

Ryan Mac (CEO of US Mint Green Ltd.) is willing to help me give stipends and internships to some of you (i.e. C.J. Sheron, Nathaniel Mullennix, Cody Sheldon, Austin Sisneros, Billy Bell, Jakob Karr etc.) who are willing to spend some time (minimum of ten hours per week working to publicize G.B.G. and K.K.K. over the internet.... I see no reason that we can't give CJ, Cody, Nathaniel, Tadd and/or Greg Deekens etc. $ 150,00 per week to blog, chat, I.M. and T.M. to promote our mission...

Another irony involves TYC whistleblower Billy Hollis, who had been formally reprimanded in 04 after he tried to alert authorities about improprieties related to Brookins' conduct. Billy has since been promoted to assistant superintendent at West Texas State School, the position which Brookins held, and works in Brookins' former office.

Hernandez and Brookins dodged prosecution for two years despite a mountain peak of evidence that they were engaging in sexual misconduct with youths under their supervision. Texas Ranger Burzynski's investigation caused sufficient concern to force both men from their jobs long before they were arrested. Yet months turned into years as Ward county district Attorney Randall Reynolds failed to return an indictment on either former TYC official. He never even presented the evidence to a grand jury.... Prosecutors are 'political'. We all joke about how do you know when "a lawyer is lying? When is lips are moving". I think it was Shakespeare who said "Let's 'kill' all the "lawyers'"! We love to talk about lawyers being snake oil salesmen and used car salesmen. Yet we always forget that every prosecutor is a 'lawyer'. Every 'judge' is a 'lawyer'. They r all trained in the Socratic method. They can (second nature) argue both sides of any issue. Yet, the moment they grab a black rope or the title 'District' in front of the 'Attorney' etc. We think "District" (prosecutor) and we forget the "Attorney"... Prosecutors lie and cheat. And they routinely accept bribes. Jan Scully (Sacto. D.A.) rarely ever brings a case against CDC guards because Jan has been bribed by the CCPOA!... When she does prosecute she'll throw the case or seek the minimum penalty.... Mary Hanlon Stone surprised me by not wanting a bribe. I don't know whether she just hated me so badly or didn't 'trust' me. Not to rat her out etc. but I must (reluctantly - but with probity) admit Mary Hanlon did not want a bribe! I can not say the same about the honorable Judge Robert Altman. Had I given him tens of thousands of dollars (he told Curt and Robert Burns etc.) I would not be in prison. And (in all candor) there were but two reasons I did not pay the bribe. Neither of which pertained to my being 'honest' or believing in the 'justice' system etc. etc. I did not give Judge Altman the bribe he sought because I'd run out of cash! And I did not trust Burns and Waite....

Do you all remember how District Attorney Nifong did Collin Finnerty and his pals on the Lacrosse team at Duke?... Nifong was a prosecutor! Nifong is Jan Scully! Nifong is 50% of American District Attorneys!.... Money talks and bull crap walks! Jan has an off-shore bank account. Jan probably has hundreds of thousands of dollars in 'cash'. I can't count (and won't name) the police officers in Atlanta, Richmond, D.C., Chicago etc. whom I've bribed.... They'll stop me for speeding. I'll hand them 2 crisp one hundred dollar bills and they tell me to 'have a nice day sir'... Police, prison guards, prosecutors and judges etc. take bribes everyday of the week.... Police chief (who has never done anything to me) Jerry Dyer (in Fresno) is known for taking bribes from pimps, dope dealers and gangsters.

I vividly recall deputy district Attorney Robert Clancy coming inside New Folsom State prison. I still say "truth is stranger than 'fiction'". And this should've been on a "law and order" episode... I had this case pending in Sacramento. And any first year law student will tell you a prosecutor is forbidden from communicating with a defendant (with counsel) outside the presence of his attorney. What D.A. do you know of who would barge into a defendants home (without a search warrant after the defendant is out on bail) to have a chat with the defendant?.... I saw Clancy walking on to the yard and I told "Atlas" (AKA Alonzo) and "Claw" that "that's my D.A., what the hell is he doing in here with Zamudio?" And Mr. Clancy walks over and says "Mr. Manning can you walk with me and Celsa (Zamudio)?" Atlas says "Gone with em Atlanta. They ain't gonna kill yo black ass". I walk and we get down near one Bldg. I'm totally paranoid. I'm wondering is he gonna claim I assaulted him? Will Zamudio hit his alarm? Is this a set-up?.... I say "Mr. Clancy I don't want to speak to you without my Attorney!" He replies "you'll get over it Sherm.... You are facing 75-years to life. I know you make money from those books". He stops and looks around to be certain it's only Zamudio, him and me. "Can your guy Peter wire $ fifty grand somewhere to make this case disappear?" I say "What? I don't have that kind of money. Are you serious?" He says "I'm dead serious. I do not accept bribes Mr. Manning. I do accept campaign contributions for my boss. And donations to charity. Peter is not an inmate. He's never been charged with a crime. If he wanted to give, donate or contribute $ fifty grand to me I might run for something one day". Now I was thinking Clancy was wearing a wire and was merely attempting to set me up on a bribery beef... He and Zamudio left and went into my cell building. They searched my cell and left... I only told one person the real details of our conversation. And this Attorney said "And.... are you gonna be able to come up with the money or not?" He was not (not one bit) even surprised.... I wasn't even gonna write (just between you and I) the fact that Kathryn Druliner wanted a bribe for her husband! He works for the Attorney General!... Now you see why I'll never get out of prison! Nor will I ever make it out alive.

If you talk with Bobby Lee Cook, Morchower, Janus or my friend Judge Michael Edward Bergin etc. (off the record) they will all tell you that judges and prosecutor accept bribes routinely. It is considered "normal" operations for the rich. Why do you think most dudes in prisons are indigent?... When O.J. had $ 10 or $ 20 million he murdered two white people ("only in America"!) and went home!! And now that he does not have a $ million bucks he's in prison (probably 4 life!) 4 a lil of nothing....

Judges sometimes accept bribes to make certain rulings! I.e. "Give me $ 100 grand and I'll allow that evidence in tomorrow. I won't dismiss the case. That'll look too suspicious. But this ruling can open the door to an acquittal". And before you say "Nah - a judge would not do that" etc. remember he or she is a "lawyer". Just a lawyer yo. And may I ask you a question? Ain't nobody here but you (C.J. Cody, Austin etc.) and me.... If you had a job (let's break it down this way) refereeing an argument and you were paid $ 400.00 per week.... Less than $ 20 grand per year etc. and I brought you $ twenty thousand (your yearly salary!) dollars in cash to rule in my favor; would you take it? I hope your answer is no. I suspect it may be yes. But either way, I'll bet you know somebody who would take it!.... Ipso Facto, there will always be a judge or two (or three etc. and a prosecutor i.e. Jan Scully, Gil Garcetti and Robert Clancy) in every courthouse who will accept bribes.

... I need $ 2500.00 to pay a clerk to make certain judge Willis (sobriquet) gets this case" an Attorney once told me... As Clancy and Zamudio were leaving the yard Alonzo ran up to

Clancy to explain to him how 3-strikes was/is "in the Bible.... When.... struck the Donkey 3 times". Clancy said" I'll have to go look at that in the Bible". I thought he should go read the book of Isaiah about Judges and officials taking "bribes".

I can recall Attorney Puckett in Dekalb County Georgia telling me "I've 'heard' over the grapevine that Attorney Mobley Childs is a "fixer"". He continued "Victoria Litlle is a very good trial lawyer but Mobley's cases never go to trial." I inquired as to 'how' and he stated "I don't know. Use your imagination or you could just call him"... It turns out that the honorable (a 'lawyer') Judge Arnold Schulman as well as deputy district Attorney Mike McDonald were basically golfing buddies with Mr. Childs. And Mr. Childs paid them ("fix") to disappear and dismiss cases. I will repeat - the same disdain we express toward "Sheista Lawyers" who "run around chasing ambulances" etc. must be applied toward the 'lawyers' wearing robes. They are crooks (many of them) and they (i.e. Schulman, Rothberg and Altman etc.) would not know "integrity" if it hit them with a right jab in the face. Nor would they know 'justice' if it hit them with a left jab in the face. Call Attorney Gerry Spence and ask him to tell you about 'Judges'....

... County Attorney Kevin Acker, who prosecutes misdemeanor and juvenile cases, offered to assist Reynolds with the prosecution, Reynolds never enlisted Acker's help. "I had 10 witnesses (against Hernandez and Brookins) and I've never been able to figure out if any of them were called "Acker said.

Burzynski grew so frustrated with Reynold's indifference that he convinced Federal authorities to assist. Reynolds was "a very weak prosecutor", Burzynski told the feds, and said he was "losing hope" that Reynolds would file charges before the statute of limitations ran out.

Burzynski had compiled a 229-page report on the abuses he found at the West Texas State School, and the TYC confirmed more than 2,100 cases of staff abusing inmates from January 2003 to December 2006. But in the end, the feds declined to prosecute.

The feds told Burzynski that Hernandez and Brookins "could only be charged with misdemeanors under federal law. Federal law requires 'bodily injury' to make a violation of civil rights a felony".

Some federal legislators were outraged. "There is no reason why a vigorous Dept. of Justice could not have gone in with a broom and cleaned up the TYC", U.S. Rep Sheila Jackson Lee (who sits on the House Judiciary Committee) said. "They are just not interested, and that is a tragedy".... And she's right, "they (over 90% of our elected officials) are just not interested".... I have written thousands (literally without embellishment) of politicians regarding crimes against children (in prisons and in juveniles etc.) and they don't reply. You'll see em on TV once or twice per year talking about cleaning up the prisons and stopping guard abuse etc. and you'll see em "if" the media decides a crime against a kid (in juvenile, jail or in prison) deserves a story or two. Politicians (like McClintock, Dan Lungren, Cantor etc.) will jump on a media story like a fly on crap. These guys (and gals) remind me of flies and leeches. Not only do they run to a story like a fly chasing 'crap', but they are full of sh-t! And they get on my nerves. They are as phony as a $ 3 bill. They don't give a darn about poor, helpless and defenseless kids in prison. They consider them "Damaged Goods" and "throw away kids". And the reason I reach out to Derek King etc. and the reason my team has to organize prisoners and students etc. is because politicians and parents ain't doing a damn thing.... I remember my teaching as a youngster minister was that women couldn't and shouldn't 'preach'. And a woman pastor told me that "God has to call women to preach because the men ain't doin nothin. If mankind don't wanna praise His name He'll make the rocks cry out He's God". Ipso Facto, 1 in 10 kids will experience sexual misconduct by a teacher during schooling. We have 23 year old police officer Bryan Weinrich (who raped a 4 year old little girl when he was 18) arrested for beating the crap out of his girlfriend. We have judges, prosecutors and police colluding (for money) to incarcerate innocent children. We have grown ass men (prison guards! Youth counselors etc.) exploiting, enslaving, beating and sodomizing boys and girls in prisons. And the only way we can get a legislator or a senator to "say" something about it is if the media says something about it. So I decided that since Limbaugh, Hannity and Coulter are not saying anything why not me. Since so many don't know, don't show or just don't care about what these kids who kill kids had happen to them before murder happened through them. Since nobody is doing anything why not use the pain, fear and loneliness which Derek felt in prison etc. as a spring board to get Him to speak up and to speak out. I decided that since most of the Republicans I see wake-up in the morning with "defeating Obama" on their minds. And since many of the Democrats I know are (also) bribe taking, coke snorting hypocrites. Since nobody gets alarmed about the hundreds of thousands of kids beat and bullied everyday - since nobody gets alarmed about the tens of thousands of kids molested and statutorily raped (in schools) every year. Since nobody is doing anything about the boys being sold as sex toys (in Texas, here in California, New York, Michigan and around the country) in jails and juveniles etc. etc. unless the bright lights of the media are trained and shined upon the issue etc. "I" could do no less than stand up and speak out. If not me who? If not now when? .... Ambassador Andrew Young, Rev. Hosea Williams, Police Chief Eldrin Bell, Rev. Moses Lee Raglin etc. etc. didn't invest all of that time, wisdom, money and knowledge into me for me to just get in jail and die. I'm still a man and I still have a voice. And "a charge to keep I have...to serve this present (these children in and outta jail, students, drop-outs etc.) age, my calling to fulfill. Oh may it all my powers engage to do my master's will". I am doing God's will. God'll do the almighty, through the least likely. He'll reach into a prison cell and get Him a dude convicted of a sex crime (Joseph) and make him a prince. He'll reach down inside a prison and use a Paul and a Silas. And "at midnight Paul and Silas prayed and sang praises unto God. And the prisoners heard them". It is midnight in America for kids. And my team and I are praying. And through Ryan, Penny, Frank and Heather etc. the prisoners (like Allen Harris, Jerry Wines, Nathan Gould, Brandon Gene Martinez etc.) have "heard" us. And through, PLN, Convictnews, Facebook and Twitter etc. we are organizing and strategizing. We use our pain, hurt and our loneliness as a springboard to launch us into the will of God... "Oh may it all my powers engage" .... I've gotta use all of my power to do this work... "If you use one tenth of the energy, brainpower and creativity to help kids as you did to con etc. you'll make history" Mrs. Patricia Kennedy told me.

And so we work and we work. And we don't wait on the media. When we get this tome into the hands, hearts and minds of just one percent of America's public school students we will revolutionize the world!.... Get this book into the hands of o-n-e percent of America's public school students and we will change the world!

There are seasons and cycles of life and... Certain things don't/won't happen out of season. There was a season and a spiritual awakening which was taking place in the 20's, 30's and 40's which got the world ready for Martin and Malcolm in the 50's and 60's.

Some things happened in this Country in the 80's and in the 90's that prepared America for an Obama in 08..... Not one pundit in 1969, 1979, 1989 or even 1999 would have predicted that millions of school kids would be volunteering for a black presidential candidate in 2007 and 2008. Nobody would have predicted that millions of 18-38 year old teens, tweenies and theenies would go to the polls in 08 declaring "I got Obama on my mind". And I prophesy that sooner or later G.B.G./HEART, Naps, Taylor Francis, Austin, C.J., Deekens and me (you'll see) are gonna mess around and spark a revolution.

Yall (Clancy, Hanlon-Stone etc.) better "Picture me rolling".... Dr. Jarman told me "Sherman to whom much is given much is expected'. You've been blessed with all kind of talent, influence and incredible capability.... I can see the look of panic on your face" he told me.

"Sherman our grief drives us to hunger for human connection." Dr. Jarman continued "I know what kind of pain and trauma you're holding on to. But you need to let it go. It'll do what God didn't allow Valley Fever to do; it'll kill you". Dr. Jarman stated "I don't know what all Dr. Yablonsky told you when you called him and he's a genius. But I'm telling you that you are an expert. The prisons are filled with experts (master cat burglars, computer hackers, Bernie Madoffs etc.).... There are physicians and psychologists in prison Sherman. There are scientists in prison.... I know you know Dr. Marilyn Windham... It is claimed (over the grapevine) that she did something with you in a dining hall. That's neither here nor there but my point is this' she almost went to prison". Dr. Jarman continued "had she gone to prison she would have, would have lost her license (she did lose it) as a psychologist. But that would not have negated the fact that she went to school all those years studying human behavior... Sherman can you count?" I replied "of course I can count Dr. Jarman". He said "And when was the last time you used mathematics?" I said "yesterday.... I had to add up my grocery store order (AKA Canteen)". He said "and you used skills in prison which you learned in the streets. You learned how to 'count' in school did you not?" I replied "Actually my mother Brenda taught me but I learned advanced mathematics at William Finch elementary school". Dr. Jarman said "so you don't let the fact that you are in prison convicted of a crime stop you from using skills you learned in civilian life. Ipso Facto had Marilyn gone to prison she could've allowed the pain and shame of her conviction to prevent her from using her 'school skills'. She would have been convicted of a 'sex' crime Sherm. So the embarrassment of losing a six figure job and falling from grace could have made her become bitter, a drunk, institutionalized and useless... And/or she could have gotten in her prison cell and used everything she learned in school, college and undergraduate school to help people. There would have been those of 'us' who would have called her a "pariah". Sherm I'm sure she would have disagreed with some of the theories and therapies propagated by some... And she would have made some enemies (i.e. psychologists working in the institution where-in she was housed). But she could have used her prison cell to catapult her ideas, talents and knowledge into an arena of hopelessness where people need it... The Joseph I read about in Genesis didn't allow plots to kill him or stop him. He didn't let slavery, being an outcast or going to prison as a 'sex' offender to stop him".

Dr. Jarman looked me directly in my eyes and told me "Sherman you have made some enemies. Some of that is due to character defects which you must correct. Some of it is because of institutional racism. And some of it is because you've criticized (rightly or wrongly) the practices propagated by some powerful people.... But you are like Michael Jordan would have been if he'd broken his leg or became paralyzed in one leg at 30. He would have been a brilliant basketball expert who couldn't play for a while or perhaps couldn't play 'ever'. He could have felt sorry for himself. He could have committed suicide or homicide. He could have gone on a coke or meth binge etc. or he could have decided to coach... It's time for you to rise up out of the ashes of your prison sentence and coach these kids. Pass on those dreams you didn't achieve (fully) because you are in jail. With the advent of the internet you can launch a masterful campaign against gangs, guns, drugs and violence right from your cell. You can do it. You've got to do it. That's why you're here".... I left Dr. Jarman that day and returned to my cell and wept. I cried the ugly cry. And when I finished crying I made the decision that G.B.G. would move forward! When they criticize me it moves forward. When they praise me (if ever) it moves forward. Whether they cry Hosanna or crucify I'm moving forward. Mr. Obama didn't wait for me to believe in his dream to launch his campaign for the highest office in the land. And (in case you live under a rock) he's there! Even though Limbaugh, Hannity and Palin called him a "terrorist" and a .... He's there! And I won't wait on Mr. Obama (Bill Cosby, Arne or anybody) to believe in G.B.G.. I will simply do the work and pray the prayers. What goes up must come down. And if I don't believe that what goes around comes around I'll stop reading the Bible. If I don't believe that one really does reap what one sows I need to stop praying. God is right and every man is a liar. And His word is clear. He knew me before He ever formed me in Brenda's womb. And destiny is inside of me. I can run around and tell you I didn't do 'this' crime! But if He is (yes He is!) really God He knows exactly what (and 'if') I did and did not do! And Habakkuk (2:3) is clear that the "vision (G.B.G.) is yet for an appointed time.... it will speak (it's speaking in this tome now!), and it will not lie.... (In prison I've had to) wait for it; (God couldn't let Valley Fever kill me because He can't lie and He promised the vision would) surely come"... Not might be, maybe or 'perhaps' but "surely". And so Dr. Jarman was a tool to ignite that fire in my belly. I was walking around here with all these backbiters (staff and convicts alike), haters, losers and angry boys and I had become depressed. I needed lifting. I needed to be bodacious and optimistic. I gotta change the atmosphere and not let it change me.

Prison can't stop me from dreaming, yearning, striving and working! So I join the late Ted Kennedy in saying "the work begins anew! Hope rises again and the Dream (vision... Habakkuk 2:3) lives on!". I won't stop! I'd love to have Tony Dungy, Bill Cosby, Michael Vick or Dr. Phil etc. to mention, endorse or at least pray for G.B.G. But -as quiet as it's kept. Just between you, me and the door post - I won't stop merely because somebody else doesn't rubberstamp my efforts. I didn't have a Cosby endorsement when I was licensed to preach the gospel. I had never heard of Mr. Tony Dungy (Michael Vick, Barack Obama or any of them) when I met Andrew Young! I didn't know them when Rev. Hosea Williams called me the "Martin Luther King Jr. of the pulpit" either.... But God ordered my steps in order to get me to a particular place (appointment(s)) by a particular time. Andrew Young didn't 'need' to befriend me and give me his home telephone number. There were thousands of 12 and 13 year old boys in Atlanta who would have loved to meet him and get to know him. Some of them were brighter than me. Some looked better than me and some had more charisma than I did. But 'they' did not have an "appointment" with Andy. They had heard and read about Elijah (Andy, Hosea, Jesse Jackson etc.) but 'they' were not Elisha. They saw Saul on TV but 'they' were not David. And so... It took me darn near 37 years to realize that what I got, who I met, where I've gone and what I know has nothing to do with me. It was in divine order. They were divine appointments. And all these great men, women, lawyers and legends whom I write about in this book etc. I didn't 'need' 'them' to get where I was or what I had. And if they don't wanna go (with me and G.B.G.) they still won't hinder me. I'm going if I've got to go all alone. I'm going if I've got to go on a wing. I'll go if I have to go on a crutch. I'll go if I have to go in a wheel chair. I heard the song writer say "I don't care how you get here". But just "Get Here if you can". And for those boys and girls being sodomized in TYC, brutalized in C.D.C. and terrorized in schools, in barrios and in ghettos etc. They don't care how help gets there. They don't care what "color" help comes in. They don't care if it's Bill Cosby, Bill Gates or Bill(y) Bell. They just need some light shining in a dark place. They don't care if the 'light' has a criminal record. 'Light' can be in jail with an 'R' in his jacket (hell you can have an "s", "t", "u" or a "v") but if I'm starving feed me. If I'm blind lead me. If I'm sick heal me. We can gossip later on about your past and the letters checkering your past etc. But when I've got an emergency I'll yell out 2 words: "Help me!" I said. "Help me!"... And... the pastors (in the streets) are too busy buying new Bentleys, Rolls Royces and airplanes etc. to give a damn about schools, juveniles and kids in the trailer parks.... A pastor (i.e. Creflo Dollar) could ask just half of his 20,000 members to launch a Heart campaign in local schools in Atlanta. I guarantee you that Ralph Bunche Middle School, Archer/Harper, Douglas and Northside High etc. could all use ten thousand prayed up, fire baptized "World (school) changers" monitoring their Halls. I guarantee you that if we got church folks who sit their butts on pews on Sunday; to sit their butts in hallways and in classrooms on Mondays etc. Arne Duncan could use their "service".... I'm tired of reading about teachers having sex with kids and coaches molesting boys. I'm tired of Catholic priests molesting altar boys... If parents would get their asses out of jail (like I'm in) and get their behinds in the school and the church etc. we would see violence, bullying, drug abuse and molesting drop dramatically.... Police can't be everywhere. But there are a hundred million parents and we can be in every school.

A kid can't play hooky or cut class if he knows that momma's best friends Louise will be at the school (with her nosey ass) watching. I can't sell dope out of my locker or in the school bathroom if I know my daddy's best friend is outside the bathroom 'monitoring' my conduct....

Prison is full of "altar boys: who bow down at the altar of a predator's cell and talk on his throne and.... It is a sad perverted environment... I am still appalled by the level of sexuality which I see amongst married guards with men. They want a man to di-k them down! They got a wife and kids yet they'll smuggle in a cell phone for a little bit of wee wee.

... Since I started writing this tome I've learned (for a fact) that C.O. Coggenshall (at M.C.S.P.) routinely paid inmates to let him watch them masturbate. He paid to see their posteriors. He loved "straight" (???) white guys. But he'd look at any male. And Coggenshall is very married to a woman....

Mike Bergin advised me to get "inside the minds of killers, rapists and molesters" because he explained that I'm "embedded with a segment of society that psychiatric universities would pay millions of dollars to study". Mike stated "do you know how much money Harvard psychiatrists would pay to interview Eric or Lyle Mendez for an hour? You've got him for tens of thousands of hours! And you are smart enough to dumb yourself down to manipulate him into thinking he's teaching and leading you". Attorney Bergin continued "I know you like a book and you are sharp enough to pull things out of Eric that a psychiatrist couldn't get even in therapy. And isn't it a fact that Eric refuses to talk with prison shrinks? You can insert yourself into his life and dig data out which can help you to help others. And prison is full of shrinks who can elucidate certain things to you if you ask them 'general' questions". Mike is a wise man...

I interviewed Dr. Lewis Yablonsky, Linda McFarlane, Bobby Lee Cook, John Burton, Doris Matsui, Murray J. Janus, Robert Navarro, Carolyn Phillips, Geri Lynn Green, Daniel Broderick and a slew of public officials (mostly telephonically) for this book... I consulted (hundreds of hours) with Dr. C. Solis, Dr. Jennifer Heitkamp, Dr. Cathy Paicez, Dr. Jaffé, Dr. J. Friedman, Dr. Jamie Davidson, Dr. A. Duran, Dr. Gregg, Dr. Handian and.... Hundreds of hours. I also have weaved in substance from thousands of hours I spent with the late, great Dr. Ty Hedblad etc. etc. As quiet as it is kept some of the things I learned from Marilyn Windham are in this book. (I still believe Mosely Collins, Geri or somebody should sue Marilyn Windham and C.D.C. for traumatizing Brandon Gene Martinez. He still suffers from PTSD due to the illicit, illegal and dangerous 'relationship' he had with her. And they don't want me to name the two correctional officers who 'caught' Brandon and Marilyn. They only punished him by moving him from 4 bldg. cell 121 to 3 bldg. and they threatened to write him up. He lost his job and everything. They did 'not' write her up!).... I've learned from watching people. I learn from listening and engaging. I certainly have had 'time' to 'think'. President Mandela told Oprah that one of the few things he missed about prison was the 'time' to "sit down and think".

... After the $ 250.00 loan to Eric Menendez had been taken care of Eric began to spend a lot of time with Marilyn Windham PhD and this was strange because Eric did not talk to prison shrinks.... I was in 'manipulation mode' one Friday evening at 8:00 pm when Dr. Windham left Eric's cell door. His celly (Henrickson) was out at the men's support group and Dr. Windham (who got off at 3"00 pm) was standing outside Eric's door for at least an hour. She talked in hushed tones. And if I crept up near the door she'd pretend to be talking about 'bodybuilding' or sports etc. She gave her self away by changing her 'tone' and 'volume' as I walked by. But (to be

259

authentic) I must officially admit that I never, personally heard her saying anything sexual, sensual or improper to Eric. Damn! But on that Friday evening as she left at 8:00 pm I asked Eric "u wanna come out n use the phone or anything?" he replied "yes - ask Mrs. Love if I can come out". I got C.O. Love to open his door and before he used the telephone I whispered "we gotta chat when you get off the telephone dude".... When he got off we went to the Shu yard together. (again I was in 'manipulation mode') "Eric - dude she thinks you did it and she's afraid of you". He bit! With his ego crushed and the pompous smirk removed he replied "she knows I didn't do it". I go "o-kay" and I began to leave the Shu yard.

...."Wait, Atlanta - what makes you think she believes I did it and she's afraid of me?".... I told him "because she is a psychologist. If she wanted a one-on-one with you Mrs. Love would let you all sit in the dayroom together. She always comes here on your day-off. And she purposely catches you in the cell". Eric said "There are a number of reasons she catches me in my cell. And believe me, fear is not one of them". I say "Oh well" and I begin (feigning disinterest and disbelief) to leave. "Atlanta - you think I'm lying don't you?" I remain silent. Eric repeats "tell me, do you think I'm lying?" I replied "Eric you know that I have a master's degree in business administration. I'm the only prisoner at CSP-Sac who is a published author. I'm one of only two guys at New Folsom who's been outside the United States (excluding Mexico). I really don't care".

He cut me off "Dude she's a freak! How do you think I got that game-boy? Where do you think my meth comes from? Why do you think I'm not borrowing money anymore?" I go "yeah right. Windham is gonna risk a six figure job for you?" He replied "I can show you some meth". I stated "you could've gotten that Lafitte". Eric says "Do you think Lafitte would bring me a 'dildo'?" I say "A what-do?" Eric says "I have a yellow dildo in my cell right now. I use it for pay. My celly uses it for pleasure". I inquire "what do you you mean 'pay'?" He states "Dr. Windham watches me insert the dildo up my ass. And I masturbate for her. And she smuggles things in to me and makes telephone calls for me. How do you think I took those photos of my asshole? Barbara Walters wanted pictures of me with the dildo too. (Author's disclaimer: I have no independent evidence to substantiate Eric's claims about Madame Walters. It is entirely possible that this psychopath was intermingling some truths with embellishments!)".... I went to his cell door and Mrs. Love opened and closed his door. He reached down underneath his bed, pulled out a pair of sneakers and pulled a ten inch dildo out. "Hey, Atlanta, you want to see me use it". I departed with all deliberate haste.

... At M.C.S.P. Lyle Menendez had C.O. Baker, Mrs. Duclos, counselor Hammonds and (then sergeant) Lt. Cherry smuggling him cell phones, drugs, porn and who knows what else. "Sex, lies and greed". Prison has it all.

What are the odds that I'd be driving in Richmond Virginia. Having just left the trial of Beverly Ann Monroe. Watching Janus and David Hicks do their thing. I'm riding down the highway thinking about some 'sins' I'm about to commit and the Menendez brothers' nefarious matricide and fatricide etc. etc. came over my radio. Never in my wildest nightmares would I have believed that I would end up in a cellblock with Eric at CSP-Sac. Then end up in a cellblock with Lyle at M.C.S.P. and then meet back up with Eric at P.V.S.P.

My assignment to learn everything I could about murderers and psychopaths was definitely fulfilled. . ... Getting inside the minds of Eric Menendez, Lyle, Daniel Henson, Marvin Johnson, Ed Stokes and Bardo etc. was spooky and it was scary. I'm still (literally) haunted by the things I saw inside the minds of these people... Ed Stokes? He paid Noah L'Hotsky to allow him (Ed) to urinate on him and to defecate on him. L'Hotsky admitted (he was my cell partner for a couple of weeks) to me that "Ed likes to piss, shit and cum on me. He'll..." Damn! And Noah was a studious and intelligent looking youngster. Noah looks like 'FeddyBear' (Anthony

Fedorov)... "only in America?" Nall, "only in prison!". ... I hope Ben Lincoln, Raider Runner (a great young man who cares about people, Micah and Sandy raised Raider right!), Michael J. Peter and Allen Harris are reading this book.... Inmate schooler (AKA "superman") was a close buddy of Eric's. Schooler got C.O. Sterkins fired. He (superman) would go on the Shu yard. And wear her (c.o,. Sterkins) panties. He'd model women's panties for her. Occasionally Eric would join Schooler on the locked Shu Yard and perform for her as she viewed them (with a bird's eye view) from the control booth. Supposedly (I did not see this with my eyes. I personally only witnessed 'superman' doing it) they would kiss and 'play' with each other on the Shu yard for her... Her husband work(ed) here. Before she got canned she told me "if I ever see my name in your books you're a dead inmate".

.... There are some cold freaks, Kinky with a capital 'K' etc. in prison. And many of them are staff... It's off the hook in here yo. And (a lot of it) if I didn't see it with my own eyes I would not believe it. And I've come to the realization that (by and large) society does not give a darn. And that can be understood "if" we were not getting "out". But 110,000 inmates (mostly young and many in gangs) get out of California prisons every year! More than 750,000 will be released across the country! It's those two numbers which ought to have people (including prosecutors, judges, guards etc.) shaking in their boots. If we keep on locking up younger and younger people for pettier and pettier crimes etc. and if these Derek Hough, Derek King and Adam Lambert looking boys continue to be savagely beat, forcibly sodomized, gang raped and traumatized in prisons etc. some of them are going to get out and get even. They are going to assassinate and annihilate the judge(s), jurors and the prosecutors (AKA "lawyers") who sent them there. I can (literally) see somebody blowing Mary Hanlon Stone's head off! I would not be surprised to read that so-and-so beat Robert Altman to death with their bare hands. I'm surprised we've not seen a "Ft.Hood" in a prison parking lot. Some jobless, hopeless, angry ex-con who was raped by a Spearman, a Tucker, a D.L. Criner or a Larry Turner etc. And the ex-con shows up in the parking lot at shift change armed to the hilt. And prison authorities and prosecutors would love being able to (erroneously and manipulatively) claim I'm threatening institutional security. And/or I'm promoting murder. That draconian and false argument would work in China.

But since my President is a constitutional scholar he will tell you (just as he recently told students in China) that free speech and the open exchange of differing opinions are foundational principles of our sacred constitution.... When the Sacramento bee ran a false, one-sided (I should have sued them for denying me equal time'. They only interviewed Mary Hanlon and Glynn. They never interviewed Comiskey and refused to interview me. I wrote the reporter 3 missives without reply!) story about me it threatened my SAFETY and security. But tens of thousands of California inmates read that 'story' and nobody tried to disallow the article inside the prisons. I wrote warden Campbell and Chief Deputy Warden Sylvia Garcia and informed them that my safety was compromised due to this inflammatory and nefarious news article. I called Paul Comiskey and he called warden Campball. The reply was concise: "If an attempt is to assault you notify staff. Unless you can prove you've been assaulted we can't move you".

Ipso Facto, Hanlon and Altman need to prove somebody has attempted to.... and (for the record) I reiterate my commitment to and my belief in nonviolent social protest and in litigation. I never support, applaud and nor do I advocate violence as a tool for protest. And if anyone reading this is thinking about assaulting staff, a D.A. or a judge etc. I understand your hurt and your pain. I can relate to your frustration. But don't let your simmering anger reach a boiling point. I promise you that violence is 'not' the answer...

The mission of G.B.G. is to reach out to thugs, losers, gang bangers, drop-outs, teens and tweenies, and get you to drop - back - in. We wanna reach (also) studious, promising and anointed youngsters like Raider Runner in Folsom. Raider has a special kind of compassion. He knows what it is like to feel unwanted and unloved. I saw Raider weep (on TV) as he talked about the loving family (headed by Micah Runner) that adopted him when he was in the sixth grade. He cried! and I immediately thought about "Angelo" who is 16 and needed to be adopted. Angelo was in the Sierra (I mention him in another part of this tome) adoption services. Who better to be a G.B.G. ambassador and to be a part of our outreach to troubled, hurting and lonely boys in group homes, foster care and in detention other than 'Raider'? I say it's a "Raider (Runner) Nation" Baby Boy. I want Heather or Penny to contact Raider and tell him he is now a celebrity and I got a j-o-b for him....

Radiation? ... (off the subject yall) but I gotta tell somebody about this. I called Attorney Geri Green yesterday but she was in the middle of the grocery store (lol) accepting a collect call.... "You've got to call me at the office Monday Sherman" she told me. But her secretary told me Friday they're in the middle of a humongous lawsuit etc. etc. So Geri, Mr. Navarro, Madame Phillips, Mosely and Robert Waters are you all reading? I was never told (at CRMC) that I was getting 'radiation' from all of these CAT scans, full body scans and other scans which I received at CRMC. I was doped up on morphine during 95% of my hospitalization. As evidenced by Dr. Smith telling me at P.V.S.P. that "you don't remember me, but I met you at C.R.M.C. You could barely lift your hand. And you were dazed on meds. But we talked".... So how could I understand any risks even "if" somebody explained them to me? All I know is that I had (literally) hundreds of scans at CRMC. Without anyone explaining radiation risks to me. It was scary and alarming when I saw (U.C. Davis Medical Dean) Dr. Mike Wilkes on TV talking about the dangers of radiation from these scans.... Does this explain my migraines, severe nausea and diarrhea? What the heck is going on? Nobody told me of these risks and Dr. DeGucchi is a radiologist who knew better... Michael Louis Kelly are you perusing this tome today?..... (Back to TYC)

... The case also languished in the office of State Attorney General Greg Abbott for two years with no action: Abbott said the matter was not in his jurisdiction; that he could not become involved unless D.A. Reynolds requested assistance.

When Burzynski's persistence eventually put the TYC sex scandal in the media spotlight; legislators (suddenly public servants! but when those lil boy inmates write their offices about rapists like Spearman and Bunnell etc. they don't reply) questioned the A.G.'s office about the lack of prosecution...

"It's the idea that these kids and their parents are less believable, and in a way require less protection from the state", stated Isela Gutierrez, coordinator of the Texas Coalition advocating justice for juveniles.

"When TYC representatives testified in their suits before these legislators, they were seen as more credible than these parents, who were low-income, sometimes had criminal backgrounds and often showed up in jeans" she said.

Lawmakers, judges and prosecutors would quickly deny any notion that justice is less important for those who wear blue jeans. Yet there is no disputing the fact that nearly a hundred TYC workers were fired, dozens more were arrested and hundreds of children languished needlessly behind bars because no one cared enough to listen, despite numerous complaints having been filed.

Nor can there be any disputing the fact that for want of prosecution by indifferent government officials, the two men responsible for years of sexual abuse of many juveniles in state custody almost walked away scot-free and untouched. The criminal cases against Hernandez and Brookins are still pending' both pled not guilty.... Mary Hanlon has been accused of sexually abusing 3 boys in jail custody. She offered to drop criminal cases against them for sex. The boys were 14, 16 and 17...: This case has been swept under the rug due to the unimaginable power Mary has as a rogue, drug addicted and corrupted prosecutor.... Mary

Hanlon Stone is a 'clear and present danger' to young boys and men. She oughta be locked up in a jail cell next to Brookins and Hernandez....

"Did you see Adam Lambert on American Music Awards on November 22?" an inmate asked a fellow prisoner. "He had a dancer in white pants and black straps that I'd love to do". Since the speaker was a 225 lbs gang banger I struggled to recall which lady dancing for Adam had on white pants and black straps. I couldn't really 'say' anything since I was ear hustling and he was not talking to me. And then he said "I would love to see him in a G-string!... And the Band 'Gloriana'? Did you see the blonde dude? I would let him f-ck me b..." This is a gang banger yall. What the hell is going on? ... I reach out to dudes like Tyson Williams, Max Steele, Ryan Andrews, (Irving Texas) and Raider Runner etc. for a reason. I reach out to Austin Sisneros and to Austin Wolfe because I know what I know. If yall come to jail you will be.... Don't come here! Because if you bring yo 'ass' to jail it will no longer be "your" ass. You feel me? Andrew Knox (W. Sacto), Kyle Love, Doug Pieper Jr. and Steven Moreno Jr. are you reading this?

You betta get yo ass back in school. You betta (sic) run to the library and get some books. Read 2 succeed and take heed what you read. Get an education!....

... If Marshall Mathers (AKA Eminem) was in prison he would be somebody's B-tch! I've got to keep it real. First of all 'Eminem' is bi-sexual! Eminem has definitely (without question) had sex with numerous men. He's on 'pipe' and he's a drug addict. Did you see his eyes at the American Music Awards? I'd pay Eminem $ 10 grand to take a drug test. He doesn't need the money but he could donate it to charity. And I'd pay $ 20 grand for Eminem to take a polygraph test and answer two questions" A. "How often do you use drugs and alcohol?" B. "Have you ever had sex with a man?"...

And for all of you kids who are 'huffing', using paint thinner and other household products to get high. Once you come to jail you will end up giving somebody some ass or a blow job just to get high. And 90% (plus) of the drug addicts (and even cigarette smokers, etc.) in prison will give up 'booty' for a pill, a smoke or a thrill!...

On 11/22/09 Keyko Torres was on News 10 in Sacramento discussing 'shopping'. G.B.G. want the dude who was standing next to her to join G.B.G.....

Gavin Dutrow and Don Kingsbury etc. join us. We wanna coalition with an International team of students in a Global movement to prevent and lessen youth incarceration etc. By promoting superior education... Hunter Brown (Wheaton Illi.), Doran Smestad, Cody Sheldon come on down.... Yall "Let's get ready to rumble!" I said lets get ready to rumble! We can do this.

Give me "A few good men" and we will transform the jangling and ragged discords of youth incarceration into an oasis of education.... I got principals (Aaron Fernander), Harvard psychiatrists (Franklin Curren MD.), former Harvard professors (Dr. Lewis Yablonsky) etc. etc. on this team. I have energetic, youthful cops (C.O. David Kelley, T. Ramsey etc.) and robbers (me! lol).... I have a distinguished panel of famous lawyers (Alan Howard, Dewey & Labeouf, Michael Edward Bergin, Mr. Ravis, Robert Navarro, Geri Green, Michael Louis Kelly, Andrew A. Bridge, Warren Ballentine etc.)....

We have intelligent, bright and concerned civilian youngsters (i.e. Daniel Bugriyev, Adam Lane, Dustin Nicolodi etc.) and.... We need you to come on now.

"Justin" was on 'Tyra' and he was (according to Madame Banks) "powdering his booty" and we have a remedy for "mantrums". I command you to put on your swat team regalia. We do not need just another "proclamation" we need "demonstration". Words without action is rhetoric. A strategy without a burden (and passion) is just ambition. And the sidelines and the benches of life are filled with ambitious and talented people. They're on the bench because they lack a burden or a passion for the action.... I know a number of jailed inmates who are better 'writers' than I am. They dot the I's and cross the T's better than I do. Some of them are degreed writers.

But the reason my name is on nine tomes is because of the drive, passion and the energy I have. And this passion is borne out of my 'burden' to make a difference.... It's not that I'm so special, talented or skilled. I just work and I'll out work my enemies.

Prisons are filled with fellas who are skilled in being able to talk a good 'game'. Their verbal gymnastics and ability to articulate is without equal. Some of them 'sound' like Malcolm, Steve Covey or Tony Robbins. They are mostly arm-chair revolutionaries.. They won't sit down and write. They won't develop a plan. They would rather 'talk' about it.

When you 'write' it, it will out live you. When you 'write' it 'somebody' is gonna read it. Even bad and mediocre books get read. Hell we wouldn't know they were no damn good if we didn't read them.... There are (indeed) thousands of jailed inmates perusing this tome right now. Lots of prisoners read. Especially guys in the Shu, Ad.seg and in solitary confinement. O.J. Simpson and Scott Peterson are (more than likely) reading this tome. I know Lyle and Eric Menendez are reading it. But (quite frankly) I don't give a damn. A bunch of evil, wicked, sadistic and bitter locked-up losers reading this to criticize is of no consequence. They're not my target audience. In fact I prefer them not to read this....

I'm not concerned about some jaded, hard-nose and pessimistic reporter reading this either. I just don't need the media for this mission. I care as much about Rush Limbaugh reading this as he cares about me listening to his show. I also am not concerned about duplicitous and perverted men like Senator Mitch McConnell, Larry Craig and Newt Gingrich reading this book.... Pat Robertson, Benny Hinn and Leroy Jenkins can pass on this tome and go look at some more kiddie porn. And we ought to lock their asses up for the crimes they have committed against children.

I'm tired of Catholic priests molesting lil altar boys. I'm tired of Catholic Bishops racketeering, covering up the molestations and hiding out the molesters. I'm tired of Benny, Jenkins and Robertson using church sanctuaries as their "my own private Idaho's". I'm sick of these con-men turning God's houses of worship into a Den of thieves. I speak with an intimate knowledge of empirical data. I know about pastoral corruption. I know what it means to talk North and walk West. I'm not writing to fake-ass, 4 Rolls Royce driving crooks. You are not my audience. Put this damn book down. You are not invited. Go get one of Benny Hinn's, Kenneth Copelands' or Creflo Dollars' books. I don't need your conning, hating plastic and deceptive spirit injected in this tome.

This book is for Tyson Williams, Omar Samy, Cody Sheldon, Billy Bell, Victor Smalley, the fellas at Homeboy Industries, Locke High School and in TYC. This book is for real people ready to deal with real issues. I am not gonna plant a seed offering into your (own private Idaho) church. Quit sending me your con letters trying to convince me to send you my tithes and my offerings. Why do you 'own' your own church? Why is your (Creflo, Jenkins, Hinn, Copeland etc.) name on the church deed? Why don't the members own the church?

You got the title and deeds to the church? It belongs to you. And you are going to hell in a handbasket. I'm a preacher whistleblower! I'm exposing you for your crookedness. You have manipulated the word of God to enrich your 'self' for the short time you're here on the planet. But your money will not buy you an air conditioner in hell. You need to fall on your face and seek repentance. You (Mason Betha) may have meant well when you got started. But you've gotten tainted. And you've gotten corrupted. And you're a con. And God can still change you. He can rearrange you.

I reach out to Shaun Rushforth. I have a j-o-b for you right now. Somebody call, email or poke Tadd Carr, Austin Wolfe, Austin Sisneros, Billy Bell, Jakob Karr, Victor, Nathan, Allen Harris (in Abbeville), Greg Deekens, Daniel Asare, Raider Runner, John Garvin, Chad Sherman,

Clay, Brett Jolliff, Alex Blench, Alex Chivescu, Keith Mullennix and Christian Nelson etc. and we have jobs waiting for them right now. Let's do this thing. We can do this!

... In 08 Dr. Phil had a dude on who didn't like his Italian nose. And he was gonna have a nose job. We want 'him' in G.B.G.. We want 'Marius', 'Brett', 'Quentin' and 'Angelo' etc. to help us transform America into a 'Raider' (Runner) Nation....

I want dudes from Derek Hough to Derek King to help us do our thing. We can do it...

Zac Efron? I was a bit skeptical when 'Max' (on TMZ.com) was complimenting Zac and saying how his parents must have raised him right etc. But I saw Zac do an interview and I (too) was impressed. He reminded me of fireman 'Jeremy' and Daniel Bugriyev. I saw so much humility. And you literally do get that feeling that Zac's parents must have raised him right.

That's a good segue to tell my troops (you youngsters) that we need to practice humility. Arrogance is such a turn-off. And arrogance is not self confidence. And humility and meekness are not weakness. When you 'know' who you are you don't need to remind me that you flew in on a private plane (Creflo). When you know who you are you can tell me "I got in my car" rather than 'always' reminding me that the car you got in was a 'Rolls' and you (do) have 3 more at home.

Arrogance is a sign of a lack of security. Once you become certain, secure and confident in who you are you don't need to announce it. Preachers (pastors and evangelists etc.) struggle with arrogance. There is something about being out 'front' which deceives us in to believing we need arrogance as a tool. And I believe that one of the main reasons Christian churches (especially 'black' churches) suffer from an absence of men is because of the arrogance of pastors. Men don't want a drill sergeant for a pastor. And men are already intimidated because women adore and worship the pastor anyway. And then we pour salt on their wounded egos by standing up and being cocky. It drives men out of the church. We ought to take a lesson from the Muslims and begin to empower men. If we begin to uplift, observe and serve the men in our church(es) they'll flock to our church. Men want to be led without it seeming like they're being led. One of the secrets of leadership I've learned in Hades (where I live with all males who are angry, bitter and broken etc.) is to lead and appear to be following. I've learned to praise, compliment and lift others. I give others credit for 'my' ideas. I'll write something and sign somebody else's name to it. If you lift, empower and enlarge other men they'll appreciate you more. And even men who don't like you, are jealous of you and... they'll help you do 'good' if you invest into their self-confidence etc. If you give them a 'vested interest' in a positive project they'll follow.

... Most men in prison are actually boys suffering from a variety of mental, psychological and spiritual deficits. And my research leads me to conclude that most of 'us' in here are arrogant because we're insecure. And most of 'us' despise reflections of ourselves. Ipso Facto, when I see arrogance in somebody else it makes me itch. I feel allergic to it etc. but when I'm in my arrogant zone, when I'm bragging about all of the triple stretch (notice I told you how long they were) Limos I've been in. Suddenly I'm not allergic anymore. I've been healed! And it's a miracle..... At 9:44 am Courtney interviewed some teens on Kmax (in Sacto) on 11/23/09. they were gathered around a thanksgiving table. "What r u thankful 4?" Courtney asked a young man.... "I'm thankful for my beautiful mother...." Courtney fell (literally) to her knees.... We want 'him' in G.B.G. Somebody call KMAX and ask Courtney who this young man is. We want him and his brother in G.B.G. with all deliberate haste. We have a stipend for him...

Certain C.D.C. employees (i.e. T.R., D.B., D.K. and "H"....) I wish I could really talk to them and tell them what I think of em. There have been times when I've met people (M.C.S.P., P.V.S.P., etc.) who have so impressed me that I wish I could really tell them what I see, think and feel...

Back to humility yo.... Bruthas we need to work on it. 'We' need to meditate on it and pray for it. It is a struggle (I know) but we can get there. I ask God to keep me humble. I ask Him to help me feel good about myself. I work on improving my Clark Kent, to remind me of my Super man. I can't do it by myself. The culture of America and even our politics lean toward arrogance, conceit and deceit.

Something in our character (defects) makes most of us wish we were 'Donald' telling folk "you're fired". But the real nature of Christ (in us) ought to lead to the desire to tell people 'you're hired". A real man is not measured by the ability to beat someone up. A man is able to build something (or someone) up. When you meet people who enjoy berating, belittling and oppressing others, rest assured that they are hurting, troubled and afflicted. People who are hurting, hurt other people. We'll go out of our way to appear to be black when we know we're white. We are concerned with public opinion. We'll tell you in a minute that we "don't care what nobody (sic) thinks' about us. But that's one of the biggest lies we've ever told.

We are obsessed by what other people 'think' about how we look, how much we weigh and.... Sometimes we'll hate about us what others love about us... I know a C.O. who is 27 and he 'looks' 16. He 'hates' looking like a lil boy. He was picked on in school and made fun of. And he didn't have a clue that the real reason the fellas were picking at him was 'jealousy'. I'd give anything to 'look' that young. To be 27 and still get carded for alcohol is the ultimate compliment. But he sees it as an insult. And every time you talk to him he'll tell you how 'bad' he is. He will tell you how many asses he's kicked etc. and he does not wear an alarm etc. etc. He (works at High Desert) ought to be on page 313 in "Blue Eyed Blonde" Book II getting $ 2 grand!... He's a good guy. But he has a complex.

Most of 'us' are suffering from arrested development in one area and an inferiority complex in another area. And we need to get healed. We need to be made whole. I've watched thousands (literally) of 'boys' get aids because of their arrested development. They were running away from their sexuality (their 'secret' was an attraction to other men). So they bedded every female they could as often as they could. And this callousness and carelessness resulted in them contracting a deadly disease.

I've watched boys self destruct because they didn't like the way they looked. Or they felt stupid. Or they couldn't read. And their feelings of shame, pain, worthlessness, uselessness and inferiority led to them abusing drugs, beating women and/or coming to prison.

Some dudes got caught in process and gave up on promise. I just wish I could have gotten to them and told them how blessed they (you) were (are).... An apple tree does not become an apple tree after it grows apples. But even when the branches are empty and you can't see anything etc. an apple tree is still an apple tree.

You are not just blessed when you get a Bentley and when you get a wife, a kid, a picket fence and a dog. But even when you're riding on Marta in Atlanta, Bart in California and on the 'bus' in Chicago you are blessed. Even when you can't get her telephone number and she won't sit next to you in class etc. you are still blessed. Paul was locked up and bound in a prison but blessed. Job was sick but blessed. You don't just get blessed when you go to Yale. Joseph was blessed when He was in jail. Don't you know how blessed you are to have eyes to see, ears to hear and legs to walk? Do you know how blessed you are to be clothed in your right mind? Michael Jackson wanted to live forever. How much money do you think Michael would have paid to have your breath and heartbeat for one more day?

Baby Boy if you could see the dangers unseen that God kept you from you would get up and do the holy dance. If you could see the stuff the devil wanted to do to you but your Daddy wouldn't let him you would shout.

As a matter of fact if you just think of the dangers you did see and didn't think you were gonna make it out of but you did. You'd have to stop and give God a clap praise right now.

The devil is not intimidated by your car. The devil is not really concerned about you getting a new house. But he's afraid of your potential. The devil is afraid, he's shaking in his boots over your potential. He does not want you to begin to operate in the realm of the holy spirit. He's not impressed with your diploma. He is afraid you are gonna break down and start praying and begin to seek the face of God. He is afraid of you. He wants you to 'think' you are a chicken. He keeps you distracted. He wants you to spend hours farting in the wind. He'll keep you tied up with television. Hooked on video games. Hooked on booze, weed or meth. He.... Do you get it Baby Boy? Only a few of you (reading) are going to really 'get this'. But I promise you that 'IF' you (Cody, Austin, Tadd and....) 'get' this it will revolutionize yo life! I'm telling you the roof will blow off of yo life if you get this. This is breakfast for champions. This... Here we go: The devil does not care whether you are hooked on meth or hooked on crack. He could care less if you're addicted to this or addicted to that. Whether you're addicted to huffing, puffing, sex, football, baseball, boxing or abusing, it does not matter. The devil just wants you to remain 'distracted'. If he can addict you to 'football' he will. If he can keep you out of church on Sundays because you've got to stay home and watch that game. If he can keep you out of school or college on Mondays because you gotta... You can be addicted to "cops" the soaps or sex. His mission remains the same. He wanna keep you thinking you're a 'chicken'. He knows that if you ever begin to focus like a laser beam and lay on your face before God you will begin to move forward. You'll go into places that eyes have not seen and ears have not heard. And neither has it entered into the hearts of men the things which God has in store for those that love Him. The enemy wants to lock up your mind and to bog you down with nothingness. As long as he can keep you 'preoccupied' with crap. As long as he can keep your mind locked up and bound it is mission accomplished. If you could see the eagle in you that the devil sees you would put down that crack pipe and get down on your knees and ask God to please show me. Show me why I was raised like I was raised. Show me why I had to go through this and go through that. Show me my mission, your plan and give me vision for my future. Show me the way.

... Can you say Amen? You don't have to be perfect. You won't always get it right. You'll fall down, mess up and Boo Boo sometimes but if you know that destiny is inside you. You'll take a licking and keep on ticking. You'll pick yourself up. Dust off your boots and take it by force.

The reason the devil is hell-bent on keeping your mind in a bind all the time etc. is because he knows what your daddy can do. He knows the majesty, the awesomeness and the marvelousness of the power of God. He knows God can take a lil shepherd boy who shovels sheep manure. A boy who has never gone to bootcamp. A boy who's not a trained soldier. Not a green beret. Not a martial arts expert. With no hand-to-hand combat skills etc. God'll mess around and give the boy a slingshot to slay 'Osama'. The enemy knows what can happen when God anoints and endows a man, woman, boy or girl with His supernatural power. God! God! God!

I know we need education. Education really is a bridge to liberation. I advocate (strongly) education! But oh Baby Baby in all of your getting get God. Humble yourself before Him and seek His will. If you will really, really seek Him you will find Him.

God is an awesome God. I know a lot of His kids are crazy, we are duplicitous, arrogant, selfish and racist etc. but there is nothing wrong with Jehovah. He is King of Kings. His son is Lord of Lords. I want you to 'know' Him. I want you to seek Him.

There is greatness, power, blessings and ability down in the marrow of your bones. You were born to win and you can do it...

... A female counselor told me "your publisher should get C.O. Hodge to do the challenge on page 313 of "Blue Eyed Blonde" Book II. And also C.O. Kelley since he's a gladiator". I told her "them dudes ain't gonna do that". She goes "tell them not to show their face(s). And this will really sell books. People will flock to the book to try to figure out who the photo is... Hell, ask the Governor (Arnold), Mark Kashirets and Buster Posey (up it to $2500.00) to do the challenge".... She crazy?

... But anybody who wants to do the challenge buts wants your face blocked out etc. Do it! You are on!....... Back to TYC...

Investigators tallied a total of over 750 complaints of sexual abuse of kid offenders from Jan. 2000 to Feb. 2007. These complaints described everything from flirting to rape, and came from all 13 TYC facilities... At P.V.S.P. C.O. Sawyer, C.O. Florez and C.O. Mendez sexually assaulted an inmate in 2008. It was reported to Dr. Duenas and to Dr. Felix Igbinosa. But Marion E. Spearman and Lt. Corley falsified documents, lied and swept the case under the rug.

I hope the hosts of smashcutstu.com are reading this. I want one of the hosts to join G.B.G. I want Kris Stump, Gene Langford, Jason Sutherland, Michael Clokely, Devin Stone, Joseph Rocha, Karther Cordero and... read this tome! Spread the word over the grapevine that this book is out. Zustin Zysman and Sean Zane need to read this book...

... Joseph Galloway told the Texas Rangers that in 2003, while locked up at the Giddings state school, guards put him in a cell with another boy who was older, bigger and stronger. The other boy was yelling to a guard, "I want some ass"....

Hold on - you'd think peace officers wearing badges would protect a kid in this position? I wish rogue, renegade and raping guards were aberrations or an anomaly etc. And I'm cognizant that (for some) it's difficult to believe that guards, cops, prosecutors and judges can be so nefarious and violent. We 'want' somebody to look-up to. We are psychologically in need of heroes and sheroes. I have always felt crushed, let down and depressed when I found out that Rev. Leroy Jenkins was a crook; when I personally discovered Leroy was a conman, a molester, and a rapist. What kind of man rapes 'anybody'? Especially his own kids?

When it became obvious, evident and apparent that Leroy has enriched himself off the backs of poor people whom he cons out of their food stamps, welfare and social security checks etc. I was crushed.... Bishop E. Bernard Jordan calls himself a "master prophet". He is actually a "master con". His motto is "a dollar a day keeps the devil away". People like E. Bernard Jordan, Leroy Jenkins, Pat Robertson and Benny Hinn etc. are incorrigible cons. And I'll use all the tough talk, mean words and angry rhetoric to describe them. But underneath my acid tongue and underneath my anger is a little boy preacher who was taught (by Dollie Manning, Brenda Smith and by my big Momma) that "boy, whatever you do don't you play with God." It hurts me to see heroes fall. I hurt when I believe in a vision or a ministry and I discover it is fraud. I can handle 'you' being gay. I can handle 'you' being an adulterer, a booze drinker or a.... I can handle the flaws, shortcomings and the weaknesses 'we' all have. I know 'we' have a 'twin'. But I cannot handle people playing with God. And some of you who grew up in the suburbs where police officers said "yes sir" and "yes mam" to your parents etc. you find it extremely uncomfortable and difficult to believe that there are men (and women) in uniform who will wake up, put on a uniform with a badge. And set up a boy to be raped by a boy. And rape boys and girls themselves. "Not a guard" you think. Well I'm not Dr. Curren, Dr. Heitkamp or Dr. Solis. So I can't really elucidate the psychological reasons which drive men to rape jailed inmates etc. I don't know what drives Marion E. Spearman, Sawyer, Mendez, D.L. Criner, Wally Tucker and... other molesters. But I do 'know' it does happen in prisons, in juveniles and in jails all across America everyday...

So the boy yelled "I want some ass" to (C.J. Sheron, Zach Freisen, Garrett McCain and Alex Chivescu etc.) Joseph Galloway. "He was hitting me on the back of the head. He was beating the hell out of me. I allowed him to sodomize me, because I couldn't fight him anymore" Joseph said. Joseph was only 15 years old at the time.

On March 28, 2007, Joseph's mother testified before the national prison rape elimination commission and said she went to the administration at the Giddings Facility to complain about her sons' treatment but was rebuffed by a case worker. "We'll handle this internally, our own way", she was told.

Mrs. Galloway said her son was also severely beaten at the Marlin unit where juvenile prisoners are processed into the system. Joseph, she said, was beaten and had his nose broken not long after he arrived.

Joseph testified about an incident in which he was forced to submit to oral sex with a female guard. He also told the commission that the guard who forced him into the cell with the prisoner who raped him had done this before. So boys were toys and human sex slaves.

Joseph, received more than 320 disciplinary write-ups during his four year stay in juvenile facilities. Those infractions, which extended his nine-month sentence, included such offenses as sitting in the wrong place in church, daydreaming and falling to sleep - even while heavily medicated.

On April 10, 2007, Joseph and 4 other plaintiffs filed a class action lawsuit in Federal Court against the TYC for failing to protect them while they were in custody. The Texas civil right project represents them.

Joseph's mom, Genger Galloway is calling for a "complete reformation" of the TYC. "It doesn't matter what these kids did to get inside", she said. "They are still kids with civil rights and they deserve justice". I concur both with her call for "complete reformation' as well as with the fact that these are kids, Americans and they have civil 'rights'. But I want "complete reformation" of juveniles and youth prisons (nationwide) for a more pragmatic and selfish reason. I have kids on the streets. I have a family out there. And in case you didn't notice - Joseph is out. 99% of the kids we send to juvenile, jail and to prison will get out. And when they've been raped, beat, abused and had their sentences extended for petty offenses etc. when they get out (I repeat quite forcefully) they will be meaner, tougher, more vicious, sicker, slicker and when they get out they'll return quicker. Something happens inside the spirit, the soul and the psyche of a scared, brutalized, beat and sodomized boy that transforms him into a savage. Animal instincts kick in and he snaps into something and somebody so changed that his own momma can't even recognize him. And you'll hear people who knew him well and watched him grow up say stuff like "that's not the Joe I know". And "that's not him".

... Joseph said "I don't care if I get $ 2 out of this lawsuit. I just want TYC to be changed forever!"... Hallelujah... I gotta steal (or 'borrow'?) Joseph's words right here. "I don't care if I" don't get an award for this tome. "I don't care if I" don't impress journalism experts with this book. "I just want" you (Brett, Maxwell Hanger, Boys, youths, etc.) "to be changed forever". Do you hear me? I can handle Oprah not calling me. I'm cool with Dr. Phil not wanting some "manipulative convict" on his show. I can handle my fellow convicts (with our bitter, broken, envious and duplicitous asses) not celebrating "K.K.K." I can accept the fact that Warden Walker is retiring and Bunnell will get me transferred again. And I will be "hit" at another prison. I can accept the fact that my "record" and my "conviction" causes a "cloud" of suspicion to hang over my head. But that "cloud" has given me the power, conviction and the alienation I need(ed) to write from a place of loneliness, pain and shame etc. which makes me better. My "cloud" is significant because just as a "shadow" has no significance unless there is some 'light' (you can't even notice a 'shadow' in the dark). A "cloud" of suspicion has no significance in darkness. Go to your window or go outside tonight at 11:00 pm and look up and try to 'see' a cloud. You can't see it in the dark. And the only time you'll 'see' a shadow is by some 'light'. And the fact that there is now some rumblings and chatter about how my "conviction" hangs a "cloud" over me means that "this" book, "G.B.G." and "NAPS" are producing some "light". Cause yall couldn't see the "cloud" over me (and you wouldn't even know my "conviction") if there wasn't some "light" (right) around me... If Joseph (in Genesis) didn't have a coat of many colors. If Joseph didn't have a dream. If he hadn't ended up becoming a "Prince" we would not even know about the "cloud" surrounding him and the 'sexual' allegation (and 'conviction') against him... Do you know how many thousands of men went to prison in South Africa convicted of "treason"? You and I will never know their names. Because typical, run-of the mill criminals are surrounded by darkness. But I'll betcha we 'heard' about Nelson Mandela. And although there are still (right now today) some folks who will tell you that Mandela bombed buildings and murdered people etc. A. It's not true. B. If it was true, how many dudes killed people in South Africa (last year) that you don't know? Matter of fact can you (C.J., Alex or Brett etc.) name one dude who went to jail in South Africa last year for treason? Probably not. We know Mandela because he was a convicted prisoner ("shadow"/"cloud") and he became South Africa's 'first' black "President" (light). People (can we be real? Ain't nobody here but you and me bro.) holler "He raped me" all the time. And California has tens of thousands of rightly (and a few thousand wrongly) convicted "rapists" that you and I will never hear about or read about because they are in darkness. And God has blessed me to be the "first" prisoner in North America to found, fund and build (G.B.G. Baby Boy) an organization (while incarcerated on a "Joseph" type offence) aimed at getting boys out of gangs, off of drugs, back in school and into college (light). If I just sat here (in 'Hades' - in darkness!) playing cards, dranking (sic) hooch, gambling and kicking back etc. you would not know me or 'see' my cloud. I wish I had more time to write about "clouds" of suspicion and "shadows". And how there can be no recognition of light unless there is darkness. And...

"I don't care if I get $ 2 (yall know I like to repeat stuff) out of this lawsuit. I just want TYC to be changed forever" Joseph Galloway said. Now let me plagiarize (lol) his words which I've stolen... "I (Sherman D. "convict") don't give a flying flip what they say. How they hate, criticize and scandalize my name. I don't care what politricians (they call this 'neology' yall) prisoncrats, jailublicans or pundits say about me, "K.K.K." ("too long! too short! too rambling! too redundant! too many names" etc.) or G.B.G. I just want you ("Brett" from Dr. Phil, Maxwell Hanger, Raider, Zach, Billy Bell etc.) to be changed (transmogrified, metamorphosized [neology], mentally vaccinated against incarceration forever!

I want you to be changed forever. To go to bed at night and sleep like a baby. To feel good about yourself. To wake up in the morning so excited that you can't hardly see straight. I want you to love yourself. Whether you have a big booty or no booty. Whether you are 'endowed' like "me" (lol) or your lady can't 'find' yours..... Be changed ... I want Joseph Hewes and Joseph Rocha - changed forever. I want the substance (the immunization and vaccination) in this tome to transform you. I want this tome to drive you to that book. I want what you read here to how change how you think there. I want your ass to go back to school. Go back to the library. Enroll in that community college. I want you to log on to Dr. Phil's "teen talk" website and to discuss your issues with some pros. I want you to go to church. Go get some help, some hope and learn how to cope.... Brian Nichols (on The Price is Right 11/24/09(and his buddies (i.e. "Cameron" who did the "worm" on TV? I want them in G.B.G. I'll give Cameron, Brian, Corey and J. Hewes stipends). I want you to never again feel like you need a gang, a boy, a man to endorse you. If you're just a damn fool and wanna join a gang and go to prison forever so be it. Quit wasting my time and put this book down. You faking the funk. You remind me of a guy I know in prison. One day he wanted to "mentor" and teach "kids" about the mistakes he'd made. At P.V.S.P. he told me about wanting to make a difference etc. Few weeks later? "I'm not supersad because.... 98% of these dudes I don't talk to anyway... I'm already argumentative. If I... I become unbearable".

... Oh, by the way, he stopped speaking to me based on something he 'heard' ("cloud"). And oh, what a blessing it was (for me) to have him stop speaking to me. When I was at P.V.S.P. his celly was a Hillbilly. I 'felt' negative, dark, evil vibes around him every time he was near me. And.... he and his celly 'endorse' each other. They validate each other. I thank God that my momma raised me in such a way that I don't need your endorsement. If there was a way for me to live in 'this' prison and 'never' speak to anyone here (literally) I'd be happy.

I don't wanna hear negativity, anger and hatred. I don't want to 'hear' this rage. I'm absolutely not interested in any prison politics etc. who did what to whom. These dudes can't 'befriend' anybody because they are their own worst enemy. Can I love you if I hate me? Can I be your friend if I don't like me?

Tyson said it best "Oprah there is nothing in there (prison) but hate, hate, hate". So much hatred (animosity, anger and envy) in here that I had a clandestine ("classified") rendezvous with Jimbo, Madame Patricia Kennedy and L.N. Johnson-Dovey (while I was in Ad-seg - falsely accused) and I said this: "Mrs. K., Johnson-Dovey and Jimbo maybe we need to re-think these live G.B.G. tours... we're in a dark place and jealously is rampant. Hell, I had guys jealous of my black-ass every time they saw me walking with Jimbo... If Joseph's 'jealous' brothers sold him into slavery to get rid of his ass. What do you all think they'll do to get rid of me?" Jimbo interjected "but Sherman you've worked you butt off to make this happen and I'll transfer anybody that sets you up. Just like Dearaujo. You know I won't tolerate any inmate setting up another". I said "yes - but trust me on this. They play dirty. And I've already got clouds. It is more powerful, pragmatic and safe to do G.B.G. Worldwide! And the way to do it world-wide is with the internet. Facebook, Myspace etc. will take us any place. And we need to make a video. We'll use C.O. Hodge, T. Ramsey, David Kelley, Daniel Bugriyev, Dustin and Adam. Adam, Daniel and Dustin will be our 'kids' and we (Dr. Duran, Dr. Solis, Dr. Heitkamp, Willie, Ford and my team etc.) will record our session. Scott Kernan can see it and add his two cents. Matt Cate and our celebrity Governator etc. and we will send the video all-over the world.

"Jimbo - kids in juvenile, schools and group homes can watch this video... We can sell it for a small fee and every penny will go to the state of California... If we wanna do a tour once or twice per year o.k. But by - and - large our out-reach ought to be over the internet... Jimbo you know Sgt. Zanini brought 'Casey' (Delta college student contemplating becoming a guard) on a tour here. Zanini brought Casey straight to Willie and me. And Casey was mesmerized. But I looked around and saw 'hate'. I want us to cancel the live tours".

... Jimbo replied "Sherman I hear you loud and clear. And Pat and I know you've never led me wrong before. Let me think about it".........

... I want to climb down inside of your brain and reach you. I ain't trying to get everybody. Hell nall. I'm just looking for a few of you who are ready to get up. I want to talk to you about your secrets. I want to talk to you about the stuff you can't even talk to your best friends about. Let's (you and me, C.J., Brian Nichols, Adam Lambeet, Corey etc.) talk about your secret pain. Your secret fears. Your conflicts. The stuff about you that you can't even explain. I want to talk to you my brother about who hurt you and how did they hurt you. Tell me about your pain. Why are you so angry? When did you become so angry? Who raped you? Who abused you? Who beat you? Who broke your spirit and made you afraid? What happened to you on the playground, in the church, at school or in the community that made you 'check out'? Why do you spend more time with video games than you do with social interactions?

What made you believe you were worthless? Who told you that you were no good? Who are you and why are you here? Who are you so angry with that you're willing to let them change how your story ends?

I came to talk to you about the little boy down inside of you. I came to talk real talk. I don't want to hear all of that mess about your ability to kick ass. I don't wanna hear about the lady you went to bed with last night. I'm not gonna talk to you about the women (Tyra, Alicia, Beyonce, Paris and...) I wish I could go to bed with tonight. I want to find my buddy who went to art school in the 90's in Atlanta (Frank Carter). I want to talk to Joey Grissett, Ronald Wright, Clay, John Caudell, Phillip Coffee and to Ralph Cannon. I wanna holler at James Emslander, Brandon A. Hughes, Joseph Latham and Gary Browning. I need to speak to 'Guadalupe' in Santa Rosa, New Mexico, Wayne Rawlings, Aaron Jackson (D. Ohio), Donald Dusk (A. Ohio) and Juan Sanchez (in W. Hollywood Sheriff's station for stat. rape in 1995) etc. I wanna talk to boys at Locke High School, McClatchy High, John F. Kennedy High School etc. I still need to find Roger White (Alto), Curtis Sykes, Harvey Lashler, Scott Johnson (Phillips C.I.), Kenneth Chandler, Ricky Sweet, John Garvin and Billy York. I want to talk to "Bad Boys" and troubled teens. I want to speak to you from a place of pain... Dr. Lewis Yablonsky calls me an "Experience Therapist". Dr. Solis calls me an "Expert on Youth criminality". Dr. A. Duran calls me an "Expert on the causes of Youth criminality". Dr. Curren calls me an "Expert communicator". Dr. Heitkamp calls me "brilliant". Jimbo calls me a "masterful manipulator" and... I got tired of reading little lightweight books which barely scratched the surface of youngsters' lives. I was livid with reporters and journalists (who've never seen the inside of a prison. Folks who don't know the difference between a juvenile, a jail and a prison etc.) writing embellished (James Frey-like "memoirs") tomes about prisons. And they'll have a half a chapter for youths. I came to bring you the inside story from the inside... When I initially got the 'vision' to write "K.K.K." I called the gang Genius Dr. Yablonsky. I had this idea of him writing a chapter etc. "I've done my work! I'm 84 years old Sherman... You woke me up with this call" he told me. "I've written 20 tomes tackling youth gangs. I've testified in more than 300 trials. I taught at Harvard. I've done psychodrama with juvenile gang members etc. Sherman I'll send you my books and you can consult with me but it's your turn now. You are the expert embedded in the story. You don't need me to write it for you"...

When I walked with Dr. Jarman he told me "I've given you and taught you everything I know for 9 years. You are the authority on what it's like to live in Hades. Your book can impact an entire nation of kids. You can do it".

And so I'm writing you from a place of pain. And I'm speaking into your spirit. You can change anything in your life which you want to change. So many guys like Ryan Hreljac, Taylor Francis, Joshua Costa and Josh Cook etc. will join me in telling you that you have so much greatness down inside of you.

... I want you to hear me today. Derek King, Alex, Allen Harris, Benjamin Harris etc. will all join me in telling you that you can get it together. Dr. Drew Pinsky can tell you that a turnaround is possible! ... If Jeff G. Howell is reading this "your secrets are safe with me. I still have 3 kites you wrote. And I have the receipt for the $ 100.00 I sent. Bye-gones be bye-gone. Let's get Justin out!"....

All of you youths reading my words etc. It's time for you to breakthrough... Gabby (in the movie "precious" .... I repeat) I want "your two roommates who were on Oprah with you to join G.B.G. today!"

In Santa Rosa New Mexico we want Guadalupe (Reyes?) to join us. Guadalupe you worked at Demy's in Santa Rosa in 1995. Where are you? I owe you an opportunity. Contact me...

I want you young boys and men to get up. Get back in school. Stay in school. Read, write and study. You have the chance (right now) to turn it all around....

When I was running around calling Dr. Yablonsky, Senator John Burton, Carolyn Phillips etc. when I was seeking wise counsel from my brilliant advisory board (including Curren, Solis, Heitkamp, A. Duran, Gregg, Jarman and Freidman etc.) regarding the writing of this book etc. I was subconsciously doing what boys do when you join gangs and follow the crowd. I was looking to be 'endorsed'. I had been beat down, lied upon and belittled for so long. I'd been in 'darkness' for so long. I'd been housed in a system designed to beat down your confidence and to break your spirit. I'd been around people who are taught, trained and bred to see the worst in me. I'd been subjected to the adversarial authority of folks from the backwoods who assume all prisoners are from the trailer parks and the hoods. And these people who run corrections (by and large) are racist, sexist, misanthropic, misogynistic and undereducated people. And they specialize in an ability to minify convicts.

I'd been in this darkness where I was consistently reminded of the Jacob, the Clark Kent, the trickster and the crook in me. And when you've been berated, belittled, lied on and psychologically diminished for so long by so many people you'll begin to 'believe' it. And you can get to a place where you say "Even though I 'know' I didn't 'rape' (stab, assault or....) that 'dude' (female or shemale etc.) I 'know' what 'I' did 'not' do! But... maybe I am just a piece of shi-. Maybe I ought to die in prison. Since I lied to Stella, cheated Don and went on the run. Maybe I deserve to die. Maybe I am no-damn good. Maybe I'm useless and worthless. I".....

I started to feel like a nobody. But..... Baby Boy always remember that you are never as bad as they (yo enemies) say you are. And you ain't as great as they (your friends), say you are. But you are a child of God.

And so I had been beat down by staff and by inmates. I felt discouraged. I couldn't find anybody to fellowship with because you can't get blood out of a turnip. And broken, angry, bitter and hateful men are jealous. And they're envious. And they will not lift you up - because they can't lift you up. They are down. Down mentally, spiritually and psychologically. How can I cheer you up when I'm depressed? How can the blind lead the blind?

So my environment is full of folks who beat each other down for sport, for pay and for play. Both physically and psychologically... So everything that would work for me in civilian life works against me in prison. Things which would promote me at Penn State, demote me in the State pen. i.e. "He's a brilliant scholar. He walked and talked with civil rights legends. He was in newspapers and on TV at 12 years of age. When most boys were playing ball he was figuring out how to buy a ball team. He led the prayer vigils for Atlanta's murdered and missing children. He's preached at some of the larges churches in America. He".... Civilian! And "He's an incorrigible criminal. He calls himself 'Reverend'. He was convicted...." Prisoner!

God revealed to me an awesome truth that I'd been missing. The blind can't lead the blind. But the blind can lead the visionless. Just because I have a sight deficit does not mean I have no vision. By the same token, if I'm paralyzed I can still teach you how I walk(ed). I can also teach you how 'not' to do what I did that put me in a wheelchair...

"You can do it better than I can and I have a Ph.D." Dr. Jarman told me "if there is a room full of standing people and one guy comes in in a wheelchair who do you think everybody will look at?" Dr. Solis asked me. "The dude in the wheelchair" I replied, thinking I had the whole message. And "By the same token if you are living in a home for people in wheelchairs. And I'm a kid who aspires to have a wheelchair. And I've been entertained on TV and with the movies about the place guys with wheelchairs live. And I'm kinda thinking that 'Oh well that doesn't look like such a bad place and at least if I've gone (been) there I'll come back to the barrio (ghetto or hood) and get respect'. And if you are in a wheelchair. And you live in the place where most guys in wheelchairs who get caught are sent to. Sherman I'll listen to you". Dr. Solis continued "Sherman, they're already listening to you. They listen to rappers who have been to prison. They listen to some rappers who are in prison. They go buy music by guys charged and convicted of rapes and murders. And most of what they are being told by rappers and others is garbage. Why not add your message to the mix? Why not add your performance to the stage? You are a master....."

I finally woke up and began to remember who I am. And whose I am. And as I began to recognize my 'Israel', my 'prince', the 'super' in my 'man' and how blessed I am, I stopped seeking endorsements. And I started seeking God. And as I sought God the enemy came in like a flood. He tried to distract me and preoccupy me. He hit me with allegations, dissension and accusations. But the Lord is a very 'present help' in the time of trouble. And now I see why in the psalms David uses the word "enemy" hundreds of times. Read Psalm 69. Read Psalm 27, 91 etc. David is always praying and singing about defeating those who are encamped against him.

And when you are in school and they 'hate' on you don't trip. They may 'hate' on you because of your hair, your weight, your teeth ("yuck mouth"), your style or whatever. But you must learn to understand 'hate'. You can't please everybody. Jesus had enemies. And if I hate your daddy I'm probably not going to be in love with you.... I wrote this book because I know what happens when kids kill(ing) kids who huff, puff, steal, rob, scam, burglarize and... It's not a pretty place....

You have so much talent and so much potential. If you will slow down and shut off the 'noise' for a while you'll find the secrets (about you) that are hidden in plain sight. This is your moment to get up. You didn't stumble upon this book. You didn't even choose this book. This book chose you.

.... 11/25/09 Adam Lambert performed on CBS. His base player had a wild hair-do with crazy hair color. I want his name and address. I want him in G.B.G.

.... Ellen did a thanksgiving show and she told a dude (in shorts and a black hat) "you're a pilgrim and I appreciate your legs". Who was he? Let's call him "Legs" or "Pilgrim" and get him this tome.

I had a chat with a female guard named Beza. Mrs. Beza is very bright and has some interesting views on fighting crime.... Nurse Emily is also a bright young lady.... C.O. Quam is a youngster who will work with T. Ramsey, David Kelley and C.O. Hodge on our youth mentoring team. We need more guards, soldiers and sailors to volunteer as part-time mentors and coaches for G.B.G.....

'Eric' was on 'the price is right' on 11/25/09. G.B.G. wants him. "Brandon" the "Black Eyed Pea" was on "Let's make a deal" on 11/25/09. I need you all (Chad Wolcott, Benjamin Alexander, Ben Whipple etc.) to find "Brandon".

.... In L.A. County jail in 1995 and 1996 (Wayside) there was "Chad" working as a porter. "Chad" lived in the "softy" dorm. Can anybody find Chad?..... Mentioning "Chad" and the "softy" dorm etc. We were returning from court on a bus one day. And the "softies" were riding with us. (A "softy" was a non-gay youngster who staff thought would be victimized in general population). One guy had Attorney Harry Weiss as his lawyer. And everybody loved Harry Weiss because Harry would smuggle packs of Camel cigarettes to his clients in County Jail. Harry was the first lawyer who told me that Gil Garcetti, Larry Longo, Altman and Mary Hanlon could all be bribed.... "And Mary doesn't only accept cash" he told me. "You know any young white boys?" I said "How young?" Harry said "No younger than ten and no older than 17. Mary beds boys". I could not believe my ears until a detective told me about Hanlon and Russell....

.... So we are on the L.A. County jail bus and this 'Weiss' client has a pack of Camels tucked down inside his underwear. And this youngster white inmate (his name escapes my memory) began to 'plead' for a cigarette. The black dude whispered "stick your tongue out for me". Dude said "I'm not gay. I have a girlfriend". There was a gate like screen separating the two of them. And the black dude said "If you want a cig stick your tongue through this screen and put it on my tongue". White guy looks around and I (always the investigator) dropped my head pretending to be nodding. And this 18 or 19 year old 'straight' C.O. Hodge look-a-like, stuck his tongue on the black dude's tongue. And that screen had to be filthy. .... One smoke.... Black guy says "You wanna nutha (sic) one?" "Hell yeah" the white guy says. "When we get to the jail they are gonna put us in the same room together to strip us out. I wanna grab your ass one time. Real quick. Nobody will see". And.... I'd pay $ 1000.00 to find this white guy. I just want to interview him for the next book!.... This non-gay, girlfriend having white boy allowed a black dude to palm his ass cheek for 'a' cigarette...

At the Georgia Industrial Institute (AKA "Alto") in the "Block" (Ad-seg) there's this 18 or 19 year old white guy in a barred cell. His name was 'Wayne'. Wayne was/is straight.... Black dude in cell next to him takes 30 minutes to talk Wayne into turning around, backing his ass up to the bars etc. Black guy reaches around through the bars and fingers his asshole...

Prison in Columbus Georgia. Andy Hines is 18. All the fellas want Andy. Andy is "a Christian" and "I don't f-ck around with that gay shit". And.... Andy is in school one day and dude talks Andy into going in the bathroom and "just let me finger that fat ass of yours please". And.... I would pay $ 500.00 right now to interview Andy. It just amazes me to see men - especially white - boys etc. who are basically heterosexual. And who under another set of circumstances (especially in 1993, 94 and 95 etc.) would have been yelling the "N" word to blacks. But they get in juvenile, jail and prison and succumb to being "undercover homos". And I'm not writing this just to clown or make fun of people. These are human beings. I'm telling this for several reasons: A. So you will know the 'actual', 'factual' way it 'is' in prison. So you will know what you'll never see on TV. Because Hollywood eviscerates prison life with inaccurate embellishments. They'll show "drag queens" and "train rapes" which are sick and do occur! But you never see the tens of thousands of country white boys' from lil country, racist and rural towns etc. who get locked up and decide to 'experiment' out of 'curiosity' with black men.... They've been hearing about them "N's" got big "di-ks" all their lives. And they decide to give it a try. And.... If they don't volunteer to help G.B.G. prevent kids from coming to prisons I'll blackmail their asses. I'll start naming names and publishing kites.... (you all know who you are! Your secrets are safe unless you refuse to help!).... And I tell it (also) so you'll know to tell your lil sisters, your aunts and your cousins etc. that that boy about whom 'they' (the ladies) are saying "He's cute! and he gotta big juicy ass!" etc. If he's Caucasian and under 30 years of age, there is better than an eighty percent chance he was having sex in prison! C.D.C. is "Brokeback C.D.C.". The prison system in your state has a "Broke-Back". And a lot of these guys get out and they'll go back to Cummings Georgia. They'll go home to Valdosta, Telfair County, Dalton or Dublin Georgia. And they'll go back to Oak Park, Sacramento etc. and bump n grind with the first 'lady' they find. And 'this' is a public service announcement to all the ladies: Beware the ex-con may have Aids! And he may be gay!.... Somebody asked me "you're not afraid people are gonna call you homophobic because of all you're writing about gays in yo (sic) book?"

I replied "Homophobic? Hell, some of them will assume I'm gay because of what I wrote. They'll wonder what 'secrets' I know about 'J' etc. But if a person closes 'K.K.K.' and the worst erroneous assumption they have about me is that I hate gays or even that I may be gay. I can tolerate those erroneous assumptions. But I have a duty to disclose the truth about the prison subculture. "I told the person "K.K.K. is raw, cutting and uncut. What I lack (for not employing a ghostwriter like Sarah Palin did) in writing skills I make up for with 'inside scoops'. America would never - ever get Eric Menendez, Lyle, Daniel Henson or Ed Stokes to say "I invite you into my bedroom". "K.K.K." is the prison "Big Brother". I am the camera on the wall inside the cell. America ain't ever seen how we live in the cells. Cameras and a few books have come inside the prison halls and on the prison yards. But they've never come inside the cell (bedroom) walls. I am inviting America inside our bedrooms and bathrooms. I want young ladies who are saying 'he ain't had no puss- in 8 years. I know he's gonna be good in bed when he gets out' etc. I want Lisa, Brandy and Jennifer etc. to know that he has his pretty, lilly white (brown or black) ass etc. sitting on a toilet, two feet away from his cell partner right now. I continued "I want boys to know that when they get here they can be as straight as an arrow! And now you're in your cell and watching TV and Andy Hines is in the cell with Cheyenne. And Caliente is on TV and the cell is your 'bedroom'. And psychologically you are accustomed to (can we just be real you all?) masturbating or having sex in your bedroom. And now your lil 3 inch penis (talking about white guys! lol) is becoming erect. And you realize you are sitting next to another 'man' (AKA Cheyenne). And you ...."

I was explaining to that guy what I want you to know. I'm not hating. Do what you want to do. I only oppose rape. If you wanna get locked up and spend the rest of your life smelling other men's farts, flexing and posturing for other men come on in. But even 'gay' guys ought to want to be 'free'. Freedom means everything!...

"Boys will be boys?" Boys will be toys! Boys will be girls! Boys will be whatever you condition them to be. And prison conditions boys to be predators, victims, helpless and useless. Boys will be perverts if you condition (and position) them to be that way...

At Pleasant Valley State Prison (un-Pleasant Valley) a short white guy ("Blue Eyed Blonde") showed me photos of him (Jacob Hill) and his 'wife'. Jacob's lady was bad. She was... They had a pretty red car. And Jacob was a cool 'wood'. And a couple of days later I was ..... Jake told Mike (a burly black dude) "Mike I got black girl booty don't I?" Mike said "Hell, nall Boy, you ain't got no ass". Jake turned around and pulled his boxers down and did a booty dance for a brutha.

.... In L.A. County Jail Christopher Parker (young white and supposedly "Bootily endowed") turned around 'in' his underwear and did a booty dance in front of numerous fellas.... "Boys will be What?" In an all male environment when you mix older boys with younger boys. When you intermingle and house (against their will) murderers, molesters, rapists and terrorists together, they feed off of each other. Association causes assimilation. And the assimilation which transpires during incarceration causes devastation....

A dude I knew in a prison in Georgia broke down and sobbed and told me "my step dad face f-cked me". ... This was a young, skinny Caucasian guy. I'd never even heart the term "Face f....". And I'd had him (s) listening to a Zig Zigler tape. And I was explaining to him how he could do anything and how he was born to win etc. And I was trying to be a black Dr. Phil, to a white brother - before we ever even heard of a Dr. Phil. And in the midst of our so-called motivational 'moment' (I'd been telling him he had to 'let go' of the pain of his past and move toward his future) he broke down and told me about this horrendous tragedy. He also told me that he'd "never told anybody this; ever 'Rev'. (he called me "Rev")".

I've come to believe that the number of boys who have been sexually molested by their fathers, uncles, brothers and cousins etc. is far greater than we could ever imagine. And most boys could never imagine. And thank the Lord that I was never molested. And I 'promise' not to be lying here. But sadly (I would not blatantly write a lie. I just would never even address it.) If I had been molested chances are very likely, I would not have 'told' it.

I can not even fathom what it would be like to be a kid and get 'molested'. Nor can I even imagine how it would feel to say "mom he molested me".... Damn that's got to be a tough nut to crack. And I've been through some tough stuff in my life. I've had my share of trials and tribulations. I've been in the storms and I've been in some rains. And life has kicked me in my gut as well as in my nuts. I've had my issue of trauma. But my God, I don't know what it feels like to be a child and to have some grown ass pervert like Garrido to rape me. That's gotta be traumatic. And I get tired of everybody claiming to be so repulsed by child molestation. Yet nobody is confessing to being a molester (not until they get 'caught'). Yet, America has (just in 'America') 24 million (almost ten percent of the U.S. population!) sex addicts. And my research shows that more than 34% of every baby born tomorrow will experience some form of sexual impropriety directed toward them (by an adult) before they are 12 years old.... Somebody is doing the 'molesting'. Somebody is sexually attracted to children. And while it is a crime and must be punished; it is also a (perverted) sickness and needs to be treated.

Until we stop throwing words, rhetoric, anger and politics at this crime (illness) and begin to fight (treat) it. We will continue a dangerous cycle of sex crimes against children which shall spiral out of control.

We don't need a new law. We don't need a new prison. We don't need more cops. All that stuff sounds good and sells newspapers. But we need more mentors, more counselors and more coaches. We need the kind of parents willing to fly gasoline into hell to save our children.... I'm always hearing from folks who got molested (and that's sad). And I'm always hearing about people who were molested. But I keep looking and I can't find anybody who is doing the molesting. I keep looking around and I'm searching here, there and everywhere and I can't find a single one who 'did' it... My advisory board members indicate that most victims of abuse become abusers. The data I've studied indicates that more than 80% of all child molesters were molested. Ipso Facto, we need to review these data with detached observational skills. And we need to engage in strategic methodologies to address the roots to halt the fruit. Simply slinging rhetoric and knee-jerk reactions etc. do not stop this madness. We need a pragmatic plan to detect, prevent, address and eliminate child molestation. We can't be in denial. We can't sweep it under the rug. Facts speak for themselves. Just as most 'crack' users are black. Most meth users are white. Most heroin users are Latino. Most pedophiles are Caucasian males. Point blank!.... Go look at all the tapes from Chris Hansen's Dateline "How to catch a predator". Count all the white molesters (vs. black and brown etc.) you see. Look on the local listings for child molesters in your county and count the white male faces versus the others...

Newt Gingrich, Larry Craig, Brian Doyle, Gary Condit, Mike Bunnell, Wally Tucker, Mike Jiminez, Joe Rikajo etc. these are the faces (often in high places) of sexual deviants. The black-ass- sexual perverts like Marion E. Spearman come far and few between (statistically). Ipso Facto, since white, powerful and politically connected men (i.e. U.S. Senators and congressmen etc.) are often sexual perverts. They've engaged in a campaign to divert attention away from detection, prevention and treatment..... How many black (or brown) Catholic priests, bishops and cardinals do you know? What color is the "Pope"?.... Ipso Facto, how many billions ($ with a "B") of dollars has the Catholic church (there goes any 'hope' that I'd get support from my Catholic brethren for this tome.) contributed to the political war chests of the Joe Liebermans and the John Kerrys? Follow the money Honey!

Many men who are gay are drawn to the Catholic church. Many Catholic church seminaries (with their so-called sworn celibacy) are like bathhouses for gay men. And becoming a Catholic priest gives them open access to pretty little lilly white boys. And these boys who are molested by men (who use their priestly Robes to 'cover' their homosexuality etc.) grow up and molest boys. And just as the priest used his robe as 'cover' etc. the molested boys (who grow up) use marriage and masculinity as a cover for their molestations... My assignment here (in "K.K.K.") is not to pull a Clint van Zandt and yell out about a 'new law', 'more police' and 'more jail time'. Nor am I challenged to pull a prisoner rights advocacy move and yell about 'treatment' only, 'less jail time' and perversion is "only a disease" etc. When we find molestation we need to lock that white (black or brown) ass up. I don't advocate these little hand slappings and secret probated sentences often handed down to the rich and famous molesters etc..... But 'if' we really wanna 'save the children' etc. we must begin to set up child predator and child abuse task forces in and out of the Catholic church. We must begin to identify victims of abuse and begin to treat them to prevent them from abusing!....

Many of you and your parents have read about the billionaire boys club. I've been asked (for years) why I never wrote anything about them since I was housed (at CSP-Sac) with two of them. Neither Ben Dosti nor Izzy Eslaminia ever borrowed any money from me like 'Eric' did.... Google the Billionaire Boys Club because I'm not gonna re-tell their story. But what kind of man puts his own father in a trunk so he can demand ransom money? And his dad suffocates because they (Ben Dosti, Izzy Eslaminia and Joe Hunt) didn't put enough holes in the trunk. Hell - Joe Hunt has written a fantasy tome with his cell partner Alan Hughes. I've heard good things about Joe Hunt. However, Izzy's dad was in some secret Israeli army. And fled the country. When I met Izzy he was trying to sell me a pack of 'razors' in 96. Izzy claimed to be a 'Muslim'. But Izzy was as gay as a $ 3 dollar bill. He was definitely doing it in the butt. A Muslim Yeah, right!....

Ben Dosti? Wow, where do I begin? Ben Dosti was caught with his asshole in Trans (I don't know Trans authentic name but he ended up celling with Eric Menendez) face. Ben was performing fellatio on Trans while Trans was performing 'fellatio' ("annallatio? neology!) on Ben's anus. Ben was sweating like a mad-dog. Superman (inmate Schooler) caught them. And I (did not actually 'see' it. I was about four feet away from the cell door) heard Schooler say "what the F?" and he said "Can I come in? Damn Ben like that?" I ran over to the door and as I got there Ben was pulling on his skivvies (underwear - tighty whities) and Trans was covering himself with a blanket. Ben says "dude can you get me out of here? She's not a regular in control. She won't know". Ben did not live in that cell... Superman told C.O. Deborah Paul to "open 106 for the telephone". And when Ben came out Schooler says "Dude you've got cum on your forehead". Ben says "F--- you"....

Chaplain Glen Shields (a damn good brother. He now pastors 'Progressive' church in Stockton Ca.) performed Ben's marriage (yes to a female!) for him. Ben (the 'on tha down lo' gay boy) is now the proud pastor of some type of ministry in civilian life. His mother was an editor for the L.A. Times food section.... How did Ben get out? The same way Izzy got an appeal bond. Because money talks and B.S. walks. And.... I can't tell you that Ben is a crook or Ben is going to hell. If God can transform Saul into Paul. If God can transform water into wine, He can change Ben Dosti. Ben may be sincere and his ministry could be authentic.

My purpose is not to shame Ben. I just want to give you youngsters an authentic inside Edition of a real life tome, written by a real life prisoner. I respect what Mumia Abu Jamal writes about. He is a political prisoner. And he writes powerfully about 'what' he writes about. And I read every tome Mumia writes.

But he hasn't written 'this' kind of tome. Nobody has because we are afraid you're gonna say "well is ole Sherm (or whoever got the balls to write it) doin it in tha butt too? He sure knows a lot about it". And we (in prison) are suffering from so much arrested, oppressed and repressed development etc. that A. We don't want you to see what's really going on. And B. we need you to believe that all we do is kick ass and take names. And C. We don't mind the "conflict" between "mom I go to church every Sunday and I've changed my life." And "Mom I'm a gangbanger for life". We're okay with that apparent conflict. But D. We can't reckon with the conflict(s) of big ole buffed men who pump iron in the day time and get buttholes pumped out in the nighttimes and (even more sadly) a large number (of the large number) of the sexually active prisoners get out and get a 'woman'. And...

I'm not supposed to be telling this, but.......

I remember LA County Jail Deputies would line up 100 naked men. And you'd have to stand in your birthday suit next to 99 (other) naked men... And seven or eight deputies are roaming around behind us "Bend over at the waist and spread your cheeks. Spread em wide or we'll be here all day... Give me 3 loud coughs!.... Turn around and lift up your nutt sack. Wipe your finger forward from your asshole to your nutt sack".... I recall (vividly) deputy Olivier telling an 18 year old white guy (Marvin Stone) "bend back over dude... what is that white stuff on the pretty pink lips of your asshole?" Then the deputy got a big flashlight and shined it on the dude's asshole... And with a gloved finger the deputy wiped the dude's asshole in front of 99 of us. "Oh - shit (no pun intented) it's freaking toilet paper!" the deputy yelled. And... he berated, belittled and humiliated this young (innocent til proven guilty beyond a reasonable doubt to a moral certainty) man in front of all of us. That was a sexual assault by staff. And I wish I'd known Attorneys Mark Merin, Robert Navarro or Geri Lynn Green back then. I assure you this boy has never forgotten that.

I tell these kinds of (authentic) stories to pull back the iron curtain, the chain linked fence and to open up the barb wired gates of the prisons and to show you what Lee Daniels would perhaps show you if he made a "K.K.K." movie or docu-drama. I don't care if you start thinking all prisoners are 'gay'. I don't care if you think (and rightfully so) that many guards are rogue, gay and crooks etc.

I want you to see what it is like to be here. If you think "ole Sherm may be" etc. You won't be the first and you probably won't be the last... In L.A. County Jail for a time Mary Hanlon thought that. She found the youngest (inmate Cervantes) Mexican cell partner (17 years old) whom she could legally put in the cell with me. She sent him there for two reasons: A. To come on to me sexually to try to corroborate her 'theory' of the case. And B. To get me to 'confess'. At about 8:00 pm the first (and only) night in the cell he said to me "I'll keep it real I wanna suck your di...".... He suffered a broken nose and required 8 stitches (he 'could' have fallen off the bunk) around his eye. The very next day he took the witness stand against me. When the judge determined he had no relevant data about my case he told Hanlon "If you wanna put him on to say Manning is violent that might go over. Apparently Manning assaulted him. But he's on record admitting that he made a sexual pass at Manning. And that Manning says he had kicked Calvario out of his car because he discovered Calvario was a man. How that'll help your case is beyond me" the judge stated...

At New Folsom State prison I met this white guy with a full beard and he (Michael Carter) was carrying a Holy Bible... He moved into my assigned cell. And he immediately shaved off his beard and mustache. "A lot of guys have told me I have pretty lips" he told me. I became suspicious... Then one day I come in and Michael has on red lipstick, t-shirt, a thong and a skirt (AKA "net bag").. C.O. Mark Brandon moved him out. And he told Brandon "I thought he was gay. Most black guys want my booty". Brandon stated "I've known Sherman a long time. He'll live and let live. But he don't (sic) get down like that".....

Prison walls without women do you still wanna bang? At P.V.S.P. C.O. Williams is an openly gay black officer. And every time he worked our building it seemed like all 200 prisoners decided to walk around the bldg. with no shirts on. "If some of them knew how they looked, child they would put their shirts back on" he said and he punctuated it with "okay".

Armando Guizar, Armando (last name unknown but PBS did a special on him. He was a notorious gangbanger who shot and killed several people. And he did not "F" around with that "gay sh-t"), Jose Zuniga, William Coker, Chuck Hedrick, Primo (Armenian) etc. etc. All would take off their shirts and find a reason to stand in front of Mr. Williams... Before I ever knew anything about C.O. D.L. Criner I mentioned him (as a Christian) to Williams. And Williams said "Criner grabbed my dick, balls and ass in the parking lot. He's bi".

Sgt. Hosman (corn-fed white boy) was in the Fresno Bee Newspaper for calling a black guard a "N". And Williams told me "Hosman may be racist but he likes black ass. He came on to me"....

At. P.V.S.P. there was this racist skinhead. He was into that witchcraft stuff. We called him Willow. He hated blacks and would kill a rapist and all of that. A legend in his own mind.... One day I "saw" (with my eyes) a black dude (a clerk) go over to Willow's cell door. The yard was out and there was barely anyone in the building. Willow was in the very last cell on the top tier. I had my mirror stuck out the tray slot so I could see his cell. I saw a white hand come out the tray slot and Willow grabs dude's penis. He fondles him a good 90 seconds. Then he pulls dude's thing into the tray slot and begins to suck him..... A racist!...

At New Folsom an inmate named Mike (I won't yet reveal Mike's last name unless he refuses to help us help kids not come to prison. Is that 'black' male? No he's white!) called me to his door and asked me to "tell Mike Henrickson to send me one of those magazines but put it in a sealed manila envelope". I delivered the message and Henrickson told me "I don't have a manila envelope but here". He gave me a magazine in an un-sealed brown paper bag. I had to look. It was a "Euro-Boy" (like a "play-girl" for gay men) magazine!! I gave it to Mike. And later on he handed me a note: "Atlanta I don't want anybody to know I'm like this. Especially my celly! I would pay you not to tell, but you've got more money than me. Do you F around? I can give you a show, a Booty dance or something to keep this hush hush". I kept the note and told Mike: "Dude, I'm cool. But your secret is safe with me. I never told his celly or anyone...

At P.V.S.P. I allowed my (next door neighbor) Tien Trung Nguyen (AKA Panther) to read several of my tomes. He read "The pursuit of happyness", "Reallionaire", "The last man standing" by Geronimo Pratt etc. He said of Pratt's book "Atlanta this is the best book I have ever read in my entire lifetime". I let him read "Fish" by T.J. Parsell. And "Fish" has a lot of prison sex in it. It is a 'graphic' (real deal) book. And Panther told me "It was off the hook. Did you look in the book since I gave it back?" Panther was a Bruce-Lee look-a-like. Very athletic and muscular. He was in the hole for writing a love letter to a female guard. And this cut-up', female loving Asian wrote in my book "Tien loves Atlanta". In one part of the book T.J. is describing sex underneath the bed with "Paul". And right by that scene Panther wrote "Atl. and Panther". First of all I'm absolutely 'livid' that he would have the temerity to write in 'my' book. ... Then to write this gay stuff. And there was a 2 page missive inside the tome: I would let you F me in my A hole if you help me get out of prison Atl...." God bless Tien and I pray for him but yall hear me... Guys in here will sell their souls for drugs, booze, a cell phone, freedom or the promise of freedom. Do you still wanna bang?

Pink-Eye on a promissory note!... I met a dude (V.G.) at P.V.S.P. who was a Caucasian. He had a black celly (R.C.) and his celly was having sex with him. This guy told me the "only reason I had sex with the dude is because he promised to help me get outta prison". I told him "V. I'm gonna write a book about you and R. And call it 'Pink-eye on a promissory note'". He went off! "I will sue you N"....

Danny Slayter, Michael Jacinto, Abel "Grumpy" Maldonado, D.J. Carpenter, Brandon A. Hughes, Brad (M.C.S.P.), Danny Macky, Nathan Gould, Martin Cheatham, Tracy Roby and Brian Thomas Cruz (AKA "red") All know about what I'm speaking about. They (Daniel Job, Jeff Glen Howell etc.) ought to all step forward and help me tell this story...

"Slit Leg"? Have you (Michael Cardenas, Henry Chan at UCSD, or CJ etc.) ever heard of 'slit legging'? Kenneth Chandler, James Lewis (Valdosta Ga.), Sam Fuick, Chris Michael Fowler (Cobb County GA.) etc. can all tell you what it is. I'm not saying 'they' did it. But they were around it.... Christopher Durbin? His parents owned a skating rink in Georgia. He's a white fella. He ran out of cigarettes and was nicking. And Chris knocked on my neighbor's door and .... My neighbor had told me "All them white boys is (sic) fu--ing dude" and I did not believe him. When Chris knocked Al told me to "get under the bed and listen". I got under the bed and Chris came in. "What's up Al?.... I need a pack of top (bugler-like tobacco) Bro" Al goes. "You got any money?" Chris says "Nall, but I go to canteen in 2 weeks". Al said "Nall? What about all that money you got on yo back 'Boy'". Chris giggled like a lil girl. "Yeah I know you wanna 'slit leg' me?" I'm wondering what the hell is 'slit legging?'. Al says Yes. Chris lays on his stomach and takes off his underwear. And he asks Al "Aren't you gonna use some lotion?" Al replies "Why do I need lotion just to 'rub my dick between your ass cheeks when it ain't going inside you?" Chris says "Lotion will make it slide better". Al says "You want me to 'f' you white boy. But I ain't puttin it in yu. Just slit leg".... John Sexton? "Try not to cum on my ass". David Ramey? "Come Daddy cum!". B.Y.? C.R.? I can name a whole lot more "straight" Caucasian males turning 'tricks' with black men in jail and going home with tales (stories) about how many "N's" they "beat down" in prison. They "beat" a dick down but.....

Vince Waldron (PFC), Kelvin Tran (Sacto), Marie Callender's bag boy (on Fox 40 bagging thanksgiving pies in Sacto), The Rubber Boy, Henry Chan, Trevor Lindsay are you reading this?

Did you all see Beyonce (Big Booty 'Beyonce') on her "I am yours" tours? She had two male dancers (grinding on my Boo! I oughta beat they ass!) on her "Get me Bodied" song. We want both dancers in G.B.G..... Ellen? Thanksgiving show? She had Andy (an Anthony Fedorov twin - lol) in high heels (red!) on her show. Tell Andy to (remove the high heels yo - we gotta pair of combat boots 4 u) come join G.B.G. We need him....

At Alto Clarence Jones was a counselor. A great man of faith and a good brutha! "What kind of system sends a man to prison for 3 Percodan pills that he had a valid prescription for? " Clarence asked me. "And to have Command Sergeant Majors, Police Majors, High school principals, Rev. Hosea Williams and a United Nations Ambassador testify for you is unheard of... I called Michael Bergin and he told me 'Clarence they'd rather call the Reverend the "F" (felon) word than the "N" word. Welcome to the New Jim Crow Jr'".... There was also a big 6ft3 coach Anthony King at Alto. He could bench press 500 lbs on a bad day.

The strongest inmate at Alto was Davenport. D.P. was in prison for raping a woman and shoving tree branches up her vagina. He cut her nipples off. And one day D.P. went off on staff. He punched a guard (K-O'ed him) and went to his cell. He held his door closed and 3 guards (600 lbs) couldn't get his door open. Sergeant Coles had just promoted to Lieutenant. And he told the guards to "back off and go find coach King. They went up C-section (A-bldg.) and got coach King. King came down and single-handedly forced the door open. D.P. swung on him and King knocked him out. King had been drafted into the NFL, but an injury felled him. King showed us pictures of his wife and she was 'bad'. I mean she was 'Beyonce Bootilicious" and......

C.O. Million was one of the most affable guards at Alto. He loved to talk politics and he worked first watch (10:00 pm - 6:00 am). C.O. Million would read your c-file and decide if he liked you or not. Dudes he liked could roam "A" building all night long under the guise of cleaning and buffing floors etc... Million would call me to control every night at 11:00 pm. He wanted to know every detail about these characters he'd seen on TV like Andy Young and Hosea Williams. To be a conservative white boy Republican he sure was fascinated by black national politics. He'd let me use the telephone (in control) to call Andy Young (404-753-2005 at that time) at home; on speaker phone. Some nights I'd call Rev. Hosea Williams 1:00 am. He never slept...

Million retired as a "captain". But prior to his celebrated retirement he stumbled upon a shocker. If I were a script writer I'd write about it. If I were an actor I'd act the part of Million out.

... One Friday night C.O. Million let coach King into the bldg. at 8:00 pm. King went up to his rec room (he got off at 5:00 pm but was dedicated to his job) with his buddies. Terry (AKA

'Cowboy') was King's favorite inmate. Terry was black and he knew my buddy Rev. Quincy Lavelle Carswell. Terry was a gambler and a 'turn out' artist. He specialized in turning out white boys. At one point he simultaneously had two gay boys (Chester and Sheffield). Chester was black and Shef was Caucasian. Coach King (along with 85% of all the guards) would sex-play with Terry, Shef and most other guys and.....

Long story short: Million creeps up to the Rec room at 10:15 pm. He opens the door and sees Terry screwing Chester and (lo and behold) coach Anthony King (authentic names) has Sheffield bent over the table and King is screwing him. King the NFL draftee. King the big muscle man. King the family man.... Maxwell Hanger? Steven Moreno Jr.? "Brett" and "Chris" are you all certain you want to continue using drugs and booze and risk coming here? .... When you come here if your celly catches the flu you'll get a cold (minimum). And if staff gets pneumonia inmates get the flu. And vice versa. And just as bacterial germs spread around the prisons, spiritual bacteria (prison is a psychological germ factory) spread around the prisons infecting most and affecting all. Unless an inmate (or staff person) vaccinates themselves against the "spiritual wickedness" (and perversions etc.) in the prisons etc. these dark spirits, thoughts and mind-sets are contagious. I have been all-over the world. I've been in churches and I've been in nightclubs. I (the homophobic writer) have been in gay clubs with my wife. I was in the Navy and JROTC. I've been in the locker rooms of Morris Brown and Georgia Tech football teams etc. and yet, I have never (ever) seen the kind of graphic and blatant 'sex playing' which I've seen in prisons. Staff and inmates alike. There is a homogenization that takes place in the prisons. It gets off on the guards as well as the guarded. And there is a process of psychological acceptance of vile and perverted jokes that come with the territory of prisons. And this psychological acceptance leads to participation. And participation leads to sex. And sex leads to disease. And these diseases being metastasized inside the prisons leads to my dis-ease with what happens to unknowing women. When they take an ex-con in and bed him down. And he injects aids, hepatitis and all kinds of diseases into them....

Please understand that Lance Corcoran, Mike Jiminez, Marion E. Spearman and D.L. Criner etc. aren't gonna admit to being perverts and/or childmolesters. I mean do you really assume Lance Corcoran is gonna say "Sherman is a great guy. And I admit that everything he said about me is true". Give me a break. If he's smart he violates policy (again) and leaks confidential (unsubstantiated or uncorroborated) data about me. His other alternative is to not respond. But he's not going to confirm anything in this tome.

But does it take a rocket scientist to figure out that if you enjoy forcing boys (and young men) to have sex. If you enjoy seeing men and lording over men etc. Prisons, jails and juveniles are the best gigs in town. And what better 'cover' for a molester or rapist than a badge and a uniform? The priest uses a robe, a collar and a Bible. A guard (D.L. Criner, Wally Tucker, Joe Rikalo etc.) use a badge, a uniform and a set of handcuffs as 'cover'. And it's open season on males.

And when prisoners are raped, "I'm a sworn peace officer. This inmate has zero credibility. I'm a married man. And I have no blemishes on my record. He's lying on me because....."

400 Boys have been molested by 152 priests in Dublin Ireland. And when priests are 'caught' they just transfer them to another parish. Ipso Facto, when guards are 'caught' (raping, beating and mistreating inmates etc.) they usually transfer the inmate...

Travis Scott (TMZ), Chris Dewan (Bibliophile), Charles Best etc. r u reading? .... At the Armani Exchange (A/X) at Arden Fair Mall (11/27/09) Bethany Church (Fox 40) interviewed a young man (at 5:37 am). And the youngster said he'd been busy and on his feet all the way up til his lunch break. I need some of you to call A/X and find out who he was. Invite him to G.B.G. today..........

Jonathan Alpert, Douglas Stave, Donald Siegfried, Attorney Debra Barron and Joshua Lipton I wanna talk to you. I need Derek King, Allen Harris, Benjamin Harris (Chester GA.), Spencer Ammons and Spencer Pratt to put on your riot gear! Chris Trinchera (CSU), Jessie Hock, Attorney Mark Redmond, Sharon Blevins and John Tu step up....

"I don't care if I get $ 2 out of this lawsuit. I just want TYC to be changed forever" Joseph Galloway said. (I'm stealing again but Lance Corcoran told you all I was "incorrigible"!) And hey Brett Jolliff, Roger Walthorn, Omar Samy, C.J. Sheron and Steven Moreno Jr. etc. listen I'd love to hear from you all. I even want to hear from Jeff Howell, Daniel Job, Andy Hines and Luke Johnson (Rich. VA).... I want you all in G.B.G. But listen, if I never get a missive from Kyle Love, Cameron Johnson, Joseph Wilson (Sacto) or Alex Blench etc. it's okay. I know I'm not a "professional writer" o.k.? I am but a "reporter". And I'm embedded in the story. And I don't need to "meet" Alex, Kyle or Cameron. I just want you (at Locke, McClatchy, U.C. Davis, Lodi and CSU Sac etc.) to be changed (helped, vaccinated and immunized) forever! I don't want you to have to see what I've seen or be what Joseph (Galloway) has been etc. A 'sex slave'.

... Alice Smith wants a change in the way TYC is operated. Also Alice said her son, Erik Rodriguez, was severely beaten by other juveniles after guards let the attackers into Erik's room. Two of the guards were fired after an investigation. "Its' not an isolated incident" said Smith's attorney, James Myart. "It's endemic to the entire system". (I want Heather or Penny to call Erik and Joseph and tell them they're in this tome. Also call Atty. Myart).... Erik had been locked up for over 20 months on a 9-month sentence. The reason for his extended stay was because he was failing a math class. "Instead of rehabilitating him, it's making him angrier and angrier". his mom said. In September 2007 TYC paid him $ 30.000 to settle his in-custody beating claim...... California prison lieutenants are authorized (by CDC) to extend prison stays for all of it's 173.000 inmates. And guards have a vested interest in our stays here. Ipso Facto, seven days per week correctional lieutenants extend the prison stays of thousands of inmates. They hold R.V.R. (Rules Violation Reports AKA "115's") hearings in which the lieutenant can extend a prison sentence by as much as 120 days (4 months) with no oversight. My own prison stay has been extended by 4 years by guards like Lt. Scarsella and Ferryance etc. And these extensions not only make prisoners angrier etc. They make prisons fuller and taxpayers wallets (and purses) emptier. This happens in Texas, in California, Michigan and allover America. And it is estimated that these prison 'extensions' (not by judges but by prison lieutenants who don't even have high school diplomas) costed California taxpayers $ 350 million last year (2009). And we have students going to jail at U.C. Davis and U.C. Berkeley etc. all because college tuitions are skyrocketing. And yet corrections extorted California taxpayers out of $ 280 million in overtime pay (in 08) and $ 350 million in prison extensions (for minor offences such as "talking back to staff" etc.). By my calculations that is $ 630 million! Over a half $ billion on corrections' extortion(s). And yet kids can't afford to pay for college tuition. That's a sin and a shame. That ought to get President Obama's attention.........

Call Don Kingsbury, John Griffin (CSU-Sac) and Nick Pelham and see what they think about these prison policies of Kangaroo courts to allow dumb prison guards to extend prison sentences........

In November 1997 another lawsuit was filed by a former juvenile over sexual advances by staff during his four-year incarceration, including by Ray Brookins. He described strip searches (Spearman? Lance? D.L. Criner? Baker? Coggenshall?) in which employees would touch (Duclos? Lt. Cherry? Rikalo?) the prisoner's genitals. "I don't think TYC did anything to help me", he said in a gross understatement....

... A prisoner in Fresno stated "I could not believe associate Warden Spearman (P.V.S.P.) forced me to allow him to finger my asshole through the tray slot in D-4. And he made me get a hard-on for him". The ex-offender continued "when I reported it to Lt. Corley they threatened to beat me and to transfer me if I didn't drop the allegations"....

... A young lady reports that "I was a page for Gary Condit when I was 15. He made me dress-up as a cheerleader and he raped me... I reported it to the speaker and was threatened"... She tearfully continued "they would ruin my life. Keep me out of college and have my family hurt. Gary Condit is a very dangerous and perverted man. If you use my name he will kill me"...

Attorneys Charles Dunn and Robert Waters can both attest to the fact that 'kids' are sexually abused in custody everyday. And the feelings of many parents whose children were and continue to be abused while in TYC custody can best be summed up in a statement by Jon Halt, whose 16-year-old son was sexually abused by another TYC prisoner. "They still treat kids like dirt" he said.... "Dirt".

Let me say (finally) about TYC that they need to hire an ombudsman for the kids. Not a white-washed, Uncle Tom like Ken Hurtle in California. But an authentic advocate who will stand up and speak out. The TYC, CYA and juveniles around this nation are chaotic and dangerous. The system is saturated with pedophiles. Not the inmates but the Spearman-like staff members who seek-out jobs in juveniles. The predators (like Bunnell, Larry Turner and Marilyn Windham etc.) who view juvenile and prison employment the same way a predator views the priesthood.... Open season on babies, boys and girls. Spiritual wickedness in high places...

We need massive class action (more) lawsuits against TYC, CYA and juveniles across this country. We need legal giants like Geri Lynn Green, Davey Turner, Robert Navarro, Carolyn Phillips and Cathy Campbell etc. etc. to come forward. I'd like to see Mark Merin, Gerry Spence, Tony Brooklier and Cupcake Brown all step-up for the girls and boys in prisons. We need lawyers willing to say "no more" to the abuse, enslavement and the sexual assaults of children in prisons. And I'm personally calling upon prisoners and ACLU (125 Broad St. 18th. Fl. N.Y. New York - 10004.... tel: (212)-549-2633) and tell them about abuse. You can write to my dear friend Linda McFarlane at just Detention International (AKA S.P.R.) at 3325 Wilshire Blvd. # 340, La. Ca. 900/0. Tell Linda I told you to write to her. She will keep your name confidential if you request it I can personally tell you that Linda McFarlane is a warrior on a crusade against in-custody rapes by staff and/or inmates. Some of you lawyers reading this ought to call Linda about lawsuits. She has hundreds of scared, defenseless inmates who need lawyers... You prisoners speak-up and speak out. Okay I'm done with TYC....

Mr. Stroup is a teacher in Indianapolis. He sends every student birthday cards and inspirational notes. "I never know which letter may help which kid. But I do know God can use a card, a letter or just one sentence out of a letter to save a life. That is why I write" he says. And (I'm stealing again but Mike Bunnell told you all I was a 'thief' and a 'con') that is why I write. I don't know 'when'. I don't know 'where'. It could be Allen in Abbeville, Benjamin in Chester, Chad Sherman in Chesterfield, Billy in Cummings Georgia or Eddie Cannon in Helena... It might be Maxwell Hanger, Sean Maloney, Jordan at Rocketown etc. It could be one boy in a juvenile, somebody at Locke, Lodi or McClatchy high etc. but one word in this un-professional (raw, authentic, un-cut) book can save or change a life.

So many of you in high school and struggling to make it to college. Some of you like Lloyd Moran (Richmond), Daniel Clay, David Hellyer, Colin Fimerty, Kyle Love etc. you think that you are invisible. You think you are just on the periphery of society and nobody is thinking about you. But no matter what you did in prison (Chris Durbin, John Sexton, Ernest Griffin, Billy Ballenger and Jimmy Peoples etc.) you (in or out of prison! In or out of school etc.) are straight in my bulls-eye target. And I write this book to see you right where you are. You do matter. You are not a nobody. You are worthy and worth a lot. And I want Billy Bell, Victor Smalley, Jakob Karr, Kupino and Nathan to dance about your "worthiness". I want the bands 'Girls' and 'Honor Society' etc. to sing about your worthiness. And I want John Butterfield and students to write about it....

I call on Daniel Asare, Eric Bulrice, Christian Lawrence and Keith Mullennix etc. to help us spread the word...

I need Penny to call Dr. Tang Ho, Dr. Ron Karn; and even Dr. Oz and tell em I said to spread the word.... You brothers in these prisons? Yeah, I know you're bitter, broken and lost. And most of you are gonna stay that way because you are jive. But make no mistake about it - even if you are locked up you can get up. Don't get it confused (Shea Berry, Daniel Job, my boy Joseph Latham etc.) prison does not have to be a career stall. It can be transformed into a way station to another level of living. It can be a gateway and not a dead-end. But you can't bull-shit your way outta jail and into a job. And then 'think' you are gonna remain free. Many of you are perusing these words (right now) in a jail cell, a juvenile or a prison... Ryan Mac, US Mint Green LTD and our core supporters advertised heavily in prison publications. So I know you all are reading. And if you are wondering "what's in 'K.K.K.' for me?" It is simple; whatever you want. Whatever you want. If you opened the book to find something to criticize you'll find a lot to criticize! If you are seeking an excuse (how about ex-cues?) for why you are. How you are you'll find that. If you seek to focus on the clouds (and forget the light which brings the shadows and clouds to sight) around Sherman D. Manning you can do that! "Who in tha hell Sherm thank (sic)he is? Dude in jail and been in jail. He had all kinds of breaks that I never had, came from a good family and you wuz close 2 Andy n Hosea. N u call yo self a preacha and look at ya in New Folsom N..." you got that Baby Boy, I hear you...

But if you really, really (with no bullshit or jive. No faking the funk or acting like a chump) wanna emerge from prison as a changed man or woman you can. But you must mentally regurgitate all the mess which has contaminated your mind doing time. You need a spiritual and psychological enema. Many of you have blown your mental booty holes (lol) out with all that garbage. We gotta get you a psychological colostomy bag. We may need to feed you some psychological antibiotics. You definitely need some spiritual B-12. All of which are available in the Bible. But let me 'warn' you not to play. You can save all of that bull shit. Miss me with your jail-house religion. I have no time for game players. I have a Ph.D degree in "Game playing", and a master's in 'game players'. I am an authority. I know how to church all day Sunday and fornicate all-day Monday. I also know how 2 get mad with God. So angry, bitter and sour that you don't even speak to God anymore. I am talking about being vexed. I know what it means to become scornful. And I know what it means to be in "conflict". This whole book (that's why I refused editing, ghostwriting and "handling" etc. I wanted it written like you are' conflicted!) is about conflict. And it 'is' conflicted. One minute I'm telling you about the awesomeness of Jehovah! And the next minute I'm talking about Ben Dosti's asshole in Trans' face! You needed a book you (Gen Y, teens and tweenies) could relate to. You are not looking 4 a "professional writer". You seek no journalistic expertise. U r just looking 4 somebody 2 be authentic. You need a flawed author (willing to admit that "I am flawed") to write a flawed, conflicted tome about our flaws and our conflicts. And you just needed a little light to shine forth in the midst of all of that massive darkness. I came to point you toward tomes and CD's by Zig Zigler, Les Brown, Tony Robbins and Na'lm Akbar. I came to tell you the truth; you must humble yourself before Almighty God. You have got to seek Him. I talk to God about my conflicts. I tell Him the truth. "God my Clark Kent keeps getting me in trouble. Lord, I love you but I like this. Lord I try to do the right thing but every time I try to do good evil is always there.

... Lord, I'll be lifted and feeling Holy and.... Then I'll look-a-round and see Tyra in a bikini and I........ Lord, I, I, I feel like it's just me but I know I'm not the only brother who looks at Beyonce and wishes she was my baby's mother... Lord I loved you before I met Veronica Waller. I loved you while she and I were fornicating. I loved you while I was lusting for Allison Brownlee and Lathasha Way. Lord I can't be the only one..."

I tell God the truth. I don't owe T.D. Jakes, Eddie Long or Rick Warren an explanation. I love them and the way they teach and preach. And I so appreciate their ministries etc. But I know 'God' for myself. And I'm not willing to buy that it was just David (and Bathsheba) or that Jonah was the only 'anointed' (and appointed) disobedient, reject, stubborn preacher.... It's me too. I don't buy that Paul was the only gangbanger and thug whom God transformed into an apostle. And even after he was born again he still had struggles, still went back and forth to prison. Still found himself preaching, teaching and writing ("hello") in prison... It's me too! You can't convince me that Thomas was the only one who was willing to die for Jesus but ended up discouraged. You won't convince me that Peter is the only one who walked and talked with Christ and was told (the word as 'we' are told in the Bible!) "Before the cock crows"... And even after all that he stood there and saw Jesus and said "I don't know him". Peter can't be the only saved, sanctified and fire baptized preacher (teacher) who broke Jesus' heart while he was saved... It's me too. You can't convince me that King David was the only preacher who was gifted, slayed giants and a man after God's own heart but ended up impregnating another man's wife... It was Rev. Jesse Jackson (himself a great man and a giant slayer) too... Jimmy Swaggart can't be the only 'anointed' preacher who picked up a prostitute.... It is me (and you) too.

... I know for a fact that 'Woody' (AKA Peyton Erbaugh) does not consider himself to be a pervert and a reprobate. But I also know Peyton has sex with men (right there at P.V.S.P.). I know you (too) have some conflicted feelings, thoughts and ideas. But if you are in prison you have a marvelous opportunity to get (Dr. Phil) real.

Get down on your knees and talk to God baby boy. Talk to Him and not them (haters)... Dudes in jail will beat you down. They'll get you down and they'll let you down. They are 'haters'....

Any man on the yard where I am will admit to you that there are "haters" and that there are "envious" men on 'this' yard. But just as it came to me that I can't find anybody who admits that 'they' are the molester etc... I also have yet to find anybody who says "Yes, Sherman I am a hater. I am jealous of other guys. I hate to see other men succeed. As a matter of fact I'm jealous of yo black ass! You thank (sic) U something cause you done wrote a book or two. But you ain't nobody Atlanta"...

I've never had one single dude admit "I am the one! I am the enemy that David is talking about in the Psalms. I'm the one encamped against God's guys. I'm the one sitting in the seat of the scornful. I'm the one sitting in the gate (in the ducat area, at the pinnochle table or in the cell etc.) speaking 'against' you".

It is always 'him' or it is 'them'. And I'm telling yall some good stuff. We can't ever get cured of cancer as long as we are in denial. A man who tells a doctor "ain't nothing wrong with me". That man doesn't then turn around and submit to chemotherapy or radiation. And without that medicine you will die. And the reason Jason and Samuel and most others are coming back to jail is because they (you and him too) are in denial. They are master haters, drug addicts, pill heads, gay boys and pathological liars. And they'll never eject the venom of the prison out of them because they are clinging on to the illogical and erroneous delusional thinking that it's "him" but not "me". Subconsciously we know that there is something wrong with "us". But some kind of way false pride and foolishness causes us to run around with our chests poked out talking about "I'm bad".

If you (my fellow convicts) have read thus far and you're still not fully persuaded that "it's me too". Then you shouldn't even be allowed to 'talk'. They should limit you to barking only because you are a damn dog. A low down dirty damn dog...

Now if I was not already in trouble with my fellow convicts etc. I will be now... California federal judges want C.D.C. to release tens of thousands of California prisoners. And 'one' prisoner absolutely opposes the mass releases. And that would be 'me'. I do not support releasing 30 or 40 thousand of us to the streets. First and foremost 'we' would be a threat to the safety and security of civilians. Any time you mass release tens of thousands of functionally illiterate, angry, depressed and dysfunctional men it is a disastrous recipe.

I'm scared of half of these dudes 'without' weapons. Put a gun in their ('our') hands and I might lock myself back up!....

Yes, I believe California prisons are killing people. They damn near murdered me with their retaliatory transfer, deliberate medical negleince, abuse and psychological terror. And yes we need to stop locking up so many people for such petty offenses. And yes we need systemic, structural change. And the system as it is poses a clear and present danger!...

A danger to me, a danger to other convicts and a danger to staff etc... And if you 'release' illiterate, unreformed, unskilled and broken men we'll return to prisons with all deliberate speed. And we will commit horrendous crimes and victimize the innocents en-route back to prison.

I do support pell grants for the incarcerated. I support education for those who seek it and job skill training. I support motivational, inspirational and informational workshops for inmates. Most especially for younger inmates without life sentences. And when guys get a GED and learn a trade etc. let em go!....

... I am far more concerned with you (youth) than I am with those of 'us' who have been locked up a long time and are still playing the same old tired games.. A congressional insider stated that "I know many congressmen, including Mr. Condit etc. who were and are a danger to kids. And they use their positions (power) to attract young girls and guys"....

"Young girls and guys" are the major focus of this tome and our work. If we are successful with G.B.G. then you (the reader) will never meet me. My goal is to prevent you from ever meeting my team or me....

Kara Kehor did a 'fur free friday' protest in Sacramento on 11/27/09. She had a dude in a black trench coat with her. We want a photo of KARA and the protesters. (We'll put em in our tomes). And we want the trench coat guy in G.B.G.

We invite the 'posties' at post 53 in Darien Connecticut to join us. Ryan Saffa and Zac Calahan need to come on.... We salute and applaud Claire Streeter and Dennis Cummings etc. these are real young studs and ladies! They are teenaged paramedics. They are fully certified... In Connecticut you only need to be 16 years old to certify as a paramedic. I'd love to see other states (i.e. Georgia, Virginia, California etc.) model Connecticut! And I have certificates and membership cards for Ryan and Zac right now. We need to highlight and celebrate teens who are doing positive and constructive things in society...

Keith Jerrolds in Georgia? Sam Fuick (Cobb county)? Joshua Orapello, John Elliot (Henrico or Chesterfield)? David Reynolds? Chad Sherman? Ricky Parnell? Clay's buddy J.R.? Wayne Snyder (Augusta Ga.)? John Garvin? John Caudell and Jodie Bear?.... All I'm gonna say is I need them to help us.... Alan Stevenson (AKA "Slim")... Alan was a cool lil youngster at Mule Creek State Prison. He celled with 'Cain' and Slim played basketball every day. And he would (indeed) fight. And "old man" had a "boy" named "youngster". Youngster (AKA David Topete) had "13" tattooed across his face. He was Mexican and "old man" was black. Slim owed "old man" $ 300.00 for heroin....

"I'm a good lookin mother f----- ain't I Atlanta?" Slim asks me out of the blue one day... He tells me in day room about his $ 300.00 debt.... "Atl. If you will loan it to me I can pay you back. Plus I got somethin in my cell you might want". I inquire as to 'what'. Slim says "too many ears out here Atl.... I'm a go lock up and you come by my cell in exactly five minutes. And I'll show it to you and if you wanna buy it just tell me. Guys routinely tried to sell me tobacco, jewelry, cell phones and dope. And you'd think that after 'years' of saying "Man, I don't do drugs" people would stop offering. Not in here! I still (right now today) get people asking me (almost daily) do I want to buy weed, meth or cocaine... I went up to Slim's cell seven minutes later and his face was in the window with the bright light on. As I approached his cell door (cell A-2-221) I see the back of his head. And I look down and he has at least 3 inches of finger in his lilly white asshole.... "Dude what are you?". He spins around with a finger across his lips shushing me... I lower my protestations.... "Slim I'm not gay bro". He replied "Cain told me you're not gay. But we all have to release our rocks. You don't gotta (sic) be gay to dick me down. I'll do pretty much anything if you help me with this Bill." I walked away from Slim's door.

David Moreno (aka 'Tino') celled with me at CSP-Sac and after 8 nights in the cell he came down off the top bunk with his boxers like a G-string and said (as he rubbed his buttocks), "You like this?"... After he put his freaking clothes back on I asked him (directly) "What makes you think I'm into men Tino?" His answer was telling "Atlanta I've been in prison 6 years and I'm 25. I've had 22 cellies, and 17 of the 22 all did something with me. Some just let me blow em. I don't tell nobody my business. You can trust me Atlanta... Please... with all due respect I want some black cock"... The next morning I persuaded Tino to exit the cell without return...

Anthony Sarabia (aka "Clumzy")...Richard Plunkett (in Georgia)?...Anyway... I can't profess to comprehend what makes a male want a male. 'We' (males) stink! We burp, fart and our feet stink. I'm absolutely 'lost' in that department. I have so many flaws and shortcomings etc. that it's not funny. And 'one' of them is I go to bed thinking about Tyra and wake up with "Beyonce on my mind". And I will never (ever) understand how a man could choose a man over Angelina Jolie...

I'm not 'angry' with gays. I allow them (even recruit them as equals) in G.B.G etc. And I've even lived with them (2 that I knew were gay!) etc. But I can't 'get down' ya'll. And the easiest way to get killed in prison is to be involved with a prison known homosexual. It's deadly in more ways than one. But who am I to judge? Some guys see this as a 'way of life'...

Erik Martin (Los Banos High School), Garrett McCain, Joseph Rocha and Justin Zysman where are you? Where is Justin Chirigotis? You fellas need to put on your riot gear. I'm coming for you and together we will change the world!... I'm not gonna pull a Rush Limbaugh or a Sean Hannity. They never allow their critics to speak... I got a message from a well known Atlanta pastor. I won't use his name: "You ought to be ashamed of yourself Rev. Manning" he writes. "If Rev. Hosea Williams could see you now he'd be disappointed. You are up there in prison and you have sold-out. You used to preach against con men and now you're afraid to expose them. You know Creflo Dollar and you know he is a crook. Creflo and Benny Hinn conned Evander Holyfield out of a quarter million dollars. They had him believing Benny healed him. But a cardiologist exposed the con. Then Creflo took $3 million in cash to 'hold' for Holyfield so his wife couldn't get the money during the divorce. When the police sought to question Creflo he fled the country. Creflo is going to hell and 'you' are going to hell for covering for him." ....My reply? No comment... Vanity Fair Magazine (September 2009 issue...). There are 4 dudes in the front area of the magazine modeling Dolce & Gabanna (Saks.com). They're playing racquetball. I want them (all 4) to take a photo for G.B.G. I need you all to find them...

A prison legal beagle wrote this: "Atlanta (aka Sherman) You are a scary brother. All you do in your books is praise the powers that be. I ain't never seen you write the fact that Scott

Kernan (CDC Chief Deputy) got caught driving drunk. And Scott gave himself a slap on the wrist (6 weeks suspension). And...Phil Garrido? 18 years? You know that CDC paroles made a monumental failure of Titanic proportions. Are you afraid to criticize Matt (Cate) and Scott (Kernan)? The Inspector General (David R. Shaw) is a friend of Matt Cate's. Matt was 'The' Inspector General and Shaw was his deputy. But even with their close friendship Shaw was extremely critical of Cate's CDC. You (Sherman) are getting as biased as the 'media'. KCRA and other Local SAC media never reminded the public that Shaw worked for Cate. And that they are pals....

"If Shaw will criticize his friend's department etc. that speaks volumes about the monumental and systemic failures of CDC's parole agents...Blood is on the parole department's hands. Every count of molestation and rape Garrido is charged with; the agent should be charged as an accessory...We'll protest guys on Wall Street getting an extra bonus. We'll hold picket signs if a molester is released into our neighborhood. And we'll call CDC and protest his release. But when there is blatant, widespread systemic parole department failure etc. Scott Kernan has the audacity to 'support' his agent's work? Kernan should resign and the parole agent should be jailed. And if McGregor Scott is a real advocate he would advise Jaycee to sue CDC and the parole agents..."

This missive was written by a female...Micha Cardenas (we need him in G.B.G.) is a researcher at UCSD. And he supports 'Electronic Civil Disobedience' to protest social injustices. I would like for Micha, Justin Berry, Zach Freisan and Ben Alexander etc. to help us launch an Internet Shame Campaign. I'd like to shame every judge who sends 'kids' to prison (for minor offenses) to be beat, raped and victimized. And I'd like to shame politicians who see 'tough on crime' slogans as political opportunity... We need to cheer and applaud Senator Jim Webb. Hell let's give Jim an award for having the balls to tackle prison (and juvenile) reform. I want Emmet Freeman (S. Lake Tahoe), Attorney Mark Reichel, Jayla Henderson, Mike Roth, Shane Ryan, Gil Hirsch and Jim Buckley to help us put the word out....

I'm calling for the immediate resignation of Judge James Wagner. Judge Wagner is a cancer that needs to be excised from the Body of Jurisprudence. He is the ultimate epitome of what is wrong with our judicial system. He ruled (2 months ago) that 14 year-old Tyler Whitt be tried as an adult. He made this ruling in spite of expert, psychological testimony stating that she is psychologically ill and immature...Will she be given a jury of her peers (kids)? Why not? If she is old enough to understand her charges and adult court proceedings etc. a group of 12 kids (13 & 14 years old) are old enough to sit in judgment of their peer. There is a reason you must be a certain age to vote and to serve on a jury in this country.

You ought to be charged as a child if you are a child. Tyler is a child.

And Steven Colver is a child molester. He was 19 years old. He exploited Tyler's immaturity and her vulnerability. Why not try that bastard (Colver) as a kid based upon some judge ruling that he has the "mind" of a "child"? We need judges who apply the law with logic and not emotion (or bribes etc.). Judge Wagner has succumbed to public outrage, outcry and the human emotions and desire to get 'revenge'. Guys like Wagner are unfit to sit on the bench. He needs to be on a park bench. Tylar's lawyer ought to file a motion seeking a 'kid' Judge, 'kid' prosecutor and a 'kid' jury...

I would not doubt that Wagner probably takes bribes like Judge Altman and Jan Scully... Altman has been known to even overrule jury verdicts via Judicial Fiat for the right amount of money...

Mentioning bribe takers etc... In my home state (Georgia) if you go to the Ben Hill county jail you'll meet Martin Hough. Mr. Hough is a bribe taking, dope peddling jail administrator. Martin and Sheriff Bobley are as racist, rotten and as corrupt as Al Capone was. They are now imitating Sheriff Joe by painting the jail pink. They're giving the cell inmates pink sheets, underwear and blankets. Martin Hough loves to see males in pink. My buddy Ballenger can attest to the fact that if you allow Martin Hough to "Blow your socks off" (aka give you 'fellatio'). He'll let you go. Yes he will! Sheriff Bobby and Martin (allegedly) run a gun running male prostitution and a cocaine enterprise. It's hard to believe since neither Sheriff Bobby or Martin can speak English. You've heard of Ebonics? I guess they speak Caucasianics. I have many friends who are country white folks and reside in rural Georgia and I can articulate (oh-teicoolaid) with the best of them. However, even I struggle to comprehend the verbal ramblings of Bobby and Martin. I've never (personally) met 'Bobby'. But Martin Hough is definitely (what we'd call in rural Georgia) a 'queer'. And he and Bobby ought to be required to wear pink uniforms and to paint their patrol cars pink. And Eric Holder ought to put Bobby Joe and Martin in cells next to each other... And that child molester Paul Robbins (at Fox 40 news in Sacramento) ought to be in a cell near them. I'm told that Paul Robins (when he was a Sacramento Radio Host) molested an 11 year old girl for 6 weeks. Her mom got her a rape examination at U.C. Davis and a warrant was 'sought' for Paul's arrest. Yet Jan Scully personally intervened on Paul's behalf. The warrant was never issued. And Paul Robins was never arrested... The single mom and her daughter were relocated to Florida. (I'd pay $10,000 for an interview with the girl and/or her mother). I'd also pay Paul Robins $2500 just to take a polygraph test. And I'll give him $10,000 if he passes. Fox 40 ought to fire Joe Orlando and Paul Robins with all deliberate speed!...

...We reach out to "Joseph" (an OCD patient and 16 year-old master pianist... His therapist is Dr. Elana Zimand), Bryce Pratt (High School Football Jock), Spencer Butterfield (H.S. F.B. Jock), Dr. Charles Sophy, Lyndell Hawkins (Tracy H.S. Vice Principal) and to Attorney Paul Gardner... The Grace Church (near Houston) gave $20 grand to it's members for 'random acts of kindness'. And I'd like to see the Grace Church give just 20 (not $20 thousand) copies of this tome to students. I want students (like Barker) at Santa Clara University in the Slurp program to have this tome. I wanna get it to great young men like Michael Dirkson and Stewart Dooley at Ballarmine College Prep School in San Jose CA. I'd like for US Mint green and G.B.G./Heart to adopt Michael's entire class. And Highlands High, Sonora High School, Burbank and McClatchy High School etc. need to study this book like a 'textbook'. And to continuously remind yourself that "There is light at the end of the school hallway.

Your pains, fears, hurts and stresses are real. It's not just a 'phase'. You are a real live human being. And "We" adults don't always get 'it'. 'We' make mistakes and 'we' fall short. But don't lock us out of your pain and your hurts. We 'may' not be able to help you. But chances are very likely that we might know somebody who can. Communicate with your parents, pastor, principal or some adult whom you can trust and I have an announcement: Sometimes people you trust will let you down. Yes we will. We are gonna be hypocrites sometimes. We lie and cheat. Sometimes we mean well but we still fail. But don't give up on us and you pray for us. (If an adult you trust harms you call 911. Even if your own daddy molests you 'report it'!).

It may be your prayers, courage actions and ingenuity etc. that changes us. Taylor Francis, Ryan Hreljac and the posties etc. are already "World Changers". And I believe Van Hansis, Chris Owens, Mick Hazen and Billy Magnussen etc. will join us and help inspire other youngsters to get on board... Adam Courtin, Jai Breisch, Shea Newberry and John Garvin etc.? Having seen the 'movement' they won't walk away...Ryan, Heather, Frank, Penny and my team will tell the world about this book. We will put it out there.

I heard a Hispanic inmate say (in espanol) that a buddy of mine is gay. Keep in mind this Hispanic guy is sickly, broken down and suffering from a number of diseases. And he spends 24/7 with his celly. "Why do you think he's gay?" I inquired. "You see how polite and proper he is. He says 'excuse me' and all that." I said "Well am I gay?" Reply: "To be honest before I got to know you ATL, I thought you might be because you got manners. But I know you ain't gay."...

Bryce? Travis? Micha? Emmet Freeman and Nate etc. If you have manners and speak English (in prison) you are gay!... Notice how President Obama crosses his legs when he sits. In civilian life that is considered to be a dignified man with 'class'. In prison, Barack would be suspected of being 'gay' for sitting that 'way'.

...Carlos Hallman and Spencer Butterfield etc. Read on...Ron Williams is a master bodybuilder. Ya'll Google the brother. He has won the Mr. Natural Universe contest but he couldn't conquer the world. He aimed to sculpt his body into a human masterpiece. "If I could build this armor around me I thought that nobody could ever hurt me again" Ron said... This big 250 lb. muscle man has a lot of secrets he was holding on to. (How about you? "It's me too.") Ron was suicidal at 13 years of age. One day when he was a little boy his mother left (him) and she never came back. He was shuttled from Foster home to Foster home. Ron was molested for 9 years. He was molested... nine years...where is "my momma"? And Ron would watch athletes and the "winners" and see how people interacted with winners. And he decided that he was going to be that guy (a winner). He began to play and excel at every sport. He masked his hurt, fear and trauma behind a tough exterior. He trained his body like a machine. "I was angry (Tyson, Vick and 2.5 million prisoners?) with God...If God loved me why did he allow all this hurt when God could have stopped it?" Ron said. And if Scott Stern (at Corcoran SATF) is perusing I want you (Scottie) to read closely..."I hated God...I didn't wanna hear about God. And one day after I'd won all the bodybuilding contests etc. I dropped to my knees and I began to weep for the first time in more than a decade...God told me "Ron you can no longer believe what people have said about you"...Thank you Jesus! Ya'll remember I was running around trying to get Dr. Yablonsky and Dr. Solis etc. to help me write "K.K.K." because (subconsciously) I had begun to believe what they say about me... Ron says "I had to release that pain and all of that hurt. The hurt was bigger than me. Pain was driving, controlling and destroying me...God asked me "Ron what do you want from me?" he said, "I won't let you down... I'm now a pastor, a motivational speaker and a personal trainer. I found my mother after all of these years and I led her to Christ"... I had to stop after the word 'Christ' and get down on my knees and talk to God. I feel the presence of the Holy Spirit right now. God is bringing somebody (you?) into the light right now. He knows who left you. He knows who abandoned you and He is still your daddy. He saw what happened to Michael Brewer. He knows how to take a disaster and make a master. He can still change water into wine. He is still God.

You can still do great things with your life. Find your place. And I had to learn that if I couldn't find my place (Tyler Perry!) I had to create my place. If don't nobody (sic) wanna publish it without polishing it then I'll publish it! ...

This book is dedicated to Jordan at Rocketown, The Cadets at Westpoint, Michael Brewer, Jeremy Jarvis, Valarie Brewer and Dr. Nicholas Namias etc. I want Ryan (to be a 'Mac') to send Michael this book so he can read it as he recuperates. God is gonna use Micheal, Jai, Craig Scott, Taylor and... In mighty ways He can use you... I'd been listening to my "God is working it out" sermon by T.D. Jakes for over 5 years before I "got" it...No matter how 'smart' you are you don't always 'get it'. Sometimes your situation can block revelation or elucidation. Sometimes you have the wrong people around you. And sometimes you just have to "wait" before you 'get it'. I thought I had it. I've heard the sermon a hundred times and still didn't "get" it till a few weeks ago! Why does God allow wrongful convictions? Why would he allow Ron to be molested? He had the power to prevent it...The greater the test the greater the reward...It might take you five years to get that...When God wants to equip you you go through tests (Joseph? 13 ½ years in prison) other people couldn't go through. "And I wanna tell you tonight

291

that some of the things that broke your heart (Joseph, Mandela, Ron, Sherman, Brewer and...) and hurt you the most, are gonna be the very things you thank god for." Jakes said. "God is going to get glory out of the pain, the tragedy, the obstacles, the opposition in your life like you have never seen before...If you faint not...touch 3 men and say whatever you do don't quit" Jakes said. There are certain things you have to go through in order to prove fit and to be meat for the master's use! Ya'll (Raider Runner, Andrew Bridge, Ron, Dungy, Vick etc) Betta (sic) read the last 3 paragraphs again...I could preach! I preached! I was politically connected! But...Andy Young and Hosea Williams could preach, teach and speak. But God introduced them to a man named Martin Luther King Jr. and they had to endure jailings, beatings, sit-ins and unspeakable racism in order to become the men they were when I met them. But my problem was that I met them (Hosea and Andy) in their glory but I never saw the story. I never saw them being beat by Bull Connor. I never saw them bearing their burdens in the heat of the day. I didn't understand that Andy and Hosea could have been (and perhaps would have been) typical, run-of-the mill 'pastors' had they not gone through the tragedies of the movement. (There is nothing wrong with being a local pastor. Pastors are pillars of the community and I am not diminishing them!) But God knew that Andy would not have the character, the confidence and the depth to be the first black congressman, first black United Nations Ambassador and 3 times Mayor 'if' he did not get the "training" he got in the movement... Hosea would not have risen to become the publisher of his own newspaper, a Civil Rights Legend, state legislator, city councilman and to feed more hungry people than any other man in America etc. If Hosea didn't get the training, experience, confidence and wisdom that he attained by working with Martin, Andy, Joe Lowery and Jesse Jackson.

They (Andy and Hosea) endured death threats; they walked through the valley of the shadow of death. They had to be there and to endure the trauma, the drama and the tragedy of watching (they were on the balcony of Lorraine Motel) Dr. King get assassinated! They (Andy, Hosea, Jesse and Ralph etc.) had to go to bed that night weeping and scared. "It could have been me." And "It should have been me." And "Why would God allow this?" Those questions haunted (shaped, built and seasoned) Andy and Hosea. And out of this training, tragedy and trauma God shaped and molded Andy into an Ambassador and Hosea into an Activist...

There is a price to be paid for every level of life... I'll repeat- I could preach. But there are many, many preachers preaching that you have never heard of, but you're reading my... Love or hate Jesse Jackson etc. he pastors no church but you know who he is... CDC is my bull Connor! Navigating my way through a racist, broken and vicious prison system is my witness to an assassination. Finding my way through this darkness has been my training my teaching and my character development. I could have been pastoring and never accused of a crime and you would have never known who I am.

I wanted glory from Andy and Hosea`s story but nobody can endow you with wisdom and experience. You have to go through it. It is God`s Resistance training. There are challenges in life. And in order for you to be prepared for the opposition and the spiritual warfare you will be confronted with etc. If you do God`s will etc. God has to put you in this gym. God has a gym. The gym can be a prison cell. The gym can be the back of the bus. The gym can be bankruptcy or watching your house burn down. Job can tell you the gym can be your sick bed...

And when you get ready to go through these tests (and this training) people around you often cannot help you. Real training is a private opportunity for you to exercise in the presence of God. And most times people around you don`t even know what you`re going through. But thank God it is a private affair because when people are working out we make some crazy noises and ugly faces. Training, exercising and working out is not a glamorous affair and the work out can last 20 years sometimes. Your limitations and struggles. It's hard to "Look" good when you're working out. It was easy for me to look good in my suit and tie at Trinity Baptist Church at Salem or at Temple of Deliverance in Memphis Tennessee. When brothers are hollering "Amen Reverend God Bless You! Praise The Lord. Preach Manning and"... But that was not the training ground. Training ground is when you get by yourself. (That does not mean the only way God can get you by yourself is to send you to prison). When you are in a place of darkness where everybody hates everybody else. Where cops hate you and robbers hate you .Where you have no support group and you are 3000 miles away from home. By yourself! I thrived at the National Baptist Conventions and at convocations etc... Last time REV. Hosea Williams introduced me before a youth congregation I got an ovation and I thrived and I (thought I did anyway- lol) was looking good in my $1500.00 suit. I had folks from all over the world in the congregation. And they would applaud support, salute and amen me. And if I'd continued on my journey I would've been somewhere in hot Atlanta or in Richmond Virginia preaching right now. And you would not be reading this. In a prison you won't get any Amens... The real challenge is when you're left by yourself not when you feel like going through it. But when you're at the end of your rope and you're tired and you wanna give up. That's when you begin to strengthen yourself and you realize that God is with you even when you're not sure that you're with yourself. You can (also) be in a room full of people and feel "alone". You're in a gymnasium filled with studs and jocks and yet you feel alone...

God had some secrets He wanted to reveal to me – He had a plan for my life. And just as a King had a dream, Jonah had a whale – I had a jail cell... There are no Free Rides in life. And nobody can say a prayer for you and endow you with instant wisdom. Even Jesus did not go from the crib to the cross. But he had to go through some things. He was led to a high mountain and he was tempted by the devil. He was God in the flesh but even Christ had to go by himself and tell the disciples to wait here while I go yonder and pray. How foolish was I (and you too) to think that just because I could preach and teach. Just because I had a gift I could/would get into glory without having to walk through a story.

Don't get it confused God can do anything! Yes He can! But how many people do you know who weighed 400 Lbs. and they went to a pastor (him) and had hands laid upon them and one hour later they weighed 150 Lbs. You've never seen it. And if they lose that weight it takes time and effort and if you become a leader it takes time and effort. You can't listen to 3 cd's and then be ready to lead. Your degree (alone) does not prepare you for leading. There is some wisdom and some teaching that will only come through the process of going to bed at night and getting up in the morning and living life.

Jesus was the only begotten "son " and he had supernatural power destiny and an appointment with the cross . But en-route to his resurrection he had to endure a crucifixion. Without going down He would have never gotten up. But even before they crucified Him He had to go through challenges, trials (training) and tribulations. He dealt with haters, plots and challengers, Christ endured "who do you think you are" and "why are you healing on the Sabbath?" And if Christ had to deal with haters and folks questioning his identity and authority etc. What makes us feel that we are going to be exalted without challenges?

I know Andrew Young, Hosea Williams, Chief Eldrin Bell and... I have preached for Jasper Williams and I've been on the news and in newspapers. I'm hooked up and cliqued in. I want to be leading and... uncle Andy I'm starting I-may (International mass alliance for youth) and...now I'm in prison and I can't get out...What happened to... "...My name is Joseph and unlike Manning I was not driving around at 2:40 a.m. roaming. I've never trolled the streets looking for a hooker. I was minding my own business. I was working in Potipher's house. And this woman falsely accused me and... Lord I'm sick and tired of being sick and tired. You gave me this dream when I was a kid. My daddy gave me a coat of many colors. And yet, every time

I turn around I'm in another mess. If it ain't one thing it's another. My brothers tried to kill me. I was sold into slavery. And now I'm sitting up in this prison for a sex crime I didn't do. Lord I feel like Ron Williams did. Why didn't you stop this from happening to me? My brothers hated me for a coat. My brothers tried to kill me for a dream. I never asked for a coat. And I never sought a dream. Why couldn't I just live a regular life and work a regular job? Now you got me sitting up in New Folsom with an 'R' in my jacket. And fellas in the prison will applaud you if you rob. They'll cheer you if you kill. But they'll hate you if you have an 'R' in your jacket. God at least you could've let me get in jail for a murder I didn't do. But you gave me a coat, a dream, a pit and now you gave me a prison. And I am getting tired…

Ya'll hear Joseph? I heard a Lil Sherman (and Ron, and Vick and you too) in "Joseph". But brothers can I remind you that God had a plan and Joseph had destiny? Joseph was in training. He was not training to be just any kind of soldier. He was in Special Forces, Green Beret, Seal Training. The harder and more prestigious the assignment the tougher and more rigorous the "training". The 'coat' was part of the assignment. The 'pit' was part of the assignment. They were strenuous training which tried Joseph in the places of his limitations. And God is more skilled than the most skilled drill sergeant. God is more skilled than the most skilled company commander. He's a master strategist and he knows what it takes to make you. Just like he knows what it takes to break you. And trials come to make you strong. And…

I wish I could teach it like I feel it. But the greater the struggle the greater the reward. If Christ had to be tried and tested in the flesh etc. what about you? "It's me too." What happened when Jesus saw Lazarus (more on this later) in the grave? "Jesus wept." I know you're big, bad and strong baby boy. I know you can bench press 315 lbs etc. But you are going to have to cry sometimes. If you just keep on living. Life will hand you something that'll bring you to your knees. You will be trained…you might experience "some" glory before you live a story. But that is just a taste so you'll know what "can be." But you will not skip the journey and arrive at the destination. And training is preparation for the destination. Joseph went thorugh hell and high water but he showed up. And…no pain no gain. No grit no glory. No story no glory. But "press forward." Press onward. Press upward. Press…

Every great man has had to learn to forget (forgive). Ron Williams had to forgive. What if Andy Young had hated all white folks because of what Bull Conner did to him? What if watching Dr. King get assassinated had injected the venom of racism into Andy? He would've never met Jimmy (Carter). He'd have never become Ambassador…Andy could have succeeded as a 'racist'. He could have gotten rich and done 'things'. I know many rich racists. But the Andrew Young that I met at Springfield Baptist Church would have never told me to "call me at home" had he not gone through the training (hurt, tragedy, sorrow, racism, etc.) he went through. And had he not forgiven…

After the plot (to kill him), after the pit and after the prison (all of which was training) Joseph was now in a palace! Thank you Jesus… Don't laugh at me today because I am in a plot, a pit, a problem or a prison because tomorrow I might be in a palace. Be careful who you laugh at today because of their hairdo, shoes, clothes, car or where they live. Be careful who you make fun of or who you bully because they're slow learners or in a special class etc. because they'll mess around and move from the hood, from the barrio and the trailer park to the suburbs…

In the palace Joseph was now baldheaded because it was a shame (in Egypt) for a man to have hair. And Joseph was the Second in Command in Egypt! And he sees his brothers (the same one's who hated on him, plotted to kill him and who sold him into slavery) and Joseph started crying…Men (Ron Williams, Andy Young, and Michael Vick) do cry. The reason why Joseph could get favor and promotion was because of his training and his forgiveness. Joseph (all those years in slavery and in prison) kept his heart clean. And Joseph was in the pit but he didn't allow the pit to get in him. He was locked up in prison for 13½ years but he didn't allow the prison to get in him. He named one of his sons Mannaseh which means "The Lord has caused me to forget." Mandela was promoted from prisoner to president because he forgave (forget) his jailers. Obama was promoted from Junior Senator to Senior President because he has a spirit of forgetfulness and he forgave Hillary. He took his former opposition and gave her a position on his team. Joseph wept so hard that everybody heard him...He wept because he could see 'why'..."I tried to do it my way. Got sent on up the highway. They got me in the system; why? Why it's gotta be like that?"... Young people start looking for your connection. Because God is training you and he is setting you up. He has somebody sitting in position to bless you. You've gotta keep your appointment. Don't let 'huffing' or banging cause you to mess around and miss your appointment...

Joseph was now in a position to kill the brothers who had wanted to kill him. Now Joseph was a prince and his brothers did not recognize him. And now his brothers are standing before him begging for food. Joseph gave them food. And he locked up Simeon so he could unblock a blessing. God will use a prison lock-up to unblock a blessing. Joseph locked up Simeon to ensure that they would bring Benjamin back.

Benjamin represents a sacrifice. God will put a "Simeon" in a prison cell to bring people back to him. What moved God and Joseph is when he saw Benjamin..."Go tell Jacob to pack his stuff because everything in your life is about to change." God sees what is in 'front' of you.

"Jacob I know you lost one son and you think you lost two. (Simeon) But I need you to trust me with Benjamin so that I can give you land you haven't possessed and houses you haven't built..." Joseph forgave his brothers and he fed his brothers. And since there was a famine in the land and they knew what all they had done to him. He blew their minds in Genesis 45:7 when Joseph told them (even though you put me in a pit, in slavery and that led me to a prison) "And God sent me (through all of that to all of this) before you to...save your lives by a great deliverance...So now it was not you (Ricardo Calvario) who sent me here but God"...Joseph had locked Simeon up. He was not punishing Simeon. He had to bound him to bless him. And some of you (right now) are all tied up and bound. Bound up in this. Tied up in that. But God can transmogrify your bounding into a blessing. And the enemies of yesterday will be the footstools of tomorrow... Whatever you are in God has sent somebody before you. There is already somebody in position who can bless you.

You're in training right now but wait. David uses the word 'wait' a whole lot of times in the psalms. "Wait on the Lord. Wait and be of good courage" and... If you ask most folk what 'wait' means they'll tell you to 'hold up' or to 'sit down'. But chilling is not waiting. Chilling is killing your destiny and delaying your promotion...I looked up "wait" in Webster's and it says "to postpone action or stay in one spot until something anticipated occurs." You can't wait unless you are anticipating something. To 'kick back' when you expect 'nothing' is not 'waiting'. Webster's also says "to remain or be in readiness or expectation." If you are not ready (you can't read, write, think etc. You are not trained) it does no good to expect anything. And if you expect something but don't get ready you're not 'waiting'. I now see why T.D. Jakes used to tell everybody to "Get, Get, Get, Get Ready." Stay ready and you won't have to get ready. Waiting is an act and it is an active word. Joseph waited 13½ years in prison. Mandela waited 27 years in prison... Paul waited in prison(s). Paul wrote his best books (alone) in prisons...

We (Ryan, Heather, Penny, Frank, Nathaniel Mullinnex, Chivescu and you too) have got to put this book in the hands of boys. And we can do it. As Kedar Massenburg says "There has been a shift and a sea change. You don't need a publisher or a producer. The internet has become The Great Equalizer!" The internet is the writer's best friend. Let's get this book to

Jason Durtchi and to (t.v. host) Julian Smith (Julian needs to go to page 313 in "B.E.B." Book II). Julian looks like (seriously) Ashton Kutcher and Van Hansis put together.

Ya'll find me Raider Runner, Lenny Younadam (Stockton), Reko (and his comrade at Dinner Party-Download.com), Rahul Malak, Andy Hines, Micheal J. Peter and the students in the Glee clubs at your schools...I am the Terri Woods of prisoners. I am reaching out of my boundaries to Joseph Rocha, Justin Zysman, David Quindt and to Pedro Armando Quant...I need to talk to Logan (Miss Daisy Design Leader), Adam (Rambotics), Justin (Rachet Rockers), Al Ostrow, Daniel Hallsell and Louis Copelin ... 'Heather' get this book to Thomas Dekker, Micha, Jamie Salyer (Sacramento, CA.), Michael Dirkson, Stewart Dooley and Adam Courtin. And I need you (Adam and Brendan, Michael, Stewart and Micha etc.) to share this tome with at least 20 students at Bellarmine College prep (San Jose), UCSD and... On March 1, 2011 the first five students who sign up 100 of your peers on the G.B.G. Facebook site will get $100.00. So I'll give away $500.00 (total). Don't try to game me because I recognize game from 5000 miles away. Each student must sign up, post a photo and state (i.e.) "Adam told me about G.B.G." or " Michael referred me" etc...

On March 10th submit (via e-mail at hallopeter@sunrise.ch) a 1500 word (or less) essay titled "What I learned from reading K.K.K." and (snail mail it to me also). We'll select the best ten: 1st place $200.00, 2nd place $175.00, 3rd place $150.00, 4th place $125.00, 5th place $100.00, 6th place $75.00, 7th place $50.00, 8th place $40.00, 9th place $35.00, 10th place $25.00... This contest has nothing to do with any other contest in this book...

Prison is the "Ass Capitol" of the world! And if you enjoy spreading your cakes (prisoners call ass cheeks 'cakes'), coughing and exhibiting your penis for men-Come on in... This book ain't really a tome. This is more of an 'argument' and a missive. This is eyewitness 'testimony' to the world's youth! John Grisham can write rings around Gerry Spence. Both Gerry and John are licensed attorneys and Gerry is a Bad-Ass Lawyer! If I had to face a jury tomorrow bring me Gerry! If I could only read one book tomorrow bring me John. John writes fiction and Gerry writes non-fiction. I've read all of both of their books. Gerry writes like he is arguing and I always end up angry! But I enjoy reading truth! Yet, I've had many buddies to send me Gerry's books back and say "not my kind of book. It's too ..." And we're not promoting this 'testimony' (a.k.a. "book") to that crowd. This is a missive! An SOS to youth! It is a mayday for youngsters... ya'll remember we want (Andy) the dude modeling the red shoes on "Ellen" on Thanksgiving Day in G.B.G. ... Ya'll call Dennis Cummings (at Post 53 in Darlen, CT.) and tell him we want Ryan Saffa and Zac Calahan in G.B.G. Ryan and Zac are a great segue into the acronym (K.K.K) for 'this' tome (a.k.a "testimony"). I named it "Kids Killing Kids" ... But Ryan and Zac are teen paramedics right? They save lives. And this missive (tome) is written to inspire you to... "K.K.K.". Nall-not to "kill" but to "keep"! The nickname (or pseudonym) for "K.K.K." is "Kids Keeping Kids". ... Look up "keeper" in Webster's and you'll discover a "keeper" is one that keeps. An attendant, guard, or warden. "One who has the charge or care of something." If you come to jail you'll be guarded by a ... thug, pervert or a molester in 'uniform'. And you'll have a "superintendent". I wrote "K.K.K." to inspire you to be a "keeper". Since "we" (the hypocritical ass adults!) have failed to "keep" you. You gotta do like Zac and Ryan (the "posties") and get certified (I'm gonna certify ya'll in this book) to "keep" yourself. I'm looking for some sons (like Taylor Francis, Raider Runner, Michael Dirkson, Stew Dooley, Spencer Butterfield, Adam Courtin, Thomas Dekker, etc.) who are willing to become "Kids Keeping Kids" (K.K.K.) to "preserve" and to "retain possession of". While the critics are arguing over how many segues I have in "K.K.K." and dealing with the controversies etc. I want my team (Ryan, Penny, etc.) to dig "K.K.K." and G.B.G. deeper into cyberspace and help create more "kids keeping kids". While they edit, polish and ghostwrite I want you to "retain possession" of your virginity, masculinity and of your mind. If we have "K.K.K." we'll fight a Phil Garrido yo. We will form "walking to school" groups of "K.K.K's" and leave "no child behind" ... We will step up to the plate (like the posties) and say "since adults are too busy yelling and acting a fool we're gonna be "kids keeping kids" outta jail, out of prisons, off of drugs and in school.

Are you reading? ...Yeah! Yeah! Yeah! I'm not writing a 'novel'. This is not some lil chill pill book to help some jail bird "escape" his reality for 8 hours. I've been there, done that and got a t-shirt my brother. I've been locked up a lil while and I know the business. I'm not hatin (sic) on the O.G.'s in jail. Hell I'm in jail. I'm just keeping it real. I know you bruthas sittin up in these prisons with me don't have a degree. Hell nearly 80% of "us" (those of us in Hades) dropped outta high school. So how dare you have the audacity, the temerity, the gall or the balls to try to critiques a tome? I'm not writing something to carry you on a plane away from your reality. If you (jailbirds) are reading this (a tome I didn't write for you) I came to confront your reality. This ain't 3 points and a poem. This is not John Grisham. That white boy can out 'write' my black ass in his sleep. This is but a missive to youngsters an sos and a mayday to say I we need some "kids keeping (preserving protecting observing and...) kids " K.K.K"...

I'm not writing for (or to) everybody You can stop by New Folsom State Prison and interview my neighbors and ask them "has Sherman ever given you one of his books to read?" Every convict will reply "no" only with "this" (K.K.K) book have I allowed some gangbangers, youngsters and board members to peruse for accuracy and opinion with (only) this to me. But a lot of guys (here) ask me can I read one of your (sic) books?" and I'll always find an excuse and I don't need their critiques but (I'll give them a newsletter!) I seek no prison companions (keep in it real) I don't make any money off of books I loan to prisoners (who hate my black ass anyway!) ... I'm writing just for a few people I'm writing to ignite the fire in the belly of Austin, Raider, Alex, Nathaniel, Keith and Christian etc. Give me just a few good youngsters I only need a few. Bring me Chivescu, Chirigotis, Heartsong, Blench, Hreljac and Butterfield. If I inspire just 25 or 30 like Julian Smith, Shaun Rushforth Hunter Brown ,Cody Sheldon, CJ Sheron Greg Deekins and Tadd Carr. If I get 25 or 30 "K.K.K" (kids keeping kids) we can transform dark nights into bright and brilliant mornings. We can help stop these kids from going to jail and start our kids to going to Vale. We can do this.

We don't need President Obama to do this. It was a long time before King, Andy, Hosea and the S.C.L.C got Lyndon B. Johnson. They worked, toiled, prayed and believed in civil rights long before they ever got a bill. We can't wait on Deacon Flip Flop or Bishop Willie Wonder our schools are falling and prisons are succeeding. Mayday... Austin, Cassius Harti , CJ, Chad Walcott, Billy Bell, Victor Smiley and Ryan etc. All I need is a few good men. I need some dudes willing to lay on their face before the Lord and holler "help me". Back in the day people really sought God. Now we have mega churches on every corner but people are still locked up and bound. As our mega churches have grown and as preachers got more Benz'/Jags and Bentleys etc. Crack use increased and bible used decreased. Prison population increased but school attendance decreased .All these nice, neat, well structured and well mannered mega churches but nobody is being delivered.

People are not seeing mind blowing miracles or supernatural interventions. The only miracles we can see are the ones faked by Benny Hinn and Leroy Jenkins. And neither Benny nor Leroy are going to schools, jails and juveniles. And if Benny or Leroy were for real I know somebody (right now) they need a hand laid upon them. But they can't write a Holyfield (like)check- they are in...Nall "we "are in prisons and it's dark, dark and dastardly in here and we need some light in here. We would love to see Bro.

I want somebody who still believes God...back in the old church they couldn't preach as good as us. They didn't have our degrees or our masters of theological explanation. Some of them couldn't even read the bible they could quote. Their choirs couldn't sing as good as us. Their musicians were not trained like ours. Their suits were not as expensive as ours. Their cloths didn't always match. Their hair wasn't weaved and dyed... we gotta lot of talent but no anointing. Them ole folks had an anointing. When they interceded for somebody a change would take place...I'm not looking for perfect boys I'm looking for Angelo, Raider, Steve Moreno Jr. and Nate .I'm looking for young men who have made some errors and played some games .But are willing to admit that our Clark Kent , our Jacob and our twin keeps getting us in trouble. I want some boys from tha hood, the trailer park and the juvenile who wanna operate in a deeper realm of the spirit .I want some boys and girls who are ready to become saturated in the spirit, intoxicated by the anointing and inebriated by Gods power. I need a Cole Zick, Devin Deuel and Michael Castro etc. Who knows that God is calling you to a higher level. I want some fellas who don't wanna be on the Chicken Frying Committee. We won't wait on a celebrity .We'll celebrate with a glass of tea and a bag of chips...

In Pierce county, Washington we just had 4 police officers shot and killed at point blank range, Execution style. We can't wait...We won't argue over doctrine, sexuality and dogma. If Justin Zysman wants to be Jewish-be that. Too many have a "form" of "Godliness" but are denying the power...I need Maxwell Hanger, the Maloney Brothers, Roger Walthorn and Omar Samy. I'll take anybody Black, White, short, tall, fat skinny or funny looking. All I need is a few good (young) men willing to seek God. Bring me Anthony Wright (Benicia CA.) Micha Cardenas and Victor Smalley. I just want some boys willing to seek God.

If I can just get a few creative, innovative and optimistic kids like Taylor Francis and Ryan Hreljac we'll create "kids keeping kids" in every school, college, church and suburb... we (CJ, Austin Wolfe, Billy Bell, Tadd Care, You and me) need a Pentecostal experience... at Pentecost when they got finished worshipping God...I said when they(they included devout men from every nation) finished they were not arguing over doctrine, racism, age, sexuality or nation-alities etc...Pentecost will drive you out of your culture. Pentecostal Worship will drive you out of your comfort zone .You'll stop trying to figure out what the next man is doing if you are really seek His face. Don't seek his hand. If you get his face you can have what's in his hand. But I need some hungry boys (Spencer Butterfield, Tom Butterfield and Garrett McCain) are you hungry? Hungry enough to seek Him... "Pastor Peter how did you get the Samaritans to come to church with the Judeans? What book did you read? What strategy did you employ? I hear Pete saying "we started praying"... at Pentecost a bunch of people had gotten into a room and started praying. If I could get me 25 or 30 of you at Rocketown. At Locke, Lodi and at the Mustard seed school to start praying until Salinas, Sacramento, Fresno and Atlanta falls under the anointing. Pray until LA. And New York start getting their worst (most incorrigible boys) young men and giving them this book. If I get a team of flawed troubled, growing and... boys still dealing with lust! Boys still dealing with trust! Boys struggling with a demon on one shoulder and an angel the other. Boys in college, school, juveniles, jails and in this and that...

I'm looking for Bill Dallas son, Josh Cook, Jason Huyck, Christopher Thompson and Kris Stump. I need some students willing to put on a G.B.G. t-shirt or baseball cap and get on a door knocking squad to tell people about "K.K.K"...I want some students (18 years old and older) to put on G.B.G. underwear and make a calendar. And put that calendar in the Frat House or the Sorority. We've got to be creative and innovative as we combat a "new kind" of "war" with hi-tech and sophisticated tactics. I'm looking for Jake Simpson, Peter Dinklage, Tim Skoczek, Jesse Lewin, Ben Finkerbinder, Jon Favream, Tony Dungy, Michael W. Smith and praying Mothers. I need some real people with real issues. Bring me   John Johnson, Josiah Poirer, Michael Wilkerson and You.

You are not an animal Come out of your spiritual cage. Come out Scott Johnson, John Garvin, Ralph Cannon and Spence Palmer. We can do this Danny Macky, Nathan Gould ,Joseph Latham and Daniel Job. Get on your G.B.G. t-shirt. Hell if CJ Sheron Austin Sisneros, Cody Sheldon, Omar Samy, Maxwell Hanger, Raider, Louis Copelin, Tadd, Daniel Sample and Joseph Latham are reading right now... You all contact 'Ryan' at US Mint Green right now. And I want Ryan to order CJ, Austin, and Joseph etc. G.B.G. clothing and send it to you. You all take photos and send them to me. We'll put them in my next book and (you can post them on Facebook etc.) use them to promote "K.K.K." We want Jeff Howell, Justin Howell, Brandon and Hugh Michael Hughes...

We want Frank Carter (Frank should be about 36 or 37 now...X-art student) and Andy Hines etc... Get suited and booted bruthas...

My team contacted Jason Sutherland. And he was too 'busy' to help. Ipso facto, his secret is now (read on) out... Here's how I met Jason. In LA County jail Jason was a tier tender (a.k.a. "run around", "porter", janitor). And Jason would come to our section door and we had 5 or 6 'freaks' in our dorm. Jason would allow freaks to reach their hands through the tray slot and fondle his penis, balls and buttocks for a nominal fee; one candy bar... I saw one dude fondle Jason's aus and then smell his fingers. He then stuck his fingers in his mouth...

Carlos Hallman, E.J. Puente, Jeff Walker etc. we need you all to help sound the alarm (mayday) in schools. We need Benjamin Harris, Allen Harris and... Sound the alarm in the hoods and in the suburbs. I don't want to see you up in here nicking or jonesing so badly that you (Tadd, Garrett etc. all of you) have your behind backed up to bars or a tray slot being fondled for candy or for this or that. I want you to stay in school so badly that I will (just as I just did Jason. And Jason is a 'white crip') sell out (the secrets) any convict or ex-convict who refuses to help me reach you. I'm risking my life telling you about Jason Sutherland's secrets. Because this is supposed to be 'hush' 'hush'. And you never question a gang bangers sexuality. But 90% of all the white crips I know are undercover gay boys! Period! They are on pipe! And no matter how solid, masculine or muscular you think you are if you come to prison you can be had... CJ, Austin, Michael Castro, Nathaniel Marshall (Malone, NY.) Jason Wilhite and Josiah Lemming etc. Stay out...Brian DeCook, David DeCook, Victor Smalley and 'Legacy' are you reading? Stay away from jail...Louis Copelin and "Angelo" ...I need you Nathan Hand, Gary Browning, Brian Boykin, John Elliot, J.R., Brett and Ricky Parnell. What you do for somebody else; God'll make happen for you. The biggest lie the devil will tell you is that you are not qualified. You need to wait until you get perfect and then 'serve'. Hell no! You start serving right now! Serving makes you better. You heal yourself by helping others heal. Serve right now! You are not too young (posties). You are not too black or white, dark or light. We need you right here, right now. We have a 15 year old girl (Alyssa Bustamante) sitting in jail in Missouri for murdering a 9 year old girl. (Elizabeth Olten) Alyssa allegedly strangled Elizabeth, slit her throat and stabbed her to death because she just wanted to know how it feels to kill. She dug two holes in the ground to be used as a grave. Alyssa tried to commit suicide at 13. And 'we' (adults) failed to catch a broken little girl and to prop her up. We did not love her and treat her. We missed it and a little girl was hurting and hurting people hurt other people. And now that 'our' failure has resulted in a "kid killing a kid" we (juvenile officer David Cook and Judge Jon Beetem) want revenge. And we insist on putting a troubled little girl in an adult prison. And we are throwing her away forever. Because all 'we' (adults) know is hypocrisy, vindictiveness and revenge. Had Judge Beetem tried Alyssa as a juvenile "we" would have called the judge "soft on crime" and...."we are throwing away the child and we are signing a death sentence for Alyssa" stated Attorney Kurt Valentine. And I say Cook and the judge should resign.

I'm sick and tired of Judge's rubbing salt into the wounds of our failures. Alyssa is our failure to detect a troubled teen. And as soon as 'we' fail we jerk our knees with hypocrisy. And we jump on the "tough on crime" band wagon. And we send another child to be enslaved as a human slave...People in prisons watch the news too. And the moment "we" hear that a Tylar or an Alyssa will be (eventually) 'coming to join us'. Predators start licking their lips and getting excited. And so the judges and prosecutors who claim to be 'tough' on crime are actually coddling predators and prisoners. They are providing prison predators with girl and boy toys! They are furthering the criminal molestations, rapes and enslavements of our kids. They are using babies as political fodder. They (the judges and prosecutors! Lawyers!) are guilty of conspiracy to commit every rape of every child whom they send to adult prisons. And every adult in America is an accessory.

Let us train the white hot light of Facebook, Myspace and cyberspace upon the hypocrisy of these "lawyers" (a.k.a. judges and prosecutors). We don't need ABC, CBS and NBC. As a matter of fact I talked to Peter in Switzerland yesterday. And I told him I don't plan to do any network news. I'm calling a blackout on ABC, NBC and CBS...I might (small chance) do a sit down with Tyra or perhaps David Begnaud (as I've said). But I'm not interested in biased, lopsided and dramatic reporters only interested in propping up judges and pulling down convicts. I don't need to be reminded of how "bad" we are. I know who I am and I know where I am. And I also know how to break the curses that have been spoken over us. I know how to fight!

...The big name media? I still recall Rev. Hosea Williams introducing me as "Reverend Sherman D. Manning". And every time I've ever talked to Andrew Young he's addressed me as "Reverend Sherman D. Manning". And Andy is an ambassador. I know some 'important' people but I've got to admit Andy is the 'only' brother I know (personally) who is 'in' the dictionary! Look in Webster's dictionary and you'll see him (Andrew Jackson Young). And yet, although a world famous politician has never questioned my "reverend-ness" the minute I got in trouble! The minute I was 'accused' of a crime. The same media who wrote stories about me as a teenager like "Boy turns playground into pulpit" (where 'they' being the Atlanta Journal Constitution-called me a "Reverend") now.. As an accused felon I never saw a single story saying "He's called Reverend by Ambassadors and Civil Rights Legends" etc. Suddenly it was "He calls himself Reverend". No I don't want to talk to Matt Lauer and that crowd any more than I want to talk to Ann Coulter. It would be an exercise in futility... Remember that Matt (NBC) played golf with President Bush. And when President Obama won the Nobel Peace Prize Matt sounded like Fox 40's Joe Orlando or a Hannity. Matt said "What has he (Obama) done? He's too young and I struggle to see how he deserves a nobel..." Matt was not being a detached reporter, journalist or an anchorman. He was being a pundit and "biased".

So just in case somebody from NBC, ABC or CBS calls my team or calls our teens, you all tell them I said "Thanks but no thanks". And oh by the way; tell them "We are aware of Sherman's convictions! We are also aware of the many false, unfounded and malicious rumors. We know what Mary Hanlon said about him. We are also aware that he "calls himself Reverend". And (Matt, Hannity, and Glenn Beck etc.) we know about his conflicts. We've met Sherman Clark Kent and Sherman Superman. We've met Sherman Jacob and Sherman Prince. We are familiar with Sherman the con and Sherman the Prince. Yes Mr. Hannity we know what's on page 313 of "BEB"II. We also know Sherman wants folks 18 and older to model G.B.G. t-shirts and panties. We are aware that he's provocative and controversial...Matter of fact Matt if you (of the "Today" show) model a pair of G.B.G. undergarments we will get you an exclusive with the Chief (sinner!) Executive Officer of G.B.G."...

I don't need network tele-vision I got world-vision. I need you (Nick Schifrin, Adam Courtin and Taylor etc.) to tele-friend. Tell somebody about us... Okay-Billy, Victor, Nathan,

Tadd, Deekens and Maxwell etc. I want you all to put the word out. I have a job for baby boomers. I want somebody (must be 50 years old or older) to make some citizen's arrests. I want them to arrest Benny Hinn, Leroy Jenkins, Creflo, Lance Corcoran, Mike Jiminez and Jan Scully. I also call for the arrest of Sheriff Joe in Arizona! Hinn, Jenkins, and Creflo are being charged with 'theft by taking', 'prostituting the gospel', 'fake healing' and 'turning the church into a Den of Thieves'. Lock em up!... Lance and Mike "racketeering, corruption, fraud" and "conspiracy". Arrest Jan for felonious "bribe taking". And arrest Sheriff Joe for the myriad of crimes he has committed! Lock them up!...

I wanna tell Victor Smalley that I believe in you. Victor I'm talking (directly) to you. You are an amazing young man with all kinds of talents. You are so special, so unique and so needed. We (G.B.G.) need you Victor. I know I'm not supposed to be personal but I'm writing 'this'. And if I die tomorrow I want to be able to say I did it my way. There is no "public option" in this tome. This (K.K.K.) is a private, personal missive to my posse. This tome (aka "testimony") is not for everybody... so yes I'm personally reaching out to Victor. I need you to dance for G.B.G. and "K.K.K." Put on a G.B.G. t-shirt and dance. Put it on Youtube and we'll send you a stipend etc... I reach out to Spencer Butterfield, Garrett McCain and the football team at Trona High School. Spencer we need you. Put on your shoulder pads and slide a G.B.G. t-shirt on and our cap and snap a photo. Put it on Facebook. Spencer (and Garrett) you are intelligent, energetic and smart enough to go places. We need you... We need J.R. Celski and Steve Weinstein... I want Tadd Carr to put on some G.B.G. gear (today!) and take five photos and post them on Facebook. Tadd (if you need it) I'll 'give' you $50.00 per photo.

I need Billy Bell. You are young, optimistic and talented. We rooted for you (B.B.) and were saddened by your injury. We want you to dance for G.B.G. and "K.K.K." Take photos in our gear Billy and put them on Facebook... I'm issuing an edict promoting Billy, Victor, Maxwell Hanger, Taylor Francis, Julian, Dirkson, Courtin, and Dekker to G.B.G. sergeants...Oprah said "You get a car! You get a car!" I say to Billy, Smith and Dirkson etc. "You get a stripe! You get a stripe!" Actually you get 3 stripes. It is now Sergeant Bell, Sergeant Smalley, Sergeant Hanger, Sgt. Francis, Sgt. Smith, Sgt. Dirkson, Sgt. Courtin and Sgt. Dekker. And as sergeants I will (personally) raise the money to pay (actually "give") you to tell others about G.B.G. and "K.K.K." Ipso facto, Sgt. Bell, Sgt. Smalley, Sgt. Hanger etc.etc. I'm ordering you to show thirty people this book this month. And tell sixty people about this book this month!... I.E. Sergeant Billy I'm instructing you to personally show (at least) one student, teen or pal (this tome) this book-every day. And turn on your computer (Ben Alexander, Chivescu, Mullennix etc.) and e-mail, text message or 'poke' two people, per day- about "K.K.K .". Can you do it? If so let me know...I'm not Rush Limbaugh. I'm not prostituting my readers. I don't need to keep all the money for myself! I'm not Creflo always chasing a 'dollar'. I don't need four rolls (I'll keep one and take the $1 million for the other three and give it to my posse!). I don't need a private jet! I'll save $30 million and buy a tour bus. I'll spread the $29 ½ million out to Omar Samy, Alex Chivescu, Nate and to Clay. I'll spread the love!...

CJ Sheron, Trevor Loflin and Alan Rafferty...you too! I need you! I need Doug Pieper Jr., Louis Copelin, Angelo and Raider. I need you guys to step up and help us... on GMA (coach John Foster R U reading?) They showed two football players from Trona High School. One of you (students) actually 'spoke' and did an interview. We want you in G.B.G.

...Suit up young man! And I've been informed that some students at Trona High School who play in "The Pit" go without eating... That's not fair! Not in America! Not when Creflo has 4 rolls and is a "World Changer". I want my readers (because I'm not unaware that 'some' of my readers are in moneyed families!) to donate money and food to Trona High School students today! Call Coach Foster and send them some food, money and books! And whoever the young man was (shown on GMA) speaking-you write me and I'll send you a check!

I need you Brandon Mathieu McGraw in G.B.G. I'm personally reaching out to Shaun Rushforth. I need Shaun to "rush" forth and help us! Mayday Shaun!...I need Hairo Torres to "rush forth" and help us! Hairo is a special soul!

I need you Joseph Rocha! You are unique and you bring a different perspective. Mayday Joseph- please help us... Justin Berry I need you! Your wit, your internet knowledge and your paradigm can help us. Justin-please "rush" forth... I need Christopher Kerney (in New Jersey) to help us! You Hunter Brown are special. You Kaether Cordero are so unique. Kaether can you hear me? MAYDAY!... Joshua Orapello we need you. We need Greg Pugh and Gary Browning too. Gene Langford was in the turnaround program in Atlanta Georgia. I need Gene and Andrew Pruitt to "rush forth"... I'm yelling to Shea Newberry, Daniel Hawlawl, Ryan Kramer, Troy Wells, Scott Kenney and Colin Hanks. This is a personal, private SOS to Scott MacIntyre and his brother. We need John Agostanelli, Angel Alcazar, David Han (Folsom CA), Paul Tharp (M.C.P.O.) and cadets at West Point... I appeal to Justin Townsend to come stand with G.B.G. Justin you need to suit up and gear up and get your pics (in uniform) on our Facebook. I want Justin's "face" in our books!

I'm calling Dr. John Diaz, Dr. Will Kirby, Dr. Drew Pinsky and Firpo Carr... We need Damien Cave, Kris Allen (Conway Arkansas) and Von Smith. Help us to tell teens that if their memories are bigger than their dreams then they're in trouble. The poorest person is the world is not the one in Trona or the trailer park. The poorest person in the world is not the one without a nickel. It is the one without a dream.

I need Dylan Heath, Eric Hutchinson, Max Steele, Brent Keith Smith in Ohio and...we need Eric Bulrice, Wil Heuser, Matt Giraud and Ryan Johnson (in CIncinatti) to "rush forth" and join us... I know Jan Acosta, Daniel Sieberg, and Matt Stuart are reading. We need you. We need John Peter, Neil Peterson (Ohio) and Wil Seabrooks. I'm calling all the students at Jesuit High School right now: MAYDAY!!

Mike Corsetto we need you yesterday! I have an announcement: Mr. Corsetto we need your time, energy and knowledge. Don't let me down Mike I'm calling you...I need Max Stassi in Woodland and Jan Acosta in Sac Town. We are calling for Ricky Braddy, Nathaniel Marshall, Jonathon Adler, Heidi Limbrunner, James Kaschak and Devin Rio...

Hey William Rains? You were abused as a kid and mistreated. William you can turn pain into gain. Your scars can be transformed into stars. I don't need a money donation for a church Will. Hell I can send you a buck or two. And I can 'rain' down a financial stipend on you. But I need to confer with you. And I have some work, teaching and leading for you to do. Start by getting some photos of yourself in G.B.G. gear. Post them on Facebook and send me copies. Then we have work for you to do. William Rains-trials come to make you strong. And "God allows horrible things to happen to us so we will never let it happen to somebody else"... I'm a thief Will, so I stole that from Oprah! My "dream" and my "vision" is to get dudes like you (Williams Rains) to take your hurt, your trauma and the stuff that hurt you and use it to help others. I want to see William helping Raider and Raider helping Angelo. I want to see Andrew Bridge working with Warren Ballentine. I envision kids around this country writing down their experiences and using what happened to them and letting it work through them.

I am calling out to Nicholas Mealey right now. I have need of your service! I have need of your experiences and your knowledge. MAYDAY!... We need John Garvin and my boy Scott Johnson in Warner Robins. I'm calling Eddie Cannon and Ralph to "rush forth". It's time for us to make this happen. We each one got to reach and teach one. We've got to do for our young people what Tyler Perry did for movies. We must make a way out of no way. We can't sit back and kick back with "kids killing kids!" We can't wait! When they (the media…"He calls himself Reverend"…) Ignore us, deny us or belittle us. When they engage in hypocrisy and try 14 year old, mentally ill children as adults. When 'they' say we are old enough to die in a war at 17 but too young to buy beer til we are 21. When they say a 14 year old is so 'sophisticated' she should be tried as a grown woman. But kids are too young (and inexperienced etc.) to sit on her (or his) jury etc. We will not sit back and chill. We are getting up and suiting up. We will make a change. If they close the courthouse doors we'll enter by a window. We're going in! We'll write-in, sit-in or pray-in…The reason students at U.C. Berkeley and U.C. Davis are protesting money spent on incarceration but denied on education is because we are sick and tired of being sick and tired.

We're willing to sit-in, lay-in and pray-in. We will seek God until we get a break-through. Let me tell you something. If I've got to go on a hunger-strike til we (G.B.G.) get the help that we need I'll do that. I won't go on a hunger-strike trying to impress a celebrity. I won't kill myself trying to reach some duplicitous politician…But Billy Bell, Victor, Maxwell,Taylor, Micha Cardenas and David Hellyer etc. I'm willing to go on a hunger strike and to lay on my face before God until He moves you (Billy, Victor, Nathan, Maxwell, Chivescu, Spencer etc.) And gets you to suit up and boot up for G.B.G… I am flawed, I'm conflicted and I'm incarcerated. But that doesn't prevent me from getting intoxicated with the anointing. I know how to get saturated in His power and inebriated with His word. I'm willing to do spiritual warfare until I get a breakthrough for you. I'm calling all angels (youngsters!) for G.B.G. Nicholas Mealey, Ital Rauch (profiler1.com), Sam Altman and Caleb Sima etc. Come out come out wherever you are. We can't kick back. Look what happened to Micheal Brewer. Not another one of us! Why sit right here and die? Why sit right here and cry? We've got to get up!

Pat Pattituchi (Sac State) and Mike Morales (American River College) this is a Hit of Reality. And I'm calling on John Romesburg. John we need you today! Suit up. We're building networks and setting up structures and infrastructure. We are creeping stealthily up on gangbangers and molesters. We are recruiting Matthew King in Seattle and Lawrence Tynes etc. Bring me Akram Sweis, Gabe Williams, Carlos Rodriguez and Ali Naqui. This is a clarion call to Douglas Stave and Curtis Sykes. Young men if we say that we have no sin we deceive ourselves…Soloman was crazy (like you and me) and almost Suicidal. David passed his weakness for women to Soloman . We all have issues and psychological blind spots. But we are coming out of our shells and working to heal ourselves…I need Mark Thew (Loomis),Dominick Lacey and Luke Sears (on xtreme home make over)… nothing silences critics like success. We will not pass our sins and our weaknesses to our kids. We'll break the curses and end the cycle. I'm looking for Jeff (homeless student…Robert Scheeler's student) and… bring me Lacey Hipp.I want Lacey to come down off of that roof in Texas and put on the G.B.G. gear and flex and pose for the cause. Lacey we need you. You are qualified to serve in G.B.G. right now. Come on Lacey.

I'm personally reaching out to Craig Hutto I know about your leg and your tragedy. But we need you to Craig you still got another leg, two arms, two eyes a head and a heart! You are qualified to serve right now. Boys need connection and direction and Craig, Tadd, Chris, Cluub and me can help them see sos! Sos!sos! We need Principal Gerald Morrow and all the students at Paul Robeson High School… I personally reach out to Alex Blench. Alex your service, expertise, brilliance and your talents are needed. I want you in G.B.G. today…

Brett Jolliff we need you right now. You are talented and blessed and worthy… Connor Carr at Rocklin High School we need you too… Jai Breisch you are uniquely qualified to serve, to teach and to preach. Come on Jai and help us. I need Adam Bettercourt and his Frat Brothers out at CSU SAC to help us… We need David Holloman to step up and step in. I'm calling

Andrew Knox in West Sacramento... Cody Sheldon what are you waiting on baby boy? Get your "gear" on and send us photos. We need your two cents Cody we gotta have your help... Austin Sisncros come on. I meant to say Sergeant Sisncros!... Michael Castro, Alex Wagner Trugman,Caleb Shockley Earl Stafford, Sean Zane, Nathan Langley (CSU SAC),Vaughn English,Zac Efron and Aaron Carter suit up!...

Jason Durtchi your service, intelligence, photo, commitment and your help are needed . I need you on the team Jason ... Ken Luring Viste, Chad MichaelMorrissette and David Hankins May Day... Mickey Blaine and Charlie Salter come on. I need Mickey Day to "rush forth "... I reach out to Charles Jackson in Fairview Ohio. I have a stipend for you. Charles don't hesitate to contact me with all deliberate haste. We need each other... I need Brain Boye and Andre Taylor (Richmond High School)... I'm calling Alex Gilbertson(in Minnesota). Get suited and booted Alex I need you to show up and " Rush Forth" today. We need Danny Gans son and Redmond O'neal... I wanna talk to Cody Cates at East Nicholas High School in Sutter County and Chelsey Ramirez... We need teachers like Josh Costa and Daniel Sample... We need you too...I want Drew Stevyns right now. Call Drew tell him we need him...I reach out to Stuart Campbell at the veggie stand in Sac Town...Stuart put yo G.B.G. gear on and take some photos at your veggie stand. We" want Stuart! " "We want Stuart!" Right here and right now. (I need Ryan Mac to send this tome to Stuart Campbell)...

We need Danny Bui (22), Kenny Scott (Spokane Washington),Christian Thorman and Michael Brezina... We need Daniel Coverston in Auburn CA. Daniel I've been looking 4 u and we need you Bro.

I need Josh Stone (N I U),Justin Zegar (today Justin),Tom Saizman, Tom Merritt and David Hanning...I'm looking 4 Greg Doggett and 4... when I write missives (like "K.K.K") I'm a projector showing movies in your mind and I want you to see G.B.G.as we "rush forth". See it in your mind. See Julian Smith hearing G.B.G. memorabilia in your mind. See it ! Dream about it and envision it. Pray for it and make it happen.

I need to reach Eric Castellanos right now...I need Ian Manshum and...Matt Fulkerson you are special. You can do great things Matt. And I want to hear from you very soon. Come on over here Matt and "rush forth".

I need Tyson Williams right now... I need Olivier Rochon and...

Adam Courtin, Michael Dirkson, Taylor Francis, Maxwell Hanger and Austin Sisncros... Cody Sheldon, Nathaniel Marshall, Ryan Saffa and CJ Sheron. Billy Bell and Victor Smalley...If I just (only) get everybody from "Adam" to "Victor". That is only 11 people! If I only get you eleven to fully engage in G.B.G. We (Michael, Maxwell, Austin etc.) will revolutionize America... I need you Austin. I am checking you out (Austin) like a college football scout checking out a player. I need you CJ Sheron. I saw how bold and stubborn you were on "Wifeswap". And I want you to be bold in G.B.G...

Jordan Simon? Boy you better get your G.B.G. gear on. We need you out in Waterloo. Jordan I want you to recruit Kelly Jansen, Zack Lynch, Cole William Lindaman, Austin Gerloff, Grant Pollock, Koby and Kyle Kwilasz. Jordan you tha man bro. Who is that standing next to you on Facebook? Sign him up Jordan as soon as you sign up 3 people I'll make you a 'sergeant'.

We want Adrian Labrado II to join...Come on Tyler Schroedor and join us today. Tyler you bring Joe Sullivan with you. We need your help today.

Ya'll find me Anoop Desai, Danny Gokey, Brendan Staudt, Brandon Widener, Josh Rineer, and Anthony Sellers. I need Dan Sellery, Justin Frazier, Joey Candillo, Andrew Hastie, Danny Henson and Jordan Simon's best friend. Whatever it takes-suit up! If you need some 'money' let me know. I'll give out as much as I can. But I need you to e-mail, text message and blog about G.B.G. Get our gear and take photos PDQ (pretty damn quick)...

...I did not know Gloria Allred was a "lesbian" and has been accused of "rape". I wrote one of my researchers about trying to contribute to this "testimony". I told her Gloria was "too" busy. She sent me several documents. One proves Gloria is a "lesbian" and one is a criminal complaint. By a 19 year old lady indicating Madame Allred used a "date rape" drug and "raped" her. Madame Allred paid $250 thousand to make the case go away. I sent all the documents to a Los Angeles attorney. He and a police officer verified the authenticity of the "Allred" documents. In light of all this-small wonder, Gloria Allred was too busy for the "kids". If her clients knew she was a "lesbian" and a "rapist" I wonder would they still hire her?...

Sergeants James Michael Avance, Nathaniel Mullennix, Roger Walthorn and Hugh Michael Hughes where are you? I need some brothers. I need some young men. I need David Proctor, Ronald Keith Dunn and Michael Sanford (Lehigh University).

I need you guys to stand-up. I need you to speak-up. I need you to rise up. We must come together and do it right now! ...I named eleven young men earlier. Why not twelve? Jesus has 12 disciples. 12 plus Jesus is 13. Well I named 11 because I'm not Jesus. And since I am one of you (conflicted, flawed and and in trouble too) I decided to appoint 11 and I make it 12...We twelve or the twelve of us can revolutionize the planet. From city to city, coast to coast, school to school and college to college we will change the world.

...I'm stepping up for change. I'm stepping up for hope. I believe in change and I 'got' hope in you. We can do this! I know we (you and me) don't always agree. I know we won't see eye to eye. You might be a Jew and I'm a Christian. I believe in Jesus and you may believe in Thor. But between you and I it doesn't make a difference. Worship who you want to worship. Believe what you want to believe. But are you ready to fight? Will you stand up for change? And will you stand up for kids? Do you want to "do" something great?

If you want in come on. Huddle up and get the "play". Let's do this thing... I used to want Matt Damon and Ashton to help us. But God showed me that all we need are a few good youths. They don't have to be famous. They don't have to attend the church you go to. They can be little or unknown. Nobody "knew" Dr. King before the "Boycotts". Nobody "knew" Hosea or Jesse Jackson. No one knew Rev. Andrew Young before the movement. But now he's in the "dictionary"!...

They might not "know" Keith Mullennix, Roger Walthorn, Daniel Bugriyev, Drew Stevyns, Stuart Campbell, Jason Durtchi, or Austin Sisneros right now. They may not know Michael Castro, Daniel Sample or Ryan Kramer just yet. They might not know David Kelley, Dustin, T. Ramsey, Heather and Penny yet. But by the time this "testimony" is over they are gonna "know". By the time they read the last page of this book they will "know" us...

Walker is retiring! I think the Governor should force every California warden to "model" Jimbo... He is the only warden in the state (I repeat) who actually does his own committees. He is the best warden in the state of California, without question...

...Whenever "Justin" finishes his mantrum and "powdering his booty" he needs to suit up. You all tell Justin we are about to "make history" by "making a difference". Tell "Marius" and "Quenten" that when the "Bromance" is over snap some photos and put them on our Facebook.

We need Plaxico Buress, TI and Paris Hilton. We need Anthony Moore and Zach Freisen...Come on yall... Tell "Brett" (from Dr. Phil) we have a stipend for him...Tell Zach Barsuglia I want him in G.B.G. We need Zach Barsuglia to recruit students as Rocklin High School to join us. As we revolutionize schools... Zach I want you to suit-up.

Roger Peck? I knew you were a good guy. And I also knew you had more in common with your dad than you'd like to admit. But you (Roger) have a right to remain silent. I like you!...

Captain Burgess? That 'might' be the name of the Chesterfield Virginia captain who's son I knew etc.etc...I want to talk to Joe Flacco, Michael Ohr and...I called Vallejo CA Mayor Osby Davis today! Mayor Davis is also a lawyer...I spoke with attorney Edmund Lee in Osby's office. Attorney Lee was gregarious, humble and very knowledgeable. We talked about the International Story that Mayor Davis "kicked off" last week. (I'm chosing not to write about the story) and he went to my website for Mayor Davis...

We have some certificates and small checks for Ryan Saffa, Zac Callahan, Michael Dirkson and for Zach Barsuglia. Zach if you're reading contact me... Corporal Day Gay, Jacob Martin (he was a "marine" on Frontline) and Sherri Miller. We need you... I need Zac Sunderland to help us start some of those internet prayer chains which he had out on the water. Pray for G.B.G. Pray that we can inspire Drew Stevyns, Corporal Dan Gay and Jacob Martin to suit-up...

Taylor Lautner and... I still want 'Max' on TMZ.com to join us. Max just seems like a good dude. We want the ombudsman (an intern) at "The Onion". And Joe Randanzo...mentioning "internships" G.B.G. / Heart (backed by NAPS, US Mint Green LTD and Dawah International etc.) is processing an "internship" program. It'll only pay $10.00 per hour (part-time...must be ages 17-28)...

Taylor Francis and Adam Courtin I "know" you are reading this right now. Hey Taylor, Adam, Julian Smith, Jordan Simon and Alex Chivescu etc. I will do anything I need to do to help you. All I want you all to do is spread the word about us. I.E. "Garrett" was on The Price is Right on 12/1/09. I want you all (everybody reading) to find "Garrett" and tell him we need him...I want you all to be provocative and sensational. We're about to "do" what has 'never' been done. Nobody believed a college dropout could start a "Facebook" and create a billion dollar company before we met Marc Zuckerburg. Nobody thought Biz Stone could take a "twitter" and Garner "tweets" around the world!... Who believed in Google? In 1990 who had ever heard of "Google"? But Sergey and Larry believed in their "dream".

And I know that having a Harvard psychiatrist head up the board of an organization led by prisoners is un-heard of...(Hell-page 313 in "BEB" Book II is unheard of...Julian Smith? D.K.? D.B.? Omar? Are you perusing?)... A youth 'preacher' who led marches, vigils and was known all-over the state of Georgia. A "boy" who turned a "playground into a pulpit." A boy after God's own heart etc. Now sitting up in a jail cell in California is unheard of. But "all things are possible to him that believeth." And if you can "see the invisible you can do the impossible." I see Taylor Francis Jordan, Simon, Brett Westcott, Cameron Brown, Dan Graves, Tyler Trosin, Taylor Congdon, Drew Ahmann, Kenny Taylor and Jordan Richards on Face book wearing G.B.G. t-shirts and caps. I see Kevin Krell, Josh Rollins and Trevor Loflin modeling G.B.G. attire. I see Josiah Lemming, Daniel Sample, Joseph Schoen, Billy Bell and David Quattlebum posing for G.B.G. calendars etc. Do you see what I see? I "see" Marius, Puerter, Brett Jolliff, Alex Blench, Alex Gilbertson, Omar Samy, Keith Mullennix and Roger Walthorn posing and modeling G.B.G. attire etc.

This is not an old fashioned, sad, indigent, wanna shutdown all prisons etc. organization. We want prisons `open`(transparent, safe, fair and rehabilitative etc) and we want cops to lock-up rapists, molesters and murderers. And we are not indigent. We are the" Faces" of a new "book". We are Joseph Rocha and Justin Zysman etc. etc. My staff said to me (R.F.)"we can sell the facesof Joseph, Justin, Blench and Jolliff! Put their faces on our product (G.B.G.) and use them to change the world". And I concur! That's why I'm calling for photos! If you've been told "you should be a model". If you've been told how "cute" you are etc. send us your photo and put it on our photo galleries. And my team will select some of your faces (i.e. Jai Breisch, Jordan Simon, Jolliff, Blench, Walthorn, Maloney and Mullennix etc.) to be on our products(tomes, shirts, caps and other garments etc.).The world will get to see your face. If you got a nice booty and/or body (that includes ladies -18 or older) we'll use their pictures also…but no nudity!…

"I hate about 30% of `K.K.K.' because it's sensational accusations… But 70% of "K.K.K." is bone chilling and gut wrenching. It's not a book! It is a Manifesto for our boys through the lens of your pen. You have painted a moving picture Sherman …and with Harvard Physicians like Dr. Alvin Poussaint reading it etc. This manifesto has the potential to make a tremendous impact" stated A- Duran PH.D…" I know that you ramble too much in this tome. But I specialized in treating kids as a psychiatrist and they read like you write…there is some transformational data in 'K.K.K.' and since you have the platform that you have I would not be surprised to see you on Tyra Banks or PBS… minus the controversial data etc. The book is breath taking" Dr. Solis stated …

I want to (again) reach out to Alvin F. Poussaint, M.D., the Faculty Associate Dean for student affairs at Harvard. I want Dr. Poussaint to continue to preach and teach the importance of education. When you educate a boy you enlighten an entire village and with this epidemic of school dropout factories etc. We need more professors of psychiatry (and professor of anything) to take inspiration from Bill Cosby and Dr. Poussaint. And to go into their trailer parks, hoods and barrios etc. and do your own 'education' Town Halls!… I want Dr. Cosby to consider making a CD and /or video to be sent to inner city and rural schools. And motivate teens to stay in school. And I want my advisory board members to hold a telephonic summit meeting with Dr. Poussaint before Jimbo retires. I want Dr. Curren, Dr. Heitkamp, Dr.Solis (Handian, Jarman, Gregg, Friedman, Houston etc.)   Warden Walker, Madame Kennedy, Johnson-Dovey, Fred Schroeder, Captain Steve Vance (ret.), Peter Andrist, Andy Young, Scott Kernan and me to tele conference (we'll record it) with Dr. Poussaint and Arne Duncan in September 2010 and our topic will be "how to keep boys in school and out of prison". I want us to discuss ways to maximize the undeserved "status" prisoners have to influence kids not to come meet us.

"Come on people" (again I advise you to read "come on people" asap). We must use this book (and "come on people "and other tomes etc.) as "the Jaws of Life" for youngsters…. I want this book inside that school in Waterloo, Fresno, Atlanta, Boston and New York etc. I envision Carlos Rodriguez, students at CSU, Hayward, Biola University and UCLA etc. Reading this and heeding this book… Infection (physical and spiritual) and darkness rage throughout America's prisons. It's raging! … I saw Robert Pattinson sitting on T.V. the other night. He looked "cool "and "classy" to the (your) civilian eye. To my cohorts he looked "soft" and "girlish" and "I would F the S out that white boy. Look how effeminate he's sitting "Michel (pseudonym) Mathis said .

I was talking to a Mexican (ex- shot caller for the Surenos) gangster the other day… We were being carnal. "Atlanta who has the nicest 'ass' you know?" I replied "it's a tossup between Tyra, Beyonce, Mariah and Alicia Keys". He replied "si" Amigo they are all booti-licious". And then he said "last night I'm dreaming that mi walk into mi cell and there is this big, juicy, round ass laying on mi bunk, his big juicy ass hole. Atlanta the lips on this ass hole were pink and pretty no odors it's (sic) smell beautiful. Mi eat it up over and over mi tongue slide in and out… then mi turn the ass over and see a big hard dick! Guess who it is Atlanta? I go "I don't wanna know" he goes "Jake Karr!"… I'm talking to a dude who is ex-military and present convict. He fought for our country in Iraq. He is a decorated veteran. He served 13 years in the Army and a Master Sergeant. He has an ex- wife and 4 kids and he tells me he watched Taylor Lautner do an interview and "said "I had to get used to putting things in my mouth every two hours : Dude is gay and I ain't never messed around but I would screw Taylor"…This would not be so bad if …This is the mind-set and the mentality of the prison without embellishment… Everybody here (inmates, guards, nurses and even chaplains etc.) Sex plays… a few nights ago I told a C.O. "I heard you were on special assignment "(for punishment) and his partner (who is married and has a 'son') said he is on special assignment. He has to give everybody blow jobs!"... he was joking. But Dr. Solis, Dr. Heitkamp or any psychiatrist can attest to the fact that every time you 'say' something (i.e."toothbrush"etc.) you 'see 'it in your mind. You can't say blue "blue Cadillac" without seeing a "blue caddy" in your mind. Ipso facto C.O. Darrell King (pseudonym) was 'seeing' C.O. Marillo (pseudonym) give men blowjobs (in his mind) as he said it ... I'm not saying that 'every' person who sex plays is gay . I'm simply saying you see what you say. And when you find a person who chose to work in an all male environment, and he continually jokes about penis, asshole, balls and... he has some curiosities and some latent potentialities. And I have a problem with the sexual 'humor' because it desensitizes us. And this desensitization contributes (strangely to staff ignoring, allowing and even promoting rapes)... to Rape.

"Kellan Lutz is so sexy I'd leave my wife for his ass!" A correctional guard told a co worker. He had a craigslist ad saying he was 'Casey' and was a Buffalo Boy seeking athletic male roommate. Lanie (on Buffalo street in the valley) is gay... I would let Kellan sit on my face. "You're gay" his coworker said.

No I'd be talking about my wife... A convict who's been in prison for 2 years (he's 27) stated I would never have sex with a dude right. I think that's sick... but 'if' I was like that I'd do it with Kellan or Brandon Lutz. Kellan gots booty... hell if Kellan was in here 'I' might be the booty bandit!...His cohort inquired "who else would you do 'if' you were that way?" He replied "Oh if I was gay? Timothy Goebels, Johnny Weir and Kris Allen." Dude states "Kris Allen is married Bro." he states "and see how he licks his lips all the time? That's a turn on... Before he won the American Idol he was broke and I would bet you my life and my kids that if a man had given Kris $1000.00 in cash and said 'let me suck your dick' etc. Kris would have dropped them trousers dude". He continued "there a married guards right in this prison who would let me suck their dicks for a grand in cash ". And he named (I'm not telling who he said but I know who they are)two guys. Did you miss it! He started out by how it was (sick) to be gay and he moved from 'sickness' and "that's not me" and "I don't get down like that" etc. And journeyed from "that's sick" to "if" I was all the way to naming people he would do. I submit that this (prison) is an environment of 'perversion'. It desensitizes, numbs us, dumbs us down. It is a cesspool of bitterness and evil...one of the greatest human rights tragedies of the21st century is what happens to boys and girls in US prisons! Rape is the weapon of choice in juveniles, jails and prisons. This weapon is utilized by gangbangers, murderers, rapists, civilian staff and guards... Five Jumbo jets of boys and girls are raped in US Prisons every day. The US prisons for kids is like the "congo" for women. The United States of America still sanctions, authorizes, supports and allows slavery. We have more than 300,000 human sex slaves in American Juveniles, jails and prisons. More than three hundred thousand slaves, human beings, teens and tweenies traded on the prison chopping block like cattle. 'Boys' locked up for minor offenses. Bought, sold and traded by veteran prison guards and convicts... I interviewed more than 5000 inmates, guards and prison(s) staff for this book and...One 18 year old boy described in detail how he was train raped by 8 gang members in LA. County Jail while jail deputies looked on. He showed me copies of missives he wrote to State Legislators, Senators, the Governor etc. He even showed me copies of unanswered missives to Pastors (i.e. Rick Warren, Benny Hinn and Kenneth Copeland etc.) Warren never wrote back and Copeland and Hinn's reply to missive(s) from a boy pleading that they pray that his celly (and the buddies of his celly) not rape him that night etc. Their replies to his cries were missives seeking monetary donations.

In LA County jail (Fulton County Jail, Rikers Island, Cook County and around the nation) this very moment there are vicious, sadistic and insidious sexual assaults taking place. TYC, LA CountyJail, CYA, CDC and prisons across America are our "congos" for U.S. children. They are the Abu Ghralbs for America's children. Every judge who sends a boy to these places filled with savagery and predators. These judges are committing crimes against humanity. That is why we (G.B.G.) use the faces of boys (i.e. Derek and Alex King… not saying 'they' were raped) to put a face on prison rapes. Kids are being threatened, beat, stabbed, enslaved, bought, sold… In America! In 2010! Right here! Right now! While we 'shop' play video games and watch cartoons.

We've had a 'war on drugs' and a 'war on crime'. Wars on this and "war" on that but we need a "war" to disrupt, dismantle and to defeat the poverty and illiteracy which lead to gangs etc. Which lead to prison etc. And just as we're able to fight wars in Iraq and in Afghanistan (simultaneously). We must likewise fight the wars on poverty and illiteracy etc. At the same time that we fight the wars on savagery (against our children) taking place inside these prisons.

We must defeat this syndicate of terror by gangs on American soil. We must employ strategic educational tactics. We must promote nonviolent conflict resolution in these schools. We must 'shame' parents into going to PTA meetings. We must become warriors for literacy. We must become proactive and get an action plan to help students at Richmond High School, Locke High etc.etc. We must support 'Race to the top' and 'Teach for America.'

"Everybody can be great because everybody can serve!! Serving is not 'rhetoric'. Serving is more than criticism…My orthodox Christian guard is a master critic. He was telling me about an 'argument' he got into with C.O. Ricky Moore (rest in peace). Moore was a good man who went out of his way to treat inmates like human beings. This guy described an argument with Ricky Moore because he felt Moore should never call an inmate "mister" or "sir". Because "you lose the right to be called 'sir' or 'mister' when you come to prison." Although police officers can be written up for not calling a 'perp' (even a child molester) "mister" and/or "sir"…He even told me that when you join the military you are no longer a 'sir' or a 'mister'. But you are your rank. (Although last time I checked you said "yes sir" to a colonel)… Look-up 'mister' and 'sir' in the dictionary. And you explain to me how one loses their 'sirness' when they go to jail… But it is zealots, fanatics and people who major in minor things that halt progress. This same Orthodox Christian (speaking about a 'dead' man) then told me how he threatened to "kick Moore's ass!" And he launched into a diatribe about meeting Moore in an alley because Moore disrespected him. And…with 'Orthodox Christians' like this. Small wonder our schools are infected with racism, rioting and bullying. I hate to say it but with so many men who attend church every Sunday. Dudes who are enrolled in 'theological seminary'! Who believe that "if you disagree with me I'll kick your ass." I'm able to comprehend how 'we' (adults) send the message to kids that "if you think Michael Brewer snitched on you beat him up. Hell throw some gasoline on him!"

We (CJ Sheron, Maxwell Hanger, Brett Joliff, Aaron Maloney etc.) can change this. But leadership and transformation won't come from the White House. It comes from your (Austin Sisneros, Michael Castro, Roger, Nathaniel and Keith etc.) house and my house. Transformation will come from social movements, grassroots and from the bottom up. …Sexual Slavery is prevalent in US prisons. And the change begins with you and with me. "Everybody can be great because…." You dudes in prisons and dudes who got out etc. can speak truth to power. You can write about it. We (who are in hades) can be incarcerated Lee Daniels' and Robert Rodriguez's. We can paint an authentic picture…

Education (yes I repeat-again) prevents incarceration. Zack Barsuglia, Dan Sellery and Jai are you reading? When we read it opens up the mind. Reading good books is the difference between a virtuous cycle and a vicious cycle. Reading is your (Zack in Rocklin, CJ is Maryland, Jai in Salt Lake etc.) "Stay out of jail free" card. We can change this country. One way to fight gangs, guns and molesters is with police and large guns. Another way to fight crimes against children is with small notebooks and pens and "everybody can be great."

We can change this country. And change this world. We can create world class schools. We need a paradigm shift from can't to can...In the days of slavery most people believed. It would never change. They thought slavery would always be but (legalized) slavery ended in America. ...Go talk to your great grandparents or anybody over 50 and they will tell you they never thought we would change the color of the man inside the White House.

But inside every great crisis is great opportunity. We (Zack, Brandon Lutz, Mikey Transorus, Billy Bell, Jakob Karr, Anthony Sellers, kids at Trona High School, Von Smith, Ross Rebagliati etc.) have a marvelous opportunity to rebuild and remake America. Dan Sellery, Dan McMullan, Josh Groban, Jake Simpson etc. We must be united and bound together by the fresh memory of the assaults on kids like Michael Brewer. We (Scott Tatum in Atlanta and Hunter Brown in Wheaton etc.) are heirs to a noble struggle for justice. And sending babies to adult jails is revenge not justice...We are bound together and united by the fresh memories of Shawn Hornbeck, Elizabeth Smart and Jaycee etc. And we must consider molesters and gang bangers "an occupying power". And we must summon all our power, creativity, ingenuity and our faith and fight!

We must be nimble and precise in how we use our power. And strategic in how we fight our enemies...we (Austin Wolfe, Austin Sisneros, Brandon Lutz, Alex Gilbertson, and Alex Chivescu etc.) are not only Americans but we (Ryan Hreljac and Tadd Carr etc.) are human beings. And that is the source, the moral source of our authority...the blood of our children is spilled on American soil and across our streets...our schools are spiraling out of control and falling off the cliff...Grandma Ora (Ora Rakestraw) has a remarkable ability to help troubled kids read. She is a foster grandparent and a warrior for literacy. We need more grandma Ora's and even kids tutoring kids...We spend $1 billion per year to incarcerate California juveniles. $1 billion with a "B". And the senate is cool with that although kids at U.C. Davis, U.C. Berkeley etc. are dropping out of college because they have no money!... Joshua Sims, Joseph UValles, Stacey Jenkins and Brian Broadway are you reading? James and Susan McClatchy fund managers and Russell Rumberger are you reading? Emily Ballesteros? Kids at Salt Lake High School? Khavin Debbs? Spencer Emmons?

Listen to me David Proctor and Maxwell. Do you want to be a prison Chippendale dancer? I'd recommend "So you think you can dance" over Prison Chippendales... Zach Freisen, Zach Barsuglia and Raider Runner etc. Run to school! Run to the library! Run to college! Run! Run away from Alfredo Tafoya, Phil Garrido and ... I'm calling Matt Whyatt, Eddie Cannon and Sam Fuick etc... We live through what we give...

Boys you must let go of those reservoirs of pain, hurt and anger. Quit hating yourself. You have not seen it all yet. Before it's all over you will be tempted in ways and areas you didn't ever think you could be tempted. But even when you fall you can get back up...you are somebody. You can get up. You (Shea Newberry, Trevor, Aaron Spool and Travis Shaw) can get up. You can build up your immunological infrastructure. ...KT Crossman, Captain Jim Whoolery, Cameron Brown and Jordan Simon we can do this. I have a vivid vision of Jordan Simon, Caleb Sima, Greg Deekens, Cameron Brown (and I) sitting down and plotting strategy. Strategies for disrupting, dismantling and defeating gangs.

We must open the door to those who abandon violence. And tell those who wreak havoc on our communities. Those days are over...

I tell guys in prison to get a GED for your kids to see. It begins the virtuous cycle. ...Joseph UValles can testify...We must devise a plan to identify potential drop-outs early. And then begin to intervene and prop those students up and prevent them from dropping out. We must teach character development and job skills...Joe Airoso, Elviar Ford, kids at Daylor High

School etc. We must come together...Gabe Williams, Carlos Rodriguez and Timothy Coleman etc. we can do this.

I want Angela Hassel and all the kids at the Mustard Seed School (for homeless kids) to look up! You are great! You (at the Mustard Seed School in Sac-town) are bright and you can be brilliant. Just read, read, read and believe. Write down your dreams. Put them on paper and plant them in your spirit....I salute Joshua Costa, Khavin Debbs, Daniel Sample, Ron Clark, Michael W. Smith, Tony Dungy and all of you who work to lift kids up! And I intend to join you...Tony Castellano (LA Jolla), Maxwell and Jordan "Ranger's Honor" I won't turn back. We won't give up. We never quit. Evan Wolfson and...

We will bring brilliant lawyers like Warren Ballentine and Andrew Bridge together to save the children...

In some states they look at 3rd grade test scores. And they use the test scores of these 8 year olds to determine how many prisons they need to build...not how many colleges but prisons!!! The schools are drop-out factories!!! And the prisons are rape factories!..Louis Dolittle are you reading?...Mike Jiminez hired 21 year old ex-con (Parolee) Raul Gomez for an internship at the CCPOA. Jiminez was in a sexual relationship with Raul. Raul Gomez is back in prison!... Attorney David Don? Robert Navarro? Attorney Sonia Mercado? R. Samuel Paz? Torry Smith (Oakland)?

I want Roderick Keith Johnson to suit up. It's not over brother...Darrel Williams (Compton), Jeffrey Stevenson, Donald Dusk (Akron Ohio), Aaron Jackson (Delaware Ohio)...I need to talk to Zane Johnston, Sean Zane, Carter White, Adam Iracheta and...Erin Haney! Nagmeh Shariatmadar, Garland E. Burrell and Judge Joe Brown? Judge Marvin Arrington?

Marilyn A. Windham PH.D plead guilty to a felony charge of having sex with a male inmate. She is a bodybuilder, crime novelist, psychologist and a rapist. And she should have gone to prison. Her attorney (Leonard C. Hart Nibbrig) says she "donated" $25 grand to Jan Scully!... I hope Curtis Lee is Reading!

C.O. Wallace Laffitte Jr. pleaded guilty to offering to sell controlled substances to a prisoner and to possessing a deadly weapon on prison grounds without authorization. He was tape recorded while offering to sell meth and weed to a convict for $500.00. He had marked money on him when they locked him up... "If I could have come up with $10 grand deputy D.A. Steve Secrest was gonna get Judge Ransom to throw out my case...ransom was not 'in' on it. But Secrest can be "bought" Wally said. When asked why he didn't turn the D.A. in Wally replied "Then my 3 year deal would have been revoked and I could have gotten 15 years"...Laffitte was caught receiving fellatio (by a male) in county jail...

Padilla should be applauded for what he tried to do for Timothy Lee Boggs...I still say Leonard is a good man...California releases 366 inmates per day!...120,000 (give or take) per year...And you could be one of them! You could be sitting up in prison (right now) having sex with Jesse James Hollywood or Steven Colver...My suggestion (if I may) is if you wanna be gay do it out there. I'm not hating. The more of you men who "do" other men (in adult consensual relationships etc.) the better shot I have with a "Beyonce" or an Alicia Keys. Hell I hope (lol) Jay Z decides to go gay!!

And I'm not buying it that all of these gay dudes just happened to become 'gay' in prison! A lot of them already had it in them! "Secrets"...Akron Ohio...dude is married. He allows a 'man' to give him a blow job. After he climaxes he says "I was thinking about my wife." He's gay... Things told to me in secret shall remain secret. Unless I call upon your ass to help divert kids away from hades and you (Jason Sutherland) are too busy...I need you Scottie Moran (Lloyd and Eric) to help us. Craig Gillstrap, David Perry, Alexander Dugdale, John Caudell and...help!)... "I needed to make bail and this dude told me he would pay my bail if I let him hug me and palm my ass." A dude stated..."I had to get out! He once rubbed across my asshole! He did not finger it." Dude? "You (know who you are) are gay!"...

Alto? J.L....you started out letting him 'slit leg' you. "you can rub your penis on my ass all you want as long as it don't (sic) go in." That was gay! Then-a week later you (J.L.) wet your pillow from slobbering as you let him "put it in"... You (are married and living in Valdosta now) are gay! ... Ya'll hear me? I'm just sayin. I will expose you. I will pull all your covers back. I will tell your family, your lady and your kids...

My goal? Easy answer? Keep kids out of prisons by any means necessary. The ends justify the means. I need Adam Iracheta (a David Archuleta look-a-like) in Texas! I need Nathaniel Marshall. Nathaniel is a miracle! He came out of a lot of storms. I'm proud of Nathaniel, Raider, Cody Sheldon and Shaun "rush-forth." Daniel Hallsell, Andrew Knox, Jordan (Rocketown) and Von Smith let's do this. We must be spiritual paramedics running into burning lives, burning schools etc. And transforming them...D.B. "you mean more to me than I've ever told you. You are special and unique! I care deeply about you. I wish I could be with you (and see you it's been so long!) Right now!"...

Michelle was on Fox 40 news on 12/2/09. She and her two sons (16 year old Raymond and his lil brother) have been at a hotel (in Sacramento) for two weeks. If anyone knows how to find Michelle, Raymond and his brother I wanna send them this tome and a check...Adam Iracheta, Steven Moreno Jr, CJ Sheron, Taylor, Cody, Nathan Niel, Austin, Maxwell etc.etc. You all take some photos (this week...Nicholas Taxera).... In G.B.G. gear and send it...Johnny O'Neal and... I decided not to use a lot of stuff...Jeff Walker (and your mom, Sharon), Will Coker, Jeremy Winters, Jeff Howell, Justin Howell, Vorhees etc. Word up! ... Love you Brandon Gene...Just keep the faith! Daniel Clay Hollifield you'll be my friend for life!!......Now we are moving into the most controversial part of this book. This is where it gets very serious (and quite frankly) dangerous. The first half of this book has been pretty nice, compelling, neat and clean. It gets ugly now. And if I did not know that I am dying I would not be writing the final half of this book. Famous trial lawyer Murray J. Janus worries that "some of those folks may try to get their 'fifteen minutes'" by suing Sherman... some of this stuff raised my eyebrows and you know I've seen it all...WOW! "...If I did not have Disseminated Valley Fever I'd be worried more about a contract hit being placed upon my head. The gangs, the serial killers, sadistic molesters and the high powered prison guards I expose hereafter are deadly. They would cut my head off just as quickly as you will take your next breath. I tried to convince myself not to write the following pages. "Some pastors and church folks will alienate you due to some of the situational semantics. And what if you miraculously recover from the cocci? The minute they transfer you out of C.S.P. Sac-you are a dead man! "I reasoned to myself. But I kept seeing T.J. Parsell, Garrett Cunningham, Michael Gorman and tens of thousands of other young (mostly Caucasian) boys bloodied, raped, sold and enslaved in prisons all across America I saw the frightened eyes of Amanda Hall, Toni Buntons and Jane Doe's who are brutally raped by guards in prisons every day. The fact that American prisons are more vicious and abusive (to female inmates). And the L.A. County Jail (California prisons and Texas prisons etc.) are more abusive to young (mostly white) boys than Gitmo and Abu Ghraib combined...My firsthand and eyewitness knowledge of what prisons do to kids made me write the second half of this book...I'm not writing to the baby boomers. They (I'm just being real) are too cynical for me. And (keeping it candid) I have given up on teaching old dogs new tricks nor shall I preach to the choir. This powerful, scathing, chilling and haunting book is to The Facebook generation...I've been writing the good for years without much fanfare. But K.K.K. is the good, the bad, the ugly and the whole truth. I should ban all persons over 40 from reading this book...Too many boys (i.e. Brett and Chris who were on the Dr.Phil show) are being arrested for petty crimes. And the rape, debauchery and sexual torture (in these prisons) which they experience torments them for life. I respect parents and I honor my elders. I love educators and I squeeze them for their knowledge. But when a brilliant man who matriculated at Harvard (Dr. Franklin Curren) tells me "Sherman you have the power to influence and to inspire the youth in amazing ways if you try." I take it to heart. Ipso facto, I have the kind of radical faith that leads me to believe that we can and we will revolutionize high schools and colleges with this (G.B.G./Heart) groundbreaking organization. Nobody believed that we could get Bloods, Crips, Skinheads, Aryan Brotherhoods, Bulldogs, Northerners, Southerners, Nazi Lowriders, Correctional Captains, Associate Wardens, Republicans, Congresspersons, senators and a tough prison warden (Jimbo Walker) to all sit at the roundtable and declare that "yes we can" impact the youth etc. with G.B.G. But yes we did.

And right this very minute I need every student, all the teens and tweenies to get busy. I am not a billionaire. And I won't bribe youth. But I will give away as much money as I can Peter (in Switzerland), our stealth supporters and I will give as many stipends, awards and scholarships as we can to motivate messengers.

We need y-o-u to use your P.C. as a mighty weapon for good, for change and for G.B.G. We join with great men like Tony Dungy and women like Donna Brazile who says "I believe in forgiveness, redemption and in second chances". And now is your time to help launch an Internet Nuclear War on child molesters, child killers, gangs, drugs and on bullying. We need your ideas, your suggestions, your input and your creativity today. You are the leaders we've been waiting for. What do you think Tony Dungy, Michael Vick, TBN second chance and G.B.G. can do to help troubled and at-risk youth to stay out of prisons? Should we do more CD's, DVD's, hostings or pamphlets etc.? Should we do more on Facebook, twitter or on Myspace? How can we marry G.B.G./Heart (more effectively) to the fraternity, sorority, student government or to local clubs? I need you to tell us what you need us to do, to help you recognize and/or avoid predators, molesters, drug dealers and gang bangers.

This book is a wake-up call. And you will get a (spiritual) "contact high" reading this book. And some of it is hilarious while other parts are chilling. And if you take action on the stuff in this book you will transform... but my concern is for what you will do when the high and the hype wear off. Life is complex and it is confusing at times. It is just not all boom boxes, video games and booty dancing. There will be times of pain, fear, tests and temptations. And as you try to navigate your way through your teens, high school and maybe through college etc. you'll face some challenges and situations that your homeroom teacher didn't prepare you for. Some of the cliques, groups and the characters you have to deal with are not easy to deal with. Sometimes you have to deal with secrets, mistakes, lies, games and with stuff your parents never told you about...And the choices and decisions you make about what to do about drugs, gangs, cliques and drama will affect you forever! I meet a lot of kids in prison (or in G.B.G., via e-mail and snail mail etc.) who messed up and ended up locked up. And they thought the same thing I thought (and you think) which was "I get this. I know what I'm doing. It's all good". And/or "I'm just going to try this one time"...or "It won't hurt to do this...it feels good...it tastes good etc..." Ya'll can I keep it legit? Ain't nuthin you can do, feel, try or taste worth you coming to prison. There are men (predators, monsters, serial killers) here in prison who can't wait to get their hands on you. This book ain't the "boogy man" crap it is real. I used real names, times and even places as I dissect the minds of monsters (i.e. Scott Peterson, Eric & Lyle Menendez etc.) whom I've lived with in prison. K.K.K. is real talk. ...Can I ask you a question? I know you look up to us thugs who are able to survive in prisons etc. But how would you like to show your naked anus (crack), penis (or vagina) and your testicles to a man every day? Michael Vick, Robert Downey and any of us in prison are routinely required to strip naked, lift our testicles, bend over and spread our cheeks for male guards. It's dehumanizing, would you like to do it daily?... I wouldn't wish prison on my worst enemy. And keeping you outta here is the cause of my life...You at Benjamin Hope Academy, Locke High School, Ralph Bunche Middle School, Harper Jr. High School, Ronald E. McNair, Lodi High School, all California Public Schools etc. I want you to go on Bing.com and Facebook today. Find me (ex-California inmate) Joseph Latham, Zachary Finney, John Neis (Las Vegas at KVBC-TV), Cong. Eddie Bernice Johnson, Justin Wheelock, David Quattlebum and David Holloman. I need you (today) to find Omar Samaha, Alex Blench, the student government president at Vista Del Lago High School, Perry Thompson (Granite Bay), Scott at magnifeast.com, Jordan Simon (in Iowa), attorney Megan Corcoran, Jake Heartsong, Chancellor Charles Reed, Tobias Lake, Garrett McCain (Sacramento, CA), Jeremy Hawes, Keith and Nathaniel Mullennix, Christian Nelson, Jeff Parshley, Ryan Hreljac, David Kelley, Eric Castellanos, Max at TMZ.com, Becky and Chris Thompson etc. E-mail them and tell them to get K.K.K. We have stipends, jobs and assignments for some of them. E-mail the Philedelphia Eagles and tell Andy Reid the book is out. Tell Channing Tatum, Greg and John Doggett, Gabe Williams (Sacto), Judges Lawrence B. Karlton and Thelton Henderson. Contact Judy Smith (Impact Strategies) and ask Judy to help us tell the world about G.B.G. and about K.K.K...we need you. Now brace yourself for the final (roller coaster) half of K.K.K...

... Today is 7/26/09 and it is 4:35 pm. I planned to be finished writing KKK 3 months ago. But I was uprooted and thrown into the hole (aka administrative segregation) on 4/15/09. Wow! And when a prisoner is placed into the 'hole 'he can take no property (i.e.television, addresses, books, manuscripts or mail etc.) with him. You take nothing. All of your belongings are put in boxes (most time officers allow your cellmate to pack your property and things often come up M.I.A. and stored in a large closet. You get nuthin. Ipso Facto the unfinished (KKK) manuscript has not been seen (by me) in more than 3 months. I still don't have it to date. And that's just another hassle that comes along with being in prison. You can be uprooted any day of the week for almost anything. A person I've helped, became angry with me because I would not help him pay for drugs. And out of Naked and Raw spite he filed a "confidential" (a way of snitching, lying and/or making an accusation against a fellow convict in secret. It's called a "1030"and when a 1030 is filed against me I'm not given the name of the confidential informant) against me. I knew exactly who he was and his allegation was ridiculous! Sgt. J. Stratton (not a fan of mine) Lt.Johnston (also hates me) and C.o. Garcia all knew it was a blatant mendacity yet they still put me in the hole. Perhaps (??) I'll revisit the allegation and all the whole drama later on. It's so dramatic and there are so many bombshells as a result of that erratic accusation made by the guy on 4/15/09 etc. that I may just write an entire tome about it.

But for all you young thugs, playas, coolios and Foolios etc. just recognize that when or if you come to jail you can be powerless. The po po can put yo ass in the hole any day of the week 4 nuthin. That's real talk. It is what it is.

But the steps of a good man are ordered by the lord! I'm so convinced that God ordered my steps that I wish I could come shout it out in your hood, suburb, barrio, school, church or university. I know some of you are atheists, agnostics, Buddhists etc. etc. and I respect you. But life has convinced me that our steps are ordained by God. And many of us fight like hell to get away from God's will. We drink up all the booze, smoke up all the weed, put needles in our veins, gangbang and shoot up the neighborhood. We act a darn fool trying to escape the ordering of our steps. And it's sometimes difficult to believe God is ordering your steps when you find yourself in a problem. It's hard to believe a divine force is guiding your steps when you end up in a pit or a prison or a mess. But the reason I re read the story of Joseph in Genesis over and over is because I'm mesmerized by Joseph. Baby boy Joseph blows my mind- Joseph's journey trips me out Joseph was a Righteous man. He was not a Crip, or a Blood, Norteño, Bulldog or

Eme.Joseph didn't fornicate and smoke weed like you and I. Joseph sniffed no glue. Unlike you and I –Joseph did not smoke, drink or chew, and he didn't hang around with them that do. And I wish I had time to illuminate and elucidate the entire story of Joseph. I wish I had the space in this potent, concise and awesome tome to theoretically dissect Joseph's story in K.K.K . But suffice it to say that Joseph and I (Sherman D. Manning) had some things in (literally) common. Joseph was a good Brutha like no other. But Joseph loved God. Bruthas got jealous of him because he had a dream (a mission, a plan, a program, a script). His own Brothers plotted to kill him. Do you think that while Joseph was being plotted on he was all Religious saying "o.k. God is ordering this plot on my life"! Do you think that when they put Joseph in a pit and sold him into slavery he said "okay God wants me to slave?" And Joseph still did the right thing and he found himself working (it's good to work young folks) in potiphar's house. Potipher happened to be a Captain (guard) for king pharaoh. And potipher's wife falsely accused Joseph of a sex crime. And (as I argue relentlessly) in prison folks convicted of sex crimes are looked down on worse than those who commit the final (murder) crime. So lets keep it real .Do you think that Joseph was so sanctified that he was sittin up in that prison saying "yes this is God. I think God has led this woman to falsely accuse me of attempted rape. God must have ordered court to wrongly convict me of this sex crime. And God has ordered the prison authorities to keep me here for 13 ½ years for something I did not do ". Can we be real? Joseph was a real life human being like you are. And you know Joseph had to argue with God. Even Job questioned God while he was suffering. Job wondered where is God when the hurting won't stop. King David seemed to be contemplating suicide in Psalms 55 when he wrote "the terrors of death have fallen upon me". Let's be real. Can't you see the young Joseph in that prison in Genesis? Look at him sitting up in that jail cell. His celly must have had him playing spades or pinochle. And over the course of living in a bathroom (cell) with another man, I can see Joseph kicked back on his bunk saying to himself "is there really a God?" I'm a living witness that Joe probably didn't say it out loud. Cause when you profess to know God and you spend your childhood claiming to your Brothers that God has this grand plan (ordering of your steps) for your life etc. And after all of that preaching and Christian stuff (Sherman, Joseph, Billy or Bob) and then you end up locked up in prison on a sex beef. You do everything you can to try not to draw any attention to yourself. It's hell living with folks in jail. The most bitter, angry, spiteful, contradictory and (believe it or not) judgmental folks you'll ever meet (I hope you never meet us) are folks in jail. Check this out, we criticize Oprah, Montel, Jesse Jackson, Al Sharpton, the NAACP, S.C.L.C. Naps, G.B.G. etc. We have an opinion (usually negative) about everything and everybody. Yet we'll sit up and write long and pitiful ass missives to Oprah, Tyra Banks, Bishop Flip Flop and to Deacon Willie Wonder. We will tell Oprah how unfair, corrupt, wicked, evil and vicious cops, courts and guards can be "Oprah they'll lock you up for a crime you didn't commit. I'm innocent...3strikes this and my public defender that". Yet the very minute we hear over the grapevine that Joseph (or Sherman, or Pete Rose, Rolando Cruz or Tim Masters) is "in here on a sex beef" we start drooling at the mouth. We can't wait to attack, beat, stab or kill "that old child molester" or that "rapist". The moment we hear about the "R" (i.e. Rapist but actually Restriction) in a guy's jacket (meaning profile or history) we forget that (although rape is a sick crime) police do lie, routinely lie, courts get it wrong and "Oprah I'm innocent". All that jive we preach about injustice, false accusations and corrupted police etc. We forget the moment we hear he's convicted of a "sex" crime...So (believe me) Joseph was a lonely man in that prison. Let me ask you have you ever had a secret hurt, a private pain or a personal battle that you could not talk to your partners, the Fellas, the Frat or the Sorority about? In your 13,14,15 or 23 years on the planet have you ever (come on and be real) had to deal with a mess, a pain, a hurt, a horror or a secret all by yourself? Lets go deeper look at Joseph. He was lonely,scared, hurt and tired. He had endured set back after set back and now he is in the big house on a rape beef. And you expect for a dude in the State Pen, who watched his own Brothers plot to kill him, was sold into slavery (like Africans),served a Captain (who liked him and trusted him) Faithfully, got falsely accused of rape, wrongly convicted and had been sittin in prison for 13 ½ years to be like "yo dude I'm cool. God ordered this for me. I know you believe the police reports and all that mess in my –c- (central) file and I know I was … but I'm cool and I'm a man of God"yea right. Can't you hear Joseph's celly (had he been stupid enough to tell his story to his celly) saying "Joe Boy u telling me you are a man of God and u all goody 2 shoes right? God planned for You Brutha 2 hate on u, try 2 kill u, sell u as a slave, leave u for dead etc. God put you in a Captain's house, caused his wife to accuse u of rape, put u in prison and u been in here for 13 ½ years and God ain't got u out yet?" But the problem (the plot) prepared Joe for the pit. The pit got him ready for Potipher. Potipher's wife catapulted him to the prison and the prison prepared him for Pharoah. And Pharoah put him in the palace. Joseph went from being a prisoner to being a Prince. But it did not happen overnight. He had to get through prison to get to the palace (the promise, the prophecy). And some people become overwhelmed by the process and give up on the promise. And as I look at my own life… My Lord… I wish I could come to where you are right now and look you in your eyes and really tell you my story… I committed a lot of sins. I even committed crimes. Crimes I never got convicted of. But God ordered my steps. I'm in prison now falsely accused. But when we do G.B.G./HEART (Helping Educate At Risk Teens) clinics I never talk about my conviction. I only talk about my crimes. It's not about how good I want kids to know I am. It's about how bad the po po says I am. I present myself to teens as the chief of sinners, a thug and a common criminal. I rarely even mention the name God to kids. Ipso facto I often call G.B.G. (Gang Bangers for God) Gang Bangers for Good. But oh baby baby if you only knew the Joseph part of my story. If I could show you just a glimpse of how God set me up. If you could be a peeping Tom or a fly on the wall and see how it all played out… One day I was on television and in the newspaper in Atlanta Georgia. I still remember the headlines of the first Atlanta Constitution (in-town extra) weekend spread about Sherman D. Manning. The headline was "Boy turns play ground into pulpit".

I still remember being a kid preacher I was licensed to preach at age 11(seriously –by Rev. Moses Lee Raglin at First Corinth Baptist Church). I was ordained (seems like a Hollywood tale or a fairy tale) at 17. At 16 years of age I traveled to New York (Pentecostal House of prayer in Brooklyn) to preach Revival and Record my first album. I remember meeting Myla Dansby on the train (she was going to attend Syracuse University) en-route to the Big Apple. We fell in love (infatuation) on the train… I came home to Atlanta and returned to N.Y. a few months later to preach at Eastward Miss.Bpt.Ch. For Dr. David Bond… Fell in love with Yvette Lewis (a beautiful sista) on that trip… At 13 I met Congressman, Ambassador and Mayor Andrew young. I began to build my Political capital like a lil Barack (in Atlanta) Obama. I got very close to civil rights legend Rev. Hosea Williams. Rev. Williams walked and talked with Dr. Martin Luther King Jr. I was very close to Rev. Williams and Ambassador Young…I travelled to Pennsylvania, Virginia, D.C., Germany, France, Switzerland etc. I was… In the promise. I was in the process. Some folks were jealous of me. Some folks plotted to kill me (literally) and the "promising" Minister, Youth leader, Civil Rights Activist etc. etc. ended up in a problem, in a pit and now (3000 miles away from home) I'm in a prison… Back up again… I (literally…Call James "Jimbo" Walker if you think I'm lying) was working in New Folsom State Prison for a Captain (i.e. potipher?) Name James "Jimbo" Walker in 2002 when I asked Jimbo to let me organize a group of convicts to bring kids into the prison and try to divert them from crime. "Get outta here" was his reply… I ended up at (as you may recall) Pleasant Valley State Prison on my death bed with disseminated valley fever. I was down to 96 lbs. I spent 14 months in a community hospital. They thought I was gonna die. I felt like Job. I felt like Joseph. I... promised God that if He would save my life I would do whatever it took to organize a group of convicts to divert kids from gangs, guns, drugs and violence... I had a dream and I saw "G.B.G." in gold letters. I woke up and spent 3 days trying to figure out words for the acronym. Dreamed again and saw "Gang bangers for God"... On my death bed, 96 pounds at Coalinga Regional Medical Center (my home away from home) I had no idea God was ordering my steps. All the hospital staff was white and Mexican (fine with me because they were good people) except radiological tech John Hutchinson. I had all white nurses for nearly a year and it just so happened a couple of travelling nurses, who happened to be black, happened to be Christians and happened to be married and happened to be from Atlanta (my home town) Georgia and happened (I'm not embellishing...this is real talk) to attend Salem Bpt. Church where Rev. Jasper Williams (a church I attended and preached at) Pastored etc. etc. They happened to decide to take a 3 month gig at C.R.M.C. and out in the country... Latasha and Will told me "we know God led (ordered/steps) us here for some reason". These two black nurses often prayed over my 96 Lbs body and...(Yall a have 2 read my book "Left For Dead" for the hole story) I ended up (although the P.V.S.P. Warden told me I could/would never return to New Folsom) transferred from P.V.S.P. (Near Fresno) to C.M.C. East (San Luis Obispo, to Vacaville. (near San Francisco), back to C.M.C. East and one morning early in 2008 I transferred to(ordered steps) New Folsom State Prison. And the egotistical, arrogant (but a good man indeed) Captian (Jimbo walker) who nearly lost his job (via a false accusation) etc. For whom I had worked now had a new title. Jimbo (aka James P. Walker) was now the Superintendent, Chief Executive Officer ... He was/is the Warden... and the same (potipher) Captian who shot down my idea for a "scared straight" like program now told (then) Captian Fred Schroeder to tell me "Yes We Can" do the G.B.G./Heart program at New Folsom State Prison in 2008... and all I can think to tell you is that I almost quit. I almost gave up I almost stopped believing God. As quiet as its kept – I (the ordained preacher) almost stopped believing in God. When your life is crumbling all around you. When people are calling you sick names(Joseph you are a rapist) . When you have to try to keep your conviction (or addiction, problem, skeleton etc.)a secret etc. When there was so much promise (prophecy) over your life (the dream, the plan, the "coat of many colors" etc). And you end up a common criminal in a Maximum Security Prison. When it seems like all hope is gone... I almost quit in the process (the false accusation, the wrongful conviction, the sentence, the hospital etc). And gave up on my promise (prophecy)... But my prison has become my stage. My prison has become my pulpit. My sentence is transformed into the most unique educational opportunity for youth you've ever seen. My prison time is transmogrified into a teachable moment. I would come back from the brink of death, organize G.B.G., convince the Senate, President Pro-tem (via a collect telephone call) to support G.B.G. get help from an associate Warden (who tried to re-transfer me out of New Folsom as Captain) Fred Schroeder etc. Who would have thought I could/would some how bring together (a team of rivals) gang bangers (skinheads, murderers, crips, bulldogs, sons of odinists etc.) and get them to work together? Who would have thought I'd be able to convince a Harvard trained physician (Dr. Franklin Curren) to hesd up my G.B.G. advisory board? Wow! I wish I could tell you I was able to magically live down any suspicions etc. That perhaps I did (may be potipher's wife was not lying) commit this crime etc. Wish I could tell yall it was my skills, will power or my credibility that convinced Fred to convince Jimbo, to convince Patricia, to convince Johnson-Dovey, to convince Steve Vance, to convince Congressmen and Senators that G.B.G. would work. But that's not how/why it happened. Quite candidly Fred, Steve and I argued vehemently over process (sporadically) but G.B.G. was bigger than Fred, Steve (and remember Steve is 6 ft 6) and me. And God ordered all of our (Fred, Jimbo, Steve, Dr. Solis, Dr. A. Duran, Dr.Gregg, Danial Bugriyev, Adam Lane, Dustin Nicolodi, Diana Smith, Johnny Willie,

Ford, Billy, Brown etc.) Steps to make this brilliant, unique, convict led and National organization (in concert with "compassion," Homeboy Industries , NAPS etc.) happen... God made it happen... After all the arguments Fred and I had. After Madame Patricia Kennedy spanked (via a verbal lashing. She's Jimbo's secret weapon against me. Mrs. Kennedy is the only person in C.D.C. who can/will give me a tongue lashing and get no back talk!) me about a pink slip (it was a joke) I sent Fred etc. It amazed me one day when Jimbo sent Fred to my office (actually the inmate ducat area) and this white Republican, who's just promoted to associate Warden etc. Fred sat down next to me shook my hand and told me "yes we can"...I'm skipping (teasing) a lot because I listen to advisors and Senator Jhon Burton advised me to keep this book concise...When I was uprooted on 4/15/09 and sent to the hole I was beyond livid. I was so angry I could not see straight. Alonso Dearaujo (a team member) blatantly lied on me and after I was in Ad-Seg a while Madame Patricia Kennedy and Jimbo came to see me for a vitek (I don't have time to explain vitek. Call Mrs Kennedy if you really wanna know) hearing. I'd refused to attend any hearings etc. Dr. Paicez and Dr. Jaffe were a tad bit disgusted with me. C.O. Parker told CCII Kennedy "you all are wasting your time, Manning will not come out for this hearing". And Dr. Paicez had already told me Warden Walker never comes to Viteks but Madame Kennedy told Parker "oh yes he will attend this committee". She came to my cell door and "are you coming out to committee?" I replied "yes". Upon my arrival at the hearing to my utter surprise CCIII Johnson-Dovey (a beautiful black woman) and Jimbo were at the hearing. "Sherman you look horrible" Walker began. "Is my word good with you?" He inquired. "I give you my word we will deal with this accusation. I can't tell you everything but Mrs. Kennedy and I know you. And we know it's a lie. This person has a history of making these type allegations. I don't know how he benefits...I appreciate all the hard work you were doing with the kids (G.B.G.) program and I know you worked your ass off. We are moving forward and"...

...Three weeks ago CO. Macias picked me up at Vacaville and stated "Dearaujo is gone." I learned he'd been caught with street drugs and he admitted to Willie and Joker (Samuel Castellanos) that he lied on me. Castellanos was so angry that he moved out of the cell on Dearaujo. "Gone where?" I asked Macias. "They special transferred his ass to Lancaster. He kicked, screamed and yelled all the way there" he told me. And one C.O. said "he'll probably get beat down the minute he gets there. He's a walking wreck. Everybody knew he lied on you". And I thought "Be not deceived God is not mocked. Whatever a man sows he shall reap." And it all comes full circle. And strangely (because I can be very vindictive) I found myself feeling sorry for Dearaujo. I was sad because I know he is a troubled soul. I prayed and asked God to help Alonso Dearaujo. Why? Because he is just another flawed human like me (and you too). We've all lied, plotted, schemed and connived. But God meant it for good...He ordered my steps even to ad-seg and...I had to be alone for months before I could finish writing a book (the one you are reading) that would give flight to the mission of G.B.G./Heart. God had some stuff he needed to show me and wanted me to see before I could finally write the book (KKK). He ordered me to write. I was (on 4/15/09) still angry with Fred, Steve and...I was mad as hell.

...Putting G.B.G. together has been the toughest challenge of my life...And the scariest! And I marched with r#ev. Hosea Williams in Forsyth County Georgia (Cummings GA.) when the Klu Klux Klan threatened us with explosives! No I'm not embellishing like James Frey. I marched in Cummings GA. It was so racist that Oprah did a show in Forsyth County!....And when Atlanta had 29 murdered and missing children in 1980 I was a lil boy preacher. I led a march and prayer vigils with Mayor Maynard Jackson, Senator Grace Davis and Atlanta Youth Against Crime. There were so many death threats on my life that the Mayor and Mrs. Davis gave me a bodyguard (Atlanta Police Officer Ed Snowden) for the march... But even that was not as scary (a strange word for me to use) as putting together a team of rapists, murderers, robbers and gangsters in a testosterone filled maximum security prison. Sometimes I had more problems with staff than the convicts. You can't cast a play in hell and expect the actors to be angels...But we did it!!

...And all I can think to tell you is "eyes have not seen, ears have not heard, and neither has it entered into the hearts of men the things God has in store" for G.B.G. , you and for me. I can tell you that no matter what you may have done, what mistakes you have made or who you may be cliqued up with-God is able to do "exceedingly abundantly above all that we ask or think, according to the power that works in us." (Ephesians 3:20).. You may be in jail, juvenile, prison, on crack, meth, oxycontin or paint but you deserve a second chance. And you can turn around. Youngsters take it from a 38 year old O.G. You may be "hard pressed on every side, yet not crushed; perplexed, but not in despair. Persecuted, but not forsaken; struck down, but not destroyed." But "all things." Not some things, most things or a few things but "all things work together for good (G.B.G.) to those who love God, to those who are called (ordered) according to His purpose". I have been called to G.B.G. Fred, Steve, Terry L Rosario, Jimbo, Adam Lane and Daniel etc. We were "called" to G.B.G./Heart! Trust me (lol) Fred would have never "called" it "G.B.G."

...But we were called and when God calls you (Joseph, Sherman, Rolando, Pete Rose, Tim Masters etc.) a false rape conviction won't stop a senator John Burton (pharaoh) from endorsing you to be a prince in prison...Why would God call Sherman D. Manning (Johnny Willie, Doc Ford, Rick Butler, Joker, Silent, Santos, and even Dearaujo)?? How dare God cal me to found, lead and preside over G.B.G.? Well let's see He called a murderer named Moses to lead the children of Israel out of Egypt. He called a drunkard named Noah. He called an adulterer who was a murderer named David. He called a traitor and a thief named Judas to be a disciple. He used a woman who had been married five times, an adulterer whom he met at the well to be a witness for Christ. He chose a man named Peter who was an ear cutting liar, who denied Christ. And after Christ himself witnessed Peter deny him at the crucifixion...as soon as Christ rose from the dead the only disciple whom he sent for by name was (Peter) the one who had denied him. Christ said "Go tell my disciples and Peter"... He called (Saul) a serial killer to become the chief Apostle...And that's what the men (Billy, Doc, Willie and all of us) on the G.B.G. team are doing-becoming men of honor. We are ambassadors for good/God...I want to tell you kids not to quit. Don't give up on the promise in the process. The process (adolescence, temptation, school, drugs, gangs etc.) can kick your ass. But even when you go through hell and high water don't quit. Don't follow the crowds or try to fit in. Bill Gates didn't fit in. Barack didn't fit in. Michelle Obama didn't fit in. They say "black" is the new "b_tch". I say "books" are the new "b_tch". Books are back in! You're reading this aren't you? Books are making a comeback!...I want you to Google Travis Wall, Kurt and Aaron (who were on the Tyra Banks show on 7/9/09), Kupono, Benjamin Manning, Alex Silva, Craig Cannon (Woodland, CA), Kyle Love, Daniel Radcliffe, Garrett Haden (Sacto), Jake Simpson, Cesar L. Chavez, Gabe Williams (Sacto, CA) Luke Sears, Atty. Kevin E. Henry, Zach Sutherland, Trevor Loflin, Dylan Vall, Justin Berry (Bakersfield, CA), Kevin Mclin, Marius and Quinten (both appeared on Tyra Banks on 7/24/09), Caleb Sima and Jai Breisch. Tell them they are in K.K.K. Send em to our www.napsusa.org, our Facebook, Myspace and twitter site(s)...When a 14 year old girl (Tylar Witt) is accused of murdering her own mother- we need G.B.G. And I need you to help us get it (this book) to inmate(s) Jesse James Hollywood and to Scott Peterson...We (G.B.G.) are still becoming...

I (repeat) almost gave up and quit...Although I am wrongly convicted I thought about all the wrong, mess, evil and dirt I did do. And I almost disqualified myself from service. But we at G.B.G. are seeds. And a seed can't grow unless it has been in and through a lot of dirt and darkness… If you're in dirt, mess, darkness, jail, juvenile, prison, detention, group homes etc.etc. today. You are still a seed and I know it looks bad. But you can't judge the day by the weather. And you must not allow what you see to cause you to give up on your dreams. When a seed is in the ground you can't see it. When folk look at the dirt over seeds in a garden it looks bad. Especially if you're hungry. But I'll make you a promise. You will bud, blossom, and bloom. Don't cave in. Don't quit or give up. God can dream a bigger dream for you than you can ever dream for yourself. Help get this book to Jordan Thomas (the Jordan Thomas Foundation), Donald Dusk (Akron Ohio), Marty Tankleff, Professor Marc Howard, Andre Segura, David Remnick, Charlie Rose, Charles Ebersol, Bill Moyers, Rev. Otis Moss, F.Lee Bailey, Professor Paul Butler, Barbara Brooks, Ian Drew , Pres. Richard Levin, Alex Seabolt, Anthony Woods (Fairfield CA. and his aide Brian), Sandra Jackson (Sacto teacher), Bev Smith and Donna Brazille. G.B.G.is depending on you computer wizards to message (T.M., I.M. and email) Chad Rettie, Senator Roland Burris, Cong. Sheila Jackson Lee, Gov. Tim Caine, Lorna Smith, Verone Kennedy, Mayor James Young, Sean Stewart, Michael Pesci, Ryan Hausley, Daniel Walsh, Judge Greg Mathis, Judge Jeanine, Whoopi Goldberg, Dr. Anthony Griffin, Jarrod Konipinsky, Tadd Carr, Christopher Krinkie, Maxwell Hanger, Michael Salazar, Becky and Chris Thompson etc.etc. Nate (Paradise Hotel-last season), Josiah Lemming, Jeff Buttle, Kyle Larsen (Sacto), Toure, John Fink, Tyler Perry, Kaether Cordero, Doug Pieper Jr., Nate Firestone, Adam Davis, Mike Delgado (El Paso Texas), Sean Farmer, Blake Koch (the magic guy for Ringling Bros. Barnum and Bailey), Gene Langford (Atlanta, GA), Ralph Cannon (GA.), Scott Coffman (Navy), Cameron Johnson (Roanoke, VA), Duane Fred Hall (U.S. Navy), Matt Charabot, Jarred Shoemaker, Zachary Boyd (Army), Matt Fiddes, Ian Drew, Gerald Posner, Derek Jones (Salt Lake City, UT), Craig Scott (Littleton CO), Ollie Valencia, The Rubber Boy, Montel, Aaron Houston, Rosey Grier, Rev. Serene Jones, Ben Tracy, Jason Huyck, Steve Henning, Jennifer Fearing, Ryan Evans (Golden CO), Chase Crawford, Christopher Savvas, Billy Magnussen, Joshua Waiter (NY), Thomas "Hollywood" Henderson (Texas), Benjamin Todd Jealous, Julian Bond, Joey Grissett (Richmond, VA), Cesar Ramirez (Oregon), Bikers Against Child Abuse, Howard Griffith Sr, Michael Vick, John Mandern (Delaware Ohio), Greg Tufaro, Jose Lari, Gotham Chopra, Ryan Hreljac, Frank Casio, Jonah Coleman, Autumn Brown, Nick Macusos, Faisal Selah (LA), T.R. Knight, Michael Urie, Prof. Antwi Akom, Andrew Knowlton, Chad Michael Morrissette (W. Hollywood), Chris Austad, James McKnight, Steven Lancaster, Zachary Finney, Wil Seabrooks, Neal Carlson, Ron Huffman, Kris Stump, Timothy Combs, Atty. Dana Cole, Matt Stuart (ABC News), Judge William O Voy, Caleb Nunes, Pete Dougherty, Danny McDermot, Matt Lanter, Logan Campbell, Michael Shackelford, Nathan hand and Gary Browning…they need this tome. And if you read that long ass list of names and didn't help by googling them please…try Microsoft's new (Bing?) search engine and find these people and tell them to get K.K.K. I need David Joiner, Curtis Sykes, Sam Fuick, Billy York, John Garvin and Scott Johnson (Warner Robbins) etc. All Georgia boys to get this book…I want you young folks to study the greats and become greater. Be a consummate student. You can raise the bar and then break the bar. You can (just as our G.B.G. has done) create what has never been done. "There is nothing (G.B.G., PLN, Jenny Triplett, Barbara Brooks, "Kat" Sanchez etc) that can't be done if we raise our voice as one". I wanna let you know whatever you believe you become. The most powerful thing on earth (God gave us) is the human mind and prayer. I call you out. And I call you to action. A man has not begun to live until he rises above the confines of his "own individualism" to "become concerned about the greater community at large." Dr. King taught that you should be the best that you can be. Even if you are a "streetsweeper. Be so good that the living, the dead and even the unborn will have to say 'there lived a great streetsweeper who swept he job well". We can heal the world. G.B.G. has found an idealogical and a spiritual Jihad against gangs, guns, drugs and violence. G.B.G. has formed a super alliance with death row inmates and prisoners across the world. We are calling Ryan Evans, Daniel Clay Hollifield, Brian Devin Graham, Alexander Dugdale, Ricky Mitchell (Summerville GA), P.O. 1st class Joel Tatum and you to help us...And although more white kids come to our G.B.G/Heart tours than blacks etc. I wanna tell black men that blacks are the most murdered generation on the planet. The most incarcerated generation on the planet. One in fifteen black males are in jail. Three in ten black men are on crack. Come on people. I'm calling a code red in the black community! I'm not mad with Bill Cosby and Dr. Alvin Poussaint. I say every pastor ought to preach about it. And all the teachers ought to teach about it. I beg (I'm willing to beg for youngsters) Russell Simmons, Kanye West, Michael Moore, George Soros, Bill Gates and Warren Buffett to help G.B.G. put K.K.K. in every U.S. school....We must sound the alarm. Your steps are ordered...It's now 1:00 a.m. and my right pinky is bleeding because it's been dragging across this paper as I write for hours. But I would not be writing "this" if I had not been in the hole. And I wouldn't be in the hole if Dearaujo had not lied on me...The lie hurt. It disrupted my life and my plans. But God ordered my steps. I thought it was a setback. But a setback is only a setup for a comeback. Maybe you've been held back a grade in school. Perhaps you are an outcast (a nerd, a jock, gay, lesbian, fat, etc) etc. Your steps are ordered. Keep pushing on, keep on trying baby boy. I would not be writing these words if Dearaujo didn't lie on me...God will use a lie to empower you with truth. God will set you up so He can get glory out of your story. You are not too young, not too white, not too skinny, you are not dumb and stupid. You are exactly where you are supposed to be. And when you learn what you are supposed to learn-you'll move on.

Join G.B.G. today as a student ambassador. We need your input, your ideas and suggestions. Along with "compassion" we provide scholarships for kids to go to college etc. Join G.B.G. today and start a chapter in your school, church, university or city. We need Rev. Otis Moss, Michael Eric Dyson, and others to promote G.B.G.

...I ordered a code red in your school, city, university, barrio or hood. We must declare a Jihad on gangs, guns, drugs, violence, illiteracy, truancy, internet predators and child molesters. We can transform America and heal the world. We are the world. We are the children. We are the ones to make a brighter day so let's start giving. Find me Justin Berry, Kaether Cordero, Ryan Evans, Jai Bresch, David E. Kelley, Benjamin Todd Jealous, F. Lee Bailey, and Tom Mesereau and we will transform the world. I've been blessed to have what I learned from Mayor Andrew Young, Rev. Hosea Williams, Mayor Jackson and Grace Davis. I was blessed with the passion and knowledge of Fred Schroeder, Jimbo, Kevin Pool, Dr. Duran, Daniel Bugriyev etc.etc. God blessed G.B.G. with a team of rivals and if just one of you reading gets out of a gang, stops doing drugs, puts down the gun and picks up a book etc. We are winning...Get this book out there. Find Daniel Job, Brandon Hughes, Hugh Michael Hughes, Joseph Latham, Jerry Wines, Chuck Pyle and get this book in jail cells, juveniles, schools, libraries, universities, law schools and churches. We (G.B.G.) need you. We are the generation we've been waiting for. If G.B.G. gets Barbara Brooks, Sasha Vodnik, Cassie Pierson, Ryan Hreljac and Jake Simpson on our side we will win. If we get Seamus Farrow and Hollywood Henderson on our side we will win. If we get Andy "the volunteer" at "Homeboy Industries" on the G.B.G. team we will change the world. Daniel Asaro (Sacto) needs this tome...young men and young ladies may I remind you that I have an intimate, in depth knowledge of wrongful convictions. I know exactly what Joseph felt like in that prison. And it haunts me to know that if I could locate Richard Martz and Bret Nelson (Bret lived in West Hollywood, was in and out of jail and his mom lives in Oregon). I could/would prove my innocence!! Ya'll remember Michael Jackson's (rest in peace) brilliant attorney Tom Mesereau? I came close to having him represent me I talked to Tom 8 or 9 times.

Arsen Serafin introduced us. And Tom did me a favor in L.A. County Jail that saved my life. But Conrad Gamble conned (extortion) my business partner out of thousands of dollars to retain Tom but Conrad kept the money! He may (I've not spoken with her) have even conned Pastor Jean Barber and others... But-no matter how many Josephs, Pete Rose, Sherman D. Manning and Tim Masters there are trapped in the bowels of prisons for so-called rapes that didn't happen etc. I am a firm witness to the fact that psychosexual deviants, pedophiles and crazed rapists (read my book "Blue Eyed Blonde" Book II) do (indeed) exist. And we must work toward prevention. Abuse victims often become victimizers. Most molesters are all in the family... I remember interviewing Ed Stokes at Mule Creek state prison. Ed had an inmate lover named Noah L Hotsky. Noah would let Ed urinate and defecate on him. Ed was an admitted serial molester. A young man whom he molested committed suicide when he found out Ed had won a new trial. Since the victim was dead, they released Ed in 2004. He told me "I'm going to some playgrounds and finding me some boys to"... I can't write my response (and re-action) in this P.G. book... Ed got out and within weeks we saw Ed on "Inside Edition". He had bought an ambulance and was using the ambulance (and an ice cream truck) to seduce boys and molest them. Ed should never, ever see the light of day again. He told me he had hundreds of victims. I got that same eerie feeling around Ed that I got everytime I was around Eric and Lyle Menendez. I got that same spooky feeling around "Arizona" at M.C.S.P. "Arizona" is the guy who stalked the actress (she played on "Mork & Mindy" with Robin Willliams) –went to her house, rang the doorbell and blew her away. He also stalked O.J. Simpson D.A. Marcia Clark by mail....I recall an inmate by the name of Bret Moore at P.V.S.P. He had one of my books ("Creating Monsters") and I autographed it for him. He was a 29 year old white guy. And I always got a weird feeling around him. Then one day he asked if he could tell me a secret. I figured he was perverted and he confirmed it. Bombshell! He told me he was wrongly convicted of child molestation. And the minute I hear "wrongly" before the word "convicted" I'm (the author) all in. But I'm also pragmatic and I listen well. I analyzed his body language, lack of congruence, his shifty eyes etc.etc. And I knew Bret was lying. He finally admitted (days later) that although "I'm not a molester I have bondage issues...I was rubbing lotion on my daughter's legs....I went to her school and kidnapped her 8 year old schoolmate and I admit I put duct tape on her wrists..." I could not take it. I had to leave. The next day I told Bret "I'm not a vigilante so I'm not going to bother you. The judge gave you 30 years and I'm not a judge. But I don't believe you're innocent and I would like for you to never approach me with any conversation again".

    ...He told his gay lover Mike (the clerk) and Mike had the temerity to approach me...Months later (I may have already written this but since I've not seen my manuscript in over 3 months, I am not certain) in Coalinga Regional Medical Center Chuck Hedrick (from Stockton) told me how they ran Bret off the yard because Montel did a show on his serial molestation...That explained why Bret asked me once how often did I watch Montel...So this book has been conditioned (salted and peppered) with the empirical data I have from not only interviewing etc. but having to live amongst and work amongst and work with child predators, fratricidal sociopaths and gangbangers for years. I like Barbara Walters. But she is absolutely wrong about Eric Menendez. I have lived next door to him and worked with him for more than 3 years (Rosario, Jimbo, Schroeder, Kennedy, etc can verify this) and even loaned him $250.00...I can truly write that I have no dog in this fight. The truth is Eric and Lyle are sociopaths. Eric is a cold-blooded, calculating, duplicitous monster without a conscience...

    And I repeat the fact that if you are under 16 years old you should never write a prisoner (unless he's family) including me. We are convicts and most of the time we're up to no good...

Can I remind you that you can turn around. You don't have to become a murderer, a statistic or a prisoner. No matter how many mistakes you may have already made your steps are ordered. That's why you have this book right now…Listen- I know it is hard as hell being a teenager. And some of you think parents and adults don't have a clue. And we (adults) most certainly think we do. We'd rather talk about it than be about it. We'd rather preach a sermon than live a sermon. And some of you are dealing with some heavy stuff. You're dealing with teenage pregnancy, drugs, nicotine and thoughts of suicide or homicide. And often we adults have castrated you when all you needed was to be circumcised. And when we castrate you spiritually, psychologically and emotionally we stunt your growth. And you act out because you've never known the power of reproduction, due to our castration.

And many of you feel you can't cry tears. And when boys can't cry tears they often cry bullets. They cry guns, cry gangs, and cry violence.

You may find yourself (at this moment) all tied up. Tied up in a gang, a clique or a mess… I remember when Jesus showed up to see about Lazarus. Lazarus' sisters told Jesus it's too late he's already dead. But it's never too late. Jesus said "Show me where you laid him down." Show me where you quit. Show me where you stopped writing or visiting him in the juvenile. Show me where you got the block on the telephone…And when they took Jesus to the tomb where Lazarus was dead. Jesus stood outside the mess, the stench and the tomb. And He called things that were not as though they were. He ordered lazarus to "come forth". And there must have been a loud sound. Mary must have said "Martha what's that sound?" Martha must have said "It's the sound of a noise that's gonna raise Lazarus from the dead." I'm telling you to come forth. Right now…And the bible says Lazarus got up out of the grave. The bible says his feet were bound (shackles) and his hands were all tied (handcuffs) up. And Lazarus stumbled out of the grave in clothes saying "I'm tied up but I'm coming out". And that's why I don't try to stop anyone from joining G.B.G./Heart or from going to church. Because even though you may still be all tied up you can still come out. Have faith that nothing just happens. I went down so that I could come up. I went without so that I could be blessed. I had to go under so I could overcome. I mourned so that I could dance. If I hadn't been lied on I would not be writing these words right now. Some brothers who have seen my wife say she's bad. "You got a fine wife" etc. But they've not seen it all. My wife has some secrets that she only shows me. Some stuff God can't show you until you become alone. Even when Jesus walked the face of this earth He left his own disciples sometimes. So He could go and pray alone. God had to get me alone…without a t.v., without a book, without the fellas blowing data in my ears. God wanted to show me something I'd never seen before. God wanted to tell me some stuff I'd never heard before. That's why I forgive Dearaujo. That's why. I forgive Conrad. I even forgive Ricardo Calvario. Bitterness and vengeance will destroy the vessel that contains it. With all the folk I have wronged, lied to and mistreated etc. how dare I sit in a glass house and throw stones? How in the hell can I give up on a crack addict, a speed freak, a prostitute, a bulldog or a skinhead when God never gave up on me?

…He orders your steps. I can't seem to get away from that word "order". I need to get Jimbo, Scott Kernan and Matt Cate to let G.B.G. make a CD for you kids to hear. I want Fred, Steve, Adam Lane, Dustin, Bugriyev, Kennedy, Smith, Willie, Doc and Billy on it. I want you to hear our voices…I need to tell you. I went to the hole, slept on a floor for 52 days without going outside so I could tell you. God got me stuck up, messed up and beat up…read my book "From the palace to the prison" …I've written non-stop from "…today is 7/26/09" til now. It's now actually 7/27/09 in the wee hours of the morning. I'm gonna ask my grandmother (Dollie Manning), Bishop T.D. Jakes, Paul Crouch, Amy Fihn, "Kat" Sanchez and Bishop Eddie Long to pray for G.B.G. and to pray for K.K.K. I'm asking Fred Moor and St. Rose Parish to pray that this book will reach who I'm supposed to reach. I'm gonna (literally) write to Barack, Michelle, Mrs. Robinson, Congressman Sheila Jackson Lee and Rev. Otis Moss and ask them to pray that K.K.K. will revolutionize the youth movement in America. We must get Craig and Marc Kielburger, Daniel Asaro, Omar Samy, Van Hansis and Ryan Hreljac this book. Ya'll help me get it to Jai Breisch, Bill Gates, Seamus Farrow and the Facebook generation. ...One of the most powerful things President Barack Obama has said since becoming president is that "when you drop out of school, you not only fail yourself. But you fail your family and you fail your country".

A 19 year old inmate asked me what I suggested He do with his life etc. etc. I told him it would be arrogant and presumptuous of me to think I could give him advice. He reminded me that I'd written all these books and he'd heard even Schroeder say how intellectually advanced I am. I told him "Every time I start to believe my own press. I.E. I'm the only prisoner at New Folsom who has gotten letters from President Mandela. I have notes from Gov. Schwarzenegger thanking me for the "wonderful gift 'creating monsters'". And I'm the only prisoner (perhaps) in California with a letter from Barack Obama's office... When I begin to feel pretty smart I'm reminded that I'm still locked up. And if I was smart enough I'd write so well that some judge would let me go." I told him "However, if I had to give you one piece of advice I'd suggest that you become as articulate with words as you possibly can. Only words can give flight to your thoughts. It is with words that you paint a picture and tell a story. And I'd suggest you spend a lot of time reading great books."

And if I ever truly become the pioneer that a few (only a few) believe that I am. I would pray that my body of work will impress upon my generation, generation Y, your generation and generations yet unborn the power and the magic of a mastery of words. If I am allowed to teach your generation anything. I should like to teach you to get back to reading!

It is 4:01 a.m. and I stopped to try to sleep. But I'm so pregnant with this word that I can't hardly see straight. I'm thinking about all the kids who are lost in the shadows. From my unusual vantage (prison) point I can read the handwriting on the wall. I can see some unusual things from my perch in the prison. I learned so very much watching President Obama as he was able to convince young people of a change we can believe in. As he was able to Barack the vote mobilizing an army of young volunteers. I learned by studying Barack, Michelle, David Axelrod and the Obama team. I watched Obama operate a campaign with military precision. He transformed stalemates into pivots. He defeated the Clinton Machine and turned blue states red. I was awed by the discipline, precision and pragmatism of our president's campaign. And as Obama grew so did G.B.G./Heart. I literally had an Obama Playbook which I used to recruit the Harvard physician, Dr. Duran, Dr. Jarman, Dr. Gregg and Senator Burton. I was blessed to be alone (my perch) as I studied the presidential race as if I were studying for a collegiate test. I ate, slept and breathed the presidential race. I grew, stretched and I learned. I was/am a student of life, and I am absolutely convinced that when Mrs. Triplett, "Kat" Sanchez, Silja, Seamus, Hreljac, Burton, Sherman, Paul Wright, Jodie Evans, Soros, G.B.G., ACLU, NAACP, S.C.L.C. and human rights watch come together and tackle war, gangs, poverty, illiteracy, classism, and racism, together utilizing The Obama strategy, we will win. Yes we can. If we get Marc Kielburger, Hreljac, Hansis, Silberman, you and I to lift up our voices as one we can operationalize an internet (via Facebook, Twitter and Myspace) Jihad against youth gangs, guns, drugs and violence. In the 50's and 60's Andy Young, Hosea and Dr. King convinced youth to get off the buses, sit in the lunch counters, build their bonfires in the streets and to go to jail for what they believed in.

If G.B.G./Heart is successful at showing Ben Jealous, Julian Bond, Kielburger, Carol Leonard, Roberta Franklin, Soros, Tyler Perry, Akon,F. Lee Bailey and Bill Gates that all of us have a vested interest in improving our educational system etc. If G.B.G./Heart can help convince Arne Duncan that making education and school fun, exciting and interesting is one of the methodologies which can be employed to lessen the drop-out rate, we'll succeed. Yes we can. If we can get Verone Kennedy to work with Caroline Kennedy, convince Russell Simmons to join the G.B.G.Roundtable with Senator Burton, Sheila Jackson-Lee, Jesse and Rev. Sharpton etc. We will succeed-yes we can.

They built bonfires in the streets. I call on you to build your bonfires on Facebook, Myspace and your place. I encourage you to use Google, Zabasearch and Bing to do a new thing. Let us focus like a laser beam on preventing the children, grandchildren and the great grandchildren of the dream, from living in poverty, illiteracy, violence and crime. Let us get together. Barack Obama's victory blew the minds of all baby boomers. They could not believe that the youth would finally show-up and showed-out at the polls. They could not envision the millions of 18-30 year old youngsters who organized, strategized, volunteered and showed up to vote at the polls. And if we can get just 10% of the kids who volunteered, campaigned and voted for Obama to help G.B.G./Heart to heal the world we will change the world. Yes we can. We must launch a full frontal assault. I say "forward march". I say to student leaders, geeks, freaks, nerds, FAT (fabulous and thick) people. Skinny and to the buff etc. Forward march. If we can get just ten Justin Berrys, ten Seamus, Daniel Asare, Sen. Burton, Gloria Romero, Barbara Brooks, "Kat", "Jasmine", you and I etc. to declare that we will fight like Bulldogs to internationalize G.B.G./Heart etc. If we move forward pragmatically with all deliberate haste. Maxwell Hanger, Ricky Lebarron, John Garvin, Ralph Cannon, Joseph Latham and...we will transform the world. We must grow up. We must stop the in-fighting and bickering. We've gotta stop holding grudges. I've had to forgive Jeffrey Glen Howell and even James Albert Enslander. They are totally forgiven for wronging and betraying me. And you must teach yourself to forgive betrayal on the highest level of your life. If you can't forgive and let it go. Your grudges will kill your spirit, quench your joy and destroy your vision. Let it go...

The youth movement must duplicate the Obama strategy. I call on all of you to use the internet to nudge and awaken all those teenagers who put our president in office. Tell them to meet G.B.G./Heart in K.K.K. Tell them to come meet our team. I want them to meet youngsters like Daniel, Adam, Dustin and Roger. I want them to meet Fred, Steve and Jimbo. Tell them to meet G.B.G./Heart on Facebook, Myspace and at our umbrella (parent) organization (NAPS) at www.napsusa.org. Tell them they do have a seat at the G.B.G./Heart Roundtable...

...My great grandfather (Grady Jackson Sr.) was the funniest man on the planet. Everybody called him "Big Daddy". And he kept everybody laughing. I'm talking about laughing from the pit of your belly. And one day when I was 17 years old I finally got (Peggy Scott...she had headlights that stood up like mountain peaks. She had a ...) Peggy to give me the time of day. I brought her to meet Big Momma (Clara Jackson...rest in the bosom of the Lord) and Big Daddy. And (all my family calls me "die" or "die boo". But Big Daddy always called me "Die V.") Big Daddy came out of the clear blue sky and told Peggy, "Miss Peggy- How you getting along? Clara Belle don't know this but I once dated a lil gal that Die V dated." My jaw dropped and I wanted to run for cover. Peggy was transfixed. He proceeded "Wanna know how I met her?... I knocked on her door one night and she said "who is it?" I said 'I'm die V' and she said you don't sound like no Die V.' I say 'you know how Die V breath smell?' She say "Of course I do.' I say I'm a blow my breath through the keyhold on the door knob and you sniff and you'll know it's me Die V.' She say 'Okay blow it'. I turned around, backed my ass up to the door knob and let out a silent fart. She sniffed and said 'Yeah that's you Die V come on in"... Peggy almost fell out laughing and I was absolutely livid. Perhaps you are wondering what this has to do with K.K.K.? I'm glad you asked and the answer is absolutely nothing. I told this (true) story just to get a chuckle. The subject matter in this book is so serious, deep and perplexing that I just wanted to lighten the moment. Can I digress a bit more and ramble? Elizabeth Hasselback is a very, very, very attractive lady. I'm extremely attracted to madam Hasselback but her politics are absolutely ridiculous. She is an undercover Rush Limbaugh. She likes Sean Hannity. And I wonder has Sean ever told Liz or Rush about how I kicked his ass in a debate in Atlanta before he went to New York? And Atl. Host "Ralph from Ben Hill" routinely kicked Sean's butt. I dare Sean to put Ralph on his New York show. Anyway I still like Liz with her cute self. Joy is my buddy. A crazy Italian sister. I have a crush on Sherri and Whoopi is my real, authentic, in the hip pocket soul sista and (believe it or not I used to really dislike Whoopi) back when she didn't wanna be called "African American" I didn't like her. But thanks to Barbara Walters I've come to see just how smart, witty, analytical and pragmatic Whoopi really is. She is deep. The kind of deep that makes my toes tingle. The kind of deep that makes the hair stand up on my ... Ok I'm getting carried away but intelligence is a turn on for me. After I make love to a woman (an adult to whom I'm married. P.G.) I wanna be able to have a conversation yo. (Ok not right after but you know what I mean.) And Whoopi has brains. I also have an affinity for Whoopi because she reminds me (so much-they even look a little alike) of my mom's best friend Betty Jean. Betty Jean was the first woman I ever saw with a gun. She was an Atlanta street cop. She's now (I won't give her last name) a special agent with the F.B.I. in D.C. with top secret clearance. We don't even know what Betty Jean does. But I wish I could introduce Betty Jean to Whoopi. And (can you hear me now).Perhaps yall wanna know what's whoopi got to do with it (K.K.K)? Actually my Big Daddy story was one of those (cheesy) segues that Whoopi uses to go to a commercial break on "the view" and since I was being humorous I thought about my sistas (lizzy liz, Sherri she/Joy B and Whoopi ...And I remember "The View" played a clip of Governor Sarah Palin as she gave her Resignation speech and my God. I thought I could ramble and engage in tergiversation but Sarah? God bless her but she was rambling in such an inconsistent way that it was actually incoherent. And after the first clip aired even Elizabeth disowned her. But (you know Liz) after the second clip Liz defended (Ann Coulter) Palins right to say what she said and... After the clip aired when the cameras showed the ladies (I love them)Whoopi (crazy black woman) Goldberg was lying on the floor (literally) in a stupor. I laughed so hard I cried... I like Star Jones and she is a brilliant Lawyer. I like Star. But what had happened wuz (you feel me)? Star went on Oprah and did an excellent job. O.k. okay I think it was "stupid" (...No- I'm in Obama school so let me re- calibrate) – Rather I think it was "unwise" (not the "s" word) and "unnecessary" for Star to lie about the weight loss. She should have told the truth but which one of us has never engaged in spurious verbiage, mendacity or prevarication? But anyway I'm still down with Star- but the day after the Oprah interview Madam Walters did the classy thing and said that she thought Star did a good job and she asked `the ladies` what they thought of Star's apology. So I'm glued to my flat screen television and anxiously anticipating some kind of lukewarm , halfhearted and/or duplicitous endorsement from Joy and Lo and behold guess what my Italian sister said? Joy said (I'm falling off my stool picturing it in my mind) "well I think I'm gonna have to take a by pass on the apology no comment." Joy you so crazy...professor Henry "Skip" Gates the Harvard Scholar. Yall remember he was arrested in his own home (in Harvard Square) by Bull Connor? I'm sorry it was actually Sgt. Jim Crow Jr who took Professor Gates' cane from him and put him in jail. ..Alright I'm kidding about Bull and Crow. But he got arrested right? And you wanna know what I have to say about it? I take a "By Pass" on it period. I don't wish to elaborate on the arrest, the beer (hope it wasn't Old Milwaukee.. I heard our President likes Mad Dog 20/20) or any of that. What I would like to say is "thank ya" to professor Skip Gates! Why because most Harvard Scholars who have been all over the world, done Oprah,Tavis Smiley, Tom Joyner, Larry King etc. They never ever respond to prisoners mail and when I wrote "creating monsters" I wrote to Professor Gates and he actually took the time to write me back. I love him for that. And let me revert back to Whoopi. I just remembered she had a talk show and I wrote to her .She(it was probably her assistant) wrote me back. And even when a celebrity has a policy that their assistants should respond to prisoner mail it says something about the character of the celebrity. Believe me most people who are half as well known as Whoopi (and a fraction as rich)do not ever respond (and their assistants are instructed not to respond) to prisoner mail. Whoopi wrote me back Denzel Washington wrote me and sent me a photo (I wonder will Lizzy liz, Madam Lisa Ling and Sherri send a Brutha a picture). And yes Professor Gates took the time to write me back and my only other comment on Brother Skip is (with all do respect) his daughter Elizabeth is... A very attractive woman. She humorously did a blog titled "My Daddy the Jail Bird". I'm done (By Pass remember) with Professor Gates and Officer the Friendly now. But (as an aside) on the subject of " lets have a conversation on Race" per se. I have very mixed and conflicting views (I wonder what Whoopi thinks) ... I mean dialogue is always better than monologue. And the lines of communication should always be open. And (stay with me I'm going somewhere) I adamantly disagree with (one of my favorite columnists) Clarence Page who feels we no longer need the NAACP. I believe we still need the NAACP. Even as I recall the historicity of the NAACP which was actually Founded by Whites, Jews and one black founder. The NAACP (Just as the ADL, ACLU and the Southern Baptist convention) still has a seat at the round table. But (having said that) the reasons I'm not very excited about some kind of National (structured) discussion about 'Race' are three fold. A. A Dr. King stated. There is a paralysis which comes from too much analysis. In my opinion too often so-called 'committees' are long on rhetoric and short on substance or action B the White friend, relatives and in-laws. I have don't need a lecture on Race. And I certainly don't need a lecture on Race. When I come in contact with Biased, or prejudiced, (and there are distinctions between them each) or Racist people (White, Black or Mexican) I'm always willing to listen, talk, teach, learn, reach, analyze, elucidate and to understand. But in my view (just my opinion now) a national discussion will be more of a photo-op than anything. C. (and most importantly) even if President Obama is supporting such a discussion (and lord knows I'm down with my President 4 sure) etc. etc. It is the fact that Mr. Obama is President, the most powerful man in the free world etc. That is precisely my strongest argument for the lack of a necessity for this National Conversation...Hold on now. I love Attorney General Eric Holder and to say that I thoroughly agreed (I did/do) with the A.G.'s statement that America remains "A Nation of cowards" as it relates to "Race". It may sound contradictory if not diametrically opposed to what I said about not needing this "National discussion" but it is not. And I can hear my soul brothers in barbershops (bobbashops) all over urban America reminding me that just because Mr. Obama is sleeping in the white house doesn't mean racism is asleep. To that, I would also fully concur Jim Crow Jr is alive and well. Go to Cummings Georgia the out skirts of Alabama, Mississippi etc. I can show you institutional and systemic racism right here in the California Department of Corruption (I mean corrections). Racism did not go down for the count with the election of our Obama. But I'll be damn if it didn't sustain a hard right to the head... But lets go deeper (as we prepare to end my lenthy, segue and get back to K.K.K. pun intended). I believe we often miss the main point of who elected Obama and the why of it all. My grand mom (Dollie Manning) is a Christian and she is not racist. She and my grandfather (James Manning) had no problem when I asked "what will you think if I marry a white woman?" They are not racist. But – since they have lived 70 years or better they have the residue of Bull Connor, Jim Crow and bloody Sunday on their psyches. My grandmother called me an expert on Politics long before I ever met Andy Young or Rev. Hosea Williams. And she usually believes my commentary. But to my utter surprise neither she, nor James, nor Dr. Jarman, nor my friend (principal) Aaron Fernander, nor Vernon Jordan, nor Andy Young etc. believed Obama would win. They wanted him to. But please notice that everybody I named is over 70 years old. And even Aaron is 50 and Dr. Jarman is 61 years old. To put it simplistically most Americans (white, black and latino) 48 years or younger began to believe (fairly early-although not initially) that Obama could Barack the vote. Even simpler! The facebook (and myspace) generation believed he could do it and because they (my generation and younger) actually (finally) took their asses to the polls he won. And – I said all that to say this: I usually am very (extremely) suspicious of anyone bold (or optimistic) enough to use the term "post racial" I really don't feel comfortable with that term. Especially when I still hear (even with a black President) white boys calling blacks "N-gers"... but you know what? Millions of people in their 60's (even though 50 is the new 30) are not comfortable (or competent) with the information super highway. I know 60 year olds who couldn't send an E-mail if their life depended on it. Ipso Facto Vernon Jordan (I love Mr. Jordan) is a learned black man. He is a distinguished Attorney and he led Bill Clinton's (I gotta letter from President Clinton! Shameless boast) Presidential transition team (read his tome "Vernon can read") Mr. Jordan told Senator Barack Obama "it's not your time. It's not your turn"... and after Mr. Obama was elected, the elegant Attorney Jordan told Whoopi, Sherri (my "girls") Lizzy and Madame Walters "how wrong was I".

Can I bottom line it? If there is to be a National converstation on "race" I suggest that only people in their (black, white, latino and others) mid fifties (I'm serious) and older participate. Because (in my humble opinion)by and large better than 90% of the Facebook generation could not give a damn about the color of a man's skin period... End of segue and end of digression...

What in the hell led (if she did it) 14 year old Tylar Whitt (of El Dorado CA.) and her 19 year old Boyfriend Steven Colver to murder her own mother? First of all what is a 14 year old doing Booty Banging with a 19 year old? That is Child Molestion. I wonder why the D.A. had not charged Steven with Molestation. He should!

Tylar and Steven remind me of an 18 (18 or 19 when I met him) year old murderer I knew named Daniel Henson.(believe it or not) Jimbo and Rosario had both the Fratricidal Eric Menendez and the Fratricidal (or matricidal)Daniel Henson on the same yard (Facility A - New Folsom) simultanensly . Daniel looks like Anthony Federov but a bit more muscular. Daniel (admittedly) murdered his mom, dad, siblings and the dog ...He shot the damn dog! He was adopted and I recall looking into his deep blue eyes and saying "you should write a book Daniel you might be able to help some troubled kid". And his reply was a jaw dropper. He told me "Atlanta I don't give a damn about any troubled teens. I'll never get out and why I did it is simple. My girlfriend and I wanted to marry. My mom tried to break us up. So I killed them all I was 16. I killed em period... If I knew how to write a book I'd probably do it for the money but...will you help me write one?" Those were his words "verbatim". Then months later he suggested (half jokingly but Daniel was a difficult read) we cell together I would never ever contemplate celling with a person whom I knew killed his own family just because Sociopaths (ask Dr. Curren, Dr. Solis or Dr. Jeff Gardere) are complex. If they were not confusing, charming, gregarious and often undetectable we'd lock them all up before they kill. I.e. Daniel once assaulted his cell partner Richard Cruz because (according to Daniel) "he kept putting his ass in my face wearing tighty whities and he asked if he could... (orally copulate)...Yet a couple of months later he and I were speaking of a guy (Jason Voltaw) who celled with Daniel and called himself a Christian etc. Jason transferred to Mule Creek and Daniel told me "I miss playing grab ass with him. That Young fine white ass I got a boner just thinking about it". I told Daniel "first of all you R starting to sound like a gay boy and that boner crap is way too much information"... I ended up transferring to M.C.S.P. and 6 months later Daniel sent Will (Robert Williams) into 2 Bldg to tell me he (too) was now at M.C.S.P. Now I had (my luck) Daniel and Lyle Menendez on the same yard with me. Not to mention Mr. Bardo (aka "Arizona")...I could write at least five more long books detailing extensive conversations with Eric (at New Folsom and at P.V.S.P., Lyle,Daniel, Bardo and Ed

Stokes alone...I can't wait to talk to Frank Darabont, David E. Kelley or Denzel (Mundy Lane productions)...Hell maybe (if I keep on hanging out with teen serial killers and cold blooded murderers) I need to talk to Dr. Phil when he does another "ask the Bishop" show... Why yall think I've loaded the G.B.G. advisory board with brilliant psychologists and psychiatrists? After all the crap I've seen heard and lived amongst I need Dr. Harvard (Curren), Dr. Jarman, Dr. Duran, Dr. Houston, Dr. Gregg and Dr. Cathy Paicez... I need them and I approach them humbly. I'm a student. I finally grew up and realized how much I don't know... Just an hour ago a Chinese psychiatrists (Dr. Chen) came to my cage and said "Mista Manning you ever see movie `Mr. John?" It very good movie brilliant actor like you in movie... I hear so much stuff about how smart you are. Mr. Manning so many Doctors love to talk to you". If a medical Doctor had told me that 2 years ago I'd be on cloud nine for days if not weeks. But today I said "thank you Dr. Chen" and told him about Harvard psychiatrist Dr. Kay Jamison Graham and some books she wrote etc. When he left I prayed and asked God to help me to grow. There is so much I don't know. I am in awe of live, knowledge and inspiration. Then my challenge (as a writer, motivational speaker, preacher and author) is to figure out ways (and I'm still learning) to present life changing information in ways (i.e. edutainment, infotainment, etc.) that are interesting, gripping and exciting to read. And it is not easy. 90% of authors have Editors, ghost writers etc. I've never (ever) had an editor, ghost writer or any of that. I really write my books me myself and I ... (But I do need a Publicist)...I remember a psychiatric social worker (Chuck Christenson) at Mule Creek. I really liked Chuck. He was 74 years old. I asked why he hadn't retired yet and he said "enjoy answer. I'm broke . I'm just not very good with money". Anyway Chuck used to enjoy reading NAPS newsletters. But sporadically (and rightfully so) he'd complain that "Mr. Manning some times you write (hilarious) like a pharmacist. The data is so powerful but sometimes it reads like an encyclopedia". I received that and worked on it... "Doc" Ford always kids me about my long, long lists of names. One day I gave him a two page G.B.G. news letter and he said "the first page was awesome. You really can write. You got a helluva way with words. But the second page (I'm laughing now) was boring as f- -k. Page two was fifty names!! Hallelujah "(lol). Doc looked at me "Atlanta" where in the hell do you get all of these names? I said "next time I send you a newsletter I'll send a broom and dust pan". He said "broom and dust pan! For what"? I said "so you can sweep up all the names I drop"... I get his point . But A. people love to see their names in print B. I use lists of names so my G.B.G. Ambassadors and interns (and you) will google people like (Doc heres to you- Maxwell Hanger, David Quindt, Min, Edward Long, Garrett Mccain, Wendy Williams, Gabe Williams, Timothy Coleman, Carlo Rodriguez, Cesar L. Chavez, David Quattlebum, Judge Lynn Toler, Judge Karen, Judge Joe Brown, Max on T.M.Z. com, Dr. Nancy Kalish, Danny Noriega, Atty. L. Lonnell Mc Millan, M.C. Hammer, Serita Jakes and)...Daniel Sample and tell them to go to www.napsusa.org, facebook.com, amazon.com, www.cafepress.com/manning or to a local book store and get this book... But life, maturity, watching President Obama (literally) and studying self has helped me to grow up and to not believe my own "press" Mr. Obama was cool, contained, controlled and composed throughout, Attacks from the Clintons, the Republicans, the McCain/Palin crap "Paling around with terrorists" and... I'm serious, I'm teaching G.B.G. a class on "Obamology". Professor Dylan Rodriguez once told me (U.C. Irvine)... call him ... that "I teach my students from your books "Creating Monsters" and "From The Palace to The Prison". My students call the lectures "Manningology"... But remember I don't believe my own press... Diddy once stated that "I stalk Russell Simmons life. I learned how to run bad boy by watching Russell Simmons" and love or hate Diddy he's successful (financially). He's worth almost $ 1 Billion. So I challenge you (Republicans and Democrats) to study, watch, Analyze and Scrutinize our President. He is a Master Communicator. He never got too high when the polls said he had it. He never got too low when

(Rush Limbooty, Coulter and even my girl Lizzy) pundits said "never" older Blacks said "not yet" and the polls said he (not time) couldn't close the deal. He was measured, composed, calm and ...When Clinton said he was too black for paling around, Farrakhan. When Sharpton (oh I didn't forget) questioned whether he was black enough. When Limbaugh and the Republican National Committee had him on a seesaw. I.E. "too black = Jackson / Farrakhan". "Not black enough = white mother". Too mysterious i.e. paling around with terrorists etc. He stood erect, with dignity and respect (no yelling or acting "stupid"... Bad calibration? lol) and handled everything they threw at him like a champ. And now comes the right Rev.Jeremiah Wright... Initially I did not have a problem with 99% of the clips the media played over and over (like my name dropping). In context, knowing and being a black preacher I was not alarmed... But secretly I must admit that I began to doubt whether or not Obama could over come the distortion. Bill Moyers interviewed a learned, calm and elegant Rev. Wright on his show. The interview went well... But later Wright seemed to have gone crazy... I still love Rev Wright though and he's a great preacher... But I began to think that maybe Vernon Jordon was right and he might not pull it off. And then come his major speech "race" and I became like Thomas when he touched Jesus and said "now I believe"... And so David slayed the giant Goliath with a rock and a sling shot. And so Obama slayed Limbaugh, Hasselbeck, Coulter, McCain, Bush, Cheney, "Blue Dog Red Necks", Bull Connor, Jr. Jim Crow Jr. and 400 years of Racism with that speech. It was a work of art. It was what I call verbal akido to the tenth degree... After the speech I told Al Augustine "he did it bro. Barack Obama will be the next President of the United States of America". And Richard Singleton (a white brother) yelled to another murderer (Ronnie Ritter) that "that'll never happen, not in this country." Barack is flawed as am I (and you) and he will make mistakes. But the Brutha is bad. He is a consummate communicator. He's able to fight you without you knowing he's fighting. He's confident but not cocky. He loves himself but is not conceited. I'm still stalking him(not "Bardo"style), taking notes, growing and learning. Every kid, every juvenile, every student and prisoner ought to study his every word and gesture. And by all means learn how to fight. I'm speaking of mental toughness, spiritual and educational warfare. Education! Information! Education! Information!... As I said earlier you youngsters have seen some bad stuff. I'm serious! You kids have seen more (at 7,8,12,and 13) before puberty than some have seen after menopause. And Dr. Phil (or the distinguished panel of G.B.G. Therapists led by Dr. Curren) can tell you that you become what you see. You become what you say. You say what you hear Ipso Facto,you become what you hear, say and see. And when kids grow up seeing vicious murderers, horrendous rapes, beatings, stabbings, crack pipes, crysal meth, heroin, gangs and... Even kids in wealthy neighborhoods see dysfunctional (yet wealthy) families. Kids in Buckhead (Hotlanta) suffer just as bad as kids in Bankhead. Inner city pain metasticizes to suburbia and vice versa. I get so many E-mails and snall mails from kids of Physicians, Lawyers and entrepreneurs who are financially well off but spiritually and psychologically bankrupt. And when I peruse (meticulously) their missives I keep saying to myself "yall(kids) have seen some bad stuff. Too many rapes, too much pornography, too many predators too many gangs and guns, and pills, needles and dope but so little hope". I tremble when I think about what you have had to see, here, say and feel, "I'm sorry" maybe no adult has ever told you that. I know we are the therapists, clinicians, pastors, professors, preachers and teachers... We think we know it all.And you learned how to kill, steal, rape, rob. And take from us. We are the village and we've destroyed the children. No child is born with the innate desire to molest, rape, maim or murder. Lets deal with the root and not the fruit. I don't quite have the training Dr. Phil has. But after 21 years of deep study in psychology and 12 years of psychoanalyzing, interviewing, observing and even worshipping with serial killers, psychosexual deviants and child molesters etc. I've learned a little bit. And adults like to talk north and walk west. We are hypocrites. And on behalf of adult

Atlanta, adult Sacramento, adult America and even adult World. I apologies to teens I'm so sorry for the devastating, confusing, painful, tragedies that we have shown you. Some of you did not make a mistake but you were born into a mistake. But can I remind you of something? Can I remind you of a miracle? Just like you mesmerized, befuddled and bemused us by declaring a Facebook Jihad against the 43 (all white Presidents) that came `before`- and electing Barack as `44`. You can rise above your circumstance, predicament or incidents and school us again. May I suggest to you that you tap into that Facebook synergistic spirit and move our culture forward. Gone and play your video games, kick back and chill. But don't let the chill kill your ambition. Your vision, your dreams and your goals. While u chattin the sistas up on the internet don't forget that we still need a cure for cancer, Aids, multiple sclerosis, hate violence and... While you are cooling out and having fun don't forget to remember that you are the world. You are the future. You are the leader we've been waiting for ... Even though you've seen some bad stuff, some hatred, hurting, violence and drugs. Even though it looks bad you can still do great things if you believe in God and believe in yourself... Wow...

On 7/27/09 Dr.Phil reared his show in which he sent two teens (G.B.G./Heart) to San Quentin State Prison for their kids program. I want you to find Chris and Brett and send them (both) this book. And I extend an invitation to Brett, his mom, Chris and his mom to (call us at 916-985-8610 ext. 3042). Come to our G.B.G./Heart tour at New Folsom State Prison... I need my interns to find Brett and Chris and make certain they get this book. And Brett can even write me and I'll send him a gratis copy. I don't want Chris writing because he's only 16. (But Associate warden Schroeder earns $114,000 per year and is a Christian. Chris can call Mr. Schroeder and ask him for a gratis copy). But Brett is 19 so I want him to write... If you could write the the perfect script for your life what would it look like ? What do you really , really wanna be? Where do you wanna go? What do you want to do? And what's holding you back? You (literally) write your own script. The stuff you do, say, hear, think and believe today determines what you'll get and where you'll be tomorrow. It is as simple as defecation. If you eat ten hot dogs and drink a gallon of milk today- you will not crap hamburgers and piss coca- cola tomorrow. You get out of it (no bun or pun intended) what you put in it. Show me a 15, 16 year old who reads at least one book per week, studies hard, asks lots of questions, plays some sports. Stays fit, eats well, goes to church, mass or mosque etc. today. I'll show you the preachers, teachers, entrepreneurs, Firemen, physicians, policemen and judges of tomorrow. Barack reads lots of books. Bill Gates reads book, newspapers and periodicals. Caleb Sima, Oprah,Gayle King and Whoopi are readers... While (I'm being a smart ass) the nation prepares to hold a "National Conversation on race". I suggest you skip (record it) the discussion and instead hold a youth G.B.G. summit, a job summit, a reading summit, a youth conference or a "conversation" on gangs, guns, drugs and violence"...

I want you to study the lives, careers, habits and the minds of successful people. Everybody in California knows famed bail bondsman, bounty hunter and businessman Leonard Padilla. (I disagree with him on some issues) He is a great man and he helps a lot of people. I plan to have a G.B.G. outside coordinator contact Mr. Padilla soon. I know Senator Burton will be donating 20 or 30 copies of this book to an inner city school in San Francisco. Maybe we can get Mr. Padilla to donate 25 copies to a Sacramento juvenile and 25 copies to a Sacramento high school. He just might do it. Yall don't make me launch another hunger strike. I'll be like "Hollywood" Henderson. When he got ready to build a youth center for kids he sat down and refused to eat until businessmen gave him the money to build it. I want folks to go online (www.napsusa.org) , buy 10, 20,100 or 1000 copies of this book and we'll inundate schools, colleges, chuches and juveniles with this book. People like Leonard Padilla know game (and con) when he sees it and he can weed through bull shit. Just like John Burton. I wonder where is

Mayor Willie Brown? We need to get Mr. Brown,Murray Morgan and Garrett McCain (both in Sacramento CA.) this book I want somebody to buy all 100 U.S. Senators this book. Because just as Sen. Burton says they all need this book. Speaking of Senate Pro Tem President (Ret) John Burton etc. He's a magical politician that all of you college and high school students would be smart to study...If you can see it you can be it. Fill your mind with the good, the clean, the pure, the powerful and the positive... Join G.B.G./Heart as an outside ambassador. We have a battery of convicts from around the nation who are inside coordinators. We need more outside and internet assistance. Its difficult getting prisoners to work together around anything worthwhile. I set up G.B.G. Reward Systems and structures in which bad people are coerced if not forced to do good.

Getting Fred (a good man) to grasp this brilliant (I'm not just tooting my own horn here. Candidly, Dr. A. Duran, Adam Lane, Dr. C Solis, Peter Andrist and Dr. Frank Curren all consulted with me on developing this system. G.B.G./Heart is a team.) Strategy was difficult at first. This was not his fault. The strategy was so complex that it was difficult to explain. And none of us agree (fully) on process. All of us agree we must do something to help save just one. My paradigm is influenced by my circumstances but not limited by them. I went into G.B.G./Heart as a pragmatist. I said "many guys will jump on the band wagon just for something to do, hoping for a pardon, a parole or a penpal." Ipso facto, I asked Fred to stipulate (and have us agree because by law we can correspond with anybody in the world) that no team member can correspond with any kid who comes here after they leave. This prevents what Mr. Burton calls "hanky panky". I told Jimbo "I need a battery of experts (psychiatrists) to monitor us." Jimbo said "Can you get a doctor or two to help?" I said "Try 7 or 8-yes."

...Ipso facto, our advisory board etc...No inmate is ever alone with a kid. Every session is videotaped to memorialize it and for security. Johnny Willie, Billy, Doc Ford, Butler, Peck and other team members all contributed great input to our program. Billy and Steve Vance tried to con (lol) me into learning to type so I could actually relieve Billy. Billy may be the hardest working convict at New Folsom. He types stuff for Captain Vance, M.A.C. (Men's Activity Council), Fundraising campaigns for the needy and tons of other stuff. But I can't type. I don't like that word "can't"/

...But the steps of our team members were ordered. And we practice and practice. ...I told Jimbo (aka Warden Walker) "I need a couple of youngster staff members like Adam Lane, Daniel Bugriyev, Dustin Nicolodi, C.O. T. Ramsey and C.O. Hodge to be silent observers when the kids come in. It's a show of G.B.G. force and unity. And the kids psychologically find comfort with these youngsters trailing us. Plus it provides more eyes and ears for you and security." Jimbo said "You want me to try to talk these staff members into helping us?" I replied 'they have all agreed already. I just wanted your opinion." And he said "dude do you ever sleep? You are manicy as hell."

...My hidden philosophy going in was 'you can't cast a play in hell (a maximum security pen) and expect (as I wrote earlier) the actors to be angels. So while some well meaning people would murmur "Don't let him join cause he is a liar. He's in it just for publicity" or "his heart ain't" right. My input was as Jesus said "whosoever will let him come." In my private meetings with Jimbo I said "as long as no kid gets raped, stabbed or assaulted the session is a success. And with 5-10 staff (including Dr. Duran and Dr. Solis) with us at all times, high powered cameras that are super-sophisticated...nobody can get raped, maimed or assaulted. And if Fred or Steve even try to get away from me I'll scream and run." Walker started laughing. "I'm serious Jimbo as long as I am in direct earshot and eyeshot of Fred and/or Steve it's good for you, good for the kids and good for me. To do a special interaction like this you go in suspicious of everybody. And we cover everybody with rules written in stone, security, strategy and transparency. I don't care if my guys lie or embellish. I don't even (just being candid) care whether the convict has ulterior motives or not. My litmus test is a can his input (be it a crook or a testimony) help the kids? B. What are the chances he might reach just one kid? If his input (good, bad, indifferent, Christian, Agnostic or Atheist) can benefit kids and if he can communicate (like a thug, a scholar or a Klansman) and the warden says he's in, he's in. The only person who can say no is you…and when you set it up so security is solid, convicts are managed, monitored and recorded it's as fool proof as it can be." You wanna know Jimbo's input? "Ok make sure you tell Fred, I'll see you tomorrow." That's Jimmy…

I want ya'll to find Phillip Brurelle (in Massachusetts), Martin "Alex" Kurzer and Ricky Harlow, Chad Newman (GA.), Joey Grissett (VA.), Christopher Durbin (GA.), Michael Wilkerson (GA.), Nathan Gould (C.S.P.), Christopher Parker (C.S.P.), Danny Macky (C.S.P.), Kyle Larsen, Garrett Cunningham (Texas), Andrew Squire (Stockton), Eric Nies, Andrew Bridge, Chris Clubb, Omar Samaha and tell them They're in KKK and GBG needs them. I need believers and doers. The good book says "the kingdom suffers violence and the violent take it by force." I need me some violent (G.B.G.) men who are ready to make a move. You can't help launch an idealogical, philosophical and technological Jihad against crimes by youth and crimes against youth if you won't bust a move. I'm looking for some sons who will stand up, square their shoulders and fight. Fight to get out of poverty. Fight to get off of welfare. Fight to get into Harvard. Fight to start a new business. Fight to win. Fight. I need some young gung ho men who can put two and two together and come up with four. I need some youngsters who can think their way out of a paper bag. Don't get it confused Baby Boy G.B.G. is a force to be reckoned with. We have the best Warden, a Harvard G.B.G. director, a great associate warden, Mrs. Kennedy, C.O. Diana Smith, CC III Johnson-Dovey, Professor Kevin Pool, Barbara Brooks, Alex Friedmann, (Award winning journalist) Silja J.A.-Talvi and you. I need some youngsters like Caleb Sima, Gabe Williams (Sacto CA), Luke Sears and Kyle Love who will stand up and fight. Fight the temptation to use (or re-use) drugs, join a gang (the only gang you're in is G.B.G.), to stab, rob or kill. I need fighters. Where are my soldiers, my fighters, my sailors, my G.B.G. (Green Beret Gangsters) and my special forces? We need you to come out of the shadows and take a stand for literacy. Take a stand for writing, for fighting. Take a stand for young entrepreneurs…

…A 2008 report by the Schott Foundation for public education concludes that "black males have consistently low educational attainment levels, are more chronically unemployed, are less healthy and have access to fewer health-care resources, die younger, and are many times more likely to be sent to jail for periods significantly longer than males of other racial/ethnic groups". The study also reported that more than 50% of black males do not graduate with their high school class and the 10 states with the lowest graduation rates –including New York, Illinois, Georgia and Michigan-enroll more than 1.6 million black male public school students, roughly 40% of that population. Other reports reveal that 75% of college age African American men are not registered at any institution of higher learning, and that one is nine black males ages 20-34 incarcerated…And by 2041 white people will be the new minority (guess the NAACP will help them in 41) in good ole America. Those dry statistics are alarming. I see why Bill Cosby, Dr. Alvin Poussaint and Ben Jealous are so concerned. This is bad. If they wanna have a "national discussion" let's have a "national discussion on education". I guarantee Mr. Obama that Arnie Duncan can count on Bill Gates, Bill Cosby, Warren Buffett, Dr. Poussaint, Professor Gates, Dr. Naim Akbar, Dr. Solis (for G.B.G.), Tyra, Wendy Williams, Whoopi, Bev Smith and Gayle King at this meeting. I'm appealing to first lady Michelle Obama to get in on this "discussion". We need an educational summit. There is a definite, direct correlation between a good education and the lack of incarceration. Educated people rarely join gangs. Rarely go to jail or prison. Oh baby boy I wish I had the touch, the talent, the skills and the know how to make this (need for your ass to learn how to read, write, think, reason, visualize, etc.) educational need as interesting as a John Grisham novel. James Patterson, Scott Turow, Verone Kennedy and Caroline Kennedy, I need some help you all...

And I need readers to text Judges Joe Brown, Greg Mathis, Lynn Toler, Pirro, Christina, Judy, James Long, Thelton Henderson and Glade Roper and tell them about this book. Judge Roper can give it to some of those youngsters in drug court out in Tulare County. (Great Whoopi like Segue? I'll take it but let me digress a moment on Whoopi girl. The only time Whoopi gets on my last nerve is when she does the 'Valley Girl' accent. I absolutely hate it.) Mentioning Judge Roper, ironically his son was fresh out of Medical School at U.M.C. Hospital (in Fresno) and Dr. Glade Roper Jr. saved my life. When my body (see "Blue Eyed Blonde" book II and "Left for Dead") was ravaged with disseminated valley fever. I'll never forget Dr. Glade Roper, Dr. Libke, Dr. Erica Kasper, Dr. John McCray, Dr. James, Dr. Fontaine and Dr. Paul Griffin. End of segue....

...I wanna holler at the twitter, Myspace and Facebook generation again about the steps of a good man. That includes ladies also. (Ladies do me a favor; you all watch 'General Hospital' day after day. Who is 'Michael'? Get his real name and e-mail it to my office asap.). If you thugs, bromantics, nerds, geeks, jocks, freaks and gangstas don't believe anything else I write. Please believe me (on everything that I love and hold dear) when I write (via tautological repetition) that the steps of a good man. Not the steps of a perfect (ain't none of us perfect bro.) man... Not the steps of the best man. But it says the steps of a good man. And wait, it did not say the jumps, the leaps or the flights. We gotta take life step by step. And you won't make it out of a gang, out of the barrio, off of prescription drugs etc. via an elevator nor an escalator. But there are steps baby girl. Leonard Padilla did not become a multi, multi, multi millionaire overnight. I need to tell Mr. Padilla's whole story in one of my tomes etc. His story is mind blowing, earth shattering, awesome and it's amazing. Mr.Padilla reminds me of Gerry Spence and of Rev. Hosea Williams in a strange kind of way. I wanna get Leonard, John Burton, Bishop Jakes, Amy Fihn and Hollywood Henderson to tape lil 6 minute clips for Warden Walker's G.B.G./Heart D.V.D.'s and C.D.'s.

But the point is success is not instant. And I can speak truth to power from an intimate point of view on the subject of wanting too much too soon. Madam Patricia Kennedy can attest to the fact that one of my strongest traits is my energy, work ethic and my focus. And Mrs. K can also attest to the fact that one of my weakest traits is my energy, work ethic and my focus. God ordered my steps back to New Folsom because I needed Mrs. K, Fred, Steve and Jimbo. See you need some folk around you who will tell you the truth. Mrs. K will tell me "You always want too much too quickly. You want instant gratification. You move, think, process and create quicker than anybody I know. It's a blessing and a curse. You can intimidate, frustrate and alienate (friends and foes alike) others if you're not careful. Slow down." And you can even utilize criticism and/or haterism to grow. People who often disagree with you and seem to disrupt you can actually propel you into your destiny. At the very back of this tome you shall peruse some (real time) G.B.G. memos, missives and newsletters that will show you how we did it. You'll see proposals, struggles, egos, attitude, testosterone, trials and tribulations. I was tempted to leave some stuff out. But I was humbled when I looked back and saw how (through the pain, fear, sorrow, setback, hurt, tears and the stress) almighty God had situated and orchestrated the events of my life to put me in a certain place, at a certain time to do this work. My journey has been hella crazy. And you can now use my messing as a blessing. You can learn from my errors and trials. One of the most unique, powerful and terrifying things about my vantage point as a criminal. A thug, a convict and a prisoner is that I've lived with every shade and grade of crook, crip and criminal you can imagine. I've seen the nuances, idiosyncratic whims, the mental tics and the... There's a great book by Steve Covey "The 7 Habits of Highly Effective People". I've learned "7 Habits of Highly Effective Prisoners." And they are lessons on how not to live life. I'm in hell remember and this book is written in B-L-O-O-D. I could be dead by the time you read this tome. I placed my life at risk by some of the contents of this book. The blood of inmate "Hollywood" Walters (see "Blue Eyed Blonde" book II) who was set up by a C.O. and murdered by a celly (Ronnie Ritter) is spread across the pages of this tome like a thick fog. The blood of my Latino buddy inmate Rocky Salazar who was murdered by his celly (Frank Christian) while the control cop played dominos is in this tome. Watching, witnessing and living murderdom mayhem, hatred and asylums is haunting, chilling and spooky. Dr. Terry Kupers (author of "Prison Madness") writes about the psychological effects of prisons and prison lockdowns. Dr. Franklin Curren told me "Being in prison Shu (segregated housing units) programs, lengthy lockdowns, prison riots and prison per se is similar to being in the war in Iraq. Inmates in MS13, Nuestra Familia and the Aryan brotherhood etc. are 'soldiers' carrying on Jihad, tribalism and mob hits inside concrete walls. Sherman residing in these walls takes a severe psychological and traumatic toll on 90% of the inmates who come here; especially the kids...Having known you (Sherman) for 11 years you are the exception to the rule. Your defiance, drive, persistence and determination has made you a man...Most people don't want to be seen near a shrink." This Harvard M.D. continued "You've made it almost cool to be around us.. And when I met you your aim was to dominate conversations in order to showcase your intellectual apparatus. However, now all you do is question, question and question. It's like we know you're a walking questionnaire. But we also know you're using these data to reach kids."

Prison smells a certain way. It sounds a certain way. It feels a certain way. And Dr. Curren was absolutely right by saying it takes a psychological toll on all of us. You should study the writings on the Menendez brothers (in this tome), on Daniel, Bardo, Stokes etc. You each will get something different out of it. But I advise you gangstas, wiggers, thugs, and studs to study this data. There is a common thread which I've detected in each and every sociopath (Eric, Lyle, Daniel, Ed, Bardo, Marvin, etc.) whom I've met. Even Lisa Ling told Oprah about a penetrating and a sort of unusual glare she saw in Eric's eyes when she was at New Folsom. (I wonder if Lisa knows the cop Celsa Zamudio who escorted her is no longer with the department). There is something hidden behind the eyes of every killer, every molester and every psychosexual deviant. And we as a nation need to study it, to prevent, detect, and ameliorate and to eliminate it...

And you ought to do any and everything you can to position yourself so that you'll never risk coming to a place like this W.I.T. Whatever it takes to not come here. Don't come here. Don't do it. Don't take a gamble on the rest of your life. Prisons are full of (credit card scammers, con artists, petty thieves, meth addicts and drug dealers) people who (good people) were felled by the desire for "instant gratification" which usually leads to "eventual incarceration". And when good people do bad things to try to get ahead etc. you end up in prison living with Menendez and me and we will ruin you for life. By the time we finish conning, playing, trapping, beating, stabbing, raping and taking you-if you do make it out you will be a 'good for nothing', corrupted , diseased son of a (excuse my French) b_tch!

...My fellow Americans I want to repeat that your steps are ordered. (call 1-800-bishop-2 and get "Nothing just Happens" by T.D. Jakes)... So I had to be lied on by Alonso, locked up by Lt. Johnston, laughed at by Sgt. Stratton etc.etc. I had to sleep on a floor for more than a month etc.etc. When I was called to a hearing before Judge Ingeeman I was escorted up a flight of steps by C.O. Bob Compton and I hadn't walked anywhere in 42 days. And my knees completely gave out and I would have completely gave out and I would have busted my butt if

Bob hadn't caught me. "Sherman dude you are wasting away. You gotta get out of C.T.C." Bob said…In the court hearing (we had court at the prison with a real, fair Sacramento Superior Court Judge) I saw that CCII Sal Goldman was there. So were Dr. Johnson, prosecuting attorney Davies, Judge Ingamin and my lawyer Robert Freeman. I'd been assured that inmates never win those hearings and in fact I'd initially refused to attend. Dr. Johnson told me it was a formality and an exercise in futility. I ended up showing up and I talked more than Mr. Davies, Freeman and Dr. Johnson…At the end of the hearing Judge Ingeeman startled the courtroom by stating "I think Mr. Manning said it best…Mr. Davies I find your petition to be lacking and I'm gonna deny your petition against Sherman D. Manning. …Now off the record Mr. Manning let me know when your next book comes out "…Sal told me "Good f_cking job dude we never lose these. You kicked their ass." They finally lost one.

But I'm still here in prison. And my job is to sound the alarm to you and to yell "Fire" with a controversially and flamboyantly titled book called K.K.K. Fire! Fire! Fire!

Christopher Kerney (W. Milford N.J.), Phillip Burelle (Fall River, MA), Seamus Farrow, Ricky Harlow, Stacey DeWitt, Kupono and David Zablotay need to hear this word "Fire". I'm yelling at the top of my lungs and this book is my bullhorn to transmit one word to Tadd Carr, Van Jones, John Fink (CSU Sac. Junior), Riley Evans (Davis CA), Musical Charits, Bill Dallas, Jason Huyck, David Quattlebum and Antwi Akom etc. "Fire". The w-o-r-d-s in this essay from hell shall continue to yell (and to dispel any myths about their being anything flip or cool about the "joint"). "Fire" in your ear in your heart and in your spirit.

I tell our G.B.G./Heart attendees that "Welcome to hell! I won't play the game of intimidation or physical confrontation with you today. That's not how we do it…Murder, rape, child molestation, psychosexual murderer, armed robber, drug addict, drug dealer etc.etc. I just named seven crimes for you. And you will see all of the aforementioned at this prison today. I'm one of them. Don't be fooled and don't get it conflicted. To be here at this level four prison means I have been convicted of a serious crime. Some guys on this team today will freely tell you about their conviction. And that's a good thing to do. I will not ever allow you up in my personal business by talking about my "conviction". To be safe, if I were you I'd assume the worst. But I will talk about crimes which I did do and got away with. And I am articulate (as are all team members)…Although I'm Sherman D. Manning the author of 9 books etc. I am not a nice guy. I have done some bad things…You are in the most dangerous position you will ever be in your whole life right now. This is real stuff…I want you to do me a favor and then I'm gonna present the other experts (Willie, Fleming, Ford, etc.) to you and they'll talk. But I want you to do me a favor and imagine that it is 11:00 pm and you are locked in a small concrete cage on your rack. It's dark, its hot, you're sweating and you're afraid. And this guy that you've never seen before in your life. This guy whom you would never ever speak to you on the streets of Sacramento, Folsom, Carmichael or Citrus Heights etc. This dude that they have locked you in this room that we are showing you-he gets up and stands by your bunk with a 6 inch blade and tells you to 'suck, f_ck or die.' What would you do? You'd fight right? Well empirical data tells us and you can feel free to ask Captain Vance, A.W. Schroeder, C.O. Ramsey or C.O. Hodge and they will tell you most guys cry and they scream. And please imagine that you are screaming and all of your neighbors (in hell) begin screaming to drown out what's being done…You can become a tier whore, used and abused. All of a sudden you belong to somebody now…I got one question for you dude and that is this: Is this how you want to spend the rest of your life? It's your decision not mine. Not Dr. Solis, not Dr. Curren, Dr. Duran and not Dr. Phil. It's your decision. Look around you and tell me this- is "this what you want to die doing?…"

That's how I generally begin my spiel. Madam A. Duran Ph.D told me once "they should give you a pardon just for coming up with the name G.B.G. and Heart". She is a great mind but let me be clear: I've a letter of commendation for G.B.G. in my file signed by the Warden. I have hundreds of Laudatory Missives (a few are in this book) from elected officials, scholars, pastors, judges and heads of state. I'm humbled and I receive them on behalf of my team.. But without equivocation my service in G.B.G./Heart must never, ever be utilized as a bargaining chip or a get out of jail free card. My conviction should be dealt with by the courts and by the evidence (i.e. Brett Nelson the last witness)-and my conviction can never be camouflaged or interwoven with my G.B.G. mission. I seek no pardon! Not based upon G.B.G. What qualified and equipped me to serve in G.B.G. were the crimes I did do, the lies I did tell and my deathbed experience...

Your steps are ordered. (I repeat) I would not (I promise you) be writing these w-o-r-d-s if I had not been disrupted, uprooted, mistreated and locked up.

Can I tell you this? God (the creator, universe or whoever you believe in) often must get you by yourself before He can bless you or give you a breakthrough. Time after time after time, the good book says "and after Jesus was alone", and "Jesus went by himself and prayed" and Christ told the disciples to "wait here while I go (alone) and pray". I think it was Abraham (could have been Isaac but it's in Genesis) who told some youngsters to "stay here with the asses" ...I had to get away by myself so God could reveal himself and show me some s-e-c-r-e-t-s...

Fire! Fire! Hell! Hell! Stay away from jail. Still, I yell...now that I've delivered G.B.G./Heart and K.K.K. to you it's time to bust a move...You are not waiting on God. God is waiting on you. Faith without works is dead. Get up and move. G.B.G. is about soldiers and soldiers move. Ya'll see the G.B.G. logo (thank you Peter)? We have swords and the good book is our sword. We deleted our knives and now we use (the word) words. It's dark out there so we need the word which is a lamp unto our feet and a light to our path.

When you get some light you can see the fight. Fight poverty! Fight crime! Fight drugs! Fight illiteracy! Fight disease! Fight! Fighting requires action and movement...The book of Psalms (in the sword) opens up (from the gate) in Psalms 1:1. By saying blessed is the man who "walks" not in the "counsel" of the ungodly...you need to walk (action) but be careful who you walk with. "Nor stands in the path of sinners". I learned to get out of the way. Folk who wanna smoke till their lungs are black, use meth, Coke or heroin etc. I get out of their way...but look at the words "walks" and "stands". And it says "nor sits in the seat of the scornful". I run from scornful people. They are like a pandemic. And if you sit (down) in the seat of the scornful it implies that you plan to (get comfortable) be there a while. Get up and move...You can't be passive or inactive if you want to succeed. Even in St. Luke (17:11-19) Jesus went to Jerusalem and passed through Samaria and Galilee. And He strolled through a village and "there met Him ten men who were lepers, who stood afar off". And they "lifted up their voices (there's nothing that can't be done G.B.G., if we lift our voice as one) and said, "Jesus, Master, have mercy on us". The bible says "so when He saw them."....Hold it, that implies that they saw Him first. That's why the book says to "Watch, keep and pray". Some of you have not, because you ask not. You've got to start looking. Open up your eyes. Wake up and start back looking for a way out of no way. Start looking for a way to learn, to teach, to reach, to beat the odds and to get up. Look for it...But oh baby, baby, baby it's so special when God sees you. I want him to see me, I want Him. So it says that "When He saw them, He said to them, "Go"......tell yourself to "go".

He didn't spit on them and make clay with dirt. He didn't even lay hands upon them. But He spoke. And that's all you need is for God (through me, through G.B.G., through K.K.K.) to speak a word for your situation. It will prevent your incarceration. You may not ever hear from Oprah, Tyra, Dr. Phil or from Obama. But God can speak to you from the lips of your momma...All you need is a word from God...WOW! I feel the roof about to blow off this place.

My toes are tingling. I feel good right now...So Jesus told these outcasts, these losers, these sick and dying men. He told them to "Go, show (yourselves) to the priests." And watch closely in the latter clause of the 14th verse and it says that "As they went". Did you get it? God is a God of action! Sometimes he doesn't heal you instantly sometimes He won't even lay his hands on you. He'll just speak a word. And even after He speaks you have to do...It didn't say "and they were healed'. It specifically and precisely states that after He spoke a word over their pain, their hurt, their health and their death that "as they went, they were cleansed". At first Jesus didn't even see them and they were chasing (walking toward the Christ) a miracle. But after Jesus saw them they walked away and the miracle was chasing them. And with every step they took they got better. And you've been spoken to by this book written in the belly of the beast, in the den of the Sodomites and termites. You have been spoken to God has used a broken, low down, stuttering, stammering, conning, conniving and crooked writer to elucidate the conditions of Hades (hell) for you to see. And it is of He and by Him that I speak and not of myself. And this book has been sent to you in your jail cell, given to you by a teacher, a preacher, a convict, a shrink or a bounty hunter just because your God is ready to speak a word over your hurt, your sorrow, your pain, Your addiction, your conviction, your affliction, your problem, your destiny and your desires and that word is= "Go"...Go!...There is still some extremely important stuff forthcoming. Teens and tweenies-read on....Status update: Have you read about the riots at (if not read on) the prison in Chino? I just learned (today at the last minute so I'm inserting this outside of chronological order.) More about the why of the riot? Why? The big "I" word meaning "integration". Wow! This is some crazy stuff. I write a lot about the backwards, 1950's ways of the California Prison System in other books (including "Creating Monsters" and "From the Palace to the Prison"). I was given some confidential (prisons are full of secrets. Ask Linda McFarlane, David Specter or Human Rights Watch) details about the riot. My confidential source has been in corrections for 38 ½ years. Are you ready for the low down? (Go view Dr. Phil's show where Brett and Chris told San Quentin inmates that "I like black people" and the prisoners told them "That (liking black people) will get you killed in prison!")...A prison guard started a debate between black and white inmates about the president (honorable Barack Obama) being black, the professor Skip Gates arrest etc. And when a latino inmate joined the black (minority) side of the debate the guard began pushing every (race) button. He threatened to force the hispanic guy to cell (bunk) with the "blacks" since he loved Barack and Gates so much. Per a federal court order C.D.C. was supposed to integrate celling (prison managers secretly oppose this due to their vested interest in prison rivalries and racism) two years ago. It has not happened. Blacks still cell with blacks and whites with whites etc...So the bottom line is "Sherman a prison guard started the riot and the media thinks it was just a gang thing. It started about Obama and Gates and then turned into an all-out riot over integration. Public estimates are around $6.5 million for the riot. Privately I'm hearing this guard is gonna end up costing tax payers $8 million....Sherman do you think your President will invite the guard and the inmates to the white house for a beer? ...Will pundits suggest a national convention on prison racism?" My source stated. I would love (I'm so tempted) to reveal the name and rank of my source. But my "word" is my bond. The person refused (claimed they didn't know it) to give me the name of the guard...WOW! And there is way, way more to this story that my source is not telling me. I've long known there are deep racist groups within C.D.C. Folk like Lt. Scarsella and Sgt. R.N. Saunders were in known militias. Both Lieutenants Massey (Ret.) and Fmr. Lt Reed (ex special investigations Lt.) told me years ago "These white people in C.D.C. will murder you if you write too much about them."...When we do G.B.G. tours I never discuss my conviction and I never discuss my political opinions of C.D.C. corruption. It is not fear but respect. Warden "Jimbo" Walker does not share my negative views of the department. Ipso facto, he asked me early on to "keep your views of the department out of our tours. I won't limit your free speech and artistic expression in your extracurricular vehicles. But when the kids are in my institution and the cameras are rolling your only job is to try to turn them around." Therefore I never (ever) use the G.B.G. Bully pulpit to argue my case or to engage in tirades against staff. But this (K.K.K) is a tome not a tour. And I want to be clear: teachers are being laid off in California. The public school system is on life supports and the plug on the life supports has been pulled. Calif. Public schools' life support system is being powered by a generator. Yet guards (the kind of vicious guards like Wally Tucker, Brumbaugh and D.L. Criner) at Chino are instigating youth prisoner riots. And the guard incited riot will cost the California John Q Taxpayer over $8 million! This kind of bull crap keeps me up at night! I am not a prison rights activist (believe it or not). I could care less about the rights of Menendez, Bardo, Peterson, Jesse James Hollywood or Manning. The rights I give a damn about are Sasha Groene, Elizabeth Smart and Sandra Cantu etc...These are our children! And why can't we get Chuck Grassley, Newt Gingrich, Mr. Issa and the freaking media to see how prisons such as Chino are (absolutely) training, schooling and are grooming the next Menendez Bros, the next Scott Petersons, the next Jesse James Hollywoods and the next Charlie Mansons. This child raping and child murdering thing is personal for me. It's very personal! When I was a kid (at home in Atlanta) we had a nationally recognized horror story in Atlanta. 29 black boys (my age) were snatched off the streets sodomized and axphixiated! I was tapped by Mayor Maynard Jackson and Senator Grace Davis (with Atl. Youth against crime) to lead 21 prayer vigils. And a march for our kids. Texas Mayor Lee Brown was with us. And I had death threaths on my life. It was the first time in my young life that I was afraid. Afraid the killer(s) would kidnap, sodomize and kill me (too). But big James Scott Manning told me not to stop marching and speaking out. He told me that what I was doing, as a boy leader in Atlanta, was just as important as what Rosa Parks did in Alabama. So in spite of the indiscreet news media giving out my home address and school name I went on anyhow. But I promised myself that when I grew up, I would work like hell to prevent any kid from having to go to bed scared of being kidnapped, molested or murdered. Until now I have failed miserably at keeping that promise. I was too busy playing games, conning, conniving and living the life of a playboy. I admit (hands down) that I failed! But valley fever, almost dying, Sandra Cantu and Casey Anthony caused my "promise" to haunt me in my own sleep. I owe this book to Sandra Cantu. I owe it to Sasha Groene, Elizabeth Smart and to every child victim. I owe this book to the 29 (twenty nine) murdered and missing boys of Atlanta that I promised to work for. This (K.K.K) cashes (G.B.G.) that check (or promissory note) that I wrote (with Mayor Jackson, Mayor Brown and Senator Davis) for kids in 1979. It took me a while and it's been a long time coming but (finally) a change has come. The creator will anoint you for "such a time as this". Esther (in the good book) was not effective until God got her to her assignment. All the tricksterism, lying, conniving and schemes I ran? It was not my time. I had the right gift for the wrong (time) occasion... So when I see hundreds of youngsters rioting over race last month (Aug. 2009) in Chino. My gift operationalizes and kicks in. And criminologists and statisticians indicate that more than 320 of the 400 (plus) participants in the riots-will be in the streets-in less than 12 months. That's what haunts me. Knowing that over 320 followers, losers, drug addicts and traumatized "boys" will be out in your community; that's frightening...My duty, expertise and calling is to paint that character sketch or the portrait of those 400 plus boys who were rioting over race in Chino last month. I've been supernaturally positioned and divinely assigned to paint this portrait for students at Locke High School, Lodi, McClatchy and at Folsom high schools etc. I am qualified (in enough dirt, low enough, corrupted and I'm in the mix enough) to paint this portrait across the canvas of your mind with professional probity; and with authenticity.

The boys (your peers, your neighbors and your siblings) who were manipulated into bloodying, battering and murdering each other at Chino last month were lost boys. Whenever I see "kids killing kids" I'm transfixed and (mentally) transported back to Atlanta in 1979. ...The boys in Chino (like some of the boys around your neighborhood) were/are lost and blind. The brain shuts down in gangs and the mental infestation of "group think" overrides...Reporters and staff are mesmerized by what Fred, Steve, Jimbo, Patricia and our G.B.G. team have been able to do. And I'm asked over and over "how did you get Senate Pro Ten President John Burton on board?" The reason Senator Burton, Peter (in Switzerland), Leonard Padilla (hopefully), Cameron Johnson, Bloods, Crips, Skinheads and captains are willing to work together in G.B.G. is because nothing unites people better than a common enemy. Fred, Dr. Curren, Dr. Solis, Willie, Ford, Billy and I all have a common enemy (="kids killing kids" Kids killing adults and the adults who molest and kill kids)...and it is this common enemy that's gonna unite you (students from Elk Grove CA.-to Atlanta GA.) with us (G.B.G.)...The boys in Chino (who may already be back on the streets by now) have no vision. Their dreams and visions have been broken and lost. And a man can lose his mother and still succeed. A man can lose his woman and still make it. But there is nothing more dangerous and more infectious than a boy/man who has lost his vision. The visionless man becomes bitter, angry and scornful. And he's more contagious than pneumonia and the swine flu combined. This book is strategically, methodically and divinely inspired to reignite your vision. Man was created by God from the soil, the dust and the dirt of the earth. Ipso facto, God fashioned man from the elements of the earth because man is the foundation (the backbone) of the human family. And if a house has a cracked window, a blown light or a broken door the government will not condemn it. But if the foundation of a house is damaged the government will condemn. That house and any building is only as strong as the foundation. So what I saw at Chino were 400 plus condemned boys!! With more than 2.5 million in prisons in America (more than 49% of whom are boys 7-19 years young) I see prisons as a mission field with (at least) 1.7 million lost, visionless, incarcerated and condemned boys. And if the boyz in the prison were not getting out we'd simply kill each other. But America is already trying (and failing) to incarcerate our way out of crime. We already incarcerate more of our people, at younger ages, for more crimes than any country in the world (including Russia!). And even with exorbitant and draconian laws (i.e. CA had 12 prisons and 19,000 inmates in 1970. CA has 33 prisons and 173,000 inmates now!) America still releases more than 65,000 visionless, bitter, uneducated condemned boys from prisons every month. Ipso facto, more than 16,000 inmates (condemned minds) will become outmates next week. And they were already uneducated and broken before they ever went to jail. Penologists, criminologists and psychiatrists (i.e. Franklin Curren MD. And Jennifer Heitkamp MD. Etc) all report that it is the poverty, lack of education and societal degradation which leads to their incarceration in the first place. Ipso facto, (if Senator Grassley and our congress would like etc.) I could gather these data under the umbrella of a blue ribbon committee. And I can issue a 'special report' signed by Harvard graduates (i.e. Frank Curren MD.), Harvard professors (Lewis Yablonsky P.H.D.) along with a large orchestra of forensic psychologists stating: (in fancy and learned semantics) the correlations and/or causality of criminal behavior. And we can all wait for the next (God forbid) Elizabeth Smart, Sasha Greene or Sandra Cantu to go missing. And while (fifteen minutes) the media trains it's halogen light on the 'issue' of crimes against our young etc. The pastors, the pundits, and the politicians can all yell "tough on crime" slogans and pass a new "One strike" and you're out law. And the beat goes on...And on and on. Or Mr. Grassley, all senators, congresspersons and we the people can get up off our lazy asses. We can get off of our knee jerk, reflex, soundbite and reactionary asses and finally decide it's time for a change to come to kids in America! I'm not gonna be invited to go on Oprah. Dr. Phil is not inviting me to go on Dr.

Phil. And Montel retired on me. But King Pharoah can't interpret the dream. Our senate, congress and the talking heads have yet to interpret (the Menendez Brothers, Scott Peterson, Huckaby, Charles Manson, Henson, Stokes or Bardo etc.) the crisis ("Kids, Killing Kids"...nightmare). Sylvia Brown and Madam Cleo have not interpreted the dream. But the bible says (ask Bishop T.D. Jakes, Rev. Rick Warren, Robert Schuller or Bishop Long. And you could just read Genesis for Yourself...) They had to go get a wrongly convicted inmate trapped in the bowels of a prison. They had to consult a dude who was locked up on a sex crime to interpret king Pharoah's dreams...

Please be advised that this gang banger for God(Sherman D. Manning) will not be one of the 65,000 inmates to get out next month. Thanks to a dude named 'Valley Fever' I'll never make it back to Atlanta! But today (in this book, with the letter to President Barack Obama and with the final missive at the very back of this book) I am finally fulfilling all of the promise (the coat of many colors...the prophecy) that Ambassador Andrew Young, Civil Rights Legend Rev. Hosea Williams, Mayor Maynard Jackson and Mayor Lee Brown etc. saw in me in 1979. I'm finally (after all of my conflicts, cons, games and my wickedness) cashing the check that I wrote across the canvas of fear-of the missing and murdered children in 1979. And when this book is published (thanks to Uncle Andy, Rev. Hosea, Mayor Jackson, Grace Davis, Dollie Manning, Brenda Smith, Dr. Curren, Dr. Solis, Fred, Jimbo, Rosario and to Peter Andrist) even my critics can write (across my jail cell and/or my tombstone) "Paid in Full." K.K.K is my (Habakkuk 2:3) debt to the Facebook generation. I seek and deserve no award-I owe this to Brett and Chris (of Dr. Phil fame) just as surely as Mike Vick owes his testimony to (and for) the humane society!! I love Tony Dungy (a great man), I believe in redemption and second chances. And I pray for Michael Vick. But let me be clear: even if (and I pray that he is) Michael Vick is sincere he deserves no award. He owes a debt to youngsters who looked up to him. And for Michael Vick (if you are reading this) and to all the Michaels (Martha Stewarts, Paris Hiltons and Michael Milkens etc.) out there reading my words: Behold- we owe a debt to the kids at Locke, Lodi High, McClatchy and at Folsom High. We owe it to them to try to keep them from becoming the condemned boys at Chino (C.I.M.) High! James Brown (in the best interview he's ever done) said (on 60 minutes) to Michael Vick: "What about the dogs Mike? What about the dogs? " And I say (along with Jimbo, Fred, Curren, Willie and Billy) to Michael (Vick, Milken and to all) "What about the kids?" (Michael, Manning, Martha, Milken, Paris etc) "What about the kids?" This is our duty, our cause and it is our debt. ...To my fellow convicts (around America), to you who are (wrongly or rightly convicted) sitting up in prisons, jail cells or even on deathrows across America. I repeat "What about the kids?" Whom we have ruined, abandoned and destroyed...I'm keenly aware of prison overcrowding, prison guard abuse, draconian and asine laws. But while we (prisoners) sit our asses in $50,000 dollar per year jail cells; paid for at the expense of the children. While we sit back, gripe, complain, sob and moan about how Oprah won't do a darn show about 3-strikes, this or that. I say to my(pitiful, sorry ass) colleagues in prisons: "What about the kids?" Bruthas-what the f_ck about our (bloods, crips, skinheads, bulldogs etc.) kids? 'Mr. Vick...it is your (and my) duty (and debt) to accept our mentoring (by the Dungys , Jakes' and the Longs') and our medicine. And we must testify to our kids. Lest they enter Hades."

I need to reach Alba Cova, Judy Smith, Alex Blench, Chris Hansen (NBC), Ray Byers Sr. (Sacto), Tom Degnan, Cody Linley, Aaron Carter, Elizabeth Graswich (Elk Grove), Laura Cole, Cong. Charles Rangel and Brett Joliff (in Ohio..we have a stipend for Brett)...I command the G.B.G. troops (in schools across this country) to help us get this check (K.K.K) into the hands (folk like Eric at Emory University and Scott at John Hopkins Univ. both of whom appeared on "Jeopardy" on 8/17/09) of teens and tweenies across the nation...

...We must abandon the practice of damanging the foundation (it takes to raise a child). And it takes a village to destroy (condemn) a child. G.B.G. via K.K.K calls upon the guards, inmates and police officers etc. to reignite the visions for our kids. We call upon you to join us as we wake up the giant sleeping in the spirits of our youths. We call upon you to each one, reach one. We call upon you to be a light shining in the dark. We call upon you (Andrew Bridge, Arthur Blank, Herman Russell, Ed Gordon, Dr. Poussaint) to not curse the darkness but light (repair the foundation via education) a candle...I'm supposed to be a hard core criminal. I've been locked up a long time. Yet I (the maximum security inmate) beg you to please light a candle for ("what about the kids?") the kids... In the words (I'm a convict so it's my nature to steal words! Lol) of John Wesley I say to Vicki Stewart, Downey Jr., Scrushy, Milken Hilton and to every inmate "pray as if everything depends on God. Work as if everything depends on us"...

Get this tome to Abraham and Winslow Norton in California...I'll apologize to TBN readers and to older readers who will be offended by some of my almost cuss words; I'm sorry. But I'm not called to Baby Boomers. I am called to boys in the locker room in the high school, playing hooky, trying that wine cooler, contemplating the use of drugs and sitting on the fence. I am called (like Esther) to be in the place, under the circumstances and in the exact position that I'm in for "such a time as this". Later on I write to youngsters (in this book) about being "under construction". And the building process of our youth is extremely important. I can't speak for (or against) Michael Vick. But I know what he saw as a kid affected his foundation. He even saw police officers who were cool with dog fighting. And these boys (and girls) at 7 and 8 are already in a gang. They've not even learned how to clean their behinds properly but they've seen (some bad stuff) drive by shootings, beat downs, murders and molestations before they turned 9 years old. And what they've seen us (the same folk murmuring about a couple of cuss words in this book) do has damaged their foundation when they ought to be under construction. And we (my generation, generation x and those older than us) are so caught up in believing 'our own press' that we've stopped listening to God. We are listening to men (who are ill equipped to tell Pharoah what the dream means) and not God. We are still laboring under a contract by a memo God gave our grandparents. He told Abraham (clearly) to go kill his own son as a sacrifice. It was only a test but God told him to kill him. And when Abraham got ready to go do God's business (I found it) He told the others to "stay here with the asses." Abraham was a man on a mission...But even though he already had his "marching orders" he kept his ears tilted toward the heavens. And when he lifted up his knife (like a gangbanger) and stretched out his hand to kill Isaac. An angel called (new orders) to him "Abraham, Abraham!" he told him "Do not lay your hand on the lad (the dogs Vick, the women Manning, the kids etc.), or do anything to him." And we are murdering too many of our sons that didn't need to die. We killed them because of what we heard, but faith is an action word and it does not come one time for a single occasion. And faith does not come from having "heard" the word. But faith (keeps coming) cometh by hearing the word. And God is calling too many of us after we've raised the knife, cocked the handle and reached for the trigger. He's telling us (New Order-did you get the memo?) "Sherman, Sherman! Do not lay your hand on that..." Blood, crip, N.L.R, Bulldog or Southerner. We need to listen for the voice of our father. And He'll speak to you from the last folk you expected him to talk through. I told you He'll raise up a murderer named Saul, transform him to Paul and send him (Paul) to a prison to write the bible we read. He's God! He specializes in using men who are flawed, damaged and conflicted like Jacob. He likes to use men with struggles, shortcomings and with conflicts. That way when He blesses we will know it had to be God. If Joseph had matriculated at Morehouse, Howard, Harvard or Yale we would expect him to become a prince. But when God bypasses the educated at Yale and uses the incarcerated in jail and says "Joseph people think you're a sex offender but you are a prince." And says "Paul you're a thug, a murderer, and a badboy.   But I'm gonna make the chief sinner the chief Apostle". We know that it's God. As I cash this check written in the blood of 29 murdered and missing children I must remind people to be careful with our kids. We must break the vicious cycle of gangs, illiteracy and of poverty. There is a new memo articulated by our President which reads in part: "When you drop out of school (you not only fail your family)...you fail your country"...We are (I repeat castrating too many boys who only needed to be circumcised. The blood of our children is on our hands. Words have tremendous power – faith (...cometh by hearing"...) and you plant seeds with words. I still hear J.B. saying to bro. Vick "What about the dogs Michael? What about the dogs?" And I couldn't sleep last night because I kept hearing (in my spirit) "What about the kids Sherman? What about the children?" And that nervous, timid and sickening feeling I felt as a boy...I was a child. Just a baby and they were threatening my life...I didn't plan to write this in K.K.K. But I'm led by the spirit to write this as a testimony. And feel free to corroborate my story. Dig back through the archives of news footage of WSB Channel 2 (Atlanta...channels 2, 5, and 11 Alive), dig through the T.V. news archives from 1979 and 1980. Then read the stories in the Atlanta Daily World newspaper, Atlanta Voice newspaper and the Atlanta Constitution Newspaper. (It's not yet in Google. We tried. It's archived in those newspapers!)..And everywhere you see Atlanta Women Against Crime, Atl. Youth Against Crime, Grace Davis, Lee Brown, Mayor Maynard Jackson, murdered and missing children etc. You'll see me...When I didn't have a fulltime body guard the Atlanta police chief told my principal (Roy J. Wolfe) that a patrol car monitored me at school. A part of my childhood was robbed. Innocence lost because a person(s) (they claim it was Wayne Williams but I don't believe it was Wayne...Dick Gregory had an interesting theory) decided to sodomize, victimize and murder boys in Atlanta...And (for "such a time as this") hearing J.B. ask Michael "What about the dogs" and some other (terminal) things in my spirit have brought the haunting fear of my childhood back to remembrance. And when I think of little girls asking mommy can they sleep in the bed with mom (because daddy, Sherman is in prison) because she is afraid (terrified) about what happened to Sasha Groene, Elizabeth Smart or Sandra Cantu. I owe this book to our kids! My sleep is interrupted by the screams and the fears of little Shermans (in Atlanta, LA, New York and in Lodi) who are terrified of being killed as John Walsh's son Adam was. Terrified that a drug dealer (and a monster who doubles as a jock) named Jesse James Hollywood will maliciously murder them. I am awakened in the night by the screams of the kids in the cities. They are afraid. Afraid of bullets and bombs. Afraid of molestation and of murder. They worry about MS13, Bulldogs, Bloods, Crips, Skinheads and EME. And when boys are afraid they lose vision.   And without vision(s) it damages the foundation(s) of boys.   And when boys' are damaged they are terrified and wanna cry.   But the Machiavellian mentality, Of the hood (suburbia, the barrios and the trailer park) won't let them cry tears. And when boys can't cry tears they cry gangs, they cry guns and they cry bullets...I want this book (this check, this cashiers check) to be deposited in your spirit. Having read these words will ignite your vision. I may not live to see the fruits of this book. But I want some (it's not for everybody but there are many whom this "check" is destined to reach and teach) of you youngsters to put yourself in treatment.   You must know that our daddy specializes in using gangbangers, Mac Daddys, thugs, boyz in the hood (barrio, suburb and the trailer park) and jail birds to do his work. As you sit in your cell, classroom, bedroom, at home, in the dorm or in the group home. I want you to know it's okay to be afraid. It is okay to be flawed. It is okay to be confused. It is also okay to cry tears. Men and boys (like Michael Vick in Leavenworth, Tony Dungy in Indianapolis, Steve crazy ass Harvey in Atlanta, Bill Cosby and even Barack Obama etc.) do cry. I am in a maximum security prison. Jimbo, Fred and Steve have 92 years in corrections and each (Ford, Willy, Billy, Jimbo, Fred and 6ft 6 Steve) of us cry. That doesn't make you a chump or a punk.

But after you finish crying you gotta wipe your eyes. Get back up and "forward march". You are no longer condemned. This powerful book has shown up to give you a stay of execution. G.B.G has come to announce your reprieve and your commutation of sentence. We are pulling you back (with these words) and shooting you into your destiny. You can get up. You know men who have R-E-A-D their way out of the slums. I have friends who have read their way off of welfare. Read their way out of gangs and read their way off of drugs. And you kids are so special and you are precious. You (in Locke High, in Jerry Pike's class at Lodi, in Atlanta, New York and in Chicago) are worth your weight in gold. You are somebody special. And no matter how bad it looks all around you it can get better. Even if yo daddy dropped out (of yo life) and dropped into prison. Bill Cosby, Tony Robbins, Tony Dungy and Dr.Poussaint (and Dr. Curren and Dr. Solis etc.) can mentor you through books, CD's and DVD's. Your mind is like a pearl. You can conquer the whole world. Jim Brown (Amer-i-can), Hollywood Henderson, Zig Zigler, Les Brown and your teachers etc. want you to believe again. Dream again. Don't let haters stop you from dreaming. Turn your jail cell into a classroom. Turn your trailer park into a library. Turn your bedroom into a learning room. Transform your high school home room into a launching pad to a university. You can do it...You are not condemned. It is not over. Read a book-say a prayer and get back in the fight...Let me digress a moment and ramble...Lydia? I do not like tattoos and I definitely don't like to see tattoos on women. So why is there something that gives me an affinity toward this lady Lydia on 'Big Brother'? I like Lydia. And (yes I'm still married and I protect my wife's privacy vigorously) Natalie? WOW. I don't like her style but as far as looks are concerned I'm all in. Natalie is very, very good looking. And I'd like for Lydia, Natalie and Kevin (especially since Kev. is a graphic designer) to all get involved with G.B.G./Heart. And mentioning graphic designs I shout out to all of the International Academy of Design and Technology students in Sacramento...and I want to reach all the students at John F. Kennedy high school in Sacto. We reach out to students at Cesar Chavez High School in Stockton. I want kids at Cesar Chavez to show this tome to Principal William Nelson. Tell Mr. Nelson he and his students are invited to attend a (filmed) G.B.G/Heart tour at CSP-Sac. Ya'll tell Mr. Nelson to contact us at G.B.G (PDP) with all deliberate speed...Andrew (he's in college at Tuft's) was on 'Jeopardy' on 8/18/09. I need ya'll to go to his wall and tell him to get K.K.K. We want tech Sgt. Michael Camillo, Wes Colter (we must have a gift for Wes) and Christopher Guzman (Sacto) to get this tome. Get it to Adam Gosney. Justin Kerr was caught trading child porn on the internet. I want our outside support team to be on the alert when people approach you about sex or nudity on the internet, call the police PDQ...You who have read my other books shall recall one of my test subjects in this Human Laboratory (Hades) named John Linley Frazier. He was a notorious (infamous) murderer. He and Eric Menendez were prison buddies. Frazier apparently committed suicide last month at M.C.S.P. (Ione). He was (no disrespect to the deceased and God bless his family) a weirdo. I met Frazier (at New Folsom) back when Jimbo was still a captain. "Sherman a youngster fresh out of C.Y.A is in the cell with Frazier and he's terrified. You wanna take Jeff (Glen) Howell for a celly?" Captain Jimbo Walker inquired...I went by Frazier's cell and he had everything (his T.V., radio, bunk, shoes) covered in plastic. It was pretty freaky. And Jeff was an 18 year old kid, up on his bunk, balled up in a knot. Frazier did not like my visit. Frazier was one of the most racist and deadly dudes in the prison. He hated Jews, Blacks and Latinos. And I went to his door and he jumped. "What the f___ do you want Atlanta? I told you I don't never (sic) want you bringing me no coffee." He thought I was serving the evening beverage. And he'd only allow my white co-workers (Menendez and Doc Ford) to serve him beverages. Nevermind the fact that the dude who made the coffee was black. I saw where Frazier was going and told him "Frazier I'm here to see your celly. And John I'm giving you a word to the wise. If I hear the "n" word coming out of your mouth as soon as the two "g's" are out of your lips my fist will be down your throat." We call that the boo game. He bought it....An hour (after Mrs. Love the control cop) stated on the P.A. "Howell pack your stuff you're moving to 109." "J" almost ran out of that cell. He told me "dude you saved my life."... Much of what I learned by studying Frazier is reflected in this (K.K.K) body of work. And the fact that C.D.C. had an 18 year old (Howell) who had less than 8 months in prison in the cell with an infamous killer, serving 'life' in prison etc.etc. This argues my point (quite vocally) about what's wrong with prisons. I submit that since Frazier evidently committed suicide he was a danger to himself, as well as others. If I'm in prison for killing people why won't I kill you? If I'll kill myself how much would it take (have taken) for me to kill (Howell) a celly? Jimbo may have (literally) saved Jeff's life...I ended up (sorry I can't embellish like James Frey) failing miserably on Jeff. I lectured him. I gave him great books to read. I even had money sent to him. But BoBo (real name Mosley) got a hold of some weed from C.O. Laffitt. And BoBo did not have the money to pay Laffitt. Jeff had a check from (Hypothekarbank-same bank that sent the $250.00 I'd loaned Menendez) me in his account. Ipso facto, BoBo (an older inmate) coerced Jeff into lying on me (Howell told C.O. Geyland I was going to assault him!) to get rid of me. I went to Ad-seg (1030) and they smoked up my money. 'This is how we do it in hell'. As an aside Jeff caused a lover's quarrel between Eric Menendez and Michael Henrickson. Mike had written "J" a kite (missive) asking if he fooled around and offering fellatio". I wanted to assault Henrickson. Then he asked me if I thought a tabloid would buy the letter. I told him that if Eric had written it he could have sold it. (I sent the missive to an attorney to keep...)...you'll recall this 'special update' was written after the book was finished. I inserted it in the middle of the tome...I got a missive from Attorney Murray J. Janus today. He always addresses the envelope to: "Rev.. Sherman D. Manning". The officer who delivered the missive stated "Janus is that that the lawyer who was on Inside Edition and Dateline right?"... I've slightly redacted the missive and changed the three names he referred to and replaced them with pseudonyms: "Dear Reverend: Very sorry to hear about your health...must say I read K.K.K. in two sittings. It is absolutely your best, most interesting book ever. I found it almost impossible to put the darn thing down...Kids love the way you switch subjects (i.e. ramble or digress as I'm doing at this moment) in your writing. Some of the contents were absolutely hilarious...I found this writing chilling and haunting. I'm glad you finally decided to write about your bogus conviction. I thought you were candid, direct and very forthcoming...I would caution you to brace yourself for litigation. I would be absolutely surprised if Mr. Doe, Mr. John and Mike don't attempt to sue you... I'll also warn you that this tome will definitely raise a lot of eyebrows. And I've every expectation that the media will come calling. I'm cognizant that you are not planning to do any interviews.. Likewise, I will of course, decline to comment without your permission. But I would advise you to reconsider doing media. And it would be great to at least do the Christian media...My daughter (also an attorney) read K.K.K and gave it a 9 ½ on a scale of 1 to 10. David Hicks (Richmond, D.A) called it "one of the most important youth books ever written by a prisoner." Aubrey Davis (a retired prosecutor) still hates your guts but he wrote 'Sherman D. Manning finally admitted to being the criminal that I always knew he was...I admit that the writing is powerful, interesting and impactful...It is a very good book written by a good for nothing 'inmate'....I'll keep you in my thoughts and prayers....M.J. "Well I guess (?) Davis was complimenting me.

Attorney Janus is a powerhouse lawyer who knows his stuff. I take his advice about the media to heart. I'm still extremely hesitant to consider doing any interviews. (I said I'd perhaps do Larry King...Dan Fitzpatrick if I could find him...perhaps Ari Shapiro or Bev. Smith...)...Dan Rather was my favorite evening anchor. And since he did the 60 minutes story on Corcoran's Gladiator beatings I would consider providing Mr. Rather with an interview.

I just don't have time for sensational bull crap and I won't be subjected to interviews all about the Menendez (Bardo, Stokes, Moore, etc) brothers...The folk who ought to be interviewed are Dr. A Duran, Dr. Jarman, Dr. Jennifer Heitkamp, Dr. Curren, Adam, Daniel and Dustin. And no one knows me better than Patricia Kennedy and Jimbo Walker. But Jimbo does not do media. .

...I want Alexander Torres and Michelle out at Cesar Chavez High (in Stockton) to tell Jay Mattioli and Hairo Torres (Hairo lives in Oregon and we do have a stipend for Hairo)...Regardless of what the tabloids may or may not write about K.K.K. I want 3 main groups to get this book. Students! You students are our main focus. My gang banger comrades, my associate wardens (i.e. Fred etc.), my youngster staff advisors (i.e. Adam, Daniel and Dustin etc.) and my team of experts (Curren, Duran and Greg etc.) have a passion for helping kids in their teens. Getting you (teens) this book is goal no.1. Getting it to youths in (and out of) detention (C.Y.A, Group homes, shelters high school dropouts etc. Kids on probation etc. we want Judges, police and probation officers to give kids this book) is goal no.2. And getting this book to kids serving prison sentences(all across the world) is goal no. 3.

I don't know how good this book is. I do know it is the realest (most authentic) book I've ever written. I know this is what Hollywood has not been able to adequately depict in the movies and on t.v. I know that truth is (not a cliché) actually stranger than fiction. And I know that I'm way out on the line (breaking out of every box and breaking every convict code.) And limb with this book. I exposed myself (my conviction) as never before. And I finally talked specifically about the monsters you've never seen on the news story in a tabloid. And even as Eric Menendez, Lyle Menendez, Becky Snead, and Tammi all try to deny the authenticity of this writing etc. How can they explain that I've published 8 tomes prior to this and never mentioned either of them before now?

I have no dog in their fight. In fact I'm more appalled by officials like Criner, Tucker, Garza and Mrs. Wheat (who are criminals etc. some of whom are key players in the $ multi-million dollar drug business in California's 33 prisons!) than I am by Eric and Lyle. And the main reason I've uncloaked Eric, Lyle, Henson, Stokes and others is because of what I see in today's youth and what I saw (Brett and Chris) on Dr. Phil. And I know (factually from all the letters I get and the crap I see on t.v.) that youngsters have bought into this incorrect, bogus and romanticized depiction of prisons which they see in the freaking movies. And as long as there is one wood in the trailer park, one brutha in the hood and one latino in the barrio who thinks going to prison (puts a notch on your belt) gives em status, we need this book!!

And although I'm hesitant to talk to media-please put the word out that I will (gratis) talk to David E. Kelley (my favorite), Jerry Bruckheimer, Mr. Spielberg and/or Mark Burnette about authentic and impacted depictions of prisons. Smart ass, know it all, care free dudes like Brett (again of Dr.Phil fame) keep me writing. Not because Brett has a damaged door or a cracked window. He's not yet condemned. He's still under construction. And his trip to San Quentin was a wake up call or his alarm. Now that Brett is awake and alert a book like K.K.K is a GPS for him. This book is a motivational tool for kids(in schools, colleges and churches) who are already doing the right thing. It will be the cheerleading session that Dr. Cosby talks about. It's the book that students at Biola University and at Tufts can read for inspiration and then pass on to buddies (siblings or to kids on the wrong path.)...And kids in crisis and in conflict can eat K.K.K. up. It is written in a conflict, about a conflict, by a conflicted convict. It is a testimony from hell. I've come to conclude (candidly) that (being real) some of the kids I meet (on our tours and doing time) could not and will not be turned around period. When they've already seen felt and heard too much; neither the Pope, Oprah, Dr. Phil or Dr. Bill (Cosby) can, could or will , turn them around. The hope for them is that this book will reach them after they fall and help them to get back up.

But when we put a hot, controversial, entertaining and thug authored book like K.K.K into the hands of a Brett there is a strong chance he will turn around. When I tell (and of course he would say "no way" and "not me" etc.) Brett (in writing) that he will (absolutely no doubt about it) either choose a man (war daddy) play gay or get raped in L.A. County jail he listens...I really advise Brett to look back at the D.V.D of his appearance on Dr. Phil. If he (Brett) looks closely he shall notice that as soon as Dr. Phil put him in the makeshift prison cell etc. The moment Dr. Phil mentioned that he'd have a bunkmate named "Bubba" Brett "licked his lips". Implication? I was watching Dr.Phil with other convicts and 3 of them (two of whom are Booty Bandit Specialists) stated "look at Brett licking those luscious lips the minute Dr. Phil mentions Bubba". And even a devout Jewish guy stated "I would bet $500.00 to $1000 that Brett would be Bretta in LA County Jail!"... I rewatched the show 3 times and the fellas were right on. He did lick the moment Dr. Phil said "Bubba". I'm certain it was just nerves but you know how it looks. And the reason I call this Broke Back C.D.C. is why are we looking at a skinny ass white boy's lips anyway? It is the nature of this perverted and perverting environment. I recall inmate Larrios (a.k.a. Chili) giving a speech one day to fellow cons about "I'm gonna leave prison same way I came in...Madre didn't raise me to be looking at some man and digging him out". Thirteen months later I went by Chili's cell and he was bowed down, upon bended knees, talking upon inmate Aranda's (a.k.a Mugsy) "microphone". Actually he was singing on it...Now Larrios is a very tall, athletic and muscular guy. He's an alpha. And Mugsy (also an Alpha male) was well known as the Latino who singlehandedly murdered a big, black Lee Haney look-a-like. Big "Bubba" had disrespected Mugsy by grabbing his ass. And Mugsy (like Chili) did not mess around. So Mugsy stabbed the guy in the heart and killed him...I wish you could have seen the look in Mugsy's eye, as he saw me catch him receiving fellatio. As I looked in it was one of those moment s you don't expect, can't prepare for and won't forget I wanted to run (literally). And then I hoped they wouldn't see that I saw...I'm gonna leave that there. Brett, Chris and all of you studs? When was the last time you ate breakfast, lunch and dinner in your bathroom? Brett and Chris can I get personal? Let's go there. Brett you are 19 and Chris you're 16. Hormones a flying. May I ask Brett and Chris how often do you masturbate? (Disclaimer: Most Christians say masturbation is wrong. Many Christians do it and deny it. I am not promoting masturbation!)...O.K.-Brett (since you're an adult over 18) let's assume you say twice per day, seven days per week...Brett if you were (and I believe you are straight) in prison right now, in the cell with Eric or Lyle. And you're on lockdown or in ad-seg. You (Brett) are locked in your cell 24 (not 23) hours per day with Eric (or Lyle). You all shower twice per week (at the same time five minutes each)...Brett you both smell each other's farts listen to each other's craps (and like Bill Clinton try not to inhale) etc.etc. You eat together and...24/7 each and every day. Brett when would you personally enhance yourself? What would you do, say or think if you wake up from a nap and Eric is enhancing himself? Do you just not enhance yourself for the duration (sometimes up to 2 years) of the lockdown out of respect to him? What if he does not reciprocate?? Brett (and Chris and all the fellas out their reading) these are things that never cross your mind when you're playing quarters, smoking weed or committing other crimes...And the key to success is the ability to ask the "what if" question. What if I get caught? What if I wreck? What if I kill somebody? What if this kills me? And I'm a half way decent looking guy. And I love good looking women (i.e. Nattalie on Big Brother, Angelina Jolie etc.)...But I want Brett and Chris to go to my website and look at my picture when you wake up tomorrow morning. And when you look at my picture in the morning ask yourself a question. Look at me and say: "Is this what I want to die doing? Ask yourself do you want to live with Sherman D. Manning for the rest of your life. Do you want a man (men) to be the first and last face you see everyday forever? Brett you told Dr. Phil that if you could write the perfect script for your life; you'd have a wife, kids and a dog. You won't get a wife (unless it's Sha Nay Nay) in the joint. You can't procreate in jail and the only dogs you'll see in here are your celly's stinky feet. Is this (prison) what you want to die doing? It's time Brett (Chris and all of you) to bud, blossom and to bloom. I see dump trucks, cranes, bulldozers and all kinds of heavy lifting equipment in your (Brett, Chris, C.J. Sheron in Baltimore and lots of kids) life right now. You are under construction. You're gonna fall down but get back up. You are not a victim. You don't need to quit. I've read an updated memo from the C.E.O. of the universe that says "You are not alone. I am here with you". I got a memo that says "You are not condemned". Your foundation is still intact. I wrote this book to tell you to "go". I wrote to tell you "forward march". You know when that little voice tells you something is "too good to be true." Listen to it. And you know when that same voice tells you "this (K.K.K.) is real talk" listen to it. I don't know Bill Cosby or Dr. Poussaint. I have no commission deal with them or promotional contract. So (be realistic) why in the hell would I advise you to read their book "come on people" if I didn't know it would transform you? Bill Cosby has $350 million! He doesn't need me. But I'm trying (Brett) to keep an "exit" sign on your butt (No Buns intended! Lol). There is so much fun you can have on the streets, with buddies and with your family without crime. Freedom is fun. Freedom is worth everything. I happen to believe (my opinion) it is okay for a person 21 or older to have a drink or two on the weekend etc. Wine is fine etc. But guess what? I would drink grape juice (only) for the next 50 years if I was going to live and could get out. I've learned you can live without anything; forever. I don't need a drink I smoked Marlboro's for twenty (a powerful addiction) years and thought I couldn't live without nicotine. But five years ago I stopped! If I were free I could would swear off (and mean it) anything forever to be free!...Yo Brett and Chris-neither of you have ever written a book. I'm fairly convinced that I'm a tad bit more educated than both of you and I've got more money-but guess what? You (Brett and/or Chris) have something I'll never have. The ability to get up (right now) and walk out the (go! Forward March!)door!...Brett and Chris should re-read the last sentence. Freedom is awesome. So I want you all (readers) to contact 23 year old Matthew Deniston (in Georgia), Jordan Benjamin and Ryan Hreljac and tell them we (G.B.G) need them. I want you all to get this book to Judge David Young and Judge Mathis. Talk about K.K.K on blogs and on social networks every day. I need the kids in the shadows to get this book. I want that young lady on the brink of prostitution or drugs to get this book. This tome should spread like wildfire across the campuses of Cesar Chavez high in Stockton, Lodi high, Locke High School, Folsom High and all the high schools in this country. It is 3:49 am and I tried to sleep (for 49 minutes) but I'm pregnant with these words. I'm in this place (Hades) "For such a time as this". This book is time sensitive. I've got to get this book out of me while I can. Peter had a dream that I (the thug) was being hailed the Tony Robbins for troubled teens. I told Peter I am satisfied just being the Sherman D. Manning of troubled youth. I'm blessed to be able to study great criminologists like Jack Levin (Northeastern university) and David Kennedy. I'm in a position to study Dr. Phil. Even the ones that get on my nerves. I read everything written by Dr. Phil, Dr. Yablonsky, Victor Frankl, Tony Robbins, Steve Covey, Les Brown, Zig Zigler etc. I study the test subjects which are readily available in this human laboratory called prison. I am able to attend formal and informal G.B.G workshops taught by Dr. Jarman, Dr. A Duran, Dr. Curren, Dr. Houston, Dr. Handian, Dr. Heitkamp, Dr. Solis and Dr. Friedman etc. I probably engage (intellectually) more shrinks than any other convict at New Folsom. I question correctional managers (i.e. Fred, Steve and Jimbo). I definitely converse with the warden (Jimbo) more than any prisoner at New Folsom. But I'm on a mission. I need information. A man can't go through what Jimbo went through being called "the comeback kid" and the "shell answer man" and come out on top; without knowing something. And my duty is to pick the warden's brain. And I'm able to write a unique, impactful and interesting book such as this because of the data I'm exposed to. The words, principles and ideas put forth in K.K.K. represent the things I've learned from mega reading, suffering, deep studies into psychology etc. The "stuff" of the missives I get from high school and college students is reflected across the pages of the book you're holding. Years of walking with and running from God are reflected in the pages you now hold. My deepest, darkest secrets are in these pages. I wrote them because of the promise I made in 1979. And because of the promise I made God when I was felled by Valley Fever. This time is what Judge Greg Mathis is talking about when he tells men to testify so that men in prison, men in juveniles, men in schools and boyz in the hood will know that they can do it too. I wrote this for Brett Jolliff (Ohio), David Quindt, Jeff Buttle, Greg Pugh (Chesterfield VA) David Reynolds (VA) Francis Ronald Wright (Chesterfield VA), Nathan Hand, Chad Sherman, Craig Gilstrap, Carl "4 Barrel" Williams, David Proctor, Brian Boykin (Richmond VA) and for Donald Dusk in Akron. I want Aaron Jackson in Delaware Ohio to get this book. I want Guadelupe Reyes (Santa Rosa?) to get this book. I pray that Tony Dungy, Tyler Perry, Michael Moore, Andy Reid, Jeffrey Lurie and Leonard Padilla will help put this book in schools. An ounce of prevention is worth more than a pound of cure. The more kids at Ron Clark Academy who are reading books like this today the fewer that will be in prison tomorrow. I fully, completely (I repeat) and I thoroughly comprehend the righteous indignation Bill Cosby feels. I can see the pain and the hurt in Mr. Cosby's eyes. You can't fake that in his eyes. And I know exactly how Mr. Cosby feels. I have never had $350 million. But I have had a whole lot (legitimately) of money (at times). And I can recall driving into Perry homes, Bankhead court or some other ghetto in Atlanta. And I recall seeing 13,14 year old girls dropping out of high school to have a baby. Boys already strung out at 12 years old. They could not write or multiply. I asked a 15 year old boy in Perry Homes in 1994 who was the President and he did not know. "Who's the Mayor?" And he had no idea. But he could quote rap songs backward and forwards. I remember guys saying they wish they could get a Lincoln (Jag or Mercedes) like mine. But they couldn't read. And I'd say to myself "Give a man a fish. Feed him for a day. Teach him how to fish-feed him for life." And I thought "If they gave Sabrina Laster, Me Me, Fe Fe, Nathaniel Burns and Chat all $1 million each. Every one of them would be broke, in jail or dead in less than a year. They're not financially literate. They know nothing about banking." And when a Cosby, a Willie Gary or a Chris Gardner sees that Locke High School lost 75% (not 7.5%) of its freshman class in L.A. it makes you wanna holler and throw up both hands! So I say to Mr.Cosby and Dr. Possaint (Dr. Naim Akbar, Cornel West, President Obama, Willie Brown and Vernon Jordan etc.) to air all the dirty laundry until they clean the laundry up. Air all the dirty laundry until they pull the clothes lines down and learn how to articulate, think, reason, rationalize and to develop a vision and a plan for a better future. If John Johnson (Ebony) could do it inspite of Jim Crow, Blatant racism and no money etc. If Earl Graves could do it I can do it too. And mentioning Mr. Johnson every boy ought to read "Succeeding Against The Odds" by Mr. Johnson. I mention Mr. Johnson in the "con confessions" part of this book. But I know a bit of the righteous anger Bill Cosby feels. When I just think about John Johnson alone I can't even fathom not reading his book. If Bill Gates writes a new book I think it is a sin and a crime not to read it. How can I not study everything Virginia Satire wrote? How can I allow Vernon Jordan, Dennis Kimero, Dr. Robi Ludwig or Oprah to write a book which I don't read? And one of the things I repeat to kids everyday is this: If anybody on the planet has been similarly situated as you are. And they were able to break a habit, get a degree or start a company, then you can do it too. If I'm addicted to something and it's costed me my house etc. all I need to do is find one person (on the planet) who was addicted and lost their house. But they broke the addiction. As soon as I see, hear or read about them I know I can...You can't read the story of Attorney Willie Gary (google him) and see how dirt poor he was and how he rose above it without his story planting seeds in your mind.

Success leaves clues…Mr.Cosby knows from experience the power of reading. He knows (as I do) that if any 12-17 year old black (white or Latino) kid (in the suburbs, the trailer park or wherever) sits down today and reads five books (in five weeks) such as the following: "Long walk to Freedom" Mandela. "Unlimited Power" Robbins. "Blue Eyed Blonde" Book II Manning etc.…If any kid (even those as poor as dirt) will read those five books back to back I guarantee you they will be transformed forever! It is impossible to internalize those five books and remain in poverty. You can't do it. So I'm not Dr.Cosby. I am a common criminal. I'm a thug and a crook. I am one of those dangerous dudes. And I don't ever stand a chance of meeting Mr. Cosby. At least you can go to his book signing and meet him. You can go to one of his "call outs" and you can meet him. I'm in jail so I'll never shake his hand. Listen to me ya'll. Sit your ass down and hear me. I have absolutely nothing to gain by kissing up to Dr. Cosby. A. He ain't gonna help me! B. (Since he's a freaking comedian and not an infectious disease specialist). He couldn't help me if he wanted to. Cosby doesn't give a damn about some nappy headed thug in prison. And he shouldn't care. Hell he didn't lock me up. Bill Cosby doesn't owe me a damn thing. And I don't owe him crap. I have read Michael Eric Dyson's book criticizing Cosby. And Dyson is brilliant. I love his writings. And having said that-I still want Cosby to continue to call people out…and I want you (students) to also call people out via this book. Find James Heath Teague (Sacto), Gerald Posner (Dailybeast.com), Tom Joyner and Doug Banks and tell em all to check out K.K.K…

I want Gabe Williams and Timothy Coleman in Sacramento to know we have gifts for them. I also wanna reach Todd Dressler in Atlanta, Attorney Steed Scott and Brian Hawn. My goal is to get this, powerful, unusual, unheard of, controversial and impactful book book into every hand that I can. We gotta get it to Attorney Andrew Bridge, to principals, teachers and professors. I want great pastors like Rev. Otis Moss (in Chicago) to please adopt a school and send 40 or so copies of this book to public school s to help kids. I know that Rev. Moss has a passion for youth and his Trinity United Church knows exactly who Christ meant by "I was in prison and you visited me not." You can visit an inmate with a book!...I'm going farther out on the limb right now but I have two advantages over Bill Cosby. A. I'm a common criminal who won't live to see freedom. So I don't have any bridges to burn. B. I don't have $350 million so nobody is gonna write a book called "Is Sherman D. Manning out of touch with poor people?" And nobody (on or off camera) is gonna accuse some jailbird of talking down to black people or wanna "cut my nuts" out. So I'm going to say what "Bill Cosby, President Obama and even Earl Graves can't (write) say. (I'm gonna go there for about 4 or 5 minutes.…) I'm sick and tired (dirty laundry) of seeing civil rights leaders enable blacks (Latinos and poor whites) to be victims. They need to hang up the victim hat and retire it. We can't afford to raise another generation of violent, obstreperous, ebonic speaking thugs who can't read, write or count. And we owe a tremendous debt to our civil rights legends (Dr. King, Ambassador Young, Rev. Hosea Williams, Rev. Jesse Jackson, Rev. Joseph Lowery etc.) for what they accomplished. I'm in awe of what John Lewis, Thurgood Marshall and even Malcolm All did. I love and salute them. And in 2009 it is not illegal for blacks to read. Nobody is lynching a kid because he can write. But since the way has been made for us to write. We now have fools who tell us you're a sissy (or a square) if you carry books and speak articulately. Rosa Parks went to jail for the right to ride on the front of the bus. But now we have lil gangsters who consider it an insult to their masculinity to sit at the front of the bus. And I'm seeing too many leaders who act like crying "racism" and crying the devil (white man) made me do it" guarantees their job security. My heart is broken because I know that these leaders know better. The focus (in 09 and beyond) must be on maximizing the rights that they (Jesse, Julian, Joseph, and Hosea etc.) fought to make possible. Teachers out to teach about it. Pastors ought to preach about it. We ought to be rapping and dancing about reading. Bring me any 7, 8, 9 year old kid (black, white or latino) and give me five weeks of reading (with him or her) and they will never be the same again. Whether that kid is in Eastgate, Bankhead Court, Compton, Watts, Buckhead, Birmingham Alabama or Birmingham England We will transform when he is exposed to great books. And I'm tired of leaders rocking people to sleep. Don't endorse my illiteracy. Don't comfort me when I'm down but help me get up. Youngsters (in 2010) won't just settle for pie in the sky, bye and bye. I hear kids saying "I want some spam where I am."

So my advice to every adult perusing this tome is to find a kid and get him excited about knowledge. Raise the level of expectation. You tell those kids how fun, exciting and empowering books are. Explain that a book can take you anywhere in the world. Let em play videos after they've read and explained what they read. Explain to them that the person who invented that video game is a reader. And explain that if they can read they don't just have to watch movies but they can make movies. If you read you can invent, create and you can do. Selling reading to kids is easy…

The way you break a cycle or break a curse off of a people, a family or a person is by radical action. And all Mr. Cosby and Dr. Poussaint are doing is trying to shock (radical) people back into action. When you love a people you want what's best for them. So I join the small chorus of voices telling people that you get what your hand calls for. I wanna be a part of the solution. And I promise you that you can get out of that gang. You can get off of drugs. You can get out of poverty. You can get out of juvenile and back into school. If you're in school you can stay there. Just believe in yourself. Go to that library and lock yourself in your room with the billionaires and millionaires who have left clues. Lock up and read "Vernon can read" by Vernon Jordan. Read "Think and Grow Rich" by Dennis Kimbro and read "Awaken the Giant Within" by Tony Robbins and you will be hooked on books… But don't read "bunk" books cause they'll bore you. But if you sit yo behind down in a room with Tony, Vernon, Kimbro or Mr. John Johnson etc. The book will come alive in your hand. And you shall transform. If anybody has ever been in the shape, place, condition or position you're in and they made a change etc. You can do it too. Find out what they did and model their success. I'm always advocating mentoring because I know the power of role models. And I have Fred, Steve, Dr. Solis, Dr. Curren and Dr. Jarman etc. Mentoring us (the G.B.G team) and we (in a sense-so far as being an example of what not to do) Mentor delinquents etc. but you can be mentored by Bill Cosby, Tony Robbins, Dennis Kimbro, Earl Graves and by Les Brown today. All you need to do is get their books and CD's. When you get my book in your room you have me in your room. You are being mentored right this minute (by Franklin Curren MD, Jimbo Walker, C.Solis MD, Fred Schroeder, Bugriyev, Adam etc.) because you are reading this book. And when you get excited and animated and e-mail, poke, TM and IM your friends about this book you will be a special envoy for G.B.G. And the more people you tell to read my book the more people we'll be mentoring. (and those of you who get a lot of people to read this book will qualify for cash prizes! Just let us know how many people you got to read this book.) And I believe in this very powerful, very unique and very distinguished team of advisors (mentors) which G.B.G. has. They know their stuff!…I need you all to find Eric Donahue (he had swine flu on Facebook). Find Channing Tatum, Tom Malinowski and Tavis Smiley and tell them about K.K.K.… Those of you who believe in God (I repeat) pray for G.B.G. God can do anything! Pray that this book will spark a revolution and a Jihad against the Taliban of gangs, molesters and the predators that are stealing the innocence of our children…I'm not smart enough to make this work on my own. It is going to take the favor of God to put this book in the hands of those that need it. I want you to pray for favor for G.B.G. All you students who have a prayer language pray in it. I don't need a donation. I don't seek a visit. I only need you to (literally) ask God to use K.K.K to set fires (not burning crosses! No pun intended) in the spirits and psyches of youngsters all across this country....Glory to God! I need 100 kids to commit (I know this sounds crazy but ya'll know I'm in jail so expect me to be crazy!) to praying twice per day (I Corinthians 4:10) over this book for 30 days. Ask God to bless K.K.K. and to "enlarge" our "territory" our circle of influence, The kids we can help to influence through this book!! (Send me an e-mail and tell me That start date of your 30 days of prayer over this book. I may publish your email in a tome..)...

..I am so blessed to have met Warden Walker, Terry L. Rosario, Patricia Kennedy, Dr.Tye Hedblad, Dr. Curren, Dr. Jarman, Dr.C. Solis and all the members of the G.B.G. Advisory board. These brilliant, distinguished scholars, physicians and correctional managers have mentored me, mentored the men on my team and taught us so much! WOW! And (you'll see A. Duran's distinguished qualifications in the newsletter later in this tome. She, C. Solis MD and Jennifer Heitkamp MD. have a strong, powerful passion for kids in the foster care system...I'm totally convinced that this book would not have been as powerful as it is without the data and mentoring which I've received from doctors like Dr. J. Friedman who works with juvenile boys daily. And Dr. Solis who treated the heads of the Child Protective Services etc. ...Dr. Duran was a mover and a shaker in C.P.S. in several states. Dr. Solis, Dr. Duran and Dr. Friedman have all been virtually godsends to G.B.G./Heart adding legitimacy, clout and credibility..) They've helped make G.B.G/Heart, this tome and me etc. better!...Dr. Phil and his wife Robin also have a strong passion for Foster Kids. And research shows that nearly 600,000 kids (more than half a million) are in America's Foster Care system. Numerous Formal G.B.G studies, surveys and workshops have corroborated what my advisory board (namely C. Solis MD and A. Duran PhD.) have pounded into my head: "The foster care system is a breeding ground for criminality and a feeding grounds to the prison system." Dr. Phil calls the foster care system a "silent epidemic". Franklin Curren MD. calls America's foster care system "broken, busted and disgusted". Dr. Jarman calls foster care a guaranteed "ticket to prison" and a virtual "get (out of society and) into jail free" card. This writer was given nightmares (literally) by some of the tales of foster care horror. That Dr. Solis and Dr. A. Duran told me...Psychiatric social worker Chuck Christenson told me when I was researching (this tome) "I was not tough enough to stay in foster care work... It almost drove me to drink or drugs." Chuck said "Mr. Manning I am still haunted by the sadistic nature of some of the abuse I saw in foster care"...G.B.G (via K.K.K) is on a mission to put the word out about what Dr.Phil calls "The silent epidemic" of almost 600,000 youngsters in Foster care in America! What I've learned about the foster care system (via the tutorial sessions by Dr. Jarman talks) live and in the flesh startles me. I want my readers to check out CASA (court appointed special advocates) and get involved with helping them. Be a guardian angel (advocate) for kids. That's why I want "Angelo" to get this book. (As I said) I saw him (Angelo) on Fox 40 trying to get a family to take him in via Sierra adoption services. He's 16 and at that age where this tome can inspire him. Foster kids suffer 7 times more post traumatic stress than soldiers in Iraq and Afghanistan! That's deep...I want you all to get this tome to Attorney L. Wallace Pate who is a civil rights lawyer who specializes in pioneering law to protect foster kids. She was helping a kid Juan Espinoza to do great things. And I was about to make a note to find Juan in LA and to ask Mr. Padilla, Senator Burton or Dr. Solis to get Juan this book. But I was absolutely floored when I glanced up at my TV and saw at the end of a Dr. Phil classic: "Juan Espinoza died tragically August 11, 2009". An 18 year old kid died? Tragically?... I dedicate a part of this tome to Juan's memory. I know Atty. L. Wallace was crushed. And as much as Dr. Phil and Robin had done to help Juan I know they had to be despondent. Let us get this tome to Sean and Beth Payton. Sean is head coach for the New Orleans Saints (Please get Sean this book!) I shout out to the "Payton's Play it Forward Foundation". And I want you to 'pay it (K.K.K.) forward' to Sean. I applaud Sean, Chris Berman and Karen Hegner (executive director for Sean). We applaud

Steve Davidson president of the Dr. Phil foundation. (Go to Dr. Phil.com and click on Dr. Phil foundation and you can help today!) G.B.G shouts out to Jerral Hancock (Army specialist), the children s advocacy center in Covington. I want you to help Hope House and the Fisher House (www.fisherhouse.org). The G.B.G. advisory board members endorse these programs as part of our own HEART platform. We salute Renee Gibbs at Youth Empowerment Program, Jerry Hamilton (Boca Ballet) and Freedom writers foundation (Erin Gruwell) and kids can free the children (Marc Kielburger)...and I can't overemphasize the impact we will make if we go online and send a donation to these groups pray for them and volunteer to help them...After Dr.Solis, Dr. Duran and Dr. Gregg etc. began to impress upon me the horrible state of the Foster Care system I took personal inventory. And I was alarmed, shocked and mesmerized to learn that at least 70% of my past (that I know of) cell mates had been in some form of foster care. That is startling and it is telling. And less than 3% of foster care kids get a college degree....and in New York more than 80% of foster kids did not finish high school. Tale after tale of abuse, starvation, psychological torture and the sexual molestations of kids in foster care are horrific. We must demand action! G.B.G/Heart (and I am certain Dr. Phil, Bill Cosby etc. will partner with a prisoner on this issue) demands that our U.S. Senate and our United States Congress reform the broken foster care system in America. It is broken...we need congressional hearings on this. I recommend that Robin and Dr. Phil, Dr. Curren, Dr. Solis, Dr. A Duran, Dr. Jarman, Atty. Allred and Atty. Pate all testify before the congress about this "silent epidemic". I wanna see Republicans and Democrats hold "town hall" meetings about foster care just as vigorously as we've held them on "Healthcare". And if we will try reform foster care it will result in less aftercare (which is mainly prison care)...I don't wanna wait around and play with this. I know it sounds (reads) like a Hollywood movie "Prisoner Org. sends delegation (G.B.G. advisors) to Capitol Hill-led by Harvard physician to testify about 'Silent Epidemic' but I told ya'll truth is stranger than fiction. Don't blame (or credit) me: Blame Robin! Dr. Phil! Dr. Duran! Dr. Solis! Dr. Heitkamp! 1979! Valley Fever! Jimbo! Fred! And G.B.G...

I want y-o-u to engage in Jihad right where you are. You in Locke High School, Northside in Atlanta, Ralph Bunche Middle School, Folsom High, John F. Kennedy High in Sacto, you kids (in Jerry Pike's class) at Lodi High Schools can/will send e-mails to your congressperson today! Write and call Madame Nancy Pelosi right now. Copy the last 3 or 4 pages of this book and send em to Mrs. Pelosi, Mr. Waxman, Maxine Waters, Sen. Brownback, Sen. Arlen Specter, to Mr. Obama etc. I want you to email, IM and TM members of the media, the congress and the senate and tell them "A group of common criminals called Gang Bangers for Good have a Heart program. They are directed by a Harvard physician and they have a distinguished team of advisors (all of whom are either PH.D. or Medical Doctors). And the G.B.G. advisors join Dr. Phil, Robin and the Dr. Phil foundation in describing Americas foster care system as a 'silent epidemic'. We'd like for our advisors (J. Friedman Ph. D, a. Duran Ph. D C. Solis MD, J. Heitkamp MD, Dr. Gregg, Dr. Jarman, Dr. Houston and F. Curren MD) to testify at a congressional hearing about ways to reform this horrible system." Recommend that they read K.K.K. and ask them to call Dr. Phil. They can call my G.B.G. advisors via (the G.B.G. secretary of state: Patricia Kennedy) 916-322-4730 ext. 3042...and let us (you and I) get this book into group homes, foster homes and into the hands of these at-risk kids. And I want kids in these group homes and in foster care to know you have rights under the law! Foster care kids bill of rights. (I'll get Daniel Bugriyev to post a link to this Bill of Rights on our Facebook site...And look on the Dr.Phil show's site...) This foster care system is a sinister story of the betrayal of 600,000 boys and girls (and cruel unusual, mind boggling tale of torture)...And G.B.G./Heart is issuing an A.P.B.(all points bulletin) in search for Andrew Bridge, Dustin Brown (Carmichael CA), Lori Bartolli, Atty. Cynthia Ribas, Joseph Canova, Patrick Tucker (at Notre

Dame), students at Chico State in the 'Hit of Reality' program and to prison inmates around the world. I want inmates to get off your asses and write letters to the Congress about reforming foster care. I want kids, students and parents to unite, write, email, telephone and contact elected officials about fixing this 'silent epidemic'. All my fellow cohorts (inmates) in jails and prisons across America who complain that we can't vote, this and that. Here is what we can do today: A. Call your family and friends and tell them to e-mail the media, the senate and the congress. And B. write a snail mail (today) about the 'Silent epidemic' and the woods, bruthas, and the essays sittin up in them tonight. The spades table, games and gambling can wait. We all claim we love the children and we hate child molesters! Well let's strike out against the molestations of children in these group and foster homes. Arm chair revolutionaries need not apply to G.B.G. If your juvenile, jail or prison wants to start a G.B.G./Heart chapter in your prison have your warden to call Warden James "Jimbo" Walker (or Capt. Patricia Kennedy at 916-322-4730 ext. 3000. Families can visit us on Facebook, Myspace or yahoo! And/or check us out at www.napsusa.org ...I wanna get this tome to Sierra McFarland (in Sacramento CA) Ericka Cuellar and to principal Verone Kennedy....I want you (the reader) to recognize this marvelous opportunity we have to join a movement for youngsters. Having prisoners, prison guards (proverbial enemies), police officers, Jail deputies, probation officers, professors, parents, pupils, athletes and entertainers all joined together for good is awesome! We need you. This (G.B.G./Heart) is a place where kids affiliate (via the internet) with boys like a band of brothers (and sisters). We train kids to be alert, aware and to think. We reach out to lost boys and girls and lost souls in general. We present kids the faces of hope, the faces of success and sensitize them to their parents, alert them to strangers and alarmed them by predators. We believe in and advocate mental self defense. We ask G.B.G. members to prove themselves by reading, writing, and by growing. We respect the G.B.G. command structure and operate with the leadership goals of a JROTC...I want to compliment you for reading this book. Especially you teens and tweenies. The fact that you are still reading shows how special you are. As G.B.G. President I am very proud of you. I'd like to send the first 1000 students who read this book a G.B.G. certificate signed by Jimbo, Dr. Curren and by me. G.B.G. is the technological, educational, and the informational O.R.A. (operational and reconnaissance agents). You have friends (via Facebook) in G.B.G. and you are getting in on something that will be big, powerful and awesome. There is "nothing that can't be done if we lift our voice as one"....I'd like for some of the G.B.G. students who have wealthy parents to send this tome to Johnathan Matheny, (his mom Bonnie), Isaac Grimes and to Simon Sue (all inmates in the Colorado Prison System)...Our special envoy wants to train budding John Johnsons, Tyler Perrys, Russell Simmons and Marcus Zuckerbergs. I want you all to locate Ricky Lebarron (Baltimore), Ricky Mitchell, Senator Tyrone Brooks, Nightline, Dateline and Ben Tracy and tell them about K.K.K. We need to coordinate (strategically and methodically) this Jihad against gangs, guns, drugs and violence. My (more than a decade) deep studies into the most dangerous (and organized) gangs in this country (to include but not limited to MS13, Aryan Brotherhood, Black Gorilla Family, N.L.R., Skinheads, Bulldogs, Nuestra Familia and EME etc.) have taught me what makes gangs tick, how they recruit, why they recruit and (more importantly) how to steal their members...One day I'm telling Attorney Murray J. Janus about some gang activity in L.A. County jail. And this seasoned lawyer who has been in some of the most sensational (drug, murder and mafia) trials in America told me: "If I were a script writer I'd write about gangs...it is fascinating (for kids, politicians, professors and even for police) to read about the power of gang members who are not smart enough to get out of jail, but are powerful enough to order (civilian) contract hits from behind prison walls." And the first time I told Atty. Janus about my dealings with Don King (also in this book) he replied "You could sell that story to a tabloid. And you could tell that story in a book…You are (for what I did to Mr. King) certifiable"…

More than 85% of kids in foster care (12 years and older) have used drugs and alcohol. Nearly 92% of kids in foster care are affiliated with a gang. How many do you think end up in prison? How many do you think end up like Juan (rest in peace) Espinoza? …Hear ye, hear ye! It is time for us to unite around the cause of kids and lets bang for justice, bang for foster care reform, bang against gangs, guns, drugs and violence…show your support. Go to (www.cafepress.com/Manning) our café shops and get a G.B.G. t-shirt, cap or coffee mug. Write the congress and the media. Spread the word about K.K.K around your campus, pad, dorm, on the internet etc. Roll up your sleeves and take action…kids go to www.boostup.org …G.B.G./Heart will have enemies. It's dangerous to oppose street gangs! But enemies are not walls, they are doors into your future. They are doors to promotion. If there is no Goliath (giant) in your life you'll remain a shepard and never be a king. No Dearaujo (J. Strattion and Lt. Johnson) NO K.K.K (not this part of it anyway)…If you have vision you will not perish. I've got visions fo G.B.G. and for you. I believe you can attract Robert Pattinson, Matthew Deniston, Derek Hough, Zac Efron and Hairo Torres to this book. Get it to the Pensacola News Journal. Get it to Peter B. Lewis, Randi Rhodes and to President Bill Clinton. Inundate foster and group homes with this book…. I wanna give a portion (to be determined) of all the profits from this tome to Homeboy Industries (www.homeboy-industries.org). And a portion to their Homegirl Café! Their motto is "nothing stops a bullet like a job". And I mention a fella (Andrew) in this book etc. He was on the Price is Right. He told Drew "I'm a volunteer for 'homeboy'". And Drew quick named him "Andy the volunteer". Andy wrote to tell me "I can tell you that there has been no other time when Homeboy was been in greater need of support. I personally am working on a project that will allow our organization to establish a partnership with an organization in Korea who would like some of our students to participate in an exchange program in their country". Ex-gang bangers going to Korea! Andy continues "I am currently working on raising funds to get this program off the ground. Sherman I would truly be grateful if G.B.G. would support my cause…you can make the check out to "Homeboy Industries"…I've sent a check representing G.B.G. but I'd love to earmark a percentage of all profits from this book to Andy's project and to Homegirl Café. I can't (yet) commit because I'm rushing to press and would have to speak with the publishing team first. But (as I say in other parts of this book) Homeboy and Father Greg Boyle (in L.A.) is the real deal. It transforms ex-gang bangers! And I encourage you to send them donations large or small. I love and fully endorse Homeboy industries. …I welcome you at Palmer High School in Colorado Springs Colorado and you at Columbine high in Littleton Colorado. All of you students who are discovering and joining G.B.G welcome. This (G.B.G.) is a big, powerful and gangsta thing we are doing for good. This is la familia. No membership dues or fees. We seek no donations. No gimmicks. We have police chiefs, senators, convicts, physicians, associate wardens, clinicians, students, boyz in the hood and girlz in the suburbs etc. in this family. We disrupt, dismantle and deprogram thugz. We do for self and kind. We are a rainbow coalition. We motivate youngsters to tap their own creativity and to lead the world. We ask Michael Vick, Paris Hilton, Martha Stewart, Mr. Dungy and Richard Scrushy to help us reach vulnerable kids with this book. We depend on students to join G.B.G and to take this gang to another level. We aim to operate G.B.G./Heart with as much precision as David Axelrod operated the Obama campaign. This (G.B.G) is (in fact) a campaign for kids. This is a campaign to promote literacy, youth leadership and mentoring through books, CD's and DVD's…tell your classmates (recruit people into this army of volunteers! Get your football team, band, cheerleaders, student government etc. in on this now…) to join us now on Facebook while we are still accepting members. I plan to cut membership off at a certain number so join now while you can...sign up to receive our monthly newsletter and success tips for teens...I want to be sure teachers like John Costa (Sacramento) and Daniel Sample (Missouri) know that their roles are urgent in G.B.G. We need Joseph Schoen, Libby Amor, Jennifer Jaimez and Diego Saavedra. And I want Michelle Gregory at the Department of Justice, Christian (on Tyra on 8/31/09), Mr. Hostetler at Sierra Child Services and kids at Palmer high school to get this book. We need to inundate lawmakers like Gloria Romero, Darrel Steinberg, and the US Congress with this book. You parents who are concerned with helping the youth of America can help by buying (at least one extra copy) a few copies of K.K.K and giving them to at-risk youth. I want lawyers to get it to clients. I want people to send judges this tome for Christmas. And I want youths and student leaders to hold G.B.G house parties and do spoken word routines using K.K.K. I want you all to get copies of this book to Mike Kroll, David Inocencio and Sandi Close at "The Beat Within" and at youth magazines. Pacific News Service, Christopher Guzman (25 in Sacto) and Atty. David Boies need this tome. Get it to Willie Gary, Floyd Abrams, Atty. Stewart Katz, Analea Patterson, Johnny Griffin and to Donald Heller. This tome can help David who wants to open an urban lounge at McClatchy High School...G.B.G/Heart invites youth submit ideas for inundating the foster care system and high schools with this book. We have some monies, stipends and gifts for students willing to go the extra mile to promote this book to students...I need creative and innovative persons who won't rest until Daniel Sample, Danny Noriega (CA.), Seamus Farrow and Caleb Sima have this book. I want students at Locke, Lodi High, and Folsom High to bust a move over the internet and find Jeff Bezos, Tyler Perry and George Soros and evangelize this book to them. I need teams of students at John F. Kennedy High, in Colfax etc. to locate Cezar L. Chavez (the youngster) and Bryan Kennedy in Oakland and evangelize this tome. You can be a G.B.G evangelist today! You have the power to find Justin Berry, Ryan Hreljac and Josiah Lemming and to tell them "Dude you are in K.K.K"...The Swiss are always peaceful in the middle of conflicts and likewise (literally) in G.B.G./Heart. Peter Andrist is the G.B.G. Swiss diplomat for G.B.G./Heart.... I want every kid who is perusing this tome to get involved today. We need you to go to work right now. Tell your parents, professors and pals that you have a new j-o-b. Tell em "Dude I work for Warden Jimbo Walker and G.B.G. " I'm serious! You have a seat at the G.B.G. roundtable. And I never have enough internet help. I need finger power to evangelize the G.B.G. mission. Find Grant who was on the "Price is Right" on 8/20/09. Grant is in the Air force Academy and we want him on our team. Norman was also on the "Price is Right" on 8/20/09. Norman is in the Merchant Marine Academy (class of 2013) in Jamesport New York. We need Norman. I have an affinity for folks in the military, OCS, ROTC and JROTC programs. G.B.G. is structured based upon a military model. We teach team members individualized training i.e. leadership, respect, tact, diversity sensitivity, ethics vs. situational ethics, discipline drill and ceremonies, the power of unity, public speaking, literacy, writing skills and mega reading. These skills are necessary to effectively participate in our G.B.G./Heart youth impact tours. I owe a great debt to Captain Steve Vance, A.W. Fred Schroeder, C.D.W. Tim Virga and A.W. Jeff Macomber for their guidance, input and intense consultation with G.B.G. as we train our core members. And I intend to make all of our 'minutes' available for students, youth leaders and other prisoners with all deliberate haste. A number of internal G.B.G. documents and edicts are 'classified'. And these documents can only be de-classified by a (G.B.G.) Lieutenant Colonel or above. (Lt. Colonel Steve J. Vance and Colonel Fred Schroeder have assured me they intended to declassify all of our documents "soon". I'm cognizant that many student leaders are anxious to peruse these documents and I'm in touch with the superiors at this Juncture....stand by)... I'd like for you to make sure that Senator Jeff Denham (Sacto), Jeff Macedo, Aaron McClear, Jackie Goldberg and Attorney Barry Tarlow are all informed that this tome (with them in it) is out....

Again I ask all of you young prayer warriors to send up fervent prayer for G.B.G. and for the contents of this tome. Ask God to help us strategically, methodically and manipulatively get this tome to teens and tweenies who need it. God can do some things that'll blow our minds if we activate His favor. He will engage the angels in a clandestine and stealth campaign to position K.K.K. in the hands of the right people, at the right time. God is awesome. Can I tell ya'll about Thomas (and Serita) Dexter Jakes? The big ole black bald headed dude you see on t.v.? Concisely: back in the early 90's you had never heard of Bishop T. D. Jakes. He was in obscurity and mediocrity. Bishop Jakes used to dig ditches for a living ...He was a ditch digger. He could preach but nobody knew him. He pastored a store front church in Charleston, West Virginia. It just so happened he was invited to preach for Carlton Pearson in Oklahoma. Pearson invited 3 preachers and Carlton had a television show. Carlton decided to play three seven minute clips etc. one of each preacher. Jakes preached about "Show me your wounds" concerning Jesus showing the disciples the nail prints in his body...And what had happened wuz-it just so happened that Dr. Paul Crouch (owner of TBN) was writing a book "I have no father but God." And Paul was struggling to decide if he should reveal certain secrets of his own personal struggle in the book. It just so happened Paul Crouch happened to come home; happened to turn on the television. When he turned it on T.D. Jakes happened to be preaching how one should "Show me your wounds" as a testimony to others. It happened to be the right sermon for the right man. Paul got on the telephone and called Carlton and "Who is that big ole, bald headed black joker on your show? I wanna meet him. Tell him I want him in California and on TBN"...Now if Paul had happened to step in the kitchen to grab a ham (seven minutes remember?) sandwich we wouldn't know T.D. Jakes today. T.D. packed up his beautiful wife Serita and the kids. They moved from West Virginia to Dallas. And now the store front (in WV) is The Potter's House in Dallas. And Jakes preached a sermon for America's first black president in January 2009...I tell Bishop Jakes' story because I want to encourage you(students, kids in foster care, kids in college and in gangs etc.) who may be digging ditches today to keep going. Nothing just happens. But success can give you an 'all of a sudden' miracle. Luck is when opportunity meets preparation and they French kiss one another. There are so many youngsters who are lost, confused, stressed and depressed. Some of you are surrounded by a classroom full of people but you are lonely. You have some secret fears, secret problems, secret pains and some secret issues you're not comfortable talking to teachers and parents about. You feel like giving up. May I ask you to please don't quit. "When things go wrong as they sometimes will, when the road you're travelling seems all up hill. Rest just a bit but don't you quit because quitters win and winners never quit." You just happened to get this book. You just happened to be reading this page, paragraph, sentence and this word. Nothing just happens. There is a reason you are where you are, who you are and reading this book. Some of the nationally recognized G.B.G./Heart supporters (i.e. perhaps Gloria Allred, Senator Darrell Steinberg, Distinguished Professor and scholar Michael Vitiello etc) don't support me. But they support the mission of G.B.G. ...Ipso facto (even as angry as I get with them sometimes) I assure you that, Senator Steinberg and all G.B.G.supporters are rooting for you. We care about how you feel, what you think and what is important to you. And G.B.G. is your opportunity to be mentored by Harvard trained scholars, corrections experts, therapists as well as clinicians. And I'd like for you to absorb the mentoring, guidance and the nuggets in this book. And as you join G.B.G. and become one of our insiders you will grow in your mind and grow in time. You will begin to recognize how important, powerful, influential and necessary y-o-u are. G.B.G. is not a regular lil organization where you sign up, come in, sit down and 'cross your legs'. We are revolutionaries! We do! We busta move baby boy. We (G.B.G.) are the authentic shot callers. We stick together and support one another. This (G.B.G.) is as unusual as our name (G.B.G.).

This is a great organization. You will not find any other inmate involved group with a Harvard psychiatrist on the team. You won't find another prisoner founded group with as many licensed psychologists, psychiatrists high level prison officials, Swiss diplomats, pastors, students etc. all on the same team. So (again) I say 'welcome'. Go tell your mom "not only do I work for Warden Jimbo Mom but I'm a gang banger!" Your mother (if you live in the suburbs) will say "you're in a what?" and she might call the police. If she does, don't trip. Get on the telephone and tell the cops "you ought to join too. Look at www.napsusa.org ….dude I think you're in K.K.K.". When you say K.K.K you'll really get their attention! But if you reside in the hood as soon as you say you're in a gang moms will say "Boy you ain't telling me nuthin new. I know yo black ass in a gang". Then you stop, show her your G.B.G cap or t-shirt and tell her you are a "Gang Banger for God". All G.B.G. members walk erect. We hold our head up. We make eye contact when chatting with you. We have a firm hand shake. We open the door for ladies. We still give up our seat for women. We groom with excellence. We read, write, rationalize and visualize. We don't allow some cult to brainwash us. We brainwash ourselves by programming our minds for success. We know the power of visualization, creative auto suggestion and self affirmations. You become what you think. And you program yourself by focusing on what you do want. Disrupt negative self talk like "I can't" and you can...I've been taught some of the super sophisticated peak performance techniques which N.L.P. (Neuro Linguistic Programming) masters teach the secret service. These same techniques were mastered by the greatest basketball player (ever) Michael Jordan... and I'll remind you that you can learn these secrets...what you say, see and hear-you become. Let me illustrate the power (and importance) of focus: this is my dot close. I need you to grab an ink pen and a Bible...I hope you have a Bible but if not-get any book. You got a pen and a Bible (book)? Okay open your Bible to Psalms 23. If you have no Bible just turn your book to page 23.... Ok, you got the 23rd Psalm? Take a look (now) at Psalms 23. Now take your pen and draw a small dot on the page. A dot anywhere on the page. Have you made the dot yet? Draw the dot on the page. Then look away from the page for ten seconds and then look back at the page....what happened? As soon as you looked back at the page where did your eyes go? Straight to the damn dot! Why? Because your attention always returns to what you last focused on! ...All that good stuff on the page ("the Lord is my shepherd; I shall not want....yea, though I walk through the valley of the shadow of death, I will not fear no evil")- you skipped all of that and put yo blue(hazel, brown or black) eyes right back on a darn dot! It's the power of "focus". I want you to see yourself succeeding, going and growing. This is 'urgent' now; when you're going to sleep focus on success. I want your last thoughts, visions, and focus to be on seeing yourself succeed. And you will (the dot) wake up refreshed and ready for success. You feel me?

...Plaxico Burress is going to prison for two years for shooting himself in a night club. (I don't support the sentence. A large fine, probation and community service would have sufficed I think.) Prisoners read a lot. I want some of you to send Plaxico a copy of K.K.K. It can help him. And I really believe great pastors like Rev. Otis Moss will tell their members to visit guys in prisons by sending them this book. Do tell!

Feed yo mind the good, the clean, the pure, the powerful and the positive. I will make you a solid promise: If you read the five books (r-e-a-d them now. Word for word and focus) I mentioned earlier (including John Johnson's) you will begin to transmogrify. It's a powerful feeling. We teach guys how to get that same (oozing) feeling of power (that we used to get from having a gun) by learning. Once it is inside your mind it will stay till the end of time. Nobody can mindjack you. Your knowledge is yours forever. And forever is a mighty long time. Get it in yo head bro. Anything Bill Cosby wants to give me? I'll take it and with "Come on People" he gives to anybody who wants to read it. His co-author is a brilliant colleague of G.B.G advisory director

Dr. Curren...Alvin Poussaint MD teaches at Harvard. I can't let Dr. Poussaint co-write a book I don't read. Are you crazy? Anything Dr. Phil wanna give me I'll take it. How could I let Dr. Phil get away with penning a tome that I don't read? Hell nall I don't agree with everything Dr. Phil says. We are diametrically at odds sometimes. But I grow, stretch and learn with every book. I disagree with 80% of what Rush LimBooty says but have read all of his books. Reading is the key to the fountain of knowledge. The key! The key! The key! I won't let Dennis Kimbro, Vernon Jordan or Les Brown write a book without me reading it...

Marion E. Spearman: He's around 42 years of age, admittedly gay, African American and the associate warden at Pleasant Valley state prison. P.V.S.P. is in Coalinga, CA. right outside of Fresno. Marion pays white guys $50.00 per hour, on Saturdays and Sundays (for 4 hours) to clean his 3 bedroom house. That's darn near 520 grand per year. But he earns $118,000 per year. And why does he pay a guy so much to just clean his house? Because there's a catch: Marion has the guy cleaning in a "speedo"! That's way out! But here's Marion. (disclaimer: This author does not know this to be factual. A correctional Lieutenant provided Sherman D. Manning with this data...) Two years ago a 16 year old white guy reported Marion to the police. He alleged Marion paid him (a 16 year old heterosexual) $50.00 per hour to clean house in the black speedo. The kid alleged Marion attempted to forcefully orally copulate. "He offered me $250.00 extra if I'd let him blow me" the kid reported. Marion had friends at the police department. And Marion paid the family $5000.00 to not press charges...Marion spends more time on the tier, at cell doors than any associate warden I've ever seen. He gets younger white inmates to provide him with visual sensations via penile demonstrations. This man is sick. He had Lieutenant Webster unassigned from building D4 because Webster caught him (red handed) fondling an inmate's private through the cell door slot. Marion told Warden Yates "Webster has to leave my building. He's in my way and he cramps my style." Webber is a very fair and Christian man. Lt. Wendy K. Meyers is also a very fair woman. She disciplined C.O. D.L. Criner for attempted brutality upon me at P.V.S.P. in C.T.C. When Marion heard about the discipline he threatened to set Lt. Meyers "fat, red-headed ass up"...I really wish Matt Cate, David Shaw, Scott Kernan or a Federal Judge would visit P.V.S.P unannounced. Senators Gloria Romero and Alan Lowenthal should visit P.V.S.P D-4. But wear a mask so you (they) don't catch Valley Fever. Enough (for now) about Marion. I just wanted to give you a break by telling you about Handkerchief Head Marion. He is a sick man. He is dishonest, a liar, abusive and a toe tapping miscreant who's heart pumps only crap. He's very unhappy and he despises being black. (...you all pray for me because an A.W. has power! And Marion is close to Bunnell. And I'm safe at New Folsom). The CCII said the governor ought to DRB me here...But Marion could have me transferred and murdered! He has the power! Eddie Watts is dead. Hollywood Walters is dead. And more inmates were murdered at P.V.S.P in 2003, 2004 and 2005 than at any other prison. And be advised that they control what the public is told. I.E. Even Arnold toured the prison at Chino 3 weeks ago. And he was lied to. They blamed it on overcrowding. Overcrowding is an insane problem of titanic proportions here. But that riot was instigated by a guard- about Obama and Gates. Unbelievable how prison P.I.O.'s (public information officers) toy with the press and feeds them lines of bull crap daily. And they buy without question. And be advised (you thugs who think it's cool to come to prison) that if we try to write the media our mail is picked up by the same staff we are writing about. Our mail is screened and processed (incoming and outgoing). They steal mail routinely. And although mail theft is a federal crime the postmaster rarely intervenes in prison mail thefts. I get a lot of mail and (i.e.) every letter I received today was at least 14 days old. That's ridiculous. Guys like Marion, Wally, DeShazio, Brumbaugh and Astorgia routinely tell their cohorts to be on the lookout for their name(s) in mail...

Have I mentioned Cupcake Brown yet? That is her real name. Cupcake was a gang member, a dope fiend and a prostitute. She was homeless and a high school dropout. She was shot twice. Fast Forward: With no high school diploma and no G.E.D. Cupcake Brown entered community college. She finished community college and then went to a 4 year college. She finished college and went to Law School and passed the bar. Now with no high school diploma, no G.E.D, with two bullets in her body and a name such as "Cupcake" etc. she is an attorney at one of the largest 25 law firms in the world Attorney Cupcake Brown. I hope my female (and male) readers and the ladies out at "Homegirl" café are reading about this phenomenal woman.

She had every reason to give up, quit and to fail. This is 'real talk' for real people and I want youths to get stories like these in your spirit and mind. And begin focusing on Chris Gardner and Earl Graves. Google them and get everything they write or is written about them and begin to model their success. Success leaves clues. Study (Google) Terrie Woods. She is a black woman who was on welfare and now owns a publishing company...I study Jimbo, Fred, Patricia Kennedy, Dr. Curren, Cosby, Poussaint, Dr. Phil, Oprah, Tyler Perry, Will Smith and David E. Kelley. I focus my mental powers and operationalize the laws of attraction in my life. This great, beautiful, wonderful, powerful, special and distinguished group G.B.G./Heart was built from the ground up with (promise, prayers, fasting, dreams, visions)the laws of attraction and N.L.P. ...and you can do it too. If Cupcake did it what about Alba? You? If Willie Gary did it what about you? If any kid has ever been in your kind of situation and went on to college, started a business, became a teacher, lawyer or doctor. You can do it too. Yes you can....

I want some of our special envoy at Lodi High School, McNair High and out at McClatchy high school in Sac town to use Bing.com and find Richard Bertges, Eric Betts (Atl. GA) and Brian Walker (in Denver Colorado) and tell them "I read about you in an awesome book called K.K.K. ("Kids Killing Kids"). Dude go to www.cafepress.com/manning and get it." Also find Dr. Susan Etok, Lottie Gatewood (Palm Beach Florida) and Al McWhorter. Tell Al and Lottie G.B.G. is extremely proud that they are mentoring Taylor Ambrose, Brianna Hollins and Raven Pierce in the "Rise and Shine" program. Tell them we want all the kids in "Rise and Shine" to have this tome. And G.B.G./Heart offers Lottie and Al honorary mentorships with our program. I'm very proud of "Rise and Shine" and I'd like to help them in any way we can... All of my thugz in the hood who used to think, (before K.K.K. showed up) it was cool to get busted and go to the joint etc. I wish you could meet a rapist whom I know named W. Brumbaugh. I want the world to know that C.O. Brumbaugh (who was trained by C.O. Wally Tucker) is a sexual deviant. Not only is he an accessory to the murder of inmate "Hollywood" Walters, but he is a perverted rapist. As he sat outside my hospital room at C.R.M.C. he told that his step dad routinely molested him. (A horrible tragedy. I'm sad for Brumbaugh the kid) Outside my hospital room Brumbaugh thought I was asleep as he opened up and confided to D.L. Criner that his step dad routinely forced Brumbaugh to perform fellatio. "Then he started to butt F (expletive deleted) me. After the 4th butt rape I told my real dad"... I couldn't get the rest of Brumbaugh's story because they came to get me for x-rays and he clammed up. Several nights later C.O. Molina told C.O. Webber that Brumbaugh was arrested for sexual battery (I could not hear if the victim was a male or female) when he was a juvenile. He also committed arson. "Well how did he get this job?" Web inquired. "Because his juvenile record is sealed and expunged" Molina replied. "C.O. Mendonsa and Jeffries filed complaints against him for attempted sexual battery. I.A. is still looking at fool. Everybody knows Brumbaugh gots (sic) issues". Small wonder Brumbaugh is in the Spearman Clique. Brumbaugh (in my view) is a cancer which needs to be excised (nonviolently) from the body of C.D.C. When you look up the word "pervert" in the dictionary you'll see a photo of Brumbaugh. He's a sick, wicked and a terrible man. He has the I.Q. of a banana. I fear for any youngster inmates having to deal with Brumbaugh. He is a loose cannon subject to snap at any moment...Chu Vue? A guard sittin in Sacramento County Jail for a "contract murder of a prison guard. The guard who was murdered is C.O. Lowe. Mr. Lowe worked at C.M.F. at Vakaville Low was a good guard and a good man. He was in uniform, in his garage, en-route to work when some gang members(suspected to be the brothers of deputy Vue. And these were Asian gang members) blew his head off at point blank range. My point? Guards are and can be extremely dangerous. I.E. Mike Bunnell: A gang member Associate Warden and a murderer. Ipso Facto I suggest you stay free... Jimmy Bounnyavong, Zachary Finney and Doug Pieper Jr all need this book... I intend to commission 100 new kids (at schools) to be State Governors(ranking as Regional Lieutenant Colonels)around the country. The G.B.G./Heart Governors must be enrolled in either high school, community or any other college. You must be between the ages of 16-25 to be a G.B.G./Heart Governor. We will select 2 students in every state .I.E. We could have the student Governor at Lodi High in CA. And one at Locke High in LA. That would be the two California Governors. Students wanting to apply for a Gubernatorial appointment must write (1000 words or less) an essay telling us why you should be the G.B.G./Heart special operations director (Lt.col.) For your state. Send it and your photo to me at the prison. Also E-mail a copy to Hallopeter@sunrise ch. Submit entries from November 1/ 2009- September 1/ 2010. (and submit them every year between Nov.1, through March 1... Governors serve for one year and are termed out after a maximum of 3 years)... There are a lot of (private) perqs for G.B.G. Governors and great responsibility. G.B.G. Lt. Colonels are like `Big Brother's` head of house hold. And G.B.G. Governors will be responsible for the facebook,myspace,yahoo sites for your region and there are a lot of inside benefits you shall receive as a G.B.G. Governor. We are excited about your forthcoming essays.

Aaron Fernander is 9 years my senior (47). As a kid I vividly recall his father owning the neighborhood grocery store. I spent many days in that store hanging around his dad and his mom (Elizabeth). Aaron's sister (Barbara) was a school teacher married to Herbert "Monk" McCall. Monk worked for Mayor Andrew Young (and later Mayor Bill Campbell). I used to play video games (pac-man) with Aaron for hours. I think I was 13 the very first time Aaron told me "I'll be a principal one day. You just watch". He graduated with honors from Albany State College. He became a teacher . Went back to school during the summer and got his Masters. And kept teaching and one day I called home and my mom said "principal Aaron Fernander". He did it just as he told me he would. And I'm extremely proud of Ralph Bunche Middle School Principal Aaron my friend... I sent him this manuscript (minus this "special update") and he wrote "boy I read the whole book on a Saturday. I couldn't stop so I read straight through. It was the best book you have ever written. And in the top 10-15 books I've ever read. And I've read a lot of books boy... I got one of my 8th grade students to read it . He read it in 3 days. He told me `this book is awesome Mr. Fernander.And I don't read a lot of books. I want a copy when they publish it and I already went online and joined G.B.G. I'll buy a few copies and put them in the school library. I want every student to read it... It will be on the bestseller list I promise you..." Well he was `right` about the `Principal` thing. And he has spent 3 decades Educating and relating to at risk teens. I was humbled by his critique. It's a blessing!

I met Congressman Floyd Flake with Eastward Baptist Church pastor David Bond in New York . Rev. Flake was flamboyant, charismatic and a learned preacher. When I met him he was not yet a congressman. But I liked him. And Bond spoke well of him and Bob Laws. Dr. Laws pastored a humongous church in New York also. Ithink some of you G.B.G. members and /or K.K.K. readers ought to go online today and find Pastor Floyd Flake (he's brilliant and his church is in Long Island New York) and tell him about this tome. And ask him to get his members to get copies and put them in the foster care system in New York. My vision is that most of you reading will commit to contacting at least 10-15 of the folks I name herein and Evangelize the tome to them. Preaching to the choir is motivational. But preaching to the lost is transformational. And I believe in a transformational gospel. So did the Lord. When Jesus met a sick person He didn't just preach to him but He healed them . When He met blind people He never read a poem. Nor did He (prosperity preachers) to sell a blessing plan. He gave them sight. He did not just preach and pray. He transformed people. I don't wanna just be about preaching, singing and dancing. I wanna do, give, assist, enlighten, empower and to transform. I love acts chapter 2. But I'm afraid too many Christians get caught up only in the sound, the dance and the 'tongues' of acts chapter 2. But be advised that after there came a sound, as of a rushing mighty wind. After there appeared to them divided tongues as of fire. After they were filled with the holy ghost and spoke in melodious tongues. After the singing,shouting, jumping and dancing. After the gospel had been preached all up in the beginning of Acts 2. Focus on what developed near and in the ending of chapter 2. Way over in 2: verse 37- the B. clause. Those who had shouted and danced asked a revolutionary and transformational question(which we the church, we the people and we the G.B.G ought to ask) "men and brothers, what shall we do?" The Lord has been here in this church the spirit is high and the revival is here. The choirs have sang and now "what" shall "we" do? I've read K.K.K. and joined G.B.G. Now what shall we "do" after all the hollering, jumping, shouting, rushing winds and tongues? Speaking of acts 2:1- all the way to 44 it was spiritual. But by verse 45 they took action. So in the last 3 verses of a chapter all about worshiping, praying, and questioning, they ended up doing. They met the daily needs of their people. And I don't want this tome to only be about the bark but I want it to create the bite. I don't want you to only be entertained but enlightened. I don't want you only enlightened but (also) educated. And after you're inspired, motivated and educated I want you activated. I want you doing things (taking action, reading books, talking to peers about this book. Taking the time to actually evangelize this tome on the internet, in your school, church, college and city). And I don't want G.B.G. to only preach, teach, speak and elucidate. But after we teach, seek, recruit, inspire and acquire members etc. I want to do for our members. I want y-o-u to be able to write to me "Mr. President here is proof that I located and contacted 25 of the folks you named in your tome. Here is what I told them about G.B.G. and K.K.K. I'm glad to do it but I'm also $100.00 short on this or that. Can you help me?" I want G.B.G. to be able to act (as in Acts 2:44-45) and help you meet your daily needs. I believe in a transformational gospel. And I will work tirelessly to try to get people like Dianne Feinstein, Leonard Padilla, Willie Brown, Senator Burton, Michael Moore, Tyler Perry and Willie Gary etc. to help G.B.G. to help you. I don't accept dues for G.B.G. We charge no membership fee and I never, ever seek monetary donations. I give money to groups (i.e. "The Beat Within", Legal Services For Prisoners With Children" and "Homeboy industries" etc.) to help them. But I am in a position to boldly tell Cameron Johnson "hey Cam I have a student member at Lodi High School who wants to go to College but has no money. What can we do to help him? I can contact LowermyBills .com and "can you help us give John Doe at John F. Kennedy High School (in Sac town) $250.00 for going beyond the call of duty to Evangelize G.B.G. "... Dr. Tye Hedblad believed in me. He was an awesome psychologist who really, really cared about people. He cared so very much. A modern day Victor Frankl. Dr. Kelly (C.S.P. Sac chief of Mental Health) loved him. So did Dr. Jaffe (chief psychiatrist). Dr.Hedblad was the most authentic, dedicated and impactful psychologist to have ever entered into hades. And he told me in 1999 "you have incredible talent, charisma and a superior intellect. You are as good of a manipulator as I've ever met. But you manipulate for the greater good. I've read your entire C-file. I'm intrigued because it is obvious to me that you did not commit this crime" Dr. Hedblad proceeded to say "but God put you in prison for a reason. You are exactly where you are supposed to be. And when you learn what you're supposed to learn, you'll move on". I had a steep learning curve. Last time I saw Dr. Hedblad Captain Jimbo Walker had dismissed my idea to bring kids into New Folsom, out of hand. I was despondent and Dr. Hedblad told me that " as manipulative, intelligent and as good of a salesman as you. No you can't quit. You should pray about it. And visualize it and take the time to master a plan to represent to Walker until you convince him. I think you have all the right stuff to build an effective group to impact youth. Don't you give up I believe you can do this". That was the last time I spoke with my mentor Dr. Hedblad. .. Upon returning to New Folsom (aka C.S.P. Sac) I wrote Dr. Kelly and Dr. Jaffe asking them to send Dr. Hedblad to see me. I had imagined coming back here to talk with him for years. Neither Kelly Ph.D. nor Jaffe MD. Replied…It took me 2 months to get a "source" to tell me. "I think you have a right to know so I'll just tell you Dr. Hedblad is dead". I dedicate G.B.G./Heart to Tye Hedblad Ph.D for always believing in me. I miss this great man so much. SO very much…It's time for you (students) to do. I want you to notify Lisa Ling about this book. Do! Heres work for you all: Contact St. John's women's shelter and Wall youth foundation (both in sacto)and tell them about K.K.K. and G.B.G. And tell them I have checks for their organization . I need you all to find out who covered the Mitt Romney campaign for ABC news. I think his name was Matt. Let me know…When Dianne Sawyer (GMA) did the Firewalk on GMA who was the guy (Anthony) who did the walk with her? Let me know. (It's work time now. Do!)Get this book to LAPD Deputy Police Chief Sergio Diaz, Sam Altman, Ryan Owens, (ABC) and Paul Navarro in New York. Get this tome to Stockton CA. student Andrew Squire, Michael Wilkerson (GA,), Kevin Mclin and to Johnny Weir. I need u 2 roll your sleeves up and get this to "Dallas" at KMAX T.V. in Sac Town and to Hugh Michael Hughes . Get inmates Brandon Gene Martinez, Danny Macky and Pedro Armando Quandt this tome. Get it to Professor Antwi Akom in San Francisco. I wanna talk to Prof. Akom .Dylan Vall creative steps(Philly) etc. Get them K.K.K. I need to chat with Kyle Larsen and John Fink (both in Sacramento). Get K.K.K. to 17 year old Jonah Coleman, Faisal Selah, Jared Klapheck and Mick Hazen. G.B.G. is very, very excited about these two student readers. And we need them to have this book. I speak of Cameron Brown and Brett Westcott at Purdue. We need Cesar Ramirez in Oregon. Pilot Cody Freisen in Colorado. I want inmates Willie Nessler and Redmond O`Neal to have this book. Justin Hartle , Attorney Anne Salisbury, Jimmy Bounyavong and Zachary Finney need this book. Go 2 work! Right now… I started this special update telling you about the race riot at Chino. (be advised that that thug Mike Bunnell also instigated a riot at Old Folsom years ago). And my main goal throughout this tome is to paint a vivid picture (unlike what is depicted in Hollywood) of the sadistic nature of the beast by adequately depicting the players in the prison (guard and inmate alike) I hope to (simply) dissuade you from entering Hades. That's why I told you about Chino and how the official media story was/is a "story" and very often the state C.E.O. (big Arnold) gets hoodwinked. Although I am in disagreement with some of the moves Arnold made as Governor. I have no reason to challenge his integrity or to assume he swept the true `reason` for the riot underneath the rug. I don't think he has a clue about what really happened or why it happened.

If I told Arnold that C.O. Thornton at P.V.S.P.is a child molester and likes kiddie porn Arnold would think I was joking. Yet, Mr. Thornton does overtime daily at C.R.M.C. and he admitted to C.O. Cornell that he got "turned on" by internet "porn" depicting "kids". Mr. Thornton also told Cornell that "when I was 24 I served a 15 year old girl twice. The b_ tch looked 30 and she was awesome in bed" and Cornell replied "15?" And Thornton said "Fif_ f_cking teen but it was only twice dude". Ipso Facto Mr. Thornton is a pervert and a child molester. And I wish some of the great citizens of Fresno or Coalinga would go to C.R.M.C. on a Monday-Friday morning and protest (non violently) the hospital allowing a child molester and a kiddie porn patron to work in a hospital! …

…I must reiterate to you kids that this is the oddest, strangest and most unusual book you'll ever read. I'm not writing it to win an award. I'm not writing it to win "friends and influence" others. It would require a level of `selling out` for me to write a tome that Matt Cate would endorse. And I happen to like Matt. He was the greatest Inspector General we ever had. But when I write about Marion, Wally and Thornton etc. it guarantees I won't ever be at the top of the CCPOA's Christmas list. It endangers me and it creates controversy. My `Warden` would even rather I not write about staff. But Rev. Hosea Williams taught me to stand up for what I believe in. And to be "unbought and unbossed". When we do G.B.G. tours I'm censored (and I understand why), monitored and limited. But when I put this sword (pen) between my three fingers it is the only opportunity I have to fully operationalize my American right to free speech and artistic expression. Jimbo is adamant and quite candid with "Sherman when the media is here it can never be about Sherman. It's about the kids. If I ever see you use a tour or a camera to promote your individual agenda or tirades against staff it is over!" And Jimbo keeps his "word". But when I write I'm not doing it to please Jimbo, Cate, Kernan or anyone. I write to elucidate Hades and create a better chance to cause kids to do a u turn. My tomes are not "sponsored" by staff, C.D.C.or even G.B.G.The tome is my thought process born out of pain and experience. And when I have a pen in my hand I'm like Rev. Hosea Williams was in a press conference. I'm like Senator John Burton was in a big five meeting. I'm like Murray J. Janus is in a courtroom. I'm a bull in a China shop. I love America and I treasure this sacrosanct right to speak truth to power. And (in case I'm deceased and my estate is sued) Janus, Blair, Berk, Mesereau, Floyd Abrams, Stephen Rohde and even Attorney Londell McMillan(yall send Atty. McMillan this tome) well defend my right to free speech. I believe Barry Tarlow, Tony Serra, Donald Masuda and the great Gerry Spence will defend me on free speech. Judge James Long does not rubber stamp everything I say but he believes in my right to say it.

I didn't seek a permission slip from C.D.C to write this tome. The California Supreme Court overturned the Son of Sam Law and held that it Raped free speech. I have a right to believe Clarence Thomas is an Uncle Tom and Rush Limbaugh is a drug addict. I believe Ann Coulter probably uses speed and I'm not afraid to voice that belief. I am a man. An American man. ..

By the time kids peruse this tome I may be dead and gone. But I want to tell every American child from deep inside my heart and soul that this book is for real. It is the real deal. I don't give a darn what you saw at the movies. Forget what you saw on "Prison Break". That's game and that is mendacity, prevarication and embellishment to the umpteenth degree. Forget what the big Homeys told you about the `joint`. Listen to all the gangsta rap you wanna listen to. But take it from a man in the mix. I'm in the prison. If I don't know anything else I know prison. I know prison guards and I know prisoners. I'm not one of those "legends" in their own "minds" who is gonna tell you I'm this and I'm that. I've never been afraid and never had my butt beat that's bogus. I have kicked some ass. On a few occasions I've been lucky enough to whip two people simultaneously! ... But I have (also) had the snot beat out of me before. Twice in prison I never thought I'd be so glad to see a prison guard. When I was getting the crap beat out of me one time I said to myself "Lord please send me a C.O." And (unlike Big Brett of Dr. Phil fame)I have been scared before. One time they put me in a cell with a 6 ft 7 brother named Diamond (Michael Young) and Diamond thought everybody was out to get him. He did a thousand pushups per day. And (Brett you reading?) Diamond told me "you can sit on my bed(bottom bunk) anytime. This down here is the living room. I ain't got no hang-ups. Do what you feel like doing. You wanna jerk off while I'm in here cool. Hell-quiet as It's kept we can even jerk off at the same time... I felt my stomach tighten. The cell door is locked. It's 9:35 pm. No guards will be by for 3 hours. And I have a giant promoting a " buddy buddy" masturbation session. Like a joint "family jerk off" I was absolutely afraid. I did not have my shank (knife) with me. And I prayed, stressed and finally spoke... "Diamond with all due respect Bro. not only will I not masturbate in the presence of another man. To each his own. But I'd consider it homosexuality as well as blatant disrespect if a celly did that with me in the cell". ..and I waited. And he (by Gods grace)took the easy way out and claimed " Bro. I was just kidding". I then (took the easy way out)pretended to believe him. I slept with both eyes open and the next day I moved out with all deliberate speed. It sounds funny now (I know yall laughing) but being candid, it is extremely frightening to sleep in a concrete cage with a stranger you don't know. And very often (more often than not) they will put a dude with a 3 or 4 year sentence in the cell with (a killer or a rapist) a dude serving life without parole. And I've known guys who murdered their (short time) cell mates just to attain single cell status. Hear ye, Hear ye: My fellow Americans you shall peruse some stuff in this tome which will turn your stomach. Some of the stuff I did (and until now I hid) will give you a negative (to say the least) opinion of me. Yet, you shall know the truth the whole truth and nothing but the truth. And some of you may think me weak for admitting past fears. Yet, when I tell what I did concerning Don King (a part of me) I still am afraid. Don King is not a joke!

But what ever happens my conscience is finally clear I never, ever, ever, ever intended to write about my case (Calvario) . I generally take every piece of advice given by Attorney Murray J. Janus. But every time he floated the idea of me just telling "the damn truth Reverend. Having seen the truth they shant turn their backs on you". He told me that trying to write to help youngsters, without telling my story was like "trying to put a puzzle together with your hands tied behind your back". So I wanna reach Maxwell Hanger, Robert Bradley Stroud, Sean Swales, Ian Manshum, Assemblymen Ted Gains, Brandon Mathieu McGrew and Joe Laggert with this book. I need you to help me get this tome to all the T.V. Judges (i.e. Judge Mathis and Judge David Young etc.) , David Hankins and to Governors . And yall know that (this is a sacrosanct edict) we must get this book to foster kids. This book will help them ! I've studied prison, prisonality (if you will), subterranean justice the prison subculture etc. I've engaged the best minds in corrections and with personal analysis, empirical data etc. I've figured out the ingredient of prisons and in (per se) figuring out the ingredients of the prison etc. I stumbled across a recipe for prison repellant. Most successes are created out of the ingredients of failures. Success is easier and less complex than we make it. Whatever I did to get fat, if I do the opposite I'll get skinny. Whatever I did to come to prison, you do the opposite and stay free...I don't know many successful gangbangers, deviants and prisoners I've interviewed . Because for the first 3 years I was too afraid to keep notes. But I do have detailed notes (including dates and times etc.) on more than 7000 interviews with more than 1000 successful prisoners. And any successful prisoner is (automatically) an unsuccessful citizen. I know what they(we)did to get here. I have analyzed the syntax and the idiosyncratic whims which run rampant in Hades. I've been guided and advised by the best minds in forensic psychology and psychiatry. I've read more than 1700 books in the past ten years as I've embarked upon this journey of discovery. I left no stone unturned as I launched my efforts to understand (inside out) this thing called prison, gangs, prison guards and the "stuff" that makes it all tick. I wanted to know why one person has a phobia about being on prison grounds.   One can barely stand to drive through those gates for a 2 hour visit with a loved one. Yet, another chooses to spend 40 years working in that prison. I needed a comprehensive, substantive and an authentic knowledge of the type(s) of prison guards. I had to know why a "straight" man would wake up one morning and decide to spend the next 40 years meticulously scanning the anus, penis, and the testicles of other men. I wanted a real comprehension of what drives one man to spend a lifetime motivating, inspiring and teaching kids as a coach. Yet another man makes the decision to spend his life caging the men whom society has condemned for life. I needed to understand the prison guard just as well as I understood the prisoner. I needed to understand how to –do- prison just as proficiently as Michael Jordan knew how –to – play basketball. But playing it (being in it and being able to figure out how/why we survive it) was still not enough. I needed to successfully take that next (unthinkable) step. I needed to also understand how to teach prison. Build a prison team (G.B.G.) and to paint a word portrait of prison just as successfully as Phil Jackson runs the triangle offense. The difficulty (and what took me so long) was/is that many great (Magic Johnson) Basketball players are not great basketball coaches . Many great speakers are not great writers. Ipso Facto. I had to learn (as an erudite because no book like this had ever been written) how to employ a kind of mental falsetto (new phrase born in Hades. I had to do what the Queen of soul did with music...) I once heard Michael Jordan say "I'm pretty much maxed out on the education of the game of basketball" and he was right; as a player, yet not as ateacher (Phil Jackson)...Back to Aretha: She maxed out on the education of the game of singing soul... She (as a couple of my embellishing friends say of me) studied the great (soul singer)and became greater. But then Aretha stepped outside her element and taught herself to sing opera. (She raied the bar)...And then she decided (after more than 40 years of singing) to learn to play piano and keyboards (and break the bar). What a woman. So it is as if a (the) Michael Jordan could learn to play like Mike then learn to physically condition himself like a Joe Weider and then learn to coach like Phil... That's a tall order .

And so I was influenced by Dr. Iye Hedblad and Dr. Jarman and I realized "I will never/ever be in a place where there are (i.e.) ten psychologists and ten psychiatrists all in the same place" And most of them feel like underachievers because they studied for twenty years and are degreed down! (i.e. Dr. Jarman has 4 separate degrees. A masters in this and a Ph.D. in that etc.) And they are extremely `limited` by what institutional policy allows them to do in a penological setting. I.E. they are disallowed (by C.D.C.) to treat PTSD. But I finally figured out that this did not prohibit me (free speech) from asking Dr. Bruce Bakeman or Dr. Jamie Davidson (author of "Sweet Release") to 'explain' to me in layman's terminology how you would begin treating an Iraqi soldier who had PTSD". And "give me an example of what the treatment would be"...If Phil Jackson were here and I stood on the prison basketball court (and Phil was prohibited by policy from "organizing a basketball team" etc.) with a ball in my hand and said: "Phil how would you teach so and so." I assure you (guaranteed) that (sooner or later) Phil would grab the ball and begin to show (teach) me how to... And I could learn more (about the game of basketball) by playing Horse with Phil (in 30 minutes) than I could learn in 4 years , on my own.

So my strategy was to not only know what led us to come to prison. I had to learn who the master prisoners were. Why? And how! Then I had to learn how to manage a prison. And what type of person wants to manage a prison. I had to strategically methodically and to subtly inject myself into the minds of master prison guards. And I figured out Terry L. Rosario, Fred, Steve, Cheryl Pliler, Patricia Kennedy, "Jimbo", Marion, Yates and... I had to study master prisons. I was able to do this by playing the prison game as a prisoner. And by reading every book written by a prisoner. But most guards weren't writing... It was not enough to play prison like Mike. I had to understand prison like Phil.. Enter Terry L. Rosario! Enter "Jimbo" etc... and perhaps no other California inmate has been able to hear guards more than I have... Most people who go to the hospital only stay a few days and even if they are prisoners/patients 99% of the time they'll be in a hospital with a T.V... But God sits behind the curtains of life orchestrating events like a puppet master... It just so happened that I went to a hospital not for 14 hours, 14 days or even 14 weeks. But I checked in for 14 months. And I had no T.V. and no radio. All I had were the 7 or 8 prison guards sittin in my room and outside my door. And I listened, and I listened, and I listened.

Hell I learned Guards`(i.e. Joe Rikalo= son= two blonde daughters etc.)Family members by name, school and age. I know the home telephone numbers of Rikalo, Criner, Garcia,

Thornton, Cornell and others. I studied these people like a science project... And to top it all off I have a team of brilliant physicians and clinicians to translate (into shorthand) complex syndrome.

It was not enough for me to play like Mike. I had to also learn to condition like Weider. Then I had to learn to coach like Phil... Being able to understand the inner workings of the minds of the Menendez Brothers was not enough. I could not organize G.B.G. and author such a tome as K.K.K. If I could only sing like Aretha. I had to raise the "bar" like Aretha. Then go back to school and learn how to sing opera. Then I had to teach myself (piano) the guard paradigm – raising the bar is not enough. I had to break (K.K.K.) the freaking bar! Breaking the bar meant coming out of my shell. Breaking the bar meant exiting my comfort zone. Breaking the bar meant learning how to read (prison).Then learning how to w-r-i-t-e (prison guards!). Then learning how to translate (teach) what I read and what I wrote and to translate it in an entertaining, inspirational, authentic and sane way. You feel me? (Some of my Christian pals won't like this example but –I'm not worthy to even tie His shoe laces!) I had to become to (about and concerning) prisons what Jesus (our Lord) was to people. Jesus saw sick people, knew why they were sick and healed them. Jesus heard folk were sick, knew they would die and then raised them from the dead. I had to see, know, heal, and to raise. It was not enough for me to be a good preacher (writer) . If being a good writer was enough to stop criminality. John Grisham would be the crime czar. But I've known guys to finish a Grisham novel and then murder their celly. I needed to do more than preach or see. I needed to prophecy. I needed a triplex paradigm of the sight world. I needed sight (elemental) I needed insight (educational). And I needed foresight (spiritual). I needed Christ to put his super on my natural. I needed to know what to say. I had to learn how to say it. And I had to be efficient at explaining why I'm saying what I say. Saying (per se) is not enough. If I had an I.Q of 200 but the public speaking skills of a boring lecturer how effective would I be? If I write a power book in German it would bless Peter Andrist but lose and confuse you. Unless you speak German. I had to fine tune the numbers of a prophet and... A lil boy sat in church next to his mom and the preacher preached. "You preach too loud" the boy yelled. His mom looked at him with a look that could kill. "You preach too long" the boy yelled and his mom grabbed him. About an hour after he yelled out "and you aint saying nothing"...The challenge is to not preach too loud or long. And to say something.

Breaking the Bar meant writing this book from my heart and not just my head. It meant breaking every rule about how a memoir should or could be written. It meant taking off every façade. It meant standing naked with the pain. Naked with the crime. Naked with the truth. Naked! Naked! Naked! It meant I had to turn the light on for you. Then I had to open the curtains. Then I had to open the shades. A news article can give you a glimpse. But K.K.K. had to do more than that. What is more difficult coaching or playing ?... Patricia Kennedy is a master manipulator. But most of the time she has no idea that she is manipulating .I've never met a prison employee who can more effectively disarm an inmate than Mrs. Kennedy. And if you asked her to explain "how" she did it she could not. Tony Robbins has earned hundreds of millions of dollars by being able to "notice what a person is doing" and packaging it as a recipe modelling and teaching it to others. That is precisely what a coach does. I am not alert smart or sharp enough to do this alone. I've been blessed to be able to notice "what" (Kennedy, Walker, Rosario, Fred etc.) people do. Then I have help (Solis, Jarman, Curren, Houston etc.) in figuring out the ingredients of what they are doing. And being able to model it and package it via recipe. I was a master con because I noticed (inflection, tonality, breathing and nuances) how Ambassador Young, Rev. Hosea William, Rev. Jesse Jackson etc. talked and emulated it. As I traveled over into the darkside of the minds of the Menendez Bros, Bardo, Henson and Stokes etc. I was able to bring certain traits, behaviors and characteristics to learned psychiatrists and to be educated on the method of the madness. The challenge for a Frank Curren is "I have this

Harvard degree I understand the pitfalls and the problem of at risk teens. I even know many of the solutions which could/would reduce youthful offenders and perhaps reduce recidivism. But I have no idea how to reach kids. Sherman you have the advantage because of your status as a convicted felon. You have a ready made and an attentive audience. Your challenge will be to take my knowledge of solutions, your knowledge of the crisis and to communicate them to young people around the world. If you pull this off Sherman you'll do for prisoners , for youths and for foster care kids. What Martin Luther Kind Jr. did for civil rights"...

And what had happened wuz I came to the conclusion that with the light of God's word, the broom (Dr. Curren , Dr. Solis, Dr. A.Duran, Dr. Gregg, Dr. Heitkamp etc.) of knowledge etc. We can (with K.K.K.) sweep up the mess (pitfall, gangs, drugs) that stands in the way of America's children. I link up (via G.B.G. with Colin Powell, Ricky Martin, Amy Finn, Matt Crouch, Tony Robbins, Pastors, Professors, Pupils and prisoners and I say let's do it!

My message to Brett, Chris, Zachary, Finney, David Zablotny, Paris Hilton, Dr. Poussaint, Alexis Graham, Keith Wright(16), Michael Vicks, Ian Drew, Charles Ebersol, Beverly Hills High students, Steve Barr, Nils Vesk, Perry Thompson, Anthony Dedousis, Chistian Nelson, Chris Shea, Ollie Valencia, Students at Vista del Lago, David Buzzetta, Ronald E. Mcnair High School Students, David Holloman, Alex Blench, Adam Bettercourt, Tom Degnan,Jake Heartsong, Jordan Simon, kevin Wehr, Zach Hall, John Simon, Jesse in Parkersburg Iowa, Redmond O'Neal, Joseph Schoen, Libby Amor, Ben Chuchla, and Daniel Sample is that "together," yes we can!

Dustin was on Tyra Banks on 8/21/09. Ya'll find him and tell him G.B.G. has a gift for him. I was interviewing an inmate who told me "I want to cut Marcia Clark's nipples off and shave a small tree branch in her --- (private). I will kill that b-tch." Initially I thought he was merely talking. But I began to profile him and he/is was a weirdo. And he will get out of prison. And I have every belief this pervert will try to get to Mrs. Clark. When you see stories like a beautiful model being viciously murdered and stuffed in a suitcase. And when you discover that her fingers were cut off and her teeth were all removed. When you learn that the only way the police were able to identify her was by the serial numbers on her breast implants you think "monster". And that is the mistake the police make time and time again. Victims also make this mistake. They always think it will "never happen to me". And the "people who do that kind kind of stuff are monsters" . And they look a certain way. I'm here to assure you that the people who do these kind of murders (mutilation and decapitations etc.)Look like Eric,Lyle, Bardo, Henson, Johnson, etc.etc. The series of sadistic murderers I've met were predominantly Caucasian fairly articulate, athletic and semi jocks. This is an over generalization for sure. But my point is that an untrained eye would never have suspected that Eric and Lyle were so-called "natural born" killers. The average person meeting Ed Stokes and/or Bret Moore would never suspect them of being pedophiles. However I'm certain that (knowing what I know, reading what I've read, and learning what I've learned)if I met Eric or Lyle tomorrow (for the first time ever) I'd have that "feeling" in my gut that says "something is not right about these guys". I would know something's wrong. If I met Marvin Johnson for the first time tomorrow I'd sense it... When I met both Ed and Bret I knew they were perverts. Pat Brown would know. So would Jack Kennedy. And the goal (through books like K.K.K.)is to teach folks (especially youngsters) to develop that "sense" that causes them to notice that they're in the presence of evil. I promise you it can be developed. Think back. Have you ever met somebody and knew they were great as soon as you stepped into their zone? U.C. Davis has the foremost neuro ophthalmologist in the Nation. Dr. Kelte. And I recall going to his office. When he walked in the room I felt greatness coming. It was not arrogance or conceit. It was a kind of silent power that spoke loudly . I've heard (and read) that Dr. Martin Luther King Jr had it. We call it "it". Well every dark spirit (not to go spiritual on you) has another kind of "it". I feel it around Rauser, Eric, Lyle, Bardo, Stokes, Moore, Henson and virtually every sadistic and/or perverted person I've ever met. You have that radar also. You're just not sensitive or listening. Ever heard of gaydar? We can all recognize the flamboyant homosexual. But the Marion Spearman's (no pun intended) will fool you if you don't listen to and feel your radar. I recall being in Richmond Virginia. Brian Devin Graham and I were in a convertible jag. Top down and we was (sic) chilling I had music blasting. I saw a funny looking cloud and I turned the music off. As soon as I turned down the music I heard the silence screaming that a tornado was imminent. A couple of seconds after I asked Brian "do you hear that (silence)? " We watched the roof blow off of a building. And just as I had to turn down the music so I could hear the silent threat. You must turn down the distractions so you can hear the silence of the demons. When you are in the presence of a very clear and present (Menendez, Arizona, Stokes etc.) danger you must tune in to the silent threats. If I blow a dog whistle you won't hear it but my dog will. But if you are watching you know when I'm blowing by watching the reaction of the dog. If I pass gas in the room with a deaf man he won't hear it. But he'll know I did by his sense of smell. If I slip a silent fart in the room with a dude with great hearing he must utilize the sense of smell to tell I passed one. When a man is paralyzed from the waste down physicians will tell you get greater strength in his arms. Blind people have powerful hearing. Some of it is biological reallocation as well as physical compensation. But some of it is merely a redistribution of his focus. You must tune in on the frequency of predators in order to identity them. Learn to listen to your feelings. And when you feel something is not right- listen, make haste and get away... "He creeps me out". The creepiness is your radar working for you. You can misread it but "it" is never wrong...

I've seen Dr. C. Solis in a lot of sad, intense and deep situations and had never seen him shed a tear. I found his tear shedding in a very unusual situation. Iwas pumping the good Doctor for psychiatric data and elucidation. And I said "Dr. Solis have you ever come across anyone either in private practice or in C.D.C. who suffered from a 'butt sniffing' fettish? The good doctor had (lol) crocodile tears flowing as he said "ah ah butt sniffing fetish ... Carl Etheridge goes by the handle "Blue". He wears a prison blue jean jacket 24/7. I've seen it 110 degrees outside and Blue will still have on that jacket . I've seen him workout in it. He keeps a large rock in his pocket at all times. Sporadically he'll wear chicken bones around his neck. We chatted all the time and I knew he was "weird". I needed a celly and almost moved with my buddy Blue ... He ended up getting a celly and the dude ran to the watch office and begged to be moved. He ended up locking up by putting himself in Ad-Seg. I saw him locked in a rec cage a few days later and inquired as to what happened. He explained that he was awakened to the feeling of air (oxygen or breath) on the crack of his anus. He thought he was dreaming. But 10 and behold Blue was standing by dude's bunk, in a blue jacket and boxers. It was midnight and Blue had apparently mastered the art of (methodically) pulling down boxers without awakening you. Blue was sniffing his crack hole! (Eric Bates writes editorials for the Scandal paper at Emery. Wonder if Eric can editorialize this?)...I went to Blue and gave him the story and he confessed! Blue told me "I been doing that for years. I had a few fights over it. It excites me man. Just sneaking and doing it while they (sic) sleep. I can't do it while they (sic) wake." I told Blue "Bru- God is my witness. If I'd moved in there and you did that I would have had to "take you out!" ... Guess what I later learned. Blue is in prison for ? Murder via semi decapitation. The police report stated Blue (literally) licked the victim's blood off of the knife...but wait...notice that "something" told me not to move with him. And I always knew he was "weird". This book is written to remind you to pay attention to that "something" you feel around certain folks. And when you hear that thought that "dude" is "weird". I would bet you my head on a silver platter that Jasmine Fiore (rest in peace and God Bless her family) had felt some nervous inklings around Ryan Alexander Jenkins. Just as a spider spits out a silk like web that he uses to transport himself from point-A to point-B. Killers, molesters and maniacs spit out a spirit or an energy which they utilize to transport themselves into your territory or confidence. Train your ears to listen for it. Train your eyes to look for it. And (of utmost importance) train your sixth sense (not to feel it because just as your nose can't unsmell unless it's stopped up. Your sixth sense can't unsense unless it is clogged up with "charm", "charisma" or "bling") to communicate what it feels to your consciousness. A clock always keeps (knows) time. A clock can't not know time unless you unplug it. However, when your clock shows 6:00 a.m. tomorrow it won't tell you (if you don't "look" at it or) if you're asleep unless (the biggy) you turn on the alarm. You hear me now? If you sleep til 9:00 and lose your job don't throw the clock out the window. The clock ticked at 6:00 a.m. The problem was you forgot to set the alarm. If you set the alarm it will sound. When it sounds you'll know "It's 6:00-get up." Your sixth sense was set at birth. It is absolutely working. But if it calls and you're listening to Limbaugh. If it calls and you're trying to convince yourself that Eric is not just flattering you. If it nudges your spirit but you're getting wrapped up in the web of dude's bull crap etc. You will miss the signal. You will not hear(feel) the alarm…

I allowed a correctional captain to peruse this tome. The captain told me "Dude I have two assurances for you. A. It's a bestseller hands down. It was like a crack pipe I couldn't put it down. That's the good news. B. You will definitely be sued! Bank on it!" I said can I use your name and quote you? "Yes and I'll have you on a bus (transfer) Monday morning if you do." Napoleon Hill was a master writer way before your (teens and tweenies) time. But Google Andrew Carnegie. You'll find that Andy was filthy rich. He was worth $300 billion with a "B". And he fully subscribed to the theory that "If I teach you how to fish I'll feed you for a lifetime." Ipso, facto he left $ hundreds of millions for libraries and foundations. He took Napoleon Hill in and told Mr. Hill "I want you to interview the top 100 millionaires in the world. Not a brief Interview like a normal reporter. I want you to live with them. Watch what they do and learn how they think. Most of them could not explain to you how they succeed if they wanted to. I will pay for all of your expenses and commission this study. This will take you at least 20 years." Ipso facto, Mr. Hill became the best-selling author of his time. "Think and Grow Rich" is a gold mine by Mr. Hill. And Dennis Kimbro wrote "Think and Grow Rich: A Black Choice." Awesome! Some of the billionaires (true story) became jealous and threatened by the book. From 1925 til 1927 it was taken off the market because some of these people did not want the "secret" of success exposed to the masses. After 1927 a very different (excluding much data but still powerful) version of the book was published. I have a copy of the original called "The Laws of Success" by Napoleon Hill. And if I had had this book on the streets I would have been a gazillionnaire! Oh baby boy this book is on Hit. It costs $49.95. I would have paid $500.00 for it…

Just as Mr. Hill moved in with his test subjects I decided more than ten years ago that "since I can't get out I may as well study. I need to know the science of prisons. The science of what drives men to join gangs, abandon family to come to Hades and hang out with all men." I was blessed to have Dr. HedBlad who was absolutely on board with my assignment. This brilliant psychologist stated "You need to view this prison sentence as an assignment. Program your brain to see yourself as a reporter or a journalist. Watch everybody and listen to everybody. And read every book written by Dr. Victor Frankl". I began with "Man's Search For Meaning." And I've read every Frankl book at least thrice. Unfortunately (the missing link) I was not reading (also) my Bible back then…But if you want to know the power of words and the power of a book. Here I am, 85 years later telling you about "The Laws of Success." And we still know about (i.e.) Carnegie Hall all because nearly 100 years ago the most successful person on the planet,

(Andrew Carnegie), commissioned Napoleon Hill to "Study the greatest success stories on the planet. Go behind the scenes and live with them. Put what you learn into a formula and write it."

...Jesus said "The poor you'll have with you always" and one of the reasons we will always have poor people is not because all of them are lazy. Not because they are doomed or "can't". But because many of those people would not read "The Laws of Success" if I gave it to them for free. Guys in jail often (especially in the hole) read more than anyone. But a lot of them are reading novels (they have their place. Entertainment is cool) The key is to get excited about books and excitement is contagious. My mom, grand mom and aunt had me reading at 3. And I saw books, magazines and encyclopedias all over the house. And Ambassador Young does not even speak to me anymore (more on that later). So I have no reason to kiss up to a man who does not even speak to me anymore. But the fact is when Ambassador Andrew Young was mayor of Atlanta I was riding with him to a speaking engagement and Andy told me that "more than 99% of the movers and shakers of the world read at least one book per week." And I never forgot it.

...So I have tried to do for youths, gangs and at risk teens, what Napoleon Hill did for those who would dare to succeed. I have interviewed, embedded myself with, watched and studied the most heinous criminals on the planet. I've infiltrated the upper echelons of notorious prison gangs. I saw/see what they do, how, where and why. And your job is to simply read it and heed it. It can't not work. This is the success system that never fails. If I am able to get this tome published in 2010 this book will be my greatest contribution to the youth of the world. This is an inside story that no outside reporter, journalist or author could ever write. If I interview Lou Ferrigno for 2 hours or even 10 hours to try to discover the secrets of 23 inch biceps, the secrets of his muscles, bulk and build. My report (article, editorial or tome) will only be as good as what he told me. A. He could have lied. B. He definitely omitted things. C. Some of what he does he can't even explain. But if I move in with Lou I can look inside his nightstand. I can snoop around in his closet. I can look inside the medicine cabinet and the cabinets. Now I know what vitamins he takes. I know whether or not he uses steroids and if so, what kind. I know what food he eats. And I can analyze the contents of his refrigerator. I can notice nuances. I.E. "Lou you urinate 4 or 5 times per hour, why?" Then he may explain that he drinks 20 glasses of so ad so per day etc. etc....

Ipso Facto, my assignment has been to package hate, rape, deviance, perversion, gangs, homicide and fratricide and put it in a tome; with a "hot button " name like "K.K.K" I kept seeing cases like Michelle Herndon who was murdered with "Propofol" (a.k.a. Diprivin) by a possessive, jealous and maniacal "friend". And in hindsight all her friends said of the killer "I should have known..There were signs". There are always "signs" and showing you Eric and Lyle Menendez as you have never seen them before is a public service that I owe kids. It is a composite portrait which will unfold as you read on.

You'll recall a multimillionaire (Andrew Luster) who was tried in Los Angeles as a millionaire serial rapist? He fled the country after his trial and bounty hunter "Dogg" brought him in. He used a date rape drug on his victims and he filmed the rapes...I had the pleasure (yeah right) of interviewing Luster 13 times at M.C.S.P. (Ione). We lived in facility C building 13. I did not get to know Luster as well as I know Eric and Lyle. But I did know him and I watched meticulously. He asked "Why don't you write a book about me and we'll go 60/40 on the profits."

Luster has an openly gay celly. Luster is one of the cockiest dudes I've ever met. And he has been able to convince (seriously) himself that it was all the women's faults. And that they "wanted" it. Luster (and his fellow members in the "Billionaire sociopath club") sleeps well at night. He reads, smokes weed, works out and goes to the library. He is agnostic. And if he got out tomorrow he would definitely do it again....Strangely (believe it or not) in my view there is a strong likelihood that neither Eric nor Lyle would kill again if set free. At least not immediately. They are a different "breed" of killers. Eric and Lyle would perhaps survive longer than most paroling inmates if they somehow got out. They could maintain for years. But when they killed again it would be a spouse, supervisor or lover. Once somebody (i.e. Becky Snead, Tammi, an employer or a close friend etc.) crossed them they'd kill them. These guys (Eric and Lyle) are narcissistic. They feel they are mentally superior to everyone. And you are obligated to be subservient in their presence. And in close relationships (i.e. mom and dad) they need to feel control. And it is a "privilege" for you to be "lucky" enough to get close to Eric or Lyle. You must "serve" and if you get close to them and become a problem, hurdle or obstacle they'll "kill" you.

How do you know a person is intoxicated? Slurred speech? Incoherence" They stumble when they walk? Their breath? Yet, a six month old baby would have no idea daddy was "drunk" because the baby has not developed the ability to "notice" the signs of intoxication. However, some persons can hold their liquor better than others. I know folks who can consume 3 long island Ice leas and walk a straight line; and speak clearly. So if they also suck on a mint they can camouflage their breath. Yet a close observer can still detect tell tell signals when a person is inebriated. I had to learn to read people with the kind of pinpoint accuracy that a jury consultant reads a jury. Ipso facto, your powers of observation may be arrested. And/or (like a baby) you might not know how to recognize the signs of a predator. But by the time you finish internalizing the comments of this tome. You will be able to set the alarm clock. I want you to wake up when you're in clear and present danger.

I also want you to feel well enough about yourself that embellished flattery will be unable to cause you to buy a pipe dream. I want you empowered to the extent that you won't need a gang to endorse you. You won't need a gun or a drug to cause you to feel like a man.

...My duty is to tell girls (over and over) that if he beats you once he'll do it again. Men don't beat women. No matter how good he is in bed. Even if he makes your toes tingle. Regardless of how good the making up is leave him. Charismatic males who are manipulative, abusive, arrogant, violent, possessive and controlling must be avoided like the plague. Leave them before they kill you...

My greatest hope and prayer is that you will help me to contact Tracy, Rob, Tony and Leonard Padilla. I pray that you'll use your computer to reach Tony Dungy, Tyler Perry, Michael Moore and Russell Simmons etc. And tell them about this book. I need students (i.e. "The Flame") to write in the school paper about this tome. I'm looking for some crusaders who will go on a mission to tell principals, professors, foster kids, juveniles and pastors about this tome. I want this book in the hands of all of those kids who wanna make a change. Of all of my writing this is the most important, candid, transformative, compelling and dangerous (for me) writing I've ever written. People will be reading this book in 2019, 2029 and even in 2059. And it will elucidate and illuminate. I want to tell you (tweenies and teens) to notice your peers. If you see a classmate, roommate or a pal acting strangely or becoming isolated step in. Reach in and win their confidence. Get them to talk to you and to open up. Perhaps they're being molested, abused, beat or stalked. You will never know til you ask. You are empowered (as a G.B.G/Heart soldier) to help walk them to a counselor or a good teacher. Go to Dr.Phil.com and click on "teentalk" go to www.napsusa.org call 1-800-448-3000 for help...

For you at-risk teens (in foster care, group homes, detention centers or schools) wherever you are this is your day. It is your time to decide you don't want to meet me. It is your decision what you do with the rest of your life. If you like hanging out with men consider tweeting them instead of meeting them in prisons. I want students at Palmer High School, at Locke High and at schools everywhere to focus on the positive...Find out what successful people do, read, think and study. Then just model what they do. You can and you will...Help us to get this treasure chest of data (K.K.K) too Brett Jolliff, Gabe Williams (Sacto), Tim Coleman (Sacto), Ian Manshum, John Matheny, Isaac Grimes, kids at Youth Empowerment, Leon Powell (Sacto) and to superintendent David Gordon. We (you and me) must inundate, schools, jails, juveniles and C.Y.A. with this book. And I want to reiterate that this book is how not to live life.

Transformation takes place every day. You have to put yourself in an environment which is conducive for learning. You stretch and exercise your mind by hanging out with positive, enthusiastic and energetic people. Excitement and enlightment are contagious. Stay away from negative people. They are toxic. If you get that into your mind (deeply), it will be a sparkplug to your life. Do not hang around, wallow around with bitter, broken, negative people. And be advised that prisons are cesspools of angry, bitter and negative people. Beware!

In my quest to acquire a more in depth knowledge of the mind, years ago I read "Change Your Brain And Change Your Life" by Dr. Daniel Amen, I found it absolutely fascinating and empowering. I learned some secrets to young minds (like yo narrow behind) and a lot about why we do what we do. I even learned a complex phenomenon that explains (somewhat) why often when an older person (like my darling Big Momma) has been married to a man (like my Big Daddy) for 60 years. When one dies the other goes shortly thereafter. When a person makes love (not a one night stand deal but in a committed relationship) there is a chemical, mental and a spiritual bond developed and the more they make love the closer these physiological bond become. And when that chemical-like, spiritual, psychological and physiological bonds disrupted by death the soul and spirit (and mind) of the widow grieves and they (too) die. That's deep. I also learned (from virtual brain scans) how severely the brain is damaged by drug use. Dr. Jennifer Heitkamp has spent hundreds of hours elucidating Dr. Amen's findings for me, to aide me in the G.B.G outreach to teens on drugs. I'm still not (yet) an expert in that department but I do appreciate the potent grips of youth addictions more clearly. I'd suggest you (at least) Google this brilliant neuro-psychiatrist (Dr. Daniel Amen) and merely view the pictures of brains that have been fried (sunny side up) and scrambled by drugs.

...I'm thinking about the Menendez brothers, Ryan Jenkins, Bardo and others. My mind goes back: to the first (ever) kid killer I ever met. In fact, this killer fits (classically) the title (K.K.K) of this tome per se. He was a kid who killed a kid in Atlanta Georgia. You would have never looked at this fellow and imagined him to be a killer. At the time of his stunning actions which left Atlanta dumbstruck and terrified. (Ya'll should Google this and/or check the archives of the Atlanta Constitution newspaper...Several of my critics suggest I play up this story and attempt to sell this tome to Will Smith. Will notoriously purchases tomes written by convicts and turns them into movies. A. I don't need to play up this story since truth is stranger than fiction. B. If brother Will Smith would like to turn this tome into a movie I will sell it to him (only him) for $1.00. The caveat? He must donate 25,000 copies of this tome to public libraries...Do tell!! Long before Eric and Lyle Menendez ever decided to concoct a tainted tale of molestation in order to justify fratricide Long before Daniel Henson decided to cut down his parents (and the dog) because they refused to let him marry at 16. Way before Marvin Johnson ever decided to cut anybody's head off and even before Bardo decided to ring a doorbell and viciously murder an actress in LA. There was an innocent and baby faced lil kid named Richard Gellner- in Hotlanta. Lil Richard Gellner is a skinny white kid who was 14 years young. Living in an upper middle class suburb outside Buckhead Atlanta. And on a hot, humid summer day Richard was cutting grass and his 15 year old neighbor (an attractive, blonde headed girl with whom he was obsessed) ended up butchered, mutilated and sadistically decapitated. News reports indicated she endured 157 stab wounds. 1st...An inside police source puts the number at 320. Her head was barely attached to her shoulders by a thin slice of muscle tissue. Her eyes were cut in their sockets. Her nipples were cut off. It was a sadistic, horrendous, evil, stunningly sinister and a terrifyingly dark murder.   Reports claimed Richard was into the witching circle, sacrifice and satanic worship.   Rumors were swirling when my distant cousin (DeKalb County Sheriff's Sergeant Smith) convinced a black captain and (jail commander) Major Melton to allow me to meet (on numerous occasions) Lil Richard. His face had never been shown on T.V. or in the papers. But having avidly followed the case as a kid leader I had this expectation of what he (a killer) would/should look like... "Hi Sherman I'm Richard" this thin, soft faced, blue eyed kid with a high pitched voice said to me. As he grabbed my hand I had the distinct feeling that this soft white hand should be in school, holding a crayon or a book.   But instead he was in an orange jail uniform, accused of having held a knife and savagely murdering his friend...I spoke with Richard for 3 hours that day.   We never even came close to discussing the case. On my fourth conversation with Richard he told me "Calvin (his lawyer was a veteran defense attorney Calvin Leiphold) is gonna have me plead guilty. We're not sure if I'll plead to temporary insanity or a straight guilty plea" in his high pitched, fast talking and animated voice. If you didn't know the contents of our discussion you'd think Richard was merely describing an episode of 'Boston Legal'.

He continued "Calvin says it's open and shut that I did it. And we can't dispute that at all. But my parents don't want my religious beliefs to come out at trial. Because they are devout Jews. Calvin thinks I can actually see the light of day if I plead." I guess you can call that a confession? It was (without embellishment) chilling. Without being melodramatic I can state with authenticity that Richard's face seemed to take on a dark glow (perhaps my fear or surprise) as he spoke. This was his first ever direct reference to the case, to me. And he asked me was I an ordained (I knew Calvin had schooled him when he said 'ordained') clergyman. "Certainly" was my reply. "Well if I tell you what I did you are held to the same standard as an attorney (i.e. Attorney Client Privilege) and can never repeat what I say right?" I nodded nervously. "Sherman do you promise to never testify against me, talk to the D.A., media or anyone about what I'm about to tell you?" I felt my stomach tighten, a lump in my throat and I sweated. "Richard we don't need to do this bro." He snapped "I want to tell you. So you'll know that Jesus you believe in (Satan I rebuke you in the name of Jesus Christ! I say) is a Crock. I want to tell you and when I'm done you might want to become one of us bro." And so I bit; "O.K. start at the beginning and tell me everything. Did you rape her also? Did you have help? Tell me every detail." And he told me the most chilling, gruesome, satanic, demonic , wicked and perverted story I had ever heard and (at 38) have ever heard. And I'd love to make myself look like the credible preacher (later turned con) and to write that I kept my word and never discussed it with anyone. However, I told famed Attorney Murray J. Janus (years later) the entire story. Attorney Janus replied "As a lawyer who's in love with the rule of law and the attorney client privilege I say to you 'never repeat this.' If I were not a lawyer I'd tell you to write a tome and get rich."... Perhaps you assume that since I did (not) keep my word and told Janus etc. Since I am writing K.K.K! And since I'll never see the light of day I may as well (make that money) tell it! And-up until about 30 minutes ago I concurred with that pragmatic rationale.   But-how can I expect youths to trust anything I say if I'm willing to sell a kid (who is being punished for his awful crime!) out just to pad my dossier? I will not write the details of Richard's monologue to me. I will say it was chilling...I will say it did not (in any way) damage my faith in Jesus! I shall admit that I'm not a drinker. But as I reflected on Richard's words to me (once) I stopped at a bar and ordered two shots of Bacardi 151 with a Coca Cola on the side...I can tell you that Richard shared (s) the same rudimentary traits, basic mental 'stuff' and eerily similar characteristics to Eric, Lyle (Menendez), Bardo and Johnson. And I believe that Clint Van Zandt, Jack Kennedy (Dr. Amen, Dr. Curren, Dr. Solis, Dr. Paicez and Dr. Jarman etc.) and Pat Brown would (indeed) recognize these common threads of psychological traits amongst the aforementioned.   It would be unwise for either Mr.Zandt or Mrs. Brown to lend credence to this author (a convict) by publicly agreeing with my findings. However, I have every belief that high profile, ex CIA agent Robert Baer and ex FBI special agent Jimmy Mattocks (who has no bridges to worry about burning) would, at least partially agree with my findings. Ryan Jenkins, Charles Manson, both Menendez murderers, Henson, Johnson, Bardo, Gellner and every serial or cold blooded killer has recognizable traits that can be discovered (early on) and (in my cases) diverted.

The psychological and psychiatric experts continue to debate whether or not there are genes and/or biological determinants which dictate a proclivity or a propensity toward violence or deviant behavior. This is the same community which is still debating whether or not there is a "gay" gene determining sexuality. I am absolutely unqualified to offer an educated opinion on the pros and cons of the existence (or not) of such genes. I shan't attempt to launch out into the deep waters of the psychiatry, knowing I have no psychological life jacket, to assist me when drowning. I don't know. And my opinion shall remain private. What I am prepared to state without equivocation redundantly to the tune of tautology is that every molester, predator, rapist and cold blooded killer has traits and characteristics which are detectable to the spirit eye and the sixth sense. I want my kids to pray, read, study and notice.

The easiest part of writing this tome (that I should have penned long time ago) is to tell an authentic accounting of what I've seen, noticed, read and learned about others. The most difficult part of writing this (K.K.K.) kind of memoir is the fact that (as surreal as it seems and as farfetched as it may be) Oprah just might (although I'm unqualified to be invited to her show. And even if qualified I'd never do her show) peruse (even in a cursory manner) this tome. And one day I'm an obscure convict. And the next day the woman I grew up watching is reading what a sorry ass man I was. And I'm about to (go for broke) dig my grave even deeper! (If I were utilizing a ghostwriter or an editor they'd insist I place the following data in the section of the tome which I refer to as 'confessions of a common'. And not here in a 'special update'. But based upon the structure of the haphazard, disjointed and non-sequential missives I receive from you youngsters etc. I decided to put this wherever the hell I want to put it! Here! ☺ When I saw a story calling Rev. Al Sharpton a confidential informant (on video) for the F.B.I (years ago) I told Lonnie Young "He's a snitch!" And we clowned Rev. Al. When I saw where Congressman Jesse Jackson Jr. cooperated in a federal investigation into Chicago politicians (to be true: especially since I was angry that neither Jesse Jr. or his father ever replied to my missives etc.) I applauded my fellow cohorts who chanted that "Jesse Jr. is a snitch!" But I successfully edited out any verbal confessions of the fact that "once upon a time the Rev. Sherman D. Manning was also a snitch." Pointing the finger of accusatory damnation toward others is always easier than "to thine ownself be true." I vividly recall being stopped by Chesterfield county detective Jeff Green at 1:00 am. I had 14 AK47'S in the trunk of my car along with $25,000 in cash! Detective Green mirandized me and (to my surprise) stated "We know you're dirty and you are small fish. We want your New York connection. I can lock you up for life right now! No bail! No bond! Zero! Or you can help me." I called noted Attorney Murray J. Janus at 1:07 am at home. He roared into the telephone "Reverend it's clients like you who call my house at one and two o'clock in the morning that costed me my first wife! This 1:00 am wake up is going to cost you $5000.00 per minute so talk fast!" I told him what Jeff proposed and he yawned "I know Jeff well and Aubrey Davis will stand-by any deal (s) he makes. But I don't like snitches! I'm a defense lawyer. I don't support this at all. You could find yourself in a body bag. But it's your decision. If you choose to cooperate I'll make certain the deal is written in stone and nobody in the media will ever know about this…We're at $15 grand and counting…put Green on the phone."… Three weeks later after much behind the scenes arm twisting by Janus with Aubrey (and perhaps Judge Gammage) the deal was set. I had to do 3 things and after the 3rd thing my guns and money (or rather my guns and Janus' money because he charged me $25 grand!) were all forgotten. Were it not for this 'deal' I had a guaranteed life sentence in prison in Virginia. Like a humble scumbag and snitch I put on a wire and did the first two obligatory chores. And on a Saturday night at 11:00 pm. I met with (then Sergeant by now he's either a captain or retired) Sgt. Jeff Green. Jeff explained all that they knew about a certain person who was always unarmed and worth millions of dollars and....When I met him at the race track gas station on Jeff Davis Hwy. I spoke into the wire that "he's got a gun under his left shoulder"...An hour after Jeff shot him he told me this: "Dude we had 16 cops out there including me. I've worked vice, patrol and narcotics for 12 years. None of us saw a gun print or a bulge. How did you know? Are you a f_cking psychic?" I lied and replied, "I just 'felt' it." To this day I've never told this story. And Jeff never knew that Tony Robbins was the reason I knew. Studying N.L.P., John Grinder and Richard Bandler etc. Deep studies into the writings of Virginia Satire and Milton Erickson MD had taught me (same thing secret service and CIA officials are taught. Ask Robert Baer. The greatest lawyers like Johnnie Cochran, Bobby Lee Cook, Meserau and Janus also have this training) the art of pinpoint accuracy observation. Congruence, breathing and the methodology of following the eyes. The cops are trained to "Watch his hands" which makes for a good cop. The CIA are trained to "watch his eyes"which makes for a great spy. F. Lee Bailey, Michael Morchower and Janus are trained to watch his "hands, eyes and his breathing" which makes for a great "interrogator and cross examiner" of crooks, cops and of spies. And I was trained to "notice what the greatest of the great do." In less than a fraction of a milli second, the person's breath shifted to his left nostril and I saw him glance (hurriedly) 'down, left' as he "thought" about his gun and (thanks to Tony Robbins, Janus, Morchower, L. Bailey and Lee Cook) I knew he had a gun...

When you all read my 'confessions of a con man' section you shall wonder if I ever got caught. Lest I be the "untouchable" James Frey I must confess that I got "caught" red handed, once.

...In a moment....I called Atlanta International Record Co. (AIR) and convinced C.E.O Alan Freeman that I was "Rev. Jasper Williams" and he should sign "Rev. Sherman D. Manning" to a recording contract. He did and I secured multiple thousands of dollars in upfront cash. The L.P. was titled "The Greatest Love of All"...One day in Baltimore Maryland I called the father (or godfather) of Motivational Speakers-The Tony Robbins of his era. I (Ambassador Andrew Young) called Zig Zigler (bestselling author and motivational speaker) and convinced Mr. Zigler to schedule "My dear friend Marc Rice (aka the right Reverend Sherman D. Manning!) to speak for your company out in Dallas, Texas." Ya'll talk about a freaking bombshell. Zig Zigler is on the motivational speakers Hall of Fame. Oprah? Larry King? Montel? Geraldo? Dr. Phil? President Jimmy Carter? President Bill Clinton? President George W. Bush? And the Honorable Barack Obama? Each and every one of them can tell you who Zig Zigler is. He is motivational royalty! "Certainly Ambassador Young and may I say I'm so sorry to hear that your dear wife of 40 years Jean died." And ten minutes later my hotel telephone rang and I buried Andy's dialect, rhythm, cadence, pronunciation and enunciation and Sherman D. Manning's speech pattern emerged in the person of one "Marc Rice Mr.Zigler; thank you so much for calling." A couple of weeks later the great Mr. Zigler and his famed wife known to the world over as "the red head" picked me (Marc) up at the Airport in Dallas in a Lincoln Town car. They took me to a hotel where the bell cap notoriously informed me that would help me to carry Mr. Zigler's luggage! Mr. Zigler humbly informed the bell cap that "sir this is Mr. Rice and I am his driver" and I laughed. After we got me checked in Mr. Zigler asked "Can we take you to our home out in Carrolton Texas?" I had imagined this house in my mind for years. Mr. Zigler talked about this house on a golf course, in speeches...It was absolutely breathtaking and surreal to be there.

The redhead baked us some cookies. These people were so generous, giving and so nice. Mr. Zigler gave me a rare copy of a book by Norman Cousins "The Anatomy of an Illness" and had me promise to mail the tome back to him when I finished. A promise I failed to keep. A beautiful home on a freaking golf course. The life! I was chauffered back to my hotel that night by an unsuspecting Zig Zigler. In my suite I worked on my speech for 4 hours. Early the following morning I got up, showered and worked out. Mr. Zigler picked me up and took me to his famed offices. A billboard read "Welcome Marc Rice." As his staffers began to assemble in a conference room in preparation for my speech Mr. Zigler excused himself for a moment and returned to beckon me from the stage. As we got outside Mr. Zigler said quietly," I just hung up with Ambassador Young (lol-the jig is up!) and he does not know a Marc Rice." We immediately got into his car and rode (silently) for 2-3 minutes. We got to a stop light and I abruptly exited the automobile. "I'll take you to your hotel" Mr. Zigler stated. I walked away. I was angry, embarrassed and floored! I'd been able to fool America's only black Governor (then Governor-now Richmond Mayor L. Douglas Wilder) into thinking I was "Andrew Young" calling him about me. But Zig ended the jig...the "analysis of a jig ended by Zig." I forgot that Mr. Zigler was/is the father of motivational speakers per se. Ipso facto, just as I learned to read body language, eyes, pupil dilation, breathing, tonality and incongruence etc. Mr. Zigler was the teacher and I'm a student. You can fool some of the people some of the time. But you can fool momma and poppa none of the time. Mr. Zigler is the poppa of the movement and he is better than me on my best day, on his worse day. He's a master speaker and a pro at the nuances of human behavior? I believe (feel free to ask him) I slipped back into Andy's speech pattern at Zigler's office...I.E. If I called someone with "this is Jasper Williams" I had to use base-like baritone and Jasper's speech pattern. And then when the person (i.e. Leroy Elliott) called me "Rev. Sherman D. Manning" I had to use a second tenor tone and scramble my speech pattern so I didn't sound like Jasper. So with Mr.Zigler I slipped because A. he's better that me. And B. My normal speaking tone is similar to Ambassador Young's and in a moment of candor I slipped back into my voice sleeve and Mr. Zigler became suspicious...To show what a Christian and a class act Mr. Zigler is, I wrote him a missive of apology from a California prison cell. And he wrote back "I forgive you!" Attorney Janus told me "You should be a special consultant for the feds on fraud. Hell I'd use you as a juror consultant. Reverend why don't you get a T.V. show similar to Ashton Kutcher? You'd punk people (especially politicians) by impersonating certain officials...I'd bet you could do telephone undercover work and bribe politicians for the Feds..." Thus far I've sent no applications to the Feds. But instead I found my skills extremely useful when entertaining demons like the Menendez Brothers, Ex-LAPD homicide cop, present inmate and G.B.G. member Richard "Doc" Ford overheard me (years ago) interviewing Eric Menendez out on the Shu-Yard one night. Eric had just smoked a joint and was opening up. Detective Ford listened in (eavesdropping) for a while. The next day Doc told me "You're the best I've ever seen and Eric is an idiot." I feigned ignorance and inquired "What are you talking about?" Doc said "I heard the confessional last night. I thought to myself 'Does Eric realize he's talking to a freaking prolific author?" You're good! You shine him on for years by not speaking to him. You psychologically cause him to seek you out. And by the time he convinces you to befriend him etc. He's out under the stars smoking a joint you bought (I'm not confessing to ever buying a joint. Captain Patricia Kennedy is perusing this tome!) him and telling you all his secrets." I laughed. I am not (at all) ashamed to admit (hands down) that I methodically, manipulatively, skillfully and willfully played Eric (and Lyle, Henson, Marvin, Stokes, Moore, Bardo, Luster and every killer I could!) for information and elucidation. It was a plot and a plan that was premeditated to the extent that I'd show Eric my 1st, 2nd, 3rd, 4th and 5th tome and say "see-you know damn well Inside Edition would be all over this if I wrote about you the inside story!

But I never even mention you." His picture I.D. card was stolen, (and between you and I) I would pay guys (i.e. "Fat Cat" Braggs) to steal the I.D. card then I'd either tip Eric off that "Dude I heard your I.D. card was stolen. Somebody is gonna sell it to the Enquirer." Or I'd buy it back and deliver it to the killer…It was a covert, psychological maneuvering for the (express) purpose of (one day) penning a tome about how not to live. And how-to recognize killers, molesters and deviants. Certainly (as you'll see later as I uncloak the hidden author by writing about my other cons etc.) I fully apologize to every victim of my impersonations, emulations and my frauds. I'm lucky (blessed) to be alive!! But (candidly) I do not apologize to the sinister, cunning, dastardly, narcissistic, abusive and duplicitous murderers and molesters whom I've deprogrammed and written about in this tome. If all of my conning, colluding, conspiring, plotting, scheming and interrogating (my fellow) criminals saves just one Elizabeth Smart (Sasha Groene, Sandra Cantu or Adam Walsh) from being kidnapped, or molested, or murdered the book is a success! If I'm a small part of causing just one boy to see beyond (and beneath) a Jesse James (aka "Scumbag") Hollywood and prevents a kids from worshipping Hollywood etc. And prevents a kid from killing for Hollywood-The Book Rocks! If just one of you will but set the alarm on your clock of observation, clock of listening to the voice of your sixth sense, then K.K.K rocks! I call upon you teens and tweenies to 'take heed" to the comprehensive data in this tome. And to be advised that just as I could not have written "such a book as this" without Eric, Lyle, Bardo, Stokes and Luster etc. I could not (also) have written this without correctional officers (S) D.L. Criner, T. Negrete, Gail Crooms, Wally Tucker, AG Guaralde, Aguierro, Ramirez, Joe Rikalo, Sgt. Fred Shelby, Sgt. C. Atwood, Arredondo, L.P., Linda Fortee, Marion Spearman (extraordinaire) and other guards who sat by my bedside and outside my room feeding me the inner workings of a guard's brain. I routinely snored, pretending to be asleep but was "all in." (I recall a female C.O. Garcia who would say when I went to the shower "Manning put in yo (sic) book a blank page and write 'taking shower' cause you can't hear us when you shower.") I could never have written this tome without my G.B.G. members or without Captain Pat Kennedy, the warden, the warden's daughter, Adam Lane, Dustin and the ever so energetic Daniel Bugriyev. Ipso facto I could not have written this book without (watching) Dr. Phil and without the G.B.G battery of advisors. Some human behavior to an untrained eye, is as impossible as it would be for you to read Braille. My advisory board members were (directly and indefatigably) able to translate the language (Braille) into layman's terminology. And as Dr. Duran says "It's our pleasure…you are in an ideal position (Hades) to write the book we wish we could write. We have neither the skill nor time to write like you." Dr. Duran concluded "The portion I read in K.K.K. (on an airplane) was a heart stopping, hair raising and a nail-biting book!" In this status update (candidly) I ask every (I hinted at it earlier) G.B.G. advisor (i.e. Curren, Solis, Friedman, Jarman, Houston Handian, Gregg, Heitkamp and Duran etc.) to buy (at least) 21 copies of K.K.K. One for yourself, and 20 for at-risk (i.e. in foster care!) teens. Cafepress will mail them anywhere in the world. If you don't like the internet or suspect someone may steal your identity call cafepress and order. Pay with a money order using a pseudonym. And I want Adam, Daniel, Dustin and Reid to order at least 3 copies. 1 for yourself and two for kids at the high school from which you graduated.

Confessions of a Conman!

"Confessions (continuing status update go and "poke" somebody about K.K.K.) of a master con! (Again never before told! And even lazy paparazzi like Max on TMZ.com could verify the authenticity of this incident) there is a reason I "own" a company. I do not take orders well. "And what had happened wuz" I was in the U.S. Navy Bootcamp. Our barracks were right next door to the Marine Corps Barracks. (A G.B.G staff advisor was Marine Corp Sergeant Adam Lane. Adam and his green beret cohorts think Navy means "never again volunteer yourself". If Sgt. Lane is reading I have 2 thoughts. A. I believe Marine means "Men Against

Real Intellect Needing Education." B. Sgt. Lane, Maynard is a #4 on that scale you should be a #2 on the scale)... I got into it with Senior Chief Petty officer Arnold. I got Arnold fired! Chief Pitts took over and he was a pal of Senior Chief Arnold's....I got an RE4 discharge. I was kicked out of bootcamp. They sent me to a detention dorm to await final discharge. I would dress up in uniform (to include white ankle leggings which only the boot camp grads and "A" school attendees wore) so I could go to the military commissary. I'd survived "marching party" as well as the severest physical punishment Navy boot camp allowed: 'short tour'. And now I have the boot. I went to the commissary and got $10.00 in quarters. I went to a pay phone and Ambassador Andrew Young called Captain French and told him " I need you to let Sherman go back to bootcamp. As you know Sherman was a star student in JROTC (for a time) Cadet Sergeant Major and a master at drill and ceremonies." Three hours and fifteen minutes later, Master Chief Petty Officer (NCOIC) Hill appeared: "Attention on deck" somebody ordered and we all popped tall. "Recruit Manning you have fifteen minutes to shit, shower, shave and put on your dress uniform."

I stood outside Captain French's door and knocked thrice (as the writing inside the hand print said) and Capt. French said "Enter". I stepped inside and stood as erect as a straight wooden broom handle. "Manning, seaman recruit reporting to duty as ordered sir." "Your orders?" he said. "The master chief said you wanted to see me sir." Captain French stated (with measured words) "Ambassador Young thinks highly of you. He is a man whom I respect highly. I've never reinstated a recruit into boot camp. However, I'm gonna send you back to day one of training. This means your 4 weeks of training thus far is rendered meaningless...Go pack your bags and report to company 048." (I will reiterate that I need to find my company cohorts Steve Coffman, Lopez, Redwine and Duane Fred Hall. Coffman is from Floyd Illinois)...

You're seeing the Faces of Killers now and the picture is rapidly becoming more clear. The awakening some of you are having may save a life. And I (again) challenge you to help us to get this "Prison Bible" to social workers, kids in foster care and so forth and so on. I want Ken Dhanini, Dr. Jim Swire, Joely Fisher and Jodie Evans (LA) to know this book is out. I want kids to begin sculpting your minds and creativity. I wanna see "Eyes of Hope" when I see you. Todd Rixon, (the teen who injured Victorio Ruvolo by hitting her with a turkey should read this tome) F.B.I. director (poke him) Robert S. Mueller III needs this book. Bryce Daniels, Atty. Alaine Hepner, Reporter Sam Bungey (Vineyards Gazette), Jenkins and associates Architecture, Steve Paris and Eddie Locascio need this tome. You are capable and qualified to launch a Cyber A.P.B. Help me find Zachary Finney, Alex Blench, David Jensen and others. I'm reminded of Master P. (send him this book) when he recorded his first CD. He travelled around the country selling CD's out of the trunk of his car and now he's worth $750 million! Put K.K.K. in the trunk of your car and tell folk about it at football games. Tell your English teachers about K.K.K. I want Ann Shulock (Sacto), Austin Teague, Patrick Boyle (surfer), (Race car owner) Arthur Luydnyk, Jeff Surface, and Macarena Hernandez to have this book. Ever heard of a photographer named Mark Smith? Heidi Fugames? We want Sam Bungey and Denoit Benizet Lewis reading this book. Deep in my heart of hearts I pray and hope and visualize that the Facebook generation, will google Ellen Eggers (Woodland, CA) Gerardo Sanchez, Maureen Black, Greg Bunker (Woodland), AL Rojas and all members off the Yolo County Justice Coalition; tell them to get K.K.K. and to pray for G.B.G. I wanna salute Attorney Mark Merin for the wonderful donation which he made (makes to the homeless folk in Sacto.). Merin is a master litigator securing hundreds of million dollar settlements for jail strip searches... I hope you'll help get this to Merin, Atty. Stewart Katz and to Daniel Job. This is a blueprint for stepping away from the prison and stepping into your destiny. As you read this and see how I've wasted so many talents and so much time I hope you pause. As you read about these sadistic killers in here K.K.K. will pull you back and then (propel) shoot you into your destiny. It's absolutely no coincidence that you are reading my words right now. My goal is to further internationalize G.B.G and to focus like a laser beam on ways in which we can subtly, slowly inject the agenda (platform and mission) to students the world over. My plan for evangelizing the world can and will work if you, me and (bare minimum) the G.B.G. advisory board members do as I've requested. In fact, if my elite board of advisors did just half of what I've asked (and just buy five copies of this book and send them to high schools) by sending this book to at-risk teens we will revolutionize the planet. So Dr. Solis, Doctors Curren, Gregg, A. Duran, Jennifer Heitkamp etc. I am strongly requesting you all please spend a hundred bucks to save lives. (If you all don't want me to tell anyone you did I promise- I won't). I just need for us to do this work. We must tackle poverty, drugs, guns and gangs as never before. We must be aware, awake and be sober. But I'm convinced my students shall take pragmatic action (busta move baby boy). And we (Al Rojas in Woodland, CA, Will Rains, Maureen Black, Arthur (race car owner) Luyundyk, Yolo Justice Coalition Members and Chico State. Students etc. will do Jihad on gangs, guns and drugs. We will not allow teachers, priests or predators to molest our children. Not another one of us! We will demand that our senate and our congress stop passing cotton candy laws. They look good and taste good. But they have no substance or ability to sustain. A new law won't remedy molestation in the homes. A new (reactionary) law won't stop school bullying or massacres. We don't need (Sen. Orrin Hatch, Sen. Grassley) a new set of air bags. We need to teach our kids how to drive. Accident prevention skills are the meat that sticks to the bones of life. It is time to hit the re-start button on crime and punishment....

I need to reach Attorney Mark Merin (Sacto-as I said), Donald Specter and Les Brown with this book. There is a lawyer (Peter) who started "The Homeless Book Club" that I wanna get this tome to. I'd hope Tony Brooklier, Stuart Hanlon and other lawyers would follow attorney Peter's example and provide books for the less fortunate. Books help you get up. I want the Alliance for Children's Rights, Sasha Vodnik (San Franciso) and inmates Brandon Gene Martinez, Abel "Grumpy" Maldonado, Nathan Gould and Jeremiah Rodriguez to have this tome. I hope people like Melissa Rothstein, Jodie Evans and Linda McFarlane will locate a few prisoners and (anonymously) send them K.K.K. ...

Bill Kristol? Karl Rove? Rush Limbaugh? Triple demons of deception trying to create Obama's Waterloo. Guys like Kristol and Limbaugh should take some of Limbaugh's drugs and rush off to communist China and stay there! I will personally pay for Madame Ann Coultier to fly over and (sporadically) entertain them. I'll send "Joe the Plumber" to make sure they have running water. And the zealot who went to a town hall meeting with a gun strapped on? We'll ship him over to guard the bodies of those three domestic predators...

Back to Manning: Attorney Morris Dees is the most famous Jewish, Civil Rights Lawyer in the United States. He sued the K.K.K. (the K.K.K.) in Alabama and won a multimillion dollar settlement. He even won the Klan Headquarters and gave it to a black family. The family transformed the Klan building into a church. A movie was made about the life of Morris Dees. He has a group called "Klanwatch" and his southern poverty law center (Montgomery Alabama) tracks and monitors hate groups and formed militias. Morris has an intimate familiarity and close acquaintance with America's Civil Rights Royalty (i.e. Andy Young, Rev. Hosea L. Williams, Jesse Jackson, Rev. Joe Lowery, Julian Bond, etc.). And one day Attorney Dees received a call from a familiar voice: "Morris, how you doin man?" He replied, "The one and only Rev. Hosea Williams! Thank you for calling sir. How are you?"... "Morris-Rev. Sherman D. Manning is in Montgomery and I'd like for you to write him a check..." One hour later I arrived at the most sophisticatedly secure office I'd ever seen, other than Don King's office. The Klan and numerous other armed militia's had been (and still are) threatening to kill Attorney Dees for years. Both

Don King and Morris Dees' offices look like prisons. Lots of cameras, metal detectors and armed guards etc. I finally got cleared to go in and a pretty lil white lady gave me a sizable check which Attorney Dees thought had all been arranged by the great Rev. Hosea Williams. And I laughed (literally) all the way to the bank. Small wonder (I repeat because it still hurts) Ambassador Young won't give me the time of day anymore. Kids be advised that no matter how much people love you if you continue to abuse them. They'll get fed up and abandon your ass. I used to (sporadically) call "Uncle Andy" at 1:00 in the morning. He did so much to help me. He made calls for me (the real Andy himself) and believed in me. But I always wanted more faster and I was willing to engage in prevarication and mendacity to get what I wanted. Spending $10 to $15 grand in one night was easy for me. Restaurants like Rounds (N.Y.), Red Lobster, Lone Star Steak House, Alekos in D.C., Ruth Chris Steakhouse, Uncle Charlies (N.Y.), The Limelight, and Jefferson Sheraton Hotel in Virginia etc. ought to have tables named after me for the dough I spent. I'd go into bars or restaurants and waitresses would run after me because of how I tipped. The Tobacco Company (actually a 4-star restaurant that has sexy ladies carrying cigar trays) in Richmond or "Betty's" etc. If my bill was $300.00 I'd tip $125.00. I remember going to an ice cream (sit down) parlor and the waitress brought me the bill. I think it was $21.00. I gave her my card, a $50.00 bill and said "keep the change darling." And her manager ran out and explained she was "only 18" and couldn't accept the tip. I was befuddled. A. I was 23. B. My female guests were 20-32. C. What the hell did her age matter? As we headed to the car one of the ladies explained "You're an ostentatious black dude and they think you're trying to pick up a white girl"...

I wasted a lot of money in the process of burning bridges. I was a vicious social climber and I had so many conflicts. A demon on one shoulder and an angel on the other. A burning desire to help hurting people. But a greed for the need to get what I wanted with speed. I had a good heart but a bad head. I feel Paul when he said every time I try to do good, evil is always there. I can feel Jacob when he was a trickster in one chapter and a prince in another. Sometimes Jacob was a conman in one verse and a prince in the next verse. This spiritual conflict often reveals itself in diverse psychological traits. This "conflict" has caused so many boys and girls to give up on their dreams, drop out of school, run away from home, use drugs and join gangs. This conflicted spirit can lead to homicide and even suicide. What do you do when you've lost confidence in your own morals? What do you do when what you've seen, heard and felt has caused you to become lonely, pessimistic, cynical and bitter? What do you do when your own role models fall from grace; before your very eyes? What do you do when you see flaws, conflicts and inconsistencies in the very folks you love, respect and look up to? What do you do when the police who arrest you get arrested? What do you do when the very substance of your belief shatters before your very eyes? What do you do when you don't know what to do?

I still remember (and I've never said this before to anyone) when Rev. Jimmy Swaggart got caught with the prostitute. I laughed and joked about it just like everybody else did. But I hid my hurt and camouflaged my pain. The truth of the matter was Jimmy let me down. We believe these myths like heroes are not supposed to die. And when someone we look up to as kids reveals themselves to be just as conflicted, just as flawed and just as human as we are it crushes our spirits and can bust our dreams. When Rev. Jesse Jackson (and I still love Jesse! Period!) impregnated a woman while he was/is married? My Lord and my God. Publicly I engaged in the same hypocrisy as others. And prison is a place which is built from the ground up on broken dreams. Prisons are filled to the rim with broken boys pretending to be men. So we will lie in wait for a star to stumble. Because lambasting another man's mistakes gives us a respite from our own failures. We love to see men fall so I laughed about that "old crook" Jesse.

But the kid on the inside of me was weeping. We all know that we have issues, conflicts and secret sins. But when the secrets of our role models surface we are crushed. I didn't tell Joe Rikalo, Sgt. Atwood and all of the staff and inmates (who were mocking Jesse and Bill Clinton) "Hey guys let's pray for Jesse. Let's pray for Jackie. He made the same kind of mistake that King David did minus having a man murdered." Instead I called him a crook. I was hurt because I grew up looking up to Jesse. He was everything I thought I wanted to be. He could preach and he could teach. And I met him in Alabama and in D.C. And I marched with him and was mesmerized by him. He was my rock star. Even my in-laws in Switzerland were in awe of Jesse Jackson. And when you look up and see your heroes fall it hurts you and angers you. And the myth is uncloaked and you know that "it's him too".

...I vividly recall perhaps the most disappointing day of my life. I grew up listening to the second most powerful pastor in Atlanta. He was on the biggest radio (WAOK-13 eight o-on your radio, tell it everywhere you go, we want people to know) station in Atlanta. They called him "The Mighty Hurricane" and Jasper (no.1) was "the Son of Thunder". Dude was bad. I'd wanted to meet "The Mighty Hurricane" since I was 4 years old...I finally got my break when I was 8. Rev. Richard Moss, Rev. Avery Sims and I were called to preach a citywide revival for this celebrated pastor. He ran ads on all the local stations about "the 3 eight year old preachers"... The sanctuary of his grand edifice had caught fire and burned to the ground. Famous gospel singer (the queen of gospel) Shirley Caesar did a concert at the Civic Center and gave him $30 thousand dollars in cash. Rumor had it that he kept the money in the trunk of his car in a large safe. He was allegedly a womanizer and had babies (by various women) all over the church. To this day he still holds services in the auditorium and never rebuilt the sanctuary. Where is the money?

We ended up doing 3 revivals for him and the more I got to know him the more I began to see, the women, the sex and the alcohol. He was my hero! ...Few years later I was at the Race Track gas station on Fulton Industrial Blvd. After I bought some gas I saw a man in coveralls, a skull cap, thick sunglasses etc. This dude looked homeless and I was tempted to give him a dollar. He had a wooden stick in his hand with a nail on the end. He (I discovered) was collecting Aluminum cans. I looked very closely and my heart dropped into my stomach when I saw who it was, "The Mighty Hurricane". It was one of the most disappointing days of my life. If you're waiting on his real name, you'll be waiting. My grand mom almost didn't believe me. Talk about falling from grace. I recall thinking that "God has fired" him. I was not mature enough to understand how that damaged and hurt me. I had no G.B.G. battery of experts to consult with. All I knew was (with the exception of perhaps Rev. Moses Lee Raglin, Ambassador Andy Young and Rev. Hosea Williams) every time I was blessed to meet and get to know a hero. I left disenchanted. And that's why I pray that Michael Vick will work and pray with G.B.G. Hell I don't need Paris Hilton's money (in fact I would refuse a monetary donation from Madame Hilton). I'd just like to see her engage lil girls and testify about how she felt in jail. I've come full circle, to a place of forgiveness and healing. I recognize that Jesse Jackson did not commit a crime against me. Nor did he lose his anointing or his calling. He simply fulfilled the scriptures that "There is none righteous no not one." He didn't do anything that I or most of your older brothers haven't done. The term hypocrite in Jesus' days meant to hide your face. Like walking around doing things with a mask on because you don't want it known that "it's me too." You can't even be a hypocrite unless you've been born again. How can you slide back (backslider) if you never slid forward? I can't put your son on punishment for violating one of my rules. If I punish a boy for a violation it means he is my son. I want to suggest that you put your faith into the message more than in the messenger. I suggest you stop selecting preachers, teachers, gangsters, athletes, actors and thugs as your heroes and sheroes. You can bee bop and booty dance without worshipping the entertainer. You like the sound of a drum but you never try to live like a drum. You enjoy the way a guitar sounds but you don't live in a "case". Learn to enjoy the rap but don't worship the rapper. People all have flaws and if you look up to us we will crush your spirit and destroy your vision.

In Hades I've come to know that prisons (jails, juveniles, etc. even women's prisons) are absolutely the angriest places on the planet. Hospitals can be sad and gloomy. Funeral homes can be spooky and cold. But there is not another place on the planet as dark, as cynical and as angry as a prison. When riots break out and people don't even know what started the fight it is an expression of the maddening and crippling grip of anger on the hearts of broken men. Any prison is subject to snap, crackle and pop at any given moment. And prison officials never respond (they react) to fights, riots and killings by working to ameliorate or eliminate the cause of the crisis. Prison officials react by "locking the angry men up in their cells to (very often) express that anger on their cell mates via rape, assault and murder...I am extremely concerned about the kids (similarly situated as Brett and Chris who were on Dr. Phil) who come here and get out. I keep going back to this issue because it is a crucial point but somebody must acknowledge if we're ever gonna stop the epidemic of "kids killing kids." If we are ever gonna eliminate the second "K" in the "K.K.K" and just let kids (K) be kids (K). We must stop sending them to prisons. And if and when we send them we'd better create a climate that does not create killers.

...In the meantime the focus of your efforts must be on you and yours. I want you to get that wind out of your jaws. I'm seeing too many angry kids! Especially boys! I see anger in the suburbs and anger in the hoods. I see anger in the trailer park and anger in the barrios. There seems to be an anger epidemic in American boys. Just think about two or three of your buddies and you'll have to admit that they are angry. White boys are angry, black boys and brown boys are angry. Angry with their parents and angry with teachers. Angry with the system and angry with the world. This anger is killing us. It has taken the wind from beneath our wings. It has clogged up our vision, and without a vision the people perish. You need a "there" to reach and strive for. The reason prisons are so dangerous and so deadly is because most people in them have no vision. They have given up. They quit. They don't even have a reason to get out of the bed in the morning. Their zeal is gone. Their zest is gone. They are wounded, bitter and broken. And all through the new testaments it seems that Jesus healed the blind more than he healed anybody. He healed some of them by spitting and making clay. He healed some of them by sending them to wash in a pool. But he was always healing blind people because without vision...you perish! You crumble! You crush! And there are millions, upon millions of (spiritually, emotionally and psychologically) blind, bitter and broken boys in the neighborhoods. We have community centers and school houses filled with blind and angry boys. Some of them are able to channel or redirect that anger by tackling other boys (aggressively) on the football field. Many will sign up for every contact sport they can so they can box it (the anger) out, fight it out, jump it out, run it out, bounce it out, run it out or work it out. That's why school boys get in so much trouble in the summertime. That sports outlet for anger is gone. And the anger (my brothers) is killing us. Why are you angry? We're angry because we don't know our daddies! Angry because they left us. Angry because somebody lied to use. Angry because somebody abused us. Angry because life is not turning out the way we thought it was supposed to happen. Somebody died who was not supposed to die. Somebody lied who was not supposed to lie. Our hope is gone. Our swagger is gone. Our belief is gone. And our vision....I told you you can lose your job and still make it. You can lose your girlfriend and still take it. But it's a dangerous thing to lose your vision. When you give up on your dream you are dead. When you have no place to go it is over. I am not there yet but the fact that I do have a 'there" to get to keeps me going. ...Bill Cosby talked about seeing prisoners mentor other prisoners and break down crying when a convict learned to read. I've witnessed hardcore prisoners in G.B.G. show some Heart. (Helping Educate at Risk Teens) when we give them a certificate (that they deserve) or when a "kid" gets it because G.B.G. gives prisoners a "there" to go to…We are angry, bitter and broken. So many of us get tired and give up in process and abandon the promise. We are troubled by the conflicts within us. But King David kept on praying and Jesse Jackson kept on preaching. When you fall you must get back up. No matter what you did or how bad you messed up. You still have worth. Your mess-up was in His will. Don't you think God had the power to prevent David from laying with a married woman? You think God couldn't prevent Jesse from his messing up? As much as I respect Barack he still has not (yet) stopped smoking. The most powerful man in the free world, not powerful enough to defeat a cancerette…Paul said he had gone up into the third heavens. And Paul said God showed him some things too awesome to utter. Some of the things he saw were so powerful that he couldn't even write them down in the Bible But (Jesse, David, Sherman, y-o-u) with that vision came a "thorn in the flesh" and Paul prayed "three times " to ask God to remove the thorn (injury, burden, ailment or flaw) in the flesh but God did not. Paul said that with that vision came the thorn in the flesh "lest I become exalted above measure." Lest I become arrogant, lest I become untouchable. God will send you a storm, a thorn, a flaw, a habit, a jail cell, a deformity or a …so you will remain humble and by the time (appointed time) you arrive at the "there" you'll be so wounded, so tired, so sore and so glad. You won't be telling folk how strong you are. But you'll be bragging about how "when I fall down He picks me up." And you won't brag about how good you are but you'll tell the bruthas how "bad" yo daddy is. God has a way of humbling you… I have driven Benz, Beemer's, Jags, Ferrarri's and when I got arrested I was wearing a $1500 suit and a $9000.00 ring and a Rolex in the 90's. And now I am in Hades.

…But be encouraged. Don't quit! Get that anger out of you. Blow it out! Pray it out! Cry it out! Work it out! If you don't get that anger under control, the anger will take you under… My concern about Chris Brown (I'm not just "hating" but we must hold each other accountable. He can/should be forgiven if/when he's really remorseful) is my brother-when you can beat a woman like that! Why are you angry? What is going on inside the mind, the soul, the psyche and spirit of a 19 year old kid to cause him to beat a woman? As low down, no good and deceptive as I've been to women. I've never. I can't fathom it. And not just Chris Brown! Boys and so-called men beat up on women every day of every week of every… This anger is volatile and can be deadly. I want to compel you to get help dealing with that anger. And the lack of goals and the abandonment of your dreams will kill you. I meet so many young men (black, brown and white alike) who have been felled, crippled, paralyzed and imprisoned by anger and by the loss of their vision. "Kids Killing Kids" are blinded by rage, hate, hurt and anger. Underneath that blindness is anger and underneath anger is hurt/sadness. You (in Schools, in colleges, in communities and in juveniles) are suffering from H.I.V. You have been infected with H.I.V and don't even know it. It is highly contagious and when your buddies, gang bangers and siblings go to prisons they acquire H.I.V. And they come home (for a while) just long enough to inject H.I.V. into y-o-u. There are 2 forms of H.I.V. one is a sexually transmitted disease. The other one is "Having Insufficient Vision." And your H.I.V. will kill you… The key to future failure is preoccupation with the past. They know not their history are destined to repeat it. But they who are pre-occupied with their history are destined to remain stuck. Don't get caught up with past failure or success. Experience is not always the best teacher. Experience can be the worst enemy. The reason older blacks could not believe Barack could win was; experience. The only way to bring radical change is to find somebody who has no experience. The reason I'm so excited about getting youngsters out at Locke High School, Lodi High school, Folsom high etc. is because every time God was ready to do something great He used an inexperienced youngster. David did not have the experience his brothers had. He was a shepherd boy. His brothers were experienced and trained soldiers. They were the Green Berets of their day. They were skilled in the use of spears, swords, and daggers! And here comes a kid named David with a slingshot. He said "Now stop this with a sword." And a young shepherd boy slayed the Giant Goliath. You'll recall that Mrs. Clinton argued passionately that she and McCain both had a lot of experience. She clowned Barack saying all he had was a "speech" (just words) he gave opposing the war. Madame Clinton and Senator McCain were master politicians with decades of experience. And here comes a kinky headed youngster with a momma from Kansas and a daddy from Kenya. And even when it seemed like Rev. Jeremiah Wright was the nail in the coffin of this inexperienced kid accused of "paling around with a terrorist." Barack told his staff "I'm gonna do a major speech on race. Even David Axelrod had some doubts. And just as David said "Stop this (slingshot) with a sword." Barack said "Stop this (speech=just "words") with experience" and the rest is his-tory. I came to use "just words" to call those things that are not as though they already were. I came to motivate you kids, you thugs, you gangstas, you jocks, studs, geeks and freaks to exhale. Get rid of that anger by any means necessary. Talk to a chaplain, pastor, counselor, madam Mary or Father Phil. But get it out of you. And I came to tell you to re-ignite your dream. You must (no matter how hard it is) not give up on your vision. You must not quit. Your H.I.V. can be cured. This tome is a pro tease inhibitor. This book is an AZT for your H.I.V. But Magic Johnson does more than take his medicine. Magic works out and he studies and he prays. Reading this tome is a mighty good beginning. I'm so proud of you and there is more. Study Tony Robbins study Bill Cosby, President Obama, Zig Zigler. Pray to the creator and work out. Work out your anger and walk out your pain. Trials come to make you strong. Trials come to teach you. God is ready to do something great so He needs you in that school. You in that neighborhood. I command that your H.I.V. be arrested. As you read this book your vision, your dreams, your hope is coming back. You are coming back to life. It's me too...

There is an actor named "Nico" and his last name begins with a "T". Find Nico and tell him about K.K.K. We need Brandon White in San Joaquin County. Help me reach Jinan Sumler (MA), Erica Guerrero (Sacto), Scott Henuset, Matt Barkley and Tom Savage. Tell them about this book. Ya'll are young and yo computer is yo slingshot. Use it for good and we can slay the giants of gangs, guns, drugs and violence...I repeat-yo mouse is the slingshot, shoot it baby boy! Shoot your slingshot. Shoot it to Nathaniel Mullinnex in my hometown! Tell Nate that G.B.G.said "come here Mr. Mullinnex we have a stipend for you." Reach out and touch Alexis Upshaw as she goes off to Georgia State to study psychology. We need Rick Upshaw as a chaperone. We need Christian Nelson to help us carry on. Ya'll we can do this.

I came to bring a light to shine in the darkness. I came like a cheerleader to tell you "let's go, let's go we got the ball". I came with a basketball and I'm gonna play it like "Mike". I came like "Phil" to coach yo ass back into the game. Get yo black, white or brown ass back up and into the game. I came to bring you, your vision back. Open your eyes Nathaniel, Keith, Brett, Chris, Alexis and C.J. open your eyes and see. See your way out of this and your way out of that. See a way out of no way. Get your butt back up and get back in the game. America loves a good come back story and tales of success. You can see if you'll just open your eyes. I came to spit on your ground and make clay with the dirt. I command you to go wash in the pool and see books on the way. See yourself succeeding. See yourself going and growing. I came to turbo charge your spirit and shoot you to your destiny.

...Slow down and get it right. There is a temptation to operate on emotions and to move with the wind. But feelings come and feelings go. You must inject some steel into your spine so you can stand the test of time. When you get rid of that bitterness and anger it will blow your mind. There are creative, innovative and potent powers buried in your mind. Tap into it and get through it. But deal with your issues. If you are using drugs you have an issue. If you are angry you have an issue. If you dropped out of school you have an issue. That's the bad news. But the good news is this: There are some people (Zig Zigler, Tony Robbins, G.B.G., Heart, NAPS, Dr. Phil, Steve Covey, Bishop T.D. Jakes, Rev. Otis Moss etc.) who may not even speak to one another (i.e. this author has never spoken to Dr. Phil or Dr. Bill Cosby etc.) But are all willing to help you. Let's be straight: Bill Cosby does not need you. Dr. Phil does not need you. With just the audience Dr. Phil has today. If he never meets yo narrow behind. If Dr. Phil, Dr. Cosby, Dr.Poussaint, Dr. Curren or Dr. Jarman etc. never meet a student at Locke, Lodi, Folsom or McNair High School etc. Three of the five aforementioned will still be Millionaires. One of the remaining two has a degree from Harvard. The other one has four degrees and even he earns over two hundred thousand dollars per year. Dr. Phil didn't pay me or commission me to write this tome. They have absolutely no need for a prisoner dying from valley fever. If I die tonight!! If I breathe my last breath this evening. The sun will still wake up tomorrow upon the eastern horizon. The light shall still punch in upon the time clock of another day... And Dr. Phil will do another show. And Bill Cosby will still own his mansion and his private plane. And Dr. Poussaint will still teach at Harvard and ... Hello? They need me even less then they need you. And they don't need you.

I wrote this book because I believe you deserve to succeed. I stated that when God's gonna do something radical and great He always chooses a youngster. I pulled Adam Lane, Dustin, and Daniel Bugriyev into G.B.G. Because the need is great...And we have churches on every corner. We have miracle workers, pastors who own (not one but) 4 Rolls Royces. And I love the church I am an apologist for the church. But I've seen people dance and shout all over the church. And can't pray off a common cold. I've seen folk go to Sunday school in the morning. Sunday evening service and to bible study on Wednesday evening and they're still in bondage. I know preachers who cheat on their wives. And I know preachers who beat their wives. So I don't intend to allow you to sing and shout and go back home and be the same again. If I have to start writing Dr. Phil sob story letters once a day until he does a show to help you I will. I can not allow you to remain the same. You in foster care. You in juvenile. You in schools or on the streets. I came to bring light. This tome is not the time for another lil cosmetic procedure. We gotta do more than put on some make-up. I'm not into rubbing deodorant under a funky armpit. We gotta get down to the core or the sore and make a paradigm shift! That's all Bill Cosby is trying to do with "call outs" and "airing" dirty laundry. I came out of the shower one day and some kind a way my towel fell over behind the bunk. Days later I kept smelling something. My clean towel smelled bad because it needed air. So air is good for dirty (and clean) laundry. We must talk about it and correct it. That's all Dr. Phil means with this is "going to be a changing (paradigm shift) day in your life". You have this book because it is up to you. I love America and I respect our lawmakers. But between you and I our politicians are not the answer. In California (read closely) we spent more money housing (over) 177,000 inmates than we spent to educate 226,000 Cal State students. Are you reading these words today? Go back and re-read those figures. Who passed the "laws" that incarcerate more than 177,000 inmates in California? Who just agreed to cut education funding again in California? Lawmakers. As a matter of fact I wanna correct myself. In several sections of this tome I ask you to send this book to lawmakers. I withdraw that request here and I ask you to send this book to everybody except lawmakers. Why? It is a waste of time. I wrote this book for youngsters who R not limited by "experience". And I love Maxine Waters, John Lewis, Gloria Romero, Jackie Speier and a couple of others. But (remember I have no bridges to burn! I am a state convict! I'm not running for Sherman the Man (ning) of the freaking year!) Most of today's politicians leave a sour taste in my mouth. Especially California (here goes my pardon!lol) Politicians! Many of them are like pimps. They prostitute their offices.

They play games and are duplicitous. Year after year, after year (in California) these college educated,overpaid and ego inflated politicians refuse to pass a budget on time. In the past ten years California Legislators (the lawmakers who are mostly millionaires) have costed taxpayers $ hundreds of millions of dollars by (because of) passing the budget late. This is on top of the already $ billions dollar(s) deficit. It happened last year,before last, before that. This year and it will happen next year. And with the money Californians have paid (in just 10 years) for the last budget we could have built 20 new (state of the art colleges) from the ground up! But tonight state senators and the assembly persons are lounging around in $ million homes with state (funded) cars in their garages. And they may or may not wobble into the capitol by 11:00 am tomorrow and be at the country club by 5:00 pm. But I'll bet you my right arm that they will not pass a budget on time next year no matter what! I'd love to see fifty 18 year olds running the State of California. Mayor Michael Sessions (18) did a pretty good job in Michigan. I say "Nathaniel Mullinnex for Governor! Go Nate! Run Nate run! Yall e-mail Eric Godbout, Luke Debettercourt (MA.) Josh Cohen and David Quattlebum and tell them I see them "in office". I think I can get David E. Kelley and Michael Fleiss to support Will Rains, Bryce Daniels, Daniel Samples, Christian Nelson and Brandon White for office! I call Rev. Mark Payton, Shively Heights Church, Rev. Lincoln Bingham, St Paul (Louisville Kentucky), Rev. Paul Morton and Father Lino Otero to help us motivate youngsters to serve. I want Jinan Sumler, Brandon, C.N.A. John Johnson (Lemoore), Casey and Ben at Sieera Vista Med Center), Josiah Poirer and you to run baby run!... If Harvey Levin is reading I want Harvey ("I'm a lawyer ") to tell Max that the challenge on page 313 in "Blue Eyed Blonde" book two is for Max also... I hope Attorney Warren Ballentine get's this book. Maxwell Hanger, Matt Barkley, and ... Ryan Jenkins was found hanging in his hotel. What a way... G.B.G. reaches out to kids at Bartlett high school, Brooks Wilson, Ryan Gough, David Jensen, Kirk Cameron, Ellen Eggers, Ken Dhanini, Lori Bartoli etc. We are on a mission to expose the horrible epidemic of 600,000 foster kids. (I repeat) and we need Ryan Kramer (donor sibling registry.org) , Becky and Chris Thompson, Tyler Perry and you to help us...

Twelve hundred inmates rioted at a prison in Burgin Kentucky weeks ago. Guess they heard about Chino California. Thirty six inmates were injured and that riot costed the tax payers $ millions. And prisons across this country (God forbid) are gonna continue to rock and roll and riot if something is not done. The mere caging of humans like animals in U.S. Gitmos and American Abu Ghraibs is a recipe for riots, rapes and murder. I reiterate the need for TBN Second Chance in every U.S. jail, juvenile, and prison. We must bring light into these dark and dingy places...

I am very excited! I've got a lot of missives from folks who heard (on the grapevine) about K.K.K. Everybody is talking bout G.B.G. and K.K.K. It's humbling and a blessing indeed. But please note I seek no applause. An award won't cure my disseminated valley fever. What will make my day is to get a missive from Nathanel Mullinnex, C.J. Sheron, Brian Hawn and/or Brandon White saying "Dear Sherman someone poked me and said I'm in a tome called K.K.K. and you have some money for me? Is this a joke?... I'll be blessed to see G.B.G./Heart out live me. If your "vision" dies with you it's not vision. I believe in succession planning. And I want G.B.G./Heart to be around for 400 years! And if you young folks step up it shall come to pass. I started G.B.G. for you to take over. I'm writing K.K.K. for the facebook generation. This tome is too fast and too all over the place for "experienced" readers! So I repeat: Don't send this to lawmakers. It's not polished by editors and falsified by book doctors or ghost writers. It's just a missive from the heart of a dude in Hades. It's just a G.B.G. testimony for teens and tweenies. It's raw, rambling and cutting. I'm not writing for an award. I'm writing for the reward of knowing that I poured my soul and spirit into this testimony to kids. I don't feel comfortable with this raw, rambling missive being critiqued by the polished masses. But I'm super comfortable with Anthony Fedorov, Ryan Hreljac and with C.J. Sheron persuing this. I don't own 4 Rolls Royces or a lear jet. I'm not pastoring a 10,000 seat mega church. I'm just a member of the TBN-second chance church. I have no blessing plan to sell you. I'm not a holy man. I am a seed in dirt. But I'm capable of understanding your hurt. I came to restore vision. I came to get you to turn your eyes around backwards and look at you. I came to lead you back to you. I came not as the light but to point you to the light... I suggest (Keith and Nathaniel Mullinnex, Christian, Brandon White, Justin Berry, David Jensen and...) You re-read this status update 2 or 3 times. I remind you to go on to Anthony Fedorovsi wall and tell him I have a stipend for him. I remind you that when we get ten or twenty students (i.e. Locke high, Lodi high, Folsom, Northside high school in Atlanta Douglas high school and your school etc.) At 9 or 10 schools to chat about G.B.G./Heart on the internet etc. Jihad will be launched. I'm not perhaps "commercial" enough for certain media. But you (right in your living room, bedroom, classroom or dorm) can blog, vlog, youtube or deluge the internet with postings about the tome. We don't need politicians. We don't need people with "experience". We don't even need "wise" people for this mission. Since we need a radical change. Since we need to do the impossible we're gonna have to see the invisible. So all I need is a few good (young) men (and ladies) and we can turn our caps backwards. It's time for us to rally! Why sit we here and die? We gotta get up. We will do it. We can do it. We must do it... Sit down today and E-mail Nils Vesk, Anthony Fedorov, Tony Robbins, Brian Hawn, Justin Berry, and Ryan Hreljac. And tell them that Dr. Franklin Curren, Dr. A. Duran, NAPS, G.B.G./Heart and our sponsors are calling them. I say to Nathaniel,Kieth (my homeboys..Yall know I still got a place in Buckhead) "follow G.B.G. And we will make you Fisher's of (young) men". Come on Brett, Chris, Dr. Phil's son who has the band, Alexis, "Living Things", Paris, Martha, J. Weir, J. Buttle, T. Goebbel, Gabe Williams (sac town), Timothy Coleman, Luke Sears and Kyle Love. Come unto G.B.G. and let's open our eyes and see. There is nothing which can't be done if we lift our voice as one . "I tried to do it my way. Got sent on up the highway. Why it gotta be like that? They got me in the system". But even in the system, at 2:21 am early October 2009. My words have come for thee my fellow Americans. My words have come to thee. I come to Daniel Sample, Joseph Schoen, Josh Costa in Stockton,Ben Chuchla and to "Angelo". I've come to bring you back to light. Don't give up on you. Redmond O'Neal and even Cameron Douglas –you can beat it. I pray that Cameron Johnson, Jennifer Jaimez and Diego Saavedra will read these words. I pray that you will get back to God. I'm not a zeolot or a fanatic. I have G.B.G. members who believe in Thor. It's their prerogative. And it is also my prerogative to tell you ain't no daddy like the one (God) I got. If you open that bible and get an 'understanding" of what you're reading. You shall be delivered. And you shall succeed. Try God for yourself. I might not be any good. And I still got a Jacob in me. But God is Awesome! God is real. I never would have made it. I never could have made it without Him. I would have lost my mind. I would have lost it all. Never would have made it without the Lord who was on my side. Redmond- you just lost your mother...I almost quit ! Redmond : I almost gave up. Redmond- I nearly gave up dude. I know you're in jail and I pray somebody will send you (Redmond O'Neal) this tome in jail. I seek no donations. I don't need you. I just want you to know that "it's me too". I believe you can rise up in that cell and transmogrify. Redmond just don't give up. I feel you (Redmond) in my spirit! I (believe it or not) actually recommend that you read "A million little pieces". It is really a powerful tome. If Cupcake Brown could turn around you can do it too. Redmond you gotta get that monkey off your back. If I don't reach anybody else in the whole wide world. Redmond you –all by yourself in the county jail cell are worth me being up in the wee hours of the morning praying for you. I can't give up on Redmond O'Neal cause somebody didn't give up on me. I know the power of the clutches of crack and meth. I know propofol . But I also know a safe place. And I link up in the spirit realm with every intercessor. And I agree in the name of Jesus that Redmond O'Neal is coming out of that. I declare you will. And to Every Redmond, Douglas and Gary Busey out there etc. You can get up. You can't give up. Please, please read good books and open your spirit. And get your vision back. There is still a dream, a hope and a vision down inside of you. You tried to drink, smoke, snort and shoot it away. But you still have a dream. "Come on people"! I am at ground zero. And ground zero is a haunting and a humbling place. And most of my co-horts would think me stupid for spending my time reaching out to some rich (Redmond) kid (in jail) who wouldn't look my way on the streets. But there but for the grace of God go. G.B.G./Heart exists for folks like Redmond and Cameron. We are that group of addicts and ex-addicts who are all in some form of recovery. If we can't tolerate, accept and love Redmond then we need to close –up shop and shut up. Who the hell am I to judge anybody? And who am I to be unwilling to forgive? Everything about G.B.G. says reach out to Redmond (Brett, Chris, you and to yours etc.) and to every person suffering from substance abuse.. Redmond O'Neal is a child of God. And I will be praying for (him) you (if you're reading. I'll write the Potter's House and to TBN (second chance) and ask them to pray for Redmond.

Somebody asked was I serious about not wanting any money from Paris Hilton. Let me be clear. Under no circumstance shall I (ever) accept a monetary donation from Paris. G.B.G.is above begging for money. And (to be clear) a lot of extremely credible people (i.e.Warden James "Jimbo" Walker, Dr. Franklin Curren and Dr. A. Durran etc.) have stuck their necks out for G.B.G. And I take their support to Heart. And the last thing I'm going to allow is some disgruntled or disenchanted person the opportunity to claim G.B.G. begged for money. We need your prayers, your ideas, your "get out the word" efforts not your money...

It's all about HEART (Help Educate At Risk Teens).Heres why: In spite of a multi $ Billions deficit more than 10% of Californias public schools are in danger of bankruptcy. That is alarming. And let me put the word out (because people all over the world are reading this book) that California is forcing college professors and school teachers to take two furlough days per month. I cannot imagine my teacher at William Finch Elementary school telling us "there will be no class Friday because we are on furlough". Yet, in the midst of furloughing educators they still have the money to pay $ millions upon millions of dollars dealing with the 4 – hour riots at Chino. It costs money to transport all those inmates to –and fro the hospital. Money to treat them at the hospital. Money to transport them back. Then they transferred (still more money, prisoner transfers are extremely expensive) hundreds of the rioting inmates to other prisons. And let us not forget that on June 21, 2009 another riot broke out between two prison gangs. The Nortenes and the Surenos. This was at the California Substance Abuse Treatment Facility. It involved more than 85 prisoners using shanks and other weapons. Sixteen prisoners (more money) were transported to local hospitals. It was premeditated because the riot broke out in five different locations simultaneously. And that one costed $2 million. If staff (the $100 grand per year toy soldiers who wear a patch on their shoulders with "rehabilitation"on it) had either prevented the riots (in civilian life we call it "community policing") and/or quelled them rapidly we could have taken that $12-15 million and used it to keep teachers and professors in the classrooms. When will we learn?

And this thing we've begun to do by paying more for incarceration than for education is ruining our country. And the state of the public school system is already sad. I get missives from high school seniors everyday (I received 13 today) who "write" on a second or third grade level. I love them and I treasure their missives (and won't embarrass them)but it bothers me . When I was in high school if you couldn't read Mrs. Jones, Mrs. Walton, Mrs. Slocum and Mrs. Warrior would not let you go until you could write a letter... So I am absolutely disenchanted with today's politicians (snake oil salesmen) who remind me of street pimps. It finally (an aha moment) dawned on me yesterday to not even waste my time, books, paper or ideas trying to convince a "politrician" to join this "change" movement. G.B.G./Heart is revolutionizing the youth and influencing minds because we're following our daddy's (God's) model: We need drastic, unimaginable and crucial change so we are getting somebody "young" and "inexperienced" to do this work. And I intend to go for broke using my cash flow for stipends, Bonuses, gifts and scholarships (G.B.G. wont accept monetary donations but we do encourage our supporters to fund scholarships! Education means everything to us!) to pull more and more students into G.B.G. . I'm calling on Tory Levitre, Jerel Benjamin, Don Renter, Rosetta Stone, Petty Officer Kyle Hatch, Jeff Bush, Dr. Stephen Grinstead, Jackie Sissel and Will Trans to stand with G.B.G. ... We need Evelyn Taft and we need Andy Roddick to stand with us... Our schools are in trouble . A young man wrote me the other day to tell me kids are now using ADHD medication to get high. They take meds which are not prescribed to them. He told me about the bullying, the drugs and even the gangs at his mostly white school. And when I think about what our kids are having to see, touch and feel due to a gang of "pimp politicians" I get upset I can't turn a blind eye to our kids in trouble. I mentioned earlier that God will put a thorn in your flesh. I know prominent and powerful evangelists who can't figure out why God allowed their son(s) to be gay... And let me tell you what I know to be true. When that pastor has a son switching around the church with his hands on his hips etc. That pastor suddenly discovers there is a lot of "other stuff" he can preach about instead of just "Adam and Eve not Adam and Steve". God will cause your thorn to give you empathy instead of arrogance. But our politicians seem to be begging for a thorn. God is never without the power to cause or allow a thorn to bring you back down.. You should have seen (yall were only 8 and 9 years old) Senators McCain, McConnell, Coburn, Grassley and Brown back 8 years ago when God allowed a thing to happen which brought us to our knees. No bickering, no partisanship etc. We had nobody talking about no prayer in the schools. I saw T.D. Jakes praying on CNN . I didn't say TBN. I said he was praying on CNN. We were together! Bush went and asked Congress for $20 billion. But instead they gave him $40 billion...

But look at them today all angry. I was talking about your anger earlier but I know where you got it from. It is learned behavior These (Grassley, Coburn, McCain etc.) guys are so angry. No wonder we have bullying in the schools You see bullying adults every day. And when Bush was our President I disagreed with him vehemently on many issues. But you never saw disgruntled Democrats showing up at town hall meetings packing guns. You didn't see this yelling and shouting like we see now... Rush Limbough, Ann Coulter and Sean Hannity are all angry. "I hope he (our President) fails" said Mr. Limbough. And he was sober that time ... But if you listen and observe you'll see Grassley and that crowd are full of anger and cynicism. Do we need another awful, horrific tragedy of titanic proportions just to make these $ millionaires in D.C. play nice and be civil? God can do anything. And He can allow anything. Perhaps we should send a spiritual epidemiologist to Capitol Hill to remind these angry politicians about the favor which God has shown us. It it a crime against humanity to abandon schools and education for incarceration. The blood of all of the "kids killing kids" is on politicians hands. And I am a student of politics. I enjoy debate and negotiations etc. But not shouting matches. And I see nobody yelling in the streets about the fact that our schools are failing and kids are suffering. The very first day of the second week of school a teen brought pipe bombs, gasoline and a gun to school out in San Matee. He set off explosives at Hillsdale High School. Who taught him how to make a bomb and why is he so angry? Kids definitely get schooled on crimes in prisons. But now a day they also learn how to conceal a body, rip out teeth and cut off fingers by watching T.V. and the internet... By August of this year (2009) there had been three teen suicides in three months at the exact same Caltrans track. Three teenagers in the prime of their youth who quit! So in trouble and so in turmoil that they quit. And the caltrans spokesman was talking about how the train operator would look directly into the eyes of these kids with their death stare and watch them die. And I lay blame for these senseless tragedies right at the door of Grassley, Brownback, Coburn and the rest of those hustlers on Capitol Hill. We need some meaningful dialogue about mental illness, depression and about suicide. Ambassador Young helped me set up a youth task force on teen suicides in Atlanta in the 90's... We need that now. I hope that mark Simon (Caltran) will read these words. And students, parents and teachers will do workshops on depression. I'm certain some of my G.B.G. advisors are willing to add their expertise and I hope "Cody" at Hillsdale, Dr. Michael Weiner, Matt Larson, parents and teachers will get this tome. The kid also had a chainsaw with his pipe bombs... I want Cody and some of you students to share this tome with Hillsdale teachers like Mrs.Sanchez and Mr. Boise. We cannot ignore this call to action. I call my troops G.B.G. to Arms. Arms? Your computer! With it you can blog, vlog and text about these issues dear to us. You can befriend a Redmond O`Neal and even pray that he'll overcome his addiction. You can write letters to the editors about politricians killing education... Fight!

Back to H.I.V. I told you there are two kinds. I also wrote in this book that too many fathers are killing or castrating boys who only needed circumcising. I spoke figuratively. But physician have now determined that circumcised men transmit HIV(the sexual disease) 50% less than men who are uncircumcised . We keep spreading this H.I.V. (Having Insufficient Vision) because our daddies never circumcised us. When your daddy circumcises you he cuts away that layer of cynicism, anger and self doubt from around your mind. When you'r circumcised you know who you are. And you can weather the storms. I wish we could have gotten to those 3 students (ironically, all of whom were from Gunn High School) with this book before they gave up. I want all the students at Gunn High to get this book. And whether you're suffering from PTSD, ADHD or oppositional defiant disorder. K.K K. is a shot in the arm. It's a tune up till you can get to Dr. Phil, a counselor or a pastor. You can still be circumcised. Are you feeling angry agitated, irritated, socially with drawn etc.? Are you eating a lot more or a lot less than normal? You may need to fill out a patient health questionnaire. But there is help available and we at G.B.G. are willing to suit up and fight with you. We're on your team. We'll defend your right to go to school(without interference from gangs, guns, drugs and violence) against all enemies.

This book has come to you to heal that H.I.V. You're never too old to get circumcised. You are facing the kinds of tragedies that fathers should talk to their sons about. You should have been taught how to handle rejection/void and depression. You should know how to feed the empty spot without a drug or a drink. If we had embraced you would not have gone looking for love (in gangs) in all the wrong places. But don't wait on a politician. Don't wait on a Judge. Just get back up and ask God to circumcise you... I want Logan Stultz , Gene Langford (Atlanta) and Caryn Elaine Johnson to have this tome. Get it to Alexandrea Martin and to Steven Jordan... But let me repeat (Whoopy) I am not seeking any dough! I know it costs a whole lot of money to drive that gas guzzling bus of yours ! Tony Robbins says "repetition forms persuasion" I did not say "truth" forms persuasion. You hear a lot of truths that you never pay attention to. But repetition causes seeds to be planted. Some of you heard (growing up) "you're stupid" and "you're a nobody". And they planted seeds in your spirit which castrated you. I came to help you erase the tape. I want to record (truths). And (to be true) watching phony, bickering out of touch and duplicitous folks like Rush, Grassley, Kristol and Tom Delay has motivated me (even more) to study peak performance and enhanced revolutionary learning. Because if I am really an iconic incarcerated scribe who's work will outlive me. I must plant seeds (often via repetition) in the garden of your church, college, school or class that will stick to your bones. I can't stop thinking about what the 3 teens at Gunn high must have seen, heard or felt that led them to snuff their own lives out. I did not know them but it is still personal to me. I did not know Sandra Cantu,

Sasha Greene, Elizabeth Smart, Adam Walsh, Casey Anthony etc. But it is personal. I did not know the 29 murdered and missing boys in Atlanta but it was personal. Martin Luther King Jr. did not know the garbage workers in Memphis Tennessee but he died standing up for those who could not defend themselves. And what I'm doing (I repeat) is not special. It is my duty as an American. And my challenge is to continue to try to communicate the complex simplistically. I wanna write about the advanced transmogrification techniques I've learned in a colorful and dynamic way...

I want you to get circumcised. I want you to talk to a parent, a pastor, a counselor etc. and utilize the web site and toll free numbers (in this book) to reach out. I want you to know that you were born to win... Hollywood was (NFL player/star) locked up on a sex charge. A sex charge... "Hollywood" Henderson was a super athlete and a dope fiend. He got so hooked he'd be trippin during games. At one game he thought a rock on the ground was chasing him. He lost his NFL career and his money. Lost his fame and his name. And Thomas "Hollywood" Henderson found himself an inmate at (small world) C.M.C. East Prison for a sexual assault he says he did not commit. And finally Hollywood kicked his drug habit. He paroled from California and returned to Texas. He had been spiritually circumcised. He was drug free and happy but flat broke. He decided to build a youth center for kids. He called a press conference and announced "I'm beginning a hunger strike until I die or until people give me the money to build this for kids". They gave him the money. He established a relationship with God and was traveling across the country talking to inmates and kids about drugs. He wrote a few books and made videos. He bought a couple of lottery tickets and one day he hit the lottery for $28 million!!

Because he was faithful, consistent and radical enough to step out on the limb. Because he didn't allow his history (I'm a dope fiend excon and convicted of a sex crime) hinder him from his destiny. Because he didn't wait on the Government for a handout. Because he didn't depend on politicians etc. God blessed and prospered him even the more. God has a habit of letting folk out of prison(s) (i.e. Joseph,"Hollywood", Rolando Cruz and Tim Masters) who were locked up on sex convictions and blessing them. And I want you to understand that your life is worth living. And you can make it. I exposed and I uncloaked myself in ways (as never before) I never thought I would. I did so because I know you (too) are tired of duplicitous, "experienced" sound bite politicians. You can relate to this tome because it's not "polished". Politicians speak (only) from written texts and talking points penned by "experienced" speech writers. They are fake, bogus and deceptive. They play the game of semantics and specialize in tergiversation. So I finally decided that the only chance I stood with youngsters (Cody Linley, Nick Hogan, Allison who's a senior at Hillsdale, Dave Salmoni, April Deguzman and Tiki Barber) was to stand naked. And to admit that "it's me too". I'm in the same boat with you. I have flaws and I've made some messes in my life. And I'm in a strange place in my life and I'm just feeling my way through certain areas of my life. I've made so many mistakes and I'm Jacob one minute and Israel the next. I got a prince in my heart and a trickster in my head. I am battling the conflicts between the demon on one shoulder and an angel on the other. I'm in the same boat as you are. But I came to tell you we don't need to give up. We have help. There is a divine force that put the universe into order. It can stand against any discording force. And that power (even in your flawed condition) will save your life... God can send you a reuber to save you like when your own brothers are plotting to kill you...You don't need to spend the rest of your life with Having Insufficient Vision! I came to arrest that blindness. I came to apprehend that visionlessness. I won't sit idly by and let you die. I can't let Redmond O'Neal throw in the towel. I won't let him give up. With all of these pastors, preachers, Christians all over the world. I believe that G.B.G. can link up with Bishop T.D. Jakes,Noel Jones, Eddie Long, Paul Crouch and the Second Chance family and we can arrest that demon. I'm crazy, radical and young enough to believe in a slingshot…

Three kids in three months committed suicide. That breaks my heart and it touches my spirit. And I want to help you not to do that. I've been sitting here in Hades and I've studied. I've studied Dr. Phil like a book. I study Judge Greg Mathis. I meditate on Dr. Cosby and Dr. Poussaint's book. I read Tony Robbins, Zig Zigler, Steve Covey and Tony Dungy's tomes repetitively. And I study the killers,rapists and molesters around me I watch, I listen, I feel and I sense. I've entered into the witching circle of darkness of Eric Menendez,Rauser, Ritter and a number of other satanic worshippers. I stepped inside the minds of vicious killers and pulled every secret, every characteristic, every trait, every habit, every nuance and even the idiosyncratic whims of Bret Moore , Bardo and Henson etc. Because having lived in darkness (H.I.V.) I knew that if I used the rudimentary principles I could learn from Dr. Phil Tony Robbins, Mr. Zigler, Dr. Curren and my battery of advisors etc. I would be enpowered to write the book of my life for you. My sole purpose in getting this into your hands (if nothing else) is to cause you to think twice next time you think about doing something that could cause you to enter Hades!

…You dudes (youngsters) who are already in jails and prisons etc. I have some words for you. (If any Adults R reading this shame on you. Close the book cause I'm going thug, tweenie nuclear for a moment:) you, who are locked up need to (remember I am you! I'm in jail too) get up off of your lazy ass. I'm sick of yo asses! U can't read, write or think. U got the nerve to call yourself some type of a gangster or a player. You sittin up in prison using indigent envelopes and u a baller! U can't even speak English! You speak Ebonics, caucasionics and Lationics . U don't know anything and won't allow anybody, To teach you anything. Your whole "life" revolve around watching cartoons, getting high and playing cards. You are the living dead. You can't be helped because you think you can see… I watch every Dr. Phil show (at least)twice. I watch at 3:00 pm and internalize. Then I watch again at 7:00 pm and take notes in my "Phil-isms" journal. I probably know Dr. Phil (lol) better than he knows himself. A celly told me a while back "I hate Dr. Phil! He's a racist". Dr. Phil is the only daytime host (I know of) with the testicles to put Al Sharpton on his show lately. Dr.Phil … is a lot of things. And "racist" is definitely not one of them. But that is typical of the institutionalized, gang,thug "I hate everybody" mentality. And for you thugz persuing my words right now I say sink or swim. If yo ass is already in jail I'm not gonna try to twist your arms or persuade you. This book is some water and you can drink it or pass the cup to your celly. I'm not looking for you to endorse me. There is a way out of no way But you have to tune in to the creative and the innovative station of your mind. You can't get there in a "crowd". Sometimes I can't think until I become "alone". And I play mental games with myself to "create". When I'm sad, mad or dealing with a complex thing I'll close my eyes and hear that southern drawl and see a big ole white bald head& say "what would Dr. Phil do"! I do the same mental gymnastics thinking of Dr. Curren, Dr. Jarman and Dr. Jamie Davidson etc. And it works for me everytime… If I had been at Chino (yall know I'm crazy) during the riot I would have curled up into a ball and cried (paradigm shift baby) like a baby! If yall had killed me my family would sue. If I lived through it I'd write E. Ivan Trujillo, Donald Specter, Michael Bien, Ann Patterson, Mark Gerragos, Tom Mesereau or Blair Beck until I found somebody to sue for me. I'd sue the guards for dereliction of duty, failure to protect etc. Sue the legislature for housing me in a system operating at 200% of It's capacity. I'd… think outside the box. Radical change is created, promoted and produced by thinkers. And when you listen to learned people (i.e. Dr. Phil, Tony Robbins, Zig Zigler, Dr. Yablonsky and Dr. Heitkamp etc.)it does the same thing for the mind which music does for the body. Just like a good beat makes you wanna get up and dance etc. When I condition my mind with the good, the clean, the pure, the powerful and the positive it puts me in the "creative" zone. And thoughts I thought I'd never think before come into my mind. It is awesome when you enter into the door of creativity. I don't mind being the odd man out. I could care less about some illiterate ass chump thinking I'm not a "man" because I won't let him call my shots... I get (I'm very serious. God is my secret Judge!) sick on my stomach listening to guys talk on the tier. The ignorance, illiteracy and the incompetence is killing us. I told a guy that "if" you just listen to news anchors and begin to emulate them you'll learn to speak". I recall telling a celly "if the Governator came into this prison right now and told you to talk (nonstop about anything) for three minutes using proper English and he would pardon you. Your ass would die in jail!

I was telling a fellow the story of Joseph (an illiterate buddy of mine) from Genesis 38,39 and 40. I told him about Joseph going to jail and coming out to be a prince in Egypt etc. And this fellow had tears in his eyes. And he reached into his pocket and handed me a pen and a piece of paper and said "please give me Joseph's address. I'm going in my cell and write he (sic) letters (sic) right now" I know yall wanna laugh. It's hilarious on one level but sad on another. This man was 46 years old and had the comprehension of a 3 year old that is sick. And this thick fog of illiteracy hangs above the prisons, jails and juveniles. If you are in prison right now I want you to write your family and even if you have to forget a "package" I want you to ask somebody to send you "Long Walk to Freedom" by Mandela "unlimited power" by Robbins. "Creating Monsters" Manning. "Succeeding Against The Odds" by John Johnson and "Think and Grow Rich" by Dennis Kimbro... Read one tome per week. And read them as if your life depended upon it. Don't scan- read. When you see a word you don't know look it up. Don't figure it out in context. Look it up. And I'll make you a solemn promise: as you are reading you shall begin to experience a metamorphosis! You will begin to grow up, transform, think, hope and move forward. I ask you to read my words and take them to heart...no excuse. U find the money 2 buy weed, pruno, tennis shoes and everything else you need. Get these books! And you all can share and take turns perusing them. Even do a book club or discussion group. But read these books and I promise you your life will change. I'm not into bullcrapping people. So I'm not gonna promise you a parole date or $millions of bucks. I don't know what the Creator's plan for your life is. But I do know you need to put "the art of war" on the shelf for a minute. And pour these five books (back 2 back) into your mind. K.K.K. is a powerful (ART) anti-retrovoral therapy for your (H.I.V.) Having Insufficient Vision. But now that you are reading and getting this 'ART' into your mind and spirit. You gonna need (ADAP)Aids DRUG Assistance Program. And your "ADAP" can be found in those five books. You will rise up and be a new man. ..I say (in this book) that guys get mad with Oprah because she won't do a show about 3 strikes. A. Oprah is not the only one with a T.V. show. And B. if you all (in Chino, C.Y.A., Stockton, Chad, Rikers Island or wherever) were to do something (i.e. begin a G.B.G. chapter at your jail or school. Read those five books and transform etc.) unique – Oprah, Tyra or Dr. Phil might be interested. But you must do it from your heart and do it for the right reason. Andrew Young once told me "if you want to know whether or not you're a Christian be willing to do a good deed and not be concerned about who gets the credit for it"...I'd love to hear what happens in,to and through you after you read all five! If Cupcake Brown and Willie Gary can make it who can't? Cupcake was a high school dropout a hooker and a dope fiend. "Come on People" ... Eric Betts, Brian Walker, (Denver Co.), Dr. Susan Etok, Lottie Gatewood, and all the kids at "Rise and Shine" need to get this (Art) tome. G.B.G. through K.K.K. is administering this ART to treat H.I.V. .You must open your eyes and see. I command you (Jason "Corey" Burgess in Susanville W.VA., Latacia Burnett, Arnoldo Rojas, Dax etc.) to open your eyes and see. With the stuff I've learned from Dr.Phil, Dr. Curren and Dr. Jarman I've used this book to spit in your dirt and make clay. I've used this book to send you to wash in the pool and restore your vision...Now enjoy the power of helping others by helping G.B.G.to help others see. You who are not in prison please use your slingshot. Find youngsters like Jose Leon and Arnoldo Rojas and tell them to get K.K.K. Twitter Ashton Kutcher (my dog) and tell him I got him and Dax some "food for thought" on page 313 of "Blue Eyed Blonde"book two! Jamie Kennedy? Page313. ..I learned (A.K.) from the best!.. We need to get this tome to (activist) Mark Rosenthal, Anthony Fedorov, Danny Noriega (CA.singer), Pastor Melissa Scott, the choir at Southeastern University (in Lakeland Florida... tell their drummer we have a stipend for him), Justin Berry and to Chris Hansen ... We (G.B.G./Heart)are social (and spiritual) epidemiologists. And since we have "vision" we can see that C.D.C.(supposedly the CA. Dept. of Corrections –doubles as the CA.Dept.of Corruption...) which is head quartered in Sacramento CA. is really the CDC (u figure it out !) headquartered in Atlanta Georgia. This CDC (prison system) needs to listen to our "director" Dr. Thomas Frieden.If you want to cure the disease (of crime, of recidivism, of riots, of H.I.V.) you can't talk to a guard (i.e. Mike Bunnell) you gotta talk to an infections disease specialist. Neither Mr. Grassley, McCain, Newt Gingrich, Rush Limbaugh, Ann Coulter, the CCPOA, Nor Jiminez etc. has a Medical degree. And you can't put out a fire (or disease) by pouring on gasoline (packing em like sardines in CDC)!We don't need a guard we need God and a doctor. I call for the Surgeon General and our director Dr. Thomas Frieden. And if we take the medicine (K.K.K.-ART) prescribed by our director (Thomas Frieden MD.) for our H.I.V.ETC. And if we follow up with Physical Therapy (our ADAP: Mandela, Robbins, Manning, Johnson and Kimbro) we will end the spread of the disease!... Yall feel me? I'm not interested in politicians at all. But I do advise you to (please) get this Medication (solution, recipe etc.) to the honorable Thelton Henderson, Clark Kelso,Judge Lawrence B.Karlton and to some patients (inmate who are hospitalized in CDC)...

    C.D.C. (Center for Disease Control?) these prisons fit the C and the D perfectly. Yet the final "C" is out of place. Prisons have become (both literally and figuratively) "centers for disease(disease as well as physical diseases). But they are not of "control". The H.I.V., mental illness, learned murder etc are all contagious. (I.e. riots!)...The disease must be treated with all deliberate speed... shifting gears: I already mentioned Rev. Leroy Jenkins in another part of this tome. But I am an apologist for preachers. There are a lot of names and stories in this book but I left a lot out. i.e. the pastors with whom I've had sexual relations with women. In the pastors study. You will neve rknow his name... But I must re-visit Rev. Leroy Jenkins. I was gonna leave well enough alone etc. But I just saw him on a news/tabloid and I am nuclear/livid! They showed him healing people. They him marrying a black woman who is nearly 100 years old. And she had just so happened to have hit the lottery for $20 million or so. And a week later Jenkins took her to Las Vegas to marry her. Come on Jenkins ! Yo (Leroy Jenkins)ass has gone too far now. I respect the elderly and protect children! And I had no intention of telling everything I know. O.K. so I sustained a serious injury in Richmond Virginia. (Foolish of me to even think that in the midst of my deception God was gonna step up and give me a miracle anyway.) So I went to Akron Ohio and had Rev. Ernest Angley to pray for me. "Man can't do it Lord, it'll take you he stated as he laid his hand on my head, no healing. I did go back to the study and meet Angley. I shant comment on that meeting. I impersonated Rev. Jesse Jackson and called Benny Hinn.Benny Hinn agreed to reserve a seat for "Rev. Sherman Manning" on the first row of Benny's church in Orlando. I flew to Orlando and Benny Hinn laid his hand on me and I was not healed. I went back and met Benny in his study, no comment. I impersonated (as I say in another part of this tome) Jesse and called Leroy . "I believe that God can do it and He will do it" Leroy told me. (yall know he's gonna destroy the video as soon as he hears about this book)... Leroy Jenkins hung up with Rev. Jesse Jackson (me) and called –me. He told me to come to the Tallahassee crusade. He asked "what" I would be wearing specifically... As I walked into his service in Tallahassee the next night he was preaching. And he spotted me entering. He feigned surprise and said "Young man, the holy spirit just told me you're Rev. Sherman D. Manning, a friend of Rev. Jesse

Jackson's. Am I right?" I said "yes". Then he launched into a long sermonette about how he had personally talked to Jesse last night. How he knew I was coming but had no idea what I looked like. The holy spirit spoke to him and told him he and I (and Jesse) would be working together closely....He laid his hand on me and yelled "Lord I lay my hands on this man." I did not get healed. Leroy explained that it might take a couple of months but healing was coming. We went out to breakfast (like 1:00 am) together. He had a black driver who was gay. At breakfast I told him about some legitimate work I was doing (Jacob/Israel-trickster on one of my shoulders and a prince on the other). I mentioned Rev. Hosea Williams and Jenkins told me "I want you to preach at my church in Delaware Ohio. I want Rev. Willliams and Jesse." I wasn't close enough to Jesse to pull that off. Plus I'd get caught if I put those two together. I was still thinking that Jenkins was authentic. As messed up as I was, I was too scared to play with God.

I flew back to Richmond and before my plane touched the ground Jenkins had left me a message at my office. He wanted me to go to a studio and record a televised message for his T.V. show. I did and I got calls from around the world. But Jenkins was manipulating the "Jesse" Angle and cashing in on it. I actually called my dear friend Rev. Hosea Williams to see if he'd go preach for him. "Rev. Manning I wouldn't preach for Jenkins if God asked me to I think he's a crook."

Rev. Jenkins began calling me daily and two weeks later I went to Delaware....I preached for him (televised) and he promised me $20 grand. Ten thousand dollars for the two speeches (ten each) at his church. I agreed to stay in town a week. He conviced me to leave my hotel and stay at his mansion since he no longer lived there. Then he tried to sell me the mansion. (I still had not received one red penny of the $20 grand). I met the older black woman (whom I saw marrying him on Inside Edition). I met a black guy by the name of "Rabbit" rumored to be a drug dealer. "When I was in prison, Rabbit visited me all the time he told me." Then he introduced me to a black gay preacher from Columbus. And I noticed Jenkins would study my reactions to see what I thought of his gay entourage. I got the distinct notion that Jenkins was what they call "bi-sexual".

He tried to get me to buy into his "healing water" business which he claimed to sell all over the world... One gentleman called to say as a friend of Jesse Jackson you should not be getting mixed up with Jenkins. He molested his own sons. He went to prison....paid his kids hush money to keep it out of the courts. And he is a bi-sexual." By the time I asked who he was he hung up on me. Rev. Jenkins picked me up that evening and took me to his place. He made some of the best homemade biscuits I'd ever tasted. I told him about the telephone call. To my utter surprise came this reply. "I did go to prison" (this was actually a day before he introduced me to Rabbit). "My sons did (also) accuse me of molestation. But that didn't send me to prison. I did give them a hundred grand to let it go because I used to sleep walk when they were kids. And it's possible I did something to them in my sleep." I had to pick my jaw up off the floor. I asked about my money and he gave me a 20 minute answer to a 20 second question. In short he claimed all his money was tied up in a lear jet he was buying and he'd send me a check in two weeks. He was buying a new mailing computer system and his present system was nice. It packed, licked, sealed envelopes for you. It was a Pitney Bowe system that he gave me. I had it shipped to Atlanta and I gave it (guess that was my payment because I never got a dime from Leroy) to Rev. Hosea Williams. He and Terrie Randolph loved it...Before I left Delaware I was certain Jenkins was a crook. And I saw him (with my own eyes) fondle the penis of that black preacher from Columbus....I left town that self same evening and never heard from Leroy again. While I was in Delaware some of what I saw turned my stomach. Jenkin's would lock up the church and practice with his "healing patients." One black woman that I saw him heal on T.V. in Illinois, was also re-healed in Tallahassee and then re-healed again. She was an amateur actor.

Rev. Leroy Jenkins (yes-he might sue me but I stand by my word) had a "smackdown", sort of "Wrestling is real" approach to healing. And now that my alarm clock is on I have no doubt that Rev. Leroy Jenkins is not only a crook but a child molester and a bi-sexual!!...(IF Jenkins is contemplating suing me?) I repeat he is a crook, child molester and a bi-sexual point blank! They reserve a special place in hell for folk like Leroy Jenkins, Eric and Lyle Menendez, Henson and Bardo!...

...G.B.G./Heart wants to produce CD's to be played for students around the world. CD's and or DVD's will be a powerful ministry tool for at risk teens who can't come to a live tour. I intend to ask "Jimbo" to assign Fred Schroeder to manage the recording and distribution of these tools. IF your school, staff, students or church would like a G.B.G. video or C.D. visit G.B.G. on Facebook, at www.napsusa.org or call 916-985-8610 (ext. 3000). If there are prisoners wanting to begin a G.B.G. chapter and your warden does not approve. You have every right to join G.B.G, online, receive our newsletters and to mentor by mail. We encourage G.B.G. prisoner members (all across this nation and even on death-row) to write letters to youngsters encouraging them not to make the mistakes you made. Some of the prisoner members send letters to principals, professors and to teachers asking them to read them to students. We send letters to pastors and to local news stations and call them a G.B.G./PSA... Many prisoners have weekly (informal) meetings using this tome as a guidebook...Every Saturday at 12:00 noon G.B.G. members (from around the world! In jails, juveniles, prisons, schools and churches etc.) are asked to say a word of prayer for all children. We pray for the well being, safety, guidance and the protection of kids. We believe in the power of simultaneous prayer. We call it Prison Corporate Prayer. If you are a believer-every Saturday (when you remember), wherever you are, whisper a prayer for kids. Let's be crazy enough to have the faith that our collective prayers will prevent molestations, beatings and murders. I want every believer to make it a habit of saying a Lil prayer for kids, at noon on Saturdays. Everybody (even on death row) can pray! Put it on your calendar –beginning this Saturday "at noon I will say a protective prayer for kids." This kind of village prayer will make a difference...

And this also means that every Saturday at noon kids will know that "There may be tens of millions of people praying for me right now." And there is a spooky kind of grace that comes upon folk when they know that they are being prayed for. I want every prisoner (as well as the family members of inmates), students and teachers etc. to commit to praying (with G.B.G./Heart) at noon every Saturday. I give prisoners hell in this tome. Because we (prisoners) get on my blankety blank nerves but I recognize as Fred Schroeder always reminds me, there is a spiritual aspect to it. We prisoners are wounded soldiers. We remind me of the high school football star who goes on to play college ball. And then we get scouted by folks from the NFL. We had a lot of hope, bright lights and a lot of promise and just before we sign the multimillion dollar contract we are felled (i.e. "thorn in the flesh") by a career ending injury. It seems to be over. Our dreams are busted and hopes are crushed into dismay. What do we do now that our injuries have led us (rightly or wrongly) to jail cells? We can lay around and wallow in despair. We can whittle our lives away at the card table, chasing pills, punks or telling war stories. We can blame our failures on the white man, Bill Cosby or even Oprah. We'll always find an amen corner when we play the blame game. Misery loves company. But we have a powerful alternative even in prison, especially in prison. We can pick ourselves up, dust ourselves off and become king makers instead of kings. The greatest football coaches (sometimes) are the playerswho lost their careers to injuries. We can become experts at passing on those dreams we could not achieve. We can view prisons as launching pads, opportunities and a platform for greatness. When I look at 7 and 8 year old gangbangers I hear President John K. Kennedy: "We (prisoners) are confronted with a moral issue. It is as old as the scriptures. (Suffer the little children and let them come unto me). And it is as clear as the American Constitution!" I argue that it is the constitutional obligation of all 3 million U.S. prisoners to become in prison(s) what we did not achieve in the streets. Let us become U.S. Ambassadors, Little League coaches for kids...become G.B.G....Billy Fleming had tears in his eyes when he told me "Sherman this means so much to me because I have fourteen grand kids out there...I want to protect them from predators"... Richard "Doc" ford wept when he told me "I arrested so many gangsters when I was an LAPD cop. ...They had looks in their eyes which were cold, lonely and haunting...Sherman we owe these children!"... Johnny "Claw" Willie told me "Allah brought you back here to New Folsom in divine order and you can't die or leave until we do this...I've been in prison 30 years, I've seen people come and I've seen them go. And I know these youngsters look up to us...who else can bring associate wardens, captains, physicians and prisoners together in such a beautiful group called G.B.G.? ...Atlanta (aka Sherman) this is Allah! He's moving by His powerful hand. Moving through you, Fred, Steve, Jimmy and all of us. This is the almighty!"

I was deeply moved by my teammates comments...Fred Schroeder (I repeat) is the same man who ordered me transferred out with all deliberate haste. But-with all of his flaws Fred loves God and Christ said" My sheep, know my voice and a stranger they will not follow." Fred knew God wanted me here. And Fred obeyed God. I know Mate Cate, Scott Kernan and the governor all have a problem with a lot of my writing. But I would hope that Scott, Matt, the Governor and the Senate (those politicians that I give hell) will commend Warden James P. Walker, A.W. Fred Schroeder, Captain Steve John Vance, Captain Patricia Kennedy Kevin Pool, Adam, Daniel, Dustin and the distinguished board of G.B.G. advisors. These people volunteer their time, guidance, knowledge and their expertise. And I think the Governor, Gloria Romero, Darrell Steinberg etc. and even the president ought to recognize the service of these civilian employees. Neither Billy, Ford, Willie or I seek any accolades. We are pragmatic enough to know it would be political suicide for any politician to praise us. We don't have a problem being in the background. In fact I told Fred that "I want you, Kevin Pool, Dr. Jarman, Dr.Curren and Adam Lane to do the media interviews etc. Fred we can't let me be the spokesman. I am too controversial! I have way too much baggage and I am an inmate." Fred Schroeder and I (the ying and yang) actually agreed. But he replied "Sherman your power is witnessing to the kids in a way only you can do... In person, on C.D. if we get it approved and on D.V.D.'s. But you are right we (Fred, Steve, Dr. Jarman. Dr. Duran, Dr. Heitkamp etc.) should be the "public face" of G.B.G. In fact we (staff) are the "HEART" (Helping Educate At Risk Teens) of G.B.G. "I replied with "Preach Fred!"... and just as President Obama helped to inspire G.B.G. We want to help inspire similar teams all across this country. Life is so unpredictable and so fragile. And I can see the looks of panic on our (prisoners) faces. Our grief (guilt, sorrow etc.which we usually disguise as anger because anger is so much more macho) drives us to hunger for a human touch. And we need to transform that hunger into a thirst to coach kids. There is no excuse for failing to reach out. Captain Steve Vance told me "Sherman I'm even willing to continue coming back to New Folsom to do G.B.G. tours after I retire in November. I won't leave you and Fred hanging. We've worked so hard to get this off the ground."

I tell my fellow convicts that I don't know what kind of pain you're holding on to in your heart. But let it go or it will destroy you. Let it go! I told Roger (Silent) to let it go. I'm always talking about "anger" because there is a demonic influence over prisons which usually reveals itself in the form of "anger". And I wanna repeat to every prisoner, juvenile and every student to let it go... Senator Ted Kennedy? Chappaquidick became his thorn in the flesh. He was riddled with scandals. Tragedy always seemed to be shadowing him. But God bless it Mr. Kennedy reached a turning point and an epiphany. He was able to rise from the ashes of defeat, tragedy and scandal. He went on to become the most celebrated Senator in our nation. And he is responsible for adding credence to the candidacy of a young and "inexperienced" politician who was running for the highest office in the land. Mr. Kennedy believes that we (yes you and me) should "see wrong and try to right it. See suffering and try to end it." That is your responsibility as well as mine. To look at Columbine, Virginia Tech and Hillsdale High and decide to pray for, write to, preach and teach and coach the kids who all too often; hail us as heroes. "The work of our own hands shall determine our destiny" Senator Kennedy stated. And so we must work, write, speak, teach and pray! (Every Saturday at noon no matter where you are)... And we each have a role (even in the prisons) to play. I might not be able to preach like Paul. I might not be able to sing like angels. But such as I have give I unto thee. Just do what you can do "to whom much is given-much is expected." G.B.G. has the kind of faith which is not just about proclamation but also about demonstration. We know that kids think "I see so much you do, I hear nothing you say." We try to show our commitment through our actions. We (Fred, Lane, Bugriyev, Willie, Ford, etc.) believe in kids. Because as Jimbo told me "Sherman a strategy without a burden is only ambition. And ambition can wane.".... I pray that folks like Justin and Mike Delgado (who was on The Steve Harvey show 3 years ago etc.) will help G.B.G. reach youngsters with their own "such as I have." I want students like Ben Bishop, Eric Bates, Wade Harsh, Alex Blench and Iman Arod (Iman and all of his classmates in the MBA course at USC) to come stand with G.B.G. as we reach out and touch youngsters. We want to say to our kids that "The work begins anew! Hope rises again! And the dream (i.e. "Dreams of our Fathers") lives on!" I declare to every kid in America, to kids all over this world (who are reading this book!)... many staff do not agree with a lot of what I write in this tome...But as it relates to the "mission" of G.B.G. and the "HEART" platform. Fred, Steve, Warden Walker, every G.B.G. advisor and the entire G.B.G. team (including Johnny, Billy and Ford) all concur with Mr. Kennedy...we shout (from the bowels of New Folsom State Prison-all the way to the Alps in Switzerland) that "the work begins anew! Hope rises again! And the dream lives on!" I invite every prisoner, every juvenile, every human being perusing this tome...

...Whatever you think about me. Please meet G.B.G. in the prayer circle (around the world) at noon every Saturday for kids. I plan to personally write to some believers I know (i.e. Zig Zigler, Tony Dungy, Rev. Otis Moss, etc) and ask them to join the G.B.G. circle of prayer this Saturday and every Saturday at noon for kids. And I invite Joshua Costa, Joshua Gurki, Lewis Hansen Moore, Nick Jonas, Julie Sena and Patrick Sanholdt to join us this Saturday at noon. All those reporters and pundits ready to dig around in my mess (Lord knows I got a lot of it!) etc. I have no problem with that. But when you finish with my mess I invite you too to whisper a silent prayer for kids at noon on Saturdays! One of Harvey Levin's reporters pointed out that he had a buddy ("Jose what up dogg") in prison who watches TMZ.com. I want "Jose", Shannon Ness, Michael Potrilli, Karishma Kumar, (all the kids at U.C. Merced), Smith Elementary School (Chicago), Principal Ronald Whitmore and Verone Kennedy to meet Fred, Steve, G.B.G. and me (in prayer) this Saturday at noon. Rev. Timothy Fleming, (Mount Carmel in my hometown), the Bridge Church (Pastor Grays in Atl.), Pastor A. Lincoln James (Trinity in Richmond), Rev. Roscoe Cooper and Bishop Noel Jones etc. meet us at noon on Saturday. I call Soloman Jackson Jr. (in Colombia S.C. we don't need a donation) to meet us in prayer...In Los Angeles where G.B.G. founding member Richard "Doc" Ford used to patrol as a street cop (before he promoted) they had 18 murders in June alone, and 7 murders in July! All 25 murders were gang killings! I think (and I'm not being melodramatic! Remember I'm not seeking your membership in a church! I seek no tithes and no offerings and I'm in jail with no bail!) 25 gang murders in less than 2 months ought to be enough (is enough) to bring us together like the 29 murdered and missing children of 1979 brought us (Mayor Maynard Jackson, Grace Davis, Rev. Sherman D.

Manning and an entire city of mourning and praying mothers etc.) together... If not now when? If not us who? I call us in these prisons. We are almost 3 million strong. To you at Pelican Bay, at Rikers Island, at Phillips C.I., In Alto, Corcoran, San Quentin, in Reidsville and in Needsville, we are in Seedsville. You are a seed. From the north and the south! From the east and the west. We must come together for our children. The village must be restored. I invite Drew Stevyns, Jacob Martin (US Marine), Kenneth Santana, Corporal Dan Gay, David Joiner, Chris Durbin, Timothy Combs, Petri Hawkins-Byrd and Marvin Speed to meet us this Saturday at noon. Just as senator Kennedy did we (who are locked up) can take our tragedies and prison. Sentences and transform them into Authentic empathy for youth. We can continue in the face of adversity and difficulty by picking others up. We (within these walls; by the power of prayer and with the pen which is mightier than the sword) can engage in a massive awareness campaign, for the 600,000 kids trapped in abusive the foster care system CPS just cut staff (in Sacto) by 200 last month. It is a tragedy that we must write about and pray for.... I invite Sherri Miller (at "All in One" in Oakland) to meet us Saturday at noon. I call kids (i.e. V. Yakubovsky and all the teens at Oakmont high school in Roseville CA), David Quindt, Daniel Job, Joseph Latham, Stuart Campbell and Josiah Lemming to meet us Saturday at noon. We have a seat at our (G.B.G/Heart) table reserved for Christians like Zac Sunderland, Matthew and Joseph Kennedy III. We want Maeve Townsend, Adam Lambert, Nurse Josiah Poirer and CNA John Johnson to meet us Saturday at noon with Christ in the school of prayer for kids. We can no longer afford to merely ride the coattails of our parents' Christianity. But we must grab the torch and the baton of service which has been passed on to us. I am making a personal appeal to lil Joe Kennedy, Maeve, Bill Burton, Daniel Sample, Joseph Schoen, Libby Amor, John Decarro, Maxwell Hanger and Alex Blench to meet us Saturday at noon. If I must go bankrupt giving stipends to Nathaniel Mullinnex, Christian, Alex, Maxwell and Libby so be it! I gotta have help from Ryan Hreljec, Mike Delgado, Alexander Dugdale, Clay, David Reynolds, David Dowdie, Gary Browning, and David Joiner! I need Sam Fuick, Chris Durbin, Chris Michael Fowler, Chris Rousche, Scott Johnson, Billy York, Ricky Lebbaron, Joe Stein, Joe Klein, Tim Coleman and Guadelupe Reyes to join us. This is a clarion call to Elder Sam Wallace, Bishop Joseph Walker, Rev. Mark Payton, Rev. Lincoln Bingham and the members of Shively Heights Baptist Church to meet us Saturdays at noon. I need Cornell McBride to meet us...Hell I want Steve Harvey to consider giving a Hoodie award (not to me) to the G.B.G. Board of Advisors. And even if he does not, he can meet us every Saturday.

After Max fulfills the challenge on page 313 (of "Blue Eyed Blonde"book II) he too (LOL-serious) can meet us at noon on Saturdays. Prayer changes things. Prayer is a potent weapon in the arsenal of humanity. I need Van Hansis, Karen Hegner, Jake Silbermann, Dustin Brown, Mr. S. Cozza (Petaluma), Dustin Brown (Carmichael), Kevin Shelton, David Jensen and Jake Heartsong (in Flo.) to meet us Saturday. Brandon White (San Joaquin, CA) we have a stipend for you. Jinan Sumler, Erica Guerrero, Tom Savage, Father Lino Otero, Cesar L. Chavez Jr., Matt Barkley, Scott Henuset, Warren Ballentine, Alexus Upshaw (homegirl!), Adam Bettercourt, Gribbon Morris (swimmer), David Holloman, Craig Cannon, Alex Sliva, Omar Samaha, Ralph Cannon and Eddie Cannon I need you. I'm calling out to the masses. No matter how much I have to give. No matter how much it costs me... I remember when Eli Nessler shot the child molester who had been molesting her kid (true story). I sat at M.C.S.P. and felt that I should write a missive to Atty. Tony Serra and ask him to give it to Willie Nessler to try to encourage Willie not to become me. I knew he was angry. And rage will destroy you. I never wrote the letter and years later when Willie beat a man to death I felt.... Who knows if my letter could/would have helped? The only thing I had to lose was a stamp. I wrote this tome (I almost named it "Act like a Child/Think like a Predator") to every potential Willie Nessler out there. I wrote it to try to save "just one". I need pushforamerica.org , Blake Koch, Luke Sears, Wes Kovarik, Nathaniel Marshall, Ricky Harlow, Kaether Cordero, Matt Chrabot, Neal Carlson, Will Seabrooks, Adam Davis, Nate Firestone, Gerald Posner Jr.(reporter), Zachary Boyd, Mayor Young (Philadelphia) and Mayor Bloomberg...All of you in prison.

"The work of our own hands shall determine our destiny." It would be beautiful if Zig Zigler would go on Facebook, Myspace or Twitter and agree to meet "the Crook (trickster)" at noon on Saturday in prayer. I still believe that the lion can lay down with the lamb. I invite Curtis Sykes, Beth Payton, Paris Hilton and even Redmond O'Neal to meet us every Saturday at noon-o-clock. I owe Willie Nessler, the memory of the fear I felt in 1979 and the promise I made (in the valley of the shadow of death) at "Valley Fever" etc. etc. I owe 600,000 kids in foster care all of the time that I have left. I call (again) Joe Kennedy III, Dustin and Maeve etc. to help (on twitter.com, facebook, backbook and any book!) CASA volunteers (Lori Bartolli) and go on to the Dr.Phil website and check out the Dr. Phil Foundation and help! I call Michael Vick, Plaxico Burress, Eric Donahue, Vernon Jordan, Dr. Robi Ludwig, Cynthia Ribas, Stephen Rhode and Mr. Padilla to join us...Find Trevor Loflin, Alan Rafferty, Bryan Kennedy, Brian Foskuhl, Joseph Canova and Sean Payton and meet us at noon on Saturday ... After all of my bullshitting, gameplaying and conning etc. I owe it to the legacy of (my mentor) Rev. Hosea L. Williams, Congressman John Lewis and Ambassador Andrew J. Young (who did so much for me) to "confront the failures of my own personal life and make a change." If John Lewis and Hosea could withstand and endure the beatings, dogs, waterhoses and the pain (for me) at Edmund Pettus Bridge I must say and do "Justice, Love Mercy and Walk humbly with God." We have a moral obligation to help our children. So I feel blessed to be able to align my voice, my prayers, my two cents and the two cents of the G.B.G team, alongside the voices of Attorney L. Wallace Pate, Robin and Dr. Phil, Senator John Burton, Death Row Inmates, Fred Moor, The SJM Foundation, U.S. Mint Green LTD., Michael Paraino and soldiers around the world...To all the 600,000 kids in foster care around this great country I repeat "The work begins anew! Hope rises again! And the dream lives on!" To all our kids in juveniles and jails. I tell you "The Work begins Anew!" ...To students at Oakmont high, Folsom High School, out at McNair, Hillsdale high, Palmer High School, Columbine in Littleton, Heritage High, Locke High school and at schools everywhere etc. I stand with you and my team at G.B.G. has you (kids) in our HEART (Helping Educate at Risk Teens). We (G.B.G.) shall never (again) abandon you. We will tell you the truth about predators, prisons, gangs, guns, drugs and violence. I call Michael Shackelford, Faisal Selah, Cozza Shelton, Clay C.J. Sheron and Justin to help us. It's time out for mantrums! It's time for us to live out the truth that "the work begins anew. Hope rises again and the dream lives on!" Saving out youth is the opportunity of our lifetime!! This is the opportunity of our lifetime!! We can come together and feed the flowers we've often robbed. This is our chance to rise from the ashes of defeat and deceit. And to teach the dream that we did not live. And to teach the love that we did not give. This is a rare, unique and an awesome opportunity for the profilers to work with the profiled, the warden to work with the ward, the doctor to work with the patient, the cop to work with the criminal, the keepers to work with the kept and all flesh shall see it together. Famed Senator John Burton, Fred Moor, Warden Jumbo Walker and Captain Patricia Kennedy are working (side by side) with Willie, Ford, Manning and Billy. And we invite Bill Clinton, Bill Gates, Mike Vick, Tony Dungy, Robin McGraw and her sons etc. to stand with G.B.G. As we help people with HIV to see. There is no "vaccine" for the sexual disease HIV (but abstinence works and condoms help). But reading, writing, prayer and education are the "vaccine" for this (HIV) "visual swine flu." I want Danny Henson (Richmond, VA), Joey Grissett, Craig Gilstrap and Francis Ronald Wright to join our team. I want Mullinnex, Christian, Sample and Schoen to send us (via snail mail and/or post them to our websites) your photos so we can use them in tomes, brochures and on the web. Send us your photos to Sherman D. Manning at CSP Sac. (My address is in this tome.) The more photos the merrier…shifting gears. I talked to Dr. Phil this morning. Dr. Phil told me that he and Dr. OZ talked Oprah into doing a cosmetic neurosurgery. This is a kind of brain survey which will force Oprah to eat healthier. I could not believe Dr. Phil would admit this to me. (Ya'll to go to opinion.com and ask her if this is for real and then come back to the book…) I affirm under penalty of perjury that Dr.Phil did tell me this! And he told me this (lol) in my sleep!... I'm joking ya'll. I've never spoken (in person) to Dr. Phil. Actually I was thinking about how hard I laughed when Oprah had Dr. Oz talking about this surgery and she said "I'm not gonna do the surgery ya'll…" I fell out. And I was dreaming that I talked to Dr. Phil and he said "Sherman I talked Oprah into doing the surgery. This is a changing day in Oprah's life." I'm just adding humor to lighten the moment…I was perusing some data by Dr. Keith Ablow, Dr.Drew Pinsky and famed therapist Dr. Milton Erickson earlier today. When I'm dealing with issues of teen addictions etc. I always call on the experts. I've come to understand how powerful an addition can be. And no Redmond O'Neal or Whitney wakes up one morning and decides "I'm ready to lose control of my life. And I want drugs to control me." People wanna "feel good." People wanna escape and anesthetize pain. And I've come to believe (especially after studying volumes of data provided by Dr. Hedblad, Dr. Curren, and Dr. Duran etc.) that most of what we try to do (as society) to combat drug addiction actually exacerbates it. A pastor yelling about how smoking crack will send you to hell is not going to magically defeat addiction. Prayer works and I believe in miracles. But God does not always miraculously heal us. Everybody is not gonna hit the lottery for $1 million and instantly be able to pay their bills. Some folk are gonna have to make payments to get out of debt. Instant miracles don't always occur. And when it comes to these drugs which are crippling and destroying kids like Cameron Douglas and Redmond etc. We have failed to recognize how devastating they can be. I've seen guys in prisons sell their souls for drugs. Even for nicotine, guys will sell a $200.00 television for 3 cigarettes. Guys who are not gay will agree to provide fellatio and anal intercourse for heroin…Eric Menendez is gay (as I explain in other parts of this tome) but he does not "burn coal" (have sex with blacks). Yet he readily offered this author sex to pay the $250.00 loaned to him for a drug debt. …So I believe we must pour tons of dollars into prevention. And then spend more on intervention. So that the estimated 1 million folks in jail for drug related offenses will stop costing kids their education…It is estimated that America spends $50 billion (with a "B") per year to house inmates in prisons for drug violations! And not only do guards smuggle dope into prisons etc. But (fellow convicts don't want me saying this) there is an orgy of psychotropic drugs being prescribed to inmates by psychiatrists. They save these drugs up and use them to get high. Many of them overdose and die on drugs prescribed to them. There is a methadone black market in prisons. You think Dr. Conrad Murray or Dr. Arnold Cline are the only Dr. Feelgoods around? Think again…fifty percent of prison inmates are (routinely) high off prescription drugs!! Ipso facto, when they are parolled they are more addicted than they were when they went to jail. I ought to write a tome "Creating Addicts". One of the reasons I've forgiven Dearaujo is because he is addicted to prescription pain killers. He is so troubled, so afraid and so mixed up. I saw him take 13 powerful pain pills (simultaneously) one day. He needs help. Not punishment but help. (Pray for Dearaujo!) …Every Saturday at noon: When we pray for youth we are also praying for youth addicts (including Redmond and Cameron)…

Prayer works! I believe that prayer brought Jaycee Duggard home two months ago. She was kidnapped 18 years ago but somebody kept praying for her…Elizabeth Smart's parents prayed her back home after she had been missing for 11 months…Sean Hornbeck and Ben (lets get them this tome) were prayed out of the claws of a pedophile…I wrote about the "alarm clock" and "act like a child, think like a predator". Well when they interviewed neighbors of the dude

(Phillip Garrido) who's been holding Jaycee for 18 years they kept saying "I got funny vibes about Phil" and…."We called him creepy Phil." I want to pound the point over and over again that: When the person seems creepy they are. When you get that "vibe" listen to it. Feel it and act on it. That "vibe" (about Menendez, Bardo, Henson and Phil) will save your life!

Studying data from the internet (a lawyer sent me his entire blog) I'm alarmed that some official didn't peruse this data and realize he was a "sicko". In Phillip's propaganda I see Jim Jones, Dwight, the occult, Rauser and Menendez! And I'll warn once more: If prisons (I.E. P.V.S.P.) don't begin to monitor the Menendez', Rauser's and their cults (operating under the guise of Sons of Odin and/or wiccans etc) there will be deaths, suicides, rapes and perhaps jailbreaks… I was educated about the Stockholm Syndrome by Dr. Hedblad and later by my advisors. And I see startling similarities in some of Eric (Menendez') propaganda and those which are propogated by the practitioners of this syndrome… C.D.C. guards are ill equipped to even recognize these practices when they see them…

Shifting gears again (I drive a non-automatic so my segues are not smooth! LOL) I've asked one of G.B.G./Hearts chief sponsors to sponsor at least 100 tomes to students. US Mint Green LTD is a powerful G.B.G. sponsor. And I love Heather and all the US Mint Green team down in Washington Township Ohio. I want US Mint Green to log on to www.cafepress.com/Manning and order 100 copies of this book. Have cafepress to send five copies to the "President of student government at Lodi High School" in Lodi CA. Have em send five copies to "President of Student Government at Folsom High School" in Folsom CA. Two copies to "President of Student Government at McClatchy high school" in Sacto CA. And send three copies to the "President of the Student Government at Beverly Hills high school" in Beverly Hills CA and I want Heather to instruct Cafepress to include the note: "your school is in this book compliments of US Mint Green LTD"…And you students reading now log on to our Facebook, Myspace or any G.B.G. site and let us know you are reading… US Mint Green can donate 80 more to Locke high school.

One of my sponsors and I were discussing the great Zig Zigler and my confession. I told him how James Nesmith (Wrightsville GA.) and Scott Johnson (Warner Robbins GA) and I used to listen to Zig all day. And my sponsor said wouldn't it be "awesome if you and Mr. Zigler did a CD, a DVD and/or a tome together specifically aimed at at-risk teens? You (Sherman) have the bully pulpit and status as both a former youth leader and as a convict. And Mr. Zigler has the credibility!" I was awestruck by the idea. To be candid, if I were Mr.Zigler I would not give Sherman the time of day!! But wouldn't it be fascinating for the kids to hear a CD or read a tome written by the father of motivational speakers and the prisoned con who almost conned him? I believe it would be a powerful, impactful testimony to teens and tweenies and it would also introduce generation Y to some of the incredible books and other data (i.e. the "I can' course and the book "See you at the top".) by Mr. Zig Zigler!

Regardless! I recommend that kids in detention centers, group homes, juveniles, at Delancey Street, Homeboy Industries, in classrooms, colleges and prisons study Mr. Zigler's materials. I met the man! I ate in his home. He took me to church with him. He is for real! He is authentic! I respect Mr. Zigler! He is for real!

And if some of these officials (i.e. especially progressives like Michael Bloomberg, Mike Nutter, L. Douglas Wilder,, David Hicks, Gov. Deval Patrick and Kevin Johnson etc.) were to begin to introduce Mr. Zigler's materials to high school students, kids in foster care, juveniles and into prisons etc. We will impact kids in a powerful way. And it won't cost a lot of money. I know Mr. Zigler well enough to know that he would discount his materials (in bulk) for schools, group homes and prisons. I believe that if my team (i.e. Dr. Franklin Curren, A.W. Fred Schroeder etc.) were to get together with Mr. Zigler etc.etc. We could get Dr. Paul Crouch, Amy Finn and TBN

Second Chance television networks around the world. I will be praying about this and we'll see what happen. But you kids at Locke, Hillsdale, Columbine, Folsom, McClatchy and Beverly Hills high school etc. ought to do two things: A. Meet us every Saturday at noon as we pray for you. And B. send Mr.Zigler an e-mail that your school would love to hear him and "the one who tried to con"… and tell him you would read a tome by his honor and by me..

…The good Lord works in mysterious ways!...Gangs? I learned a new term from Judge Greg Mathis today. "Wangster." I hope they put it in the dictionary. According to Judge Mathis a "wangster" is a so-called gangster who has no money! They'll crip walk and throw up gang signs but don't have a pot to piss in or a window to throw it out! I guess I need to start a W.B.G. "Wang Bangers for Good?" LOL!

I hope Sandy (my friend who works in the office of the president at Ebay) is reading this. If she is "Holla". I hope Jake Shears at Scissor Sisters and "Living Things" are reading. We break out of every box with this book. We are coming for you to make you (thugs and gangsters) "fishers of men." I take sups like Brett and "Chris" who were on Dr.Phil and put them in charge of something in G.B.G. I learned this tactic from Rev. Hosea Williams and from Andrew Young when he was running for mayor. They (Andy and Hosea) learned it from Dr. King. Andy would always put a young and "inexperienced" person in charge of though the youngster had flaws they would usually excel! Their pride was on the line!

Mayor Kevin Johnson just announced he will be giving away a "youth of the month" award for Sac teens 12-18 years old every month. A $200.00 check! I love it! And I'm (check our website to find out) going to see if I can get some of our sponsors (i.e. US Mint Green) to help G.B.G. to (likewise) give a youth of the month award monthly! I'd like to give $75.00 per month to youths 15-19 years old. Every month! Any youth who signs up ten or more G.B.G./Heart student members, send me a list of students you signed up along with an essay (1000 words or less) on any subject. And my team will decide on a monthly winner. We'll announce on facebook, myspace, yahoo, usaservice.org (and always on www.napsusa.org questions? E-mail (hallopeter@sunrise.ch) If you are under 17 (15 or 16) you must present parental permission to participate in the G.B.G youth of the month.

I want to establish more stipends and help more people like John Cushard, David Holloman and Andrew Knox. We can definitely use input from Tony Romo, Joseph Schoen and Daniel Sample. I want Mr. Sample to be one of our "outside" Senior Vice Presidents. We have positions for Cameron Brown and Brett Westcott. I want Cam and West to put on G.B.G. t-shirts and hats on campus and recruit when they "pass out compliments." I want Kevin Shelton to work with us. We need you (out at Lodi High, McClatchy High, Locke etc) to go on to Facebook and Myspace and tell Zach Friesen, C.J. Sheron and Chris Thompson that a revolutionary group G.B.G./Heart needs them. Find me Daniel Clay Hollifield (in Richmond, VA.), Alex Dugdale and Tadd Carr. We have a stipend for Michael Parker in Walnut, CA. I need somebody to go on the web and notify students at Palmer High School (Cole Springs), Columbine and to tell Craig Scott we need him. We must locate Brian Hawn, Kupono, R.Gibbs at Youth Empowerment program, Nils Vesk, Jimmy Bounyavong, Maxwell Hanger and Omar Samy. Let's put Maxwell and Omar in our photo gallery.

This youth outreach must be unique, technologically sophisticated and well orchestrated… I would love for some of you teens and tweenies to get my grand mom's video of me in the march in Forsythe County with Rev. Williams and put it on youtube. I'd like some of you to get my "Keep on Dreaming" speech in which Rev. Hosea Williams introduced me and put it on youtube.

We need a special envoy for G.B.G. ,,,We need Brian Devin Graham, Danny Henson (Richmond, VA), David Reynolds, Chad Sherman, Sierra McFarland and Daniel Radcliffe.

G.B.G./Heart is a band of brothers for good. We are all growing. We train for success. We condition our minds to win. We prime our brains for positivity. We study Tony Robbins, Les Brown, Zig Zigler etc. We use humor, practical jokes and even Ashton Kutcher-like (or Jamie Kennedy) punk-ing to infotain and edutain...I need to reach Sean Farmer, Brian Boykin, Frank Carter (ATL), Gene Langford (ATL.), Marvin Stone, Drew Stevyns, Jacob Martin (US Marines) and Sherri Miller. We must rise to our best ideals. We must be creative and innovative as we engage in a methodical and massive awareness campaign about foster kids. G.B.G. wants unlikely participants (i.e. Mr. Kutcher, Jamie Kennedy, Paris and Michael Vick) to help us in this crusade for kids in crisis. We need Stuart Campbell (Sacto), Zac Sunderland, Solomon Jackson Jr., James Heath Teague, Jeff Allen Walker, John Fink, Ron Huffman, Michael Urie, Tyler Schuurman, Christopher Cluub (Oregon) and Eric Bates. I need Brenda and Kyle Love and Cody Freisan. We must do the almighty through the least likely. We believe ordinary men can do extraordinary things. If we have the right mental attitude and if we believe. I want Phillip Brurelle, Mary and David Coleman, Josh Panno, Kaether, Megan Ward, Mike Sieff, Laticia Burnett, Joel Tatum, Derek Jones (Utah), Jai Breisch and Marc Kielburger to peruse this tome.

John TU, the owner of Lower my bills, Erin Gruwell and Caroline Kennedy need this tome. I want to reach out to Ian Drew, Azziza Davis, Travis Wall, Garrett McCain, Charles Ebersol, Jordan Thomas, Sandra Jackson and ask you all to help us tell the world about this silent epidemic. Our American foster care system is a producer of "kids killing kids." It's time to call out the freaking troops. It is time for us to realize that Dr. Martin Luther King Jr. was right when he said "Everybody can be great" because "everybody can serve." G.B.G. is an "everybody" organization!... Trivia? In 2002 I used to see a group on the Spanish channel late at night. The group was all girls with uno guy. They were dancers. It almost looked like a group of 19 or 20 year old cheerleaders. And uno night they all sat a (I'm serious) bottle on the stage and they danced above the bottles. I think the one lucky guy's name may have been "Enrique". Who knows the name of the group? Let me know asap...I spoke with Warden "Jimbo" Walker today and he told me "I'm thinking about promoting CCII Johnson-Dovey to associate Warden Sherman." I said "I hope so; she'll be the only black A.W. at New Folsom!" lol. He asked "are you done with that controversial and flamboyant 'K.K.K.' tome yet?" I said "Anything you suggest I tell the youngsters?" He said, "Yes tell them if they don't wanna stay in school, off drugs and out of gangs that I have a cell for them always and forever!"

I hope Nathaniel Mullinnex (youth V.P.) is perusing this tome. I have assignments for Nathaniel, Keith and for Christian. I want pastors Mark Payton and Lincoln Bingham to get involved with our International efforts. I wanna reach Todd Dressler and Andrew Pruitt in Atlanta. I want John DeCarro to get this book. I wanna get it to students at Biola University, Sam Bompas, Megan Spaulding and to Lt. Gov. Garamendi. Let's get this tome to Tyrone Brooks and Grace Davis. We must reach Glenn Close, Adam Bettencourt and Alex Blench. I have a guy in the Navy who was on a novel "PBS" special from Manassas Virginia. (Christopher Altus?) If you know him tell him he has a stipend! (I repeat) Brandon White, Ben, Casey, Jeremy, Matt Barkley, Chris Stall, Shannon St. Louis and Marc Zuckerberg. Let me hear from ya'll. Adam Gosney, Wes Cotler and Andrew Tufts. Chad Newman, Keith Jerrolds, David Hartline and Jimmy Peoples (all Georgia boys). Richard Kenneth Chandler, Daniel Masterson and Hairo Torres. Ya'll send Zac Efron, Tatum Channing and Derek Hough to page 313 of the "Blue Eyed Blonde" book II.

Feed your mind the good, the clean, the pure, the powerful and the positive. Look up and live....Tech Sgt. Michael Camillo, Hugh Michael Hughes and Christopher Guzman (Sacto) let us hear from you...You can if you think you can...Alex Youshock is now being tried as an adult. He is the kid (17 "K.K.K.") who took the chainsaw, explosives, sword etc. to Hillsdale high a month or so ago. Now he's facing (overkill) life in prison. He was very withdrawn similar to the VA Tech killer. But (knee jerk reaction) since the village failed (to raise) him now we react with severe overkill! We wanna show how tough we are on crime and make an example out of him. Although we are too unwise to realize that just as the death penalty is not a deterrant to crime; giving Alex life (although no one was hurt) is not going to deter the next withdrawn, shy, loner kid (whom we fail to treat and care for) from going off and trying something!

Cody Sheldon, Michael Castro, Scott McIntyre (and his brother), Mick Hazen, David Jay and Josiah Lemming let me hear from you. And let the work begin anew to engage in a youth Jihad to expose the silent epidemic. I've been accused of understanding social intelligence and I wanna use it to work with technological wizards such as 19 year old Ben Alexander. As he returns to college perhaps we can structure, channel and direct Ben's internet savvy and use it for good. I'd consider making Ben one of the youngest G.B.G./Heart Vice President's ever. We need Ben and I think he needs us. Ben is a great violinist also...

...Redmond O'Neal (and all youngsters dealing with addictions etc.) I want you to know you have to survive this. You've gotta overcome this! Whatever it takes. I believe in the Lord Jesus Christ. But whoever you believe in Redmond. If you gotta call Budda, Moses and Thor call them! We have lost too many. Not another one of us. We've got to get that monkey off of your back. I declare that it is so. I link up with Paul Crouch, Amy Fihn, Bishop Jakes, Zig Zigler and prayer warriors (at noon this Saturday) all over the world and we pray for you. I'm even asking Nick Jonas, Dr. Phil and Robin, Serita Jakes and Vanessa Long to meet us Saturday at noon. I know that the prayers of the righteous availeth much. And I command Redmond to be set free from those drugs. And likewise I believe that some youngster who has been abused will read this and instead of using drugs to fill up the void. You will report the abuse. You will know it was not your fault and you will get psychological, social and spiritual help. And once you are converted "strengthen the Brethren". We need you. We are rooting for you...

This strange and unique book you are reading is just as "all over the place" as youth are. And I want you delivered. Come off that dope and come out of the gang. Having the advantage of studying the most prolific predators as well as notorious gang leaders etc. I've come to the conclusion that the gang shotcaller", sexual "predator" and the occult "leader" share some of the same basic traits, methodologies and even "gifts" if you will. I promise you that Phillip Garrido, Bret Moore, Eric Menendez, Lyle Menendez, Bardo, Stokes, Henson, Jim Jones etc.etc. all look for youngsters who are loners. The more isolated you are the less opposition. They are masters at reading the social "constructs" of people. If you are not close to your family, teachers and don't have strong social networks they can enter into your confidence zone unchallenged. I hate to say this but every great salesman knows this also. You move in and win the person's confidence. The moment anybody wins your confidence they can sell you anything; including sex, their philosophy or their gang. Young people I'll repeat; the minute an adult asks you to keep a secret run! No adult has any business (not a preacher, a teacher, a boy scout leader etc.) asking a kid to keep any secret. And remember that if you isolate yourself (in school, at the mall, in the park or wherever) you set yourself apart as an ideal target for a gangleader, an occult leader or a predator. I'm teaching you what they don't teach you at Harvard (LOL) but they need tp. Joshua Walter, Jake Simpson, Francis Graham, Mark Peterson (Kansas), David Buzzetta and Megan Nerwinski get this tome. And we need folks like Mayor Larry Langford, Jonah Coleman, Nick Mancusos, Frasier Esty, Jamie Constantino (in Stockton), Perry Thompson (student-Granite Bay High School), Steve Barr and his staff to get this book. We must inundate public and private schools with this tome. I know a lot of kids in private schools hooked on drugs being abused and even in gangs. They need this book. Jeff Parshley, Dustin Johnson (Seattle), Chris Shea, Ollie Valencia, John Simon (Parkersburg, Iowa), Jordan Simon, Attorney Megan

Corcoran, Jennifer Portman and Joe Kennedy III need this book. I want kids doing spoken word projects with this tome, with Zig Zigler's works and with Dennis Kimbro's work. I want youths in jails and in juveniles speaking "K.K.K." out loud! Speak "see you at the top" out loud. I want kids in foster care to read and re-read this book until you internalize it. I'll be asking people whom I believe care about you (i.e. Attorney Andrew Bridge, Cameron Johnson, Dungy and Andy Reid etc.) to help us get this tome and other positive and life changing materials to your school, church or prison. And I want you (kids! I'm not worried about adults. We think we know it all: We're too cynical and too traditional!) to get this medicine (data) in your heart, your head and in your spirit. Read and re-read this. Condition your mind for success. Just before you go to sleep at night think "I can." Think "I will." You literally "program" yourself to succeed. As soon as you wake up "I can" and "I will"... One of the greatest things I think Oprah did was to make it almost "cool" to talk to a shrink (Dr. Phil) and I try to set that kind of stage in Hades, with the little influence that I have. And I want you to know you don't have to be nuts to seek out wise counsel. Get help wherever you can.

...I hope we (G.B.G./Heart) can get Judy Smith (Impact strategies. I want Heather and US Mint Green to send Judy this tome) to help us launch this awareness campaign. Judy, Kyle Larsen (Sac-Town), John Fink, Chris Kainkie, Marayam Guzman and Paula Duncan need this tome. Let's get it to kids at Sheldon High School in Elk Grove. Let's contact Mick Hazen and Ben Manning. You kids launch a viral marketing campaign for K.K.K. Contact Pastor Johnathon McNight and tell him I need him to meet me on Saturdays at noon. Tell Matthew Deniston (in Georgia), Destini Chunley (a junior at Lodi) and Mr. Jerry Pike we need them. Perhaps Ben Alexander and/or Justin can lead the viral awareness campaign for us. We want to "poke" every student we can about G.B.G. We want students at Lodi, Locke, Beverly Hills and McClatchy high to tell everybody to go get "K.K.K." ...Again I say to David Jensen, Jake Heartsong, Clay, Justin (on Tyra 8/26/09), to Christian, Keith, Nathaniel and Alexus: "The work begins anew! Hope rises again and the dream lives on!"

Dr. Curren explained to me that someone is infected with the sexually contracted H.I.V. every 9 ½ minutes. I told him someone is infected with (having insufficient vision) HIV perhaps every 9 ½ seconds. It's killing us and we need healing. We need vision....I wanna shift back to Phillip Garrido: My stomach turns as I think of this case. I do wanna commend local T.V. host Walt Gray for interviewing these guys anytime they're willing to talk. It turns out he had been sentenced to 50 years for rape in Nevada. He only served about 9 years. Mistake no.1 If a man really does a rape and gets a fair trial and gets fifty years. Let his ass serve fifty years! A neighbor called the police on 11/30/2006 and reported to the Contra Costa deputies that "strange" activity was going on involving "children". They told the deputies that he was creepy and "addicted to sex" etc. The deputies went to his house on 11/30/06 and determined "no criminal activity" was taking place. They never searched the "village" in the back yard where Jaycee and two kids were being held captive as slaves. Sheriff Warren E. Ruff apologized and admitted "organizational" and "work product" failure. He did not fire the deputy. He should have. And Jaycee's family should sue the sheriff and sue C.D.C. The C.D.C. (CA Dept of Corrections) is responsible for parole agents. And parole agents "searched" Phillip's house 8 times per month, for 8 years! More than 784 parole searches by C.D.C. and they never found Jaycee. Jaycee should sue C.D.C. with all deliberate haste. I recommend Tom Mesereau, Blair Berk, James Brosnahan or Gerry Spence. There was a multi-agency task force led by C.D.C. I call it a Multi-Agency task failure of titanic proportions. 784 "sexual offender compliance checks" but they did not discover the "villages" and "tents" in the back yard. And C.D.C. blames their blunders and dereliction of duty on the "craftiness" of Paul. I want to ask C.D.C. parole agents a question: seven words. "Are you smarter than a fifth grader?" Every agent who visited that house ought to be fired and arrested. And C.D.C. has the audacity and the unmitigated gall to try to be arrogant in the face of such a gigantic failure. Take paroles away from C.D.C. They can't prevent 4 and 5 hour riots which cost tax payers $ tens of millions. So you know they can't run paroles....whatever anybody wants to think about me I'm okay with that. I've earned the right to be "suspect". But regardless of what my baby boomers want to say about me. I think we should demand accountability from law enforcement authorities who failed Jaycee. Her hurt, her pain, her molestations, her psychological torture and her PTSD is on the hands of the Contra County Sheriff's department and on the California Department of Corrections!! Phillip had so many red flags you'd have to be color blind not to see them. But my assignment as a "convict" author who has lots of time on my hands for analysis....(P.S. "time" is a segue for Mandela and Oprah...President Mandela told Oprah that prison gave him time to sit down and think....Oprah said "But did you really need 27 years to think?" LOL) the Atlanta Constitution". And Boston's "Christian Science Monitor" wanted to talk to me while we were in the throes of the crisis of Atlanta's murdered and missing children. Yet after the crisis was over I couldn't get a call back from the local ghetto paper. And nobody is talking about all those boys gone missing in Atlanta. My assignment is to recognize that although Phillip and Nancy Garrido were international sensations last month. Everybody wanted to talk to Weave (and Beth Hassett. Nobody was talking about Weave in July. But Linda out at Just Dentention told me about weave a year ago!) Margaux Rooney, and psychologists etc. But as soon as the trial is over we'll forget again. Edie Lambert and the great reporting she and Walt Gray did will be as forgotten as Grace Davis and Sherman D. Manning. So my assignment (with all the time I have) is to utilize by bully-pulpit and my platform to use Phillip as a teachable moment for the "kids" of today, tomorrow, next year and the next century..." He (Phillip Garrido) looks like a guy that would be mowing the lawn next door" one courtroom observer said of the child molester! Youth Lesson: (I repeat) kid's he's not the lone man in a black trench coat with red eyes and a tail. He is usually an everyday, normal looking guy...and P.S. Sandra Cantu (Melissa Huckaby) and Nancy Garrido have taught us sometimes it is a woman. Beware! Watch, keep and pray!... " He's as normal looking as anybody I've ever seen" stated another observer. You feel me? But a cute lil police officer by the name of Allison Jacobs (U.C. Berkely police officer) along with officer Lisa Campbell taught the defining message of this book: "I had a weird uneasy feeling" officer Allison stated. End of story! If I get kids (around the country and around the world) to internalize those six words: "I had a weird uneasy feeling". This book will literally save lives! ... The kids made no eye contact (red flag), answers seemed rehearsed (red flag), kids seemed subdued (red flag) and robotic (red flag). And Jaycee's two little girls (whom she had by her molester/slave owner) have only known "one backyard" all their lives. There will be lingering scars and psychological wounds....After Hurricane Katrina in New Orleans there had been 40 young adult suicides, in less than 8 months in 2009. All brought on by the "bad stuff" kids had to "see" in Hurricane Katrina. The youngest of the 40 was 11 years old. This is so sad. Psychologists estimate there are 45,000 folks in New Orleans suffering from mental illness due to Hurricane Katrina- nearly 5 years ago. But the media moved on! Thank God for Brad Pitt! –Jaycee? There are 2.3 million kids sold in the human sex trade every year! I recommend every parent, pastor, professor and pupil go get "Call and Response" a DVD by Ashley Judd. There is a "sexual earthquake" involving kids in America. And there are some very powerful, businessmen, judges, lawyers, physicians even police officers participating in it. To the extent that Justin Berry had death threats upon his life for appearing on Oprah to discuss it! Every parent should remove webcams from your kids room forthwith!...

Scott Kernan (with whom I disagree on several issues)-under secretary of C.D.C. said something I agree with: "We should focus on the offenders" involving child sexual assaults. The "craftiness" of a Garrido, Stokes or a Bret Moore needs to be studied over, and over and over again. Time and again (I'm gonna say what Scott can't say) C.D.C. psychiatrists and psychologists are privy to data that ensures them a child predator (about to be released) will reoffend. But they are crippled and paralyzed by red tape and rendered uncapable of taking action...I was at Mule Creek when Ed Stokes was released and several psychiatrists and psychological experts knew he would re-offend. But they were powerless...

...Back to the two sheroes: Allison Jacobs and Lisa Campbell-it was their maternal instincts that cracked the case. Emphasis on the word instincts! Allison and Lisa did what years and years of investigations by sheriffs, parole agents, police and even the FBI could not do. They said "something" about this guy, this picture is out of place. I encourage parents all over this world to begin teaching kids to "set" the "alarm clock" on your "instincts." I'm gonna try to get this book to Victor Carter, Dorreal Fluker, Allison, Lisa, Chief Roy Wasden, Attorney Johnny Griffen, McGregor Scott, Doug French, Sheriff Warren Rupf, Jason Gomes and to teachers around the world. And I want them to teach it. I want youngsters like Brandon Crouch, Josh Costa, Andrew Bridge, Joe Kennedy III and Nathaniel Marshall to spread the word about these techniques: "Instincts". I am calling on Fred Kollar, William Taylor, Ala Fadel (Algeria), Ben Alexander, Brian Hawm, Clay and Alexander Dugdale. Ya'll get this tome to inmate M. Powers (aka "sparfy") Brandon Gene Martinez, Pedro Armando Quandt etc... It's time for all of us who "say" we have a passion for "youth" to put up or shut up. We gotta "crap" or get off the pot. Fred (Schroeder) asked me "Sherman what if Jimmy could only get the Governor or Matt (Cate) to agree to allow you to do a C.D. or DVD for these kids if you'd do it for free?" I replied "Fred: When Valley fever kills me I must leave something for my family and that is what my artistic expression via my tomes, texts, memoirs and fiction will do. But-if we could get somebody like Zig Zigler or Tony Robbins to help us, I would sign a contract! Mr.Zigler does this for a living! It would be unfair to ask him to do it for free! But all of my profits from any C.D. or DVD would go to any youth program earmarked by the Governor. I'd agree not to receive one red cent!" And I meant it. It would be presumptuous of me to speculate on who would or would not want a donation from me. But I would like for Ron Clark of the Ron Clark Academy to consider receiving a contribution from me.... As an aside I'm aware of a series of serious death threats against my life by persons at R.J. Donovan, High Desert, Lancaster and various prisons around the state. And I would ask the Governor to order me a D.R.B. to CSP-Sacramento where I am safe. However, if C.D.C. transfers me and I'm murdered. I believe the nation will take notice. I would hope David E. Kelley, Grace Davis, Roland Burris, Mr. Rangel, Mrs. Waters and even Dr. Poussaint would take notice of my murder...I want Ben Jealous, Julian Bond, former Atlanta Police Chief Eldrin Bell (a one time friend of mine), Chief T.J. Scipio, Keith and Nathaniel Mullinnix, Christian Nelson and Cameron Johnson to help us put the word out! We need Brandon Crouch, Scott Coffman, Frank Carter, Keith Jerrolds, Ralph Cannon, Christopher Rousche and Spence Palmer to help us G.B.G./Heart needs some "young" and "inexperienced" soldiers in the army of this battalion! We need some teens who can use a "slingshot" (P.C.). Bring me Ben Alexander, Justin Berry, Daniel Sample, Chris Thompson, Keith, Nathaniel and Christian and we will change the world!! "Before I formed you in the womb (in Atlanta) I knew you; before you were born I...behold, I cannot speak, for I am a youth. ....Do not say, 'I am a youth,' for you shall (C.J. Sheron, Nathaniel, Keith, Ben, Justin, Daniel, Joshua, G.B.G etc.) go to all to whom I send you, and whatever I command you, you shall speak," ...Ya'll can I tell ya'll a secret? I was scared in my flesh to tell ya'll some of the stuff I tell you in this tome! Stuff about the Menendez brothers, stuff about Stokes, stuff about Spearman, Bunnell and even stuff about me but "...Do not be afraid of their (Marion, Wally, Criner, Eric, Lyle, Phillip etc.) faces, for I am with you to deliver you....Then (Jeremiah 1:5-9) "the Lord put forth his hand and touched my mouth (and pen) and the Lord said to me. "Behold, I have put my words in your mouth"... Are ya'll reading this? I tried to do it with my words and my skills and my intellect but I kept coming up short. And in my flesh I almost went ballistic when Jimbo, Fred, Mrs. Kennedy and Steve let them roll me up and put me in AD-seg on a lie....but "all things work together for good" ...all things! And sometimes (I repeat for Redmond, Cameron and others). He has to get you alone so he can reveal some secrets and show you how "bad" He is. He'll get you alone in a divorce court, in a jail cell, in a rehab or in a detention hall because He wants to touch your mouth and to put His words in your mouth...I don't know why I feel such a sense of connectedness to Redmond O'Neal? I'm not certain what is telling me it's "time" to reconnect with my best friend Emmet Brown .(Last time I saw Emmett was at his dad's funeral.) I'm not sure why I'm led to Judy Smith and Impact strategies. I don't know why I want US Mint Green to get this tome to Attorney Johnny Griffin (Sacto), Stewart Katz, Tony Serra and to Mark Merin...There is something very special about Christopher Thompson (Stacy Smedley's brother). And we need to get this tome to Chris. He'll know why when he reads it. I feel a pull to my homeboys in Georgia (Nathaniel, Keith, Christian Nelson, Christopher Durbin, David Joiner, Sam Fuick, Eddie Cannon, James Nesmith and John Garvin etc.)... But I sense and I feel that if you the reader will poke, e-mail or text message the folks I name in this book and tell them "You are in a book "K.K.K". Go to www.cafepress.com/Manning and get it. We will revolutionize schools. As we build the G.B.G./Heart database, websites and magazines etc. We need your photos of you and yours etc. We want Ben with the violin, Anthony singing, Noriega dancing and you too. Snail mail photos to me at my office (located in a gated community with 24 hour security in Represa, CA.) ASAP. And/or you may e-mail them to me also.

I want unique ideas from folk like the Mullinnex brothers, Christian, Daniel Sample, C.J. Sheron, Nathaniel Marshall, Danny Noriega, Nate (Paradise Hotel), Cole (the Secret Millionaire), kids at Locke, Folsom, McClatchy and Lodi High Schools about what we can do transmogrify, revolutionize and transform schools, teens and tweenies. What do you (Ben, Nate, Cole or Chris etc.) feel we should do to inundate schools and libraries with this book? We need your ideas with all deliberate haste. And I wanna hear from Brandon White as well as Brandon Crouch. We wanna hear from student leaders from Birmingham Alabama to Birmingham England. Let's locate Francis Ronald Wright, Craig Gilstrap, John Jody Bear, David Proctor, Chad Sherman and David Reynolds (Chesterfield County) and tell em G.B.G. has something for them. We need Scott Johnson (Warner Robbins GA), Billy York, Kyle Love and Cody Freisen. We need Daniel Job, Hugh Michael Hughes, Jerry Wines, Zach Freisen and Paula Duncan. We need Cody Sheldon and Garrett Cunningham forthwith.

Bring me Sean Farmer and Phillip Coffee and we will break out of every box. G.B.G. is bigger than me. It is bigger than my team. Bigger than Bugriyev, Lane, Nicolodi, Willie or Ford. It is bigger than New Folsom State Prison and bigger than Jimbo. Utilizing usaservice.org, Facebook and myspace G.B.G. can revolutionize your place. I wanna do a "practice" workshop (with Fred, Steve, Bugriyev, Lane, Nicolodi, the G.B.G. team etc.) and film it. And have Scott Kernan, Mr.Cate and the Governnor to review it and send the film all over this world to change youth. It won't cost a dime to make the film. Adam, Daniel and Dustin will be our "youth" (i.e. Brett and Chris) and the team will do our spiels. We need no "security" approvals because Adam, Daniel and Dustin already work at the prison! And (if Mr.Kernan will approve) this 90 minute DVD can go to Locke, Folsom, McClatchy, Lodi and help youngsters all over this world. I believe (Kernan, Governor, Cate, Romero, Walker, Schroeder are you reading?) I can get Mr. Zig Zigler to record a five or ten minute message to youngsters and we'll put that on our G.B.G./Heart film... Let's do it. (call 916-323-6001 and 916-985-8610 and ask for the G.B.G./Heart film).. It is time. We have all wallowed for far too long. We have locked up almost 3 million people in America. 49% of them are 7-19 years young. We have dropped the ball. We sat around here from 1991-2009 farting in the wind while Phillip held Jaycee captive...I was/am livid with the parole agent and the police. But the more I think about it I am livid (with nuclear anger) with yours truly(=Sherman D. Manning). I don't have to answer to a parole agent or to a sheriff. I blame me. In 1991 what was I doing? It is eerily haunting for me to admit that I think I was attempting to con Mr. Zig Zigler at the same time Phil Garrido was kidnapping Jaycee. If I had done my job (as a citizen and as a man) in 1991 perhaps? Well what if I'd done my job ("ask not what your country can do for you. But ask what you can do...") in 2001 and wrote a book that uncloaked my conviction and unmasked Menendez, Stokes, Moore etc. etc. And if I'd sent this book to Jason Gomes, Wes Kovarik, Angie Gladfelter or somebody who knew Phil or Nancy. Just maybe the alarm clock that aroused the maternal instincts of Lisa and Ally would have led to the rescue in 2001 instead of 2009. But in 01 I was sittin on my mad with the world because....I was just doing what I do! Just minding my "own" business and living my "own" life. What if Senator Ted Kennedy just minded his "own" business and never asked to see Michael Johnson's (asst. Dep. Sgt. At Arms for the U.S. Senate) report card? What if Jesus minded his "own" business and never died on a cross? I came to wake you out of your slumber and remind you that you are (you in Dallas, Atlanta, Miami, Pensacola etc.)your brother's (and sister's i.e. Jaycee) keeper. The fact that she was held captive by a monster for 18 years is a failure of you and me to see. We had H.I.V. (Having Insufficient Vision)...The fact that neither the police, parole agent, deputy, neighbors etc. could see Jaycee, two lil girls, a swimming pool, a compound, a trampoline with a teddy bear etc. We couldn't see beyond, beneath, around and between the shrubbery and trees because of our H.I.V.....We couldn't see. I've never raped anybody or molested a child. But the hurt, the fear, the pain the tears, the molestation of Jaycee is on my hands, my heart and my conscience. How dare I call myself a man who loves God and cares etc. and yet I've slept, night after night for 18 years. While Jaycee was held captive, as a human slave in the freest country on the face of the planet? I am embarrassed! I am ashamed! An I wanna say to every inmate, in every jail cell and every prison all over this earth Jaycee's 18 year captivity is your fault and it is my fault. When was the last you (or me) wrote a missive to a politician, a pastor, a parent or a teacher that said "Here are some things to look for in a predator. Since I was molested..." or "Since I know a molester" etc? Jaycee's captivity is a direct result of that same "village" it takes to "raise a child." That "village" which turns it's head and "Destroys abandons and neglects" a child...I'm troubled today and I'm calling on people in high places and low, in jailcells and classrooms to step forward and save the children. I want C.N.A John Johnson, Fireman "Jeremy Hudson", Denver Whitney, Casey and Ben at Sierra Vista Med. Center, Kiley Kennedy, James Wetick, James Mattocks and even Jamie Kennedy to come stand with us.. God will judge America by how we treat the powerless and the least amongst us.

     ...And I want Tobias Lake, Peter Severson, Ben, Nate, Keith, Alexus and all the Upshaws to help put the word out "Like a good neighbor (pun intended) "K.K.K." is there"... From yo jailcell (Michael Jacinto, Abel "Grumpy" Maldonado, Armando Guizar and every inmate) you can articulate profound and lofty truths to transform youths (between you and me only). I've raised hell for years about prisons and rightfully so. But the fact that I (a convicted felon) can lay back in a jail cell or a hospital room and write and publish a tome is a testimony to the greatness of America. It causes me to love this country and to appreciate the constitution. And I want to serve as an inspiration to release you from your hesitation. I want you to read, to draw, to write, to teach and to preach. I want this tome to agitate you to act. There are publications (Prison Legal News, Convict News, The Beat Within in San Franciso etc.) willing to publish your writings, drawings etc.. I command you to write, to teach, to preach. You can be a beacon on a hill. You can be a light shining in the dark. The internet has made all things possible. I reach out to Roberta Franklin, Carol Leonard, Sasha Vodnik, Cassie Pierson, Peter B. Lewis, All Of Us or None, George Soros and to Todd Dressler (the Dresslers in Atlanta GA). I don't need your money! I need your attention, effort and your action. It is time! "Come on people (prisoners, parents, pupils and profesors)"...come on in that prison, classroom, college and even in the trailer park. You can do it! I am writing this tome because of a debt I owe to Ambassador

Andrew Young, to Rev.Hosea Williams, to Flip Schulke, James Scott Manning and to Dollie Mae Manning...till the day I meet my maker I won't stop praying for G.B.G. and "K.K.K" to spread like wildfire. Oprah said (I repeat) "God allows horrible things to happen to you. So that you (in that jailcell or wherever) will never let it happen to somebody else."... I was there with Mayor Maynard Jackson, Lee P. Brown and the Murdered and Missing Children. I still remember the fear and I must never let it happen to somebody else. Recently my nightmares about being chained to my hospital bed, the flashbacks I have of patients coding and dying in my room. My terror from Valley Fever was now added a new companion. I'm waking up in the middle of the night seeing that "one back yard" that Jaycee and those kids had to see for 18 years....I'm seeing Phillip, Stokes and Bret Moore. That's why I'm putting this white spot light on predators. No matter what it costs me. All that it takes for evil to rage is for good men (neighbors, folk who feel something "odd") to remain silent. In light of 1979, in light of Bret Moore's kids, Sandra Cantu, Haleigh Cummings, Sasha Groene, Casey Anthony and Jaycee. I can't keep quiet. And I must never let it happen to somebody else...Go online to Aaron Carter, Biz Stone, Phillip Coffee, John Sexton, John Garvin, Matt Stuart, Derek Hough, Cody Linley and poke them for G.B.G. Ya'll saw "America's Smartest Model" (Andrew?) tell em I said holla. I can't and won't keep quiet! I need Gary Browning, Ricky Parnell, Brian Foskuhl and Ronald Keith Dunn all in Richmond VA. I need Clay's pal Joey. I need their input and their expertise forthwith. We need Matthew Deniston and you. Shine this white hot light on every pervert in America. I want prisoners in record numbers to write to the prison law office in San Quentin. Write to stop prisoner rape in LA. And report being raped by staff or by inmates. I want boys at C.Y.A. in Stockton, Chad and around the country to write confidential/legal (sealed) letters to Attorney Melissa Rothstein at "Just Detention" in LA about any in custody rape(s). I want students to contact the police (immediately) about sexual contact or advances by teachers, coaches or any adult! Never falsely accuse anybody! But if it happened report it today! ...I believe that the contents of this book (which is a tad bit longer than senate president Pro-Tem John Burton wanted it to be! LOL) will help kids all over this world! And I want Maxwell Hanger, Zac Friesen, C.J. Sheron, Nathaniel, Christian, Keith and Daniel Sample to contact me forthwith! I want Wes Colter, David Quindt, Hugh Michael Hughes, Durbin, Cannon, Sykes, Johnson and Ricky Mitchell (Summerville GA) to let me know you're reading! I reach out to Sherri Miller ("All In One" Oakland), Petri Hawkins-Byrd, Kennet Santana and to every teacher. This tome is dedicated (also) to every teacher in this world. I pray that public school teachers and principals will read the power of hope, direction and guidance off of these pages. I pray that Biz Stone and Marvin Stone will spread the word of K.K.K. I need Drew Stevyns, Levi Morton (philly officer), Jacob Martin, Zac Sunderland, Stuart Campbell (at the veggie stand) and Ricky Harlow to help us... If you know of a person in jail who wants to be their brother's keeper and write to help youth etc. Go to my websites and tell us about them. We may try to help spread their writings etc. I also suggest you contact Prison Legal News, Convict News and "The Beat Within". I intend to utilize everyday of my life to do, say, sing, write or pray something to use prison as a platform to teach kids what not to do...Jaycee, her two kids and their 18 years in captivity are but another "thorn in my flesh" to keep me writing, and writing, and writing...This (18 years) was not ("one back yard") supposed to happen; not in America! ...29 murdered and missing children? Not in America! Adam Walsh? Sasha Groene? Jeffrey Dahmer, Garrido, Manson etc. Cantu, Haleigh and Casey? Jaycee?Not in America. While we were sleeping an enemy (amongst us) has done this dastardly thing. An enemy has done this!... We gotta get this tome to F.B.I. Special Agent Chris Campion... The same car Phillip Garrido used to abduct (which was described to police 18 years ago) Jaycee in sat in that "one back yard" for 18 years. Nobody saw it because of H.I.V. (Having Insufficient Vision)!... I want employees at Papa John's in Chester VA,

Chesterfield County and near Cloverleaf Mall in Virginia to peruse "K.K.K." and drop me a line today....I'll probably need to cut way back on the amount of newsletters we publish near the end of this tome. But the letter to President Obama and the letter to Gen Y (after that) are urgent...I want to provide a way of escape for America's 3 million inmates also. You (inmates) can write, draw and pray! And your writing, drawing and praying can help shine a white hot light on predators long after the media has forgotten about Jaycee.

You gang bangers can write to progressive mayors (i.e. Kevin Johnson has a gang task force) like Gavin Newsome, Michael Bloomberg, Michael Nutter and Cory Booker and offer insight into preventing kids from joining gangs. We (inside these prisons) are the experts on gangs, predators, crimes, violence and on cons. You can use your expertise to help make America a more perfect (and safe) union! ...I hope Joshua Orapello, Jerry Wines and Charles Best all get this book. I want pastors to read it and to heed it. This tome is a powerful tool to teach kids why not to join gangs. It's not that I'm so bright and smart. One of the (quiet as it's kept) secrets which have made this tome so potent, useful and unique has been the brilliance of those I've been blessed enough to study. Warden James P. Walker would have never sat down and cooperated with me writing a book! Neither would Terry L. Rosario, Cheryl Pliler, Susan Hubbard, Fred, Steve, then CCII now A.W. Johnson-Dovey, CCII Sal Goldman, or Captain Patricia Kennedy... But the smartest thing I've done (in addition to positioning myself to study sadistic murderers, child predators and serial killers etc.) has been to study prison guards and prison managers...I recall a meeting with Captain Jimmy Walker, Captain Steve Vance, Dr. Hedblad and Chief Deputy Warden Terry L. Rosario in the 90's. I looked at Vance, Walker and Rosario and realized they represented over 87 years of managing and overseeing molesters, maniacs and murderers... For years I studied these guys like an S.A.T. test. I watched the way they walked, talked, acted and reacted. I learned volumes in the "art and skill of manipulation" from "Dad" aka Terry... And this book reflects the paradigm, styles, characteristics and traits which I've garnered from meticulous analysis of these managers. I.E. Jimbo is the most ubiquitous warden in California. And he has the uncanny ability of making everybody think they "know" him. Many inmates are allowed to call him "Jimmy" and they feel special. I call him "Jimbo" so I feel "special". And even though "we" think we "know" him so well... I recall noticing a wedding ring on his finger 6 mos ago, and I told Willie I didn't know Jimbo's ass was married." C.D.C. would be wise to try to talk Walker into hanging around another 2 or 3 years at least... I learned "monitoring", "modeling" and even "mirroring" people from Ambassador Young, Rev. Hosea Williams, N.L.P from Tony Robbins and my assignment now is to take what I've learned from watching the worst of the worst (Marion E. Spearman, James Yates, Trimble, M.C. Davis, etc.) as well as what I've observed from the best of the best (Terry L. Rosario, Cheryl Pliler, Jimbo, Virga, Kennedy, Fred, Steve and Jeff Macomber etc.) and reducing it to writing. Ipso facto, as I analyze even the idiosyncratic whims and nuances of those (of us) whom they've "kept" etc. These combination(s) of data make ("K.K.K.") one helluva read. One could call this tome the "unauthorized biography of Eric, Lyle, Bret, stokes, Bardo, Leroy Jenkins, Dwight York etc." As well as the "unauthorized biography of the managers of C.D.C."... These lessons should be taught to kids at Franklin High School in Stockton and at schools across the globe... We must keep G.B.G. diversified and authentic. We want Jai Breisch, Craig Scott (Littleton, Colorado), Christopher Eavy (or Eavey in Chesterfield VA), Josh Orapello, Michael Hawkins (VA) and all "young" and "inexperienced" soldiers in JROTC programs, "upward bound " and schools across the world! Bring me Nathan Hand in Richmond, John Caudell and Wayne Rawlings. We also need Wayne Dillard, Brian Boykins and you. Let's get this tome to Sean Hornbeck, Anthony Lonnick and to Shea Newberry. I want prisoners (who messed up "bad" like Willie Nessler etc.), Nathan Gould and Christopher Parker to have this tome. The more copies of this tome we get into classrooms, churches and prisons etc. the better! I was asked if "select" businesses could do P.S.A. ads for G.B.G. and K.K.K. The answer is to explain the phenomenol success of our G.B.G. and "why are so many teen boys in and out of custody joining G.B.G.?" Dr. Jarman explained to me that "Sherman not to burst your bubble (lol) but it's not really about you. When boys and young men hear "Gang Bangers for Good" initially the "good" is irrelevant. They want to belong to a "Gang". And by the time they realize that the founders are in the joint it takes them on a mystique and a magic for them." Dr. Jarman continued "There is something powerful, enticing and magnetic about "boy" time. We like to get together in the "boy" scouts. We like to get together and shoot basketball, play baseball or football. We'll wrestle each other or box each other. Even golf (Gentleman Only Ladies Forbidden) brings boys together... Promise keepers have enjoyed awesome success at bringing boys together. T.D. Jakes has enjoyed incredible success at bringing boys together in his "manpower" revivals... G.B.G is the prisoner/prisoner workers version of "Manpower". Just as T.D. Jakes feeds Manpower into the prisons via television. You're feeding G.B.G. into the streets via books and (hopefully) CD's and D.V.D.'s...And we are voyeurs by nature. That explains why girls and boys can't wait to see what you write about what's going on inside the Gated Community." Dr. Jarman concluded by stating "and even prison employees can't articulate what it feels like to go to sleep every night in a jail cell. That explains the success of numerous prisoner tomes by Rubin "Hurricane" Carter, Mandela, Mumia and even Manning...Your challenge is to elucidate and illuminate the prison with such dastardly detail; that having seen (read) the truth boys shall choose education over incarceration." That's just a taste of Dr. Jarman's mental repertoire. He's bad! Yes he is! I've learned so very from Dr. Jarmon, Dr. Jamie Davidson, Dr. C. Solis, Dr. Franklin, Curren and everyone else on my advisory board. And be advised that these psychologists and psychiatrists were hand-picked to serve on our board. I credit the Governator, Matt Cate, Scott Kernan, Jimbo Walker, Dr. Jaffe and Dr. Kelley for hiring these therapists in the first place. CSP-SAC has the most awesome group of "shrinks' in the state. They don't come any more brilliant than Dr. Jennifer Heitkamp, Dr. Gregg, Dr. A Duran and Dr. Handian...Embarking upon G.B.G. as well as 'K.K.K." I was in over my head. And it dawned upon me that therapists, parents and kids all over the world could be reading this tome. And "it better be good" a correctional counselor told me...

I interrupted the normal "flow" of this tome with a "status update" because this is not a normal or regular book and this is not a regular or normal time. This book (with a heck-uv-a name like K.K.K.") came to interrupt regular programming. I came to shake up some people, places and things. When kids are joining gangs at seven years old! It's time to step out of our comfort zones. When boys don't carry books and won't mind their teachers at school. But they'll carry a sword, chainsaw, explosives and guns to school. It tells me that these kids don't need another "regular" tome. Three points and a poem ain't gonna cut it. So I came to bust up in yo school, church, college or jail cell. I came with my thug bruthas (Jason, Joker, Silent, Doc, Billy and Willie etc.) and we came to tell you like it is. We are not soft core. We are hard! Just like pimping ain't easy, thugging ain't easy surviving in a maximum security penitentiary where folk who have murdered, molested, raped and decapitated etc. ain't easy...Doc, Silent, Joker, Hillbilly, Johnny Willie and Fleming Billy all told me to keep it real. Billy said "Sherman I've got 14 grand kids out there. I don't want a molester, murderer or a predator to destroy their lives and futures.. "K.K.K." has the potential to help them." He continued "if you combine everything you've seen, heard, felt, learned and experienced from the team, staff and from the clinicians-what a book." Former LAPD Homicide Cop Richard "Doc" Ford told me that "if you just write about the cellies you've had it'll be a freaking best seller! You've had some of the most interesting, dangerous, craziest and heinous cellies in the world... Some of them were only in the cell with you overnight, but still... And don't just write about the times you kicked ass. Do include stories like that guy who chased you around seven building with the mop (actually a broom)"... Doc continued "I guarantee you police officers and profilers will read "K.K.K.". They may never tell you they did. But they have to. If I were still a homicide detective or a sergeant and if I heard about a book "K.K.K." by a prisoner, I'd be all over it!"

Richard Butler spent more than 100 hours elucidating the "structure", chain of command and the inner workings of white prison gangs for G.B.G. and "K.K.K."... Rick was willing to share secrets about the internal occurrences of A.B., N.L.R. and Skinhead activity which aided me in seasoning the contents of this tome with data that could/would save white kids lives...

Johnny "Claw" Willie methodically and meticulously provided this writer with collegiate like courses on the black gang structures of North America. My years of close observation and sporadic participation in gangs and gangsta crimes had provided me with a (kind of) high school diploma on black gangs. My avid study of the 20 books written on gangs by the (gang genius) great Dr. Lewis Yablonsky had provided me with a (kind of) Masters degree (or T-6) in black gangsterdom. But hundreds of hours of lectures and monologues by, and dialogues with, Johnny Willie qualifies me for a doctorate degree in Black Crips, bloods, Black Gorilla Family, 415 etc. etc. And a myriad of Latino convicts would only speak to me if I agreed to use pseudonyms. One of them (a Mexican gang "general") indicated to me "Atlanta I know you expect to die from Valley Fever pretty soon." My heart began to pound as he peered into my eyes with a death stare." "And I'm not threatening you essay but you gots family in Atlanta. And point blank, if you use my name it will get me killed. And before I die somebody in your familia..." he paused. I stated "Mi amigo don't go there. You have my word on everything I love including God. Your name in my Libro will be Charlie". With that, "Charlie" shook my hand and told me things that rattled me. And I'm not "all that" but it's gotta be deep, dark and dastardly to rattle me. One day after a two hour conversation with Charlie Dr.C. Solis could see pain and terror written across the canvas of my face. I think that other than Mrs. Kennedy, Jimbo and perhaps Fred- C.Solis MD. knows me better than any staff. He walked up to me in my "office" (the ducat area) and said "Breathe...now you get a taste of how I felt when I had the head of a certain CPS as a patient. The stories can haunt you. I want you to take a walk around the track with me." And as Dr.Solis and I made our journey around that track. I flashed back to the walks Lt. Jimmy Guyton and I used to take to relieve stress and "chop it up". I recall Lt.Guyton telling me one day "Manning I don't know what in the hell you are doing in prison. I mean I know your charges but after 24 years in corrections I know when a man don't (sic) belong in jail. You're out of place Bro." And years ago I recall (the master manipulator aka "Dad") Terry L. Rosario telling me that"You are the most brilliant inmate I've ever encountered in 30 years! (He was embellishing which was trademark T.L.R.!)...If I were you I'd learn to shut up." I did the opposite and opened up my mouth with (LOL) "Who you tellin to shut up?" He replied "Sherman if you, with the ability to write and articulate that you have, were to be quiet you'd become a master of the universe of the prison...Try listening, looking and absorbing –you've got the gift of gab. If that could get you out why are you in my prison?" I was floored and Chief Deputy Warden Rosario told me something which helped propel me into (eventually) writing this- "K.K.K.".... Terry said "I'm glad I'm the Chief Deputy Warden and not the inmate; make no mistake about it...but since you are you and I'm me....having watched you over these years, knowing what I know...If you were to shut up, pull information out of staff, convicts, psyches etc. You could do the unthinkable.

"....While other inmates are manipulating staff to smuggle drugs in, cell phones and money. While inmates are playing my female staff to have sex in mop closets for a two minute thrill...If I were Sherman D. Manning I'd be conning, conniving, manipulating staff and inmates for information. You have the ability and the con. You can't con me or Jimmy (then captain-now Warden) or Steve. We are not sources. But there are vulnerable, gullible and even "naïve" staff at every prison... If you would put your ego on the shelf and shut the F (expletive deleted) up kid, you could write a book that would blow the public's mind... It would not have to be written nicely or neatly. If you just told what you see, what you hear and what you feel it would blow people's minds"...From that day forward I began to be quiet. I looked, I listened and I questioned. It drew me way out of my element. It (literally) revolutionized my life and resulted in me finally writing (this) the book of my life... "Sherman I'll never be your source". Fred told me a few months ago. "Prison management becomes guarded when you come around. We know you are sneaky, superstitious and stealthy...but with what you are doing with G.B.G./Heart, as a Christian and as a man I am proud of you. You are finally doing what you are supposed to do. And I am truly praying for you". So stated associate warden Fred Schroeder...

The Latino Gang General shared intimate details about Eme, Nuestra Familia, Bulldogs, southerners and others that rocked me to my core. I learned how little I really "knew" about Mexican gangs. There is a human sex trade inside prisons that the public has never even heard of. I knew about "boys", "punks", "queens" and "war" daddies. But the level of organized crime and the deeply entrenced, methodical and strategic planning involved with "selling ass" in Mexican prison gangs is mind boggling. I found out from Amigo "Charlie" (and I corroborated his data by speaking with several high level persons who had the "keys" to the yards etc.) that more than 60% of the Latino inmates, (under the age of 30) that I saw on the yards were "owned" as sex slaves by "shotcallers"...Charlie said "You know Tino (real name David Moreno), Casper (real name Voorhees), Paya (real name Trujillo) and Cricket (real name Tovar)?" I said "Yeah I know them all." He said "A. Each of them is hooked on heroin. B. Each of them is owned. C. Each one of them has a G-string in they (sic) locker"... I personally spoke with Tino and eventually he admitted to me "Atl. I'm a "bitch" I got turned out behind drugs...Every Mexican you see in prison can be had for the right price." Tino looked directly at me and said "You would suck a (deleted –d- word) for the right amount of money or drugs." I replied "You lost your mind." Tino says "If I had five thousand dollars in cash, gold, or dope how many dudes on this yard do you think would let me d--- them down dude?" I said "A whole lotta booty would become tooty fruity" and he laughed. I said "But Tino are you gay? Did you ever think about sex with men before you came to prison?" He said "Atl. don't use my f__ name (I did and I am....He ain't "Charlie")...I know you write books dude but nah. Before I came to prison I never thought about no man screwing me....I still hate getting f---. But when I'm high I kinda enjoy kissing and sucking"... after a two hour chat David Moreno (aka "Tino") reminded me to "Don't use my name Atlanta. I gots a lady on the streets dude" ...I made the (selfish) decision that utilizing the authentic names of "screw" boys who will get out and carry diseases to women etc. was more important than feigned allegiance I had/have to any "self" reported prison "boys." Ipso facto, (as you shall see) I also had to recall that as that great man Dr. Tye Hedblad prepared to risk his job-testifying for me in Sacramento Superior Court. He said to me one day "Sherman if you ever get the courage and the intellectual integrity to pen a tome which includes your frauds and shenanigans etc. You may not ever be at the top of Don King's Christmas list. And you'll probably never preach for Jasper but A. You'll write a bestseller and B. You will actually help young men all over this earth" ...Dr. Hedblad knew all of my secrets. All of them and it is safe to say that (at that time) I absolutely (i.e. see "From The Palace to the Prison", "Creating Monsters", "Blue Eyed Blonde", "Blue Eyed Blonde" Book II etc. etc.) had no intention of writing about my dealings with Zig Zigler, Don King, Leroy Jenkins etc.etc. And I would have bet you my life that I would not ever (under any circumstances write about my conviction) write about Ricardo Calvario. But even years after that conversation with my "saint" of an advisor, Dr. Hedblad, Dr.

C. Solis stated to me "Mr. Manning no matter how much you write; dancing around your conviction anesthetizes and dilutes your power as a writer. It's like Stevie Wonder suddenly getting his sight back but trying to play the keyboards in freezing weather with mittens on his hands!! No matter how good he could see; how would he sound playing his harmonica with gloves or mittens on? " Dr. Solis is "deep" … "We'd all applaud Stevie's new found vision but we'd rather hear a blind Stevie; and Wonder what it would be like for him see….than to hear him try to manipulate instruments wearing mittens….We are all glad that Mr. Manning is bright enough to found G.B.G. and we are glad you have the ability to see that prison can be a platform." Dr. Solis continued "And by law neither Dr. Heitkamp, Dr. Curren or I can ever discuss your case (conviction). But your refusal to address it puts gloves and mittens on the fingers of your writing…Just think about that…" And he walked away and my heart pounded and it pounded. And when you read my "Confessions of a Con Man" and the details of my conviction etc. You can thank (the late) Dr. Tye Hedblad, CDW (in some sense), Terry L. Rosario, Dr. Jarman and Dr. C. Solis for manipulating me to "take off the gloves!" … Without their masterful pushing, prodding and suggestions etc. I would have taken my "case", my crimes and my cons to the grave with me. I still recall giving Dr. Solis a hundred pages of (what I thought were) the best of this tome (which excluded my "case", my crimes and my cons) and he brought them back 3 days later and said. "Philosophically, psychologically and even penologically it's good writing. It is very interesting and kids will read it…But" and the but made me nervous…."It would not give me chills. It would not keep up at night. Let's face it: you are not as great a writer as John Grisham or James Patterson. You'll probably never be that good." (there went my ego!) "But " Dr. Solis continued "What would make me suggest to President Obama if I were on his staff; to read your writing etc. would be if you had the audacity, temerity, guts and the nuts to take off the mittens…" He then ran a psychological bulldozer over what vestiges of ego I had remaining. "Even your missive to the president is okay. A seven on a scale of one to ten. I did not speak to Dr. Solis for two weeks after that…and O.J. Simpson put on the gloves. And in this tome I finally took them off!!! And I wanna tell every young man reading my words today. It is t-i-m-e. Every young man (from Redmond O'Neal to Redmond Doe –from Cameron Douglas to Cameron Joe) it is time for you to take off the gloves! Take off your façade, mittens or your mask. We brothers have learned how to hide ourselves for as long as we can remember. We were taught not to cry. We were taught not to let girls see inside of us. We learned as toddlers that boys didn't do this and boys don't do that. And if you did you are a sissy, a punk or a chump. And we were given all of these varying definitions of what it meant to be a man. And we went through grade school with those gloves on our emotions. We went all the way through high school with that same pad lock on our spirit. Some of us graduated from college still locked up in the prisons of our masks and facades. We walked down the aisles and married her still wearing those gloves. And the masks, gloves and the mittens are killing us. The locks on our spirits are driving us to drink, to shoot, to drug, to kill and to crave. There is a spirit of anger (that I mentioned earlier) that has locked boys-to-men and males who wanna be fathers. And prisons are the colleges which produce masters and doctorate degrees in anger. Because somebody told Sherman, and Redmond, and Cameron and John Doe that men don't cry… And we have arrived at this particular point in our lives having mastered the art of camouflaging our emotions and when boys don't, can't or won't cry tears we cry bullets! …And we have almost 3 million boys who were supposed to be men. Locked up in angry juveniles, jails and prisons in America. And our anger (for not being able to live up to society's expectation….not being able to marry, have two kids, a house and a white pickett fence… Not being able to live our dreams!) has led us to meth, coke and smoke. Our anger has led us to con, rob, kill and to steal. And if I accomplish nothing else with G.B.G. or "K.K.K." I came to set a fire to that anger. Just as the real "K.K.K." utilized "Fire" to burn crosses. I want you (in that school, in that college, in that prison) to ask God to help you to "Burn Baby Burn". Burn down that anger, Burn off that pain. Burn out of that façade. Burn off those gloves. It is killing us. we can't be men. We can't be fathers. We are boys camouflaging as men. We have locked up our potential and buried our destiny. There is nothing worse than a locked up mind and an incarcerated spirit. And I get missive after missive from males in foster care, in schools and even in colleges who are trapped in the prisons of addictions, poverty, illiteracy and alcohol.... There are males in their teens and twenties who drive nice cars, have sexy ladies and some of them have kids. And tonight as they lay in bed next to their woman; they are more locked up at home than Charles Manson is in prison. They are more imprisoned in their apartment then an inmate at San Quentin...The spirit of restlessness, shame and sorrow has disguised itself as anger amongst men. If our anger were visible it would appear as a black, tar and an evil substance. The silent epidemic of anger keeps showing up in Columbine, showing up at Virginia Tech, showing up at Hillsdale High School and in massacres, murders, rapes and...When we actually look inside the mind of a Menendez, or a Manson or even a Henson we see anger....You can't empty a shotgun into your mother's face and head without being angry! You can't rape (what is rape? It is brute-blunt force! It is selfish! It is angry!) without anger! There is anger in robbery, anger in riots and anger in killing... When Los Angeles rioted after Rodney King it was anger beneath the pain. Anger spreads across the neighborhoods and even cities like the wildfires of Auburn CA. Anger is more contagious than swine flu. Anger is underneath shame, underneath embarrassment and behind guns, bullets, knives and blades. Alex Youshock was just an angry little boy who woke up and tried to defend his "honor" with a sword, a bullet, a knife, explosives and in this and that..... The two boys at Columbine were angry.... The "K.K.K." (Klu Klux Klan and "Kids Killing Kids") were angry when they rolled up on innocent families and set fires just because people were black...And these "riots" we see in prisons (in Chino and in Philadelphia, Illinois, Michigan etc.) are sparked by anger... It is time for you to confront your anger. You gotta get it off your chest and get it out of your system. Your anger has alienated, devastated and almost eliminated your existence. Almost three million of us are locked up in physical prisons because our anger was more important than our love (for women, love for family or even love for freedom) was. Why are you angry? And who are you so angry with that they are worth you changing how your story ends? ....Underneath the surface of every uprising we see in the schools, the streets or even in the prisons is anger...(As I mentioned). It is what Lisa Ling saw when she told Oprah that Eric Menendez had the most "piercing" or penetrating eyes she'd seen. Therein lies the anger. He's angry. Prisons are like disaster zones filled with the matter of men who are riddled with anger....A buddy of mine was getting his hair braided underneath the canteen area one day and there were 7 or 8 of us standing around him. All joking and having fun and out of the blue he jumped up yelling "I need my space! Ya'll crowding me out! I need my space man!" If there was a devil in the flesh he looked like him. I'd never seen him like this before. And later he told me "this is what decades of pain, death and anger will do to you." I realized how close he was to "snapping". And since you are reading right now this is "Captain's Mast" and in G.B.G. I'm the commanding officer. Baby Boy I'm calling you to attention. It is time for you to snap to. Even you bruthas in church have been faking the funk. You go to church with a mask on. You are angry with the preacher, and angry with your teacher. You go to bed angry and you wake up angry. You have covered up your emotions, your heart and your soul. You have layered defenses to keep people out. And in the process of hiding you've lost your soul...When boys can't (won't or don't) cry tears we cry blades, bombs and bullets. I have come into your house, your class, your cell and into your space to bring you to a point of release. You are not a mistake. You are not a waste. The reason you are reading this right now is because there is a divine plan for your life. If it was not meant to be you would not see the words you are seeing right now. The seeds of greatness, the seeds of potential, the seeds of destiny are within you right now. I'm up at 2:26 A.M. writing this. And you are reading this because there is a reason for your life. You are exactly where you are supposed to be. And when you learn what you are supposed to learn; you'll move on. You can't drink that anger out. You can't smoke that anger out. You can't eat it out. No matter how much sex you have it won't rid you of your anger. You must call upon forces that are bigger than you and greater than me to release that anger. Dreaming of your father and visualizing your mother won't rid you of that anger. If you will move that rock you'll see the worms. As soon as light hits those worms they start running. My assignment is to shine a light underneath the rocks of your anger. And beneath the anger and madness we will find the sorrow and the sadness. That scared, hurting and sad little boy is beneath the rock of anger. You are conflicted and you are perplexed because underneath the skin, the flesh and blood, the muscles and the bone etc. You are a spiritual being. And until you get your spirit right you'll be all wrong. There is a yearning, a hunger, a thirst inside your spirit man that seeks your daddy. And not the one who impregnated your mother but your daddy in heaven. And whatever we pour into the void won't fill it but spirit. "When my father (fleshly) and my mother forsake me, then the Lord will take care of me" (Psalms 27:10). If you continue reading Psalms 27 you'll see "I would have lost heart" if I had not "believed" that I would see (even though right now you have H.I.V.) the goodness of the Lord in the land of the Living." Your daddy is ready to take care of you because you can't even take care of yourself. There are 3 million of us in physical prisons and 30 million of you in (emotional, mental and spiritual) psychological prisons. Our mothers and our fathers (or our lovers, siblings or our hopes and dreams) have forsaken us and this has hurt, troubled and saddened us. And since we think men don't cry we've buried our pain underneath the rocks of anger. And we are almost about to lose heart. You are almost out of breath. You are almost about to faint. But your daddy sent me here (right where you are) to tell you to release that anger and look up. God has got your back and He'll take care of you. Let all of the pain, sorrow and the hurt go. Let it go! Let it go! Let it go!

And when you call out to your daddy He will answer! I promise! Do it! And after you get your business fixed with our daddy you can take off the gloves. Take a spiritual breath. And then wake up and live-It is such a relief to let it go! You may need to go back and re-read the last 3 pages again. These pages are soaked in spiritual medication but you gotta get it. We have gone to too many barbecues, baseball games and after partys to not get it. Some of us even went to church services but we were still all covered up. You can't dance it away baby boy. You can't even shout that anger out. Your daddy has to put his super on your natural. And you have to surrender and ask Him to "take care of me"...I am in Iowa calling Ben Alexander to come forth. G.B.G. is providing that meaningful, social interaction that Peter's son "Ben" sought on the internet. Come on Ben, Tadd Carr, Guy Heinz, Ryan and Nathaniel etc. It's time to lower our layered defenses and be men of substance and men of honor...I walked out on Zig Zigler because he (did not have H.I.V.-he could see) saw through my mask and my disguise. And he was about to see me. And the most important point I need to tell you is that the moment you cry out "ABBA" God will step in and you go into rehab. It is urgent and critical for you to know you might not be instantaneously and miraculously healed. It might take you a year of watching Dr. Phil, going to church, getting counseling, reading Kimbro, Zigler, Tony Robbins and Manning. But the moment you humble yourself enough to cry "ABBA" divine forces are dispatched and you go into a process of healing. I don't know how long your healing will take. But I do know a mighty good Doctor who has never lost a patient. And I do know there is room at the cross (in the course, in the class and in rehab) for you. Though millions have come there is still room for one. There's plenty good room for you to weep, to mend, to grow and to heal. I came to invite you to rehab with G.B.G. I came to bring some light into some mighty dark places. I came (with my homeboys) to pull you back so that the creator can propel you into your destiny... Brian Walker (Denver CO), Carlos Rodriguez (Santa Ana), Gabe Williams, Timothy Coleman (Sacto) and Brandon White etc. Can I talk to ya'll in private? The sailor (Christopher-from Manassas Virginia) on the PBS "Carrier" special, Cole on "the Secret Millionaire" and Matt Stuart at ABC. As G.B.G. Commander in Chief coming to you from my command post in the prison I have to tell you that you can't get "around" God. I've studied peak performance techniques. I've studied what makes the great great, and even greater. I believe in Neuro Linguistic Programming. I believe in the success system that never fails. I continue to load my mind with the writings of Victor Frankl, Napoleon Hill, Tony Robbins and Les Brown. But the missing element was my Daddy. I tried to do it on my own. But even when my pockets were over flowing with money. Even when I was being chauffeured around New York City in a limousine. I still had a hunger that food would not fill. I had a pain that liquor couldn't kill. I tried to do it with my strength and will. But "lean not to thine own understanding. But in all of thy ways acknowledge (ABBA) the Lord and He (ABBA) will direct thy paths." My brutha (from another mother) the spirit of your Daddy (ABBA) is in your DNA. And you can never be happy and at peace until you acknowledge Him. I promise you this is real talk. You can get excited without him. You can have fun without Him. You can kick the can down the road, carouse around and enjoy a level of success without Him. But the peace, joy and the rest that your soul seeks can only be found in Him.... Most males are even angry with God...When the Governor toured the prison at Chino, after the riots I saw anger. Broken glass, busted T.V.'s, broken windows. That was broken dreams, busted hopes, and broken lives. That was anger compounded by anger. When you get it off your chest. When you ask God to lead, direct, love, forgive and heal you. That is when you enter rehab and in the fellowship of brothers (i.e. we in G.B.G.) who are being transparent and are growing together. You must do the toughest thing for a boy or even a man to do. What is the toughest thing for us (the fellas) to do when we take the ladies shopping? What is the toughest thing for us to do when we are already dressed and she's still in the mirror? (Psalm 27:14) "Wait..." Ya'll feel me? When you enter into rehab for anger, drugs, alcohol, violence or whatever you must know that the God of verse 10 is gonna "take care of me" when my momma, daddy, my lady or my buddy forsake me. We must know that since I'm in rehab ABBA in verse II is gonna "teach me" His way and even "lead me". And the God of verse 12 is aware of jealousy, envy and haterism but He shall not "Deliver me to the will of my adversaries; for false witnesses have risen against me,"...and the bruthas who have come against me are so violent they don't just do evil, think evil or do violence. But they..."Breathe out violence." The mark of a truly angry man is one who can "breathe out violence" In these juveniles, in C.Y.A., in these jails and in prisons you can listen to men talk and we're so angry that even when we call ourselves being "cool" it sounds angry. If you are spriritually in tune you can literally "smell" it on our breath. We wake up in the morning angry with the world. We go to bed at night angry. We use anger as a shield and anger as a weapon. I'm so afraid that if I allow any intimacy (not "sex", they do that all the time but I'm speaking of in-to-me-you-see) you'll see how hurt, how sad, how afraid and how broken I am. So I'm so damned angry that I "breathe" out violence. My anger is so deeply entrenched inside me that I've internalized it. So much to the extent that I can't (in flesh) live (breathe) without it....It's deep my brothers and you know I'm right. You've got to bring it up and bring it out. And I keep getting stuck on this anger thing because it's killing boys and men. And I won't tell your mom, your school, your probation officer or your parole agent; but (quiet as it's kept) I've seen hundreds of you go to "Anger Management" and paint or wallpaper over your problem. But you're still not "there". You are still messed up. It's deeper than a class baby boy.

You should keep going to class. But you must also get down on your knees and talk to God…And when God delivers you you still get to "Wait on the Lord". Those 4 words almost drove me to the cemetery. My need for instant gratification and my drive to have it "now" almost killed me. But no matter who lays hands on you you can get anointed with oil from head to toe. You can speak in other "tongues" and get tingling in your spine. You can go to Harvard, Morehouse or Yale but you still got to "W-a-i-t on the Lord"… And you will get tired. You will get weak. I promise that you will get discouraged. But after you learn to wait you can "be of good courage, and He (not yo homies and not the sistas) shall strengthen your heart"; but don't forget the B clause of verse 14. It is but a friendly reminder and re-read (internalize) the last five pages twice and you will revolutionize your life!

There are so many hurting, crippled and paralyzed boys, males and men. And we have been attacked with a spirit of jealousy. This envy amongst men is tearing at the very fabric of our being. It happened in the beginning. Cain got angry, bitter and jealous and he murdered his brother Abel. Joseph's own brothers wanted to murder him because he had a dream… When Dr. Martin Luther King Jr. was alive black preachers, leaders and school teachers fought him. Those of us who came along after he was assassinated have a tendency to believe that they celebrated him while he was alive. They did not. Preachers from Alabama to Illinois worked against him. I've been blessed to walk and to talk with his closest friends (Andrew Young and Hosea Williams) and they explained to me that after he was assassinated everybody lauded him. But there is a spirit of jealousy running rampant amongst men in families, in ministry, in companies and in jail cells. Very few of us (men) will applaud another brother unless he's throwing, shooting or hitting some type of ball. I've even found psychiatrists and psychologists who are jealous of Dr. Phil because he's on TV and they're not. They don't know the Phil before the Dr. They don't know the trauma of his childhood. They don't know he was homeless and dirt poor.

But we don't feel empowered celebrating other men. We are jealous, envious, bitter and rotten to our core. And this envy, jealousy and hate is robbing us of our joy and destroying our destiny. I can't reach my peak, hit my stride or climb this mountain. Because I am more committed to keeping my foot upon your neck and holding you down. Than I am to climbing and gaining ground. But the only way I can keep another man down is if I stay down with him. So we have prisons, colleges, schools and cities filled with angry boys, trying to be men. And we're all at the bottom of the mountain. Because we refuse to applaud, support, praise and lift each other up. When we started G.B.G. I saw a spirit of jealousy unlike anything I'd ever seen. Folk you thought would support, encourage and endorse you will turn on you like a snake when you try to raise something up. They will sabotage you, hate on you and even defecate on you because of a jealous spirit.

I didn't even plan to write this book the way it is written. I wish I could tell you that a controversial title like "K.K.K." was pre-planned by Judy Smith and Impact Strategies etc. it was not! And even though this disjointed, disruptive and powerful book is reaching boys and men whom it seemed couldn't be reached. I can't (won't and don't) take the credit. You can't really plan power or manufacture authenticity. But people like Bishop T.D. Jakes and (my homeboy) Bishop Eddie Long etc. Even Bishop Noel Jones has been teaching, preaching and prophesying about how God will do the almighty through the least likely. And this book is "that" that the prophets have spoken about. And my momma (Dollie Mae Manning) has been praying for me. And she knew that I couldn't even die until the prophecy spoken over me was fulfilled. This (tome) is "that" that they prayed into fruition. And I had to leave and to abandon everything that was familiar to me to write this book. I had to move the slab of that solid rock of anger to write this. I had to watch the worms of bitterness. Pride and ego run out of my way. I had to open my mouth and let Him speak to me and through me. The first miracle (and I do mean a literal miracle!) is not how good, how deep or how powerful this book may be. The first miracle is that I wrote it. I promise you (in the name of Jesus Christ) I planned to never, ever ten thousand times never write this book. I'm comfortable writing about them, they and theirs. But this man you see in me letting you see into me was not supposed to be. But the spirit of the Lord is upon me and he hath anointed me to write what I am writing. This was not a part of my tome draft. I didn't plan the personal confessions, the stuff on anger and on jealousy were not a part of my plan. But God looked down and saw the trauma of DJ AM. He sees Redmond O'Neal, Cameron Douglas and Gary Busey. And He knows how and when to orchestrate the steps of a Michael Vick and hook him up to a Tony Dungy. And He will bring Cameron Johnson, Leonard Padilla, Tony Dungy, Joel Rowe, Tyler Gentry and all of us together when He's ready. And I am just the trumphet. He chose to blow this music through. I am just as flawed and conflicted as Redmond and Cameron. But in the throes of the conflict Daddy reminded me of who I am. He let me know that I am bought with a price and paid for. He reminded me of my assignment and showed me how to do it. And the reason Tyler at Purdue, Scott Henuset, Tadd Carr and petty officer First Class Joel Tatum are reading this is divine. There are boys and men who never even knew my name and you've got this book and you can't get away. This is not even the type of book you normally read. But a Matt Damon, Deion Sanders, Magic Johnson, Derek Jones, Chad Michael Morrissette (W. Hollywood, CA) and Chris Austad are lead to this tome. Lawyers like Keith Wattley, Johnny Griffin, Don Samuels, Clyde Blackmon and Donald Heller are hearing about this writing. And I am not writing for me this whole thing is so much bigger than myself. I'm not taking up an offering or begging Dungy, Cosby, Vick, Hilton or Professor William Julius Wilson for a donation. I am not selling a blessing plan. All I want to do is Pull you Back (Jake Heartsong, Jordan Simon, Joe Kennedy and Matt) and help propel you into your destiny. I came for bloods, crips, MS13's and for Jason Gomes. G.B.G is for Michael Parker (Walnut CA), Maxwell Hanger, Run Huffman, Chris Krinkie and Kyle Larsen. We came to bring together a band of brothers. We are all in rehab and we prop each other up. I came for John Fink, Collin Finnerty and John Burris. I want Joshua Orapello, Greg Pugh (Richmond VA), Nathan Hand, Luke Johnson (Richmond VA), Willie Nessler and John Caudell to come join the brothers. I came for Shea Newberry, Michael Hawkins and Shawn Hornbeck. We have a seat at the G.B.G table for you. And we have work to do. We are called to service and in various stages of rehab. We don't wait til we're well to serve others. But as we crawl we pull others with us. When we can walk we pull our brothers who crawl. When we get strong enough to run we pull the walkers with us. We want you too! We want Brett Miles, Jarrod Konipinsky, Hayes Johnson (Texas), Zac Sunderland, Ryan Hausley, James Dauphin, Daniel Walsh, Timothy Combs, Paul Butler (Harvard), Kaether Cordero, Neal Carlson and Ricky Harlow. We are transforming from boys to men. We are being healed of our H.I.V. (Having Insufficient Vision). And we are spreading the word about light, vision and sight all across this world. We are HEART (Helping Educate At Risk Teens) at Davis High School, Folsom in Colfax, in Pittsburgh, Antioch and in Auburn. There is no stopping what can't be stopped. We intend to spread the "vision" and light or sight of G.B.G. from school to school (church to church, jail to jail and prison to prison) around the world. Stop!...take notice of where you are. Confront and challenge the man (or boy) in your mirror. Am I angry? If so, with who? And why am I angry? And what can I do (today) to begin to release my anger? Who are some of the people (i.e. teacher, pastor, counselor, coach, psychologist?) I can talk to today about my anger? "I am committing myself to releasing this anger out of me. I will pray it out! I will talk it! I will cry, read, meditate and visualize it out! I will be free from it! I must get free!" This is a crucial place. This is your moment. I don't want to see you suffer anymore. It is time for you to come out of it. This potent tome is teen intervention. This is to the MTV generation. This is for the Facebook and the Myspace generation. This is for the teens and tweenies. Wake up the sleeping giant within you. You can make it. You can take it. There is a reason you are still here. There is life after this and life after that. Life after dope and life after crack. You can still do well. It is not over. You are not done. You still matter. You have worth. You are a child of God! I got faith for you til you get enough for yourself. I got belief in you. I won't let you quit. I won't let you give up. I came through all of this hurt, sorrow, anger and pain just to write you this. You've got to come through. You've got to get up. You've got to see. You can do it. You'll come through it. We'll (G.B.G. you and me) do it together. Yes we can! Yes we can!

Redmond O'Neal, Cameron, Tadd Carr, Radovan Mahocek (you and you too)... say this: "I still have a future, God's not through with me. I still have a tomorrow, just you wait and see"...Repeat that ten times....we must get that anger out of you. And we must eliminate all jealousy. It is a curse that will destroy us. Out of all of my messes, flaws and conflicts. Jealousy was not one of my curses. Early on (that's why mentors, role models and teaching is so important) I had powerful men to build self esteem and confidence in me. Rev. Moses Lee Raglan assured me that "A lot of older pastors will be jealous of your oratory and your gift. But stay humble and don't worry about haters." And my daddy James Scott Manning was (still is) big, and he was bad and tough. And he was a man. He lived like a man and let us watch him. I never saw jealousy or a spirit of intimidation in him. My daddy didn't cut other men down or try to rain on their parade. He showed me how to be a man. And I was blessed by Andy Young and Hosea Williams. They were not petty, cracker jack or jealous men. If you could preach, speak, teach or sing they'd give you your propers. Andy routinely bragged on what a great preacher Jasper was. Hosea routinely told me I could "preach rings around most youngsters." And my seeing and hearing these great men applaud other men rubbed off on me and taught me to applaud other men. I.E. that big old, b;ack, bald headed joker in Dallas; T.D. Jakes can preach!

...Noel Jones can preach and my homeboy with the 50 inch biceps, Eddie Long can preach! And God has used Jakes, Jones and Long to minister to a bitter, broken, angry, modern day Jonah at NewFolsom State Prison. TBN is so important, such a blessing and such a light. Even my white, Republican associate warden (Fred Schroeder) says "that T.D. Jakes can preach"... And I want you boys, kids and men to begin to develop self esteem. I want you to practice praising, applauding and complimenting other men. You must study, read, pray and develop a certainty of self that enables you to bless other men. There are some creative and innovative forces down inside of you that will only come forth when they are called by another man. It takes a greater man to make another man great! (re-read that)....Bishop Long was going through some storms in his life and he was riding with Bishop Jakes. And Long told Jakes "I feel like quitting I feel like a failure." And Jakes slammed the brakes on his car and pulled to the side of the road. And Jakes told Long "don't you ever call yourself a failure." And Jakes began to speak some things which God has done through Long that Long had forgotten about. And it encouraged my homeboy with the 50 inch biceps! Because when you got 50 inch biceps, drive a Bentley and you pastor 20,000 people it can get lonely. And powerful men need power. And pastoring can be lonely and it drains you. But nobody could have spoken renewal, revitalization, rejuvenation and new birth into Bishop Long's spirit except another man. And there are so many of us who just need a word of encouragement, of blessing and acknowledgement from another brother.

My uncle Melvin Jackson was/is the best wall paper hanger in Atlanta. A brilliant interior decorator. And he used to take me with him in to Bert Lance, Mike Thevis and William Orkin's (a.k.a owner of Orkin exterminating) home. And uncle Melvin used to speak esteem, encouragement and power into my mind. And I am a better man because James Scott Manning,

Rev. Moses Lee Raglin, Command Sergeant Major James A. Smith and so many men spoke blessings into my mind... I remember one of the top auto-salesmen in Atlanta; Carl "Four Barrel" Williams. He was pulled out of car sales by M&M products company (owned by Cornell McBride. I.E. Stay soft fro) and I remember Carl introduced me to the Great Bernard Bronner (BB Cosmopolitan Curl...owner also "upscale" magazine)... and Carl and Mr. Bronner spoke confidence and blessings into my mind. They would not allow me to be jealous or intimidated by anyone. And there are so many boys and youngsters (Tadd Carr, Michael Parker, Nathaniel, Keith and Christian) who are destined for greatness. But could end up destroyed if some "other brother" does not blow a blessing in their ears. I came from my office (in the same place Paul wrote much of the New Testaments) in the prison to say to the Mullinnex brothers, Christian Nelson, (the son of "Nellie"), Cameron Douglas, Cameron Johnson, Douglas Stave, Daniel Clay, Daniel Radcliffe, Luke Sears, Luke Johnson, Michael Vick and you (too) that greatness lies within you. You were divinely created and wonderfully built by God! You are somebody! Wherever you (in jail, school, Harvard or Yale) are- you are somebody. And it may stun you that in a tome to teens and tweenies I'll applaud some O-G's. I will. To Dr. Bill, Cosby, Tony Dungy, Dr. Poussaint, Dr. Phil, Zig Zigler...thank you. In mysterious ways God has planted you guys on the trail of my life to help bring me to this critical moment...Thank you Mr. Cosby for calling me out and reminding me of my responsibility. Thank you Mr. Dungy for reminding me that God could still use me to mentor. Thank you Dr. Poussaint for helping inspire the "E" part of HEART (Helping Educate At Risk Teens). That you for helping me be authentic and real Dr. Phil. Thank you Mr. Zig for cancelling my gig. It helped me. I thank Senate President Pro Tem John Burton for supporting me from the beginning...

I wanna say thank you to these men. Some of whom didn't even know they were reaching, teaching and mentoring a dude in Hades. And I learned a term from Wendy Williams called "Friend in my Head." And some of the aforementioned have been "friends" in my head. And I wanna take this moment to tell all 3 million of you in prisons. I wanna tell all 750,000 of you who will get out next year. To the 65,000 (plus) of you getting released next month. I want you to know that Dr.Cosby, Dr. Phil, Tony Dungy or even Tony Robbins can be a "friend", a coach or a mentor in your head. You can use the creative power of visualization to use Cosby, Phil or Dungy to help you deal with your anger, jealousy and self esteem. Great men have great vision. You must develop your spiritual vision. You need sight, insight and foresight. G.B.G welcomes you and yours. We want your input, outlook and your testimony. There are some of you feeling this book like you've never felt before, do tell! Do tell! Tell Luke Johnson (on Jeff Davis) in Richmond VA, (tell John Burris, Leo Terrell or Johnny Griffin my estate might need them.) I want you to join G.B.G. so we won't see history, we will be history. G.B.G. is unheard of and you need to get in where you fit in.

"K.K.K." is a "secular" spirit filled tome. It is interactive and unique. I have prayed (over and over) over this book and these words. There is medicine in these words...I want ten readers to go to zabasearch.com and get a home address for Marion E. Spearman. When you find Spearman's address post it on my website. And I want people to begin to protest in his front yard (non-violently) ... Back to Garrido. He didn't wake up one morning at twelve years of age and become a sexual deviant. A cursory examination of Garrido's criminal record shows the following. He began hearing voices early on. He had a motorcycle accident which his dad claims made him "nutty as a fruitcake." He began abusing LSD early on. If we had intervened before he raped Katherine Callaway there would have been no Jaycee. At his trial when he had raped Katherine his attorney told the judge he was a nut and needed to be "committed". But the prosecutor objected and hired a psychiatrist to declare that Garrido did not need to be institutionalized. This man had admitted to parking by elementary schools and masturbating while viewing little girls. He started a church in a bathroom and invented a box into which God talked. What did he need to do to convince the D.A., the courts and police that he should not be free?...

Our lawmakers are absolutely lost! And because of a misdiagnosis a "new law" that was supposed to be about violent repeat offenders. We ends up incarcerating a million petty thieves. To the tune of $billions! At the expense of our kids education....

...There is a pain, a void, an aching and a plague of low self esteem afflicting boys in this country. And I submit that we don't need a new law. What we need is to restore "vision" in our babies and in our boys. This will require $ billions of dollars being invested, in today's youth on education. And we can't seek instant gratification. It is going to take time to dig us out of the mud. But we can do it. And I want to go deeper than lawmakers and talk to preachers. Bishop Noel Jones said years ago that he wished older preachers and pastors would have leveled with him. There were some preacheristic pit falls he would have danced around. If preachers had taken the time to be candid. I wanted to run to Bishop Jones and shout "amen". There were so many pressures, problems and pitfalls that I faced as a teen minister etc. that none of the O-Gees ever talked to me about. And that is why "fathering" (on another level) is so crucial. There are boys reading this book right now who have never had a man (or a father) to talk to them (you) like this. And when a boy's father has dropped out of the home and dropped-in to prisons etc. We need other "men" (in the village) to step up and step in. We have to mentor boys if they're ever going to be men. And we must stress the essentials of self worth, self esteem, education and motivation to these boys. We can do it....

I had a meeting with Dr.C.Solis and Dr.A. Duran and they told me that Bill Cosby went to Detroit last month. He went on a door-to-door campaign for education. I asked Madam Duran were there any civil rights leaders with him? She said no. I wondered where was Rev. so and so! Where was Bishop Flip Flop and Deacon Willie Wonder? The Detroit School System is $259 million in debt. Less than 31% of high school freshman in Detroit will promote to 10th grade. Detroit Schools are like war zones. They look like California prisons. Kids like 15 year old Ebony Patterson are afraid of being shot at school. This is disturbing. This is haunting and I want Madame Tyra Banks, Bev Smith and Steve Harvey to talk about it. We must train the hot white light of the media upon the Detroit schools system until a change comes. I want preachers to preach about it ("Education is free-get it") and singers to sing about it. We need policy makers with "vision" to (finally) make the connection between a great gradual education preventing an eventual incarceration. I am not asking Republicans to not be republicans. They can still shout about "tough on crime." I'm okay with that. But behind the scenes we need lawmakers with (sight, insight and foresight) "vision" to sit down and lead a massive effort to overhaul U.S. education. That (I'll admit) is wishful thinking but what you can do (right where you are) is begin to get an education. You don't need to wait on a new law or some money. Rob your library! Go read everything you get your hands on. I promise that when you begin (I repeat) to read "Come on People", "See you at the Top", "Succeeding Against the Odds", books by Tony Robbins, Tony Dungy and Les Brown etc. You will be healed from HIV. You will rise up and experience a metamorphisis. You have the power to tap creative, amazing and innovative forces and to transmogrify your life. You can't read "What makes the Great Great" by Dennis Kimbro and not be transformed. Don't take my word for it. Go to the library or a book store and read any book by Kimbro, Robbins, Zigler or Dungy and watch what happens inside you when you read it. I'll say like T.D. Jakes to "get, get, get, get ready! Get Ready!"... You will be astounded, amazed, mesmerized, befuddled and bemused by what will happen in, to and through you when you read this stuff... I recall being in Richmond Virginia with Peter Andrist. I began to imitate Rev. Hosea Williams, Andy Young, Jesse, Dr.Martin Luther King Jr. and Tony Robbins. Peter (literally) turned red and got goose bumps. "You should travel all over America and emulate Dr. King at schools" he told me. He continued "It is so fascinating it is surreal." Then Peter blew my mind with "I could take you to a University in Switzerland where nobody spoke English. And they would get excited to hear you do the "Mountaintop" speech… I took Peter up on his challenge (almost literally) on one of my trips to Switzerland. I surprised everybody when I asked to go to a convalescent home. (Don't applaud me. That was the "Israel" in me. It was the boy Dollie Manning raised me to be…. My wife has photos taken of me that day at the nursing home (in this book)… Peter's mom (great woman) Magrit volunteered at a nursing home. She took me with her and I spent 6 hours going from room to room visiting with the elderly. At that time I did not speak swiss-german. And in a rec room (7 old ladies and 4 men) Peter told me to "Do Dr. King." And I broke out with "well I don't know what will happen now. We've got some difficult days ahead. But it really doesn't matter with me now… I've been to the mountain top"….by the time "mountain" rolled off my lips every person in the room was applauding…. And they could not understand a word I was speaking! …. Peter was right! Excitement, Enthusiasm and positivity are contagious….When I was 7 years old I went to the cemetery (near our house) and a white family was burying their loved one. They had a small podium and I asked if I could have it. They looked surprised and a white lady said "What will you do with it son?" I told her I was going to put it in my back yard and "preach" behind it. She gave it to me. And I can recall a number of occasions I'd be in the back yard preaching and neighborhood dogs and cats would freeze and look transfixed as I preached. Excitement (I repeat) enthusiasm and positivity are contagious. Ipso facto, if you read Zig Zigler, Tony Robbins, Les Brown, Dungy, Cosby and Poussaint you will get excited. And you will transform…I want every young man (white guys also, just do it!) to get a lil book called "Visions for Black Men" by Dr. Naim Akbar! …And (no I have no deal for kickbacks! LOL….I don't even know these guys!) call -1-800-bishop2 and get a CD from Manpower titled "A Prince in Egypt" by T.D. Jakes. Then call "New Birth Missionary Baptist Church in Lithonia GA. You need to get a CD by Eddie Long called "Passion for Life." If you get these two CD's you can "Get, Get, Get, Get Ready!" I'm not gonna beg you to get them. But I do want you to finally confront your anger. Get rid of your jealousy. Challenge the inferiority complexes that run rampant amongst boys. I want you to rise up out of the ashes of mediocrity, illiteracy and addictions. And I challenge you to take a bet on yourself, your future and your destiny. I want you to release that anger and that jealousy. I want you to take a bet on the boy, (girl, lady) or the man in your mirror. You're not just reading this by accident. You are where you are for a reason. You have this book in your hands for a reason. It would be fantastic if you join G.B.G. all that's well and good. And I hope you do. But-even if I never meet, hear from or see yo narrow ass. It's all good. Damn Sherman D. Manning.

All I really, really want you to do is to get yourself together. I'm done with the lofty and profound dissections for now. I'm not writing this tome for an award or a commendation. I don't need to meet you. You can't cure my valley fever. And you can't get me out of jail. But the one thing you (y-o-u) can do is be wise, intelligent, pragmatic or smart enough to know that "this dude Sherman is in hell! A living hell! He's done time with the worst of the worse. (Eric & Lyle, Bardo, Henson, Stokes, Bret etc.) And if Sherman ain't good for nothing else. He can school my young ass on how not to go to (jail) hell! If my white (brown or black) ass don't do nothing else! I'm "A" read and heed "K.K.K" ….you feel me? R-E-A-D this damn (ya'll excuse my French) book! Do it now! This book is a debt I owe! Do ya'll hear me? I owe the ones who loved, taught, led, influenced and invested so much into me. I had absolutely no excuse for ending up where I am. (Although you'll read about the big secret- the wrongful conviction etc…but-why was I out roaming the streets at 2:40 am? And if I had not been so selfish, greedy and arrogant etc. I could have handed Calvario a fifty dollar bill and I would be in Atlanta today!!! I would be at home!) Rev. Hosea Williams (you all should read his fascinating story told by Andy Young in the book "An Easy Burden") gave me so mush! He gave me his knowledge, his time and his experience. I got closer to him than his own kids. I knew him. The same man you see on the photograph, on that infamous balcony (at Lorraine Motel-in Memphis) with Andy, Jesse, Ralph Albernathy and Dr. King... The closest two men to Dr.Martin Luther King Jr. (Hosea and Andy) and the last two men with Dr. King on this earth wore Andy and Hosea. And they gave me their home telephone numbers. Their time and their knowledge look: Andrew Young was the first black congressman in the U.S. He was United Nations Ambassador. And I called him (at home) just like he was a schoolyard pal. And after all the time, wisdom, books, money and credibility Andrew Young and Hosea Williams invested in me. I had the temerity to reward them by getting locked up in Hades!!! ...I owe the contents of this potent tome to the memory of that civil rights legend ("Unbought and Unbossed") Rev. Hosea Williams! And I likewise owe this tome to the legacy of Ambassador Andrew Young! And (in some sense) to Congressman John Lewis...And if you (Uncle Andy) are reading this book right now.... Here's ("K.K.K.") to you! To Hosea! And to John Lewis! For all of your time, help, credibility and energy. It was not in vain. It has been a long (via cons, schemes, plots, frauds, Valley Fever and...) time coming. But finally (with this book to youngsters) a change has come to (from, by and through) Sherman D. Manning...I apologize for my mistakes, my errors and for my sins. And this book is my letter to all of my younger brothers (black, brown and white alike)...I told the story of Peter and the Dr.King speech not to make myself (look or sound) good! You will probably never hear me speak. I told it just to explain why you are excited right now! you can't hear a Martin Luther King Jr. speech and not be moved. He was so powerful, so anointed and so "chosen" that even the emulation of him, by me is enough to excite folks who don't speak English! When President John F. Kennedy first saw (and heard) Dr. King speaking on television. It is said that President Kennedy stated "Damn he's good." ... (He might destroy the video after this book but perhaps someone can surreptitiously request it before. He's informed that I snitched him out...Norville?) Somebody ought to get the video from my speeches at Leroy Jenkins' Church. It was an all-white audience that cheered furiously as I spoke in my "Dr. King" mode....I hope Heather or somebody will put it on youtube...I'm sending this (missive/tome from my Heart from Hades) writing to all of those students in Detroit, at Locke, Purdue University, McClatchy High, Heritage High School and to teens everywhere. This writing is for Kris Stump, PJ Lukac, Brian Walker (Denver), Craig Scott, Jai and to all the youth. I want you all to get delivered. I want you to get down to the business of living. You must rise to the toughest challenge of your life. You can do better. You can put the crack pipe, meth, heroin, prescription drugs or the bottle down. Your destiny will not be hindered by your history. Your tomorrow shall not be assassinated by your yesterdays. Your future shall not be damaged by your past. Everything you went through has brought you to now. And no matter what (abuse, pain, violence, discrimination or limitation) life has hit you with, you are still here. And I know Somebody who believes in you. A thug by the name of Sherman D. Manning believes in you. Yes I do! And I know a couple of others (Dr. Curren, Dr. Solis, Dr. Heitkamp, Dr. Duran etc. to name a few) who believe in you. I promise y-o-u that Bill Cosby, Tony Dungy, Dr. Alvin Poussaint, Zig Zigler, Les Brown, Tony Robbins, Fred Schroeder, Steve Vance, Patricia Kennedy, Warden Jimbo Walker, Scott Kernan and even Matt Cate believe in you.... In a strange (historical and a "crazy" kind of way) we are (police, prison guard, politician and prisoner) a diverse group (Senator Burton, Mr. Padilla, Mrs. Romero etc.) of people who have confidence in you. We'll meet you every Saturday at noon in prayer. And we will look for you in schools, and in the bookstores, libraries, churches and in companies. You will transform and you will come forth. You will rise above every obstacle, hurdle and set back. I speak as (the chief thug, chief sinner) commander in Chief of G.B.G./Heart! I speak from the Heart (Helping Educate at

Risk Teens) we (G.B.G.) see, predict, pray for and prophecy great things for you, to do, be, give and live; in your future. My team (Doc, Jason, Silent, Joker, Billy and Willie etc.) and I are excited for you. We are cheering you on and applauding you. We have our G.B.G. caps turned backwards. Adam Lane, Dustin, Daniel Bugriyev, Fred, Kennedy and Steve believe there is nothing you can't achieve. You (Danny Noriega, PJ Lukac, Ben Alexander, Brian Walker, Arcadian Broad, Shawn Hornbeck, Greg Deekins, Ryan Nelson, Lance Mosely, C.J. Sheron and David Hellyer etc.) can do it. As you read the rest (meat) of this book you can go and you can grow. Willie Gary, Bill Cosby and Cupcake Brown (no pun intended. But "only in America" could somebody named "Cupcake" succeed!) did it. You can do it too! According to Andrew Young, the fact that you are reading this means you are destined to succeed. I'm not writing this by myself. A team (the "A" psyche team of G.B.G.) of brilliant therapists (led by the Harvard psychiatrist Franklin Curren MD), correctional experts (led by Warden Jimbo Walker), convicts and others contributed their hearts, souls, minds, knowledge and their expertise to this powerful writing. I did not do this by myself. First and foremost was God through Christ. To, for and about God I say (like Marvin Sapp) "I never would have made it....I never could have made it without you. I would have lost my mind I would have lost it all without you." Thank you Jesus. To Dollie Mae Manning, James Scott Manning, Brenda Smith, Rev. Hosea, Mayor Andy and all of those who cheered me on. So many of you all believed in me when I couldn't even believe in myself. You pushed, prodded and moved me forward. You ushered me into my destiny. And God's delays are not God's denials. The fact that I sat down and (with the help of my teammates and advisors etc.) wrote this book is a powerful testimony of God's power and mentoring. Had Andy, Hosea, Rev. Raglin, Uncle Melvin and James not invested their time, encouragement, wisdom and knowledge into me I would never have written this book. And because they kept on praying for and believing in me. Because Zig Zigler didn't kick me out of his car (even though I messed up). I can't kick you out of the G.B.G. car. Even though some of you messed up and you've been in trouble. I know that you are just like a tea bag. You're not worth a whole lot unless you've been through a lot of hot water... You are somebody! And my team and I are committed to this major campaign to restore vision. The HIV (Having Insufficient Vision) virus cannot stand in the face of education. We pull you back and release you into your destiny. By the time you finish this book there's gonna be a change in you. When you finish reading this book you're gonna feel differently, walk, talk and see differently. I'm so excited for you I can't hardly see straight. I feel a change coming. I feel change in the schools. Change in the colleges. Change in the prisons and change in the air. There is a spirit of change being unleashed into your atmosphere. You (Joey Grissett, Ronald Wright, John Jody Bear, John Sexton, Scott Johnson, Daniel Clay, Cody Sheldon, Josiah and Christian etc.) are changing before your very eyes. You can because you think you can. If you can see it you'll be it. What is growing in your mind will grow in time. You'll read your way out. You'll think your way out. You'll speak your way out. You'll study your way out. You'll pray your way out. There is nothing that you can't do if you believe you can. You didn't choose or find this book-it chose and found you. I didn't even plan this book. The book planned me. The prayers of the righteous availeth much. Those prayers Dollie, Clara Jackson, Brenda, Rev. Raglin, Rev. Williams, Rev.Young, Deacon Stanfield, Pastor Jean Barber and Rev. John McClure prayed over my destiny, ushered me into G.B.G. This is bigger than me. I command you to see I curse the HIV and you must see. You'll see a way out of no way. You'll see a bridge over troubled water. You'll see how to rise above it.... I see a change coming for you (Redmond, Cameron, John, Nate and you too) today. You shall come forth. You must come forth. You will succeed. I do believe there is a reason that you are reading this right now. There are more than 6 billion other people on the planet; doing other things right now. Why are you reading? I'm crazy enough to believe that some mother's prayers have prayed you to this book. And when you finish this book "A change is gonna come." This is the magic moment for your life. You can wake up the giant, the power and the strength inside of you. You can break loose from the shackles which have held you captive. You can break the psychological chains that are holding you back... Perhaps you assumed I was done with "anger". Well ass-u-me! Don't assume.....since I reside in Hades. Since I live in the place that a wicked man like Phil Garrido will be coming to. Since I live in the place that manufactures rage etc. I'm not done with anger. Schools don't teach about it. Preachers don't preach about it. Speakers don't speak about it. And yet our babies, males, boys and men are suffering from an anger tsunami. We are filled to the rim with rage and running over. Anger is the fuel that feeds our fights, mayhem, murders, riots, arguments and abuse. It takes anger for a Chris Brown to assault, beat and abuse a woman. When I look at a woman, I see beautiful queens of the universe and mothers of the earth. I see Tyra Banks, Shateecia Smith, Madam Oprah and Queen Gayle King. How could any man raise a hand and slap Tyra? Rape Oprah? Kill Gayle? He has to be angry. Certainly there are a myriad of dysfunctions, demons and disorders that lead to rape. And even underneath (or inside) anger there is fear and hurt. But no psychologist will argue that anger is not in it. It may not begin or end it. But show me a violent act and anger is in it... If I do nothing else with the time I have left on the planet. If I never see Uncle Andy again. If I never shake the hand of Zig Zigler or Tony Robbins etc. I owe it to Andy, to Zig, to Hosea, to Yvette, to Teeka, to Yak, to Dollie and to every woman ("I'm every woman") to dissect the subculture of the boys that live with me in Hades. I must tell the truth.... Now is that time for an authentic, probitistic, realistic and comprehensive character sketch of 3 million males in jails. My testimony may kill me and it may reveal to be that "one" who broke the code.   But even associate Warden Fred Schroeder admitted that "I can't corroborate any negative things you may write about staff. I wish you would not write about staff... But I agree that Hollywood romanticizes prisons in ways. That appeals to kids. ...Sherman it's time for the truth to be told about prisons. Having seen (read) the truth our boys will choose education over incarceration"... A 19 year old inmate told me "Atlanta I know you write books and stuff. If I tell you a secret will you promise on your faith not to put my name in your book?" He conned me and it worked. That word "faith" secured his anonymity. "My celly raped me" this guy said to me. "I'm afraid, confused, embarrassed and I don't know what to do." I told him how sorry and troubled I was to hear that. "He got me high and stuck his tongue down my throat." He indicated "If I kill him in his sleep I'll never go home. I parole in 9 months. If I tell I'm a "snitch" and a "fag". What do I do Atl.?" We talked for two hours I will not reveal his name. Nor will I reveal all of the advice I gave him. I will say that I gave him Linda McFarlane's address to which he could write "confidentially". And I will reiterate that males are raped in every jail, every juvenile, every prison, in every state in America. The crimes are about anger, control, power, and rage. They are rarely reported, routinely ignored and rarely prosecuted...Ladies are also raped in jails and prisons every second, of every minute of every day. And these victims of abuse, violence and rapes are routinely paroled back into society and their hidden pain, secret sorrows and private rapes lead to public disorders. And public dysfunctions....I would also caution every youth to remember: guards own the gates! And many guards themselves will take you, rape you and forsake you too... Mark Salling, Kevin MChale, Benji Schwimmer, Steven Anderson, Jason Mraz and Jason Gomes need to help G.B.G. put the word out. I want Michael Carandang, Josh Ross, Zac Freisen, Silas Miers, Alex Seabolt, Bradford Cox, Asher Book, Kyle Haycock, Aaron Schroeder (grad student in San Diego), students at Aplington-Parkersburgh High School, Alex Hornbuckle, kids at Skyline College, Keystal Callaway Jaime, Chief Howard Jordan and Trevor Donovan to come stand with G.B.G. It is urgent that we come together and tackle this anger, HIV and the rage in boys in America. We need Garrett Carlisle, Matt and Jack (on Tyra Banks

Show 9/2/09), "d" and Weston. We are calling John Jessup, Ivan (dancer), Neil (dancer), Kupono and Travis Wall. I'm calling Ryan Neilson, Greg Deekins, and Maxwell Hanger. And to all of you kids who are in torment, pain and are hurting. You've been beat, abused or raped. You must tell somebody! If you've got to e-mail Dr. Phil or Tyra etc. do so. You don't have to be on their show(s) to utilize their resources. But having the horror heard helps heal the hurt! Re-read those eight words over and over. Tell somebody!... I'll ask the G.B.G. advisory board to (also) put some data on our Facebook sites etc to help victims. We certainly need systemic change in these prisons to combat the victimization of youths. But my assignment is to A. Keep you outta jail. And B. help you who have been hurt to deal with it. If you don't deal with the hurt of your yesterday it'll end up hurting your tomorrow. ...One of the reasons prisons are such cesspools of dysfunction and rage is our refusal to deal with the custody rapes. Ipso facto, we have 3 million males who are raping, being raped, have been raped or thinking about rape. And the violence and volatility of the raped, the raping and the rapees (to be) contaminates, aggravates and annihilates the very oxygen in the prisons....Males run to a gang, a clique, a cult or any cover to try to cover their (literally) asses and avoid rape. But even in the gang (as I've explained) they find that the young-Gee must give it up to the O-Gee. And by the time the youngster is older he's adapted to "doing it in the butt," dropping "it like it's hot" and male "bonding." So much so that he's no more good for any woman....The prison literally contaminates the mind, aggravates sexuality, infects the spirit and rejects normality. There is nothing cool, calm or collective about a prison. The recipe for dysfunction, disease and failed males is made up of the ingredients of the prisons. We (in the prison) are trained to hate, programmed to abuse and taught to kill. We are filled with rage and running over with anger. We have mastered the art and skills of rage, hate, anger and violence. Prison is an incubator for molesters, rapists and murderers. We are the epitome of abuse and a replica of rage....By and large, when you put us in prison you may as well lock the door and never set us free. Without a miracle (and certainly God can do anything) if you set us free we will rape, rob, steal and kill.... When we are here we will do just as Phil Garrido did. From Hades he wrote lengthy, convincing missives about how he'd changed his life and...When three members of the parole board were either careless enough or naïve enough to believe him. He got out and graduated from rape and kidnapping to abduction, molestation and enslavement... His first victim went to his parole agent who said "Yes he is a sick puppy. And we know he is going to reoffend." That statement (alone) is enough for me to say Jaycee should call Mark Merin, Tony Serra, Johnny Griffin, John Burris, Stewart Katz or Tom Mesereau and sue! ...Behold-I know ten inmates who will be released from prison in 2010. And I will bet you my eyes that nine of them will reoffend within 3 months. Six of the nine will commit sex crimes. But they will get out. Prison manufactures sexual deviants (as quiet as it's kept). Many prison employees are sexual deviants. I.E. Sergeant John Sanders (at CMC East) is a known sexual deviant. He raped a male inmate last year. And Linda McFarlane had to demand he be treated. And he was kept at CMC East, under Sgt. Sanders direct supervision (in LOU) after Sanders raped him! Linda, Psuyin and "Stop Prisoner Rape" were his only help. Warden Marshall did what the "good ole boys" do; he covered it up. These kinds of in custody rapes by staff take place everyday of the week... My fellow convicts will hate me (even more) for writing this: But I want to tell women that once any male has been in jail for more than a year; Run baby run! I don't give a damn how good he looks. He may have 100 inch biceps. The camera may be in love with his eyes. But be advised that (if he was in prison) the gang was in love with his ass. I could care less what he looks, smells, seems or feels like-run! How many ex-convicts do you know who can afford weekly psychological counseling from Dr. Phil, Dr. Jeff Gardere, Dr. Jarman or Dr.Curren? Do you know a dude getting out of jail who has an extra $1500.00 per month to pay for psychological intervention? I didn't think so-run! ...My message to Tyra Banks, Larry King, Geraldo (Tavis Smiley, Charlie Rose, Doug Banks, Steve Harvey, Bev. or Tom Joyner etc.) is this: Put the word out to these mommas, sisters and families etc. Tell the teachers and the preachers to do any and everything they can to keep their boys out of here!... What I used to like about Tim Russert was he was a numbers man. I like philosophy and I love psychology. I belive in sociology and politics etc. But strictly looking at numbers: more that eighty two percent of all California inmates who got out last year reoffended within a year. More than 93% of us who get out return within five years. What else do I need to tell you? If your son, boy, boyfriend, buddy or neighbor is headed for Hades I encourage you to do anything within the law to keep them out of prison. It does not take a rocket scientist to discover prisons manufacture madness. If you lock me up in a cell with Phil Garrido for five years. And if you don't murder his perverted ass what do you think I'll be like in 2014? Let me crap, shower, shave, eat and sleep in the room with Garrido (or Stokes, Bret, Eric, Lyle, Bardo, Manson or Henson etc.) for five years. Wake me up in October 2014 and tell me I'm free. What kind of man will I be? It doesn't take Dr. Phil, Dr. Gardere or Dr. Curren to figure out that association causes assimilation. "Birds of a feather flock together." Blessings and curses run in families. Most dope addicts (in prison) cell with the other addicts. Perversion can be learned behavior. Most abusers learn from their abusers. And the only way you can secure a "single" cell in prison is to "rape" (but even it must be proven. C.D.C. is known for claiming a "rape" never happened!) or "murder" a celly.

...Jam a jail with Garridos, Brets, Stokes and Bardos and you have (what we have) perversion upon conversion upon perversion...Tyra? (I repeat!) Once we have been locked up you may as well throw away the key. I wouldn't trust an ex-offender with my daughter even if the "pope" endorsed him. I've seen so many secret Garridos (listen to the eyes. How can anybody look at Phil's eyes and miss it? He may not admit it. But I'll bet my life that when Dr. Phil saw Phil's eyes Dr. Phil saw "it"!) and Stokes in here that is not funny. I'm speaking of the Garridos who don't make the news or are not yet discovered. Prisons are filled with "wierdos." And the prison can't reform them. Forensic psychologists can't transform them and parole agents can't inform the public about them....Scott Kernan defended his parole agent's miserable failure! And Scott Kernan is a very good man. When he was Warden at Mule Creek he was almost as good as Rod Hickman and Jimbo Walker. I actually like Scott a lot. Having said that- I assure you that Scott knows this parole agent should be fired. From a management standpoint (pragmatically) the decision was made to show a United Front. I understand the decision and I disagree with the decision....However, a police captain explained that "his" county had 350 sex offenders. 349 more offenders than agents to patrol the offenders. California has 111,000 former inmates and 173,000 present inmates. (284,000 "lost boys"....multiply $50,000 per year times 173,000 then multiply $40,000 per year times 111,000 then add them up...Small wonder teachers and professors are being laid off in California!)... I want P.J. Lukac, Jason Jenkins, Johnathon Simon (U.C. Berkeley), Chris House (Graphic Design student at Sac City College), Dr. Barbara Ziv, Jason Mraz and Jason Gomes to read this. I am absolutely alarmed by what I'm seeing, hearing and feeling in Hades. It's the best kept secret in criminal justice: the rape epidemic behind bars! Which exacerbates and aggravates the troubled boys who come here for petty crimes. I'm not gonna dilute the potency of my argument by debating the pros or cons of 3-strikes. I'll let the prison revolutionaries and the Phil Garridos argue three strikes. But I will say that in my view it would be better if it were all or none. You can't continue to lock up 18 year old boys (with 4 and 5 year sentences) in the same prisons with Garrido, Menendez and Stokes. And be surprised when you release a 22 year old offender. And he dresses up like Santa Clause. Goes to the mall and molests little boys. Prisons are a recipe for violence, deviance, psychological disorders and maniacal behavior. Read "Prison Madness" by Dr. Terry Kupers. I also recommend a tome by a former sex crimes D.A. called "It Happens Everyday. Inside the World of a Sex Crimes D.A." And I want to repeat (to mothers, ladies, sisters, dads, etc.) rapes, violent sexual assaults and sexual slavery takes place every day in prisons. One estimate says a California Caucasian (inmate) is raped every 19 minutes. Every 19 minutes! Parents: Do anything you can to keep your kid out of prison!!! Don't believe the hype! "Prison Break" was a joke! Do whatever the hell you can to save your sons. Take them to church! Fast and pray! Take them to a deacon's house! Put their names on the altar. Take them to see the pastor (one on one). Find a man in your family (who has never been to jail) and ask that man to mentor him. Buy him books by Dr. Phil, Zig Zigler, Les, Robbins, Cosby or by me. Pray for them. Put olive oil in their shoes, hang chicken bones around their neck (LOL)! Keep them out of here! By any means necessary!... Can you imagine your son (boyfriend, neighbor or brother) locked in a cell tonight with "Blue"? He is awakened to the feelings of a cool draft about his anus. And he looks around to discover "Blue" (with 21 inch biceps-who does 1200 pushups per day. Has and will use a shank. And is incarcerated for murder by knife) sniffing his buttocks. "Blue" has surreptiously pulled his boxers down. What would your son, buddy or brother do? Does he murder "Blue"? \If he kills "Blue" he kills his (own) future. If he tries to kill "Blue", "Blue" could kill him too. Does he break it down and give it up? What does an Anthony Fedorov, Clay Aiken, Garrett Cunningham or a T.J. Parsell do with a celly like "Blue"? You parents should require your boys to read "Fish" by T.J. Parsell. If Tyra, Dr. Phil or Bev don't want to call my name I'm cool with that. But (they can forget mentioning me) I plead with Tyra Banks, Dr. Phil etc. to tell teens and tweenies (like Brett and Chris) to read the "Fish" book by T.J. Parsell. It should be required reading for every American male! (I'm willing to personally send Dr. Phil two copies and he can give one to Brett and one to Chris)... America, mothers (cause most of the brothers are in here) ya'll better save these boys. Keep them out of prison! Ya'll ought to line up and bus in with Dr. Bill Cosby. Next time Dr. Cosby goes anywhere ya'll better run along with him. And if you're in a church that does not mentor young men get out now! We have got to intervene and prevent our boys from entering this machine. Prison is a machine designed to destroy any and everybody that comes in contact with it. It is fail proof. It works over and over again. Mark Christiansen, Zac Sunderland, Maxwell Hanger and David Hellyer you all need to help us spread the word. We need to initiate and orchestrate the kind of technological awareness campaign (similar to the Obama campaign for the presidency) to deter our boys from jails, juveniles and prisons. And we must promote education, curiosity, information and creative visualization. These are the vaccines for HIV. I am adamant and solid in my clarion call to you to save the boys and keep them from becoming toys for gangbangers in prison. Put the word out! Fix the broken foster care system.. Reinvest in education and that's the way to prevent incarceration. This is the cause of my life! I breathe to put the word out!...

Back to anger! I recall a show Montel aired with a black girl who had been set on fire by a man. Her face was burned beyond recognition. I could barely look at her. I felt ashamed with myself. And I remember thinking about how angry the guy was who set her on fire. Years ago Oprah aired a show where a black girl was nearly murdered (disfigured beyond recognition) and Oprah reunited her with the white paramedic who saved her life. Her face was blown apart. She's had many reconstructive surgeries. I wondered about the anger of the perpetrator....Here at New Folsom we had a guy who was in prison for putting an infant into the microwave and cooking her to death. He was disturbed, on drugs, etc. But also angry. So angry he should never be free. His eyes tell a certain story about his anger and ruthlessness...I also interviewed a guy in here who put a baby in a pot of boiling water. And he boiled her to death. And I noticed in the boiler, microwaver, both Menendez brothers and every psychopath etc. Exaggerated feelings of self importance and achievement. They are void of empathy and they're grandiose.

You can't convince Eric, Lyle, Henson, Stokes or Garrido (whom I've not met) that they are not "special". And when a guy like Eric is interviewed by Barbara Walters or Montel (even though I support interviewing so people can "see" behind the masks) it enhances their delusions of grandiosity. I'm a living witness that they feel that we circle around them and we're lucky to be allowed to share the planet with them.... And the pragmatic problem with prisons per se is there is no intensive personality reconstruction taking place. (Any prison psychologist will tell you their caseloads are too full and prison authorities limit their therapies. They are not even allowed to treat PTSD and if C.D.C. points to DMH as a model that is a joke. I've been to DMH due to my PTSD D.M.H. does not treat PTSD...) So even they pass time away with no treatment, no meaningful social interaction and no education. And (I reiterate) when they are left to be schooled by us (the thugs) they get meaner, tougher, sicker and slicker and when they get out they return quicker...Dr. Thema Bryant-Davis (she teaches psychology at Pepperdine. Hope her students get her this tome) strongly advocates reinvesting into the rehabilitation of the 7-19 year old kids in prison! I argue that these kids in prison are like kidnap victims. The traumatic loss of a family hardens them. They (kids in prison) are relentlessly controlled by prison gangs and predators. And when a child is in prison and he is afraid etc. His brain is overloaded and he begins to reconstruct his belief system. He takes on a new persona and a new identity! I once told Dr. Jamie Davidson (author of "Sweet Release") that prisons seem to implant an invisible magnet inside the boys who come here. And when they get out they are lost dogs and puppies searching for their masters. And their masters are prisoners and prison guards. Dr. Davidson replied "that's deep Manning. You ought to write a book about 'that magnet' and if you just put a hundred copies in high schools you will save lives!"... I'm praying that folks like Dr. Bryant-Davis, Dr. Jeff Gardere etc. will take heed to advice given by Attorney Robert Navarro (years ago) and come talk to the real "experts" on the prison subculture. If we are ever going to break the cycle; come talk to the guys who walk the walk. I've accumulated a Mountain Peak of data from young, scared (mostly Caucasian) boys I've met in prison. And their tales of horror have haunted me. This is why I'm on this campaign to reduce "anger" in our boys. Because it takes unspeakable anger to rape, control and to enslave these boys in prisons. And the public needs to know what's going on in here... These boys come in here and it's like they're up against the Taliban. They are outnumbered, out ranked, out smarted and over powered. And they may as well be "slaves". They are programmed into a quiet, submissive and frightened obedience...These boys are captive, captured and imprisoned within the prison.... This tome (missive) is to teens and tweenies but (also) for parents and professors. I want Greg Hardesty, Robert King, Michelle King, Cong. Bill Dela Hunt, Verone Kennedy and Joe Clark to read this book. And I want us all to pay close attention to Ally Jacobs words about Phil Garrido. She said he had those "penetrating blue eyes" same as Lisa Ling said of Eric Menendez. And Ally said "I got a weird and uneasy feeling". I tell you (again) listen to your instincts. And Ally said of the little girl "it was like she looked into my soul." WOW! Ally knows not only the art of reading people but she knows how to "listen to intuition."...

I want parents to give their kids little classes on what to do if they are touched inappropriately. Tell them to "yell" kick, scratch, etc. Yell "help" and yell "fire" and yell "this is not my daddy." And take it a step farther. Just like we used to do fire drills and tornado "drills". Do abduction "drills". Do role playing with your kids. Have em do "show and tell" and show you what they will do if grabbed by a stranger. These "drills", "role playing" and "show and tell" can save their lives!!

When you teachers notice delusional thinking, grandiosity, pathological lying etc. in 11 and 12 year old kids etc. Don't overlook it. Call their parents. Devise a plan for intervention. We must begin to engage in intensive personality reconstruction, therapy and counseling early on so we can have a shot at preventing the next Garrido, Stokes or Menendez....Thanks to the internet (I repeat) parents, teachers and students can log on to Dr.Phil.com and click on "teen talk' and/or look at the Dr.Phil Foundation. And access the help data located on his site. Check out the other websites I mention in this book and put these resources to work for your school, students, and your family today! This could save a child's life! This is real talk ya'll..I did a survey with all of my G.B.G. advisory board (including Franklin Curren MD, Dr Jarmen, A. Duran Ph.D, Dr. Gregg etc.) I asked them what did they think was the no.1 cause of boys (17-22 etc.) who get released and end up returning. "What do you think happened to them while they were locked up that drives them to come back after they get out?". And they all concurred with Dr. Curren: "Sherman it is called modelling"... These boys come in here frightened and crippled by fear and they automatically begin to walk, talk, think and act like those around them. Initially they are faking. Fake it till you make it. But sooner or later "prisonality" becomes ingrained into their identity. And just as abduction victims "bond" with their captors etc. Young boys in prison bond with booty bandits, butt sniffers (like "Blue"), predators and gang leaders. And a kind of Stockholm Syndrome takes hold of the mind, mentality and the identity of the prison boy. Gangsters and predators become their daddies, their siblings and their "friends". And the worst part of housing youngsters with gangsters (other than the fact that they will be recruited, raped and enslaved etc.) is that process of assimilation that I talk so much about....

I was housed (a couple of weeks) in a psyche unit (E.O.P./Ad-Seg). And many guys there are truly disturbed. And I recall seeing a guy who had to put on a special jumpsuit (with no opening in the front. No zipper and no way for him to even take a leak) which was zipped up in the back by staff. And they put a pad lock on it! I noticed that the window of his cell door was covered with cardboard with a small one inch space left for peeking inside. I asked what the jumpsuit was for and was told he was known for pulling out his penis and masturbating in front of women. So the space suit prevented him from pulling it out. And if a female looked in his cell (because of the cardboard on the window) he could not "bust her eyes." I recall thinking about how humiliated I'd be walking around with this suit on. And every day the guy wearing the suit would strike up conversations (out loud) about his "suit". I.E. "I ain't never getting out. Other men have women to look at on the streets. All I got is these women in here to look at." And day after day he defended his "suit" wearing and tried to "normalize" it. And I witnessed him (slowly but certainly) convince two or three guys that it was actually "pretty cool" to be wearing that "suit." One guy said "I used to look at you as a freak but now you really a stud. You got the balls to whip it out on any female" etc. etc. I later confirmed he's doing a life sentence for child rape and an assortment of other perverted crimes.

But just listening to a pervert justify and try to normalize a perversion. And to listen to the tacit approval etc. was a metaphor for what prison does to destroy people forever. We reside in an abnormal environment. And you must be or (at least) act abnormal just to survive in here. And repetition is the mother of skill. We do it for so long that "it" becomes "us".

I'd be wasting time engaging in an argument aimed at (old "dogs") the senate etc. Explaining the need for "programs", education and rehabilitation in prisons. They (politicians) don't give a damn about right or wrong. They just want to win the next election.

Ipso Facto, I can be of greater service by warning you to stay out of prison!... And if you are already locked up (and are getting out) I say study, pray, read and visualize. When the prison is awake you should sleep. When they are asleep you wake up. Do anything you can to stay out of the prison mix. It will rub off on you and ruin you....when you get out go to church! Get pastoral counseling. Get in any program you can. And go to the public library. Read everything you can by Hill, Robbins, Zigler, Covey, Brown, Kimbro and Cupcake Brown. Get motivational CD's and listen to them. And stay away from the hood, barrios and the trailer park! Join a G.B.G. chapter in your area (or start one!)...

I want Michael Sanford (at Lehigh), Jim Miller (C.E.O. Jackpot Rewards), Kyle Haycock, Dr. Alicia Salzer, Dr. Jeff Gardere, Aaron Shroeder (grad student in San Diego), Asher Book, Trevor Donovan, John Jessup, Matt and Jack, "d", Weston, Brandon Davis, Garrett Carlisle, Alex Hornbuckle, Skyline College Students, Krystal Callaway, Jaime and Samantha Moody to get this book. We need to get it to Mike Wilkerson, Billy York, Sam Fuick and Brian Boykins etc.

We must inundate high schools with this book. We must get the data in this book to students at Christian Brothers High School, St. Francis, Green Dot schools, Christian Lawrence and Biola University...... Get it to Travis Wall, Benji Schwimmer, Neil (dancer), Ivan (dancer), Jeff Buttle, Seamus Farrow and to Kevin McHale. People like Ryan Hreljac, Nils Vesk and Ben Alexander are brilliant enough to do informational Jihad via the internet and promote G.B.G. And the sky is the limit as to what I'm willing to give, allocate or donate to students willing to utilize the internet to inundate schools with data about this book. Just do it!! Ben, Nathaniel Mullinnex, Christian, Ryan, C.J., Zac and Alexus I can't do it without your help. Crank up those search engines and climb on to those walls and tell everybody about "K.K.K." Having seen this scribed Portrait of the Prison they must turn around... Align yourself, your school, your church, your club and your mind with G.B.G./Heart. Make a contribution to yourself, your family and to your country by being a part of this G.B.G. Awareness Campaign. Help us raise the awareness about the silent epidemic of nearly 600,000 foster kids in America! Help us likewise, raise an awareness about 1.3 million (plus) kids being beat, sodomized, traumatized, humiliated, devastated and enslaved in prisons in America.... I must admit to (Ben Alexander, Nathaniel, Keith, Christian, Justin Berry, C.J. Sheron, Brett, Chris, Ryan, Brandon White, Brian Walker, Eric Bates, Brandon Stafford, Ron Clark Academy, Jimmy Stovall, Steve Barr etc.) teens and tweenies that without you we can't do it. It won't happen unless we electrify youngsters. If we are successful at convincing (folk like Brett and Chris on Dr. Phil) our youths (Hairo Torres, Chelsey Ramirez, Nick Pelham and Daniel Asare etc.) that they are the solution even as they grow, we will win. One of the defining moments of my life was an awakening to the fact that my physician could have (God forbid) cancer. Even while he successfully treats my cancer. A soldier who is a double Amputee can still teach me about weapons and about warfare. Ipso facto, even while I'm in conflict I'm still qualified to teach. The biggest myth (passed on erroneously) is that I can't "serve" til I no longer need "serving" (to be served). I don't teach because I'm well. I teach because I'm better than I used to be. And there is a healing that comes through helping. So we take narrow ass guys like Brett and Chris who are still struggling. And G.B.G. gives them an assignment. And we hold them accountable. And they get to be a part of the solution. And they get to become ambassadors, a special envoy and a part of an innovative organization directed by a Harvard trained psychiatrist. We say to Brett, Ben, Nate, Christian, Chris etc. to "follow me and I will make you fisher's of men." We say to students at every high school to give us your time, talent, intellectual muscles, ideas, visions and your creative intelligence and we will change the world together. One prayer will change the world together. One prayer (every Saturday at noon), one book, one idea and one campaign at a time. We tell Brett and Chris to get G.B.G. caps, t-shirts and coffee mugs and throw up Heart "signs" everywhere they go. And we plan (in the future) to ask some of my mentors to recognize outstanding and "upward bound" youths in G.B.G. I intend to write to Tyra Banks, Steve Harvey, Dr. Cosby, Dr. Poussaint, Leonard Padilla, Willie Brown, John Burton, Gloria Allred, Arianna Huffington, Michael Moore, Judge Mathis and William Julius Wilson and ask them to recognize our student volunteers... Judge Greg Mathis broke down and cried, on T.V. the other day when a kid named Brandon gave him flashbacks of his troubled past. Brandon left Oakland trying to escape gangs, drugs and violence. Brandon's uncle utilized tough love minus the love. I was glad that a man with authority, prestige and power demonstrated that men do and can cry. I'm reaching out to men and demanding that we take our boys back and teach them to be men. I hold prisoners accountable also. Especially those of us who run to chapel every Sunday and claim to be born again. If we have been changed by our trials, changed by God or changed by education etc. We must strive for authenticity instead of popularity. And I'm here with you. I'm in the mix. So I don't buy the bull.... We all (especially in prison) claim to be so outraged by child molesters. But we are opportunistic hustlers willing to sell our mommas for meth and crack. We are frauds. I remember when a powerful celebrity was charged with a number of child molestation charges. Ninety percent of the prison population thought he was totally and completely guilty. And inmate and staff alike ran around talking about how "sick" he was. Yet, during his trial (prior to his exoneration on every charge) I found black, white and Mexican inmates admitting that they would love to be his cellmate. To beat him or assault him for being a so-called molester?" No! For his unspeakable wealth!... I recall C.O. Duclos admitting that she would smuggle him drugs for the right amount of money. Prisons are places of contradiction. The guards are often as wicked as the guarded....

(This could get me murdered! Especially since he still corresponds with prisoners whom he met inside). Suge Knight (in my view) is not only a crook, a dope fiend and a hustler. Suge is a homosexual!!!! When he was at MCSP C.O.Baker smuggled him food, Cuban cigars, weed and meth I never saw Suge do meth. The meth was for the white boys with whom Suge had sex. I'm told Suge took it in the backside. I can't confirm or deny that. But we caught him receiving fellatio from a 19 year old white inmate. Suge referred to him as a "her, she" and that "b_tch." Associate Warden Mike Bunnell was routinely seen conversing in whispered tones with Suge... When I was at P.V.S.P. C.O. Pieper thought I was dying (so did many of us) and he confided that his family suspected that Bunnell may have had (old Folsom capt.) Captain Doug Pieper murdered! "My aunt Evette and her son Doug still fear for their lives. Bunnell is a very dangerous man" Mr. Pieper told me.... But Suge never did anthing wrong to me. I just dislike bullies. And especially bullies who feel they are above the law. And (even worse) bullies with sexual secrets. I am mindful of the fact that Suge probably will come back to prison. And if Valley fever has not defeated me he may (literally) try. I also know several prisoners (at M.C.S.P., Donovan, High desert etc.) who call and correspond with Mr. Knight. So be it. I eat, sleep, live and breathe G.B.G. And all that it takes for evil to rage is for "good men to remain silent." How dare I call myself a student of Rev. Hosea Williams (who's motto was "unbought and unbossed") and Andy Young etc. When they risked their lives for the rights I enjoy. How am I a student of these fearless men if I'm gonna write "K.K.K." and be afraid to speak the truth? And compromise my mission. The mission of G.B.G. is bigger and more important than me. And only when a dream, a goal or a mission is bigger than the dreamer. Only when "a man has found something worth dying for is he fit to live"... I remember the F.B.I. warned Rev. Hosea Williams (in the 90's) that they'd received a number of credible death threats on his life. He refused bodyguards (although he always had a 38) and one night he advised me to stay away for a while. I refused (although I was absolutely afraid!) and said "if they get you they gotta get me Doc." It reminded me of one of our famed Forsythe County marches. Dynamite and explosives were reported stolen and speculation was the K.K.K. stole it. It was rumored they would bomb us on our march. My grandmom told me not to march. I told her I wouldn't.... After the march with Rev. Williams she asked if I'd marched. "No, sure didn't." and Dollie turned on her VCR of the footage from the march that clearly showed her baby grandson marching with my mentor Rev. Hosea Williams...Hosea told me "so what if they kill me. They killed Malcolm and Martin. I'll be in good company if they kill me."... Ipso facto, if Suge gets Bunnell to orchestrate a transfer and I get "hit". I know who my Redeemer is. And getting this awareness message to boys, foster kids and gang bangers is more important than my life! "A charge to keep I have"... I squandered it before. But not this time.... "To serve (that's what G.B.G. is all about) this present age. My calling (had it in 1979. Blew it! Wasted it!) to fulfill. Oh may it all my powers engage to do my master's will." I gotta engage all of my power in this awareness campaign. An old black hymn says "I'll go! If the Lord wants somebody. Here am I, send me... If don't nobody else go. I'll go!!" ...Talking about Suge, gangs and even Chris Brown won't help my standing amongst my fellow prisoners. But I don't give a damn. If I don't tell it who will? I must tell you (Boyz in the Hood, suburbs, barrios, and in the trailer parks etc.) that I heard prisoners rooting for Chris Brown. And I am appalled! What if it was your mother, your sister or your daughter that he beat the hell out of? But understand that prisoners wanted Chris to come to jail so they could leech off of him. But other than that they were down with Brown. And as he entered court I heard teen girls chanting "We love you Chris." I was sickened to my stomach. But again that mentality is a reflection of the failures of our fathers. And the failures of us as men. We did that! And Chris had the temerity to be upset with Oprah for merely saying "he needs help." And Chris had the audacity to retort "After all I did for Oprah in Africa. I sang for her school etc." If he did it from his heart, for the kids, what did they have to do with anything? I'm not anti-Chris. He's a great talent. But so was Ike Turner and many other woman beaters.

If Chris repents, confesses and then (he's got to deal with that anger....Perhaps anger with his father!) gets some serious counseling from a Dr.Phil, a Dr. Gardere or a Dr. Solis etc. then he can move on! ...Some of my pals in the prison wanna remind me (obviously they don't know me) that some folks are in the prison for crimes they did not commit...(for the record) I know many people who plead guilty to crimes they did not commit. Hell I know somebody intimately who has done that. Any defense attorney (Mesereau, Janus, Serra, Griffin, Masuda or Balsier etc.) can authentically tell you they've had clients whom they knew were innocent-plead guilty due to fear of a trial. That's why (love or hate him) when I heard folk alarmed about a certain celebrity paying to make a sex case go away etc. I said to Attorney Janus "they're living in a dream world." If the best criminal lawyer in the state (A. Janus, A. Morchower or Deana Cook etc.) looks you in your eyes and says "I know you did not do this. But jurors in this area are very conservative to be frank, people have been found guilty on less evidence. If we go to trial you may get convicted. Even the fact that you have such a great lawyer can be held against you by juries. You're facing 20 years! ...However for $2 million the case goes away!" If you have $50 million and they want $2 million=you pay! If you are poor they don't ask for (institutional racism and classism) $2 million. They ask for a guilty plea and 2 years, Being able to "call you a felon is more powerful than being able to call you a n----er (sp-c or we-back)" says presidential advisor (and Harvard graduate) Van Jones....

Having said that, I still submit that most of us in here did something. And the reason I'm so adamant, stern and indifferent toward us (Boyz in tha prison) is because of what I see, hear, taste and feel in us; in Hadez.. Yes-God can do anything! Yes a human being can re-create, revitalize, transform and experience New Birth even in prison! It can happen and it does happen. Give me one book by Zig Zigler, one by Tony Robbins, one by Dr. Poussaint, one by Dennis Kimbro and the Holy Bible and I can show any 18,19,20 year old boy in prison, in the hood, in the suburbs, on crystal, crack or heroin how to revolutionize their life. In 30 days or less...I know I'm right! If my Governor, Cate and Kernan were to allow my team (G.B.G) to develop 30 two hour D.V.D.'s to be shown to troubled youth (i.e. in Detention, C.Y.A. or Sacto County Jail) over a 30 day period etc. I'd stake my life on the fact that more than 80% of the viewers would be changed for life! But with this tome its my assignment to compile everything I've learned from brilliant minds (i.e. Franklin Curren MD, C. Solis MD, Jennifer Heitkamp MD etc) in psychiatry, the top minds (Jimbo Walker, Rod Hickman, Kernan Cate, Fred, Steve, Rosario and Kennedy etc.) in corrections etc. And to pool the data I've observed (first hand) from the worst (Menendez, Stokes, Henson, Bardo, Frazier, Moore etc.) of the worst etc. and to use it in this book to revolutionize youngsters (again I must apologize to the Great John Burton for making the tome a little longer than planned. But just as attorney Janus suggested "Rev. this tome could be your one shot at righting your wrongs and reducing to writing, a record which can transform teens and tweenies!") …We must reach them prior to prison. Prison (aka Hades) is tarnished by a spiritual (and mental) infection! This book offers intervention which is prevention. I am blessed (better than blessed) to have been afforded the opportunity to meet the folk I've met. I was overlooking the uniqueness of my journey until Attorney Janus hit me with it: "I'm sorry that you're in prison and I'm very sorry that they expect your Valley Fever to kill you." Atty. Janus said: "But there comes a time when you are called to take lemons and make lemon-aide. I recall Attorney David Hicks (now Richmond District Attorney) and I were trying the Beverly Ann Monroe Case (of Dateline fame). And the Menendez brothers story broke." Atty. Janus continued "I remember you asked me about the Menendez care…Who would have ever thought, sitting in Virginia that you would (one day) be sitting in Sacramento, in prison with Eric Menendez? And that after that you'd go to the lone and entertain Lyle Menendez? And you'd get to know Bardo, Frazier, Henson and others. And you'd get to know the top corrections officials in California. And along the way you'd meet Harvard trained psychiatrists. Along with brilliant, book publishing psychologists like Dr. Jamie Davidson. Not to mention the notorious Dr.Marilyn Windham (who drove a red Mercedes and was known for having sex with prisoners in mop closets!)… Atty. Janus finished with "my daughter (Atty. Deanna Cook) can draw up your will. And I'll want 20% of all sales of the "K.K.K." book. And $100 grand from the movie rights.You know Will Smith will buy it. What really tickled me was the fact that Janus was not laughing!!! …But it was hours after that conversation that the power of his words began to take on a new kind of magic. I thought Terry L. Rosario. I thought about Steve Vance. I recollected hundreds of hours of conversations with Mrs. Patricia Kennedy, Fred Schroeder, Dr. Hedblad, Dr. Curren, Dr. Jarman, Dr. A. Duran and Dr. Solis etc. I reflected upon every eerily similar feeling I'd gotten around Eric, Lyle, Marvin, Brett, Ed Stokes, Bardo and the other misereants….And I thought back to that day in Powhattan Virginia. I thought back to Janus, Monroe and Hicks. And the waterworks started. I wept and wept and I wept. And I thought back to Oprah: "Sometimes God allows horrible things to happen (to you) so that you will never allow it to happen to somebody else." And it dawned upon me that every powerful person (Williams, Young, Zigler etc.) whom God had allowed me to meet and to know. Every great thing I'd done. And every fraud I'd done. I lies I'd told (Stella, Yvette, Marv and Lathia etc.) …. My mistakes, errors, the manipulations and the scams. The stuff they say I did and stuff I really did do… Nothing just happens! Nothing just happens! No-thing! None of it-just happens! I could live in denial. The choice was mine! ….From this book, as you can see (I made) a choice! (as an aside-I hope Will Smith, David E. Kelley or Jerry Bruckheimer etc. will get footage of me at the late Bishop Gilbert Patterson, Rev. A.Lincoln James and Leroy Jenkins churches to use in any film!) As Johnny Willie told me after a G.B.G. roundtable meeting. "Atlanta you got me all the way out on the limb. Your black ass (sic) got me sittin round the table with sworn enemies. I'm talkin to guys I'd a never talked to, because of you! …Willie continued "I'm having nightmares Atlanta literally nightmares about bein (sic) surrounded by snakes. I'm doin this for one reason. Cause you came to me with a death stare in yo eyes. And when you said "Uncle Willie I can't do this without you," I knew you was (sic) sincere. I felt my soul shake…" Willie continued "You told me we would be history and not just see history! You told me we was gon change lives. So now I know you mad at Steve and Fred. But don't let that anger bog you down or stop you. If we gonna do it let's do it right and real. You gotta come out the closet with yo secrets. You gotta talk about your case, your crimes, yo life and yo truth! You started this Atlanta! And it's on you to do what you know is right to do. If you stay humble Allah will bless you. I love you boy." …Later Willie and I were awaiting Fred Schroeder for a G.B.G. meeting. We were walking the track and Willie pointed to a group of guys (enemies! Including Silent, Joker, Jason, Billy, Doc, Butler etc.) and said "them white boys n Mexicans ain't my friend (sic). And they ain't yo friend! But they standing there waiting on a G.B.G. meeting because of you. You touched they souls n brought them together. You can't let them dudes down. They don't even like you but they look up to you. They aint gon tell you that. Because we are too bitter, too jealous, too angry to tell a fella con that we look up to you. But Atlanta these guys look up to narrow black ass…"

I had no idea that those would be the last words I heard from Willie for months. This was the same day God allowed Dearaujo, J.Stratton, Garcia (I.S.U.) and Lt. Johnston to send me to ad-seg to be alone! Alone with Willie's and Murray's words. Alone with my thoughts, my visions, my dreams and my God. No-thing just happens! (I'll repeat) I would've and could've never written this part (and "confessions of a Con Man" etc. of this book if I hadn't become alone!) of the book if God didn't allow it. Willie's words to me had the kind of effect that Bishop Jake's words had on Bishop Long when Jakes slammed on his breaks. Pulled the car to the side of the road and told Long "don't you ever call yourself a failure." …

And with this tome I don't come by myself. But I come with convicts, Wardens, Harvard psychiatrists, young staffers (Bugriyev, Lane, Nicolodi, etc.) and we come to pull the car, the van or the school bus, over to the side of the road. And we (Patricia Kennedy, Dr. Curren, Willie, Doc, Billy, Fred, Steve, and the rest of our team) tell you (juveniles, students, teens and tweenies etc.) don't call yourself a failure! You are somebody! We came to tell Gabriela Rodriguez (and her hubby wearing the "Alcatraz-psycho ward" t-shirt), Nathaniel Frank, Ben Ownby, Alex Effron, Bruce Marks, Kids at Stillman College (Ala), Rocky Mountain College (Montana), Washington State University, St. Francis high and Grant High School etc. You are not a failure! You are somebody! …This is your reveille! Use this book to bring light. A book (i.e. "K.K.K.") is a passport to take you anywhere in the whole world! A book (i.e. the Holy Bible) will even take you into the heavens! A book is a doorway into places which you may never go in the flesh. This book beckons Alex Chivescu, ((also the Gen. Laborer wearing goggles and a facemask at the Cliff Spencer Furniture maker), Matt Cash, Chris Cash, Simon Perez (Oakland) Ryan Rathjen, Chad Burton (Oakland), Paul Norton, Karen Bricker (librarian) and Teresa Payne. And we call on Ryan Hreljac, Van Hansis, David Hellyer, Luke Sears, C.J. Sheron, Scott Czeda and Chris Austad. We call every young man to come take a stand. We (G.B.G.) can "never leave a soldier (teen or tweenie) behind on a battlefield! "G.B.G. can't leave anybody behind. We aim to scoop you up and pull you back. And this book (as well as the books of Zig Zigler, Tony Robbins, Dennis Kimbro, Dr. Poussaint and Les Brown's etc.) is written to shoot you into your destiny!… (on a lighter note) The same C.O. Baker (at M.C.S.P. he and his siblings are known as the Baker brothers!) who smuggled dope into Suge was known as "Booty stick". (No joke) He would take his billy club (state issued baton) at breakfast in the chow hall. And he'd rub the baton between inmates butt cheeks! I promised myself if he ever did it to me I would knock him out cold! He did it to a known homosexual named Daniel Masterson and (to his credit) Daniel wrote everyone including the President about Baker. After Sylvia Garcia, Roseanne Campbell and Bunnell swept it under the rug for so long. Finally Senator Diane Feinstein got involved. And Baker was suspended for 30 days and assigned to drive a "trash truck." But (the Green Wall! They stick together!) officers held a cookout and raised $3500.00 for Baker so he wouldn't lose his house.

And his fellow guard (led by Mike Bunnell) i.e. C.O. Pogue harassed and retaliated against Daniel til Bunnell locked him up and transferred him to Salinas Valley....

... I gotta admit that if I'm going to a battle field and I gotta fight. I don't need guys who've been to school and been to seminary. But I want some thugs who have learned how to fight and been to the cemetery. And my G.B.G. soldiers know how to do warfare. And we did not come into your college, classroom, home room or juvenile to play pitty pat. We came to do warfare. We know how to fight! And if you are going to evade the prisons that we live in. You must abscond from militias and abandon gangs. You must believe in yourself and have confidence in your abilities. You have to develop self esteem and grow in your own personhood... Guilt, anger and inferiority are a potent brew. And prisons, jails and juveniles are brewing factories! ... You (youths) can get a whole new feeling and such a rush from helping others etc. you'll get lightheaded! .... Ben Franklin always said "Well done is better than well said." We want youngsters to do something to equip yourself against gangs. You have the gun (your brain) and the power. Your mind is faster than a speeding bullet and more powerful than a locomotive! We are calling on youngsters in college, in schools and in the hood to support "The Jane Doe no more initiative." We want you to engage (with G.B.G.) in Gorilla tactics and methodologies against gangs, guns, drugs and violence. We want kids (in record numbers) to support the Shawn Hornbeck Foundation (log on)! We want kids and parents to follow your "gut". We want kids to learn by studying F.B.I. agent Lynn Willett. Lynn is known as a human polygraph machine. When she initially interviewed Shawn Hornbeck and Ben Ownby's molester (Mike Devlin, like Garrido a loner! And like Garrido 6 ft 4!) She noticed "his pulse increase when he talked about Shawn." And the hair on the back of my neck stood up."... You may never read people the way Lynn, Janus, Zigler or Robbins can. But you can train yourself to listen to your gut, intuition and your instincts!... G.B.G. considers Shawn Hornbeck a hero! Shawn Hornbeck is a hero! Because he survived!! Shawn (and Smart, Ben and Jaycee) is a hero!... You may never master the circular interviewing techniques that Mark Merin, Barry Tarlow, Janus and Willettt have mastered. But you can notice "he's not making eye contact." And (if you look closely at Garrido in court on T.V.) you can notice that Blah, Penetrating and eery look and run from it! You are powerful. you have so many things you can do to prepare for your destiny. You (Shawn, Ben, Jaycee etc.) can not be replaced! G.B.G. is "calling all angels!" I (and my team) won't give up! You (wherever you are reading today) don't give up!" Shawn Hornbeck said "There's nothing like a mothers and a fathers love." And when Shawn said that I (the jail bird! The bigshot prisoner!) wept! I wept for (and with) Shawn, Adam Walsh,C. Anthony, Sasha Groene, Elizabeth Smart, Ben, Jaycee and so many others! I wept for their parents! I wept for their pain. I wept! I wept! And I returned from my pain to my friend (anger!) and I learned from my pain. I turned my pain (and anger) into power. I prayed! And after I prayed I wrote (write!). ....I'm calling all angels! I won't give up! You (even prisoners and prison guards, police and professors, parents and pupils etc.) don't give up!" Shawn didn't give up! We can't give up! It knocks me off my feet when I realize that (love him or hate him) Mr.Obama is so right! We can all serve! And Dr. King (better still Jesus Christ) was right! "Everybody can be great because everybody can serve!! In a strange kind of way God (to Him be all the glory and praise) used a broke down, reject, disoriented and disobedient preacher (S.D.M.) from Atlanta. And while he (like Jonah) was/is trapped in (a whale) jail. God used me to write (Patricia Kennedy, Fred, Steve, Jimbo, Bugriyev, Lane, Dustin, Willie, Billy, Roger, Curren, Jarman, A. Duran, Gregg, Houston and Handian etc.) the names of some (convicts, staff, psychologists and psychiatrists etc.) folk (whom you never knew existed) into history and to help you etc.etc. etc. a long time ago Rev. Hosea Williams told me "I'm glad you know history! I'm delighted that you can quote Shakespeare...But Rev. Manning are you willing to use your life, your pulpit and your pen to write your name into history the way Shakespeare wrote his name into history?" He told me "I hold the Civil Rights record for more arrests than any civil rights leader alive! Andy, John Lewis, Dr. King, Joe Lowery and us went to jail so your ass (sic) could read. And you could write! You have no excuse not to take this baton of power, of freedom and of manhood and to write yo (sic) name in history! And I do mean history!!! "

...That is why I am adamant about G.B.G. and this is in my Heart (Helping Educate At Risk Teens)! I can't even die until this is done. I must go tell it on the mountain, in the valley, in the barrios, trailer parks, hoods etc. over the hills and everywhere... You can transform. You can be great! You can serve! I'm more convinced than ever that we who messed up and have been benched (jailed) by the game of life. We can coach! We can teach! We can preach! We can inspire! We can motivate! We don't have any excuses! With bibles free and years to read. With Dr.Phil on T.V. twice per day, five days per week. With Tyra Banks and books galore! With a black president and a body builder Governor! If a comedian named Al Franken can walk from stand-up to the senate. If a working woman named Nancy can Pelosify the speakership of the House! What can't be done? I came to call yo ass up off the bench of your prison cell. I came to call you to coach and to teach. We need you to lead and to preach. I call those things (people) that are not as though they (you) already were! I came to slam the breaks on the car, bus, van, motorcycle, bicycle or tricycle and as Jakes told Long and Willie told me. It's time for you to see that you are not a failure! You have a job to do right in that school, college, hood, barrio, trailer park, juvenile, jail cell or prison. You have a job to do! You are not a mistake! You are not a failure! You succeeded in getting this damn book. And you're still reading. If you take action on what you are reading (whether I'm the chief priest or the chief sinner) you'll transform into a winner. There is no poverty in your spirit! You can be changed from the inside out! If you look up you can get up. Be like a doggon timex man. Take a licking and keep on ticking. We fall down but we get up! (as Shawn Hornbeck says) "At the end of every tunnel there's always a bright light." Shawn ain't a philosopher and he's not speaking theoretically! This is an 18 year old kid who has walked through the valley of the shadow of death! He was viciously assaulted, kidnapped and subjected to terror too graphic for me to even write down on paper. Yet, from the ashes of terror, fear and pain Shawn rises up. And his history affects my destiny. And by affecting my destiny he influences your future. And you are where you are, reading what you are reading and you can't get away. Because nothing just happens! No-thing just happens! Shawn is a walking, talking, breathing, living and giving miracle! And when he sat down to do an interview with CBS. He didn't have any idea that his story would receive glory in "K.K.K." And that even when he turns 28,38,48, 68, 88 and long after he's gone his story will get glory through a tome written in a California jail cell! Typed and printed in Massachusetts. And published in Switzerland! But no-thing just happens!

In prisons gang bangers control the gang, control their sex slaves by fear, terror, and threats of retaliation!... A youngster white (and many black and brown) inmates live out a script written by the shot callers! And the script is so ingrained into the mentality of inmates (as I mentioned before) that we roll up mattresses, stack boxed up on our bunks and wear tennis shoes inside our cells etc. Even when (or if) we are out of the gang and out of the game. This is a form of programming and the institutionalization that feeds the magnet that brings us back; when we get out...on the streets (in a sense) we are like Pavlov's dogs. We are looking for a mattress (but instead have a bed) to rollup and a box to stack up. And when we fail to find it on the streets. We reoffend and come back "home" we have locked up minds and incarcerated spirits...But thanks to Rev. Hosea Williams, thanks to Dr.Bill Cosby, Dr. Phil, Dr. Curren, Dr. Davidson, Dr. Hedblad yes-thanks to Shawn Hornbeck. I've come to tell you that you can write your own script! You (Brett and Chris on Dr. Phil) still have the opportunity (as teens and tweenies) to write your own script and direct the (real life) movie of your (own) life! (I'm not bragging) but if a dude in a jail cell can reach out (via the internet and books) and touch you wht can't you do? As Zig Zigler is famous for saying "You can change who you are. You can change where you are. You can change how you are. By changing what (books, magazines, data) goes into your mind."

I came to lead you (David Joiner, Chris Michael Fowler, James Nesmith, John Garvin, Billy York, Scott Johnson, Christopher Rousche, Richard Kenneth Chandler, Ricky Sweet, Spence Palmer, Brian Graham, Daniel Clay, Gary Browning, Chad Sherman, David Reynolds, Ricky Parnell, David Dowdie, Ronald Wright, Chris Eavey, Alexander Dugdale, Brian Foskuhl, Jeff Schroeder, Jessie Godderz, Kevin from Chula Vista, Jimmy Stovall, Eddie Cannon, Ralph Cannon, Craig Cannon, Nils Vesk, Perry Thompson, Jamie Constantino, Autumn Brown, Frasier Esty, Jonah Coleman, Faisal Janjua, Lavelle Hawkins, Mick Hazen, Jared Klapheck, Joseph Brown Jr. Nick Hogan, Dante Stallworth, Chris Powell, Andrew Procknow, Nicole Lucas-Waddell, Ben Cooper, Fred Lange, Justin Berry, Jerry Box, Brian Hawn, Eric Domingo, Samantha Moody, Trevor Loflin, Garrett Carlisle, Trevor Donovan, Alex Hornbuckle, Asher Book, Kyle Haycock, Joseph Schoen, Libby Amor, Redmond O'Neal, Ben Alexander, Nathaniel is staring you in the face. The answer is in your mirror. The answer is beating in your chest. Your miracle is in every breath that you take. You are a freaking miracle! Don't look for the miracle! You (after all you've been through) are a miracle. And if y-o-u will use your search engine! Use your mouse! Use your ingenuity! Use your creativity to tell somebody else to read this book! You (Ben, Mick, Sample or whoever) will make a miracle for somebody else! When you use your (computer, facebook, myspace, e-maiil, telephone or stamp! Word of mouth! Church! School or club!) resources to turn somebody (else) on to this book! You create and initiate a miracle for somebody else! My toes are tingling! My spine is tickled! The hair stands up on the back of my neck as I think about Shawn (Ben, Nathaniel, Christian, Sample and Schoen etc.) Reading this book and telling others to "read this book!" ....The reason I offer small stipends and lil scholarships for folks like Alex Chivescu, Maxwell Hoch, Maxwell Hanger, Alex Bleach, Alex Seabolt, Ben Cooper(Davis Ca), Brandon Stafford, Jimmy Stovall, Alma Flores, Shawn, Christian, Nathaniel, and Keith etc. is so that they will join the Clarion Call for G.B.G. and this HEART (Helping Educate At Risk Teens) message shall spread all over the world! When Ben Alexander (in Iowa), Nathaniel Mullinnex (in Atlanta), Alex Chivescu (in Massachusetts etc.) start telling Perry Thompson (in Granite Bay) and (Christian on Tyra on 8/3/09... Diego Saavedra, Mike Caradang, V. Yakubovsky at Oakmont High School, Michael Sanford at LeHigh, Matt and Jack, "d" and Weston on Tyra on 9/2/09) kids at Aplington Parkersburgh High about "K.K.K." ...when kids read this book in their situation. They will never come to this place of devastation... I believe that once you've tasted better bad is not good enough. Anymore I believe that if Mr. Hostetier (Sierra Child services) gets this book to Angelo and if Angelo logs on to the website of the Shawn Hornbeck Foundation. I believe that when we connect Alex Chivescu with Alex Seabolt. When we get Alex Hornbuckle, Joe Simon, and Christian to get involved with Shawn's foundation! To click on to Dr. Phil's "teen talk" to get involved with "the Jane Doe No More Initiative." To use the innovative creativity of the internet brilliance etc. of Pete Alexander's son Ben. To interact socially with G.B.G./Heart to utilize Ben Alexander's know-how to tell Ben Ownby's story. And to somehow use what was Ben (Alexander's) pit fall as an asset. To bring people together we would have never gotten together. To tell the stories of Justin Berry, Shawn Hornbeck, Ben, Sasha Groene and even Caylee. To utilize the internet as a tool to get kids to see. How to recognize a predator and to not become prey. We can use the G.B.G. community to say things in a way. That will attract attention and will get a mention while in school, at home or even in detention... with Ben Alexander, Ben Cooper, Mullinnex, Alexus, Carlisle, Sample,

Chivescu and you too. We will do Gorilla warfare against gangs, guns, drugs, predators and violence. We (G.B.G. you and me) can do this. Yes we can! ...Yes-we-can! ...Prior (P.P.P.P.) planning prevents poor performance! This book is your passport into a world I never want you to see. It is a reminder for you to be all that you can be. We aim to do intervention and cause prevention. now that you are reading and we have your attention...since I have your attention I've come to speak a word like Paul. I've had to ask the creator to give me a double portion of power for this hone. Because I'm writing to people who have seen so much hell and your yesterdays are disturbing your tomorrows. I'm writing to people who wanna keep going back to Egypt. I'm writing to people with an Egyptian mentality. God had to put me in a situation so I could sit at the feet of Dr.Phil, Dr. Curren, Dr. Solis, Dr. Duran, Bishops and teachers and preachers. He knew I needed Harvard, Morehead, Stanford and Yale to push (troubled teens and tweenies) you into your destiny. He knew I needed the wisdom of Andy Young, the fearlessness of Hosea Williams and the passion of Robbins to impart vision. He knew this HIV (having insufficient vision) was a curse that needed to be broken. And the spiritual D.N.A. is inside of you to move into vision. I see vision for the barrio and vision for the hood. I came to remind you teens and tweenies that you have all the gifts and talents you need to survive. But you can thrive and develop the drive to keep hope alive. You are not a failure. You are not a loser. I came to tell Brett, Chris and you to come out of Egypt. Come out of drugs, smoke and booze. There is work for you to do. I came to call you into service.... God used Moses to bring them out but he used Joshua to bring them in my assignment (with this tome)is to bring you out. I came to remind you that destiny is inside of you. And we want to align you with Dr. Phil, T.D. Jakes, Zig Zigler, Tony Robbins and others to bring you in. my mission is to speak (write) these words into the atmosphere. And once these words ("K.K.K.") have been spoken into your atmosphere the HIV will begin to disappear. Your sight, your might, your vision and your mission shall be restored. G.B.G. (my team and me) have come to pull you out of that mental, psychological and spiritual darkness. Light is coming back! And might (power and strength) comes with light! ...I came to shine the whit hot light of vision on to your destiny the same way John Walsh shines light on criminals! Come out, come out wherever you (Brett and Chris) are! I came to speak to the winner in you and to call you out. Just as Shawn Hornbeck can relate to Jaycee better than you and me. The G.B.G. team and our advisors can relate to you too. We understand your yesterdays and believe in your tomorrows. Shawn gave some advice to Jaycee that'll work for you and me. He said "You have to keep looking to your future and believing it will be better than your past." ... we who live (convicts) work (guards) and teach (therapists) in prisons are in the Ph.D program. I'm in the prison (P), Hades (h), degree (d) program. My team and me a qualified to lecture at Lodi, Locke, Harvard, Howard, Morehouse and at Yale about this hell (Hades) that "Kids Killing Kids" leads to. And we predict that massive outbreaks of vision are taking place right now. There are some Josephs (Pete Rose, Hurricane Carters, Rolando Cruz, Chris Ochoas, and Nelson Mandela's) getting out of prisons today. And because of Dr. Curren, Dr.Solis, "K.K.K" and G.B.G. there are some youths beginning to see. That education is the authentic bridge to lliberation. Education prevents devastation. Education is a vaccination to prevent incarceration. Education removes the scales from your eyes. Education regenerates the (mental) optic nerve and restores vision/sight and light... We (G.B.G.) came to bring vision. I wish you'd see you the way I see you. I see some Craig Kielburgers! I see some Craig in Brett, in Chris, in Nate and in you. I came to sound the alarm and awaken the giant within you. Wake up in that homeroom. Class room, bedroom, juvenile, or jail cell. Now is the time to rise and see. We are living in an age where you can be all that you believe you can be. Now is time to have faith in God and to believe you can see. You become what you believe. You are shaped by your beliefs not by your circumstances. I believe vision is being restored, unleashed and released in your class, school, college and in your community. And I want you (no matter how young or old you are. Even though you're still not "there"yet) to start cheering your buddies, girlfriends and boyfriends on. You can re-preach, re-teach and re-speak what you read in this book! Time and again I'll re-preach what I heard T.D. Jake's, Paul Morton, Noel Jones and Eddie Long preach.

I re-teach the lessons I learn from Dr.C.Solis, Dr. Franklin Curren, Dr. A. Duran, Dr. Jarman and Dr. Jennifer Heitkamp, Dr. Phil can't preach (LOL) his message with my flavor! I want students, teens and tweenies to re-speak what I write. And when you speak this data into the atmosphere you're going to change entire schools, churches and cities. And more and more people are gonna wanna borrow this book! But don't loan it to en (LOL). Send their butts to www.cafepress.com/manning to get their own copy. And see, youth (y-o-u) see. If we (G.B.G.) do nothing else except awaken your sight and your night vision etc. We will succeed! Life can be scary, dark and it can be spooky but there is a crack in every night. And if you look lard enough in the dark you'll see the stars. And along with night comes stars. And with stars comes the light from the moon. And when you see the moon you know that morning is coming soon. And the sun will rise again. And ain't no need to worry. What the night is gonna bring it'll be all over in the morning. The sun is gonna shine in this place. And make you feel like you can run this race... But the key to Shawn Hornbeck's survival is the key to cure your HIV. You must hope through the night. Hope attracts light! The law of attraction is operationalized when you hope, when you believe and visualize creatively. You must creatively visualize! Create a vision with your eyes. See it you can be it. If (when) it grows in your (mind) it'll grow in time. Negativity is toxic! But positivity, excitement, enthusiasm and vision are contagious! Let vision, creativity, excitement and innovation break out and catch on in your class, college, city and in you. You can do what you believe you can do. Your future (in god's hand) is up to you...I see sight (vision, a bright future and destiny) in you. I really, really do. You don't just have to watch and see history. You can do and be history...Yes you can!

G.B.G. came in "K.K.K." to kickstart your hope again. And we know you can win. There are millions of you (kids and students) holed up (in schools, colleges and dorms) and plotting to succeed and you believe we came to say keep at it. You can do it. Just stick to it! Study! Read! Write! Saturate your mind with hope, light and knowledge. If you are out of school get back in. if you dropped out drop back in. Plot, think, dream, strategize and visualize your success. You are clever enough to do it... I hate to admit that I smoked cigarettes for almost 20 years. ... And one of the few commercials that really reached me was the one with a woman. And she had a hole in the base of her neck. And they showed her putting a cigarette to the hole and smoking. That miserable and worst case scenario was more effective than the surgeon general for me. Ipso facto, Dr. Curren (of Harvard fame), Dr.Solis, Dr. Heitkamp, and Dr.Duran never cease to remind me that (as it relates to G.B.G.) they are the surgeon general. But Silent, Doc, Billy, Willie and me (you see). We are that wounded woman with a hole in our neck. We put the cigarette to the hole and then the story is told. In our hole (void, darkness, and in our Hades) you can see the results of gangs, guns, drugs, and violence. I came to put a magnifying glass on your potential and ability. I came to focus on the power of your vision. I came to turn the light on and to (awaken the giant within) open your eyes. I came to remind you of your potential, power and your passion. I came to focus like a laser beam on the holes in our (G.B.G. team) necks. I came to shine the light on the flesh over your hole. I came to speak hope, life, light and vision into your life. This is your day to recommit. You can rise to the challenge and go into your destiny. You are a rising star. I see a gold mind (mine) in you. You will read, write, learn, go and grow. This is your season to discover the reason. Your reason for being is all in seeing. Seeing who you are and who's you are today is the first day of the rest of your life.

A crack is coming in the midst if your night. I see a bright future for you. I see you budding, blossoming and blooming. I came to disrupt, dismantle and to destroy gangs. You are the caller of your own shots. I want you to get up now and move forward. Move stealthily away from gangs and bitter, toxic people. I believe in you. You are so precious. You are worth more than your weight in gold. You are somebody! ...Inissa Garcia (Washington State Univ.), Ben Alexander, Nate, Brett and Chris etc. you are special. I want you to dig, search, and delve into the secrets that Napoleon Hill, W.Clement Stone and John Johnson all tapped into. I want you to find vision! When you get a vision you'll get provision....the G.B.G. team and me-we are elite in home personal development trainers. We are Doug Williams when he retires from the Redskins (as quarterback) and returns to gambling to coach. We came to show you how to use books, cans, and brooms to work out and build muscle. We came to remind you of all the tools, instruments, power and the potential you already have and aren't using. We want you to elevate your mind and get yourself together. Exercise your right to dream and to visualize. Pick up a book. Push up a pen. Sit up and read. And stretch your mind. You can if you think you can... Gangbangers (and some prison guards) are the architects of the torture program in prisons. This cesspool is filled with the waters of hatred, rage and racism. I stand before you (in this book) with the hole of anger in my neck. And I smoke from the cigarette of violence and the cigar of ruthlessness. It's to be or not to be. You can see or close your eyes (HIV) and be me. To be baby boy, or not to be.... G.B.G. is calling (Elite home trainers in Sacramento....I.E. "Brad" at Elite) Brad (in sac-town), Jason Huyck, Jeremy Pearsons, Christopher Durbin and sam Fuick. We are "Calling all Angels" and asking you to help spread the word about our awareness campaigns. With the internet you can be Jerry Bruckheimer, David E. Kelley, Spike Lee or whoever you want to be "K.K.K." doesn't need the nation. But Jai Breisch, Craig Scott, C.J. Sheron, Christopher Thompson, Andrew Bridge and students all over the world. You can beam G.B.G. and "K.K.K." from one side of the planet to the other with Facebook, Myspace, vlogs and with blogs. And we are depending on you (Keith Mullennix, Christian Nelson, Alex, Ben and y-o-u!) to use every form of digital footprint (including youtube and sprint) to tell pastors, professors, parents and pupils about "K.K.K." I want ya'll to hollaback! ...I'm getting ready to touch some nerves but your destiny means everything to me. If even the roughest and toughest gangsters can't empathize with Adam Walsh's dad (and mother and siblings) John. I can't even relate to you yo. I mean there ought to come a time when prisoners and police, guards and the guarded, bloods, crips and skinheads ought to share (and care as Americans and as human beings) the Fellowship of Grief, sorrow and pain. We ought to be joined together in the University of Suffering when a Caylee Anthony, a Sasha Groene, an Adam, a Jon Benet etc. is kidnapped, or molested or murdered. And if a brother can't feel a parent's pain your soul is stained and you are dead. And I've met a lot of dead dudes in prisons....

Why are you angry? (again-the ultimate question) who are you so angry with that you'll allow them to change how your story ends? (I've never told this; ever!) I was angry with Brenda Smith! (this is private but I gotta tell this to empower and to inspire thousands of angry little boys wanting to be men. I never thought I'd tell it!) I was angry with her because when she married Harold she took both my beautiful lil sisters with her but she left me with my (Dollie a/k/a my "mother") grandmother ...Leaving me there was the biggest blessing (Psalm 27:10) Brenda ever could have given me. She didn't even fully understand that God led her to leave me where I could grow and prosper. But she did exactly what God wanted her to do. And for decades I was angry at her. And before we reconciled I was hurt, bitter and angry-and every time a woman loved me I did the same thing (to the women) that I thought my mother did to me; I left her. Marva Respres? I left! Left...Yvette (a queen) Lewis? I left her. Stella Bryant (to be continued later in the book) I left. I had no idea why I left (except Meine beautiful stealthy Sabine) every woman that I got close to. I rebelled, retaliated and I left them like I thought Brenda left me. But Brenda Smith is (indeed) any mother and I love her and she loves me. And it took me 3 decades to understand the root (source) of my anger... and I'm a better man because of it. For a time I thought it was mostly African American men who were angry with a chip on our shoulders because (of a myriad of real, embellished and imagined reasons)... But having acquired a variety of authentic Caucasian (predominately female I confess) friends I've come to notice that most white boys (sometimes for the very opposite reason(s)) are just as hurt, bitter, insecure and as angry as blacks and browns. And we males confuse anger with masculinity. So the bigger, badder and the madder I can be the more man I think I am. But deep in my core it's a sham. I told you prisons are cesspools of anger. The guards and the guarded compete to be the angriest. But God says that "Anger rests in the Bosom of fools!" I am tired of fools. I have come (as commander in chief of G.B.G.) in "K.K.K." to make a citizens arrest! I came to arrest that anger. I keep coming back to it because it keeps coming back to you. I came to arrest your anger. Dr. Curren calls it an emotion. I call it a demon. Call it anything you want to call it but it's eating at your core. It's sapping you of your joy. Robbing you of your peace. It is destroying your relationships. And I arrest that anger. I apprehend that anger over your mind and your spirit. I pull you back and shoot you into your destiny. I see you becoming a man I see that shell cracking. You're getting your understanding back. And that anger is dying. The moment you recognize that it is crippling your freedom is within your view....

Churches are full of women and prisons are filled with men! Because the enemy knows are filled with men! Because the enemy knows if he attacks (imprisons, locks up and entangles) the foundation (man) he'll destroy the family and here are (I repeat) almost 3 million (but keep in mind that many of us drop-out dads father 4 and 5 kids so you gotta multiply x times 3 million!) Three million cracks in the foundations of American families! But in the foundations of (now) a dream! And if you are young God is giving you a vision! And II Corintians 5:7 tells you and me too that "for we walk by faith, not by sight." and it may seem (in different parts of this book) that I use "sight" and "vision" interchangeably. But don't be fooled a blind man can walk because we don't walk by sight... Faith is the substance of things hope for. How can you hope for a thing you have not pictured? Black convertible. Red convertible. Blue tooth brush...I assure you that you pictured a black convertible, a red convertible and a blue toothbrush as soon as you read it. You didn't see it but you envisioned (that's not "sight" bro.) it... And Faith is the evidence of things not (felt? Smelled? Known? no) seen...so we walk by vision.... The greatest gift to a man is his vision not sight. Visions enemy is sight! If you (this will cause a metamorphisis right now! if you get it!!) get caught up (defined, imprisoned and limited) by what you see you'll quit before you get the victory. When I said if you can see (I meant picture or image or visualize with your mental or spiritual eyes) it you can be it. I meant imagine, visualize and spiritually recognize...vision shows you what could be; sight shows you what is. Did you get that? Don't trust your eyes but fine tune your vision....Barack Obama won the presidency because he kept selling vision, dreams, change and hope. ...If my Harvard trained director (Dr. Franklin Curren) of my board of advisors. If my battery of expert psychiatrists and psychologists (Dr. Jennifer Heitkamp, Dr. Solis, Dr. Duran and Dr. Gregg etc.) ... If all of the correctional geniuses (including C.D.W. Terry L. Rosario, Fred, Steve and Warden Jimbo Walker etc.)...If my team of rivals (bloods, crips, skinheads, EME, etc.) accomplish nothing else etc. etc. If Senator John Burton, the family foundations, Leonardo Padilla, Senator Feinstein, Maxine Waters, Murray Janus and all or supporters accomplish only one thing with this book! It'll be worth every chapter, every page, every paragraph, every sentence, word and letter if we get you to recognize your need for vision!... With my Harvard led them I tell you that males with vision become boys. Boys with vision (discipline, education and spiritually) become men. Genitalia determines male ness. A male with a little game and the animal instinct becomes a boy. But I misspoke earlier by stating prisons are filled with men. But prisons are filled with boys who don't know how to be men. We have sight, but no insight or foresight. And our visions have been replaced with doubts, anger and with a nightmare. But I came to bring light. I bring light so that you can experience a spiritual oasis. Whether you believe in god (Allah, Budda, or whoever) I came to bring light. You could be (if you'd dare to envision and to see) a doctor, a lawyer, a teacher, a coach, a leader, an entrepreneur and a man (amen)! Vision is the source of confidence...with my sight I see what my physicians (i.e. Dr. Andrew R. Elms) have told me. "Your chances for survival for more than a year are limited. Meningitis is as serious as it gets Mr. Manning." That is with sight. With my vision I see G.B.G. having enough HEART (Helping To Educate At Risk Teens) to help Chris Mullennix's sons Nathaniel and Keith. Nathaniel Mullennix can become a recipient of stipends, scholarships and grants from G.B.G. in my vision. He's my homeboy! Chris raised him and Keith right. And the universe has aligned capacity and the mental apparatus to help operationalize the G.B.G. awareness campaign over the internet. I feel that in my vision. I have visions for employing the artistic expressions of Hossein AZIZ, Alex Seabolt and Chris Thompson. Vision tells me Leonard Padilla, Cameron Johnson, Jamie Fox, Robert Downey Jr., Michael Moore, Tyler Perry, Steve Lopez and Steve Barr will be involved. I sense the destiny of I. Hodges (at "California Family Fitness" in Natomas CA), Brad (at "Elite" in Sac town), Kyle Love, Pastor Billy, Zig Zigler and Emmet Freeman (in South Tahoe CA) being involved with our mission. There are people (right this very minute) who had no plan, no desire and no intention of ever getting on board with some so-called "prisoner" group. But when G.B.G. initiates the challenge by "calling all angels" to prevent the next "missing child." There are some students, parents and teachers at Beverly Hills high school, Lodi, Columbine, in Folsom, Jamie Costantino (Stockton), Michael Sanford, Daniel Sample, Schoen, Fedorov, Jeff Schroeder and Maxwell hanger who are going to line up to be a part of our HEART. I envision Dr. Thomas Bryant-Bryant, Dr. Gardere, Alex Effron, Teresa Payne, Emmet Freeman and John Simon climbing on board and telling Nate (the intellectual mechanix), Keith and Chris "I join". And we (G.B.G.) will continue to honor my vision for G.B.G. by never begging people for their money. And we (G.B.G.) will continue to bless (financially, socially and spiritually) and empower our ambassadors (and our special envoy i.e. Nathaniel and Keith Mullinnex, Perry Thompson, Garrett McCain, Matt & Jack, "d", Weston, Alex Hornbuckle, Chris and thousands of teens and tweenies all across the world. I envision (by faith) that the seeds which have been planted by promise keepers, Manpower, through T.D. Jakes, miles Munroe, Eddie Long and Noel Jones etc. are resulting in the vision of boys (in and out of prisons, schools and colleges etc.) and the dreams of men being restored! I have a vision that some of the word, the vision and the prophecy that some of the word, the vision and the prophecy which has been and is being preached by Jakes, Jones and Long is budding, blossoming and blooming right here right now.

My hair stands up on the back of my neck and my toes begin to tingle when I think (sight) of all the boys housed in jails, juveniles, and prisons who are just passing the time away. Their anger reverberates in the prisons and they've become radioactive and destructive. But because of an intensive personal reconstructive process spoken into existence by a T.D. Jakes, an Eddie Long and a Noel Jones when most pastors had abandoned prisoners. Because God would choose to use a Dr.Phil to help a con, a crook and a fraud (S.D.M.) to get real because a Paul Crouch was willing to listen to the voice of his vision. And TBN pumps the word into these dark and evil prisons. And because the entrance of the "word" brings light God sat back in Zion and used a big Ole, Bald headed black joker named Jakes. God birthed a vision in Jakes in West Virginia. God connected (my homeboy) Long with the 50 inch biceps with Jakes. And some kind a way God orchestrated the events of a long, a Jakes, a Jones... And (for the record for you seeing boys in the prisons etc.) I noticed that there is a common thread between these men...Long was homeless! Jakes digged ditches and was nearly homeless! Dr. Phil was a homeless son of an alcoholic. Paul struggled with addictions. Jones was abused in (a place of safety) church as a boy. And neither Jakes, Crouch, Phil, Jones or Long have ever ever heard of a nappy headed joker, born in Atlanta, locked up in California... named Sherman D. Manning. And even if I never meet or greet, Phil, Crouch, Jakes, Jones or Long. There is nothing that they can do to withdraw the hope, the power, the prophecy and the Vision that they have deposited into my mind, my soul and my destiny. Even at my lowest state...yes (ya'll can verify I ain't embellishing my testimony just to sell a book! Call Paul Griffin MD in Coalinga CA 559-955-5555) when Dr. Griffin told me I would die!!! At that juncture Dollie had not heard from me (Mark Merin, Stewart Katz, Keith Wattley?) in 9 months. P.V.S.P. refused to call her and... as I went in and out of consciousness I could see, hear, and feel T.D. Jakes sweating like a bulldog, preaching that "God" would "rearrange governments" because Dollie (in Atlanta) refused to stop praying for me. And my faith and my vision reminds me that no-thing just happens. And revival broke out at New Folsom and God brought me back to plant G.B.G./Heart. And when (ever) I die it won't die with me. I envision Nathaniel, Keith, Alex Chivescu, Shawn, Emmet and Ryan Rathjen have been awakened to a cause greater than a girlfriend... Empowering young minds with the "game", strategies, tools, awareness and the vision in this book is a mission like a magnet for teens and tweenies... and just in case Bishop Long, Bishop Jakes and Bishop Jones take a peek at this book. I want to tell you (on behalf of all of us at G.B.G.) thank you for letting the creator use you to impart light, visions and dreams. That's all I wanna say; thank you! ...And to my thugs (bloods, crips, skins, nuestra familia and shot callers etc.) in these prisons (with me) all over America I have come to bring light! ...I'm not gonna speak in tongues. I'm not going on a 30 day fast to get you (thugs) to get on board. This (G.B.G.) aint for everybody. Some of you boys with anger reverberating in your cell can go on and keep your shank. I hate to admit (real talk) it but the worse you (boys) are. The more men with vision (rising up in the prisons to coach our younger brothers) stand out and get noticed. The darker you are the more "kids (thinking about) killing kids" can see our light shining in the dark. A man is not measured by his physical ability to beat someone up. A man (i.e. Nate Mullinnex, Chris Thomason, Anthony and Alex etc.) is measured by his spiritual and mental ability to build something up... If you in jail and you still think you a man cause you can kick ass and take names. Do me a small favor and pass this book to another brother. I don't wanna waste your time cause I know you got people to beat and a cell(hell)to meet. Give this book to somebody else. You can throw it down if you want but the "cover" will pull somebody else...

I came to bring...I want you to close your eyes for thirty seconds and think of something that makes you happy. Do it now! Now whatever it was you thought of that makes you happy I want you to close your eyes one mo again and (for thirty seconds) think about it! Did you do it? Well the book ("K.K.K.") is a success! I said "think". I never said "see". So when you thought, if you "saw" you see how to have vision. And vision (brothers in the jail, brothers in C.Y.A. Brothers in juveniles, bruthas in the prisons, the suburbs, the hoods, the barrios and trailer parks etc.) is the ultimate key to bring you out! Vision is a magnetic, powerful and a mighty tool. Vision gives men a "there" to go to. Vision causes boyz to be men! Vision will kepp them in the early morning you will wake. Vision has caused me to spend many a night, writing and re-writing this book all night long...Dr.Curren, Dr. Heitkamp, Dr. Solis, Dr. Duran, Dr. Jarman, Dr. Jamie Davidson, Jimbo Walker, (Nicole's mom). Patricia Kennedy, Fred Schroeder, Steve John Vance and my entire G.B.G. team will rest better tonight if just one of you discover (or rediscover) ignite (or reignite) your vision. I promise you (every one of you in schools, in universities or wherever you are) that Scott Kernan, Matt Cate, Walker or Schroeder have never met a man who got locked up with "vision". Their entire careers have been spent guarding angry boys who often had collisions for lack of light (word) and lack of vision... Warden James Jimbo Walker looked at me and it seemed like I could feel him looking into the depths of my soul. There was power in this look and (come to think of it) he'd never looked at me in this way in more than twelve years. "Sherman you are working your ass off with this kids program. And I have a sneaky feeling ("vision") that some way, some how your dream will be realized... Mrs. Kennedy, Fred, Steve and all of us believe that kids all over America are going to hear, see and read about "Gang Bangers for Good" and the HEART program! Awesome!" I must admit I was wowed hearing this from the warden and then Dr. Jarman said to me "Sherman son keep on doing what you're doing!" Dr. Franklin Curren told me "Make it happen!" and as I was laying on my face before God it seemed like I could see Rev. Hosea Williams saying "It show took yo ass long enough to get into your destiny. You had to go through hell and high water. You took the long, by hook, fraud and crook-route but I'm proud of you. You are finally doing what you are supposed to do." And I started weeping. It takes a greater man to make another man great. And (in my vision) Rev. Hosea Williams was slamming on the brakes like Bishop Jakes. He was pulling his car to the side of the road. Rev. Williams was telling me what Bishop Jakes told Bishop Long "Don't call yourself a failure. You are somebody. You might be in prison but the prison is not in you and because of your vision. God is using G.B.G. to cause many youths to see"... I wept! I cried what Oprah Winfrey calls the ugly cry. I cried till (TMI?) snot ran and tears rolled. I felt a burden and a bondage lifting. And then I saw something in the spirit that made me understand what Paul meant when he said he saw (vision) some things so powerful he couldn't even write them down in the Bible. I understand the thorn in the flesh like I've never understand it before... all of my mistakes! All of my errors! My sins! My scams! My frauds! My weaknesses! My wickedness! All of my falls and my faults! No-thing just happens. Every trial and tribulation. All of my fears, tears, my hurts and my pains that I learned to transform into rage, ruin and anger. Not one bit of it could cause me to escape the destiny, that had been spoken into me, before my daddy ever met my mother. No matter how far away I ran from Ninevah I still had a "there down inside of me. And when valley fever sent a death angel to get me God told death to wait a while. He said "not yet" because "he still never got to "there." I left my home in Georgia I ran (from Ninevah) to Virginia! And when Ninevah came calling me in Virginia. I (literally) headed for the Frisco Bay. I came all the way to California (like Jonah) trying to get away from my Ninevah ("there"). But my journey has taught me how real (authentic) "you can run (from Ninevah) but you can't hide" is. I ran from Rev. Moses, Les Raglin, Rev.Hosea Williams and Ambassador Andrew Young because they kept reminding me of my ("there") destiny. I went as far away from Ninevah (literally) as I could get... And even while I was smoking and joking, laying and playing, carousing around at 2:40 am in Tarshish ("away from the presence of the Lord"). I declare that my "there" reached out and touched me and said "I got a whale (jail) prepared for you." And my "there" brought me to Hades and I promise you I was angry...I stopped talking to God! I stopped talking about God. I began (in the "prison") to live like God did not exist...And of all the people, a half white/half Mexican dude (Brian Thomas Cruz) moved in the cell with me and (out of the blue) he hooked up a wire to his T.V. and put it on TBN and (this half white and half Mexican dude) said "I want you to see my favorite preacher ("there") Bishop T.D. Jakes. We watched Jakes at 3:00 p.m. and Bishop Eddie Long (from my home) at 5:30 p.m. and my "there" started calling, and calling, and calling. And I ran and ran and I ran. And when life keeps punching you and punching and when vision ("there") keeps calling you and calling you and calling... You fellas who have fought or even wrestled with other brothers know what it means when you concede and say "I give"...

And laying up in that hospital room looking at Nurse Rose when she repeated "Dr. Griffin wants me to tell you that in his medical opinion you will die..." I went back to P.V.S.P. and insisted that they call Dollie and Dr. Ngvyn (Merin? Katz? Michael Bien? Masuda? Collins?) refused to give me the "oxygen" that Dr. Griffin wrote that I needed. And I battled with death and ("there") visions all night long. It was the longest, most traumatic, most painful and most terrifying night of my life... and as Jakes (I had no t.v., no books and no radio) preached to me and "there" called me. And I saw G.B.G. and I...told God that "I give". Thank you Jesus! I didn't say thank you Jesus! I didn't say thank you Jakes I said thank you Jesus! I told him "I give"... and I came to tell Alex Chivescu, Ryan Rathjen, Feddybear, Nathaniel Mullinnex, Emmet Freeman, Christopher Thompson, Benjamin Whipple, C.J., Zach, Ryan Hreljac, Shawn, Ben Cooper, Ben Alexander, Garrett McCain, Andrew Procknow (and your son), Andrew Knox, and Jonah Coleman etc. (and you too) your ("there")vision is calling you. The only reason you have this book in your bedroom, school or jail is because your vision (to be or not to see) is calling you. You do have a "there." And you're to stay in school or get back in you're to go to the library, bookstore or to synagogue or wherever. You are to walk into your destiny. Dope, Meth or booze won't get you there. You need your vision...can I tell you another secret that (if I didn't write it I'd think it was a Hollywood script!) will blow your mind? (I mention it in another part of this book) but your ("there") will always find you and God will send you witnesses to verify your destiny ("there")....Nurse Will is from Birmingham Alabama He happened to go to Atlanta (my hometown). And he happened to have a Chevy Tahoe and.... Nurse Latasha is from Jackson Mississippi and she happened to have a Chevy Tahoe. And she happened to go to Atlanta...will happened to take his (Alabama) Chevy to have it serviced. At the same time Latasha happened to take her (Mississippi) Tahoe to be serviced. They happened to both be travelling nurses and happened to marry....and they happened to attend Salem Baptist Church (Rev.Jasper Williams) and they attended New Birth Church (Bishop Eddie Long). And they happened to take a gig at a country hospital in Coalinga California where I happened to be dying... And so when I think about the fact that he loved me enough to send Will and Tasha to Atlanta! When I think that he loved me enough to feed them at Salem and at New Birth. When I reflect upon the fact that he flew them from Atlanta to Coalinga just to tell me that my "there" (Ninevah) was calling me I can't keep quiet! Yeah! Yeah! Yeah! It caves me to jump and to shout! It makes me pump my fist! I've got to clap my hands and stomp my feet! I'm not playing church but I've got something to shout about!! That's why I wrote this book! That's why we have G.B.G.! Not to get you to write a check or join a church. But to remind you thugs, you ganstas, you boys and men that you have a "there" to get to. You have a "vision" and a dream. You may only Clark Kent but you have a telephone booth (a "there") that you can go to. And when you get in your element (vision) nobody can defeat you in your element...You might be able to out "sing" Kobe Bryant. But he'll wear you out (in his element) on a basketball court. You might be able to out "dance" T.D. Jakes. But put him in (his element) a pulpit and he will preach you crazy! You be able to out "run" Aretha Franklin. But she can sing (her elements) the yellow pages and make a church go crazy... There is power, anointing, creativity, destiny and majesty in a man when he discovers his "there" and gets his "vision". I would that all of the facebook generation discover your "vision". Not your scam, not your plot and not your scheme (I'm an expert on schemology) but your "vision" will bring you out! Your vision will bring you out! Your vision will raise you up on mountains. Vision is the wind beneath your wings! This book is salted and peppered with seeds designed to cause you to unleash your creativity. This is a vision workshop! It is a seminar and a clinic to spark Reinvention Brainstorming sessions at Washington State University, Locke High Schools and at schools across the planet. My team and I have Ph. D in thugology and on the results of visionlessness. And we know the power of 'modelling'. (We've modeled and mimicked thugs, criminals and dope dealers for decades!) Ipso facto, in light of our darkness, madness and failures etc. (with a little prodding and direction from Harvard psychiatrists etc.) Ipso facto, simply reversing our mentality is a roadmap for intensive personal reconstruction. It takes energy to create energy. And light creates, motivates, stimulates and attracts light. Create, motivates, stimulates and attracts light. You will discover powerful "aha" moments, motivation, excitement and stimulation as you read this book right? But I want to warn you that this high (and it is a high! I'm high right now! And I don't drank, drug, smoke or chew; and don't hang around with them that do.) Will wear off. Motivation is like showering, it wears off. You must shower daily right? These "aha" moments and moments of clarity will wear off. But these strategies, methodologies (some of which I've gleaned from other learned minds and merely recalibrated it with a teen and tweeny twist.) And insights you're learning is potential power. Power is the ability to take action on what you're learning. I'm teaching an agricultural message to you metropolitan boys. But Nataniel, Keith, Christian and even Michael Sanford (and his frat bros. at Lehigh) must remember that this book is like a bucket full of seeds. If you go buy corn seeds today you won't eat corn tomorrow. You plant then you must watch them day after day. If you plant them, monitor them, feed (water) them you will produce corn! A whole lot of you have the problem I struggle (but I'm growing) with; the desire for instant gratification. If you plant great corn seeds today but insist on eating corn tomorrow. You will end up stealing (by hook, crook or scam) somebody else's corn. And it'll taste cool. You can kick back with the fellas and laugh about how easy you stole it. "Plus I still got the corn I planted that's gonna grow sooner or later." But actions plant seeds into the karma bank. And I get 3 million witnesses (i.e. G.B.G) that you will get caught! Even John Gotti got caught! Even John Gotti got caught! Ask Bernie Madoff won't you get caught….so your theft of someone else's corn will get you locked up. And you'll even miss out on all the seeds you did plant. Then your ass is in prison mad at Oprah because she won't do a show on the seeds you lost!!.. This book is a bucket of seeds and potential. Schools manufacture (or garden) seeds and potential. But successful gardeners learn to watch, water, fertilize and garden their seeds. You must take the seeds in this book and plant them in the garden of that great mind you have. Then garden, feed, monitor and water those seeds with patience, hope, creative visualization, goals, a plan and with enthusiasm. And if you take action on what has been planted the corn, the ideas, the vision and the dream will grow. You garden these informational and strategic seeds with positive self affirmations! Talk to yourself and tell yourself "I can succeed I do believe. I will develop my talents, skills and my intellect! I see myself going and growing." The most successful folks on the planet (Zig Zigler, Tony Robbins and the late W. Clement Stone etc.) mastered "self talk" they have learned how to talk to themselvesin ways that excite and ignite themselves… I repeat –this book is full of seeds. Dream seeds and vision seeds. Seeds to keep yo yo butt out of prison! But you must paint, tend and water these seeds. When you close the book to take a break you reflect (water and feed the seeds) on what you read. "I gotta listen to my instincts. Watch the eyes and body language. I've got to pay attention to my gut . If it seems too good to be true it is … if he looks eery, spooky or comes toward me I run, yell, scream "help" and scream "fire". Fire gets everybody's attention!... if girls call me "man pretty" like they do Ashton Kutcher, the boys (in the gangs in prison) are gonna want me to play pretty ("girl pretty") in the cell. "Talk to yourself. I've learned to brain wash myself with hope, enthusiasm, positivity and with faith. And when Courtney Kirkwood, Daniel White (Washington State Univ.) and folks like Mr. Hodges (CA. Fit. Ctr in Natomas) begin to sprinkle their seeds, plans and visions with faith, positivity, enthusiasm and with hope they'll discover a potent brew for success. These seeds contain the recipe for revolutionizing your life! …be certain to fertilize, water, watch and tend to the garden of your mind everyday! …Look-talk about seeds or potential etc. what if (i.e.) Nathaniel Mullinnex never hears about this book? Will he get the $250.00 stipend we can give him? What if Alex never hears about this book? Can he get a G.B.G/Heart scholarship? If David E. Kelley, Will Smith or Spike Lee never hear about "K.K.K." can they turn it into a movie? No! No! No! But if you (lots of y-o-u) will sit down with those seeds (potential) and plant them into Facebook, Myspace and the internet generation etc. If you take action(s) and e-mail, text mail, snail mail, and/or call people and say "Dude you are in a book called "K.K.K." etc." The moment you tell them they are in the book, you have their attention. Tell them the book's title is "K.K.K." and they are all in. And if you plant the seeds that leave a powerful digital footprint leading to G.B.G. and to "K.K.K." I see you being a part of a powerful team of doers. I see Ben Alexander, Ben Cooper, David Hankins, Alex Dugdale and even Justin Berry taking a leadership role in telling the world about the silent epidemic of nearly 600,000 foster kids. I see Brian Hawn, Chris Thompson, Sean Farmer and even Seamus Farrow taking a leadership role in using this book as a tool to educate fellow teens and tweenies about the muted epidemic of the sex slavery and the degradation of incarceration. The campaign (per se) will lessen the number of "kids killing kids" and (by definition) it'll reduce the number of kids going to prison...I want "Angelo", Emmet Freeman, Kyle Love, Ben Ownby, Gabe Williams, Timothy Coleman and Carlos Rodriguez etc. to participate in G.B.G. Heart outreach and prevention tactics; to prevent a Bret, a Devlin, a Stokes or a Garrido from victimizing, abducting and molesting them... My assignment for you is to begin daily to plant, water, tend and feed the seeds! Do you understand? ......You see the six periods after "understand"? Right before the six dots? I stopped at "understand" and gave the last fifty pages (up to the word "understand") to a 28 (youngster) year old psychologist (Dr. Houston) and asked him to critique it. I also gave it to a facility captain who doesn't want his name used. The captain said "I read all 50 ½ pages and I've read your other books. Dude this is your best writing ever. I'd let my sons read this stuff. I wouldn't want em (sic) writing you letters in prison. But I would want them to read it...I don't support what you wrote about C.O. Baker...Bunnell? No comment but don't use my name Sherman." ...Dr. Houston's opinion was urgent to me because A. He's young! B. He's brilliant and C. he is an avid reader! ..."Mr. Manning I read it all. First the negative." I got nervous...He said "As a reader I'd wonder if you didn't have some kind of deal with Bishop Jakes, Jones and Long. If I didn't know you as I do I'd wonder if they didn't ask you to promote them. That's the negative.... "I could live with that. For the record (I affirm) I've never met Jakes or Jones. And I'm pretty certain Long doesn't remember me. And as much as I love their preaching(s). I criticize each of them for not answering prisoner mail!! Dr. Houston convinced "Other than that suspicion I think it is awesome! Mr. Manning if you figure out a way to market and promote this book I can see it on New York Times Bestseller list... if I were you I'd make sure that Oprah, Tyra Banks, Larry King and all the talk show hosts get it. there is no other book out yet, like it. It will be a hit!" I was shaking when Dr Houston finished...

Marketing: I'm where Master P. was when he threw out the rule book and sold C.D.'s and tapes (Gorilla Marketing) out of the trunk of his car....Ipso facto, I'm (right now) commissioning youngsters to take an Amway or Herbalife approach to this book! I need college students, high school students, teachers, professors, pastors and the family members of prisoners to promote and sell this book. Students? If you devise a strategy (i.e. using Facebook, Myspace, Yahoo!, Ebay etc.) to sell this book etc. for every 100 books you sell we'll give you $150.00!! Period! You work it out and/or just have the buyer tell Cafepress that "Alex Chivescu told me about "K.K.K." We need all of you who say you have a passion for youth to tell others about this book....I want groups like "Recycled Percussion" (Manchester, New Hampshire) and "Living Things" to talk about "K.K.K" at concerts. I want clubs like "Uncle Charlies", the "Pyramid", "Twisters" (Richmond VA) and the "Limelight" in New York to talk about "K.K.K." If a few pastors like Rev. Timothy Flemming, Bishop Joseph Walker, Brandon Crouch etc. talk about "K.K.K." we will revolutionize the youth. I pray that Russell Simmons, Michael Moore, Tyler Perry and others will hear about "K.K.K." and put it in libraries, schools and the inner city. But I can't bank on them. I am taking a bet on Nathaniel Mullennix, Alex, Christopher Thompson, Kyle Love, Maxwell Hoch, Maxwell Hanger, Michael Shackelford, Jesse, John Simon, Alex Hornbuckle, Daniel Whife, Faisal Janjua, Vinny Deal, Gary Schaffer, Jessica Valeriay and Myshelle Hamlin. I believe students at Wakefield High School (Arlington, VA), Locke high and schools across this country can promote this book like Don King promotes boxing. This book is Tamiflu for spiritual swine flu. This is AZT for HIV. And I need you and you to tell somebody else to get this book.

A thirteen year old girl sent me a missive stating she is a prostitute...I gave her missive to a female pastor to respond to. She's too young to be a prostitute. I think she is a prostitot! And I adamantly oppose all prostitution period!

Derek King? Alex King? When Derek and Alex were 12 and 13 (in 2001) they murdered their dad in his sleep. They slaughtered him with a baseball bat. They went to prison and grew up in prison. They were recently released and G.B.G has reached out to them. (No reply at press time). Derek now says "If I define myself as a murderer and an ex-con that's all I'll ever become. I must move past it." He wouldn't specify way they did it but he did say "my anger kept building and building." And this is why I've written over and over about "anger". It can drive a 12 and 13 year old to slaughter a sleeping dad! "Anger" drove (I repeat) Willie Nessler (a child molest victim) to beat a man to death with his bare hands. Ipso facto, I'm commissioning a task force (led by my advisory board) on "anger" focusing on boys= preteens, teenies and tweenies. I'll update the task force findings in April, 2011 on Facebook. In the meantime I encourage boys and teens dealing with anger to log on to the Dr. Phil show and click on "Teen Talk". I shout out to D.J. Strong's mom in Seattle Washington. She made a sign and stands on street corners begging for money to send D.J. to college. "How could I not do it?" she says. "To me its automatic. You should go to the ends of the earth for your kids.".. I concur! And if D.J. is reading I have (just a small stipend) $250.00 to help you achieve your dreams! I also have $350.00 for the King Brother's trust fund!...I want teens to speak out at peace conferences etc (in his schools, churches and colleges) about G.B.G./Heart, non-violence and education.

You write your own destiny! You are the script writer of the film of your life and like Paul (or perhaps Saul prior to becoming an apostle) I sit on my perch in prison and I see great things in the future for Alex and Derek! I see marvelous success for Nathaniel Mullennnix, Keith, McCain, Hornbuckle, Simon, Jai, Shackelford, Redmond, Cameron, Gabe Williams, Tim Coleman and for all of you who will plant the seeds (you are a S.E.E.D.-Student Educating Elevating and Developing) in this book. If you will go get a book by Zig Zigler, Les Brown, Tony Robbins, Dr. Poussaint, Dennis Kimbro and W. Clement Stone etc. you will turbocharge.

The revolution which has already begun inside you. I see greatness all down in the marrow of your bones. I see great things Hairo Torres, Ship, Alex, Anthony Fedorov, Josiah Lemming, Cody Sheldon, kids at Ron Clark Academy, Washington State University, Green Dot Schools, at Christian Brothers High School, C.J. Sheron in Maryland, Dan David, Marcus Dixon, Hodges (CA. Fam.Fitness in Natoma, CA) Luke Sears, Brandon White, Brian Kennedy, Brian Walker (Denv. Colo.) and for all of you youngsters who will plant the seeds of this book. Plant the seeds your parents, teachers, professors and preachers give to you. You are a rising star no matter where you are. Your scars can be transformed into stars. Never give up on yourself of on your dreams. These can be miracles when you believe. Belief and faith unleashes some kind of an invisible force which propels you toward your destiny. This is a massive moment in your life. This is a chance for you to choose chaos or community. You can choose (today) to get (intimately) involved with an awareness campaign to demand action for the (nearly 600,000) foster kids in America! You can use your internet skills to promote "The Jane Doe No More" initiative. You can be your brothers keeper. Check out the Shawn Hornbeck foundation, www.napsusa.org, and deal with your anger....Study Cupcake Brown, Willie Gary, John Johnson and Earl Graves to see how/why they succeeded. I'm "Calling all angels! I won't give up! You don't give up!" This is your chance (Justin Berry, Ryan Hreljac, Christian Lawrence, kids at Biola University and at Lehigh etc.) to use your wall, your website, your cliques and your connections to help NAPS, G.B.G, the Shawn Hornbeck foundation and other groups. You are only a mouse click away...I'll see you Saturday at noon in prayer... Pay close attention to the missive to the president and to kids after that!! ...Andrew Lnn, Joe Wilson (Sacto), breakdancers in "No youth left behind" (we have something for "No youth left behind") ..."K.K.K." is a prescription for transformation written with (Harvard scholars, psychologists, therapists and gangbangers) for teens and for tweenies! Greg Deekins, Tadd Carr, Brenda Love and her son Kyle....I am a super salesman for G.B.G. and I need you to be supersalesmen for K.K.K. I wanna work with Travis (Travis at mygreenhouse.com), Billy Magnussen, Dillon Chase, Michael Rady, Tom Degnen, Josh Groban, Superintendent Johnathon Raymond, Attorney John Burris, and Josh C. Brown and father Michael Manning.....I want to operationalize some pilot programs to teach kids some basic "Face Reading" techniques taught by F.B.I. special operatives. I'm of the firm belief that we can't over teach or over educate our precious children. I want to present some of the methodologies (in this book) to Ron Clark Academy, Verone Kennedy and to Aaron Fernander. I also want our advisors to train some high school (i.e. Lodi High School, Folsom high, John F. Kennedy high and Locke high etc.) students and college students etc. And then send these students to do talks to kid 5-12 years old and these will be sort of Dr. Phil (Junior) get real talks for kids. Kids are extremely impressionable and they catch on quickly. I want them "role" playing and doing "show and tell". We must tweak their instincts. I believe we will see a beautiful explosion of awareness in grade schools if we all do our part. Prison is this weird social experiment that we must use to the advantage of citizens. If I were governor I'd require crooks (i.e. credit card scammers and hackers etc.) to advise the police, gratis. If you were a landscaper on the streets you'd be scaping land (gratis) in prison. You would work! Professional public speakers turned cons, turned master impersonators etc. (like someone we know intimately) would teach public speaking strategy, literacy and communications skills in prison!

How dare we allow prisoners sit on their hind pots (butt) and leech off of taxpayers? It's time for a change. And I won't wait on permission from public official nor will I engage in penological food fights. I will operationalize my plan, with the rights I still have (under free speech and with second and third) party to the internet...to activate plans to help kids. My plans will (by definition) be transparent and they will be subject (per se, due to my perch) to the scrutiny (as it should be) of law enforcement, psychiatrists and psychologists. However, I want to warn those who make a living off of crime and punishment not to try to deter my action plan with bogus fodder, innuendo, propaganda and general bull...I am not a politician! Ipso facto, I need no votes. Ipso facto, I'm already at the bottom. I'm considered scum, a thug a "felon". No scare tactic or smear campaign will deter me. People have every right to believe, disbelieve, entertain or ignore my work. But I don't have a right not to try or not to work. I am an American. I am an American! I am an American!....If Joe Wilson can be heard (a distinguished member of the U.S. Congress! Also Joe is Jim Crow Jr.) disrespecting our president by yelling "you lie." I can be heard telling our president "you" speak the "truth" when you say we all can serve! If Mike Duvall (distinguished focus on the family member goes to church every Sunday State California Assemblyman) can write laws and be heard in the assembly. While (simultaneously) touting himself as spanker in chief (of 19 year old female lobbyists etc. and I'm hearing Duvall was also into S&M and I don't mean Sherman and Manning!) on hidden Mike etc. Then my team and I can and will be heard in this place! And if attorney John Burris happens to take a look at Mike Bunnell, my valley fever, Marion, Brumbaugh and my PTSD etc. Burris might bring Bunnell, Tucker, Negrete, Marion and Yates to their knees! As a matter of fact (if Mr. Burris is reading) I will give Mr. Burris 50% (it's normally 35%) of any settlement! Plus I'll give 5% to the "Jane Doe No More" initiative! That leaves me with less than 45% for me and the tax man! I'll go one step farther (this is how bad I want them for pain, suffering, torture, cruel and unusual punishment! And for refusing to contact my family for 9 months. Allowing a crystal meth addict to work on me. Sitting outside my room betting on my death! And under RLUIPA for systematically denying me chapel access for 14 months etc!) I'll also give John Burris (or a Johnny Griffin, Don Masuda, Mark Merin, Michael Bein, Tony Serra, Tarlow, Mesereau etc.) ten percent of any movie rights as we sell (tell) my story! Mr. Burris (I believe in you!) if you want it you've got it! If not bring me Riordin, Brooklier, Wattley, Blair Berk or Brent Newell etc. Help me! Help!...

Linda McFarlane told me that over 60% of allegations of sexual abuse inside (male and female) jails, juveniles and prisons involve staff members rather than other prisoners. You all should re-read that sentence. It seems to me like lil girls and women in these prisons might need the Jane Doe No More Initiative, Oprah, Tyra, Robin Roberts or somebody...And one of the persons (few persons who fight to expose this silent epidemic) who helps in-custody rape victims told me that "prison authorities will fight tooth and nail to keep "K.K.K." out of prisons if you Cassie Pierson and legal services for prisoners with children...perhaps even Paul Wright and prison legal news etc.) will step up and sue my warden or official attempting to keep this tome out of prisons or jails. This book is not a threat to safety and security. No more than a newspaper, a magazine criticizing prison guards etc. and no more than eye witness news. Nothing in this book promotes violence against staff or violent uprising. I promote freedom of expression, artistic expression and (unlike Congressman Joe Wilson or Mike Duvall) civil discussion and litigation. Violence is never the answer! ...But guards (in my "opinion") like Sgt. John Sanders (at CMC East) ought to be exposed for raping inmates! Call 213-384-1400 ask Linda, Attorney Rothestein or psuyin who Sgt. Sanders raped... There is a silent epidemic of folk in positions of power (i.e. psychologists and guards etc..) like Dr. Marilyn Windham manipulating, coercing, and paying inmates for sex. Long before Dr. Marilyn Windham was discovered (reported) having sex with an inmate in a mop closet at C.S.P. Sacramento. She had manipulated and coerced Brandon Gene Martinez and this author for sex and "peep" shows. Her misconduct and rape(s) had been reported to Dr. Menutti who was (a brilliant man) felled by a brain tumor prior to completing an inquiry. ...C.O. Duclos was caught by Lt. Cherry (then a sergeant) while she sexually fondled inmate James Albert Emslander!... Upon learning I was transferring back to M.C.S.P. Duclos protested to Mike Bunnell (who called Marion E. Spearman and concocted a ploy to keep me away from M.C.S.P.) about my return. In a meeting Spearman, Brumbaugh, Lt. J.D. Bennett and Sgt. Martinez told this author "Duclos does not want you back at M.S.C.P." and Spearman stated "Your writing about staff sex including about me (A.W. Spearman) makes people not want you at they (sic) prison! Like that lil sexual situation between C.O. Mendez, C.O. Sawyer, Flores and you know who! Manning you can end up like inmate Walters and Watts if you don't stop writing bout this shit."... It should be noted that Walters and Watts are both dead.

I have watched and witnessed (with my own eyes) correctional officers (i.e. Wally Laffit, Wally Tucker, D.L. Criner, Menendez, Sawyer, Flores, Sgt. John Sanders and W. Brumbaugh etc.) commit sexual assaults and/or perpetrate sexually humiliating acts upon incarcerated inmate(s). And Spearman wanted to reach some type of "deal" for me to exclude him from this book. My reply to Marion E. Spearman is "we're not gonna negotiate or equivocate. It's not personal it's just business. You (Marion E. Spearman) are a cancer of wickedness which needs to be excised from C.D.C

...Furthermore, any implications that I have a vendetta against you (Spearman) merely based upon your sexuality etc. is preposterous. My reputation of being fair and unbiased toward gay, lesbian and bisexual Americans is unblemished and without taint!!"

I would hope that Cole Clemens, Mollee Gray, Christopher Aguilar (in L.A.), Vilma Leake, Melanie Oudin (my homegirl), Rachel Cameron and Yvonne Walker etc. will tell Carla Kettner, Craig Silverstein, Josh Berman, Taboo, Mario Lopez and Criss Angel. About "K.K.K."... on 9/10/09 (fifteen minutes into her show) Wendy Williams took a question from a white gentleman with sort of brownish red hair) about the Desperate Housewives of Atlanta. I want this gentleman (name unknown) to receive a G.B.G. stipend. And I want him as a special envoy in New York! (Hope Ben Alexander, Keith or Nate Mullinnex etc. will call Wendy's producers and find him)...I want students at Chapmen University and out at Lehigh to get this tome. I'm "calling all angels" and I need you all to use your mouse to inform students at Lehigh, Locke, Duke, Lodi, Emory, Pepperdine and Purdue etc. about this book. Put the word out to students and professors at Washington State University etc. that we mention them in "K.K.K." I want to reach out and touch Jake Heartsong (in Pensacola Florida), Kevin Shelton, Joe Klein (West Hollywood) and even Bob Heartsong and tell them about this tome.

Ralphe Bunche principal Aaron Fernandez wrote: "The temptation (for some "principals") will be to think "K.K.K." too incendiary a title for kids but my experience as an educator for 30 years is that whenever we (as parents or adults etc.) attempt to shield a book, a film or a C.D. from kids it only promotes whatever we're attempting to hide. I think "K.K.K." is a marvelous book for teens." This book is not a silver bullet against gangs and predators etc. But if it plays a small part in preventing the bludgeoning of one kid it is worth it! If just one teen (like "Angelo" c/o the Sierra Adoption Agency etc.) trapped within America's 600,000 foster kids gets support etc. the book is worth it. If this book shines such a white hot spot light upon the violence perpetrated against teens in prison(s) and prevents one kid from going to Hades it is worth it. If one child, teen or tweenie learns to read faces, watch eyes, listen to their instincts and to feel their gut etc. This book is worth everything we've put into it. The sleepless nights, tears, prayers, isolation and the frustrations etc. They are worth everything that has been put into it... I need youth (Ben Alexander, Brandon White, Kris Stump, Christian Nelson, Nate and Keith, Hreljac, Chris Thompson, Luke Sears, C.J. Sheron, Kyle Love, Dillon Chance, Josh Groban, D.J. Strong and Chris Durbin etc. to help us get this book to attorney Barry Maxwell, Derek Cressman, Alex King and to Derek King. I want you (Andrew Bridge, Christopher Guzman, Cole Clemens etc. to be Hip (Having Intellectual Power) as we use G.B.G./Heart and "K.K.K." to heal HIV (Having Insufficient Vision) in schools all over this earth. If you (Ben, Keith, Nathaniel, Christian and Alexus etc. my hometeam) will help us to get this book into the hands of lawyers like Robert Waters, Stewart Katz, Mark Merin, Barry Maxwell, Tony Brooklier and Tony Serra etc. The sky is the limit as to what we can do. (special note: If you hear of any prisoner being disallowed this book contact the prison law office, local NAACP, ACLU, "Stop Prisoner Rape", Keith Wattley and/or Atty. Mark Merin...Also contact prison legal news and tell them inmates are being denied these constitutional rights! The more copies of this tome we get in jails, juveniles and prisons etc. the better! ...We support free speech, artistic expression as well as non-violence!) ...I'm calling on James Drake (and his teammates at Sheldon High School), Mario Lopez, Travis (at mygreenhouse.com) and Zach Freisen to help spread the news about this book...Assemblyman Jeff Miller (lied) claimed that he "forgot" what Mike Duvall was saying when Duvall was caught on tape admitting (to assem. Miller) to having sex with and "spanking" a 19 year old. Miller claimed "I don't remember what Duvall was saying." And Miller is on the Ethics Commission. Small wonder such inattentive (deceptive, crooked, corrupted) lawmakers can't pass a timely budget and can't clean up "corrections". And when a hillbilly redneck like Joe Wilson, a forgetful (unethical) Jeff Miller and a spanker (Mike Duvall) can propogate their opinions etc. Yes, I deserve to be heard. And I (in spite of Marion E. Spearman, Brumbaugh, Tucker and D.L.Crine etc.) insist on being heard. I want students at Pleasant Grove high school, Archer/Harper, Northside High and at Palmer high school to hear me too. I've come to bring sight, vision, awareness and candor. I hope Lisa Israel, Judy Smith, Jacob Heartsong, Daniel Job, James Nesmith, David Quindt and even Jeff Glen Howell will help us put this powerful book in the hands of many! ...I dedicate this tome to No.12 on the football team (and to the entire team) at Oakmont High School. I dedicate it to students at Whitney, Davis and at Galt High School. We send this tome to every student at Yale University in New haven CT. And I want the student who wears No.12 at Oakmont High (in CA) to help us tell Yale (on Facebook) that "K.K.K." is out! G.B.G./Heart shouts out to all the great students at Bella Vista high school and we draft football players (i.e. Marques) like Brandon to become Broncos for G.B.G. and we also invite every student at Rancho Cordova high school to get involved today... I want folks like Casey Chapman, Ruehl, Brandon Gilda, Char Ghio (A.D. at River City High) wtc. to get involved with our Heart Programs. We support Colusa, Maxwell, turlick, Oakdale, Ripon Christian, Roseville, Pioneer, Dixon, Antelope, Kennedy, Delta, Downey, Bear River, Capital Christian, Chico, Pleasant Grove, Rocklin, Grant, Beyer and East Union High school students. We applaud Modesto Christian, Sheldon, Union Mine, El Dorado high schools coaches, players and students. And I believe in the power of sports to teach teams and teens life coping skills. Kids at Fort Hill High School, Mr. Will Brown (principal), Weston Ranch, Florin High and Ceres high should all look into our stipends, essay contests and our student ambassador programs. Tokay high, Summerville and Yuba City high students as well as Golden Valley high students and staff are invited to get involved with our fledgling grants and stipends. We intend to jolt football players, cheer leaders, band members as well as pep squad. Prisons are filled with ex-football players, boosters and coaches. And we intend to flex our muscles and touch the nerves of the Joe Wilsons and Mike Duvals of politics. We offer a pragmatic approach to politics. We encourage kids to run for public office. We will support 18 and 19 year olds who run for public office. We went teens and tweenies to establish platforms to address wrongful convictions, rapes in prisons and the treatment of youthful offenders by Americas Judicial System. I encourage principals like Will Brown (at Foot Hills high) to join Aaron Fernander, Verone Kennedy and other principals and discuss these (real life) G.B.G./Heart issues with students who are headed (rapidly) into the real world.

If they can drive a car at 15, join the Marine Corp at 17 and launch military bombs at 18 etc. They can read "K.K.K" as teens and as tweenies. They are intelligent enough not to agree with my writings (and opinions) on every single issue. I hope they disagree with Glen Beck, Hannity, Coulter and Limbaugh on some issues. I certainly don't expect teens, parents and professors to concur with me on all issues. And I argue in support of kids rights to dissent and to disagree... even with me.

I want to hear the voices of Christian Norton, Shannon Murphy, Nathan Fletcher, Lionel Woodyard (Atl. GA), Brandon Gilda, Rachel Cameron, James Drake, Anthony Carabella, James O'Keefe and Christian Nelson etc.. And my duty is to tell the truth (as I see it) from my vantage point. Always influencing youths with truths to steer them away from Hades... Chris Brown forces me to revisit him. He had the audacity to tweet that Wendy Willams looks like a man. A. He must not know about the large Wendy Williams prison Fan Club. B. My cohorts and I view Chris Brown as effeminate (Kutcher would say "man pretty") and girlish. I have no doubt that the fellas at L.A. County Jail would dress Chris up at look as womanish as Wendy (who is all woman!) in jail. And Chris would be somebody's girl in prison. He's proving to be a bully of women. And I encourage all real ladies to run from sissified, violent and assaultive boys like Chris. And if he ever comes to prison. I know some (non-G.B.G. because we are non-violent!) convicts who want a formal, vocal apology from Chris (for Rihanna, Madam –o- and for Wendy)! ...

As quiet as it's kept the culture of this runs rampant in D.C. politics (as well as in Sacramento etc.) is more corrupted, rampant and wide spread in prisons. The Dr. Marilyn Windhams of C.D.C are myriad! Go ask c.o. Linda Forte (pay no. 1326) about psychologists Lumpkin and Martin at P.V.S.P Both Dr.Martin and Dr. Lumpkin use the C.T.C. as a "My own private Idaho" type of infirmary. Dr. Lumpkin and Dr. Martin are known sexual predators. Both of them routinely sexually fondle inmates in C.T.C Dr. Lumpkin is known as a freaky deaky. C.N.A. Ashley and Carmen both allege that Lumpkin has fought civilian child molestation charges. I'm not certain about those allegations but I know Dr. Silverstein, Dr. Bruce Bakeman, Dr. George and Dr. Murphy have all received complaints about Dr. Lumpkin and Dr. Martin's sexaal escapes with demented inmates, in mate workers and patients in C.T.C... But with D.L. Criner and Gail Crooms working (sporadically) C.T.C. and with Marion E. Spearman covering for Lumpkin and Martin etc. small wonder sexual crimes against inmates get swept under the rug... I'll make sure Spearman gets you transferred (i.e. Donavan, Pelican Bay etc.) and murdered if you mention the sexual complaints against me "Dr. Martin stated. And Dr. Hoffman was with him.

I wish I could get a Flamboyant Mississippi Lawyer like Dennis Sweet to come to California and sue Attorney Sweet would deliver a bone crushing defeat to these backwoods gay cowboys... Dr. Martin, Dr. Lumpkin and Marion ought to do a cheer. They should chant "say it loud we gay and we proud!" (pun intended!) ... But these people are vicious, violent, vindictive, powerful and they are deeply entrenched within the anus of c.d.c. to California kids I say stay away from prison. By any means (legal) necessary... I want you kids to remember that this book is not about you believing everything I believe. I am a flawed man. The most urgent task for this tome is to heal your H.I.V.(Having Insufficient Vision).I want you (like my niece Jazmyne of whom I'm very proud! And like my sweet niece Ke Ke) all joining "upward bound" and other extracurricular groups that help elevate your minds. I want you boys to stay out of juvenile, jail and prison by any (legal) means necessary. That is the main goal of K.K.K. !

A buddy of mine made fun of me when I told him I speak well of John Walsh in this book. "I won't read it"he said. "What has John Walsh did for me?" He asked. I replied "Walsh has done a lot for me. Since I have two beautiful sisters (Shanteeka and Shanteecia) on the streets. Since I have a daughter (Kimberly), a son, a wife etc. I am glad he locates murderers, rapists and molsters! I salute John Walsh! We may disagree on a variety of issues but John Walsh won't get a disagreement from me for shining a white hot spot light on predators!" He almost choked. But be advised this same bother supports Chris brown fully. And he feels Rihanna deserved what Chris did... No man should ever hit a woman. Never! When a woman hit me I restrained her when she got out of hand I ran! Period! If James Scott Manning or Dollie caught me doing what Chris Brown did they would attack me and disown me. Chris Brown is a chump!

And (hear me) I'm tired of the media acting like politicians and celebrities are off limits and not to be questioned. I want to see the media call politicians (and celebrities) who prey on people sexually –what they are! With the same disdain that we talk about that bastard Phil Garrido...

You all recall congressman Gary Condit! It still believe he paid the straggler to murder Chandra Levy. In my opinion Gary Condit is a murderer! That's only my opinion. But I know for a fact that Gary Condit snorted cocaine and he's a rapist. As you read about my own "bad boy "behavior in the "Confessions of a Conman" section of this book you'll see I lived in the D.C. Virginia area for a long time. I wined and dined with movers and shakers. And I saw the kind of unspeakable crimes that Rev.Hosea Williams and Ambassador Andrew Young warned me about. At a party that some couriers from Dupont Circle took me to D.C. I saw Gary Condit snort cocaine. And a young 18 year old girl told him "you raped me" and Condit replied " you wanted it"…

The ex.mayor of my hometown Mayor Bill Campbell was a well known cocaine addict. I watched Bill snort lines of cocaine. Bill is another one of those politicians who who are on "pipe" (not crack) but "men". He frequented "blacks", "backstreet" and the "armory" in Atlanta. I never personally saw him have sex with a man. But I saw him snort coke. And Bill Campbell was a known crook and known to frequent gay clubs…

Congressman Mike Pence is as gay as a $3 bill. Mr. Pence is known to pick up male hustlers in D.C. He used to frequent the "frat" house. "Mr. P's"and "the Chesapeake house" in D.C… Mr. Zell Miller? Ex. Governor of my home state of Georgia? A known cocaine abuser, womanizer and an under case racist. I knew Zell well and he is as wicked as hell…

California: Mike Duvall? The teenage woman spanking is but a tip of the iceberg. I am told by a person who spoke on the condition of anonymity due to being unauthorized to speak on this matter. The sources claims that Duvall is known to have sexually assaulted a number of teenaged females. And due to his deep connections, wealth and power he has evaded prosecution without a scratch. It is sin and a shame what politicians are allowed to get away with because of their status. I would hope that private investigations, persons with cell phones cameras etc. will begin to follow these politicians when they leave the Capitol . I f the public thinks it's just Condit, Marion Barry (who I like) , John Edwards and Duvall. They are Bozo the clown philandering drug abuse and wild sex runs rampant amongst politicians many of them (Condit, Pence, Duvall etc.) are scumbags, deceptive and perverted hustlers!

I'm convinced that the reason a murderer, a gang member and a violent man like A. W. Mike Bunnell was able to keep his job after he killed or had Doug Pieper killed etc. is because of Bunnell's "good ole boy" ties to California politicians period!... C O. Pieper (at P.V.S.P.) lives in fear of his life (because he has the "Pieper" name and blood). And he fears Bunnell could have Mrs. Pieper and Doug Pieper slaughtered … One powerful inmate gang member at P.V.S.P. stated to me "Atl." I have 4 years left. After what Bunnell did to me at M.C.S.P –when I get out I'll get my crew to murder Bunnell… Believe that I do not agree to him "hitting" Bunnell. Violence is not the way ever!As I reflect upon all of Marions Lies, Cruelty and abuse administered by the hands of Marion. I am surprised some ex-con has not murdered him… I say don't bother him physically. Go to zalasearch.com and get Marion E.Spearman's add. d tele… Put the data on my (personal- G.B.G.does not support my decision). But I want people to conduct telephonic warfare by calling him. Then show up at his house to protest and to yell (nonviolently) at Marion for stealing the the spirit and hope of the inmate…

I've heard for years that Rush Limbaugh not only abuses prescription drugs. My New York source claims Rush abuses cocaine. I know Ann Coulter uses cocaine and Ann approaches politics with a "casting couch approach. My contacts allege (and it is authentic) Ann is a master fellatio artist… When I debated Sean Hannity (the first time) in Atlanta he used coke at the station police chief T.J. Scipio, ex. Police chief Eldrin Bell, (APD Ralph Batts and ex.Dekalb narcotics officer Mike Scanrick etc) and (radio host) "Ralph from Ben Hill" can all attest to the fact that Sean Hannity was busted having sex with a male hustler, in Atlanta, in the 90's and Sean Hannity had street drugs on his person and Sean Hannity was let off the hook. He bribed the cops … and Attorney Mobley Childs got a "possession of child pornography" charge "fixed" and expunged from Seans record!I know I'm right .ask Atty. Steed Scott, Atty.

Victoria Little or ex. Special Agent Alexander Hamilton about Sean Hannity. He is a self absorbed, coke head, perverted homosexual with pedophile tendencies. And the main stream media gives there guy a pass. They don't and won't write about it. And it is this type of media bias, hypocrisy amongst "so called" role models etc. This has turned our kids against politicians and celebrities. The reason we've lost respect for even the presidency (much to my dismay) is because the same kids (which a few will try to persuade not to peruse a tome written by a felon etc.) who hear us talk north, watch us walk, west. How does a 14 year old kid feel watching America's brilliant, shining first African American President speak. And seeing some stomp, jumping, tobacco chewing, hillbilly, red neck yell out "you lie". Yet Joe will teach parliamentarian rules at schools to kids... In an ERA where a sitting Governor Elliott Spitzer rides to office on the backs of pimps, prostitutes. And dope peddlers whom he prosecuted (and waged a crusade against) as Attorney General. Then he's caught with his hand (or private) in the proverbial "cookie jar". This causes kids to feel betrayal on the highest level of their lives candidly. The more Spitzer's, Sandfords, Campbells,delays, Cuminghams, Abramoffs, Madoffs and Duvalls who get busted , caught, disgraced and/or jailed etc. The more relevant are the future. You can make your school, your college, your city and our world better greatness and destiny are inside of you. I sense destiny inside of you. I sense an awe and a spark inside of you. You Joe Kennedy (third), Matthew Kennedy, Connor Briard, Zack Hall, Matt Berry, Garrett McCain, Alex Hornbucke and Kyle Larson are world changers. And my goal is to climb down inside your minds and to motivate you to succeed.

I have a hole in my heart which has driven me to write the hole compels and inspire me to break away from the norm and to will my way forward. My task is to find, train, inspire, lead and to incite you into your destiny. I want John Fink, Tadd Carr, Christopher Krinkie, Anne Salisbury and Isaac Grimes to press forward. I want kids at Palmer High School, Jonathan Matheny,Alex Blench, Sean Swales and Ian Manshum to help spread the G.B.G.mission. It will be up to you all (Nathaniel, keith, Alex etc.) to get this tome to Jeffrey Lurie, Aaron Carter, Derek Hough, Omar Samaha and to bloggers. I need Brett Jilliff, Attorney Megan Corcoran, John Simon, Atty Marc Grossman and Attorney Timothy Kent Hobbs to know this book is out: I need Att. Michael Alder, Judge Thelton Henderson and Judge Lawrence Karlton to know it is out. I have called out some extremely dangerous thugs in this book. And Mike Bunnell, Spearman and those other miscreants are vindictive. So I need you all to be vigilant!... C.D.C. is an empire run by mostly thugs. If Mr. Obama saw the level of entrenched corruption violence, racism and the hate groups within C.D.C. he might elect to shut down C.D.C. Before he shuts down Gitmo. How dare C.D.C. allow a racist thug like Sergeant R. N. Saunders and Lt. Stephen Luke Scarsella to work in C.D.C. ?

How dare Sgt. K. Scott (a bonafide member of a racist hate group!) propagate racial hatred via the "son of odin" at P.V.S.P. ? These guys (Sgt. K. Scott and his crew) are racist, wicked and backwoods enough to try to assassinate Mr.Obama. I mean that: I have heard Sgt. K. Scott (before Barack won) state "I'd hang him if I got my hands on him"... Lance Corcoran is a known cocaine abuser. Lance Corcoran defends the likes of Mike Bunnell and Marion... Chief Deputy Warden Max Lemons testified before the State Senate that he had "walked prison yards with rapists, molesters and murderers ". But he was more afraid of "Bunnell, Corcoran and Mike Jimenez than he was of prison inmates! Mr. Lemon had 24 hour armed guards because he feared retaliation by the guys in green (correctional officers!) ... Again I say google Mike Bunnell... small wonder I've had books stolen by staff. They steal letters, photos, letterhead etc. etc. In violation of my constitutional rights to free speech and artistic expression. These backwoods, hillbilly and Jim Crow Jr. rednecks don't understand "son of sam". You don't quench my speech because you disagree with me. You don't steal a photo because you dislike it. This is the United States of America. And no Joe Wilson you don't yell out simply because you disagree!

The CCPOA (in my view)is a Mafia like organization filled with drug addicts. The CCPOA President is an undercover homosexual and a speed head. Mike Jimenez hired a paroler under the guise of wanting to rehabilitate him. The only thing Jimenez wanted to rehabilitate was his... blank – blank Jimenez had sex with this paroler. And they had wild sex together! And they did crystal meth. And thanks to Jimenez enabling him he returned to prison! Lance, Mike,and the CCPOA have been complicit in setting me up and transferring me to P.V.S.P., C.M.C. etc. And now they want me at Donavon. I have "hits" on me by inmates staff refuse to document (i.e. "launch pad", "raven" P. Brinson, Etheridge and at least 30 other guys. Including the ex-parolee who worked for Jimenez...). I have staff who want me d-e-a-d! Due to my outspoken criticisms of this monster factory. New Folsom has very few programs but (thanks to Cheryl K. Pliler, Terry L. Rosario, CC(third) Patricia Kennedy, A.W. Jeff Macomber, Tim Virga and A.W. Johnson-Dovey etc.etc.) it's safe for me. It would be fair for Governor Arnold, Gloria Romero, Rod D. Wright, Kernan, Hubbard and Cate to D.R.D. me to New Folsom State Prison... I need my readers to call (510-271-0310) Attorneys Keith Wattley, Thomas Master, Alexis Wilson Briggs, Michelle Iorio and ask them to ask Scott, Matt, Gloria and Rod to D.R.D. me to New Folsom! (www.theuncommonlaw.com) . If any inmate is being denied a copy of this book(which is no more of a threat to safety and security than "nation" newspaper or the Sacramento Bee Newspaper etc.)call Alexis! Call(510-280-2621)Attorney Donald Spector, Susan Christian and Millard Murphy. The prison law office fervently defends my right to free speech so does F. Lee Bailey. I imagine that if you all call Attorney Floyd Abrams, James Brosnaham, Gerry Spence, Willie Gary orTony Serra they will all file amicus briefs in support of my free speech. Call the ACLU (202-393-4930)... They will defend my free speech on principle... Call Barry Scheck (212-364-5340). Call Murray J. Janus (804-143-1400)... No inmate shall be denied this book merely because I call out C.D.C. officials for the thugs that Max Lemon, James Mattocks and the courts said they were, and I say they are. I adamantly oppose inmate on staff, staff on inmate and/or inmate on inmate violence. I say (and write)over and over to never use violence to advance your cause. Murderers and molesters like Bunnell, Spearman, Scott and Corcoran don't fear violence. They have machine guns...They fear scribes, litigation, information and organization... My death will make me a martyr. I'll never get the glory in life that my story will get in death. But I'd rather die on my feet than live on my knees. Nelson Mandela did not serve 27 years in prison for me to live on my knees. Dr. Martin Luther King Jr. was not assassinated for me to muzzle my opinions. Andrew Young, Julian Bond, Vernon Jordan,Rev. Hosea Williams ("unbought and unbossed") and John Lewis did not endure beatings, bites, batons and water hoses for me to allow I.S.U. to manipulate my rights and prevent me from being heard... Mr. Willie Brown believes in my right (as an American)to be heard.

I equate the CCPOA to the Taliban and they need to be rectified forth with... G.B.G. supporter John Burton is now the chairman of the California Democratic party! Kudos! And he was speaking two weeks ago about the so-called Boston Tea Parties taking place... "How dare these idiots disrespect the President of the United States" Burton stated "these idiots have the audacity to compare our President to a Nazi and they're questioning where he was born "etc. Burton continued "calling President Obama a communist makes me think they must be smoking tea rather than drinking the tea!" I love Mr. Burton. He reminds me of Rev. Hosea Williams. And Mr. Burton supports the G.B.G. Mission. He does not support or concur with all of my opinions, beliefs or writings. But I'll betcha Mr. Burton, Willie Brown, Donald Specter, Atty. Richard Seltzer and Robert Waters support my American right to express (non-violently) my opinion! I am somebody! I am an American.

...And I will continue to speak out and speak up for a variety of people. I am not a Caucasian. Yet, I argue forcefully for the thousands of Caucasian boys raped inside the Los Angeles County Jail every year. We need to shine a white hot spot light on L.A. County Jail. It is the Abu Ghraib of American jails. Go ask Jason Sutherland, Ricky Sweet or Juan Sanchez about L.A. County Jail. Scared white inmates slit their wrists and hang themselves to get out of L.A. County Jail... I.S.U., Lance Corcoran and Gary Condit don't give a darn about the young white males raped in L.A. County Jail so why not me? I am pleading with Tyra Banks, Lisa Ling, Laura, Dr. Phil, Bev. Smith, Tavis Smiley or somebody to do an intensive/extensive story on the nightmare of being young white and locked up at L.A. County Jail. You are an "endangered species." I want Paris Hilton, Martha Stewart, Richard Scrushy or somebody to say something.... John Dannenberg, K.Chandler, Don Samuel, Steve Smith, Dennis Sweet, Bloggers, students, activists etc. "There but for the grace of God go I" into the L.A. County Jail as a Caucasian male! Steve Lopez, Andy Furillo, Benoit-Denizet Lewis speak... attorney Larry Hopkims, youth law center (San Franciso), Van Jones, Rose Braz etc. Speak up to and for the rape victims trapped inside of L.A. County Jail.

Where is the outrage from judges and from prosecutors? How dare a D.A. stand up and argue for victims of rape who are (i.e.) prostitutes etc.? Because "even a prostitute does not deserve to be "raped." But these same prosecutors will (and do) turn a deaf ear and a blind eye to white boys who are penetrated, traumatized, sodomized and victimized in L.A. County Jail every day of the week? I repeat: Read "Fish" by T.J. Parsell. I repeat: Call Dr. Terry Kupers in San Franciso. Call Linda McFarlane at "Just Detention."

I'm calling Attorney Kyra Kazantzis, James Zahradkai, Gerry Spence and Rose Braz (not for me) on behalf of each and every 15-28 year old white make in L.A. County Jail... After Stewart Katz or Mike Meria sue C.D.C., P.V.S.P. and Bunnell for me they ought to file a class action law suit for every Caucasian-aged 15-28 in L.A. County Jail. The jail (per se) is a clear and present danger to every white guy. And the PTSD alone is enough to require compensation!

...I want every G.B.G. member, supporter and student to please (public service) send an email, post a blog or a tweet or write a missive to Nancy Pelosi, the media and/or to President Obama about the state of emergency for white inmates at L.A. County Jail. Write Lisa Ling, Dr. Phil and Tyra today! I demand action!...Captain Scott Jones (at Sacto County Jail) is a Bunnell. Captain Jones set inmates up to be raped as punishment! Jones is also known to be into kiddie porn! Where is Rush Limbaugh, Ann Coulter and Hannity? Why are they not drinking tea and partying about the $ hundreds of billions dollar failure of the American penal system?

Let's drink tea, wear a sign and yell out "you lie" to every U.S., State and local legislator who will lose sleep about Abu Gharib and stay up late figuring out how to shut down Gitmo...But who are sleeping well (right now-this very minute) while white boys are raped in L.A. County Jail!! I know I.S.u. and prison authorities are brainwashed into suspecting every move I make as sinister, manipulative and as suspect. So be it! But...what could my "Angle" possibly be for pleading with Tyra banks, Tom Joyner, Tavis, Charlie Rose, Moyers, Brian Williams, Lisa Ling and....to please take a closer look at what it is like to be young, white and male in L.A. County Jail?

I know T.J. Parsell, Linda and everybody at "Just Detention International" will stand with me in my unified call to shut down L.A. County Jail, release every white male or protect them while they are in jail. Rape is not a part of the penalty! Paris and Martha can you say amen? Dateline, Sixty Minutes, 48 hours, 20/20 and Nightline where are you? Rape is not a part of the penalty! ...

Youngsters: Prison is a bad place. It is filled with duplicitous, bitter, angry, evil, and broken boys. What can go wrong will go wrong in prison. (Keith Morrison? Hollaback) I told my mom "You'd think I'd be used to it by now." And she replied "if you ever get used to it then you are broken also." I am still amazed by the Hearts of Stone which I see and live with everyday. Guys running around with college "books" but bitter souls. They have lied, cheated, angled and envied for so long that even if Jesus Christ walked in here (in the flesh) they'd hate on Jesus and accuse him of rape.

These are ragged men. They'll never love you or me because they hate self. These are scumbags who are rotten to the core. The sin, the hate, the lies, the anger is bone, spirit, heart and soul deep... If I get sweaty and begin to smell a bit I can jump in the shower and soap will clean me up. I can use deodorant and spray on cologne and I'm good for a day. But if I have a sore or a wound and it is open, infected and smelly. I can shower but the smell won't leave because an infection is bone deep...the gents I live with (many if not most) are rotten to the core. You can't wash this madness away with soap. Bring me some gasoline and a match and I'd have to burn the place and the people down...Pathological and chronic lying is rampant in prisons. People tell one lie to cover another. And will look you straight in your eyes and tell you how much integrity, honor and loyalty means to them. It is a cesspool. I'm getting to the point that when certain individuals come around me and occupy my space I feel a heat of anger and sin. I don't wanna go too deep into it (demonology) because people get scared when we write about Lucifer as a being in people but suffice it to say that prisons give vent to satanic forces and we are a door way for the devil. Everybody is mad, upset, angry or envious of somebody for some reason. Everyone of us in here is trapped in a burning house (Hades) but we'll never get out. Because we are too busy hating one another. We are lying on, stealing from and setting each other up. So busy fighting each other that we have no time to look for an exit. We are so busy making evil deposits into the Karma Bank that when the karma truck parks in our front yard with H.I.V., aids, cancer, a life sentence, our ladies leaving us etc. we wonder why?

We are so under developed spiritually that we have the temerity to think that I can lie on you, abuse you, set you up, hurt you for no legitimate reason(s). Refuse to admit it. Refuse to seek repentence from God and man and yet wonder-why I'm gonna "die in prison".

I say to every wicked, woman beating, Chris Brown supporting, racist, bigoted, classist, duplicitous, cold, vicious and heartless convict (we who are here) that we deserve to be neglected, forgotten and abandoned by society. I don't blame them for overlooking us. If we are so demented, so hateful, so spiteful, so mean, angry and envious that we'd rather kiss a prison guard's ass than shake a fellow convict's hand etc. We ought to die here. These guards earn $70 grand (and some over $225 grand) per year and go home every night. But I'll run into the chow hall and slave (for $.18 per hour) for the po po. I'll cook the "boss man" cheese burgers and fries. And all but feed him. But I charge my fellow captive inmate. Because I've been programmed, hypnotized and brainwashed to take from my fellow prison mates but give to the "master." If you wear blue (and are locked up too) I'll charge yo ass for a bag of frozen water (ice!). It doesn't cost me a damn thing but I just don't feel right bringing you a bag of ice or a burger for free. But the minute that dude in green asks me for a burger I'll give him two. I'm brain dead. I'm so lost I may as well walk around with my eyes closed. I'm in an evil place! ...Young people please hear ye! Hear ye! I'm talking to you (Nathaniel, Keith, Alex, Chris Thompson, CJ Sheron, Ben Cooper, Ryan Hreljac etc.) kids; don't come to prison. It is more deadly, deadening, hardening and demeaning than your worse nightmare. I could never dream a dream more nightmarish and horrible than prison my call, duty and my mission is to restore your vision. I want you to see a bright future and never subject yourself to the madness of the prison machine. I've met people (staff and convict alike) who go to church each and every Sunday. And are filled with larceny, envy, anger and deception on Monday cold and deadly men who can give you a testimony about their so-called conversion that'll send chills down your spine...

A person with H.I.V. who does not know he is infected can do for more damage than one using protection. A person with HIV (Having Insufficient Vision) who thinks he is "saved" and a Christian and not "infected" is a dangerous, deadly and duplicitous man. I assure you some of these vile creatures are reading right now (you know who you are) and you ought to be ashamed. You ought to fall on your face before God and tell him "I'm not gonna get up until you change my life." God can do anything! David committed a lot of sins. So did Saul but David listened to Nathan! I need you youths to listen to Sherman make a u-turn and move away from the prison (crime, drugs and gangs). You can turn around baby boy: yes you can! Yes you can! I want Christian Nelson, Jonah Coleman, Kids a Locke, Autumn Brown, Torey Van Oot, Josh Cook, Nathaniel Frank and you and u2. I want you to read this book like Tyra Banks read Barack Obama's two books. Use a ruler, a highlighter dissect my running ramblings turn my words inside out. Question me. Question my assumptions, theories and my ideas. Question everything. Analyze and scrutinize this tome. Blog, Vlog, wall and tweet about "K.K.K." and "G.B.G.". I want Maxwell Hoch, Maxwell Hanger, Faisal Janjua, Nick Hogan, Anthony Federov and Marc Kielburger to get, analyze and scrutinize this book.

This is all I got yall. I wrote it for Jerry Wines, Pedro Armando Quandt, Brandon Gene Martinez, Johnny "Claw" Willie and for the kids. It's my last best chance to redirect you away from the prison. I want the Michael Jackson dancers (who also worked the memorial) to get this tome. The fella who seated Janet at the burial? Get him this book. I want Shawn Hornbeck (a hero) Ben, Jai Breisch, Alex and Derek King and Van Hansis to read this book and drop me a line. I need Kurt and Aaron (on Tyra), Sean Kennedy, Chad Rettie, Shane Hoschar, Tadd Carr, Garrett Haden and Garrett McCain to peruse and analyze this book. I want Jarrod Konipinsky, Hayes Johnson, Zac Sunderland, Judge Marvin Arrington and Thelton Henderson to peruse this tome with avid interest. I shout out to "project rise" and to Ryan Hausley. I want Erin Gruwell and Daniel Berlant to read this book...I hope great lawyers (i.e. Timothy Kent Hobbs, Marc Grossman and F. Lee Bailey) will peruse this tome and get on board in my fight against P.V.S.P. Bunnell, Spearman and my disseminated Valley Fever...I hope Casey Chapman, Char Ghio, Tony Deville, Will Brown, Christian Norton, Lionel Woodyard and Attorney Dennis Sweet will read this and share it with kids. I'm telling Andrew Pruitt (Atl. GA), Frank Carter (ex-art student Atl. GA), Mike Delgado, Sean Farmer, Donald Dusk, Aaron Jackson (Delaware Ohio), Joey Grissett, James Drake, Anthony Lonnick, Cole Clemons, John Burris, Tom Degnan, Travis, Lisa Israel, John Neis and Tony Dungy to get this book....

...I challenge youths (my boys Nathaniel, Keith, Christian Nelson, Christian Norton, Brett, Chris and even Dr. Phil's son in the rock band etc.) to join G.B.G. This is not about me. It is about retired wardens like Terry L. Rosario, Cheryl Pliler, Jimbo Walker, psychologists, students, mentors and mentees meeting up on Facebook, Myspace and at www.NAPSUSA.org and using G.B.G./Heart as an elite anti-prison unit...our group of soldiers (Nate, Keith, Alex, Chris and you) will identify, destroy and dismantle these homegrown domestic terrorists (i.e. Stokes, Bret Moore, The Menendez Bros., and Phil Garrido etc.) who are harming babies, children and kids. We will tackle illiteracy, anger, gangs, guns, drugs and violence strategically. We will use our Facebook and Myspace sites as the G.B.G. Nerve Center and New Folsom State Prison (and your school, church, YMCA, Police Station, office, etc.) is my command post. G.B.G. is a (per se) counterterrorism group of kid commandos, prisoners, guards, counselors, psychologists, ministers and police etc. And we are extremely serious about defeating our enemies. C.O. Diana Smith and CCIII Patricia Kennedy have both told me that if I would commit just half of my energy and brainpower (like I did to doing frauds, cons and scams) to devising methodologies, plots, schemes and strategies to identifying predators, molesters and the gangs that prey upon the youth, I could leave a legacy. And I call upon my partners in crime (wrongly convicted and the rightly convicted), guards police, pastors and entrepreneurs to download your ideas (for change) on our web sites. I tell the G.B.G. team that every thing we (the convicts) do, say and write will be scrutinized, dissected and analyzed but I love that. Cameras keep people honest out of fear or necessity. And when we know that our suggestions, ideas and strategies are on the internet for F.B.I. Agents, profilers, pastors, parents, psychologists and even Dr. Phil to scrutinize etc. it forces us to come (write) real, authentic or not at all…..

And I believe in Romans chapter 4. I call those things that are not as though they were. I'm prophesying (that although they don't support me and they don't support my politics and beliefs etc.) that Tony Dungy, Bill Gates, Bill Cosby, Les Brown, Michael Vick and Richard Scrushy etc. Even Paris Hilton shall come forth and support the G.B.G. "mission thoroughly." G.B.G./Heart will contribute to and work in concert with Bill Coibion, Founder of "shoulder to shoulder" which mentors boys. G.B.G. will contribute finances, tomes, data and essays to "Shoulder to Shoulder" because we want more moms like Angela Murchison to be able to say "My son is coming out of his shell and less violent. He is losing some of that anger and he's less violent. His grades are improving and he is discovering who he is now. He is now in criminal justice in high school." I want that kind of testimony for kids across this country and G.B.G. working with "shoulder to shoulder", in concert with "Freedom Hall" and other youth. I call upon every teen at Martin Luther King Jr. Technology Academy (Sacto.), Monticello High School (in Virginia), Foot Hills High etc. and at schools around the world to join G.B.G. (on yahoo!, Facebook and Myspace etc.). I call upon Christian Norton, Ryan Hreljac, James O'Keefe and Garrett McCain to join us and to help us to change the world…I (again) thank God for what he has done to my life through T.D. Jakes, Eddie Long, Noel Jones, TBN and Second Chance God is an awesome God. And (in spite of my blemishes, sins and my flaws etc.) I promised God that if he did a certain thing I would holler about the awesomeness of Jehovah til the day I die. He is an awesome God. He rules and he super rules. I thank him for how he blessed me through Tyra Banks, Tyler Perry, Bill Cosby, Tony Dungy and others. He has sent people my way (CCIII Patricia Kennedy, Jimbo Walker, Rosario, D. Smith, Scott Kernan, Matt Cate, John Burris, Carolyn Phillips , Cupcake Brown etc.) who have helped me find myself. And now I have vision. The cause of my life is to fight H.I.V. and restore vision to young men. I'll fight the good fight. I'll load the Karma Bank with authenticity, energy, love and with service. I will rectify the wrongs and live out the authentic meaning of my destiny. …Rev. Hosea Williams shall look down upon me and be proud that I got my vision (my kick, my drive, my hope and my destiny back!) back after the selfish and criminal ways I abused the leading, befriending and the mentoring of Ambassador Andrew Young. I pray he'll call 916-985-8610 ext. 3042 and tell CCIII Kennedy to "tell Sherman I forgive him now." I want to do Andy, Dollie, James, Moses Lee Raglin, Eddie Long, T.D. Jakes and Noel Jones proud. "Sherman got his groove" back.

"K.K.K." will be perused, ridiculed, discussed, written about, scrutinized, analyzed and dissected all across America. I feel it in my spirit. And I've prayed the prayer of faith over this tome….It is "Manpower" for convicts! It is eye opening for kids it is abrasive, disjointed, scathing, abrupt and candid just like me. But it will change lives….You can't defy the laws of gravity. You can't put the candor, the hurt, the shame, the transparency, the sweat, prayers, visualization and tears I put in "K.K.K." and have it be mediocre. I have asked (and am re-asking even now) Bishop Jakes, Potters House, Bishop Long, New Birth, Mt. Carmel (Atl. GA), A Lincoln James, Noel Jones, Tyler Perry, Tony Dungy, TBN, Brandon Crouch, Mike Barber, Amy Fihn and believers across the world to pray for this book. You can't speak the "word" over a body of work like this and have it return void.

I see vision being restored in the lives of Maxwell hanger, Brett, Chris, Derek, Alex and for teens and tweenies around the globe. Having read this book they can't (won't and don't) walk away and be unchanged. I ask attorneys Carolyn Phillips, John Burris, Mark Merin, Grossman etc. to purchase at least ten copies of this book and have Cafepress mail them to Locke, Lodi, Ranch Cordova and Beverly Hills High School students etc.etc. And I reiterate my call to every believer (around the world)to ask God to use this book to restore "vision" to teens everywhere. I need me some prayer warriors (i.e. Zig Zigler, Tyler Perry, etc.) who believe in a God of Favor. I want the same God who transformed Tyler from a homeless victim of sexual abuse to a multi-millionaire, filmmaker, writer and actor etc. I want that same God to take this book and use it to marvel, mesmerize, reach and to teach boys to be men, of vision.

...As you (Nathaniel Mullennix, Alex, Christopher Thompson, CJ, Brett Jolliff, Alex Blench, Christian Norton and Ben Cooper etc.) read my cantankerous criticisms of certain folks (i.e. Bunnell and Spearman etc.) remember the main mission of this book is to rid you of HIV (Having Insufficient Vision) and to pull you back; and to shoot you into your destiny. We can do it. ...Yes we can!

I had an intensive (finally) meeting with associate Warden Johnson-Dovey and Warden Jimbo Walker today. The meeting was lively, enlightening and inspiring. Mr. Walker strongly advised me to stay positive and he said "You know your constitutional rights to free speech and artistic expression...Sherman I'd never attempt to stand between you and your construction." He continued "Hell I don't know what all you are writing about. But I do know you. And you know I support C.D.C. even in my sleep. So if you insist upon being negative etc. just know that (for the record) I don't support it. Mrs. Kennedy, Johnson-Dovey etc. none of us support anything you elect to write about staff; period!" Walker concluded "You know I'm always straight with you so I'm telling you that I will not vouch for you or be associated (in any way) with your politics, propaganda or with your criticisms of C.D.C. when it comes to the kids, helping them and telling them you guys story etc. We are with you guys 100%. That's where our support begins and ends point blank..."

I guess it can't get any clearer than that. Mr. Walker is a great man with a quick mind. And I concur with his decision to have nothing to do with my "politics, propaganda" or "criticisms" of C.D.C.

And since it is clear that I'm standing alone I want to (again) speak freely. Jaycee Dugard's sadistic imprisonment should have never happened. Phil Garrido's parole officer is Eddie Santos. I don't know the man. I do know that on9/14/09 KCRA interviewed a source within C.D.C. who refused to show his face. And I know exactly who that man was/is. And this anonymous C.D.C. official (afraid to be identified because he knows the Bunnells, Corcorans and Mike can cause you to disappear! ...I won't reveal his identity but I know him well. And he indicated that Eddie Santos did not do his job. And he stated C.D.C. is "covering up" his mistakes. And he stated "we're supposed to be protecting the public but we did not do our j-o-b with Garrido." And I concur fully. And Gordon Hinkle had the audacity to defend Eddie Santos...Matt Cate was a great inspector general. 1-10 I gave him a 9 ½ as I.G. and as director I give him (thus far) an 8. I support Mr.Cates agenda as well as Scott Kernan (as I've reiterated on a number of occasions)... But I don't support Eddie Santos. I believe in accountability and responsibility. This parole cover-up reminds me of Chicago Style "Good Ole Boy" politics. Eddie did not kidnap, molest and imprison Jaycee. Phil is responsible for those horrendous crimes. The only crime Eddie Santos is guilty of (is the same crime deputies, the sheriff, legislators and the congress are guilty of with regard to white male jail victims in L.A. County Jail!) is failing to protect her, detect the compound (in the back yard) and to rescue her. Mr. Santos should be fired with all deliberate haste. His direct supervisor should also be fired. And every parole officer Garrido had over the last 18 years must be fired. And every participant in that multi-agency task force who visited that house and cleared Phil ought to be fired! And I wish (for once) we would do something about this. I wish all those willing to play dress up paint signs, protest and throw a Boston Tea Party etc. would throw a Boston Tea Party in California outside the parole office. I would (personally) like to see an internet campaign to fire Eddie Santos. I don't support the bastardization of Mr. Santos. Don't hurt him or harm him. But do fire him. I wish an army of flag toting, Boston Tea drinking citizens would e-mail the governor, Sen. Gloria Romero, Rod Wright, Dianne Feinstein, Jackie Speier and Nancy Pelosi and demand that Eddie Santos be fired. That's not vindictiveness it is justice. All these candidates for governor ought to unify their voices calling for Santos to go. And I'd like for every gubernatorial candidate to explain what they will do to change parole supervision and to change C.D.C. This is serious....And sell Garrido's house and give the proceeds to Jaycee....

My mother (Brenda Smith) is doing well. Brenda got her groove back. And I'm so proud of her. I'm still her baby boy. She should tell Harold Smith to "Look at me now." And Brenda and Dollie (as was Clara Jackson) are strong black women. And they are living legends in my life. They both prove that you (ladies) can come back from the pain of a divorce and a break up. And you can get up. My momma is a survivor! And now she's thriving and very successful. I love her so much...

Today I (a convict) broke down and sobbed like a baby. I was thinking about (the 24 year old Yale student viciously murdered by an angry psychopath!) Annie and Jaycee. And I reflected upon an angry man I'd spoken with today etc. but in the midst of my weeping I became cognizant that what really broke my spirit was/is the fear of never being with my family again. My dream has been to stand in a pulpit in Atlanta (one more time). And to see Brenda, cat (Dollie), Reggie, James, Teeka and Yak as I preached my comeback sermon. I would have given my right hand to be able to preach at home one more time. But the reality of my illness (Valley Fever thanks to Bunnell, Spearman and gross medical neglect) causes me to conclude that I might not make it back. I won't be going home. I will die here. Lord have mercy. And all the folks I've wronged shall never see me confess and repent. I won't ever look Andy Young in his eyes and apologize. I'll die in Hades....

But in lieu of seeking your sympathy or even compassion, I simply ask (re-ask) you to pray that Almighty God will use every chapter, page, paragraph, sentence, word and letter (in this tome) to (in some way) help teens and tweenies. This little light (tome) of mine. I'm gonna let it shine. I want this book to shed some light in some mighty dark places. The darkness and voids which suck our kids into gangs, calls them to drink, drugs and addiction. The darkness which perverts, infects and deranges the mentality of our kids and compels them into crime. I want these pages to reach the unreachable. I want to be an instrument to restore the gleam and the sparkle back into the eyes of our young. Jesus said to "suffer the little children and let them come unto me." I want to assist them in getting to Jesus, getting to education and getting to inspiration....

I need to take a moment to practice what I preach. I mention Jakes, Long and Jones. But-the temptation for men is "I don't want to put dudes on a pedestal because we all human." But the moment a Michael or a Kennedy dies we preach their lives into the heavens. But we always wait till they're gone to recognize how great they were. And "the greatest thing a man can do is to make another man greater."

I want to preach their funerals while they are with us. T.D. Jakes-God has used you, your messages and your television ministry to "transform" me by the renewing of my mind. Bishop Jakes you are a gifted preacher, a magnificent brother and a role model. I applaud you. I salute you. I lift you up in prayer. God is using you to change the 3 million Americans in prisons Baptist Church! God is exploding through you (Dr. Jakes) in manpower and using you to build brothers up. I wanted to nod, wink, applaud and salute you, Bishop Eddie Long and Bishop Noel Jones while you are alive. Thank you for being a ministry to me at the most critical and crucial time of my life...I hope readers shall download this "praise" and e-mail it to Jakes, Jones and Long.

...I'll never meet Bill Cosby, be on Tyra or talk to Dr. Phil. Because of my predicament, position and my condition my dream of meeting Tony Dungy shall not be fulfilled on this side. I won't meet Tyler Perry or the bishops etc.etc.

But because God worketh miracles by, with and through pens and on (this) paper etc. "K.K.K." can be hailed as a national treasure (for youths) long after I'm gone. Tyra can see it! Oprah could hear about it. Teachers, students and inmates will read it. and many shall heed it. This (tome) book is my moment to shine the light (lit in me by Christ, brightened by Andy and Hosea) bright. This is it! This is my moment to leave this powerful, bodacious, candid and mighty weapon in the arsenal of weaponry for kids. Having read this tome they will never be the same. There comes a time when the stars just seem to line up and after all of these years of playing games, being angry, conning and conniving I finally faced my authentic self. I faced theme that I couldn't, wouldn't and didn't see (H.I.V.-having Insufficient Vision) for over a decade. Deep down in the confines of our bodies there are still little kids inside all of us. You can buy a one year old Jaguar but if it has 200,000 miles on the engine it is diminished. Some of us are beat down, stressed and depressed at 40. The numerical age is young but we are already worn out. But in spite of our mileage, the wear and tear each of us 38, 48,78, 88 and even 98 year olds are still kids inside. That innocent, excited, curious, energetic and effervescent lil boy is still inside my 38 year old body. I was a boy at 7,17,27 and even 37. I still have that kid in me. And you do too. But traditions, customs and society told us to stop laughing, questioning, touching, tasting and feeling...and I had lost myself. I knew I was in there but I was too timid, distrusting, ashamed and afraid to look. But "I'm starting with the man (teen or tweenie) in the mirror. I'm asking him to change his ways. No message could have been any clearer. If you wanna make the world a better place take a look at yourself and make a change". A "look" at "yourself" can revolutionize your life. A look at your habits a look at your anger. A look at your friends. A look at your talents, gifts and at your skills.

...I had to decide that even though the prison prevented me from playing in the football game of life I could reinvent, renew and transform myself (as an erudite) into a coach. If I could not be "king" (player) I'd become a "king maker." I'd become the go-to guy for greatness, inspiration and motivation...my dream of working with Jim Brown, Hollywood Henderson and others can't happen. But this book is my truth. It comes from a hole in my heart. It comes from a place of pain, seclusion and an overwhelming sense of destiny.

I must engage in succession planning to leave G.B.G. to Drew Stevyns, Thomas Kaplan (at Yale), Travis Payne, Gene "Junior" Watson Jr. (N.Y.), Josiah Lemming and Alex Chivesvcu. I command you all to be soldiers in the army of G.B.G. "We got to fight although we have to cry. We've got to hold up the blood stained banner. We've got to hold it up until we die." ...I've set this unique, special and powerful organization up and I leave it to Ben Cooper, C.N.A. John Johnson (Lemoore CA), Anthony Federov and Johnny Weir.

And I order Nathaniel, Keith, Christian Nelson and Christian Norton etc. to build upon the work of my hands. I pray that teens will burn up some of that marvelous energy, wit and ambition. And you will seize G.B.G. and via the power of the internet you shall cause us to be a force to be reckoned with. I have certain visions, dreams and pictures for how I see G.B.G. looking. And I must pray, attract, compel and propel G.B.G. into it's destiny. I need Drew Stevyns, Hairo Torres, the Texas Tenors and recycled percussion to help promote G.B.G....

This is our moment to shine. School by school, church by church, street by street etc. we should spread the word about this tome. Tell somebody today, use the internet to launch an international awareness campaign about G.B.G. and "K.K.K". Now is the time to put up or shut up. I put my heart, soul and my spirit into these words. Young people-the anointing upon this writing is contagious. You'd better be careful how long you read this book cause this blessing will rub off on you. This blessedness is contagious. I feel it right now…Garrett McCain, Brenda and Kyle Love, Stacy Smedley and Christopher Thompson "We want you"… Let's get "K.K.K." to Ken and Elizabeth Green (Kansas City, MO), Ken Cappalletty (Ohio), Mary and Robert Ott, Niki Schwartz, Rev. Daniel Ring and to Thomas Kaplan…I want Garrett McCain, Ryan Hreljac, Gabe Williams, Timothy Coleman, C.J. Sheron, Jake Heartsong, Ben Cooper, Maxwell Hanger, Adam Lambert, Jeff Buttle, Josiah Lemming, Chad Michael Morrissette, J.G. Howell, Luke Sears, Greg Deekins (VA.), Tadd Carr, Anthony Fedorov and Daniel Clay Hollifield (etc.) to send me your photos for our (up and coming) photo gallery. Hurry…

I spirit of enlightenment, power and a forwardness being unleashed upon youths. I can feel it coming in the air tonight. If you're breathing you're blessed. Greatness is inside of you Hugh Michael Hughes, A. Voorhees, Alan Stevenson, Jason Sutherland etc. etc…I remember when I was a boy in Atlanta. My mom (Dollie) and I would be at First Corinth Baptist Church every Sunday morning whenever I did not have to preach. And I used to love Sunday Morning service. I'd be standing next to Dollie and Rev. Moses Lee Raglin would do his favorite prayer hymn. And a "hymn" in a black church is a powerful worship tool. There is usually no instruments during a hymn. And we hold the notes a long time inflecting here and there for emphasis. I.E. "The Church is a mourning" would sound this way in a hymn: "The chuch is een moa-oan-ning-the chuch is moa-oaning." It's crazy to write it but the sound (and feel) of a hymn is unique and unmistakable…I loved it when Rev. Raglin would do "a charge to keep I have." He'd begin "Eh-eh-e-a-eh-ay chaaaarge-i-i-toooo-ooo keeeeep-ahm ahn I (hold note) I have ahh aha ae-aa-aah good-I –eh, I , I toooo glooo-a-reee-efy…" After the church sang a few verses of the hymn we'd fall silent for a while.

Then you'd hear the women in the soprano and alto and all tha bruthas in Falsetto…Not even a word just a note. We'd all begin……"Oooooooo" it sounds like "who" (or whooooo) without the 'w' and 'h'. Just a beautiful soft high key moan. And as we moaned Rev. Raglin would begin with "most holy God our father"… We'd be "ooooo" and he'd go "It's once and again that a few of your children have bowed down before your holy throne." And he'd take us into the heavens in prayer. And there was a sound, a sense and a spirit in that church. I don't even have an adequate group of "words" which I can write out to explain to you that feeling I'd get in church. Such a warm, strange, pulsating sensation. I felt God in that church…If my governor told me right now "Sherman if you let us chop off your right hand! We will drive you to a Baptist Church (in shackles and chains) I promise (on everything dear to me) I would let them chop it off. Lord have mercy I'm so so so not racist. (with a Caucasian wife and two of my best 3 friends in the world are white … and…you know!) But I've never gotten that feeling in a white church. And (quiet as it's kept) I didn't get that feeling at some black churches (believe this!) just as I describe to you how wicked, dark, hot, evil and eerie a prison "feels". There is no doubt that when you walk into an atmosphere where there are hundreds of people on one accord, praising God, worshipping and praying etc. It feels like favor…Whitney Houston, Aretha Franklin, Tyler Perry and Gayle King know exactly what I'm talking about. Neither weed, coke or speed can match the high you feel when you are drunk in the holy spirit. Every now and then when I'm alone I can worship, pray and fast. And I can go back to that feeling…

I hope just some of you will go to church and feel it…. When I write about God 2 youngsters I have two fears: A. I hope I've not been so secular, carnal and profane that it makes you uncomfortable to hear (read) me writing about Christ. B. I fear you may do what I used to do which was to "hear" but not "listen". And I'd feel they are lying about their faith. And many times I thought they're "just brainwashed or embellishing... Stuff could not be happening the way they claim it is." Let me be frank. Some of them are lying and conning. Period! The flipside is this: Some of the stuff I've watched God strategically orchestrate and masterfully manipulate has blown my mind. I'm not looking for a "gang" of bible toting zealots. But I do want some teens, tweenies, parents and professors who have faith in a higher power. (If you don't that's yo right and I'm still down with you anyhow!) I want a prayer wing of the G.B.G. program. My vision is to (one day) have a round the clock prayer team that keeps G.B.G./Heart in prayer...I.E. Monday-McGregor Scott prays for G.B.G. for ten minutes at 8:00 am at 9:00 am. Macy Bell prays for G.B.G. for ten minutes at 10:10 am. Dollie (in Atlanta) prays for G.B.G./Heart for ten minutes and so forth and so on. Every hour at least one person (up to thousands around the world) has G.B.G./Heart in prayer. We have got to get this kicked off ASAP!

I'm a graduate student of Human Behavior and I'm still mesmerized by you and me. Wanna shout out to Beverly Foy, Asst. U.S. Atty. Laurel White, Atty. McGregor Scott, satirist Joel Stein and Atty. Robert Waters. I really pray that attorneys Scott, Merin, Waters, Burris or Carolyn Phillips will help me bring Bunnell, Spearman and the egregious medical dept. of C.D.C. to it's knees. Attorneys Robert Waters, Katz, Merin, Burris, Carolyn, Navarro or Analea Patterson what must I do? Do you want my tome profits? Cupcake Brown, F.Lee Bailey, Griffin or Michael Bein help me...

I am determined to work with Drew Stevyns, Garret McCain, Cameron Brown, Brett Wescott and David Hellyer. G.B.G. needs energetic, animated and as enthusiastic as Brett Westcott and Cameron Brown. I need some of you (right now) to e-mail, text mail or call Cameron and Brett out at Purdue. And tell them that an innovative, creative group of Ph.D's, psychiatrists, prisoners, pastors, entrepreneurs and students (G.B.G./Heart) need their help. I commission Brett and Cameron to write www.napsusa.org on their sign as they pass out compliments on Wednesday. I'm willing to give monetary stipends or a bonus to Brett and Cameron. Brett, Cameron (and Gabe Williams, Timothy Coleman, Ben Cooper and Tadd Carr etc.) can drop me a line for immediate reply. We will use the photos of Drew, Brett, Cameron, Gabe, Tim, Ben, Tadd, Nathaniel and Keith etc. in or photo gallery. I can't be any more direct than this: Daniel Sample, Michael Sanford, Kyle Haycock, Alex Hornbuckle and Cesar Ramirez (in Oregon) we want you. And (as long as you are 17 or older. Otherwise you need parental permission) all you need to do for a stipend or help is ask. Richard "Doc" Ford reminded me that "Atlanta" you and I spend $thousands per year on Canteen, packages and special purchases. It would be hypocritical of us to not be willing to donate a few $thousand dollars per year to help struggling students who are willing to work on our G.B.G. web sites and to promote our campaign." Doc said "Sherman our internet campaign and our tome "K.K.K." is far more important than the tours. The book is the backbone of our mission. It is a portable and compartmentalized reminder to youths of what Billy Fleming, Rick Butler, Johnny "Claw" Willie, Dr. Curren and G.B.G. said." Doc Ford continued "Atlanta if you need me to get my wife to send five or ten copied of our tome ("K.K.K.") to schools (i.e. Folsom or Rancho Cordova high school etc.) let me know. You know my burden for those troubled kids and the guilt I feel as a former distinguished and so-called decorated LAPD detective." Doc stated (with candor) "I don't always agree with your propaganda or your politics. And I don't really have time for the disputes you have with C.D.C. staff. But even Warden Walker admits that you are the driving force of G.B.G. and you willed, prayed and visualized it into existence and it is a blessing to be a part of it."

Doc Ford stated "Long after you and I are in hell trying to buy an air conditioner (LOL) kids in schools, colleges and churches will be reading about the ex-police officer, guards, cons and psychiatrists etc. who came together for good. It's a blessing." When I saw tears trickling ever so softly down Ford's cheeks I was taken aback.

Doc told me "and Atlanta no matter what society thinks about us. No matter what dirt, wrong or crimes are in our past. They can't deny the fact that a group of convicts were candid, transparent and concerned enough to come together and found an International organization to mentor youths by showing them our errors… to my way of thinking our web site is far more important than in-house tours. With this book and the internet we can reach hundreds of millions and (yes) billions of people…" Men always try to cover pain or tears with humor, jokes or idle chatter. So I turned the subject to Eric Menendez. No one at New Folsom State Prison knew Eric as well as me other than former LAPD detective Richard "Doc" Ford. For more than 3 years Eric, Doc and I were the 3 evening workers in the building. Eric, Doc and I would spend from 6:00 p.m.-9:00 p.m. outside on the Shu Yard alone. And nobody knows about Eric Menendez's homosexuality, drug addiction and his demonized religious beliefs (better than me) except Doc. And nobody (or inmate) has loaned Eric more money and bailed him out of drug debts like Ford and Manning. I reminded Doc of Eric Menendez anal offer to me on the Shu Yard and Doc said "I'm a cop. I don't forget anything. I was hoping you forgot so I could put that in my (LOL) book!" But Doc also said "You can casually mention it because all our telephone (Doc is always pragmatic! It's the cop in him) calls are monitored and recorded. So every time you and I got on the telephone and had money sent to Tammie and Becky for Eric I.S.U. knew about it. You remember when you had 3 checks sent to 3 different inmates from that Swiss (Hypeothekarbank) Bank and I.S.U. withheld the checks for 3 months. The captain had to get the checks. They record that crap." Doc concluded "But I am not interested in bad mouthing Eric or anything like that. And I have no interest in discussing his sex scandals, Henrickson or any of that with the media. I don't have the time. I don't want to be on t.v. I've been there, done that and got a t-shirt!

I inquired "But Doc let me just ask if the National Enquirer asked you if I loaned Eric money, if you and/or I saw him do drugs and copulating Henrickson etc. what would you say?" He stated "since I don't want to be involved I can't confirm or deny any of that; period…" Let me reiterate the fact that I did not do, begin,start or form G.B.G. on my own. It was Richard "Doc" Ford, (my dear friend and brother) Johnny "Claw" Willie, William ("Billy") Fleming, (then captain) A.W. Fred Schroeder, Steve, Dr. Solis, Dr. Curren, D. Heitkamp, Dr. Duran etc.etc. It was the belief and support of Senator (now chairman of the Democratic Party a.k.a. Bull in a China Shop) John Burton, Fred Moor, Rod Wright etc.etc. It was just not just me. I am not (as CCIII Patricia Kennedy reminds me) an organization. It takes "People to make up an organization. And if you let your ego get in the way you will fail the kids…what is more important-proving you are "right" or reaching troubled youth?" Madame Kennedy stated.

"Sherman you drive people nuts (LOL) in a prison hierarchy. You start at the top (Warden) and work your way down. People feel like you go over their heads to get things done. They don't know your history. They can accept that a former police officer will still sporadically act like a cop in prison. They will accept that a professor turned prisoner will still use a professional lingo in jail etc. But-and that's a big but trying to get testosterone filled, arrogant administrators to "understand" that Manning is a college educated black man from America's black mecca (Atlanta) and Manning used to hobnob with political and civil rights royalty. You called Ambassador Andrew Young at home. You're well traveled and you like white women. And now your in jail with a crazy conviction that even Rosario said you didn't do. It is a tough pill to swallow. Some of them hate you."

CCIII Patricia Kennedy concluded "That's the bad news. But the good news is you are finally he will!),Valley Fever, wisdom or what. But even Jimmy admits you are growing…and as long as you're humble, sincere and use that great brain of yours for something other than talking about Bennell (LOL…but that's Mrs. K. Jimbo and Johnny Willie love to hear me get chewed out. Even associate warden Johnson-Dovey likes to hear me get chewed out) you can do great things." …Before she retires (in 8 or 9 years) she should be warden Patricia Kennedy. She is a candid, decent, intelligent and an honest person. And honest people are far and few between in C.D.C. These people specialize in lies.…

I am so grateful. Even being sick with this valley fever and facing my own physical mortality. Even in the face of the envy, viciousness, evil and "meanness" I reside within. Even though I know a few people like Johnny Willie who could and should be forced if just one Tony Serra, Kent Russell, Ephraim Margolin or a Gerry Uelmen would look at his case. In the midst of this madness knowing that I won't make it home.

I feel a peace which surpasses all understanding. I'm watching God as he mesmerizes, hypnotizes and bemuses me by showing me his awesomeness. I am running to the t.v. and begging T.B.N. to show me more "manpower", more Jakes, Jones and more Long. And I'm sensing a messianic move that eye hath not seen and ear hath not heard. And I'm walking in the light and in the knowledge of the fact that divine providence, the universe and almighty God has always been in control. He had a divine and a permissive will for my life. And even when men thought evil upon me. When they smiled in my face and stuck daggers in my back. When they broke bread with me, shook my hand and winked their eye-but they secretly wished I was dead. When I realize the intense level of hatred, "anger" and rottenness in these prisons etc. I realize that "If it had not been for the lord that was on my side I would have been swallowed up."

I like Kanye West. He has not done a darn thing for me but I like Kanye. So I am biased. But he was 100% wrong, drunk and in error when he jumped on the stage and took the mike etc. etc. But when I looked I saw that little "boy" inside Kanye who still does not understand why God allowed his mother to die at the hands of a black doctor…"I need to take time and analyze how I'm gonna make it through the rest of this life…I allowed my hurt (aha) to cause her hurt" he said. And that "hurt" and/or "fear" is what lies underneath that "anger" that we boys are addicted to. We are so angry…I felt that demonic anger emanating out of Kanye. Kanye needs to go sit down with Bishop Jakes, Bishop Long or Bishop Noel Jones. And he also should go see Dr.Gardere, Dr. Phil, Dr. Curren, Dr. Davidson or Dr. Jarman…]

Let me repeat: we are so angry. We got wind in our jaws we go to bed angry. We wake up mad at the world. We make love to our women angrily. We are angry enough to beat Rihanna we are angry enough to spit on Whitney and….we need to be healed. Brothers (yes I'm talking to you in that school at Locke, Monticello and at Lodi etc.) We won't talk to anybody. We won't reach out to anybody and won't let anybody reach in. We need to get that wind out of our jaws and release that anger. Having the horror heard (Kanye) helps heal the hurt. … I've come like Paul who was in a hole (Hades=prison) baptizing, healing and preaching and teaching etc. I've come to arrest that anger. I have a warrant for the arrest of your anger. I'm gonna ride that anger until I break it down. I have come to bring light. You don't need to believe in me; to receive the ability to see. You don't need to eat what I eat or think like I think. All you need to do is reach out and grab this release. You a muslim? You a Catholic? You Jewish? You Pentacostal? You don't believe in Jesus? (I do! And he's real!) You can call on the lord. Call him Jesus, Abba, Jehovah, Allah or Pah Pah. I don't give a darn. But as long as you're calling on the divine force that put the universe into order; that can stand against any discarding force. As long as you're calling up the force that is light and is love. I say release that anger. You gotta let it go bro. it is driving you mad. It is destroying you and killing you. I arrest that demon. I curse and I rebuke it and I speak (visualize and "faith") your release into existence. By the time you finish this book you're gonna see a change in you. By the time this book is over. You will feel a burden of hot, hateful anger coming out of you. And I suggest that you get real and be sincere. And lay on your face before God. I suggest that you cry out to our daddy and begin to see, envision, imagine and feel deliverance... "Whatsoever things ye desire when ye pray believe that ye receive them and ye shall have them". I repeat that powerful, revolutionizing, transmogrifying verse every day of my life!

...I believe I have Michael Sanford, Brett Westcott, Cameron Brown, Tadd Carr, Maxwell Hanger, Garrett McCain and youth around the world on the internet chatting about "K.K.K." and G.B.G. . I see it! Jason Segel vendettaness, vindictiveness and brutality... Analca Patterson? McGregor Scott? James Brosnahan,, Robert Waters,... Rogue and criminal Warden Mike Bunnell discovers I've written and published a tome discussing his criminality. He (conflict of interest) punishes me by sending me to "Pleasant Valley so you can catch Valley fever and write a book about that". I write everybody telling them (at M.C.S.P.)what Bunnell said. I identify an enemy at P-V-S-P- on facility –A- Bunnell sends CCI Costa and instructs Costa to pretend "Ray Sanchez" was not at P-V-S-P-...I refuse the transfer-Bunnell oders Captain Robinson to get I.S.U. to cell extract me and forcefully (on video camera) transfer me to P.V.S.P- . At P-V-S-P- I'm terrified of Valley Fever. I tell Dr. Postolo. He even writes down (I have his notes) that I stated Bunnell sent me to P-V-S-P- to "catch valley fever and write a book about that". The Mayo Clinic states Valley fever kills Blacks worse than anyone else ... In light of all of this I'm still felled from disseminated valley fever 3 ½ months after I get to P-V-S-P- where my enemy is housed... For weeks as my stomach bloats, I'm short of breath and passing out etc. C.O. Wally Tucker,D.L. Criner and CC I Freeland etc. refuse to let me get Medical treatment. Nurse Hall asks Physicians (for 3 weeks) to see me and they refuse... when Nurse Hall finally convinces R.N. Bond to see me Bond says I'm faking, only have gas and sends me back to die. Nurse Hall re-sends me to see R.N. Bond and Dr. Benjamin. Dr. Benjamin finally orders an x-ray of my bloated belly. He reads the x-ray and concurs with nurse bond declaring "all that is just gas". He gave me an enema!!! He laughed at me and asked me did I think "Bunnell gave me gas". He sent me back to die... At the building C.O. Wally Tucker and D.L. Criner teased and taunted me about Bunnell, rape this and rape that... Did I use my enema? I nearly died before a Psychiatrist sent me out...At UMC hospital Judge Glade Roper's (Tulace County superior court) son Dr. Glade Roper told me the "gas" was 6 liters of valley fever fluid which was about to kill me ... "What kind of prison allowed you to walk around with your abdomen distended like this? This did not happen overnight? Doctors Roper,McCray, James and Libke told me ...World renown Gastroenterologist Dr. Sheik told me "there are only 27 cases in the world like yours this case is clearly deliberate gross medical negligence ... If you survive this you should own C.D.C... Robert Sillen asked the Governor to shut down P-V-S-P- due to valley fever one year ago Mr. Manning "...

Dr. James stated "it seems like they (prison authorities) wanted you to die at P-V-S-P"... C.O. Pieper told me "I can't prove Bunnell killed my uncle Doug Pieper. But I know this Bunnell sent you to P-V-S-P- and Bunnell convinced Yates, Spearman and staff not to contact your family for nine months... You're mad at Joe Rikalo for not letting you go to the chapel . Rikalo was following orders". C.O. Linda Forte told me "all of us know exactly why you were sent to P-V-S-P- you are supposed to be dead". Dr. Paul Griffin stated "yours is the worse case of deliberate medical negligence I've ever seen. And the stress (alone) from them not letting you use the phone, see t.v. or read and write nearly killed you. I have no desire to go to court... But I would testify that they were cruel and unusual to you".

Nurse will said "my wife and I both witnessed C.D.C. attempt to murder you". He whispered we'll fly up from Atlanta to testify that staff tried to murder you. .. We also know about the girl addicted to meth... Mr. Brosnahan, Blair Berk, Mr. Water, Mark Merin, Masuda, Johnny Grifflin how about I give you 75% of any settlement... Carolyn Phillips, Robert Navarro, Cupcake Brown, Tom Mesereau, Tony Serra, Mr. Scott etc. I'll give you 75% ... I just want to march physicians, nurses and officers to the stand andlet them testify about what Mike Bunnell did to me and to my family Help me please...

David Goldman, Scott Bauman (Ohio), Cody Sheldon, Alex Wagner Trugman, Reggi Beasley, Samson Beren and Kenny Hoffpauer etc. I need you at G.B.G...John Arnold (billionaire) Todd Kent , Andrew Schrader, Nicholas Lyman and Chris Eaton we need You. I hope Judge Greg Mathis knows how much he means to G.B.G. .. Former LAPD Homicide cop Richard "Doc" Ford told me "Judge Greg Mathis is one of the greatest inspirations to our team on the planet. We must send him "K.K.K"... I concur fully ... Brett Westcott, Cameron Brown and Andy (the volunteer) I hope you all will E-mail Judge Mathis and tell him about "K.K.K... G inane Javier (sacto) , Alan Rafferty, Don Reisinger(cnet), Dave Salmoni, L. Miranda(the west side story) and kids at Santa Barbara College we need you too... Ryan Sherman is entangled in a sexual relationship with ccpoa president Mike Jimerez. It is off the hook. Wendy Williams would love it ...

I want you all to locate Trevor Loflin, Ero Carrera, Caleb Sima, Caleb Peek, Dr. Luis Rubio and Justin Berry... You all find Stephen Memory, Andrew Rauscher, Alex Mandel, Rev. Alice Baber Banks (Christian Fellowship Ministry Church in Del Paso Heights)and her members. G.B.G. needs Christian Fellowship Ministry Church to adopt G.B.G. and pray for us.

I want Dylan Heath, Jay Cohen, Bill Dallas, Mark Dallas, Francis Graham,Mark Petterson, Stephen Alford (Atl.GA.), Kaether Cordero, Ari Shapiro, Daniel Sample and Rebecca Delgatto Rottman to get this book...

"The whole head is in a sick condition and the whole heart is feeble ". We need help. We need help. We really need help.

...I'm looking for John Hancock ("Hands on Disaster), Marc Young ,Ben Chaput, Gary Hardwick, Thomas Hollywood Henderson and Michael Vick... I reach out to Jason Yeager (Christie Prairie Texas), Kevin Fox (Wilmington Ill:), Lester Neblett, Jason Word(Sacto), The Clark Brothers and living things. I want Jeffrey Buttle, Mario Punteri, Rev. Otis Moss, Chris Casimie, Jonathan Phillips, Aaron Eby, Louis Copelin (Folsom), Doug Pieper Jr. and Ben Tracy. I need every reader to please find these people and tell them about this book. I need doers......

Chad Michael Morrissette (west Hollywood) Justin Wilson, Dan Continello, Omar Samy Kasey Edwards, Daniel Watts, Christopher Elliott (sacto), Robert Santillanez, Matt Martinez (Carmichael CA.), Ted Russert, Ryan Andrews (Irving Texas), Mark Green (CA.), Nicholas Evans (CA.), Kevin Babcock, David Zimel, Alex Ruoff, Lawrence Becker and Mike Barber we need you. And I will give just about anything for or to you all who will use your computer to locate those special people... It is so important to G.B.G. that we reach Barbara Becnel, Cesar L.Chaves, Eric Cline, Jonathan Kisamore and Eric Jona. And I do not pick names out of a hat (lol). Each name (really) is a special and important person whom we need to get this tome to.

Mike Bunnell (ya'll know him by now right?) Cora stood against Moses and God killed him. God wanted to kill Aaron but Moses prayed for Aaron... I don't know what God has planned for Bunnell. But I do know what Bunnell planned for me. And I need to get justice. Judge Thelton Henderson, Gloria Romero, Dianne Feinstein etc. I need somebody to help me break the back bone of this machine. They must be stopped...

Lets get Howard Bragman, Jason Huyck, Brenda Franklin, Warrick Dunn, Sasha Vujacic, Kevin Jeffries and David Deluz this book... I want Garrett McCain and Christian Norton (and all of my teens) to start turning your voice into a vehicle for change. We are one! We are the future...

All of you with this tome sput your entire lives walking toward an appointment you didn't even know you had. You are now in the right place at the right time. I need you to act... The (a) word doesn't work when you hear it. The word works when you do it... Ya'll feel me? Let's get this "word" to Kenny Hoffpauer, Chancellor Tom Crow, Professor Chris Golston, M. Gerald Schwartzbach, Sam Hayes (n.y.), Josh Sommer, Max Steele, Thomas McDonell and Gary Hunter... Nathaniel (in Atlanta GA.)Are you reading right now? If you (Nathaniel, Keith and Christian) R perusing this I need u 2 use your search engines and find Collin Orcutt,(Nate how difficult could it be 2 find Collin Orcutt?)Andrew A.Bridge, Brent J.Newell, Francis Papica (LA. CA.), Aaron Moskowitz (San Francisco), Urban poole, Bradley Thomas, D.J. Swearinger, Tony Hunter , Brandon Walker and Nicholas Taxera ... I have a stipend for Nick Taxera!

This book and our G.B.G. platform can transform the youth of this world. But we must get it to certain people divinely aligned to receive it like Michael Adams (and no. 85 for the Cardinals), Levi Turner, Justin Carter, Justin Snyder, Frank Therance, Tru Watkins etc...We must make it happen prison is my platform to reach into schools, jails, colleges, hoods, suburbs, geeks, freaks and needs after reading this book you must go into your community and transform it. You are the kingdom and it has come on thy street and thy school... This book shall program your mind with the software of change. This is a change you can believe in. Once we cure that H.I.V. there is prevision for yo vision... Hello Christopher Clubb, David Sommers, Ryan Collins, Dr. Lisa Boesky and Joe Clark... There are 1.1 million students in New York City. Nathaniel, Keith and Christian ya'll gots work to do!!Reach them... Paul Pruden, Jeff Axten, Christal Amour and Carlos Rodriguez I need ya. G.B.G. believes emotional gymnastics and mental acrobats strengthen the minds of men. Your mindis like a pearl and a jewel ... I need Carlos Rodriguez, Christina Ortega, Andrew Knox, Drake Bell, Josh Peck, Antonio Guzman, Rick Klein, Anthony Fox, Jason Shaner, Prof. Marc Howard, Chris Simpson, Ryan Jasinski, Nicholas Passeck and Justin Long...

Dr. Jarman consistently reminds the G.B.G. team about the power of modeling. And thanks to Wardon Walker we have great men around us (i.e. Captain Scottie Shannon and Lt.Jimmy Guyton) to model. And I want Angel Alcazar, David Han (folsom), Joseph Han, Damien Cave and Jake Silbermann to join our mentoring program... If your memories are bigger than your dreams you are in trouble. The poorest person in the world is not the one without a nickel it is the one without a dream. I want G.B.G. members around the world to dream, hope, yearn and to strive.

We reach out to Nurse Randy Greene, Ben Jurney, Ben Woodside, Matt Engen, Christopher Durbin and Eddie Cannon. Prisoners leave a trail of tears in this University (Hades) of pain. This is a field of suffering and anger. And Jimmy Walker has motivated us to lift up our minds above the walls of the prison. And to see the suffering of the kids in the cities. And through G.B.G. via the internet and this powerful tome we reach out and touch you with our stories.

.   We want Kyle Sevey, Mayor R. Rox Parris, Adam Pani Adrian Lamoi, Alex Flores (sacto), Guy Farris, Travis Fitzsimmons, Scott Miller, Justin Townsend, Robert John Burke, Shane Kippel, Juan Morrira, Joshua Daniel (k96685), Daniel Henson (p28214), Danny Magee, Brendan Moran, Kris Applegate, John Stevens, Martin McEntee, Richard Alcarez, Jason Durtchi and Dr. Alex Valclavik to get this tome. We must get it to Kris T. Jernell, Alex Seabolt, Alex Holgan, Christopher Savlas, Andrew Theiss, Nick Pelham, Tyler Schroeder, Phillip Pohle, Duncan Wong, Joey Chima, Zach Harris and to the Schoettlerneufeld tire retread center... It is a great company! John Romesburg, Pat Pattituchi, Nic Buron, John Decaro, Teen Youth Court Coordinators, G.T. Dave, Benjamin Whipple, Devin Rio, Peter Snow etc.

We must reach out to the students at the Ted Ginn Academy in Cleveland and bring them into our camp...We never touch people so lightly that we don't leave a trace of our spirit... I wanna touch David Jay, Jay Manual, Oz Contreras and Amy Frank. I want to reach Dr. Zweigh, Dr. Milton Frank Mytler Perry. We will teach students to move from promise to power. But we gotta reach Jon Hilsenrath, Joshua Kaizuka, Chris Bergaus , Ted Russert and Evan Williams... Dr. C. Solis wants me to recommend teens read a book called "Good Enough Mothering" and also "Sweet release". We need to reach Greg Doggett, Arik Jensen, Alex Higgin Botham (sacto), Nick Bradwell, Zane Starkewolf, Eric Blinden, Ted Shaw, Daniel Cowart, Brian Greene, The Rubber Boy and Tyra Banks. ...We can do this. God won't take us to what he can't take us through. Our God is awesome. Yes he is... T.I. needs this book. We must reach Dave Hamrick, Bret Boardwine (Ohio), Clayton Johnson, Marc Hamilton(ASU Student in AZ.) Azim Khamisa and Dr. Charles Ware.... Don't forget the kids dying in foster care. Putting kids into foster care is like trying to put out a fire by pouring gasoline on it. We must make a change in foster care... I want Louis Levy, Fabian Hambuechen, David Hellyer, Adiso Banjoko, Jamie Johnston, Adam Ruggiero and Matt Damon... Prison is an easily accessible social structure in which some can function with a level of acceptance and adequacy. Some of us perform in the social system of prison more effectively than in larger society. We need to break this curse here and now... I want to reach Attorney Charles Geerhart, Austin Sisneros (Utah), Eric Flores (Roseville CA.), and all the students at Riverton high school in Utah. We have a stipend for Austin Sisneros....

If I can influence or persuade just 25 % of you students reading this to locate only 40 % of the names in this book we will revolutionize America. We can do it.

I aim to tell a certain story about the Bunnell's of C.D.C. So that my authentic tale of attempted murder and madness shall compel you to stay the hell out of jail..."It's an abominable circumstance and grieves me very greatly" president Jimmy Carter said of what he calls white America's "racism" toward President Obama. President Carter must have been chatting (lol) with Detective "Doc" Ford (who's also Caucasian). Doc told me that Joe Wilson was/is racist and that many of the good ole white boys just can't stand to see a black President. White Black and Brown Christians must pray that God will unleash his Angelic beings to be with the secret service as they protect President Obama. I've asked all of the G.B.G. members as well as our board of advisors to pray for Sasha and Malia's father... We must disrupt, dismantle and destroy hate groups in America. And perhaps we can begin in these racist ass prisons. By remaining Bunnell, Sgt. K. Scott, Wally Tucker, D.L. Criner(black) and Marion E. Spearman(black). D.L. and Marion are more dangerous to black inmates than any klansman will ever be.Dudes like Ward Connerly, Shelby Steele and Clarence Thomas are more of a threat to blacks than Joe Wilson, Glen Beck and Ann Coulter can ever be...I'd much rather deal with Jim Crow and Bull Connor (any day) than a Handkerchief Head Criner or an Oreo Spearman...

I studied the mind of Ecoterrorist (mentioned later in this book. He just committed suicide) John L.Frazier (here) at New Folsom for years. I learned a lot about racism, hate, murder and madness by interacting with this man who murdered up to 8 people. Frazier was on death row and had his death sentence commutated. Former Sergeant R.N. Saunders used to smuggle sensitive racial material to Frazier. And the contents of this tome are tainted (affected or painted) by the things I learned from this maniac John Frazier. But I'd rather deal with a Frazier than a Spearman anyday. I prefer that racist Sean Hannity of over Ward Connerly hands down...

It is 4:00 am and I've (again) had zero sleep. I've been praying. I have been praying for G.B.G./Heart... I'm under qualified to lead it I am a flawed fellow. It will take the miraculous hand of God to do it. We need his favor. I am going to reach out to congressman Bob Inglis and to congress woman E. Bernice Johnson. I need help. I'm in a dangerous situation surrounded by broken and fragile men. Rotten, evil, filthy and dangerous men jealous, duplicitious and dastardly men. But I still believe God. And Jim gonna write 200 letters next week to Andy C. ("the volunteer" from Ohio), Austin Sisneros in Utah, Christopher Thompson etc.etc. And I am going to ask them to pray for G.B.G. . To pray for me and to pray for this book. I'm even gonna ask Tony Robbins,Zig Zigler and Rev. Otis Moss to pray for us…

I got valley fever yall and "before I was afflicted I went astray, but now I keep your word" (psalm119:67)…And 71 says "it is good for me that I have been afflicted, that I may learn your statutes". When Dearaujo was stealing my clippers he didn't know that all this was gonna be "good for me". Even the guys who plotted, schemed and helped him concoct the story did not know about the power of our God! I had cc (two) Sal Goldman nodding and agreeing today as I explained to him that God transformed that messing into an awesome blessing . Goldman saw me laying on that cold and hard floor for nearly two months. But man thought evil "toward" me but (Joseph told his hating brothers) "God meant it for good"

Joe Wilson turns out to be (as President Carter implies) a confederate flag toting klansman. And young folks ought to let it be known that we are not going to support a klan platform. I have no time for racist black folks or the Joe Wilson, Coulter, Hannity or Limbaugh.

I hope Barck consistently deprograms and examines his secret servicemen to insure against infiltration and/or undercover klans in the secret service …Mr. Obama must listen to President Carter (and Morris Dees) be diligent, prayerful and diligent…

Marion E. Spearman? Wally Tucker? D.L. Criner? And the infamous Mike Bunnell? I am willing to take a polygraph test by an unbiased F.B.I.expert . I will answer every question about these guys at my expense…I will also pay for Bunnell, Criner, Tucker and Spearman to all be polygraphed right now today! Why not find out who is being honest?… I will pay! And there is absolutely no rule(s) prohibiting Bunnell, Spearman or me from taking polygraphs. I am certain that distinguished lawyers like Carolyn Phillips (in Fresno), John Scott, Sean Musgrave, Robert Navarro, Analea Patterson (Orrick Herrington & Sutcliffe), John Burris or Tony Brooklier will assist me in arranging the polygraphs…

I want to litigate Mike Bunnell's attempted murder (of me), the gross deliberate medical neglect,cruel and unususual punishment , retaliation and medical malpractice so badly that I'll accept a law student's (Carter White?Susan Christian, Millard Murphy, Barry Scheck,F. Lee Bailey, Willie Gary) assistance. I just need to get it before the court. Having seen Bunnell, Spearman, Tucker, Criner, Dr. Benjamin etc. etc. No court can deny me a trail. This is as close to an open and shut case as you can get…Analea, Robert Waters, Cupcake Brown, Carolyn Phillips or Joshua Kaizuka what if I agreed to pay your 60 %? We know the great attorney Michael Louis Kelly is readingis book… Attorney Kelly?…

Oh yes I forgot to tell you (Brett, Chris, Rick's son Michael and John Butterfield etc.) All that when I titled this book K.K.K(kids killing kids) I was not talking about the kids who set Michael Brewer on fire etc. setting him on fire … Nor was I talking about the kids who killed 15 year old Albert (the honors student)in Chicago. I was not talking about 14 15 16 year old kids who kill "other" kids. No! I'm talking about (and I know I made you all wait a while before I elucidated this) about teens (kids) and tweenies (young Thomas's) who kill kids(didymas). I'm talking about the millions of kid Clark Kents and Lois Lanes who have killed Superman and Superwoman. I'm talking about kid sauls who've killed their paul.Im talking all the young Josephs who were trapped inside the prisons of poverty, illiteracy, gangs and drug abuse (Michael, Brett, Chris) and they killed themselves before they made it to the palace. I'm talking about all the boys and girls who allowed their cracks and flaws (didymas)to destroy their greatness and strengths (prince) … You can (read closely) kill yourself! You can take the gun of doubts, disbeliefs, impatience, addictions or gangs etc. And kill your self (future dreams and vision).You can take the knife of illiteracy and kill your education and die in incarceration. You can take the stick of inferiority and kill the eagle in you and die a chicken. You can kill Didymas, and Didymas is Thomas is twin- is You…Kids(Didymas)killing(entrapping, incarcerating, paralyzing, neutralizing and even murdering)Kids   (Thomas) is killing off an entire generation(Literally and Figuratively).....I need Private Joseph Foster, Shaun Rushforth(USC), , Steven Morero Jr.(Long Beach) and Connor Owen, etc. to help me (with that great tool, the "internet.") Stop this madness, this epidemic, this pandemic of kids killing kids. Together we(Taylor F. in Menlo Park, Adam and Brendan, etc.)can stop this pandemic of kids killing kids.   We can do it, Yes we can!...

This Book (Right where You are) is Christ coming back for You...Even though you messed up (Brett, Chris, Michael, Chuck, Saul and all Yall) and you are scared to screw up. Even though Church folks wrote you off and called you doubting. Brett, Chris or Doubting Michael. God has come for you in K.K.K.to say Nicholas Jonas, Steven Morero Jr., Esteban Nunez etc. put your hand in my side. It is me. I came back for the boy inside of you. I came back because I see inside the Meth Addict, Crack Addict, Rapist, Murderer, Thug, Con and the Burglar. I came back for You. Already saw me but Brett, (Didymas) you need to see me in my Glory. You (Brett,Chris, Rick's Baby Boy, Michael need to see me, so you'll know that behind every C rucifixion there is a Resurrection. Behind every going down there is a getting up. A setback is a setup for a comeback. Brett you need to see me because you and Chris and Michael may end up in jail, in prison, or on Dr Phil and find yourself thinking that it is over. But having seen Me, you'll be able to see that you can get off the booze, drug or Gang Train... I have come for You boys in this time. (Written by a Joseph and a Paul in a prison) so you could see me. Because your will Be what you see. I care for Michael Vick through Tony Dungy, Tyson through Oprah, etc. and I am coming for You through K.K.K. You can turn around... that ain't for everybody, that's Christ's talk. For just a few of you (and you too) will embrace it. You opened this book one way. (Precious)and you shall close it.(Changed!) Transformed all the way down to your toe jam.) Another way..It has been a long time coming! But because of what You read, You heard, You visualized, and your Momma prayed for etc. , finally A Change Has Come to Brett,Sharon Moreno and to you.... I have come for You(Didymas). Ya'll feel me?

I will print the G.B.G. newsletters in the following pages but first I'd like to showcase some persons, companies and activists that I'd like for you to look up, look into, check out and possibly patronize etc... Check out Madam Barbara Brooks (also a G.B.G executive advisor) of the sentencing and justice reform advocacy. "Yes we can change 3-strikes law!" Mrs. Brooks can be reached via yeswecanchange3x@aol.com or 530-32908566... U.S. Mint Green (locate witnesses, family, friends, addresses etc) P.O. Box 751944 Washington Township, Ohio 45475...   PrisonWorld   Magazine   etc.   Cont.   Jenny   Triplett   678-233-8286 prisonworldradiohour.com ... prisonvoice.com (G.B.G. Advisor) at Convictnews.com or write Convict House, P.O. Box 1477 Ontario, CA.91762 (G.B.G. gives convict news magazine rave review and encourages the families of juveniles and inmate to convictnews.com out immediately) ...We give a loud shout out to attorney F. Lee Bailey for the great program he founded in Minnesota in which he gets business owners to sponsor youth inmates eligible for early release. This famed Lawyer tells chambers of commerce around the country "some of you should offer inmates some social interaction. Have him at your homes so he can see the long range wisdom of not holding up as gas station but instead acquiring a skill that makes him employable and down the road would allow him to have the stability of a family, a steady job and an increasingly forgiven reputation for the sins of the past. And here's the gold in the pot at the end of the rainbow "Lee Bailey continued" each one of these inmates who succeeds is an inspiration to those who do not believe it possible to leave a prison and be anything other than a candidate to return "G.B.G. amens Mr. Bailey and we invite him to join famed attorney Murray J. Janus, Senator Burton and others as a G.B.G. sponsor we'd also invite Lee Bailey to come and speak to G.B.G./Heart Staff, Advisors and members… since2007, Trinity Broadcasting Network (TBN), the largest Religious Network in the world has been quietly spreading a faith- based rehabilitative tv program for prisoners . TBN'S Second Chance program is poised to expand nationwide Alabama, South Dakota, Texas, Pennsylvania Florida and correction corp. of America (CCA) have already signed up for the free in-house television shows, and Ohio, Mississippi and South Carolina plan to begin pilot programs. TBN pays for all costs associated with the programming. Second Chance consists of up to four faith – based tv channels TBN ,the most popular faith-based channel in the United States, the church channel, TBN Enlace USA, a Spanish language channel airing faith based stuff from America and Latin American Countries, and JCTV (A vehicle for G.B.G), a faith-based entertainment channel targeting 13-29 yr old prisoners. Prisoners are never required to watch the programming. Prison experts G.B.G/Heart and expects such as Holyoke College Criminology and Sociology Professor Richard Moran notes that several studies and empirical data indi-cate a correlation between watching tv and violent behavior. Violent programs engender violence while inspirational programs have a positive effect. Offenders need a fundamental shift in how they perceive the world, transitioning from a vengeful mindset to one of grace, forgiveness, and self-control. Profess- or Moran noted, "At a time when budgetary limitations disallow many program opportunities for in-mates, the availability of 24 hr messages of hope is a powerful encouragement to all in corrections. TBN broadcasts are less intrusive than institutional Faith-based programs(e.g. "God Pods"), which have re- ceived Court approval provided no government funds are used in the religious component of said programs." The director of TBN second chance is Amy Fihn. In a missive dated April 28, 2009 she wrote in part. "Dear Sherman Thank you for sharing information about G.B.G.. It sounds like a great program to impact troubled youthful offenders in a profound way to help change negative mindsets that may even-tually land them into Adult Prison Institutions…with the interest and involvement of people like you, we believe we can begin to effect positive change inside America's Correctional Facilities. The Red Tape and levels of bureaucracy can be quite challenging…we would greatly appreciate you remembering the TBN Second Chance Initiative in your prayers. Keep up the good work and continue to be a vessel for the Lord to use in your environment for His glory." So wrote Madam Amy Fihn (619-276-7020, www.TBNsecondchance.org) A blessing, free TV! I'm embarrassed that it took me 3 months to write Amy back. But as C.O. Klausing told me, "dude, I have never seen anybody that gets as much mail as you do." But (eventually) I answer each and every missive. And as convicts, the G.B.G. team is uniquely positioned to offer expert commentary on the power of television in "our" captive environment. One of our members is a son of Odin and he told me "it's not my faith that I support C.D.C. doing the second chance deal is especially for free." I told Amy that I intend to get with Billy, Fred Schroeder, and Dr Curren and we will write a G.B.G. missive to the governor as well as to President Obama expressing our avid support for TBN second chance. Warden Walker, Associate Warden, Fred Schroeder, Billy and this writer all know Scott Kernan (C.D.C.'s Deputy Director) personally. We believe our missive will be well received (will send Matt Cate, Scott Kernan, and Senator Gloria Romero copies) by the bureaucratic bosses. And I intend to invite Amy, Dr. Paul Crouch's son and some of the JCTV staff to come and speak to the G.B.G./Heart team. I think Jimbo, Mrs. K, Adam, Dustin, Daniel Bugriyev (whose dad is head Russian chaplain for California and has a passion for youth), C. Solis MD, A. Duran PHD, Jennifer Heitkamp MD, Dr. Gregg, Dr. Jarman, Frank Curren MD, Doc, Willie, Billy, and our entire team will be blessed by an inspirational speech by Amy. And Peter (Andrist) wants G.B.G./Heart to do a DVD to show on TBN second chance. I plan a teleconference with Peter, Fred and Madame Kennedy to work it out.   Then Billy and I will sit down and dot the I's and cross the t's. G.B.G./Heart stands firm in spirit, prayer, commentary and in action with Amy Fihn, second chance and with TBN. Their mission, their offer, and their plan coincide solidly with the G.B.G. heart mission by helping rebuild inmate lives and reduce recidivism. I encourage all outside G.B.G. Ambassadors to do online petitions in support of Second Chance. Email or Snail Maid your Governor, Congressman, and the Senate and ask them to push for this positive programming in all prisons with all deliberate speed. And be sure to visit www.TBNsecondchance.org. You mail also email TBN second chance at TBN.org and then log on to our blogs,(http://shermanmanning.blogspot.com) and tell us that you did and pray the prayer for faith for this awesome program today.

I need some tech savvy, internet geeks(and HS, college, etc.)to use Facebook(like never before)to shout out "extra, extra read all about' K.K.K'." I need Y/O/U/ to use your Twitter page status updates, pokes, My Space and even Craig's List.org to tell others about Second Chance, about G.B.G. heart and our parent company NAPS(National Association for Public Safety), visit www.cafepress.com/manning today. And go back and reread the book and you will get what you are supposed to get. Email Dr. Phil (also go to Dr. Phil.com and click on teen talk), Tyra, Judge Matthis, Judge David Young, The LA Times, The NY Times, The Atlanta Constitution, Connect with kids, Boys and Girls Clubs of America and the local YMCA and tell them about K.K.K.. Send this book to Bernie Madoff, Martha Stewart, Michael Vick, Russell Simmons, Earl Graves, to Vanity Fair, Ebony, Time magazine and to Newsweek.

K.K.K. deserves to be perused, studied, analyzed and scrutinized by young people all across this Earth. Get it to Ryan Harlow, Van Hansis and Mayor Michael Sessions. You can get a "contact (G.B.G.)" from this book. Share it with Will C. Brooks, Neil Carlson, James McKnight and Jason Huyck. (yall find Jamie Kennedy, Michael Delgado (who was on Steve Harvey's TV show) from El Paso, TX Jeremy, the firemen at Coalinga Fire Dept., John Johnson a CNA in Coalinga, California, Chris Austid, Ashton Kutcher, Adam Lambert, Blake Koch, Matt Chrabot, Scott Cozza from Petaluma, California and Luke Sears and tell them there is a challenge for them on page 313 of "Blue-Eyed Blonde." Book 2. And since Jessie on Big Brother is so arrogant and cocky, etc.. Find Jessie online and send him to page 313 of "Blue-Eyed Blonde" book to also. And Paradise Hotel 2008? Nate, tell him to check out page (313)... Check out Microsoft's new "bing" search engine. I support anything Bill Gates is involved with due to Bill and Melinda Gates strong advocacy (and financial support) of bettering public schools and education in America. Please tell Microsoft that G.B.G./Heart strongly endorses bing and K.K.K. (you'll be surprised to learn that even gigantic companies like Microsoft will sponsor 100 or 1000 copies of a book like this to be put in schools. Every company (quid pro quo) that I've profiled here is encouraged to at least buy a couple of copies of K.K.K. and send it to a prisoner. Thank You!) Go bing and yahoo.....see group www.yahoo.com/group/publicsafety. This yahoo site is the G.B.G. parent company. E-mail me at hallopeter@sunrise.ch or at publicsaftey.yahoogroup.com ... I'll remind you to be certain to have your family ulsit(or ya) convicthouse.com . And check out Madame Jenny Tipiplet on the radio (WWW.ARTFIRST.COM) on Thursdays @ 10 pm est (9 pm cst, 8 pm mst, 7 pm pst)for the live show. The show is archlued in mp3 format and placed on the site for your convenience. They have a prison roundtable, discussions etc. I expect that G.B.G. advisor Dr. A. Duran may be Jenny's guest one day and possibly me. G.B.G. supporters Peter Andrist may call in from Switzerland and G.B.G./Heart will definitely be sponsoring the weekly show. Call Jenny in my hometown at 678-233-8286...Tell her G.B.G./Heart sent you ...Justin Berry was on Oprah. He's a young internet wizard. G.B.G. needs (you to go online) to find Justin. If we had 3 Justin's and 3 Ryan Hreljac we would turbo charge our Internationally recognized group. Find Evan and Melissa of "so you think you can dance" Fame, Danny, Noriega and Hairo. We need them yesterday. Christopher Clubb (Oregan), Laura Bledsoe and Tyler Schulrman... We endorse an internet company called loopt. It's a great site for locating old friends. It's C.E.O. is Sam Altman (soon 2 B a G.B.G. advisor.)... Go to the loopt website and tell Sam G.B.G.- K.K.K. spoke well of him and our pals out at Stanford University.... Finally. I hope our sponsors will send this book to inmates like Bryce Dixon(Flo), David Monroe (s.p.), Ernest Morgan (S.Q.) and Michael Tyler (all at San Quentin)... I hope Texans like Rev. Floyd Williams (Antioch Bpt. In Houston), Donna Orr and Jill Hegna will get contact highs from this book... My closing (epilogue) "letter to President Obama" will come on the very last few pages of this book ...

Letter to the President of the United States

TO: The Honorable Barack Obama

Dear Mr. President; If I didn't know that Dr. Bill Cosby was persuing this tome I'd be tempted to preface this missive with `what up Brutha Prez?' But I can hear Mr. Cosby and my old English Professor (Madam Warrior) saying "how dare you assault the English language" and my darling Grandmother (Dollie Manning) saying "boy you show Mr. Barack respect"... Greeting to First Lady Michelle,to lil Sasha and Malia. The G.B.G./Heart team, staff, members, TBN Second Chance, NAPS and our supporters are praying for you. And we mean it when we say "we are praying that God will . . . . At this time I've been rushed back to U.C. Davis Hospital (from Wakaville) and admitted. Dr. Andrew Elms (a youngster) stated "Mr. Mr. Manning you have meningitis. It means your cocci (valley fever) has run to your brain. We'll try to reverse it but in all candor you could be dead in less than a year." This is not the first time a physician has told me I'm headed for the pearly gates. But it was still chilling. "From your charts I see you've been put up one hell of a fight against this disease. It appears that C.D.C. has risked your health and safety time and again. I see where they just had you next door to an inmate who has a contagious infectious disease knowing valley fever compromises your immune system and it appears that a 'carefully orchestrated' cover-up took place at P.V.S.P. by medical staff. I hope your family is suing P.V.S.P." 'Just Detention International' (formerly known as "Stop Prisoner Rape") has worked closely with G.B.G./Heacy in our efforts to draw international attention to the thousands of (mostly white girls and boys) kids who are raped in detention centers all over America (and world wide) each year. Linda McFarlane (JDI'S Deputy Executive Director) wrote to me this "It sounds as if things have been stressful with trying to finish the book and getting it published. I am so sorry to hear that you are having nightmares and a reaccurrence of the trauma reaction." Linda Marvelled at my ability to work through pain and wrote "you are working hard and keeping positive. I am so impressed with all you do." Mrs. McFarlane continued " I am so sorry to hear that your illness is causing you so much distress. It must be frightening to be incarcerated and to be so ill with all your positive work and waiting. You certainly have a legacy to be proud of and I sincerely hope that you are around to see the effects of your work.. Melissa (Attorney Melissa Rothstein-JDI'S staff lawyer) does not do private legal work, so she would not be able to prepare your will for you. All the best, Linda." Never thought I'd be preparing a will at age 38. But that was before I met a Fella named "Valley Fever." I recall Dr. Quintana (at Mercy Bakersfield Hospital) telling me "Mr. Manning it is crystal clear you should have never gone to P.V.S.P and when you arrived, according to your records, you specifically informed (Dr. Postolov) A physician that you were sent there to catch valley fever. And having history of asthma ands a compromised immune system they not only did not transfer you; they didn't even test you." Back in the late 90's Dr. Johnson (at CSP-SAC) had insisted I take an AIDS test because my immune system was so low. After 3 negative kids AIDS test Dr. Johnson said "something that is not H.I.V. is causing your immune system to be low." And years later Dr. Quintana would reiterate (after another negative AIDS test) "I'm cognizant that you're not a participant in any "Risky Behavior" but I'm just harmed that C.B.C. is sending you back to P.V.S.P. with a vulnerable immune system. I don't blame you for refusing to go back." I was refusing to return to P.V.S.P. due to my valley fever Lt. Ellis and C.O. D Jones (who worked at the hospital) were very sensitive to my concerns and did not want to send me back. I told Dr. Quintana (and Lt. Ellis and Jones) how Marion E. Spearman had farced me to sleep in a cell with cell with no mattress, blankets, food or running water for 6 days. "Dr. Quintana a C.O. forced me to ingest a pill he got out of his personal belongings. I threw up for days Marion and Sergeant Grey destroyed the appeal Marion is a black man from my hometown. He grew up in the ghetto called Carver Homes. He has a vendetta against me" Dr. Quintana inquired "He's Black?" I told Dr. Quintana that my psychologists stated "The near psychological torture of being in a hospital for 14 months with no tv, telephone, visits, recreation or Religious Activity, constituted severe cruel and unusual punishment" Dr. Bruce Bakeman wrote a memo insisting that my stay at P.V.S.P was causing severe P.T.S.P. and could lead to Liability.

As I write this I have no dog in this fight. I finally left P.V.S.P. and I'm dying and will never see Marion again. But I state here and now (with all deliberate integrity) that I've met severely corrupt, racist, vicious and wicked officials (I.e. Mike Bunnell) working in these prisons. But beyond the shadow of a doubt Marion E. Spearman (associate warden at P.V.S.P), my homeboy and fellow African American is the most dangerous and deadly man in corrections. He is ruthless, reckless and duplicitous. When I was assaulted (the first time) by C.O. Williams "(and his partner) and then by C.O. Mendez and his partner etc. I was bloody and battered. Captain Shannon videotaped my bloodied body and stated "something happened to his man." Nurse Glenn Pickett wrote morning was obviously assaulted." Marion had Lt. Bennett and Kenneth Scott to destroy the tape and doctor the reports. Dr. George and Dr. Mullan requested my immediate transfer out of P.V.S.P.. "Inmate Manning is suffering from major depression and severe PTSD after enduring the longest hospital stay of any P.V.S.P inmate and his physician (Paul Griffin MD.) feels stress, Alvne can kill him. We (Dr. George and Mike Mullan) recommended an immediate transfer out of this institution." Marion destroyed the report! I had to go on a hunger strike to convince A.W. Ron Henson to finally transfer me out. I was assaulted (again) by C.O. Mullin as I exited P.V.S.P "This is for Mr. Spearman... If you write anything about his sexuality and the rumor about him and Yates..." Attorney Cassie Pierson (in San Francisco) wrote "Sherman you should own C.D.C. After all that has happened to you at P.V.S.P. I read Dr. Bruce Bakeman's memo and I spoke to Mavreen MA Honey; you've been tortured...Bunnell and CCI Costa Kalsifred documents (I had an enemy -Ray Sanchez on facility at P.V.S.P when I arrived there) just to get you to P.V.S.P in the first place." McGeorge school of Law distinguished professor and scholar Michael Vitiello wrote to a large Sacto Law Firm that "meaning endured deliberate gross medical negligence at P.V.S.P." and Professor Vitielle worked tirelessly to try to fid a reputable attorney and it's quack physicians. I'm too sick so I gave up.... "Hey Die (my nickname) this is Keke Reggie's daughter I have not seen you in so long but I'm 14 now.. I really miss you and I hope you get out real soon." I'm dedicating this missive to all the young and bangers out in the streets. To you youngsters smoking weed, is using meth, dropping out of school and just acting a damn fool.. Read on.. "All Cat's ("Cat" is my mother in Atlanta) sisters and brothers have been in the hospital within the last month. First your aunt Boot (Marderie Cat's oldest sister) had an operation, she had heart failure. Then Annette (Cat's youngest sister and my god-mother) had cancer.. Then we almost lost uncle Melvin (my favorite uncle); he was real low sick (she does not say from what. So I have to wait 13-14 days on Lee to receive and reply to my inquiry as to "What's wrong with him). Then uncle Roy (Cat's oldest brother) was found unconscious at his house.." Yall feel me young gangstas and playas? Imagine that you are sitting up in a cage and the C.O. calls your name "Hurck", "Sheron", Ben Chuchia" or "Diego Saavedra and he hands you a cutter and you anxiously open it expecting to read who just had a baby, who enrolled in college and who is getting married etc. And instead you read were all of you Aunt's and uncles- All of them- nearly die4d within the last month. DAMN... And that letter is neither fiction nor embellished. It's what my niece sent to me and I was/am numb absolutely numb.

...Redmond O'Neal was (a rarity- they usually don't let you attend) Allowed to go to his mom's Farrah Fawcett) funeral in shackles and chains. So when you guys like Brett and Chris (and you) are out there acting a fool perhaps you should ask yourself "Is there anything I'm doing, worth me going to prison?" And having to receive "Dear John" letters and letters detailing family disasters that you can do nothing about. Who's shoulders are you going to cry on? If you cry on your cellies shoulders (I'm just being authentic) he'll interpret that as a sign that you want to talk on his microphone!! Did you all see the movie "Brokeback Mountain"? I call this "Brokeback C.D.C.". It's getting worse everyday. Fellas get this: they stopped allowing all girly magazines (and no I'm not promoting porn. I do know it is sin) a few years ago. Prisoners (read closely) can possess no frontal nudity. Anal nudity is allowed...I'm not Dr. Phil and I'm not Dr. Curren. But to my poquito way of rationalizing and analyzing I think no frontal (women's private) nudity in an all male environment. But all men do have an anus and we are only allowed anal nudity? Are they trying to create homosexuals? They have placed (dehumanizing and unsanitary) timers on every prison toilet in California. You can only flush a toilet twice every fifteen minutes. Flush a third time and it shuts off for one hour. So I can only see "but" porn. Now I'm being forced to inhale "butt" waste?

...Let's go deeper (no pun intended) now at P.V.S.P. in ad-seg Marion E. Spearman (the warden's gay lover) forces cell mates (two men) to shower together!! What the hell is going on? ...I know Matt Cate (C.D.C. director) and Scott Kernan (deputy director) and they are consummate professionals. I wonder do Scott and Matt know what Marion is really doing out in Coalinga CA.? ...More importantly I wonder if you young studs, jocks and playas have ever contemplated what it's really like living amongst "Kids Killing Kids". Does Brett or Chris wanna come and cell up with the Menendez brothers, Marvin Johnson, Ed Stokes or Mr. Bardo? Eric and Lyle...nevermind that thought. I really hope Chris Shea (Sacto), Jeremy Hawes (twin cities), Joseph Latham (Latham should be 23 or 24 and he was at Mule Creek State Prison in 2004), Jennifer Jaimez (Sacto), Josh Costa (CA. teacher) and Daniel Sample will get this book...Christian was on Tyra Banks's show on 8/3/09. He identifies himself as a "racist" and I really want Christian to read this book. Because I can see him in prison! I need readers to activate a G.B.G. Gorilla Army and google, bing, zabasearch and locate the folks I name in this book and tell them they are in this book. Don't tell them what I say. Make them (LOL) read it for themselves.

...Michael (Eminem look-a-like) was at the L.A. Fitness club (in Bridgeville PA.) during that tragic shooting and I want Michael to have this book. It will help him...."Doc" Ford (G.B.G. member) and I are giving away $hundreds of dollars (you'll see it at the back of this book) to students to try to inspire you all to read, write and study. Tell others on your twitter, Facebook and Myspace page about the money. If it's wildly popular we will do it again. And if I'm dead-Peter will take my place...the show must go on! Lot's of you all (LOL) write to ask if the contest on page 313 of "Blue Eyed Blonde" book II (for those 18 and older) is serious. In a word "yes!"...I want principal Salome Thomas-El and his student to get this tome. I promise you readers that if you will take the time and e-mail folks like Sandy Close, David Innocencio, Al Gore, Lisa Ling, Caroline Kennedy and teachers like Daniel Sample (in Missouri) and recommend this book then Linda's prediction that this book will be my "legacy" shall come true. I want Michelle out at St. John's women shelter (Sacto) to have this tome. (And Michelle if you're reading drop me a line and "doc" and I will send the shelter a check with all deliberate haste). If Jim Vargas (Sactowall Youth Foundation) is reading I have a check for you foundation today! ...Ashton Kutcher, Steve Bing (Hollywood CA), Jim Nicholson (Seattle), Jai Breisch, John Breyault (Sacto), Ari Shapiro, Breaksk8, Cameron Douglas, Murray Morgan, Yvonne Walker (SEIU) and every high school principal needs this book. G.B.G./Heart and K.K.K. could very well be the final curtain call of my life but I promise you the data in this tome can change lives. It is from my heart not just my head. If you all will find Kevin Mclin, Peter Gramatas, Pedro Armando Quandt, Ben Tracy (NBC), Londell McMillan, Arthur (who was on the Wendy Williams show on 7/30/09) and scream "K.K.K." to them then K.K.K. will do it's job. I have a dream that G.B.G. monitors will be in every high school and students will learn how to identify a predator and a molester from what they read in this book!... One of my members to me (seriously) I should be in the universal world ccp record (Dan Rollman-universal records.com you all should contact Dan for me) for singlehandedly mailing more letters than any prisoner in California and maybe the world! The C.S.P. Sac mailroom estimates I've sent 1500 letters (this year) to people, politicians and parents about G.B.G./Heart and if (when) I find just 20-30 people (students) half as committed as Daniel Bugriyev and Adam Lane etc. We will transform schools...find me Kyle Larsen (Sacto), John Fink (Sacto), Tadd Carr, Cesar Ramirez (Oregon), Derek Jones (Oregon), Chris Stall (Sacto), Shannon St. Louis, Emily Messick etc. I have G.B.G. stipends (shall but better than nothing) for Kyle, Fink, Stall and for St. Louis. We have money for Brett Westcott, Cameron Brown and Maxwell Hanger. And for any student struggling, trying to stay in school or go to college etc. If you are indigent and you contact me I will do all I can to help you. I'm bold enough (I've got more time on my hands than you do) to write to Steve Bing, George Soros, Leonard Padilla, Tyler Perry and even Kevin Trudeau (since he knows where all the free money is!) and ask them to help you! I'll do anything to keep you out of prison university! "He that loves reading has everything within his reach." A G.B.G. advisor showed me a report which states that it costs $291,570 to raise a child (nearly three hundred grand) from 2008-till their 18th birthday. 32% of that is housing...so I can house you for 18 years on the streets for less than $90 grand. But-I can only house a kid for 2 years in a California prison for that same $90 grand. What the hell? Did you read that? ...Mentioning money: CA. prison guards are the best paid guards in the nation. Due to California's budget crisis they took a (similar to a furlough) ten percent pay cut. But did they? Every guard I know simply works 2 days overtime and they more than compensate for the 1-%. Too bad teachers don't have ample overtime the way CA. prison guards do. I know many guards earning $160,000 per year!! ...I need an army or internet savvy youth to employ the move-on.org and the David Axelrod/Obama strategy to get this tome to Josh Groban, Timothy Goebbel (now a college student), Johnny Weir, Jeff Buttle, Josiah Lemming and to Boink magazine....

I wanna let you know that you don't know what you can get away with until you try. Gen. Colin Powell says "Look below surface appearances and don't keep from doing so (just) because you might not like what you find" Powell's power, however, does not emanate from his positions, but instead, from his convictions. In a freaky kind of way my conviction (literally as a maximum security common criminal) has qualified me and prepared me for my position as G.B.G./Heart president...And may I warn you that I'll be dropping more (explosive) bombshells during and after my "letter to Barack"...

I saw "Angelo" on Fox 40 part trying to get adopted. He is a part of the Sierra Adoption services. I'd like for Mr. Hostetler to get this tome to Angelo. And I wanna give Angelo a $250.00 G.B.G./Heart check to help him on his way...and perhaps in my death (legacy) I can do what I could not do in life. (I have no dog in this fight and no vested interest in this; but to attorneys Kent Russell, EphraimMargolin, Gerald Uelman, Donald Heller, Johnny Griffin or to any lawyer I say this:) I want somebody to help Johnny Willie with his case. He's done 30 years in prison. And I never do this kind of appeal (for anybody) in a book. I've not asked you to get me out have I? And-there are many, many guys I know in jail (who are paroling soon) who should never be free! Never, ever, ever! But any half way decent attorney like Stuart Hanlon or Chris Darden could vindicate Johnny Willie's rights. I'm pleading with some lawyers to help

Willie. He's at C.S.P. Sac-A-8-cell #101...God's grace is painted across the canvas of despair. And regardless of my personal struggle or plight I must tell you I have seen God's grace...It is a far better place I go to than I have ever done. It is a far better place I go to than I have ever gone..I want my legacy to be about the transformation of generation y, teenies and tweenies. When you know you are near death you develop a kind of candor and boldness that a 38 year old, planning to live to be 98-won't have. I can say some things (in K.K.K) that I would not be writing if I was gonna live. The A.B., N.L.R., Nuestra Familia and the Green Wall would murder me for some of the data in this book. And please call former special F.B.I. director James Mattocks and ask him how dangerous C.D.C officials like Mike Bunnell are. Bunnell is a murderer I believe Bunnell had Captain Doug Pieper murdered! (see "Blue Eyed Blonde" Book II)... And I'm in the position, due to my conviction (as a common criminal on my way to the pearly gates)...to elucidate what Dr. Cosby, Dr. Poussaint and brother Barack are talking about. White kids in suburban look up to prisoners! Jesse James Hollywood (a murderer) has a cult following. I used to read some of the missives sent to Eric Menendez. He got letters (unsolicited) from preachers, teachers and politicians who would not even answer my letters. He got marriage proposals from college students! He got letters from gays, lesbians and straights. A guard (I won't call his name) who used to screen Scott Peterson's mail told me Scott got hundreds of letters per month. And Scott routinely writes an older gay (businessman) in Hollywood who sends him money. Scott writes graphic, hardcore gay porn to this guy. And guy's claim to fame is murdering a woman and an innocent child. Manson has a fan club! And I get some rather unique missives at times. Kids often think we (prisoners) have status. And so I (admittedly) manipulative my ready-made (undeserved) status to speak truth to power to what Cosby, Poussaint and Barack are so adamant about. And the advantage I have over President Obama is I don't have to worry about a civil rights icon getting angry with me for "talking down to black people." I don't have to worry about Rev. Jackson (and I still love Jesse!) threatening to (LOL) cut my nuts off! Mr. Cosby catches hell because he is perceived to be too rich and to proper to understand ("It's a black thang you can't understand") poverty etc. But although I was not poor I spent years working in the hoods (Perry Homes, Hollywood Court etc.) and organizing poor people with Rev. Hosea Williams. And I marched with Jesse Jackson in D.C. (in Eastgate projects). And yes I have photos of Jesse and I. And yes Jesse has never written me back. So I understand the frustration and humiliation of being locked in (prison), locked out (of the power structure) and forgotten about. I am "the" people. And from my vantage point in Hades and my perch in the prison, I can also say "Come on people." Unlike Barack I need not fear political suicide or appearing as an elite. How in the hell can a prisoner, a common criminal-be elite or out of touch? Hell I should get one of Steve Harvey's hoodie awards cause I'm "hood" certified! ...And-I feel what you all are saying when you feel that "education is the bridge to liberation" is just a tired cliché. But it's authentic and it is on point. Education defeats classism, discrimination and even racism.

Show me a man (or woman) who can read, write, count, think and reason and I shall show you a Thurgood Marshall who can walk into an all white court house and litigate (victoriously) the rights for black folks etc. You black folk reading (right now) would be on the back of the bus and unable to vote had there been no educated black folks... I heard Vernon Jordan talking about racism a few years ago. And he explained that at the time the top 3 fortune 500 companies (including "American Express") had black C.E.O.'s and those white folks (the good one's and the bad one's) would never put a man in charge of billions of bucks if he was not qualified! Rich folks don't put people in charge of their money as a public service. Mr. Jordan pointed out that he has sat in boardrooms with staunch racists. And he was not there because they liked him. He was there because they respected him; he was competent. Dr. Keith Black (who is black) is the world's greatest neurosurgeon. And some of his patients don't like his skin color but they adore his brain power. If you are competent you can not be denied. People who don't even like you will seek you out if you are competent. (get "The Pursuit of Happyness" by Chris Gardner and read about his racist client J.R.) ...Ya'll think holding a gun (I've held many) glues you a feeling of power? Knowing how to solve a problem, build a company, figure out a solution, a remedy or a formula etc. makes you feel hella high. And you can transmute that high you get from weed, guns or gangbanging into the desire for knowledge. The more you learn the more you will earn. Libraries are the most dangerous places on the planet because you can go into a library and figure out how to do anything in the world!! But quit acting a damn fool thinking you are cool. There is nothing cool about an ignorant fool running around (I see white boys and latinos doing it also) saggin and can't read or speak "English." What does s-a-g-g-i-n spell backwards??

I know exactly why prisoners can't have the internet. It's not porn etc. officials are worrying about. It's a pimp (Partner In Major Progress) they are worried about. Glue me 24 hours of internet use and I would turn America upside down.. A. I would e-mail and find every person I've named in this book. "C.J. Sheron (in Maryland) you are in a brand new tome called K.K.K. written by a jailbird. B. I'd build the G.B.G./Heart Facebook, Myspace and twitter following. C. I'd organize a Jihad against gangs and illiteracy...I'd organize! Organize and organize. But many of you only use your computer for porn. What a waste. You can change the world with (i.e. usaservice.org) the internet. And this is what Dr. Bill Cosby is so passionate about. Competence...you think Mr.Cosby is airing dirty laundry? Well wash that soiled sh-t! Wash it! You think Mr. Cosby is being tough? I recall mayor Maynard Jackson telling a group of black students that he was tired of seeing "shuffling and grinning negroes" who drop out of school and get on welfare. And you thought Cosby was being tough? You all (Cameron Glass, Maxwell Hanger, Daniel Job and Andrew Knox) need to come see me before I kick the bucket. And I shall show you that most of us (in Hades) can't read and write over a 7th grade level. Many are functionally illiterate. Ignorance, shucking and giving thuggery is a recipe for incarceration... to you "Woods" who speak caucasionics (white e-bonics i.e. "rite" instead of "right") and all you ebonic masters I say learn to speak proper English. Folks can look at you and assume you're a "fool"; but then you open your mouth and confirm it. the power of life and death, success and failure; even the power to get to the White House is in the tongue- if you can speak.

I'm being real. It pisses me off to see 16, 17 and 18 year old kids who can't talk. I heard a sexy young lady (21) on Judge Judy saying "I "lended" him the money" and "we "rid" around. I cringed...

Legacy? If I have to look down from the heavens and see G.B.G./Heart at it's peak. I want to witness a revolution. I want to see a battalion and a squadron of youngsters transformed into a team of "special forces" against illiteracy, truancy and gangs. "The kindgom suffers violence and the violent take it by force." And "the grand essentials of happiness are something to do, something to love and something to hope for." G.B.G. fits that bill for me. May I repeat "there is nothing that can't be done if we lift our voices as one." Dr. King enjoyed his greatest success when he was able to convince white brothers that they (too) had a vested interest in the black plight. And when he was able to inspire white students to join the movement they (together) revolutionized the planet. What Harvard trained physician Franklin Curren, A. Duran Ph.D. and our entire prisoners, police, students and pastors to work together and to echo the Heart sentiment. We reach out to Aaron Levine, Adam Kuperstein, Travis Guyer, Brett Miles, Rev. Andre Schumaker, Timothy Combs, Antwi Akom, Jason Wilhite and Alan Rafferty. We wanna pair them with Bugriyev, Lane, Nicolodi and others. We want to have Charlie Miller, Eric

Castellanos, David Kelley and Ari Shapiro talking about G.B.G. Some of the stuff in this book is jaw dropping. And I would caution my family that someone may wish to sue my estate after I'm gone. But I fully stand by the contents of this tome...G.B.G. seeks some elite operatives to engage in our unconventional warfare (Jihad) against the incarceration of America's children. We need "Dallas" at Kmax in Sacramento to help us. We want Alice Huffman, Ben Todd Jealous, Josh Walter, Ryan Evans (Colorado), Frank Carter (artist in Atlanta), Christopher Clubb and Marc Kielburger all working (together) in G.B.G. our job and duty is not to lead youngsters. We inspire youngsters to lead themselves. We call on youngsters to master your mind(s). Learn to read like Beethovan composed music. Learn to write like Shakespeare wrote poetry. And think I need some thinkers out there. Bring me Ryan Hreljac, Karen Chapski, Tyler Schuurman, Eric Nies, Mark Gross and Ernest Griffin and we will do Jihad. My duty is to inspire, motivate incite and propel you to excel and stay out of jail. We need to ally Congressman Edolphus towns, Run Huffman etc. with Captain Cedric Simon (Jail commander) and even utilize this book to incite Jihad...We need Bryan Kennedy, David Hellyer and Tobias Lake and we will do warfare against the perils which catapult kids into prisons. David V. Adams SR, Carol Biondi, H.Thomas Boyle, J. Mario Molina M.D., Algelica Huston and Russell Simmons can help us. So can Michael Moore (see Michael Moore in "Blue Eyed Blonde" book II), Stewart Hills (Davis, CA) Jerry Pike and all his students at Lodi High School. Mentioning Lodi High School I want all the Lodi students to know we have a $500.00 check to help you all start back printing "The Flame" newspaper! And perhaps students in Mr. Pike's journalism class can all become G.B.G. ambassadors. I prophesy that our G.B.G./Heart shall stage a coup d'etat against street gangs, child molesters and (also) the illiteracy which leads youth to commit crimes. "This is G.B.G!" This is coup d' etat, jihad and it is warfare. I'm committed (with break out of every box, transform my ownself by the renewing of my mind daily. I will manipulate my bully pulpit (Hades) to testify to youngsters. I'll work with the determination of a Medgar Evers, a Martin Luther King Jr. and a Thurgood Marshall. I am as dedicated to keeping youngsters out of jail as Mother Teresa was to caring for the poor...I reveal the secrets of the infamous Menendez brothers as a testimony to my captive audience about the backwards, desperate and perverted happenings within the "prison subculture." This place weirds you out: "Atlanta (aka Sherman) I know you don't f_ck around and I respect that but for the $250.00 you loaned me can I give you a blow job or some ass? Heck you can even play with my ass on the Shu-Yard. My celly (Mike Henrickson) is even willing to do a threesome....Flush this kite (missive). E. ..."Guess who wrote that missive? Eric Menendez! I declare that to be authentic under penalty of perjury... I sent the missive to a famed lawyer (for safekeeping under the attorney/client privilege.). Prison is like a bathhouse ...and this stress atmosphere retards rationality and creates killers..."I'm gonna kill that n_gger Obama, when I get out if he wins!" stated "Raven" at P.V.S.P. I don't know his real name but he ("Raven") was the inmate plumber (facility 'A') at P.V.S.P and he is extremely violent. Do I think the secret service will allow him to murder the President? Of course not. But is he dangerous and irrational enough to try? Absolutely! And these (Raven) are the kinds of people you will be locked in a cell with, every night if you come here. The psyche is damaged by just being in prison. It is exacerbated by ad-seg within the prison. This is a 24 hours Taliban. This is Gitmo! ...I'm the face of the signature illness (PTSD). My 14 month hospitalization causes terrible debilitating flash backs. PTSD causes invisible wounds. And my duty is to show you my wounds, my hurt, my dirt and my pains. And it is from a place of woundedness that I reach out to your wounds. And you can turn your scars into stars..."So you think you can dance?" I say to you gang bangers-so you think you can bang? Come here to Hades and you'll find yourself banging against a man's private part...(Disclaimer: Senator Dianne Feinstein is not an official sponsor of G.B.G. In the back of the tome some memos have her listed as "sponsor". G.B.G.

anticipated (too soon) support from this great senator. However, at press time she had not agreed to sponsor. Our official sponsors do include Famed senator John Burton, Swiss philanthropist Peter Andrist, Harvard Grads and a battery of licensed psychologists. Dr. Phil never responded to our offer to team with him...and G.B.G./Heart President Sherman D. Manning does still have a copy of the first loan check he sent to Eric Menendez. At this time Eric's wife resided with Lyle's wife Becky Snead. The check was written from Hypotherkarbank in Switzerland-to Becky Snead for Tammi and Eric. And prison investigators recorded Manning authorizing the check telephonically. Prison I.S.U. also recorded Eric stating to his wife that the check was for her. ...My initial plan was to never expose the Menendez secrets til I got out of prison! Attorney Murray Janus asked me on several occasions why I never wrote about these two guys. I've penned 8 tomes which never mention them. A. Had I written about them while residing with them I could be killed. B. I planned a big tell-all tome to be published upon my exoneration about all of the killers and perverts whom I'd resided with in prison. But my plans were diverted and altered when I learned I'd probably not live very long. And that I would never get out of prison...Ipso facto, I had to finally let the cat out of the bag and tell you what you will never see in a Hollywood depiction of prison. I'm certainly not the smartest dude in prison. If I were I would not be (duh) in prison. Yet even my enemies will tell you I read 3 or 4 books per week. Time and again I've been forced to mail 300-400 books home to be donated to inner city libraries. I can truly state I've read almost everything written by, for or about prisons, gangs and thugs. And never have I read one that really told it like it is. Dr. Lewis Yablonsky (Harvard prof.) has authored 19 books about gangs and prisons. He is 84 years old and considered the foremost expert on gangs in North America. Dr. Yallonsky even wrote a preface for the notorious "Tookie" William's "Blue" Rage, Black Redemption." Dr. Yablonsky's brother is an F.B.I. special agent and during a telephonic interview in 2009 Dr. Yablonsky stated "Sherman you are the "experience" therapist. You are the "real life" expert. You know more about gangs, child predators, serial killers and the inner workings of a prison than I'll ever know. You have been able to look inside the mind of a killer; up close and personal...if you'll write what you've seen you'll blow the minds of wanna be gangsters."... I've read Jack Abbott's book thrice. I read Rubin "Hurricane" carter's (great book) book 6 times. Read all 19 of Dr. Yablonsky's books. I've read books by cops, killers, pastors, F.B.I. profilers and many others. And I've still never read a book which truly tells kids how it feels when you are caught, tried, sentenced, convicted and then the lights are out and the cell door is locked, and you are trapped in a cage with Eric, Lyle, Marvin, Bardo, Stokes, brett or even Sherman. I want to tell you: Eric Menendez (be advised that due to the author's illness and frequent hospitalizations this tome is not printed in chronological order) is obsessed with John Walsh, Geraldo Rivera and Edgar Cayce (the deceased author). Eric stated "I'm glad Adam (Mr.Walsh's son) was molested and murdered. They should have cut his penis off and shoved it up his anus, John hates prisoners." Yet, he never missed an episode of AMW. It was as if he expected to see himself on AMW. He never really explained to this writer why he hated Geraldo. But he certainly believes he has the gift that Edgar Cayce (supposedly) had. And he predicted to this writer, in 2001 that he would be on the Montel Williams show. And reluctantly I admit that-he was.....

Years ago in my hometown Bishop Joe Price introduced me to one of the weirdest people I've ever met. (Joe Price had been introduced to me by Conrad Gamble!) Joe introduced me to minister Dwight York. Minister York headed the United Nation of Nuwabian Moors. Dwight had a compound outside of Atlanta with many families living there. Dwight believed in aliens, astroplaning, sex with girls as young as 6, sex with boys as young as 5. Dwight told me his religion was a combination of Islamic, Jewish, Christian and the native American faiths. He believes in U.F.O.'s as well as reincarnation. I was told I was one of the few outsiders allowed inside of the compound. I saw kids dressed (literally) as cowboys on (black kids) one occasion, Indians on one occasion and as muslims on another....As I prepared to make my fourth visit to Dwight's compound a civil rights legend told me "Dwight is claiming to be a type of Messiah. He has sex (which he'd never told me) with children, he calls himself "Doc", "Dwight" and "Abba". He's a cult leader." And then it dawned on me how strange the people I'd met there acted. I never re-visited the compound. Years later I'd read where Dwight received 135 years-to-3 life sentences in prison. Even more startling to me was the fact that Eric G. Menendez had memos, publications and pamphlets by Dwight. "He's a fantastic leader and a prophet." Eric told me. I never informed Eric that I knew this monster, as I reflected upon Tony Alamo, Wayne Bent (Strong City), Branch Davidians, Heaven's gate, Jim Jones etc. The personality of both Eric and Lyle began to unfold in my mind. Congresswoman Jackie Speier me Jim Jones and she warns "Jim Jones and Jonestown can happen again- we've got to be more vigilant!" I fully concur with her statement and I add to that "Jonestown is happening in prisons across America. Under the guise of 'Sons of Odin', 'Wiccan' etc. Just as Osama Bin Laden manipulates and mutates the Islamic faith etc. high profile prisoners i.e. Eric Menendez are hijacking religions, manipulating lesser intelligent inmates (and staff) and creating a culture of occultism in prisons!" One would think C.D.C. would have taken a closer look when Eric carried the entire prison to be locked down (C.S.P-Sac) due to staff finding a computer in his cell....one would be inclined to think C.D.C. would have gained some notion about the leadership and influence of Eric when inmate Mike Taylor and Eric were discovered drafting escape plans on the Shu-yard at C.S.P. Sac. Long lines of makeshift rope were found hidden inside the mattress of inmate Taylor. Taylor refused to finger Eric and Eric was eventually cleared of all charges.

Correctional officer Wally Laffitt routinely smuggled speed and weed in to Eric, Taylor and Henrickson. Henrickson's civilian lover (Tom) and Tammi also participated in the drug running....Eric was corresponding with Larry Birkhead (of Anna Nicole Smith fame-although at that time I'd not heard of Madame Smith) years ago. Larry identified himself as bi-sexual and wanted to visit Eric. Eric indicated he would advise Larry to obtain a fake Lawyer's business card or law student's I.D. and visit Eric as an attorney (in a private attorney room) and be able to "give each other hand jobs underneath the table",

...Eric is leading a personality driven movement from behind bars. He's successfully convinced his members to reject everything and go with the flow of the group. Eric G. Menendez (the vicious killer who even claims to have had intimate relations with lawyer Leslie Abramson) has all of the hallmarks of a cult leader...trying to better comprehend how/why people are seduced into cults even inside prisons, I went to Dr. Franklin Curren (chairman of G.B.G.'s advisory board-whom we go to for input and expertise etc.) and he explained that the occults affect the 'frontal lobe' and anesthetizes it. The frontal lobe is the 'executive chambers' of the brain. It's where all decisions are made. C.Solis MD. added "even in 'gangs'. We often discover that charismatic and flamboyant personalities can gain manipulative access to persons' minds and the brain shuts down (i.e. in gangs and cults) and all decisions are made for it (you)." Piggybacking off of what Dr. Curren and Dr. Solis explained, one can better comprehend why it is that inmates (especially youngsters) who enter Hades are never the same again. Experts like to give syndromes fancy titles like "learned helplessness" and "institutionalization" and even "PTSD." When in a sense-it's pretty elementary to conclude that when a 17 year old Jeffrey G. Howell enters prison. He's young, naive, scared, skinny, undereducated and addicted. And he comes to Hades where Eric, Sherman, Henson and Johnson reside. And he must cell with one of us. He will take on our identity (fake it til you make it) and learn to act, think and react as we do. And upon his release from prison he will be fully indoctrinated in the prison mentality. Having had all decisions made for him by staff and/or gangs and wardaddys etc. Upon his release from prison he will be a criminal....Eric is responsible (in my view) for an inmate committing suicide at C.S.P. Sac just prior to Lisa Ling visiting the prison Eric had been caught in the chapel with the clerk. (a.k.a "Irish") making long distance and out of country telephone calls over the chapel telephone. (it was common knowledge that Johnny "Boy" Chico, Irish, Henrickson and Eric would have sexual rendezvous in the chapel; routinely). It is alleged that Eric was orchestrating another attempted escape via telephone meetings...Upon being caught Irish lost his job and Eric did not keep his word (stating that he would take the rap and claim Irish knew nothing etc.) and Irish committed suicide!!!

At P.V.S.P. upon being brought drugs by C.O. Garza, Eric's celly "Spot" sold some to an inmate in building #3 who subsequently went to his sell and murdered his cell partner. Also at P.V.S.P. Eddie Watts was provided drugs in the visiting room (which had allegedly been set-up by Eric and C.O. Wheat) and inmate Viafanova (aka "Twin") ratted Eddie out. Eddie was placed in a holding cage by then captain Marion E. Spearman. Eddie told Spearman the drugs were for Eric and "I just swallowed them I need my stomach pumped." Marion laughed and disregarded Eddie's plea for help. And Eddie died in the holding cell with Spearman looking on.

I have no vested interest in what happens to Eric, Lyle, Johnson, Stokes etc.etc. I'll never see them again. But as a human being who knows how Many youngsters (i.e. Joseph Miller, Howell, Latham, Johnny "Boy" etc.) come to prison with short sentences and are manipulated by "master manipulators" like Eric and Lyle etc. I am duty bound to sound the alarm. And quite frankly I should have my ass beat for being to selfish, too timid and too afraid to speak out prior to being given a (medical) death sentence. And even on my way to the dusty grave I shall not attempt to paint myself as a saint. I was/am a chief of sinners! I'm a thug, a gangster and a common criminal!

I had to improvise and disguise myself in order to survive in Hades. In a real sense I denied the Christ just as did Peter at the fire... Moving away from the Menendez Monsters back to the man in my mirror, I have sinned. Dam I have sinned. And in the process I stone a similar letter. I'd been told by a reliable source that "if you catch a new case they can't transfer you until the case is adjudicated, and that could take years!!!The Clayton County Sheriff laughed at his letter and refused to fly to California and testify. However, Mary Hanlon Stone (as expected) encouraged D.A. Jan Scully to push for 75- years to life ...After telling Dr. Hedblad the whole story he agreed to testify for me. Attorney Janus tried to get me to admit to the Judge why I wrote the letters. "The Judge is pragmatic enough to understand your fears. You were driven to write these. The case can be dismissed". I fought the caes (without transferring) for five years... Sadly, I had a celly (Michael Sajatovick) also transferring to gladiator school. He spat upon Mr. Rosario to (temporarily) halt his transfer. But when the D.A. refused to 'charge' him, this writer advised him to write a threatening letter to Governor Gary Davis. He did and it stopped the transfer. I don't know how much time Michael received for the threat. But it is sad and it is sick that convicts are so afraid of being transferred to certain prisons that they will risk getting life sentences- just to avoid certain prisons. ..Happens every day! Quite candidly? Last year (2008)I was about to be transferred to Donovan where I knew I'd be murdered! And I went crazy with fear. Wrote an irrational threatening letter to a lawmaker. Tow CHP Officers (who insisted I not use their names) came to interview me stating "obviously you have no intention and no capability of carrying this threat out. Why are you wanting this B.S.?...

Prior to my departure from P.V.S.P. inmate Rauser (a/k/a "Angel",ex-bpt.preacher-present high priest in Wiccan – ex- Menendez pal from C.S.P SAC.)And Eric Menendez were trying to raise $5000.00 to "take over C.D.C. by organizing Christians, Muslims,Jews and wiccans vader one united banner!! "Who introduced me to Mike Bunnell? Eric Menendez! Who introduced me to Dr. Marilyn Windham? Eric G. Menendez. I recall (vividly) Lonnie Young and I catching Eric Menendez, Johnny 'Boy" Chico, Hendrickson and inmate schooler(aka "superman"-superman ended up getting C.O. Sterkin fired for performing freak shows in the control booth etc.) having a 4 way sexcapade in Eric's cell. It was a very unusual sight. As well, it was a normal site Sex runs rampant in prisons. Many muscular inmates are commonly referred to as "Lee Haney in the daytime and LIL Mrs. Muffet at night. Superman in the daytime and wonder woman at night". I challenge reporters to interview people like Terry Rosario (who is retired) and ask him how often inmates (i.e. Menendez etc.)are caught in illicit sexual triangles ...I call upon Tony Jury, Whit Johnson , Jeremy Hawes, Chris Shea (sacto), Brandon Hughes and Huggh Michael Hughes to stand 'shoulder to shoulder' with G.B.G. and break the cycle of criminality which leads youth to prisons... I studied David Holmes for two years and tried to figure out what made him tick. David dressed up as Santa Claus (in Cobb County) and took lil boys to mall bathrooms to molest them. David, likeBret Moore has a number of tell tell hallmarks which are (absolutely) identifiable; if one knows what to look for. Bring me Omar Samaha, David Holloman(sacto),Adam Bettencourt (sac-state student), Alex Blench, Glen Close(puppies behind bar), Principal Paula Ducan (Sheldon High School-Elk Grove), Marayam Guzman, McClathy, High School Students (sacto), Stewart Hills (Davis...we have a $350.00 stipend for Srewart) Destini Chunley, Joshua Panno and David Coleman. I'm calling people out in K.K.K. to come together. I need you all to help us help schools. The California Public School system is on life supports. And the Governor has shut off the electricity powering the life supports. The life supports are running on a generator. The University system is operating on an I.V. and we must reverse the curse. I call upon Rachel Ruff (sacto), Jordan Benjamin and Andrew Rauscher to join us. G.B.G.is real! We trust God. The bible makes faith. The bible doesn't make sense! I need you to get this tome to Barbara Becnel, Atty. Don Masuda and Atty. Donald Heller. Get it to Christopher Miller, Ernest Sonnier, Alba Cova, Ericka Cuellar, Michael Miller (United Methodist Church is sacto), John Singleton, Anthony Morrison, Nathan Gould, Judge William Ovoy and to your Congressman. I need you to get Hal Lifson, Rachelle Spector, Phil Spector, Christopher Durbin (GA.) Jonathan Karp, Alexander Dugdale, John Francis and Amy Fisher this book. This unique, unconventional, unorthodox and unusual tome is written to pull you youngsters (thugs, jocks,nerds, freaks, geeks, outcasts etc.) back (with the truth about what goes on inside Hades) like a slingshot; and then shoot you into your destiny! I want you to be able to recognize a coach named James Spencer Hagelston who doubles as a perverted child molester. I want you better equipped to recognize an Ed Stokes or a Bardo standing outside your door. I want Ladies to recognize a thug, a liar and a con man named Sherman D.Manning promising to marry you and to love you til death do us part. K.K.K. is written to pull you back –cause you to do. A double take ("is this too good to be true?)And to shoot you into your destiny! Bring me Bryce Dixon, Donna and C.J.Sheron (in Md.) Justin Berry and Kyle Love. I needGarrett McCain (student), Sandra Jackson (teacher) and Charles Ebersol to help us do jitlad on gangs. We must deprogram kids coming out of prisons just as we deprogram kids coming out of war. Prison is a war zone. We need to support Lorna Smith, Charles Best and all of those who work to keep Youngsters from going to jail in the first place.I want Army Spec. Zachary Boyd, Dr. Jeff Gardere, Dr. Nancy Kalish, Ricky Harlow and Black Koch to join us. We can't continue to paint and wallpaper over the problems our Youth are facing. We must take action. Bring me Michael Vick and Michael Milker. I need Bill Dallas and David Zablotny to get this book today. G.B.G./Heart is staging a miracle as we pull you back and shoot you into your destiny...What I've come to understand from great minds like Dr. Yablonsky as well as Dr. Franklin Curren is the power of my positionas a convict. In a moment of candor Dr. Curren told me "the reason you can be more effective with at-risk youth than I or Dr. Yablonsky can ever hope to be is because of your status as a state prisoner. Someone who is here and in the mix nothing I learned at Harvard can qualify me to speak truth to power with the kind of conviction and compassion that you have". I'm humbled by my trails,blessed by my battles and bettered by my circumstances...G.B.G. is looking 4 some soldiers to join us as we bang for education, bang for literacy and bang for good. This (G.B.G.) is the real deal. We R LA. Familia baby! This is the family! We are a strategic response unit 2 gang, guns, drugs and violence. G.B.G. is a provocative megaphone which we can use to support "David" out at McClathy High School as he opens an urban teen lounge. We wanna work with Deputy D.A. Kristine Reed and teach youngsters how to overcome even psychological rapes which gang leaders commit everyday. Bring me Break sk8 and Wes Kouariv and it's Coup D. Etat! K.K.K

Is written to infuse some steel into your spine and to open up your mind. Let us create an online community to fight against child porn, child rapes and child crime. Alex Blench, Justin Berry and Maxwell Hanger can train on-line sharpshooters to work in concert with AMW.com etc. to bring down child predators... The reason I offer funds to David Holloman, Craig Cannon and to Adam Bettencourt etc. is because we must employ unique tactics to acquire unique talent. And G.B.G. is the facebook generation and a 'flatscreen organization. We stand with SEIU Pres. Yvonne Walker, California teachers and all educators. Bring me Zachary Finney, Van Hansis and Mick Hazen and we will change the world. Let's bust a move against violence, hate, rapes and molestation. G.B.G./Heart is the real deal. We do warfare! Don't get it confused-we fight baby boy. And yea though we walk thru the valley of the shadow of death we will fear no evil for God is with us (G.B.G.). "For by you I can run against a troop, by my God I can leap over a wall... He is a shield to all who trust in him... It is God who arms me with strength, and makes my way perfect. He makes my feet like the feet of deer, and sets me on my high places. He teaches my hands to make war, so that my arms can bend a bow of bronze... I have perused my enemies (drug dealers, rapists, molesters and murderers) and overtaken them... I have wounded them, so that they could not rise, they have fallen under my feet. For you have armed me with strength for the battle... As I lay 96Lbs on my death bed I thought "I am poured out like water, and all my bones are out of joint... My strength is dried up like a potsherd, and my tongue clings to my jaws; you have brought me to the dust of death. For dogs have surrounded me; the congregation of the wicked has enclosed me... I can count all my bones. They look and stare at me"... But I want G.B.G./Heart to remember that "blessed be the Lord my rock, who trains my hands for war, and my fingers for battle. My loving-kindness and my fortress, my high tower and my deliverer, my shield and the one in whom I take refuge, who subdues my people under me". I want you to think big. I want you to dream big. Read big, pray big. Imagine and hope big. I want you to utilize, facebook, myspace, bing and google like never before. Reach out and touch Steve Bing, David E. Kelley, Michael Moore, Russell Simmons, Ashton Kutcher and Caroline Kennedy and tell them about this tome, G.B.G./Heart and about NAPS. And let singers Danny Noriega (CA.), Joslah Lemming, Nathaniel Marshall, Daniel Sample and Jason Hike know there are stipends with their names on them... I want principals like Paula Duncan, Ron Clark (Ron Clark Academy) and Joshua Costa to know I'm willing to try to get this tome into their schools. And I will donate money when I can. I believe in education!...I say in this book that Bill Cosby gets on my damn nerves. And he does. But Bill Cosby is right: I f the K.K.K were coming black parents would hide their children. But we don't hide them from gangbangers and crack dealers. More then 65,000 people will get out of prison this month! 82% of them have no High School diploma. Hello! These are nearly 1 million black men in prison. Damn! As much as I love Jesse Jackson, Al Sharpton and everybody else –wow. We need to declare Jihad on illiteracy. One million black men in prison! As mad as I get with that fat ass drug addict Rush Limbaugh and that megalomaniac Sean Hannity etc. We can't blame Rush and Sean for this one. They are not pulling black boys out of school. The Black Panthers are not hooking white boys up on crank and heroin. We are doing it to ourselves. We must wake the hell up, put down the crystal meth and ever-clear. Put down the beer and hold a damn book near. You can read your way to success. You can read your way out of the gang, out of the trailer park, out of the juvenile, out of the damn dope. It's not cliché and it's not a con. You can transform the jangling discords of yesterday's failure into an oasis of today's success. I have never seen a bridge that a book wouldn't cross. I have never seen a mountain a book wouldn't climb. I have never seen a battle a book wouldn't win…Although Tony Robbins doesn't answer my mail anymore I still recommend every kid read "unlimited power" by Robbins. And go get "come on people" by that damn Bill Cosby and Alvin Poussaint Md. I want this tome reframe the fight and the gang. We can change the narrative right here right now. Don't you ever allow anybody else to tell you it's cool to be a fool. Cool to go to jail and be screwed by other men. Reading is cool. Malcolm could read. Martin could read. Barack can read Michelle, Sasha and Malia can read. Ryan Hreljac can read. You can do it too. One of our supporters from Morocco (EL Malki Said) wrote "Sherm you have an emotional intelligence that is off the charts… No one is capable of painting a character sketch like you do… You've got the midas touch". I hope he is just half way right. And as we reach out to 25 year old Dustin Johnson and to Andrew Goddard and his son etc. our message is clear. The character sketch of the average prisoner is that of a void loser. And to get in the winner's circle one must get in the library… To politicians I say don't confuse the airbag with the solution. Prisons used to be airbags for lawlessness and crime. Yet now they're being depended upon as babysitters, warehouse and as permanent keepers. California cut funding by more than 20% to the university system in the past 2 years. That is a recipe for the creation of murderers and rapist. I wish citizens would show up at town hall meetings demanding that we restore spending on education. But in this bubblegum generation where sophisticated adults get together, yell, holler and fight like animals (over health care) etc. small wonder the village fails to raise peaceful and educated kids. I would suggest that kids look past the violence and hypocrisy you see in adults. And choose to lead, follow or get out of the way. You are a great generation with marvelous potential. I believe in young people. And you have been called to this book. This book choose you. And some of my adult cohorts will take offense to a few of the words (i.e. "ass" which is in the bible) I utilize in this tome. But at the end of the day, the one's who will reject this tome merely based upon 2 or 3 words they claim (deceitfully) not to use – they were gonna reject it anyway. They would want me to beat you over the head with the kind of lofty semantics which you'd never read but I'm in critical condition. And when one is in critical condition one has no time to butter people up. This is a crucial moment and I won't miss this opportunity to use Hades as a vehicle to meet you at the front gate, and try to persuade just one not to come and reside here. Hear ye. Hear ye…..

I saw C.O. J. Purdie a little while ago. I hadn't seen dude in 7 years. He says "U still writin books dude? Am I in one?" Then he launches into "did you ever get the balls to write about your buddy Eric Menendez?" I thought to myself "if you only knew". I said nothing to him about K.K.K. He did add "everybody is talking about the Gang Bangers For Good program. Sounds pretty cool dude".

I was reflecting on Sergeant J. Stratton and Lt. Johnson and how unfair they treated me. Even Captain Jeff Lynch (Jeff is actually pretty cool but he goes along with the crowd. Rarely have I found a "Jimbo" who will blatantly go against the crowd!) could have decided not to place me in the hole on Dearaujo's Mendacity. But I believe that some of you will actually end up thanking Stratton, Dearaujo and Johnston for mistreating me. Had not it been for them (I repeat) you would not be reading this. And let there be no doubt about the fact that I know (in the fabric) of my being that lives will be revolutionized not just by what I've penned But the input, opinions and expertise of Dr. Curren, Dr. Solis, Dr. A. Duran, Dr. Jennifer Heitkamp, Dr. Jarman, Dr.

Gregg, Warden Walker, A. W. Fred Schroeder, A. W. Jeff Macomber, C.D.W. Tim Virga, C.D.W. Terry L. Rosario Sr., Captain Patricia Kennedy and others-which are (collectively and specifically) represented in this book will transform, enlighten and elucidate.

Each time I go back and re-read this unfinished book I get mesmerized. I'd love this book even if I didn't write it... And we need you to I.M.,T.M. and E-mail (for G.B.G.) folks like Sherwood Cathern (Bayside church of South Sacramento), Mayor Cory Booker and Mayor Michael Bloomberg and tell them about K.K.K. Mayor Booker is working tirelessly on a re-entry program to help keep ex-offenders out of prisons. Perhaps Mayor Bloomberg can donate a thousand copies of this book to help Cory's program.

I want you to know that God will restore to you the years that the cankerworm, the palmerworm and the locust ate up. Your life is not over no matter how lonely you may be it's not over baby boy. I know how easy it is to give up. Some of you have gotten hooked on drugs or alcohol and you want to stop. But it's easier said than done. And you are one of the tens of millions who will never be on Dr. Phil or on Oprah. It seems like everybody else has been blessed and been on t.v. But you wonder, silently, "what about me?" Well I wrote this book for the bad boys and the bad girls. I wrote this book for the teens and tweenies whom society has given up on. You who have been written off, thugged out or locked up. You can turn around. There is medicine in this book for you. I don't know what page you change is on. But if you really read this book you better believe a change is gonna come... Again I don't know what page it's on but a change is gonna come. I've instructed G.B.G. allies (and am asking them right this minute) to contact T.D. Jakes, Eddie Long, Bishop Earthquake Kelley, Rick Warren and even the Pope and ask them to pray that this tome (K.K.K.) will stir you up and change you. I've personally written the Potter House, Dr. Paul Crouch, Amy Fihn, TBN and all Second Chance staff and asked them to pray that my gift will be unleashed in this book. And I believe that there are some good students out at Lodi High School, McClathy High School, Folsom High School, Colfax High, Columbine, Virginia Tech, CSU Sacramento, UC. Davis, Morehouse, Spellman, Biola Univ., Purdue and at Union theological sem. Etc. Who will use this book to witness to their partners and pals who have gone astray. I believe that the chairman of African studies out at Washington and Lee University will share this tome with his students. Professor Marc Howard (who wants to become a Lawyer) and Marty Tankleff need this book. It is an interactive book. And I want all of you reading to take 45 seconds and go to T.D. Jakes.org and just click on "contact us" and write "Bishop Jakes-Sherman wants you to pray that the new book K.K.K. will revolutionize teens and tweenies". I met Bishop Eddie L. Long when I was a boy preacher. Rev. Hosea Williams introduced us. Long does not remember me but I need to dream of getting out and going to preach for Long, William Smith, Bishop Jakes and Noel Jones etc. That won't happen now. But if you will make certain that Smith, Long and Jones know about (via the power of the internet) this tome my testimony will help transform youth.

I'm writing to thugs, wanna be thugs, lil gangstas, those slingin on the corner as well as lil rich kids strung out on meth. This book is passing by the street corner in the trailer park, in the suburbs, the barrio or in the hood etc. And just as Jesus walked up to a fisherman named Peter and said "follow me and I'll make you fisher of men". I step up to you who are slingin, bangin and slammin and I say to you – come home. The greatest thing about being a prodigal son (or daughter) is that a prodigal always knows his/her way back home. And has a certified thug, as a certified supplanter and trickster I know the business. I know the game. I know some scams your parents and teachers will never know. And I've come –not with 3 points and a poem. Hell you can write your own poetry. I don't come with a nice little, neat message about "just say no" or "Jesus loves you"(although he does !) etc. I come as a thug with an IED! K.K.K. is an improvised Explosive Device designed to explode in your spirit. This book has been prayed over upon my death bed. I have written so many pastors, prayer warriors and mothers etc. with one message: I need you (Amy, Linda, Bishop, and Reverend etc) to pray that K.K.K. will reach the unreachable and teach the un-teachable in the schools, colleges and in the hoods". And can I tell you all a secret? After having my body ravaged from valley fever etc. Then being set up and thrown into the hole. I must admit that "I wuld have lost heart"…I "would have fainted". I would have (psalms 27:13) given up. If I had not believed that "I would see the goodness of the lord in the land of the living". That's why you have this book right now. Because I didn't give up. And I believe that this will be an authentic new beginning for a new gang. Your scars are about to be transformed into stars. Adam Lane, Daniel Bugriyeu, Dustin Nicolodi, Fred, Franklin Curren M.D. And all of us at G.B.G. have come to make you fishers of men. We didn't come to condemn you or to ridicule you. We came for those who may never make it on the radio or on t.v. I came for the least likely and the left out. I came for youngsters who are struggling to navigate your way through life. You are somebody. You can come out of that prison of destruction, prison of alcoholism, prison of prostitution, prison of crank and prison of crack. Prison of this and prison of that. This book is standing outside the door of your mind. And just as Jesus stood outside the mess. Stood outside the stinky stuff and called Lazarus out of the tomb. This book (and our team i.e. Dr. Curren, "Jimbo", Willie, Ford etc.) which is written from the same place (a prison) that Paul wrote Phillipians from etc. stands outside your problems, your addiction and your mess. And we (the team of rivals) tell you to "come forth". I say "Come on people." Come on youngsters! I know it's hard to resist joining a gang and it can be deadly getting out of a gang I've witnessed partners like my buddy "Fats" who got out and dropped out of a Mexican gang, and gangbangers murdered him and left him in the trunk of a car. But God will help you, he'll keep you and he'll hide you.

He (G.B.G.) who "dwells in the secret (where gangs can't find you) place of the most high shall abide under the shadow of the almighty." Come on people! If you are G.B.G. baby you can say of the lord that "He is my refuge and my fortress." And in these ghettos, trailer parks and barrios you need a refuge and a fortress. God is so awesome that when the gangs, the po po, drug dealers (or whoever) are trying to get you God will do what you homeboys won't…They say they got your back but they'll end up snitching like a rat. But God will "cover you with his feathers, and under his wings you shall take refuge; his truth shall be your shield and buckler." And the night cometh when no kid can see. It is dark out there in the cities, in the hills, in the schools and in the streets. But no matter how dark it gets you don't need to become a Menendez, a Bardo, a Peterson, a Marvin or a Manning. For "you shall not be afraid of the terror by night, nor of the arrow (or bullets) that flies by day, nor of the pestilence that walks in darkness, nor of the destruction that lays waste at noonday. "Let me tell you students something. And this ain't what I read in a book. My distinguished scholars on the G.B.G. team did tell me this. But years of being in the mix have proven to be that "A thousand may fall at your side, and ten thousand at your right hand; but it shall not come near you…" And when it really gets bad, dangerous and spooky (Psalms 91:11-12) in yo life God will "give his angels charge over you, to keep you in all your ways. In their hands they shall bear you up, lest you…." trip over a beer can, an I.E.D. or a crack pipe.

I command you to take up the helmet of (you a soldier right?) salvation and the sword of the spirit, which is the word of God."

And I wanna reach out to the Facebook generation because I understand some of what you feel. Just like I used to watch folks on Oprah and on Tyra and thought to myself that (her guests) should have been me. Just as I'd watch preachers preach about guys in jails and I said, that should be me. There are millions of you sitting at home thinking Daniel Radcliffe, harry Potter, the American Idol and/or the Jonas Brothers ought to be you. And yet you sit there in relative obscurity and your boredom, frustration and your alienation leads you to start taking risks and doing things you should not do. You send that naked photo, sample that drug or lay out of school trying to be cool. But I've come (to you) like a thief in the night telling you to turn around...

...A month ago at a state prison in Chino there was a riot. It started with black and Hispanic gang members going at it. 60 inmates (mostly youngsters) had to be hospitalized on the streets. 271 inmates received mild to medium injuries. Prisoners set the prison on fire. 2 inmates died from stab wounds. And when you are in prison and a riot breaks out you must participate! If you don't you'll be raped, sodomized or murdered...

L.A. County Jail is the most violent jail in America. Inmates have been known to murder guys, behead them and to stuff dead bodies in the trash can. I was in L.A. County (and nearly murdered had not it been for famed Attorney Tom Mesereau) for over a year. And I give eye witness testimony to you that a jail riot is the scariest thing you'll ever see. Hollywood has never adequately depicted the horror, senselessness and the terror of a jailhouse riot. ...And all those 17-21 year old kids at Chino had to see their belongings (televisions, radios, family photos etc.) destroyed in the fires of hatred. Damn I wish I could get Denzel (Mundly Lane Films), David E. Kelley, Spike Lee or John Singleton etc. to do an authentic film (or even a PBD "Frontline" special) about "Prisons: American Gitmos/Abu Ghirabs from the inside/out!"

Let me move back to Jakes and Long for a moment. Obviously I'll never meet Bishop Long again, nor shall I ever meet Bishop T.D. Jakes but I would like for somebody to tell Jakes and Long to stay on t.v. They will never know how many guys didn't commit suicide because at 3:00 p.m. they saw Jakes preaching. Or at 5:30 p.m. they saw Bishop Long preaching. That's why G.B.G./Heart rote a personal missive to President Obama asking him to help get TBN (Second Chance) into every U.S. Prison, jail and juvenile. These gospel programs are bright lights shining in some mighty dark places...

I let Franklin Curren M.D. peruse the first 100 pages of this tome and I was startled by his critique. This man went to Harvard! And I am but a lowly prisoner. Dr. Curren stated "Sherman it's coming along quite well. I've never read a book like K.K.K. ...Let's face it. The title alone turns heads and raises eyebrows. And I'm certain the contents will be controversial for some. But at a minimum-it will create a dialogue. You have mastered the ability to translate the data you've obtained from the learned and the unlearned and to reduce it to writing...kids (youngsters) will be glued to the pages of this book-just as they were to "Prison Break" and to "24".

I want you thugs, rebels, outcasts, jerks, nerds and geeks to know that I still believe that you are the head and not the tail. You are the first and not the last. I don't care who gave up on you or who said you're a failure I came to tell you that you can get back up. Your life is worth living. You have worth and you matter. Get up! I want you(the reader) to go on the internet and find Christian Nelson, Keith Mullennix, Nathaniel Mullennix, and Joe Gastring and tell em to get this tome. There is a 21 year old young lady named "Star" who visits Charles Manson; find her and tell Star to get this book. G.B.G. can employ Keith and Nate Mullinnex, Christian Nelson, Kaether Cordero, Kyle Love, Zach Freisen and Hugh Michael Hughes if you will find them. And if you are willing to volunteer for G.B.G/Heart let us know. And if you would like one of the paying G.B.G./Heart jobs let us know. And if you know a student who is trying to go to college but needs some financial assistance let us know. We might be able to give them a mini-scholarship, a stipend or a donation. Put the work out. Tell Mark Petterson (Univ. of Kansas) that we have something for him.

What you see on "jail", "cops" and a lot of the other prison shows is a crop. I used to watch "Prison Break" and can tell you "only in Hollywood." Prison is not like that and I want guys like Michael Parker (Walnut, CA.) and Maxwell Hanger etc. to see what I see. I'm cognizant that some parents won't want you reading this book because I'm in jail. I know some parents with think I'm being too candid or too whatever. But the mess I've seen in hell qualifies me to write with conviction, integrity, authenticity and with a specificity unlike anything I've ever read. And the nice, neat and professorial tomes which you've half perused over the years have not worked.

I must awaken you. I cannot over-emphasize the fact that if you are a white male 15, 16, 17, 18 etc. years old etc. you can/will be housed in the buildings and cells with 30, 40, and 50 year old cons. And you will be forcefully raped and enslaved. And if you wonder why your buddy (who is 20) who did 3 years (and got out) never mentioned being raped etc. Easy answer: He is ashamed and embarrassed! David Reynolds (in Virginia), Chad Sherman and Chuck Sherman don't wanna admit to you that they gave it up to a Booty Bandit in jail. Do you really think your pal Douglas Stave, Marvin Stone or D.J. Carpenter is going to say to you "Yes-They locked me in a cell with a dude who had been in prison for 27 years and he f-cked me in my a—hole and he made me s-ck his d-ck and I was afraid if I told it he'd kill me and then I'd be labeled a snitch and a b-tch."

Did you really think your buddy was gonna scream more homosexual confessions from the roof tops of the schools, the universities or the hoods? I saw bulked, yoked up (i.e. "Jessie" and "Russell" on "Big Brother". In the joint; however, "Big Brutha" is a dude named "Bubba"). White boys as they relinquish their shoes, shirts, watches and their butts! I recall one Robert Pattinson look-a-like being told in L.A. County Jail to "Gimme yo underwear you pretty lil wood. U got on boxers or briefs?" White guy said "Boxers". Bubba said "pull yo pants down and pull yo boxers up like a G-string". After the guy complied the dude told him to take them off and "Give em to me so I can sniff em when you make bail". And he did exactly that in L.A. County Jail. I'm a black man – so I have no dog in this fight. But- if I were a white U.S. Senator, congressman or legislator etc. I would demand that the L.A. county jail be shut down forthwith .L.A. county jail in 2010 to white guys is what the Edmund Pettus Bridge was to Rev. Hosea Williams and Cong. John Lewis in the 60's. L.A. count jail is a white mans worse nightmare. I saw a Derek Hough look-a-like raped by 4 mexicans and 3 black gangsters in L.A. county. L.A. county jail is akin to absolute torture. It is so horrendous that the L.A. county sheriff asked Jesse Jackson and Cardinal Mahoney to come and speak to jail inmates to try to stop the violence. I think (I'm guessing) Lisa Ling may be doing a special on L.A. county jail. If she does I hope she'll speak with Dr. Lewis Valblonsky, Jeffrey "Allen" Walker, Nathan Gould and Christopher Parker. I had a celly who resembled Zac Efron who told me day one "I'm only 19 and I've never been f-cked. But I know I gotta put out. U got everything I need, I was wondering if I could just s-ck u everynight and….". I declined and he relocated the following day. I met a fellow (Michael Carter) who was carrying a Bible and he had a full beard, etc. and he loved T.D. Jake's preaching etc. And I moved him into the cell (A-7-109). When I came out of the shower Michael had cleanly shaved his face and legs. Michael had on lipstick and a skirt. He used his see through laundry bag to make a skirt. And he told me what all he wanted to do to me…three minutes later C.O. Mark Brandon was dragging him out of the cell.

I just wanna know if David Proctor, Ricky Parnell, Gary Browning (VA.), Ashley Hamilton and Redmond O'Neal really want to come to the Big House. And to all of those gullible "disciples" like "Star" I encourage you to send (K.K.K) this tome inside juveniles and group homes as a wake-up call. I want Zac Efron, Hough, Shia Labeouf, David Archuleta, Adam Lambert and Robert Downey Jr. to have this book. I know there is stunning news in this book. I know some people will close this book not thinking highly of me. But can I be candid? I don't give a Flying Flip what they think of me. The advantage of being a maximum security prisoner, unable to see the light of day is I don't need a vote. I think Tookie's book is awesome and should be required reading for all youth. And I wanna reach out to Barbara Becnel (who worked with Tookie). But pragmatically I have an advantage over Tookie: I seek no pardon! And I'm not on death row pleading for a stay of execution. Rappers (i.e. Eminem and all of them) can kiss my ass! I'm way past thinking that a Damon Dash or a Jay-Z is gonna run to my rescue and help me. As quiet as it is kept nobody who refers to women as "B-tches" and "whores" needs to help me anyway. When you have no respect for women I question your sexuality. Because deep studies into psychology have led me to conclude that most hardcore gangbangers are (themselves) in denial about their own homo-sexuality anyway. So I don't give a damn about this tome causing me to be unpopular. I am a convicted felon anyway!

But if one Daniel Clay Hollifield, Wayne Rawlings, Brian Foskuhl, Chris Shea, Jeremy Hawes, Chris Thompson, Brian Devin Graham or Marvin Stone will read these words and be helped- my work is done. If some of you get this back to Ed Westwick, Nick Jonas, Chace Crawford, Michael Manson and to Van Harris my work is done. I wish you could see what I have to use for an ink pen as I write this (in long hand). Ever seen a see through Bick? Pull the pen filler out of the case and you have what I'm writing with; no case. My 3rd finger is blistered and swollen. My pinky is bleeding and my hand is cramping. Paper is limited so I've had to use the back side of other documents etc. to write this. I'm reminded of Dr. Martin Luther King Jar .writing his famed "Letter from a Birmingham Jail Cell" on toilet paper because he (too) had no paper. I can't die till I write this book. U got to get it 2 Chance Crawford, Daniel Job and to Ashton Butcher. I want all 3 million of Ashton's twitter pals to have K.K.K.

Please make no mistake about prisons and sexuality. Many staff persons are also predators. I have sympathy for every female prisoner in the world. Ladies are routinely raped by staff in prisons. It is an epidemic of titanic proportions. Some staff just humiliate prisoners sexually for laughs. I recall a white inmate at P.V.S.P named "Chuck" (Charles Hedrick from Stockton). Chuck had "white pride" tattooed across the backs of his arms. He considered himself a gangster. He was cooler than Eminem. And on day Chuck was caught in someone's cell giving a tattoo. And C.O. Deathridge (now a sergeant at Salinas Valley) along with Wally Tucker decided to strip search Chuck in front of the entire building. Then they (Deathridge and Tucker) forced Chuck to pull his boxers up in his buttocks like a G-String and leave them there for 30 minutes with his nose on the wall. I recall (vividly) C.O. Wally Tucker, D.L. Criner and C.O. Deathridge telling inmate pompa to do a strip tease in the day room. Pompa got naked and began sobbing. Tucker (literally) forced him to bend over while Tucker shoved a gloved finger up his anus. Criner forced him to "open yo mouth and suck on this flash light like it's a d-ck". These are staff members! And if you wonder why we didn't do anything….A. I'm not James Frey (who supposedly won every fight) and B. tell who? In these prisons guards r like a mafia. They stick together…I.E. Facility A- (P.V.S.P) Sergeant was Kenneth Scott. K Scott's supervisor was Lieutenant Scott (his wife). Mrs. Scott's supervisor was Captain Beels who was related to Scott's by marriage.

We had (at P.V.S.P.) thugs guarding us. There were staff members caught stealing $1 dollar sodas. There were staff members caught smoking weed by the state police. There was Johnny Brown, T. Negrete, Arredondo, Timm and Asturgia (all rumored to be meth addicts). Sgt. Scott and C.O. Deshazio are bonifide members of racist hate groups. Sergeant K. Scott and C.O. Deshazio were caught on video tape calling me "N" this and "N" that. And "we wish you would have died from valley fever". And Marion E. Spearman witnessed this misconduct and swept it under the rug. Small wonder Wally Tucker and Sgt. Deathridge (and Criner and Gail Crooms) can sexually assault inmates (routinely) and get away with it. I've got one more on tucker for you. Brace yourself: Wally Tucker brought a dildo (an actual sex toy) to work and placed it on inmate Pompa's bunk! And Tucker called Crine, Crooms, Deathridge and K. Scott in to show them. We all saw it and Pompa wept. Tucker claimed he was gonna 'hot trash' (destroy) it. I believe (and this is speculation) Tucker might have been intimately acquainted with that dildo.

But these are the kinds of officiers John Jody Bear, Daniel St. John (in Richmond, VA.), and you will be guarded by if you come to prison!!

Somebody asked me "do u realize if u did get out the A.B. or the Mexican mafia might have you killed?" I replied "If valley fever wasn't killing me they'd kill me in here. Especially if I left C.S.P. SAL" And I will admit that naming names of real life murderers (in real time) is a dangerous thing to do. This twisted slippery puzzle called prison- must (finally) be told as a testimony to kids. The unholy alliance between Eric Menendez, "Angel" (Rauser), "Spot", Henrickson, Tom, C.O. Garza, C.O. Wheat etc. must be exposed. And (I repeat) I should have my ass beat for allowing Eric to hoodwink and deceive Madame Walters, Montel and everybody else. Deon C. ("Fatcat") Braggs still has missives written by Eric seeking speed for sex etc. etc. And these are high powered correctional officials (now retired) whom I could send Keith Morrison (NBC), Ben Tracy or Geraldo to talk to about the Menendex Sexcapades...and for the few non-thinkers who assured the Menedez Bros. were rich etc. I have an announcement: the state paid for both of their lawyers during the second trial. Use gumption and ya'll recall that the parents were rich and since Eric and Lyle murdered the parents obviously they did not inherit the money and most of their family want nothing to do with them. When Eric and Lyle do get money it is from fan mail, their spouse (i.e. tammi grooms animals and she wrote a LiL to me.), From drug sales and/or from sex. If you have money you can buy a blowjob or some tail from Lyle Menendez or Eric any day of the week. Eric is more into the wiccan and son of odin than Lyle is. Eric enjoys sex with men more than Lyle does. Eric could be described as a "Bottom" in bed. He wants to be dominated and manhandled. Lyle prefers being the masculine on in bed. Eric has never had sex with a woman. Lyle claims the only time he's been with a woman was after they murdered their parents and he fled the country. And he had a prostitute. If anybody wants to know about Lyle's sex in prison here are a slew of witnesses: Jerry Wines, Jeremiah Rodriguez,Daniel Job, E.J. Puerte, Charles Pyle, Larry "Lunchmeat" Lewis, C.O. Duclos, C.O. Baker or C.O. Warren. For updates on Eric's prison bromances call C.O. Garza, C.O. Wheat, Michael Henrickson, Eric Wilson, Joseph Miller and Joseph Sweerey.

Some of my readers need to contact Nina Morgan (and her son in Atlanta), Mr. S. Alford (with Atlanta Public Schools), Vista del Lago High School Students and Jerry Brucheimer and tell them about this book.

I need James Lewis (Valdosta GA.), John Garvin, Keith Jerrolds, Roy Cherry and Ralph Cannon (all Georgia boys) to know about this book. And those of you who wanna know more must get "Blue Eyed Blonde" Book II. And I encourage all of you who are being turned off and repulsed by some of the contents of this book to-stay out of jail. You'll never have to witness or entertain any of the sadistic and perverted behavior of which I speak if you simply stay out of jail. My job, duty and responsibility is to tell you the truth about what you'd hear "If prison walls could talk"! It is 11:38 pm right now. There are 64 cells in a prison building. Approximately 100-128 inmates. And gay sex (some forceful, some via intimidation and some induced by drugs etc.) is taking place in (at least) 30 of those cells. Sixty or more inmates (hard core criminals with bulging muscles) are in bed with one another. And 95% are having unprotected sex. The 5% who use protection (except guys like Eric who gets Garza and Wheat to bring him condoms) are using sandwich wrap. They put cellophane plastic over their "microphones" (privates) and insert "mikes" covered with cellophane into lubricated "speakers" (backsides). This is alarmingly dangerous. Especially considering that more than 65,000 of the guys screwing their cellies this month, with get out next month. And they will bring their Hepatitis, HIV and Aids to the streets with them. And who will pay for their healthcare? This prison state which we have created is a monstrosity which has not been thought out. I would hope that the contents of this tome will reach the desks of Michael Bloomberg, Cory Booker, Mike Nutter, Shirley Franklin, Congressman Bobby Scott and Dick Durbin. And I would hope that people like Nina Morgan in my hometown will discuss K.K.K (with her son) as she drives to walker wrestling etc.etc. I hope Andy C. ("the volunteer") will contact his friends in the moment and talk about K.K.K.

I want A. Markham (in Pensacola, Fla.) to have this book. If you will talk about it and use it we can divert kids from juveniles, jails and from prisons. And always remember that the goal is not to build me up. We wanna build the book up! Don't evangelize me. Evangelize the book. Evangelize the mission of G.B.G/Heart... If (you guys think I'm kidding or embellishing about the corruption of guards call fmr. F.B.I . Director James Mattocks. These guys stick together and will murder (i.e. Notorious Mike Bunnett) you if you break the code...when C.O. Wally Tucker and D.L. Criner get angry with an inmate (AKA YA'Bone) they forced a flamboyant homosexual (AKA "BellaDonna") to move in the cell with Ya'Bone and falsely accuse him of rape. Criner and Tucker paid BellaDonna a carton of Camels to lodge the complaint. Moreover, they paid "primo" to give BellaDonna two black eyes. Moreover, the investigations Lieutenant (Lt. Corley) is a personal buddy of Tucker's. And Marion E. Spearman (openly gay) is rumored to be sexually entangled with Criner (along with C.O. Williams. Notwithstanding the fact that Spearman was caught performing fellatio)...And Spearman was in charge of Corley etc....Ipso Facto, when an inmate perturbs or offends staff in anyway (especially youth dentention facilities etc) staff can/will find a way to set an inmate up. They can pay to have you raped. They can pay to have you accused of rape. And the inmate always loses.

When D.L. Criner pulled a 38 on me and threatened to murder me, inmate Ojeda was in the very next bed. And Ojeda (a paraplegic) told me "I think I crapped on myself...but Manning you know I can't say what I saw. They could murder me. I'm at their mercy Bro. If you get a lawyer to call me when I get out then I'll tell everything man!!...I can only hope that after I'm dead and gone A Donald Masuda, Mesereau, Tonny Serra or a James Brosnahan shall persue this tome and nail (via litigation and non-violently!) Bunnell, Criner, Tucker and the rest of those thugs to the cross. And I remind you who are screwing up in school and at home etc. that if you're foolish enough to come here you are powerless in here. Write Al Sharpton, Jesse Jackson, Pat Robertson or any of them and I can assure you they will not write you back!

Back to Brutha D.L. Criner (the gunslinger), Wally Tucker etc. (Full disclosure: this writer did not witness the following incident but was told this by a veteran correctional officer..) Correctional officers D.L. Criner, Macias and Wally Tucker entered Facility A-Bldg. 2 and handcuffed an inmate to his bunk (with mechanical wrist and leg restraints.) Criner (who is as black as midnight on top of an ace of spades) pulled the inmates underwear down and sprayed whipped cream over his anus. Tucker then sprayed whipped cream down his spine and into each of his ears. As Tucker, Criner and Macias laughed inmates were paraded by the cell to view this guy lying spread eagle on his bunk... "Hey Twin" Criner said to inmate Viafanova "Go get me some baby powder and sprinkle some powder on Deuce's (the inmate's pseudonym) ass on top of the whip cream; cause Tucker didn't bring no cherry". Twin replied "his asshole is the cherry". Although I did not witness this particular incident I do believe it occurred. Down in Georgia there were 3 guards who were brothers (the Moody Bros.) working in a prison called "Alto". And they were known as the Minnesota Wrecking Crew for assaulting inmates. Criner, Tucker, Macias, Deathridge, W. Brumbaugh and Marion E. Spearman etc. have the same kind of reputation. They don't fear being caught because 99 ½% of inmates are afraid to repeat their egregious misconduct. And although I'd love to be able to tell Oprah, Tyra Banks, Michael Moore or Jerry Bruckheimer that (like the untouchable and undefeatable James Frey) I stood up and fought Criner and Tucker etc. that would be blatant embellishment if not out right prevarication. (on only two occasions I was lucky enough, in L.A. county jail to stop guys from train raping 2 guys.) Like a little cowardly wimp- most times I (too) saw sadistic staff abuse and looked the other way. And all that it takes for evil to rage is for good men to remain silent. Although Harvard scholars and and expert panel of physicians are landing and celebrating this book etc. Though C. Solis Md, A. Duran PhD etc. call me "courageous" for penning this tome. I aint doing nuthin special. Service is the price you pay for living on the planet. My refusal to talk about my conviction (refusal to show youth my wounds), refusal to write what I knew about Eric, Lyle, Bardo and Stokes etc. was selfish, cowardly and it was fraudulent. And (to be candid) if Valley Fever was not propelling me to the cemetery; with deliberate haste etc. I would still not be writing about all this stuff now. Peter, Attorney Janus and Dr. T. Hedblad (a saint) encouraged me long ago to uncover those hidden treasures and write about them. The ever so candid Murray J. Janus once stated to me "Rev. your secrets (good, bad and indifferent) still go to the grave with me..but if you were to man up and write about the Menendex Bros., your calvario situation, you could make a major impact on a segment of society that most activists can only dream of reaching." Attorney Janus continued: "I don't think you realize what a powerful, colorful, unusual and complex life you've lived. The only reason I've never put you in contact with a David E. Kelley, Bruckheimer, Geraldo or some other persons who could do something with your story is because you refuse to tell your story." And please note that the show "Matlock" was modeled after famed Georgia Attorney Bobby Lee Cook. And Mr. Cook introduced me to Mr. Janus as "the greatest trial lawyer in Virginia". Ipso Facto, I should have (immediately) taken Janus' words to heart. So this tome is past due. And this tome is my debt to kids. Everytime I see and Eddie Jaramillo, A Pedroia, a teacher molesting a child etc. I cringe because I know that had I written this book 8 years ago, that child might not have been molested. How or why so? Because if a 12-19 year old kid had read about Ed Stokes, Marvin, Holmes, Bret (and all of the other psychosexual molesters featured in this book) or other predators, etc. They might have been able to get away from a molester. Sure that is a big "might" but that "might" could mean the difference in life and death. I don't (I repeat) believe my own press. I know this is not the best book every written. John Grisham can out write me in his sleep. But I can say (humbly and honestly) there is not another (more candid, chilling, detailed, scathing and direct) book (for teens and tweenies) on the market like this book. K.K.K. is my stage and I intend to tear this stage apart. In this book I let it all hang out. This is the hand writing on the wall. This is the final curtain call. This book has been in the spirit of my heart (Helping Educate At Risk Teens), the fabric of my soul and birthed in my belly. This book is the climax of my debt to young people. This is what I can give to the cause of kids can free the children (Marc Kielburger), the NAACP (Stephanie Brown-Yartn & college coordinator), students at Ronald E. McNair High School and to The Freedom Writer's Group (Jom Tu and Erin Gruwell etc.)...A portion of the profits from this tome with go to helping kids go to college.

I pray that Paris Hilton, Richard Scrushy, Brad Falke, students at Vista del Lago High, Pastor Robert Smith (New Bethol in Detroit), Francis Graham, Megan Nerwinski and Travis Wall will get this book. I want Ray Clark Academy students to get this book. I write from a place of pain, fear, concern and disdain. I am awed by the power of Generation Y. I'm disdained by my generation, as well as the hypocrisy of the village (i.e. Baby Boomers etc.). I'm sick and tired of being sick and tired. We will never win the minds of students like Chelsey Ramirez (Sacto), Kyle Love (Auburn), Ben Whipple, Alex Seabolt or Max Hanger with our hypocritical bull shit! Those youths are from (Missouri) the show me state. And how can Rush Limbaugh speak to this generation if he's hooked on drugs and obese? How dare Hannity tout the morals of democracy when he can't even have a civil dialogue (vs. monologue)? How dare a prisoner (Sherman D.

Manning) be called a "prolific author" when he has been too timid, too cowardly to write (directly about his own (wrongful) conviction! Generation Y, teenies etc. want somebody to be real. Youngsters can handle the truth. They can relate to candor and to reality...and (in this tome) I had to go back to the place (my conviction) where I gave up and move the stome away. When Mary and Martha finally gave up on Lazarus they buried him and covered the buried place with a stome. And all of us have some secret pains, secret failures, secret stinky stuff that we've given up on and buried. We have covered the embarrassment, hurt, shame and pain...and Jesus told them to (I talk more about this later) "Show me where you laid" Lazarus. And when they showed Him where they quit and gave up. He said "Roll the stome away". And with this bodacious, outrageous and controversial book I had to roll the stome away. I had to uncover my pain, my fears, my shame etc. I had to roll the stome away for all the world to see. Lazarus was dead. And he was stinky. And I had laid my embarrassment and my shame to rest. I covered it up! But then Jesus showed up at my hospital bed and told me to "show me where you quit. Show me where you gave up. Show me where you disqualified yourself from service. Show me where you gave up on you goals, your visions and your dreams". And I replied (As did Martha- and just as Mary of Yau Yangsters) by telling the Lord "By now my mess, my secrets, my conviction is stinking. It has been buried for so long". But the Lord let me know the same thing he told Martha (and the same thing He's telling you thugs, gangbangers, N.L.R., Crips, Bloods, and Arian Brotherhoods etc.) etc. He said "Take away the stome". He would not show me what he could do with my stinky stuff (i.e. G.B.G. and K.K.K) until I uncovered it. And because I uncovered my secrets (as you'll see in the calvario story) the master is using G.B.G and K.K.K to reach, inspire and teach at-risk youth who would have never been reached with a lecture, a speech or a song. Wherever this tome falls short (i.e. tautology and ramblings etc.) I take the blame. And wherever this book succeeds (the team lead by Harvard Physician Franklin Curren etc) G.B.G and Christ gets the fame. God gets glory from my story. I will never sit on the stage inside Harpo Studios in Chicago Illinois. And 299 million, 999 thousand of you will never sit in Harpo Studios either.

And So I write to the last knowing you can be first. I write to the least likely knowing you can do the Almighty. I write to the Boyz in The Hood and the Girlz in The Suburbs. I want this book to be the wake-up call. Let K.K.K cause reveille at your frat, your sorority, your youth group, your school or in your hood. I want you to get on the telephone and poke folks on Facebook etc. and tell them "Dude check this out; I'm reading a book written by gangbangers, Harvard psychiatrists and convicts who will never get out. Dude u have got 2 get K.K.K in your hands 2 day". I want book clubs to discuss K.K.K and perologists can scrutinize it. But I'm confident that youngsters will know that this book is keeping it real! I have uncovered my stinky stuff and transmogrified it into a testimony for the myspace generation!

In this tome I train my documentarian, eyewitness and author's lense toward the kids who kill kids, adults and others; whom I know in Hades. I testify to Perry Thompson and all the students at Granite Bay High School. This book is for the kids who mya not attend church, synagogue, mosque, or mass every Sunday. This is for those studs, jocks, outcasts, nerds and even jerks in the cities all across America who don't necessarily peruse tomes penned by learned scholars...Hades, hell or the prison has become the canvas across which I've painted this authentic (haunting, chilling and breathtaking) tale about maniacs, murderers and molesters. I kept most of this book P.G. but its still raw, candid and real. Inmates David Buzzetta, Willie Nessler and Johnny O'Neal need this tome. Yall get this to Sandy Close, Leslie Neale, Juvies, Suspect Entertainment and to Father Greg Boyle. If Father Boyle is reading G.B.G is willing to help "Homeboy Industries" out. Let us know what you all need. We also want to help "Delancey Street" out. And we wanna help highschools to fund their student newspapers and radio shows etc. G.B.G is willing to donate money to any legitimate youth media outlet. Go to our Facebook and Myspace sites and e-mail me. Michael Castro, Perry Johnson and Jason Castro? I have $100.00 for Michael, Perry and Jason. All they need to do is read this book from beginning to end. The moment Perry, Michael, Jason and C.J. Sheron finish reading this book they simply need to send me a snail mail telling me they read the whole book. And I will send each of them a hundred bucks! Do tell...I'm announcing my retirement from book writing in K.K.K I will continue to blog, tweet and to do our internationally published newsletters. But I won't write another book after this. This book is that gateway, that special portal which can lead youth to a better life. This is that tome which can pull you back and then propel you into your destiny. For many of you this book is going to be an angel on your roof top. I am a firm believer that (deep down) people know the truth when they hear it. And because your heart has been hardened this book is written to speak through the hardened crust of the gang and to meet you in your heart...Carlos Rodriguez (ex-Santa Ana dancer) and Jeffrey Buttle need to join our heart program...and one of the things I've learned about life is trials come to make you strong. And the teacher doesn't talk while the test is taking place. And I encourage all student (youth/civilian) G.B.G Ambassadors to get involved by writing your senators and the President about the tragedies taking place in the Congo. I want kids to research whats going on in the Congo and then write letters about if. I've found that when we give at-risk teens something to do they grow and transform in the process. It's the same strategy we use in allowing prisoners to mentor. I want kids who are in the throes of struggle to participate in positive activities right now. Log on to the kids can feed the children website and get involved. Send me an e-mail and let us know that you're doing. I am convinced that empowerment comes from helping others. The reason Glenn Close' "puppies behind bars" has prisoners weeping is no matter how hardcore one may be- it feels good to help others. I've seen G.B.G team members sobbing when we mentor, teach and reach folks. And (as quiet as it is kept) sometimes (every now and then) I fight tears when I read missives from troubled youth who read my books or are impacted by our work. So if you get nothing else out of this book please do something for others. Help somebody else. You have the power to influence the world. Use your computer, your e-mail, your voice and your opinion. Don't sit back set a new gold standard for motivating youngsters to get involved in your community, school, church and in the world.

Drugs: Damn! What can I say? An addiction is so, so freaking powerful. Cameron Douglas is on house arrest for drugs and while on house arrest his girl gets busted smuggling him ten dime bags of heroin in the handle of an electric tooth brush. It is almost hilarious. I can't un-addict you with this book. As powerful as this book may be it can't rid you of your addiction. I can tell you if you have not tried drugs don't waste your time. Be strong, independent and powerful enough to avoid falling for drugs. It is as simple as a decision. Just as you made the decision not to jump off of a bridge last week; decide not to even experiment with drugs. I'm a living witness you can be the life of the party while you're sober. And if you have an addiction talk to a local pastor or a school counselor. Log on to Dr.Phil.com and click on "Teentalk" and ask for help. Go to my websites and blogs and we'll post some data to help you get clean. And I will repeat- Addiction is a powerful problem. Its like a magnet to fill a void. But thousands have stopped abusing drugs. And I know that you can do it. And if Redmond, Cameron Douglas, David Buzzetta or Lindsay Lohan is reading this book. I urge you to go to Dr. Phil's website. Dr. Phil (also) gets on my darn nerves also but he's good and he does care. I want Mayor Larry Lanford, Rev. Robert Campbell (New Beginnings Church), Rev. Otis Moss, Brandon Weible, Alan Rafferty and Andrew Tauscher to get this book. This book is our (G.B.G team: including Dr. Currenr, Dr. A. Duran, Adam Lane, Daniel Bugeiyey, Dr. Jarmon etc.) crusade against gangs. It is a campaign to reach every child, every secrets (in this book) unfold like a Spanish fan not just to entertain you or get a chuckle but I wrote this jaw dropping book about the (authentic) sissified characteristics of gang bangers lest you be misled. I Sherman D. Manning do hereby affirm to you (the Facebook Generation) under the penalty of perjury that most of the gangbangers you see getting out of prisons etx. Have been banging buttholes and banging poles (sword fights-pun is intended) in prisons. Don't let them deceive you the jig is up and the cat is out the bag baby boy. I come in a way no Harvard scholar can come. Not one reporter can come with the viewpoint I have. I have eyewitness testimony live from Broke Back C.D.C.! Live from Broke Back Depts. Of corrections! Them same thugs u looking up 2 with saggin pants, bandanas, tattooed from head 2 toe, wearing a fake bling, bling etc. There were having sexual intercourse with men in prison. That's it and that's all. And I have more respect for an admitted homosexual (although I believe homosexuality is a sin) than I do for a so-called gang banger who is pumping iron during the day time and pumping peter in the night time. And I declare to you (no embellishment) I have seen dudes who can Bench press 500 lbs. squatting down on the top of their cell partner at night. That (alone) ought to be motivation enough for you to stay off drugs and keep yo ass out of jail. When Dr. Phil (get the dvd and watch it) sent Brett and Chris to San Quentin State Prison. One of the black inmates told Brett he'd like to screw him. And his bendediction to Brett was "you take care of yo ass cause I believe we'll see you again" and he meant it. And I'm not picking on Brett at all. Hell Brett might be as awesome as James Frey (pun intended) who never lost a fight. But I promise you- I assure you that if Brett is is L.A. county jail he will be walking bow legged! They will rape Brett (If Brett is reading I'm gonna give him some game) tell the sergeant you are gay! It's your only chance. They have (90% white boys) gay and scared Caucasians in the gay tank but you (Brett? Chris?) must lie and pretend to be gay. It's a white guy's only chance in L.A. county jail. Message sent!

I strongly recommend all my Caucasian readers read two books: "Creating Monsters" (www.cafepress.com.creating) and a book called "Fish" by T.J. Parsell. Damn: I went back and re-read the last 29 pages of this tome and I scared myself. I said to myself "these fools (Eric, Lyle, A.B., N.L.R The Green Wall, Criner, Spearman etc.) are gonna put a hit out on yo black ass!" I almost (keepin it real yall) tore up a lot of this book. But I can't. This (K.K.K.) is my final curtain call. It is put up or shut up for me. If you all wanted a peachy lil tome you'd go to Walmart. This book is a crusade against predators, molesters, gangbangers and the drug dealers who are destroying the village. Why do you think I'm offering a $ hundred bucks for some folks to read this book? It ain't because I'm independently wealthy or have money to burn. It is because I must be creative and innovative as I sound the alarm. All I'm looking for is 'just one'. If one young man drops out of a gang, drops back in school, gets off dope and develops hope- this crusade is not in vain. Please read this book and heed it. Send it to Melissa Huckaby, Scott Peterson and Charles Manson. Somebody ought to send Eric (P.V.S.P. in Coalinga) and Lyle (M.C.S.P. in Ione) copies. (When you do post a message on our Facebook site letting us know you did). Helping Educate At Risk Teens by transforming my mess into a message is now the cause of my life. Utilizing (even bizarre strategies) unique methodologies to put this book into the hands of kids allover America now consumes me. I live for this. And I have come to believe that I am alive for this moment. Martin Luther King Jr. (and hell no I'm not comparing myself to Dr. King) was receiving death threats on his life. He went to Memphis and gave the famed "Mountaintop" speech…"I've been to the mountaintop and I've looked over and I've seen the promised land. I may not get there with you. But I want you to know tonight that we as people will get to the promised land. I'm not worried about anything. I'm not forcing any man. Mine eyes have seen the glory of the coming of the Lord" Dr. King said. Well I have not yet been to the mountaintop. I have not looked over. But I have dreamed and visualized G.B.G Academies all over the world. I see kids training in G.B.G. similar to the JROTC program intermingled with "upward bound". I envision this book in schools, libraries, juveniles, jail cells and in prisons. And I may not live to see it. But it must become true. And there are forces and guards who will (i.e. Marion, Mike Bunnell, The Green Wall, Brumbaugher) spit on my grave when I die. There are very clear and present dangers. But no lie can live forever. And no threat shall muzzle the mouth that speaks truth to power.

I was born to be a youth activist and leader. I wasted my substance with bull. I lied, cheated, scammed and conned. But in strange ways, all of my dirt qualified me to be that "experience" therapist which Dr. Yablonsky spoke of. I can say some things Bishop Jakes and/or Bishop Long can't say. I can get away with some profanity and with some sailor's vernacular because of my thug status. Because I'm on the battlefield. Thugs can't con me because you can't slick a slickster. I'm a master of the game. Paul understood murder, lust, anger, hatred and violence so well because of his former status as sau. Channelling, redirecting and manipulating all of the wrong, game, cons and frauds I've perpetrated and using them as a bully pulpit etc. to reach youngsters is the cause that keeps me going. I go to bed (whenever I do get sleep), wake up in the morning and I even shower thinking of ways to use G.B.G to reach troubled teens. I'm not as smart as I would like to be because if I was I'd find that breakthrough before I did. I need to find a way to reach the kids who don't watch Oprah, won't watch Dr. Phil and don't go to church. I want to reach that Jesus got criticized for dining with (tax collecters and prostitutes etc.). Kids who are well don't need a doctor. Well kids r ambassadors and recruiters for G.B.G.. The kids who have been written off, strung out and acting a damn fool etc. That's my crowd. Kids who have been victimized and traumatized by a vindictive, judicial system- my crowd.

I wanna introduce them to "the save America act". I want Jeff Parshley, Christian Nelson, David Quattlebum and Nathaniel Mullinexx to come stand with us. Bring me John Decarro, Pepper Marshay and Chris Austad. For the toubled ladies you (too) have a seat at the Heart (Helping Educate At Risk Teens) table. I wanna reach Girls Gone Wild. Many of you have been abused, beat and raped. Many young ladies are dealing with addictions and afflictions. I want you to log on to www.mercyministries.org. I believe Nancy Alcorn (at Mercy Ministries) can help you. She specializes in helping troubled young ladies.

I want readers to contact John Vetter, Mayor Booker, Mayor Bloomberg, Mayort Nutter and Mayor Franklin and tell them we shout out to them in K.K.K.. I want every person (strange request) who believes in God to take a minute and pray for G.B.G. and for K.K.K.. Pray that God with strategically, methodically orchestrate avenues to get this book into the hands of troubled kids. Ask God to let this book be an IED for gangs and predators. I need some of you to not only pray-but fast and ask God to use this book as an awesome vehicle for transformation. I see this book in homeless shelters, churches, public libraries, juveniles, high schools, college dorms, coffee shops, synagogues, on death row and It shall come to pass if we will have faith.

If you are a youngster and in prison (reading this). There is a way for you to transform right where you are. Shot callers will come calling. They will try to break down your defenses and strip you of your personality. They aim to break you, take you and then to remake you. Talk to the chaplain and call your family. Try to find at least one compassionate staff member (i.e. a psychologist, psyche tech, nurse, physician etc.etc. there's always one) in whom you can confide. Ask them to put you up on game and express your fears. But show no weakness with fellow prisoners. I hate to go here- but even if you get beat down do not fight back. Do everything you can to avoid physical altercation but if they start you try to finish it. Channel and redirect your fear into fight. Don't jump in to basketball games or other contact sports at least for a couple of weeks. You need to watch the games to see who the bullies, bandits and shotcallers are. Don't inject your opinion into disputes or debates which don't involve you. And pray…And pray…And pray…

The best remedy is to stay out of prison. I mentioned (earlier) a racial riot at the California Institution for Men(Chino). It turns out that the state (which is cutting education funding) must pay $6.5 million to pair the damage the riots caused. If I were Arnold, Matt Cate or Scott Kernar I'd fire the watch commander along with every guard working during the riot. Had they adequately supervised and monitored the dorm there is no way the riot could have lasted that long, been so severe and caused such damage. But when guards are playing dominos, using cell phones, performing fellatio (i.e. Marion E. Spearman) or asleep etc. a riot can be deadly. And this $6.5 million does not include the $ hundreds of thousands of dollars it costed to treat all of those prisoners at local hospitals. The state will invent the money to repair the prison. But teachers have to teach 40-50 students per class due to a financial tsunami facing California's education system. What a shame.

And if you were at Chino you would have been rocking and rolling in that foolish riot. And many guys serving 2, 3 and 4 year sentences will acquire new charges for longer sentences as a result of participating in an unavoidable riot. And I'm being told this riot lasted for four hours! What were the correctional guards doing for four hours? I can recall (like it was yesterday) the very first riot I had to participate in at L.A. County Jail. It resembled the L.A. riots after the Rodney King beating. One moment I was playing cards with a white inmate and the next minute I was tackling him because it was whites against blacks. I recall breaking Alan Stark's jaw (AKA "Turtle") in a riot. And six months later Turtle and I were in a holding cell together. I thought he was going to try to murder me but instead we shook hands and talked about the riot. Turtle asked "Sherm do you even know y we was (sic) rioting?" I had no idea. But on a more serious level I'm absolutely certain that participating in mere senseless, shameful and obstiepesas riots damages us (the participants) for life.

I may not get there with you. "But I have to believe that even though I have lied, cheated, mistreated and wronged so many people. I must believe that the God (Israel) in me and what I learned from Rec. Hosea Williams, Grace Davis, Mayor Maynard Jackson and Ambassador Andrew Young will result in the success of G.B.G/Heart. I may not live to see it but in spite of my stinky, evil and my dead stuff etc. I still believe that Jesus Christ of Nazareth will stand outside of my mess and (raise it up) create a message. I see Master P., Channing Tatum, Tom Malinowski (HRW), Alice Kessler, John Deccaro, Nancy Alcorn, John Vetter, Seamus Farrow, Eli Pariser, Mike Turney Jr. and Luke Sears operationalizing G.B.G/Heart all over the world...anger, control, revenge, hostility, bitterness and racism are the ingredients that make up a "successful prison". Reverse discrimination (whites r the underdog), hatred and...the stuff of the prison. And my goal is to do, teach, write, say or to pray something to divert 'just one' of your from this place. Hades suffers from an egregious spiritual infection. So I've channeled all of my manipulative skills 4 good/God.

Dr. Franklin Curren gave me a certificate/which was signed by C. Solis Md, A. Duran PhD., Gregg Phd., Jennifer Heitkamp MO, Jarmar Phd. And others) which read in part: "...you have been successful at bringing together a team of rivals all willing to work toward diverting kids away from crime...you will go down in history as a pioneer among mentors and youth leaders...no other person incarcerated or free has worked with more drive, energy and determination than Sherman D. Manning...the G.B.G/Heart advisory board awards you the National Prison Leader of The Year Award effective September, 2009"...wow! A Harvard educated physician along with a battery of therapists awarded me with that certificate.

I hope that Captain Daniel Hahn (Sacto P.D.), Captain Jerry Cooper, Chiefs of police and prosecutors across America will promote the contents of this book. The that Bloods, Crips, Skin heads, members of Nuestra Familia etc. all provided data, interviews and background for this book makes it more credible. The fact that a symphony of psychiatrists, wardens and correctional experts screened this tome makes it unique. The fact that no editor, no professional book doctor and no ghostwriter helped with this book makes it even more palatable for real teens seeking real answers. I want kids at Granite Bay High School, Futures High School (Sacto), Kirsten Dunst's brother, P.J. Crowley and Becky Thompson to get this book. Kids who have run away from home or are being victimized by adults need to (immediately) contact the National Center for Missing and Exploited Children…If you need to talk etc (I repeat) go to DrPhil.com and click on "TeenTalk".

I want to award the G.B.G. National Youth Ambassador Award (if I'm alive) in April 2009. I'd like to give one kid (aged 15-22) a $5000.00 scholarship along with a $750.00 cash award and a trophy…visit us on Yahoo, Facebook, Myspace or www.napsusa.org to learn more.

We really, really need people (especially students) to volunteer to help us blog and maintenance our websites. If you are technologically endowed and will help us (stop playing space monkey) and e-mail us today! We need Maxwell Hanger, David Hellyer, C.J. Sheron, Brian Hawn, Chris Shea, Nathaniel Mullinnexx, Christian Nelson, Craig Scott (Littleton Co.), Keith Mullennix, Cody Freisen, Jeff Parshley and Andrew Knox today. Please take an hour and e-mail the folk I've named throughout this book. I'm willing to award and recognize those of you who will take an hour and find 10-20 people (in this book) and tell them about K.K.K. Just e-mail hallopeter@sunrise.ch and tell us who all you contacted.

This tome uncloaks the Menendez Brothers and illuminates prison as their own "private Idaho". It uncloaks gangs and reveals word portrait of the prisoner predator as never seen before…As I reflect back upon one of my many conversations with Eric G. Menendez I recall how awestruck he was when I told him that I knew the right Rev. Leroy Jenkins personally. Although I never told Eric I preached for Leroy (or that Leroy tried to sell me his mansion in Delaware Ohio…OR that Leroy Jenkins has me on his television show. OR that Leroy Jenkins cheated me out of $20,000..) I did tell him that I knew Leroy well. I slept in his house. Leroy bakes a mean homemade biscuit. Leroy Jenkins is an undercover homosexual. And Leroy even molested his own kids. One would assume that since Eric claims his dad molested him, he'd hate Jenkins after I told him about Jenkin's alleged molestation. Not so, Eric wanted to write him and reach out to him etc. Are yall ready to here how I met Jenkins? I was foolish enough to believe he had healing powers. So I conned the con thinking the con was authentic. I called Leroy Jenkins pretending (I affirm under penalty of perjury. It was aired on T.V. on Leroy's Show!) I was Rev. Jesse Jackson! And I told Jenkins that I (Jesse) was sending "Rev. Sherman D. Manning" to his Tallahassee Crusade. Leroy and I were close until he tried to get me to call Paul Crouch (owner of TBN) and perpetrate a fraud on Dr. Crouch to get him (Leroy) on TBN. Then I found out his famed leg extension healing was as fake as that head of black hair Jenkins had. (I did meet a fabulous minister named John Mandern who was remodeling Jenkin's house). Leroy Jenkins is a master con! But I guess I (pretending to be Jesse) conned the con. But anyway Eric wanted me to put him in contact with Leroy via personal introduction. I declined. But Eric seemed as interested in Jenkins as he was with Cayle, Jim Jones and Dwight. He studies cons, cult leaders and psychics.

"…a part of me loves being in prison. I was never a celebrity at home. I dropped out of school and disappointed my parents. Never lived up to their high standards. The first time I ever signed an autograph was as an inmate. Hell I get all the speed, sex and food (smuggles in by guards like Garza, Wheat and Wally) I want. I have two cell "phones" Eric once confided in me. Woe. I hope Paul Crouch Jr. and his son (who's doing well at L.A. Film School) both get this book. I want Tatum Channing to get it…I did (I'll mention again) boot camp (U.S. Navy) in San Diego. I want my naval buddies (camp 048) Lopez, Duane Fred Hall and Scott Coffman to (our company commanders were S.C.P.O. Beuchamp and Franklin…Coffman's first name might have been Steve. He was from Floyd Illinois…Please find them!) get this book. And if Duane, Coffman, Tatun, Van Hansis and Jake Silbermann are reading- go to page 313 of B.E.B II ("Blue Eyed Blonde" Book II)… at Coalinga Regional Med Center I had C.N.A. John Johnson. Somebody please get John this tome. And get it to my fireman (Jeremy) at Coalinga Fire Dept.

Andrew R. Elms Md. Just left my room: "If we get a miracle we might be able to defeat this meningitis" he told me fat chance. God can do anything! God is awesome!! But I know I'm dying due to all the mess I've done this is it! My curtain call. But these words, in this book will live on forever. Dr. Donald Templer (author and psychologist) once told me "your power is in your books Mr. Manning…spend less time talking and more time writing. You never know who will read your books bro. Paul did his best writing from prison!" And although I'll never be on Oprah, Dr. Phil (told yall I wouldn't do Oprah anyway) or Tyra etc. Madam 'O' Gayle, Dr. Phil, Tyra and Tyler are all readers…and I'm so serious about this book and its mission. (The cause of my life) that here's a message to Tyler Perry: "Mr. Perry if you will order 1000 copies of this book and donate them to (i.e. Archer High School, Douglas High, North side High etc. All in Atl. GA or Beverly Hills High in CA) schools I will donate 100% of all the profits (of those 1000 books) to Oprah's Angel Network. That is how important it is to get this book in teen's hands forthwith".

If my grand momma (Dollie Manning, whom I love with everything) is perusing this tome. I say to her "Cat I'm so sorry. I let you down. You raised me right. It's not your fault. I am very sorry. I love you and I miss ya!".

And lest some of you assume I only speak negatively of the Menendez monsters etc. and try to put myself on a platform (obviously you've not read this book in full) I remind you that "woe is me, for I am undone". I could easily bring big shot pastors down in this "tell all" (actually "tell some") book. But rather than deflect attention from me I've taken full blame I.E. There is a Famous Pastor (in or near Illinois) with whom I have run trains on women…on two occasions this pastor and I rain train on women in the pastor's study of his church. (And I'm sending him a copy of this tome. And I know he's sweating and his heart is beating fast right now!) And he still pastors that very large church. And he (Pastor X) has not lifted a finger to help me. In fact he put a block on his telephone so I can't call him. He's a master preacher. But I won't reveal his identity. The point is me. I was so full of crap that I had sex in the church. (as quiet as it is kept) Pastors across America (From Atlanta GA to LA California, from Chicago to Virginia) routinely have sex in church! If I were to name names you'd have to pick your jaw up off of the floor. Famed, prestigious and noted pastors. I used to wonder why God allowed them to remain free and in power. But I finally learned that they (too) are all in their own private jails and prisons. I recall a powerful pastor in Illinois once telling me when I was only 18 "Manning whatever you do stay single…I see why Jasper divorced Roberta. Marriage is a prison per se man. I hate goin home every night" he told me…and I'm a living witness that who you hang out with affects your moral code. The closer you become to people whom you admire and/or look up to. And the more you see your heroes' (mentors or even popular friends) flaws and scars etc. the more you begin to compromise your own moral code. Usually a kids initial disappointment and/or denial. From there one moves to acceptance. And (more often than not) inside that acceptance come tolerance. With tolerance comes emulation. When I first preached for a certain big shot pastor out of town. I recall sitting in a restaurant with him (on Kedzie) and hearing him say "Manning you're a bad ass". Then he corrected himself by restating it with "Manning you're a bad actor". But I knew he'd said "ass". And to me that was profanity. And not only did I not use profanity. I found it unbelievable that he used it. Weeks later I was with the most famous pastor in the state of Georgia and we were talking about a record producer who (believe it or not) had ripped me off. And in this pastor's study Rev. "So and So" said to me in a loud voice "F-ck him Manning! F-ck him! Damn him! You don't need that cracker!" And I had to pick my jaw up off the floor. Rev.

Moses Lee Raglin and Rev. John McClure etc never talked that way in my presence. So I was flabbergasted to hear this famed pastor. And it troubled me...slowly but certainly I became them. That's why I'm so adamant and forceful in advocating that youngsters become G.B.G Ambassadors! I'll pay them if I have to! Because I know the power of mentoring. I know the power of cliques! I know the power of role models. And if (this must become so) G.B.G/Heart can inspire just a small number of core volunteers to prognosticate the G.B.G/Heart mission- it will revolutionize youngsters. We must start student by student, juvenile by juvenile, teacher by teache, thugh by thug, drop out by drop out indoctrinating youngsters to the contents of this tome. I aim (with the help of these brilliant therapists, experience convicts as well as correctional experts etc.) to indoctrinate youngsters into a mindset that leads away from a jail cell and keeps them out of hell. I intend to be but a small part of influencing great (private eyes) folks like Jay Salpeter, Paul Ingels and Scott Rose etc. and allying them with Jamie Costantino (Jamie is an ex-gang member in Stockton and we need Jamie on the G.B.G team as an outside supporter!), congressman Anthony Weiner, John Verdi, Anthony DeDovsis (out at Harvard) and with Scott (Scott owns www.magnifeast.com)...to the Thugz I say "The Lord God has given me the tongue (and pen) of the learned, that I should know how to speak (and write) a word". Wow! If I don't do nuthin else with this year or less I have remaining on this planet..to young gangbangers, thugz, players, students and/or youths- If I do zero else I wanna just "Speak a word" over your situation, your mess, your classroom, your school, your jail cell, your prison etc. over you! (Isaiah 50:4-5) I came (in K.K.K to speak a word "in season to him who is weary". I get letter after letter from kids in crisis, kids in college, kids in trouble who are "weary". They try to drink, smoke or shoot their "weariness" away. But I can attest to the fact that through G.B.G and as I write K.K.K God has been awakening "me morning by morning, he awakens my ear to hear as the learned (my advisory board led by Dr. Franklin Curren). The Lord God has opened my ear". God opened my ear! And for those of you who will (as did Dr. Curren, Dr. Solis, Dr. Duran etc.) be surprised that a prisoner could/can write a book like this; I say "The Lord God" gave me "the tongue of the learned". It's not me! All the con, trickery and bull you read about (in this tome) is me. Woe is me. But the good, the clean, the pure, the powerful and the positive in this book is God...point blank...exclamation point!

I want Dr. Leslie Price (sacto), Daniel Berlant, Jason Huyck and Bruce Lisker to get this book. Get it to livingthings.com (the band in England), Eric Bryant (tell Eric in LA to pray the prayer of faith over K.K.K) and to Dr. Michael Serafin (Marysville CA). Get it to Dr. Quintana and Dr. Fontaine (at Mercy Bakersfiled). K.K.K is a mosaic of the inside view of criminal predator's minds. No other book (in print) takes the reader inside the minds, private lives and inside the jail cells of infamous monsters (i.e. Menendez, Bardo, Moore, Stokes and Johnson) like K.K.K. And (I hate to go here) if anyone doubts my former close association with the Menendez Bros. etc. etc. contact Chief Deputy Warden Terry L. Rosario, Scott Kernan, inmate "Fat Cat" Braggs, C.O. Mansky, C.O. Larry Crane, Teuers, Criner, etc. etc. and verify my housing to see if it jibes with Eric & Lyle's housing. Ipso facto, Eric and I worked together for more than 3 years, on third watch (in building 1 and 7)...when Eric and I worked together(simultaneously with the time I loaned him the $250.00) our guard supervisors were C.O. Love, C.O. Mansky, Crane, Criner, Teurs, Keene, etc. etc. and when I transferred from CSPSAC to M.C.S.P. Ione the first inmate to pull me out of my cell (in Bldg one) was Lyle Menendez to tell me "my brother told me all about you". Lyle had a myriad of questions about who all Eric was having sex with. Did Michael (Henrickson) have a nice ass? Was Eric working out. How much was Eric using drugs and did I ever screw Eric. Later when Lyle cane into a little money (a grand from fan mail) he asked me to talk Chucky (AKA Charles Pyle from Sacto) into celling up with him. "I need someone broke so I can be the alpha male. Chucky's young, naïve and blonde. I'll buy him a T.V. as long as he sucks me off every night and eats (TMI?) my ass-hole up. I'll even suck him from time to time". I actually delivered the message to Chucky (minus the sexual proposals). And Chucky indeed moved with Lyle. And Lyle indeed bought Chucky a T.V. and (P.S.) when I asked Chucky about their sexcapades Chucky said "I don't "really" mess around. But dude (Lyle) has got it bad. He is voracious". I said "you mean like a voracious reader?" Chucky said "I mean a nymphomaniac". I said "since ya don't "really" mess around, how would you know?" Chucky laughed and walked away.

G.B.G/Heart and the message in K.K.K. means as much to me as healthcare means to Senator Ted Kennedy. Getting this book to America's Youth is as important to me as getting his letter from a Birmingham Jail cell to preachers was to Dr. King. And Dr. King took some heat for some of the contents of that controversial missive. Some black pastors were angered by Dr. King's missive. Just as some prisoners, guards and gangbangers will be appalled by the contents of this tome. If I were not sick (my days on earth would be very limited) I would definitely expect gangbangers to murder me for the things I've said about their hidden and camouflaged sexuality. I more than crossed the line. Jessie on Big Brother reminds me of a gang banger. Here is a guy (Jessie) who must remind you (every fifteen minutes) that he has 18 inch arms. Who wears a t-shirt with a picture of himself on it? Jessie is narcissistic, a sissy, a chump and in prison he would be a ...I won't even go there... But these gang bangers are as unsure of themselves as Jessie. And they wear their "pride" on their chests just as Jessie wears his picture. And they can't read, write or count. And they will take a life with less thought than you'll give to going to the bathroom. We must get this book (speaking 'a word') to youngsters in places like Locke high school (in Los Angeles). Locke high school lost 75% of its freshman class via drop-outs last year. But it ain't just Locke. All across this country school yards resemble prison yards instead of college quads. And more than 95% of all U.S. high schools reported serious violent incidents in 2008. I wanna pass this word (K.K.K) into the hands of Brandon Stafford, Jimmy Stovall, Alma Flores, Debra Watkins and assistant principa Alexander. I'm extremely impressed with Green Dot public schools and C.E.O. Steve Barr out at Locke last year 600 students fought and police had to break them up with riot gear. So Locke was preparing them for (C.M.I) Chino. The cycle must be broken. And I want all 600 of those fighting students to read this book. And I say (just as Locke cheerleaders chanted at a basketball game) to Locke high students "Lets go, Lets go-we (you, me, and G.B.G) got the ball." Let's go Brandon, Jimmy Barr, Faisal Selah, Seamus Farrow and all Locke high students. I'm going to do my best to press this tome into the hands of Locke high students. And (strange-I know-but real) the first 3 Locke high students to snail mail me a missive: "Dear Sherman I read all of "kids killing kids" and passed it on to a friend" I'll send them (you) $100.00 each...Yes- the first 3 letters I receive from Locke high students; I'll post them on our website and send all 3 students $100.00 each...To you at Locke High School (and at Beverly Hills High, Archer/Harper Ralph Bunche Middle School, McClatchy High School etc.) I remind that you are somebody. You may (or may not) have been born in the slums. But the slum was not born in you. It matters not where you came from but where you are going to go (Let's go, Let's go, we got the ball!) in your mind and you will go in time. Read everything you get your hands on. Read like a maniac! Read like a mad man! Read ("Fish" by Parsell, "Long Walk to Freedom" Mandela, "Come on People" Cosby, "Creating Monsters", "Blued Eyed Blonde" Book II Manning, "Reallionaire" Gray, The Holy Bible! Etc.)-Read...Read stuff you even disagree with. Reading opens the mind and takes you places. Locke high I promise you that you can read your way out of no way! Read! I want at least 50 students at Locke high to form a special envoy for G.B.G/Heart. I want you to get your parents on board and for you to pall this book all around the football team, to the basketball team, to the band and to cheerleaders. I want yall to share this book with white students. I want you all to discuss, critique and to analyze this tome. I'm even adding a dedication to all Locke high school students in this book. I'm in much prayer for every student, every parent and every teacher at Locke. If I only get this tome to every student (and we at G.B.G can/must do that! If I gotta call on Daniel Bugriyev, Adam Lane, Dustin Nicolodi and M. Reid and ask each of them to order 2 or 3 copies each and have them sent to Locke High School...and all of the G.B.G advisors i.e. F. Curren Md, C. Solis Md and J. Heitkamp Md etc earn more than $150,000 per year. I'm certain Dr. Curren, Dr. Heitkamp and Solis can all afford to purchase 10 copies each and send them to Locke High School in L.A.) At Locke my work is done. And I want Paul Crouch Jr, Amy Fihn and all the folks at Second Chance to just pray that Locke high school will be saturated with this book.

I am intimately familiar with what's going on in a school like Locke. I speak from a place of strong love, great hope and expectation. James Earl Jones says "Language is just an instrument or a tool". And I intend to use the 26 Alphabets as a vehicle for the transmogrification and the revolutionization of teens and tweenies. And I want you kids in Locke high school, Bevery Hills High, in Watts, Compton and in the suburbs to start back dreaming. You need to have a dream baby boy and disappointment is the gap between expectation and reality. But develop consistency in the midst of the process. I want you to read (at least 30 minutes per day. I read for hours every day.) Every day. Whether you're in the hood, the burbs, a jail, a barrio or wherever. Read everyday and you'll learn to love it and you'll grow. And I want you to stop feeling intimidated by success, books and knowledge. You will master it one step (one day, one book, one page, one paragraph, one sentence, one word and one letter) at a time. I promise you that you can do it...kids- can we be real? I don't need you. I'm not looking for you to join a church or to buy my CD. This book will not (I promise you. If you think I'm lying call Arnold and ask him.) win me a pardon. Nor will this book cure my valley fever. The only reason I am writing to you (in Locke, Folsom High, McClatchy High, Heritage High, U.C. Davis, SCUSAC etc.) is because I owe it to you to tell you the truth about Hades. It's my destiny to show youth my wonds, my mess, my errors, my crimes and my scars so you can reach for the stars...I love Jesse Jackson, Al Sharpton, Rick Warren and many others in ministry. They have helped me tremendously (even though they don't write me back). But I'm not called to the kids already in church and in ministry. I'm called to the Lost youth. I'm called to the truant geeks, freaks, nerds and thugs. I'm called to the Jacobs and the Sauls. I'm called to Jordan, Blake, Redmond O'Neal and Cameron Douglas. I steal from (I'm a convict so yall know I'm a thief! LOL) great minds like Tony Dungy (you sll should peruse Tony Dungys tome) and I translate the verbiage into my "thugology". I sit my ass back in my hospital bed and in prison and I study Bill Cosby, Dr. Alvin Poussaint, "Come on People", Chris Gardner, "The Pursuit of Happyness", Tony Robbins, Steve Covey, Dr. Phil, Dr. Yablonsky, Dr. Curren, Dr. Duran, Dr. Gregg etc. I study monsers like Eric & Lyle, Marvin, Bardo, and Stokes etc. and I'm able to interrogate brilliant minds like Dr. Jarman, Dr. Houston etc. And I mix these philosophies, strategies, and mentalities together. And I create what Dr. Jarman and Dr. Curren call a "tome of Gumbo" which is as palatable to the kids at Locke high school as it is edible to students at (although they need a lot of water) Beverly Hills High School. This is that book baby boy! Yeah! Yall "feel me"? And as an aside- Jimbo will not accept any "gift" from an inmate. But just as my publisher gave Arnold "Creating Monsters" etc. the publisher will be giving Jimbo, and the board of advisors (led by Frank Curren Md.) copies (grafts) of this book. And I want them (Solis, Duran, Heithkamp etc. I repeat) to pay it forward. I want them to go to www.cafepress.com/Manning and order some copies of this book to be mailed to Locke high school...These monsters (i.e. Eric and Lyle) have been my human guinea pigs. And as Dr. Solis says "every time I see you I know I'm about to be pumped for information, explanation and elucidation...but it always makes me glad I went to medical school". The coach of the Philadephia Eagles has two sons who were locked up on drug charges. I want them to have this tome. I want the owner of the Philly Eagles to get this book. And since the "Eagles" gave Michael Vick a second chance Mike needs this book. And I do recall Mike stating he found Christ back when he was in jail. So it would be nice for Michael Vick to take (just a couple $ thousand bucks) a tad bit of that $1.6 million contract and donate some copies of this book to Philadelphia public schools and/or to Mayor Michael Nutter's re-entry program. And I'd like to see Michael make a donation to TBN's Second Chance program.

I want L. Garrison, Adam Cragg, Attorney Billy Martin and Paris Hilton to have this book. I even want Brittney Spears to get this tome. I invite Jamie Costantino, Andrew "the volunteer", Father Greg Boyle, All Homeboy Industries members, kids at Futures high school, and kids at Locke to attend a G.B.G/Heart tour. Hopefully my health won't prohibit me from making it back to do a few more G.B.G/Heart interventions. I wanna see Steve Barry, Tony Robbins, Nils Vesk, Eric Bryant, Debra Watkins and others. I want Brandon Stafford, Jimmy Stovall, Coach Andy Reid and Tony Dungy to get this book. Lets get it to Steven Spielberg, David E. Kelley and every principal. This tome covers the United States of prisons. This tome can trigger united youth actions all across the world. Johnny Machione needs this book..."I like to hear success stories so that other men in prison can do the same thing" states the Honorable Greg Mathis. Judge Mathis is the realest judge on T.V. . He's been locked up (like a lot of kids at Locke) in juvenile before. He dropped out of high school. His mother had to visit him in jail to tell him she was dying from cancer. Judge Mathis gives a damn about youth. I have an autographed photo of Judge Mathis on my prison wall. He inspires much of what I do, say and write...Bill Cosby calls "come on people" a cheerleading session. Well "K.K.K" is a pep rally! (Mentioning Dr. Poussaint and Bill Cosby: I'd like for them to please donate 100 copies of "Come On People" to Locke High School...I want students to e-mail Dr. Poussaint at Harvard and tell him what I said in K.K.K)...I want Sam Bompas, students at Kash career college (Sacramento), Delta college (Sacto), Clint Van Zandt and students at Ronald E. McNair high to have this book. Get it to Ayana Kleckner and to Evan Williams...teens? I'm not your mom and I'm not your dad. I'm a common criminal. And I know yo parents get on your last nerves sometimes. I know they think they know it all. But I must admit to you that they know more than we think they know. And even when they say "No", won't let you go and punish you. They love yo black (white and brown) ass. They love you! Believe that. And even though you have acquaintances, family or siblings in jail etc. you can break the cycle. You may already be in the mix. Get out right now. Just make up in yo mind "I'm gonna turn around". You can program yourself for success. You can set yourself up to succeed against all odds. You can light up your community, your school or your classroom. Light it up with love, concern and with the determination to pull yourself up by your own bootstraps kick yourself in the ass and say "Not another one of us...I can't go to prison like my daddy did. I gotta break this curse off of my life. I gotta read my way out of the slums. I can R-e-a-d my way into collefe, into a career and into success...If Judge Mathis could do it-I can"...Can I talk to you youngsters like (as if) I know your parents aren't reading? Can I get down, raw and candid with you? Can yall 4 get that I'm a church boy 4 a minute and just remember I'm a convict?

Listen to me: Is this what you want to die doing? Do you wanna die on meth or on crack? Do you wanna die in the back of a patrol car? Do you wanna die on welfare and illiterate? Pick yo ass up off the ground. The ground is no place for champions. People died for your black ass to read. You white folks don't have the right not to read. You (teens) are the leaders we've been waiting for. You are the kids we need to cure Aids and cancer. You are the kids we need to cure racism and hatred. More than 50 new (armed militants) hate groups have been formed in the last 20 months; because of the Barack that you all put in the White House. The work is not done. It's not finished. We're not there yet. So we need you to stay off drugs, in school and out of prison. Don't bring your back side to Broke Back prison. Prison is Dream-Death Row. Prison is a Death

Row for vision and destiny...I wanna speak directly to students at Locke, Folsom, Columbine and McClatchy high school. I need to speak directly into your spirit and tell you what I see. I've seen too many boys and girls get caught up in this vicious monster factory. I've personally watched (with my own eyes) the deaths, the murders, the assassinations and the crucifixions of kid's dreams, hopes, futures and ambitions in Hades. That's the why G.B.G/Heart and getting K.K.K into your school, college and city is the cause of my life...I'm sounding the trumpet to you. Call me the prison czar. It's my duty, my debt and my responsibility to call Jessie Godderz, John Gonzalez (Philadelphia Inquirer) Nils Vesk, pastors, police, guards and gangsters and to demand that we tell u the truth. The truth, the whole truth and nothing but the truth. My goal is to see you in the college quad and not the prison yard. Let me see you in "Green Dot" uniforms and not "black and white" prison uniforms. Let me see you with books in your hands and not with cuffs on your wrists. I wanna see you on vacation and out on the stroll but not on probation or on parole. Let me see you on America's Rich and Famous and not on America's Most Wanted. And remember that even if you are not rich in money. You can be rich in mind. I'd rather be on the bus and be free. Than to ride to the prison in a Mercedes...this tome is for 11 year old Damon Weaver, Brandon Stafford and for Maxwell Hanger. I pray that G.B.G/Heart (Helping Educate At Risk Teens) metastasizes through the hoods, barrios, trailer parks, schools, colleges and churches like a positive (inoperable) cancel spreading through a body. I've been losing a whole lot of sleep in my effort to put forth this book to challenge you to go. I aim to pull you back (like I said) and to shoot you into your destiny!!

I prophesy that the data inside this book shall trigger mentorship, Big Brother and teen programs all across America. I prophesy that the stuff I've been taught by Warden Walker, Dr. Curren, Dr. Yablonsky, Dr. Duran and Dr. Heitkamp etc. will trigger youth groups across America like wild fires in California. I pray that what I've been taught by Johnny, Willie, "Doc" Ford, Billy, Joker, Silent and others will trigger transformation and education all across this darn nation. Let K.K.K wake up the sleeping giant within your. I've seen too many young tears and too many youth fears. I can't take any more of this devastation caused by the incarceration of our young. I need for you to get up. I want to push you toward success and away from mess. I pray that people like Joe Kennedy III, young Matthew Kennedy and Caroline Kennedy will help Heart to speak a word with K.K.K. You can do it. You are Superman. Go into your phone booth and transform. The library is your phone booth. Books are your kryptonite. Fill your mind with hope, faith and knowledge and you will be armed and dangerous! I need u 2 b armed and dangerous enough to promote education instead of incarceration. We can promote Yale over jail. We can do it.

This (book) is my duty, my debt and my job. I would never, ever have told the Calvario story if I didn't know it was my duty, could save lives and could help somebody. I have written 8 books before this one never telling the Calvario, Don King, Rev. Hosea Williams or Ambassador Andrew Young stories. I have never written about the Menendez brothers! I refused to build my writing career and be known as "that guy who wrote a tell all book about the Menendez Bros". And my own jaw dropping confessions? I planned to take them to my grave. But here I am fully exposed (by my own self inflicted wounds and exposure) and uncloaked as a sinner, con and as a crook. I want to thank you youngsters for inspiring me to write this. Thank you for receiving this book with an open heart...I don't need any sympathy. I need no camaraderie. I don't need to fraternize. All I need is for you to pull yourself together. Read this book and pass it on.

I want Shea Newberry to get this book. I met Ben (from the lab) and Casey (transporter) at Sierra Regional Medical Center (San Luis Obispo) and I want them to have this book. Fox aired "The Secret Millionaire" last summer with a father son team. The son was Cole Bing or Google Fox and find Cole and tell him about this book...Rachel Morningstar Hoffman's pal Cole (also) was on Dateline. Cole lives in Clearwater Florida; get him the book. I want Jennifer Portman (Rep. The Tallahasee Democrat) to have this book. Get it up to Beverly Ann Monroe (and her daughter) in Richmond Virginia. Nate was on (FOX) " Paradise Hotel" last year. Get Nate this book. Get it to the Philadelphia Daily News, Emile Hirsh, Ted Murphy, Stan Brock, Jessie Godderz and to Chris Hansen. Write about K.K.K on the walls of your Facebook pals. Get it to Nathaniel Marshall, Tatum Channing and to at-risk teens all across the world.

And I'm reminding Daniel Bugriyev, Adam Lane, M. Reid, Dustin etc. to spread the word on twitter.com, myspace.com etc. about this book. There is absolutely no rule prohibiting a Dustin Nicolodi from writing (on a wall) "Dude I'm reading a new book "K.K.K". you should go to www.napsusa.org or www.cafepress.com/Manning and get it!"

Let me thank you (all you college and high school students) for writing me with so many suggestions which are reflected in this book. And as you read this haunting, candid, earth shattering and chilling tale remember it is happening every day of the week. I would hope Joel Stein (L.A. columnist), Mark Arax, Mr. Rothchild (L.A. Times), The Atlanta Daily World, The Atlanta Voice and Magic Johnson get this book. I hope the Scissor Sisters, Green Day, Rev. Smith and Rev. Otis Moss will all get this book. I want teens to evangelize this book. I want you all to turn the internet upside down and spread the contents of K.K.K like a wildfire in Santa Barbara. I want you all to find Trevor Loflin, Jai Breisch, Ryan Hreljac, Seamus, Joe Kennedy III and even Mike Tyson and tell them about this book. I want Russell Simmons to get it...most pastors and elite churchfolks will reject (its too candid so don't waste your energy) this book. They are well. But I want you to get it to the sick (Jacobs, Sauls, tricksters, gang bangers, drop outs etc.). Spread the word.

In-custody graduate to more violent and sadistic criminal activity upon their release from prisons. "I'm not a liberal" states C.Dolis MD. "But irrefutable data points to the conclusion that once youngsters enter penological institutions they are ruined for life... more than 90% of kids under the age of twenty one who are locked up today will get out in much less than five years. And more than 82% of them will reoffend in less than one year. Arguably, a large number of that 82% will return with life sentences in prisons... "Dr. Solis concluded "with the California prison system operating at 200% of capacity with more than 172,000 inmates in 33 prisons here. Data suggests that almost 80,000 of those inmates are under the age of 21... Perhaps 55,000 of these kids in custody are psychologically traumatized to the extent that (without expensive enhanced therapy) they've been transformed into violent criminals; for life"...Mr. President! This keeps me up at night. And let me be clear: I've made it clear to the Justice Department (namely pardon Attorney Ronald L. Rogers) that my service in G.B.G./Heart (in my view) does not qualify me (or my team members) for a pardon (regional, federal or otherwise) from prison. As a matter of fact the office of the U.S. President does not even have the judicial authority to pardon a state inmate. I write this because (as a bad/boy) I'm cognizant of the fact that we (inmates) often have ulterior motives, discover "jail house" religion and seek favor with politicians...If I'm ever released from prison it will be because the courts determine that my conviction was unlawful. Ipso facto my service with G.B.G./Heart is immaterial to the conviction and shall never be "considered" by a court of law. I write this to elucidate my intentions to you. Lest we be misunderstood. You have this convict dedicating a tome to a president and claiming that crimes against young inmates and their plight keeps him (me) awake at night. I'm certain that Glenn Beck, Limbaugh and Hannity would call it insanity etc. that I'm not positioning myself to seek favor from our president. Having said that sir-I seek no favor. I seek action! We need no more blue ribbon committees or commissions etc. We need your administration to do something in light of kids killing kids. Help stop the judicial tsunami and stop sending our kids to these cesspools. And we must tackle America's eyesore; our prison system like never before. If we are to prevent the 250,000 kids who shall be released in 2010 from (juveniles, jails and prisons) becoming "Criminals for Life". We must reverse the curse and with your help (i.e. supporting TBN Second Chance, doubling the money we spend on educating our kids, changing sentencing laws, reinvesting in community policing and pell grants etc.) We can do this. If not now when? If not you who? If not why not?

Mr. President we must develop programs to help kids develop self esteem, self worth and self assurance so they won't feel the need to join a gang (unless it's G.B.G.). We must address youth crime and punishment and make prison (for kids) the last resort. We must also address the rape epidemic in prisons forthwith. When we take a child's freedom, the government takes on the sole responsibility of protecting that child's safety. With more than 2.5 million folks behind bars (49% of whom are between the ages of 7-19 Mr. President!) in America, keeping kids killing kids (kids killing parents, kids committing crime-period) safe is a humongous job. Prisons and juveniles (nationwide) are failing miserably at this job. This myriad failure has resulted in a virtual tsunami of infectious disease as well as rampant violence in the prisons. The failure is in part, rooted in the unparalleled secrecy and the prison guard code of silence. This "code" has resulted in a culture of corruption, impunity, violence and retaliation against inmates who dare to report the sexual assault. In the worst juveniles and prisons, officials facilitate and/or participate in sexual assault, grant perpetrators impunity and respond to kids cries for help with derision..."After being raped by a prison guard in Texas, I was devastated and terrified. I felt certain that filing a formal complaint with the perpetrator's colleagues would only have made my situation worse" states Garrett Cunningham. In December 2009 (via the G.B.G./Heart Facebook site, www.napsusa.org and www.cafepress.com/manning) G.B.G./Heart shall launch a cyber effort to inundate the congress and senate with e-mails and telephone calls asking them to address prison rape. We want everybody (even the person perusing this presidential missive) to snail, e-mail and to call 202-224-3121 (http://www.house.gov/house/memberwwwbystate.shtml#CA the house of representatives on 12/1/09. We'll repeat our calls and e-mails on 1/3/10. We are mobilizing twitter nation, the facebook generation, criminal justice, law schools, human rights, defense lawyers, students, pastors and parents to form focus groups, monitors and citizens task forces to receive and respond to abuse victims' cries for assistance. "Just Detention International" executive director Louisa Stannow and Deputy Executive Linda McFarlane (also a G.B.G./Heart advisory director-psychiatrist Franklin Curren explains that "survivors of rape experience fear, shame, guilt, tension, anxiety, exaggerated startle responses, anger, depression, impaired concentration and memory, and rapid mood swings. For some victims, eating and sleeping patterns are disrupted also."

G.B.G./Heart Director of training C.Solis MD. states that "Incarcerated survivors are at high risk for sustaining long-term psychological difficulties due to the absence of adequate Mental Health treatment in the wake of an assault...I.E. addiction, depression, and judicial identions." G.B.G./Heart special advisor A. Duran Ph.D. adds "Inmates-especially youngsters victimized in multiple assaults and/or are under continuing control of the perpertrator(s) can develop complex PTSD- severe psychological harm as a result of repeated, prolonged trauma." Dr. Jarman elaborated on the subject of serious post trauma. Psychiatrist Jennifer Heitkamp (G.B.G./Heart distinguished special advisor) is an expert psychiatrical problems behind bars and she explains that "PTSD is not on the correction department's list of major mental illnesses etc. It is often overlooked, disregarded wrongly treated as a non-urgent illness"... J. Friedman Ph.D. (G.B.G./Heart special advisor) states "Inmate counseling sessions usually occur in earshot and/or view of corrections officers, who sometimes even acquiesced or participated in the rape. Moreover "he continues, "once a victim reports information about the rape, the counselor is obliged to report this to prison managers. Ipso facto, the victim seeking mental health help becomes the proverbial "rat" or "snitch", risking severe reprisal from the assailant, his gang or buddies...and experts nationwide agree that prisoner rape is perhaps America's most seriously under-reported crimes."

President Obama: In my tome "Creating Monsters" I interviewed a high ranking prison official (who spoke on the condition of anonymity) and the person stated that "in my 24 years in the department I've investigated hundreds of rapes. Inmates raped by gangs, cellies and even by staff...An inmate is raped in California every nineteen minutes." I was startled and thought the person misspoke. Their reply to my animated inquiry: "In jails (i.e. Los Angeles County) juvenile detention, CA Youth Authority, female prisons and CA state prisons (combined) an inmate is raped every nineteen minutes! ...That's the best estimate by two experts...These experts are at the top of their fields hired in secret....They interviewed 250 inmates and 25 staff. The report was withheld from the legislature and ultimately shredded." My requests for more data were met with silence. At that juncture (I think it was ABC) ABC News (World News Tonight) as well as Nightline were doing major stories on prison rapes... "Sherman if you use my name or even my gender when you write about this I will be forced to destroy you."

My inside view, unique vantage point and unusual access to predators and prey have given me a strange and spooky qualification to testify from Hades. I can read the handwriting on the wall... Mr.Obama: Prisons produce killers, rapists and molesters. This is the devil's workshop our kids come here and attain status, creds and so much ("game") instruction in how to commit more crime etc. that they enter prisons as high school drop outs and exit with masters degrees in psychosexual deviancy, murder and mayhem...Mr. President I vividly recall listening to a convict (Marvin Johnson) explicitly and specifically tell an inmate (Gregory Swokla) how to cut a person's head off with precision!!! Marvin is convicted of decapitating two persons. My buddies (Lonnie Young and Johnny Willie) and I were befuddled. I told the fellas (rather quietly) that "they teach surgeons how to cut in a matter of hours. But it takes a lifetime to teach us how not to cut, kill and maim...Dr. Johnson?" I recall sitting I my cage (cell) one night along in the dark. My neighbors were two Hispanics and "Colombia" (his nick name) methodically gave his celly a lecture on how to rape a celly. He routinely referred to the tome "The 48 Laws of Power," manipulation, intimidation and psychological brainwashing. It could have been confused with a lecture at Princeton by Professor Cornell West if it were not so evil. He talked about "grooming" the celly, the carrot and the stick, when and how to use violence and specific methods (to use) to keep the C.O.'s from hearing. Colombia explained that 9:30 pm. Is court time. That's when you put your t.v. on the Mexican channel which shows a lot of sexual shows. And you simultaneously show him pornography to excite him etc . share a stick of weed (easily availablein all U.S. prisons...Colombian specifically told him correctional officer Wally Laffitt brought weed, speed and crack to inmates...It should be noted that officer Wally L...ended up being ratted out. They arrested him and found counterfeit money, drugs and an unregistered gun on him. He had 19 years in the dept...fired em and he actually went to prison for two years.) With him and some pruno (prison manufactured alcohol). You secretly put psychotrophic drugs in the hooch which acts like a date rape drug...He even explained that Dr. Marilyn Windham would help you get any psyc. med you want as long as you 'bust her eyes'. Which means show her your "package". A couple of years ago Dr.Marilyn Windham was caught having sex with a inmate in a mop closet...The red convertible drivin Dr. Windham was charged with rape. The results of her arrest are not available...Colombia had alternative plans i.e. what you do if he does not 'get down' (meaning smoke marijuana), what etc. How to decide which strategy (grooming, fighting) to employ on your celly. Mr. President it's extremely disrupt (and at times impossible) for a frightened inmate to convince staff to give him "single cell status." I recall Dr. Brad Lumpkins ar Pleasant Valley state prison who was famous for telling inmates (including this writer) to "rape or kill your celly and we'll give you single cell status." He even told inmate Ronnie Ritter this cell partner "Hollywood" Walters. (Dr. Lumpkins was not the only accessory; C.O. Brumbaugh told Ritter "Your new celly is a child molestation") and Ritter murdered Walters that self same night. Ritter fed Walters pruno mixed with drugs. When Hollywood passed out Ritter strangled him to death and stuffed him underneath the bunl. Ronnie stated "Yeah I killed his ass and at least I'll get single cell status for ten years". I'm reminded of a thin and effeminate Michael Gorman (New Folsom- Bldg-A-7) in ad-seg. He kicked, banged and yelled all day pleading to be moved out of the cell "F_ck or fight" an officer (G.W.) told Michael. The next morning C.O. Mequita discovered Gorman Face down, dead and nude with a t.v. guide shoved up his anus. Gorman wasa 21 and was paroling in less than a year. Mr. President our starving schools feed prisons!! The California State Criminal justice budget has grown to over $13.6 billion for 08-09 from $7.2 billion in 2000 and $3.1 billion in 1990. Yet, only one new school has been built in the last 44 years. Yet, brilliant, young California teachers like Joshua Costa may lose their jobs. Prison guards are tenured.

Mr. President what kind of people drain its education system while simultaneously preparing to lock kids up instead? We don't guarantee kids a free (as does Switzerland) seat in a university, but we will guarantee them a bunk in a prison. We can't/won't put a free book ("The Audacity of Hope"?)in kids hands but we will put handcuffs on their wrists. In my view, watching politicians pump up the already bloated prison budget while cutting admissions in the State University system is like watching a horror movie in which the panicked heroine, thinking she has eluded her pursuer, has actually locked herself in a room with the killer...These prisons which routinely house 17 year olds with 57 year olds cause permanent damage to America's children. Depression, anxiety, sleeping disorders, psychotic breaks: every symptom one might reasonably expect a victim of torture to manifest. A. Duran Ph.d. notes "Sherman while it's technically illegal to confine an inmate in a Shu (Security Holding Unit) who has a mental illness, this is of no consolation to the thousands of prisoners who have become mentally ill as a result of being put in a shu and 75% if the guys isolated in those dark shu's today will get out of prison. And they take their anger and dysfunctions to the streets." On the subject of torture again, in 2005, Army Reserve specialist Charlie Graner was convicted of torture, maltreatment and cruelty in Iraqi prisoners at Abu Ghraib. In 1998 when Graner was a guard at the maximum SCI-greene prison in Pennsylvania-a facility where 98% of the inmates are black and 97% of the guards are white- he was accused of employing methods strikingly similar to the ones he later used at Abu Ghirab. Maximum security prisons like SCI Greene (GA. State Prison at Riedsville, Rikers and Pelican Bay etc.), while doing nothing to reduce recidivism, do serve as effective training academies for sadists like Graner (and many guards). One wonders: If producers of prison reality tv wanna do a show on prisons as schools for crime, why don't we do a series on Graner and the Shu-Abu Ghraib connection? G.B.G. member (and prisoner for 30 years) Johnny "Claw" Willie sums torture up more eloquently than reams of statistics: "Put a dog in a cage and then come by and kick the cage or poke that dog with a stick every day. What happens when the dog comes out of that cage?"

Mr. Obama: When you gave that historic speech in Chicago the night that you won the election etc. I heard you say to those who did not vote for you that "I will be your president too." Ipso facto, there are nearly 3 million of us unable to vote. And we do have voting families and friends etc. but we (prisoners) need you to be our president too...I have no personal dog in this fight (tome). I'll never meet you sir. I will never be free, period. I am a chief sinner. I'm the lowest of the low. I'm a thug and but a common criminal. He that has ears let him hear. Behold, I only testify of that which I am certain...An inmate in Orange County Jail on domestic battery and child porn charges was falsely labeled a child molester by guards, and as a result was savagely beaten to death by other prisoners. The victims parents sued Orange County for $60 million for failing to protect their son, but settled for $600,000 before trial. Computer technician John Derek Chamberlain, 40, was awaiting trial at the jail on October 5, 2006. At 1:00 pm that day, his lawyer, Jerry Sterling, called the jail and advised them that John was in fear for his life because he'd overheard threats from dudes who thought he was a child molester…Prison guard routinely manipulate (via embellished propaganda or mendacity) inmates, one against another. So jail officials ignored Jerry's request to have John moved to protective custody. John was dragged to a blind spot in the dorm. Mr. President-Twenty prisoners beat him for 30 minutes; he was stripped naked, scalded with hot water. (Please note this was a county jail not a state prison. Many would/could be bailed out and returned to the community with all deliberate speed. These were not guys sentenced to life terms whom society would never see again.) he was kicked, punched and stomped. They spat on him and urinated on him. Three jail guards were nearby but did not intervene as they were preoccupied watching TV and sending text messages. (It should be a federal crime for a jail or prison guard to text or use a cell phone in an institution). Chamberlain was pronounced dead at the scene.

Chamberlain's family filed a lawsuit in U.S. District Court alleging that jail guard Kevin Taylor had told inmate Jared Petrovich, a gang "shot caller", that John was a molester and "needed to be beaten." Taylor further told Petrovich that prisoners in the dorm would be rewarded for the beating by being allowed to watch a televised Dodgers vs. Mets playoff game. The suit alleged that Orange County officials should have known that child sex offenders were frequently targeted, severly beaten and were even targeted by guards. (Never mind the presumption of Innocence). Furthermore, guards should have noticed the lengthy, boisterous and fatal beating because they were in the area watching TV and could hear Chamberlain's cries for help. The lawsuit also alleged the guards gave inmates time to wash off blood to prevent their being identified. The parties settled in March 2008. The settlement included written recognition that Orange County and its employees denied the allegations. But a special grand jury report released in 2008 found wrongdoing by jail staff and the board of supervisors created an office of Independent review to examine complaints at the jail.

Seven prisoners have been charged with homicide. Two have admitted that guards Taylor and Jason Chapluk instigated the attack by falsely claiming John was booked on molestation charges. Taylor's defense was that he was watching t.v. (on the job) and heard and saw nothing inside F-barracks during the 30-minute period in which John was savagely murdered. After the murder Taylor altered the jail log to reflect his willingness to have moved Chamberlain, which he falsely wrote that Chamberlain had "declined". Details emerged that at 6:30 p.m. John had been taken to a partially hidden cubicle where a lynch mob doused him with scalding water, beat him with shoes, kicked his head and punched him- all while he lay screaming for help on the floor, curled into a protective ball. One inmate hit John so hard that he broke his own hand. Another, holding onto a bunk for leverage, stomped on his skill. Orange County guards have an infamous history of arranging fatal beatings at the jail and using prison gangs as enforcement. John's murder was the fifth such death at the facility in a month where deputies were accused of instigating such attacks. Conspiracy to commit murder carries a 25-life sentence. But Orange County is a hotbed of wealthy "tough-on-crime"conservatives, and it remains to be seen if any guards will do a single day in the pen for their complicity in the murders. Finally, it's said that the sheriff has been arrested and fired for a battery of offenses (including forced sex on a male inmate, drug smuggling and possession of kiddie porn). I asked Dr. Solis, Dr. Curren, Dr. Heitkamp, Dr. Duran and Dr. Friedman to comment on this incident as it relates to public safety. They issued a joint special report too lengthy to publish in this tome. I have thoroughly reviewed the 29 page report and after considering the report at length, I have come to the conclusion that the 70 or 80 inmates (some locked up on petty theft and disorderly conduct beefs etc.) who merely witnessed this savage murder will carry psychological baggage (for life) back to the kids, parents and the elderly in the neighborhoods. And more than 95% of county jail inmates are released in less than a year. Mr. President: I declined to comment on professor "Skip" Gates' arrest for disorderly conduct. However, let us imagine that Skip Gates had been arrested by Sgt. Jim Crow (in the 60's)rather than sgt. Jim Crowley in 09. And let us imagine that a young, impressionable, undereducated (i.e. high school attendee) Louis Gates, merely locked up (rightly or wrongly) for allegedly yelling at Sgt. Jim Crow ("Boy don't you talk back to the po-lice. Hold your head down and keep your mouth shut") etc. After perusing (meticulously) this report by psychological and psychiatric experts Mr. President, what keeps me awake at night is not merely the 'potential' that a young Skip Gates arrest may or may not have been the result of racial profiling. I'm more troubled by the severe, atrocious psychological impact the jail experience would have had on a young Skip. Had a 116 or 17 year old Skip witnessed the savage, animalistic and tortured beating (who can say that some combination of peer pressure, fear, intimidation and immaturity might not have led Skip and participate in the filing?) And murder of Johnnie Derek Chamberlain etc. I would be inclined to believe that (having witnessed such brutality) the 16 year old "Skip" that we knew in his youth would not be the (brilliant, learned and distinguished) Harvard professor Henry Gates we know in his middle age. We know that faith comes by hearing and hearing. By the word. And violence is also learned behavior. And certain things we hear, see and experience in adolescence affect how we think, feel and act as adults. (i.e. President Obama-you were raised by your darling grandmother as was I. And you still remember your beautiful grandmother having a drink of whiskey and a cigarette at the end of the day. And you still smoke. And my darling grandmother smoked Winston 100's for 40 years. And I smoked for 20 years. And when my grandmom stopped two years later I stopped. It was the toughest battle of my life.) so the teachable moment for this writer is not necessarily about race, color or creed. Had Skip been white and the cop black it still would have no bearing on what Skip saw at Orange County Jail. And I write earlier to generation y and to the teenies that "Ya'll have seen some bad stuff" because I know that what kids see can determine what they'll be. And when our children see drug addicted parents, drop out dads, older siblings who don't go to school, molestation, rapes and murders, etc. It will affect their destiny. We are programmed and limited by what we see. Our beliefs create our destiny. What we see affects what we believe. Mr. President: After reviewing the report by G.B.G./Heart staff advisors I am perplexed, distressed and troubled by what our at-risk kids (killing kids) have had to see. I have no sympathy for Eric (Menendez) and Lyle the killers. There is no justification for emptying a shotgun in your mother's (and father's) head. I can't fathom it. Nor do I have sympathy for Dandol Henson, Bardo, Marvin Johnson or any of the other homicidal maniacs whom I've had to live amongst. But the advantage (as farfetched as that may sound) that I have (as a student of psychology, a journalist and as an author) has been the ability (and willingness) to study, watch, notice, analyze scrutinize and to engage so-called "Natural Born" killers (sociopaths) up close and personal. F.B.I. profilers will never-ever understand Eric, Lyle, Stokes, Bret or Bardo the way that I do. Any reporter knows that when you are embedded with the troops in Iraq you will understand soldiers better than a reporter (at home) will ever know them. And I've had the double blessing (or bonus) of having a team of brilliant experts (C.Solis MD, Frank Curren MD., Jennifer Heitkamp MD, Jarman and A. Duran Ph.D. etc.) who would, could and did (do) elucidate for me the inner workings of the human brain etc. and though these experts would never discuss another inmate with me. They are always willing to answer questions like why people do what they do etc. and I am a thug, a thief and a robber. And I routinely rob these learned physicians (and therapists) of knowledge it took them 20-25 years of schooling to acquire. Ipso facto, there is no sympathy for what they did (murder and molestation etc) but (for me) there is a measure of sympathy for what they (as kids) had to see. Behold, I don't but the story the Menendez brothers told the court about their dad molesting them. For various reasons I don't buy it (their story remains fluid. Eric has told this writer that actually Lyle molested him. Yet inmate Deon Braggs (aka "Fat Cat") stole a missive sent to Eric, by Lyle, via an attorney stating that Eric should stick to the "strategy" of blaming "me" as an appellate strategy. Also Eric convinced Barbara Walters that Lyle made him do it. Barbara Walters was so charmed by Eric that she paid $75 grand for his appellate attorney. Although ABC standards and practices dept. advised madam Walters not to do so. Eric stated Barbara had a friend to author a check written to his wife Tammi)... However I am absolutely convinced that Eric, Lyle, Daniel, Stokes, Johnson, Bret (although there is widespread disagreement among scholars about the existence of genes and/or biological determinents etc.) had to see some bad (wicked, greedy, sadistic and diabolical) stuff as kids...Eric is charming, affable and gregarious. But there is something (you can't really see or touch it) about him that feels evil. It's spooky. I remember going to sleep one night saying to myself that I felt dark and evil by having to sleep in the same building with him. He told me once that he astroplaned in his cell. And he was totally serious and congruent. I mentioned earlier that for a time he was atheist, then agnostic, then devout Catholic, then into mystics and now he's a high priest in the Wiccan faith. He is building clerk in building #5 at Pleasant Valley State Prison. C.O. Garza and Mrs. Wheat were in love (not sexually) with him. Garza and Wheat smuggled meth to him. His celly "Spot" always agreed to take the fall if Eric was ever caught...

But there was always something just underneath the surface I can feel around any killer. And I believe (with every fiber of my being!) that I can detect a child molester within 5 minutes of seeing, speaking with or being around him. One by one, person by person without fail I can tell. I still recall telling my P.V.S.P. celly Omar Hernandez ("Dopey") that "there is something strange and perverted about that Bret guy" way before any of us knew. Ipso facto, I still recall telling Wayman Berry "see Ed Stokes" and that sixth sense was why I knew Pete Rose (at M.C.S.P in Ione) was not a pervert. Although we'd read in newspapers how Pete had molested a lil girl and detectives said he met the profile of a predator I told Chuck "He is not a child molester." Three years later D.N.A proved that all the profiling, gossip, innuendo and even the testimony was wrong. Pete spent 9 ½ years in prison for a molestation he did not do. Yet Mr. Pedroia will only spend one year in county jail for a molestation which he did do.

President Obama: Hundreds of thousands of kids 7-19 years old (in Cook County, Georgia New York, California and D.C. etc.) will enter jails (juveniles and prisons) this year. Most will be arrested for mild to medium violations i.e. disorderly conduct, weed, booze, scams and assaults. But what terrifies me is what they see will affect what they will be. Once they arrive in Hades and we conmen, thugs, predators, psychosexual deviants and murders bite our infectious teeth into their spirits and dig our perverted claws into their flesh they will never be the same again. And they will (750,000 this year) get out. Please remember that the Caucasian brother who sadistically tied Jimmy Lee Byrd to his truck and dragged him until his head came off his shoulders etc. was a good boy. He grew up playing with black kids and befriended them. He went to Hades (Texas prison system) for a few years and experienced a sociopathic metamorphosis. In Hades (in states like Texas and California) whites and blacks are enemies. Segregated in cells but integrated on the yards. And we teach "our own" to hate "them." and a white inmate who does not join a gang will be somebody's "girl". (although 50% of them in gangs are still undercover gays!). He'll be "in the hat"... Nevertheless when the Caucasian youngsters exited the Texas department of "corrections" his father said "something happened to him in prison that changed him." His dad was afraid of him. Mr. Obama: having come here

(Hades)and seeing (racism. Riots, train rapes and murders) what they have to see most of them are "changed" into "criminals for life." Mr. President: Just as faith cometh by hearing doubt (rape, murder and molestation etc.) cometh by hearing and hearing by the words of Satan. Here in Hades where the Menendez brothers and I live "there is none who does good, no not one." In Hades our "throat(s) is an open tomb; with their (our) tongues they (we) have practiced deceit." (behold Mr. President) "the poison of Asps is under their (our) lips....whose mouth is full of cursing and bitterness. Their (our) feet are swift to shed blood. Destruction and misery are..."In prison our feet hasten to mischief, our hands move to do evil." President Obama: In Hades "the whole head is in a sick condition and the whole heart is feeble." (Behold) I repeat that "the whole head is in a sick con..."In prison and we (con-victs) affect and infect everything and everybody we come in contact with. The most bitter and scornful folks you will ever, ever meet are those of us who are locked up in prison....kids come here everyday for the smallest offense. And some show up with 2-3 year sentences. And we recruit them to commit gang hits, sell dope, steal, stab and kill and many young "short timers" (five years or less) enter Hades and never get out...(I hate to say it; but that's good for the public...) and the one's who do get out are never the same. You become what you see. And what do they see in (me) Hades?

...But President Obama if groups like "Shoulder to Shoulder" (in Del Paso Heights, Ca), NAPS, Second Chance, G.B.G./Heart, Homeboy Industries and "Just Detention International" can get a lil bit of the residue of the Obama magic, we can focus more on programming our kids for Morehouse, Harvard and Yale, instead of prison, juvenile and jail. If wrongly (and rightly) convicted prisoners, our families and our friends could get a call back from Tina Tchen, Valarie Jarrett or Emanuel etc. If we the President, we the police, we the prisoner, principals, professors, pastors, teenies and tweenies will work together we can stop the epidemic of kids killing kids: yes we can!

Sincerely

G.B.G./Heart-President, founder and prisoner Sherman D. Manning

...Dear facebook generation: I told you all I'm a thug, a crook and a common criminal right? I forgot to tell you I am also a liar. Remember I told you my missive to Mr. Obama was the end of the tome? I lied; some of you reading this actually attended a G.B.G./Heart workshop at C.S.P. Sac (New Folsom) in Represa. You met the team and you met me. And I either lied to you by omission or by commission. I usually tell kids (or I'll imply) that I am a murderer. For more than a decade I lied about my conviction. Then I began to speak metamorphically about it. I.E. "I'm in Joseph's (Genesis Chapter 39) predicament." But in all of my writings (some of it powerful like "Blue Eyed Blonde" book II and "Creating Monsters"). I never had the temerity, the guts or the nuts to w-r-i-t-e about my conviction. I'm not writing to parents ("the village") right now. The president may or may not have perused my missive to him (I'm told I may be the first California prisoner to have received a missive from Obama's White House.) I don't know we sent it to Robert Gibbs. But even if he did he's done now. I am writing to the youth. Let me preface by saying a D.C. reporter (Mike Doyle at McClatchy news) asked me if I'd be a youth leader when I got out. I stated "Mike I won't be getting out of prison ever." My reply to his next question was both startling and hilarious to Mike. He inquired "But if you were going home and you're speaking to a group of parents etc. What would you say to moms and dads Sherman?" I replied "Keep your kids away from me!" Mr. Doyle (who knew all about my conviction. In fact he killed the story because I didn't want him to state my conviction) said but Sherman you've never been convicted of a child molester! Why in hell would you tell a parent to keep their kids away from you?" I replied "Easy answer Mike, I am in Hades. And no man who has been in Hades should ever be trusted with your kids! ...Mike if some of my fellow cohorts (who are going home) heard me tell you this they would stab me. But I would tell parent to act like a citizen but think like a predator. I'd tell kids to act like a child but think like adults….so then when that adult (teacher, preacher, priest, coach, uncle or cousin etc.) begins to heap compliments, gifts, accolades on you and win your confidence etc. Beware Mike I'd tell kids the moment an adult (who is not your parent) asks you (a kid) to keep a "secret" you run, yell "fire", scream, shout and get away! …Mike the child molester only has power as long as his secret is kept. The moment his secret is told he becomes a powerless little perverted B_tch!!!

…But Facebook Generation-I've never written about my conviction. I wrote and talked about my crimes (stuff I did do and got away with) but not my conviction. The only reasons I'm now willing to fully disclose the conviction and the crime(s) are threefold. A. I'm not getting out! So my fear that people would assume I did it (the conviction) is now meaningless. B. When I was on my deathbed I promised God!!! C. Famed Lawyer Murray J. Janus was livid to learned I picked up a female prostitute on Santa Monica Blvd. at 2:40 AM. She got in the car and I discovered she was a man. I demanded he get out of my car. "Not unless you give me $50.00." I gave him an ass whipping. He went to a payphone and told the police I had a gun and was "threatening people". He changed his mind and called back and said "He raped me". … Murray sent Attorney Barry Tarlow and Blair Berk to see me. "They know Ricardo is lying and is a speed freaking hooker. There was no rape and we'll prove it" Tarlow told me. He wanted a lot of money. Peter wire transferred the money from Switzerland to Conrad Gamble. Conrad kept the money and never paid Tarlow. I was too embarrassed (being charged with raping a grown ass man!) to try to borrow money from my contacts etc. for legal fees. Even Atty. Tom Mesereau told me the case against me was bogus…. (Bishop Eddie Long is now accused of having sex with young men via coercion etc…) I could not run my family in dept by letting them mortage their houses etc. to pay my legal fees!

And since I know there was no rape and folks like Murray Janus and David Hicks (and Michael Edward Bergin) had shown me that the courts do work etc. I threw caution to the wind and told my folks "keep the money cause I'm gonna need it when I get out. I may need to sell a jag or something til I get out of debt". To be true, I was certain of two things: A. I would walk on this bogus case. And B. Conrad would be killed no matter what it cost (and so David had Uriah killed?) me I would pay to have him killed. You don't steal from me and you don't steal from people whom I love… But just as God did not cause me to (or even allow) rape Ricardo. God wasn't gonna allow me to be a murderer. I could write every detail but suffice it to say I was convicted by an all white jury, without a Lawyer in Santa Monica Supreme Court… That's (the so-called "rape") what I was innocent of. But lest I come across as an innocent victim let's talk about what I did do. I've earned a lot of money (legitimately) in businesses. And I've also conned, connived, cheated and (the instant gratification Mrs. Kennedy was speaking of) deceived good women… Where do I start? Perhaps I'll start with the most dangerous con I've perpetrated. How many people do you know who are sick enough, bold and foolish enough to hustle Don King? (I hope tmz.com or max is not reading this. Cause just as I didn't want 2 b known as the guy convicted of "rape". I also didn't wanna b known as the guy who hustled the biggest hustler in New York!) many believe Mr. King is in the mafia. I can attest 2 the fact that he's not because if he were I'd be d-e-a-d… Remember how Conrad ripped me off? (Check out Galatians git)… Neither my wife, nor Peter nor anyone (except Murray J. Janus…under the Attorney Client privilege I admitted it to him after I did it… Janus stated "Don King? You are certifiable".) That great man Ambassador Andy Young does not even speak to me anymore. He knows I'm not a "rapo". That's not it. Here's why he no longer speaks to me. I'd lost $ fifty grand in a bad investment. And I was supporting a wife and six different women in five different states. I was in Baltimore Maryland and I called Don King at home: "Hey Don this is Ambassador Andrew Young". Mr. King says to me "yes Ambassador I'd recognize your voice anywhere". I

(Ambassador Young) convinced Don King to write Rev. Sherman D. Manning a check for $ 15,000 grand. It was written on either (I only had the check a bout ten minutes) the Chase Manhattan or the Chemical Bank... I cashed it with all deliberate speed. And when Ambassador Young didn't show up at the LA. Guardia Airport to do lunch with Don a week later. Don called Andy and I was away in Switzerland. And nobody knew (except now Andy, Don and me) about my foolish scam but me. Sadly if I'd called Andy he would have loaned me $ 15 grand... I lost a dear friend (Andy) and created a powerful enemy (Don King). Be lying if I told you I was not afraid. D-o-n King? I could (can) imitate Andy, Rev. Hosea Williams, Rev. Jasper Williams and Cong. John Lewis to the point of exact emulation!... (I'll digress and lighten the moment because it's creepy to be actually, finally coming clean. It's scary but in an unusual kind a way I feel a load lifting!!)... Anyone who knew civil rights legend Rev. Hosea Williams knows he had a very distinct, raspy and unique voice. He sounded exactly (seriously) like Don King on the telephone... Terrie Randolph was Rev. Williams personal secretary for 16 years (at that time). One day when I knew "Doc" (that's what I called him) was out of the office I dialed 373-5751 (it's now 222-9999) and Terrie answered "Rev. Williams office". I said (lol) "Terrie "she said "yes sir Rev. Williams". I said "I want u 2 take all (lol) the phones off the hook (anytime Doc was having a big meeting or something he'd tell staff 2 take all the phones off the hook!!!!") and get all the staff n yall meet me downtown in 30 minutes on the steps of City Hall! We gonna have a press conference. "Terrie said" you want everybody there Rev. Williams? "I yelled "did I stutter white woman or am I speaking and Terrie said "everybody; yes sir" and I slammed the phone down without saying goodbye just as Hosea would have... They say a criminal will always return to the scene of the crime and I believe it... I had 2 c it with my own eyes. I parked my car 4 blocks from City Hall at 2:30 pm and peeped (from a far off) and I counted 13 folks (including Terrie and Mrs. Julia Ambles) standing on the steps of city hall with the press awaiting civil rights legend Williams...At 5:17 my pager went off and I saw "373-5751-911" oh lord... I called ... "Hey Doc how u doing? Rev. Williams yelled to the top of his lungs "you bastard. Rev. Manning when Terrie told me what happened I said that wasn't anybody but that "Jack Logged preacher (lol) Rev. Manning ... I said "Doc what r u talking about I've been out of town all day". He said "out of town my ass. Ya ought to be in hell. You costed me $10 grand in lost work with that stunt... As long as yo ass hole points toward the ground don't you ever call me or come by here again!" Click! He hung up on me... Three weeks later he testified as a character witness for me... (So did Ambassador Andrew Young, Command Sergeant Major James A. Smith, 6 Pastors and 3 city councilmen ...) Hosea loved me and he admitted I only got stopped because I'd been on t.v. with him calling the Dekalb County Police Department "racist!.. Open season on Blackmen"... I totaled a Ferrari and injured my neck. Dr. Mike McDonald (call em up at Morehouse Medical Associates) wrote me a prescription for percodan. Rather than take the entire bottle I grabbed 3 pills and took em with me on my way 2 Marva's house. Officer "Jim Crow-ley". O.K. I'm kidding about Crowley... But Officer Weaver stopped me for speeding. I was indeed speeding. When he came to my door he said "you're that Manning n-gger who hangs out with that Hosea n-gger? And ...What r those 3 pills on the dash?" I replied "percodan ... I have a valid prescription at home. I'll give you my Physician's number. That's why I have this neck brace on"... Weaver said "lil Hosea u r going 2 jail" and I hauled ass my first and only police chase. Finally he did a pit maneuver and wrecked me. And he beat me severely... Did I tell yall that this common criminal (that would be me) also was an escape artist?

No joke ...They took me to Decatur (Georgia) city jail. All white staff and understand that Hosea is known across the country. And there was not a police officer anywhere in Georgia who didn't know his face or voice... Put me in a lil holding cell with a rather Mayberry looking twin jail door. An old white jailer with a mouth full of scoal came and told me "u gon go see that judge in

30 minutes. U gotta look pretty 4 the judge. After that we gon beat yo black ass so bad "Hosea" won't even recognize u." When he left I began kicking the door with every ounce of my strength. I utilized every mind trick I'd ever learned in karate school. My goal was to kick so loud that maybe the judge would hear me... No dice. I put mu buttocks at the edge of the steal bench and extended my legs and feet and kicked with all my power (and f-e-a-r)... The thin lock broke and I ran out of the basement of the Decatur jail... And I ran and ran. I asked a guy at a gas station for a quarter. Called Hosea. He told me he would call T.J. Scipio (one of the few black Dekalb county police officers) because "Rev. Manning those white boys will shoot u and kill u... Don't move..."Ten minutes later T.J. Scipio (who is now a Chief of police in a small town) pulled up and saved my life. T.J. said "Rev. Manning I know these white boys want u bad. But don't lie 2 me. Did they really threaten 2 beat u?"... How many African American men do u know who escaped from a white jail, lived 2 tell it and had the "escape" charge dropped by a white judge? That was a testimony to the power of Rev. Hosea L. Williams and an awesome God. Who (as sinful as I was) still loved me... Even in my lowest state... Perhaps I should stop now but oh no I'll tell my own (authentic) story. So that when this Valley Fever wins the battle over my body nobody will be able to say I was to cowardly to tell youth the truth, the whole truth and nothing but the truth. If nuthin else, my story can serve as a 'real life' example of how not to live... Don King? This man is worth a $Billion dollars. He could have had me killed for my fraud ...I'd be lying if I claimed I'm glad 2 by dying from valley fever. I am not. But (to be candid) I am glad about one thing. And that is I won't have to one day (maybe) get out of prison and then register as a sex offender (for the rape of a man that I did not do) for life...I'd be crippled... Everywhere I go people r looking at my face on a web site as the dude who raped Ricardo?... I could have not withstood this kind of invalid, untrue, shame and humiliation. I used to pray that Ricardo Calvario would wake up one day and say "I was angry .Sherman D. Manning did not rape me". Perhaps he does not know the penalty 4 perjury is like a $200.00 fine. And that the statute of limitations is over. He can not be charged with anything! Nothing! If he called media, John Burton, Padilla or Tyra Manaila and admitted that "Sherman D. Manning did not rape me!" He could not even be fined. It is to late!... After a trial with no lawyer I'm talked into paying attorney Robert Thomas Burns... Pay him and he guarantees new trail... Atty. Janus told me (telephonically) that some of what Burns was doing sounded "suspect" ... He deceived me and ripped me off. I now hear (but the "bar" refuses to confirm or deny) that Robert Thomas Burns may actually be disbarred... I'm told by Murray that my "sentence" is illegal due to an illegal enhancement. In short Mr. Calvario claimed that after the rape (which never happened) I supposedly "laughed" and "named twenty different diseases" that I had just given him. And based upon my supposed "laughter" and the naming of my so-called "twenty" diseases those were "aggravating circumstances" which gave rise to a "judicial justification" for sentencing me to the "maximum" term ... Chief Dep. Warden (ret) Terry L. Rosario read the entire case and told me once that "you were a helluva guy out there. Brilliant... But a thug. You did a lot of dirt... But after really reading this case I do not believe you raped Ricardo any more than I did"... It is 6:04 am now and I've written (read and re-read) all night long 2 u youngsters. No sleep. I could not stop until I told you the big "secret" which has been hanging over my head like a thick "fog" hanging over this prison. Now you see why I've always refused media interviews etc. Because I did not want the "interview" to be a sensational interrogation about the stuff I did not do. Writing this has been creepy but (in a way) it's a catharsis I may not live another 365 days. (Not to mention the prisoners who will try to murder me for breaking the convict code if I transfer to Donovan, High Desert etc.) But (mark my words) if I do live a while I shall not ever write another book, another chapter, another paragraph, page or even a sentence about my "wrongful" conviction. I won't discuss the specifics of the case again. It is out there and I'm done with that ... But back to the dirt I did do... Earl Graves is the

publisher of Black Enterprise Magazine... I lied, conned and manipulated him. I called Mr. Graves as "Rev.Hosea Williams"... Make the "check out to I-Max for Rev. Sherman D. Manning". Mr. Graves sent me the check in Virginia... That great man Mr. John Johnson was founder and publisher of Ebony Magazine. I "Rev. Hosea Williams" called Mr. Johnson (one of my heroes) and had him to send "I-Max" and Manning a check... Arsenio Hall's famed pastor Rev. Cecil Murray (pastor of F-A-M-E the oldest Black Church in LA. And also Atty. Tom Meseren's pastor) got a call from me as "Rev. Williams" and Rev. Murray also mailed me a check. You know what young people? God probably saved my L-i-F-e by letting me go to jail in a "Joseph predicament". I am absolutely certain I would have been murdered. Just as I wanted (and planned to) to kill Conrad for ripping me off... And I love the lord all the way down to my shoe laces. I do love God. And David loved God also when he had sex with another man's wife. King David (the paslmist) loved God when he had the woman's husband murdered... And I don't justify my evil intentions by invoking David. I'm simply saying if I (a man) could love God, (preach every Sunday etc.) and still desire to kill a man about my "money" etc. What about an atheist or agnostic for example? Sooner or later somebody would have killed me about their "money"... But Quincy Jones told "Rev. Williams" that Mani I'm already sending Jesse Jackson a check every month. I can't do it Rev.

 ... Amos Waller (the late pastor of Mercy Street Baptist Church in the windy city) Dr. Joseph Wells (guarantee you President Obama knows him – one of the largest churches in Chicago), Rev. Leroy Elliott (ended up becoming my friend), The late television pastor Gilbert Patterson (he televised my sermon "The Lord is Good". I wish I could hear the (.D. before I die) Clay Evan's Brother Rev. Pharis Evans (Gary Indiana), late recording artist Rev. Milton Bivason, Rev.A. Lincoln James (pastor of the largest black church in Richmond VA.) etc. and others. Each of the aforementioned (yall betta be glad I aint getting out! Lol) distinguished pastors have one thing in common. Each of them received a call from another Rev. Williams stating (i.e.) "hey Leroy this is Jasper Williams and one of my sons in the ministry is in Chicago Sunday and I want you to preach him for me". Leroy replied "Jasper I'll let him preach all 3 services Sunday". After I left Chicago that night (en-route to a large black N.Y Church "Southern Bpt. Church" that was without pastor), rather than wait for Jasper to call him Monday (as planned) Leroy Elliott decided to call Jasper (ouch). "Jasper that negro Manning preached his ass off. He got "it" boy" and Jasper said "Rev. Manning was in Chicago?" LOL... Leroy called me (next day in N.Y.) and when I answered the telephone in my suite in N.Y. Leroy said "is this Jasper Williams?" I said "Leroy its Manning". He said "na" man I dialed 404-792-0303 this ain't Dr. Williams! Somebody playing with me!" My throat went into my stomach and Leroy said "hah,hah,hah I got u back boy!... Manning listen buddy I forgive you but Jasper don't (sic). Man you can preach. You don't have to use Jasper like that. You'll make people doubt your "calling" to preach... Come back and see me man I love you bru"... Jasper Williams is perhaps the T.D. Jakes of the Baptist Church... Artha Franklin's (the queen of soul) Father was Dr. C.L. Franklin. He was the fore most Baptist pastor of his era. Jasper preached just like him. When he was murdered Artha called "Jasper my Father would only want you to preach his funeral." And Jasper went to Detroit and preached "a good soldier in the Army of Christ." Jasper was the man. His name opened church doors around the country. And I could mimic his telephone voice. What was sad is that A. I preached all over Georgia, Florida and in New York without playing the Jasper con. B. I'm a gifted preacher and C. Nobody called Jasper (the first, second, third time) when I preached for him. But although I preached for him twice on my own I still had to speed up my appointments by conning. As Mrs. Kennedy said "instant gratification"

 All this is fodder for unflattering and irritating inquires. But when you're already in Hades and can't get out how can the whole truth hurt me? Lest I emulate James Frey ("A million little pieces") and write a flattering cacophony of lies for my own ego. Sadly James 'book is powerful! (Although I disagree with his atheism. And I believe he did have sex with the priest!) A tome like his (even if fiction) paints a compelling picture about why one should never use drugs... (As an aside- if yo ass goes on Oprah you better tell her when, where and how you embellished!) Oprah does not interview folk in prison with my conviction! But by a freak Madam "o" called Jimbo wanting an interview I would never do it. No way: I love Oprah so much. Her soul is right. She motivates me... "God can dream a bigger dream for you than you can ever dream for yourself". And when she went and got my homeboy out (Marcus Dixion wrongly convicted of rape... Marcus is from Rome Georgia. I preached at Pine hill Bpt. Church in Rome... Hate 2 admits that "Jasper" also set that up!) of prison! I loved it!... "Sometimes I wake up in the morning and I can't believe it's me"... And (my favorite... Ann Curry asked didn't Oprah get "tired") "when I think of Harriett Tubman and all those slaves with no money, no resources and no voice. And how they kept on working for our people. They didn't get tired... I don't have the right to get tired". Love that! But as bad as I've treated women (read on...) I would not do Oprah for $ 1 million! She would shred my black ass 2 pieces! ... If I could find Dan Fitzpatrick (he did my first radio interview at 11 years of age) I'd do Dan's show. I've been on Larry King so I'd do Larry's, Rev. Smith, Tavis Smiley and Charlie Rose. David Begnard, Nick Janes and Adrienne Bankert are my favorite local reporters. David is very dramatic and I would do neither. Although Adrienne is very sexy! Hey I'd do Ellen!!!

By the way the "Greater Southern Baptist Church asked me to be their pastor. $72,000 (more than twelve years ago), plus a house and a car. Problem no.1 the women I had with me (nay nay) was my wife. (I'd met her in Chicago at a barbershop). And no.2 I was too wild and too much of a philanderer to pastor. I never wanted to pastor... women? (Goodbye Oprah!) Wow! I'm not Wilt Chamberlain (2000 women or "James Frey"?) ... But I had some women. And I never hit a woman physically. No way! But I was abusive (verbally), unfaithful and ... conning... I won't tell every story. But I shall tell the worst of the worst. Estelle Bryant (aka Stella) became infatuated with my preaching. She began to ask me to come to pen. She lived in Harrisburg with her 12 year old daughter Mahoghany (I'm so, so sorry Stella and Mahoghany! But God got me back so I got mine!) I flew to Harrisborgh and I dined her. She had worked at "Hershey" for 16 years. She was 10 years older than me. (Many say she should have known better).. But I was wrong. She wanted to marry. She told me if she quit Hershey she'd get $thousands from her credit union. I told her to quit and we'd go to Richmond and I'd start a church and eventually marry. She quit her j-o-b. Gave me all the money. White buddy of mine (Joshua- a skateboarder and his girl Lori... Josh had a blue volkswagon van. Anybody know where Josh and Lori are? Baltimore? Richmond?)went with Stella, Mahoghany and I to Richmond... Stella and I put Mahoghany in school (we were staying in a hotel) and I was buying radio time etc. etc. and after 2 weeks I sent Stella and Mahoghany to go buy breakfast... I called me a cab, left Stella a $100 bill, got in a taxi and flew to Chicago. Stella never saw me again. I lost sleep. I felt so bad. But never bad enough to find her and send her that money back. If someone had done to one of my little sisters what I did to Stella I would kick his ass from one side of Atlanta to the other... I just went back and perused the last ten pages. I almost ripped them up. I was a sick man. I am so embarrassed. This is the first time I've ever really written about me. Woe is me for I am undone. Writing it is sickening (yet cathastic) and then reading it turns my stomach.

...Stella was a beautiful lady. And Mahoghany was a good girl and I left them in a strange town-alone. I was too much of a coward to man up. Afraid that if a person got too close to me they could find out where I was blind. And everybody has some blind spots. I left them... But as sad, mad and hurt as she was it was actually good for her sake that I left her. I would have ruined her through and through...

Some of you young females are hurting because he left you. But when people walk away from you let them walk. You can't make em stay anyway. But your destiny is not tied to the one who left you. It means their part in your story is over. Let them walk. Develop the gift of good bye. Let them go... I'm sure Stella cried and she hurt and... I ended up in Hades. ... And she is probably happily married and doing well. She probably slept in a queen or king size bed last night. Well I didn't sleep at all last night. But when I do I sleep in a bathroom. I live in a cage. She should be glad I left. And you ought to be glad when a hoodlum (like me) leaves. You don't need to be hooked up to a loser-let him (or her go!) ...I am sorry for all the dirt I did do. And I am ashamed to (finally) write it. and I would have to be Bozo the Clown to assume that I'm the only thug, conman and crook. There are some conmen, thugs, cowards and crooks reading right now. My word to you? Easy; look at me... You guys out there running around like you're invincible. You slinging and gunrunning and banging? Look at me. There is no status to be gained from coming to prison. Cameron Johnson has status! He's free! Bryan Kennedy, Rebecca Delgato Ruttman, the kids at Creative Steps (in Philly) Ari Shapiro and Joshus Panno have status... (You all help G.B.G. do gorilla activism by getting this book to Willie Nessler, Cameron Douglas, Redmond O'neal, David Coleman and his mom Mary Coleman... Linda McFarlane- even if I'm dead before K.K.K. is published-make sure they get this book!....) ...Also (ya'll get "Bobcat" Johnny O'Neal a copy of this tome. He's a prisoner and one of the few I'd probably trust as a celly-to not set me up..)... Prisons are for losers, legends in our own minds. Status is getting a j-o-b and building a career. My big brother Reggie Manning has never had as much money as I have. He's not as educated as I am. He's never flown to Switzerland or owned a convertible Jaguar... but A. he's free! He has never gone to prison! He lives at home with his beautiful wife Stacy. He raises his daughter Keke. That is status...

Prison creates deviant and irrational thinking... Eric Menendez? He (literally) walks around the prison as if he's done the nation a favor. I got angry with him once and told him that. "You're not a celebrity Eric. You are infamous. You viciously murdered your own kith and kin. It was premeditated. You emptied- reloaded and blew your mom's face off. And come in here like you shit gold and as if you've done the nation a favor...married to Tammie but in love with Mike Henrickson...You're sick dude" ... And when Madame Walters came to interview him? He began to think he was John Gotti. He even told me he thinks Barbara Walters likes younger men! I.E. him... He used to always say Barbara told him she hated Star Jones... I said they seem very friendly on the show. "Oh no-Barbara says she is only there because they need a token black. Barbara hates Star Jones!" ... Prison ain't cool...maybe some of you thugs who are in the Facebook Generation will call a lawyer (Mesereau, Blair Berk or Donald Masuda) after I tell you this part of the story. Even though I just finished writing to you about how wicked, how distinguishing, how dirty and how low I'd become. (An I tell ya'll what happened? There is a temptation to forget that I wrote that my steps are ordered when I began to tell you what a con and a crook I had become. And so "...and I shall seem to be a deceiver to him; and I shall being a curse on myself and not a blessing"... All biblical names had a meaning Abram? God changed his name to Abraham because Abra-ham meant "Father of many nations." And Genesis chapter 27 explains clearly that "Jacob" means "sup planter, trickster and conman." In verse 19 Jacob manipulated his own father. He did some bad stuff. How low can you go? You know your father is sick, blind and dying and you call him and claim to be Jasper when you're really Sherman... Jacob told his own dying daddy (27:19) "I am Esau your firstborn; I have done just as you told me....that your soul may bless me." Jacob had a twin (the first born) brother named Esau. Esau had a blessing coming from their father Isaac... Jacob had already tricked Esau out of his birthright. Now he was using con, game, deceit and manipulation (because of the desire for "instant gratification") to fool his own daddy into giving him (Jacob) his twin brother's blessing…   Some of the folk I called, when I pretended to be Jasper, Andy and/or Hosea (conning for a blessing), had slight suspicions that "is this really Ambassador Young?" In verse 21 Isaac (too) was a bit suspicious. "Come near, that I may feel you, my son, whether you are really my son Esau or not." Guess what Isaac said in 22? "The voice is Jacob's voice, but the hands are the hands of Esau." So Isaac being conned by his own son, about to die- gave Jacob Esau's blessing… Later on Esau said "Is he not rightly named Jacob (trickster)? For he has supplanted me two times. He took away my birthright, and now look, he has taken away my blessing"… And over in Genesis 33:24-28 the conman, crook and the liar wrestled with an angel all night long. And he said I (the liar) won't let you go until you bless me. And the angel in 27 says "What is your name?" Don't give me that Jasper, Andy or Hosea stuff. I heard you tricked your own daddy out of yo brutha's blessing. You been wrestling and pleading all night long. So come real or not at all. What is your name?... "He said, "Jacob"… He said "Sherman". He said "C.J.", he said "Seamus", he said "crack addict", he said "meth abuser". Remember the literal translation of the name Jacob is "con" or "trickster". And in 28 the angel said "your name" even though you lied! Even though u conned! Even though u stole! Even though u a bulldog, Aryan brotherhood, Nuestra Familia or a crip etc.. He (a spokesman 4 God) said "Your name shall no longer be called Jacob, but Israel" can I tell you all what "Israel" means? Israel means "prince". This angel demonstrated the awesomeness and the audacity of God. He transferred a crook, a crip, a liar, a blood, a trickster, a southerner, a sup planter and a hood rat into a "prince" overnight. But- God himself confirmed the name change in Genesis 33:9. Guess what God did to the dude who had just tricked his brother out of a birthright and a blessing? Guess what the creator of the universe did to a dirty and low down man who had put on his brothers clothing, used his brother's cologne, put on his brother's gloves and disguised his voice to sound like Esau and tricked a sickly and dying man? Guess what God did in 33:9? I'll tell you. God appeared to Jacob and in God "blessed him". You thought (like I did) he was gonna curse him didn't you? In verse ten God said to this imposter/impersonator "…your name is Jacob; your name shall not be called Jacob anymore, but Israel shall be your name." So he called his name Israel (prince)." And while folk r murmuring, hating and wondering why God would (will) decide to bless, anoint and to use a conman and a sup planter. While folk r hating and talking about gangbangers. God has never been without the power to anoint, use, call and transmogrify to a gangbanger for crips. A gang banger for bloods etc. into a Gang banger for God (G.B.G.) and when God decides to use the disobedience of a broken, jackleg, head strong, reject and stubborn preacher named Jonah people start scratching their heads n gossiping. But I've noticed that as long as Jonah is in a whale people are cool with that. But when the whale spits him up and God picks him up people trip… U mean to tell me he is a G.B.G.? U want me 2 believe this trickster is a prince? That does not sound fair. Why would God do that? I can't see that. Are you ready to see the answer? …"For he (God) says to Moses, "I will have mercy on whenever I will have mercy, and I will have compassion on whomever I will have compassion… God who shows mercy." For the scripture says to the Pharoah (Romans 9:17) "For this very purpose I have raised you up." God is so awesome that oh baby, baby the foolishness of the power of God. He (literally) raises up Sauls so he can make Pauls. He'll raise up a bull Conner so he can show himself through a Martin Luther King. He'll send a rosa to park(s) down in a jail cell so he can raise up a whole race of people to sit on the front of a bus. He is God." He said, "…I have you, and that my name may be declared in all the earth. Therefore he has mercy on whom he wills, and whom he wills he hardens."

        …When I was at M.C.S.P. a rogue associate warden (see "Blue Eyed Blonde" Book II and "Left for Dead" www.cafepress.com/manning) named Mike Bunnell decided to transfer me to Pleasant Valley State Prison so I could "catch Valley Fever and write a book about that." You should google Mike Bunnell. He was angry because I had mentioned him in a book. Bunnell once had an affair with CCPOA president Mike Jimenez. Bunnell is a murderer! Google him today... they extracted me and forced me to P.V.S.P. Three months later I was nearly dead. I was deliberately denied medical attention. (P.V.S.P. is one of the most corrupted prisons in the country. Folks like associate Warden Marion E.Spearman, Lt. J.D. Bennett, Brumbaugh, Wally Tucker, D.L. Criner and....corrupted! Spearman forced me to sleep in a cell without a mattress, no clothing, no food and no running water for 6 days. No running water...at a hospital C.O. Garza got Spearman's permission to place me in five point restraints for 3 days. A medic named "Ross" who worked for Dr. McClay pleaded with Garza at Comm. Regional Med. Center to unhook me. Marion had my "appeals" shredded...on another note-Marion E. Spearman was caught performing fellatio on James Yates...P.V.S.P. is a mess!)... I was chained to a hospital bed for 14 months. No t.v. No telephone. No books. Cruel and unusual officers like C.O.T. Negrete (a meth addict), Johhny Brown, Criner and Wally Tucker sat outside my door bragging about how much money (overtime) they made off of me and betting on my death. The physicians had to call the prison several times because Criner, Negrete, Tucker and Johnny Brown were verbally assaulting me. Tucker physically took my manuscript (which Dr. Griffin got the warden to authorize due to my sensory deprivation..."Stress can kill him. And he's been laying here with nothing for 7 months" Paul Griffin Md. told them.) and the nurse said my blood pressure was "dangerously" high. Six nurses told me "I know you're gonna sue these people when you get out"... C.O. Criner pulled a gun on me and threatened to kill me. Sgt. Hudgins controlled him. I appealed all of this and Marion E. Spearman (singlehandedly) had Lt. Herrera to shred the appeals.

Federal receiver Rob Sillen had told Governor Schwarzenegger and the honorable Thelton Henderson that P.V.S.P. should be shut down a year before I went there; due to Valley Fever deaths. C.O. Figueroa (who's widow is a Fresno City Cop) died from Valley Fever. Lt. Webster (a good man) nearly died from Valley Fever. Xavier Garcia did die and many others. P.V.S.P. is still open and expanding. Money for a valley fever vaccine was disapproved.... You'd think there would be a a loud symphony of lawyers suing for staff and inmates....Keep thinking... Keith Wattley, Robert Navarro or Carolyn Phillips? Perhaps you'd assume Thomas Master, Anarea Patterson, Alexis Wilson Briggs or Michelle Iorio?...

I wish I knew where Carol Leonard was. She warned me about Valley Fever and P.V.S.P....RLUIPA? Religious land use and institutionalized persons act?? I was systematically disallowed to worship in the Hospital Chapel for 14 months. It was empty 95% of the time and locked. And not one time was I allowed to go in and worship... On Easter Sunday C.O. Grady (good man) asked the senior man (a Christian) "can we take Manning into the chapel so he can use a hymnal and worship?" I saw Satan in C.O. Joe Rikalo as he absolutely refused. 14 months with no chapel access and no chaplain? I asked that the prison chaplain be allowed to come and see me. Especially when physicians told me I would die... "Per Marion, per Yates-No!" That is unconstitutional!... After that denial, needing spiritual rejuvenation and conversation I signed myself out of the hospital (I was 96 lbs. had been there 9 months!) AMA. Why? Spearman and Yates refused to allow me to call my 76 year mom and refused to call them for me. Refused to tell my family I was away sick. And refused to allow me to go to the chapel or send the chaplain. Dr. Griffin wrote on my AMA papers that "It is my opinion that without oxygen and amphotericin B you will die"... My goal was to get to the prison and call my momma. I got to the prison and was held in the prison infirmary where Dr. Nguyen A. refused to allow me to use the telephone and B. refused (absolutely) to provide me with oxygen (blatant-deliberate medical negligence). "Do no harm?" The following day a nurse told me I was dying and the "Doctor won't allow us to provide the oxygen you need although we do have oxygen... Let me call an ambulance. Go back and I will call your mother." I went back to the hospital. The nurse did not call as she said she would but Paul Griffin MD. took care of it...

I stayed at numerous hospitals during my 14 month hospitalization but longer at C.R.M.C. than any other. One hospital knowingly allowed a known crystal meth addict to perform numerous invasive procedures on me while high. The radiologists (Dr. D.) is having an affair with her (K.) and he also gives her prescriptions for drugs to get her high. And while performing a five minute procedure upon me that went horribly wrong I saw her jumping, shaking and scratching. The procedure (picc line) took 4 hours. The picc line bled out that night risking my life. I'm giving the hospital time to apologize to me or I will take it to the media and to the courts. You feel me?...

...Steps? Ordered? Hospital? Alone? I was a preacher who loved God. I was born again and strayed away. I "journeyed to a far country, and there wasted his possessions with prodigal living." (reference St. Luke 15:11-32). I became a playboy. But wait: go back to the "trickster" Jacob. God clearly told him "your name is" prince. You are no longer a (Jacob) trickster. But even after that God would vacillate by (interchangeably) calling him Jacob (trickster) in one verse and Israel (prince) in another verse   He was transformed from a trickster to a prince. But he still has some con in him. And even after God himself stated "You are no longer Jacob!" All through the Bible you never read he is the God of Abraham. Isaac and Israel." Never! It always says he is the God of "Abraham, Isaac and Jacob (trickster)." Your God id not the God of the very best of you. But he is the God of the gangster in you.-You got that? O.k. let's go deeper:

Prodigal Living..."But when he had spent all...sent him into his fields to feed swine. And he would gladly (was hungry) have filled his stomach with the pods that the swine ate," ... Now watch very closely. Verse 17 is on hit. Verse seventeen will revolutionize, transmogrify, transform and renew your mind if you "see" it. It says "But when he came to himself..." When a Christian is tricking, conning and conniving and he knows the Christ. And he sinks so low that he'll leave a Stella in Virginia or trick his daddy out of his brother's blessing etc. he is not in his right mind. He is in fact dead... I was dead. And some of you have done some stuff like I did. As quiet as it is kept some of you have raped, or robbed, or shot, or banged or killed. And you are (as was I) responsible for your actions. No cop outs baby boy in the flesh. Do the crime do the darn time. But there is a spiritual explanation to explain your situation. There is destiny inside of you. There is a divine plan for your life. Your steps have been ordered!... I was dead. And so were you. When the prodigal son finally came to his senses and went home his daddy said in verse 24: "For this my son was dead and is alive again. He was lost and is found." I was so lost I was restless. I became a busy body and a fraud...

The church loves to talk about Paul. But they forget about Saul. As God changed Jacob's name to Israel- God changed Saul's name to Paul. But before he was Paul he was a murderer! He persecuted Christians. He persecuted the church. Saul was a gang banger, a thug and a savage. Stoning Stephen to death and throwing people in jail just for calling the name of Christ. Half of the Bible was written by thugs, tricksters, bangers, murderers, accused attempted rapists and prison inmates. And even after Saul was transformed into Paul he said " O wretched man that I am! Who will deliver me from this body of death?" After Paul was transferred into a fire baptized Apostle he still said "For I know that in me..." In my flesh. In my trickster. In my killer! In my blood! In my crip! In my bulldog! In my N.L.R.! In my Saul!... "(That is in my flesh) nothing good dwells.... But how to perform what is good I do not find. For the good that I will (want) to do, I do not do; but the evil I will not to do, that I practice."... Lord I love you and I was changed on the road to Damatcus and you gave me a new name. And you gave me an anointing. And I am now an apostle but every time I try to do good, evil is always there, hindering me on my way. It is not me Paul but me Saul... "but sin that dwells in me" the apostle....

-I stopped talking to God. I stopped reading the bible. Behold, the biggest mistake I ever made in my life was to stop talking to God! I called myself mad at God. I testify to you (Facebook Generation) from my perch (bunk, hole) in Hades. ...I don't care how wrong you are etc. Oh baby, baby, baby, baby- if you believe this whole tome is but a figment of my imagination, it's all good. If you believe. I've embellished, so be it. if you believe it's all a crock of crap, so be it. But I plead with you, and you and you to believe this one thing! Not talking to God is the biggest mistake you can ever make! Don't ever, ever, ever (ten thousand times never) stop talking to yo Daddy...I stopped speaking to him. and what's even worse-he stopped speaking to me. So I was in a "far country." Both literally and spiritually. I am an award winning preacher and God let me get caught up 3000 miles away from home, for a crime he knew I did not commit. I could handle me knowing. But my problem was the fact that I knew that he knew. And yet he allowed me to be put in a pit, put in a problem and put in a prison. And I was humiliated, embarrassed and ashamed... I stopped talking to him and about him. I felt like the joke was on me. I'm a preacher all the way down to my toe jam. I love the Lord God and.... "Joseph-what happened to your coat of many colors? Joe dog what happened to the favor of God upon yo life? Where is yo God now? I thought u said I had a dream. Yo Joe u been in this joint 13 years bro. U can't even make bail and get outta jail. Joe maybe I would have believed your dream if God would have just let u go 2 a pit. But he let u get in a problem, a pit, and a prison on a rape beef and..."

I thought to myself "I sacrificed my childhood preaching for him." I remember one Sunday all the kids were going to the fair and it was my only opportunity but I had to go preach. ....First 16 years of my life I fasted and prayed and preached and I walked with God... And now he let me go to prison for this? I am not gonna talk to him. Oh lord...I stopped talking to my daddy...I would sneak a look at T.D. Jakes or Eddie Long on t.v. and say to myself "That ought to be me- But I am in this hole! I am in Hades." I wanted to ask Abba...(same thang yall wanna ask him) "What about me?" ...Ambassador Andrew Young said on t.v. "I think Rev. Manning is a "great" young man with a promising future." Lord- what happened to the promise? Why did you leave me? I'm not supposed to be here... But "write the vision and make it plain on tablets, that he may run who reads it. "Are u ready 4 the bombshell? If you get the next 9 words into your concsciousness you will never have 2 come to Hades...9 words baby girl. (Habakkuk 2:3) ...Take a deep breath. Here we go: "For the vision (dream Joseph, promise Sherman....u been impersonating Hosea, Andy and Jasper. You been tricking people out of other folk's blessing because u didn't know this) is yet for an "appointed time"; but at the end it will speak, and it will not lie. Though it tarries, (while u in a problem, or in a pit or in a prison) w-a-i-t (Joseph, Sherman, Blood, crip, B.G.F, N.L.R., EME etc.) for it; because it will surely come, it will not tarry"... My God.... Go back and re-read the paragraph beginning where I wrote "...next 9 words..." Re-read that.... This is some good stuff.. This stuff is so potent and so awesome I can't even hardly write it. But God is such an awesome God that even in yo lowest state he is still in charge...(I've been awake 2 ½ days now writing, praying and reading. I can't stop till I write the vision and make it plain). God will use your mistakes, your struggle, your pain, your disobedience, your cons, your banging, your hurt and your sorrow as a sign for somebody else. When jack legged Jonah found himself in the belly of a whale and he couldn't say he was "innocent". He disobeyed God. If you could have gone down in the water and told him that "God is gonna use your disobedience. Your whale as a sign for his only begotten son" Jonah would have said you must be trippin. You must be out of your mind. But hundreds of years later Jesus said just as Jonah (a sign) went down in the belly of a whale for 3 (ordered) days so shall the son of man go down into the earth for 3 (ordered) days. Jonah had to go down when he did and he had to come up when ("appointed time") he did. If you could have gone to Robbins Island prison in South Africa, in the 60's and told inmate Mandela "Hey Nelson-I know you were in a problem, a pit (your trial) and now you're in a prison. I know you have a life sentence for treason. But God is gonna use your prison sentence as a sign for even generations unborn. Even though you are in prison with a life sentence and black people can't vote in S. Africa. God is gonna open your prison cell in 27 years and you will be the first black president" Mandela would have thought you needed to take a few pills and go 2 c Dr. Phil.

If you could have gotten to a lil nappy headed boy with the middle name "Hussein" in 1970... When he had to entertain only "Dreams of my Father" because he didn't know him... "Hey Rock-Dog you I know u go by "Barry" and some call u "Barack" but rock dog u r blessed by God and highly favored. U r gonna be used as a sign for generations unborn. Yo mother is from Kansas and yo daddy is from Kenya. U will go 2 Harvard and the windy city and end up in D.C. Mr. President"... Barack would a thought you was smoking some good sh-t...

-I stopped talking to him for years. But God can't lie. And he can't let u die til his promise comes true. So he got me alone...alone...96 lbs. Right at the door of death. So close to death I could feel the death I could see the bright lights you see before you see the pearly gates and ....Hallelujah...I'll tell it all in another book, on a C.D. or (TBN Second Chance) on t.v. ... But I called him... And I understand David now because he knew he messed up. He had laid with a married woman and got her pregnant. And he was a king. And you know they were murmuring and ..."Call his self a child of God and a king. Now he has committed adultery and got the woman pregnant"... Rev. Jesse Jackson? A married preacher? "I knew he was a crook"... And now David has had the woman's husband killed... "I knew Sherman D. Mannning was a phony first time I saw him. He looked like a crook. All that "Boy turns playground into pulpit" crap was game. Look at how he did Stella. I know he was a no good fella"... But what I learned from David was after all his dirt and shame, he knew exactly who he needed to talk to and Dave said "Against you, you only, have I sinned, and done this evil in your sight"...

...In that hospital room I cried out to the God of Abraham, Isaac and of Jacob and he heard me. Hallelujah! That's why I don't spend one minute trying to convince anybody about my relationship With God. I just wanna point you into your destiny... And he spoke to me, gave me G.B.G. and I made him (not you) some promises! If I hadn't gotten valley fever I wouldn't have talked to him. If I hadn't stated back talking to him I would not have started writing this book. And if I hadn't gotten lied on by Dearaujo you would not be reading this part of the book. O-R-D-E-R-E-D. I had to go down when I did how I did and almost die. I had to mess up how I messed up. God has never been without the power to stop a man from messing up and look: I'm getting ready 2 blow yo mindBro. And the Lord said Simon (can u hear me now?) in deed Satan has asked (the devil can't get you lest God allow. He asked God to allow him to test job... Peruse St.Luke 22:31-32) for you that he may sift you as wheat. Jesus continued "but I have prayed for you, that your faith should not fail; and when (appointed time" ordered steps) you have returned to me, (not if you return to me), strengthen the Brethren". Jesus is so awesome he already knew (predestined) that Peter would deny him! Wow! He knew David was gonna. He knew Jonah was gonna. He knew Jacob was gonna. He knew about me and you too but watch... "that your faith should not fail". Faith comes by hearing and hearing by the word of (not men) God. I almost died because my faith almost failed me. Because I was not talking to God. And I was not hearing (faith comes by h-e-a-r-i-n-g) God. And if the devil can keep you from talking, hearing and reading. "The word is a lamp unto my feet and a light unto my path". Life is dark. Drive down a dark road at night with no head lights and you will wreck. I kept wrecking and ending up in jail because I had no lamp and no light. I had the gift of preaching and speaking. But you can be the best driver in the world and if I put you on the curvaceous slopes of Switzerland or the meandering road, of California to drive with no lights at night you will wreck. I wrecked because I let the devil con me into leaving my sword (the word) on the shelf and... The reason you are reading these words right now is because of what he told (me and David and...) Peter "when (not if) you have returned to me, (at 96 Lbs when the death angel came to get me Jesus said "not yet he has not returned") strengthen (K)your (K) Brother(K)... Strengthen (G) your (B) Brethren (G)... Hello? Can yall hear me now? Read it. John 9:3... You read it...

Jesus told Peter that your "faith" won't fail you. If u have no hope, u need no faith. Faith is the substance of things hoped for. Faith is the bridge between where I am and where I wanna go... I was not building faith because I was dead, in a far country, and not getting the faith (word). So I started trying to solve all my problems (pits and prisons) with my plans (flesh). But if u try 2 solve all yo problems with yo Buddies plans or a checkbook you will fail. There is some stuff you can't deal with in the flesh. Flesh handicaps, hinders and limits you to build faith you have to comprehend that your life (you) under construction. And being under construction prepares you to do warfare. No Army goes to the battlefield without training... And training your faith in the boot camp of life is painful. You get real sweaty, tired and funky when u under construction. But the greater the battle the greater the spoils. I might look rough right now (blood, crid) but I'm under construction. Sooner or later I'll be a G.B.G. but I'm in training. When they wanna build a building real high they dig (construction) the foundation real low. Show me the foundation and I'll tell you how high the building will be, by how low they dig the foundation. I see some cranes, bulldozers and heavy lifting equipment in your life. You are under construction. If you spend time with God and get in the word you will be armed and dangerous. All I need is a few folks who are ready to do battle against illiteracy, jihad against child molestation, battle against High School dropouts and prison dropins battle... G.B.G. is about battling baby! You have been taught to look "past, present, future", wrong. The G.B.G. methodology is future, present, past. Look into your future (ahead), bring it (the future) into the present and watch it come (to) pass you... All the reporters, pundits and critics who will talk smack about this book (mark my words) yall send them to John 1:9 and, and, and I kept telling you earlier that "yall have seen some bad stuff". I didn't even know why I kept hearing that in my spirit. But you are limited by flesh. And we keep saying I'll believe it when I see it. But Christ is saying you'll see it when you believe it. So in your flesh psychologically and emotionally you are affected, limited and hindered by what you have seen. But you can ask God to supernaturally "show me what I've never seen before". Because even though you are limited by the confines of your hometown. Even though you are limited by what you have seen in the suburb the barrio, the trailer park or the ghetto- God can show you something you have never seen before... People who meet you while you are in the ditch (lowest state) don't understand you are under construction. Build your faith and God will blow your mind... When you stop building (feeding your spirit, mind, faith food etc.) You'll forget what God has already shown you before... "And the Lord turned and looked at Peter (as Peter denied him), then Peter remembered the word of the Lord"... Yall have seen (gangs, beatdowns, contract hits, drive by killings, murder, poverty, racism and classism) some bad stuff... Lazarus died in St. John 11. And Jesus went to Bethany and told em to "show me where you laid him". Jesus wouldn't show them what they'd never seen before until they showed him where they gave up. Jesus "groaned" in the spirit and he was "troubled". 11:35 "Jesus wept" they still didn't understand how awesome God is. If we did like Peter and "remember" what we already know. Remember you started with a drop? One drop of sperm resulted in a head with a brain, 2 eyes, 2 ears, 1 nose, 1 mouth, 32 teeth, 2 arms... One drop. What can't we believe? Jesus wept. Jesus told them to take away the stone. And they were still in flesh and Martha said "Lord, by this time there is a stench, for he has been dead four days". And Jesus lifted up his eyes and said, "Father, I thank you that you have heard me". He started out with "thank you" and "I know that you always hear me, but because of the people who are standing by ". Sometime when Jesus got ready to do a miracle he would put people out. Be careful who you allow to stand around you when you need a miracle. And your faith will fail you if you don't feed it. Remember and move from flesh to visualization (prophecy and promise). You must see it in your mind and you will see it in time. This man was a mess. He was dead 4 days and already stinking. And our Lord was calm, cool and collected. He only wept because of their unbelief he said show me where you laid him and I'll raise him up. I'll show you what you've never seen before. I just raised up a dead boy in Main. I'm getting ready to lay my body down and raise it on the 3rd day. While yall were here weeping I was in Main healing the sick and raising the dead... "I said this that they may believe that you sent me"... He said loudly "Lazarus, come forth". And he who had died came out... God is able to show you some things you have never seen before. But get out of your mind and quit trying to do it in your flesh and activate the "super" on your "natural". And God will show you some stuff you have never seen before that eyes haven't seen and ears haven't heard". God will show up outside that which is dead. He will show up outside that which is sick and he will show up outside your mess, your dirt, your gang and all of your stinky stuff and he will fix it, heal it or raise it up. U can't c what u never "seen" but in "flesh" unless u hallucinating. U mess around and tell Dr. Phil, Dr. Curren, Dr. Handian, Houston or Heitkamp that u r "seeing things" and they'll try to put your butt on keyhea (forced meds). But Bill Cosby, Dr. Alvin Poussaint, President Barack and even G.B.G. all talk about parenting, Fatherless boys and dropout dads. And that is because (in flesh) you can't "see" (unless you're crazy) what you've never "seen". Ipso facto, boys who don't know (see) their fathers don't know how to be a man   or a father. And when you don't "see" your father it will even (cause you to) destroy your sons. And my "people perish for lack of vision"... Jesus even (have you ever "seen" anybody talk to "clothes"!) spoke to the grave clothes and told them to "loose him, and let him go". And the reason Cosby, Dr. Poussaint and Obama want boys not to just see a momma is because... "Then many of the Jews (skeptics, critics and nonbelievers)... "Who" had "seen" the things Jesus (your Father) did, "believe" in him". Did you miss it? Oh baby, baby, baby... I know Bill Cosby gets on your nerves and you think he's blaming the victims (fatherless boys) etc. As quiet as it's kept sometimes he gets on my nerves. I want him to tell me a joke so I can laugh around my problem (trickster). Barack said "any fool can make a baby but only a "Father" can raise a child". Why are they so adamant? Barack "knows" what it's like to only have "dreams" of your Father. They want men to "see" Fathers because "after" the critics (he's blaming us. Racism did it I don't "believe" I've never "seen" this before) they had "seen" Jesus "do" it they "believed". That's good stuff. If you can "see" it you can "be" it. "Come on people".

Look (see) into the future, bring it into your present and watch (see) it pass by. That's what Paul did. He was in "prison". Yes he was. He had been in "problems" and in "pits" and now he was in "prison". You can also be in a prison of poverty, a prison of ignorance, a prison of an addiction etc. But listen to "critics"... Sherman I remember what you did (past). I remember when you conned (trickster). Noah you were a drunkard. Moses you gang banging murderer. David? Call yourself a preacher, a king and a psalmist. I remember what you did. And Paul (shul) your behind sitting up in prison (Joseph, Silas, Nelson Mandela) and Paul this aint your first time in jail (Sherman) you killed people Paul. You locked folks up for going to church and now your in prison. And while in this prison guess what Paul said to Hannity, Limbaugh and Beckman? "Brethern (bloods, N.L.R., B.G.F.) I do not count myself to have apprehended; (I am an apostle and I was a murderer. But I'm still not there in the flesh. I have not attained perfection in this "body" of death) but one thing I (David, Moses, Noah and yes- Manning) ". In Philippians 3:13-14 you will see what Paul, in a jail cell has taught G.B.G. to do ready? Read: I am "forgetting those "things" (murders, banging, dope) which are behind and reaching (seeing my future, bringing it to my present) forward to those things which are ahead. I press" you Brothers in suburbia, kids in the hood, the school and the barrio. You need to "press". Get your ass up and "press" your way back into school. "Press" your way out of the hood, the gang and the pain. Stop being a victim, a sissy and a wimp. Get the "word" in your life so you'll be armed and dangerous. And get your "swagger" back so you can "press". The ex killer, in the jail cell said "I press toward the goal (the dream and the vision) for the prize of the upward call of God in Christ Jesus". No matter where you are or what you did your daddy is "calling you". Can I tell you a secret? As author of this tome with the flashy, controversial and ostentatious (K.K.K) title that everybody is talking about. I fully intend(ed) to write such a book that will spark a revolution and a metamorphosis in "your" life... And you who began perusing this tome on page one, won't close this book and (ever) be the same person. And I don't even know on what page (in you) the change began –but I see some heavy equipment (cranes, bulldozers etc.) outside your mind. I see some things on you that I've never seen before... Even though you are in a more (a problem, a pit or a prison) forget what got you in there and focus (see) on what's gonna get you out. When Paul and Silas were in prison (hole) they were teaching, preaching, writing ("hello you hear me now?) And baptizing folk in the prison (perverts, suburbs, dorms etc.) God can use you (Joseph) in a hole (a jail, the ghetto, the school, the club) just like he can use you on a mountain. I need you Bruthas to "press" . If you can see it you can be it. See it in your mind and you'll see it in time. Your yesterday has been killing your tomorrow. That's what Poussaint, Cosby and Barack have been trying to get you to see. Its not about blaming anybody. I'm not mad because you're a rich kid. I'm not blaming your parents for spoiling you. Ipso Facto, I'm not blaming the poor. I'm proclaiming to you that what you saw affects what you see. You've been allowing your history to hinder you from your destiny your yesterday (past, limitation, lack of education) is killing your tomorrow – but press. I'm looking for some sons, who will stand up, square their shoulders and press!!!

Sherman D. Manning – President and Founder of Gang Bangers for God (good) Founder of HEART (Helping Educate At Risk Teens), motivational speaker, expert on youth criminality, gangs, institutionalization and recidivism. He's an entrepreneur and chief executive officer of A&M Enterprises. He's the Founding President and Chairman of (NAPS) the National Association For Public Safety...

To apply for a "compassion" (G.B.G./Heart supported) scholarship contact Fred Moore at 419-874-1333 or E-mail publicsafety@yahoogroups.com. To join G.B.G. as an Ambassador (student, parent,teens, tweenies etc.),intern, volunteer or a paid employee also E-mail the Yahoo address. Visit www.cafepress.com /manning, www.NAPSUSA.org etc. Any book store (in the world) can order this book for you... Help put the word out over Twitter, Facebook, myspace and all over the place about G.B.G./Heart. The Christopher Clubb, Daniel Sample, Joseph Schoen, Redmond O'Neal, Dustin Burns, Steve Harvey, Dan Rollman and everybody to join G.B.G./Heart....press....

Richard "Doc" Ford and Sherman D. Manning are giving away $500.00 each to help students buy books etc.etc. If you are between the ages of 16-22 you should write an essay about this book and submit it. "Doc" will select the top five essays and give $100.00 (each) to the top five Sherman will select the next top five and give $100.00 (each) to those five individuals so-ten essayists will receive $100.00 each for the best essays on K.K.K. submit your (1500 words or less) essay to hallopeter@sunrise.ch and send a duplicate to (post it) groups.yahoo.com/group/publicsafety-include yoru age, a photo, tele. No. and your snail mail address. ...(Important) from the top ten we will select one person to receive an additional $500.00 G.B.G./Heart stipend... All submissions must be made by March 1, 2011.... Winners will be announced on May 6, 2011 at groups.yahoo.com/group/publicsafety on Facebook and on Myspace... We will also ask convictions and prison world magazine to publish some of the essays in their magazines...

....I want readers to locate Jordan Simon and Jesse (Jesse works at "The Pizza Ranch" in Parkersburg Iowa) in Iowa. We have stipends for Jesse and for Jordan Simon... I shout to paster Jean Barber, Bethel Mission and to elder Sam Wallace in Decatur Ga. Love yall so very much. Although John Walsh pisses me off a lot I can't help but salute him. He helped find that two bit chump Jesse James Hollywood. And I want somebody 2 send "Hollywood" this book in the prison! "Hey Hollywood. How ya like John Walsh now?" Hello Damian Stohr and hi to Greg Johnsson (St. Louis Post Dispatch). I hope Jennifer Portman (The Tallahassee Democrat) is reading. I want Joe Kennedy III, Matthew Kennedy, the Editor at the Philedelphia Daily News etc. to read this.... Somebody please get this to Paul and Jan Crouch at TBN in Santa Ana, CA I know Paul and Jan disagree with some of the cuss words etc. in this book (so does my mother). But I still say Paul and Jan Crouch (at P.O. Box A, Santa Ana, CA 92711-2101 via Amy Fihn and Second Chance, TD Jakes, Eddie Long and P.T.C. etc.) have saved lives. Prison riots (I speak from a perch in the prison! I represent 3 million voices of TBN and Second Chance Baptist Church inside these prisons!) have been prevented! Prison suicides and murders have been stopped. All because Paul Crouch decided to quit his job and mortgage his house to buy TBN more than 35 years ago. I tremble, I weep, I wail when I think about where California's 33 prisons, 173,000 inmates and America's 3 million inmates would be without TBN lord have mercy! And I prophesy that people (i.e. Michael Vick, Tony Dungy, Andy Reid, Willie Gary etc.etc.) are gonna sow seeds into TBN and Second Chance like never before. I'm so convinced that I will sit down tonight and write Amy Fihn and tell her so. I want juveniles and prisoners to get "I have no father but God" by Paul Crouch... K.K.K. and the stuff of this tome has been tried and tested in the biggest human laboratory in America (U.S. Prisons!). And my test subjects have been (Manning, Sauis, Tricksters, The Menendez Brothers, Bardos, Crips, Bloods, Aryan Brotherhood etc.) convicts and my instructors are (Frank Curren MD, Jennifer Heitkamp MD, etc.) Harvard trained physicians etc.etc. I want Green Dot public school students, mayor Nutter, Cory Booker, Mayor Bloomberg, Caroline Kennedy, principals, teachers and students to read and heed "Kids Killing Kids".

I dedicate it to Locke high school students, teachers and parents. I also dedicate it to Beverly Hills high, Archer high, Northside high, Folsom High, McClatchy, Colfax and Lodi high school students and staff... I wanna get it to Judge Lawrence B. Karlton, Judge Thelton Henderson, Josh Pruyn, Harisevugan, Jordan Simon, Attorney Megan Corcoran, Professor Kevin Wehr, David Keith, Mike E. Bergin and to Clay Hollifield. Let's get it to Connor Briard, Zach Hall, Matt Berry and all Lakeside Little League players in Granite Bay CA. Let's find Judy Smith (Impact Strategies) and ask Judy to help G.B.G./Heart launch an international, calculated and concerted campaign against gangs, guns, drugs and violence. If we get Tony Dungy, Andy Reid, Michael Vick, Homeboy Industries, Homegirl Café, Shoulder to Shoulder, Just Detention Int., PLN, Compassion and Kids Can Free the Children all on the G.B.G./Heart team we will win and make a change... I need you (youth) to contact senators, congresspersons, pastors and the media about the contents of this book. Getting people like Megan Corcoran, Jake Heartsong (in Pensacola Florida), Ryan Hreljac, Cameron Johnson, Leonard Padilla and Senate President Pro Tem John Burton on the same team for youngsters is the cause of my life... What keeps me awake at night is what I know will happen to Brett and Chris (both of whom were on black San Quentin gang banger told Brett to "Take Care of yo Ass" ...And that gangbanger and San Quentin staff could have also told Brett that (like Motel 6) "We'll leave the light on for you"...

To telephonically order any book by G.B.G.President Sherman D. Manning call (toll free) 1-877-806-1659... If you (or someone you know) need help getting out of a gang call 1-323-526-1254 (make that call for gang help and for gang tattoo removals and for jobs today). To contact TBN second Chance call 619-276-7020. For 24 hour counseling call 1-714-New-Hope...(G.B.G. invites Jeffrey Lurie to donate 100 copies of K.K.K to Harper Jr. High School in Davis, CA)... (Important Notice:) For teen drug, teen suicide and teen violence intervention go to www.DrPhil.com and click on "Teen Talk". And go to www.napsusa.org... The G.B.G. convict team notes the great work Superbowl coach Tony Dungy does as he says "I've visited a lot of prisons and I know that there are a lot of young men who have made mistakes and deserve a chance to make a comeback. They need mentors..." Pro. Football Quarterback Michael Vick just got out of Federal Prison (in Leavenworth) and (like G.B.G.) he speaks to kids: "I'm a living example of what not to do" Mike says. And that is what each G.B.G. team member represents. And Warden Walker's Harvard directed G.B.G./Heart team invites Tony Dungy, Mike Vick, Andy Reid and Jeffrey Lurie to help G.B.G./Heart to impact troubled teens all over this world. G.B.G. does not seek monetary donations! We don't need your money. We need Mr. Dungy, Mr. Vick, Mr. Lurie, Richard Scrushy etc. to pray for our team and to let us use your testimony (i.e. on CD, D.V.D. and on TBN/Second Chance) to inspire, impact and to warn youngsters about crime... Locke High School students (students at Lodi High School, Beverly Hills High, Harper Jr. High, Folsom High, Robert E. McNair High and all high schools) and McClatchy high school students should do 4 things: A. Apply for a G.B.G. scholarship, job or stipend. B. Spread the word (via Facebook and Myspace etc.) about this book and about G.B.G. C. Write an essay about K.K.K. and submit it forthwith. D. Volunteer to be a special Envoy/G.B.G. Ambassador today....

Jan Scully took another bribe a month ago Michael Weiss allegedly ran over Leroy Fisher was an elderly security guard. Michael was charged with first degree murder. He gave one hundred thousand dollars (to an offshore account) to Jan Scully. She then had the charge reduced to Second degree murder. Weiss then posted a $400 thousand bail. Andrew Weary (a great young man...Ryan and Heather send Mr. Weary this tome) was crushed and hurt that Weiss charge was reduced. All the patrons at 'Badlands' were crushed.

Justice is irrelevant. Truth does not matter. He who has the money has the power. He who has the gold makes the rules.... In court-the law is a lying can tell. All that matters is who tells the best and most convincing lie. They should lock Scully up with all deliberate speed. (If Weiss denies this he can contact my office. I will listen to his claims he's innocent til proven guilty.)...On 12/2/09 "Michelle" (homeless mom) was on the news with her 2 sons. Raymond (16) and his younger brother. They'd been staying at a 'hotel' (on a homeless voucher) for two weeks I want Raymond to have this tome. And I want to send Michelle a check who knows how to find them?

In El Dorado there is a youth (Christian) organization called "Young Life" on Vine Street. They showed (on the news) 3 or 4 of the youths who have been helped by young life. I want all of those fellows (including the guy who said he'd been attending since 7th grade and is now a sophomore in college) to have this book.

Let's get it to Matthew Riley, Scott Jones and Danny Dubois....Evan Low? He is only 26 years young. He is a brilliant young man. Evan is the youngest, only Asian and first openly gay Mayor of Campbell, Campbell CA. Mayor Law is a trailblazer and I can see him being a US Senator one day. I'm very proud of Evan and I shall send him this tome. I want Evan to work with G.B.G./Heart. We need his imput, energy and enthusiasm.

I am in the Epicenter of Hate and Ground Zero for violence and I intend to work with firm determination to prevent people like SPC Chris Toppin, Matt Fulkerson, Zach Bursuglia and Raider Runner from coming here. I am calling upon every person to work with us join our internship programs. We want Adam Iracheta, Tomas Plancarte-Benson, Daniel Tingen, Greg Finkelstein and Chad Phillips etc. to join our internship program (sponsored by US Mint Green Ltd).

I met with Dr. Curren on 10/5/10 and told him (Shakespeare) "History will vindicate me. I will write history." Mark Zuckerberg says people don't remember you by accusations etc. "You get remembered by what you build." Build G.B.G.

We will engage in marathon teleconferences, summits, prayers, fasting and visualizing etc. as we launch this massive campaign to dismantle, destroy and defeat gangs. We will transform the jangling discords of poverty and illiteracy into an oasis of hope and inspiration. We will shine the white hot spot light (via our blogs and vlogs etc.) on gangs, guns, drugs and violence. We will find a way to reach and to empower Jacob Tenbrink, Austin Sisneros, Von Smith, Jakob Karr and Victor Smalley...

We will call upon leaders (from my friend Ambassador Andrew Young, Alvin F. Poussaint M.D., Evan Low, Fred Moor, Arne Duncan etc. to Aaron Fernander, Daniel Sample and Joshua Costa etc.) to help us revolutionize American schools from Georgia to Michigan and from California to Mississippi. We will run into American High Schools like Spiritual Paramedics and chase out hate, horror and violence by any means necessary. We can do this. Yes we can!.......

Sherman D. Manning, 2010

Afterwords

On 10/10/10 I spoke with former District Attorney Michael Kraut. We discussed his recent appearance on Dr. Phil and this tome. Attorney Kraut asked me to "send me a copy of K.K.K. ...I'm very familiar with Bob Blasier." I've asked Mr. Kraut to get this book to "Danny" (Danny and Bonnie were back on Dr. Phil last week)! I hope Danny (perhaps while he's at LA-Hacienda, MyFriend's place or the Mark Houston Academy etc.) will read K.K.K. twice. We want Danny in G.B.G. and Bonnie in HEART! (We're praying for Bonnie's mom Paula). I hope Mike Kraut will join Bob Blasier and help get K.K.K. in schools (i.e. Locke High etc.) around the world... We want Mark Indelicato, Loni Coombs, Blake (who runs support groups on Facebook and he knew Tyler Clementi), Jake (who was on Dr. Phil's bullying special in October 2010), Isaiah (cyberbullied) and James (18) to get K.K.K. If Andrew Gossett, Netzach Miller, Henry Joost, Ariel Schulman and Nev get K.K.K. we will change the world.... Every dream starts with only "one" believer. K.K.K. is my dream. Peter Andrist was my "second" believer! Will you (Rich Phomvongsa, Matthew Gadbots, Harry Taylor, Dr. Andrew Gordon, Dr. Steve Salzman or Fabio of "the Amazing Race" etc.) be a believer? Keith Hartman, Ryan Blakemore, Matt Easley and Jeff Gerber etc. we can stop these killings, beatings and bullying. If we bring together a John Kwasniewski with a Blasier and a Kraut (that's hella Clout) we will win ... yes we can!!!

See G.B.G. on Facebook

Sherman D. Manning, 2010

Index

Hubbard, 31, 71, 79, 414, 462
Huckaby, 341, 408, 506
Hudson, 194, 199, 201, 412
Huffman, 43, 88, 97, 138, 320, 405, 423, 489
Hughes, 106, 107, 110, 113, 127, 132, 178, 181, 192,
    224, 233, 236, 272, 278, 280, 299, 305, 321, 363,
    405, 411, 413, 470, 493, 498
Hunter, 61, 62, 79, 88, 91, 95, 97, 229, 234, 235, 236,
    263, 297, 302, 310, 476
Hurst, 61
Hutchinson, 61, 109, 167, 302, 317
Hutto, 140, 141, 148, 185, 222, 234, 303
Huyck, 43, 48, 53, 60, 69, 86, 98, 119, 136, 137, 139,
    148, 196, 200, 298, 320, 336, 446, 475, 481, 511

J

Jackson, 26, 66, 94, 106, 114, 133, 134, 136, 148,
    149, 167, 169, 176, 187, 192, 201, 203, 211, 223,
    230, 231, 235, 236, 252, 255, 258, 266, 272, 286,
    292, 300, 304, 305, 311, 315, 318, 320, 321, 324,
    325, 330, 339, 341, 343, 349, 350, 366, 367, 375,
    380, 381, 382, 384, 395, 396, 399, 405, 413, 424,
    429, 451, 465, 468, 487, 488, 493, 494, 499, 502,
    508, 509, 513, 527, 534
Jacobson, 60
Jake, 44, 60, 72, 73, 76, 86, 88, 92, 97, 127, 128, 130,
    132, 134, 137, 139, 147, 176, 184, 233, 235, 239,
    240, 276, 298, 307, 310, 314, 319, 321, 368, 400,
    404, 406, 407, 423, 440, 445, 457, 470, 476, 499,
    510, 538, 541
Jakes, 25, 47, 48, 74, 99, 113, 143, 152, 153, 157,
    162, 168, 219, 227, 231, 232, 235, 286, 291, 295,
    323, 329, 334, 335, 341, 357, 386, 390, 392, 406,
    415, 422, 424, 426, 440, 442, 444, 448, 450, 451,
    466, 468, 473, 496, 498, 507, 527, 533, 538
Janes, 61, 528
Janus, 32, 79, 86, 90, 98, 107, 109, 112, 113, 116,
    118, 122, 123, 127, 128, 130, 133, 138, 150, 151,
    165, 168, 195, 197, 212, 213, 222, 240, 254, 259,
    260, 312, 345, 354, 364, 365, 374, 375, 377, 438,
    439, 441, 447, 462, 479, 490, 492, 503, 524, 526
Jarman, 27, 28, 29, 31, 37, 39, 43, 44, 47, 48, 53, 59,
    67, 69, 83, 84, 92, 155, 225, 256, 257, 272, 273,
    307, 324, 327, 329, 346, 348, 351, 352, 353, 366,
    367, 374, 378, 386, 393, 394, 398, 415, 418, 431,
    439, 441, 445, 449, 473, 476, 480, 495, 513, 517,
    521
Jarrad, 61
Jarvis, 184, 199, 291
Jason, 43, 48, 53, 56, 60, 69, 83, 86, 87, 89, 93, 95,
    96, 97, 98, 106, 119, 127, 128, 131, 132, 135, 136,
    137, 139, 148, 149, 151, 160, 166, 174, 183, 196,
    197, 200, 211, 223, 224, 233, 234, 235, 236, 247,
    252, 268, 286, 296, 298, 299, 304, 305, 311, 320,
    328, 336, 394, 410, 412, 415, 423, 429, 432, 440,
    446, 463, 470, 474, 475, 476, 481, 488, 494, 505,
    511, 520
Jay, 53, 55, 250, 251, 311, 346, 406, 475, 477, 511

Jenkins, 99, 106, 112, 121, 131, 152, 169, 235, 264,
    268, 297, 301, 310, 369, 373, 375, 379, 387, 395,
    396, 414, 417, 428, 432, 439, 509
Jensen, 92, 379, 387, 388, 400, 407, 477
Jiminez, 98, 110, 111, 116, 164, 165, 173, 216, 240,
    243, 251, 277, 282, 301, 311, 395
Job, 112, 132, 163, 180, 181, 236, 251, 266, 280, 283,
    285, 292, 299, 315, 317, 321, 379, 400, 411, 458,
    488, 500, 501
Joe, 63, 89, 93, 97, 100, 109, 113, 116, 129, 131, 140,
    144, 148, 167, 168, 170, 177, 180, 188, 197, 202,
    204, 206, 209, 215, 218, 219, 229, 233, 246, 247,
    249, 269, 277, 278, 282, 290, 292, 300, 301, 304,
    306, 310, 311, 315, 329, 334, 365, 366, 378, 380,
    382, 400, 401, 407, 410, 418, 423, 434, 442, 443,
    455, 456, 457, 458, 461, 462, 474, 476, 477, 478,
    490, 498, 515, 516, 531, 533, 538
Johnson, 32, 34, 45, 52, 61, 87, 88, 92, 95, 107, 113,
    114, 116, 128, 129, 135, 139, 147, 175, 179, 181,
    185, 188, 196, 204, 212, 215, 223, 224, 226, 233,
    234, 235, 236, 238, 260, 272, 283, 297, 298, 299,
    302, 311, 314, 320, 336, 340, 349, 351, 355, 358,
    362, 366, 368, 373, 374, 385, 387, 388, 391, 394,
    400, 403, 404, 406, 410, 411, 412, 413, 414, 423,
    425, 429, 443, 446, 448, 455, 465, 469, 477, 481,
    483, 485, 491, 492, 493, 495, 505, 510, 511, 516,
    518, 521, 527, 529, 538
Johnson-Dovey, 29, 70, 79, 117, 122, 155, 161, 182,
    199, 271, 307, 317, 333, 405, 414, 462, 467, 473
Johnston, 89, 185, 195, 311, 314, 335, 440, 477, 495
Joiner, 119, 127, 128, 130, 132, 133, 188, 212, 214,
    216, 220, 227, 234, 320, 400, 411, 443
Jolliff, 83, 129, 130, 131, 132, 141, 142, 147, 155, 158,
    163, 174, 177, 181, 195, 196, 225, 231, 239, 240,
    265, 283, 303, 306, 349, 373, 467
Jonas, 92, 147, 194, 235, 399, 406, 479, 497, 500
Jones, 43, 59, 85, 97, 129, 151, 152, 163, 177, 179,
    197, 216, 221, 222, 227, 281, 320, 326, 336, 389,
    392, 399, 403, 405, 406, 422, 424, 426, 438, 445,
    448, 453, 463, 466, 468, 469, 473, 483, 486, 491,
    496, 509, 513, 527, 529, 539
Jordan, 40, 85, 88, 91, 116, 133, 135, 152, 156, 159,
    194, 203, 211, 220, 226, 236, 257, 268, 284, 291,
    304, 306, 310, 311, 312, 314, 320, 327, 348, 351,
    358, 359, 365, 368, 391, 401, 405, 406, 423, 430,
    462, 487, 493, 513, 538
Joseph, 24, 26, 27, 28, 38, 45, 48, 49, 52, 60, 62, 68,
    76, 89, 92, 98, 100, 103, 110, 120, 125, 132, 137,
    143, 147, 148, 149, 150, 151, 154, 157, 163, 170,
    173, 175, 176, 177, 181, 183, 188, 192, 194, 197,
    198, 199, 200, 202, 203, 206, 208, 209, 210, 211,
    214, 216, 230, 233, 234, 235, 236, 238, 239, 246,
    250, 253, 256, 257, 266, 268, 269, 270, 271, 272,
    283, 285, 288, 290, 291, 293, 294, 295, 296, 299,
    302, 306, 310, 314, 317, 319, 321, 325, 342, 350,
    353, 356, 368, 388, 392, 394, 400, 401, 404, 422,
    443, 453, 476, 478, 479, 485, 492, 501, 523, 527,
    533, 536, 537